The Plays and Poems

Of

WILLIAM CARTWRIGHT

Edited with Introductions and Notes

By G. Blakemore Evans

MADISON

Published by THE UNIVERSITY of WISCONSIN PRESS—1951

COPYRIGHT, 1951, BY

THE REGENTS OF THE UNIVERSITY OF WISCONSIN

PRINTED IN THE UNITED STATES OF AMERICA
BY THE WILLIAM BYRD PRESS, INCORPORATED, RICHMOND, VIRGINIA

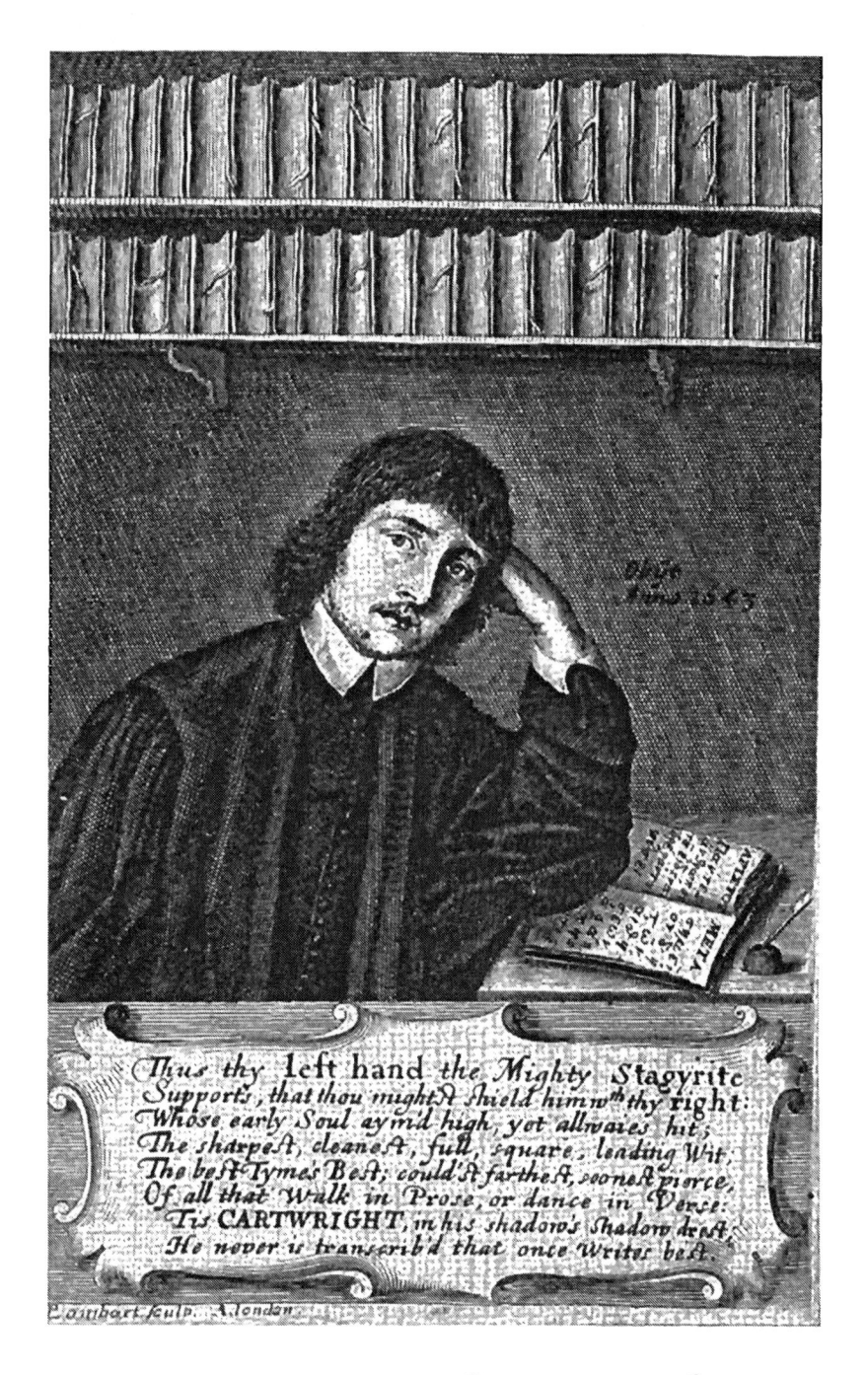

> Thus thy left hand the Mighty Stagyrite
> Supports, that thou might'st shield him wth thy right:
> Whose early Soul ay'md high, yet allwaies hit;
> The sharpest, cleanest, full, square, leading Wit:
> The best Tymes Best, could'st farthest, soonest pierce,
> Of all that Walk in Prose, or dance in Verse:
> 'Tis CARTWRIGHT, in his shadow's shadow drest,
> He never is transcrib'd that once Writes best.

William Cartwright.

Frontispiece of *Works* (1651). The signature of William Cartwright is from the Oxford Subscription Book, under February 24, 1631/2.

To
MY PARENTS
—*whose child this is.*

FOREWORD

Si quis emergat poetaster, vel criticus
Qui notas fecerit aut animadversiones aliquot,
Deleatur d, alii legunt sic, codex meus sic habet,
Phœbus audit, literarum decus, sidus, oraculum.
—Robert Burton, *Philosophaster*

THE PRESENT edition of Cartwright's plays and poems has been the frequently interrupted work of some years, and I have come to look upon it with a tolerance and indulgence which others may find difficult to understand. But though in danger from time to time of being suffocated by the Cartwrightian aether, I have, I hope, avoided the pitfall of exaggerating Cartwright's position or merit as a writer. Mindful of this danger, I have eschewed for the most part the role of critic and interpreter and have confined my discussion to historical and bibliographical problems, the essential business of an edition. On the other hand, where I have thought that praise was justified I have allowed myself the license of an occasional comparative.

The text of the plays and poems here presented is based on the earliest authoritative copy, printed or manuscript. The general editorial principles will be found fully described in the General Introduction, Chapter V, "The Text." In the matter of annotation I have made no attempt to gloss words and phrases which will be clear to anyone with some knowledge of Elizabethan and Caroline drama. Of more value, it seemed to me, was the tracing of Cartwright's general relations with his period, his sources, and his influence. A good deal of material of this kind has here been offered, but the task is endless and the result merely the reflection of a limited knowledge of an ample field. I am also conscious that a number of allusions which ought to have been caught, explained, and illustrated may have been overlooked. These, humbly, "I bequeathen" to the next editor of Cartwright! The Textual Notes represent the usual not too happy compromise between reason and inclusiveness. Finally, the statement on page 72 that the list of variations there given between copies of the *Works* (1651) contains "most of the principal variants" is not as truthful as it should be. Too late for inclusion in that list a group of nine more variations was discovered in sig. L. They are included, however, in the Textual Notes to *The Siege*.

I must thank the following libraries for their generous permission to make use of manuscript materials in their collections: the Bodleian Library, the British Museum, the Folger Shakespeare Library, the Harvard College Library, and the New York Public Library. I have also to thank the University of Texas Library for allowing me to use its unique copy of the *Works* (1561) containing the cancelled leaves in *The Lady-Errant*.

The library staffs of the institutions already mentioned, and those of the Huntington Library and the University of Illinois Library, have all served me with their accustomed unfailing courtesy. Particularly I should like to mention the thoughtful kindness of Miss Eva Faye Benton and Miss Isabella Grant of the University of Illinois Library.

My continual indebtedness to other students in the field of seventeenth-century drama and poetry must be only too apparent. I have tried to acknowledge a small part of this debt in my footnotes. But other more personal debts remain which make it a pleasurable obligation to follow Bottom's advice: "Call them generally, man by man, . . . and so grow to a point."

My sincere thanks are due to Professor T. W. Baldwin for his permission to make full use of his Restoration prompt copies of *The Lady-Errant* and *The Ordinary*, and to Dr. William Van Lennep for first drawing my attention to the prompt copies and then most unselfishly allowing me to exercise his prior claim on Professor Baldwin's permission to use them. Professor Willa McClung Evans has been more than generous in placing at my disposal valuable manuscript material connected with Henry Lawes. She was also kind enough to secure for me the permission of Miss Naomi Church of Beaconsfield, Buckinghamshire, to incorporate readings in my Textual Notes from Lawes' autographed collection of manuscript songs now in her possession. To Miss Erma R. Gebhardt I owe a special debt of gratitude for her generosity in allowing me to make use of her unpublished B. Litt. thesis (Oxford, 1932), an edition of Cartwright's *Ordinary*, with valuable critical introduction and notes. My only regret is that I heard of Miss Gebhardt's work only after my own was in nearly final shape for the press. And although, even then, I was able to profit greatly from Miss Gebhardt's scholarship, an earlier knowledge of her thesis would I am sure have further enriched my own work on *The Ordinary*. To Professor William A. Jackson, Curator of the Houghton Library, I am indebted for advice in the interpretation of the bibliographical material on the *Works* (1651) in my chapter on "The Text."

Dr. Sina K. Spiker, editor of the Wisconsin Press, under whose expert care my manuscript has been prepared for the printers, has also earned my wondering gratitude for her patience with one who seems to have done his worst to try it severely. Having a specialist's knowledge in seventeenth-century English literature, Dr. Spiker has also been able to make a number of important criticisms and suggestions.

For friendly interest and encouragement in pursuing Cartwright to the point of print I must thank particularly Professors Ruth Wallerstein and Mark Eccles of Wisconsin, Miss Livia Appel of the State Historical Society of Wisconsin, and Professor Douglas Bush of Harvard.

In addition to the debts already recorded I have received information and critical advice from a number of other friends and colleagues, among them, Professors Edgar W. Lacy, Robert Shafer, Alexander H. Schutz, Robert W. Rogers, Earl R. Wasserman, and Dr. William Bond, Curator of Manuscripts at the Houghton Library. That my best return can consist only in naming them is certainly a poor measure of their kindness to me. My father, Professor M. B. Evans, with parental fortitude, read over the page proof for me.

My wife, with untiring and Laconian patience has aided me in the dull duties of typing, proofreading, and index-making. But she already, without the further futility of words, understands the full weight of my debt to her.

Finally to Professor Hyder. Edward Rollins of Harvard, under whose kindly and learned care this study received its first form as a thesis, go my affectionate and respectful thanks. I can express my debt to him very simply: what may be of value in my work is his, by precept and by example; the inevitable errors, confusions, and ignorances—they poor things are mine own and must, regretfully, "be booked with the rest."

G. Blakemore Evans

University of Illinois
September, 1950

CONTENTS

List of Abbreviations xiii

GENERAL INTRODUCTION

Life of William Cartwright 3
The Plays 22
The Poems 33
Influence and Later Reputation 46
The Text 61

WORKS

The Lady-Errant 81
The Royal Slave 165
The Ordinary 257
The Siege 355
The Poems 441
Doubtful Poems 564

NOTES

Critical Notes 575
   The Lady-Errant, 575—*The Royal Slave*, 588—*The Ordinary* 610—*The Siege*, 661—*The Poems*, 676—*Doubtful Poems*, 764
Textual Notes 769
   The Lady-Errant, 769—*The Royal Slave*, 776—*The Ordinary*, 799—*The Siege*, 807—*The Poems*, 809

APPENDIX

Moseley's Preface 829
Metrical Analysis of Stanza Forms 834
Bibliography of Cartwright Publications . . . 836
List of Manuscripts 839
Index 843

LIST OF ABBREVIATIONS

References by date alone in the Textual Notes are identified in the Critical Notes under *Text*.

AC, *The New Academy of Complements* (1671)
Addit., Additional (MS.), British Museum
B, Bedford MS. of *The Royal Slave*
B.M., British Museum
Bod., Bodleian Library
C., Collier, *Select Collection of Old Plays* (1826), Vol. X
Chalmers, *The English Poets* (1810), Vol. VI
D., Dodsley, *Select Collection of Old Plays* (1744), Vol. X
DNB, *Dictionary of National Biography*
E, Egerton (MS.), British Museum
F, Folger MS. of *The Royal Slave* (MS. 7044)
G, Gebhardt, Thesis, *The Ordinary*
Goffin, *Life and Poems of William Cartwright* (1918)
H., Hazlitt, *Select Collection of Old English Plays* (1875), Vol. XII
Harl., Harleian (MS.), British Museum
L, Drexel MS. 4041, New York Public Library
LA, Lawes' autographed MS.
Mal., Malone (MS.), Bodleian Library
MC, *The Marrow of Complements* (1655)
MLN, *Modern Language Notes*
NED, *New Oxford English Dictionary*
P, British Museum MS. of *The Royal Slave* (Addit. MS. 41,616)
PB, *Parnassus Biceps* (1656)
PC, prompt copy (of *The Lady-Errant* and *The Ordinary*)
PMLA, *Publications of the Modern Language Association of America*
R., Reed, *Select Collection of Old Plays* (1780), Vol. X
Rawl., Rawlinson (MS.), Bodleian Library
S, Bodleian MS. of *The Royal Slave* (Arch. Seld. B.26)
SD, stage direction
TLS, London *Times Literary Supplement*
WI, *Wits Interpreter* (1655, 1662, 1671)
Works (1651), Cartwright, *Comedies, Tragi-Comedies, With other Poems* (1651)

GENERAL INTRODUCTION

COMEDIES
TRAGI-COMEDIES,
With other
POEMS,

BY

Mr WILLIAM CARTWRIGHT,
late Student of *Christ-Church* in *Oxford*,
and Proctor of the UNIVERSITY.

The *Ayres* and *Songs* set by Mr *HENRY LAWES*,
Servant to His late MAJESTY in His
Publick and Private *Musick*.

———— *nec Ignes,*
Nec potuit Ferrum, ————

LONDON, Printed for *Humphrey Moseley*, and
are to be sold at his Shop, at the sign of the
Prince's *Arms* in St *Pauls* Church-yard, 1651.

The title-page of *Works* (1651).

I

LIFE OF WILLIAM CARTWRIGHT

Sownynge in moral vertu was his speche
And gladly wolde he lerne and gladly teche.
—CHAUCER

As WITH so many of his contemporaries, the main outlines of William Cartwright's life are well known, but for the more intimate detail of personal interests and character, we search very nearly in vain. On the whole a large number—perhaps even a surprising number—of so-called "Lives" of Cartwright have been written, the first appearing in 1651, seven years after his death, the latest and only authoritative sketch in 1918. A brief preliminary survey and criticism of the most important biographies, especially those of the seventeenth-century writers, will help us to define and evaluate our materials and expose the core of interdependent matter which runs through each account.

The earliest attempt at a memoir of Cartwright appeared in the first collected edition of his *Works* (1651),[1] and though the author was also the publisher and the whole notice perilously near to a publisher's "puff," the essential importance of this account as the *fons et origo* for all later writers cannot be overestimated.[2] In an age hostile to poets of a learned and Anglican persuasion, Moseley felt called upon for his own sake to offer some sort of apology for Cartwright, for his beliefs, for his profession, and for his poetry. Unconsciously perhaps, Moseley drew a pen personality of considerable charm and vividness. Much more than the actual meager

---

1. *Comedies, Tragi-Comedies, With other Poems*, By Mr William Cartwright, ... London, Printed for Humphrey Moseley, ... 1651. Referred to throughout as *Works* (1651). The Preface entitled "To the Reader," occurs in signatures [¹a3]ʳ–[¹a6]ʳ.

2. This statement may be readily verified by a glance at Moseley's preface as it is reproduced in Appendix A, where all the echoes and borrowings of other seventeenth-century writers are noticed.

factual information, it is this savor of personality that gives the memorial its lasting value, a value amply recognized by later biographers. Though not altogether free from slight inaccuracies, the main outlines of Moseley's preface are generally correct, with one important exception.[3]

In 1668 David Lloyd published his *Memoires*.[4] Among the more than 250 lives which the volume boasts there is a biography of Cartwright with the imposing title, common to most of the lives, "The Life and Death of Mr. William Cartwright." Altogether, it is a strange production, based for the most part on Moseley's preface and drawing heavily upon the large number of commendatory poems which introduced the 1651 edition. The few new details which Lloyd offers are, without much exaggeration, either wrong or garbled, and only serve to make what was already confusing enough, worse confounded. There is no doubt, however, that Lloyd, though he may never have known Cartwright personally, had a first-hand and intimate acquaintance with his poetry; and I have pointed out in the notes to the *Poems* numerous instances, scattered throughout his book, of direct and unblushing plagiarism. On the whole, however, though Lloyd affords us several new and interesting glimpses into Cartwright's personal life, it is impossible to give anything he says more than doubtful credit.[5]

Omitting the brief notice of Cartwright in Edward Phillips' *Theatrum Poetarum* (1674),[6] we come to the important figure of Anthony Wood. In the same year, 1674, Wood published his *Historia et Antiquitates Universitatis Oxoniensis*. Part of the project included, more or less as an appendix, an account of Oxford writers, among whom Cartwright received consideration.[7] Much of the actual data for this life was collected for Wood by John Aubrey during the

---

3. Moseley, probably influenced by two contributors to the commendatory poems prefixed to the 1651 *Works*, E. Nevill and John Berkenhead, says that Cartwright died at the age of thirty. The conflicting accounts of his birth date will be fully discussed later. See also my note, p. 833.

4. *Memoires of the Lives, Actions, Sufferings, and Deaths of those Noble, Reverend, and Excellent Personages, That Suffered by Death,/ Sequestration,/ Decimation,/ Or otherwise, for the Protestant Religion,* . . . 1668, pp. 422–25.

5. When, for example, we find Lloyd taking almost twenty lines from Cartwright's poem on Jonson, turning them into prose, and applying them to the attainments of Mr. Dudley Digges (*Memoires*, p. 426), it is not unreasonable to be cautious in accepting his characters of other people. The example cited is only one of a number of similar cases.

6. P. 190; printed in 1675.

7. II, 274.

years 1671–72.[8] Wood himself, an indefatigable antiquary, seems to have been able to add very little to the facts already known and those supplied to him by Aubrey. The life as it is found in volume two of *Athenae Oxonienses* (1692)[9] appears to be but a slightly expanded version of the Latin life of 1674. Actually, however, the English version, printed in 1692, is probably the earlier and furnished the basis of the Latin translation, which was carried out, and apparently not too well carried out, under the eye of Cartwright's friend John Fell, then Bishop of Oxford. The most noticeable difference between the two accounts is found in the bibliography of Cartwright's compositions; the list in the Latin text is extremely perfunctory, cryptic, and misleading.[10] Besides the official memoir, Wood's *Historia*[11] gives an account of the presentation of Cartwright's *Royal Slave* before the king and queen during the Oxford visit of 1636.[12]

In the same year with the first volume of Wood's *Athenae Oxonienses* (1691), Gerard Langbaine published his important *Account of the English Dramatick Poets*.[13] This work is too well known and appreciated to require much comment. Langbaine, unlike Lloyd and Wood, acknowledges his debts to earlier writers and begins his account with a careful statement of the conflicting reports of Cartwright's birth. In addition to the memoir, Langbaine gives a bibliography of Cartwright's works, a great improvement on the 1674 Wood bibliography, and a number of useful comments on the sources and history of individual plays. In 1699 Charles Gildon "improv'd and continu'd" Langbaine's *Account*; actually he greatly abbreviated much of the old material and introduced numerous errors. Cartwright suffers with the rest; in particular his four plays are absurdly misdated, an error which is faithfully repeated through-

---

8. '*Brief Lives*,' ed. A. Clark, I, 148. The Cartwright material is collected from three Aubrey manuscripts; see the editor's footnotes and introduction. One of the manuscripts is dated 1671 by Aubrey.

9. 1721 ed., II, 34–36. The third edition (1813) edited by P. Bliss has also been consulted.

10. Langbaine (see below), who had access only to the Latin edition of 1674, is misled into quoting Cartwright's "November" under its Latin title.

11. I, 344–45. Wood's account is borrowed almost verbatim from Archbishop Laud's description.—*Works of William Laud*, ed. J. Bliss (1853), V, 152–54.

12. The short account of Cartwright in William Winstanley's *The Lives of the most Famous English Poets* (1687, p. 162), contains nothing new.

13. Pp. 51–56. This Gerard Langbaine must not be confused with another Gerard Langbaine, a friend and contemporary of Cartwright's, who served with him on the "Council of War."

out the eighteenth century by each of the so-called dramatic handbooks.

Almost nothing new was added to the work of the seventeenth-century writers during the next 250 years. Among men who in this time interested themselves in Cartwright we may mention Oldys, Cibber, Chalmers, Campbell, Cunningham, Hunter, Bullen, and Gerber;[14] but it is not until the publication in 1918 of R. Cullis Goffin's account—as an introduction to his edition of the *Poems*—that we find any serious attempt to add fresh material.[15] By careful research Mr. Goffin was able to settle with finality the vexing problem of Cartwright's birth and parentage, and to present for the first time a relatively full picture of his home environment. Though we shall later[16] have some occasion to criticize Mr. Goffin's text of the *Poems*, it must be understood that his work on Cartwright's life leaves other investigators very little to offer that is at all new. The extent of my own debt in the remainder of this chapter is sufficiently obvious.

WILLIAM CARTWRIGHT was born in Northway,[17] Gloucestershire, near Tewkesbury, about December 23, 1611.[18] His family, at the time

---

14. William Oldys' manuscript notes on Langbaine's *Account* are preserved in the British Museum (Addit. MSS. 22,592-22,595). A transcript of these notes with additions by Malone, Steevens, and Percy is in the Bodleian Library (Malone MSS. 129, 130, 131, 132). Oldys adds one short anecdote connected with Cartwright's death, but gives no authority for it. There is also an unusually well documented life of Cartwright in *Biographia Britannica*, II (1748), 1179-81. Other accounts are the following: Theophilus Cibber, *The Lives of the Poets* (1753), I, 277-81; Alexander Chalmers, *The English Poets* (1810), VI, 511-12, and *The General Biographical Dictionary* (1812-17), Thomas Campbell, *Specimens of the British Poets* (1819), III, 303-4; G. G. Cunningham, *Lives of Eminent and Illustrious Englishmen* (1834), III, 267-68; Joseph Hunter, *Chorus Vatum Anglicanorum* (1848), IV, 231-37 (British Museum, Addit. MS. 24,490); A. H. Bullen, in *Dictionary of National Biography* (1887), IX, 232-33; F. Gerber, *The Sources of William Cartwright's Comedy "The Ordinary"* (Berne, 1909).

15. *The Life and Poems of William Cartwright* (Cambridge, 1918).

16. See Chapter V, "The Text."

17. Northway is in the parish of Ashchurch, which in turn is in the hundred of Tewkesbury. See Sir Robert Atkyns' *The Ancient and Present State of Glocestershire* (1768); and, for a slightly fuller account, S. Rudder's *A New History of Gloucestershire* (1779).

18. The exact date and place of Cartwright's birth have long been uncertain. Lloyd (*Memoires*, p. 422) gave August 15, 1615, at Burford, Oxfordshire, Wood (*Historia*, II, 274, *Athenae*, II, 34), following Aubrey ('*Brief Lives,*' I, 148), gave the date of his baptism as September 26, 1611, at Northway, near Tewkesbury, in Gloucestershire; Moseley ("To the Reader"), while offering no exact dates, tells us that Cartwright died at thirty, a statement which was

of his birth, was apparently well to do; at least we are informed by Aubrey[19] that his father, also named William,[20] enjoyed an annual income of three hundred pounds and the services of "two able-bodied manservants."[21] On his mother's side Cartwright was descended from the Coles, another Northway family, likewise of respectable fortunes.[22] The general relationships within the Cartwright family and their connection with the Coles appear in the accompanying genealogical table, published in the *Visitation of Gloucestershire, 1623.*[23]

---

probably suggested to him by the commendatory poems of John Berkenhead and E. Nevill, prefixed to the 1651 *Works*. Sir Robert Stapylton, also in the commendatory poems, says he died "not one and thirty." Up to the publication of Mr. Goffin's edition of the *Poems* in 1918, most biographers had agreed in accepting Wood's account. Mr. Goffin, however, has settled the matter by turning up the actual baptismal entry in the parish records of Ashchurch. I have reckoned December 23 as the date of birth, following the method used in determining the date of Shakespeare's birth.

19. '*Brief Lives*,' I, 148.
20. Lloyd (*Memoires*, p. 422) gives Cartwright's father's name as Thomas.
21. Goffin (*Poems*, p. xiii) quotes from *Men and Armour for Gloucestershire in 1608*.
22. Goffin, *Poems*, p. xiv.
23. Ed. by J. Maclean and W. C. Heane, *Harleian Society Publications* (1885), p. 38. Goffin reproduces this table, not very correctly (*Poems*, p. xiv). The table as given by Messrs. Maclean and Heane differs in a few slight particulars from two manuscript copies in the British Museum (Harl. MSS. 1041, fol. 104; 1543, fol. 137), one of which must have formed the basis of their text. Since the differences are unimportant, I have thought it best to reproduce the table as printed in their edition. A similar genealogical table for the Cole family may be found on page 43 of the *Visitation*. In a second *Visitation of the County of Gloucester, 1682-1683* (pp. 34-36), we find a continuation of the above table with the addition of two sisters: "Dorothy, born 1616" (this must be the sister Howes whom Aubrey, '*Brief Lives*,' I, 148, speaks of as being four years younger than Cartwright); and "Mary, born 1618, ob. 1620." We also learn that Cartwright's mother died in 1620, and that "Thaxton, 2 son," was born in 1613. Goffin (*Poems*, p. xiii) suggests that the Thomas Cartwright who, according to Foster's *Alumni Oxonienses* (I, 245), matriculated at Christ Church on October 21, 1642, at the age of sixteen, was a younger brother of the poet. He is described as the son of William Cartwright of Greekeland, county of Gloucester. Like the poet, he was elected to Christ Church from Westminster, where he went as king's scholar in 1640 (*The Record of Old Westminsters*, ed. G. F. R. Barker and A. H. Stenning, 1928, I, 168); the Oxford and the Westminster records agree on all points. If Goffin's suggestion is correct, this Thomas Cartwright must have been the son of William's father by his second marriage, since his first wife died in 1620. Aubrey ('*Brief Lives*,' I, 148) mentions this second marriage, and says the second wife brought the poet's father "100 *li.* per annum, in Wiltshire." A Latin poem by Thomas Cartwright of Christ Church appears in *Epibateria . . . Mariae ex Batavia Feliciter Reduci* (1643), sig. C4ᵛ. Cartwright himself has a

Cartwright Genealogical Table from *Visitation of Gloucestershire*, 1623

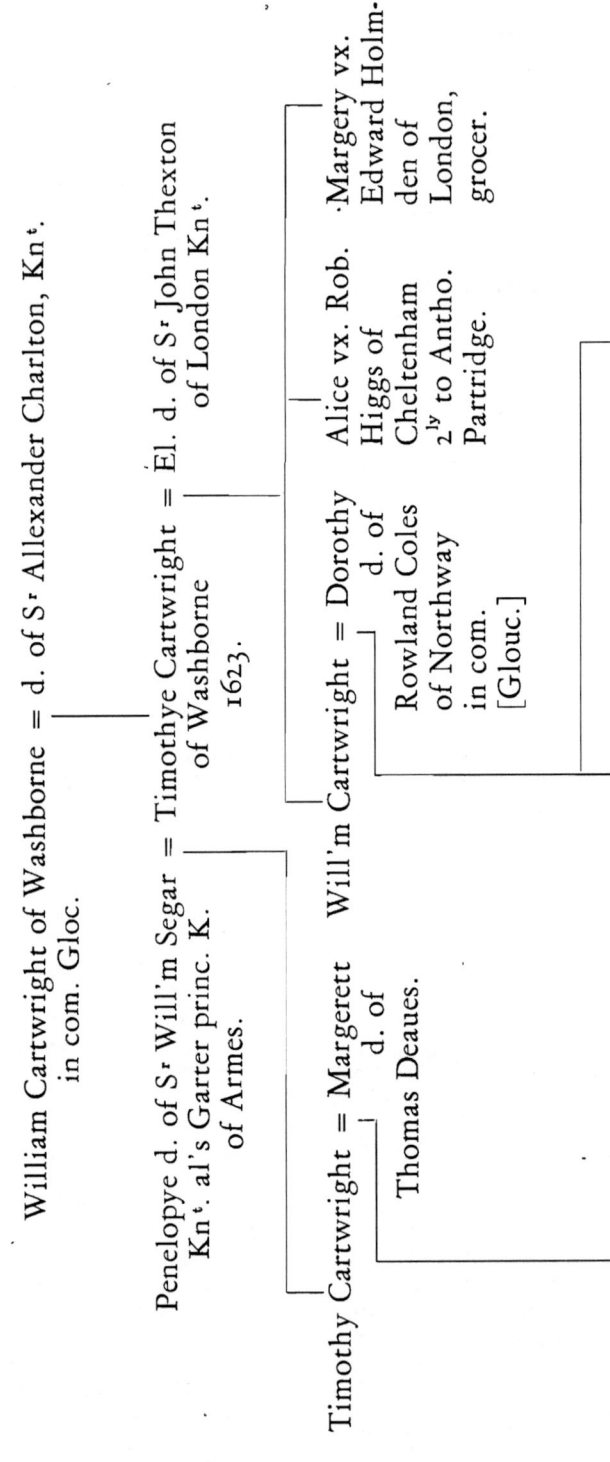

William Cartwright of Washborne = d. of S᷃ʳ Allexander Charlton, Kn᷃ᵗ. in com. Gloc.

Penelopye d. of S᷃ʳ Will'm Segar Kn᷃ᵗ. al's Garter princ. K. of Armes. = Timothye Cartwright of Washborne 1623. = El. d. of S᷃ʳ John Thexton of London Kn᷃ᵗ.

Timothy Cartwright = Margerett d. of Thomas Deaues.

Will'm Cartwright = Dorothy d. of Rowland Coles of Northway in com. [Glouc.]

Alice vx. Rob. Higgs of Cheltenham 2ˡʸ to Antho. Partridge.

Margery vx. Edward Holmden of London, grocer.

Thomas Cartwright 1 yere old and more aº. 1623.

Will'm Cartwright 13 yere old 1623.

2 Thexton Cartwright.

Such evidence of family connections and worldly position makes the sudden, and quite unexplained, reverse of fortune which befell the family a few years later difficult to understand. All we know is that by the time Cartwright reached school age his father had moved to Cirencester, where he was reduced to the necessity of keeping an inn,[24] a venture which lasted only a year, or little more, and turned out to be merely a further source of loss.[25] Living thus in comparatively reduced circumstances, young William was sent to the free school,[26] where he received his grounding from a certain Henry Topp, a former student of Oriel College, Oxford.[27] So promising was his progress under Master Topp, although the man's reputation as a teacher seems to have been slight,[28] that his father, upon the advice of friends, procured for him a king's scholarship at Westminster. Here he was fortunate to come under the care of Lambert Osbaldstone, a man of great and widely acknowledged learning.

Although no Westminster records exist for the next few years, we know that Cartwright was elected to a studentship at Christ Church, Oxford, where in 1628[29] he was entered as a gentleman

Latin and an English poem in the same collection.

24. The character of Goodstock in Jonson's *New Inn* suggests an interesting parallel: "He pretends to be a gentleman and a scholar, neglected by the times, turns host and keeps an Inn." Like Cartwright's father he too "was bred a scholar in Oxford" (*Works*, ed. Gifford-Cunningham, II, 337, 339).

25. Aubrey, *Brief Lives*, I, 148.

26. Early education at the local free school is not in itself a mark of poverty. Shackerley Marmion, whose father was Lord of the Manor at Aynho, received all his pre-university training at the free school at Thame, Oxfordshire.

27. Cartwright could not have received instruction from Henry Topp until 1622, in which year Topp was appointed to the school at Cirencester (Goffin, *Poems*, p. xv). This makes it unlikely that he entered Westminster until 1623 or 1624, though Wood implies ("so great a progress did he make in a short time") that he was not long under the tutelage of Topp (*Athenae*

II, 34). Wood gives the name as William Topp; Goffin makes the correction (*Poems*, p. xv). Bliss in his edition of the *Athenae* (III, 83) had, however, already pointed out Wood's error in his note to the life of Thomas Master, an Oxford friend of Cartwright, who also worked under Topp.

28. Goffin, *Poems*, pp. xv-xvi.

29. *The Record of Old Westminsters* (ed. Barker and Stenning, I, 168) gives the following notice under Cartwright: "elected to Ch.Ch. Oxon. 1628, matric. Feb. 24, 1631/2; B.A. 1632; M.A. 1635." The lapse of time between Cartwright's election to Christ Church and his university matriculation is apparently not unusual. Some of the confusion in dates among later writers is perhaps due to a contradiction in Wood's two accounts. In the *Historia* (1674), II, 274, we read: "atque inde ad Aedem istam accessit, anno CIƆDCXXXI." But in the later *Athenae* (II, 34-35) Wood writes: "was elected Student of *Ch. Ch.* in 1628." Langbaine (*Account*, 1691, p. 51), not having the *Athenae*, follows the *Historia*: "and in

commoner.[30] Such an election was an honor eagerly sought after and is in itself eloquent of a brilliant and successful career in the school. One aspect of this studentship which must have appealed strongly to Cartwright's father was that it covered more than half the expense of fees and residence at the university.

Before passing to Cartwright's Oxford career it may be worth noticing that his family had already formed strong connections with the university. Both his father, William, and his uncle, Thexton, Cartwright,[31] were Oxford men, having entered Balliol College in the same year, 1604, and it seems reasonably certain that the great traveler John Cartwright, author of *The Preachers Travels* (1611), himself an Oxford man, was likewise some relation of the family.[32] Cartwright's approach to his future home was, therefore, finely tempered by years of home training and association.

The Christ Church which Cartwright entered in 1628 was, even in the first quarter of the seventeenth century, beginning to acquire the reputation of the "poet's college," of a "nest of singing birds" as Dr. Johnson, with much less justification, later called Pembroke. Even in the nineteenth century we find Beddoes still referring to Christ Church as the mother of such poets as Corbet, Cartwright, and Cowley. Of Cartwright's early years here we learn very little. We are told that as an undergraduate he was "put under the Tuition of *Jerumael Terrent*, [and] went thro' the Classes of Logic and Philosophy with an unwearied industry,"[33] "sitting," says Lloyd, "sixteen hours a day at all manner of knowledge."[34] And Lloyd continues:

---

the year 1631 was chose Student of *Christ-Church* College in *Oxford*." He in his turn is followed by the anonymous writer in the *Retrospective Review* (1824, IX, 161), who remarks that "he was chosen student of Christ's [*sic*] College, Oxford in the year 1631."

30. Both Cartwright's father and his uncle, Thexton Cartwright, were entered at Oxford as "pleb." The change is peculiar in the light of the reduced circumstances in which his father was then living. See *Alumni Oxonienses* (ed. J. Foster), I, 245.

31. Goffin (*Poems*, p. xiii) notices that Cartwright's uncle, Thexton Cartwright, is not included in the genealogical table given above. The entry in Foster's *Alumni Oxonienses*, however, is quite explicit as to the relationship.

32. Wood, *Athenae* (ed. Bliss), II, 114. Wood writes that John Cartwright "seems to have been descended from the Cartwrights of Washbourne in Glocestershire.

33. *Athenae*, II, 35.

34. *Memoires*, p. 424. The "sixteen hours" need not be taken too literally. Apparently Lloyd considered sixteen hours the minimum for serious academic labor, since it turns up again in "The Life and Death of Mr. John Gregory" (*ibid.*, p. 87): He "awaked

His soul naturally great and capable, had, he said, three advantages to fill it; great spirited Tutors, choice Books, and select Company; it was his usual saying, That it was his happiness that he neither heard nor read any thing vulgar, weak, or raw, till his minde was fixed to notions *exact as reason*, and as *high* as *fancy*.[35]

If we may accept this report of Lloyd's as genuine, these remarks are of great interest and value, since they give us a sudden glimpse of the hidden days at Westminster and the undergraduate life at Oxford. His reference to "select Company" seems indeed literal truth, and it must have been at about this time that he became an active member and leader among a "knot of the choicest *Oxford* Wits always together, as Mr. Sugge, Mr. Cartwright, Mr. Masters, Mr. Berkenhead, Mr. Stotevile, Mr. Waring, [and] Mr. Newman."[36] Presumably Lloyd again refers to the same group when he speaks of "a Club of great Wits at *Oxford* that met twice a week to consult this Oracle [i.e., Mr. John Gregory]."[37] Only two small facts, however, are known with certainty for this period. In 1629, as Mr. Goffin tells us, Cartwright was one of the leaders in a student "protestation to the King against the discipline maintained by the Dean and Chapter";[38] and, in 1630, the poet made his first appearance

---

his large Faculties to sixteen hours Study every day for many years together."

35. *Ibid.*, p. 422.
36. *Ibid.*, p. 425.
37. *Ibid.*, p. 88.
38. *Poems*, p. xvii. Goffin's source for this information is the *Calendar of State Papers, Domestic Series, 1629* and *1640/1*. (He everywhere refers to this collection as *Clarendon State Papers*.) In volume two for 1629 (p. 99), under November 17, we find mention of a protestation made by the students "on certain differences between the Dean and Chapter of Christ Church, Oxford, and the students of that house. The disputes turned principally on the amount of allowances made to the students." The "allowances" under question seem to have been the privilege of the so-called Westminster Supper, which the dean and chapter were trying to abolish (see H. L. Thompson, *Christ Church*, 1900, pp. 59-61). Under February 2, 1630, Crosfield (*Diary*, ed. F. S. Boas, 1935, p. 41) records: "The Students of Christ Church their overthrowe in their suit against ye praebends, concluding it was noe Colledge, but a Cathedrall." Does this refer to a settlement of the above dispute, or to some other case? The second entry in *Calendar of State Papers, 1640/1* (p. 460), noted by Goffin, reads as follows: "Declaration of Jasper Mayne, William Cartwright, and Henry Killigrew concerning their proceedings against the Dean and Chapter of Christ Church. Whereas we have constituted Mr. John Mylles our delegate under this Form,—That we gave him power to proceed against the Dean and Chapter of Ch[rist] Church by all lawful means, for procurement of our rights from them,—We here protest that we gave him this power in those general terms upon this interpretation both privately and publicly made to us, that by lawful means was meant our petitioning his Majesty, our founder and Visitor; and that the reason why the

in print. Two years later, June 5, 1632, Cartwright received his B.A.; he then continued his studies for the M.A., which was granted on April 15, 1635.[39]

The next two years, 1636–37, were important and busy ones for Cartwright, and, had the times been kinder, the events which then occurred might well have led to advancement at both court and university. As it was, however, they did nothing but offer "promise of increase."[40]

The last of the great royal progresses took place in 1636, and though the town of Oxford was rather grudging in its reception, the university behaved splendidly. Among the entertainments arranged for the benefit of the royal party, Cartwright's *Royal Slave* was

---

form was conceived in such general terms was that our way of proceeding might not be discovered to the Dean and Chapter. And therefore if any other means be used we utterly disclaim it." Goffin apparently takes this declaration to refer to the same affair that was in agitation in 1629. There are several points against such a view. In the first place, the general term "student," among whom Cartwright is not particularized, has been reduced to three individuals; secondly, one of these individuals, Henry Killigrew, was not a former student of Westminster, and hence would not have been concerned in the matter originally; and third, a period of ten years and more has elapsed since the first case. Finally, it must be pointed out that Cartwright's part in the original affair of 1629 is purely hypothetical. We can only suppose that he was one of the "students" concerned. A full knowledge of the facts, especially those of the 1640/1 affair, would be most valuable, but it is useless to make any further guesses. One thing, however, must be mentioned in all fairness to Mr. Goffin. In 1638, through the influence of Laud, Charles wrote an extremely severe letter to the authorities of Christ Church ordering once for all the discontinuance of the Westminster Supper.—Thompson, *Christ Church*, pp. 60–61.

39. Wood, *Fasti*, ed. Bliss (1815–20), I, 478. Wood does not enter Cartwright among those receiving the B.A. in 1632; see, however, Foster's *Alumni Oxonienses*, I, 245.

40. Goffin (*Poems*, p. xviii) suggests that perhaps Cartwright, once well launched on his academic career, "was able to revive something of his father's old rank," and adds that "an estate was bought at Leckhampton, near Cheltenham, Gloucestershire." His authority for this second statement is very slight. Aubrey ('Brief Lives,' I, 148) only says that he called upon Cartwright's sister Howes (née Dorothy Cartwright, born 1615/6) at Leckhampton, and later adds "Old Mr. Cartwright lived sometime at Leckhampton, Gloc., wher his daughters now live." Aubrey's last remark might mean only that old Mr. Cartwright lived with his daughter's family at Leckhampton. So far as Mr. Goffin's initial suggestion is concerned, I greatly doubt whether men in Cartwright's academic position had very much extra money for "family rehabilitation," and we know that even as late as 1640 (see note 38 above) Cartwright was at loggerheads with the officials of his college over some matter, of which the root was probably money.

chosen as the climax of the celebration, a choice which seemed at the time to reflect real credit not only on the young author but on the university at large. Opinions were unanimously favorable, even extravagant, one writer going so far as to assert that "his Majesty and all the Nobles com'end[ed] it for the best y^t ever was acted."[41] Cartwright's cup must indeed have overflowed when in November of the same year the queen commanded a second performance, this time at Hampton Court. He himself went to London to supervise the production, receiving a honorarium of forty pounds for his pains and, what was vastly more important, a renewal of the indispensable royal favor. Thus, though *The Royal Slave* was not the earliest of Cartwright's plays, being antedated by *The Ordinary* (c. 1634) and probably by *The Lady-Errant*, it was the first to receive more than academic recognition.

The next year, 1637, promised to throw a beginning of preferment in Cartwright's way. Through poor management and careless work the Oxford press had fallen on evil days.[42] Among his other reforms, Laud, then chancellor of the university, was anxious to improve these conditions, and in the Statutes of 1634 provided for

a Person set over the Printers, who shall be well-skill'd in the Greek and Latin Tongues, and in Philological Studies, with the Title of *Archi-typographer*, whose Office is to supervise and look after the Business of Printing, and to provide, at the University Expence, all Paper, Presses, Types, etc., to prescribe the Module of the Letter, the Quality of the Paper, and the Size of the Margins, when any Book is printed at the cost of the University, and also to correct the Errors of the Press.[43]

Apparently the man suggested for this new and inclusive office[44] was

---

41. From a letter by George Evelyn reprinted in *Memoirs of John Evelyn*, ed. W. Bray (2d ed., 1819), I, 662.

42. Percy Simpson, *Proof-Reading in the Sixteenth, Seventeenth, and Eighteenth Centuries* (1935), pp. 170–76. I have drawn heavily on Mr. Simpson's account in treating this matter. It should be noticed, however, that Miss Erma R. Gebhardt, in an unpublished thesis (B. Litt., Oxford), had earlier discussed the appointment and its bearing on Cartwright.—"An Edition of William Cartwright's *The Ordinary:* With Critical Introduction and Notes" (1932), pp. i, viii.

43. A paraphrase of the Latin original from John Pointer's *Oxoniensis Academia* (1749), quoted by Simpson (*Proof-Reading*, p. 170). It so happens that we possess several fragments of the proofs of first and second editions of *The Royal Slave* possibly corrected by Cartwright. The minute corrections show an unusual understanding of such matters.

44. Actually, the *Architypographus* did not discharge all these duties himself. In *Collections* (VI, 7), Thomas Hearne writes: "The Architypographus is to be a Governour & to praeside over the rest, & he is to manage, as a Scholar, all things for the Honour and Credit of the University" (quoted by Simpson, *Proof-Reading*, pp. 170–71).

Cartwright, for there is preserved among Laud's letters one to the vice-chancellor, dated May 19, 1637, in which he writes:

> I like your proposal very well for Mr. Cartwright, and am glad to hear that he is so passing fit for the Greek, and every way else so well deserving for this or a better place. I have not leisure to write a letter to the heads, which may lie ledger against that time; but I am very heartily willing to give my consent, that when the voidance shall come, Mr. Cartwright may be the successor, and to that end I give you free and full power to move the heads, or to do any other act fitting or conducent to the good success of this business. And so much I pray let Mr. Cartwright know, and withal give him thanks for his fair respective letter to me. One thing is considerable, I take it, the statute requires that somewhat should be done with the bedel of law in relation to the learned press; but my memory does not hold it perfectly what it is; and therefore you shall do well to consider it. And now upon a sudden considering Gayton's sufficiency,[45] it is come into my head to ask this question. Why may not all three esquire bedels join in the learned press, though perhaps but one of them need be the chief manager: for aught I know, this may be very well worth your considering.[46]

Interpreting this letter, Mr. Simpson suggests that "Cartwright was evidently a prospective candidate for the esquire bedelship of law when it fell vacant, on the understanding that the post of architypographus should be joined with it."[47] A slightly different interpretation, however, is equally possible. In the first place no mention is actually made throughout of the office of *Architypographus*, and it seems difficult to believe that Laud is speaking of more than the esquire bedelship of law in that part of the letter which makes direct mention of Cartwright.[48] Apparently Cartwright had made application for the position in his "fair respective letter," and it must surely be to this position that Laud refers when he writes of "voidance" and "successor"; there could be no question of any such provisos in a new office. Laud then suddenly half-remembers a clause in the new Statutes of 1634, in which it is provided that upon the "first avoidance" the bedelship of law shall be "annexed" permanently to the office of *Architypographus*,[49] and suggests, there-

---

45. Edmund Gayton was esquire, or upper, bedel of physic and arts combined, and seemingly not very highly "considered" by Laud.

46. *Works of William Laud*, ed. J. Bliss (1853), V, 170, quoted by Simpson, *Proof-Reading*, p. 173.

47. *Proof-Reading*, p. 173.

48. If Laud is speaking only of the bedelship of law, it is difficult, I admit, to explain the reference to Cartwright's knowledge of Greek; classical learning was not apparently a prerequisite for the position. See the *Laudian Code* (1634), Title XVIII.

49. *Oxford University Statutes*, trans. G. R. M. Ward (1845), I, 206.

fore, that since Cartwright is now in line for the one office, he should also become the new overseer of the Oxford press. If this reasoning seems a little tortuous, the letter itself is too vague and confused to allow any final opinion. Whatever else is doubtful, it appears clear that Cartwright was at least suggested for the post of *Architypographus;* whether he was ever actually promised it is another matter. At any rate no vacancy occurred in the bedelship of law until thirteen years after Cartwright's death, and no *Architypographus* was appointed until 1658.[50]

Since nothing very immediate could be expected from the hoped-for office of *Architypographus,* Cartwright, in 1638, took holy orders, most probably at the suggestion of his friend and patron, Brian Duppa, then Bishop of Chichester. Four years later, on October 13, 1642, a year after Duppa became Bishop of Salisbury, he was appointed to the succentorship in that cathedral.[51] During this time Cartwright made a very high reputation for himself as an orator, becoming "the most florid and seraphical Preacher in the University."[52] And on the king's return to Oxford after the battle of Edgehill (1642), it was Cartwright who, by command, was chosen

---

50. Simpson, *Proof-Reading,* p. 173.

51. Something of the extent of Cartwright's debt to Duppa may be gathered from some lines (possibly by W. Towers) in a commendatory poem prefixed to Thomas Washbourne's *Divine Poems* (1654), sig. [A7]ᵛ:

Cartwright is Wit throughout, but I read o're
More then his four playes, his last pious four,
And then his several Gratitudes unto
Him, whose head taught him, and purse fed him too;
Who gave him to buy books, and gave him skil
In each of them, to choose out Well from Ill,
The Learned, Pious, Constant *Duppa,*

I owe this reference to G. E. Bentley, *Shakespeare & Jonson* (1945, II, 279-80), who assigns the lines to Washbourne.

In connection with Cartwright's appointment as succentor it should be observed that he must have possessed a beautiful speaking and singing voice. Indeed, I strongly suspect that no small part of his fame as a preacher is attributable to this gift. Among the commendatory poems to the *Works* (1651), we find a number of significant references.

John Fell speaks of the voice that did "Charm th' attentive Throng"; and Ralph Bathurst of Trinity recalls his "conquering presence" and his "numerous strains" like "Almighty Thunder." His friendship with Henry Lawes is also pertinent in this connection. Gilchrist in his note to Cartwright's poem in *Jonsonus Virbius* (1638), amusingly affirms that Duppa appointed him his "successor in the Church of Salisbury." While we are on the subject of Cartwright's voice, we may notice a curious reference to his eyesight in the commendatory poem by "B: C:" (sig. [***8]ᵛ):

Though he had not much more than *Homer's* sight,
In verse hee'd *Homer's* and *Eustathius* light.

Does this mean that Cartwright suffered from very poor vision, was, in fact, almost blind? There is no hint of this handicap in any of the other poems or memorial lives.

52. Wood, *Athenae,* II, 35.

to preach the sermon of "victory."[53] Only one of Cartwright's sermons has been preserved. It bears the fanciful title, *An Off-spring of Mercy, Issuing out of the Womb of Cruelty, or, A Passion Sermon* (1652).[54] Although in no way remarkable, this sermon has the merit of an easy, if ornate, style and of clearness in form and presentation. It is, moreover, not noticeably overstocked with the learned lumber which clutters up so many of even the best seventeenth-century sermons. Like his verse, Cartwright's prose is too rhetorical, too full of the glitter of words and pointing of conceits. But the style

---

53. Aubrey, 'Brief Lives,' I, 148. "A Prayer of Thanksgiving for His Majesties Victory over the Rebells at Edge-Hill," published without attribution in *Private Formes of Prayer, ... also a Collection of all the Prayers Printed since these Troubles began* (Oxford, 1645), may possibly be by Cartwright.

54. The title-page reads: "AN / Off-spring of Mercy,/ Issuing out of the Womb of / Cruelty./ OR,/ A Passion Sermon,/ PREACHED AT/ *Christs-Church* in *Oxford*, [rule] By that late Renowned Or- / nament of the University,/ *William Cartwright*. [rule] . . . LONDON,/ Printed by *A. M.* and are to be sold / by *Iohn Brown* at the guilded Acorn/ in *Pauls*-Church-yard, 1652." The sermon was entered on the Stationers' Register on June 12, 1652, by A. Miller. The British Museum copy is dated "July 15." The publisher assures us that it is "no bastard Posthume, because its printed according to a Copy written with the Authours own hand." His tribute to Cartwright is a curious one: "Reader, The best description I can make of *Oxfords Cartwright* will be but as an heap of noysome dirt before the Gates of the Stately *None-such*." As a specimen of Cartwright's prose style we may quote the concluding paragraphs (pp. 29-31):

"Thus was it his determinate counsell, that the Old Testament should be swallowed up in the New, that all those Ceremonies of sacrifice should be buried in that immaculate sacrifice that he himself delivered, and that the Sepulchre of *Moses* so long hid from the world, should be found at last in our Saviour Christ. Thus did the Sun of Righteousnesse set with more grace and sweetnesse, then either he did rise or run his course with, and enlightning his thorns in so many pointed Rayes, of that his greatest work, His death made glories and circles of lustre for all the rest of his actions: Thus when the Jews by divine fore-knowledge had brought the Deity to that despicablenesse, that they occasioned those miracles, That He should be impleaded and condemned who is Judge of all; He laden with curses, that scatters blessings as Sunne-beams over the face of the world; That health it self languisht, and the very impassible [*sic*] suffered. God (who is wont to take his rise where men stop) was pleased to strike miracles out of these, greater then these. For behold, *An Off-spring of Mercy, issuing out of the womb of Cruelty*; A bundle of new miracles as farre beyond the former, as they are opposite to them, A condemnation that absolves us; A curse that blesseth us; A sicknesse that recovers us; and a death it self that quickens us; So much was his love stronger then death, who though He were a Son, yet learn'd he obedience by the things he suffered; and being made perfect he became the Authour of eternall salvation to all them that obey him.

"Among which number, O Lord, write our names, for his sake who this day suffered to blot out that hand-writing that was against us. *Amen*."

is not utterly vicious, and in the hands of an experienced orator it must have rung with the urgency of genuine eloquence. So Jasper Mayne exclaims:

> But these thy looser Raptures must submit
> To thy rare Sermons, and much holier Wit;
> In whose rich Web such Eloquence is seen,
> As if the Romane Orator had been
> Sent forth to preach the Gospell; ...
> Thou wert a Poet, but thy Sermons do
> Shew thee to be the best of Preachers too; ...
> What holy Craft did in thy Pulpit move?
> How was the Serpent mingled with the Dove?
> How have I seen Thee cast thy Net, and then
> With holy Cosenage catch'd the Souls of Men? ...
> Thou to all Hearers wert all Things, didst fly
> Low to the People, to us Scholars high;
> Hadst Milk for Children, and strong Meat for those
> Whose Minds, like thine, to Mens perfections rose.[55]

Or hear John Fell, later Bishop of Oxford:

> Or view him when his riper thoughts did bear
> His studies into a Diviner Sphere:
> When that his Voice did charm th'attentive Throng,
> And every Ear was link'd unto his Tongue.[56]

To his contemporary Abraham Wright, Cartwright appeared as one of the "*Prime Masters* of this Nation in their several *Waies* of Preaching," and in his book, *Five Sermons, in Five several Styles; or Waies of Preaching* (1656) the third sermon is "in Dr. Maine's and Mr. Cartwright's Style."[57] Wright's imitation is on the whole very clever and manages to reproduce most of the external characteristics of Cartwright's manner. The pairing of Mayne and Cartwright is enlightening in view of the close friendship which we know to have existed between the two men. Despite his seniority Mayne seems to have been very much under Cartwright's influence. The relationship will become clearer when we examine Mayne's two plays in a later chapter.

Sometime during 1642 Cartwright was made Reader in Meta-

---

55. *Works* (1651), sigs. [¹b5]ᵛ–[¹b6]ʳ.
56. *Ibid.*, sig. ¶1ᵛ.
57. Pp. [39]–65. Chalmers (*English Poets*, 1810, VI, 512) confuses this sermon of Wright's with Cartwright's one published sermon, 1652, which he tells us appeared in Wright's *Five Sermons* (1656).

physic to the university. No record of the appointment remains, since the lectureship was unendowed, but we find ample evidence of Cartwright's tenure in the numerous references to his excellence in the office of lecturer:

> When *Aristotle* ran as smooth as *Virgil*, and his Philosophy melting as his Plays, and his Lectures on that obscure Book which *Aristotle* made not to be understood as clear as his Poems; the abstractions refined, what was rugged for many ages, lost its horror and pleased, and the thornes of Philosophy turned Roses by him, that the Theatre was thin to his School, and Comedy was not half so good entertainment as his Philosophy.[58]

Though he may have lectured well, he was not to lecture long. In the very year of his appointment, civil war fell upon Oxford, and lectures and most other academic pursuits gave place to more urgent and practical matters.

In common with the other members of the university—undergraduate, graduate, and faculty—Cartwright now began to appreciate the stark reality of civil war. From all accounts Oxford was at this time, and for some time to come, a very uncomfortable and dangerous place in which to live. The university itself was in a position of great difficulty, since the townspeople, almost to a man, were strongly for Parliament, and though the officials and most of the students were equally ardent in the royal cause, they were never able to feel much sense of internal security. Clashes between town and gown were frequent, even after Charles had set up his standard in Oxford, and any true cooperation was never attained.

Foreseeing the necessity of a refuge and center of operations, Charles ordered the university to place the town in a state of defense. The proclamation was issued on August 13, 1642. In the general commotion which followed, Cartwright seems to have taken a leading part, being appointed one of the so-called "Council of War,"

---

58. Lloyd, *Memoires*, p. 423. Aubrey ('*Brief Lives*,' I, 148) records that Cartwright wrote a "treatise of metaphysique" and makes a note to remind himself to ask Dr. Thomas Barlow about it. Apparently he forgot or Barlow knew nothing, for we hear no more of this work. Perhaps Moseley had something similar in mind when in his preface "To the Reader" (sig. [¹a6]ʳ) he writes: "... his *Poems* you see come first to hand, ... You may gain more, of higher use, hereafter." Probably, however, he was thinking chiefly of Cartwright's Latin poetry and religious writings.

Miss Gebhardt (Thesis, *The Ordinary*, p. vii) calls attention to an entry under "Receipts, 1641-42" which reads: "Recipta in usum Bibliothica, A Graduat: & Scholar: finarum Wᵐ Cartwright 0:10:0." Miss Gebhardt considers the reading "finarum" questionable.

a group of twenty-seven from the various colleges, whose duty it was "to order all things that were to be done on the University behalf in joining with the Troopers, for the finding of Maintenance for them during their abode here, and for providing of arms for the safety of the University."[59] In compliance with the statute, "trained" bands, made up of "priviliged men of the University," in which the "schollers were promiscuously bothe Graduates and Undergraduates; a great many of them Masters of Art, yea devines allso," were assembled.[60] In the exercise of these trained bands Cartwright must have taken an active part, for when, two months later, Lord Say took over the city for a short time, he and two other men were arrested and imprisoned "for utteringe of some wordes, &c., but especially for trayninge at the Universitie's musters."[61] According to the invaluable Twyne, however, the imprisonment did not last very long, for upon payment of "200 *li.* baile a peice taken for them," they were released with a warning "not [to] come to the Universitie unlesse by order from my lord Saye."[62] Even the last proviso did not long affect Cartwright, for it became void soon after, when Charles, on October 28, took over the town as his headquarters. Lluellin has described the scholar bands in his satirical poem, "The Spy of the Buttery":

> The *East* line *common souldiers* kept,
> The *North* the *Honest Townesmen* swept.
> The *West* was man'd by th' *Loyall Schollers,*

---

59. Wood, *History and Antiquities of the University of Oxford*, ed. John Gutch (1796), II, 447. A contemporary, anti-royalist pamphlet, *University Newes, or, The Unfortunate proceedings of the Cavaliers in Oxford* (1642), tells how the bad behavior of the 250 troopers sent by Charles to protect the town and university alienated both the town and a large number of scholars, reducing their "trained band" from 500 to only 300.

60. *The Life and Times of Anthony Wood*, ed. A. Clark (1891), I, 55. In *True News from Oxford* (1642), a pamphlet in the form of a letter from a "Scholar in the University to a brother of his in *London*," this band of scholars, styled "heroicke Cavaleers" by Lord Lovelace and Lord Wilmot, is seriously ridiculed. Among other things they are accused of having fled from the training field upon the news of an approaching band of troopers. It admits, however, that a few held their ground.

61. *Life and Times*, I, 62. Wood's reference to "utteringe, &c." is made clear by the lines immediately preceding his account of Cartwright's arrest: "Mr. [Humphrey] Floyd of Oriell College kept as prisoner at the Starre, for some wordes uttered by him to this effect that 'if he were able he had rather lend the kinge a thousand pound then one penny to the parlament.'"

62. *Ibid.*, I, 62. The information was added in a note by Twyne to Wood's manuscript. The bail seems extremely large, amounting to something like five thousand dollars by modern standards.

> Whose *Gownes* you slave are *blacke* as *Colliers*.
> They taw'd it faith, their *Gunnes* would hit,
> As sure as they had *studied* it.
> They ramm'd their Bullet, they would ha't in,
> *Bounce* went the *Noise*, like *Greeke* and *Latine*. . . .
> These Knaves talkt much o th' *siege* of *Troy*
> And at this *siege* they leapt for Joy.[63]

Cartwright's short life was now fast drawing to a close. In April, 1643, he was appointed Junior Proctor to the university, a position of some little dignity and responsibility; but he did not live to complete his year of office.[64] On November 29, 1643, he fell a victim to a new disease then raging in Oxford, the "camp disease" or, as Moseley quaintly calls it, a "fatall choice *Feaver*." He was buried near the choir in the south[65] aisle of Christ Church cathedral, apparently, as later report informs us, without any epitaph to mark the spot: "Pitty 'tis so famous a bard should lye without an inscription."[66]

Cartwright did not die alone; among others Dudley Digges and Thomas Master were struck down at almost the same time and by the same sickness.[67] Thus at a single blow Oxford lost three of those

---

63. *Men-Miracles with Other Poemes* (1646), pp. 57-58.
64. Wood, *Fasti*, ed. Bliss, II, 56.
65. See Wood's plan of the church reproduced in *Wood's City of Oxford*, ed. A. Clark (1890), II, 550. Bullen (*DNB*, IX, 232) gives "north" aisle and is followed by Gerber.
66. Aubrey, '*Brief Lives*,' I, 148. As in the case of Cartwright's birth, there is some confusion concerning the exact date of his death. Wood (*Athenae*, II, 36) gives the date as above, November 29, and the date of his burial, December 1; but Mr. Goffin points out (*Poems*, p. xxvi) that the Register of Deaths, preserved at Christ Church, gives the "7th" of December as the date of his funeral. It is just possible that Wood is right about the date of his death and that because of the troublous state of affairs, or the prevalence of the disease among others, the funeral was postponed. See also the following note.
67. It should be noticed how often these three names appear together. In a letter from Arthur Trevor to the Marquis of Ormond, dated December 9, 1643, from Oxford, we find the following statement: "The sickness still continues here. Sir *Peter Wyche* the Comptroller of the King's houshold dyed yesterday: and this morning his Lady. His successor is not known. My Lord of *Danby* I hear is likewise dead: and three of the most famous men of this University, *Cartwright, Diggs*, and *Masters*, died here this last month." See *A Collection of Letters, 1641-1660*, ed. T. Carte (1739), I, 26. This letter might be extremely valuable in determining the exact date of Cartwright's death if we could be sure of what the writer means by "this last month." Unfortunately, checking the dates on which Digges and Master are supposed to have died, we find that the *DNB* gives October 1, 1643, for Digges, and August 31, 1643 (Wood, *Athenae*, Dec. or Jan., 1643), for Master.

five whom Griffith a little later celebrated as "Numina . . . *Oxonii Tutelaria*."[68]

A single glance at the hundred and more pages of elegaic verse which introduce the collected edition of his *Works* (1651) is more than enough to establish the fact that Cartwright's death aroused very sincere grief. But interest went even higher. Lloyd records that "the King and Queen enquired very anxiously of his *health in his last sickness*."[69] And another writer tells us that on the day of his death King Charles appeared in black, and, when asked the reason, replied that "since the Muses had so much mourned for the loss of such a son, it would be a shame for him not to appear in mourning for the loss of such a subject."[70] Aubrey adds: " 'Tis not to be forgott that king Charles 1st dropt a teare at the newes of his death."[71]

Cartwright as a man must have appeared to his contemporaries as a person of engaging charm and force. Genuinely learned, a master of four languages besides English, he still retained a "Candor and Sweetness that made him equally *lov'd* and *admir'd*";[72] deeply read, he saw life largely as a reflection of his reading and never thought to read much between the lines. His religion, with its strong Anglican affiliations, was practical and of rather mixed loyalties—his political devotion to the cause of Charles vying with an intense hatred of the Puritan Aeolists, both tempered by his first academic love. Whether we may now wholly approve of such a character in each of its perhaps rather superficial aspects is really not a question of great moment. To those who knew him best, his friends and teachers, he seemed "the utmost man could come to."[73]

This survey of Cartwright's life may conclude with what Lloyd assures us were his own dying and prophetic words: "I see the seeds of miseries that will continue an age; and a blot upon our Nation and Religion that will last with the world."[74]

---

68. William Griffith's remark may be found in his "Praeloquium" to R. Waring's *Amoris Effigies*, edition of 1671. John Gregory and John Berkenhead are the two others mentioned.

69. *Memoires*, p. 422.

70. Oldys' manuscript notes to Langbaine's *Account of the English Dramatick Poets*. No source for the anecdote is offered.

71. '*Brief Lives*,' I, 148.

72. Moseley, "To the Reader."

73. Lloyd, *Memoires*, p. 423. He ascribes the words to John Fell, then Dean, and later Bishop, of Oxford.

74. *Memoires*, p. 424. Mayne, who credits Cartwright with prophecy (commendatory poems, sig. [¹b5]ᵛ):

Witness thy *Royall Captive*, where we do
Read thee a Poet, but sad Prophet too.

And Lloyd (p. 442, side note) calls *The Royal Slave* "his Prophesie" (?copying Mayne). There is confusion here perhaps with Strode's *Floating Island*.

II

THE PLAYS

What makes so many scholars then come from Oxford and Cambridge, like market-women, with dorsers full of lamentable tragedies, and ridiculous comedies, which they might here vent to the players, but they will take no money for them.—SHIRLEY.

CARTWRIGHT'S DRAMATIC interests were confined to two genres: Platonic drama and Jonsonian middle-class comedy. "Tragical-historical-pastoral" seem to have offered him no lure. Jonsonian middle-class comedy will be discussed in the Introduction to *The Ordinary*, but the matter of Platonic drama is so much a part of the very warp and woof of three of his four plays that it demands special discussion here.[1]

Structurally, Cartwright's Platonic plays show two distinct trends in the development of the Cavalier drama. Two of the plays, *The Lady-Errant* and *The Siege*, have well-developed comic underplots; the third, *The Royal Slave*, is "all of one piece," with a minimum of comic relief. As Mr. Harbage points out, the exclusion of the comic underplot—a heritage from Fletcher's school of tragicomedy—was a step in the direction of the Restoration heroic drama.[2] Cartwright, however, favored the comic element, and *The Siege*, which is perhaps his latest play, makes use of an unusually prominent comic underplot. Moreover, an analysis of scene arrangement shows a progressive freedom in breaking with the continental and Jonsonian theory of linking or "connection" of scenes, a freedom which is particularly reflected in comedy and which finds widest

---

1. Mr. Alfred Harbage has treated the whole body of Platonic drama at length in his *Cavalier Drama* (1936), and Miss Kathleen M. Lynch's study, *The Social Mode of Restoration Comedy* (1926), is for this earlier period most valuable. Mr. Harbage's *Thomas Killigrew* (1930) and Miss Lynch's article, "Conventions of Platonic Drama in the Heroic Plays of Orrery and Dryden" (*PMLA*, XLIV [June, 1929], 456–71) should also be consulted.

2. *Cavalier Drama*, p. 68.

expression in *The Ordinary* and *The Siege*.[3] By means of this greater freedom, interest in a double denouement is sustained to the very end of the latter play, a point which marks a considerable advance in dramatic structure over *The Lady-Errant*.

When we examine the subject matter and settings of Platonic plays, we are at once struck by their eternally repetitive nature. All, as Mr. Harbage points out,[4] have much in common with Greek romance and its later imitators. Like the widow's cruse, Greek romance offered a never-failing spring of famine rations in a time when sturdier fare was scarce. Cartwright's settings afford perfect examples of this exotic fashion—Cyprus, Persia, and Byzantium. His plots, moreover, in accordance with a custom which may be traced indirectly to Aristotle, deal exclusively with exalted persons and illustrious actions. These characteristics, however, might with equal propriety be identified with the earlier tragicomedy of Fletcher; indeed, on the mere basis of subject matter to distinguish sharply between Fletcherian tragicomedy and the tragicomedy of the Platonic genre is impossible.[5] Only in the *treatment* of the subject matter, as it is "oriented" and metamorphosed by the doctrines of the Platonic love cult, can we perceive distinctive characteristics.

It is of course an error, and one too easily made, to suppose that the doctrines of Neoplatonism were strange to English drama before 1633, when Walter Montague's *Shepherd's Paradise*, the play which introduced the type, was first performed. Traditions of Neoplatonism had found full expression in the nondramatic poetry of England certainly from the time of Spenser, if not before, and it was inevitable that echoes of this philosophy should, almost from the first, find their way into serious English drama. What was essentially new in Montague's play and in the host of offspring to which it stood parent, was the use of Neoplatonic theories, especially those dealing with love, as a motivating agent for the entire "manners" of the drama. Not only do the characters discourse in Neoplatonic accents, but the whole action of the play grows out of situations brought about by *living* in Neoplatonic terms. Good "Anglo-Saxon attitudes" are lamentably wanting, and, as Miss Lynch observes, such

---

3. The figures for each play, indicating the number of times the stage is left vacant, are: *The Lady-Errant*, 8; *The Royal Slave*, 11; *The Siege*, 18; *The Ordinary*, 19.

4. *Cavalier Drama*, p. 28.

5. See some comments on Cartwright's *Royal Slave* and *The Siege* and their connection with Fletcherian tragicomedy in F. H. Ristine's *English Tragicomedy—Its Origin and History* (1910), pp. 143-44.

action as the play presents has to depend largely upon argument and syllogism. With Fletcher plot and action were paramount; with the Cavalier dramatists plot and action were merely the vehicles for the expression of a philosophical and ethical code.[6] The play was not the thing.

When we examine Cartwright's plays in the light of this general criticism, we find that in all essentials of tone and atmosphere, if not in structure, they are perhaps more representative than the plays of any other dramatist. As regards structure we have already seen that Cartwright was something of a reactionary, clinging, except in *The Royal Slave*, to a strongly developed comic underplot. It is also true that his plays are constructed with greater attention to unity and finish than is generally the case with other Cavalier dramas. This care for dramatic form was likewise an inheritance from earlier playwrights, particularly Jonson and Fletcher,[7] whom Cartwright honored above all others. For this reason Mr. Harbage's description of the Platonic play as sprawling, with fortuitous and illogical action and lacking in dramatic build-up to a denouement, does not apply too seriously as a particular criticism of Cartwright.[8] On the other hand, his plays reveal all the faults incident to overmuch reliance on the props of rhetoric and argument. Like those of the other dramatists, his characters say too much and do too little; and even the little they do tends to stamp them as lifeless puppets rather than as human beings. Again, when we examine the most typical plot characteristics of Cavalier drama, we are forced to call Cartwright old fashioned. Here are no pirates or freebooters, no woman in disguise who serves her lover as a page, no child recovered after being lost at birth.[9] In the Platonic drama, however, manner was everything, and this manner is preeminently Cartwright's. His plays, moreover, give the most thorough and reasoned discussion of Platonic love doctrines to be found in drama—perhaps a doubtful distinction, but, for the moment, important. I feel forced

---

6. Harbage, *Cavalier Drama*, pp. 43–45.

7. It was also probably from Fletcher that Cartwright acquired his taste for lush natural imagery. Writing a little before 1660, Samuel Holland (*Romancio-Mastix*, 1660, p. 102) pictures Cartwright in the Underworld among the champions of Shakespeare and Fletcher, who are described as "surrounded with their Life-Guard, Viz. Goffe, Massinger, Decker, Webster, Sucklin, Cartwright, Carew, etc."

8. *Cavalier Drama*, pp. 41–42.

9. *Ibid.*, pp. 31–33. Any one of these, except perhaps the first, might be paralleled in the earlier drama, but in Cavalier plays they tend to become chronic.

to offer, therefore, a tedious brief compendium of Cartwright's Platonic-love philosophy as it is developed in the three tragi-comedies. The classification is purely arbitrary.

Love.—Love is a strong desire to be united to what is fair and beautiful by the most perfect means that nature yields or reason teaches. Love is both eternal and without beginning. Love is common to all creatures, but honor is peculiar to man. Love, because it is essentially good, must be diffusive; unconfined to a single point, it can spread its influence over all nature, retaining its vigor and chastity unimpaired. The sphere of virtue is especially proper to woman, since a woman's soul consists of love and sense; a man's soul of sense and reason. Love in a woman's soul performs the office of reason in a man's soul, i.e., produces virtue; hence a woman's soul is "ripe" when very young, while the soul of man has to gain virtue through the exercise of reason. As reason governs man, so love—the prime mover of the universe—governs woman. It is the duty of a good man to worship woman, for, gifted with inherent love, woman was born to rule. Souls frame the body; therefore the beautiful must needs be good. There are no sexes in the mind. Pure love can enter only the virtuous mind; therefore a lover must be virtuous. All love has its complement preordained by the Gods.

The way of true love.—True love consists in the perfect union of souls; it loves not the person but the virtue. The eyes are love's entrance ports. In the eyes love kindles a fire by which reason purges out all grossness and makes the flame of love burn clear as a divine idea of the mind. A lover must love those qualities of excellence in his mistress which he finds wanting in himself; woman is, therefore, the complement of man. Love strikes very suddenly, but the approach to love must be gradual; trial and difficulty refine love. Beasts and plants both move to propagate their kind, but human love must be higher and must move to make itself immortal. Immortality is accomplished by each dying in himself, or herself, to live in something created out of both their deaths. Any pure love must be returned by the admired one because it is an offspring of her own beauty. True love is able to create a presence in the mind so that the absence of a lover is no let to happiness. Souls in love are governed by reason to suppress passion and to move in a regular motion toward the loved one; anything else which the soul may strive for is but a digression, not a true journey of the soul. Love will not disappoint; once lovers have expressed their love of hearts through their eyes, the rest may be left to the care of the deities. The course of true love once begun is inevitable. Before love all stations in life are equal; the love of a princess is not preferred before the love of a chambermaid.

Lets in love.—Desire alone blinds us. The God of Love is not blind; he is pure sight, the sight of the soul. Love itself is never indiscreet, only the lover is indiscreet. A vaunted favor violates a pure spotless honor, but a favor seen does not. To kiss a mistress against her will in an excess of passion destroys the communion of spirits, for sensuous love, typified by a kiss, is, like the love of beasts, devoid of reason. If chastity is injured the mind suffers, for chastity is but an attribute of the mind. Jealousy, though an apparent enemy of love, really arises not from distrust but from a proper care of the beloved. Only jealousy in excess is a curse. The senses, however, are not to be completely banished, for as we must please the mind and soul so must we also feed the sight and touch. Temperance in pleasure—the middle road—is all.

The joys of friendship.—True friends are one in mind and sense; think with each other's thoughts, hear and see with each other's ears and eyes. In the absence of his friend, a friend may even be loved by his friend's mistress—platonically. The friendship or love of a wife for someone other than her husband is really a compliment to the husband, inasmuch as what she admires in the other man is but a reflection of those virtues for which she loves her husband. Even after death the happiness of the survivor is a source of joy to his dead friend.[10]

A word should be said about Cartwright as a dramatist. If we define a dramatist as one who, while he holds the mirror up to nature, makes his characters act and speak like men and women and chooses his situations where they may most strike "home to our business and bosoms," Cartwright will cut but a sorry figure. At best, his plays are the expression of a fashion:

---

10. If the reader is further interested he may consult the characteristics of the Platonic love doctrine as they are listed in Miss Lynch's "Conventions of Platonic Drama in the Heroic Plays of Orrery and Dryden," *PMLA*, XLIV (1929), 461–70.

> But this 'tis when women sit at the helm of state,
> They square all Court entertainments to the fashion
> Of the last Romance they heard.[11]

From the standpoint of drama this fashion had nothing to commend it. Even the ethics it preached was warped—if not immoral, at best amoral. To call Cartwright a rhetorical puppet-master is harsh. Yet his characters are worked by ethical strings instead of muscles. They speak, from a single mouth and with a single voice, words which are pitched in a uniformly high, resounding tone.

> ... in florid impotence he speaks,
> And, as the prompter breathes, the puppet squeaks.
>
> —*Pope.*

Not as in great dramatic figures do their thoughts and actions arise from internal struggle or suffering. All is external—on, but never under, the polite surface. And it is this condition of externality, more than anything else perhaps, that distinguishes and disgraces not only Cartwright but all his fellow Cavalier dramatists.

If, on the other hand, we are able to overlook, if not to forgive, these weaknesses, we may yet find something to praise. In the eighteenth century Cartwright seems to have had a reputation for being one of the few dramatists of his time who invented his own plots.[12] Although this was very largely a misconception, such a judgment is an indirect tribute to Cartwright's adroitness in managing and combining his materials. His plays are always thoroughly, if a little

---

11. William Chamberlayne, *Love's Victory* (1658), V, vii. Miss Lynch considers D'Urfé's *L'Astrée* (its last part was published 1627) as the original source of most of the court Platonic love cult (*PMLA*, XLIV, 459-60).

12. See John Ferriar's "Essay on the Dramatic Writings of Massinger," printed in Gifford's *Plays of Philip Massinger* (1840), p. xxix. In a footnote Ferriar later adds: "Cartwright and Congreve, who resemble each other strongly in some remarkable circumstances, are almost our only dramatists who have any claim to originality in their plots." Although I doubt the real originality of either writer, the comparison with Congreve is interesting. Ferriar refers, I suppose, to Congreve's failure as a "natural" dramatist, to his inability to paint more than the externals of character. As Leigh Hunt remarks: "Congreve's characters can all of them speak well, they are mere machines when they come to act. Our author's superiority deserted him almost entirely with his wit. His serious and tragic poetry is frigid and jejune to an unaccountable degree." (*The Dramatic Works of Wycherley, Congreve, Vanbrugh, and Farquhar*, 1871, p. lxxiii). In many respects this criticism might be applied to Cartwright. Further "remarkable circumstances" of resemblance between these two men I cannot suggest, except a possible borrowing from *The Royal Slave* in Congreve's opera, *Semele*, which will be pointed out in the note on line 1573SD.

stiffly, constructed, and his eye is usually alert for theatrical effect, which if not a virtue *per se*, is an important part of good play-making. Whether the general morality of *The Ordinary*, his only comedy, can be defended I doubt, but no one will deny that there are in it moments of wit, if not humor, and scenes of considerable comic force. Thus, within the rhetorical limits already set down, Cartwright is capable of good, even compelling, verse. Indeed, in this respect he is not at all inferior to any of the more fashionable Cavalier dramatists, and he has at his command a finer turn for courtly expression and compliment than many a professed courtier. But his highest praise lies in "finished excellence," his plays are consciously and painstakingly constructed, his power of clear expression is always under perfect control, his verse is carefully wrought and "filed"—in a word, "good form" is the keystone of his work.

Cartwright's blank verse, which, from the viewpoint of manner, has been characterized as rhetorical in the extreme, may technically be compared best with that of Massinger and Shirley, particularly in its high percentage of run-on lines and light, or weak, endings. *The Royal Slave*, for example, shows 51 per cent of run-on lines and 14 per cent of light and weak endings. Where Cartwright and Shirley differ most from Massinger, apart from their characteristic verse movement, is in their relatively slighter use of double or feminine, endings.[13] In point of mere technique, Cartwright is superior to most of the other court dramatists. Suckling, Carlell, and D'Avenant are slipshod by comparison, though sometimes more moving.

Until very recently it has been generally taken for granted that none of Cartwright's plays was revived after the Restoration. This view was based on purely negative evidence: the complete lack of performance records. How untrustworthy such evidence is appears from the recent discovery of Restoration prompt copies of both *The Lady-Errant* and *The Ordinary*.[14] Through the kindness of Dr. W. B. Van Lennep, who directed my attention to these prompt

---

13. Figures for a metrical analysis of *The Royal Slave* in percentages are as follows: run-on lines, 51.2; weak endings, 3.7; light endings, 11.4; double, or feminine, endings, 28.8; divided lines, 10.6.

14. Even before these prompt copies were brought to my attention, I was able to postulate a Restoration performance of *The Ordinary* on the strength of a prologue and epilogue "To the Ordinary," printed in a *Collection of Poems* (1673), pp. 163–68. (See the Introduction to *The Ordinary*.)

copies, I have been privileged to examine them and to make full use of the new material which they offer.[15] Since Restoration prompt copies of pre-Restoration plays are rare—only two others[16] being known to me—it will be worth our while to examine these in some detail. Unlike surviving pre-Restoration prompt copies, which are all in manuscript, these prompt copies make use of a printed text, that of the *Works* (1651)—the only text for *The Lady-Errant* and *The Ordinary*. Two distinct kinds of editing must be carefully distinguished in the deletions and changes which are freely made in both plays. Before a play could be acted by professional players, it was necessary to secure the license of the Master of the Revels.[17] This official was interested in a play solely for its moral and political aspects. Profane allusions to the deity, other oaths, and indecent references generally must be formally deleted (even if later restored by the actors), and any dangerous political opinions or tendencies summarily "exploded" before they could exercise their seduction on the audience. Late in 1671, when *The Lady-Errant* and *The Ordinary* came up for consideration by the authorities, Sir Henry Herbert, nominally at least, was still Master of the Revels, and both licenses are signed by him, while the license to *The Ordinary* is entirely in his autograph.

After the Revels Office was finished with a play, censorship as it is generally understood seems to have ended, and matters thereafter seem to have rested entirely in the hands of the theater manager or reviser and the actors, in the present instance the Duke's Company

---

15. The volume containing the prompt copies is the property of Professor T. W. Baldwin of the University of Illinois. Dr. Van Lennep's help and advice have been invaluable in dealing with this material.

16. James Shirley's *The Sisters* (1652), preserved at Sion College, London (see *Poetical and Dramatic Works of Sir Charles Sedley*, ed. V. de Sola Pinto, 1928, I, 300); and Shackerley Marmion's *A Fine Companion* (1633), in the British Museum, Grenville collection (see *Dramatic Works*, ed. Maidment and Logan, 1875, p. xviii).

17. Immediately after the Restoration, considerable trouble ensued between the two new royal patentees, Thomas Killigrew and William D'Avenant, and the representative of the old regime, Sir Henry Herbert, Master of the Revels since 1623. After a good deal of recrimination and letter writing, Sir Henry was reinstated in his old position. A letter from Humphrey Moseley, 1660, has been preserved, in which he denies that he has reached any agreement with Mr. Rhodes of the Cockpit playhouse (later taken over by D'Avenant under the title of the Duke's Company) to act any plays belonging to him. (See *The Dramatic Records of Sir Henry Herbert*, ed. J. Q. Adams, 1917, pp. 87ff.) Some agreement must later have been reached with Moseley, since both *The Lady-Errant* and *The Ordinary* were his property.

under D'Avenant.[18] These men looked at the text with eyes very different from those of pious old Sir Henry, to whom "i'faith" was a parlous oath maugre royal assertions to the contrary. The play is the thing, and every effort must now be bent to make it good entertainment.

Two different handwritings and at least four different inks can be distinguished in both *The Lady-Errant* and *The Ordinary*. One hand is that of the prompter who is responsible for indications of scene settings, lists of needed properties, stage directions, and calls. The other hand belongs to the actual reviser. He it is who remodels speeches by omissions and additions, reassigns speeches, and is generally responsible for cuts and rearrangements. Both hands may be observed at work in the pages reproduced from the prompt copy (facing pp. 86 and 260). It is possible that a third hand (also that of a reviser) may be seen very occasionally in *The Ordinary*.

With the stimulus of a practical aim always in the foreground, long rhetorical speeches are shortened, figurative and fanciful language pruned and obsolete words replaced by a more current idiom, whole scenes cut out or shifted, dances introduced wherever possible —even where apparently impossible—parts altered, and, finally, some of Herbert's deletions restored. In short everything was done to adapt the play to the theatrical demands of the moment—a species of opportunism which has its justification, we are told, in the size of the box-office receipts. In all fairness to these Restoration adapters, however, it must be allowed that Cartwright does not suffer by their attentions. The changes made are nearly always improvements. Indeed, they are the sort of changes which almost any intelligent modern reader feels time and again like making himself. A more detailed account of these playhouse alterations will be given in the separate introductions to *The Lady-Errant* and *The Ordinary*.

In conclusion, we must glance briefly at F. G. Fleay's suggestion that Cartwright had some hand in completing and preparing for the press Fletcher's *The Bloody Brother*.[19] Later writers, Oliphant for

---

18. It seems probable that Cartwright's plays first came to the notice of the Duke's Company during their performances in Oxford during the Act in 1669 or 1671. (See W. J. Lawrence, *TLS*, Jan. 16, 1930, p. 43.) It is perhaps worth noticing that Ralph Bathurst, who had earlier been a friend of Cartwright's, was at this time president of Trinity College. He was especially known for his patronage of the drama.

19. *A Biographical Chronicle of the English Drama* (1891), I, 203-4.

example,[20] do not so much deny as ignore the suggestion. According to Oliphant, the play must be most deplorably minced up, by the approved rule-of-thumb method, between Fletcher, Massinger, Jonson, and an unknown.[21] The lines assigned to the "unknown" (particularly III, i, 1-55) are assuredly not by Cartwright. Indeed the only passages in the whole play (I, i, 45-85) which bear any resemblance to Cartwright's usual style are unanimously assigned to Massinger by the critics, except Fleay, who provisionally gives them to Middleton.[22]

Although I do not in any way desire to press Cartwright's claim, I feel bound to point out an interesting coincidence which lends at least negative support to Fleay's theory. The first mention of *The Bloody Brother* in Herbert's records, under the title *Rollo*, comes on January 17 (or 24), 1636/7, on which occasion the play was revived and presented at Hampton Court.[23] At the time, therefore, or shortly before, Cartwright was actually on the ground, since his own *Royal Slave* was the entertainment which (on January 12) immediately preceded this performance. The evidence is negative and may mean nothing, but it is at least worth noticing. Two quarto editions of *The Bloody Brother* were issued, the first in 1639 at London, the second, with the title *The Tragœdy of Rollo Duke of Normandy*, a year later (1640) at Oxford. The Oxford edition seems to have been Fleay's principal reason for connecting Cartwright with the play. In that text the acts are divided according to the neoclassical theory of entrances and exits, a method which Cartwright observes in all his plays. To draw any conclusions from this fact, however, is unsafe. Too many others, particularly the academic playwrights, employed the same system. Another point in connection with the Oxford edition which might be wrested into evidence for Cartwright is the assignment of the play solely to John Fletcher. *The Bloody Brother* was entered in the Stationers' Register under the initials "J.B.," whereas the 1639 London quarto purported to be by "B.J.F."[24]

---

20. E. H. C. Oliphant, *The Plays of Beaumont and Fletcher* (1927), p. 459.

21. In an earlier study (*Englische Studien*, XV [1891], 354-55) Mr. Oliphant includes Middleton as a collaborator.

22. "Metrical Tests as Applied to Dramatic Poetry," Part II (*New Shakspere Society's Transactions*, first series, 1874, p. 60). But see his later *Biographical Chronicle of the English Drama*, p. 203, where he also assigns the scene to Massinger.

23. *The Dramatic Records of Sir Henry Herbert*, ed. J. Q. Adams (1917), pp. 57, 76, Fleay, *Biographical Chronicle of the English Drama*, p. 203.

24. Oliphant, *The Plays of Beaumont*

Cartwright's championship of Fletcher as a dramatist who needed no collaborators is well known. Gayley, indeed, accuses Cartwright of originating the myth which turned Beaumont into a mere editor of Fletcher's too exuberant plays.[25] Finally, an examination of the Oxford quarto shows that, in spite of the superficial care exercised in scene division, the text is poorer than that of the 1639 London edition; bad line division is particularly noticeable. In fact, it is not the sort of text which we should expect from the meticulous Cartwright. There are, moreover, several stage directions given wholly in Latin, a practice foreign to Cartwright's known usage. Hence, although no definite verdict can be returned in a case of this kind, my own judgment makes me dismiss Fleay's suggestion as probably only another example of the literary mare's-nest, a Shandean hobby-horse gone wrong.

---

and Fletcher, p. 458. Whether anything can be made out of the identity of titles between Sir Henry Herbert's *Rollo* and the *Rollo* of the Oxford 1640 edition I do not know. At any rate, I will not "make" it. The coincidence between Cartwright's "military dinner" in *The Ordinary* (II, i) and the Cook's description of the wonderful dishes which he will prepare for the ducal table in *The Bloody Brother* (II, ii) has often been pointed out. All authorities assign this scene to Fletcher. Cartwright took the hint for his "military dinner" from *Neptune's Triumph* (1624) of Jonson, who had in turn borrowed the idea from Fletcher.

25. C. M. Gayley, *Beaumont, the Dramatist* (1914), p. 209. See also W. J. Lawrence, *Pre-Restoration Stage Studies*, 1927, pp. 356–57, 358.

III

THE POEMS

SEVENTEENTH-CENTURY POETRY, like the poetry of all ages, may be studied as a true perspective of its time. Though less strikingly objective and impersonal than eighteenth-century verse, the poetry of seventeenth-century England forms a close commentary upon the trends of thought, religion, and politics in an age which began with God at the center of man's universe and ended with new universes, men wiser in their own conceit, and a strange God—from Spenser and Hooker to Rochester and Locke.

Cartwright's role in this great story was only a slight one, but such as it was, it is mirrored faithfully in his poetry. Before, however, we can appreciate or even understand the poetry, it will be necessary to give our attention to some of the more important influences which, working together—not always very harmoniously perhaps—formed Cartwright's poetic style. Many sources of influence might be suggested, but the most essential may be conveniently reduced to four or five.

Men of Cartwright's type, reactionaries, found themselves facing an increasingly unfriendly, even hostile, world. Harassed by their environment, each man according to his nature felt the urgent necessity of reassertion to create a new faith in the old order. Such a need might find its intellectual expression in two directions. Either the individual sought to reassure himself by probing into the very roots of his personality, as did Sir Thomas Browne in *Religio Medici*; or he turned away from himself to find reassurance in a reaffirmation of the old creed and the old values. The second attitude led to a conplete absorption in the "way of the world," usually interpreted in terms of the "good old days." Of this type were most of the poets of the thirties and forties, including Cartwright, none of them men of great depth of thought, but rather of a fierce activity of mind. Curiously enough, the greatest champion of the "defensive school," because he combined in himself the essentials of both the contemplative and the active attitude, was John Milton, the iconoclast of "forms," who while he cried out against formalism in all its manifestations, defended one of the great dying "forms" in his *Paradise Lost*.[1] Thus in a sense Cartwright and Milton are brothers, though either might have been dismayed by the realization. This defensive attitude toward art and poetry already marks the middle seventeenth century as a thing apart from the later days of the sixteenth, when Sir Philip Sidney could tell the poet to "look in thy heart, and write."

Apart from the inescapable influence exerted upon Cartwright by his academic training and his life in the university, two other literary influences must be reckoned with: Ben Jonson and John Donne. The closeness of Cartwright's relationship with Ben Jonson cannot be questioned. He was "sealed of the Tribe of Ben," and Jonson himself is reported to have said, "My Son *Cartwright* writes all like a Man."[2] Their acquaintance presumably dates from Cartwright's days at Westminster School, where we may picture Ben, himself an old Westminster boy, keeping a fatherly eye upon promising young scholars and poets. Jonson's influence can best be seen in the classical polish, neatness, and impersonal tone of much of Cartwright's verse, and his indebtedness to Jonson the dramatist is abundantly clear in his one comedy, *The Ordinary*. Finally, Cartwright's fondness for the heroic couplet may be traced to the same source. Jonson stood for Cartwright as the great academic ideal of the true poet, a man in whom matter, form, and manner were merged in a perfect trinity. Donne's influence is both less direct and less important. From him Cartwright learned a too free use of the so-called metaphysical conceit. As used by Donne himself the metaphysical conceit became "the very opening of the mouth" of self-expression and emotion. But in the blundering hands of his imitators it all too often lost its emotional potentiality and became an actual barrier to personal expression and feeling. In other words, Cartwright frequently employs the metaphysical conceit with all the fervency of a rhetoric handbook.

One other formative influence may be noticed. The society in which most of the "polite" poets moved, and on the fringes of which

---

1. We may recall in Scott's *Woodstock* (Chapter XV) how old Sir Henry Lee, a typical member of the old order, was delighted by some lines in Milton's *Comus*, until he learned by whom they had been written.

2. See Humphrey Moseley's preface "To the Reader," sig. [¹a5]ʳ.

Cartwright at various times dallied, was essentially a mannered coterie, an artificial synthesis of propriety and hypocrisy. That the literature of such a society should be steeped in convention is inevitable, and convention is one of the keynotes of Cartwright's verse. It is seen in his choice of subjects, in his exaggerated characters, above all in his "philosophy of compliment." In short, Cartwright's verse has all the impersonality and some of the polish and ease of Jonson, the metaphysical conceit gone stale of Donne, and the conventionality of the born courtier, all tempered by the mental attitude of an age on the defensive.

Cartwright's exact position among his contemporaries cannot be too dogmatically decided. To make him, as Mr. Goffin seems to wish,[3] a member of the metaphysical school is, I believe, to set the emphasis in the wrong place. And it is worth observing perhaps that Sir Herbert Grierson includes nothing of Cartwright's verse in his *Metaphysical Lyrics and Poems of the Seventeenth Century* (1921). Mr. P. W. Souers speaks of Cartwright as a leader among the Cavalier poets.[4] This statement too, I feel, needs qualification. Cartwright's poetry judged as a whole is of a very different kind from the poetry of Carew, Suckling, or Lovelace, the three most typical members of the Cavalier school. In these poets there are a deftness of touch, an appearance of spontaneity, and, in the cases of Suckling and Lovelace, a roughness, partly assumed, which are almost entirely lacking in Cartwright. There is, moreover, a lack of serious moral fiber in the men themselves that one does not associate with Cartwright. If Cartwright stoops at times to the fashionable immorality of convention, it is because he was an imitator, not a habitué. He is always "stable,"[5] with a full continuity of tone and accent which reminds us at times of the younger Milton. Despite Moseley's assertion that poetry was Cartwright's recreation and never his business, we cannot escape the feeling of conscious workmanship and artistry in all Cartwright's verse. Such is not the case with the Cavalier poets: even the "hard-bound" Carew does not give us this sensation. Furthermore, we may be sure of one thing;

---

3. *Poems*, pp. xxxii–xxxiv.

4. *The Matchless Orinda* (1931), p. 255. Paul Saunders ("William Cartwright—A Naive Sensualist," *Anathema*, Vol. 1 [1935], No. 2) also describes Cartwright as a Cavalier poet. See my discussion of his article later in this chapter.

5. As the eighteenth-century critic Henry Headley remarks (*Select Beauties of Ancient English Poetry*, 1787, I, xxxvii): "Good sense and solidity are the most prominent features of his poetry."

Cartwright would have been deeply chagrined had we failed to recognize this artistry and conscious "rectitude":

> For thou to Nature had'st joyn'd Art, and skill,
> In Thee *Ben Johnson* still held *Shakespear's* Quill:
> A Quill, rul'd by sharp Judgement, and such Laws,
> As a well studied Mind, and Reason draws.[6]

Admittedly in the choice of subject matter and in other points of convention Cartwright shows all the characteristics of the typical Cavalier poet, particularly in his plays. His political sympathies likewise were all on the Cavalier side. Yet in spite of these obvious affinities, I feel that it would be at least partly misplacing the proper emphasis to call Cartwright a leader of the Cavalier school, even a late leader. He was with them, but not of them. If it is really necessary to "place" him anywhere, he is most thoroughly at home, I believe, in that small group of academic poets among whom we may class Randolph, Corbet, Hall, King, Strode, Mayne, and, in some respects, Cleveland and Cowley. Without exception these men all stem from Father Ben, show more or less of Donne's ingenuity without his passion, and borrow more than a little of the court tinsel of convention. Here, if he must reign somewhere, Cartwright can reign nearly unchallenged.

Cartwright's minor poetry falls naturally into four classes: occasional verse, love poetry, humorous verse, and translations from the classics. But before we examine each of these groups separately something may be said about the general metrical form of Cartwright's verse.

Like other poets of his time, Cartwright employs a wide range of stanza forms.[7] Almost never indeed is the same form repeated, and the stanzas themselves vary from as many as twenty lines to the triplet, neither extreme appearing more than once. Within the stanza Cartwright obtains his happiest effects by a judicious use of the two- and three-stress line. His handling of long irregular stanzas, for example in his "*Ariadne* deserted by *Theseus* . . . in the Island *Naxos*," shows him a master of poetic and musical rhythms, a fact which Henry Lawes recognized when he chose this particular poem to introduce his first book of *Ayres and Dialogues* (1653). The same poem likewise met with Milton's special approval:

---

6. From Jasper Mayne's commendatory poem, prefixed to the *Works* (1651), sig. [¹b4]ᵛ.

7. See the complete metrical analysis of all Cartwright's stanzaic arrangements in Appendix B.

> Thou [Lawes] honour'st Verse, and Verse must lend her wing
> To honour thee, the Priest of *Phœbus* Quire
> That tun'st their happiest lines in Hymn, or Story.

And Pepys sang it to Lawes' setting one morning as he went by water to Erith.[8] It is perhaps worth noticing that Cartwright has no verse in the sonnet form, either English or Italian.

Although more than half of Cartwright's poems use one stanza or another, the great bulk of his verse is composed in the heroic couplet, with occasional use of the four-stress line. Here again we see the influence of Jonson. Cartwright's couplets have a smooth but strong flow and considerable polish:

> No Myst'ry there blocks up the way, no sowre
> Nor rugged Verse that must be scann'd twice o'r;
> But his soft Numbers gently slide away,
> Like Chrystall waters, Smooth, and Deep, as they.
> *Euterpe* was his Muse, Ease and Delight
> Lead us along; we Read as He did Write.[9]

As a rule Cartwright uses the closed couplet, or at least does not employ an excessive number of run-on lines.[10] When we read Pope, or even Dryden, we are conscious of the couplet with its neat turn, it ceaseless antithesis and periphrasis, in a word, its tantalizing perfection. But in Cartwright the couplet, though largely closed, is used as an instrument to fashion a whole; not to express a single thought, but as a link in the development of an idea. We read not from couplet to couplet, from gem to gem, but, undisturbed by the click and snap of a mechanism, are carried through to the end of a full thought-paragraph. Cartwright's fondness for the couplet may be seen even in the stanzaic poems. Rarely indeed, even in the most involved stanzas, does he use anything but couplet rhyme.

The group of occasional poems may best be discussed under three heads: royal or personal panegyric and elegy, verses devoted to religious occasions and experience, and literary criticism in the form of commendatory poetry.[11]

---

8. See the notes to this poem, p. 721. Goffin (*Poems*, p. xxxvii) points out that Cartwright overuses the monosyllable in his lyric verse, a practice which tends to weaken the line.

9. From Ralph Bathurst's commendatory poem, prefixed to the *Works* (1651), sigs. **1v–**2r.

10. "A Translation of *Hugo Grotius's* Elegy on *Arminius*" is an exception. It employs a very high percentage of run-on lines, in one case as many as six consecutive lines.

11. All questions of texts, sources, parallels, et cetera, will be found discussed in the notes to the *Poems*.

Like Dr. Johnson, Cartwright "dedicated to the royal family all round." There are, in all, eleven English poems addressed to various members of the reigning family[12] and many references to them in other poems. Each of the more numerous than dignified royal births is chronicled, until, upon the appearance of a sixth child, even the stalwart Cartwright becomes a little querulous:

> Though all Your Royall Burthens should come forth
> Dischargd by Emanation, not by Birth;
> Though You could so prove Mother, as the Soule,
> When it doth most conceive without controule;
> Though Princes should so frequent from You flow,
> That we might thence say, Sun-Beames issue slow. . . .

On one occasion only did Cartwright miss an opportunity of paying his respects to the throne. When in 1641 Oxford published *Euchoristica Oxoniensia*, congratulating Charles on his safe return from Scotland, Cartwright contributed no verses. The best of his royal eulogies are "To the King, on the Birth of the Princess *Anne*"[13] and "On the *Queens* Return from the Low Countries," the last, especially, containing some extremely fine lines.

Among his panegyrics and elegies to private individuals Cartwright has perhaps more than the usual share of successes. As Mr. Souers points out,[14] in writing verse of this type it was Cartwright's custom to reconstruct an idealized portrait of the individual. Some of his portraits are frankly unpleasing—for example, the long and fulsome eulogy on Lucy, Countess of Carlisle, and a later poem "On the Lady *Newburgh*, who dyed of the small Pox." Others, however, possess considerable charm, at times considerable poetic virtue. Such are "To Mr *W. B.* at the Birth of his first Child," "An Epitaph on Mr. *Poultney*," "The death of the Right valiant Sir *Bevill Grenvill* Knight," "On a vertuous young Gentlewoman that dyed suddenly," and parts of "To the memory of a Shipwrackt Virgin." It would not be difficult to enlarge this list, and it can be added truthfully that no one of Cartwright's poems in this genre falls below the common

---

12. This does not include the special dedication to King Charles prefixed to *The Siege* (*Works*, 1651, sig. G1) nor the doubtful verses, "On the Prince Charles death" (Folger MS. 646.4, pp. [158]–59) here printed for the first time. There are in addition nine Latin poems also addressed to members of the royal family. What is probably Cartwright's earliest published work (Latin) was a poem of this type. It appeared in *Britanniae Natalis* (1630), an Oxford publication in honor of the birth of Prince Charles.

13. Particularly the second part, "To the Queen."

14. *The Matchless Orinda*, p. 266.

standards of such poetry—poetry which, never of a very high order, can easily degenerate into a rant of hyperbole not worthy the name of verse. Cartwright's use of the courtly compliment is unsurpassed even by avowed court poets. No one could better the delicacy of such couplets as

> Things twice seene loose; but when a King or Queene
> Commands a second sight, they're then first seene,[15]

and

> Pardon, thou Soul of Goodness, if I wrong
> Thine Ample Vertues with a sparing Tongue,
> Alas, I am compell'd, speaking of thee,
> To use one of thy Vertues, Modesty,[16]

or

> Forgive, thou all of goodness, if that I
> By praising blemish, too much Majesty
> Injures it self: where Art cannot express
> It veyls and leaves the rest unto a Guess.[17]

Cartwright's small body of religious verse is not very impressive. He was not by nature, I believe, a deeply religious man. There is nothing in him of the mystic. On the other hand, I am not prepared to say, as Mr. Goffin seems to hint, that he failed to take his entrance into the ministry seriously.[18] All we can learn from his writings and from contemporary accounts points him out as a man who, once embarked on an undertaking, would strive with soul and body to carry it through honestly. In "Consideration," the first example of religious verse in the 1651 volume, written probably in 1638 before entering holy orders,[19] we find an early expression of what later,

---

15. From the third prologue to *The Royal Slave*, ll. 24-25.
16. "On Mrs *Abigall Long*, who dyed of two Impostumes," ll. 57-60.
17. "On the Lady *Newburgh*, who dyed of the small Pox," ll. 57-60.
18. *Poems*, p. xxx. Goffin bases a good part of his inference upon a misreading of a line from "A New-years-gift to *Brian* Lord Bishop of *Sarum*" (ll. 11-12):

> "But being the Canon bars me Wit and Wine,
> Enjoying the true Vine."

The *Works* (1651), the only textual authority for this poem, reads "Enjoyning."

19. It is perhaps worth noticing in connection with Moseley's statement, "here is but one Sheet was written after he entred *Holy Orders*; some before He was twenty years old, scarce any after five and twenty," that so far as it is possible to date any of the poems all those which were written *after* 1638 (and they far exceed a single sheet) *follow* this poem in the *Works* (1651). (The poem on Stokes would seem to be an exception, since the book which Cartwright is eulogizing, *The Vaulting*

under the influence of Vaughan and Traherne, came to be known as the "philosophy of the child."[20] This short poem and some lines in the best of his religious poems, "A New-years-gift to *Brian* Lord Bishop of *Sarum*," constitute almost the whole of Cartwright's personal poetic utterance. It is true that occasionally a personal note seems to be struck in the love lyrics, but how much is the true voice of Cartwright and how much the personal impersonality of convention we can only guess. The three short poems on the Nativity, the Circumcision, and the Epiphany were set to music, probably by Henry Lawes. The *Works* (1651) concludes with a highly conventional and artificial poem entitled "Confession," an obvious tailpiece, which one cannot avoid feeling was written expressly for its present position. It "confesses" nothing.

Some of Cartwright's best verse, written "all like a man," is to be found among his elegiac and commendatory poems to literary men. There are, in all, seven such poems: two addressed to Fletcher, and one each to Jonson, Killigrew, Kynaston, Spelman, and William Stokes.[21] As a general rule this type of verse is worthless either as serious criticism or as poetry, truth being cast to the four winds in favor of friendship and rhyme. The many commendatory poems prefixed to Cartwright's own *Works* (1651) are in most cases only too good examples of the common order. " 'Tis," says Donne, "the pre-eminence / Of friendship only to impute excellence," two lines in which he penned the general epitaph of commendatory verse. Very rarely, however, in the case of writers like Jonson, Carew, and Cartwright, the genre rose above its fate and developed into a valuable, and one of the earliest, instruments of criticism.

To substantiate Cartwright's claims as a critic, we cannot do

---

Master, was not published until 1641. Cartwright's poem, however, was not among the other commendatory verses then printed, which possibly suggests that it was written earlier upon seeing Stokes' manual in manuscript.) Though Moseley's arrangement may be more the result of luck than good guidance, it is quite possible that he possessed special information, or was setting up from a manuscript arranged for him by a close friend of Cartwright's, like Brian Duppa, or even from Cartwright's autograph. Moseley ("To the Reader," sig. [¹a4]ʳ) writes: "from whose own *Manuscripts* you have this *Impression*." I do not, of course, suggest that too much weight can be attached to the position of "Consideration" in the *Works* (1651), but it should at least be taken into account in dating individual poems.

20. There is another echo of this same "philosophy" in "To the Memory of the most vertuous Mrs *Ursula Sadleir*" (ll. 49-54).

21. The poem on William Stokes will be noticed later among Cartwright's humorous verse.

better than to analyse and contrast the two poems on Fletcher and the poem on Jonson.[22] The main thesis which Cartwright maintains in both the poems on Fletcher is that Fletcher as a dramatist could stand alone, without the advice and collaboration of Beaumont. The poem on Jonson has no particular ax to grind except in so far as it defends Jonson against the charges of plagiarism from the classics and tries to palliate Jonson's late failure as a dramatist.

Fletcher was admittedly of too exuberant a fancy, but he was capable of acting as his own critic without any aid from Beaumont; witness his *Faithful Shepherdess*. He combined in his genius art, language, and wit [note the omission of nature], and could raise the various passions at will. His scenes are well timed, strong, and vigorous, and do not drag to their conclusion. No one can anticipate the denouement from the first scenes of his plays. Light and shade [comic and tragic elements?] are so used that each is revealed, but not overstressed. Business [the unravelling of plot by intrigue and counterplot] grows continuously to the climax and then works to the denouement in a regular falling movement. Each of the characters is perfectly sustained throughout the play, in mental reaction and speech, outward motion and appearance. Fletcher's muse occupies a place just between "*Johnsons* grave, and *Shakespeares* lighter sound." It is quite distinctive and knew how to please all palates [referring perhaps to tragicomedy]. Fletcher truly understood the passion of love. Jonson's love-scenes by comparison are cold and frosty. He could write comedies as well as pastoral and romantic drama. Shakespeare's wit [observe the point of comparison] was dull compared with his, old-fashioned, and now considered obscene and bawdy. Fletcher's comic vein was as free as Shakespeare's, but was free from his scurrility. It came unforced, "cleane, chast, and unvext." Fletcher was no plagiarist, nor did he write merely for money. Hence his productions have more than a mercenary inspiration to give them life. Of all that was ever produced by ease, wine, or wit Fletcher's writings are the best [the motivating agents are worth noticing].

If we turn from this sketch of Fletcher to the elegy on Ben Jonson,[23]

---

22. It is presumably of poems like these by Cartwright and others that Dryden is thinking in his "Prologue to the University of Oxford" (1674) when he writes:

With joy we bring what our dead Authors writ,
And beg from you the value of their Wit·
That *Shakespear's*, *Fletcher's*, and great *Johnson's* Claim
May be renew'd from those who gave them Fame.

A contemporary notice of the poem on Jonson appears in the commendatory verses of William Stanton, prefixed to the *Works* (1651), sig. [****2]ʳ:

O could we mourn thy Fall with such a Verse
As thou didst powre on honour'd *Johnson*'s Hearse!
An *Elegie* so high and wisely writ,
It shews who is and who is not a Wit;
Which had He liv'd to read, He had defi'd
All the mad World, having Thee on his side;
For Thou so praisest Him, thy *Eulogy*
Still dwels on Him, and yet rebounds to Thee;
Thine and His Temples jointly Crown'd: elsewhere
Thou outwrit'st Others, but thy own self there.

23. Headley (*Select Beauties of Ancient English Poetry*, 1787, II, 158) characterizes this poem by saying: "There is a masculine flow of good sense in this panegyric that places Cartwright very high both as a poet and a critic."

Cartwright's critical powers become increasingly evident. Observe particularly how the two men are contrasted and distinguished. Modern criticism and taste would not perhaps unreservedly endorse all of Cartwright's judgments, but no one can deny the essential truth of his insight into character and production.

> Ben Jonson is the Father of Poets. Present-day poetry when judged by his laws appears like the ravings of a lunatic. He exhibits such realistic portraits in his characters that each observer takes the character to be his own. He anticipated the present generation in his delineation of "manners" to such an extent that "manners" of today form a comment on his plays. It is merely a question of "living o're" his models. His use of language is such that its parts work inevitably into a whole and he always finds the exact word for the context. The soul of Jonson's works is "proportion'd *decencie*" [decorum]. His plots are so particularly excellent that they almost "untie" themselves and never require the services of a "deus ex machina" to "cut" them. He chose uncongenial subjects for many of his plays and never took the road of least resistance to popular favor. He was not prodigal of his intellectual wealth, but knew when to conserve and when to dispense it freely [compare Fletcher]. Jonson, unlike the writers of the present day, who pour out all they have, and themselves too, into a single play, transcribes not himself but his age [manners]. Hence his plays depict the "common *life*, theirs [but] their *owne*." His characters never constitute libels upon particular persons, but they strike at the vice and spare the individual. His sharp attacks on vice do less harm than the quiet acceptance of those who condone or excuse it. His plays are all moral and promote morality in the reader and spectator. Jonson owed nothing to the advice of others. Judgment and right sense were his only guides. A "stout *beauty*" was his grace, but, since such severer pleasures in their very nature partake something of a sterner cast, his muse, yet fair to behold, carries a spear in her right hand. His slowness in composing is a virtue, for he wrote not for "sodaine *pay*" but for posterity. He was read almost as a classic during his own life time. No blame must attach to him for rifling the treasures of antiquity, for he made his cullings flourish anew in a fresh and living soil. Although Jonson's last plays fall short of the high standard of his early ones, they will nevertheless be appreciated in the years to come.

The remaining three poems to Kynaston, Spelman, and Killigrew add nothing to Cartwright's reputation as a critic, the closing lines on Killigrew's future reputation being particularly unfortunate:

> And if Mens approbations be not Lot,
> And my prophetique Bayes seduce me not;
> Whiles he, who straines for swelling scenes, lyes dead
> Or onely prays'd, you shall live prays'd, and read.

The consideration of the second principal group of Cartwright's poems, the love lyrics, brings our discussion to the edges of that small world where occasional superlatives may be used without apology. In a note to Jonson's "Celebration of Charis" Gifford writes:

> There is a considerable degree of ease and elegance in these effusions; and indeed it may be observed in general of our poet's lyrics, that a vein of sprightliness and fancy runs through them which a reader of his epistles, &c., is scarcely prepared to expect. In the latter, Jonson, like several other poets of his age, or rather of his school, who also succeeded in lyrics, sedulously reins in the imagination, and contents himself with strength of sentiment and thought, in simple but vigorous language and unambitious rhyme.

With only slight qualifications this criticism of Jonson may be applied to the two extremes of Cartwright's pen, and it is a comparison which would have given Cartwright, the "Son of Ben," a peculiar satisfaction. While it is true that his occasional verse shows a fondness for intellectual ingenuity not often found in Jonson and that his lyrics have perhaps a more studied air, the essential lines of the comparison hold good and form at the same time one of the most revealing evidences of Cartwright's true literary affiliations.

"A naive sensualist" is the title conferred upon Cartwright in an article by Mr. Paul Saunders.[24] Mr. Saunders deals solely with Cartwright's love poetry and hence sees him in a very one-sided light. For example, to style Cartwright "the laureate of the body" is going rather far. But Mr. Saunders displays a genuine regard for Cartwright as a lyricist, and his remark that he "had the misfortune, as far as posthumous fame is concerned, to be born in the most brilliant age of English poetry," is worth pondering. The phrase "a naive sensualist" is in many ways a peculiarly happy one, but not quite as Mr. Saunders means it. It expresses for me the paradox of Cartwright's love poetry. For while these lyrics give every outward evidence of a conventional, abandoned type of sensualism, they were written, I am convinced, by an essentially temperate man. They are the expression of the poet's reading rather than of his living, a means of escape from the reality. This view will explain what Mr. Saunders characterizes as a "blunt" quality in Cartwright's sense imagery. He lacked the delicacy of experience.

Among the best of these love poems we may single out such almost perfect verses as "To *Chloe*, who wish'd her self young enough for me," "No Platonique Love," "Falshood," "A Song of Dalliance," "*Lesbia* On her Sparrow," and "A Valediction." Mr. Bullen considers "A Song of Dalliance" the finest of all Cartwright's

---

24. "William Cartwright—A Naive Sensualist," *Anathema* (1935), Vol. I, No. 2.

lyrics and slyly suggests that many more poems of this type would go far to explain his great contemporary reputation. Within the impersonal and conventional limits of Caroline love poetry, they are all lyrics of a very high order, marked by a finish and simplicity which may rival the work of greater masters. Two songs in the plays also deserve special notice, "Wake my *Adonis*, do not dye" from *The Lady-Errant*, and "Come my sweet, whiles every strayne" from *The Royal Slave*. The first song was set to music by Dr. Coleman, the second by Henry Lawes, whose fondness for Cartwright's verse has already been noticed.[25] "The *Ayres* and *Songs* set by Mr *HENRY LAWES*" appears on the title-page of Cartwright's *Works* (1651), and settings for several poems, in addition to those already mentioned, including "To *Cupid*," "To *Venus*," and eight lines from "The Teares," have been preserved.[26]

The two remaining divisions, humorous verse and translations from the classics, do not require much comment. In the first group I include such poems as "On the great Frost. 1634," and "A Bill of Fare," neither of which can be classed as purely humorous verse. Only two of Cartwright's poems, "The Chambermaids Posset" and "On Mr *Stokes* his Book on the Art of Vaulting," deserve this title.[27] The other two are brought under this head, however, because they illustrate Cartwright's ingenuity at work on subjects capable of a "witty" treatment. "On the great Frost. 1634" is Cartwright's nearest approach to "Clevelandism." "On Mr *Stokes*," properly a commendatory poem in the bantering vein, contains humorous passages which make us wish that Cartwright had written more verse of this sort, and wasted less time on the fatuities of compliment.

Most sixteenth-century and seventeenth-century translations of classic poetry are more remarkable for vigor than fidelity. To this general rule Cartwright, I believe, forms something of an exception. His translations, while they retain all the Elizabethan vigor, sacrifice little of the text. The translation of Horace's "Audivere Lyce" is perhaps the best.[28]

---

25. See also Lawes' commendatory poem to Cartwright, prefixed to the *Works* (1651), sig. **1^r.

26. Full data on the musical texts may be found in the notes to each poem.

27. Perhaps we should also include "Now thou our future Brother" from *The Ordinary* (IV, v).

28. We must include among the translations two not of classical origin: "Love inconcealable," from the Italian of Stigliani, a near contemporary, and "A Translation of *Hugo Grotius's* Elegy on *Arminius*."

Some lines by Henry Vaughan, Silurist, may introduce a fitting conclusion for this chapter:

> I'll tell them (and a *truth* which needs no *Pass*)
> That *Wit* in *Cartwright* at her *Zenith* was.
> *Arts, Fancy, Language,* all conven'd in thee. . . .[29]

Here Vaughan unerringly places his finger on what is perhaps Cartwright's principal characteristic both as a man and as a poet —his wit, wit not as we understand the term today, nor quite in the highly laudatory sense in which Vaughan meant it, but simply as that capacity or power to do well whatever he set out to do. Thus he wrote as good Platonic plays as could (or should) be written. His occasional verse is all that such verse in the nature of things should be. His love lyrics challenge comparison with those of any of his immediate contemporaries. His critical verse stands almost alone. Why then does he remain a second-rate or third-rate figure? One answer is that he contented himself with second-rate sources of inspiration. Nothing that he did well required much more than a capable talent. When he aimed higher, as in *The Ordinary*, when he matched himself with the masters of comedy, he failed, but his failure is more interesting than his successes.

---

29. *Works* (1651), sig. [*12]^r.

IV

INFLUENCE AND LATER REPUTATION

How many after being celebrated by fame have been given up to oblivion; and how many who have celebrated the fame of others have long been dead.—MARCUS AURELIUS

MUCH HAS been said directly and indirectly about Cartwright's great contemporary reputation: "great" is not, I believe, an exaggeration. In the 1640's superlatives were used in profusion; used also, one fears, in some confusion. Indeed what was once said of Francis Quarles, that "he had to die before Milton could become known," is in a somewhat similarly ironic sense true of Cartwright. For there can be little doubt that, before the publication of *Paradise Lost*, the *Works* of 1651 was a more widely read volume than the *Poems* of 1645. Cartwright had a large and sympathetic audience; Milton had "fit audience though few."

I do not intend to repeat all the eulogies heaped upon Cartwright during his lifetime. They are quoted at length in the first chapter. Our immediate concern is with the all too numerous fashionable "labels" which later decorated his posthumous *Works* (1651).[1] Long "bills of excellence" might be quoted from these eulogies, and it would not be difficult to extract from them an idealized portrait both of the man and of his abilities which would find few rivals in any period of the world's literature. Setting aside, however, the obviously biased interest of these verses, something of good faith surely may be allowed to the sheer weight of corroborative testimony.[2] Here was a young man who appealed to his friendly con-

---

1. It has not been thought worth while to reprint these fifty-four commendatory poems in the present edition. A list of the contributors may be found in the bibliographical discussion of the *Works* (1651) in Chapter V, "The Text."

2. Miss Gebhardt (Thesis, *The Ordinary*, pp. xxii–xxiv) points out that all was not praise and cites William Towers' defence of *The Siege* in the commendatory poems, sig. [*10]ʳ. She also draws attention to the several sets of verses which were prefaced to Rich-

temporaries as a type, a type which, in the fast-changing onrush of seventeenth-century thought and event, represented all the old virtues, as they understood virtues—loyalty to the king and to the established church, a morality practical rather than visionary, and a philosophical attitude which Bacon damns as "sophistical." In a word, Cartwright typified "authority." No wonder that men like Henry Lawes, Izaak Walton, Alexander Brome, Henry Vaughan Edward Sherburne, and James Howell, to name only those who were not of his immediate academic circle, men who were heart and soul champions of a falling order—no wonder that such men should salute Cartwright as a fellow spirit. While he was alive he had actively followed the cause of king and church. He had died in the cause. Now he might live again *for* the cause. Here also was a man whom they could whole-heartedly endorse without the stigma morally and politically inherent in the overt worship of more popular figures. This attitude will go far to explain the tributes of Sherburne, Brome, Howell, and Vaughan, to whom I suspect Cartwright was personally almost unknown.

ard Brome's *A Jovial Crew* (1652), in several of which uncomplimentary remarks are aimed at Cartwright and Moseley, especially on the score of the number of commendatory verses attached to the *Works* (1651). John Hall remarks on "some itching Academicks" who have recently taken up playwriting, whose

> Products were
> Lame and imperfect, and did *grate* the eare,
> So, that they mock'd the stupid Stationers care,
> That both with *Guelt* and Cringes did prepare
> Fine Copper-Cuts, and gather'd Verses too,
> To make a Shout before the idle Show.

"J. B." writes sarcastically of books which need

> Regiments of *Encomiums*,
> On all occasions, whose *Astronomie*
> Can calculate a Praise to *Fifty three*,
> And write blank Copies, such, as being view'd,
> May serve indifferently each *Altitude*.

And he adds that it will do no good for "the *Stationer*, when all th'*Wits* are past,/ [to] Bring his own *Periwig Poetry* at last." James Shirley also has a flight at the "Fifty two" commendatory verses and then adds some all too trenchant criticisms aimed obviously at Cartwright:

> *Learning*, the File of *Poesie* may be
> Fetch'd from the *Arts* and *Universitie*.
> But he that writes a *Play*, and good, must know,
> Beyond his Books, Men, and their Actions too.
> Copies of Verse, that make the *New Men* sweat,
> Reach not a *Poem*, nor the *Muses* heat;
> Small Bavine-Wits, and Wood, may burn a while,
> And make more noise, then Forrests on a Pile,
> Whose Fivers shrunk, ma'invite a piteous stream,
> Not to lament, but to extinguish them.

In fairness to Cartwright's contemporary reputation I think it should be noticed that the real point of these attacks is not Cartwright but Humphrey Moseley, a rival publisher, who in this same year published a collection of five of Brome's plays. John Hall's voice is moreover not an impartial one, since by this time he had avowed Puritan leanings and was a Cantabrigian to boot; and Shirley, whose voice we listen to with more respect, is here repeating the unkind sentiments regarding academic playwrights to which he had given expression in *The Witty Fair One* (1633), IV, ii.

On the other side, I do not wish to underestimate the sincerity of much of what these poems say, and say repeatedly, of Cartwright's literary abilities. Such virtues as he possessed as a writer are strongly marked, clear for all to read. They were, moreover, qualities that appealed very forcibly to the mid-seventeenth-century mind—impersonality, wit, polish, easiness, natural language, all combined with a slight but reassuring savor of the lamp. In the words of the anonymous poet whose verses are engraved under Cartwright's portrait, he had "The Sharpest, cleanest, full, square, leading Witt," and was "The best Tyme's Best, . . . Of all that Walk in Prose, or dance in Verse." We may dismiss the commendatory poems with two exceptionally pleasing stanzas from the verses by John Finch:

>   Whats best cannot be prais'd;
> The single lustre of the Sun
>   Cannot by Croud of Stars be rais'd;
>   Nor can the Spring disclose
> Colours, or Sweets, but are undone
>   In presence of the Rose.
>
>   Who can adorn that Face
> Whose matchless Beauty once display'd,
>   All Ornament doth grace?
>   Write fair and mend, you blot;
> Imperfect Silver may crave aid
>   Of Gilt; Gold needs it not.

And some of the couplets of kindly Izaak Walton:

> I cannot keep my purpose, but must give
> Sorrow and Verse their way; nor will I grieve
> Longer in silence; no, that poor, poor part
> Of natures legacy, Verse void of Art,
> And undissembled teares, CARTWRIGHT shall have
> Fixt on his Hearse; and wept into his grave.
>   Muses I need you not; for, Grief and I
> Can in your absence weave an Elegy: . . .
>   Sing on blest Soul! be as thou wast below,
> A more than common instrument to show
> Thy Makers praise; sing on, whilst I lament
> Thy loss, and court a holy discontent,
> With such pure thoughts as thine, to dwell with me,
> Then I may hope to live, and dye like thee,
>   To live belov'd, dye mourn'd, thus in my grave;
> *Blessings that Kings have wish'd, but cannot have.*

It is worth while, perhaps, to point out two slight instances of the regard in which, even several years after his death, Cartwright's name as a poet and critic was cherished. In 1647 when the first folio of Beaumont and Fletcher at last appeared it contained two long commendatory poems by Cartwright, an honor accorded to no one else. And again, in 1650, when the fifth edition of Barten Holyday's translation of Persius' *Satires* was published, Cartwright's name was subscribed to some verses which, as early as 1616, had been ascribed to "I. Knight." Small straws, but at least straws which indicate the breeze of popular opinion.[3]

Further and rather more substantial evidence of Cartwright's popularity may be seen in the unusually large number of drolls or dialogues, nine in all, which the enterprising anthologist filched from his plays during the fifties. These drolls appeared in two miscellanies, *The Marrow of Complements* (1655) and *Wits Interpreter* (1655), both of which also contain a number of his lyrics and songs. In addition, poems by Cartwright appeared in ten other miscellanies before 1660.

Apparently the *Works* (1651) was well received by the book-buying public, for a year later another publisher, A. Miller, brought out an edition of one of Cartwright's sermons. And as late as 1656 Moseley was planning to publish a collected edition of Cartwright's Latin verse. Although "promised to be printed very speedily,"[4] the collection never appeared.

Cartwright's great reputation did not last long. Like the chameleon, it fed for ten years or less on the air promise-crammed. But the Restoration breathed a new air. The king was dead! Long live the king! It was, however, a different king and a strange age, an age in which men, freed at last from the uneasy restraints of the Puritan rule, sought forgetfulness of the past in the creation of a loud and clever present. Many of the things which Cartwright had looked upon as sanctities were gone. As a poet Cartwright went with them. Even wit as he and his fellows had understood it was challenged, and Clevelandism became synonymous with catachresis. Shadwell quite definitely dates Cartwright when in *Bury Fair* (1689) he makes Oldwit, a champion of the good old days, cry:

---

3. See the notes for a fuller discussion of these two points. It is possible that Jasper Mayne also had two poems in the 1647 folio.

4. The edition was advertised at the end of John Collop's *Poesis Rediviva* (1656). A list of Cartwright's Latin verse is included in Appendix C.

No Wit! Ounds, now you provoke me. Shall I, who was *Jack Fletcher*'s Friend, *Ben Johnson*'s Son, and afterward an Intimate Crony of *Jack Cleaveland*, and *Tom Randal*, have kept Company with Wits, . . . live to be Depos'd by you? . . . I, that was a Judge at *Blackfriers*, writ before *Fletcher*'s Works and *Cartwright*'s. . . .

Curiously enough Cartwright's reputation as a writer of Latin verse seems to have survived better than his reputation as an English poet. Joseph Hunter observes[5] that "He, Randolph and Cowley are the only Englishmen named by [James] Du Port [one-time Greek professor at Cambridge and later vice-chancellor of the university] when he is celebrating those who had excelled in Latin verse." Hunter refers to the following couplet in Du Port's *Musae Subsecivae seu Poetica Stromata* (1676), page 75:

> Randolphus placet, immo Cowliusque,
> Cartritusque, alliique forsan Angli.

We may now turn for a while from Cartwright's reputation to his influence—a rather more tenuous theme perhaps. In the notes and separate introductions to the plays, a number of later borrowings from Cartwright are pointed out. Among those named as debtors are Shadwell, D'Urfey, Settle, Lovelace, Sedley, Southerne, Katherine Philips, Dryden, and Congreve. Other names might easily be added, as a glance at the Index will show. With three exceptions, however, these writers lifted and left, and to speak of influence would be misleading. The three exceptions are Katherine Philips, Settle, and Dryden. Settle's case has been sufficiently stated in the Introduction to *The Royal Slave*, but Katherine Philips' and Dryden's debts to Cartwright deserve rather more careful consideration. First, however, we must retrace our way a little.

Mr. Mark Van Doren, in writing of Dryden's occasional poetry, brings out well one important function of Cartwright as a poet when he remarks: "The main line of descent from Jonson to Dryden had been through men like Cartwright and Waller."[6] This is to assign to Cartwright a rather more dominant position than is commonly allowed him, but that he exerted a strong influence on his

---

5. In his *Chorus Vatum Anglicanorum* (British Museum, Addit. MS. 24,490, fol. 237). Hunter is mistaken, I think, when he asserts that these three are the only Englishmen mentioned. On page 76 More ("Morusque noster") and Buchanan (to be sure a Scotsman) are both named. Leicester Bradner in his *Musae Anglicanae: A History of Anglo-Latin Poetry, 1500–1925* (1940), does not mention Cartwright.

6. *The Poetry of John Dryden* (1920), pp. 137-38.

writing contemporaries, and through them on later writers, is illustrated by the strongly Cartwrightesque manner of many of the more than fifty commendatory poems prefixed to the *Works* (1651). And on some of the early poetry of a major figure like Henry Vaughan (himself a contributor to the 1651 volume) the influence of Cartwright's manner is as clearly stamped. But the direct influence of Cartwright is best seen in the work of three people: two, Jasper Mayne and Martin Lluellin, his personal and adoring friends; the third, Katherine Philips, a younger disciple worshipping a great shade.

Jasper Mayne, whose name is coupled with Cartwright's by Abraham Wright in his *Five Sermons, in Five several Styles; or Waies of Preaching* (1656),[7] seems to have fallen thoroughly under the spell of the younger and more forceful poet. A number of close parallels between Mayne's *Amorous War* and *The City-Match* and Cartwright's plays are pointed out in the Notes. In his occasional verse also Cartwright's influence may be felt. A comparative study of the well-known lines to Shakespeare signed "I.M.S.," usually assigned to Mayne, with Mayne's later, more compact, if less poetical, verse is revealing, since the earlier verses were presumably written before he was exposed to Cartwright's stronger personality.

Martin Lluellin's little volume of poetry published in 1646 under the quaint title *Men-Miracles* bears not only silent but vocal testimony of Cartwright's influence. His name constantly recurs among the seven commendatory poems, one writer, "W.B." affirming:

> In every sheet I view, methinks I see
> Thy *Cartwrights* Ghost appeare; For such was he.

A doubtful compliment for Cartwright! Another contributor, "E.G.," in ecstasy describes how the Spirit of Poetry went from Chaucer to Spenser and from Spenser to Jonson:

> Not *rested* untill *now*, *Randall* it brush'd,
> And with the fulnesse of its weight it crush'd.
> It did thy *Cartwright* kisse, and *Masters* court,
> Whose soules were both transfused in the sport.

And "J.C." asserts:

> Does not the shade (bright shade of *Cartwright* know)
> What fruite we misse 'cause he would have it grow?
> That *sigh'd for Genius* once againe we see
> Up from the dust, live and put forth in thee.

---

7. See above, p. 17.

Lluellin himself has two poems on the death of his friend, only one of which appears in this collection.[8] Of all his poetry, the series addressed "To my Lady Ch." is most in Cartwright's vein, but couplets such as the following may be found throughout the volume:

> Your bright approach cleares all, and forbids they
> Should *dread* a *Night*, who doe but *change* their *day*.

> We misse not the *Perfections*, but their *Place*,
> Tis the same *Beauty* in *another Face*.

> He like old *Enoch* to His Blisse is gone,
> 'Tis not His Death, but his Translation.

Last in the "school" of Cartwright, is Mrs. Katherine Philips, the "Matchless Orinda." Mr. Souers, in his detailed study of this ingenious lady, declares unequivocally that "Katherine was in reality Cartwright's disciple," and again, "Cartwright was in every sense Orinda's master, her master not only in manner but in matter."[9] From him she received her flair for "witty gallantry," and on the Platonic doctrines developed in his tragicomedies she based in large part her "philosophy of friendship." She even went to the length of calling some of her special circle of friends by names borrowed from his plays: Cratander (John Berkenhead), Charistus (John Owen), Lucasia (Mrs. Anne Owen). Mr. Souers quotes an interesting echo from *The Lady-Errant* in one of Orinda's letters:[10]

---

8. His other poem appeared in the *Works* (1651). A passing reference to Cartwright is made by George Daniel in "A Vindication of Poesie" (about 1647) where he is grouped with Godolphin, one of the Beaumonts, and Montague (see *Poems*, ed. A. Grosart, 1878, I, 31).

9. *The Matchless Orinda*, pp. 256–57.

10. *Ibid*., pp. 257, 260–63. The quoted passage occurs in *Letters from Orinda to Poliarchus* (1705), pp. 59–60. As Mr. Sours observes (p. 59) a number of the contributors of commendatory verses to the *Works* (1651) were friends of Orinda (Henry Lawes, John Berkenhead, Francis Finch, Henry Vaughan, Sir Edward Dering), hence presumably the invitation to the inexperienced, twenty-year-old Katherine Philips to join in the chorus. Actually she was only a little over twelve when Cartwright died, but this does not prevent her from calling him her "much valued Friend" (sig. ['a6]ᵛ).

A second curious example of Katherine Philips' intimate knowledge of *The Lady-Errant* has recently come to my attention. In a belated reading of the *Letters from Orinda to Poliarchus*, I noticed the frequent use of the name Calanthe (in one passage referred to as the "Priencess [*sic*] *Calanthe*" [p. 46]), a name which it seemed to me was used as a second pseudonym for Anne Owen, in place of the usual Lucasia. On again consulting Mr. Souers' study, I found that he also considered the two names as referring to the same person (pp. 126, 136–37). But what he could not then

And thus it is that the thing call'd Friendship, without which the whole Earth would be but a Desart, and Man still alone, tho' in Company, grows sick and languishes, and *Love once sick, how quickly will it die?*

Compare (I, v):

> O my *Olyndus*, were there not that thing
> That we call Friend, Earth would one Desart be,
> And Men Alone still, though in Company.

Among Orinda's poems those which seem most strongly to bear the stamp of Cartwright's manner are "Upon the double Murther of King *Charles* I," "A Sea-Voyage from Tenby to Bristol," "Mr. *Francis Finch*, the Excellent Palaemon," and "On the Death of the Illustrious Duke of Gloucester." The Matchless Orinda stands as one of the few connecting links between Cartwright's world and the world of Charles II and Dryden.[11]

Dryden's knowledge of Cartwright seems to date from his days at Westminster School, where like Cartwright himself he was admitted as king's scholar. Here he is reported to have fallen strongly under the influence of Dr. Busby, then headmaster, a man who not only had known Cartwright personally, but had acted the leading role (Cratander) in *The Royal Slave*, a characterization for which he received extravagant praise.[12] It is not surprising then to think that we detect echoes of Cartwright in Dryden's earliest published poem, "Upon the Death of the Lord Hastings" (1650),[13] or that Dryden and Howard's *Indian Queen* (1664) bears such obvious marks of *The*

---

have known was Katherine Philips' reason for equating the names. That reason is to be found in *The Lady-Errant*, where the original name for the character known as Lucasia was Calanthe (see a full discussion of the problem in the General Introduction, Chapter V, "The Text," and in the Introduction to *The Lady-Errant*). Katherine Philips' knowledge of this technical change in character-names, at some stage in the textual history of the play before its publication in 1651, suggests that she herself may have had a hand in making that change. Perhaps, either as actor or director, she was connected with a private performance of *The Lady-Errant*, probably before May, 1648, at which time Moseley entered for his copy on the Stationers' Register. On this hypothesis it is possible to explain the substitution of a name so like that of Leucasia, the heroine of *The Siege*, as an intentional borrowing (by Katherine Philips?) from another of Cartwright's plays. But still we do not know why Calanthe was considered unsatisfactory in the first place.

11. *The Matchless Orinda*, p. 264.
12. See the Introduction to *The Royal Slave* for further comments on Dr. Busby's performance.
13. See Mark Van Doren, *The Poetry of John Dryden* (1920), p. 4. See also my note to Cartwright's poem, "An Epitaph on Mr. *Poultney*."

Royal Slave. Nor does Dryden ever seem to have forgotten his early study of Cartwright, although so far as I know he never mentions his name. In a mature poem, "To the Memory of Mrs. Killigrew" (1686), there are, it seems to me, definite recollections of Cartwright's very beautiful elegy, "To the memory of a Shipwrackt Virgin."[14] And in as late a play as *Don Sebastian* (1690) Dryden remembers *The Royal Slave* well enough to make an obvious borrowing from it in the first act.[15] Mr. Souers makes an even larger claim for Cartwright's influence on Restoration drama and on Dryden in particular. He writes: "It might not be too uncritical to affirm that, if Olyndus and Charistus had not spoken as they did, Celadon and Florimel (or any other of Dryden's clever pairs) would never have appeared upon the stage."[16] This is, I think, somewhat to overstate Cartwright's claim at the expense of the whole body of Cavalier drama, but the general implications of the statement are worth pondering in the light of Cartwright's position among the Cavalier dramatists.

Any discussion of Cartwright's influence in the Restoration must take into account the recently discovered revivals of *The Ordinary* and *The Lady-Errant* in 1671, even though these failed to establish more than a passing interest and somehow eluded all the surviving theatrical records.[17]

With the coming of the eighteenth century Cartwright is a forgotten figure, almost a forgotten name. Writing in 1691, Langbaine still spoke with considerable enthusiasm of William Cartwright as "A Person as Eminent for Loyalty and Learning (his years consider'd) as any this Age has produc'd." But though Langbaine had certainly read Cartwright—whom had he not read!—one suspects that it is the voice of Wood and Lloyd, not the voice of personal conviction, which speaks. Among compilers of dramatic handbooks, indeed, his reputation remains unchanged and, I am afraid, his works unread.[18] It is true that five of his poems were gathered up into the 1716 and 1727 editions of the so-called Dryden's *Miscellany*,[19] but in

---

14. See my notes to this poem for a fuller discussion.
15. See the Introduction to *The Royal Slave* for a full statement of the extent of Dryden's borrowing.
16. *The Matchless Orinda*, p. 264.
17. See above, Chapter II, and the separate introductions to *The Ordinary* and *The Lady-Errant*.
18. After Langbaine, beginning with Gildon (1699), the handbooks give absurd dates for Cartwright's plays.
19. See Earl R. Wasserman, "Pre-Restoration Poetry in Dryden's *Miscellany*," *Modern Language Notes*, LII (Dec., 1937), 552-53.

the literary world generally he suffers the fate of even the best Caroline poets, except Waller and Denham. In the first half of the century only two persons, outside the handbooks, seem to have noticed Cartwright's existence, Alexander Pope and Aaron Hill. Pope's interest in Elizabethan poetry, particularly Donne, and his weakness for purloining whole lines from seventeenth-century verse, is well enough known. Thus in his scheme of the English poets by "schools," Cartwright is placed among the followers of Donne, a position which indicates that Pope found little in Cartwright except metaphysical wit. This opinion is strengthened by two comments on Cartwright which he made in Spence's hearing.

> Cartwright and Bishop Corbet are of this mediocre class of poets [he has just been speaking of Crashaw, Stanley, Randolph, Sylvester]; And Bagnel, the author of the Counter Scuffle, might be admitted among them. . . . He mentioned Cleveland and Cartwright as equally good or rather equally bad.—What a noise was there made about the superior merits of those two writers?[20]

Neither remark strengthens our faith in Pope's critical powers; especially when he rounds the second off with the statement that "Donne is superior to Randolph; and Sir W. Davenant a better poet than Donne."[21]

Aaron Hill's "use" of Cartwright is rather more extensive.[22] Hill, who in general seems to have been a picker-up of unconsidered Elizabethan trifles, helped himself to at least three of Cartwright's poems, one of which, his version of "*Lesbia* On her Sparrow," he acknowledges. The other two, "The Gnat," based on Cartwright's poem of the same name, and "Belinda's *Grave*," based in part on "*Corinna's* Tomb," are less actual versions of Cartwright's poems than poems on the same theme which make use of ideas and phrases from Cartwright's originals. Hill and Cartwright also translate two of the same epigrams of Martial, though the translations show almost no similarity. Significantly, however, Hill's translations

---

20. J. Spence, *Anecdotes of Books and Men*, ed. S. W. Singer (1820), pp. 22, 144.

21. It seems probable that Pope actually read the 1651 *Works* with some care, for, although he does not seem to borrow directly from Cartwright, he imitates the closing verses of Izaak Walton's commendatory poem (quoted above) in his "Epistle to Dr. Arbuthnot" (ll. 404-5):

"O grant me thus to live, and thus to die!
Who sprung from kings shall know less joy than I"

22. I was led to examine Hill's verse by a reference to his version of "*Lesbia* On her Sparrow" in Earl R. Wasserman's *Elizabethan Poetry in the Eighteenth Century* (1947), p. 180.

appearing in his collected works just before "Belinda's *Grave*," are in the same order as Cartwright's, and one employs part of the same Latin title ("In Pompeios").[23]

Moving on into the later eighteenth century we hear little of Cartwright until the seventies, though he figures in *Biographia Britannica* (1748), and Theophilus Cibber includes him in his *Lives of the Poets* (1753), even going so far as to quote, incorrectly, a lyric from *The Ordinary*. Cibber, or whoever really wrote Cartwright's life, knew the play through the offices of Dodsley, who had included *The Ordinary* in his *Select Collection of Old Plays*, published in 1744. Zachary Grey quotes extensively from the plays in his *Critical, Historical, and Explanatory Notes on Shakespeare* (1754). On the other hand, Dr. Johnson, so far as I know, never mentions Cartwright, nor cites him as an authority in his *Dictionary*; and George Coleman in his very superficial essay, *Critical Reflections on the Old English Dramatick Writers* (1761), written as an introduction to Coxeter's edition of Massinger, has nothing to say about him. With the coming of the "black letter" editors, of course, references to Cartwright become more frequent—not perhaps evidence of renewed popularity. Malone, for example, in his clever attack on Macklin's forgery of a pamphlet called "Old Ben's *Light Heart* made heavy by young John's *Melancholy Lover*" makes use of some of Cartwright's verses to Jonson, as quoted by Langbaine, to expose the deceit. And Farmer is pleased to refer to him as "this now forgotten poet."[24] Slightly more concrete evidence of awakened interest is found in the proposals published in 1779 for a complete new edition of Cartwright's plays and poems. This advertisement appeared in *The Playhouse Pocket-Companion* (1779):

Printing by SUBSCRIPTION, In Two neat Pocket Volumes, Price Seven Shillings, The PLAYS and POEMS of WILLIAM CARTWRIGHT, Student of Christ

---

23. See *Works of Aaron Hill* (1754), III, 313 ("Belinda's Grave"); p. 312 (the two Martial epigrams); III, 153–54 ("*Lesbia's Lamentation*, on the Death of her Sparrow; altered from *Mr. Cartwright*"); pp. 160–61 ("The Gnat").

24. *An Essay on the Learning of Shakspeare*, 1767 (*Plays of Shakspeare*, ed. Steevens, 1793, II, 10). Farmer refers to Cartwright only indirectly in connection with W. Towers' commendatory poem to the *Works* (1651), in which Towers says that Cartwright is not like those "whose little *Latin* and no *Greek* Confin'd their whole Discourse to a Street-phrase." Steevens, a little later, in his "Appendix to Mr. Colman's Translation of Terence," bent only on demolishing Farmer's argument and patently without having read the original, remarks: "Surely, Towers, having said that Cartwright had *no* Greek, is no proof that Ben Jonson said so of Shakespeare."

Church, Oxford, and Proctor of the University; Who flourished in the Reign of Charles the First. Carefully revised and corrected from the last Edition, in 1651; With Notes, Critical and Historical, and an Essay on his Life and Writings. By the Author of the Critical HISTORY of the ENGLISH STAGE, prefixed to this Work.[25]

Unfortunately, like the Cheshire cat, this proposal merely smiled and vanished. But the bare suggestion is a valuable indication of the newly awakened interest in earlier English drama and poetry.[26]

On the continent Cartwright was known by name, if by nothing else. As early as 1733 a short notice of his life and works, taken from Wood, appeared in one of those tremendous "Universal Lexicons" which seem to have been the chief delight of eighteenth-century Europe.[27] And somewhat later Lessing includes him in his "Geschichte der englischen Schaubühne."[28] In France, however, I have found no notice of Cartwright before 1813, again in a "Biographie Universelle."[29]

John Nichols' *Collection of Poems* (1780-82), Henry Headley's *Select Beauties of Ancient English Poetry* (1787), and George Ellis' *Specimens of the Early English Poets* (1790) are the first later eighteenth-century anthologies to contain any of Cartwright's minor poetry. Headley's collection also contains some good critical remarks and several useful notes. Neither Goldsmith's *Beauties of English Poesy* (1767) nor Lamb's later *Specimens of English Dramatic Poets* (1808) notices him. In 1805 Gifford included John Ferriar's essay on Massinger in his edition of that dramatist's works.[30] Ferriar, unlike Coleman, makes a number of references to Cartwright, who here figures beside Jonson, Fletcher, and the other major writers. He is, I believe, the only minor dramatist named at all, nor from Ferriar's manner of speaking of him could we guess his true

---

25. Printed on sig. [a2]ᵛ. The projected edition is noticed by Goffin (*Poems*, p. xli).

26. See also Hill's version of Cartwright's "Lesbia on her Sparrow," which appeared in *The Public Advertiser* (1787), No. 16622.

27. *Grosses vollständiges Universal Lexicon* (1733), V, 1171-72.

28. *Sammtliche Werke* (1823), XV, 230.

29. *Biographie Universelle* (1813), VII, 238-39.

30. Gifford himself, of course, knew Cartwright's work well and makes numerous references to it in his illustrative notes, particularly in his edition of Jonson. Because of his commendatory poems to Jonson and Fletcher, Cartwright also received some notice in Gilchrist's edition of *Jonsonus Virbius* (1816), and in the three editions of Beaumont and Fletcher's works (1750, 1778, 1812) which appeared before the great Dyce edition of 1843.

status. Such preferred treatment, if uncritical, is highly refreshing to the starved appetites of Cartwright apologists.

Leaving the editors and anthologists for a moment, it should be noticed that Coleridge, about the turn of the century, read Cartwright's poems and at least one play (*The Lady-Errant*) with sufficient enthusiasm to jot down in his commonplace book six passages.[31] Some of these quotations, all of which were attributed to Coleridge himself by James Dykes Campbell, are so much altered by Coleridge as to suggest that he either quoted from memory or purposely adapted the lines with some view to metrical experiment.

In 1810 Chalmers included a complete reprint of Moseley's collection (1651) of Cartwright's minor poems in his *English Poets*.[32] And Campbell, in 1819, admitted selections from the poems in his *Specimens of the British Poets*. From then on Cartwright's small, but representative, place was assured in all but the most selective anthologies.

The earliest essay devoted entirely to an appreciation of Cartwright's poetry appeared in 1824 in the *Retrospective Review*, that champion of lost literary causes. The type of criticism of which this essay is a product is well illustrated by the following quotation:

> Sufficient, we are in good hopes, will be rifled from the present little book, (which may be ranked as a violet, humble, but sweet smelling,) to serve our reader to make his breakfast pleasant.

The bulk of the essay consists of long quotations from what the author considers Cartwright's best lyrics. His choice in the main is good, and there is a sincerity in his intentions which makes his

---

31. See *Poetical Works of Samuel Taylor Coleridge*, ed. James Dykes Campbell (1907), "Fragments" 64, 96, 98, 111, 113, 118. The fact that the first five of these "Fragments" were actually by Cartwright was pointed out by E. H. Coleridge (*Complete Poetical Works of Samuel Taylor Coleridge*, 1912, II, 996). The identification of the sixth passage (118) I owe to the kindness of Professor Earl Wasserman, who also called my attention to Coleridge's interest in Cartwright.

My friend, Dr. Charles Patterson, has recently pointed out to me that Coleridge also knew both *The Royal Slave* and *The Siege*. His daughter, Mrs. Sara Coleridge, states that lines 10–13 of the Hampton Court "Prologue" to *The Royal Slave* "was a favourite quotation with Mr. Coleridge; he used it more than once in reference to those same newspaper writings, ... which are here restored to the Public" (*Essays on his Own Times*, ed. by His Daughter, 1850, I, "Preface," [xi]). A quotation (slightly adapted) from *The Siege* (ll. 86–94) appears in the same collection (II, 599–600).

32. Cartwright's poems were not included in Anderson's similar *British Poets* (1793).

work refreshing in spite of its obvious weakness. He promises the reader a later article on Cartwright's plays, but no such article appeared. Probably, he had read the plays in the meantime!

I have found only three references to Cartwright in early nineteenth-century American literature, all in Irving. Two occur in *The Sketch Book* (1820), where he uses the little rhyme of "Saint *Francis*, and Saint *Benedight*" from *The Ordinary* as a motto for his essay on "Christmas Eve," and some later lines of Moth, the antiquary, to introduce the story of "Rip Van Winkle." The third serves as a motto to "An Old Soldier" in *Bracebridge Hall* (1822).[33]

With the turn of the half-century, we come to the modern era of specialized criticism in all fields of English literature. And to carry our miniature Cartwright allusion book further is unnecessary. Most modern readers will be content to consider Cartwright adequately summed up by that Caliban of critics, Swinburne, when he unkindly dubs him "that typical Oxonicule, the Rev. William Cartwright."[34] Few I am afraid will allow him the praise lavished on him by Charles Kingsley in his *Plays and Puritans*, but because the words are so pleasant and the intention so good, I will allow myself to quote some passages from the six-and-a-half pages of the original:

> And yet there is one dramatist of that fallen generation over whose memory one cannot but linger, fancying what he would have become, and wondering why so great a spirit was checked suddenly ere half developed... Cartwright must always rank among our wondrous youths by the side of Prince Henry, the Admirable Crichton, and others, of whom one's only doubt is, whether they were not too wondrous, too precociously complete for future development.... This superabundance of euology [referring to the commendatory poems prefixed to the *Works*], when we remember the men and the age from which it comes, tempts one to form such a conception of Cartwright as, indeed, the portrait prefixed to his works (ed. 1651) gives us; the offspring of an over-educated and pedantic age, highly stored with everything but strength and simplicity; one in whom genius has been rather shaped (perhaps cramped) than developed: but genius was present, without a doubt, under whatsoever artificial trappings; ... It is impossible to open a page of 'The Lady Errant,' 'The Royal Slave,' 'The Ordinary,' or 'Love's Convert,' without feeling at once that we have to do with a man of a very different stamp from any (Massinger perhaps alone excepted) who was writing between

---

33. *The Ordinary*, III, i, 1006-13, 1050-54 and I, iv, 371-75. Irving evidently knew the 1651 *Works*, since his quotation in "Christmas Eve" retains the original seventeenth-century spelling. The other quotations are given from one of the modern reprints of the play.

34. Quoted by F. S. Boas in *Shakespeare and the Universities* (1923), p. 266.

1630 and 1640. The specific gravity of the poems, so to speak, is far greater than that of any of his contemporaries; everywhere is thought, fancy, force, varied learning. He is never weak or dull; though he fails often enough, is often enough wrong-headed, fantastical, affected, and has never laid bare the deeper arteries of humanity, for good or for evil. Neither is he altogether an original thinker; as one would expect, he has over-read himself: but then he has done so to good purpose. If he imitates, he generally equals. The table of fare in 'The Ordinary' smacks of Rabelais or Aristophanes: but then it is worthy of either; and if one cannot help suspecting that 'The Ordinary' never would have been written had not Ben Jonson written 'The Alchemist,' one confesses that Ben Jonson need not have been ashamed to have written the play himself: although the plot, as all Cartwright's are, is somewhat confused and inconsequent. If he be Platonically sentimental in 'Love's Convert,' his sentiment is of the noblest and purest; and the confest moral of the play is one which that age needed, if ever age on earth did. . . . The 'Royal Slave,' too, is a gallant play, right-hearted and lofty from beginning to end, though enacted in an impossible court-cloud-world, akin to that in which the classic heroes and heroines of Corneille and Racine call each other Monsieur and Madame. As for his humour; he, alas! can be dirty like the rest, when necessary: but humour he has of the highest quality. 'The Ordinary' is full of it; and Moth, the Antiquary, though too much of a lay figure, and depending for his amusingness on his quaint antiquated language, is such a sketch as Mr. Dickens need not have been ashamed to draw. The 'Royal Slave' seems to have been considered, both by the Court and by his contemporaries, his masterpiece. And justly so, . . . True it is, that the songs are excellent, as are all Cartwright's; for grace, simplicity, and sweetness, equal to any (save Shakespeare's) which the seventeenth century produced: but curiously enough, his lyric faculty seems to have exhausted itself in these half-dozen songs. His minor poems are utterly worthless, out-Cowleying Cowley in frigid and fantastic conceits; . . . Are we to gather from this fact that Cartwright was not really an original genius, but only a magnificent imitator; that he could write plays well, because others had written them well already, but only for that reason; and that for the same reason, when he attempted detached lyrics and addresses, he could only follow the abominable models which he saw around him? We know not; . . .[35]

And so Kingsley runs on, defying modern critical estimates at every turn, but lighting up certain facets of his subject which too easily tend to get lost in the cooler element of academic niceties.

Today Cartwright's greatest debt is probably owing to Miss Margery Allingham, who, by quoting one of his poems in her excellent detective story, *Dancers in Mourning* (1938), brought him to the attention of a reading audience of thousands.

---

35. "Plays and Puritans," *Works* (1890), XII, 61-66. I owe my knowledge of Kingsley's criticism to Miss Gebhardt (Thesis, *The Ordinary*).

V

THE TEXT

... the dull duty of an editor.—Pope

Let us now be told no more of the dull duty of an editor.
—Dr. Johnson

CARTWRIGHT'S WORKS do not raise any large textual problems. There are in general no questions of priority of texts. The collected *Works* published in 1651 is the sole authority for three of the four plays and for about half of the minor poems. The remaining poems, with but one or two exceptions, all appeared during Cartwright's lifetime, many of them in editions with which he was closely associated. The one play published independently of the *Works*, *The Royal Slave*, was printed in 1639 and 1640 at Oxford, probably under the personal supervision of the author. These facts make the establishing of a text a relatively simple matter.

The general method may be briefly described. In every case, unless otherwise stated in the notes, the text presented is that of the earliest printed edition, of which, wherever possible, four copies have been collated. The seventeenth-century orthography has been preserved; "long s" has been modernized. Punctuation I have not considered "as wholly in my power," and I have differed from the original only when some change was necessary to clear the sense. Emendation of any sort, that devil of supererogation, has been pursued in the same spirit. All changes are recorded, the more important ones discussed in the notes. Finally, in the important matter of variant readings, I have tried to be as complete as space or reason would permit. Mere variations of spelling, unless of special interest, have been ignored. Even such variant spellings as "then" and "than," "whither" and "whether," have not as a rule been noted. On the other hand, variants in punctuation where they suggest a different reading of the text have been recorded. The spelling in the variant readings when more than one text is included under a single entry is always that of the first cited edition or manuscript. Further details in connection with these general statements will come to light in the course of the following discussion.

The following copies of the *Works* (1651) have been used in preparing the texts of *The Lady-Errant*, *The Ordinary*, and *The Siege*: (1) the editor's personal copy (the copy-text); collated with (2) a copy in the Harvard College Library (14424.3.1*); (3) and (4) two copies in the University of Illinois Library. For *The Royal Slave*: (1) the Library of Congress copy of the 1639 quarto (PR 1241.L6) has been used as the copy-text; collated with (2) the Bodleian copy; (3) a copy (97469) in the Huntington Library, San Marino; (4) the University of Illinois copy (formerly the Hoe copy). For the *Poems*, except for those based on the *Works* (1651) or printed from manuscript, I have not tried to indicate the exact copy-text. Copies in the British Museum, Bodleian, Houghton, Folger, and Huntington libraries have been consulted and collated. In establishing the text of those poems which depend upon the authority of the *Works* (1651) the same four copies already listed above have been used (my own copy as copy-text), plus two supplementary copies (Bodleian copy, Antiq. f.E $\frac{1651}{5}$, and a copy in the possession of Professor T. W. Baldwin) for the text of "On a vertuous young Gentlewoman that dyed suddenly."

1. The *Works*, 1651.[1]

The copyright for the *Works* was entered in the Stationers' Register on May 4, 1648, three years before the publication of the volume:[2]

Master Moseley. Entred for his copie under the hands of Sr Nath. Brent and Master Latham warden a booke called *Poems & Playes* (vizt) *The seige, or, Love's Convert, The Lady Errant; The Citty Cozener, or, The Ordinary*, being Trage-Comedies, by Mr Wm Cartwright . . . . vj^d

---

1. The following bibliographical account of the *Works* (1651) is reprinted essentially unchanged, by permission, from an article of mine in *The Library*, 4th Series, XXIII (June, 1942), 12-22. A parallel study of the *Works* (1651) by Mr. J. Periam Danton may be consulted in *The Library Quarterly*, XII, No. 3 (July, 1942), pp. 438-56. Miss Gebhardt (Thesis, *The Ordinary*, pp. xxv-xxx), also includes a bibliographical account of the *Works* (1651). I should like here to record a special debt of thanks to Mr. William A. Jackson, Librarian of the Houghton Library, Cambridge, Massachusetts, for his continual assistance and encouragement in this study.

2. *A Transcript of the Registers of the Worshipful Company of Stationers; from 1640-1708*, ed. G. E. B. Eyre (1913), I. 295.

It will be noticed that this entry makes no mention of *The Royal Slave*, a play of which two earlier editions (1639, 1640) had been published for the Oxford bookseller, Thomas Robinson. Presumably Robinson refused to sell his right in *The Royal Slave*, since his initials, combined with Moseley's name, appear on the separate title-page to the play in the *Works* (1651).[3] How long before 1648 Moseley had been planning an edition of Cartwright's works we do not know. Not long, I believe, though Mr. John Curtis Reed in his article on Moseley says "he had the copy for ten years."[4] What Moseley actually says, however, is that "One had the Forhead to affirm, that himself made Verses this last Summer, which our *Author* wrote (and whereof we had Coppies) Ten years since," a statement which clearly refers to the manuscripts of perhaps three or four poems and is ambiguous even in reference to those. Nor do the many commendatory poems help us in this matter. Those of the poems which it is possible to date were all written within a year, or at most two years, of the date of publication.[5]

---

3. No entry relating to *The Royal Slave* appears in the Stationers' Register. Had Moseley purchased Robinson's rights the transactions would almost certainly have been entered. See the entry of a similar transaction between Moseley and Robinson under December 12, 1646.

4. "Humphrey Moseley, Publisher," *Oxford Bibliographical Society* (1927–1930), II, 70. Mr. Reed fails to notice the entrance of the *Works* (1651) in the Stationers' Register.

5. A closer scrutiny than I have been able to give these commendatory poems might perhaps yield more positive results. The type of evidence which such a search might afford is well illustrated by Cartwright's two poems to Fletcher, which must have been written at least four, and probably eight, years before the appearance of the Beaumont and Fletcher first folio in 1647. The following is a complete list of the contributors: K.P. [Katherine Philips]; Monmovth; T.P. Baronet; Edw: Dering Baronet; Io: Pettus Knight; Robert Stapylton K t.; Io. Ieffryes Esq.; Jasper Mayne, W: Barker; Edw: Sherburne Esq.; Iames Howell; Jo. Leigh, *Esquire*; I.C. [John Castilion] B.D. *of* Ch. Ch.; Fr. Finch, è Soc. Int. Templ.; Io. Finch; Thomas Baines; Will: Creed; Rob: Waring, John Berkenhead; W. Towers; Henry Vaughan. *Silurist*; Ios. Howe; M. Lluellin; Rich. Goodridge; Io. Fell. A.M. OXON, Iohn Raymond; Robert Gardiner ex ho. M. Templi; W. Waring Esq; A greater Lover of the Author's Memory than his own; Hen. Lawes; Ralph Bathurst. Trin. Col. Oxon.; Mat. Smalwood; Tho. Vaughan. è Col. Iesu. Oxon.; Fr. Palmer Student of Ch. Ch. Oxon.; Geo: Hill; J: Cobbe; Rich: Iles; E. Nevill; Wil. Stanton Esq.; R. Mason; Fra: Vaughan; Hen: Davison; Tho. Severne Ex aede Christi. A.M. Oxon.; H.B. [Henry Bold] F. NC. Oxon.; Wil. Bell; I.P.; Alexander Brome; Tho: Philipott; C.W. [Christopher Ware]; Tho: Cole *ex Aede Christi*, Oxon.; B:C: Oxon.; Rich: Watkins. A.M. C.C. OXON.; R.Hill; Iz. Wa. [Izaak Walton], *The Stationer*. Hum. Moseley.

Treated as a problem in the printer's art and without any reference to contents, the 1651 volume may be described as follows. It is a compact octavo, signed : [‡Portrait]¹, [¹a]–¹b⁸, *¹⁸ (two sheets folded one inside the other, with a pair of conjugate leaves, sigs. [****4] and [****5], inserted between sigs. *8 and [*9]), ¶⁴, **⁸ (sig. [**7] being cancelled), ****¹⁴ (including a sheet signed ***, inserted between sig. [****3] and [****6]), ²a–²b⁸, c–e⁸, f⁴, g–k⁸, A–U⁸ (plus a cancel-insert of three leaves signed U, V2, and [U3], placed between sigs. [T8] and U), X². This collation represents, I believe, the ultimate intention of the printer, but a number of variations in the arrangement of the preliminary matter (sigs. [¹a] to **** inclusive) and four important variations in the body of the volume occur.

In order to explain the confused arrangement of the preliminaries it is necessary to understand the exact make-up of each of the quires and something of the order in which they were printed. Quires [¹a] and ¹b are, with one exception, perfectly normal, each consisting of a single sheet of eight leaves. The exception occurs in sig. [¹a7]ᵛ which appears in two states (both otherwise from the same setting of type): (1) with the signature 'T.P. Baronet' and (2) signed with a rose and harp, both crowned, followed by "Baronet" (rare).⁶ Quire * is anything but normal. It is made up of two sheets plus a quarter sheet, and it seems to have been the printer's intention to have these two and a quarter sheets bound together in a single gathering, signed *—*8, plus the unsigned quarter sheet (actually sigs. [****4] and [****5]), inserted in the middle of the quire (between sigs. *8 and [*9]), plus [*9]–[*16]. Such an arrangement was certain to lead to confusion. In my own copy of the *Works*, for example, this quire, plus an extra pair of conjugate leaves (sigs. [****2] and [****7]) inserted between sigs. *4 and [*13], is sewed as two gatherings, each of ten leaves. Other variations may also be found. Another peculiarity about quire * remains to be noticed. In some copies sigs. *8 and [*9] are not conjugates, but are printed on separate leaves. This variation seems to be the result of an error originally made in the signature of the poem ending on sig. [*9], an error which was caught soon after printing began. Some copies still retain the offending leaf, although marked with the customary

---

6. Miss Gebhardt (Thesis, *The Ordinary*, p. xxix) notes that the same crowned rose and harp appear later in the volume as ornaments, for example on sig. [²a2]ᵛ.

knife-slash for cancelling. It is signed "I.B." instead of the usual "John Berkenhead."

The quire signed ¶ consists of a half sheet, or four leaves, only. At the bottom of sig. ¶ there is a printer's direction to the binder (usually cropped): "Place this half sheet between one Star and two Stars." Quire ** is normal, except that sig. [**7] was meant to be cut out after binding, and, when left in through carelessness, is always found marked with a knife-slit as a cancellandum. The two poems thus cancelled appear later, that on sig. [**7]ʳ by Hen: Davison on sig. [****3]ᵛ, and that on sig. [**7]ᵛ by Rich: Watkins in a considerably enlarged version on sig. [****6].

Quire **** is actually made up of two differently signed sheets. The make-up of the quire is explained by a second printer's instruction: "Place the sheet with three Stars in the middle of foure ****." The sheet signed *** is perfectly normal, consisting of eight leaves, but the gathering signed **** contains only six leaves, all unsigned except the first. The missing pair of conjugates, sigs. [****4] and [****5], has already been accounted for in the quire *, inserted between sigs. *8 and [*9]. In spite of the fact that only the first leaf of the gathering **** is signed, it is possible to determine the correct sequence of the other seven leaves by a study of the watermark and catchwords. In all copies which I have been able to examine with this problem in mind the watermark appears either on sig. **** and not again in the first half of the gathering, or on sigs. [****2] and [****3] and not on sig. ****. Such watermark positions indicate that the pair of conjugate leaves which was taken from this sheet to complete sig. * represents (as we have assumed above) sigs. [****4] and [****5]. Turning now to the question of catchwords, we find that, disregarding the catchwords on sigs. [****4] and [****5], the only catchword which then appears in the gathering agrees with the first word on sig. ***. This fact makes it fairly evident that the leaf bearing this catchword must be sig. [****3] and its conjugate sig. [****6]. Thus only one pair of conjugates remains to be accounted for, which by elimination must be sigs. [****2] and [****7].

We are now in some position to suggest the probable order in which the preliminaries were printed. The first quires to be set up were, I suppose, those signed *, **, and ***, in the regular order indicated.[7] The next were presumably quires [¹a] and ¹b, the use of

---

7. The reappearance of identical type-headings in each sheet shows that no two sheets were in type at the same time.

the alphabet or some other symbol in the second being necessary to distinguish this quire from the others signed with a star. In this case, moreover, although quire [¹a] is unsigned, no instructions to the binder would be necessary since quire [¹a] contained the general title-page and the preface, and quire ¹b would naturally follow the first quire. These five sheets represent, I believe, the preliminaries as originally planned, but more and more commendatory poems kept pouring in, some from such important men as Izaak Walton and Henry Vaughan, and additions had to be made. The order of printing in the remaining three gatherings must remain hypothetical. All that can safely be said is that probably the gathering signed **** was the last to be printed, since it contains matter which supplements quire *, and the revised version of the poem cancelled on sig. [**7]ᵛ, as well as a second copy (from a different setting of type) of the poem on the recto of sig. [**7]. The order, therefore, would be gatherings ²* and ****.[8] The remaining quire, signed ¶, is certainly a late addition, but whether later or earlier than gathering **** there is no means of knowing. The fact that the quire contains a half sheet only might certainly be interpreted to mean that it was the last to be printed.

I can offer no satisfactory explanation for the printer's method of arranging some of the quires in double gatherings. Once embarked on the method, however, his reasons for inserting the gatherings where he has are clear enough. Only three quires in the preliminaries could admit inserted matter without breaking into the text of a poem: quires *, ***, ****. The second half of the gathering ****, however, had to be placed at the end of the preliminaries; hence it could not itself be inserted. Thus after quire ²* had been inserted in quire ¹* and quire *** in quire ****, nothing further could be inserted except in quire *** which was already a double quire.[9] Thus quire ¶,

---

8. There is one fact which does not square with the theory of the late addition of the second sheet (²*) in quire *. The catchword on the verso of sig. *4 agrees with the first word on sig. *5 (the first leaf of ²*) and does not agree with the first word on [*13], its conjugate and part of the middle pair of leaves in ¹*. This would point to the conclusion that the second sheet in quire * was originally planned as a part of that gathering and was not inserted as an afterthought.

9. The isolated position of quire ¶ might also be made into an argument for considering it to be the last printed part of the preliminaries. Why, we may ask, if it was not printed after all the arrangements had been made for inserting quire *** in quire ****, did the printer not make a single final quire by combining the two late additions, placing quire ¶ in the middle of quire ****?

although only a half sheet, had either to be placed within quire ***, a proceeding certain to lead to trouble, or to be made, as it was, a separate quire.

The make-up of the body of the volume, the text, is, with four notable exceptions, entirely normal. The quires are signed in two series: ²a–²b⁸, c–e⁸, f⁴, g–k⁸ (paged as 1–148, first two leaves without pagination), and A–U⁸, X², plus a cancel of three leaves, signed U, V2, [U3], inserted between sigs. [T8] and U (paged as 1–320, first leaf unpaged, second leaf wrongly paged as 1, with the page numbers 301–6 repeated in the cancellans).

The first variation occurs in sigs. [²b8], c4, and [c5], all of which appear in a cancelled state.[10] The reason for the cancel is clear enough. Each of the three leaves in its first form refers to *Lucasia*, one of the principal characters in *The Lady-Errant*, by the name *Calanthe*. Apparently at one time Cartwright used *Calanthe* throughout,[11] but he later changed his mind and altered the title in all but a few places. As we know, such confusion is not uncommon in other seventeenth-century plays. But this explanation disposes of only a part of the question, for sig. [²b8] occurs not in two states only, but in three, each representing a new setting of type. State A has already been sufficiently explained; states B and C, which are textually almost identical and of equally common occurrence,[12] afford us a good example of duplicate setting used presumably as a simple time-saving device. The question at once arises, why duplicate setting of sig. [²b8] but not of sigs. c4 and [c5]? The answer would seem to be that the error in the last two cases was caught by the proofreader almost as soon as printing started, while the faulty

---

10. I owe my knowledge of a cancelled state of sigs. c4 and [c5] and of a third state of sig. [²b8] to Mr. William McCarthey of the Widener Library, Harvard University. The possibly unique examples of the cancelled state are preserved in the University of Texas Library, Austin, Texas. Miss Gebhardt notices the existence of these leaves from a reference in a bookseller's catalogue (Thesis, *The Ordinary*, pp. xxxiii–xxxiv).

11. The name *Calanthe* occurs again three times in the play, in each case abbreviated as '*Cal.*', on sigs. [c6]ᵛ (as speech-heading to a song), d3ᵛ and [e6]ᵛ. All three slips remain uncorrected in all copies I have seen, although the third is corrected in the list of *Errata*. See above, Chapter IV, "Influence and Later Reputation," note 10.

12. Distinguishing marks for state A have already been given above. States B and C may readily be distinguished by the variant spellings of "I'll" in the first line (recto). In one (which I call state B) it is spelled "I'le"; in the other (state C) "I'l." A complete list of the variants of the several states of sigs. c4, [c5], and [²b8] will be found in the Textual Notes.

sig. [²b8] escaped notice until the impression was either completed, or nearly so.

Before proceeding to the three remaining problems, it will greatly simplify our approach if we discuss here the *Postscript* which Moseley printed on the last leaf of the preliminaries (sig. [****8]ʳ). This *Postscript* appears in two forms. The usual form, or six-line *Postscript*, reads as follows:

Postscript.

We shall not trouble you with an *Index*, for already the Book is bigger than we meant it, although we chose this Volume and Character purposely to bring down it's bulk. The *Printer's* faults (such as they are) must lye at his own door; for the written Coppy was very exact. But (to save you that labour) the next Page tells you his ERRATA.

The second form, or ten-line *Postscript*, is very rare.¹³ Both forms are from the same setting of type, with a slight rearrangement of the first line in the six-line form.

Postscript.

This *Impression* hath stood at the *Printers* Threshold ready to come forth; but staid for three sheets of our *Author's* Manuscript (remaining in the hands of an *Honourable Person*) which till last week we could not recover; aud [*sic*] we would not publish a lame *Edition*. We trouble you with no *Index*, for already. . . .

Both forms of this *Postscript* are interesting, the second, and earlier one especially so, since they throw light on the apparently separate, but actually closely connected, problems of the cancellans following sig. [T8] and of the Index which Moseley carefully tells us does not exist, but which nevertheless occasionally puts in an appearance.

The peculiar problem of the Index was first noticed, I believe, by Bliss in his edition of Wood's *Athenae* (1817). In spite of Moseley's statement to the contrary, an index was actually set up and some copies printed off. It occupied the last two leaves of the half sheet signed X, sigs. [X3] and [X4]. Occasionally copies of the *Works* appear containing fragments of it in the form of stubs, and a single copy in the Bodleian Library, possibly unique, preserves the two leaves intact.¹⁴ They are printed recto and verso and are unsigned

---

13. I have seen only two copies, one in the Bodleian Library, the other in the Folger Shakespeare Library, Washington, D.C.

14. These leaves are reproduced by J. Periam Danton in "William Cartwright and His *Comedies, Tragi-Comedies, with other Poems* . . . 1651," *The Library Quarterly*, XII (July, 1942), 449.

and unpaged. Page references are given for the *Poems* only, and the four plays are listed at the end on sig. [X4]ᵛ.

Leaving the Index for the moment, let us examine the question of the cancellans which was inserted following sig. [T8]. The cancellans is made up of three leaves, each of which occurs in two distinct states representing two settings of type. The first, which we will designate as the "uncensored" issue, occurs rarely and is signed U, U2, and [U3]. The second state, which may be distinguished as the "censored" issue, is the common one and represents the publisher's final intention. It is signed U, V2, and [U3]. Two of the poems on these leaves gave offence to the Commonwealth authorities, who ordered the complete deletion of certain lines and stanzas. As a result the "censored" issue contains large blanks where the offending lines have been cut out. Although the two distinct settings of type are easily enough explained by supposing that the orders of the censor did not reach Moseley until after the original type had been redistributed, Moseley's reason for resetting the poems so as to leave blanks where the lines had been deleted is not so clear. To have run the text together would undoubtedly have disturbed the initial text distribution, which in the original was so ordered as to fill the three leaves. But almost anything would have been less unsightly than the blanks. Perhaps Moseley retained them as an outward and visible sign of disapproval and as a warning to his "loyal" readers of the forced omissions. A number of copies containing the "uncensored" issue of the cancellans either were sold surreptitiously or had been already distributed before the authorities caught the peccant lines.

In his ten-line *Postscript* Moseley mentions "three sheets of our *Author's* Manuscript . . . which till last week we could not recover." Even if we had no further evidence there would be little cause for hesitation in identifying the poems contained in these "three sheets" with the two censored poems, "On the *Queens* Return from the Low Countries" and "Upon the death of the Right valiant Sir *Bevill Grenvill* Knight,"[15] together with a third poem, "On a vertuous young Gentlewoman that dyed suddenly," all of which appear in the cancellans discussed above. But the identification rises to certainty when an examination of the cancelled Index shows that these poems were not included in it. Here, then, is Moseley's true reason

---

15. Both these poems had been published earlier at Oxford: "On the *Queens* Return" in 1642, and "Upon the death of . . . Sir *Bevill Grenvill*" in 1641.

for withdrawing the Index, not to save space but to save paper and the trouble of setting up and printing off a new and corrected one. Even so, it is a little surprising that he should decide to scrap a whole index because of three slight omissions towards the end. Is this perhaps another example of the good Moseley's business "rectitude," or is some less worthy motive lurking in the corner?

One problem yet remains. As in the case of each of the four plays, there is a separate title-page to the *Poems* (sig. [M5], verso blank), reading: "POEMS / Written by / Mr WILLIAM CARTVVRIGHT, / Late Student of *Christ-Church* in / OXFORD, and Proctor of / the *University*. / [rule] / The AYRES and SONGS set by / Mr HENRY LAVVS, Servant to His / late MAJESTY in his Publick / and Private Musick. / [rule] / LONDON, / Printed for *Humphrey Moseley*, and / are to be sold at his shop at the Sign of / the Princes Armes in St *PAVLS* / Churchyard. 1651." This title-page, however, occurs in two distinct states, in part from different settings of type.[16] The wording of both is identical, only the arrangement in the second "section" has been altered. Both states are conjugate with sig. M4, which is the same in all copies. In state A, which is that found in almost every copy, the second "section" is arranged thus:

The AYRES and SONGS set by
Mr HENRY LAVVS, Servant to His
late MAJESTY in his Publick
and Private Musick.

State B, which is exceedingly rare, is as follows:
THE
AYRES & SONGS
Set by
Mr HENRY LAVVES,
Servant to His late *Majesty* in his Publick
and Private Musick.

Which of these two, we may ask, represents the earlier state of the title? Any answer, of course, involves a second question, why are

---

16. It has been pointed out to me by Mr. William McCarthey of the Widener Library that Moseley employed identical type-settings in part at least in all five separate titles. These same type-settings also appear in both the variant titles to the *Poems*. A study of all the separate titles seems to indicate that the poems and plays were actually set up in the following order: *The Ordinary*, *The Siege*, the *Poems*, *The Lady-Errant*, and *The Royal Slave*.

I have seen only two copies of state B of the separate title to the *Poems*: one in the British Museum (Grenville copy); the other in the Houghton Library, Harvard.

there two states of the title at all? Several theories suggest themselves, but only two seem worth serious consideration: an accident to the forme, or a trial title-page. In the case of an accident to the forme, a by no means uncommon happening, it was frequently necessary to reset a whole "section" which had either become loosened or dropped bodily from the frame. Such an explanation, however, fails to take into account the change in type sizes and the considerable respacing in both the upper and middle "sections." We would naturally suppose, moreover, that the type-setter would restore the forme with as little trouble as possible. One thing, however, is clear: whatever the actual reason for the alteration, it must have been made during the printing of the sheet since neither state is a cancel. On the whole, the theory of a trial title-page seems more nearly to meet the facts. As we have already noticed, Moseley used the same type-settings for certain parts of all the five separate titles.[17] When, therefore, the compositor came to set up a title-page for the *Poems* he had ready to his hand the type-page earlier used for both *The Ordinary* and *The Siege*. The single word "Poems," however, takes up but one line of type space, unlike "THE / ORDINARY, / [rule] / A Comedy," and "THE / SIEDGE: / Or, / Love's Convert, / A TRAGI-COMEDY." Seeing this difficulty, but failing to look far enough ahead, the compositor, after placing "Poems" in large capitals in approximately the same position as the first word of the other two titles, and without disturbing the lower "section" in any way, moves what was formerly the middle "section" up close under the word "Poems." He then places the same rule below this "section" which had before been above it. He is thus left with a comparatively large empty middle "section" which he proceeds to compose as in state B above. The rest of the forme being completed, he begins to print off. Now after several sheets have been pulled either the compositor himself or the proofreader sees that the resulting title-page is unsatisfactory. The upper "section" is patently crowded, and undue prominence is given to an aspect of Cartwright's poetry which has no immediate connexion with the present volume. The type-page, therefore, is reset, the upper "section" respaced and enlarged, the middle "section" reduced and smaller type employed. The result is state A, and we may observe that the process has finally produced a title-page which is as a whole much more in keeping with the general format of the other separate titles.

---

17. See note 16, above.

Like most seventeenth-century books, different copies of the *Works* show slight variations in text, page numbers, et cetera, the result of corrections and changes made by the proofreader while the volume was going through the press. I have examined some twenty-five copies and, although I have attempted no exhaustive collation, the following list will, I believe, be found to contain most of the principal variants:

 sig. [²a8]ᵛ *Flo.*] some copies read *Elo.*
 sig. d1ʳ howsoever] *some copies read* howsoeve
 sig. e1ʳ could stoop] *some copies read* could stould stoop
 sig. g2ᵛ *88*] some copies read *8*
 sig. g4ʳ *91*] some copies read *19*
 sig. D1ᵛ *Sahpho*] some copies read *Sappho*
 sig. D3ᵛ You'r] *some copies read* Your
 sig. G2ʳ *Parentage*] some copies read *Parente*
   faire] some copies read *fair*
   force] some copies read *fierce*
   la lampe . . . la lampe] some copies read *le lampe . . . le lampe*
   vint] some copies read *venst*
   en frappa] some copies read *ene frapa*
   blessa] some copies read *bleça*
 sig. L2ʳ again upon] *some copies read* ogain upon
 sig. L3ᵛ when 'twas] *some copies read* when twas'
 sig. [L8]ʳ monstrously] *some copies read* monstruously
 sig. [T6]ʳ *295*] most copies read *592*

Three uncorrected errors in pagination may also be noticed:

 sig. I2ᵛ *129*] read *126*
 sig. [Q7]ʳ *259*] read *249*
 sig. [T5]ʳ *593*] read *293*

The Plays

In preparing the texts of the four plays, lines have been numbered continuously through each play, excluding prologues and epilogues, which have been numbered individually. Stage directions are not included in the line numbering. Except where they stand at the opening of a scene they are referred to in the notes by the number of the immediately preceding line followed by "sd."

For a complete discussion of the text of each play see the separate introductions.

The Poems

The first collected edition of Cartwright's minor poetry appeared in the *Works* (1651). The *Poems* occupy sigs. M5ʳ–X2ᵛ, plus the cancellans signed U, V2, [U3] (in the uncensored issue, U, U2, [U3]), following sig. T8. The separate title-page which occurs in two states, has already been discussed (see above, p. 70).

Moseley's collection includes eighty-eight poems. Only two definitely attributed poems have since been added, one of which, "November," was certainly known to Moseley, but was omitted for political reasons.[18] The other, "A Song of Dalliance," was first reprinted by A. H. Bullen[19] from one of the two seventeenth-century miscellanies in which it appeared after the publication of the *Works* (1651). One other poem "On one weepeing," printed by Goffin from a manuscript, is given in a very much shortened version by Moseley with the title "The Teares." The completeness of Moseley's collection probably reflects special help from Cartwright's Oxford friends and particularly the interest of Brian Duppa. Even when, as in numerous cases, an earlier printed edition of a poem existed, Moseley seems without exception to have used an independent manuscript source. This important fact gives Moseley's edition an added textual value.

Moseley does not include Cartwright's Latin poems since it was his intention to publish them later in a separate edition. This edition is advertised at the end of John Collop's *Poesis Rediviva* (1656) under the title, *Poemata Graeca et Latina a Gulielmo Cartwright e C.C.C. Oxon.*, "promised to be printed very speedily by H. Moseley." So far as we know, the book was never published.[20]

Even after the appearance of Moseley's collected *Works* (1651), a number of the poems and songs from the plays were reprinted in seventeenth-century miscellanies, and one or two were issued in separate editions. These publications are all listed in the notes to each poem.

---

18. In his preface "To the Reader" Moseley says: "And (take it on his word who never *subscrib'd* to a Lye) there's nothing kept from you but only one short Paper of Verses: what that is, and why it is not here, we need not tell you; for it hath been twice already Printed, though above our Power to bring it with its fellows." Moseley raises an interesting point when he claims the missing poem has already been printed twice. See my introductory note to "November."

19. *Speculum Amantis*, 1902, pp. 10–12.

20. There is no entry of it on the Stationers' Register. I have not seen the advertisement but quote it from Goffin (*Poems*, p. xli), who gives Oldys as his authority. The Harvard copy of Collop's *Poesis* does not contain the advertisement, but the last leaf, where it would presumably be found, is missing.

Cartwright's English poems were first reprinted as a whole by Alexander Chalmers in his collection *The English Poets* (VI, 513–48) in 1810.[21] Chalmers' edition is merely a reprint of Moseley's text, with the spelling and punctuation somewhat modified. Except in one or two cases no effort has been made to collate it for the present edition.

The first attempt at a modern critical text of the complete *Poems* appeared in 1918, from the press of Cambridge University under the editorship of R. Cullis Goffin. This edition is prefaced by an excellent introduction, to which I have had repeated cause to turn in the course of the preceding chapters. I regret that it is impossible to speak so highly of Mr. Goffin's text. His textual theory, if rather restricted, is good, but too frequently his practice fails to support the theory. If any justification for a new text were needed, I have only to ask the reader to glance at the variant readings. Among these variants Mr. Goffin's name is too prominent. On the other hand, much praise is due to Mr. Goffin for turning up manuscript copies and recording some of the later appearances of the poems in seventeenth-century miscellanies and in other poetry collections. This earlier spadework has made my own digging much easier, and for it I am profoundly grateful.

The present edition of the *Poems* follows the same editorial principles used in preparing the text of the plays. Each poem is given from the earliest printed text unless otherwise stated. Of this text, wherever possible, four copies have been collated. In a few cases only, it has seemed preferable to use a manuscript source. The variant readings, under the restrictions laid down at the beginning of this chapter, aim at completeness. Mr. Goffin's choice of variants seems to have been purely selective,[22] almost "haphazard." A good number of supplementary manuscripts and printed texts[23] have been

---

21. Proposals for a new edition of the plays and poems, "Carefully revised and corrected from the last Edition, in 1651; With Notes, Critical and Historical, and an Essay on his Life and Writings," were made in *The Playhouse Pocket-Companion* (1779), sig. [a2]ᵛ, by the "Author of the Critical HISTORY of the ENGLISH STAGE, prefixed to this Work." Although according to the advertisement it was "Printing by Subscription," this edition never saw the light. If we may judge from the author's "Critical History," the loss was not irreparable.

22. I suppose Mr. Goffin intended it to be understood that his variant readings are selective only. All he says is, "In the following pages, variant readings are given in footnotes" (p. xliii).

23. Appendix C offers a complete bibliography of all the known publications, printed before 1700, which contain works by Cartwright.

added to those given by Mr. Goffin, in particular three manuscripts,[24] two of "Falshood" and one of "A Sigh sent to his absent Love," which offer widely different versions from the printed 1651 text.

Following Cartwright's acknowledged poems, I have included in this edition eight poems of doubtful attribution. Seven of the poems, the so-called Splendora series, were first claimed for Cartwright by Miss Willa McClung Evans in an article entitled "To Splendora" (*PMLA*, LIV [June, 1939], 405-11). The principal evidence for associating the poems with Cartwright is found in the sixth of the series, "To Splendora weeping," the eight lines of which are in fact part of an acknowledged poem, "The Teares" (*Works*, 1651, p. 214). The same eight lines, still attributed to Cartwright, likewise appear in Henry Lawes' *Ayres and Dialogues* (1653, p. 21). Miss Evans also feels that the "subject-matter, imagery, vocabulary, and metric patterns" of the poems strengthen Cartwright's claim.

While there is, I believe, a fair possibility that the Splendora poems may be Cartwright's, I feel that the evidence needs a certain amount of qualification. In the first place, the appearance of the acknowledged Cartwright lines in the Splendora series is as evidence open to question, since seventeenth-century verse writers made little of *meum* and *tuum*. Moreover we may call to mind Moseley's warning in his preface "To the Reader":

Had you miss'd this *Impression*, 'tis odds you had seen none, or none entire: for, certain *Plagiaries* . . . began to plunder Him; which would have forc'd us to an *Action of Trover* for recovery of stollen *Wit*. They knew he was dead; and therefore One had the Forhead to affirm, that himself made Verses this last Summer, which our *Author* wrote (and whereof we had Coppies) Ten years since. Were his name worth spelling, you should have it. . . . Such Pick-Poets hereafter may rob, but cannot steal, for now this Book is every *Reader's*: . . .[25]

Indeed, we might pursue a very similar line of argument and claim the whole series for the author, probably Strode or Carew, of "On a Gentlewoman Walking in the Snow," since the last poem in the Splendora group, "To his Mrs Walking in ye snow," seems

---

24. A list of all the known Cartwright manuscripts may be found in Appendix D.

25. Note also the following lines from Francis Vaughan's commendatory verses (*Works*, 1651, sig. [****3]^r):

Cartwright, till now, we could have dress'd thy Shrine,
For 'twas but stealing some good Peece of thine;
Swear it our own, subscribe our names unto't,
And heretofore they made no bones to do't,
Who having robb'd thee, cry *'tis Scholar's Wit;*
And then the needy Gallants think th'are quit. . .

to be little more than an expanded version of that poem (see the Notes, p. 765). Goffin, for example, follows this line of reasoning when he prints as Cartwright's the poem entitled "On one weepeing," an expanded version of "The Teares." It should be noticed, perhaps, that "To his Mrs Walking in ye snow" and "On one weepeing" are from the same Bodleian MS. (Malone 21, fols. 78–79 and 52, respectively).

Turning now to the questions of "subject-matter, imagery, vocabulary, and metric patterns," it seems to me we must still take neutral ground. The subject-matter of the Splendora poems was, as Saintsbury on a similar occasion remarks, *publicissima*, and the imagery, some of which may indeed be compared with Cartwright's, can as easily be paralleled in other poets. Nor is the vocabulary more peculiarly Cartwright's than it is the vocabulary in general poetic use in the period. And it should be noticed that double epithets like "soule-inchaunting," "sence-amazing," and "dew-bepearled" are not typical of Cartwright. The metrical patterns, with one exception, are confined to the four- and five-stress couplet, the exception, "To Splendora A morning Salutation," being composed in a nine-line stanza. Arrangements of this sort are common enough in Cartwright, who was fond of irregular stanza forms and seems to have enjoyed experimenting with them. He employs two different nine-line stanzas, each once, though eight- and ten-line stanzas were his favorites. The Splendora stanza differs from Cartwright's, an argument in its favor, since Cartwright very rarely (three times in all) uses the same stanza form twice. Metrically only one point is here against Cartwright's authorship. That is the use of a one-foot line as the third verse of each stanza. Nowhere in his acknowledged work does Cartwright employ less than two major stresses in a stanza line. Finally, it may be observed that the rhymed couplets of the other Splendora poems are composed with a greater use of enjambement than is usual in Cartwright. Perhaps for this reason "To Splendora hauing seene and spoke with her through a window," a poem in which this tendency is less pronounced, seems to me most in Cartwright's couplet style.

In what has been said above I have tried to show why we must accept the evidence in favor of Cartwright's authorship of the Splendora poems with some caution. But it has not been my intention to disprove his authorship. Occasionally the tone and texture of the poems do strongly suggest Cartwright, or at least an imitator, and no modern edition of his works should omit them.

The eighth poem, "On the Prince Charles death," is, I believe, here printed for the first time. Its attribution to Cartwright rests entirely on the slender evidence of the initials "W.C." which immediately follow the title in the manuscript, though the verses as a whole are very much in Cartwright's more conceited manner. No serious claims are made for it.

THE LADY-ERRANT

INTRODUCTION

1. The Text

THE LADY-ERRANT was published for the first and only time in the *Works* (1651), having been entered on the Stationers' Register by Moseley May 4, 1648. There are no textual complications apart from the different states in which certain leaves (sigs. [²b8], c4, [c5]) occur (see the General Introduction, Chapter V, "The Text," p. 67). A transcript of the separate title-page and a signature collation may be found in the notes to the play. The present edition, based on a collation of four copies, reproduces the 1651 text, except where certain editorial changes have been necessary. All such changes are recorded in the Textual Notes. Alterations, additions, and deletions made by the Revels Office and the Restoration players for the 1671 revival of *The Lady-Errant* are given among the variant readings in the Textual Notes. The Restoration prompt copy is designated as *PC*.

Of the three lyrics which *The Lady-Errant* contains, two appeared in later seventeenth-century publications (see the notes to each lyric) and all, including also the Prologue and Epilogue, were reprinted by Goffin in his edition of the *Poems* (1918).

2. Date of Composition and Stage History

No definite date of composition can be advanced for *The Lady-Errant*. It has by some been thought to represent Cartwright's earliest dramatic venture, a view which would place it before March, 1635, by which time *The Ordinary* was almost certainly written. Others, however, have suggested that *The Lady-Errant* was composed after and as a result of the success of *The Royal Slave*. With one possible exception,[1] Cartwright's contemporaries make no mention

---

[1] John Berkenhead apparently mentions *The Lady-Errant* in his commendatory verses (sig. [****4]ʳ:

Where are such Flames, such Puissance and Sway,
As thy CRATANDER, or LUCASIA!
His Soul would fill a Globe, yet big as 'tis,
Hers would *informe* as great a World as His.

Unfortunately, even this reference is not certain, since the description of Lucasia rather better fits the character of Leucasia in *The Siege*.

of the play, and the evidence of style and construction affords small help, though the fact that *The Lady-Errant*, unlike *The Royal Slave*, contains something like a separately developed comic underplot links it with *The Siege*, which, whenever begun, is surely the last play which Cartwright completed. Actually, however, this link with *The Siege* would lend support to an early date, since that play on Cartwright's own authority was a revision, by royal command, of an earlier and unsatisfactory draft. Again, as Genest long ago pointed out, *The Lady-Errant* "begins well—promises much, and ends very flatly,"[2] a description which might be applied to many a piece of prentice work.

Miss Gebhardt, who seems to favor a later date, advances as evidence the tone of the Prologue and Epilogue, which, unlike those of *The Ordinary* and *The Royal Slave*, make no apology for youth or inexperience, and have, in fact, the polish and assurance of a writer confident of his success.[3] To this, of course, it may be objected that it is not experience, but inexperience, which dictates this tone, and that Cartwright learned the wisdom of at least assuming, if not feeling, a proper diffidence later.

The name of the heroine of *The Lady-Errant* presents a problem which if we knew more might give us a clue to the date of the play. The heroine's name was originally Calanthe, but for some reason it was changed to Lucasia, a change so carelessly carried out that vestiges of the original name still were lying about in the manuscript from which Moseley set up his 1651 text.[4] But the problem is really twofold: first, why change the name at all; and second, why change the name to Lucasia, a name so similar to Leucasia, the heroine of *The Siege*? Miss Gebhardt points out that Calanthe is the name of the heroine in both Ford's *Broken Heart* (1629) and Samuel Harding's *Sicily and Naples* (printed at Oxford in 1640, but written some years before) and concludes that perhaps "Calanthe may have appeared too popular a name for a heroine around 1638."[5]

---

2. *Some Account of the English Stage* (1832), X, 54.
3. Thesis, *The Ordinary*, pp. xxxv–xxxvi.
4. See my discussion of this point in the General Introduction, Chapter V, "The Text," p. 67.
5. Thesis, *The Ordinary*, p. xxxviii. It should perhaps be noticed that the heroine's name both in Ford's and in Harding's play is Calantha, not Calanthe. Miss Gebhardt speaks of "around 1638" because it was in that year that Harding, then a young man of eighteen, received his B.A., but the preface to the 1640 edition of Harding's play would seem to suggest that it was composed at an even younger age.

This answer, as I am sure Miss Gebhardt would admit, does not carry much weight. Nor does it suggest any solution to the other question, why having decided to alter the name, Cartwright chose Lucasia, supposing Leucasia of *The Siege* was already in existence, or if Leucasia was yet to be born, why she was later christened with a name so similar to an earlier brain child's.[6]

I should like to make one further suggestion, a suggestion which would set the date of the play between 1633 and about 1635. The opening lines of the Epilogue read:

> Though we well know the Neighbouring Plain
> Can strike from Reeds as high a Strain,
>   And that the Scrip, and Crook
>   May worst our Poet's Book. . . .

By the "neighbouring Plain" Cartwright must certainly be glancing at Cambridge, and the "Scrip, and Crook" which threatens to "worst our Poet's Book" refers presumably to a rival pastoral play either presented at Cambridge, or at least composed by a Cambridge writer and presented perhaps at Court. The Prologue adds two points: the audience viewing Cartwright's play is an aristocratic audience accustomed to Whitehall entertainments, and Cartwright's play, unlike some other play, gives no offence to the "Weak or Stubborn . . . Being the Female's Habit is / Her owne, and the Male's his"; in other words "each Sex keeps to it's Part." Is there a play which can fairly be said to answer all the demands of this interpretation? First, we can dismiss the question of a pastoral play acted at Cambridge. In the ten years from 1630 to 1640 Cambridge (as compared to Oxford) presented relatively few plays, mostly Latin comedies, and no pastorals.[7] We must look, therefore, for the play among those acted at Court. Only one, Montague's *Shepherd's Paradise* (1633), seems to fulfill all the points in the hypothesis. Walter Montague was a Cambridge man, a commoner at Sidney Sussex College. He received his M.A. from Cambridge in 1627, though not in any sense an academic figure like Cartwright. His play, *The Shepherd's Paradise*, is a long and, one may add, tedious pastoral romance and was presented at Whitehall in January, 1632/33. It was, moreover, the play which served to set off the whole Platonic love-cult

---

6. See a possible explanation for the choice of Lucasia in the General Introduction, Chapter IV, "Influence and Later Reputation," note 10.

7. This statement is based on information taken from Alfred Harbage, *Annals of English Drama, 975–1700* (1940).

drama, of which Cartwright's play is an example. And finally, and most important for our present inquiry, it was acted entirely by women, Queen Henrietta and her maids being the performers. This last fact gave rise to a good deal of criticism at the time and serves to give point to Cartwright's defense that here no women are masquerading as men. I submit this as at least a possible interpretation of what seem to be obvious topical allusions in the Prologue and Epilogue. If it is at all sound, *The Lady-Errant* would have to be dated within a year or two of Montague's play while such allusions might still be fresh enough to be caught by the audience.

Fleay[8] supposes that *The Lady-Errant* was performed at Oxford in 1635 or 1636, before the Elector Palatine and Prince Rupert. Now it is true that Prince Rupert visited Oxford with the royal party in August, 1636, and attended a performance of one of Cartwright's plays, but he saw *The Royal Slave*, not *The Lady-Errant*. Of an earlier visit of either Rupert or his elder brother I can find no trace. Although Fleay's suggestion seems invalid, there can be no doubt, judging from the tone of the Prologue and Epilogue, that as already noticed, the play was performed before an aristocratic, if not royal, audience. Mr. Nicoll strangely enough, ignoring the evidence of this Prologue and Epilogue, thinks *The Lady-Errant* was never performed;[9] and Mr. Schelling, going to the other extreme, asserts that not only *The Lady-Errant* but also *The Ordinary* had been presented before royalty.[10]

The following lines, already noticed in part, make it seem certain that the female roles in *The Lady-Errant* were actually played by women:[11]

> And that each Sex keeps to it's Part,
> Nature may plead excuse for Art.
>
> As then there's no Offence
> Giv'n to the Weak or Stubborn hence,
> Being the Female's Habit is
> Her owne, and the Male's his. . . .

---

8. F. G. Fleay, *Biographical Chronicle the English Drama* (1891), I, 48.

9. A. Nicoll, *Stuart Masques and the Renaissance Stage* (1938), p. 139.

10. F. E. Schelling, *Elizabethan Drama 1558-1642* (1908), II, 90. There is absolutely no evidence for such a statement so far as *The Ordinary* is concerned. Of course, neither Mr. Nicoll nor Mr. Schelling knew of the newly discovered Restoration prompt copy of *The Lady-Errant*.

11. F. G. Fleay (*Biographical Chronicle of the English Drama*, I, 48) seems to have been the first to call attention to this fact.

INTRODUCTION

The joint appearance of male and female actors in a regular play at this early date is, to put it conservatively, very unusual. That the women who took part were members of the gentry or nobility and not professional actresses, no one will question. The performance of the Queen and her maids in Montague's *Shepherd's Paradise* (1632/33) has already been discussed, but in that, all the roles were played by women. The participation of men and women in the masques of the period, while affording something of a precedent, is scarcely comparable. There is, indeed, a reference in Richard Brome's *Court Beggar* (1632) which suggests that women actors were less uncommon than we now suppose: "and his mother can play her part; women-Actors now grow in request." This, it will be noticed, dates about a year earlier than the performance of Montague's play. Probably, however, Brome is referring to the playing of French women comedians which set London talking in 1629, and so outraged Lawyer Prynne.[12]

Mr. Nicoll thinks that in writing *The Lady-Errant* Cartwright was composing with scenery in mind and points to the "Grove" and the two trees in III, i, as evidence. Such a supposition is unnecessary, since there are a number of earlier plays making similar or greater scenic demands and yet clearly not involving, as in *The Royal Slave*, the use of actual scenes.

Certain changes were made in *The Lady-Errant* for the 1671 revival by Sir Henry Herbert and the players of the Duke's Company. Herbert's license, which in this case is only signed by him, reads:

> March: 9: 1671: This Play Called The Lady Errant
> may bee Acted by the Dukes Company of Actors
> as Lycenced by
>
>   Henry Herbert
> Millb: Westm^r   M.R.

So far as the Revels Office was concerned *The Lady-Errant* afforded very little opportunity for an exercise of authority.[13] Occasional

---

12. Fleay (*ibid.*) remarks that through an imperfect reference in Ward's *English Dramatic Literature* he was at first misled into the belief that Prynne in his criticism of the French actresses was actually referring to Cartwright's *Lady-Errant*.

13. It seems a little uncertain what fee Sir Henry asked for licensing The *Lady-Errant* and *The Ordinary*. The usual fee for a new play was two pounds. If, however, they were considered as old plays, as indeed they were though they had not before been licensed, the fee was only one pound. See *The Dramatic Records of Sir Henry Herbert*, ed. J. Q. Adams (1917), p. 121.

oaths and mentions of the deity were crossed out. But this is all. More of a problem, however, faced the professional censors, whose business it was to make the play "go" on the stage. According to modern taste the revival of *The Lady-Errant* is difficult to understand. We naturally ask, why not *The Siege* or *The Royal Slave*? Actually, it seems quite possible that *The Royal Slave* was revived. *The Siege* is another question. In a number of essentials *The Siege* is much more in the manner of Restoration heroics than *The Lady-Errant*. It is, moreover, a better play. Two things, however, might conceivably have militated against its revival: the prominence of the comic element—an element considerably cut in *The Lady-Errant* (see below); and the serious plot itself, which exhibits an attempt upon the life of a lascivious monarch by an outraged virgin. We have only to recall the fate of such a play as *The Maid's Tragedy* during the reign of Charles II to appreciate the difficulty here. *The Lady-Errant*, on the other hand, is a perfectly harmless and "moral" play, but I fear it brought the actors little more than enough to pay for the expenses of production, and, as Downes in another case remarks, "Expir'd the third Day." Presumably the decision of the company to produce *The Lady-Errant* rested upon some moderate success which had attended the revival of *The Ordinary* some months earlier.[14]

In an attempt to speed up the action of the play, the theater censors omit four entire scenes: II, v; IV, iii and iv; V, i (a long comedy scene, ll. 1705–1826). Possibly another short scene (V, iii) was also meant to be cut. These, however, represent the only serious omissions. Some of the longer speeches are slightly cut, and an effort to bring Cartwright's language up to date can be traced in a number of minor changes: "The Means advis'd" (l. 9) becomes "The Means most easy"; "pricking" (l. 381) becomes "riding"; "share in their meat" (l. 462) becomes "eate at their tabl[e]." Many of Cartwright's figurative or metaphorical expressions are either ironed out or cut out: "Politique dore" (l. 3), for example, is changed to "gates of State," and "wheels o'th'State" (l. 64) to "gouernment." With the laudable intention of lending variety to the entertainment three new dances are introduced: the first, a "Dance [o]f 8," in the second scene of Act II; the second, a solo jig by "Nicias,"[15] just before Eumela's song in Act III, Scene iv; the third, a "Grand dance," climaxing the play in the last scene of Act V.

---

14. Herbert's license for *The Ordinary* is dated "January 15. 1671."

15. It is a curious coincidence that "Nicias" is the name of one of the characters in Cartwright's *Siege*.

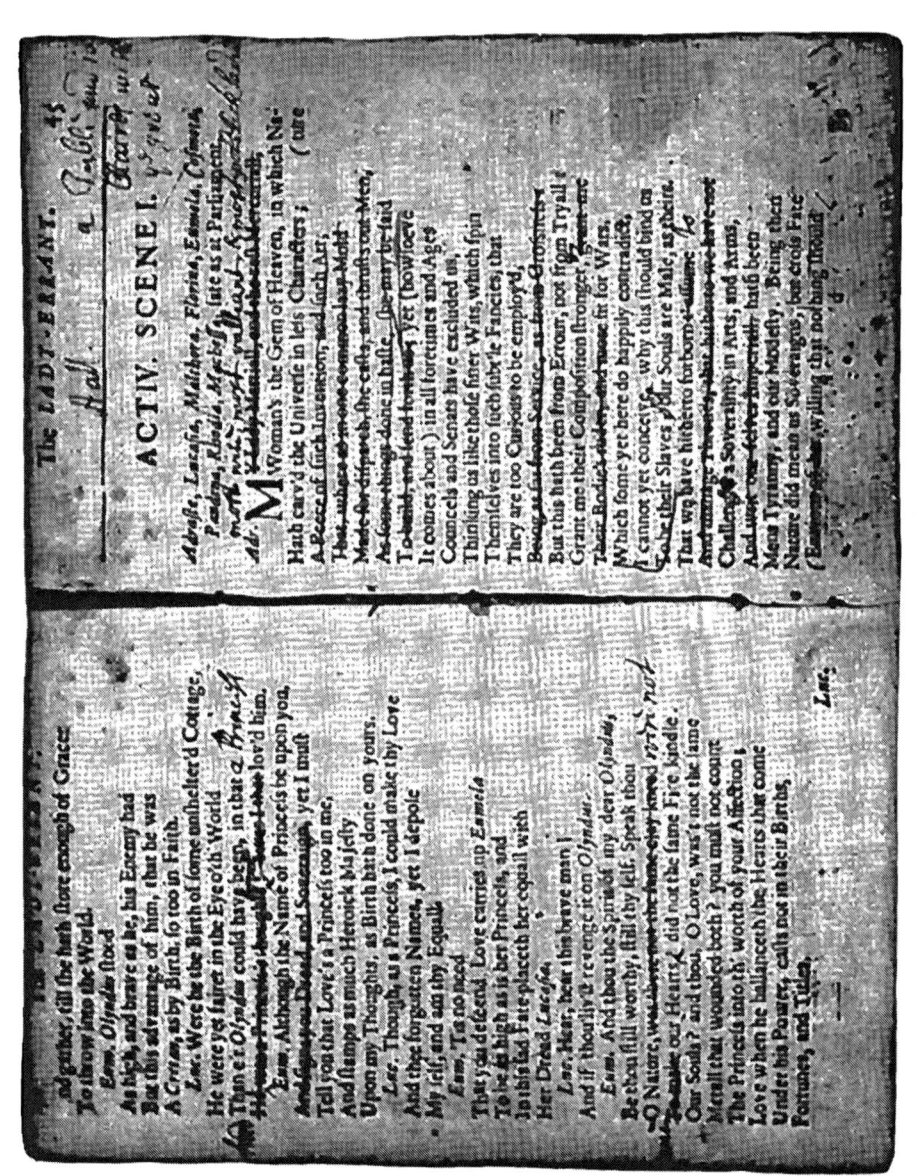

Two pages from the Restoration prompt copy of *The Lady-Errant*, showing the prompter's hand, the reviser's hand, and deletion by crossing through and circling. Reproduced through the kindness of Professor T. W. Baldwin.

The scenery indicated in the brief notes at the beginning of some of the scenes appears to have been of the simplest. No setting is noted until the first scene of Act II, when a "Hall" is called for. Only two other scenes are distinguished. A "Grove" first appears in Act II, Scene vi, and seems to serve until the first scene of Act IV, when the "Hall" is again needed. Finally, in Act V, Scene ii, the setting is marked "Pallace." It will be noticed that none of these settings makes any demands that could not readily be met by old stock pieces. Apparently, the Duke's Company were not disposed to make too much of an initial outlay, on the whole an understandable diffidence.

3. Sources

No direct source for *The Lady-Errant* is known. Cartwright probably received his initial hint for a female commonwealth from Aristophanes.[16] Three of Aristophanes' comedies deal with the question of female interference in the affairs of state: *Lysistrata*, *The Thesmophoriazusæ*, and *The Ecclesiazusæ*. Only the last two concern us here. Mr. Schelling thinks that Cartwright used *The Thesmophoriazusæ* "for his suggestion."[17] In my opinion *The Ecclesiazusæ* affords the closer parallel. Both plays were almost certainly well known to Cartwright, in whose mind they must have formed an inseparable pair. Another treatment of the same theme, likewise stemming from Aristophanes, and surely familiar to Cartwright from his school days, may be found in Erasmus' *Colloquies*, under the title "The Assembly, or Parliament, of Women."[18]

Ward, ignoring Aristophanes, suggests that Fletcher's *Sea-Voyage* (1622) was Cartwright's inspiration for the central idea of a female commonwealth.[19] The suggestion has been repeated again and again. Actually the connection between the two plays is slight. A female commonwealth may be found in both, but each is conceived of and developed in an utterly different manner. In Fletcher, the members of the woman's commonwealth, finding themselves deceived by

16. Both Fleay (*Biographical Chronicle of the English Drama*, I, 48) and Hazlitt (*Play-Collector's Manual*, 1892, p. 127) note that one scene is taken from Aristophanes. Their reference here is vague, for both are merely echoing Genest (*Some Account of the English Stage*, 1832, X, 54): "... in the comic scenes, the women form a conspiracy against the men, with a view to get the affairs of the state into their own hands —this is borrowed from Aristophanes."

17. *Elizabethan Drama, 1558–1642*, II, 46.

18. See the Notes (IV, i) for further discussion.

19. A. W. Ward, *English Dramatic Literature* (1899), III, 139.

men and by force of circumstances confined to a deserted island, abjure the company of man on pain of death. Cartwright, on the other hand, following the lead of Aristophanes, makes the principle behind the forming of the woman's commonwealth political, when the women decide that they will take over the reins of government which too long have been usurped by overweening man. On one point alone Fletcher and Cartwright agree: all men must be completely banished from the female state.[20] Such an idea, of course, finds no echo in Aristophanes. For a common source, however, we have only to turn to the well-worn legend of the Amazons.

Although no definite source for Cartwright's conception of the character of Machessa, the Lady-Errant, can be indicated, the springs from which she rose are not difficult to trace. Burlesques of the ridiculous stories and popular heroes of knight-errantry are common, from *Don Quixote* and *The Knight of the Burning Pestle* to Holland's *Romancio-Mastix* or Butler's *Hudibras*. Once given the idea of satire, the rest follows.[21] Again, given the Amazon tradition and the long line of its descendants from Hippolyta to Bradamante and Britomart, the conception of a warlike and "mankind" woman is not a remarkable invention.[22] Machessa's only new characteristic is her heroic resolve to "disobliege our Sex" from the obligations which past generations of knights-errant had heaped upon it.

Other sources and literary parallels are discussed in the notes.

---

20. This point is not very clearly worked out in Cartwright's play.

21. Cartwright did not even invent the term "Lady-Errant." Earlier uses may be found in Shirley's *The Ball* (1632), V, i, and in Randolph's *The Jealous Lovers* (1632), II, vi.

22. A "martial maid" plays a considerable role in Fletcher's *Love's Cure*.

THE LADY-ERRANT.

A

Tragi-Comedy.

Written by
Mr WILLIAM CARTVVRIGHT,
Late Student of *Christ-Church* in
OXFORD, and Proctor of
the *University*.

LONDON,
Printed for *Humphrey Moseley*, and
are to be sold at his shop at the Sign of
the Princes Armes in St *PAVLS*
Churchyard. 1651.

The Prologue.

SAcred to your Delight
   Be the short Revels of this Night;
That Calme that in yond Myrtles moves,
   Crowne all your Thoughts, and Loves:
And as the fatall Yew-tree shews   [5]
No Spring among those happy Boughs,
So be all Care quite banisht hence
Whiles easie Quiet rocks your Sence.

   We cannot here complain
Of want of Presence, or of Train;   [10]
For if choice Beauties make the Court,
   And their Light guild the Sport,
This honour'd Ring presents us here
Glories as rich and fresh as there;
   And it may under Question fall,   [15]
Which is more Court, This, or White-Hall.

   Be't so. But then the Face
Of what we bring fits not the Place,
And so we shall pull down what ere
   Your Glories have built here: [20]
Yet if you will conceive, that though
The Poem's forc'd, We are not so;
And that each Sex keeps to it's Part,
Nature may plead excuse for Art.

   As then there's no Offence   [25]
Giv'n to the Weak or Stubborn hence,
Being the Female's Habit is
   Her owne, and the Male's his:
So (if great things may steer by less)
May you the same in looks express: [30]
Your Weare is Smiles, and Gracious Eyes;
When ere you frown 'tis but disguise.

The Persons.

Demarchus	King of *Cyprus*.
Dinomachus	King of *Crete*.
Charistus	Son to *Dinomachus*.
Philondas *Pæstanus*	Two Lords of *Cyprus*, the one Husband to *Florina*, the other to *Malthora*.
Olyndus	A young Lord of *Cyprus*, left at home by reason of sickness.
Lerinus *Ganyctor* *Iringus*	3. Courtiers left at home.
3 Priests	Belonging to *Apollo*'s Temple in *Crete*.
Adraste	Queen to *Demarchus*.
Lucasia	Daughter to them.
Florina *Malthora*	Two Ladies sadly bearing the Absense of their Lords.
Cosmeta *Pandena* *Rhodia*	Three busie factious Ladies, and contrary to the two former.
Eumela	A young Lady Confident to the Princess.
Machessa	A Lady-Errant for the time.
Philænis	Her Page.

The Scene Cyprus.

The Lady-Errant.

ACT. I. SCEN. I.

Cosmeta, Pandena, (Rhodia between them) busily discoursing in the Myrtle Grove.

   Cos. AND if you see not Women plead, and judge,
Raise, and depress, reward, and punish, carry
Things how they please, and turn the Politique dore
Upon new hindges very shortly, never
Beleeve the Oracle.
   Rhod. Could I see't 'twould prove [5]
An Antidote against old Age, and make me
Grow younger still without Expence or Art.
   Pan. You sin past pardon *Rhodia*, if you doubt it.
   Cos. The plot's most firm and strong.
   Pan. The Means advis'd.
   Cosm. The carriage hitherto successefull; we [10]
Gain daily to our side.
   Rhod. Doe they come in?
   Pan. As to a Marriage; Offer money, Plate,
Jewels, and Garments, nay the Images
Of their Male-Gods.
   Cosm. The very name of Rule
Raises their Blouds, and makes 'em throw their Wealth [15]
Away as heartily, as if they were
Young Heires, or old Philosophers.
   Rhod. Why then,
There's one care sav'd *Cosmeta*.
   Cosm. What's that pray?
   Rhod. I was preparing strong Preservatives
Against our Lords came home, for fear of fainting [20]
At their Arrivall.

Pan. They'd have smelt indeed
Of Labour, Sweat, Dust, Man, and Victory.
   Cosm. And such grosse Rustick sents, that a Court nose
Without the patience of a Stoick, could not
Have possibly endur'd them.
   Rhod. I believe [25]
They'd have encreas'd the Bill, and some would weekly
Have dy'd of the Lords Return from the *Cretan* War:
What growth's your Plot of Madam?
   Cosm. O it ripens
Past expectation! See, Besides our selves   { *Puls out a*
Eleven Court-Ladies on the Roll already;   {   *Roll.*   [30]
Hyantha then sends word, that ten, or twelve
Very substantiall Countrey-Ladies have
Subscrib'd three days ago.
   Pan. My Province here,
The City-wives, swarm in, strive, and make means
Who shall command their Husbands first.
   Cosm. And then [35]
Of Countrey Gentlewomen, and their eldest daughters,
More than can write their Names; 'Tis now past danger.
   Rhod. But, Madam, how'l you gain the men at home?
   Cos. For that brace & half of Courtiers there, *Ganyctor*,
Lerinus, and *Iringus*, they are mine, [40]
Fast in the Net, if I but pitch it only.
   Rhod. Look where they come, pray sweare 'em presently.

ACT. I. SCEN. II.

Ganyctor, Lerinus, Iringus.

   Cosm. I'll give 'em but my hand to kiss, and 'twill
Bind 'em as fast, as if it were the holiest
Of the best *Sibyls* Leaves.
   Pan. Favour your tongues; [45]
Let's lie in Ambush here a while, and listen
What they discourse of.
   Rhod. Why of Women I warrant y'.
   Cosm. Peace *Rhodia*, peace, close sweet *Pandena*, close!

Irin. *Lerinus*, this hath been the worst Spring that
I ever knew.
   Lorin. Faith it has', for *Flora* [50]
Still challeng'd it before, but now *Bellona*
Hath got the time: Roses and Violets were
The fruit o'th' Season formerly, but now
Laying, and raising Sieges: Building up
And pulling down of Castles; Manning, and [55]
Demolishing of Forts have sign'd the Months.
   Gan. Where beauteous Ladies slumber'd, & were guarded
By the enamor'd Lizards (as if *Cadmus*
In envy had reserv'd some Serpents teeth
And sown 'em there) hard watchings and rough Guards [60]
Fill and make up the field.
   (*Cosm.* Most smoothly said,
And like a Cowardly Poet.)
   Irin. There's a feare
The Women too will rise at home.
   Ler. Their fingers
Itch to be tamp'ring with the wheels o'th' State.
   Gan. 'Tis very well my Lord *Olyndus* then [65]
Is left at home.
   Ler. How does his Lordship now?
Still angry that his Majesty would not let
His Sickness go against the Enemy?
   Irin. He finds the hardest Wars at home, he hath
Visits, and Onsets, that molest him more [70]
Than all his griefs. He now complains of health;
The eager Ladyes do besiege him hourly,
Not out of love so much, as want of men;
Any thing now, that wears but Breeches only,
Is plotted, and projected for as much [75]
As a new Fashion, or an Office 'bove Stairs.
   Ler. They do call this their time of Persecution,
Swear they are living Martyrs.
   Gan. Then the Punishment
Must make 'em so; I'm sure the cause will never.
   Ler. A man is striven for as eagerly [80]
As the last loaf in a great depth of Famine.
   Irin. You won't believe what I shall tell you now;

Pandena and sweet *Rhodia* at this instant
Both love me, hate each other, eager Rivals;
The one enshrines her Mellons in pure Chrystall, [85]
And as the fruit doth ripen, so her hopes
Of me doe ripen with it——
   (*Pan.* Monstrous fellow!)
   Irin. The other counts her Apricots, and thinks
So many kisses grow there; lays 'em naked
And open to the Sun, that it may freely [90]
Smile on her vegetable Embraces.
   (*Rho.* Good! do you hear this, Madam?)
   (*Cos.* Peace and let him on.)
   Irin. The one presents me, and the other presents me
Gums, Spicknard-boxes, Fruits, and early Roses,
Figs, Mushrooms, Bulbi, and what not? I am [95]
More reverenc'd than their Houshold-God, and taste
Their store before him still.
   (*Cosm.* Close yet for my sake.)
   Irin. And proud *Cosmeta*——
   (*Pan.* Nay you must hear't out too.)
   Irin. She, that, if there were Sexes 'bove the Moon,
Would tempt a Male Idea, and seduce [100]
A Separate Hee-Substance into Lewdness,
Hath smil'd, glanc'd, wink'd, and trod upon my toes,
Sent smooth Epistles to me, whom I let
Pass unregarded, as a suing Beauty,
And one that makes my triumph up——
[*As he speaks* Cosmeta *and the other two Ladies approach.*
Fair Ladies [105]
You make my Triumph up in that I see you.
   Cosm. What? have you been at the Wars then Captain?
   Irin. Madam
I've stood o'th' shore, and wisht well to our Fleet.
   Cos. If that be all, pray how comes so much Crest,
And Scarfe, and Boot to be misplac'd on you? [110]
   Gan. Is't not a time of War, dear Lady?
   Pan. You follow
The times then, though you won't the Camp.
   Ler. 'Tis fit
We should be in the Field-fashion however.

Rho. 'Cause you intend the Wars at home perhaps.
Irin. Troth the beleagering of you, Lady, will [115]
Hardly deserve the name of a Siedge; you'll yeeld
So easily on the first approach.
Cosm. You doe
Mistake her, Sir, she means, that you intend
To take great Towns at home——
Pan. Demolish Castles,
And high-built Pyes at once——
Rho. Gaine Sconces 'twixt [120]
The first and second Course——
Cosm. And in the vertue
Of the large *Cretan* Jar kill men at Table.
Irin. No Lady, we do stay at home to make 'em.
Pan. The Wars indeed'll exhaust the Kingdom much.
Cos. And fit tis that should some way be supply'd. [125]
Irin. You won't corrupt me, Madam! pray forbear.
Cos. No, Sir, I will not do the State that harm;
For the Corruption of one Coward must
Needs be the Generation of another.
Ler. I'll warrant th' Issue will be truly valiant. [130]
Rho. And how so Captain *Stay-by-it?*
Pan. Madam, he
Can neither fight nor speak: I'll tell you how.
That you're a Coward, Sir, is granted: Thus then;
Either your Father was valiant, or was not.
Irin. A very sure division, Lady, that. [135]
Pan. If he were valiant, and you a Coward,
'Tis your Sons course next to be valiant;
But if he were not valiant, and that
You are a Coward of a Coward, then
Your Lineall Issue must be valiant needs, [140]
Because two Negatives make an Affirmative.
Cosm. A most invincible Argument!
Irin. This shall not
Serve I assure you, say what e're you will
You shall not reason me to your Bed-side.
Rho. No, Sir. [145]
Cos. Not though we send you Mellons?
Pan. Ripen'd Hopes?

Rho. Apricocks, Figges?
Pan. Vegetable Embraces?
Cos. And smooth Epistles? Go you vile abusers
Of what you cannot compass; 'cause you nourish
Desires, you will discharge the sin on us. [150]
Irin. Ladies you're much deceiv'd: had you the Aphorismes
Of th' Art perfect, that each word should go
With a designe, that not an Eye should be
Lift up, or cast down without mystery——
Ler. Could you force sighs, faigne passions, manage looks, [155]
Season your jests, speak with a Manner still——
Gan. Should you consult a Decade of Chambermaids,
And sadly advise with your Chrystall Oracles,
In which Attire your Beauties would appear
Most strong; in what contrivance your sweet Graces [160]
Would be most fierce, and overcome Spectators,
You should not have one look to quench the fire.
Ler. You shall be Vestals by compulsion still——
Irin. You shall make Verses to me e're I've done;
Call me your *Cælius*, your *Corinnus*, and [165]
Make me the Man o'th' Book in some Romance,
And after all I will not yield.
Rho. You're got
Into a safe field of Discourse, where you
Are sure, that Modestie will not suffer us
To answer you in a direct line.
Cosm. You were [170]
Wont to go whining up and down, and make
Dismall Soliloquies in shady Woods——
Pan. Discourse with Trees——
Rho. And Dialogue with Eccho's——
Cos. Send Messages by Birds, make discreet Thrushes
Your trusty Agents 'twixt your Loves and you—— [175]
Rho. Which Loves you call'd Nymphs——
Cos. When indeed they were
Milkmaids, or some such Drudges. This your rating
And prizing of your selves, and standing off,
Comes not from any bett'ring of your Judgements,
But from your Mouth's being out of taste.
Pan. Pray y' what [180]
Employment are you fit for?

 Ler. Ile assure you
None about you.
 Cos. Their whole Employment is
To goe Embassadors 'twixt retir'd Ladies——
 Pan. To ask how this great Ladies Physick wrought——
 Rho. Give an account o'th' vertue of her Drugs. [185]
 Cos. Make perfect Audit of the Tale of sighs
Some little Dog did breath in his first sleep:
Goe you Reproach and Refuse of your Countrey.
 Gan. You speak most valiantly Heroick Lady.
 Ler. Pray *Venus* you permit the Lords to rule [190]
The Common-wealth again, when they come home.
 Pan. Know Sir, they shall not——
 Cos. And you shall consent,
Ayd, and assist us in't in spight of you,
Willing or unwilling, all's one.
 Irin. Wee'll leave you.
 Gan. Your Company grows dangerous.
 Ler. 'Tis half Treason [195]
To hear you talk.
 Pan. Before you 'tis very safe. *Ex. Gan. Irin. Ler.*
You'll never dare t' engage your selves so much
I'th' Army, as to inform the King of't.
 Rho. Come,
Let us away too.
 Cos. We will vex 'em through
All sorts of Torment, meet 'em at each Corner, [200]
Write Satyrs, and make Libels of 'em, put 'em
In Shows, & Mock-Shows, Masques, & Plaies, present 'em
In all Dramatique Poetry: they shall
Be sung i'th Markets, wee'll not let 'em rest
'Till themselves sue to be o'th' Female *Covenant*. [205]

Act. I. Scen. III.

To them *Eumela*.

 Pan. But hold, here comes *Eumela*.
 Cos. Lady Secretary
Unto our future State, God give you joy.

Eum.   You bestow Offices, as City Mothers
After their Travail, do give Flowers between
Their House and *Juno*'s Temple, to the next [210]
They meet, or as you do your Ribbands, to
Entangle, not Reward.
  Pan.   Then you are Wise
And Politique still——
  Rho.   Of the Male-faction Lady?
  Cos.   And you will suffer by Prescription still?
But to be serious now; what do you do? [215]
  Eum.   That which you would, if you should come to Rule:
Wake, Sleep, Rise, Dress, Eat, Visit, and Converse,
And let the State alone.
  Cos.   Y'are very short.
  Eum.   Indeed I am somewhat now in haste; I'm going
To meet a pair of Ladies, that would willing [220]
Keep their own Sex, and not turn Lords.
  Pan.   You mean
Florina, and *Malthora*, those that are
Sad now, that one day they may be in History
Under the name of Turtles.
  Cos.   What Dialect may
Those Ladies grieve in? *Dorick* or *Ionick*? [225]
Doe they make Verses yet?
  Eum.   Their Manners are
A kind of *Satyr* upon yours; though they
Intend it not, the people read 'em so.
  Rho.   'Cause they have laid aside their Jewels, and so
Blinded their Garments——
  Cos.   'Cause they eat their sweet-meats [230]
In a black Closet, they are counted faithfull,
The sole *Penelope's* o'th'time, the Ladies
Of the chaste Web i'th' absence of their Lords.
  Eum.   Your sadnesse would be such perhaps, if you
Would take the pains to shew the Art of Mourning. [235]
  Rho.   Is there another way of grieving then?
  Eum.   This is not grief, but stands to be thought grief:
They are not of such vaunting popular sorrow;
Their Tapers are not dy'd in dismall hue,
And set in Ebon Candlesticks; they wear [240]

No sad black Sarcenet Smocks, nor do they smutch
Their women, to be serv'd by mourning Faces;
This were to grieve to Ostentation,
Not to a reall friendship.
   Pan. Is there friendship
Think you 'twixt man and wife?
   Eum. You'll say, perhaps,   [245]
You, and your Husband, have not been friends yet.
   Pan. Madam, you prophecy.
   Eum. I might be thought t'have done so,
Had I foretold a truth to come, but this
Is History already.
   Cos. If they do not this,
Nor wear the day out in a hoodwinkt room,   [250]
Where there's no living thing besides the Clock,
Nor yet take Physick to look pale, what doe they?
   Eum. They grieve themselves, their Doctor grieves not for them:
They do that in the Absence of their Lords
That you would in the Presence of your own.   [255]
   Cos. You see we look as fat, and fair as ever——
   Eum. Your Kitchin's warm, your Box, and Pencils fail not.
   Pan. —We are as long in dressing as before—
   Eum. And have the same Romancys read, the same
Letters brought to you, whilst y'are doing it.   [260]
   Rho. —Sleep, and take rest, as then, and altogether
Speak as much wit as we did before the wars.
   Eum. And to as little purpose.
   Cos. Fie *Eumela!*
That you should be so obstinate, as to hear
Wealth, Honour, Pleasure, Rule, and every good   [265]
Knock at your door, and yet not let 'em in.
   Eum. Madam, I know my Looking-glasse wo'n't shew
The altering o'th' State, when it presents
The changes of my Face, and that I cannot
Order the Kingdome, as I do my Hair.   [270]

                  Enter *Florina* and *Malthora.*

   Pan. Yonder's your business; Madam, there are three
Sad things arriv'd, two Ladies and a Lute.

Cos.   But shall I write you down before you go
The thirteenth in the Rowl of the Asserters
Of Female Liberty?
   Eum.   If Liberty be the thing [275]
You so much stand for, pray you give me mine;
I neither grant, nor yet deny; I will
Consider.
   Cos.   We dismiss you, Madam, then
Unto your serious Counsell.
   Eum.   Fare you well.

                    Exeunt Cosm. Pan. Rho.

Act I. Scen. IV.

*Eumela goes to Florina and Malthora who
are sate in the Grove.*

   Flo.   O come, *Eumela*, thou dost know, without thee [280]
Our thoughts are Desarts, Rocks, and Sands, and all
That either Nature's absent from, or hath
Reserv'd unto her self alone.
   Eum.   I bring you
Noise, Trouble, Tumult, and the World; but if
There were that power in my worthless presence, [285]
That I could cast a day upon your thoughts,
You should not think of Places that are sacred
To Night, and Silence: Visits still, and Feasts
And the whole Ring and Throng of Mirth should stir
In your delighted Souls.
   Mal.   Prethee *Eumela* [290]
Is there no secret ancient Grove, that hath
Stood from the birth of Nature to this time,
Whose vast, high, hollow Trees seem each a Temple,
Whose paths no curious Eye hath yet found out,
Free from the Foot and Axe.
   Eum.   If I could tell you [295]
It were found out already.
   Flo.   Hast thou read
Of any Mountain, whose cold frozen top
Sees Hail i'th' Bed, not yet grown round, and Snow

I'th' Fleece, not Carded yet, whose hanging weight
Archeth some still deep River, that for fear [300]
Steals by the foot of't without noise.
   Eum. Alas!
These are the things, that some poor wretched Lover
Unpittied by his scornfull Shepherdesse
Would wish for, after that he had look'd up
Unto the Heavens, and call'd her Cruell thrice, [305]
And vow'd to dye.
   Flor. I prethee pardon me;
I live without my self.
   Eum. But I have read
Of a tall secret Grove, where loving Winds
Breathing their sighs among the trembling Boughs,
Blow Odes, and Epods; where a murmuring Brook [310]
Will let us see the Brother to our Sun,
And shew's another World there under water.
   Mal. Prethee let's go, and find it out, and live there.
   Eum. Our Ancient Poet *Linus* somewhere sings
Of some such thing.
   Mal. Thou alwaies dost deceive us; [315]
Thou told'st us of an Eccho too, and when
Thou brought'st us to it, thou had'st put *Philænis*
Behind the Wall, to give us all the Answers.
   Flor. Yes, and thy bringing in my Father's Dwarf
With Bow and Wings, and Quiver at his back, [320]
Instead of *Cupid*, to conveigh us Letters
Through th' Air from hence to *Crete*, was but a trick
To put away our sadness. But I had
Almost forgot what we came for, I prethee
Take up the Lute there, and let's hear the Ode, [325]
That thou did'st promise us; I hope 'tis sad.

        The Ode sung by *Eumela.*

   To carve our Loves in Myrtle rinds,
     And tell our Secrets to the Woods,
   To send our Sighs by faithful Winds,
     And trust our Tears unto the Flouds, [330]
       To call where no man hears,
       And think that Rocks have Ears;

To Walke, and Rest, to Live, and Dye,
And yet not know Whence, How, or Why;
To have our Hopes with Fears still checkt, [335]
To credit Doubts, and Truth suspect,
   This, this is that we may
   A Lover's Absence say.
Follies without, are Cares within;
Where Eyes do fail, there Souls begin. [340]

  Mal. Thou art a harmless Syren fair *Eumela.*
  Flor. 'Tis very true indeed; thou feed'st at once,
And dost correct our follyes: but wert thou
As we, thoud'st do the like.
  Eum. For Love's sake tell me
Why should you seek out Groves, where the bright Sun [345]
Can make no day, although he throw upon 'em
Whole flouds of Light, Places where Nature will
Be blind in spight of Him? Why should you fancy
Caves fit to write sad Revelations in?
Or why a Lover stretcht on shaggy Moss [350]
Between two Beds of Poppey to procure
One Minut's slumber?
  Flor. These, *Eumela*, are not
The Journyes but Digressions of our Souls,
That being once inform'd with Love, must work,
And rather wander, than stand still. I know [355]
There is a Wisdom to be shewn in Passions;
And there are stayd and setled griefs: I'l be
Severe unto my self, and make my Soul
Seek out a Regular Motion, towards him
Whom it moves to, and thou shalt shortly see [360]
Love bleed, and yet stoop to Philosophy.

Act I. Scen. V.

Olyndus and Charystus *toward them.*

  Eum. Madam I must away; *Olyndus* yonder
Is hasting towards me.

Mal. Farewell *Eumela*,
Be ever happy.
   Flor. And may some good God
Cherish thy Loves, as thou dost cherish others. *Ex. Fl. & Ma.* [365]
   Eum. My Lord *Olyndus*, what's your bus'ness to me?
   Olyn. Vertuous *Eumela*, you must doe me the favour
To give this Letter into th' Princess's hands
With all the speed and secrecy you may.
   Eum. I carry with me Night, and wings my Lord. *Ex.* [370]
   Cha. O my *Olyndus*, were there not that thing
That we call Friend, Earth would one Desart be,
And Men Alone still, though in Company.   *Exeunt.*

ACT. II. SCENE I.

Machessa, Philænis, *and after a while* Cosmeta,
Pandena, Rhodia.

   Mac. Give me my Javelin; hangs my Fauchion right?
Three Ladyes sayst thou? So! go fetch 'em in now. [375]
What? goes the Tilting on I mention'd? Is there   { *En. Pan.*
No Just, nor Turnament yet granted out?   { *Cos. Rho.*
   Cos. You're well appointed Madam.
   Mach. How I hate
That Name of Madam, it befits a Chamber:
Give me the words o'th' Field, such as you'd give [380]
To fairer Ladyes pricking o'r the Plains
On foaming Steeds. But I do pardon you.
Shews not this Scarf and Fauchion far more comely,
Than paultry pyebald Ribbands, and young Bodkins?
   Pan. You wear a rigid Beauty, fierce Delights. [385]
   Rho. Your Pleasures threaten, and your stubborn Graces
Tempt, and defend at once.
   Mach. Why now y'are right.
And what say'st thou, my little Noon-tide shadow?
My trusty Pigmy?
   Phil. Now indeed, and truly——
   Mach. Hell o' these simpring Protestations! [390]

Thou sinfull Inch of short Mortality,
Give Ear to my Instructions: here I swear
By th' Sacred Order of my Lady-Errantry,
If thou effeminat'st thy discourse once more
With these precise, minc'd, Little-Sisters-Vows, [395]
Thy breath is forfeit.
   Phi. By that bloudy Fauchion——
   Mach. I there's a Wench, spit from the mouth of *Mavors!*
Bellona was thy Nurse.
   Phi. —And that fierce Javelin,
I'd rather see a Plume o'rshade your back
With a large, generous Carelesness; than a bunch [400]
Of fidling Feathers hang before you, just
As modest fig-leaves do in naked Pictures.
   Mach. Thou little 'Vantage of Mankind, thou Grain
That Nature put into the Scales to make
Weight to the World, thou tak'st me very much. [405]
   Phi. The Sable Fan, which you wore last upon
Your white Lawn-Apron, made you shew just like
The Ace of Clubs, with a black spot i'th' middle.
   Mac. Why how now little Mischief? is't not knavish
And waggish, like a very Page o'th' Court? [410]
   Cos. What use do you mean her for?
   Mach. Have you not read?
To summon Knights from th' tops of Castle wals.
   Pan. I fancy those brave Scythian Heroines;
Those Noble, valiant *Amazons* like you.
   Mach. Nature did shew them only as my Types. [415]
   Cos. There's nothing wanting but adventures: We
Shall quickly now requite the Errant Knights
That help distressed Ladies to their wishes.
   Mach. I'l disobliege our Sex. If that you find
Any imprison'd, or inchanted [420]
Tell him *Machessa*'s his deliverance.
Said I *Machessa?* Hold! that word *Machessa*
Sailes through my Lips with too small breath. I'l have
A Name that Mouths shall travell with: let's see?
Wee'l put a Prologue to it: So! I have it; [425]
It is concluded—*Monster-quelling-Woman-*

Obliging-Man-delivering-Machessa,
She, She is his deliverance: tell him so.
   Ph. Do she that can; I would you'd change your Name;
'Tis longer than your Self, and if it were   [430]
Some three foot shorter, 'twere as high as I am. [*One knocks.*
   Mach. See who 'tis knocks; you do not know your Office;
Bellona, hear my Name, and send Adventures.

Act. II. Scen. II.

To them *Ganyctor, Lerinus, Iringus.*

   Cos. The Courtiers Madam; work for us! remember.
Pray stand aside as soon as we begin.   [435]
   Gan. Save you *Machessa*.
   Mach. I've a Name besides,
By which I mean Posterity shall know me;
The word is grown: 'tis *Monster-quelling-Woman-
Obliging-Man-delivering-Machessa.*
   Irin. Sweet *Monster-quelling-Woman-ob-*and so forth–   [440]
Wee've brought a business to you.
   Cos. Valiant Captain,
What is th' Affront that's most in fashion now?
   Irin. Why doe you ask me Lady?
   Pan. 'Cause y'are wont
To receive most, and so can tell the newest;
Which now perhaps you come to have redrest.   [445]
   Rho. What is the strength o'th' Subject think you Sir?
   Ler. Why what know I?
   Cos. Who should Sir, if not you
That have so oft been beaten by all sorts,
And all degrees of men?
   Pan. Which Lady now
Sends you most Favours?
   Rho. Which most Mellons?
   Cos. Which   [450]
Most Gums, and Spikenard Boxes?
   Rho. Who presents you
With the best Figs?
   Pan. The plumpest Bulbi?

Gan. You,
And you, and you; you will not worry me?
    Cos. By your Periwig, Captain, but we will.
    Pan. By your [455]
False Teeth we will.
    Rho. And your glasse-Eye we will.
    Ler. For *Jove*'s sake, Madam.
    Irin. S'heart I'm not breath-proof.
    Cos. Alas, we han't begun yet.
    Gan. Let's beseech you.
    Pan. We will not be beseech'd.
    Cos. Think upon Rest,
As a past pleasure of your youth——
    Pan. You shall not
Be idle quietly in the Presence Chamber. [460]
    Rho. You shan't tell lies in quiet to the Waiters.
    Cos. Nor, when you've done, share in their meat in quiet.
    Pan. Wee'l meet you at the *Bath*——
    Cos. You shall not wash
Without disturbance.
    Pan. At the Theater too——
    Rho. You shall not misconceive good Comedies [465]
Without vexation——
    Cos. And at *Flora*'s Park——
    Pan. You shall not cheat at little Horse-races
Without discovery.
    Rho. In th' Temple then——
    Cos. You shall not kneel in quiet at the Altars——
    Rho. Wee'l hearken, and observe——
    Pan. You shall not have [470]
So much free time, as to appoint a meeting
With her kneels next y'——
    Rho. If that y'are bid to Supper——
    Cos. Wee'l stay you, though y'have got a warrant to
Ride post to eat.
    Ler. Good Madam, be content.
    Pan. And if y'are set——
    Irin. Hell, and Furies——
    Cos. You [475]
Shall rise, and prove perfidious to the hot

Cramm'd Fowl upon your trencher.
 Gan. Wee'l subscribe——
Are you content?
 Rho. And when y'are weary of
All this——
 Cos. Wee'l doe all this again.
 Pan. Wee'l keep you,
As they doe Hawkes——
 Cos. Watching untill you leave   [480]
Your wildness, and prove inward.
 Gan. Hear y' Madam——
 Ler. We will subscribe.
 Cos. Come quickly then, lest that
We take a toy, and will not let you. { *Mach.* steps in and
 Mach. Stay.   { *draws till they all*
The Gods have destin'd this should be the first { *pass out.*
Of my Adventures—go—y'are free.
 Irin. Our thanks   [485]
Will be too small a Recompence. [*Exeunt* Gan. Irin. Ler.
 Mach. The Deed
Will pay it self; Vertue's not Mercenary:
Or, if it be, mine is not. So; I do
Begin to come in Action now. To do
And suffer, doth engross whole Nature, and   [490]
I will engross both them; I'l set all free,
But only Glory; her I'l Captive lead,
Making her Trumpet only sound my Name,
That is, the Sexe's. I am all their Fame.
How goes your Bus'ness on?
 Pan. Vertue and Fortune   [495]
Joyn in it both.
 Cos. *Eumela* is come over,
Hath undertook the Machin, and hath promis'd
To bring it to that pass, that neither Queen,
Nor Princess shall gainsay't. *Florina*, and
Malthora both have given in their Reasons,   [500]
Which I have answer'd, and convinc'd.
 Mach. If that
It come to any danger, let me know it.
           Exeunt Mach. Phi.

Act. II. Scen. III.

To them *Eumela*.

Rho. *Eumela* welcome; does your bus'ness thrive?
Eum. Too fast.
Cos. What? have you sent to th' Ports?
Eum. All's safe.
Machessa's ours you say——
   Pan. Yes, and *Philandra*. [505]
   Eum. *Cleora* and *Earina* busie Sticklers,
Oenone and *Hermione* sent as Emissaries
To try the farther Cities—*Paria* hath
A pretty stroke among the Privy Chamber.
   Cos. You've lost no time.
   Eum. Nor will, *Cosmeta*— [510]
Psecas, and *Dorcas*, *Cloe*, and *Plecusa*,
Phillis, and *Glauca*, swore this morning all
As I was dressing.
   Rho. On what Book I pray?
   Eum. On the Greek Epigrams, Madam, or *Anacreon*,
I know not which: they bind alike.
   Cos. What hopes [515]
Have we o'th' Women of *Lapythia*?
How stand the Dames of *Salamin* affected?
   Eum. Why *Lycas* sent to give them a fair Largess
Of Loaves and Wine, & then, whiles that well cheers 'em,
Eugenia brings 'em a most promising Answer [520]
From some corrupted Oracle, and so leads
The superstitious Souls to what she pleaseth.
This is a ground, a thing suppos'd. The Plot
Is wholly now upon *Florina*, there
It knits, and gathers, breaks, and joyns again; [525]
She's Wise, and Noble—we must find a way
Not thought on yet to gain her.
   Pan. But the Queen
And Princess——
   Eum. They perceive the business ripens,
That it doth move the limbs, and can for need
Shift, and defend it self, and therfore doe [530]

By me make promise of a generall meeting
As soon as may be: i'th' mean time, we have
Full leave to gather any Contributions,
Gold, Silver, Jewels, Garments, any thing
Conducing to maintain the Publique Cause. [535]
  Omn. Goddess *Eumela!*
  Eum. Goe, fall off, the Princess
Is at hand—I'l goe mingle Counsels.
Exeunt Cos. Rho. Pan.

Act. II. Scen. IV.

Lucasia to *Eumela.*

  Luc. *Eumela* you are come most opportunely.
  Eu. This to your Highness from my L. *Olyndus.*
[*delivers the Letter.*]
  Luc. You're happy that your Love is with you still, [540]
That you can see, and hear, and speak to him.
Venus doth favour you more than the whole
Kingdome *Eumela; Mars* for her sake's kind to you.
  Eum. I must confess it happy: but *Olyndus*
Cannot be brought to think it so; he fears [545]
His sickness will by some be constru'd Love;
Which, if his Valour in his Country's danger
Durst give the upper hand, ev'n at the Altar,
Though *Venus* did her self look on, hee'd pull
Out of his Breast, and cast aside, as some [550]
Unhallow'd part o'th' Sacrifice.
  Luc. His King
Hath found him truly valiant. E'r I open
This Paper, you must state one Point, *Eumela,*
Suppose me busie in the holy Rites
Of our adored *Venus:* if by chance [555]
I cast mine Eye upon some Princely visage,
And feel a Passion, is the Goddess wrong'd?
Or the Religion lesse?
  Eum. Our Loves what are they
But howerly Sacrifices, only wanting
The prease and tumult of Solemnity? [560]

If then i'th' heat and Achme of Devotion
We drink a new flame in, can it be ought
But to increase the Worship? and what Goddess
Was ever angry that the holy Priest
Increas'd her Fires, and made 'em burn more clear? [565]
 Luc. True, but suppose the Face then seen doth never
Appear more after, is not that a sign
The Goddess is displeas'd?
 Eum. That it a while
Appears not, is to cherish, not extinguish
The Passion thence conceiv'd: as Persecutions [570]
Make Piety stronger still, and bring th' Afflicted
Unto the glory of renowned Martyrs.
 Luc. But is there then no hope but that? Alas!
This man perhaps might perish in some War
As now (But O ye Gods avert the Fate!)   [*to her self.*] [575]
And then th' unhappy sighing Virgin fall
From that her feigned Heaven.
 Eum. It cannot be;
Venus destroyes her Deity, if She shew
And then delude: She will not lose what once
Sh' hath made her own; She that knits hearts by th' Eyes, [580]
Will keep the knot fast by their Entercourse;
If you have once but seen, and lov'd, permit
The rest unto the Deity. Will it please
Your Highness to peruse the Letter? 'tis
Of moment I presume: why blush you Madam? [585]
And, while I ask you, why look pale?
 Luc. *Eumela*,
The supposition's truth; lately, thou knowest,
I did assist at *Venus* Sacrifice;
He, whom I saw, and lov'd, saw, and lov'd too,
And now hath writ—but let *Olyndus* tell him [590]
I will not see him, though he were the Soul
Of all Mankind.
 Eum. I will.
 Luc. Hear me—yet if
He have a true undoubted Friend, he may
Send him, I'l meet him in the Myrtle Grove,
And tell him more.

Eum. I will obey.
Luc. But stay— [595]
And yet that's all.
Eum. I go. [*Exit* Eumela.
Luc. The Soul doth give
Brightness to th' Eye, and some say, That the Sun,
If not enlight'ned by th' Intelligence
That doth inhabit it, would shine no more
Than a dull Clod of Earth: so Love, that is [600]
Brighter than Eye, or Sun, if not enlight'ned·
By Reason, would so much of Lustre lose
As to become but gross, and foul Desire;
I must refine his Passion; None can wooe
Nobly, but he that hath done Nobly too. [605]

Act. II. Scen. V.

To her *Florina* and *Malthora*.

Mal. Your Highness here alone?
Luc. But so long only
As gives you leave to ask. What? sad *Florina*?
I'd thought your Soul had dwelt within it self,
Been single a full presence, and that you
Had set your self up your own Trophy now [610]
Full of true Joy.
Flo. 'Tis hard to cast off that
That we call Passion, we may veyl, and cloud it,
But 'twill break out at last. True Joy is that
Which now I cannot have.
Luc. How so *Florina*?
Flo. True Joy consists in Looks, and Words, and Letters, [615]
Which now an Absence, equall to Divorce,
Hath wholly barr'd us of.
Luc. Looks, Words, and Letters!
Alas they are but only so much Air
Diversly form'd, & so the food of that
Changeable Creature; not the Viands of [620]
True constant Lovers.
Flo. But, if I see not,

Is not my Joy grown less, who could not love
'Till I first saw? and if I hear not, can
I have the perfect Harmony of pleasure,
Who something ow to words that I first yeelded? [625]
    Luc. Who ever yet was won by words? we come
Conquer'd, and when we grant, we do not yeeld,
But do confess that we did yeeld before.
But be those Senses some Contentments, Madam,
You must not yet make them the great, and true [630]
Essentiall Joy that only can consist
In the bright perfect Union of two Spirits.
    Mal. But seeing those Spirits cannot work, but by
The Organs of the Body, 'tis requir'd
That (to the full perfection of this Joy) [635]
Bodies should be near-Neighbours too.
    Flo. I must
Confess that I subscribe unto the Princess,
And somwhat too to you: the Presence may
Conveigh, and fill, and polish Joy; but yet
To see, or hear, cannot be Joyes themselves. [640]
And where this Presence is deny'd, the Soul
Makes use of higher, and more subtle means,
And by the strength of thought creates a Presence
Where there is none.
    Mal. Alas! how we doe lose
Our selves in speculation of our Loves, [645]
As if they were unbody'd Essences!
    Luc. I would
Eumela now were here; Shee'd tell us, All
Is the same Joy, as Love from sight, or thought,
Is the same Love; and that Love's turning to
Either of them, is only but a Needle [650]
Turning to severall points, no diverse flame,
But only divers degrees of the self-same.
Come Madam let's away and seek her out.   [*Exeunt.*

Act II. Scene VI.

Charistus, Olyndus.

Cha.   Not see me, say you, though I were the Soul
Of all Mankind?
Olyn.   They were the words return'd— [655]
But if he have a true undoubted friend,
Send him, I'l tell him more.
Cha.   Have I deserted
My Country, now in danger, where I had
Took Honour Captive, and for ever fixt her
As an Intelligence unto my Sword, [660]
To move and guide it? have I scorn'd my Fortunes,
And laid aside the Prince? have I contemn'd
That much priz'd thing call'd Life, and wrestled with
Both Winds and Flouds, through which I have arriv'd
Hither at last? and all this not to see her? [665]
Olyn.   Doth She betray, or undisguise you to
The State? Doth She forbid you, Sir, to love?
Affection is not wanting, where 'tis wise.
She only doth forbid you that you see her.
Cha.   Only forbid me to be happy, only [670]
Forbid me to enjoy my self; What could
She more, were I her Enemy? *Olyndus*
Hast thou at no time told her, that there was
A *Cretan* call'd thee Friend?
Olyn.   Why doe you ask?
Cha.   Perhaps Sh' hath found this way to send for thee. [675]
Olyn.   Though I have thought it worth the boasting, that
Charistus is my friend, yet by that Word,
Sacred to Noble Souls, I never had
So much accesse to tell her any thing,
Much lesse my Friendship.
Cha.   Thou shalt goe *Olyndus*. [680]
Olyn.   When my eyes see her, yours doe; when I talk,
'Tis you that talk; we are true friends, and one,
Nay that one interchang'd; for I am you.
Cha.   'Tis true thou art my friend, so much my friend,
That my self am not more my self, than thou art. [685]

If thou dost goe, I goe —— But stay —— Didst not
Thou say mine eyes were thine? thou didst: if that
Be so, then thou must love her too, and then——
Olyndus, thou must stay.
   Olyn. She loves you so,
(As my *Eumela* doth informe me) that   [690]
No humane Image can deface the Print
That you have drawn i'th' Tablet of her Soul.
   Cha. If that She loves me so, why then She must
Love thee so too; for thou and I are one.
   Olyn. Why then, Sir, if you go your self, the issue   [695]
Will be the same however, so, when She
Loves you, Shee'l love me too.
   Cha. We are both one
In hearts and minds *Olyndus*: but those Minds
Are cloath'd with Bodies, Bodies that do oft—
I know not what — yet thou hast an *Eumela*,   [700]
A fair *Eumela* trust me — Thou must go—
But use not any Language, Gesture, Looks,
That may be constru'd ought above Respect;
For thou art young and Beautiful, & Valiant,
And all that Ladies long for.
   Olyn. When I prove   [705]
So treacherous to my Friend, my self, my fair
Eumela, mark me with that hatefull brand
That Ignominy hath not discover'd yet,
But doth reserve to sear the foulest Monster
That shall appear in Nature.
   Cha. I beleeve thee: [710]
Yet something bids me still not let thee go.
But I'l not hearken to it; though my Soul
Should tell me 'twere not fit, I'd not beleeve
My Soul could think so.
   Olyn. How resolve you then?
   Cha. Do what thou wilt. I do beleeve —and yet   [715]
I do—I know not what—O my *Lucasia*!
O my *Olyndus*! divers waies I bend,
Divided 'twixt the Lover, and the Friend.   *Exeunt.*

ACT. III. SCENE I.

Olyndus to Lucasia *in the Grove.*

Olyn. May't please your Highness, Madam—
I have a friend so much my self, that I [720]
Cann't say he's absent now, yet he hath sent me
To be here present for him: we enterchange
Bosoms, and Counsels, Thoughts, and Souls so much,
That he entreats you to conceive you spake
To him in me; All that you shall deposite [725]
Will be in safe, and faithfull Ears; the same
Trust you expect from him, shall keep your words,
And the same Night conceal 'em: 'tis *Charistus*
The noble *Cretan*.
   Luc. When you said your Friend,
The rest was needless; I conceive him all [730]
That makes up Vertue, all that we call Good
Whom you *Olyndus* give your Soul to; yet
I'd rather court his Valour, than his Love,
Did he shine bright in Armour, call for Dangers,
Eager to cut his way through stubborn Troops, [735]
Ev'n this my softness, arm'd as he, could follow
And prompt his Arm, supply him with fresh Fury,
And dictate higher dangers. Then when Dust
And Bloud hath smear'd him (a disguise more worthy
Of Princes far, than that he wears) I could [740]
Embrace him fresh from Conquest, and conceive him
As fair as ever any yet appear'd
To longing Virgins in their Amorous Dreams.
   Olyn. Fury could never from the Den of danger
Awake that horror yet, that bold *Charistus* [745]
Durst not attempt, stand equall with, and then
Conquer, and trample, and contemn.
   Luc. Revenge
And Hate I do confess, may sometimes carry
The Soul beyond it self to do, and suffer:
But the things then are Furious, not Great, [750]
And sign the Actor Headlong, but not Vertuous.
   Olyn. He that can do this, Madam, and Love too,

Must needs be vertuous; that holy Flame
Clean and untainted, as the fresh desires
Of Infant Saints, enters not Souls that are [755]
Of any foul Complexion. He that Loves,
Even in that he Loves, is good: and as
He is no less an Atheist, that denies
The Gods to be most happy, than the Man
That dares Affirm there are no Gods at all; [760]
So he's no less an Heretick, that shall
Deny Love to be Vertuous, than he
That dares Affirm there is no Love at all.

   Luc. But he hath left his Country now, when that
Her Wealth, her Name, her Temples, and her Altars, [765]
Her Gods, and Liberty, stand yet upon
Th' uncertain Dye; when Danger cals his Arm,
And Glory should arrest his Spirit there;
And this to Court one, whom he knows not, whether
She may think Vertue a meer Airy word, [770]
And Honour but a blast, invented to
Make catching Spirits dare, and do high things.

   Olyn. That you are Vertuous, is a knowledge, that
All must confess they have, but only those
That have not Eyes: For if that Souls frame Bodies, [775]
And that the Excellence of the Architect
Appear in the perfection of the Structure,
Whether you have a Soul enrich'd with vertues,
Must be a blind Man's doubt: Nature dares not
Thrust out so much deceit into the World; [780]
'Twould make us not beleeve her works were meant
For true firm Peeces, but Delusions only.

   Luc. Though I must not agree t' you, to pass by
What you have said, If I were Vertuous,
You must confess him so far ignorant yet, [785]
As not to know whether I'd Love, or no.

   Oly. This Knowledge is of more Extent than th' other.
For being that to be lov'd is the Effect
Of your own worths, you must love all mens Loves
As a Confession of your Graces, that [790]
Your selves have drawn from them. That which your Beauty
Produceth, is a Birth as dear unto you,
As are your Children.

Luc. Should there more than one
Love us (if this hold) we must love them too,
And so that Sacred Tye that joyns the Soul [795]
To one, and but to one, were but a Fable,
A thing in Poetry, not in the Creature.
  Olyn. One is your Trophy: and he Lov'd as That;
The Rest but Witnesses: thus Princes, when
They Conquer Princes, though they only count [800]
Those Names of Glory, and Renown, their Victory,
Take yet their meaner Subjects in, as fair
Accesses to their Triumphs, who, although
They are not the main Prize, are somewhat yet
That doth confirm that there was worth, and force, [805]
To which the Main did justly yeeld.
  Luc. Be't then
That I do love his Love, I am not yet
Bound to accept it in what shape soever
It doth appear; the Manner, Time, and Place
May not be relish'd, though the thing be lik'd. [810]
  Olyn. For these he doth expect your Dictates, with
As much Religion, as he would the Answers
Of Sacred Oracles, and with the same
Vow of Performance.
  Luc. You must tell him then,
He must go back, and there do Honorably; [815]
Succour his Country, cheer the Souldier, fight,
Spend, and disburse the Prince, where e'r he goes,
Get him a Name, and Title upon *Cyprus*.
I will not see him 'till he hath Conquer'd, till
He hath rid high in Triumph, and when this [820]
Is done, let him consider then, it is
My Father, & my Subjects, and my Kingdom
That he hath Conquer'd.
  Olyn. I am an Agent only,
And therefore must be faithful.
  Luc. But withall
To shew that I reject him not, you may [825]
Tell him, that being he hath such a friend,
Whiles he is absent I will love *Olyndus*
Instead of him.   [*Exit* Lucasia.
  Olyn. But that my Friend is in me

I should have deem'd it Sacrilege, to have had
A thought like that suggested. My *Charistus*, [830]
Were he not something carefull in his Love,
(I will not call him Jealous) were beyond
The Lot of Man: I must not tell him all,
Some may be hid; yet how shall I unriddle
The Mystery of this Answer? But the knots [835]
That Love doth tye, himself will only find
The way to loose——

Act. III. Scen. II.

To him Charistus.

——And here *Charistus* comes.
Souls once possess'd, as his, are most impatient,
They meet what they should stay for.
    Cha. Dear *Olyndus*,
Pardon that I expect not, but make hast [840]
To intercept my Doom. Others perhaps
May wait the punctuall Minute, and observe
The just and even Period: but *Charistus*
Doth love too slow, when time, and Sun can bind him
Unto a regular Motion.
    Olyn. Would you had [845]
Been there your self! would you had drunk in all
The Looks, Words, Graces, and Divinities
That I have done! I'm like the Priest that's full
Of his inspiring God, and am possess'd
With so much rapture, that methinks I could [850]
Bear up my self without a Wing, or Chariot,
And hover o'r the Earth, still dropping something
That should take root in Kingdoms, and come up
The Good of people.
    Cha. Let me ask thee then
As we do those that do come fresh from Visions, [855]
What saw'st thou there?
    Olyn. That which I see still, that
Which will not out; I saw a Face that did
Seem to participate of Flames, and Flowers;

Eyes in which Light combin'd with Jet to make
Whiteness be thought the Blot, and Black hereafter [860]
Purchase the Name of Innocence, and Lustre.
The whole was but one solid Light, and had I
Not seen our Goddess rising from the Flouds
Pourtray'd less fair, less Goddess, I had thought
The thing I saw, and talk'd with, must have been [865]
The Tutelar Deity of this our Island.
 Cha. That I should let thee go! that I should be
So impious to my self, as not to break
Her great Commands, and so become a Martyr
By daring to be happy 'gainst her will— [870]
But on *Olyndus*.
 Olyn. You may think this
The Height, the Achme, and the All of her:
But when I tell you, that She hath a Mind
That hides all this, and makes it not appear,
Disparaging as 'twere, what ever may [875]
Be seen without her, then you'l thus exclame;
Nature, thou wert o'rseen to put so mean
A Frontispeece to such a Building.
 Cha. Give me,
O quickly give me the whole Miracle,
Or presently I am not.
 Olyn. Think, *Charistus*, [880]
Think out the rest, as 'tis, I cannot speak it.
 Cha. Alas! what should I think?
 Olyn. Conceive a Fire
Simple and thin; to which that Light we see,
And see by, is so far impure, that 'tis
Only the stain, and blemish of the World; [885]
And if it could be plac'd with it in one
And the same Tablet, would but only serve
As bound and shadow to it: Then conceive
A Substance that the Gods have set apart,
And when they would put generous Motions [890]
Into a Mortall Breast, do take the Soul
And couch it there, so that what e'r we call
Vertue in us, is only but a Turning
And Inclination toward her from whom

This Pow'r was first deriv'd.
   Cha. What present God [895]
Lent thee his Eyes, and stood blind by, whiles thou
Did'st gaze, and surfet on these Glories?
   Olyn. Others
Do Love the shape, the Gesture, and the Man,
But She the Vertue. Mark *Charistus*. She
Saies She could Court you ring'd about with Dangers, [900]
Dote on you smear'd, and stiff with hostile Bloud,
Count and exact your wounds, as a due sum
You are to pay to Valour; All which when
I told her was in Love, she said I did
Present a Spark, when She desir'd a full [905]
And glorious Constellation — to be short,
She saies you must go back, do honourably,
Get you a Name upon the *Cyprian* Forces;
And bids you when y'have done all this, consider
It is her Father, and her Subjects, and [910]
Her Kingdom that you Conquer——
   Cha. And her self
That I shall lose by doing so. If I
Return, and *Crete* be Conquer'd, then She will
Count me Spoyl, and Luggage; and my Love
Only a Slave's Affection. If I Conquer, [915]
And *Cyprus* follow my Triumphant Chariot,
My Love will then be Tyranny, and She,
How can She light an Hymeneal Torch
From her lov'd Countries Flame? I am rejected,
Charistus is a Name of scorn.
   Olyn. What Fates [920]
Dare throw that Name upon my Friend? To shew
That She rejects you not, because there is
That Trust, that Faith, and that Confusion of
Charistus and *Olyndus* 'twixt us, in the mean
Whiles he is absent, tell him, saith She, that [925]
I'l love *Olyndus* in his stead.
   Cha. How! Man
Th' hast dealt dishonourably. This the Light?
And this that Fire that makes that Light a stain?
   Olyn. This I foretold my self: my good *Charistus*

Let not your Anger carry you beyond [930]
The bent of Reason; can I give account
Of others Passions? did I first conceive
The words my self, then speak 'em?
   Cha. O ye Gods!
Where is the Faith? where the *Olyndus* now?
Th' hast been a Factor for thy self: I'd thought [935]
I'd sent a Friend, but he's return'd a Merchant,
And will divide the Wealth.
   Olyn. Far be that Brand
From your *Olyndus*! far from your *Lucasia*!
She hath a Face hath so much Heaven in it,
And this *Olyndus* so much Worship of it, [940]
That he must first put on another Shape,
And become Monster, e'r he dare but look
Upon her with a thought that's Masculine.
   Cha. Peace Treachery! I am too cold; my anger
Is dull and lazie yet. I'l search that Breast, [945]
And dig out falshood from the secret'st Corner
In all thy Heart, here in the very place
That thou hast wrong'd me.
   Olyn. There is nothing here
That my *Charistus* knows not. Pray you open,
And search, and judge; and when you find all true, [950]
Say you destroy'd a Friend.
   Cha. It is your Art
I see to wooe, but I will make you speak
Something that is not Flattery.
   Olyn. *Olyndus*
Ne'r lov'd the Man as friend yet, whom he did
Fear as an Enemy. 'Tis one part of Valour [955]
That I durst now receive, conceal, and help you,
Here in the Bosome of that State, which hath
Cast out a spear into the *Cretan* Field,
And bid you War.
   Cha. Thou hast already here
Betray'd my Love; thy falshood will proceed [960]
Unto my Person next. I'd thought I'd been
Clasp'd in Embraces, but I find I am
Entangled in a Net.

Olyn. Y'are safe as in
The Bosome of your Father, take this Veyl
Of Passion from your Eyes, and you'l behold [965]
The same *Olyndus* still.
   Cha. The same Deceiver,
The same false perjur'd Man. Draw, or by Heaven,
That now should Thunder and revenge my wrongs,
Thou shalt dye sluggishly.
   Olyn. Recall your self,
And do but hear——
   Cha. What words a Coward will [970]
Fawn on me with, to keep an abject life,
Not worth the saving.
   Olyn. Witness all ye Gods
That govern Friendship, how unwillingly
I do untye the Knot.
   Cha. Draw quickly, lest
It may be known I am the *Cretan* Prince, [975]
And so my juster Fury be not suffer'd
To scourge a timorous and perfidious Man.
   Oly. Though thou stand'st here an Enemy, and we have
The Pledge of all the *Cretan* State, yet know
Though all our Island's People did look on, [980]
And thou proclam'st thy self to be the Man,
They should not dare to know the Prince, untill
I'd done this Sacrifice to Honour.
   Cha. So!

> *They fight, and wound each other dangerously, and then retire,* Charistus *to* Lucasia's *Myrtle, and* Olyndus *to the next adjoyning, and leaning there speak.*

   Oly. I have not long to stay 'mongst Mortals now,
And then you may search all those Corners that [985]
You talk'd of in my Heart. But if you find
Ought that is falshood towards you, or more
Than Reverence to *Lucasia*, may I want
The Honour of a Grave——Hear O ye Gods,
(Ye Gods whom (but a while) and I am with) [990]
Lucasia is as spotless, as the Seat
That you prepare for Virgin Lovers!

Cha. I
Have wrong'd thee, my *Olyndus*, wrong'd thee much,
But do not chide me; there's not life enough
Left in me to make use of Admonition. [995]
  Olyn. If you survive, love your *Lucasia*; 'twill
Make your *Olyndus* happy; for the good
Of the surviving Friend, some holy Men
Say doth pertain unto the Friend Departed.
  Cha. Vertuous *Lucasia*! and hadst thou *Olyndus* [1000]
Not been so too, my Gods had fought for me;
But I must dye——*Olyndus*. [*Charistus faints.*
  Olyn. Heavens forbid
That my *Charistus* perish! I have only
Strength left to wish: If I can creep yet to thee
I'l help thee all I can. [*Olynd. sinks.*
  Cha. And I will meet thee; {*They creep one to the other and so embrace.* [1005]
Let us embrace each other yet. The Fates
Preserve our Friendship, and would have us equall,
Equall ev'n in our Angers: we shall go
Down equall to the Shades both, two waies equall,
As Dead, as Friends. And when *Lucasia* shall [1010]
Come down unto us (which the Heavens forbid
Should be as yet) I'l not be Jealous there.

Act. III. Scen. III.

To them as they lye groveling, and embracing thus,
Machessa *and* Philænis.

  Phi. O me! Good Heavens! had you the Balsam, Lady,
Now that you told me of, 'twould do some good.
  Mach. This is *Olyndus*, that the honour'd Stranger; [1015]
Brave Spirits are a Balsam to themselves:
There is a Nobleness of Mind, that heals
Wounds beyond Salves — look not, but help *Philænis*,
Gather the Weapons, and the rest up quickly;
Where two are wrong'd, I ought to succour both. [1020]
            {Machessa *carries 'em out.*

Act. III. Scen. IV.

Lucasia, Florina, Malthora, Eumela.

Lu. Madam, ne'r fear your Dream, for that is only
The reliques of your day-time thoughts, that are
Preserv'd b'your Soul, to make a Scene i'th' Night.
  Eum. Have you not dream'd the like before?
  Mal. Yes thrice.
  Eum. Why then *Pæstanus* now hath perish'd thrice, [1025]
Or else y' have sometimes dream'd in vain.
  Flor. Eumela,
I told her this, and that her troubled Sleeps
Were one Love still waking.
  Luc. Wee'l divert
This anxious fear. Reach me the Lute *Eumela.*
Have you not heard how *Venus* did complain [1030]
For her belov'd *Adonis*? The young Poet,
That was desir'd to give a Language to
Th' afflicted Goddess, thought her words were these.

The Ode.

Luc. *Wake my* Adonis, *do not dye;*
    One Life's enough for thee and I. [1035]
      Where are thy words? thy wiles?
      Thy Loves, thy Frowns, thy smiles?
      Alas in vain I call;
    One death hath snatch'd 'em all:
    Yet Death's not deadly in that Face, [1040]
    Death in those Looks it self hath Grace.

    'Twas this, 'twas this I feard
    When thy pale Ghost appear'd;
    This I presag'd when thund'ring Jove
    Tore the best Myrtle in my Grove; [1045]
      When my sick Rose-buds lost their smell,
      And from my Temples untouch'd fell;
        And 'twas for some such thing
        My Dove did hang her Wing.

> *Whither art thou my Deity gone?* [1050]
> *Venus in Venus there is none.*
> *In vain a Goddess now am I*
> *Only to Grieve, and not to dye.*
>   *But I will love my Grief,*
>   *Make Tears my Tears relief;* [1055]
>   *And Sorrow shall to me*
>   *A new Adonis be.*
>
> *And this no Fates can rob me of, whiles I*
> *A Goddess am to Grieve, and not to Dye.*

Flor. Madam, they say 'twas in this very Grove [1060]
The Goddess thus complain'd.

Act. III. Scen. V.

To them Philænis *with a couple of Napkins.*

Eum. How now *Philænis*?
Are you turn'd Sewer to the Lady-Errant?
  Phi. Lady I'm sent to wipe away the Bloud
From these two Myrtles.
  Eum. Bless me! what Bloud *Philænis*?
  Luc. I hope the Song will not prove ominous. [1065]
  Phi. 'Tis fit we have some Wars at home too, else
My Lady would have no employment left.
  Luc. What Wars? whose Bloud?
  Phi. A pair of froward Lovers,
Olyndus, and the Stranger, fought, it seems,
Here till they almost kill'd themselves: and when [1070]
Neither did fear, but both did faint, it seems
Olyndus lean'd there, and the Stranger there,
And with their Blouds besmear'd the Trees a little;
We did not think your Highness should have seen it.

> *They rise amaz'd, the Princess repairs to the Tree where* Charistus *bled, and* Eumela *to the Tree where her* Olyndus *bled.*

  Luc. Is this *Olyndus* way of mingling Souls? [1075]
  Eum. Is this the Others Enterchange of Breasts?

  Luc. O Heavens! durst your *Olyndus* thus?
  Eum. O Heav'ns,
And O ye Gods too! durst that other this?
  Luc. Did he then stay behind for this *Eumela*?
  Eum. And did he leave his Country to destroy   [1080]
One worth it all, here in our very Bosoms?
  Luc. H' has ruin'd one, whose like if Nature will
Shew to the World again, she must lay up,
And gather, till she hath store enough of Graces
To throw into the World.
  Eum. *Olyndus* stood   [1085]
As high, and brave as he, his Enemy had
But this advantage of him, that he was
A *Cretan*, as by Birth, so too in Faith.
  Luc. Were he the Birth of some unshelter'd Cottage,
He were yet fairer in the Eye o'th' World   [1090]
Than e'r *Olyndus* could have been, in that
He was a Princess's thoughts; 'twas I that lov'd him.
  Eum. Although the Name of Princess be upon you,
And signs you Dread, and Soveraign, yet I must
Tell you that Love's a Princess too in me,   [1095]
And stamps as much Heroick Majesty
Upon my Thoughts, as Birth hath done on yours.
  Luc. Though, as a Princess, I could make thy Love
And thee forgotten Names, yet I depose
My self, and am thy Equall.
  Eum. 'Tis no need   [1100]
That you descend, Love carries up *Eumela*
To be as high as is her Princess, and
In this sad Fate placeth her equall with
Her Dread *Lucasia*.
  Luc. Hear, hear this brave man!
And if thou liv'st revenge it on *Olyndus*.   [1105]
  Eum. And thou the Spirit of my dear *Olyndus*,
Be thou still worthy, still thy self. Speak thou
O Nature, was there not the same clay knead
To make our Hearts? did not the same Fire kindle
Our Souls? and thou, O Love, was't not the same   [1110]
Metall that wounded both? you must not count
The Princess into th' worth of your Affection;

Love when he ballanceth the Hearts that come
Under his Power, casts not in their Births,
Fortunes, and Titles.
   Luc. Would some powerfull God   [1115]
Would change our Persons, and make thee *Lucasia*,
And me *Eumela*, that I might avow
The justice of my Love in spight of State.
   Mal. Forbear *Eumela*.
   Flor. 'Tis the Princess speaks.
   Eum. Nor Prince, nor Subject speaks, but Love in both.   [1120]

Act. III. Scen. VI.

To them Machessa.   *They leave their Trees, and repair to* Machessa.

   Flo. Here's one can tell you all.
   Luc. Say, good *Machessa*,
How doth the Stranger?
   Eum. Lives *Olyndus* yet?
   Mac. Both live, but wounded much, yet hopes of both;
For they are Friends, and as their Minds have clos'd,
Their wounds may shortly too.
   Luc. How fell they out?   [1125]
   Mach. I heard the Stranger, Madam, thus confess,
As our *Olyndus* did embrace him; Thou
Wert honourable, my *Olyndus*, ever;
But I was foul, and Jealous: then *Olyndus*
Fell on his Neck, told him 'twas only heat,   [1130]
And strength of Love; and vow'd he'd never tell
The cause and ground o'th' Quarrell: but the Stranger
Swore by his Gods, and Altars, that he would
Go find, and tell, and ask the Deity
Forgiveness first, then him — I heard no more   [1135]
But only sighs from either.
   Luc. 'Twas too much —
That I should throw away my grief for one
That durst have such a thought! *Charistus*, you
And I are both deceiv'd in one another;   [*aside.*
And, poor *Olyndus*, deerly hast thou paid   [1140]

For both our Errors ——
    ——*Machessa*, as you love me
Be carefull of *Olyndus*, for the other——
My care hath been more than he's worth already—[*aside*.
  Flo. *Eumela*,
The Princess is much troubled, pray heav'n your freedom
Did not offend her Highness.
  Eum. I hope it did not: [1145]
Madam, if too much Love made me forget,
And pass the bounds of Duty, humbly, I beg
Your Graces pardon, beseeching you t'impute
My folly to my Passion.
  Luc. Call't not Passion,
'Twas Reason to Contest: Love's Kingdom is   [1150]
Founded upon a Parity; Lord, and Subject,
Master, and Servant, are Names banish'd thence;
They wear one Fetter all, or, all one Freedom.
  Eum. There was some Spirit spake within me, 'twas——
  Luc. Alas! excuse it not: all that do Love,   [1155]
In that they love, are equall, and above none,
None, but those only whom the God denies
The honour of his Wound — *Eumela*, hear me,   {*Whispers*
Charistus is grown foul, and thy *Olyndus*   *her.*
Is now my Martyr, for my sake he bleeds,   [1160]
And I, for this, will make *Charistus* know,
That he, who doubts his Friend, is his own Foe.
                            Exeunt.

ACT IV. SCENE I.

*Adraste, Lucasia, Malthora, Florina, Eumela, Cosmeta,
Pandena, Rhodia, Machessa,* sate as at Parliament.

  Adr. My Lady Martiall, and the rest Mercuriall,
Woman's the Gem of Heaven, in which Nature
Hath carv'd the Universe in less Characters;   [1165]
A Peece of such Invention, and such Art,
That, where as in one common lazy Mold
Made for dispatch, she casts, and thrusts out Men,

As some things done in haste, she may be said
To build, and send forth us; yet (howsoever [1170]
It comes about) in all foretimes and Ages
Councels and Senats have excluded us,
Thinking us like those finer Wits, which spin
Themselves into such subt'le Fancies, that
They are too Curious to be employ'd, [1175]
Being as far from Service, as from Grossness:
But this hath been from Errour, not from Tryall:
Grant me their Composition stronger, grant me
Their Bodie's ruder, and more fit for Wars,
Which some yet here do happily contradict, [1180]
I cannot yet conceive, why this should bind us
To be their Slaves; our Souls are Male, as theirs.
That we have hitherto forborn t'assume
And manage Thrones, that hitherto we have not
Challeng'd a Soverainty in Arts, and Arms, [1185]
And writ our selves Imperiall, hath been
Mens Tyranny, and our Modesty. Being then
Nature did mean us Soveraigns, but cross Fate
(Envious of her, willing that nothing should
Be perfect upon Earth) still kept us under; [1190]
Let us, i'th' name of Honour, rise unto
The pitch of our Creation. Now's the time;
The best and ablest men are absent, those
That are left here behind are either Fooles,
Or Wise men overgrown, which is all one. [1195]
Assert your selves into your Liberty then,
Stand firm, and high, put these good Resolutions
Forth into Action: then, in spight of Fate,
A Female Hand shall turn the Wheel of State.
   Om. Inspir'd *Adraste*!
   Om. Most divine *Adraste*! [1200]
   Adr. If that you relish this let Mistris Speaker
On to the rest.
   Om. On, on, on, on, on, on!
   Eum. Most Willing, most Agreeing, most Potent,
And most free Ladies, *&c.*——
'Tis fit all things should be reduc'd unto [1205]
Their Primeve Institution, and first Head;

Woman was then as much as Man, those Stones
Which *Pyrrha* cast, made as fair Creatures as
Deucalion's did: that his should be set up
Carv'd, and Ador'd, but hers kept down, and trampled, [1210]
Came from an ancient Injury; what Oracle, and
What voice from Heaven commanded that?
   Cos. Most true!
Observe that Ladies.
   Pan. *Sibyl*'s Leaf by *Juno*!
   Eum. He that saies Woman is not fit for Policy,
Doth give the Lie to Art; for what man hath [1215]
More sorts of Looks? more Faces? who puts on
More severall Colours? Men, compar'd in this,
Are only Dough-bak'd Women; not as once
Maliciously one call'd us Dough-bak'd Men.
   Cos. 'Tis no single
Voice; the whole Sex speaks in her.
   Eum. Some few yet [1220]
Do speak against our Passions, but with greater;
Rail at our Lightness, but 'tis out of Humour;
Rather Disease than Reason; they being such
As wipe off what they spit. For Heav'n forbid
That any should vouchsafe to speak against us [1225]
But rough Philosophers, and rude Divines,
And such like dull Professions. But wee'l now
Shew them our Passions are our Reasons Edge,
And that, which they call Lightness, only is
An Art to turn our selves to severall Points. [1230]
Time, Place, Minds, People, all things now concur
To re-estate us there where Nature plac'd us:
Not a Male more must enter *Cyprus* now.
   Cos. No, nor an Eunuch, nothing that hath been
Male heretofore.
   Pan. No, nor Hermophrodite; [1235]
Nothing that is half Male. A little Spark
Hath often kindled a whole Town; we must
Be cautelous in the least.
   Eum. That then they may not
Regain the Island, all the Havens must
Be stor'd, and guarded.

Cos. Very fit they should. [1240]
Eum. Next to the Havens, Castles out of hand
Must be repair'd, Bulwarks, and Forts, and Sconces
Be forthwith rear'd.
Cos. 'Tis time we were about them.
Eum. Arms then must be bought up, and Forces rais'd;
Much, much is to be done——
Pan. Why let *Machessa* [1245]
About it straight.
Eum. I see agreeing Minds,
Your Hearts and Courage very ready, but
Where is the Nerve and Sinew of this Action?
Where shall we have the Mony to do this?
Cos. Wee'l give our hair for Cordage, and our finest [1250]
Linnen for Sails, rather than this Design
Shall be once dash'd for want.
Pan. There's much already
Come in——
Cos. And more doth dayly.
Pan. Hearts and Purses
Concur unto the Action.
Cos. We have Notes
Of the particular Contributions. [1255]
Eum. Her Majesty would have you read 'em, that
She may know what to trust to.
Cos. From the Temple   [*She reads.*
We do expect ten dozen of Chalices,
But they are hid, or else already gone——
Eum. This is not what you have, but what y'have not. [1260]
Cos. We tell you this, that you mayn't take it ill,
That we ha'n't borrow'd some o'th' Holy Plate.
Well then, to what we have—— First from the Court
Ten Vessels of Corinthian Brass, with divers
Peeces of *Polyclet*, and *Phydias*, [1265]
Parrhasius, *Zeuxes*, and *Protogenes*,
Apelles, and such like great Master-hands.
Eum. Statues, and Pictures do but little good
Against the Enemy.
Cos. Pray y' hear it out:
Rich Cabinets then, which, though they do contain [1270]

Treasure immense and large, have nothing yet
Within them rich'er than themselves.
   Eum. What hold they?
   Cos. Pearls, Rubies, Emralds, Amethysts, and Saphirs,
Crysolits, Jaspers, Diamonds, two whereof
Do double the twelfth Caract: besides Sparks   [1275]
Enough to stick the Roof o'th' Banquetting House,
And make it seem an Heav'n.
   Eum. Well, on *Cosmeta.*
   Cos. Twelve standing Goblets, two more rich and massy,
The one bears *Bacchus* sitting on a Vine,
Squeezing out Purple liquor, Th' other hath   [1280]
Silenus riding on his patient Beast,
And Satyrs dancing after him. More yet,
Twelve other less engraven with less Stories,
As Loves, and Months, and Quarters of the year,
Nymphs, Shepheards, and such like— This from the Court.   [1285]
   Eum. What from the City?
   Pan. Purple Robes, and Furs   [*Pan. reads.*
In great abundance— Basons and large Ewers,
Flagons, and Dishes, Plates, and Voyders, all
Rich and unwieldy. And besides all this,
Gold Chains, and Caudle-Cups innumerable.   [1290]
   Eum. The Contribution's much——
   Pan. But yet not ended——
Twelve City Ladies send us word, they have
Twelve Iron Chests, and rib'd with Iron too,
Wherein they do suspect there lies a Mine,
That hath not seen the Sun for six *Olympiads.*   [1295]
   Eum. Let 'em be got in suddenly; we must
Be hot and eager in our undertakings.
The Wealth's enough; the East was overrun
By the bold *Macedonian* Boy with less.
Was't not *Machessa*? But I pray you nothing   [1300]
From the poor Country Villagers?
   Pan. Very little;
Hoop-rings, and Childrens Whistles, and some forty
Or fifty dozen of gilt-Spoons, that's all.
   Eum. Let it be hastily deliver'd all
Into her Majesties Treasury.

Cos. Under favour, [1305]
We think *Machessa* would be very fit
Both to take in, and to disburse.
   Eum. It is not
For any private Interest that She asks it,
But for the Publike good.
   Pan. Perhaps. But yet
The People will think better, if it be [1310]
Entrusted in a Subject's hand, and Hers
Especially who never had a Husband—
   Cos. No, nor a Child as yet.
   Adr. Why be it so;
You shall dispose't *Machessa*.
   Mach. I consider
The trust you give me; see the weight, and Nature, [1315]
The Price and Moment of the Cause; Know next
My Order binds me not to be endow'd
With any Wealth or Utensill, besides
My Steed, my Habit, Arms, and Page; To which
When I prove false, let him that weaves my Story [1320]
(Whether he be a Courtier, or perhaps
A Scholar that writes worse) bring me no higher
Than to scratch'd Faces, and such Suburb brangles.
Truth is the Essence of our Order, we
Who are Errants cannot deceive and Be. [1325]
   Adr. Let us away: though the Male-Gods may frown,
The Female part of Heaven is sure our own. [*She whis.* Eu.
   Eum. Noble *Machessa* all your deeds I see   { *Ex.* Adrast.
Tend to the Scope of Honour.   Luc. *&c.*
   Mach. Were she seated   *Manent* Eu.
Upon the top of some high craggy Rock, [1330]   Machessa.
Whose Head were in the Country of the Thunder,
Guarded with watchfull Dragons, I will climb,
And ravish her from thence, to have my Name
Turn'd o'r from Age to Age, as something that
Ought to outlive the Phœnix, and dye only [1335]
With Men and Time.
   Eum. Though you Court Danger thus,
I hope you will not scorn bright Glory, if
She come an easier way.

Mach. I look to her,
Not to her Cloaths, and Habit.
    Eum. Will you be
Famous in History then? fill swelling Volumes   [1340]
With your sole Name? be read aloud, and high
I'th' *Cyprian* Annals? and live fresh upon
The Tongue of Fame for ever? will you stand
High on your Steed in Brass, and be at once
The stop of Strangers, and the Natives Worship,   [1345]
By one fair Peacefull Action?
    Mach. Brave *Eumela*,
To say I'l do't is lazy; it is done.
    Eum. 'Tis the Queen's sute besides,
And She shall thank you.
    Mach. Honour is my Queen,
And my Deeds thank themselves. But say, *Eumela*,   [1350]
Quickly, what is't?
    Eum. Why only send this Wealth,
That's put into your hands, unto the Army,
And so defeat this folly that they here
So eagerly pursue.
    Mach. By Heav'n I'll first
Scatter the Ashes of my Ancesters,   [1355]
Burn and demolish Temples, or pull down
The Statue of our Goddess, whiles her self
Stood with the proudest thunder to defend it;
You ought to thank me, that you have propos'd it,
And yet still live.
    Eum. But pray you reason it.   [1360]
    Mach. Follies of idle Creatures! who e'r heard
Of Ladies Errant yet that stood to Reason?
But you that brag of Books, and Reading, and
I know not what unnecessary Learning,
Tell me, did brawny *Hercules*, who wand'red   [1365]
I'th' Lion's skin, and Club, or well-set *Theseus*
That trod his steps, e'r do the like?
    Eum. No. Women
Ne'r came to such a pitch of danger yet
As to be banish'd all: then who e'r trusted
Theseus, or *Hercules* with ten Drachmas? who   [1370]

Could know their Minds that way? This single deed
Will make *Machessa* go beyond his *Pillars*,
And th' other's Fame. They quell'd but single Robbers,
You will defeat thousands of Rebels. They
Help'd some poor Village, or some Town perhaps, [1375]
You will redeem a Nation.
  Mach. Thou say'st something;
But I shall break my faith.
  Eum. To whom? to those
That have before broke theirs unto their Prince?
  Mach. They'l curse me too.
  Eum. As bold *Machessa* hunts not
The Praise of People, so she can contemn [1380]
Their Curse, when she doth well. Consider too
Nations will curse you more if you assist 'em.
  Mach. But 'tis against my Order to deceive.
  Eum. 'Tis more against your Order to assist
Rebellious Persons 'gainst their King. Besides, [1385]
Doth not your Oath enjoyn you to relieve
Distressed men? who more distressed now
Than is the King, and th' Army? fear not words;
You are not Treacherous unto them, but faithfull
Unto your self. Why stands this Helmet here? [1390]
Why do you wear this Fauchion? to what use
Carry this Javelin?
  Mach. Not to help women; no,
Men are my Oath. All shall be sent *Eumela*,
The King must have it: wee'l be famous——
  Eum. But
You must be secret 'till it all come in. [1395]
  Mach. And you'l assist me in the sending of 't?
  Eum. Take you no care for that, 'tis done.
  Mach. But will
The Queen not take it ill?
  Eum. 'Tis her great fear,
You'l scarce be brought to yeeld it up. Away,
Go, and delude 'em on, y'are safe, and may [1400]
Deceive in Conscience now.
  Mach. *Bellona* bless thee!   [*Exit* Machessa.
  Eum. But how shall we now conveigh it to 'em?

Act. IV. Scen. II.

To her Philondas *and* Pæstanus *as having stoln from the Army.*

—Heav'n's of the Plot! No fitter men. *Jove* bless me!
My Lord *Philondas*, and my Lord *Pæstanus*!
This your appearance to me's like the first [1405]
Appearance to a new admitted Priest,
And I am quite as doubtfull now as he,
Not knowing whether 't be my fancy, or
The God, that makes the Vision.
   Phil. Dear *Eumela*,
Thou know'st we do appear to Ladies still [1410]
In very flesh and bloud. Though we may talk
Of spirituall Love, my Lord, and I, you know,
Could ne'r creep in at Key-holes yet; I'm sure
We pay for th' opening of the doors, *Eumela*.
   Eum. My Lord you make *Pæstanus* blush.
   Pæst. I hope [1415]
I am not so ill bred *Eumela*.
   Eum. Troth
The Camp hath spoyl'd you both. The *Cretan* Ladies
They say are far beyond our *Cyprus* Dames.
   Phi. Yes to cleave Logs, and carry Burthens.
   Eum. But
I mean for Beauty.
   Phil. In whose Eyes, *Eumela*? [1420]
In the Town-Buls?
   Eum. They say the Gods have chang'd
Shapes, to come down, and visit 'em.
   Pæst. 'Twas that
They might be like 'em then.
   Phi. For *Jove* could never
Be a fit Husband for 'em, till he had
Got horns, and hoofs.
   Eum. Saw you no Children there? [1425]
   Pæst. What then *Eumela*? ha'n't you read of Creatures
That have Conceiv'd by th' Air?——
   Phi. Don't think of any
Such thing as man? The Wind and Sun *Eumela*,

Get all the Children there; that makes 'em bluster,
And rage so furiously when they are old. [1430]
   Pæst. Come, we lose time; where is *Malthora* prethee?
   Phi. Answer him not; by *Venus*, these young Husbands
Are as impatient as a hungry Courtier,
Or a rich Heir come newly to his Means;
Do you hear me ask for *Florina* yet? [1435]
   Eum. 'Tis not in fashion, Sir, to love your Lady——
   Phi. At least you ought not to profess it.
   Pæst. I
Dare swear, though none professeth less, yet none
Loves more than you my Lord.
   Phi. 'Tis i'th' dark then;
Day-light and Love are two things. But, *Eumela*, [1440]
What do they do for Men now we are absent?
Do they take Physick, or else Pray?
   Eum. My Lord,
Their Griefs are in your places.
   Phi. Have their sighs
Got Limbs, and Bodies? Can their sadness give 'em
Comfort at Midnight?
   Eum. They possess it with [1445]
A kind of sweetness, are so tender of it,
That should they part with it, they'd think they had
A second loss.
   Pæst. How can they pass away
Their time with that?
   Eum. Why 'tis as necessary
To them as Friend, or Confident.
   Pæst. But tell me [1450]
How does *Malthora* bear it?
   Eum. Sir, she finds
That solitude in her self, that others do
Look for in Desarts.
   Pæst. Come my Lord, let's go
And help 'em to sigh for us.
   Eum. They're to come
Hither my Lord: pray stand behind these hangings [1455]
Till I discover the whole Scene; In quickly.
Here, here they come.
                        Ex. Pæst. *and* Phi.

Act. IV. Scen. III.

To Her Florina, Malthora.

Mal.   Bless me *Eumela*! I
Must get me Mens apparell, and go see
How all things stand abroad; I did but close
Mine Eyes, and presently me thought the Ghost   [1460]
Of my *Pæstanus* did appear before me,
Wounded, and bloudy, and as soon as I
Went to embrace him, vanish'd into air.
   Eum.   You are so fearfull, Madam, and do fancy
Danger and death so strongly, that if he   [1465]
Were at this instant present here before you
You'd not beleeve your Eyes. Madam *Florina*
What's that you look on so?
   Flor.   It is, *Eumela*,
The Picture of my Lov'd *Philondas*, as
He had his Armour on, (and O the Heav'ns   [1470]
That he should ever be in such a Habit)
But Fates would have it so; 'twas young *Protogenes*
Took it before he went. Me thinks it sometimes
Doth move, and alter Colour, and endeavour
To get loose, and come out.
   Eum.   Have you the Picture   [1475]
Of your Lord Madam too?
   Mal.   Yes here, *Eumela*,
Drawn by the same hand: is't not very like him?
   Eum.   Methinks they're neither true: I've both their Statues,
Though not in Armour, and as I remember
They don't agree with them.
   Flor.   Pray y' let's examine   [1480]
To pass the time a while.
   Eum.   I've newly put 'em
Both into Habits, and me thinks they look
So fresh, and lively, that I might mistake 'em,
But that I know they're absent; look you here.   *She draws*
Does not this look more like *Philondas* far,   *the hangings*   [1485]
And this more like *Pæstanus* than the Tablets?   *and shews*
You must not come too near: I'l leave y' a while   *'em.*
To view, and judge.   [*Exit* Eumela.

Flor.   Good Heav'ns! my Lord *Philondas*!
Mal.   My dear *Pæstanus*!
Phil.   I am come you see
A prety jant here to fulfil the longing   [1490]
Of a young Novice-Husband.
Pæst.   The first day
That *Hymen* joyn'd us, brought not truer joy
Unto my Soul than this.

Act. IV. Scen. IV.

To them Eumela.

Eum.   My Lords, the Queen
Is come to make a visit to your Ladies:
What will you do?
Phil.   Go and conduct her in.   [*Ex.* Phil. Pæst.   [1495]
Eum.   Now Madam? does your Husband vanish, when
You offer to embrace him?
Mal.   O *Eumela*
He's gone already. This his short appearance
Is only as th' appearance of a Star
To one that's perishing in a Tempest.
Flor.   'Tis   [1500]
Only to let us die with some more Comfort.
Were they to stay *Eumela*——
Eum.   This disjoyning
Of Bodies, only is to knit your hearts;
You'l form their Pictures in your Thoughts perhaps,
And once or twice more look behind the Hangings.   [1505]
Mal.   Peace good *Eumela*! here's the Queen.

Act. IV. Scen. V.

To them Adraste, Philondas, Pæstanus.

Adr.   *Charistus*,
Heir to the *Cretan* Kingdom lost say you?
Phi.   Yes, and suspected to lye hid in *Cyprus*.
Adr.   And this is that doth stop the War?

  Pæst. This, and
Th' Equality of Forces.
  Adr. Do our men   [1510]
Awake, and rouze themselves?
  Phi. Rich noble Spirits,
And Minds that have kept Altars burning still,
To Glory break out dayly, shewing how
Peace and Religion did not sink, but calm 'em:
This blast will swell 'em big, and high, and make 'em   [1515]
Ride Conquerours o'r the Flouds.
  Adr. They do not sleep then?
  Phi. No, nor watch lazily; the World will see,
He, whose blest goodness hath kept War from us,
Hath not took Courage from us too; When his
Sad study'd Councels did remove the danger,   [1520]
They did not then remove the Mind. The Arm
Of this days *Cyprus*, if provok'd, will strike
As deep as *Cyprus* six Olympiads backwards,
And the unquiet *Cretan* shall appear
But as he did of old, our Exercise,   [1525]
More than our Foe: a people that we suffer
To breath, and be, to keep our selves in breath.
  Adr. What doth the King?
  Pæst. More than the meanest Souldier,
Yet still comes fresh from Actions: his Commands
Are great, but his Examples greater still.   [1530]
  Phi. With his uncover'd head he dares the Thunder,
Slights hail and snow, and wearies out a Tempest,
Then after all he shakes himself, and gives
Rain, as the Heavens did before, but with
A more serene Aspect. He doth exact   [1535]
Labour, and hardness, hunger, heat, and cold,
And dust, as his Prerogatives, and counts them
Only his serious Pleasures; Others Wars
Are not so manly as his Exercises,
And pitch'd Fields often are more easie service   [1540]
Than his meer Preparations.
  Adr. 'Tis enough;
Y' have spoke a Composition, so made up
Of Prince and Souldier, that th' admiring World

May imitate, not equall. Come, my Lords,
I have a business to employ you back with. [1545]

Exeunt.

ACT. IV. SCEN. VI.

Lucasia, Eumela, Charistus, Olyndus.

Luc. I must confess, had not this Action been
Tainted with private Interest, but born
From zeal unto the Publique, then it might
Have been read Valour, as it is, it will
Be stil'd but Fury.
   Eum. Madam it had then [1550]
Been only Valour, now 'tis Love and Valour.
   Luc. Where those Religious Names, King, Country, Father,
Are trampled over, can you call it Valour?
   Cha. If trampled o'r for you. To hazard all
These holy Names, of Subject unto King, [1555]
Of Prince to Country, and of Son to Father,
And whil'st I spar'd to shed the smallest drop
Of Bloud, that might be once call'd yours, to have
That ignominious Name of Coward hurl'd on me,
And take up all their Places; what else is it [1560]
But to esteem your self a Prize, that doth
Absolve me from all these, and make me stand
Above the rate of mortals.
   Olyn. Father, Country,
State, Fortunes, Commonwealth, th' are Names that Love
Is not concern'd in; that looks higher still, [1565]
And oversees all these.
   Luc. Is it not Love then;
For that, as it is Valiant, so it is
Just, Temperate, Prudent, summons all those Noble
Heroick Habits into one rich Mass,
And stamps them Honour.
   Eum. But that Honour is [1570]
A Valour beyond that of Mortals, striving
Who shall possess most of this Mole-hill Earth.
   Olyn. That Honour is a Justice, that doth see
Measures, and Weights, Axes, and Rods below it.

    Eu. A Temperance not concern'd in Meats, and Wines. [1575]
    Olyn. A Prudence that doth write *Charistus* now
A better Patriot, than the sober'st Statesman
That plots the good of *Crete*.
    Luc. If he that cares not
For things, be th'ence above them; if he sees
More nobly, that doth draw the Veyl before [1580]
His Eyes to Lower Objects, then *Charistus*
Soares high, and nothing scapes him.
    Cha. Fair *Lucasia*,
I am not so immodest, as to challenge
The least of these my self: but yet in that
I love your Vertues, they are all mine own. [1585]
    Luc. And yet you fear'd I was anothers, whom
I durst not publiquely avow. Do y'think
My Love could stoop to such Contrivances?
Or if I meant a subject of such worth,
I needed to pretend a Prince?
    Olyn. It is not [1590]
Lucasia's Love, that dares not call the Eye
Of Day to try it: But where Love's engag'd
To such a Treasure as your self, what can
Be thought secure? It stands and watches still,
And fears it's very helps; could any love [1595]
Lucasia and be careless, 'twere a fault
Would make him not deserve her.
    Luc. Could you then
Think I could be so impious unto Love
As to divide *Eumela* and *Olyndus*?
Or else so treacherous unto Friendship, as [1600]
To part *Eumela* and my self? Being Hearts
Are Temples, and both sorts of Love most Sacred,
To have wrong'd either had been Sacrilege
Worthy the horrid'st Thunder.
    Eum. Love drinks in
All that may feed suspicion, but is deaf [1605]
To what may clear it; 'tis engag'd so much
To th' Object, that it views the Object only,
And weighs not what attends it.
    Luc. Where the Heart

Offends, you blame the Passion. Love it self
Is never undiscreet, but he that Loves.
  Cha. Wisdome and Love at once were never yet
Permitted to a God, I must not then
Presume they meet in me. If Love admits
Discretion, if it Ponder, and Consider,
Search, and Compare, and Judge, and then Resolve,
'Tis Policy, not Affection: give it Eyes,
Counsell, and Order, and it ceaseth. What
Though it first brake from out the Chaos? 'twas
To make another in the Creature. Distance,
Figure, and Lineament are things that come
From something more Advis'd; Love never leads,
It still transports. The Motions which it feels
Are Fury, Rapture, Extasie, and such
As thrust it out full of Instinct, and Deity,
To meet what it desires.
  Luc. Alas! it self
Hath Eyes, but 'tis our Blindness that doth veyl them:
If Love could not consist with Wisdome, then
The World were govern'd by one generall Madness.
  Olynd. 'Tis not deni'd but that we may have Wisdom
Before we Love, as men may have good Eyes
Before they fix them on the Sun: but dwell they
A while upon it, and they straight grow blind
From those admired Beauties.
  Luc. But if Love
Do not consider, why then doth it fear?
Why doth it form *Chimæras* to it self,
And set up Thought 'gainst Thought? why is't alike
Tortur'd with Truth, and Falshood? why afflicted
As much from Doubts, as Certainties?
  Cha. This is
Not from Distrust, but Care; Love is not perfect
Till it begins to fear. It doth not know
The worth of that it seeks, unless it be
Anxious, and troubled for it: And this is
Not any thought of Blemish in the thing
It loves, but only Study to preserve it.
  Lu. Who puts a Snake 'mongst Flowers to preserve 'em?

Or who pours Poyson into Crystall that
It may be kept from cracking? Jealousie
What art thou? thou could'st not come down from Heav'n;
For no such Monsters can inhabit there.
   Eum. Nor can it spring from Hell; for it is born   [1650]
Of Love, and there is nought but Hate.
   Luc. Pray y'tell me
Who joyn'd it unto Love? who made them swear
So firm a Friendship?
   Olyn. The same Deity
That joyn'd the Sun and Light, the same that knits
The Life and Spirit.
   Luc. These preserve each other: [1655]
But that doth twine and wreath it self about
Our growing Loves, as Ivy 'bout the Oak;
We think it shelters, when (alas!) we find
It weakens, and destroys.
   Eum. It is not Jealousie
That ruins Love, but we our selves, who will not   [1660]
Suffer that fear to strengthen it; Give way
And let it work, 'twill fix the Love it springs from
In a staid Center.
   Luc. What it works I know not,
But it must needs suppose Defect in one,
Either Defect of Merit in the Lover,   [1665]
Or in the Lov'd, of Faith; you cannot think
That I give Others Favours, when your self
Boast such a store of Merits.
   Cha. O *Lucasia,*
Rather than be so impious as to think
That you want Faith, I must confess a want   [1670]
Of Merit in my self; (which would there were not.)
And being it is so, I was compell'd
To fear lest one more worthy than my self
Might throw me from my happiness. Consider
That you are born t' enrich the Earth, and then   [1675]
If you will have one Love and not be Jealous,
You must convert your Eye upon your Eye,
Make your own Heart Court your own Heart, and be
Your self a servant to your self.

Luc. But doth not
This Passion cease at last?
  Olyn. It ceaseth to [1680]
Disturb, but still remains to quicken Love;
As Thunder ceaseth when 't hath purg'd the Air,
And yet the Fire which caus'd it still remains
To make it move the livelier.
  Luc. Were it quiet, [1685]
What Hand, *Charistus*, would More sweetly move
The Orbs of this our Island? who fetch in
More frequent Conquests? and who more become
The Triumphs than your self?
  Cha. Beleeve *Charistus*
Dreams; Errours, false Opinions, slippery Hopes, [1690]
And Jealous Fears are now his Spoyl, his Captives,
And follow Love's Triumphant Chariot, which
His Soul sits high in, and o'rlooks the vain
Things of this lower World.
  Luc. *Lucasia* did
Only retire, not flie; Let's to the Grove, [1695]
And by the Consummation of our Loves
Under those Myrtles (which as yet perhaps
Preserve the blushing Marks of those your Angers)
Appease th' offended Goddess.
  Olyn. This your Union
Will make your Kingdoms joyn; *Cyprus* and *Crete* [1700]
Will meet in your Embraces.
  Eum. Our Hearts are
Love's ord'nary Employment: 'tis a Dart
Of a more scattering Metall that strikes you;
When he wounds Princes, he wounds Nations too.
                                          Exeunt.

ACT V. SCENE I.

Pandena, Cosmeta, Rhodia, meeting *Machessa*
and *Philænis*.

  Cos. Lady *Machessa*, opportunely met. [1705]
  Pan. What store of Arms prepar'd?

Mach. The Country's layd;
Spits, Andirons, Racks, and such like Utensils
Are in the very Act of Metamorphosis;
Art is now sitting on them, and they will
Be hatch'd to Engins shortly.
    Pan. Pray y' how doth   [1710]
The Muster-Roule encrease?
    Mach. As fast as *Chloe*
Can take their Names; we shall be all great Women.
    Phil. Pray y' what Reward shall you and I have Lady?
    Mach. Why I will be the Queen o'th' *Amazons*,
And thou o'th' *Pigmies*.
    Phil. I, but who shall place us   [1715]
In the *Amazonian*, and *Pigmean* Throne?
    Mach. Who but our Swords *Philænis*? when we have
Setled the Government here at home, we will
Lead out an Army 'gainst those Warlike Dames,
And make 'em all our Vassals.
    Phil. These left handed   [1720]
Ladies are notable Politicians.
The King of *Monomotapa* you may
Be sure will be your Enemy, or else
The Book deceives me. But the *Agags* they
Will sure be for you.
    Cos. Who may the *Agags* be?   [1725]
    Phi. Why a black ugly People, that do turn
The inside of their Eye-lids outward, that
They may look lovely; if they catch the *Amazons*,
They sowce 'em straight, as we do Pig, by quarters,
Or else do pickle 'em up for Winter Sallads.   [1730]
    Mac. How did you come by all this Knowledge *Phil*?
You are a learned Page.
    Phil. Lady, do y' think
I never read to th' Women in the Nurs'ry?
But will you lose one of your Breasts? 'tis pitty
That your left Pap should be burnt off.
    Mach. Why Gyrl?   [1735]
What use will there be of it?
    Phi. To give suck.
You must go seek out some brave *Alexander*,

And beg some half a dozen of Children of him,
Or else you'l be no true bred *Amazon*.
   Pan.   Must they have *Macedonian* Fathers then?   [1740]
   Phil.   I think the *Amazonian* Queen doth swear
To no such Article when She is Crown'd;
But ord'narily they do so; yet howe'r
Your Grace may send for the three Courtiers,
That you deliver'd from these Ladies here,   [1745]
They would be glad to be employ'd in any
Such State-affairs. But I'd almost forgot
The *Pigmies* Conquest.
   Rho.   Have you read of them too?
   Phil.   Though some say that their Souls are only stopt
Into their Bodies, just as so much Quick-silver   [1750]
Is put into hot Loves, to make 'em dance
As long as th' heat continues; yet, beleeve it,
They are a subt'le Nation, a most shrew'd
Advising People.
   Cos.   How'l you then subdue them?
   Phil.   By Policy, set Hays, and Traps, and Springs,   [1755]
And Pitfals for 'em. And if any do
Dwell in the Rocks, make holes upon the top
As deep as Cups, and fill 'em up with Wine;
You shall have one come presently, and sip,
And when he finds the sweetness, cry *Chin, Chin*:   [1760]
Then all the rest good Fellows straight come out,
And tipple with him till they fall asleep;
Then we may come and pack 'em up in Hampers,
Or else in Hand-baskets, and carry 'em whither
We please our selves.
   Mach.   A notable Stratagem!   [1765]
You'l never leave your Policies *Phil*.
   Phi.   But yet
We must draw out some Souldiers howe'r.
   Cos.   There's no great need of Souldiers; Their Camp's
No larger than a Ginger-bread Office.
   Pan.   And the Men little bigger.
   Phil.   What half Heretick   [1770]
Book tels you that?
   Rho.   The greatest sort they say

Are like stone-pots with Beards that do reach down
Unto their knees.
   Cos. They're carri'd to the Wars then
As Chickens are to Market, all in Dorsers,
Some thirty Couple on a Horse.
   Phil. You read   [1775]
Only Apocryphall History. Beleeve me
They march most formally: I know't, there will
Be work enough for Souldiers.
   Mach. Wee'l train up
All the young Wenches of the City here
On purpose for this Expedition,   [1780]
And 't shall be call'd the Female War.
   Phil. I fear
They won't be strong enough to go against 'em;
They have an Enemy doth vex 'em more
Than Horse or Man can.
   Mach. Who, the Cranes you mean?
I'l beg a Patent of Her Majesty   [1785]
To take up all that fly about the Country,
For the *Pigmean* Service.
   Phil. I, but who
Shall's have to Discipline 'em so, that we
May fly 'em at them off our fists?
   Mach. They fly
In a most war-like Figure naturally: [1790]
However we may have a Net cast o'r
Th' Artyllery Yard, and send for th' Gentleman
That bridles Stags, and makes 'em draw Caroches,
Hee'l exercise 'em in a Month or two,
And bring 'em to it easily.
   Phil. We must carry   [1795]
Six or sev'n hundred of Bird-Cages
And Cony-Coopes along with us.
   Mach. For what?
   Phil. T' imprison Rebels, and there feed 'em up
With Milk, and Dazy-roots. I will so yerk
The little Gentlemen.
   Cos. You must not play   [1800]
The Tyrant o'r the Wretches.

Phil.   You shall see   [*Draws her Sword.*
How I'l behave my self. This foreside blow
Cuts off thrice three, this back-blow thrice three more,
This foreright thrust spits half a dozen of 'em,
Bucklers and all, like so many Larkes with Sage   [1805]
Between them; then this down-right cleaves a stubborn
Two-footed Rebell from the Crown o'th' head
Down to the twist, and makes him double forked
Like a Turn Stile, or some such Engin. Others
I'l knock pall-mall, and make the wretched Caitiffs   [1810]
Measure their length upon their Mother Earth,
And so bestride 'em, and cry Victory.
  Mach.   And what'l you do, when you are seated in
The Throne, to win your Subjects Love *Philænis*?
  Phil.   I'l stand upon a Cricket, and there make   [1815]
Fluent Orations to 'em; call 'em Trusty
And Well-beloved, Loyall, and True Subjects,
And my good People: Then I'l mount on Horseback,
Shew 'em my little Majesty, and scatter
Five or six hundred single pence among 'em,   [1820]
Teach 'em good Language by cleft sticks, and Bay-leaves,
And Civilize 'em finally by Puppet-Plays.
  Cos.   Most studi'd, and advis'd!
  Pan.   The heart of Wisdome!
  Rho.   And Soul of Policy!
  Mach.   Come little Queen,
Wee'l go and make her Majesty acquainted   [1825]
With all the Plot; 'twill take her certainly.   *Exeunt.*

Act. V. Scen. II.

Adraste, Lucasia, Charistus, Olyndus, Eumela, Florina,
  Malthora, in Myrtle wreathes.

  Adr.   Was all the Treasure ship'd?
  Eum.   All, but the Pictures,
And Statues, they'r reserv'd. I saw the Luxury,
And wealth of *Cyprus* sail. The Souldier doth
By this time gaze upon't.
  Adr.   The news, *Charistus*,   [1830]

Of your Adventures here, I dare presume
Hath joyn'd both Armies now. Me thinks I see
The *Cyprians* standing here, the *Cretans* there,
And, in a space between them, both Kings meeting
In a most strong Embrace, and so provoking [1835]
Clamors and shouts from both sides, and a joyfull
Clattring of Weapons.
   Cha.   Beautious Queen, your Vertues
Are greater far than Fame; and you your self
Greater than them! Though Gold and Purple do
Adorn your head, yet you have Wove your self [1840]
Far richer Diadems from your Royall Acts,
And made your self Immortall by producing
Immortall things. But though your wreath of Vertue
Hath made what e'r the Sun beholds in all
His course enamor'd by you, yet if I [1845]
May pull one single one from out the rest,
There's none, for which you have more Altars rais'd
Unto your Name, than for that Noble Love,
Whose flames you keep still burning in your self,
And cherish in all others.
   Adr.   Sir, you have Conquer'd [1850]
A Princess, and in her a Queen: I am
Th' addition to your Triumph. We ow much
To you *Olyndus*.
   Olyn.   I can challenge nothing
But my *Charistus* Friendship. 'Tis to him
You ow these seeds of Peace. Although his Father [1855]
Appear'd so tender of him, that when he
Came hither secretly to view the Rites
Of *Venus*, which *Lucasia* then perform'd,
The aged Man hasted to th' Oracle
To know what Fortune should attend his Son, [1860]
And, for an unexpected answer, did
Banish those Priests for which our King now fights:
Yet for all this, ev'n in this heat of danger,
H'hath made another Venture, and the Kingdom
Now grieves his second loss.
   Adr.   Do you know the answer [1865]
That the God gave to his enquiring Father,

For which the King did banish all the Priests?
   Olyn. I may repeat it now, th' Event assures me
It meant you no Misfortune. It was this;
      Charistus *shall his Country save,*   [1870]
      If he become his Enemies Slave.
   Adr. I hope th' Event will not fulfill it.
   Olyn. 'Tis
Fulfill'd enough to make an Oracle true.
   Adr. I hope you have no Enemies, and for Slave
The Gods avert it!
   Olyn. He's *Lucasia*'s Servant,   [1875]
There's that fulfill'd; *Cyprus* is now reputed
The *Enemy* to *Crete*; but as for true
And reall Enemies to you *Charistus*,
The World hath none so Barbarous; your Vertues
Have under this disguise shew'd so much Prince,   [1880]
That they betrai'd you still to any Eye
That could discern.
   Cha. Honour'd *Olyndus*, you
Outdo me still. Friends should be alwaies equall:
You must take off, and pare your Vertues, that
You may go even with me. I ow much   [1885]
To you, *Eumela*, too.
   Adr. Her service hath
Preserv'd the Kingdom, and refounded *Cyprus*.
   Cha. Two Scepters are her Debters.
   Adr. But, *Eumela*,
You might have told me sooner, that *Lucasia*
Began to feel a Passion; you ne'r knew   [1890]
That I destroy'd true vertuous Loves; it is
A pleasure to me to perceive their Buddings,
To know their Minutes of Encrease, their Stealths,
And silent Growings; and I have not spar'd
To help, and bring them on.
   Eum. You have so favour'd   [1895]
Agreeing Souls, that all the World confesseth
Your own is perfect Harmony. But where
The God is Blind, should not the Creature be
Silent, and Close? That which is bred by whispers
Would dye if once proclam'd.

    Luc. If it were any, [1900]
It was a fault of Trust; 'tis more Injustice
To betray secret Love, than to make known
Counsels of State. *Cupid* hath his Cabinet,
To which, if any prove unfaithfull, he
Straight wounds him with the Leaden Shaft, and so [1905]
They live tormented, and dye scorn'd.
    Adr. No more;
'Tis well: I meant not to Accuse, but Praise.
Have you set some to watch, and signifie
The King's Return?
    Eum. Three peacefull Courtiers,
Lerinus, and *Ganyctor,* and *Iringus,* [1910]
Desir'd that they might bring the News, and so
Are gone unto the Port.
    Adr. My Ladies, you
I hope will clear up now.
    Flor. I have too much
Joy to express it.
    Mal. Could you see my heart,
You'd view a Triumph there.

Act. V. Scen. III.

To them *Philænis.*

    Phil. And't please your Highness [1915]
There are three Ladies wait without, who, if
You have a vacant Ear, are come t' inform you
Of something neer concerns the State.
    Adr. The old
Vexation's busie still — *Pandena* and
Cosmeta, and the other — are they not? [1920]
Tell 'em they may come in — How shall we do,
Eumela, now to stop their Clamour?   [*Ex.* Phi.
    Eum. 'Tis easie;
There's nothing yet provided; the Return
O'th' King being now so sudden, 'twill amaze 'em,
And make 'em kneel for mercy to you, if [1925]
You do but threaten to disclose the Plot.

Act. V. Scen. IV.

To them Cosmeta, Pandena, Rhodia.

Adr. Your business Ladies?
Cos. Please you to dismiss
Those Faces that have Beards?
Adr. Fear not, they shall not
Betray your Counsels.
Cos. Please your Highness then,
There's fear that our Design will come to nought, [1930]
Our Trust is falsifi'd.
Adr. How so?
Cos. We came
To ask *Machessa* about Weapons, and
She presently demands, how many cases
Of Knives, what Forks we have, Tosting, or Carving?
Pan. Talk we of Swords, she asks what Crisping Pins [1935]
And Bodkins we could guess might easily be
Rais'd through the Common-wealth?
Rho. We spake of Armour,
She straight replies, send in your steel Combs, with
The Steels you see your Faces in, wee'l quickly
Convert 'em into Greaves, and Gorgets.
Cos. If [1940]
This be not treason 'gainst the Female State,
Beleeve not Policy, nor me.
Eum. Why she
Was your own choice; you cri'd her up as one
That having neither Child, nor Husband, would
Take to her self the Commonwealth as both. [1945]
Cos. We do suspect your sadness sweet *Florina*.
Rho. And your retir'dness too *Malthora*, (as
Demure as you stand here) is deep engag'd.
Pan. Nor is *Eumela* free.
Mal. Whence do you gather it? [1949]
Cos. Pray y' why those Myrtle wreaths? why your Gates drest?
And your Doors Crown'd?
Flo. In hope our Lords will shortly
Enter, and Crown 'em more.

Cos.   Most evident!
Can there be bolder Falshood? Did we not
Agree to keep out Husbands from our City
And our Minds too? And yet behold there are   [1955]
Garlands and Flowers prepar'd; and they to be
Receiv'd as Lovers. Husbands are at best
But a sad kind of pleasure; one good Look,
And a Salute's enough at any time
For the Good-man o'th' Family.
   Flo.   Pray y' allow   [1960]
Affection more Expressions; Love doth cease
To be, when that it breaks not out into
Those signs of Joy; as Souls cease to be Souls
When they leave off to shew their Operations.
   Pan.   This is no time for vain Philosophy,   [1965]
We are to have a fine State of it shortly,
When Ladies once begin to utter Axioms,
And raise a Faction 'gainst the seven Sages.

Act. V. Scen. V.

Machessa.

   Mac.   And't please your Highness, three Embassadors,
Sent from the *Cretan* State, do crave admittance.   [1970]
   Adr.   Usher 'em in.   [*Ex.* Ma. [*Eum. whispers the Qu.*
   Cos.   There's life you see i'th' bus'ness;
Let's yet be true. The fame of our Exploit
Already makes us sought to. There's an Honour
Not usuall too i'th' Number of 'em; when
Arriv'd there three before from the same State?   [1975]
And't please you, let *Pandena*, *Rhodia*, and I,
Manage their Entertainment?
   Adr.   Do so.
   Pan.   It shall
All be to th' honour of the Female State.
   Cos.   Prepare your self *Pandena*; here they come.

Act V. Scene VI.

To them Machessa *ushering* Lerinus, Iringus, *and* Ganyctor,
as Embassadors.

  Ler. Most Gratious, most Renowned, and most Beautious. [1980]
  Cos. Pray y' be not troublesome; We're taken up
Wholy with the Affairs o'th' Kingdom now.
  Irin. When will your Ladiship have a Vacancy?
  Pan. You are Impertinent; True Politicians
Do never use to answer on the sudden. [1985]
  Rho. It is not now as heretofore; the times
Are grown more wise, and more reserv'd; there are
Matters on foot far greater; you must wait——
You are Embassadors.
  Gan. We should not think so,
But that you're pleas'd to tell us so; your usage [1990]
Hath a far different Dialect from your Tongue.
  Cos. Were there not Women in your Kingdom fit
For this Imployment? I perceive your State
Is utterly unfurnish'd, that it cannot
Send forth three Female Agents.
  Irin. 'Tis not, Madam, [1995]
The custome of our Master to commit
His Kingdom's secrets to a peece of Chrystall;
That were not to Negotiate, but Betray.
  Pa. You shall meet Women here, that are not Crystal,
Those that will find out you, and hide themselves. [2000]
  Rho. You shall not need the help of an Interpreter
When we give Audience; Speak what Tongue you will
You shall be understood, each one of us
Hath more than one.
  Ler. We easily beleeve it,
Though you should speak none else besides your Native. [2005]
  Cos. Pray stand you by, and wait a while.
  Ler. We obey.
  Cos. Now will they think the better of us; 'tis
The way to bring our selves in Credit by
Neglecting of 'em thus. I'd have 'em know
We were to be saluted at their coming. [2010]

Pan.   Their State is very unhappy, that it is
So unprovided: I beleeve these are
The very wisest in the Kingdom; for
They have no Manners.
   Rho.   You guess rightly, Madam;
The greatest Counsellors and Lawyers scarce   [2015]
Know how to make a Leg.

Act. V. Scen. VII.

To them *Philænis.*

   Phil.   Arm, arm, arm, arm,
The King, and Lords are within sight. Here Madam,
Pray take my Sword, and Helmet.
   Cos.   Worthy Gentlemen,
Do y' come to proffer aid from th' *Cretan* King
To help us 'gainst the Men?
   Irin.   No Ladies: we   [2020]
Come but to tell you that the King is Landed,   { *They discover*
We are your fellow-Subjects.   *themselves.*
   Cos.   Fellow-Villaines
Among your selves. *Eumela*, we may thank
You for all this.
   Pan.   But Sister of the Sword,
Great Lady Stickler—   [2025]
   Mach.   Be patient pray y' a while—Take you this Helmet,
And you this Fauchion Sir, and you this Lance;
Embassadours still must be dismiss'd with Presents.
   Rho.   Where is our Plate?
   Pan.   Our Wealth?
   Cos.   Our Jewels?
   Mach.   Folly!
Did not my Order bind me to assist   [2030]
Distressed men?
   Cos.   Who would e'r trust a Woman?
   Mach.   The Queen will give y' a fair account.
   Adr.   'Tis no
Time to debate things now. The truth is, all
Was ship'd, and sent the King, as one great Present

From all the *Cyprian* Women. If you do [2035]
Desire that he should know how it was rais'd,
For what intended, by what means diverted,
I'l bid him spare his thanks, and tell him 'twas
Not Bounty, but Misfortune that directed
This vast Supply to him.
  Cos. We hope your Highness [2040]
Will be so Gratious to us, as to let us
Make the best use yet of our Evils. 'Twill
Be something, if that, which was meant Sedition,
May now be took for Contribution,
And we esteem'd Relievers of the Army. [2045]
  Adr. I do engage my Royall word, you shall
Be put in th' Annals, as good Members of
The *Cyprian* Commonwealth. But heark, the noise!
The Horses, Trumpets, Priests! They come! stand off.

Act. V. Scen. VIII.

To them *3* Priests of *Apollo* with wreaths of Lawrell,
    Demarchus and *Dinomachus* hand in hand, *Pæstanus,*
    Philondas, Souldiers.

> *The* Priests *standing on one side, and the* Ladies *on the other, leaving a free space between 'em, in which* Demarchus *and* Adraste *first meet. Then* Dinomachus *and* Adraste *receive* Charistus *and* Lucasia, *Then* Philondas *meets* Malthora, *Then the King and Queen joyn* Olyndus *and* Eumela, *The rest then salute, and receive one another with Welcome; While they all thus meet, the* Priests *on the one side, and the* Ladies *on the other, sing thus enterchangeably.*

1 Priest.   Apollo, *who foretell'st what shall ensue,* [2050]
            None speaks more Dark than thou, but none More true;
            If Heard, Obscure; but yet if Seen, most Bright;
            Day's in thy Visage, in thy Sayings Night.
Pr. Cho.   *Day's in thy Visage, in thy Sayings Night.*

1 Lady.   Venus *makes good what he Decrees,* [2055]
            And Love fulfils what he foresees,

	Thus Gods help Gods, thus Mortals ow .	
	Much to the Bayes, much to the Bow.	
La. Cho.	*Much to the Bayes, much to the Bow.*	
2 Priest.	Phœbus *as Præsent shewes us future things,*	[2060]
	Our Trivets Counsell give, our Trees teach Kings,	
	And whil' st our Oracle instructs the State,	
	What e'r the Priest shall say the God makes Fate.	
Pr. Cho.	*What e'r the Priest shall say the God makes Fate.*	
2 Lady.	*What are your Trivets to Loves wings?*	[2065]
	They Teach, but these do Conquer Kings:	
	Venus *to Fate adds all the bliss,*	
	She that makes Doves, makes Kingdoms kiss.	
La. Cho.	*She that makes Doves, makes Kingdoms kiss.*	
La. & Pr.	*Thus then the Myrtle and the Bayes we joyn,*	[2070]
Chorus.	*And in one Wreath* Wisdom *and* Love *Combine.*	

   Dem. I never raign'd till now. You needed not
Have sent that Ample Treasure; I had all
Wealth in your Loves. Come, Great *Dinomachus*,
As they joyn'd Voices, so let us joyn Hearts.   [2075]
   Dino. Sir, your Embraces vanquish far beyond
Your Sword, though happy; you march Conquerour
More by a Glorious Peace, than if your Arm
Had scatter'd Deaths still as you pass'd; your Throne
Grows hence; y'have gain'd what e'r you have not ruin'd;   [2080]
Your Pow'r rules *Cyprus*, but your Fame the World.
   Dem. Hate only is between th' Ignoble, when
The Good dissent, tis only difference,
No malice; Vertue flames in both, and so
Each must the other Love; their Discords are   [2085]
More blameless than th' Embraces of the Bad;
'Tis to stand off, rather than bear a Grudge.
And if they fight, when e'r they do lay down
Their Weapons, they lay down their Anger too.
As we affect then to seem good, and are so,   [2090]
Let one Oblivion wrap up what hath past
On either side.

Dino. But I must first ask Pardon;
I've wrong'd a Deity. Great *Apollo*, be
Thou still propitious. Here I do restore
Thy Blameless Priests. What was but only Darkness, [2095]
I thought Contrivance; and the Priest not Loyall;
Because the God was pleas'd to be obscure:
But now th' Event lends light to that, and Me;
   And my Charistus *doth his Country save*
   By being thus become his Enemi's Slave. [2100]
Peace rest upon 'em both; *Apollo* spoke it,
And *Venus* hath perform'd it.
 Dem. As they joyn'd
To make us happy, so let us pay back
United Thanks, and joyn their Deities in
A double Feast. It is not Mens Lot only [2105]
To need each other; ev'n the Pow'rs themselves
Give and take help. Affection brings about
What Counsell cannot. Thus the Gods have lent
Love unto Wisdome for an Instrument.
        Exeunt Omnes.

The Epilogue.

Though we well know the Neighbouring Plain
   Can strike from Reeds as high a Strain,
     And that the Scrip, and Crook
     May worst our Poet's Book;
Like Fayries yet we here could stay   [5]
Till Village Cocks proclaime the Day:
And whiles your Pleasure is the Theam,
    Feed and keep up the Dream.

But Sleep beginning now to shed
   Poppies on every Bed,   [10]
Love stay'd his hands, and said our Eyes
   This Night were made his Prize:
And now (instead of Poppies) flings
These wishes on you from his wings.

The Calm of Kingdoms new made Friends,   [15]
When both enjoy their Hopes, and Ends,
   The like in you Create,
   And make each Mind a State:
The thoughts of Princes, when they do
Meet Princes to coyn Princes too,   [20]
Possess your Breasts with Fire and Youth,
   And make each dream a Truth:
The Joyes of Friendship after Fight,
   Of Love's first happy Night,
Of Lords return'd, make you still greet,   [25]
   As when you first did meet.
And, quitted thus from Grief and Fear,
Think you enjoy a Cyprus here.

THE ROYAL SLAVE

INTRODUCTION

1. The Text

THREE EDITIONS of *The Royal Slave* were printed in the seventeenth century: two, at Oxford in quarto, in 1639 and 1640, during Cartwright's lifetime; the third, in octavo, in 1651 as part of the collected *Works*. No entry for *The Royal Slave* was made by Moseley on the Stationers' Register (see my discussion of this point in the General Introduction, Chapter V, "The Text," p. 63). The play has never been reprinted. A transcript of the title-pages and a signature collation of each edition may be found under *Text* in the Notes. The second edition (1640) was printed from the first (1639), and the third edition (1651) from the second. According to Mr. Goffin, the second quarto affords the best text.[1] In one sense this is true, since it corrects many of the typographical errors of the first edition. On the other hand, it adds nearly as many more of its own, and gives every evidence of having been set up from the first quarto. These considerations leave the ultimate authority of the first quarto unchallenged.

We are in the unusual position of possessing several fragments of the proof sheets for both the 1639 and 1640 quartos. They consist of sheet A (imperfect), G (sigs. G2^v and G3^r and the first two lines of text on G1^r and G4^v), and I (sigs. I1 and I2) of the 1639 edition, and sheet B (sigs. B1^v and B4^r) of the 1640 text.[2] There is, unfortunately, no way of knowing whether the corrections are made in Cartwright's own hand. Mr. Simpson is rightly noncommittal on the point, although we know that Cartwright had a strong interest in all affairs relating to printing.[3] Another writer, Mr. F.

---

1. *Poems*, p. 205.
2. These fragments are all in the Bodleian Library, except those of sheet G, which were formerly in the possession of the late G. Thorn-Drury, but have since been sold. Mr. Percy Simpson discusses all the fragments, except those of sheet B (1640), in his *Proof-Reading in the Sixteenth, Seventeenth, and Eighteenth Centuries* (1935), pp. 83–84. My statement of details does not always agree with Mr. Simpson's. The Bodleian also possesses a letter from Mr. Simpson concerning the fragments of sheet B which turned up too late to be included in his book (the letter is preserved with the fragments).
3. See Chapter I, pp. 13–15. In the

Needham, is less cautious and ascribes the hand in at least one of the fragments (sigs. I and I2) to Cartwright.[4] My own search has disclosed one Cartwright signature (see frontispiece).[5]

Apart from the interest which attaches to these proof corrections as possible examples of the author himself at work, the actual corrections do not amount to much, but consist largely of changes in the punctuation and occasionally in the spelling. In the proof of sheet A (1639 quarto), for example, only two verbal changes are made. The eighth line in the first prologue originally read "Not to boast Colour, but to confesse." The second "to" is deleted by the corrector. Again, in line one of the second prologue, we find "After the Rites" altered to "After our Rites." Curiously enough the heading of the dramatis personae reads "The Persons of the / Play speakers," and is uncorrected, although it appears correctly in the published copy. The corrections in sheets G and I are all trifling. One correction in sheet B (1640 quarto) is interesting because it seems quite unnecessary, even wrong. In lines 55–56 the uncorrected proof reads "The King loves no Garbidge-tubbes." The corrector carefully added an apostrophe in "loves," thus "love's," a change which appears in the final copy, and is reproduced in the third edition.

In addition to the printed editions five manuscripts of *The Royal*

---

letter referred to in the last note, Mr. Simpson notices that the type of "e" used in the corrections of sheet B (1640 quarto) is the same as that used in the correcting of the proofs of the first edition (1639), and he "inclines to think it was the press-corrector's."

4. *Bodleian Quarterly Record*, IV (1924), 77–78. The blank outer forme of sheet I preserves an interesting little document. It is a challenge from Nicklis Swanne to Robert Milles, citizen of London, "to play with [me] at eight severall weapons here under-named at the kinges Armes in Holly-well, on Saturday next, being the second day of the moneth [ffebruary] betwixt one and two of the clocke in the after noone." The challenge contains a number of spelling corrections, etc., which Mr. Needham is inclined to attribute to Cartwright, without, however, any authority.

5. Aubrey (*Remaines of Gentilisme and Judaisme*, ed. James Britten, [Folk-Lore Society], 1881, p. 69) records a volume formerly in Cartwright's library which contained manuscript notes in his hand: "When I was of Trin. Coll. there was a sale of Mr. Wm Cartwright's (Poet) bookes, many whereof I had; amongst others (I know not how) was Dr. Daniel Featly's *Handmayd to Devotion;* wch was printed shortly after Dr Heylins Hist. aforsd. In the Holyday Devotions he speakes of St. George, and asserts the story to be fabulous; and there was never any such man. Wm Cartwright writes in the margent 'For this assertion was Dr. Featly brought upon his knees before Wm Laud A-Bp. of Canterbury.'" (Quoted by Goffin, *Poems*, p. xix.)

Slave have been recorded: (1) Bodleian Library, Arch. Seld. B. 26; (2) manuscript in the possession of the Duke of Bedford; (3) Folger Shakespeare Library, MS. 7044 (formerly in the possession of B. Dobell); (4) British Museum, Addit. MS. 41,616 (from the Petworth collection); (5) Heber MS. 1043. The first four of these manuscripts have been used in preparing the present edition, though the readings of the Bedford MS. are given on the authority of the late G. Thorn-Drury, who at one time prepared, or had prepared for him, a collation of the Dobell (now Folger) and Bedford MSS. These collations, unpublished, are now in the Widener Library at Harvard, and those of the Bedford MS. have been included among the variant readings. Mr. Harbage lists the Petworth-British Museum MS. as two distinct manuscripts.[6] The so-called Heber MS. which contained a list of the actors for the initial performance at Oxford (1636), has dropped from sight.

The Bodleian MS. of *The Royal Slave* (Arch. Seld. B. 26) is bound in a volume containing several entirely unrelated manuscripts. The leaves containing Cartwright's play occupy fols. 103 through 135 (33 folio leaves, the chain-lines running perpendicularly, fols. 132ᵛ through 135ᵛ being blank). The leaves measure 26.1 by 17.85 cm., and have been considerably cropped in binding, so much so that most of the catchwords have been cut away. Fol. 103ʳ, which serves as a title-page, reads: "The / Royall Slaue / A / Tragi-Comedy." On the verso of the same leaf is "The Persons." The list of dramatis personae is followed by "The Prologue to the King / and Queene" (fol. 104ʳ) and "The Prologue / To the Vniversity" (fol. 105ʳ). The "Prologue at Hampton-Court" and its fellow epilogue do not appear in any of the manuscripts. The text of the play begins on fol. 106ʳ and runs through fol. 131ʳ. "The Epilogue to the / King & Queene." (fol. 131ᵛ) and "The Epilogue to the / Vniversity." (fol. 132ʳ) follow. The manuscript is written in a clear hand, showing both secretary and Italian characteristics. Punctuation is extremely uncertain, often absent. The Bodleian Manuscript Catalogue dates the manuscript 1636–38, upon, I believe, the authority of Malone. It is designated as *S*.

The Folger MS. (MS. 7044) is contained in a volume labeled "Miscellanies Vol. 24" originally from the Shadwell Court Library and formerly owned by William Woodward. It contains 26 leaves,

---

6. "Elizabethan and Seventeenth-Century Play Manuscripts," *PMLA*, L (1935), 689.

numbered 1 through 26, measuring 28.5 by 18 cm., and has been badly cropped in binding, so that many of the catchwords and some whole lines have been cut off. The title-page (fol. 1^r) reads: "The / Royall Slaue./ A / Trage-Comedy. / The Scene / Sardes." The verso of fol. 1 contains "The Persons." "The Prolouge / To the Kinge and Queene." follows on fol. 2^r and "The Prolouge to the Vniversity, by a Preist / discouer'd at his Deuotions, as before." on fol. 2^v. The text of the play begins on fol. 3^r and runs through fol. 25^v. "The Epilouge / To the Kinge and Queene." appears on fol. 26^r and is followed by "The Epilouge / To the Vniversity. / By / Arsamnes." on fol. 26^v. The Folger MS. is the only manuscript which contains the descriptions of the scenes or "appearances." These have been written in by a second hand which shows much stronger secretary characteristics than the almost pure Italian hand in which the body of the manuscript is written. It is designated as *F*. A reproduction of fol. 25^r appears on the opposite page.

The British Museum MS. of *The Royal Slave* (Addit. MS. 41,616) is the first of the four miscellaneous items bound together in a folio volume. It is carefully written in a predominantly Italian hand, and each page has a neatly ruled margin around the four edges. It is roughly the same size as the Bodleian and Folger MSS. There are 24 leaves, both fol. 1^r and fol. 24^v being blank. The title-page (fol. 1^v) reads: "*The / Royall Slaue* / A / Tragicomedy / The Scene / Sardes./ Acted before the King / at Oxford." Fol. 2^r contains "The Persons." On the verso of fol. 2 follows "To the Kinge & Queene / theire Ma:^{ts}. / The Prologue." The text begins on fol. 3^r and runs through fol. 23^r. Fol. 23^v is blank. "The Epilogue." appears on fol. 24^r. It should be noticed that the Prologue and Epilogue to the University are here missing and that this manuscript omits more stage directions than any of the other manuscripts. It is designated as *P*.[7]

The Bedford MS., according to the Thorn-Drury collation notes, is a small folio of 35 leaves, bound in a modern green cover. The title "The Royall Slave" appears on the recto of fol. 1, and it is repeated as "The Royall Slave / A / Tragi-Comedy" on fol. 2^r. Of the four

---

7. W. W. Greg (*Dramatic Documents, Commentary*, 1931, pp. 363-64) describes this manuscript as "a calligraphic copy, evidently literary, and perhaps prepared for presentation," and suggests that the absence of the Prologue and Epilogue to the University "points to its being a presentation copy for the Court."

| also now ye
| are with the
| guilt keepe[?]
| and a showre of
| teares falling
| on this altar
| puts out the
| flame /

The Gods desire it not
            Act. 5. Sc. 7
        To Them
        2 Preist
2d Preist Stop, stop Arsanes.   the scean appeares
Heaun is not pleased with the Sacrifice   altered
The glorious Sunne hath veyl'd his face in Clouds   scean [?]
Not willinge to behold it, and the Skyes
Haue shed such numerous teares as haue extinguisht
The fire though fully kindled
        Atos. Thou hast now
The voyce and visage of the Gods good Preist
The Heauns were neuer more Serene. The Gods
Haue iustify'd my care Cleander
        Arsam Happy newes
Death sends thee backe vnto vs; this comes not
From any humane Powr, 'tis not my hand
That spares thee blest Cleander 'Tis Som: God,
Some God reserues thee vnto greater workes
For vs, & for thy Country
        Cleat: Beinge then
You so interest of G[?] thus diuide
That life they lend me, one halfe shall be yours,
The other Ephesus, that mine Actions
Wearinge both Gratitude and Piety,
Like to some well wrought Picture, may at once
Behold both you and that. It shall nere be sayd
The Gods reuiu'd Cleander to a time
To make him fall more fowle
        Arsam Thy fayth hath been
So firme and tryd, thy Moderation
So stayd, that in a Just reward I must
My selfe conduct thee into Greece, and there

Fol. 25r of Folger MS. 7044 (reduced).

manuscripts here collated, this one, on the whole, is the least trustworthy, frequently offering readings which look like obvious guesses on the part of the scribe. There is a regular tendency to expand elided forms, and there are occasional signs of bowdlerizing. It is designated as *B*. Since I have had access only to those readings of *B* recorded in Thorn-Drury's collation notes (Widener A 1832.5*), the omission of a reading from *B* in any given textual note does not necessarily imply that *B* agrees with the copy-text.

A study of the mass of variant readings recorded in the Textual Notes to *The Royal Slave* reveals a great number of minor variations in the texts of the several manuscripts, but it is their number rather than their textual significance individually which is impressive. From this study, however, it is possible to establish certain definite points concerning the interrelationship of the four manuscripts, and the relationship of the manuscripts to the printed text of 1639.

The interrelationship of the four manuscripts.—(1) None of the four manuscripts here collated is directly derived from any of the others. (2) None of the manuscripts shows evidence of being more authoritative than another, though *B* (Bedford MS.) seems to be textually the least dependable. (3) Although none of the manuscripts is directly derived from any of the others, it is obvious that *S* (Bodleian MS.) and *B* can be traced back, probably at several removes, to a common original; there is also a definite connection, though less clearly marked, between *F* (Folger MS.) and *P* (British Museum MS.). (4) The omission in *P* of the Prologue and Epilogue to the University and of a certain amount of stage business suggests that this manuscript represents the earliest state of the text now extant.

The relationship of the manuscripts to the printed text of 1639.— (1) The first quarto (1639), which is the ultimate source of the 1640 and 1651 texts, is derived from none of the four manuscripts here collated, and shows a large number of readings appearing in none of the manuscripts. (2) Of the four manuscripts, *F*, quite apart from the scene descriptions put in by a later hand, has most in common with the printed text. (3) Certain important omissions, common to the four manuscripts, distinguish them from the printed text: (a) the descriptions of the "appearances," except in *F*, where they have been written in afterwards by a second hand; (b) the Prologue and the Epilogue to the King and Queen at Hampton Court; (c) the second stanza of the Priest's song in Act I, Scene ii; (d) the Ladies' "solemne march" and the verses from Claudian in Act V,

Scene v; and (e) the procession and Priests' song in Act V, Scene vii. (4) The omissions noted above suggest that the manuscripts represent an earlier state of the play than that appearing in the 1639 quarto.

In addition to those already described, three other manuscripts must be noticed. (1) British Museum Egerton MS. 2725 (fols. 115–16) contains the first two prologues and epilogues and the first stanza and chorus of the Priest's song in Act I, Scene ii. It is not derived from any of the four principal manuscripts discussed above. It is designated as *E*. (2) New York Public Library Drexel MS. 4041 contains the text and musical setting of three songs from Act I, Scene ii (both stanzas), Act III, Scene i, and Act V, Scene vii. This manuscript was brought to my attention by Miss Willa McClung Evans, who is responsible for rediscovering it.[8] It is designated as *L*. (3) Henry Lawes' autographed collection of manuscript songs (now in the possession of Miss Naomi Church of Beaconsfield, Buckinghamshire, England) contains "Come from the Dungeon" (I, ii) and "Come my sweet" (II, iii). Again I owe the knowledge of this manuscript to the kindness of Miss Willa McClung Evans, who got permission for me from Miss Church to make use of it in my collations. It is designated as *LA*.

A complete list of the texts of all the lyrics from *The Royal Slave* which appeared separately in later seventeenth-century miscellanies (or singly in manuscript) will be found in the notes to each lyric. Mr. Goffin reprints the lyrics, with one exception, together with the three prologues and epilogues, in his edition of the *Poems* (1918).

It should be clear from what has been said in the preceding paragraphs that an editor has no real problem in choosing a basic text. The 1639 quarto, which there is some reason for believing Cartwright actually saw through the press, remains unchallenged as the best authority and has been reprinted here, changes being made only when it seemed certain that the 1639 text was at fault. Four copies of the 1639 quarto have been collated. All changes, including a complete list of variant readings, mere differences of spelling excluded, from the second (1640) and third (1651) editions and the manuscripts are recorded in the Textual Notes. The variants also include the readings of all the later separate appearances of the lyrics.

---

8. See her discussion of the manuscript in *Henry Lawes, Musician and Friend of Poets* (1941), pp. 129–34.

2. Date of Composition and Stage History

Although today *The Ordinary* is the best known of William Cartwright's plays, to the seventeenth century and to Oxford and the court particularly, *The Royal Slave* was the summit of Cartwright's dramatic labors.[1] Even if present-day taste finds in this play relatively little of interest, the judgment of Cartwright's contemporaries should still be listened to with respect. Their opinions are delivered in no measured terms. According to George Evelyn, brother of the diarist, "his Majesty and all the Nobles com'end[ed] it for the best y^t ever was acted,"[2] and Gerrard reports that it was "generally liked, and the Lord Chamberlain so transported with it, that he swore mainly he never saw such a play before."[3] Crosfield, in his *Diary* (August 30), writes: ". . . ye Royall Slave was acted wth good applause of King & Queen."[4] And as Archbishop Laud observed, "It was very well penned and acted, and the strangeness of the Persian habits gave great content; so that all men came forth from it very well satisfied."[5] Especially significant, however, is Queen Henrietta's command for a second production in London at the Court's expense—an invitation so far as I know quite unprecedented before this time.[6]

Today these heaped-up praises seem rather absurd. But two additional circumstances bring the problem into sharper focus: scenery and costuming by Inigo Jones and music by Henry Lawes. In the collaboration of these two popular artists can be seen the explanation for a large part of the play's success. Such a view if carried too far, however, would reduce Cartwright to a position little better

---

1. There are, for example, nine references to *The Royal Slave* in the commendatory poems prefixed to Cartwright's *Works* (1651), as compared with five for the other three plays combined.

2. From a letter reprinted in *Memoirs of John Evelyn* (ed. W. Bray, 2nd ed., 1819), I, 662.

3. From a letter of George Gerrard's to Edward, Viscount Conway and Killultagh (Sept. 4, 1636), *Calendar of State Papers, Domestic Series, 1636-37*, p. 114.

4. *The Diary of Thomas Crosfield* (ed. F. S. Boas, 1935), p. 92.

5. *Works of William Laud* (ed. J. Bliss, 1853), V, 153. Wood has the same remark, copied almost word for word from Laud (*History and Antiquities of the University of Oxford*, ed. J. Gutch, 1796, II, 411). According to David Lloyd (*Memoires*, p. 422, marginal note), Brian Duppa is supposed to have remarked in regard to *The Royal Slave*: "Cartwright finds *Wit*, and we *Money*." What Duppa meant, I don't know.

6. The invitation asking Jasper Mayne to produce his comedy, *The City-Match*, at court is not exactly comparable, since that play had not been formerly presented before the court at Oxford.

than that of a successful opera librettist. Actually this view overstates the case and ignores certain things which are excellent in both the conception and the composition of *The Royal Slave* as a play. Facts, moreover, come to Cartwright's rescue. On the evening before the presentation of *The Royal Slave*, William Strode's *The Floating Island* had been performed, likewise with the full scenical and musical assistance of Jones and Lawes. The performance was not a success, although the scenes seem to have been even more sumptuous than those for *The Royal Slave*. All the blame was laid on the play, one testy but noble spectator remarking, "it was the worst that ever he saw but one at Cambridge";[7] while even Wood records that it "had more of the Moralist than Poet in it."[8] The point to be observed is that it took more than mere spectacle and sound to please the court; something was still demanded from the play. What this something was may be summed up as follows: an exotic, usually serious, plot dealing with exalted and unreal characters, moving in an atmosphere falsely moral and saturated with the doctrines of a sentimentalized and sophisticated Neoplatonism, the whole tricked out in a many-colored rhetorical coat. Though bordering on a mock-criticism, the definition is in general fair, and it may be applied with a minimum of change to almost any of the serious plays of the court dramatists in the decade 1630–40. Of this genre, Cartwright was a past master, and his *Royal Slave* remains one of the best and most representative plays of the type. These considerations should discourage sufficiently any temptation to regard Cartwright as a mere librettist; on the other hand such a comparison suggests another aspect of the production. As Mr. Baskervill has pointed out, "the regularly placed masque scenes and antic dances in Cartwright's *Royal Slave* of 1636 foreshadow heroic opera with its elaborate scenery."[9] But it seems to me that the comparison goes even deeper than this, and that it is no exaggeration to compare Cartwright's whole verse manner with that of operatic recitative. Declamation and a general atmosphere of heroics is the soul of both. Moreover, the very nature of the motivating agent—Platonic love—

---

7. Reported by George Gerrard as a remark of Lord Carnavon's in his letter to Viscount Conway, cited above (*Calendar of State Papers, Domestic Series, 1636–37*, p. 114).

8. *History and Antiquities of the University of Oxford*, II, 408. Actually Strode's play is far from bad, though not very well calculated for court palates. The subject, which treats of the temporary deposition of a king, may also have given offense.

9. *The Elizabethan Jig* (1929), p. 161.

was basically sympathetic to such a treatment, a treatment both ethically exalted and a little unreal. In many respects *The Royal Slave* may be looked upon as an extension of the masque into the field of drama, a collaboration which left the drama very much on the defensive. Scenery, singing, and dancing are all brought over in a body, while the tempo of the play must be radically altered to adapt itself to a new environment. Signs of this invasion by the masque may be seen in many plays, but *The Royal Slave* is perhaps the best example of the finished product. All in all, the final effect of this performance must have been very close to that of continental heroic opera of the period, in which, it will be recalled, much of the dialogue was spoken, not sung.

Miss Willa McClung Evans, in her book on Henry Lawes,[10] gives an interesting discussion of Lawes' musical settings based in part on her recent discovery of a manuscript containing three of the songs in the New York Public Library.[11] She suggests a theory of collaboration between Cartwright and Lawes, a collaboration very like that between masque writer and composer.

> That Cartwright's songs formed an integral part of the plot and helped to define the nature of the characters also suggests that Lawes' services were taken into account by the playwright in planning the structure of the comedy. The story of Cratander's struggle to master his own passions and ambitions forms the outline of the play, each of the main incidents presenting the hero overcoming various weaknesses, and each weakness being symbolized in a song to which the doughty Cratander turns a deaf ear. The pleasure seventeenth-century audiences took in music made Cratander's lofty indifference appear the nobler.[12]

The only argument which might be brought against early collaboration between Cartwright and Lawes in the working out of the main lines of the play is the condition of the four manuscript copies of *The Royal Slave*. These copies presumably represent some state of the text before the London performance, since they all omit the Prologue and Epilogue to their Majesties at Hampton Court. They also omit

---

10. *Henry Lawes, Musician and Friend of Poets* (1941), pp. 128–35.

11. MS. Drexel 4041.

12. *Henry Lawes*, p. 128. I cannot quite agree with Miss Evans when she suggests that there is any struggle in Cratander to master his passions or to overcome his weaknesses. He has neither passions nor weaknesses; therein lies his principal defect as a dramatic character. I also feel that she carries the pattern too far when she makes the song in Act III, Scene i, appear as a temptation directed at Cratander. Apart from these very minor points, however, the interpretation and its development are most persuasive.

the whole processional business and song in Act V, Scene vii, and the second verse of the song in Act I, Scene ii.[13] Now it might be argued from these omissions that Lawes came late on the scene and simply composed music for what he found ready to hand,[14] and that later when a court performance was projected he took the opportunity to get Cartwright to introduce fresh material. On the other hand, all that the evidence necessarily suggests is that some of Lawes' work in connection with the play came as an afterthought.[15]

It is not known when Cartwright began to compose his *Royal Slave*; presumably, however, not before 1634 and certainly not after August of 1636, in which month the play was presented before Charles I and his court as the culmination of the entertainments offered on that occasion—the last of the great royal progresses. Cartwright's play was performed on Tuesday, August 30, in the great hall at Christ Church.

An interesting letter (July 15, 1636) from Archbishop Laud to the vice-chancellor has been preserved concerning the initial arrangements for the two plays to be put on at Christ Church. It appears that certain difficulties were being experienced by the authorities in making the other colleges pay their share of the total expenses of the Christ Church plays.[16] Since this letter has been generally

---

13. For a list of the principal omissions in the manuscripts, see above, pages 167-70. See also the Textual Notes and my note on Act V, Scene vii.

Miss Evans (*Henry Lawes*, p. 132) says: "The final song is essential to the action of the climax." Artistically this is true, but the song would nevertheless appear to have been an afterthought. It is perhaps worth noticing in this connection that Drexel MS. 4041, which contains Lawes' setting for this final song, also contains that for the second stanza of the song in Act I, Scene ii. Thus these two "omissions" are here related. When, however, Lawes published his setting for this song in Act I (*Select Ayres and Dialogues*, 1659, etc.), he printed the setting for the first stanza only.

14. The absence of the scenic descriptions in all the manuscripts (except in *F*, where they have been roughly inserted after the completion of the manuscript) would likewise suggest that Jones did not get to work on the play until after it was completed. But again the evidence might bear other interpretations.

15. Lawes' only comment on *The Royal Slave* occurs in his autographed manuscript (p. 75), following his setting for "Come from the Dungeon": "This songe was sunge in A playe cald ye Royall Slaue, written by Mr William Cartwright, present by the Scollers of Christchurch in Oxford before their Majestyes. 1636." Not an enthusiastic comment, perhaps, but compare his comment on *Comus* in the same manuscript. See in Miss Evans' *Henry Lawes* (p. 103, transcribed p. 101n) a facsimile reproduction of the page from Lawes' autograph manuscript containing this comment. Miss Evans also quotes his comment on Cartwright's song (p. 134).

16. Crosfield in his *Diary*, July 25 (quoted in *Works of William Laud*, ed. J. Bliss, 1853, V, 145), records the vari-

ignored in other accounts of the occasion, certain portions of it are worth quoting:

Sir, Since I writ last to you, the dean of Christ Church came to me, and acquainted me with two things, which are very necessary you should both know and remedy.

The one is, that the university seems to be unwilling to contribute to the charge of the plays, which are to be at Christ Church. Now this charge, as by reason of their building, they are not able to bear alone; so I must needs acknowledge, there is no reason that they should, whatever their ability be: for the king is to be entertained by Oxford, not by Christ Church. And that he lies there, is but for the conveniency of the place, where there are so many fair lodgings for the great men to be about him. Indeed if Christ Church men will say they will have no actors but of their own house, let them bear the charge of their own plays in God's name: but if they will take any good actors from any other college or hall, upon trial of their sufficiency to be as good, or better than their own, then I see no reason in the world, but that the whole university should contribute to the charge. . . .

The other is, that since the university must contribute to this charge . . . I hold it very fit, that all the materials of that stage, which are now to be made new, and the proscenium and such apparel whatever it be as is wholly made new, shall be laid up in some place fit for it, to which the vice-chancellor for the time being shall have one key, and the dean of Christ Church the other, that it may not be lost, as things of like nature and use have formerly been. And if any college or hall shall at any time for any play or show that they are willing to set forth, need the use of any or all of these things, it shall be as lawful and free for them to have and to use them as for Christ Church. . . . And to the end these things may be kept with the more safety and indifferency to the university, I think it very fit that an inventory be made of them, and that one copy thereof remain with them, at Christ Church. . . . For my part I think it fittest that an inventory should be kept in the university registry. . . .[17]

Only one point in the letter need detain us here. Whether the clannishness of the Christ Church students evaporated before the chancellor's threat we do not know. The only actor in the Oxford performance whose name has survived was Richard Busby, a senior member of Christ Church. He played the leading role of Cratander, the royal slave, a characterization in which he is reported to have taken the palm from Roscius himself.[18] A manuscript recording the names of all the actors has been reported; it is unfortunately lost.[19]

Late in the afternoon of the day on which Cartwright's *Royal*

---

ous amounts which each of the colleges had been assessed in the time of Elizabeth: Christ Church 2,000 pounds; Magdalen 1,200 pounds; New College 1,000 pounds; etc.

17. *Works of William Laud*, V, 144–46.
18. Wood, *Historia et Antiquitates Universitatis Oxoniensis* (1674), I, 344.
19. W. C. Hazlitt, *Play-Collector's Manual* (1892), p. 200.

Slave was given, the king and court had already witnessed one theatrical entertainment, George Wilde's *Love's Hospital*, produced at Laud's own expense in the refectory of St. John's College.[20] The prospect of a second play cannot have been very bright, especially after the failure of Strode's play the evening before. But expectation was agreeably surprised. Wood, as usual, is our principal source of information:

> The Play ended, the King and Queen went to Christ Church, retired and supped privately, and about 8 of the clock went into the Common Hall there to see another Comedy called 'The Royall Slave,' made by Mr. Will. Cartwright of that House. It contained much more variety than that of 'Passions calmed.' Within the shuts were seen a curious Temple, and the Sun shining over it, delightful forests also, and other prospects. Within the great shuts mentioned before [see the account of Strode's play, pp. 408–9], were seen villages, and men visibly appearing in them, going up and down, here and there, about their business.[21] The Interludes thereof were represented with as much variety of scenes and motions as the great wit of Inigo Jones (well skilled in setting out a Court Maske to the best advantage) could extend unto. It was very well pen'd and acted, and the strangeness of the Persian habits gave great content. All men came forth very well contented, and full of applause of what they had seen and heard. 'It was the day of St. Felix,' (as the Chancellor observed,) 'and all things went happy.'[22]

---

20. *Works of William Laud*, V, 147, 152–53.

21. The fourth "appearance," described simply as "a Wood" in the printed texts (IV, iii), is thus particularized in MS. *F*: "Act 4. Sce: 3: here appeeres (with variation of the Scene) a wood and a landschap. &c."

22. *History and Antiquities of the University of Oxford*, II, 411–12. Although this account of the performance is often quoted, the corresponding account in the *Historia* (1674, I, 344), seems to have been ignored. Since it is fuller in some respects than the English version, I have thought it worth while to make the following translation of the most important section: "Arranged within the rear of the Proscenium, behind the leaves (which indeed it should be noticed had then been used for the first time), fastened moreover with bolts so skillfully that they could be drawn apart as quickly as possible, extended, close by, a very broad and quite delightful outlook: for green forests and a splendid temple illuminated by the rays of the sun from above, fed the eyes of the spectators; and certain villages appeared and certain men were seen walking about to and fro, attending to their business. Finally Inigo Jones, who, indeed, arranged with the greatest genius possible all sorts of spectacles, especially those masques of the courtiers which were celebrated with dances, had taken care that part of the play should be ornamented with lively appearances of places and people and with the rest of the apparatus. Equal thanks also were due to Master Busby, to whom Roscius should yield the palm in acting; as many as were present took so great pleasure from this circumstance in the first place, and secondly from the very well trained actors and from the Persian costumes which were full of strangeness, that they declared that they had never heard or seen anything more beautiful." It should be noticed that at least one detail in this description has been appropriated from the passage describing

INTRODUCTION

This passage from Wood and another almost immediately preceding it, which describes the scenic properties for Strode's *Floating Island*, have received much attention from historians of the stage. Although it is beyond the scope of the present study to discuss these scenic arrangements in detail,[23] it will, nevertheless, be useful to emphasize one or two of the more important facts. In the first place, Wood's account is supplemented by short scenic descriptions in the play itself, which Cartwright, in each case, refers to as "appearances." Although this word has exercised the critical mind from the time of Malone,[24] Mr. Nicoll's explanation of it as "related to the Spanish *apariencia*, technically employed for a scenic perspective,"[25] is fairly satisfactory.[26] In all, Cartwright records five different scenes and one partially altered scene (V, vii), making a total of eight changes—two scenes, "The Court" and "A Temple of the Sun," being used two and three times respectively.[27] Both Miss Campbell and Mr. Nicoll agree in assigning to these Oxford performances the first introduction of flat wings on the English stage,[28] an innovation of the greatest importance since it allowed for a much more frequent change of scene within a single play. Wood describes the Christ Church stage as follows:

> It was acted on a goodly stage, reaching from the upper end of the Hall almost to the hearth place, and had on it three or four openings on each side thereof, and partitions between them, much resembling the desks or studies in a Library, out of which the Actors issued forth. The said partitions they could draw in and out at their pleasure upon a sudden, and thrust out new in their places according to the nature of the Screen, whereon were represented Churches, Dwelling-houses, Palaces, &c, which for its variety bred very great admiration.[29]

---

the performance of Strode's *Floating Island*, a passage which in the *Historia* is reduced to almost nothing.

23. The two best discussions are to be found in Allardyce Nicoll's *Stuart Masques and the Renaissance Stage* (1938), pp. 138–40, and L. B. Campbell's *Scenes and Machines on the English Stage During the Renaissance* (1923), pp. 189–91, 210. A. H. Thorndike's *Shakespeare's Theater* (1916), p. 193, may also be consulted.

24. *An Historical Account of the Rise and Progress of the English Stage* (1790), p. 70.

25. *Stuart Masques and the Renaissance Stage*, p. 139.

26. It is not altogether satisfactory, however, since it fails to account for the use of the word in the last "appearance," where there is no question of a change in "scenic perspective."

27. *The Royal Slave* is the first printed play to preserve a complete description of all its scenes. The phrasing of the descriptions in the Folger MS. (*F*) deserves notice; see especially Act IV, Scene iii.

28. *Scenes and Machines on the English Stage During the Renaissance*, pp. 179, 189; *Stuart Masques and the Renaissance Stage*, p. 138.

29. *History and Antiquities of the University of Oxford*, II, 409. The descrip-

With the aid of this account and a little study of Inigo Jones' plan for the staging of D'Avenant's *Salmacida Spolia* (1640), we may gain a very fair idea of the type of apparatus used, except that in his Oxford work Jones was faced with the necessity of allowing for a larger number of changes in the scene, a difficulty probably more than offset by the comparative simplicity of the Oxford "scenes" when compared with the extravagant sumptuousness of those used at court.

Unfortunately none of Inigo Jones's designs for either *The Floating Island* or *The Royal Slave* has survived. Again, however, it is possible partially to remedy the loss by reference to some of Jones' other published masque drawings. Nicoll's *Stuart Masques* contains a number, mostly unattributed to particular masques, which may be studied with advantage; for example, "A City Square," Figure 52 (*Royal Slave*, second appearance); "A Palace," Figure 104 (*Royal Slave*, third appearance); "A Woody Landscape," Figure 53, or "A Forest Scene," Figures 37, 50 (*Royal Slave*, fourth appearance); "*A Fortified Town in The Queen of Aragon*," Figure 101 (*Royal Slave*, fifth appearance). The "strangeness of the Persian habits," moreover, is not entirely lost to us, since Jones' sketch for "A Noble Persian Youth" in D'Avenant's *Temple of Love* (1634) is yet extant.[30] D'Avenant's own description of the costume is worth quoting:

> The Page retires, and the noble Persian youths make their entry, apparelled in Asian coats of sea-green embroidered, that reached down above their knees, with buttons and loops before, and cut up square to their hips, and returned down with two short skirts; the sleeves of this coat were large without seam, and cut short to the bending of the arm, and hanging down long behind, trimm'd with buttons as those of the breast; out of this came a sleeve of white satin embroidered, and the basis answerable to the sleeve, hung down in gathering underneath the shortest part of their coat; on their heads they wore Persian turbans silver'd underneath, and wound about with white cypress, and one fall of a white feather before.[31]

One phase of the performance still remains to be dealt with—the "Interludes," which according to Wood "were represented with as much variety of scenes and motions as the great wit of Inigo Jones (well skilled in setting out a Court Maske to the best advantage)

---

tion is taken, of course, from the account of Strode's *Floating Island*. We also know that a regular proscenium was designed for the occasion (see Laud's letter to the vice-chancellor, quoted above, p. 175).

30. Nicoll, *Stuart Masques and the Renaissance Stage*, Fig. 176.

31. *Dramatic Works of Sir William D'Avenant* (ed. Maidment and Logan, 1872), I, 298.

could extend unto."[32] At first sight it would seem that Wood here refers to regular entr'actes, special dances and music placed between each act or major change of scene. While such a view is possible, several fairly substantial arguments can be brought against it.[33] In the first place the Latin version of Wood's *History and Antiquities*, the *Historia*, makes no mention of any such interludes, simply asserting:

> Denique quamlibet, Ludi partem vividis locorum & personarum Imaginibus, reliquoque apparatu adornandum curârat *Ignatius Jones*, qui quidem spectacula omnigena, maxime vero larvata illa quae cum choreis celebrantur, Aulicorum ingenio quam optime accommodabat.[34]

It is, moreover, remarkable in the English account that Jones is mentioned only at the end in connection with these interludes. His name occurs nowhere else in any of Wood's accounts of the two Christ Church plays. This might not unreasonably lead us to suppose that in his use of "Interludes" Wood is referring to the various scenes of the play itself. In the second place, the warrant issued for paying the expenses in the later court performance mentions very specifically the number of dancers employed as twelve, a number only just sufficient to take care of the four Ephesian slaves, the two strumpets, and the six martial ladies of the masque and antimasque in the last act.[35] Finally, entr'actes of the type here postulated are unknown in English drama before the Restoration.[36] Therefore, although no final judgment of the problem is possible, the weight of evidence, in spite of Wood, seems to discourage any theory of special entr'actes.

---

32. *History and Antiquities of the University of Oxford*, II, 411.

33. The unusual shortness of *The Royal Slave* (1608 lines) might be advanced as an argument for the presence of the entr'actes.

34. I, 344. It seems reasonably certain that the comma after "celebrantur" should follow "Aulicorum." See my translation of the passage above, p. 176n.

35. This is, of course, a negative argument, since it is clear that for the rest of the performance the six martial ladies and, except for one other scene (II, iii), the two strumpets were free. It supposes, moreover, that the four Ephesian captives were acted by dancers. This difficulty, however, is not great; the roles are such as to offer considerable opportunity to dancers and in one place at least demand a knowledge of the art. It is, therefore, worth observing that the number of dancers mentioned in the court warrant agrees exactly with the number required by the final masque scene.

36. The earliest "intermède" of this kind occurs in Dryden's *State of Innocence* at the end of the first act. See W. J. Lawrence, "Dryden's Abortive Opera," *TLS*, Aug. 6, 1931, p. 606.

The customary second presentation "before the University and Strangers" took place three days later (September 2), but did not mark, as was so often the case, the end of *The Royal Slave*.[37] And it must have been with a rare feeling of delight that Cartwright received the royal command for a third performance at court. The queen's wishes were made known to the university through correspondence with Laud, then chancellor. The facts of the whole transaction are best given by Wood:

> In November following, the Queen sent to the Chancellor that he would procure of Christ Church the Persian attire of the Royall Slave and the other apparell wherein it was acted, to the end that she might see her own Players act it over again, and whether they could do it as well as 'twas done by the University. Whereupon the Chancellor caused the Cloaths and Perspectives of the Stage to be sent to Hampton Court in a Waggon, for which the University received from her a letter of thanks. So that all of it being fitted for use (the author thereof being present) 'twas acted soon after, but by all mens confession, the Players came short of the University Actors. At the same time the Chancellor desired of the King and Queen that neither the Play, or Cloaths, nor Stage, might come into the hands and use of the common Players abroad, which was graciously granted.[38]

The letter of thanks from the queen which Wood mentions has been preserved, as well as two other letters, one from Lord Pembroke, then lord chamberlain, the other from the Earl of Dorset, both assuring the university that their "commands" respecting the scenes and costumes will be most faithfully carried out.[39] The queen's letter, indeed, should be quoted in full, both as an important document in the history of the theater and as a pleasant reminder of the close relations existing between court and university before the civil war:

Henretta Maria R:

Trusty and Welbeloved, We greet you Well. The Cloathes together with ye whole furniture and Ornaments belonging to that Play wherewith wee were so much pleas'd att our last being in Oxford wee have Received: and doe acknowledge

---

37. Wood, *History and Antiquities of the University of Oxford*, II, 412.

38. *Ibid.*, II, 412–13. Wood's account is taken largely from Laud (*Works*, V, 153–54). Langbaine (*Account of the English Dramatick Poets*, 1691, p. 55) embroiders the account a little: "The Sentence was universally given by all the Spectators in favour of the *Gown*: tho' nothing was wanting on Mr. *Cartwright's* side, to inform the Players as well as the Scholars, in what belong'd to the Action and Delivery of each Part." It may be noticed that in the *Historia* (I, 344) the queen is made to send for *both* the costumes and the scenery.

39. *University Register*, R., fols. 138^v, 138^v–139^r.

for no contemptible Testimony of your Respect to Vs y⁰ Vnfurnishing your Selfe of such Necessaries meerly for our Accommodation. A thing which wee doe not only take very kindly, but are Ready to Remember very Really, whensoever you will furnish Vs with any Occasion wherein our Favour may bee vseful unto you. In y⁰ Meane time you may be confident that no Part of these things yᵗ are come to our hands, shall be suffered to bee prostituted vpon any Mercenary Stage, but shall bee carefully Reserv'd for our owne Occasions and particular Entertainments att Court: With which assurance, together with thankes, and our best Wishes for y⁰ perpetuall Flourishing of your Vniversity, We bidd you hartily Farewell. Given vnder our hand at Hampton Court y⁰ sixt day of December. 1636.[40]

The correspondence is completed by two letters from the University: one to Laud (in Latin), thanking him for his delivery of the university's letters to the queen;[41] the second to the queen (in English), thanking her for all her "favours."[42]

With this last letter our information, at least so far as it concerns Oxford, is exhausted. Presumably the scenes and costumes were returned with the poet, when the performance was over, quite "unprostituted" in the public theater. When we turn to the London performance itself, however, we again find ourselves in possession of unusually full information regarding it. We have already seen from Wood's account that one of the chief reasons for the court performance was to compare the respective merits of the royal players (the King's Men) with the young university amateurs. Apparently no expense was spared to give the professional actors every chance of making a favorable comparison:

April 11, [1637]. Westminster. Warrant to pay 154 l., being the charge of the alterations and additions made in the scene, apparel, and properties employed for setting forth the new play called the Royal Slave, lately acted at Hampton Court, together with the charge of dancers and composers of music, the same to be paid as follows, viz., to Peter le Huc, property-maker, 50 l.; to George Portman, painter, 50 l., and to Estienne Nau and Sebastian la Pierre for themselves and 12 dancers, 54 l.[43]

---

40. Printed, presumably from the original, in *The Bodleian Quarterly Record*, II (1918), 151–52. There is also a transcript of the letter in the *University Register*, R., fol. 138ʳ, to which a heading is added declaring that the letter was read before in convocation on December 19, 1636. See also *The Works of William Laud*, V, 153–54 (note).

41. *Works of William Laud*, V, 158–59.

42. *University Register*, R., fol. 140ᵛ.

43. *Calendar of State Papers, Domestic Series, 1636–37*, p. 563. Another version, reprinted by C. C. Stopes ("Shakespeare's Fellows and Followers," *Shakespeare Jahrbuch*, XLVI [1910], 99) reads "ye charge of ye alterations, reparations, and additions" and "Estienne, Nan, and Sebastian," omitting the names of the property maker and painter. This warrant is dated April 4, 1637.

In addition to this, the players themselves were given an extra bonus of twenty pounds, over their regular fee of ten pounds:

> Theis are to pray and require you out of his Ma^ts Treasure in your charge to pay ... the Company of his Ma^ts Players the summe of Two hundred and tenne pounds (beeing after the usuall and accustomed rate of Tenne pounds for each play) for One and Twenty Playes by them acted before his Ma^ty at Hampton Court ... And that you likewise pay unto them the summe of Thirtye pounds more for their paynes in studying and acting the new Play sent from Oxford called The Royall Slaue which in all amounteth to the summe of Two Hundred and Forty Pounds: ... 12th of March 1636.[44]

Finally, to complete the expense sheet we must include the honorarium of forty pounds given to Cartwright, as author and production manager,[45] making a not inconsiderable total cost for the London performance of 224 pounds, or, translating it into approximate present-day terms, well over $5,000. If we compare this figure with the large sums spent on the great court masque productions, it does not seem very impressive; on the other hand, so far as we are able to judge from the rather scanty contemporary information we possess, for the production of a single play it is unparalleled.

These unusual expenses immediately raise two questions: first, why were the King's Men given twenty pounds more than customary

---

44. Reprinted "From the Original" in Peter Cunningham's *Extracts from the Accounts of the Revels at Court* (1842), p. xxiv. The statement in the warrant that ten pounds was the "usuall and accustomed rate" of payment for each play is not strictly true. Ten pounds was the regular rate for plays at the Blackfriars or the Cockpit, but twenty pounds was the normal fee for all plays acted at Hampton Court. See C. C. Stopes, "Shakespeare's Fellows and Followers," *Shakespeare Jahrbuch*, XLVI (1910), 95, 96, 101). As it happens, however, the warrant is correct for the season which it covers (1636–37), since the plague had closed the theaters in London. For this reason the players must have remained at Hampton Court and were unable to claim the usual extra ten pounds per play given them as compensation for their time lost in the regular London season. Thus it is correct to say that in the case of *The Royal Slave* their bonus was twenty, instead of ten, pounds. Two other much shorter versions of the warrant exist. One, dated "15 March 1636," may be found in George Chalmers' *An Apology for the Believers in the Shakspeare-Papers* (1797), p. 509 (note). The second, dated "March 16th 1636" is reprinted in C. C. Stopes' article (p. 99) referred to above. See also Gerald E. Bentley, *The Jacobean and Caroline Stage* (1941), I, 52–53, for the most recent summary of the materials.

45. *The Dramatic Records of Sir Henry Herbert* (ed. J. Q. Adams, 1917), p. 57: "*The Royal Slave*, on thursday the 12 of Janu.—Oxford play, written by Cartwright. The king gave him forty pounds." Since Sir Henry Herbert's manuscript is lost, the only authority we have for this entry is Malone's transcript in his *Historical Account of the English Stage* (1790), p. 235.

for performing Cartwright's play; and second, why was such a large additional outlay (154 pounds) necessary for the "alterations, reparations, and additions . . . made unto ye scene, apparell, and propertyes"? In answer to the first question, we can only suggest that a bonus was given on the consideration that the play once learned was an otherwise dead loss to the actors, since, even if the type of drama it handled had not been "caviare to the general," the play itself, as well as the scenes and costumes, was included in the Oxford prohibition concerning the "common players." The second question admits of an even less certain answer. One thing should be noticed, however. If, as most authorities seem to agree, the scenes used at Oxford introduced a wholly new type of flat wing, a certain number of alterations would have to be made in the stage equipment at Hampton Court to accommodate the innovation. It is, moreover, not impossible that the new flat wings were found quite impracticable, and that, rather than alter the basic stage arrangements of the Great Hall, it was thought cheaper to have some of the old angle-type wings made. Work of this sort would require the combined offices of the property-maker and painter, thus accounting for at least one hundred of the 154 pounds. Also it seems probable that the first part of the last scene in Act V should be considered as an addition made for the London performance. In the four play manuscripts this scene begins with the Second Priest's speech, "Hold, hold *Arsamnes*" (l. 1574), omitting the execution procession and the priests' song.[46]

The court performance took place on Thursday evening, January 12, 1636/7,[47] and, as we have already seen, failed to measure up to the standard of the amateur Oxford presentation. While the blame seems to be thrown on the actors, the ungrateful suspicion haunts one, that, with its novelty worn thin, a second performance of *The Royal Slave* would be a severe tax on any audience. Only one small notice of the occasion has been preserved:

Upon Twelfth-night, the Royal Slave, which had been acted at Oxford before their majesties the last summer, was acted by the king's players at Hampton Court. The players had procured from the university all their apparel and the scenes, which the university did not altogether approve of; yet they lent them, but with a letter to my lord chamberlain, that because they had provided that entertainment only for their majesties against their coming to Oxford, they humbly

---

46. See the earlier discussion of this point, pp. 173–74.

47. *The Dramatic Records of Sir Henry Herbert*, pp. 57, 76.

besought, that what they had done for the entertainment of their majesties might not be made common upon the stage. And this was the request of the university in general.[48]

We should notice here the university's repeated insistence that neither the play, stage, nor costumes were to come into the hands of the professional actors; in all, this note is sounded from seven different sources. The university's solicitude for its property may best be understood, perhaps, in the light of a phrase which constantly recurs in the Duchess of Newcastle's biography of her husband: "His Majesty was pleased to keep [them] with him for his own service." Historians of the stage have seen in these demands of the university evidence that not altogether unsimilar scenery was even then in occasional use in the public theaters, a theory which, of course, receives support from various other sources.

Three years after the London performance (1639) *The Royal Slave* was published at Oxford. Even then, seemingly, it had not lost its appeal, for the very next year saw the issue of a second edition—an unusual honor for an academic play. In 1655 a prose droll based on Act III, Scene iv, was published in *The Marrow of Complements*, with the title "*A Complementall Contestation. . . . A Dialogue (supposed) betweene* Alberto *and* Sophrinda."[49] A further testimony of its popularity may be seen in the number of manuscript copies which have survived. Five manuscripts are definitely known.[50]

In the light of the evidence afforded by the recently discovered prompt copies of *The Lady-Errant* and *The Ordinary*, it seems not unlikely that *The Royal Slave* was also revived during the Restoration. Unlike the other two plays, *The Royal Slave* had been licensed once

---

48. From Edward Rossingham's letter to Sir Thomas Puckering, Jan. 11, 1636/7 (reprinted in Thomas Birch, *Court and Times of Charles the First*, 1848, II, 266). The date of the performance (Twelfth Night, or Jan. 5) given by Rossingham does not agree with the date set by Sir Henry Herbert (Jan. 12); Rossingham's letter, moreover, dated Jan. 11, was apparently written before the performance recorded by Herbert. These facts have led to the suggestion that there were actually *two* performances. See M. S. Steele, *Plays and Masques at Court* (1926), p. 265, who, however, thinks it unlikely. Laud (*Works*, V, 153) complicates matters by stating that "the play was acted at Hampton Court in November following." Whether or not this confusion of dates points to two (or three) performances it is impossible to decide; at any rate only the date given by Herbert receives corroboration from a second source. See the bill presented by the King's Men for plays acted 1636-37, reprinted in *The Dramatic Records of Sir Henry Herbert*, p. 76.

49. Pp. 54-56.

50. See above, pp. 166-69.

already by Sir Henry Herbert, on the occasion of its first London appearance in 1636. Whether in a case like this the business of censorship had to be gone through all over again, or whether the Revels Office was satisfied with the formality of a fee, is not, I believe, certainly known. Since, however, the charge for a revived play was only one pound, as compared with two pounds for a new play,[51] it seems probable that it was only a question of renewing the former license.

Later allusions to *The Royal Slave*, if we except those in the commendatory poems prefixed to the *Works* (1651),[52] are not very common. It seems probable that George Rivers had Cartwright's play in mind when, in *The Heroinae* (1639), he writes: "Unkind Fortune, that deal'st with us as the Persian [*sic*] with their Slaves, crownst us for a Sacrifice!"[53] An imitation of the same passage by Lovelace is given in the Notes. Katherine Philips, a devoted disciple of Cartwright's, has what appears to be one reference to *The Royal Slave*;[54] in addition, she borrows the name *Cratander* for one of her circle of philosophical friends, John Berkenhead. We may also notice a reference in the epilogue to Settle's *Cambyses* (1671):

> But maugre all your spight, Poets of late
> Stand stoutly unconcern'd at their Play's Fate;
> Provided, 'tis their destiny to gain,
> Like the fam'd Royal Slave, a third dayes Reign.

Cambyses was Settle's earliest play, partly written while he was still a student at Oxford. The influence of Cartwright's play can be felt throughout the tragedy, particularly in I, iv, and V, iii.[55] Finally, there is Dryden's debt to *The Royal Slave* in *Don Sebastian* (1690), I, i.[56] At the opening of Dryden's play it appears that Muley-Moluch,

---

51. See *The Dramatic Records of Sir Henry Herbert*, p. 121.

52. The writers who there allude to *The Royal Slave* are Jasper Mayne, John Leigh, R. Hill, John Berkenhead, W. Towers, Ralph Bathurst, Matthew Smalwood, William Bell, and Thomas Philipott.

53. P. 72.

54. *Poems* (1678), p. 30, "To Mrs. Mary Carne, when *Philaster* courted her" (ll. 1–13).

55. Compare also the following words from Settle's "Epistle Dedicatory" (sig. A2ᵛ): "Then, as that God, the Sun, which they ador'd, lends his kind Rays to all lesser lights," with *The Royal Slave*, III, iv:

> Doth not the Sun (the Sun, which yet you worship)
> Send beames to others than your selfe?

There seems to be rather garbled reference to *The Royal Slave* in an anonymous court epilogue to Settle's *Empress of Morocco*, printed in *A Collection of Poems* (1673), p. 171.

56. The general influence of *The Royal*

the Emperor of Barbary, has promised a "sacrifice of Christian Slaves" as a thank-offering for his recent victory. When he comes to view the captives to make choice of the victims only a "Company of Portuguese Slaves" is produced for the occasion by Mustapha, Captain of the Rabble:

> *M.-Mol.* These are not fit to pay an emperor's vow;
> Our bulls and rams had been more noble victims:
> These are but garbage, not a scarifice.
>
> . . . .
>
> *M.-Mol.* But are these all? Speak you, that are their masters.

Sebastian, Alvarez, Antonio, and Almeyda, all disguised, are finally introduced:

> *M.-Mol.* Ay: these look like the workmanship of heaven;
> This is the porcelain clay of human kind,
> And therefore cast into these noble moulds.

The lot finally falls on Sebastian, who declares himself and defies Muley-Moluch:

> *M.-Mol.* What shall I do to conquer thee?
> *Sebast.* Impossible!
> Souls know no conquerors. . . .
> *M.-Mol.* Thou talk'st as if
> Still at the head of battle.

Muley-Moluch is so overpowered by the courage and magnanimity of Sebastian that he pardons everybody—for the time being.

The points of resemblance to *The Royal Slave*, I, ii, are obvious, both in situation and phrasing. Compare particularly the first twenty-five lines of Cartwright's scene with the lines from Dryden's play quoted above.[57]

3. Sources

The Royal Slave has always been considered the most original of Cartwright's four plays, and, so far as I know, only one attempt has been made to point out some of its sources.[58] The originality,

---

Slave on the structure and atmosphere of Dryden and Howard's *Indian Queen* (1664) should also be noticed.

57. Both settings and situations in Thomas Morton's *Columbus* (1792) suggest some acquaintance with *The Royal Slave*.

58. See a short article by W. G. Rice, entitled "Sources of William Cartwright's *The Royall Slave*", MLN, XLV (1930), 515-18. Mr. Rice stresses Cartwright's indebtedness to Massinger's *The Bondman*, compares Cratander with Marullo and Atossa with Cleora, and points out how Cleora, like Atossa,

however, is more apparent than real, and some very definite sources were drawn upon.

For convenience of classification, *The Royal Slave* may be said to belong to a small group of dramas best called "custom of the country" plays—plays which draw their principal motivation from some law or custom, usually exotic, peculiar to a race or country. To this genre belong such plays as Shakespeare's *Midsummer Night's Dream* and *Measure for Measure*, Fletcher's *Laws of Candy* and *The Custom of the Country*, Massinger's *The Old Law*, and Edward Howard's *Woman's Conquest*. Cartwright's play deals with a pretended Persian law under which it was incumbent upon the reigning king, as a thank offering for victory, to choose from the prisoners of war a mock king, who, after enjoying the full power and privileges of kingship for three days, should then be sacrificed to the sun god. A little reading in Sir James Frazer's *Golden Bough*, particularly the fourth volume, *The Dying God*, will show that the implications of such a law have roots deep in the folk history of centuries. The general pattern behind the custom is the sacrifice of the king by proxy for some supposed benefit to his people, the outgrowth of an actual practice of putting the king himself to death at regular intervals, varying with cause and country. In *The Royal Slave*, to be sure, this custom is shorn of all its deeper significance—almost certainly it had none for Cartwright—and appears merely as a sacrificial law supposedly indigenous to Persia.

The source of Cartwright's law seems to lie in classical history. A similar custom among the Persians is actually recorded by Dio Chrysostom, an author to whom Cartwright might have had ready access. He writes:

'Have you never heard about the Sacian feast held by the Persians, against whom you are now preparing to take the field?' And Alexander at once asked him what it was like, for he wished to know all about the Persians. 'Well, they take one of their prisoners,' he explained, 'who has been condemned to death, set him upon the king's throne, give him the royal apparel, and permit him to give orders, to drink and carouse, and to dally with the royal concubines during those days, and

---

pleads "in behalf of the preserver of her reputation and safety." I feel that Mr. Rice somewhat overstates the case for Massinger, but the parallels noticed above, and one or two others which I have not listed, are interesting and may well be significant. Mr. Rice likewise points out the passage from Dio Chrysostom quoted below and suggests that perhaps Cartwright knew Chrysostom's works in an edition published at Paris in 1604 (another edition 1623).

no one prevents his doing anything he pleases. But after that they strip and scourge him and then hang him.[59]

Failing a first hand knowledge of Dio Chrysostom, Cartwright may well have derived his information from a fat little volume by Barnabe Brissonius called *De Regio Persarum Principatu*.[60] Brissonius discusses this Sacian feast and quotes not only Dio Chrysostom, but also Athenaeus. At any rate, from whatever source Cartwright drew his knowledge, there can be little doubt that the passage quoted above from Dio Chrysostom was the ultimate spring of his fantastic law.

For his political plot, which serves to bring the sacrificial law in play, Cartwright also turned to ancient history to some slight degree. Arsamnes, the Persian king, is represented as just returned from a victorious campaign against the Ephesians. History, indeed, records such a campaign under the great Darius, directed more especially, however, against the Ionian cities as a whole, to punish the burning of Sardis after their revolt from the Persian yoke.[61] At this point, however, history fades completely into the background, and the third element of the plot, Greek romance, enters.

The particular romance in question is a little-known work by

---

59. Dio Chrysostom (trans. J. W. Cohoon, 1932), I, 199. Frazer (*The Dying God*, 1911, pp. 113–14) discusses this passage and gives a further reference to Athenaeus (*Deipnosophists*, trans. C. D. Yonge, 1854, III, 1021-22). The reference in Athenaeus is not, however, so important for our present purpose, since he fails to mention the final execution of the mock king; on one point he is, nevertheless, more circumstantial than Dio Chrysostom, specifying five days as the length of the mock king's reign. See also Strabo (*Geography*, trans. H. L. Jones, 1928, V, 263, 265), who mentions two differing origins for the feast of Sacae.

60. Ed. of 1710, pp. 398–400. It is possible that Cartwright was led to this book, as I was, by a reference to it in John Cartwright's *Preachers Travels* (1611), p. 83. Since there is nothing in this last account, which gives a more or less contemporary description of Persia and the surrounding countries, that might have been used in the preparation of *The Royal Slave*, it is difficult to show that Cartwright did, or did not, know the book. More germane to Cartwright's immediate needs was Sir Thomas Herbert's then lately published *Relation of Some Yeares Travaile* (1634), which contained a quite detailed account of Persian customs and religion. Here again, however, no definite evidence that Cartwright knew the work is to be found. Indeed, *The Royal Slave* as a whole shows only the most superficial knowledge of Persian beliefs and customs, a knowledge which can have been little better than common knowledge among educated men of Cartwright's day.

61. Sir Walter Raleigh (*History of the World*, 1687 ed., p. 389a) gives a good account of the attack on Sardis and the subsequent Persian revenge.

Theodorus Prodromus, which in its late Latin translation bears the title *Rhodanthes et Dosiclis Amorum*.[62] Except that the novel, like Cartwright's play, opens with a scene in prison, the first part of the story, a typical Greek romance, need not concern us here. It deals principally with the earlier lives of the three chief characters, Rhodanthe, Dosicles, and Cratander, who, being fellow-prisoners, amuse themselves, if not the reader, with a detailed account of their several misfortunes. Not until near the end of the book do we find the episode which caught Cartwright's imagination.

The situation is this. Bryaxes, a barbarian ruler, after slaying his immediate inferior, Mistylus, seizes the spoils which Mistylus had earlier won. Among the prisoners are Rhodanthe, Dosicles, and Cratander. Placing them in two ships, one for the men and one for the women, Bryaxes sets sail for his capital, Pissa. The vessel bearing the women captives is shipwrecked, and only Rhodanthe escapes, but Dosicles and Cratander arrive safely at Pissa. Bryaxes now decides to placate the Gods with a human offering from his spoils of war and Dosicles and Cratander are haled forth to furnish the sacrifice. After a long interchange of arguments about the propriety of the whole performance, Bryaxes undergoes a change of heart and would spare the victims were it not for the anticipated wrath of the Gods. Suddenly, just as the sacrifice is about to take place, the blazing funeral pyre is extinguished by a rainstorm. This is interpreted as an omen of the Gods' displeasure at the sacrifice and Dosicles and Cratander, amid general rejoicing, are set free.

The larger outlines of Cartwright's indebtedness here are clear enough, but his debt is even more specific. Throughout the play it is possible to trace close paraphrases of passages from Theodorus' novel. Although an exhaustive list of these borrowings may be consulted in the Notes, a single example may be given here.

> *Arsamnes.* True. Tell me, wert thou then to pay thy vowes,
> What wouldst thou sacrifice? the best, or worst?
> *Cratander.* The best, unto the Best. If I had destin'd
> An Oxe unto the Altar, he should be

---

62. Paris edition (1625), translated into Latin by Gilbertus Gaulminus. On the general question of Greek romance, a number of perhaps merely family resemblances between Heliodorus' *Aethiopica* and *The Royal Slave* may be noticed. See Underdowne's translation (revised by F. A. Wright in the "Broadway Translations"), pp. 284-85, 291-92, 294, 301-3, 316.

Faire, and well fed; for th' Deity doth not love
The maymed, or mishapen, 'cause it is
A thing so different from himselfe, deformity
Being one of Natures trespasses. . . .

Bryaxes. . . . Verum age, si bovem sacrificare velles, an non opimum eligeres? *Dosicles.* Omnino eligerum. *Bry.* An non optimo mulso victimarum carnes irrigares? *Dos.* Ita facerem: nam optimum optimo tribui expedit. *Bry.* An pulchros Dei amant? *Dos.* Amant. *Bry.* An ipsa Pulchritudo, pulchrum quidpiam non est? Si pertendis, deformes igitur non amant. *Dos.* Non amant: Deformitas namque malum est.[63]

The relative importance of the three sources in the development of *The Royal Slave*, though a matter impossible to decide finally, may nevertheless bear a guess. In all probability the order in which they have here been treated represents the progress of Cartwright's approach to his composition. Beginning with the central idea of a sacrificial law, it was not a great step to the adaptation of a little Persian history to afford the imperative exotic background peculiar to seventeenth-century tragicomedy. Theodorus' novel, though obviously of considerable importance, seems to have been used rather because of an essential likeness between it and Cartwright's already formulated plot than as a source of direct inspiration.

Cartwright's method of assembling his dramatis personae is typical of most seventeenth-century authors (*pace* Jonson!). Nearly all the names which he uses are well known in history, but they are arranged without much relation to time. A glance at Sir Walter Raleigh's *History of the World* (1614) is enlightening in this respect. Within a few pages [64] we find Arsamnes mentioned as a minor Persian king, Atossa as the daughter of Cyrus and wife of Darius,[65] Praxaspes as a favorite of Cambyses, Masistes as a son of Darius, Orontes as a son of Cambyses, Hydarnes as a Persian satrap, Hippias as a prince of Athens, Leocrates as a ruler of Athens, and Mandane as a daughter of Astyges.[66] One point may be noticed in Cartwright's favor: he

---

63. *The Royal Slave*, I, ii, 137–44; *Rodanthes et Dosiclis Amorum* (1625), pp. 320–23.
64. Ed. of 1687, pp. 381–92.
65. Atossa is one of the principal characters in *The Persians* of Aeschylus. The play itself, however, has no connection with *The Royal Slave*.
66. Raleigh (*History of the World*, p. 471) of course mentions a Philotas. Since we know that Cartwright took the name of his principal character, Cratander, from Theodorus' *Rhodanthes et Dosiclis Amorum*, it seems likely that he also took the name Stratocles from the same source, where it occurs as the name of a pilot or ship's captain (p. 44). A Phocion is mentioned in D'Urfé's

has at least kept the Greek and Persian names separate, a care not too rigorously affected by his contemporaries.

In conclusion, one direct borrowing from an earlier contemporary play, Fletcher and Massinger's *Beggars' Bush* (about 1622), should be noticed. In Act IV, Scene iii, the four slaves, having planned to murder Cratander, disguise themselves as beggars and meet in a wood through which they expect Cratander to pass alone. Unable to decide who shall actually do the deed, they agree that they will ask the next passenger to choose which of them is fittest to become a Persian priest, the one chosen to become the sacrificer of Cratander. Already knowing of the plot, Cratander is himself the first to pass. He quickly recognizes the slaves and gives them in charge. In Act II, Scene i, of *Beggars' Bush*, we find a meeting of the principal beggars, all apparently in their professional gear. They are unable to decide who shall become their new ruler, but agree to put the question up to the first stranger that passes and to abide by his decision.[67] Though Cartwright has avoided any verbal parallels, the general atmosphere and conduct of the two scenes is so similar that there is no reasonable doubt of their connection.

L'Astrée (ed. H. Vaganay, 1925, I, 142). In his *Cambyses* (1671), Settle introduces a Prexaspes, "His [Cambyses'] Favourite," a Mandana, "A Captive Princess," and an Atossa, one of the "waiting Ladies to *Phedima* and *Orinda*."

67. Actually, the whole situation is the result of a trick arranged in the preceding scene (I, iii) between Gerrard, disguised as Clause, and Florez. The basic situation is to be found earlier in Peele's *Arraignment of Paris* (1584), II, i, where it appears to be Peele's addition to classic myth. The beggar disguise, however, links Cartwright with *Beggars' Bush*.

THE ROYALL SLAVE.

A Tragi-Comedy.

Presented to the King and Queene by the Students of *Christ-Church* in Oxford. *August* 30. 1636.

Presented since to both their Majesties at *Hampton-Court* by the Kings Servants.

OXFORD,
Printed by WILLIAM TURNER for
THOMAS ROBINSON. 1639.

THE PROLOGVE
to
THE KING
and
QVEENE.

The first Appearance,
a Temple of the Sun.

> *One of the Persian Magi discover'd in a*
> *Temple worshipping the Sunne, at the*
> *sight of a new Majesty leaves the Al-*
> *tar, and addresseth himselfe to the*
> *Throne.*

From my Devotions yonder am I come,
Drawne by a neerer and more glorious Sun.
   Hayle ô ye sacred Lights; who doe inspire
More than yond holy and eternall Fire.
   A forreine Court lands here upon your Shore, [5]
By shewing its owne worth to shew yours more:
Set here as Saphires are by your Queen's veines,
Not to boast Colour, but confesse their staynes.
No matter now for Art, you make all fit;
Your Presence being still beyond all wit. [10]
   Whiles by such Majesty our Scene is drest,
   You come both th'Entertainer and the Guest.

THE PROLOGVE
to the
VNIVERSITY.

A Priest discover'd as before.

After our Rites done to the King, we doe
Thinke some Devotion's to be paid to you.
But I could wish some Question hung up there,
That we by Genuine sounds might take your eare.
Or that our Scene in Bodley's Building lay, [5]
And th'Metaphysickes were cast into a Play.
To please your Palates I could wish there were
A new Professour, Poet of the Chayre.

   But as where th'Earth cannot ascend, we know
The Sun comes downe and cheeres her here below: [10]
So we (the Stage being ayr'd now, and the Court
Not smelt) hope you'le descend unto our sport;
And thinke it no great trespasse, if we doe
Sinne o're our Trifle once againe to you.

   'Tis not the same as then, that glorious Prease [15]
Did passe both for the matter, and the dresse.
For where such Majesty was seene, we may
Say, the Spectators only made the Play.

   Expect no new thing yet; 'tis without doubt
The former Face, only the Eyes put out. [20]
But you adde new ones to it, being sent
As for our grace, so for our supplement.

   We hope here's none inspir'd from late damn'd bookes,
Will sowre it into Tragedy with their lookes;
The little Ruffe, or Carelesse, without feare [25]
May this securely see, securely heare.
There's no man shot at here, no Person's hit,
All being as free from danger, as from wit.
And such should still the first adventures be

Of him, who's but a Spy in Poetrie. [30]
   No Envy then or Faction feare we, where
All like your selves is innocent and cleare.
The Stage being private then, as none must sit,
And, like a Trap, lay wayte for sixpence wit;
So none must cry up Booty, or cry downe; [35]
Such Mercenary Guise fits not the Gowne.
   No Traffique then: Applause, or Hisse elsewhere
May passe as ware, 'tis only Iudgement here.

The Prologue to their Majesties at *Hampton-Court*.

Most mighty King,
    and
Most gratious Queene:

The rites and Worship are both old, but you
Have pleas'd to make both Priest and People new.
The same Sun in yon Temple doth appeare;
But they'are your Rayes, which give him lustre here.
That Fire hath watch'd e're since; but it hath been [5]
Onely Your gentler breath that kept it in.
Things of this nature scarce survive that night
That gives them Birth; they perish in the sight;
Cast by so far from after-life, that there
Is scarce ought can be said, but that they were. [10]
Some influence yet may crosse this fate; what You
Please to awaken must still come forth new.
And though the untouch'd Virgin Flow'r doth bring
The true and native Dowrys of the Spring;
Yet some desires there are perhaps, which doe [15]
Affect that Flower chaf'd and sully'd too:
For in some bosomes stucke, it comes from thence
Double-perfum'd, and deeper strikes the Sense.
And we are bid plead this; fore-seeing how
That which was fresh ere-while may languish now. [20]
  Things twice seene loose; but when a King or Queene
  Commands a second sight, they're then first seene.

The Persons of the Play

Speakers

Arsamnes, King of Persia.

Praxaspes,
Masistes, } His Lords.
Hydarnes,
Orontes,

Molops, A Gaolor.

Cratander, the Royall Slave.

Philotas,
Stratocles, } 4. other Ephesian Captives.
Leocrates,
Archippus,

Phocion, } 2. Cityzens of Ephesus disguis'd.
Hippias,

3. Magi, or Persian Priests.

Atossa, Queene to Arsamnes.

Mandane, } Her Ladyes.
Ariene,

Servants.

Mutes

Masquers, 6. Ladyes.

Musitians.

2. Strumpets.

The Habits *Persian*. | The Scene *Sardis*.

Act. I. Sce. I.

2ᵈ Appearance, a City in the front, and a Prison on the side.

Philotas, Stratocles, Leocrates, Archippus singing in the Prison, Molops harkning without.

Mol. These wicked Ephesian Captives, are most everlasting Tipplers; I charm'd my fleas with 'em last night, and left them too I'm sure well to live, and yet they're at it againe this morning. [5]

Slaves within. Hem! hem! hem! A pox on our Gaolor, &c.

Mol. So! now they're tuning their Pipes. O the Religion of these Greekes! they sing and drinke downe the Sunne, and then they sing and drinke him up againe. Some [10] drunken Hymne I warrant you towards now, in the prayse of their great huge, rowling, Tunbellyed god *Bacchus* as they call him. Let's hearken a little.

The Slaves song within.

'A pox on our Gaolor, and on his fat Jowle;
'Ther's liberty lyes in the bottome o'th' Bowle. { *Mol.* That's I. That's I. [15]
'A figge for what ever the Raskall can doe, { *Mol.* I againe
'Our Dungeon is deepe, but our Cup's so too. good, good.
'Then drinke we a round in despight of our Foes,
'And make our hard Irons cry clinke in the Close.

Mol. Wondrous good Ifaith! These fetter'd Swannes [20] chant it most melodiously before their deathes. Sure there is a great deale of pleasure in being hang'd; for I have observ'd it e're since I was a little one, that they alwayes sing before they goe to't. But here's that will spoyle your voyces my Friends. [25]

Phil. Who's there?

Mol. Your friend at a dead lift; your Landlord *Molops*.

Phil. Now grand Commissioner of fate; what wouldst thou have Heyre apparent to *Pluto*?

He opens the dore, and the Slaves enter.

Mol. Come forth; and if you can endure to read, her's a Persian line in my hand will instruct you. {*shews 'em a halter.*} [30]

Stra. Guardian of Ragges and Vermin, Protectour of halfe-breeches and no shirts, what's thy Raskalship's pleasure?

Mol. Good words Sir, good words: I am your Destiny, do you not see your Thread of Life here? [35]

Leoc. Yes, yes, 'tis of thy wives owne twisting, good *Molops*, I know the Promotion of your Family: she came from the Web-errantry of highway-Inkle, to the domestique turning and winding of home-bred Hempe, and thence gets [40] a three-halfe-penny Legacy at the departure of every wrong'd Sinner.

Archip. And as for thy selfe, had not that weighty bulke of thine crack'd so many Gibbets, that the King began to feare his Forrests, thou had'st never been preserv'd to whiffle [45] plagues as thou usher'st us to the Barre, and take away the Judges stomackes as often as they come to eate upon Life and Death, and celebrate the Funerals of distressed Gentlemen.

Mol. You dying men may be impudent by your places, [50] but I'd wish you to compose your countenances and your manners both, for the King is comming to visit you.

Phil. What mak'st thou here then? though I easily beleeve thou hast an ambition to be seene in good company, yet prethee be gon, and don't discredit us. The King loves [55] no Garbidge-tubbes.

Mol. The King shall be inform'd of the fowle words you give his Officers.

Stra. Why what can he doe? he won't let us goe and conquer us againe, will he? [60]

Leoc. But good honest Landlord, what's the Kings intent to honour us with his Royall visit?

Archip. To assigne us perhaps some three or foure hundred stripes aday a peece, to take downe my Landlord's bo-

dy, and make him in case to suffer what he hath beene long [65]
adjudg'd to.
   Mol.   No, Saucines, 'tis to make one of you King.
   Arch.   Then, Saucines, know your Masters.
   Mol.   Be not mistaken: 'tis not any way to honour you,
but to make himselfe sport. For you must know, that 'tis the [70]
custome of the Persian Kings after a Conquest, to take one
of the Captives, and adorne him with all the Robes of Majesty, giving him all Priviledges for three full dayes, that
hee may doe what hee will, and then be certainly led to
death. [75]
   Phil.   Will he allow so long? I'd give my life at any
time for one dayes Royalty; 'tis space enough to new mould
a Kingdome. His Majesty useth us wondrous reasonably; I'd
as liffe deale with him as any man I know. But who's to have
our cloaths, Sirrah, when we have done? [80]
   Mol.   'Tis a small fee that the State hath entayl'd upon
my Place an't please you.
   Phil.   By my troth I guess'd so: I was wondring how
their Courtiers could goe so brave with so little meanes.
   Stra.   Well, what must be, must be. I was affraid I should [85]
have dy'd a silly foolish old *Animal*, call'd Virgin. But now,
have at one of the Ladyes e're I goe: I have a strong desire
to leave some Posterity behind me. I would not have the
house of the *Stratocles* decay for want of Issue.
   Leoc.   If I have the fortune of't, I'le Revell it all night; [90]
Kings, they say, ought not to sleep for the good of the people.
   Arch.   Sirrah Gaolor, see you send Mistris Turne-key your
wife to take us up whores enough: and be sure she let none
of the young Students of the Law fore-stall the Market.
   Mol.   Peace, the King approaches: stand in your rankes [95]
orderly, and shew your breeding; and be sure you blow nothing on the Lords.

Act. I. Sce. 2.

To them

*Arsamnes, Praxaspes, Hydarnes, Masistes,
Orontes, Priests; after a while Cratander.*

Arsam. Are these the fairest, and the handsomest
'mong all the Captives?
Mol. There is one more which I set apart; a good per- [100]
sonable fellow, but he's wondrous heavy and bookish, and
therefore I thought him unfit for any honour.
Arsam. Goe call him forth; there's none of all these has
A Forehead for a Crowne; their blood runnes thicke,
As if 'twould blot a sword. (*Enter Mol. with Cratander.*
         See, there comes one [105]
Arm'd with a serious and Majestique looke,
As if hee'd read Philosophy to a King:
We've conquer'd something now. What readst thou there?
Mol. I beleeve hee's conning a Hymne against the good
Time. [110]
Crat. 'Tis a discourse o'th' Nature of the Soule;
That shewes the vitious Slaves, but the well inclin'd
Free, and their owne though conquer'd.
Arsam. Thou dost speake
As if thou wert victorious, not *Arsamnes*.
Crat. I not deny your Conquest, for you may [115]
Have vertues to entitle't yours; but otherwise,
If one of strange and ill contriv'd desires,
One of a narrow or intemperate minde
Prove Master of the field, I cannot say
That he hath conquer'd, but that he hath had [120]
A good hand of it; he hath got the day,
But not subdued the men: Victory being
Not fortunes gift, but the deservings Purchase.
Arsam. Whom dost thou call deserving?
Crat. Him, who dares
Dy next his heart in cold blood; him, who fights [125]
Not out of thirst, or the unbridled lust
Of a flesh'd sword, but out of Conscience

To kill the Enemy, not the man. Who when
The Lawrell's planted on his brow, ev'n then
Under that safe-protecting Wreath, will not [130]
Contemne the Thunderer, but will
Acknowledge all his strength deriv'd, and in
A pious way of gratitude returne
Some of the spoyle to Heav'n in Sacrifice;
As Tenants doe the first fruits of their Trees, [135]
In an acknowledgment that the rest is due.
   Arsam.   True. Tell me, wert thou then to pay thy vowes,
What wouldst thou sacrifice? the best, or worst?
   Crat.   The best, unto the Best. If I had destin'd
An Oxe unto the Altar, he should be [140]
Faire, and well fed; for th' Deity doth not love
The maymed, or mishapen, 'cause it is
A thing so different from himselfe, deformity
Being one of Natures trespasses: he should
Be crown'd then, and conducted solemnly, [145]
That my Religion might be specious,
'Twere stealth else, not Devotion.
   Arsam.   Bravely sayd.
But (t's pitty) thou hast reasoned all this while
Against thy selfe, for our Religion doth
Require the Immolation of one Captive; [150]
And thou hast prov'd that he is best bestow'd
That best deserveth to be spar'd.
   Crat.   I could
Tell you, the Gods have neither appetite
Nor entralls; that they doe not hunger after
Your Cookery of sacrifice, and that [155]
A graine of Incense, or a peece of Gumme,
If offer'd with Devotion, may redeeme
A destin'd Hecatombe. But this would be
To deprecate my fate; which by your Sun,
Your Sun that doth require me, I expect [160]
With the same minde, as I would doe my Nuptialls.
   Arsam.   And so't shall come, thy shape and vertues doe
Enrich and furnish thee for Heav'n. I would
Or thou hadst fled, or I not conquered.
Adorne him with the Robes. But thou must sweare [165]

First to be faithfull to the State.
  Crat. I sweare.   (*He kisseth the Scepter.*

The Priest's song whiles he puts
on the Robes.

'Come from the Dungeon to the Throne
'To be a King, and streight be none.
'Reigne then a while, that thou mayst be
'Fitter to fall by Majesty.   [170]

Cho: 'So Beasts for sacrifice we feed;
      'First they are crown'd, and then they bleed.

'Wash with thy Bloud what wars have done
'Offensive to our God the Sun:
'That as thou fallest we may see   [175]
'Him pleas'd, and set as red as thee.
'Enjoy the Gloryes then of state,
'Whiles pleasures ripen thee for fate.

Cho: 'So Beasts: &c.

  Arsam. Now then, *Cratander*, I doe here indulge thee   [180]
All the Prerogatives of Majesty
For three full dayes; which being expir'd, that then
Thou may'st fall honourably, I intend
To strike the blow my selfe.   (*Ex. Arsam.*
  Crat. I neither take
New courage from the Power, nor suffer new   [185]
Feares from the Death that waytes it: both are things
That have two eares, by which they may be taken;
So that they are indifferent in themselves;
And only good or bad as they are order'd.
Off with their shakells Sirrah: you my Lordes   [190]
Take order they be quickly well attir'd,
That they may come to Court, and doe us service.
'Tis next of all our Royall pleasure, that
Battle be re-inforc'd by the next Sun,
To make our Conquest perfect: all's not safe   [195]

Till the Snake leave to threaten with his tayle.
Our Reigne is short, and businesse much, be speedy.
Our Counsels and our deeds must have one birth. *(Ex. Crat.*

   Mol. If you'l make use of any Ornaments, I've a couple
of Jack-chaynes at your service: Come Gentlemen, please [200]
you to follow, I'le give you ease of your Irons suddenly.

   Phil. Sirrah be quicke, that my foot may be at liberty to
kicke thee.   *(Ex. Mol. and Slaves.*

   Prax. Whether tends the minde of this ambitious wretch?
H'hath thoughts so hasty, and so large, as if [205]
Hee'd over-runne the whole world in a breath.

   Hyd. I like the courage of the man: methinkes
H'hath given a tast, how worthy he is of
A longer Kingdome.

   Masist. You'l obey him then?

   Hyd. I don't obey
Him, but the King; as they that pay their vowes [210]
Unto the Deity, shrowded in the Image.

   Masist. True, 'tis the King's will he should be obey'd,
But hee's a Slave; the man lookes personable,
And fit for Action, but he is a Slave.
He may be noble, vertuous, generous, all, [215]
But he is still a Slave.

   Oron. As if the sullying
Must turne all purer mettle into drosse;
Or that a Jewell might not sometimes be
In the possession of a private man.

   Mas. What? you too for the rising Sun, my Lord, [220]
Though't be but a Meteor cast from the true one?
If that the conquer'd Hart must lead the Lyon,
I'le teach my wishes to runne thwart unto
That large successe you looke for.

   Prax. Be my feares
No Omen to the Kingdome, ô yee Gods, [225]
But I suspect, this Comicke folly will
Sport our free Monarchy into a Nation
Of cheated Slaves. But peace; the Queene.

   Oron. We two
Will goe, and see his carriage.

   Prax. Doe my Lords;

And 'cause you wish his State so well, pray see [230]
The Slaves provided of their cloathes. (*Ex. Oron. Hyd.*

Act. I. Sce. 3.

To them

Atossa, Mandane, Ariene.

  Atos. Y'have seene
This Three-dayes King my Lords? I cannot sport
At th' Miseries of men: methinkes I feele
A touch of pity, as often as I view him.
How doe you thinke hee'le beare his State?
  Mas. As Schoole-boyes [235]
In time of Misrule, looke big awhile, and then
Returne dejected to the Rod.
  Mand. I wonder
No woman's chosen Queene for company.
These Male wits are but grosse and sluggish; fayth
You'd see a delicate Comedy, if that [240]
A she wit might but Impe his Reigne.
  Prax. O Madam!
Your Sexe is too imperious to Rule;
You are too busy, and too stirring, to
Be put in Action; your Curiosity
Would doe as much harme in a Kingdome, as [245]
A Monkey in a Glasse-shop; move and remove,
Till you had broken all.
  Arie. Thinges then it seemes
Are very brittle, that you dare not trust us.
  Prax. Your Closet and your Senate would be one;
You'd Gossip at the Councell-table, where [250]
The grand contrivance of some finer Posset
Would be a State affaire.
  Mand. I never knew
But this one difference yet 'twixt us and you:
Your follies are more serious, your vanities
Stronger, and thicker woven; and your Councels [255]
About the razing of a Fort or City,

Contriv'd as ours about a messe of spoon-meat;
So that you laugh, and are laugh'd at againe.
  Atos. I hope you doe but exercise, your wits
Are not at sharpes?
  Mand. Wee'le venture how he will, [260]
Foyles, or bare poynts we care not.
  Atos. Cease the strife.
How's this *Cratander* qualify'd, my Lords?
What vertues has he?
  Mas. No great store of vertues;
Hee's a tough fellow, one that seemes to stand
Much on a resolute carelesnesse, and hath [265]
A spice of that unnecessary thing
Which the mysterious call Philosophy.
Here comes a couple can informe you better:
They have observ'd the thing.

Act. I. Sce. 4.

To them
Hydarnes, Orontes.

  Atos. My Lords, what thinke you
Of this new King? what doth he do? what is he? [270]
  Hyd. Hee's one that knowes, and dares preserve his own
Honour, and others too; a man as free
From wronging any, as himselfe; he beares
A Kingdome in his looke; a kingdome that
Consists of Beauty, seasoned with Discretion. [275]
His Graces are virile, and comely too:
Grave, and severe delights so tempering
The softnesse of his other pleasures, that
A settled full content doth thence arise,
And wholly take up the beholders thoughts. [280]
  Arie. Why then hee'le turne the Scene; we did expect
Something that would have saved us the labour
Of reading Play-bookes, and Love-stories.
  Oron. See,
How you're mistaken Madam: he doth carry

All things with such a State, and yet so free [285]
From an insulting Pride, that you'd conceive
Judgement and power put into the Scales,
And neither overpoysing, whiles he shewes
Rather that he can rule, then that he will.
   Mas. Th' afflicted ne're want prayses. O how false [290]
Doth th' Eye of pity see! the only way
To make the Foule seeme gratious, is to be
Within the ken of death; he that e're while
Would have beene thought a Monster, being now
Condemn'd to die, is thought an Hero.
   Mand. Truly, [295]
I thinke you have not yet beene neare your death.
   Mas. I've beene but seldome with your Ladyship.
   Atos. Away, let's goe and view againe; he promiseth
Something that is not sport: If he doe well,
And keepe his vertues up untill his fall, [300]
I'le pay a good wish to him as hee's going,
And a faire mention of him when he's gone.
                    (*Ex. Atos. Mand. Arie.*

               Act. I. Sce. 5.

                To them
               Arsamnes.

   Arsam. How doth our new King beare his Royalty?
   Prax. If he goe stil on thus, his three daies folly
Will fill your Annalls.
   Mas. He is growne the talke [305]
And sight of all the Court: h'hath eyes chayn'd to him,
And some say hearts; nor are they meane ones, such
As he may steale without being miss'd, but those
The theft of whom turnes sacriledge.
   Arsam. I hope
Atossa is not in the Rowle; he dares not [310]
Be favour'd by my Queene.
   Hyd. Her pure Affections
Are sacred as her Person, and her thoughts

Soaring above the reach of common Eyes,
Are like those better Spirits, that have nothing
Of Earth admixt, but yet looke downe upon [315]
Those numbers of Inhabitants, and where
They see a worthy minde oppress'd, vouchsafe
At least to helpe with pitty.
   Arsam. Doth she then
Seeme to compassionate his fortune? we
Must watch his Actions narrowly.
   Prax. He may [320]
Grow insolent else past remedy: but yet
Your Majesty hath a preventing eye.
He may, when that his Channel's full, discharge
His streames on all that's round him, rushing forth
With a strong headlong Torrent, as mischeevous [325]
As uncontroulable, th' ungratefull waters
Choaking ev'n that which gave 'm life; but yet
You can kill evils by first seeing them.
   Oron. All this hath taken up but one Eare only;
The other, and the softer is reserv'd. [330]
Religion, and your word (which, equally
As that, is binding) are both past for three dayes:
To cut him off before, were to abridge
Your Triumph, and Devotion.
   Arsam. He must live
And Reigne his time prescrib'd; but he must not [335]
Performe the Actions he intends. Let then
All the delights and pleasures, that a Slave
Admires in Kings be offer'd. Though an hundred
Still watchfull eyes beset his head, yet there
  Is one way left; Musicke may subtly creepe [340]
  And rocke his senses so, that all may sleepe. (*Exeunt.*

Finis Act. I.

Act. 2. Sce. I.

3ᵈ Appearance, a stately Palace

Cratander.

Cra. Perish their Tables, and themselves: a Throne
May stand without those tumults of delights,
That wayte on big and pompous Luxury.
I'le crosse their expectation, and quite banish   [345]
All that their weaker mindes do thinke delight.
Kings pleasures are more subtle, then to be
Seen by the vulgar; they are Men, but such
As ne're had any dregges, or if they had,
Drop'd 'em as they were drawing up from out   [350]
The groveling Prease of Mortalls. To offend
Beyond the reach of Law without controule,
Is not the Nature, but the vice of Pow'r;
And he is only great, that dares be good.

Act. 2. Sce. 2.

To him
Praxaspes, Masistes.

Prax. He weares a serious looke still; we may hope   [355]
As soon to calme a Tempest with a song,
As soften him.
  Mas. Beasts and hard Rockes have both
Been mov'd; and by his Country-man. Let's try.
That we may some way, Sir, expresse our service
Unto you, with intent you may not feele   [360]
Bare honour only without the delights,
We have provided you a taste of our
Best Persian Musicke.
  Crat. That's an innocent pleasure;
Sphears make it, and Gods heare it.
  Prax. Boy come in.

Act. 2. Sce. 3.

To them

*Two women and a boy, as he is preparing
to sing, Atossa, Mandane, and Ariene
appeare above.*

Prax. ·Your last new song, that which I gave you Sirrah. [365]
  Atos. See yonder where he sits; let's stand and see
How hee'le behave himselfe; the Lords have vow'd
To try him to the utmost.
  Mand. I begin
To feare that he is mortall.
  Prax. Come begin.

Boy singes.

1

Come my sweet, whiles every strayne   [370]
  Calls our Soules into the Eare;
Where they greedy listning fayne
  Would turne into the sound they heare;
    Lest in desire
    To fill the Quire   [375]
    Themselves they tye
    To Harmony,
Let's kisse and call them backe againe.

2

Now let's orderly conveigh
  Our Soules into each other's Brest,   [380]
Where interchanged let them stay
  Slumbring in a melting rest.
    Then with new fire
    Let them retire,
    And still present   [385]
    Sweet fresh content
Youthfull as the early day.

3

Then let us a Tumult make,
  Shuffling so our soules, that we

    Carelesse who did give or take,   [390]
    May not know in whom they be.
     Then let each smother
     And stifle the other,
     Till we expire
      In gentle fire   [395]
    Scorning the forgetfull Lake.

 Crat. I did expect some solemne Hymne of the
Great world's beginning, or some brave Captaines
Deserving deeds extoll'd in lofty numbers.
These softer subjects grate our eares: But what   [400]
Are these my Lords? shee Minstrells?
 Mas. Consequences,
Which we out of that duty which we owe you
Thought a fit present, that you might not want
Any delight that Persia yeelds.
 Crat. I have
No humane thought about me now, forbeare.   [405]
 Prax. You are no Statue Sir? or if you were,
These yet methinkes might melt you.
 Crat. If you will
Needes put your selves to th' trouble of Procurers,
Bring me a Kingdome in one face, or shew me
A People in one body; then you might   [410]
Happily worke on mine Affections.
There I durst powre my selfe into Embracements,
Loosing my selfe in a Labyrinth of joy.
As 'tis, you only make me colder, by
Surrounding me with these your hostile flames.   [415]
 Mas. I hope you doe conceive it our Affection,
And duty to your Scepter.
 Crat. Let me aske you.
Was't not enough you try'd me with those baytes
Of wines, and meates, cull'd from the spoyle of Nature,
But you must bring vice in another fashion?   [420]
 Prax. Will you then let your dayes passe sluggishly,
And reape no pleasure from your Pow'r?
 Crat. 'Tis one
To punish such offenders as your selves,

That will abase your honour to so vile
And abject an imployment. If you offer [425]
The like againe, you shall perceive, that Kings,
How short so e're their Reignes be, have long hands.
This Act, what e're you stile it, is flat Treason.
Our Honour is abus'd in't. O the foreheads
Of women once growne impudent! that these [430]
Can stand so long, and heare their infamy
Debated quietly, expecting when
They shall be call'd to their reproach! what fled?
And left the Prey behind to tempt me? Ho!
Who waytes without? Conveigh these wicked creatures [435]
Unto the Gaolor *Molops:* give him charge
To use them as he would doe Enemies.
My Country would twice suffer, should I yeeld
Unto their vices too. But Greece is not
Only preserv'd in me: had they perhaps [440]
Carry'd these Creatures to the wilder knot,
Headlong *Archippus*, or bold *Stratocles*,
Easie *Leocrates*, or prone *Philotas*,
Their Present might have hit. But hearke, they come:
I'le step aside, and watch their actions. *Exit.* [445]
  Atos. What doe you thinke Mandane? is he mortall?

{ *Prax. and Mas. steale out, and leave the two women with him.*

Act. 2. Sce. 4.

*Philotas, Stratocles, Leocrates, Archippus,
in rich Persian Habits.*

  Str. How far do we out-shine the Persian Court?
See what good cloaths can do. I thinke there are not
Foure properer Gentlemen walke the streets.
  Phil. The Ladyes certainly must love us now. [450]
  Leoc. But are you sure they'le passe this way?
  Arch. Yes, yes.
Let's to our stations, and be ready to
Accost 'm at the first approach.
  Atos. *Mandane,*
Doe you and *Ariene* step downe to 'em,
And try their Courtship.

 Mand. All I thinke be safe.   [455]
 Arie. Cratander is hard by; ne're fear; let's down. *They descend*
 Str. I wonder none passe by yet: sure they'le send
Tickets unto us, to invite us to
Their Lodgings the back-way.
 Arch. Ne're doubt it Man,
They'le come themselves; for proofe behold. (*Ent. Mand. Arie.*
 Leocr. Halfe booty;   [460]
Equall division Gentlemen.
 Phil.⎫
 Str. ⎬ Agreed, agreed.
 Arch.⎭
 Phil. Nay, start not Ladyes, we are men.
 Arie. 'Tis well
You tell us so before hand, we might else
Thinke you disguised Satyres, come on purpose
To put the Nymphes to flight.
 Leoc. We are not hairy;   [465]
We have no Tayles, I'm sure.
 Arie. Truly if Satyres
And you were in one Market-towne, I thinke
You might see one another for nothing.
 Str. Doe you
Take us for Monsters then?
 Mand. Pray heav'n we don't
Discover 'em in your Manners.
 Arch. We are come   [470]
Not to disturbe, but heighten your delights.
 Mand. Can you shew any trickes then?
 Arch. Love-trickes Lady.
 Arie. Can you run through a Hoope? or fetch up mony
With your eye-lids backward?
 Mand. Can you peirce your Tongue,
Or cut your Throat, and yet live after it?   [475]
 Str. Do y'thinke us Tumblers then, or Jugglers?
 Mand. Both;
And truly these would please us farre above
Your Love-trickes.
 Leoc. Shall I draw some Ribbon then
Out of my Throat? Shall I cast a Lock upon

    Your pretty cheekes, or seale your lovely lippes [480]
Up?
    Arie. What will content you when you have done?
    Leoc. A kisse.
    Mand. We doe not use to grant such favours *gratis*.
    Leoc. What will you take to give one then?
    Mand. A Muffler.
    Phil. I perceive you are well skill'd [485]
In the whole course of Love, you but keepe off
To make delights more sweet.
    Arie. You would doe well
To doe so too.
    Phil. Why Madam? doe not feare me:
I snore not in my sleepe; this Nose of mine
Will not proclaime.
    Mand. 'Tis something Trumpet-like; [490]
I would not trust my selfe with such an Instrument.
Methinkes 'tis somewhat guilty.
    Phil. How I love
This pretty, pettish, froward, wanton anger?
Give me a Pleasure that I struggle for.
That Favour's genuinely sweet, that's wrested. [495]
    Str. Feare him not Madam; I'le be your defence;
My soule is link'd and chayn'd unto your Tongue.
    Arie. You speake in a fit dialect; you rellish
O'th' Language of the place whence you came lately.
But to be serious now awhile, pray speake, [500]
What doe you see in us fit for desire?
You cannot love us possibly.
    Str. By this kisse.
    Arie. Stand off.
    Arch. And this.
    Mand. Your Oath's not good in Law.
Tell us, what wrong hath either of us done you,
That you should seeke thus to revenge your selves? [505]
    Phil. You are too scornefull, we too easie; come
Let's hurry 'em to some place of secrecie,
Where all their scoffing shan't prevaile: you two
Quickly seize her.
    Arie. \
    Mand. / Helpe, helpe.

Act. 2. Sce. 5.

As they carry out the Ladyes,
Cratander meets them.

Crat.   Yee Villaines hold.
What is the matter? why this violence?
   Leoc.   A little Love-sport only; we were arguing
Pro, and *Con* out of *Plato*, and are now
Going to practise his Philosophy.
   Arie.   What they stile Love-sport only, and misname
An arguing out of *Plato*, would have prov'd
A true and downe-right Rape, if that your presence
Had not become our Rescue.
   Crat.   Wicked Villaines,
That in your miseries can't forget your vices,
Acting those crimes to day, which e're the Sun
Thrice set, will elsewhere be your Torture. Cannot
The chayne and hunger kill those seedes of evill,
But even in the midst of your misfortunes,
Your sports must be the robbing of faire honour,
And Rapes your Recreations? which, an't please
The Gods, you call Philosophy. Leave the place;
Infection's busie where you breath; the next
Attempt installs you in the Dungeon.   (*Ex. 4. Slaves.*
   Mand.   Most worthy Sir, your Noblenesse hath showne
A minde beyond your fortune: though it be not
Reall as we could wish it, yet beleeve it
You hold a perfect Royalty in the hearts
Of those, whose honours you have now preserv'd.
   Crat.   I owe this duty to your vertues Madam.
                                        (*Ex. Mand. Arie.*
These Slaves must be repress'd; the giddy People
Are ready to transpose all crimes upon
Him that should moderate them; so perhaps
Their faults might be accounted mine. Besides
Snares are laid close in every path for me;
And if a King but stumble, 'tis a Precipice:
When all eyes see't, a blemish is a Monster.
Pure vertue then, and thou faire honour, give me

Leave to cōtemplate on your Beauties; let {*As he is musing, Atos. from above throwes him a gold chayne.*}
The strength of my Imagination dwell
Upon the sight of your Divinities.
What? more temptations yet? ha? whence? from whom? [545]
The heav'ns I hope don't drop downe follies too:
No arme out of the cloudes! a chayne? why this
Is but an Exprobration of my late
Distressed fortune. 'Tis rich yet, and Royall;
It cannot be the wealth of any, but the Throne. [550]
Fall out what will, I'le weare it, 'till I know
From whence it came; and if it prove a Mettle
That some foule drossy minde could not endure
Should longer dwell with it, I then will cast it
With as much scorne and anger from my shoulders, [555]
As now I doe receive't with admiration.

Act. 2. Sce. 6.

To him

Hippias, Phocion.

Hip. Looke, there he walkes alone considering;
Let's to him while we may; good day *Cratander*.
Crat. Good *Hippias, Phocion!* you are welcome; how
Dare you trust your selves in an Enemies Court? [560]
Pho. We passe disguis'd to see what will become
Of our Affayres; and being the future state
Of Ephesus depends on you, are come
Only to give you notice of it, for
We doe presume you're not to be intreated [565]
To doe us good.
Crat. Alas! I am not, after
The period of three dayes; this makes the time
Which even now I thought an age, seeme short
And too contract for my desires.
Pho. When you
Should raise your Country struggling in the dust, [570]
The time is short, and too contract; 'tis long
Enough to lead an Army out against it,

To crush those Reliques of an halfe-life, that
Her doubtfull body faintly breaths; you may
With that right hand spin three dayes to the space [575]
Of many Olympiads.
  Crat. What is your meaning?
  Pho. Have we endur'd the hate, and felt the fury
Of violent *Arsamnes* so long? have we
Suffer'd his sword untill it did grow blunt,
And rather broke, then wounded? have you try'd [580]
The weight and strictnesse of the Persian chayne
So long, and aske us now, what is your meaning?
Come, come *Cratander*, I could chide you, but
That I beleeve you only hide the good
That you intend your Country, that it may not [585]
Be disappointed; you may safely tell us
You will betray the Persians into our hands,
That we may gather forces, and prepare
Against their comming.
  Crat. Oh! is this your Errant?
Here, take your chayne againe, it cannot binde. [590]
  Hip. How e're don't exprobrate our Poverty,
Though all our wealth hath been the Persians spoyle.
  Crat. Why you threw't in before you, to make way
Unto your Suit.
  Hip. Is it not lawfull to
Salute the Persian Mock-King, thinke y', unlesse [595]
We bring a Guift? I'd thought the name of Ephesus
Had priviledg'd our accesse. Thinke on the honours,
The long continuing honours, that you shall
Receive at home; thinke on those numerous teares
That you shall wipe away from flowing Eyes, [600]
At the first sight of Liberty.
  Pho. Your approach
Will entice Cities out of Houses; th' aged,
And the young too; the Matron, and the Virgin,
All mingled in a blest confusion,
Will in a solemne full Procession come, [605]
And with that great Religion bring you in,
As if their Captive Gods were brought them backe.
Come then a King home, that went'st out a Slave.

Crat. I am so still; no sooner did I come
Within the Persian Walles, but I was theirs. [610]
And since, good *Hippias*, this pow'r hath only
Added one linke more to the Chayne. I am
Become *Arsamnes* Instrument: I've sworne
Faith to his Scepter and himselfe, and must
Aske his leave, e're I doe betray his Country. [615]
   Hip. You're free enough against us. O the justice
Of an unnaturall Sonne! yet aske your selfe;
Ought that be ratify'd that's done by force?
   Crat. As if the valiant could be forc'd by any.
   Pho. You shall not change your fortune, you shall only [620]
Passe to another Empire; and for that
Right may be violated.
   Crat. Empires are
Desir'd for glory; be all wickednesse then
Farre absent, for in that there can be none.
   Pho. You are resolv'd to reason your selfe then [625]
Into a measur'd unthankefulnesse? what can
Hinder this good t' your Country, but your selfe?
Fear'st thou the Thunder, and the Gods? the anger
O'th' Grecian Pow'rs will be upon thee, if
Thou not restor'st them to their seats. On then, [630]
Thou undertak'st their cause, thou fight'st their warre.
   Crat. I cannot tell what powers you pretend;
Tell me of Justice and Fidelity,
These are the Grecian Gods.
   Pho. Be then thy name
Blasted to all Posterity, and let [635]
Our wretched Nephewes, when their Soules shall labour
Under the Persian Yoake, curse thee, and say,
This slavery we owe unto *Cratander*.
   Crat. Pray stay, I will goe with you, and consider.
How am I streightned! Life is short unto me: [640]
And th' good man's End ought still to be a businesse.
We must dy doing something, least perhaps
We loose our Deaths; we must not yet doe ill
That we misplace not Action: If I strike
On this hand, I'm a Parricide; if on that, [645]
The same brand waytes me too: how doe I tremble,

Like to the doubtfull Needle 'twixt two Loadstones,
At once inclining unto both, and neither!
Here Piety calls me, there my Justice stops me.
It is resolv'd; Faith shall consist with both; [650]
  And aged Fame after my Death shall tell,
  Betwixt two sinnes, *Cratander* did do well.   *(Exeunt.*

Finis Act. 2.

Act. 3. Sce. I.

*Philotas, Stratocles, Archippus, Leocrates,
Molops, in drinking Chaplets, after the
Grecian manner.*

Phil. Set a watch at the doore, to keepe out sleepe;
He's mortall that offers to betray so much weaknes
As to winke. Here *Archippus*. [655]
  Arch. May not a man winke without mortality,
When he lets it goe downe? Here *Stratocles*.
  Phil. I doe state winking in that case divine.
  Str. Come thou uneven lumpe, thou heape of sinnes in
proofe; we will liquor thy Keyes, open thy Cages, and give [660]
thy meager Tenants a Play day, Raskall. Bring the Jarres
nearer. As I hope for fortune, I thinke my soule will passe
into a frogge. Now for a hundred Throats; to thee *Molops*.
  Mol. You Grecians I thinke have sponges in your mawes;
'tis but setting your hands to your sides, and squeezing your [665]
selves, and presently you drinke as much as before.
  Leoc. Off with thy Cup Landlord, and talke not; wee
learn'd it from the Teat, foole.
  Mol. Have at thee, *Archippus*.
  Arch. I doe not like these healths at randome; let's have [670]
a sober methodicall order for a while.
  Phil. What? shall we drinke by dice then, and let fortune
name the heyre to the Cup?
  Str. Or shall we drinke our Mistresses names, and soake it
Alphabetically? [675]
  Leoc. If we drinke names, let not the Letters passe for

single ones, but as they would in number: I doe pronounce *Alpha* no letter till it begin to multiply.

Mol. I never thought Drinking such a Mystery before; a blockhead can't be drunke, I see. [680]

Phil. Right; shallow braines can ne're attaine to't; that makes your fooles, and your old governing Philosophers continue so sober still. The veget Artist, and the vigorous Poët, whose braines are full and forging still, will streight get a pleasant madnesse from that that will but warme those [685] colder Rheumaticke Sages, whose noses alwayes drop like Still-snoutes.

Str. The noblest drinking methinkes is the Postures.

Arch. Let's have 'em.

Leo. A match. [689a]

Phil. Bring the Pots in play. But where's the wenches, [690] and the Musicke you promis'd us, good *Molops*.

Mol. For wenches, the Towne will not yeeld any at this time; and I durst not venture my single wife amongst you all. For Fidlers, I have provided them, they stand ready without. [695]

Leoc. Call 'em in sweet *Molops*.

Strat. Well, what shall those Raskalls play, whiles we drinke the Postures?

Phil. The Battle by all meanes.   *Ent. Mus.*

Str. Strike up the Battle then. Thinke your selves all in [700] service now, and doe as I doe.
Take your Bowes Gent: and make a stand.
Right! draw your shafts now, & nock 'em.
Very good! now smooth your feathers.   [705]
Well done! Present, and take ayme.
Here's to thee *Leocrates*.

{ *They take their pots in their left hands.* *They take their cups in their right hands, & fill.* *They blow off the froth.* }

Leoc. Have towards thee *Philotas*.

Phil. To thee *Archippus*.

Arch. Here *Molops*.

Mol. Have at you Fidlers. [710]

Str. Now draw your Bowes and let loose all.   { *They drinke all together.* }

Mol. The other charge, good fellow Souldiers.

Phil. Let's have a Song betweene, and then have at you.

Leoc. Fidlers, employ your Throats and sing awhile; you shall drinke with 'em after. [715]

Str. Sing that which I made in the Prison; 'tis seasonable enough.

Song.

1. *Now, now, the Sunne is fled*
   Downe into Tethys bed,
   Ceasing his solemne course awhile. [720]
2.   *What then?*
   'Tis not to sleepe, but be
   Merry all night, as we;
Gods can be mad sometimes, as well as men.
  Cho: *Then laugh we, and quaffe we, untill our rich noses* [725]
        Grow red, and contest with our Chaplets of Roses.
1. *If he be fled, whence may*
   We have a second day,
That shall not set till we command?
2.   *Here see* [730]
   A Day that does arise
   Like his, but with more eyes,
And warmes us with a better fire, than hee.
  Cho: *Then laugh we, &c.*
1.2. *Thus then we chase the night* [735]
    With these true floods of light,
This Lesbian wine, which with it's sparkling streams,
    Darting diviner Graces,
    Cast's Glories round our Faces,
And dulls the Tapers with Majestique Beames. [740]
  Cho: *Then laugh we, &c.*

Str. Well said! now the other charge to the honour of *Cratander*.

Phil. I feele a rumbling in my head, as if the Cyclops were forging Thunder in my Braines: But no matter, give it me: our ancient Orpheus sayes it, Perpetuall drunkennesse is the reward of Vertue. [745]

Act. 3. Sce. 2.

To them

Cratander.

   Crat. Which the most vitious have: must I still meet
Some thing must greeve me more than your misfortunes?
The Chayne and Fetter were your Innocence. [750]
   Phil. We don't fire Temples Sir: we kill no Father
Nor Mother, 'tis not Incest to be merry.
   Crat. But to be drunke is all. Doe but consider,
(If that at least you can) how Greece it selfe
Now suffers in you; thus, say they, the Grecians [755]
Do spend their Nights: Your vices are esteem'd
The Rites and Customes of your Country, whiles
The beastly Revelling of a Slave or two,
Is made the Nations Infamy. Your wreathes
Blush at your Ignominy: what prayse is't [760]
When't shall be said, *Philotas* stood up still
After the hundreth Flagon; when 'tis knowne
He did not so in warre? you're now just fit
To teach the Spartan boyes sobriety;
Are all good Principles wash'd out? how e're [765]
Be without vices, if not vertuous.
That I should have authority to command
Vices, but not forbid 'em! I would put you
Once more into his charge, but that you would
Make even the Dungeon yet more infamous. [770]
   Mol. Gentlemen heare me; *Cratander*   (*Ex. Crat.*
Speakes well, and like a good Common-wealth's-man.
   Arch. Out you dissembling Raskall; are you of *Cratander's* faction?
   Mol. Good Gentlemen don't kicke me: I shall leave all [775]
my drinke behind me, if you doe.   (*Ex. Mol.*
   Phil. Must we still thus be check'd? we live not under
A King, but a Pedagogue: hee's insufferable.
   Leoc. Troth hee's so proud now he must be kill'd to make
a supper for the immortall Canniballs, that there's no Ho [780]
with him.

Arch. I never thought he would have beene either so womanish, as to have been chast himselfe, or so uncivill as to keepe us so: but hee talkes of lying with surpriz'd Cities, and committing Fornication with Victory, and making Mars [785] Pimpe for him.

Str. These are the fruits of Learning; we suffer all this meerely because he hath a little familiarity with the Devill in Philosophy, and can conjure with a few Notions out of *Socrates*. [790]

Arch. In good troth I take it very scurvily at his hands, that he will not let me deserve hanging. I'd thought to have done all the villanies in the world, and left a name behinde me: but hee's severe forsooth, and cryes out Vertue, Mistris Vertue. [795]

Phil. Diseases take her; I ne're knew any good she did in Common-wealth yet. I wonder how he dares be so impudent, as to be good in a strange place.
Did not you marke his Rhetorique cast at me?
I was the Butt he shot at.—What prayse is't, [800]
When't shall be said *Philotas* stood up still
After the hundreth Flagon, when 'tis knowne
He did not so in warre?—meere, meere upbrayding:
And shall *Philotas* this? this from *Cratander*?

Act. 3. Sce. 3.

To them
Praxaspes, Masistes.

Prax. Whence this deepe silence? are you sacrificing [805]
To your dumbe Gods of Greece? where are your Cuppes?
Your Loves, your Madnesse?

Leoc. Do not Ravish me;
I will cry out a Rape, if that you come
Within twelve foot of me; we must be modest,
Modest an't please the Gods.

Mas. Fy! fy! We look'd, you should [810]
Have left at least a dozen of great bellies
A peece behinde you upon every Tribe.

Where are your Spirits? had I been in your case,
Nature e're this had been inverted. But
You thinke on your last end, as if the world [815]
Were to expire with you.
   Str. O! we must walke
Discreetly, looke as carefully to our steps,
As if we were to dance on ropes, with Egges
Under our feet: we have left off shackles,
To be worse fetterd.
   Prax. Can a brest of large [820]
And ample thoughts tamely endure the ring?
And be led quietly by th'Patient Nose,
When Licence is Religion? One whose dull
And sluggish temper is call'd wisdome, one
Whose indiscretion kill'd with some formality, [825]
As Quicksilver with fasting spittle, doth passe
For a grave governing Garbe. This heavy lumpe
Dulls all your active fire.
   Mas. You understand not:
For to what end is Liberty indulg'd?
To be oppress'd by a severer Rule? [830]
One newly taken from among your selves,
To make your state worse by his Tyranny?
But you shew what you can endure.
   Phil. By Heav'n
We doe enslave our selves; We can b'as free
As is *Cratander*, though not so malitious. [835]
   Mas. You are as things of nought with him; for tell me;
When call'd he *Stratocles* to Coun*̂*cell? when
Ask'd he *Leocrates* his advice? *Philotas*,
Archippus, names excluded from his thoughts,
But when he meanes to shew that he hath anger. [840]
   Phil. What Star wert thou borne under *Stratocles*?
   Str. That which all Governours of Market-townes are,
Some lazy Planet, I beleeve.
   Phil. Thou 'wert wont
To exercise upon a throat or two,
To keepe thy hand in ure; now shew thy selfe: [845]
Let's slit this graver weazen.
   Prax. Now I see

You have some man about you, now your blouds
Run as they should doe, high and full; you slept
Meerely till now. If that *Cratander* should
Quit scores with Nature e're his time be out, [850]
The King must chuse againe; the dead you know
Ne're goes for Sacrifice.
   Leoc. Must one of us
Peece up his Reigne then?
   Prax. There's no other way;
The Gods themselves require't.
   Leoc. My Hanches quake,
As if that *Molops* were to season them, [855]
And put 'em streight in paste for the great Gods.
   Phil. Who e're
Succeeds him, shall allow the rest what e're
Nature or Art can yeeld. Nothing shall be
Unlawfull, but to sleepe and mumble Prayers.
   Arch.   *Cratander is disco-*
   Strat. } Agreed, agreed. } *ver'd over-hearing*
   Leoc.   *them.*
   Phil. Then fill me out an Oath. [860]
All I presume will binde themselves with this
Good common looser of all cares, but what
Do tend to Liberty, to doe the like.
   Str. The motion's worthy; crowne the Goblet then.
   Phil. Would 'twere his bloud. By Truth her self th'Ofspring [865]
And childe of Wine, *Cratander* dyes e're halfe
The glasse of his short Tyranny run out.
This thē to the infernall Gods. (*powrs some on the ground*) & this
To our just angers, Gods as great as they. (*he drinkes.*
Good *Omen*! so! the thickned streames run black; [870]
'Twas bloud methought I dranke: 'twere Lazynes
To say, he shall be dead; hee's dead already.
Drinke and prepare for Pleasures. (*They all drinke.*
   Omnes. Liberty. (*Exeunt.*

Act. 3. Sce. 4.

Cratander, Atossa.

 Crat. He must be more than Man that gaynes it backe
Without my will.
 Atos. Your Justice must restore it. [875]
Will your severer Majesty triumph,
With soft spoyles of a Lady's Cabinet?
 Crat. As I would not feigne Favour, and be-ly
A Jewell or a Twist, to gaine the name
Of Creature, or of Servant unto any; [880]
So by your Beauty, (for if Persians may
Sweare by their Sun, I well may sweare by that)
Where honour is transmitted in a true
Mysterious Gage of an Immaculate minde,
I will defend it as some sacred Relique, [885]
Or some more secret pledge, drop'd downe from Heav'n,
To guard me from the dangers of the Earth.
 Atos. But in that
You make it common, you bereave it of
All that you call Divinity.
 Crat. He that vaunts
Of a received Favour, ought to be [890]
Punish'd as Sacrilegious Persons are,
'Cause he doth violate that sacred thing,
Pure, spotlesse Honour. But it may be seene,
And yet not prostitute. I would not smother
My Joyes, and make my happinesse a stealth. [895]
 Atos. How your thoughts flatter your deceived Fancy
Into a State, that when you leave to thinke,
Dyes, as your thoughts that kept it up! what is't
That you call joy and happinesse?
 Crat. I must
Confesse, I have no Merits, whose just heat [900]
May extract ought from you, call'd Love: yet when
I doe consider, that Affection
Cannot looke vertuously on any thing
That is resplendent, but a subtle image

Purely reflecting thence, must needs arise, [905]
And pay that Looke againe; I doe take leave
To say, the carefull Deities provide,
That Love shall ne're be so unhappy, as
To want his Brother.
   Atos. Why? I never spent
A sigh for you; you never had a kisse, [910]
Nor the reversion of one yet.
   Crat. Such Love
Is but Love's Idoll; and these soft ones, that
Confine it to a kisse, or an embrace,
Doe, as the superstitious did of old,
Contract the Godhead into a Bull, or Goat, [915]
Or some such lustfull Creature. Be it far,
Be't far from me to thinke, where e're I see
Cleare streames of Beauty, that I may presume
To trouble them with quenching of my thirst.
Where a full splendor, where a bright effusion [920]
Of immateriall Beames doe meet to
Make up one Body of perfection;
I should account my selfe injurious
Unto that Deity, which hath let downe
Himselfe into those Rayes, if that I should [925]
Draw nigh without an awfull Adoration;
Which my Religion payes to you: but being
You like not the Devotion, be content
To slight the Sacrifice, but spare the Altar.
   Atos. I am so farre from ruining that Breast [930]
In which there lives a sparke of chaster honour,
That I would hazzard this so priz'd a trifle,
Which men call Life, that it might live there still;
And prove that Love is but an Engine of
The carefull Pow'rs, invented for the safety [935]
And preservation of afflicted goodnesse.
Conceive not hence a passion burning toward you;
For she that speakes like woman, is a Queene.
   Crat. I can distinguish betwixt Love, and Love,
'Tweene Flames and good Intents, nay between Flames [940]
And Flames themselves: the grosser now fly up,
And now fall downe againe, still cov'ting new

Matter for food; consuming, and consum'd.
But the pure clearer Flames, that shoot up alwayes
In one continued Pyramid of lustre, [945]
Know no commerce with Earth, but unmixt still,
And still aspiring upwards, (if that may
Be call'd aspiring, which is Nature) have
This property of Immortality
Still to suffice themselves, neither devouring, [950]
Nor yet devour'd; and such I acknowledge yours.
On which I looke as on refin'd Ideas,
That know no mixture or corruption,
Being one eternall simplenesse; that these
Should from the Circle of their chaster Glories [955]
Dart out a beame on me, is farre beyond
All humane merit; and I may conclude,
They've only their owne Nature for a cause,
And that they're good, they are diffusive too.
   Atos. Your tongue hath spoke your thoughts so nobly, that [960]
I beare a pity to your vertues, which
E're night shed Poppy twice o're th'weary'd world,
Must only be in these two Registers;
Annalls, and Memory. Could you but contrive,
How you might live without an injury [965]
Unto Religion, you should have this glory,
To have a Queene your Instrument.
   Crat. There's nothing
Can wooe my heart unto a thought of life,
But that your presence will be wanting to me,
When I'm shut up in silence: yet I have [970]
A strong Ambition in me to maintaine
An equall faith 'twixt Greece and Persia:
That like a river running 'twixt two fields,
I may give growth and verdure unto both.
Praxaspes, and *Masistes*, potent Lords, [975]
Are both 'gainst my designes; so that I shall not
Obtaine an Army; for they thinke I have
That vile minde in me to betray this Kingdome,
To which I've sworne fidelity; when by
Your selfe, by all that's good, my'intent is only [980]
To perfect great *Arsamnes* Conquest, and

In that be beneficiall to my Country.
In which if that your Majesty will descend
To act a part, after the Scene is shut,
I'le downe t'Elysium with a joyfull minde, [985]
And teach our Grecian Poëts your blest name
And vertues, for an everlasting Song.
   Atos. Were it against my selfe, I'de not deny it.
Walke in, I'le follow you. In great designes   (*Ex. Crat.*
Valour helps much, but vertuous Love doth more. [990]

Act. 3. Sce. 5.

To her

Arsamnes.

   Arsam. Was't not enough that you perus'd his Actions,
And surfetted your Eyes upon his follies,
Seeing, and seene againe, but you must cast him
A Chayne, an Emblematicke Chayne?
   Atos. 'Tis not
The veyle that hinders the quicke busie Eye [995]
From reading o're the Face, but Modesty.
He hath a weake defence, that doth entrust
The preservation of a chaster Love
Unto a silken Cloud.
   Arsam. I stand not much
Upon the commerce of your Eyes, but 'tis [1000]
Your Chayne.—Your Favour—that—. Do'y'thinke 'tis fit
A Queene should send one linke unto a Slave?
   Atos. Doth not the Sun (the Sun, which yet you worship)
Send beames to others than your selfe? yet those
Which dwell on you loose neither light, nor heat, [1005]
Comming not thence lesse vigorous, or lesse chast.
Would you seale up a Fountaine? or confine
The Ayre unto your walke? would you enjoyne
The Flow'r to cast no smell, but as you passe?
Love is as free as Fountaine, Aire, or Flower. [1010]
For't stands not in a poynt; 'tis large, and may,
Like streams, give verdure to this Plant, that Tree,

Nay that whole field of Flow'rs, and yet still runne
In a most faithfull course toward the bosome
Of the lov'd Ocean.
   Arsam. But when you divert [1015]
And breake the Streame into small Rivulets,
You make it runne more weake, then when it kept
United in one Channell.
   Atos. If it branch
Into a smaller twining here, and there,
The water is not lost, nor doth it quit [1020]
The former Name; this is not to destroy,
But to enlarge the streame: did it dry up,
And leave the Fountaine destitute, indeed
You'd reason to be angry.
   Arsam. But what should make you
Present him with a guift? you might have smother'd [1025]
A good opinion of him in your Breast,
(As some digressing streames flow under ground)
And so have rested; but you shew it now,
And make the world partaker.
   Atos. Who would stifle
An honest Fire? that flame's to be suspected [1030]
That hides it selfe. When that a man of valour
Graceth his Country with a good attempt,
You give a Sword, an Horse, a Mannoure, nay
Sometimes a whole Province for reward. We have
A sense of Vertue too, as well as you: [1035]
And shall we be deny'd the Liberty
To shew we have that sense? A Favour is
The Almes of Love; I doe not passe away
My heart in Charity. Vertuous *Cratander*
Shewes forth so full a Transcript of your life, [1040]
In all but his misfortunes, that methinkes
You may admire your selfe in him, as in
Your shade. But yet let chast *Atossa* rather
Not be at all, than not be wholly yours.
   Arsam. Thou art still vertuous my *Atossa*, still [1045]
Transparent as thy Crystall, but more spotlesse.
Fooles that we are, to thinke the Eye of Love
Must alwayes looke on us. The Vine that climbes

By conjugall Embracements 'bout the Elme,
May with a ring or two perhaps encircle   [1050]
  Some neighbouring bough, and yet this twining prove,
  Not the Offence, but Charity of Love.   (*Exeunt.*

Finis Act. 3.

Act. 4. Sce. I.

*Atossa, Mandane, Ariene, other Ladyes,
and Women of divers sorts.*

  Atos. That we have naturally a desire
To preserve Honour is a Principle
Not questionable, but by those that would   [1055]
Corrupt, and rob us of it: that you prize
Your Chastity more than wealth, and thinke your Cabinets
Cheape and unworthy, if compar'd t' your mindes,
I'm so assur'd, that I need only tell you
The danger, not intreat you to avoyd it.   [1060]
The Slaves next night intend a Rape upon
Your Honour, and your Wealth; to tell your Husbands
Were to procure a slaughter on both sides.
If we avert the ryot, and become
Our owne defence, the Honour, as the Action,   [1065]
Will be entirely ours: which may be done
Only by flying to *Arsamnes* Castle.
A thing so easy, that 'twill only be
To take the Ayre for fame: and when we doe
Returne, our Husbands shall strew prayses in   [1070]
Our wayes, which we will tread on, and contemne.
  Omnes. Let's fly, let's fly, let's fly.
  Atos. How I doe love
These worthy, noble thoughts! the Action
Will make our Tombes not need an Epitaph,
When we shall live still fresh in History.   [1075]
The sacred Gods of Marriage will present
Themselves unto you night by night for this,
And personally thanke you in your Dreames,

For thus preserving their Rites undefil'd.
But time is short, I must away, to make [1080]
Provision for our flight. If any doe
Desire a further satisfaction
In this our grand designe, we leave our Ladyes
Mandane here, and *Ariene*, who
Can give a full relation of our businesse. [1085]
    Omn. Away, away, to the Castle, to the Castle. (*Exeunt.*

Act. 4. Sce. 2.

Cratander, Hippias, Phocion.

    Crat. Vrge me no more, I am sure my Countrey
Requires not Perjury.
    Pho. Ought any word
Be kept with Enemies? no path is foule
That leades to liberty.
    Crat. O *Phocion!* [1090]
Such men as you have made our Grecian faith
Become a Proverbe t'expresse Treachery.
An Oath's the same in Persia, and in Greece:
And bindes alike in either.
    Hip. But consider
Wee're thrall'd and yoak'd; the hard gaines of our sweat [1095]
Must be sent in to serve their Luxury.
Tribute, and taxe, and payment, will still keepe us
As in a siege: to take the Aire perhaps
Will be a charge unto us.
    Pho. Nor is't Ephesus
That only dreades this slavery; *Claros* too, [1100]
And *Colophon*, nay *Magnesia*, and others
That joyn'd i'th'warre do feare a share i'th'Tyranny.
    Crat. Your forces are so weakned, that you cannot
Regaine a perfect Liberty: your Friends
Begin to fall off too: all that you can [1105]
Expect now, is to settle these your evills,
And live protected as a weakned friend
Under the Persian shelter: still preserving

Your Lawes and Liberties inviolate.
A thing perhaps yet rather to be wish'd for, [1110]
Then compass'd.
  Hip. Yet methinkes you might procure it,
Having such command.
  Crat. What may be done in so
Short space, shall all be to your good: goe then
And deale discreetly with the Army: tell them
The tempest that is falling on their head, [1115]
Unlesse the Persian shield them. When you have
Perswaded them to this, conduct your Forces
Towards *Arsamnes* Castle, where the Queene,
And Ladyes now expect me. But be sure
You come not within sight of *Sardis*.
  Pho. Why? [1120]
Shall we not march beyond the Fronteirs then?
  Crat. By no meanes, for you'le cut off all retreat.
Now, when you see the numerous Persian come,
You may securely fly without the losse
Of any; this will quell the future rising [1125]
Of those, whose frowardnesse is not content
Either with th'Calme or Tempest of Affaires.
We must comply with Fortune, now wee're conquer'd.
Permit the rest unto the Gods and me.
  Pho. Hip. Successe attend it.   *(Ex. Hip. Pho.*
  Crat. So; my next care now [1130]
Must be t' avoide those Slaves, who, I o'reheard,
Have a designe upon my life. But let
Even the plotting Destinies contrive,
And be themselves of Councell, all their malice
Shall only shew an idle fruitlesse Hate, [1135]
Whiles Wisedome takes the upper hand of Fate.
                           (Exit Cratander.

Act. 4. Sce. 3.

4th Appearance, a Wood.

Leocrates, Archippus, after a while Philotas, and Stratocles, all foure disguis'd in beggars habits; one having a leg, another an arme ty'd up:

all some counterfeiting trick of such maunding people. Leocrates and Archippus peepe out of the woods side at severall places.

Leoc. Holla!
Arch. Holla!
Leoc. *Archippus?*
Arch. *Leocrates?* Ne're be afraid man, 'tis I, the very same. [1140]
Leoc. 'Fore *Mercury* I did not know thee: thy comming forth out of the wood with that raw arme, and those totter'd cloaths, makes thee shew like *Actæon*, newly reviv'd after his worrying.
Arch. Where's *Stratocles*, and *Philotas?* [1145]
Leoc. They're looking Bur-leaves perhaps for Excoriation; or else robbing some Gibbet to accommodate themselves with decent weeds.
Phil. Holla!
Stra. Holla! [1150]
Arch. Hearke: I heare 'em; they are hard by; let's answer 'em. Holla!
Stra. O are you there?
Leoc. Save thee Brother *Stratocles*: Joy to thee Valiant *Philotas*; I commend you that you keepe your wordes: I'm [1155] glad we are so punctuall.
Stra. D'ye thinke we have no Religion in us? 'tis a most corrupt time, when such as we cannot keepe touch, and be faithfull one to another.
Leoc. But are you sure *Cratander* will passe by this way? [1160]
Arch. My Lord *Praxaspes* sayes he loves this walke.
Str. But wee've done ill to leave our weapons yonder.
Leoc. Pish! he won't passe by this houre, hee's busie yet: Wee'le fetch 'em as soone as wee can agree who shall doe the deed. [1165]
Phil. Who shall doe the deed sayst thou? why thou, or he, or he, or I.
Leoc. Do thou then if thou hast a minde to't.
Phil. No faith, thou shalt have the whole honour of it to thy selfe; I will not rob thee of an inch of it: I am not envi- [1170] ous, *Leocrates*, not envious.
Leoc. Well; the next Passenger is to decide it then; hee

[Act IV, Scene iv]

that shall be judg'd the fittest to make a Persian Priest, must do the deed.

Str. What else? dost thou thinke we will be so base, as not to stand to Covenants? [1175]

Phil. You have all made your selves very unfit to bee Preists methinkes.

Str. Why so *Philotas*? do you not see woodden legs, and Crutches, wry Neckes, and lame Armes, maym'd limbes, and blind sides? [1180]

Phil. Good faith, we may be all taken for an Hospitall broke loose.

Arch. And we have wood enough among us to—. As I hope for Mercy *Cratander*.—by the ball of Fortune here hee comes: Soule of my life what shall we doe? { *Cratan. is discover'd walking toward them.* } [1185]

Str. Not a sword, not a knife among us! all left behind us in the wood! that we should be all manicled now, out of a most unlucky Policy! We shall never have him alone againe: make toward him and be hang'd, that hee may resolve the Question howe're. [1190]

Act. 4. Sce. 4.

To them
Cratander.

Leoc. Blesse thy senses and thy limbes, faire Master: doe a courtesie to a company of poore distressed Persians; 'tis not mony we aske, nor cloaths; only thy Judgement, thy Judgement, man of Understanding. [1195]

Crat. What's your request?

Leoc. That out of thy great Wisdome, soule of Learning, Thou'd'st be pleas'd to tell us freely, which of us foure is fittest to make a Persian Priest. [1200]

Crat. I am not well skill'd in your Persian Rites, I know not what Man, or how qualify'd Your Temple may admit of, but I have Two or three Servants within call here, they Shall umpire this your variance. Ho! *Sisarmes*, { *As Cra. views thē narrowly, they fall to their Postures.* } [1205]

Ho! *Artobazes*, draw nigh quickly; seize   *(Ent. Servants.*
These foure pernitious Raskalls: did you thinke
You could ly hid? 'tis not your leg good *Stratocles*,
Nor your close arme *Leocrates*, that can
Disguise you from mine eye. I can tell you   [1210]
Who dranke my death, who were your grand Abettors,
In this designe. You now would know who's fittest
To make a Persian Priest: Malitious fooles,
Is it not all one as to aske me, who
Is fitt'st to Sacrifice me? But you see   [1215]
I live, and will doe, to your Punishment.
Goe, away with 'em; take them as they are.
Let 'em not alter either Cloaths, or Posture,
But lead 'em through the City thus to *Molops*;
And give him charge to keepe 'em so, untill   [1220]
He heare our farther Pleasure.   *(Ex. Crat.*

  Serv. Come along, Gentlemen, wee'le try your stumps,
How many miles a day you can halt.

  Str. Sirrah, be civill, or else before *Jove* I'le pull off my
wooden leg, and break your Pate with it, though I dy for it.   [1225]
                                   (Ex. Serv. and Slaves.

Act. 4. Sce. 5.

Hydarnes, Orontes, Praxaspes, Masistes.

  Hyd. Wee're like to have an honest Court of't shortly.
  Prax. You speak, my Lord, as if 'twere not so now.
  Hyd. 'Tis honest now, and shortly will not have
The Pow'r to be otherwise.
  Mas. Why *Hydarnes*?
  Hyd. There's not a woman left man; all are vanish'd,   [1230]
And fled upon the sudden.
  Mas. What? I hope
They have not chang'd their Sexe all in a minute?
They are not leap'd into rough chinnes, and Tulipants?
  Hyd. There's scarce a face without a beard appeares.
  Mas. A signe there are few Eunuches in the Palace.
  Hyd. My Lords,   [1235]

This is not to discover what's become of 'em.
They've taken weapons with 'em too they say.
  Prax. They have no Sacrifice to performe, that I
Can tell of, neither if they had, would they
Take armes, that were t'invade the Deity. [1240]
The Sword's no Instrument of their Devotion.
To them a Messenger.
  Mess. My Lords, you must make haste with all your forces
To th'Queene and Ladyes in *Arsamnes* Castle:
They now are likely all to be surpriz'd,
By the remainder of the Greekes.
  Prax. Cratander, [1245]
That damned Villaine hath entic'd 'em thither,
Meerely t' entrap 'em. Let us to the King;
Wee'le on although against revolted Slaves.
  We fought with Men before, but now with Vice;
He calls for death that must be conquer'd twice. (*Exeunt.* [1250]

Finis Act. 4.

Act. 5. Sce. I.

5th Appearance,
A Castle.

*Atossa, Mandane, Ariene, with divers other
  women in warlike habits, discover'd on the
  Castle walls, with Cratander fully seated
  in the midst.*

  Crat. Most vertuous Queen, you make me search my self,
To find the worth which you do so far prize;
As thus to hazard for one man, whose life
Is under value, that which others would not
For a whole Kingdome, Reputation. [1255]
  Atos. Where Goodnes is to suffer, I would willingly
Become the Sacrifice my selfe to free it.
  Crat. Had great *Arsamnes* beene in danger, had
Your whole Line beene in jeopardy of ruine,

You could have done no more; Your pity hath [1260]
Thrust you into Heroick Actions, farre
Beyond the eager Valour of try'd Captaines;
Which I can never worthily admire,
When I consider your reward will only
Be, to be rank'd in story with a Slave. [1265]
    Atos. I do't not to the Man, but to the Vertue.
The deed's reward enough unto it selfe.
    Crat. 'Twould be a peece of exemplary Ingratitude,
To bring you into any danger hence:
You're safe as in your Court; your Subjects shall not [1270]
Run any doubtfull hazard, in the Chance
Of an uncertaine Battle: their first step
Shall be Victorious: and when your Eloquence,
Guarded with Beauty, shall procure the freedome
Of our Enthralled City, the Ephesians [1275]
Shall know a Goddesse greater than their owne,
And you depose our magnify'd Diana;
Having Shrines in every Breast out-shining hers.
As for my selfe, I shall live still in those
Good benefits my Country shall receive. [1280]
This day instating me in Immortality:
While raising thus our City by my fall,
I shall goe downe a welcome shade, and dwell
Among the Ancient Fathers of my Country.
    Atos. Leave the Conditions to me: but peace; [1285]
Expect we quietly a while, they come.

Act. 5. Sce. 2.

To them below
Arsamnes, Hydarnes, Orontes, Praxaspes,
Masistes, and others in warlike habits.

    Prax. Can you containe Sir? looke how proudly hee
Sits in the midst, hemm'd in on every side
With Beauties, which his wheeling eye runs o're
All in a Minute.

Mas.   Here's a delicacy [1290]
That ne're was practis'd by a Captive yet,
Nor heard of since the Custome first began,
That Conquer'd Slaves should personate their King.
   Arsam.   The Luxury and Ryot of arm'd Love!
O that mine eyes could dart forth peircing Lightning! [1295]
That I could shoot some quicke invisible Plague
Into his boyling marrow. Hee is seated
So, that a Dart or Arrow cannot reach him,
Without the danger of a Persian breast,
Worth all his Nation. But why name I worth, [1300]
Where I see so much Infamy? O *Atossa*!
Is this your amity to Vertue? this
The Pity that you lend afflicted goodnesse?
There's worke enough now for my sword, although
The Enemy approach not. Credulous woman, [1305]
Descend, *Arsamnes* calls thee; if he be
A Name regarded when *Cratander's* by.
   Atos.   Most vertuous Sir, you may expect perhaps
Atossa's breast growne strange, and wrested from
Her wonted faith; but witnesse O thou Sun, [1310]
Whom with a pious eye I now behold,
That I have neither try'd t'unty, or loosen
That sacred knot: but what I've condescended
To ayde thus farre, is only a faire likenesse
Of something that I love in you.
   Arsam.   If then [1315]
Your Loyalty be still intire to me,
Shew it, and yeeld *Cratander* up to us.
   Atos.   As his designes are honourable, so
Are our intents, with which there needes must stand
A resolutenesse: it cannot be Vertue, [1320]
Unles't be constant too. Th'approach o'th' Enemy
Forbids me to say more: On to your Victory,
Your wonted art to Conquer; they're the Reliques
Of a few scatter'd troopes, the fragments of
The last meale that your swords made; on, and when [1325]
You have subdu'd them wholly, we will plant
Fresh Bayes upon your browes, and seale unto you

A peace, as everlasting as our Loves.
   Sould. within.   Arme, arme, arme, arme.   { *Ex. Arsam. Lords, &c.*
  Omn.   Mithra and Victory.   *as to the Battle.*
  Atos.   Let us be resolute now my Ladyes, and   [1330]
At their returne shew them that they have something
Left yet to Conquer; Breasts, that are not shaken
With their loud noyse of Trumpets. See, they're comming:
This was a Race, no Battle; Let's prepare.

Act. 5. Sce. 3.

To them below

Arsamnes, &c. as from the Chase.

  Arsam.   What? fly upon the sight of us? to 'appeare   [1335]
Was here to overcome, a looke hath done
The businesse of the sword; your feares may sleepe
Securely now; Open the Castle gates.
  Atos.   But you must grant us some Conditions first.
  Arsam.   Must we be Articled with by our women?   [1340]
What is't, an't please the Gods, that you require?
  Atos.   *Cratanders* life.
  Crat.   It is not in your Pow'r
To grant it great *Arsamnes*: your Queene speakes
Out of a tender pitty to no purpose.
  Atos.   Heare me *Arsamnes*: whom the raging sword   [1345]
Hath spar'd, why should the peaceable destroy?
All hate's not ended in the field, I see:
There's something still more cruell after warre.
  Arsam.   Alas! you know not what you aske; the Gods
Permit not that he live; he falls to them.   [1350]
  Crat.   You must not heare her, Sir, against the Gods,
Who now expect their solemne Feast and Banquet.
  Atos.   If they are Gods, Pitty's a Banquet to 'em.
When e're the Innocent and Vertuous
Doth escape death, then is their Festivall.   [1355]
Nectar ne're flowes more largely, then when bloud's
Not spilt, that should be sav'd. Do y'thinke the smoake
Of humane Entralls is a steame that can

Delight the Deities? Who e're did burne,
The Building to the honour of the Architect? [1360]
Or breake the Tablet in the Painters prayse?
'Tis Mercy is the Sacrifice they like.
   Crat. Let not Affection call a Curse upon you,
While you permit it to take place of your
Religion.
   Arsam. See, he will not live *Atossa*; [1365]
To doe the unwilling man a courtesie
Is but a specious Tyranny.
   Atos. Alas!
He would be neare the Gods, he would leave us.
You must not, shall not kill him, my *Arsamnes*.
Speake *Ariene*, call to him *Mandane*. [1370]
   Arie. You owe him, Sir, the honour of your Court;
Slaves had defil'd our Husbands beds, and we
Brought forth a Race of unlike Children, to
Blemish your Realme, and us; when now by him
Wee're all preserv'd immaculate and spotlesse, [1375]
As tender Votaries.
   Mand. Consider next,
No heated rage hath snatch'd a sacred Goblet
From any Altar, to profane it with
The streames of bold intemperance; no cryes
Of Virgins came unto your Eares; you've liv'd [1380]
This while as safe, as if you had beene guarded
By the revengefull Thunderer.
   Arsam. I may not
Afflict him with a Court'sie; it can't be
A Guift, that he must be compell'd to take.
   Crat. 'Tis the best time to fall, when there are most [1385]
Requests made for our preservation.
Though, great *Atossa*, I could wish that your
Blest Pray'rs were spent in gaining a good peace
For hopelesse Ephesus. The Gods that doe
Require my ruine, would accept their safety. [1390]
   Arsam. He durst not be so bold, unlesse h'were Innocent.
   Atos. Will you be so ungratefull then, *Cratander*,
As after all to cast away your selfe?
Forbid him good *Arsamnes*, by these Teares

I aske you:—but I am too womanish. [1395]
   Oron. Your Majestie is not Rock: you had a Nurse
That was no Tyger; looke but up upon her.
   Hyd. Can you deny ought, when the Soule is powr'd
Out at the eyes in a Petition?
   Arsam. Cratander, live; we doe command thee, Live. [1400]
   Crat. Beare witnesse ô yee Gods, that I doe suffer
This as his Servant too. And yee the Soules
Of my deceased Country-men, who fell
In the last Battle, if there yet be sense
In the forgetfull Urne, know that it was [1405]
No stratagem of mine to be detayn'd
Thus long from your Society. Now to you,
Arsamnes: Good Kings equall those in Lawes
Whom they have overcome in war; and to
The Valiant, that chiefe part of good, to which [1410]
We all are borne, sweet Liberty, is pleasing
Ev'n in the Enemy. Your Queene, and others
Her Ladyes here, with the most beautifull
Part of your Royall Court, are in my pow'r.
But farre be't from me t'injure but the meanest: [1415]
Only one life I'm so much Master of,
(Since you have put it in my Pow'r) that I
Must give it backe againe, if it must be
Beyond the Ephesian safety: the Altar comes
More welcome than the Throne, if this shall bring [1420]
Freedome to me, and Slav'ry to my City.
   Atos. Here I must dwell, *Arsamnes*, ty'd by great
And solemne Vowes, (our Gods do now require it)
Till you shall grant that the Ephesians may
Still freely use their antient Customes, changing [1425]
Neither their Rites nor Lawes, yet still reserving
This honest Pow'r unto your Royall selfe,
To command only what the free are wont
To undergoe with gladnesse. I presume
You scorne to have them subject as your owne, [1430]
And vile as strangers. Tyrants conquer thus.
   Arsam. It is a time of Mercy; you have only
Call'd forth those Favours which were freely comming.
These generous thoughts have added to our Conquest.

It is no Victory, that's got upon [1435]
The sluggish, and the abject. Descend then;
And when wee've joyn'd our hands, as Pledges of
Our hearts combining so, let us returne
To th'Celebration of an equall Triumph,
In an united marriage of our joyes. [1440]
  Crat. There, I confesse a Conquest, where I finde
He that subdu'd my body, gaines my minde.
              (*Ex. Arsam. and Lords, as to the Ladyes.*

Act. 5. Sce. 4.

Molops, Philotas, Stratocles, Leocrates,
            Archippus.

  Mol. Nay, remember you kick'd me Gentlemen.
  Arch. Faith Landlord *Molops*, I'd have
sworne thou hadst beene of a better Nature, than to re- [1445]
member Pot-quarrels.
By my troth I should have kick'd my Father in that humour.
  Mol. Well, you collogue now: say I should present you to
Arsamnes and *Cratander*, what would you doe?
  Leoc. Only welcome their returne with a Dance, that so [1450]
we might friske into Liberty.
  Mol. Yes, and kicke me againe.
  Str. Dost thou thinke we are Rogues and Villaines?
  Mol. Well, with all my heart, but upon this Condition,
that you unty neither Leg, nor Arme; you know *Cratanders* [1455]
charge.
  Phil. Dost thou thinke wee'd bring thee into any danger?
We have study'd the Figure, and the Measure already.
  Mol. You must let the two old women dance with you.
  Phil. Who, the two whores that *Cratander* committed? [1460]
  Mol. The very same. They are wondrous sutable now:
for you must know, that when such slippery Eeles doe come
under my fingers, the first thing that I doe, is to strip 'em, and
to put 'em into other cases. You'le make a most perfect
Gobline's Masque among you. [1465]
  Str. Why? they will fall in peeces, if they stirre but any
thing violently.

Mol. No matter for falling in peeces; I'le pawne my word to you, they shall not sweat.

Leoc. Any thing, good honest *Molops*, we are content. [1470]

Mol. You, within there, Polecats; do y'heare? I have procur'd so much of the Gentlemen, hold your breaths be sure, and remember you doe not drowne the Musicke with your Coughing. (*Exeunt.*

Act. 5. Sce. 5.

6th Appearance, the Court againe.

Arsamnes, Cratander, Atossa, Lords and Ladyes as Victorious; to them after a while Molops.

Ars. Whiles thus we're joyn'd we are too hard for fortune, [1475]
Scarce Heav'n it selfe can hurt us, for it will not.
There's no care now remaining, but t'invent
New pleasures. Let the houres wheele swiftly away
In sports and Dances. Then we pay the Gods
Best thanks, when we doe shew most sense of joy. [1480]

To them Molops.

Mol. I have an humble suit to your Majesty in the behalfe of some distressed people.

Arsam. Let's heare't: what is't?

Mol. There are halfe a dozen of sinners at the doore, foure of them are the Captives which your Majesty refus'd: [1485]
two of 'em are of another Sexe, but would willingly joyne with'em, and present you with a Dance, in congratulation of your happinesse.

Arsam. Goe, bring 'em in, let Prisons this day know
The joyes of Palaces. We will receive (*Ex. Mol.* [1490]
All the delights the world can yeeld us. Hearke.

The foure Slaves as they were sent to Prison, and the two whores are presented by Molops. They dance in their Cripple Postures.

Atos. I hope your Majesty will not deny
To grace a Company of younger Ladyes,
With the like favourable eye.

Act V, Scene vi]   THE ROYAL SLAVE   247

Arsam. They doe
Honour our joyes in condescending to   [1495]
Be Actors in their Celebration.
  The Ladyes in a solemne march, present themselves all in
    war-like habits, and dance: the whole Dance expres-
    sing these verses of Claudian.
      Insonuit cum verbere signa magister,
    Mutatosque edunt pariter tunc pectora motus,
    In latus allisis clypeis, aut rursus in altum
    Vibratis, grave parma sonat mucronis acutum
    Murmur, & umbonum pulsu modulante resultans
    Ferreus alterno concentus plauditur ictu.
Arsam. I see that *Sardis* hath it's *Amazons*:
An Army of these would subdue the world.

Act. 5. Sce. 6.

To them
1. Priest.

1. Priest. The fire is fully kindled, and the people
All in their festivall attire; there wants   [1500]
Only the Sacrifice, and your selfe to kill it.
  Arsam. The voyce of Ravens in the dead of night
Conveighs not harsher notes into mine eares.
I've pardon'd him.
  1. Priest. You cannot, unlesse you
Will be more impious in preserving him,   [1505]
Than you were valorous in conquering.
  Arsam. Will not the Gods receive an Hecatombe
Of Oxen in exchange? may we not finde
The Destiny's in Beasts entralls? we will choake
The fire with weighty lumps of richer gummes,   [1510]
And send perfum'd clouds up into their seates
In one continued thankefulnesse, if that
They'le spare this humane Sacrifice.
  1. Priest. To promise
The fairest Captive, and redeeme him with
A Beast, or Teare of some relenting Tree,   [1515]
Is not to worship, but delude.

Arsam. *Cratander*,
The Gods recall my courtesy; I stand
Doubly ingag'd, to Heav'n, and to thee;
But thou canst easier pardon; for I know
Thy Vertue's such, that thou hadst rather suffer [1520]
Thy selfe, than Heav'n should be violated.
Being then this sword must cut thy pretious thread,
If Statues may preserve thee, and thou thinkst it
A life to florish in faire memory,
I'le people all my Kingdome with thy Images, [1525]
To which they shall pay vowes, as to those Gods
Who now require thy company.
  Atos. Yee Powers,
Why are you growne thus cruell unto Vertue?
'T will be a wish hereafter to be foule.
I cannot see him die, and live my selfe. [1530]
Pray you defer his death a while, don't post him
Away; perhaps the Gods may spare him yet.
  Crat. I know that divers mindes are here contain'd
Under one silence, all expecting how
I'le beare this sudden accident. T'accuse [1535]
Or Gods, or Men, 's the part of him that would
Live longer. If I looke on the desires
Of some here, whensoever I shall fall,
I shall be thought t'have liv'd too little: if
On the Actions I have done, I've liv'd enough: [1540]
If on the injuries of Fortune, too much:
If on mine honour, and my fame, I shall
Live still; he gaines by death that doth die prays'd.
Others have longer kept an Empire, but
None better left it. To speake more, were but [1545]
A sluggard's Policy, to defer his suffrings.
On to the Altar.
  Arsam. Art thou willing too?
Curs'd be my Victory! and thou my Sword
Be never henceforth happy, if there be
Another Sacrifice to fall like this. [1550]
Witnesse yee Gods, how I unwilling pay
My vowes in kinde. Most vertuous *Cratander*,
(Worthy of Heav'n, but yet to tarry longer,
And make Earth happy by thy presence,) looke;

Act V, Scene vii] THE ROYAL SLAVE

These teares I pay thee as a sad farewell. [1555]
I feele the blow my selfe that I must give thee.
  Crat. These teares doe neither befit you to pay,
Nor me to take; be then *Arsamnes*, on.
  Arsam. I feele a numnesse seize me; I am stone;
I shall not lift mine arme against thee. Sure [1560]
The Gods desire it not.   (*Exeunt.*

Act. 5. Sce. 7.

7th Appearance, the Temple again discover'd, an Altar, and one busie placing fire thereon.

Enter Molops bearing the Sagar, then the 4 Slaves, 2 by 2; next the 4 Lords, then 4 Priests: after them Cratander alone, then the King and Queene, next Mandane and Ariene, last the Masquers: they all solemnely goe round the Stage, and having placed themselves, Cratander standing by the Altar, a Priest singes the first song.

1. Priest. *Thou ô bright Sun who seest all,*
    Looke downe upon our Captives fall.
    Never was purer Sacrifice:
    'Tis not a Man, but Vertue dyes. [1565]
Cho. *While thus we pay our thankes, propitious be;*
    And grant us either Peace or Victory.

After the Song, *Molops* delivers the Sagar to *Arsamnes*, and *Cratander* kneeles downe at the Altar; then another Priest sings the second Song.

2. Priest. *But thou ô Sun mayst set, and then*
    In brightnesse rise next morne agen.
    He, when he shall once leave this light, [1570]
    Will make and have eternall night.
Cho. *Good deedes may passe for Sacrifice, ô than*
    Accept the Vertues, and give backe the Man.

8th Appearance, the Sun eclipsed, and a showre of raine dashing out the fire.

Whiles the last Chorus is singing, the Sunne appeares eclipsed, &c. After the Song Arsamnes prepares to give the stroke, but is interrupted by the Priest.

2. Priest. Hold, hold *Arsamnes*;
Heav'n is not pleased with your Sacrifice.
The glorious Sun hath veyl'd his face in clouds
Not willing to behold it, and the skyes
Have shed such numerous teares, as have put out
The fire though fully kindled.
  Atos. Thou hast now,
The voyce and visage of the Gods, good Priest.
The Heav'ns were never more serene. The Gods
Have justify'd my care, *Cratander*.
  Arsam. Happy newes,
Death sends thee backe unto us; this comes not
From any humane pow'r; 'tis not my hand
That spares thee, blest *Cratander*, 'tis some God,
Some God reserves thee unto greater workes
For us, and for thy Country.
  Crat. Being then
You so interpret it, I'le thus divide
That life they lend me, one halfe shall be yours,
The other Ephesus's, that mine Actions
Wearing both Gratitude and Piety,
Like to some well wrought Picture, may at once
Behold both you, and that. 'T shall ne're be said,
The Gods reserv'd *Cratander* to a crime,
To make him fall more foule.
  Arsam. Thy faith hath beene
So firme and try'd, thy moderation
So stayd, that in a just reward I must
My selfe conduct thee into Greece, and there
Continue thee a King; that what was meant
For sport and mirth, may prove a serious honour;
And thy Three Dayes passe o're into a long
And happy government; to be rul'd by thee
Will be as freedome to them; 'twill not be
Accounted slavery to admit a Prince
Chosen from out themselves: thy Vertues there
May shine, as in their proper Spheare. Let others
  When they make warre, have this ignoble end
  To gaine 'em Slaves, *Arsamnes* gaines a Friend.

FINIS.

THE EPILOGVE
to the
KING & QVEENE.

Crat.   *Those glorious Triumphs of the Persian Court*
Are honour'd much in being made your sport.
The Slave though freed by th'King, and his Priest too,
Thinkes not his Pardon good, till seal'd by you:
And hopes, although his faults have many beene, [5]
To finde here too the favour of a Queene.
For 'tis our forward duty that hath showne
These loyall faults in honour to your Throne.
Great joy doth bring some madnesse with it still;
We challenge that as title to doe ill. [10]
   Can you expect then perfect motion, where
'Tis the Digression only of our Spheare
Which wheeles in this new course, t'expresse the sense
Of your approach, it's best Intelligence?
O were you still fix'd to it! your resort, [15]
Makes us desire an everlasting Court.
And though wee've read you o're so long, that we
Begin to know each line of Majesty,
We thinke you snatch'd too soone, and grieve, as they
Who for an halfe yeare's night, part with their day. [20]
And shall, till your returne, though you appeare
In favours still, thinke darkenesse in our Spheare.
   Your sight will be preserv'd yet, though you rise:
   When e're you goe, Great Sir, hearts will have eyes.

THE EPILOGVE
to the
VNIVERSITY.

Arsam.　Thus cited to a second night, wee've here
Ventur'd our Errours to your weighing Eare.
Wee'd thought they'd have beene dead, as soone as borne;
For Dreames doe seldome live untill the morne.
　　There's difference 'twixt a Colledge and a Court;　　　　[5]
The one expecteth Science, th'other sport.
Parts should be Dialogues there, but Poynts to you:
They looke for pleasing, you for sound, and true.
We feare then we have injur'd those, whose Age
Doth make the Schooles the measure of the Stage:　　　　[10]
And justly thence for want of Logicke darts,
May dread those sturdy Yeomen of the Arts.
　　We are not trayn'd yet to the Trade, none's fit
To fine for Poet, or for Player yet.
We hope you'le like it then, although rough fil'd;　　　　[15]
As the Nurse loves the lisping of the child.
　　The Slave (then truly Royall, if you shall
By your smiles too redeeme him from his fall)
Hopes you'le dismisse him so, that he may sweare,
One Court being gone, he found another here.　　　　[20]
　　Though rays'd from Slave to King, he vowes he will
　　Resume his former Bonds, and be yours still.

The Epilogue to their Majesties at *Hampton-Court*.

The unfil'd Author, though he be assur'd,
That a bad Poet is a thing secur'd,
Feare's yet he may miscarry, for some doe
Having just nothing, loose that nothing too.
His comfort's yet, that though the Incense fly [5]
Foule and unwelcome, and so scatter'd die,
Neither the blot nor sinne can on him stand,
Being the Censer's in another hand.
For though the Peece be now mark'd his, and knowne,
Yet the Repeaters make that Peece their owne. [10]
Being then a new Reciter some way is
Another Author, we are thus made his.
Wee therefore hope nothing shall here be seene
To make the Slave appeale from King or Queene:
From your selves here, t'your selves at Oxford; *grace* [15]
And favour altring with the time and Place,
So that some thence may deeme it happy fell
There only, where you meant to take all well.
'Tis then your Countenance that is the price
Must redeeme this, and free the Captive twice. [20]
He feares ill fate the lesse, in that if you
Now kill him, you kill your owne favour too.
   How e're he will not 'gainst injustice cry;
   For you who made him live, may make him dy.

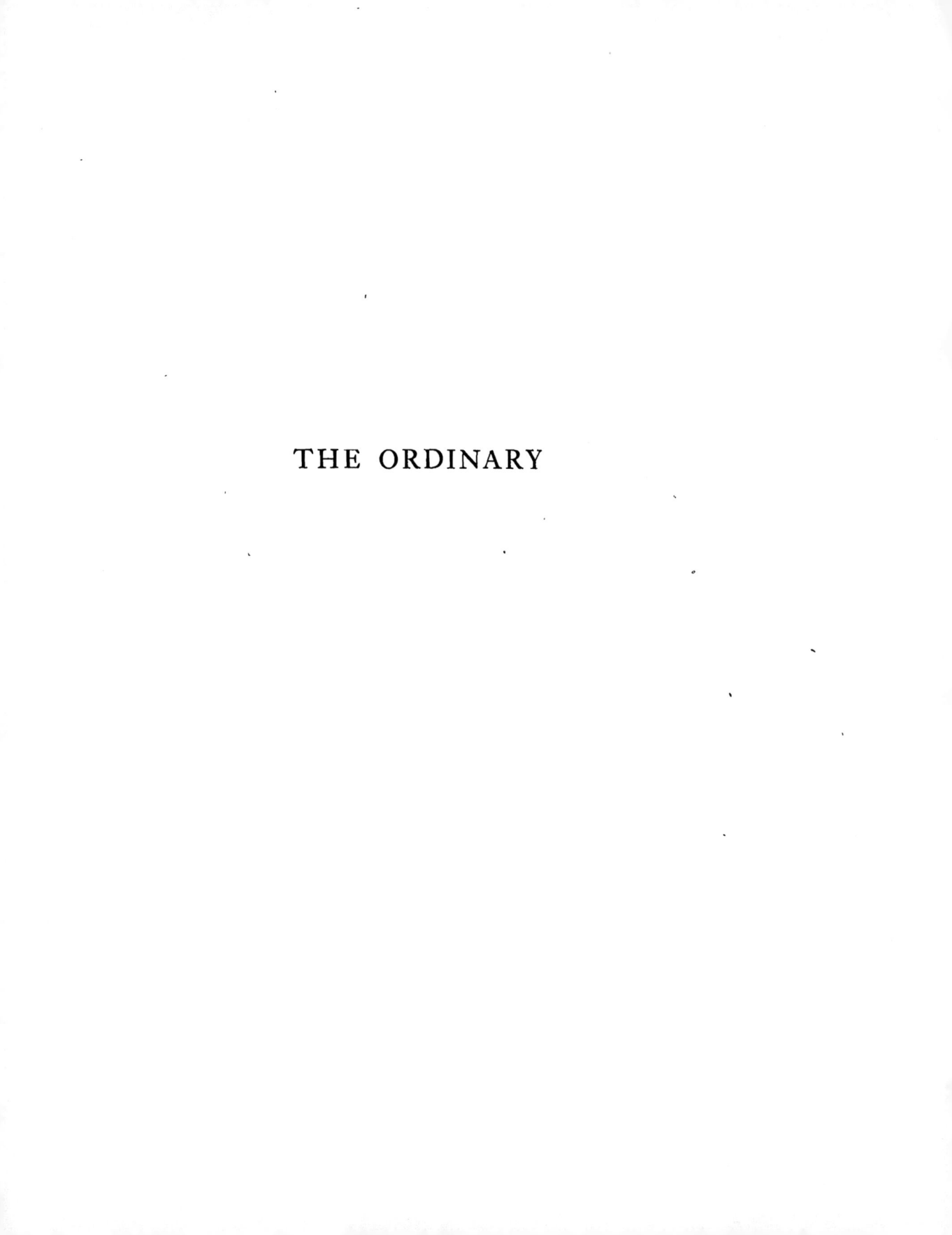

THE ORDINARY

INTRODUCTION

1. THE TEXT

THE ORDINARY was first printed in the *Works* (1651), after being entered by Moseley on the Stationers' Register on May 4, 1648, under the title "*The Citty Cozener, or, The Ordinary,*" and designated as a tragicomedy in common with *The Lady-Errant* and *The Siege*. A transcript of the separate title-page and a signature collation may be found in the notes to the play. *The Ordinary* was reprinted for the first time by Robert Dodsley in the tenth volume of his *Select Collection of Old Plays* (1744). Dodsley modernized the spelling and punctuation. Each of the three successive editors of Dodsley's collection, Reed (1780), Collier (1826), and Hazlitt (1875), retain Cartwright's play. Reed's edition (1780) includes some excellent notes, some of which were contributed by Steevens and S. Pegge. They were reprinted in the two later editions and are incorporated in the notes to the present edition. A fifth edition of *The Ordinary* appeared in 1810 in the third volume of *The Ancient British Drama*. It is, however, merely a reprint, with no attempt at editing, of Reed's 1780 text, notes and all.[1]

My own text has been based on a collation of four copies of the 1651 edition. Any variations from that text are recorded in the Textual Notes. Of the modern editions, it has been thought sufficient to collate only Dodsley's and Hazlitt's in their entirety, Dodsley's as representing the earliest edited text of the play, Hazlitt's as representing the culmination of an editorial tradition. In each case, however, where Dodsley or Hazlitt differs from the 1651 text or where they differ from each other, the variant has been traced in the two intervening editions of Reed and Collier. The text of the 1810 reprint of Reed has been ignored. The readings of the various editors have been recorded in the Textual Notes. Dodsley is desig-

---

[1]. Miss Erma R. Gebhardt's text ("An edition of William Cartwright's *The Ordinary*. With critical introduction and notes." Unpublished B. Litt. thesis, Oxford, 1932) is a reproduction of the 1651 text with occasional editorial corrections. Miss Gebhardt's more important readings are recorded in the Textual Notes, designated as *G*.

nated as *D*, Reed as *R*, Collier as *C*, and Hazlitt as *H*. Obvious corrections made in the 1651 text are not as a rule traced through the later editions.

All of the five lyrics in *The Ordinary* appeared later in seventeenth-century miscellanies. For texts see the notes to each lyric. Goffin reprints all the lyrics as well as the Prologue and Epilogue in his edition of the *Poems* (1918). The readings of these texts are recorded among the variants of the modern editions of the play. Also included with the variant readings is a complete transcription of the deletions, additions, and changes made for the Restoration revival of *The Ordinary* in 1671.

2. Date of Composition and Stage History

The Ordinary[2] represents Cartwright's only excursion into the field of pure comedy, a step which he himself admits was a venturous one, and which some later writers have described as fatal. But the voice of critical opinion has not been entirely unanimous. William Oldys, for example, in his manuscript notes to Langbaine's *Account*, writes: "*The Ordinary* is an excellent play; and finely exposes the Puritanical spirit of the times," a remark which may be scored against Ward's judgment that the play is "one of the least enjoyable productions of its kind."[3] My own opinion is that Cartwright's comedy may be compared favorably with almost any nearly contemporary production in its own genre of realistic, middle-class comedy. Certainly among the other writers who devoted their major literary energies to plays in the Platonic or cavalier mode, Cartwright can hold his head high. Comedy, however, was not the forte of these men,[4] but it seems to have served very largely as a kind of safety valve for what they considered their more serious work.

---

2. In Moseley's entry of the *Works* (1651) in the Stationers' Register (May 4, 1648) the play is called *The Citty Cozener, or, The Ordinary*, and is wrongly designated as a tragicomedy. See *A Transcript of the Registers of the Worshipful Company of Stationers; from 1640-1708*, ed. G. E. B. Eyre (1913), I, 295.

3. A. W. Ward, *History of English Dramatic Literature* (1899), III, 140. Miss Gebhardt (Thesis, *The Ordinary*) draws attention to a criticism of *The Ordinary* made by Charles Kingsley in "Plays and Puritans" (*Works*, 1890, XII, 65). "As for his humour, he, alas! can be dirty like the rest, when necessary: but humour he has of the highest quality. 'The Ordinary' is full of it; and Moth, the Antiquary, though too much of a lay figure, and depending for his amusingness on his quaint antiquated language, is such a sketch as Mr. Dickens need not have been ashamed to draw."

4. A. Harbage, *Cavalier Drama* (1936), p. 72.

However this may be, there are several scenes in *The Ordinary* any one of which, considered in itself, must have offered extremely good theater. Among the most notable are the *flite* between the widow and her three unwilling suitors (I, ii); the mock quarrel of the Clubbers (III, iv); and the reported confession of Sir Thomas Bitefigg. Each of these scenes is worked up with considerable verve, and the situation is exploited to the full, perhaps a little overexploited.

It seems probable, from internal evidence, that Cartwright completed *The Ordinary* sometime before March 26, 1635. In III, i, the antiquary, Moth, pledges himself to Mistress Potluck in "this tenth of our King," and Charles came to the throne on March 27, 1625.[5] On the evidence of the separate title-page to *The Ordinary*, which reads "Written by / WILLIAM CARTVVRIGHT, / M.A. Ch.Ch. Oxon." instead of, as in the case of the four other separate titles, "Written by / Mr WILLIAM CARTVVRIGHT, / Late Student of *Christ-Church* in / OXFORD, and Proctor of / the *Vniversity*," Fleay suggests that the play was written and presented, in honor of the occasion,[6] when Cartwright received his M.A. (April 15, 1635). The suggestion is sound and conflicts with none of the rather meager facts. Certainly the play seems to have been first presented before an academic audience; whether it was later revived for the royal party during the Oxford sequestration we do not know.

During the Commonwealth *The Ordinary* met with a not uncommon fate. Certain portions were lifted out of their context and, with a few changes and additions, turned into drolls, or more properly speaking, dialogues. Three such dialogues made their appearance in John Cotgrave's *Wits Interpreter, or the English Parnassus* (1655). Two of the three adapt the scene between the widow,

---

5. First pointed out by S. Pegge in his note to the passage in Reed's Dodsley (1780), X, 250. Miss Gebhardt (Thesis, *The Ordinary*, pp. xxxvi–xxxvii) suggests that lines 24–30 of the second Prologue to *The Royal Slave* glance back at, and apologize for, the anti-Puritan and possibly personal satire of parts of *The Ordinary*. If this is so, it definitely places the composition of *The Ordinary* before that of *The Royal Slave*.

6. Fleay, *Biographical Chronicle*, I, 48. Miss Gebhardt (Thesis, *The Ordinary*, pp. xxxiv–xxxv), presumably following out Fleay's suggestion, observes: "The writing of a play was no longer required of a candidate for the Master's degree but there is evidence that he occasionally presented one." She then notices two poems by Martin Lluellyn in his *Men-Miracles* (1646), one entitled, "To my Lord B. of Ch. when I presented him a Play" (p. 77); the other, "To *Dr. F.* Deane of Ch. Ch. now Vice-Chancellour of *Oxford*, upon the Same occasion" (p. 80), which begins:

Not that I begge degree, as understood,
To bring a *Trifle* and receive a *Hood*.

Mistress Potluck, and her unwilling admirers (I, ii); the third is based on the scene between the booby, Andrew Credulous, and Mistress Jane (IV, iii).[7] Three more such dialogues were printed in *The Marrow of Complements* (1655),[8] two again dealing with the Potluck-suitor scene. Since all these dialogues may be consulted in full in the notes to *The Ordinary*, it will be sufficient to notice here, as an example of the general type to which they all belong, a single title: "A Sportive Complementall Interlocution (The Adolescent being willing for ever to frustrate her hopes whom he hath (seemingly) assented to Marry.) A Dialogue supposed betweene *Juvenillio* and *Thais.*"

The Ordinary was revived after the Restoration, and a prompt copy for this revival has recently been discovered. The play was licensed to be acted by the Duke's Company late in 1671[9] by Herbert, whose license, written entirely in his own hand, reads:

> This Comedy, called th [*sic*] Ordinary
> the Reformations observed
> nay [*sic*] bee Acted, not otherwise.
> January 15. 1671
>
>   Henry Herbert
>   M R.

Herbert's moral blue-pencil found more to work on in *The Ordinary* than in *The Lady-Errant*. Here again, however, the play was politically harmless, and his principal efforts had to content themselves with oaths and bawdry. Like the Constable in the play itself, Herbert would have "no Advowtry in my Ward But what is honest." Even then Homer nodded, and we find a line like, "Pox!— Plague!— Hell!— Death!— Damn'd luck!" (l. 1634) left unscathed, while only two lines below a quite harmless "Heaven" is ruthlessly expunged. Only a single deletion in either *The Ordinary* or *The Lady-Errant* shows evidence of Herbert's characteristic method of cutting (ll. 107–9).[10] Sir Henry was by this time an old man, and it is likely

---

7. Pp. 81–83, 84–87, 88–90. The first of these has three speakers so that it cannot strictly be called a dialogue.

8. Pp. 59–61, 72–73, 88–91. In addition to these a few words are taken from one of Moth's speeches (ll. 999–1000) and inserted in "An Amorovs Dialogve, Managed betweene John Medly a Tyler. and Jone Simper-Sudds a Farmers Daughter" (p. 48).

9. Although the Duke's Company is not mentioned in the present license, it is specifically named in Herbert's license for *The Lady-Errant*.

10. I owe this information to Dr. W. B. Van Lennep.

88 The ORDINARY.

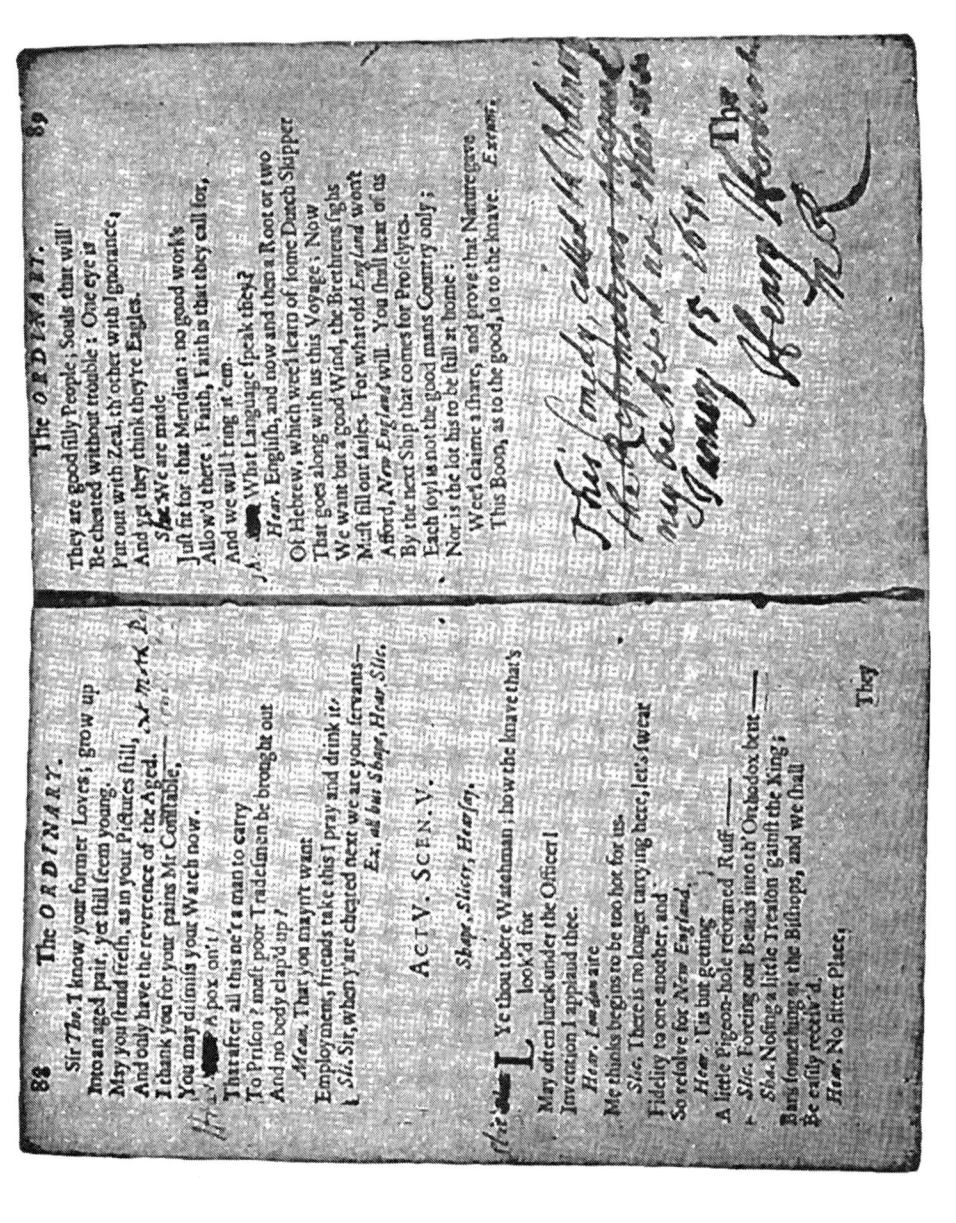

Sir *Tho.* I know your former Loves; grow up
Into an aged pair, yet still seem young;
May you stand fresh, as in your Pictures still,
And only have the reverence of the Aged.
I thank you for your pains Mr Constable.
You may dismiss your Watch now.

Hear. A pox on't!
That after all this ne'r a man to carry
To Prison? must poor Tradesmen be brought out
And no body clap'd up?

Mean. That you mayn't want
Employments, friends take this I pray and drink it.

Sli. Sir, when y'are cheated next we are your servants—
Ex. all but Shape, Hearsay, Slic.

ACT V. SCEN. V.

Shape, Slicer, Hearsay.

L— Ye'tho' there Watchman; how the knave that's
look'd for
May often lurck under the Officer I
Invention I applaud thee.

Hear. I wonder are
Me thinks begins to be too hot for us.

Slic. There is no longer tarrying here; let us sweat
Fidelity to one another, and
So relieve for *New England*.

Hear. Us but getting

A little Pigeon-hole restored Ruff———
Slic. Forcing our Beards into th' Orthodox bent———
Slic. Nosing a little Treason 'gainst the King;
Bait something at the Bishops, and we shall
Be easily receiv'd.

Hear. No fitter Place;

They

The ORDINARY. 89

They are good silly People: Souls that will
Be cheated without trouble: One eye is
Put out with Zeal, th' other with ignorance,
And yet they think they're Eagles.

Shap. We are made
Just fit for that Meridian: no good work's
Allow'd there. Faith, Faith's that they call loss,
And we will ring it em.

Hear. What Language speak they?

Shap. English; and now and then a Root or two
Of Hebrew, which we'el learn of some *Dutch* Skipper
That goes along with us this Voyage; Now
We want but a good Wind, the Brethren's fights
Must fill our sails. For what old *England* won't
Afford, *New England* will. You shall hear of us
By the next Ship (hat comes for Pro slyte—
Each soyle is not the good mans Country only;
Nor is the lot this to be stull at home:
We'el claime it there, and prove that Nature gave
This Boon, as to the good, so to the knave. *Exeunt.*

This Comedy called the Ordinary
the Reviewed may bee Acted
may bee Acted new 26 1669
January 15. 1671
The
Henry Herbert

Two pages from the Restoration prompt copy of *The Ordinary*, showing Sir Henry Herbert's autograph license, the reviser's hand, and reassignment of roles. Reproduced through the kindness of Professor T. W. Baldwin.

INTRODUCTION

that the principal work of the office fell to the lot of his deputy assistant, Edward Hayward. This particular passage, however, dealing with the church and religion, was well calculated to catch his eye. On the score of morality as a whole, it is safe to say that as much bawdry was left untouched as was censored. Whether the quite extraneous scene (IV, iv) between Shape, the Mercer, and the Chirurgion was deleted by Herbert because of its moral implications or by the players in an effort to shorten the play, I cannot say. The odds, however, are on the players. As a censor of Restoration comedy Herbert's sensibilities to the "terrible double entendre" must have been anaesthetized. Thus, on the whole, his deletions reflect perhaps more distaste for the rather raw physical terms which Cartwright, as a representative of an earlier and less "refined" society, occasionally employs, than for actual indecency.[11]

The Ordinary as a play was naturally better fitted for the Restoration stage than *The Lady-Errant*. In spite of its length only two scenes are wholly omitted: the one noticed above (IV, iv)—a scene which cannot properly be said to form any integral part of the play, and a short scene (V, i) between Sir Thomas Bitefigg and his daughter Jane. In the last act the order of some of the entrances is altered. Lines 2376-2434 are inserted following line 2256. This change is I believe a real improvement, since it allows the action to run uninterruptedly to its natural climax. In the original the later entrance of Mistress Jane, the wife-to-be of Meanwell, disturbs the bustle of the final action. It is a little difficult to account for the omission of Priscilla's rather immodest song in III, iv—a song in the typical Restoration manner. The deletion, moreover, seems to be undoubtedly the work of the players. Probably it was merely replaced by a popular topical song. Surprisingly enough, Moth's speeches, which one would expect to find heavily cut, escape almost untouched. The role of Slicer was apparently played by one of the principal comedians, and the lion's share of Shape's part, particularly in the reported-confession scene (V, ii), is given over to him.

In the matter of scenery *The Ordinary* need not have put the Duke's Company to any particular expense. No scene was called for which was not presumably in common stock. I do not quite understand the distinction made in the prompt copy between the first and second

---

11. The fact that we do not know to what extent Herbert was himself responsible for these deletions makes it difficult to be entirely consistent in our discussion of them.

scenes of Act I. The action in both according to the text seems to pass in the same place; yet the scenes are marked "New hall" and "New Ordinary" respectively. I also do not understand the exact meaning of "New" as applied to these scenes, unless it refers to a newly made stage set. Only two other changes of scene are called for, both exteriors: Covent Garden and Red Lion Fields. That stock scenery was used, at least in part, is shown by this last scene in Red Lion Fields. No hint of such a location is found in the play.

A prologue and an epilogue for the revival of *The Ordinary* have been preserved. They are printed in *A Collection of Poems Written upon several Occasions* (1673),[12] with the headings "Prologue *to the Ordinary*" and "Epilogue *to the Ordinary*." Before the recent discovery of the Restoration prompt copy, I was not altogether certain that these verses should be attributed to a revival of Cartwright's *Ordinary*. Judged by internal evidence alone they might have been written for almost any play, and Richard Brome's *The Damoiselle, or the New Ordinary* (printed in 1653) was in many respects a more likely candidate. In the light of our present knowledge, however, there seems to be no doubt that this prologue and epilogue represent part of the 1671 revival of Cartwright's play.[13]

3. Sources

The Ordinary is certainly the least original of Cartwright's four plays. Indeed a study of its sources has already served as the subject of a German doctoral thesis by Friedrich Gerber,[14] and Miss Erma Gebhardt has added substantially to Mr. Gerber's findings.[15] Even

---

12. Pp. 163–68. Both Prologue and Epilogue are reprinted in the notes to *The Ordinary*.

13. These verses are immediately preceded by a seemingly related "*Prologue at Oxford*" (p. 161), in which two lines from the "Prologue *to the Ordinary*" are repeated (see the notes). It may be observed that the prologues and epilogues of both *The Lady-Errant* and *The Ordinary* appear to have been completely ignored by the Restoration players, at least none of them bears any mark of deletion or alteration. But in view of the topical nature of such productions, this was only to be expected.

14. Friedrich Gerber, *The Sources of William Cartwright's Comedy* "The Ordinary" (Berne, 1909). Almost half of Mr. Gerber's study is devoted to a discussion of the ordinaries of seventeenth-century London; pages 39–82 deal with Cartwright's play. A later, briefer study of Cartwright's indebtedness to Jonson in *The Ordinary* may be consulted in Mina Kerr's *Influence of Ben Jonson on English Comedy, 1598–1642* (1912), pp. 93–100.

15. I regret to say that Miss Gebhardt's thesis (see note 1, above) only came to my notice just as I had completed my manuscript for the press. For this reason my acknowledgements to her work are less complete than they

so, the full extent of Cartwright's indebtedness has not been reckoned up; nor does the present study, though it piles up a further tale of debts, pretend to exhaust the subject. In apology for Cartwright, it can only be said that a similarly unkind study might be made of a great majority of the comedies produced during the 1630's.

It is generally agreed that in *The Ordinary* Cartwright is following in the footsteps of his revered poetical father, Ben Jonson. Perhaps it would be more truthful to say that, like other "sons," he is following *after* Jonson. Judged by Jonsonian "humour" standards it might be difficult to single out from the list of stock dramatis personae any very specific "humour" characters, though, with some apology to Jonson, Moth, the antiquary, and Sir Christopher, the curate, might be so dignified. Assuredly the general plot conception of the comedy is Jonsonian, for it is based more or less directly on an adaptation of *The Alchemist* (1610); moreover, the realistic tone and London setting both reflect Jonson's influence, though perhaps at second hand. On the other side, it must be admitted that Cartwright does not seem to pay any particular attention to "that connexion [liaison des scènes] which the Incomparable *Johnson* first taught the Stage,"[16] or to the unities of time and place. In such sins of omission, however, Cartwright's usage was the rule, not the exception.[17]

The Alchemist (1610) has already been mentioned as one of the important sources of *The Ordinary*.[17a] Without doubt the central idea

---

would otherwise have been; though in cases where Miss Gebhardt has supplied me with new information I have inserted it and credited her with the discovery. And on points of importance where we have independently arrived at the same conclusion I have also tried, so far as was possible, to make reference to her study.

16. Quoted from Shadwell's address "To the Reader," prefixed to *The Royal Shepherdesse*, 1699 (*Works*, ed. M. Summers, I, 99).

17. In his *Essay on the Dramatic Writings of Massinger* (printed in *The Plays of Philip Massinger*, ed. William Gifford, 3rd edition, 1840) John Ferriar writes: "Cartwright, who was confessedly a man of great erudition, is not more attentive to the unities than any other poet of that age." It is to be presumed that Ferriar does not include Jonson in this sweeping criticism. Ferriar several times in the course of this essay couples the names of Cartwright and Jonson, speaking of them as of equals.

17a. Another play, *The Fary Knight, or Oberòn the Second*, which depends even more extensively on *The Alchemist* than Cartwright's, must be noticed here. It has only recently (1942) been printed by Professor F. T. Bowers, who attributes it with great likelihood to Thomas Randolph. Mr. Bowers suggests 1622–24, with preference for 1623–24, as the date of Randolph's original version and believes that the play was first performed as a school production at Westminster. While we do not know the exact date of Cartwright's entrance at Westminster, it is reasonably certain that it must of using an ordinary as a base of operations for a gang of sharpers and confidence men is taken with little change from Jonson's play, though there, to be sure, the "ordinary" is only an empty house, vacated by the owner under threat of the plague. Cartwright was not content, however, to borrow only the frame for his play from this comedy, but saw fit to appropriate several other major incidents and numerous minor details. The extent of this borrowing will be made clear in the notes.

In his book, *The Cavalier Drama*, Mr. Harbage notices a certain similarity in plot construction and material between Cartwright's *The Ordinary*, Jasper Mayne's *The City-Match*, and Cowley's *The Guardian*.[18] All three plays are from a common stock—realistic pictures of London middle-class life—and all contain certain common elements: a pair of bravoes who live at an ordinary and who quarrel with the proprietor of the house (in Cowley, as in Cartwright, it is a widow); and a poetaster as one of the bravoes (a penny-poet appears among the "Clubbers" in *The Ordinary*). One or two other minor congruities[19] and a single verbal parallel[20] are

---

have been not later than 1624 (see the General Introduction, p. 9n). If the lower limit of Mr. Bower's date is allowed, Cartwright almost certainly saw *The Fary Knight* and may even have taken part in it, since he did not leave Westminster until 1628. Any influence of this play, therefore, on Cartwright's work would materially strengthen Mr. Bowers argument and such influence may possibly be found in Act IV, Scene ii, of *The Ordinary*, where Have-at-all, on the lookout for a victim on whom to try out his magically acquired valor, waylays the unfortunate Moth, gives him a thorough drubbing, and is about to run him through when interrupted and pacified by Slicer and Hearsay. In the same way in *The Fary Knight* (V.ii. 1405-1506), Losserello, who likewise thinks he has been rendered courageous (or at least invulnerable) by magic means, falls foul of Politico, takes him prisoner, and is about to execute him when he is prevented by Snap, one of the two servants of Craft, the Cheater.

Though so far the evidence for some kind of relationship between the two plays seems satisfactory enough, the whole problem is considerably complicated by the revamping which *The Fary Knight* underwent at the hands of some later writer with heavy borrowings from Shirley's *Young Admiral* (acted 1633, printed 1637) and *The Traitor* (1631). After a careful weighing of the evidence, however, Mr. Bowers concludes that "There is no evidence (although the theory is quite possible) to show that the augmenter added any part of the plot, or any entire scene, not present in Randolph's version," though "some of the dialogue in his [Losserello's] combat with Politico must have been added by the augmenter" (p. xli).

18. P. 74. Miss Gebhardt (Thesis, *The Ordinary*, pp. xliii-xliv) points out that Mayne's *City-Match* is modeled directly on Jonson's *Silent Woman*.

19. There is a gull in Mayne's *City-Match* named Timothy, whose father, like Andrew's in *The Ordinary*, has imprisoned the father of the hero for debt; Timothy, however, though he is thor-

noticed below. In neither, however, does the principal action take place at the ordinary, and the romantic plots, though stereotyped enough, bear no close resemblance to the Meanwell-Jane episode in *The Ordinary*. If there is any question of borrowing involved, the culprit would not seem to be Cartwright. Cowley's *Guardian* is certainly much later, having been first performed for Prince Charles on his Cambridge visit of 1641,[21] and *The City-Match* was written not earlier than December of 1634[22] and probably at least a year later, since there is evidence that it was composed in connection with the royal Oxford visit of 1636.[23]

Gerber draws attention to what he considers a similarity between the Meanwell-Jane love plot and the Jasper-Luce episode in Beaumont and Fletcher's *The Knight of the Burning Pestle* (1607).[24] I can see no reason, however, for comparing the two plays, apart from the almost ubiquitous situation, common to both, in which a father favors a foolish, wealthy suitor while his daughter loves a poor but honest man, whom after many crosses and counter-crosses she marries with her father's consent.

Gerber further suggests that Middleton's *Your Five Gallants* (1607/8) may have influenced Cartwright:

The general conception of Meanwell might have been suggested by this play.

---

oughly gulled, is finally honorably married to the hero's sister. Mayne's play also has two money grubbers, Warehouse and Seathrift, who may be compared to Simon Credulous and Sir Thomas Bitefigg.

20. *The City-Match*, I, iii (Hazlitt-Dodsley, XIII, 214):

"Yes, and I
To sleep the sermon in my chain and scarlet."

Compare *The Ordinary*, I, i:

"I shall sleep one day in my Chaine, and Skarlet
At *Spittle*-Sermon."

21. It is interesting to notice that in his revised version of *The Guardian*, which he called *Cutter of Coleman Street* (1661), Cowley omitted both the scene at the ordinary, where the two bravoes dispute with the proprietress over their rent, and the character of the poetaster. Perhaps the notoriety which Cartwright's widow-suitor scene had received from the various dialogues or drolls published during the Commonwealth caused the first of these changes.

22. This date is afforded by a reference (V, ii) to the great frost which gripped the country on December 10, 1634. See Cartwright's poem, "On the great Frost. 1634."

23. Wood, *History and Antiquities of the University of Oxford* (ed. J. Gutch, 1796), II, 413: "Mr. Jasper Maine's Play called the 'City Match,' though not acted at Christ Church before the King and the Court as was intended. . . ." Sir Sidney Lee (*DNB*, XXXVII, 162) would seem to be mistaken when he asserts that Mayne completed *The City-Match* in 1639. Cartwright's influence on Mayne's *Amorous War* (about 1637), has already been noticed.

24. *Sources*, p. 79.

Here, Fitzgrave, in order to win Katherine, the wealthy orphan, who is courted by five gallants, disguises himself as a scholar, and assumes another name. He then mingles with them, learns all their foul intentions, and sees their reprehensible life. To save Katherine from their snares, and to secure his object, he contrives to lay bare all their wicked plans and shameful deeds. He succeeds, by unmasking them in the presence of their respective courtezans, of Katherine, and other persons. In spite of the difference in the details, a few of the general features are similar in both plays.[25]

Though what Mr. Gerber here says is generally true, the very truth of his synopsis tends to destroy the validity of his conclusion. In the first place, Meanwell is already a member of the gang when the play opens and is primarily interested in revenging himself upon the old miser, Simon Credulous, who has caused the ruin of his father; and in the second place, Meanwell has no particular desire to expose the practices of his fellow "complices" to further his love affair with Mistress Jane; that he does so follows purely from the chance of circumstances.

Genest long ago drew attention to the resemblance between Cartwright's scene between the Chirurgion and the Mercer (IV, iv) and two scenes in *The Knave in Graine* (1640), "New Vampt.... Written by J. D. Gent."[26] Miss Gebhardt[27] has collected a number of suggestive verbal parallels between the two scenes (in one of which the situation is closely parallel) and Cartwright's. Her conclusion is that "either *J. D.* wrote two scenes on suggestions obtained from *The Ordinary* or that Cartwright made up one scene from two scenes of *The Knave in Graine*, or from an earlier play which served as a common source." On the whole Miss Gebhardt favors the position that Cartwright and J. D. used material from a common source. In this connection it should be noticed that the general situation can be paralleled in a number of earlier nondramatic analogues, the closest being "How *Scogin* deceived the Draper" in *Scoggin's Jests* (about 1565). The several other analogues are discussed in the notes and an interesting later analogue in Lucas' *Lives of the Gamesters* (1714) seems to lend support to Miss Gebhardt's view of a common source.

---

25. *Ibid.*, pp. 60–61.
26. *English Stage* (1832), IV, 110; X, 115. *The Knave in Graine* also centers one of its two main plots (the one to which "New Vampt" certainly refers) on a group of sharpers who make their headquarters at an ordinary they call "The Leaguer."
27. Thesis, *The Ordinary*, pp. lvi–lxii. Two or three of Miss Gebhardt's verbal parallels are pointed out in the notes.

Finally, some interesting coincidences between the plot of Molière's *L'Avare* (1668) and the Meanwell-Jane love episode in *The Ordinary* deserve to be noticed. In both plays we find the rich, avaricious father and the young lover who, rejected by his mistress's father, returns in disguise and enters into his service, pretending to aid him in his plans for marrying his daughter to a rich but despised suitor, while he really plots to win her for himself.[28] Molière, as Jonson before him in *The Case is Altered* (about 1599), made free use of Plautus' *Aulularia*. The resemblances, however, between *The Ordinary* and *L'Avare* cannot be explained by reference to the *Aulularia*, since none of the common factors is found there. Though I would not suggest, of course, any first-hand connection between Molière and Cartwright, the coincidence is worth observing.[29]

Shadwell, apparently, also noticed the similarity between the plot of *L'Avare* and parts of *The Ordinary*, and turned it to account in his adaptation of Molière's play, *The Miser* (1672). Retaining the common elements already noticed, Shadwell added several new characters and situations, some of which at least seem to have been suggested by *The Ordinary*. In Molière, for example, the unwelcome suitor, whom Harpagon, the miser, wished to force his daughter to marry, was a more than middle-aged man. Shadwell, however, changes the proposed suitor into a young and foolish "cit," Timothy, the son of a scrivener, whose name, Squeeze, sufficiently describes his nature; thus in Cartwright Sir Thomas Bitefigg is glad to arrange a match between his daughter and the son of Simon Credulous, an arrant old money grubber. Such a change led Shadwell to depart from his original very considerably, for it was necessary in some way to dispose of Timothy. Again Shadwell seems to have turned to *The Ordinary*, where he found Andrew Credulous married by a trick to Mistress Jane's amorous waiting-woman. This situation solves the difficulty, and, with the aid of two cheating gamblers,

---

28. We may also compare the attitude of Valère, who pretends to agree with everything the old miser says, with that of Meanwell in II, v.

29. I have at times been tempted to believe that Molière was acquainted with some of the English dramatic writers of this period, perhaps from contact with English refugees during the Commonwealth rule. Massinger's *The City Madam* (1632), for example, offers some interesting parallels with Molière's *Les Précieuses Ridicules* and *Tartuffe*, and one of the earlier editors of Massinger, not I think Gifford, pointed out a very interesting verbal parallel in one of the plays, to which I have unfortunately lost the reference. Such things, of course, afford no proof of influence.

who are an addition to Molière and remind us strongly of the "complices" in Cartwright's comedy, Timothy is safely, if somewhat ignominiously, married to a former courtezan.[30] If these parallels are not in themselves sufficient to prove Shadwell's debt to Cartwright, Shadwell was good enough to suggest a verbal borrowing which seems to clinch the case. When Andrew Credulous is at last introduced (V, iv) with his newly wedded wife, Priscilla, old Simon Credulous flies into a rage and cries out:

> D'y'see?
> Your Chamber-maid Sir *Thomas*; out you whore.

And Andrew, showing for once a little back bone, answers:

> Take heed what you say Father, shee's my wife.

So Shadwell's Squeeze exclaims (V, i):

> Oh Villian! marry a Whore, out of my sight.

And Timothy answers:

> A Whore Sir, I vow to God I scorn your words, do you marke me, she's as Pretty a civil young Lady, and I am sure I had her Maiden-Head, had I not my dear?[31]

The sources which have been discussed so far are only the most general ones. It would be possible to take the play scene by scene and point out sources, or at least analogues, for almost every situation and character. But enough has already been said to show that *The Ordinary*, like the majority of the contemporary comedies, is very largely derivative. The remainder of this source and analogue material will be found dealt with at length in the notes.

---

30. The arrest of old Squeeze by the constable and watch, who was seized in an attempt to "commit carnal copulation with one Mrs. *Lettice*," may be compared both with the arrest (IV, v) of Andrew Credulous, who was taken "In dishonest Adultery with a Trull," and with the mistaken arrest of old Credulous (V, iv).

31. It is perhaps worth noticing that Shadwell seems to have another reminiscence of *The Ordinary* in his late play *The Scowrers* (1691). Just as Slicer, Hearsay, and Shape disguise themselves and mingle among the watchmen, pretending to be looking for themselves, so in *The Scowrers* (V, 1) Ralph, who has been caught by the constable and watch after a "roaring and scowring" match, pretends to be one of the rescuing party and sends the watch off after the culprits in the wrong direction.

THE ORDINARY,

A Comedy,

Written by
WILLIAM CARTVVRIGHT,
M.A. Ch. Ch. Oxon.

LONDON,
Printed for *Humphrey Moseley*, and
are to be sold at his shop at the Sign of
the Princes Armes in St *PAVLS*
Churchyard. 1651.

The Prologue.

'Twould wrong our Author to bespeake your Eares;
Your Persons he adores, but Judgement feares:
For where you please but to dislike, he shall
Be Atheist thought, that worships not his Fall.
   Next to not marking, 'tis his hope that you   [5]
Who can so ably judge, can pardon too.
His Conversation will not yet supply
Follies enough to make a Comedy;
He cannot write by th' Poll; nor Act we here
Scenes, which perhaps you should see liv'd *elsewhere;*   [10]
No guilty line traduceth any; all
We now present is but conjecturall;
'Tis a meere ghesse: Those then will be to blame,
Who make that Person, *which he meant but* Name.
   That web of Manners which the Stage requires,   [15]
That masse of Humors which Poetique Fires
Take in, and boyle, and purge, and try, and then
With sublimated follies cheat those men
That first did vent them, are not yet his Art,
But as drown'd Islands, or the World's fifth Part   [20]
Lye undïscover'd; and he only knows
Enough to make himselfe ridiculous.
   Think then, if here you find nought can delight,
   He hath not yet seen Vice *enough to* write.

Dramatis Personæ.

Heare-say	— An Intelligencer.	⎫
Slicer	— A Lieutenant.	⎪ Complices in
Meanewell, Littleworth disguiz'd, a decay'd Knights Son.		⎬ the Ordinary.
Shape	— A Cheater.	⎭
Sir *Tho. Bitefigg*	— A covetous Knight	
Simon Credulous	— A Citizen.	
Andrew	— his Son, Suter to Mrs *Jane*.	
Robert Moth	— An Antiquary.	
Caster. ⎫ *Have-at-all.* ⎭	— Gamesters.	
Rimewell	— A Poet.	⎫
Bag-shot.	— A decay'd Clerke.	⎪ Clubbers
Sir *Christopher*	— A Curate.	⎬ at the Ordinary.
Vicar *Catchmey.*	— A Cathedrall Singing-man.	⎭
Mrs *Jane*	— Daughter to Sir *Thomas*.	
Priscilla	— Her Maid.	
Joane Pot-lucke	— A Vintners Widow.	

Shopkeeper. ⎫ Officers.
Chirurgeon. ⎭ Servants.

The Scene,
LONDON.

Act. I. Scen. I.

{ *Hearesay, Slicer,* }
{ *Shape, Meanewell.* }

Hear. WE're made my Boys, we're made; me thinks I am
Growing into a thing that will be worship'd.
Slic. I shall sleep one day in my Chaine, and Skarlet
At *Spittle*-Sermon.
Shap. Were not my wit such
I'd put out monies of being Maior. [5]
But O this braine of mine! that's it that will
Barre me the City Honour.
Hear. We're cry'd up
O'th' sudden for the sole Tutors of the Age.
Shap. Esteem'd discreet, sage, trainers up of youth.
Hear. Our house becomes a place of Visit now. [10]
Slic. In my poore judgement 'tis as good my Lady
Should venture to commit her eldest sonne
To us, as to the Inns of Court: hee'l be
Undone here only with lesse Ceremony.
Hear. Speak for our credit my brave man of War. [15]
What, *Meane-well*, why so lumpish?
Mean. Pray y' be quiet.
Hear. Thou look'st as if thou plott'st the calling in
O'th' *Declaration*, or th' *Abolishing*
O'th' *Common-Prayers*; cheare up; say something for us.
Mean. Pray vexe me not.
Slic. These foolish puling sighs [20]
Are good for nothing, but to endanger Buttons.
Take heart of grace man.
Mean. Fie y'are troublesome.
Hear. Nay fare you well then Sir.   [*Ex. Hea. Sli. Sha.*
Mean. My Father still
Runs in my mind, meets all my thoughts, and doth

Mingle himselfe in all my Cogitations, [25]
Thus to see eager villaines drag along
Him, unto whom they crouch'd; to see him hal'd,
That ne'r knew what compulsion was, but when
His vertues did incite him to good deeds,
And keep my sword dry —— O unequall Nature! [30]
Why was I made so patient as to view,
And not so strong as to redeeme? why should I
Dare to behold, and yet not dare to rescue?
Had I been destitute of weapons, yet
Arm'd with the only name of Son, I might [35]
Have outdone wonder. Naked Piety
Dares more than Fury well-appointed; Bloud
Being never better sacrific'd, than when
It flowes to him that gave it. But alas,
The envy of my Fortune did allow [40]
That only, which she could not take away,
Compassion; that which was not in those savage,
And knowing Beasts; those Engines of the Law,
That even kill as uncontroul'd, as that.
How doe I grieve, when I consider from [45]
What hands he suffer'd! hands that doe excuse
Th' indulgent Prison; shackles being here
A kind of Rescue. Young man tis not well
To see thy aged Father thus confin'd,
Good, good old man; alas thou'rt dead to me, [50]
Dead to the world, and only living to
That which is more than death, thy misery:
The Grave could be a comfort: And shall I ——
O would this Soule of mine —— But Death's the wish
Of him that feares; hee's lazie that would dye. [55]
I'le live and see that thing of wealth, that worme
Bred out of splendid mucke; that Citizen
Like his owne sully'd Wares throwne by into
Some unregarded corner, and my Piety
Shall be as famous as his Avarice; [60]
His Son whom we have in our Tuition
Shall be the Subject of my good Revenge;
I'le count my selfe no child, till I have done
Something that's worth that name: my Braine shall be

Busie in his undoing; and I will [65]
Plot ruine with Religion; his disgrace
Shall be my Zeales contrivement; and when this
Shall stile me Son againe, I hope 'twill be
Counted not wrong, but Duty. When that time
Shall give my Actions growth, I will cast off [70]
This brood of Vipers: and will shew that I
Doe hate the Poyson, which I meane t' apply. *Exit.*

Act. I. Scen. II.

Mrs *Potlucke*

Pot. Now help good Heaven! 'tis such an uncouth thing
To be a widow out of Term-time —— I
Doe feele such aguish Qualmes, and dumps and fits, [75]
And shakings still an end —— I lately was
A wife I do confesse, but yet I had
No husband: he (alas) was dead to me
Even when he liv'd unto the world; I was
A widdow whiles he breath'd; his death did only [80]
Make others know so much. But yet ——[*Enter Hear.*
 Hear. How now?
So melancholy sweet?
 Pot. How could I choose
Being thou wert not here? the time is come,
Thou'lt be as good unto me as thy word?
 Hear. Nay, hang me if I er'e recant. You'l take me [85]
Both wind and limb at th' venture, will you not?
 Pot. Ay good Chuck, every inch of thee, she were
No true woman that would not.
 Hear. I must tell you
One thing, and yet I'm loth.
 Pot. I am thy Rib,
Thou must keep nothing from thy Rib, good Chuck; [90]
Thy yoak-fellow must know all thy secrets.
 Hear. Why then I'l tell you sweet. [*He whispers her*
 Pot. Heaven defend!
 Hear. 'Tis true.

Pot.   Now God forbid; and would you offer
T' undoe a widdow-woman so? I had
As leive the old Vintner were alive againe. [95]
   Hear.   I was not born with it I confesse; but lying
In *Turky* for Intelligence, the great Turk,
Somewhat suspicious of me, lest I might
Entice some o'th' *Seraglio*, did command
I should be forthwith cut.
   Pot.   A heathen deed [100]
It was: none but an Infidel could have
The heart to do it.
   Hear.   Now you know the worst
That you must trust to, come lets to the Church.
   Pot.   Good Mr *Hear-say*, Nature ne'r intended
One woman should be joyned to another. [105]
The holy blessing of all wedlock was
T' encrease and multiply, as Mr *Christopher*
Did well observe last Sabbath. Ile not do
Any thing 'gainst Gods word. I do release you
Of all your promises, and that it may not [110]
Be said you lost by loving me, take this.
Perhaps I may get you a contribution
O'th' women of the Parish, as I did
The broken-bellied-man the other day.
   Hear.   Seeing you needs will cast me off, let me [115]
Intreat this one thing of you, that you would not
Make me your Table-talk, at the next Gossiping.   *Exit.*
   Pot.   Indeed I pitty thee poor thing, or rather   [*En. Slic.*
I pitty thee poore nothing. Good Lieutenant
How dost thou? Thou art mindfull of thy Promise? [120]
   Slic.   What else my jolly wench?
   Pot.   Good sweet Lieutenant
Give me but leave to aske one Question of you,
Art thou intire and sound in all thy limbs?
   Slic.   To tell the very truth, ere now I've had
A spice o'th' Pox, or so; but now I am sound [125]
As any Bell. (Hem) Was't not shrill my Girle, ha?
   Pot.   I do not aske thee about these diseases;
My question is whether thou'st all thy parts.
   Slic.   Faith I have lost a joint or two; as none

Of our Profession come off whole, unlesse [130]
The Generall, and some sneaks.
  Pot. My meaning is
Whether that something is not wanting that
Should write thee husband.
  Slic. Ne'r feare that my wench;
Dost think the King would send me to the wars
Without I had my weapons? Eunuchs are not [135]
Men of imploiment in these dayes; his Majesty
Hath newly put me on a peece of service;
And if I e're come off (which I doe feare
I shan't, the danger is° so great) brave Widow
Wee'l to't and get Commanders.
  Potl. If you can [140]
Leave me, I can leave you: there are other men
That won't refuse a Fortune when 'tis proffer'd.
  Slic. Well, I must to his Majesty, think on't;
So fare thee well. Thine to his very Death,
That is a Month or two perhaps, *D. Slicer.* [*Ex. En. Sha.* [145]
  Potl. Kind Master *Shape*, you are exceeding welcome.
Here hath bin M︎ʳ *Hearsay*, and Lieutenant
Slicer: You may ghesse at their businesse, but
I hope you thinke me faithfull.
  Sh. I beleeve
The memory of your Husbands ashes, which [150]
Scarce yet are cold, extinguisheth all flames
That tend to kindling any Love-fire: 'Tis
A vertue in you, which I must admire
That only you amongst so many should
Be the sole Turtle of the Age.
  Potl. I doe [155]
Beare him in memory I confesse; but when
I doe remember what your promise was
When he lay sicke, it doth take something from
The bitternesse of Sorrow. Woman was
Not made to be alone still.
  Sh. Tender things [160]
At seventeen may use that plea; but you
Are now arriv'd at Matron: these young sparkes
Are rak'd up, I presume, in sager Embers.

Potl.   Nay don't abuse her that must be your Wife;
You might have pitty, & not come with your nicknames,   [165]
And call me Turtle: have I deserv'd this?
　Sh.   If that you once hold merits, I have done;
I'm glad I know what's your Religion.
　Potl.   What's my Religion? 'tis well known there hath
Been no Religion in my house e'r since   [170]
My Husband dy'd.　　　　　　　　*Ent. Slic. Hearsay.*
　Hear.   How now sweet *Shape*? so close
Alone w' your Widow.
　Sh.   Sirs dare you beleeve it?
This thing, whose prayer it hath been these ten
Yeares, that she may obtaine the second tooth,
And the third haire, now dotes on me, on me   [175]
That doe refuse all that are past sixteen.
　Slic.   Why faith this was her sute to me just now.
　Hear.   I had the first on't then. A Coachman, or
A Groome were fitter far for her.
　Slic.   You doe
Honour her too much to thinke she deserves   [180]
A thing that can lust moderately, give her
The sorrell Stallion in my Lords long stable.
　Sha.   Or the same colour'd Brother, which is worse.
　Potl.   Why Gentlemen ——
　Hear.   Foh, foh! she hath let fly.
　Potl.   Doe y' think I have no more manners than so?   [185]
　Sha.   Nay faith I can excuse her for that: But
I must confesse she spoke, which is all one.
　Slic.   Her breath would rout an Army, sooner than
That of a Cannon.
　Hear.   It would lay a Devill
Sooner than all *Trithemius* charmes.
　Sha.   Heark how   [190]
It blusters in her nosthrils like a wind
In a foule Chimney.
　Potl.   Out you base companions,
You stinking Swabbers.
　Hear.   For her gate, that's such,
As if her nose did strive t' outrun her heels.
　Sha.   She's just six yards behind, when that appears;   [195]
It saves an Usher Madam.

Pot.   You are all
Most foul-mouth'd knaves to use a woman thus.
  Sli.   Your playster'd face doth drop against moist weather.
  Sha.   Fie, how you writh it; now it looks just like
A ruffled boot.
  Slic.   Or an oyld paper Lanthorn. [200]
  Hear.   Her nose the candle in the midst of it.
  Sha.   How bright it flames? Put out your nose good Lady;
You burn day-light.
  Pot.   Come up you lowsie Raskals.
  Hear.   Not upon you for a Kingdom good *Joane*,
The great Turk, *Joane* —— the great Turk.
  Slic.   Kisse him Chuck, [205]
Kisse him Chuck open-mouth'd and be reveng'd.
  Pot.   Hang you base cheating Varlet.
  Slic.   Don't you see
December in her face?
  Sha.   Sure the Surveyer
Of the high-waies will have to do with her
For not keeping her countenance passable. [210]
  Hear.   There lies a hoare frost on her head, and yet
A constant thaw in her nose.
  Sha.   She's like a peece
Of fire-wood, dropping at one end, and yet
Burning i'th' midst.
  Slic.   O that endeavouring face!
When will your costivenesse have done good Madam? [215]
  Hear.   Do you not heare her Guts already squeake
Like Kitstrings?
  Slic.   They must come to that within
This two or three yeares; by that time shee'l be
True perfect Cat: They practise before hand.
  Pot.   I can endure no longer, though I should [220]
Throw off my womanhood.
  Hear.   No need, that's done
Already: nothing left thee, that may stile thee
Woman but Lust, and Tongue; no flesh but what
The vices of the sex exact, to keep them
In heart.
  Sha.   Thou art so leane and out of case [225]
That 'twere absurd to call thee Devill incarnate.

Slic. Th' art a dry Devill troubled with the lust
Of that thou hast not, flesh.
   Pot. Rogue, Raskall, Villaine,
Ile shew your cheating tricks Ifaith: all shall
Be now laid open. Have I suffer'd you   [230]
Thus long i' my house, and ne'r demanded yet
One penny rent, for this? Ile have it all,
By this good blessed light I will.
   Hear. You may
If that you please undo your self, you may.
I will not strive to hinder you. There is   [235]
Something contriving for you, which may be
Perhaps yet brought about, a Match or so;
A proper fellow; 'tis a trifle, that;
A thing you care not for I know. Have I
Plotted to take you off from these to match you   [240]
In better sort, and am us'd thus? As for
The Rent you aske, here take it, take your money;
Fill, choake your gaping throat. But if as yet
You are not deaf to counsell, let me tell you
It had been better that you ne'r had took it.   [245]
It may stop some proceedings.
   Pot. Mr *Hearsay*,
You know you may have even my heart out of
My belly (as they say) if you'l but take
The paines to reach it out; I am sometimes
Peevish I doe confesse; here take your money.   [250]
   Hear. No.
   Potl. Good Sir.
   Hear. No, keep it and hoord it up.
My purse is no safe place for it.
   Potl. Let me
Request you that you would be pleas'd to take it.
   Hear. Alas 'twould only trouble me; I can
As willingly goe light, as be your Treasurer.   [255]
   Potl. Good Mr *Slicer* speake to him to take it,
Sweet Mr *Shape*, joyne with him.
   Slic. Nay, be once
O'rerul'd by a woman.
   Sha. Come, come, you shall take it.

Potl. Nay Faith you shall; here put it up good Sir.
Hear. Upon intreaty I'm content for once; [260]
But make no Custome of't; you doe presume
Upon my easie foolishnesse; 'tis that
Makes you so bold: were it another man
He ne'r would have to doe with you. But marke me,
If e'r I find you in this mood againe, [265]
I'le dash your hopes of Marriage for ever.
                    Ex. all but Hear.

Act. I. Scen. 3.

To him,
Meanewell, Andrew.

And. God save you Tutors both.
Mean. Fie *Andrew*, fie;
What kisse your hand? you smell, not complement.
Hear. Besides, you come too near when you salute.
Your breath may be discover'd; and you give [270]
Advantage unto him you thus accoast
To shake you by the hand, which often doth
Endanger the whole arme. Your Gallant's like
The Chrystall glasse, brittle; rude handling crackes him.
To be saluted so were to be wounded. [275]
His parts would fall asunder like unto
Spilt Quicksilver; an Eare, an Eye, a Nose
Would drop like Summer fruit from shaken Trees.
Mean. For the same reason I'd not have you dance.
Some Courtiers, I confesse, doe use it; but [280]
They are the sounder sort, those foolish ones
That have a care of health, which you shall not
If you'l be rul'd by me. The hazard's great,
'Tis an adventure, an exploit, a piece
Of service for a Gentleman to caper. [285]
Hear. A Gallant's like a Leg of Mutton, boyl'd
By a Spanish Cooke; take him but by the one End
And shake him, all the flesh fals from the bones,
And leaves them bare immediately.

And. I would
Not be a leg of Mutton here.
   Hear. I saw [290]
In France a Monsieur, only in the Cutting
Of one crosse Caper, Rise a man, and come
Downe, to th' amazement of the standers by,
A true extempory Skeleton;
And was strait read on.
   And. Sure this man, [295]
Good Tutor, was quite rotten.
   Mean. See how you
Betray your breeding now! quite rotten! 'tis
Rottennesse perhaps in Footmen, or in Yeomen,
'Tis tendernesse in Gentlemen; They are
A little over-boyl'd, or so.
   Hear. He is [300]
A Churle, a Hind, that's wholesome; some raw thing
That ne're was at *London*: One in whom
The Clown is too predominant. Refin'd
People feele *Naples* in their bodies; and
An Ach i'th' bones at Sixteen, passeth now [305]
For high descent; it argues a great birth.
Low blouds are never worthy such infection.
   An. Ay, but my Father bid me I should live honest,
And say my Prayers, that he did.
   Hear. If that
You cannot sleep at any time, we do [310]
Allow you to begin your Prayers, that so
A slumber may seize on you.
   Mean. But as for
Your living honest, 'twere to take away
A trade i'th' Common-wealth; the Surgeons
Benefit would go down: you may go on [315]
In foolish chastity, eate only Sallads,
Walk an unskilfull thing, and be to learn
Something the first night of your wife; but that's
To marry out of fashion.
   An. Here's no Proofes,
No Doctrines, nor no Uses. Tutor I [320]
Would fain learn some Religion.

Hear.   Religion?
Yes to become a Martyr, and be pictur'd
With a long Labell out o' your mouth, like those
In *Foxes* Book; just like a Jugler drawing
Ribband out of his throat.
   An.   I must be gone.   [325]
   Mean.   Obedience is the first step unto science;
Stay and be wise.
   An.   Indeed I dare not stay
The Glyster works you sent to purge gross humors.   [*Ex.*
   Mean.   Being you will not take your Lecture out
Good morrow to y' good *Andrew*. This soft foole   [330]
Must swim in's Fathers wealth. It is a curse
That Fortune justly makes the City's lot,
The young Fool spends what e're the old Knave got.
                              Ex. Mean.

Act. I. Scen. IV.

To Hearsay, enter Slicer and Credulous.

   Hear.   Sir let me tell you this is not the least
Of things wherein your wisedome shewes it self,   [335]
In that you've plac'd your Son in this good sort.
   Cred.   Nay nay, let me alone to give him breeding;
I did not hold the *University*
Fit for the training up of such a Spirit.
   Slic.   The *University*? 't had been the only way   [340]
T' have took him off his courage, and his mettal,
He had return'd as Slaves doe from the Gallies,
A naked shorn thing with a thin dockt top,
Learnedly cut into a Logick mode.
   Hear.   A private Oath given him at first Entrance [345]
Had sworn him Pilgrim unto Conventicles;
Engag'd him to the hate of all, but what
Pleaseth the stubborn froward Elect.
   Slic.   But we
Following another Modell doe allow
Freedome and courage, cherish and maintaine   [350]
High noble thoughts ——

Hear. Set nature free, and are
Chymists of manners ——
   Sli. Do instruct of States ——
   Hear. And Wars: there's one, look on him ——
   Slic. Doe but view
That searching Head ——
   Hear. The very soule of Battell,
True steele.
   Slic. H' hath been an Agent some few years   [355]
(A score or so) for Princes, and as yet
Doth not write forty.
   Hear. I confesse I can
Discover th' Entrailes of a State perhaps,
Lay open a Kingdoms Paunches, shew the bowels
And inwards of a Seigniory or two;   [360]
But for your deeds of Valour, there is one,
Although I speak it to his face, that can
Write a Geography by his own Conquests.
H' hath fought o'r *Strabo*, *Ptolomy* and *Stafford;*
Travell'd as far in arms, as *Lithgoe* naked.   [365]
Born weapons whither *Coriat* durst not
Carry a shirt or shooes. *Jack Mandevil*
Ne'r saild so far as he hath steerd by Land;
Using his Colours both for mast and saile.
   Cred. I'd thought h' had been Lieutenant.   [370]
   Hear. That's all one.
   Slic. I've worn some Leather out abroad; let out
A heathen Soul or two; fed this good sword
With the black bloud of Pagan Christians;
Converted a few Infidels with it.
But let that passe. That man of peace there hath   [375]
Been trusted with Kings Breasts ——
   Hear. His name is heard
Like Thunder, and that meer word, *Slicer*, hath
Sufficed unto victory.
   Slic. He's close,
Reserv'd, lock'd up. The secrets of the King
Or *Tartary*, of *China*, and some other   [380]
Counsels of moment have been so long kept
In's body without vent, that every morning

Before he covers them with some warme thing
Or other you may smell 'em very strongly;
Distinguish each of them by severall sents —— [385]
  Hear. A grove of Pikes are rushes to him, hail
More frights you, than a shower of Bullets him ——
  Slic. The Dutch come up like broken beer; the Irish
Savour of Usquebaugh; the Spanish they
Smell like unto perfume at first, but then [390]
After a while end in a fatall steame ——
  Hear. One Drum's his Table, the other is his Musick.
His Sword's his Knife, his Colours are his Napkins,
Carves nourishing Horse, as he is us'd to do
The hostile Pagan, or we venison: Eates [395]
Gunpowder with his meat instead of Pepper,
Then drinks o'r all his Bandeleers, and fights ——
  Slic. Secrets are rank'd and order'd in his belly,
Just like Tobacco leaves laid in a sweat.
Here lies a row of Indian secrets, then [400]
Something of's own on them; on that another
Of China Counsels, cover'd with a lidd
Of New-found-land discoveries; next, a bed
Of Russia Policies, on them a lay
Of Prester-Johnion whispers ——
  Hear. Slights a tempest; [405]
Counts lightning but a giving fire, and thunder
The loud report when heaven hath discharg'd.
H'hath with his breadth supplyd a breach.
When he's once fixt no Engine can remove him.
  Slic. 'Twould be a Policy worth hatching, to [410]
Have him dissected, if 'twere not too cruell.
All states would lye as open as his bowels.
Turkey in's bloudy Liver; *Italy*
Be found in's reines; *Spaine* busie in his Stomack;
Venice would float in's Bladder; *Holland* saile [415]
Up and down all his veines; *Bavaria* lie
Close in some little gut, and *Ragioni*
Di Stato generally reek in all.
  Cred. I see my Son's too happy; he is born
To be some man of Action, some Engine [420]
For th' overthrow of Kingdomes.

Hear.   Troth he may
Divert the Torrent of the Turkish rule
Into some other Tract; damme up the streame
Of that vast headlong Monarchy, if that
He want not meanes to compasse his intents.   [425]
   Cred.   The Turkish Monarchy's a thing too big
For him to mannage; he may make perhaps
The Governour of some new little Island,
And there plant Faith and Zeale: But for the present
M' ambition's only to contrive a Match   [430]
Between Sir *Thomas Bite-figg's* only Daughter,
And (if I may so call him now) my Son;
'Twill raise his Fortunes somewhat.
   Slic.   We have got
One that will doe more good with's tongue that way
Than that uxorious showre that came from Heaven,   [435]
But you must oyle it first.
   Cred.   I understand you.
Greaze him i'th' fist you meane: there's just ten Peeces,
'Tis but an earnest: If he bring't about,
I'le make those ten a hundred.
   Hear.   Thinke it done.   *Ex. Cred. & Ent. Sh. Mean.*

Act. I. Scen. V.

Hearesay, Slicer, Meanewell, Shape.

Our life methinks is but the same with others;   [440]
To couzen, and be couzen'd, makes the Age.
The Prey and Feeder are that Civill thing
That Sager heads call Body Politick.
Here is the only difference; others cheat
By statute, but we do't upon no grounds.   [445]
The fraud's the same in both, there only wants
Allowance to our way: the Common-wealth
Hath not declar'd her self as yet for us;
Wherefore our Policy must be our Charter.
   Mea.   Well mannag'd Knav'ry is but one degree   [450]
Below plaine Honesty.

Slic.   Give me villany
That's circumspect, and well advis'd, that doth
Colour at least for goodnesse. If the Cloake
And Mantle were pull'd off from things, 'twould be
As hard to meet an honest Action as   [455]
A liberall Alderman, or a Court Nun.
   Hear.   Knowing then how we must direct our steps,
Let us chalk out our paths; you, *Shape*, know yours.
   Sha.   Where e'r I light on Fortune, my Commission
Will hold to take her up: I'l ease my silken   [460]
Friends of that idle luggage, we call Money.
   Hear.   For my good toothlesse Countesse, let us try
To win that old Emerit thing, that like
An Image in a German clock, doth move,
Not walke, I meane that rotten Antiquary.   [465]
   Mean.   Hee'l surely love her, 'cause she looks like some
Old ruin'd peece, that was five Ages backward.
   Hear.   To the great Vestry wit, the Livery braine,
My Common-Councell Pate, that doth determine
A City businesse with his gloves on's head,   [470]
We must apply good hope of wealth and meanes.
   Slic.   That griping Knight Sir *Thomas* must be call'd
With the same lure: he knows t' a crum how much
Losse is in twenty dozen of Bread, between
That which is broke by th' hand, and that is cut.   [475]
Which way best keeps his Candles, bran or straw.
What tallow's lost in putting of 'm out
By spittle, what by foot, what by the puffe,
What by the holding downwards, and what by
The extinguisher; which week will longest be   [480]
In lighting, which spend fastest; he must heare
Nothing but Moyties, and Lives, and Farmes,
Coppies, and Tenures; he is deaf to th' rest.
   Mean.   I'l speak the language of the wealthy to him.
My mouth shall swill with Bags, Revenues, Fees,   [485]
Estates, Reversions, Incomes, and assurance.
He's in the Gin already, for his Daughter
Shee'l be an easie purchase.
   Hear.   I do hope
We shall grow famous; have all sorts repaire

As duly to us, as the barren Wives [490]
Of aged Citizens do to St *Antholins*.
Come let us take our Quarters: we may come
To be some great Officers in time,
  And with a reverend Magisterial frown,
  Passe sentence on those faults that are our own. *Ex. Om.* [495]

Act. II. Scene I.

Have-at-all, Slicer, Hearsay, having rescued him
in a Quarrell.

 Have. 'Tis destin'd, I'l be valiant, I am sure
I shall be beaten with more credit then,
Than now I do escape. *Lieutenant* hast
Bethought thy self as yet? hast any way
To make my Sword fetch bloud?
 Slic. You never yet [500]
Did kill your man then?
 Have. No.
 Hear. Nor get your Wench
With child I warrant?
 Have. O Sir.
 Slic. You're not quite
Free of the Gentry till y'have marrd one man
And made another: when one fury hath
Cryd quit with t'other, and your Lust repair'd [505]
What Anger hath destroyd, the Title's yours,
Till then you do but stand for't.
 Have. Pox! who'd be
That vile scorn'd Name, that stuffs all Court-gate Bils?
Lieutenant thou mayst teach me valour yet.
 Slic. Teach thee? I will inspire thee man. I'l make [510]
Thy name become a terrour, and to say
That *Have-at-all* is comming, shall make roome
As when the Bears are in Procession.
Heark hither *Franke* ——   *They consult.*
 Hear. That's good, but ——

Slic. How think'st now?
Hear. Nay he will pay you large—lie. [*aloud*
Have. Pay, what else? [515]
Hear. Make him beleeve the Citizen's his Guest,
The Citizen that he is his.
Slic. Concluded;
Would you fight fair or conquer by a spell?
Have. I do not care for Witchcraft; I would have
My strength relie meerlie upon it self. [520]
Slic. There is a way though I ne'r shew'd it yet,
But to one Spaniard, and 'twas wondrous happy.
Have. Think me a second Spaniard worthy Sir.
Slic. Then listen. The design is by a dinner;
An easie way you'l say, I'l say a true; [525]
Hunger may break stone walls, it ne'r hurts men.
Your cleanly feeder is your man of valour.
What makes the Peasant grovel in his muck,
Humbling his crooked soule, but that he eates
Bread just in colour like it? Courage ne'r [530]
Vouchsaf'd to dwell a minute, where a sullen
Pair of brown loaves darken'd the durty Table;
Shadows of bread, not bread. You never knew
A solemn Son of Bagpudding and Pottage
Make a Commander; or a Tripe-eater [535]
Become a Tyrant: he's the Kingdoms arm
That can feed large, and choicely.
Have. If that be
The way, I'l eat my self into courage,
And will devour valour enough quickly.
Slic. 'Tis not the casual eating of those meats, [540]
That doth procure those Spirits, but the order,
And manner of the meal; the ranking of
The dishes, that does all; else he that hath
The greatest range would be the hardest man.
Those goodly Juments of the Guard would fight [545]
(As they eat Beef) after six stone a day;
The Spit would nourish great Attempts; my Lord
Would lead a Troop, as well as now a Masque;
And force the Enemies sword with as much ease
As his Mistrisses Bodkin: Gallants would [550]

Owe valour to their Ordinaries, and fight
After a crown a meal.
   Have. I do conceive
The Art is all in all. If that you'l give
A bill of your directions, I'l account
My self oblig'd unto you for my safety. [555]
   Slic. Take it then thus. All must be Souldier-like;
No dish but must present Artilery.
Some military instrument in each.
Imprimis sixe or seven yards of Tripe
Display'd instead o'th' Ensign.
   Have. Why, you said, [560]
Tripe-eaters ne'r made Tyrants.
   Slic. Peace Sir, Learners
Must be attentive and beleeve. Do y' think
Wee'l eat this? 'tis but for formalitie;
Item a Coller of good large fat Brawn
Serv'd for a Drum, waited upon by two [565]
Fair long black Puddings lying by for drumsticks;
Item a well grown Lamprey for a Fife;
Next some good curious Marchpanes made into
The form of Trumpets: Then in order shall
Follow the Officers. The Captain first [570]
Shall be presented in a warlike Cock,
Swiming in whitebroth, as he's wont in bloud;
The Sergeant Major he may bustle in
The shape of some large Turkey; For my self,
Who am Lieutenant, I'm content there be [575]
A Bustard only; let the Corporall
Come sweating in a Breast of Mutton, stuff'd
With Pudding, or strut in some aged Carpe,
Either doth serve I think. As for Perdues
Some choice Sous'd-fish brought couchant in a dish [580]
Among some fennell, or some other grasse,
Shews how they lie i'th' field. The Souldier then
May be thus rank'd. The common one Chicken,
Duck, Rabbet, Pidgeon. For the more Gentile,
Snipe, Woodcock, Partridge, Pheasant, Quail will serve. [585]
   Hear. Bravelie contriv'd.
   Slic. That weapons be not wanting

Wee'l have a dozen of bones well charg'd with marrow
For Ordnance, Muskets, Petronels, Petarrs;
Twelve yards of Sausage by insteed of Match;
And Caveari then prepar'd for wild-fire. [590]
   Hea.   Rare Rogue! how I do love him now me thinks.
   Slic.   Next wee'l have true fat, eatable old Pikes;
Then a fresh Turbut brought in for a Buckler,
With a long Spitchcock for the sword adjoyn'd;
Wee'l bring the ancient weapons into play. [595]
   Have.   Most rare by heaven.
   Slic.   Peaches, Apricocks,
And Malecotoons, with other choiser Plums
Will serve for large siz'd Bullets; then a dish
Or two of Pease for small ones. I could now
Tell you of Pepper in the stead of Powder, [600]
But that 'tis not in fashion 'mongst us Gallants;
If this might all stand upon Drum heads, 'twould
Work somewhat better.
   Have.   Wil't so? then we'l have 'em
From every ward i'th' City.
   Slic.   No I'm loath
To put you to such charge: for once, a long [605]
Table shall serve the turn; 'tis no great matter.
The main thing's still behind: we must have there
Some Fort to scale; a venison pastie doth it:
You may have other Pies instead of outworks;
Some Sconces would not be amisse, I think. [610]
When this is all prepar'd, and when we see
The Table look like a pitch'd Battel, then
Wee'l give the word, Fall to, slash, kill, and spoile;
Destruction, rapine, violence, spare none.
   Hear.   Thou hast forgotten Wine, Lieutenant, wine. [615]
   Slic.   Then to avoid the grosse absurdity
Of a dry Battel, cause there must some bloud
Be spilt (on th' enemies side I mean) you may
Have there a Rundlet of brisk Claret, and
As much of Aligant, the same quantitie [620]
Of Tent would not be wanting, 'tis a wine
Most like to bloud. Some shal bleed fainter colours,
As Sack, and White wine. Some that have the itch

(As there are Taylors still in every Army)
Shall run with Renish, that hath Brimstone in't. [625]
When this is done fight boldly; write your self
The tenth or 'leventh Worthy, which you please,
Your choice is free.
   Have. I'l be the gaming Worthy;
My word shall be Twice twelve; I think the dice
Ne'r mounted any upon horseback yet. [630]
   Sl. Wee'l bring your friends & ours to this large dinner:
It works the better eaten before witnesse.
Beware you say 'tis yours: Confession is
One step to weaknesse, private Conscience is
A Theater to valour. Let's be close. [635]
Old *Credulous*, and his Son, and Mr *Caster*
Shall all be there.
   Have. But then they will grow valiant
All at my charge.
   Slic. Ne'r fear't; th' unknowing man
Eates only Flesh, the understanding Valour;
His ignorance i'th' mystery keeps him coward: [640]
To him 'tis but a Meale; to you 'tis vertue.
It shall be kept here.
   Hav. No fitter place; there is
An old rich Clutchfist Knight, Sir *Thomas Bitefig*,
Invite him too; perhaps I may have luck,
And break his Purse yet opèn for one hundred. [645]
A Usurer is somewhat exorable
When he is full: He ne'r lends money empty.
   Slic. Discreet, and wisely done; I was about
T' have prompted it.
   Hear. Stout Mr *Haveatall*
Lets be sworn Brothers.
   Have. Pox! thou fear'st Ile beat thee [650]
After I've eaten. Dost thou think I'l offer't?
By my next meale I won't: nay I do love
My friends how e'r: I do but think how I
Shall bastinado o'r the Ordinaries.
Arm'd with my sword, Battoone and foot Ile walk [655]
To give each rank its due. No one shall scape,
But he I win off.

Hear. You shall have at least
Some twenty warrants serv'd upon you straight;
The trunck-hose Justices will try all means
To bind you to the Peace, but that your strength [660]
Shall not be bound by any.
   Slic. Surgeons will
Pray for your health and happinesse, you may
Bring 'em to be your Tributaries, if
You but denie to fight a while.
   Have. My teeth
Are on an edge till I do eat; now will [665]
I couzen all men without opposition.
I feel my strength encrease with very thought on't.
Sword, sword, thou shalt grow fat; and thou Battoon
Hold out I prethee, when my labour's done,
I'l plant thee in the Tower-yard, and there [670]
Water'd with wine thou shalt revive, and spring
In spight of Nature with fresh succulent boughs,
Which shall supply the Commonwealth with Cudgels.
Thou I first meet after this meal I do
Pronounce unhappy shadow; happie yet [675]
In that thou'lt fall by me. Some men I will
Speak into Carcasse, Some I'l look to death,
Others I'l breath to dust, none shall hold back
This fatall Arm: The Templers shall not dare
T' attempt a rescue; no mild words shall bury [680]
My splitted spitchcock'd ——
   Slic. Oliv'd, hasht ——
   Hear. Dri'd, powder'd ——
   Have. Rosted fury.
                                           Exeunt.

Act. II. Scen. II.

Meanwell, Moth.

   Mean. If what I speak prove false, then stigmatize me.
   Mo. I nas not what you mean; Depardieux you
Snyb mine old years, Sans fail I wene you bin [685]
A Jangler, and a Golierdis.

Mean. I swear
By these two *Janus* heads you had of us,
And your own too, as reverend as these,
There is one loves you that you think not on.
   Mot. Nad be, none pleasaunce is me ylaft, [690]
This white top writeth my much years, I wis;
My fire yreken is in Ashen cold,
I can no whit of daliance: If I kissen
These thick stark bristles of mine beard will pricken
Ylike the skin of Hownd-fish. Sikerly [695]
What wends against the grain is lytherly.
   Mean. Me thinks y'are strong enough and very lusty,
Fit to get heyres; among your other peeces
Of age and time, let one young face be seen
May call you Father.
   Mo. Wholsom counsel! but [700]
The world is now full Tykel sykerly;
'Tis hard to find a Damosel unwenned;
They being all Coltish and full of Ragery,
And full of gergon as is a flecken Pye.
Who so with them maketh that bond anon [705]
Which men do clypen spousaile, or wedlock,
Saint Idiot is his Lord I wis.
   Mean. This is
No tender and wanton thing, she is a stay'd
And setled widow, one who'l be a Nurse
Unto you in your latter daies.
   Mo. A Norice [710]
Some dele ystept in age! so mote I gone
This goeth aright, how highteth she say you?
   Mean. Mrs *Joane Potluck*, Vintner *Potluck's* widow.
   Mo. *Joane Potluck* Spinster. Lore me o thing mere.
Abouten what time gan she brendle thus? [715]
   Mean. On Thursday morning last.
   Mo. Y' blessed Thursday,
Ycliped so from *Thor* the Saxons God.
Ah benedicite I might soothly sayne,
Mine mouth hath itched all this livelong day;
All night me met eke, that I was at Kirke; [720]
My heart gan quapp full oft. *Dan Cupido*
Sure sent thylke sweven to mine head.

Mean.   You shall
Know more if you'l walk in.   *Exit Meanwel.*
   Mo.   Wend you beforne;
Cembeth thy self, and pyketh now thy self;
Sleeketh thy self; make cheere much Digne good *Robert*:   [725]
I do arret thou shalt acquainted bin
With Nymphs and Fawny, and Hamadryades;
And y'eke the sisterne nine Pierides
That were transmued into Birds, nemp'd Pyes,
Metamorphoseos wat well what I mean.   [730]
I is as Jollie now as fish in Seine.   *Exit.*

Act. II. Scen. III.

Hearsay, Caster, Shape.

   Hear.   Can I lie hid no where securely from
The throng, and presse of men? must every place
Become a Theater, where I seek shelter?
And solitudes become markets, 'cause I'm there?   [735]
Good Sir, I know your tricks: you would intrap;
This is your snare, not your request.
   Sha.   Take heed,
He's nois'd about for a deep searching head:
Ile pawn my life 'tis a trick.
   Hear.   Leave off these Ginnes,
You do not do it handsomly; you think   [740]
Y'have met with fooles I warrant.
   Sha.   On my life
A spie, a meere informer.
   Cast.   As I hope
For fortunes, my intentions are most faire.
   Sha.   A Gamesters Oath: he hath some reservation.
   Hear.   Yet did I think you true——
   Cast.   By all that's good,   [745]
You do me wrong to think, that I'd wrong you.
   Hear.   When I lay Agent last in new *Atlantis*
I met with, what you now desire, a strange
New way of winning, but yet very sure.
Were not the danger great I'd ——

    Cast. Do you think
I will betray my self, or you, whom I
Esteeme above my self? I have as yet
One hundred left; some part of which ——
    Sha. Faith Sir,
These times require advice; if it should come
Unto the Councels eare once, he might be
Sent into other Kingdoms, to win up
Monies for the relief o'th' State, and so
Be as it were an honest kind of Exile.
    Cast. If I do e'r discover, may I want
Monie to pay my Ordinary, may I
At my last stake (when there is nothing else
To lose the game) throw Ames Ace thrice together.
Ile give you forty pound in hand ——
    Hear. I may
Shew you the vertue of 't, though not the thing;
I love my Country very well. Your high
And low men are but trifles: your poyz'd Dye
That's ballasted with Quicksilver or Gold
Is grosse to this ——
    Sha. Profer him more I say.
    Cast. Here's fifty ——
    Hear. For the bristle Dye it is
Not worth that hand that guides it; toies fit only
For Clerks to win poore Costermongers ware with.
    Sha. You do not come on well.
    Cast. Here's threescore ——
    Hear. Then
Your hollowed thumb join'd with your wriggled box,
The slur, and such like are not to be talk'd of;
They're open to the eye. For Cards you may
Without the help of any secret word,
Or a false hand, without the cut or shuffle,
Or the packt trick, have what you will your self;
There's none to contradict you.
    Cast. If you please
But to instruct me here is fourescore pound.
    Hear. Do y'think 'tis money I esteeme? I can
Command each Terme by Art, as much as will

Furnish a Navy. Had you but five pound
Left you in all the world, I'd undertake
Within one fortnight you should see five thousand. [785]
Not that I covet any of your drosse,
But that the power of this Art may be
More demonstrably evident, leave in
My hands all but some smaller sum to set,
Something to stake at first.
   Sha. Hee'l tell you all [790]
If you but seem to trust him.
   Cast. Here I'l lay
Down in your hands all but this little portion,
Which I reserve for a Foundation.
   Hear. Being y'are confident of me, and I
Presume your lips are sealed up to silence, [795]
Take that, which I did never yet discover;
So help you Fortune, me Philosophie.
(I must entreat your absence Mr *Shape*.)   *Exit Shape.*
I do presume you know the strength and pow'r
That lies in Phancie.
   Cast. Strange things are done by it. [800]
   Hear. It works upon that which is not as yet.
The little Æthiop Infant had not been
Black in his Cradle, had he not been first
Black in the Mothers strong Imagination.
'Tis thought the hairie Child that's shewn about [805]
Came by the Mothers thinking on the Picture
Of Saint *Iohn Baptist* in his Camels Coat.
See we not Beasts conceive, as they do fansie
The present colours plac'd before their Eyes?
We owe pyed Colts unto the varied horsecloth; [810]
And the white Partridge to the neighbouring snow.
Fancie can save or kill; it hath clos'd up
Wounds when the Balsam could not, and without
The aid of salves; to think hath been a cure.
For Witchcraft then, that's all done by the force [815]
Of meer Imagination. That which can
Alter the course of Nature, I presume
You'l grant shall bear more rule in petty hazzards.
   Cast. It must, it must: good Sir, I pray go on.

Hea.   Now the strong'st fancies still are found to dwel [820]
In the most simple; they being easiest won
To the most firm beliefe, who understand not
Who 'tis they do believe. If they think 'twill
Be so, it will be so; they do command,
And check the course of Fortune; they may stop [825]
Thunder, and make it stand, as if arrested,
In its mid journey: If that such a one
Shall think you'l win, you must win; 'tis a due
That nature paies those men in recompence
Of her deficiency, that what e'r they think [830]
Shall come to passe. But now the hardest will be
To find out one that's capable of thinking.
   Cast.   I know you can produce an Instrument
To work this your design by. Let me owe you
The whole and entire courtesie.
   Hear.   I've one [835]
Committed to my custody but lately,
The powerfull'st that way, I e'r found yet;
He will but think he shall b' abus'd in such
A Company, and he's abus'd; he will
Imagine only that he shall be cheated, [840]
And he is cheated: All still comes to passe.
He's but one pin above a Natural: But ——
   Cast.   Wee'l purchase him; I'l take up for't; old *Simon*
Shall have my Farme outright now: what's a peece
Of durty Earth to me? a clod? a turf? [845]
   Hear.   Because I see your freer nature's such,
As doth deserve supplies, I'l do my best
To win him o'r a while into your service.
   Cast.   If I should strive to pay you thanks, I should
But undervalue this great courtesie. [850]
Sir, give me leave to think & worship. Stay;
First will I beggar all the Gentlemen
That do keep Termes; then build with what I win.
Next I'l undo all gaming Citizens,
And purchase upon that: the Foreman shall [855]
Want of his wonted opportunities,
Old *Thomas* shall keep home I warrant him.
I will ascend to the Groom Porters next.

Flie higher Games, and make my mincing Knights
Walk musing in their knotty Freeze abroad; [860]
For they shall have no home. There shall not be
That pleasure that I'l baulk: I'l run o'r Nature;
And when I've ransack'd her, I'l weary Art;
My means I'm sure will reach it. Let me see
'Twill yearly be —— By Heav'n I know not what —— [865]
 Hear. Ne'r think to sum it, 'tis impossible;
You shall ne'r know what Angels, Peeces, Pounds,
These names of want and beggary mean; your tongue
Shall utter nought but millions: you shall measure,
Not count your moneys; your revenews shall [870]
Be proud and insolent, and unruly;
They shall encrease above your conquer'd spendings
In spight of their excesse; your care shall be
Only to tame your riches, and to make them
Grow sober, and obedient to your use. [875]
 Cast. I'l send some forty thousand unto *Pauls*;
Build a Cathedral next in *Banbury*;
Give Organs to each Parish in the Kingdom;
And so root out the unmusicall Elect.
I'l pay all Souldiers whom their Captaines won't; [880]
Raise a new Hospitall for those maim'd People
That have been hurt in gaming; Then build up
All Colleges, that Ruine hath demolish'd,
Or, interruption left unperfect.
 Hear. 'Twil
Never be done I think, unless you do it. [885]
Provide the wealthiest Gamesters, there's but one
Thing that can do us wrong, Discovery.
You have no enemie, but frailty.
 Cast. Night
And silence are loud names, compar'd with me.
 Hear. I see the tide of Fortune rowling in [890]
Without resistance. Go, be close, and happy.
            Exeunt.

Act. II. Scen. IV.

Andrew, Meanwell.

And. Vpon my Conscience now he cheated me;
I could have never lost it else so strangely.
   Mean. What is a paltry cloak to a man of worth?
It barr'd men only o'th' sight of your body: [895]
Your handsomnesse will now appear the better.
   And. He was as like our Mr *Shape*, as could be;
But that he had a patch upon his Cheek,
And a black beard, I should have sworn 'twere he:
It was some body in his cloaths I'm sure. [900]
   Mean. Some cunning Cheater upon my life won
His cloak and suit too.
   And. There it is for certain.
Pies take him, doth he play for cloaks still? Surely
He hath a Fly only to win good cloaths.   [*Enter Sha.*
   Sha. The Pox and Plague take all ill fortune! this, [905]
The second time that he hath cheated me:
My very best suit that I had!
   And. How now?
What lost your cloak, and suit? A jest I vow;
I vow a pretty jest: 'odsnigs I guess'd so;
I saw him have it on; it made him look as like you, [910]
As like you —— 'Tis a Rogue, a meer Decoy.
   Sha. A Rogue, a meer Decoy? and yet like me?
   And. Nay hold, I mean he is a Rogue, when that
He hath his own cloaths on. D'y'think that I
Would call him so, when he is in your suit? [915]
   Sha. No more of that good *Andrew*, as you love me
Keep in your wit.
   And. Speak Tutor, do I use
To quarrell? speak good Tutor.
   Mean. That wit *Andrew*
Of yours will be th' undoing of you, if
You use't no better.
   And. Faith I thought I might [920]
Have broke a witty jest upon him, being
I've lost my cloak.

Mean.   True, but he has lost his too:
And then you know that is not lawfull wit.   [*Enter Hear.*
  Hear.   Here's Mr *Credulous*, and old Sir *Thomas*,
They have some businesse with you.
  Mean.   Bring 'em in.   [925]
  Sha.   My businesse lies not here Sirs, fare you well. [*Ex. Sh.*
  A.   For Gods sake don't you tell old Sim on't now.

Act II. Scen. V.

To them, Sir *Thomas Bitefig, Credulous.*

  Mea.   God save you good Sir *Thomas.*
  Sr *Tho.*   Save you Sir.
  Mean.   You'r welcome Mr *Credulous.*
  Cred.   Come hither;
Whither do you steal now? what? where's your cloak?   [930]
  And.   Going to foiles ev'n now, I put it off.
  Mea.   To tell you truth he hath lost it at Doublets.
  Cred.   With what a lie you'd flap me in the mouth?
Thou hast the readiest invention
To put off any thing —— thou hadst it from   [935].
Thy mother I'l be sworn; 't nere came from me.
  Mean.   Peace as you love your self; if that the Knight
Should once perceive that he were given to gaming,
'Twould make him break the match off presently.
  Cred.   Sr *Thomas* here's my Son; he may be yours,   [940]
If you please to accept him.
  And.   Father don't
Give me away for this: try me once more.
  Sr *Tho.*   I like his person well enough, if that
You'l make him an Estate convenient.
  Mean.   He hath more in him Sir than he can shew;   [945]
He hath one fault, he's something covetous.
  Sr *Tho.*   Mary a very commendable fault.
  Cred.   He is descended of no great high bloud:
He hath a House, although he came of none.
His Grandfather was a good Livery man,   [950]
Paid scot and lot, old *Timothy Credulous*
My Father, though I say it that should not.

Sr Tho. I don't regard this thing, that you call bloud:
'Tis a meer name, a sound.
  Mean. Your Worship speaks
Just like your self; me thinks he's noble, [955]
That's truely rich: men may talk much of Lines,
Of Arms, of Bloud, of Race, or Pedigree,
Houses, Descents, and Families; they are
But empty noise God knows, the idle breath
Of that puff nothing Honour; Formall words, [960]
Fit for the tongues of men that ne'r knew yet
What Stem, what Gentry, nay, what vertue lies
In great Revenues.
  Sr Tho. Well and pithy said,
You may work on my Daughter, and prevaile,
For that yong stripling: 'Tis a foolish wench, [965]
An unexperienc'd Girle, she'd like to have been
Caught by Sir *Robert Littleworths* Son, if that
I had not banish'd him my house: a youth
Honest enough I think, but that he's poor;
Born to more Name than Fortune.
  Cred. He is safe [970]
For ever wooing. I have laid his Father
Out of harm's way; there's picking meat for him:
And God knows where he's gon; he hath not been
Seen this long while; he's sure turn'd vagabond;
No sight of him since th' Arrest of his Father. [975]
Andrew addresse your self to good Sir *Thomas.*
  And. 'Slid Father you're the strangest man —— I won't.
  Cre. As God shall mend me thou'rt the proudest thing ——
Thou canst not complement, but in Caparisons.
  And. What's that to you? I'd fain say something yet; [980]
But that I can't, my losses do so vex me.
  Cred. Come think not on't my Boy, I'l furnish thee.
  And. Sir, though ——
  Cred. Nay, to't I say; help him Sir, help him.
  And. Sir, though without my cloak at this time ——
To morrow I shall have one —— give me leave [985]
Barely to say —— I am your servant Sir ——
In hose and doublet.
  Cred. I'l do what you told me.

Hear. Take heed: if that you do't hee'l guesse you'r giv'n
To idle spendings, and so crosse the match.
I will invite him as to my self.
   Cred. Do so. [990]
   Hear. Sir *Thomas*, if you'l please so far to grace us,
As be a guest to morrow here, we shall
Study hereafter to deserve the favour.
   Sr *Tho.* Although I do not use to eat at Ord'naries,
Yet to accept your courtesie, good friends, [995]
I'l break my wonted custome.
   Hear. You shall have it
With a free heart.
   Sr *Tho.* If I thought otherwise,
I do assure you, I'd not venture hither.
                                           Exeunt.

Act. III. Scene I.

Moth.

   Moth. Harrow alas! I swelt here as I go;
Brenning in fire of little *Cupido*. [1000]
I no where hoart yfeele, but on mine head.
Huh, huh, huh, so; ycapred very wele.
I am thine Leeke, thou *Chaucer* eloquent;
Mine head is white, but o mine taile is green.
This is the Palyes where mine Lady wendeth. [1005]

     Saint Francis, *and Saint* Benedight,
     Blesse this house from wicked wight,
     From the Night-mare and the Goblin,
     That is hight good fellow Robin.
     Keep it from all evill Spirits, [1010]
     Fayries, Weezels, Rats and Ferrets,
        From Curfew time
        To the next prime.

Come forth mine Duck, mine Bryd, mine honycomb.
Come forth mine Cinamon.   *Enter Mrs Potluck.*

Pot.   Who is't that cals? [1015]
Mo.   A Knight most Gent.
Pot.   What is your pleasure Sir?
Mo.   Thou art mine pleasure, by dame *Venus* brent;
So fresh thou art, and therewith so lycand.
  Pot.   Alas! I am not any flickering thing:
I cannot boast of that slight-fading gift [1020]
You men call beauty; all my handsomnesse
Is my good breeding, and my honesty.
I could plant red, where you now yellow see;
But painting shews an harlot.
  Moth.   Harlot, so
Called from one *Harlotha* Concubine [1025]
To deignous *Wilhelme*, hight the Conqueror.
  Pot.   Were he ten *Williams*, and ten Conquerors
I'd have him know't, I scorn to be his Harlot.
I never yet did take presse-money to
Serve under any one.
  Moth.   Then take it now. [1030]
Werme kisse! Thine lips ytaste like marrow milk;
Me thinketh that fresh butter runneth on them.
I grant well now, I do enduren woe,
As sharp as doth the *Titius* in Hell,
Whose stomack fowles do tyren ever more, [1035]
That highten Vultures, as do tellen Clerkes.
  Pot.   You've spoke my meaning, though I do not know
What 'tis you said. Now see the fortune on't;
We do know one anothers Souls already;
The other must needs follow. Where's your dwelling? [1040]
  Mo.   Yclose by *Aldersgate* there dwelleth one
Wights clypen *Robert Moth*; now *Aldersgate*
Is hotten so from one that *Aldrich* hight;
Or else of Elders, that is, ancient men;
Or else of Aldern trees which growden there; [1045]
Or else as Heralds say, from *Aluredus*:
But whence so e'r this Yate ycalled is
There dwelleth *Robert Moth* thine Paramour.
  Pot.   Can you be constant unto me as I
Can be to you?
  Moth.   By *Woden* God of Saxons, [1050]

From whence comes Wensday, that is Wodensday,
Truth is a thing that ever I will keep,
Unto thylke [day] in which I creep into
My Sepulchre; I'l be as faithfull to thee,
As Chaunticleere to Madam Partelot. [1055]
   Pot. Here then I give away my heart to you,
As true a heart as ever widow gave.
   Moth. I *Robert Moth*, this tenth of our King
Give to thee *Joan Potluck* my biggest crumpe Ring:
And with it my Carcasse entire I bequeathen [1060]
Under my foot to Hell, above my head to heaven:
And to witnesse that this is sooth,
I bite thy red lip with my tooth.
   Pot. Though for a while our bodies now must part,
I hope they will be joyn'd hereafter.
   Moth. O! [1065]
And must we part? alas, and must we so?
Sin it may be no bet, now gang in peace.   *Ex. Potluck*
Though soft into mine bed I gin to sink
To sleep long as I'm wont to done, yet all
Will be for naught; I may well lig and wink, [1070]
But sleep shall there none in this heart ysink.   *Exit*

Act. III. Scen. II.

Credulous, and *Shape* dogging him.

   Cred. So now the Morgage is mine own outright;
I swear by the faith of my Body now
It is a pretty thing, o' my corporal Oath
A very pretty thing. Besides the house, [1075]
Orchards, and Gardens: some two hundred Acres
Of Land that beareth as good Country corn,
For Country corn, as may be.
   Shap. As I'd have it.
   Cr. How now good friend! where dost thou live? dost thou
Know *Caster's* Farme?
   Shap. Yes Sir; I fear 'tis gon: [1080]
Sure *Caster's* Farme is cast away.

Cred.   A jest!
Good troth a good one of a Country one;
I see there's wit there too. Then thou dost know it.
  Shap.   I am affraid I shall not know it long;
I shall lose my acquaintance.   [1085]
  Cred.   'Snigs another!
A very perillous head, a dangerous brain.
  Sha.   God blesse my Master, and the Devil take
Some body else.
  Cred.   Um! that's not quite so good
As th' other two; that some body else is me:
(Now you shall see how hee'l abuse me here   [1090]
To mine own face) why some Body else good Brother?
  Sha.   The rich gout rot his bones; an hungry, old,
Hard griping Citizen, that only feeds
On Heyrs and Orphans goods, they say must have it:
One that ne'r had the wisdom to be honest;   [1095]
And's therefore Knave, 'cause 'tis the easier Art.
I know he hath not given half the worth on't.
'Tis a meer cheat.
  Cred.   'Slid Brother thou hast paid him
To th' utmost, though he hath not paid thy Master.
Now is my wit up too: this Land I see   [1100]
Will make men thrive i'th' brain.
  Sha.   Would he were here,
Who e'r he be, I'd give him somewhat more
Into the bargain: a base thin-jaw'd sneaksbill
Thus to work Gallants out of all. It grieves me
That my poor Tenement too goes into th' sale.   [1105]
  Cred.   What have I done? now wit deliver me.
If he know I am he, hee'l cut my throat;
I never shall enjoy it: sure it was
Your Masters seeking friend; he would ne'r else
Have had to doe with it; he that bought it is   [1110]
A very honest man; and if you please him
Will deale with you. I may speak a word
In your behalf: 'twont be the worse for you.
  Sha.   I'm going Sir unto him; do you know
Where I may find him?
  Cred.   What if I am he?   [1115]

Sha.   I am afraid he is not half so honest
As you do seem.
   Cred.   Faith I'm the same; I try'd
What metal thou wast made of: I perceive
Thou wilt not flinch for th' wetting; thou mayst be
My Bayliff there perhaps.
   Sha.   And't please your Worship.   [1120]
   Cred.   So now the case is alter'd.
   Sha.   I do know
It was my Masters seeking, you would ne'r
Have had to do with't else. He sent me to you
For the last hundred pound, by the same token,
That you invited him to th' eating house.   [1125]
   Cred.   (O this simplicity! he does not know
Yet what an Ordnary means.) I was now coming
To have paid it in.
   Shap.   I'l save your Worship that
Labour an't please you: let me now begin
My Baylifeship.
   Cred.   'Snigs wiser yet than soe.   [1130]
Where is thy Master?
   Shap.   Sir, my Master's here
I thank my stars; but Mr *Caster* is
At an Horse-race some ten miles off.
   Cred.   Why then
I'l stay till he returns; 'twill be by dinner.
   Sha.   Your best way's now to send it; if by chance   [1135]
The race go on his side, your Worship may
Faile of your purchase.
   Cred.   'Snigs and that's considerable.
Here, here, make haste with it; but e'r thou goest
Tell me, is't a pretty thing?
   Sha.   O' my corporall Oath,
A very pretty thing: besides the house   [1140]
Orchards, and Gardens, Some two hundred Acres
Of Land that beareth as good Country Corne,
God give you luck on't.
   Cred.   Right as I did say,
Ev'n word by word. But prethee stay a little;
What Meadow ground's there? Pasture in proportion?   [1145]

Sha.   As you would wish Sir; I'm in haste.
Cred.   Nay Bayliffe
But one word more, and I have done; what place
Is there to dry wet linnen in?
Sha.   O twenty
To hang up cloaths, or any thing you please.
Your Worship cannot want line-room. God be wi' you.   [1150]
Cred.   But this once and ——
Sha.   I must be gone —— The Race.   [*Exit Shape.*
Cred. Little thinkst thee how diligent thou art
To little purpose. 'Snigs I pitty him;
What haste he makes to cheat himself! poor foole!
Now I am safe the wretch must pardon me   [1155]
For his poor Tenement; all's mine. I'l sow
One ground or other every month with Pease:
And so I will have green ones all the year.
These Yeomen have no Policie i'th' world.   *Exit.*

Act III. Scen. III

Priscilla, Meanwell.

Pris.   Pray y' entertain your self a while, untill   [1160]
I give my Mistris notice of your presence.
I'd leave a book with you, but that I see
You are a Gentleman: perhaps you'l find
Some pretty stories in the hangings there.
Mean.   Thank you sweet-heart.
Prisc.   (A very proper man)   [1165]
If't lye in me to doe you any pleasure,
Pray you Sir use me, you shall find me ready.   [*E. Pr.*
Me.   I make no doubt of that: these Implements,
These chamber Properties are such ripe things,
They'l fall with the least touch. From twelve to twenty   [1170]
They thinke that others are to sue to them;
When once they've past these limits, they make bold
I cannot say to wooe, that's somthing modest,
But aske downright themselves.   *Ent.* Mrs *Jane.*

Jan. Leave us *Priscilla*,
And wait without a while.
   Mean. Faire Mistres pardon [1175]
The boldnesse of a stranger, who uncivilly
Thus interrupts your better thoughts.
   Jan. May I
Demand your businesse.
   Mean. Under favour thus.
Not to use farther circumstance faire Virgin,
(And yet lesse faire 'cause Virgin) you are one [1180]
That are the thought, the care, the aime, the strife,
I should not erre if I should say the madnesse
Of all young men; all sighs, all folded Armes,
All o'r-cast looks, all broken sleeps are ow'd
Only to you.
   Jan. I'm sorry I should be [1185]
A trouble unto any: if I could
Afford the remedy as well as now
I doe your grief, assure your selfe that cure
Shall be the birth of my next Action.
   Mean. That cure is my request. If that this were [1190]
Mine own sute, I had us'd no circumstance.
Young Master *Credulous* a proper man
(For sure he shall be rich) one whom the whole
List of our City-Virgins dote on —— you
Conceive the rest I know.
   Jan. Alas, what ailes him? [1195]
I'l not be slack to doe him any good.
   Mean. 'Tis in your power. He is very much
If you will know't —— But sure you will not grant
If I should tell you ——
   Jan. If you thus presume
That I am hard, you only aske denyall: [1200]
Your expectation's cross'd except you faile.
   Mean. If you will know it then, he is in love.
   Jan. I pitty him indeed poore heart: with whom?
   Mean. Even with your beautious self.
   Jan. 'Tis not well done
To scoffe one ne'r did injure you.
   Mean. I vow [1205]

By all that's good, by your faire selfe, I am
As tender of you as that blest one is
Who e'r he be that loves you most. If I
In any case abuse you, let me be
More miserable than *Little-worth*. [1210]
  Jan. Is he become expression? is his Fate
The period of ill wishes? sure he never
Deserv'd so ill from you.
  Mean. I don't reflect
Upon his ruin'd Fortunes, but your coldnesse.
And sure I may call him unhappy, whom [1215]
You doe neglect.
  Jan. That man, where ere he be,
Is happier than your selfe; and were he here,
You should see him receiv'd and your self scorn'd.
  Mean. I doe not thinke so Lady; sure you would
Make more of me than so. I'l bring the man, [1220]
And so confute you.
  Jan. It may be I might
Love you the better somthing for that Office,
If he might enter here.
  Mean. Nay I could tell
Y'had cast him off: alas you need not hide it,
I have it from himselfe.
  Jan. Doth he think so? [1225]
Could I but see him ——
  Mean. If his sight can bring
But the least joy unto you (as perhaps
You'l take some pleasure in his misery)
You shall enjoy it.
  Jan. I doe feare you promise
Only to raise my hopes a while, and then [1230]
To triumph in their Ruine.
  Mean. That you may
See how my breast and tongue agree, I'l leave
This Ring with you till I return again.
  Jan. My *Littleworth*! foole that I was: could I
Not all this while perceive 'twas thee? why didst thou [1235]
Deferre my joy thus long by suffering me
To stand i'th' Cloud?

Mean. Alas! I ghess'd I'd been
Infectious to thee now; that thou wouldst look
On a disease more mildly than on me:
For Poverty is counted a contagion. [1240]
  Jan. I call this kisse to witnesse (which I wish
If I prove false may be the last to me
Which friends pay dying friends) I ne'r will be
Others than thine.
  Mean. I like the vow so well,
That the same way I'l seale my promise too. [1245]
If I prove not as thou (that is most constant)
May this kisse be, that I may wish it worse
Than that which is due to departing souls,
The last that I shall take from thee. I am
Sent here, but yet unknown to them that send me, [1250]
To be anothers Spokes-man. The man is
That foolish Son of Mr *Credulous*:
Thou must pretend some liking; 'twas thy Father
Granted me this accesse to win thee for him;
Be thou no way averse. 'T shall be my care [1255]
So to bring things about, that thou shalt be
Mine by consent in spight of misery.
  Jan. Be secret, and Love prosper thy design. *Ex. Jan.*
  Mean. Happy that man that meets such faithfulnesse.
I did not think it had been in the Sex. [1260]
I know not now what's misery. Peace: my Fair [*Musick*
Is hallowing the Lute with her blest touch.

        A Song within.

  1.   *Come, o come, I brook no stay:*
       He doth not love that can delay——
         See how the stealing Night [1265]
         Hath blotted out the Light,
       And Tapers do supply the Day.

  2.   *To be chaste is to be old,*
       And that foolish Girle that's cold
         Is fourscore at fifteen: [1270]
         Desires do write us green,
       And looser flames our youth unfold.

Mean. 'T cannot be her, her voice was ne'r prophan'd
With such immodest numbers.

> 3. *See the first Taper's almost gone,* [1275]
> *Thy flame like that will straight be none;*
>   *And I as it expire*
>   *Not able to hold fire.*
> *She loseth time that lies alone.*

Mean. 'Tis the breath [1280]
Of something troubled with Virginity.

> 4. *O let us cherish then these Powr's*
> *Whiles we yet may call them ours:*
>   *Then we best spend our time,*
>   *When no dull zealous Chime,* [1285]
> *But sprightfull kisses strike the Hours.*

Mean. What dost thou mean?   [*Enter Priscilla.*
Pris. Only to please you Sir.
  Mean. Sweetest of things was't thou? I faith I guess'd
'Twould be no others melody but yours. [1290]
There have been many of your sex much given
Unto this kind of musick.
  Pris. *Sappho* was
Excellent at it: but *Amphion* he
He was the man that out-did all; 'tis said
Of him, that he could draw stones with the sound [1295]
Of his sweet strings. I'd willingly arrive
At some perfection in the Quality.
  Mean. I do acknowledge your desires most prone.
This for your trouble.
  Pri. I am not mercenary,
Your acceptation is reward enough. [1300]
  Mean. You have it then.
  Pris. Beauty go with you Sir.
                        [*Exeunt several waies.*

Act. III. Scen. IV.

Credulous, Hearsay, Slicer, to them Sir *Thomas Bitefig, Haveatall, Caster,* as to the Ordinary.

Cred. You're welcome friends, as I may say ——
Hear. You do forget.
Cred. —— That am a guest as well as you.
Slic. Most noble sons of Fortune, and of Valour,
You grace us with your presence: you must pardon [1305]
Our small provision.
Hear. No variety here
But you most noble guests, whose gracious looks
Must make a dish or two become a feast.
Have. I'l be as free as 'twere mine own.
Cast. Who thinks
On any thing that borders upon sadnesse [1310]
May he ne'r know what's mirth, but when others
Laugh at his sullen wrinkles.
Have. We will raise
A noise enough to wake an Alderman,
Or a cast Captain, when the reck'ning is
About to pay.
Cre. Hang thinking, 'snigs I'l be [1315]
As merry as a Pismire; come let's in.
Slic. Let's march in order military, Sirs.
Ha. That's well remember'd most compleat Lieutenant.
Ex. as to the Ordnary.

Act III. Scen. V.

Rime-well, Bagshot, Vicar Catchmey, Sir *Christopher.*

Rim. Come my most noble order of the club.
'Cause none will else, let's make much of our selves. [1320]
His letter may procure a Dinner yet.
Bag. Cheer up Sir *Kit,* thou lookst too spiritually:
[I] see too much of the Tith-pig in thee.
Ch. I'm not so happy: *Kit's* as hungry now

                    As a besieged City, and as dry   [1325]
                    As a Dutch Commentator. This vile world
                    Ne'r thinks of Qualities: good truth I think
                    'T hath much to answer for. Thy Poetry
                    Rimewell, and thy voice Vicar *Catchmey*, and
                    Thy Law too *Bagshot* is contemn'd: 'tis pitty   [1330]
                    Professions should be slighted thus. The day
                    Will come perhaps, when that the Commonwealth
                    May need such men as we. There was a time
                    When Coblers were made Church-men, and those black'd
                    Smutch'd Creatures thrust into white Surplisses,   [1335]
                    Look'd like so many Magpies, and did speak
                    Just as they, by rote. But now the Land
                    Surfets forsooth. Poor Labourers in Divinity
                    Can't earn their groat a day, unlesse it be
                    Reading of the Christian buriall for the dead: [1340]
                    When they ev'n for that reason truly thank
                    God for thus taking this their Brother to him.
                      Catch. Something profane Sir *Christopher*.
                      Chri. When I
                    Levell my larger thoughts unto the Basis
                    Of thy deep shallowness, am I prophane?   [1345]
                    Henceforth I'l speak, or rather not speak, for
                    I will speak darkly.
                      Catch. There's one comfort then
                    You will be brief.
                      Chri. My briefness is prolix;
                    Thy mind is bodily, thy soul corporeal;
                    And all thy subtile faculties are not subtile,   [1350]
                    Thy subtilty is dulness. I am strong.
                    I will not be conceiv'd by such Mechanicks.
                      Rime. I do conceive you though Sir *Christopher*,
                    My Muse doth sometimes take the selfsame flight.
                      Chri. Pauci, pauci quos æquus amavit [*Iupiter*]. [1355]
                    But Quadragessimall wits, and fancies leane
                    As ember weeks (which therefore I call leane,
                    Because they're fat) these I do doom unto
                    A knowing ignorance; he that's conceiv'd
                    By such is not conceiv'd; sense is non-sense   [1360]
                    If understood by them. I'm strong again.

Rime. You err most Orthodoxly sweet Sir *Kit*.
Chri. I love that though I hate it: and I have
A kind of disagreeing consent to't.
I'm strong, I'm strong again. Let's keep these two [1365]
In desperate hope of understanding us.
Ridles, and Clouds are very lights of speech:
I'l vaile my carelesse anxious thoughts, as 'twere
In a perspicuous cloud, that I may
Whisper in a loud voice, and ev'n be silent [1370]
When I do utter words; words did I call them?
My words shall be no words, my voice no voice;
My noise no noise, my very language silence.
I'm strong, I'm strong: good Sir you understand not.
  Bag. Nor do desire; 'tis meerly froth, and barme, [1375]
The yest that makes your thin small Sermons work.
  Chri. Thou hold'st thy peace most vocally. Again.
  Catch. I hate this Bilke.
  Chri. Thou lovest 'cause thou dost hate.
Thy injuries are Courtesies. Strong again.
  Cat. Good *Sampson* use not this your Asses jaw-bone. [1380]
  Chri. Thou'st got my love by losing it; that earnest
Jest hath regain'd my soul. *Sampson* was strong;
He kill'd a thousand with an Asses-jawbone, {*Ent. a Serv.*
And so will I. 'st, 'st — good friend d'y' hear? {*as passing by*
Here is a letter friend to Mr *Meanwell*. [1385]
  Bag. Any Reversions yet? nothing transmiss'd?
  Rime. No gleanings *James*? no Trencher Analects?
  Ser. Parly a little with your stomacks Sirs.
  Catch. There's nothing so ridiculous as the hungry:
A fasting man is a good jest at any time. [1390]
  Ser. There is a Gentleman without, that will'd me
To ask if you'l admit of him among you,
He can't endure to be in good company.
  Catc. You'r merry *James*; yes by all means good *James*;
Admit quoth he? what else? pray y' send him in. [*Ex. Se.* [1395]
Let's be resolv'd to fall out now; then he
Shall have the glory to compose the Quarrel,
By a good dozen of pacificall Beere.
  Rime. Bag. Agreed, agreed.
  Chri. My Coat allows no Quarrell.

    Rime. The Colour bears't if you'l venture the stuffe, [1400]
The tendernesse of it I do confesse
Somewhat denies a grapling.
    Chri. I will try,
Perhaps my Spirit will suggest some anger.   [*Ent. And.*
    An. Save you boon sparks: wil't please you to admit me?
    Chri. Your Worship graceth us in condescending [1405]
To levell thus your presence humble Sir.
    And. What may I call your name most reverend Sir?
    Bag. His name's Sir *Kit*.
    Chri. My name is not so short,
'Tis a trissyllable, an't please your Worship:
But vulgar tongues have made bold to profane it [1410]
With the short sound of that unhallowed Idoll
They call a Kit. Boy learn more reverence.
    Bag. Yes, to my Betters.
    And. Nay friends, do not quarrel.
    Chri. It is the holy cause, and I must quarrell.
Thou Son of Parchment, got between the Standish [1415]
And the stiff Buckram bag: thou that maist call
The Pen thy Father, and the inke thy Mother,
The sand thy Brother, and the wax thy Sister,
And the good Pillory thy Couzen remov'd,
I say learn reverence to thy Betters. [1420]
    Bag. Set up an hour-glasse; hee'l go on untill
The last sand make his Period.
    Chri. 'Tis my custome,
I do approve the Calumny: the words
I do acknowledge, but not the disgrace.
Thou vile ingrosser of unchristian deeds. [1425]
    Bag. Good *Israel Inspiration* hold your tongue;
It makes far better Musick, when you Nose
Sternolds, or *Wisdoms* Meeter.
    Catch. By your leave
You fall on me now Brother.
    Rim. 'Tis my cause,
You are too forward Brother *Catchmey*.
    Catch. I [1430]
Too forward?
    Rim. Yes I say you are too forward
By the length of your *London* measure Beard.

Act III, Scene v]   THE ORDINARY   317

   Catch.   Thou never couldst entreat that respite yet
Of thy dishonesty as to get one hair
To testifie thy Age.
   Bag.   I'm beardlesse too;   [1435]
I hope you think not so of me?
   Chri.   Yes verily,
Not one hairs difference 'twixt you both.
   Rim.   Thou violent Cushion-thumper, hold thy tongue,
The Furies dwell in it.
   Catch.   Peace good Sir *Kit*.
   Chri.   Sir *Kit* again? Thou art a *Lopez*; when   [1440]
One of thy legs rots off (which will be shortly)
Thou'lt beare about a Quire of wicked Paper,
Defil'd with [un]sanctified Rithmes,
And Idols in the frontisepiece: that I
May speak to thy capacity, thou'lt be   [1445]
A Balladmonger.
   Catch.   I shall live to see thee
Stand in a Play-house doore with thy long box,
Thy half-crown Library, and cry small Books.
Buy a good godly Sermon Gentlemen ——
A judgment shewn upon a Knot of Drunkards ——   [1450]
A pill to purge out Popery —— The life
And death of *Katherin Stubs* ——
   Chri.   Thou wilt visit windows;
Me thinks I hear thee with thy begging tone
About the break of day waking the Brethren
Out of their morning Revelàtions.
   And.   Brave sport Ifaith.   [1455]
   Rime.   Pray y' good Sir reconcile them.
If that some Justice be i'th' Ordinary now
Hee'l bind them to the peace for troubling him.
   Bag.   Why should he not good Sir, it is his office.
   An.   Now 'tis o' this side; o for a pair of Cudgels!   [1460]
   Rime.   Peace Inkhorn, there's no musick in thy tongue.
   Catc.   Thou and thy Rime lye both; the tongue of man
Is born to musick naturally.
   Rime.   Thou thing,
Thy belly looks like to some strutting hill,
O'rshadow'd with thy rough beard like a wood.   [1465]
   Chri.   Or like a larger Jug, that some men call

A Bellarmine, but we a Conscience;
Whereon the lewder hand of Pagan workman
Over the proud ambitious head hath carv'd
An Idoll large with beard Episcopal, [1470]
Making the Vessel look like Tyrant *Eglon*.
   Catch. Prophane again Sir *Christopher* I take it.
   Chri. Must I be strong again? thou humane beast,
Who'rt only eloquent when thou sayst nothing,
And appear'st handsome while thou hid'st thy self, [1475]
I'm holy 'cause prophane.
   And. Couragious Raskals,
Brave Spirits, Souldiers in their daies I warrant.
   Bag. Born in the field I do assure your Worship:
This Quarrelling is meat and drink to them.
   Rime. Thou lyest. *Bag.* Nay then I do defie thee thus. [1480]

[*Ba. draws his Inkhorn and* Ri. *catcheth off Sr* Chr. *hat and spectacles.*]

   Rime. And thus I am prepar'd to answer thee.
   Ch. For the good S^{ts} sake part them; I am blind,
If that my Spectacles should once miscarry.
   Rime. Caytiff, this holy instrument shall quaile thee.
   Bag. And this shall send thee to thy couzen furies. [1485]
   Chri. I feel a film come o'r mine eyes already,
I must look out an Animal conductive,
I mean a Dog.
   And. Pray y' beat not out his eyes in
Anothers hands. *Chri.* Most strongly urg'd.
   Catch. Your words
Are meerly wind. *James* ho! what *James*! some beer. [1490]
They're mastive Dogs, they won't be parted Sir,
Without good store of Liquor.   [*Ent. Serv. with beere.*
   And. I will souce them.
   Ser. Drink t' 'em Sir, if that you'l have 'em quiet.
   An. Is that the way? here's to you my friends; a whol one.
   Ba. Were't not for that good Gentleman thou'dst smoak [1495]
      (for't.
   Ri. Had I not vow'd some reverence to his presence,
Thou hadst been nothing.
   Bag. 'Fore *Mars* I was dry;
This valour's thirsty: fill to my Antagonist.

Rime. No, mine own dish will serve: I'm singular.
Few vessels still do well; I carry this [1500]
To drink my beer, while others drink their sack.
I am abstemious *Rimewel*: I hate wine
Since I spake treason last i'th' Celler. Here
Give me thy hand, thou child of fervency.
Didst thou mistrust thy spectacles? [1505]
It was no anger, 'twas a Rapture meerly.
  Chris. Drink, and excuse it after. *James* your help.
Come Man of voice keep time while that I drink.
This moisture shall dry up all injuries,
Which I'l remember only to forget; [1510]
And so hereafter, which I'm wont to call
The future-now, I'l love thee stubbornly.
Your beer is like my words, strong, stinging geare.
  Catch. Here little Lawyer, let's be friends hereafter;
I love this reconcilement with my heart. [1515]
  And. 'Tis the best deed that e'r I did: O' my conscience
I shall make a good Justice of the Peace,
There had been bloud-shed, if I had not stickled.
  Ser. More bloud been spilt I warrant than beer now.
  And. That Inkhorn is a deadly dangerous weapon: [1520]
It hath undone one quarter of the Kingdom.
  Chris. Men should forgive; but thou art far, yea far
From it O *Bagshot*; thou'rt in love with hate;
Blesse me! I see the Fiend still in his looks;
He is not reconcilable with drink; [1525]
Hee'l never love truly, till he eat with me.
The nature of his Spirit asketh meat:
He hath a Woolf in's breast; food must appease him.
  And. Cold meat will doe it, wil't not?
  Rim. Any thing——
That may imploy the teeth.
  And. Goe *James* provide; [1530]
You are not merry yet.
  Catch. To satisfie you
In that point, we will sing a Song of his.
  And. Let's ha't; I love these Ballads hugeously.

The Song.

1. *Catch.*   *Then our Musick is in prime,*
              When our teeth keep triple time;   [1535]
              Hungry Notes are fit for Knels:
                  May lankenes be
                  No Quest to me.
              The Bagpipe sounds, when that it swels.
    Chor.   *May lankenes, &c.*   [1540]

2. *Bagsh.*   *A Mooting Night brings wholsome smiles,*
              When John an Okes, and John a Stiles,
              Doe greaze the Lawyers Satin.
                  A Reading-Day
                  Frights French away,   [1545]
              The Benchers dare speak Latin.
    Chor.   *A Reading, &c.*

3. *Rim.*   *He that's full doth Verse compose;*
            Hunger deales in sullen Prose:
            Take notice and discard her.   [1550]
              The empty Spit
              Ne'r cherish'd Wit,
            Minerva loves the Larder.
    Chor.   *The empty Spit, &c.*

4. *Chr.*   *First to break Fast, then to dine,*   [1555]
           Is to conquer Bellarmine:
           Distinctions then are budding.
              Old Sutcliffs *Wit*
              Did never hit,
           But after his Bag-pudding.   [1560]
    Chor.   *Old* Sutcliffs *Wit, &c.*

  And.   Most admirable; a good eating Song.
  Chri.   Let us walk in, and practice it; my Bowels
Yern till I am in charity with all.
  And.   A Christian resolution good Sr *Christopher.*   *Ex.*   [1565]

Act. III. Scen. VI.

Meanwell with a letter in his hand, *Hearsay, Slicer.*

Mea. Sweet Sir I am most passionately yours, [*Mean. reads.*
To serve you all the waies I can. *Priscilla.*
Very well Penn'd of a young Chambermaid;
I do conceive your meaning sweet *Priscilla*:
You see I have the happy fortune on't; [1570]
A night for nothing, and intreated too.
 Slic. Thou dost not know how I do love thee; let me
Make use of this, thou'lt have the like occasion.
 Hea. Thou art the fawningst fellow *Slicer* —— *Meanwel*
Heark here.
 Mean. For Gods sake be contented Sirs; [1575]
I'm flesh and bloud as well as you. Lieutenant,
Think on your Suburb Beauties; sweet Intelligencer,
I will by no means bar you of your Lady.
Your sin I assure you will be honourable. [*Exit Mean.*
 Slic. Pox o' your liquorous lips; if that she don't [1580]
After this sealing forty weeks deliver
Something unto thee as thy act and deed,
Say I can't Prophesie.
 Hear. If I don't serve him
A trick he thinks not of ——
 Slic. Did'st mark how he
Did apply himself to the Knight all dinner? [1585]
I am afraid he plaies the cunning Factor,
And in anothers name woes for himself.
 Hear. Let it go on; let it work something farther.
'Tis almost ripe enough to crush; he hath not
Crept high enough as yet to be sensible [1590]
Of any fall.
 Slic. Now is the time or never.
This night you know he and his Doxie meet;
Let me alone to give them their goodmorrow.
If that we carry things but one week longer
Without discovery, farewell *London* then; [1595]
The world's our own. He ne'r deserves to thrive

That doth not venture for it. Wealth's then sweet
   When bought with hazzard. Fate this Law hath set;
   The foole inherits, but the wise must get.

Act. IV. Scen. I.

Credulous, Hearsay, Slicer.

Cred. *My Name's not* Tribulation, [1600]
   Nor holy Ananias:
I was baptiz'd in fashion,
   Our Vicar did hold Bias.
   Hear. What, how now Mr *Credulous*? so merry?
   Cred. Come let's be mad; by yea and nay my Son [1605]
Shall have the Turkish Monarchy; he shall
Have it directly: the twelve Companies
Shall be his Kickshaws.
   Hear. Bashaws Sir you mean.
   Cred. Well Sir, what if I do? *Andrew* the great Turk!
I would I were a pepper corn if that [1610]
It sounds not well: do'st not?
   Slic. Yes, very well.
   Cred. I'l make it else: Great *Andrew Mahomet,*
Imperious *Andrew Mahomet Credulous,*
Tell me which name sounds best.
   Hear. That's as you speak 'em.
   Cred. Oatemeleman *Andrew, Andrew* Oatmeleman. [1615]
   Hear. *Ottoman* Sir you meane.
   Cred. Yes *Ottoman.*
Then Mrs *Jane,* Sir *Thomas Bitefiggs* Daughter,
That may be the she Great Turk, if she please me.
   Sli. The Sign o'th' half Moon that hangs at your door,
Is not for nought.
   Cred. That's the Turks Armes they say; [1620]
The Empire's destin'd to our house directly.
Hang Shop-books, give's some Wine, hay for a noise
Of Fidlers now.
   Hear. The Great Turk loves no Musick.

Cred. Does he not so? nor I. I'l light Tobacco
With my Sum-totals; my Debt-books shall sole
Pyes at young *Andrew's* Wedding: cry you mercy;
I would say Gentlemen the Great Turks Wedding.
My Deeds shall be slic'd out in Taylors Measures;
They all imploy'd in making Mrs *Mahomet*
New Gowns against the time; hang durty wealth.
   Sl. What should the Great Turks father do wth wealth?
   Cred. 'Snigs I would fain now heare
Some fighting News.   [*Ent. Cast.*
   Slic. There's one will furnish you I warrant you.
   Cast. Pox! —— Plague! —— Hell! —— Death! ——
       Damn'd luck! —— this 'tis! ——
The Devill take all Fortunes: never man
Came off so; quite and clean defunct by Heaven ——
Not a peece left.
   Cred. What all your Ord'nance lost?
   Cast. But one to bear, and lose it! all the world
Was sure against me.
   Cred. 'Snigs how many fell?
   Cast. He threw twice twelve.
   Cred. By'r Lady a shrewd many.
   Cast. The Devill sure was in his hand I think.
   Cred. Nay, if the Devill was against you, then ——
   Cast. But one for to be hit in all the time ——
And that too safe enough to any ones thinking;
'T stood on eleven.
   Cred. 'Slid a mighty slaughter;
But did he stand upon elev'n at once?
   Cast. The Plague take all impertinencies, peace.
   Cred. These Souldiers are so cholerick there is
No dealing with 'em; then they've lost the day.
   Cast. 'Twas ten to one by Heaven all the while.
   Cred. And yet all kill'd at last? hard fortune faith.
What news from *Bruxels*? or the *Hague*? d'y' heare
Ought of the Turks designs?
   Cast. I'l make thee news
For the Coranti Dotard.
   Cred. Ay, the Coranti,
What doth that say?

    Cast. O hell! thou foolish thing
Keep in that tongue of thine, or ——
    Slic. Good now peace,
He's very furious when he's mov'd.
    Hear. This 'twas.
You must be ventring without your Fancy-man.
    Cred. What Officer's that Fancy-man, Lieutenant?
Some great Commander sure.
    Cast. Pox! let it go;
I'l win't again: 'twas but the Reliques of
An idle hundred.
    Cred. 'Snigs and well remember'd.
You did receive the hundred that I sent you
To th' Race this morning by your man, my Bayliffe?
    Cast. Take him away, his wine speaks in him now.
    Cred. Godsnigs the Farme is mine, and must be so.
    Slic. Debate these things another time, good friends.
                                Enter Haveatall.
Come, come, have Patience. Od's my life away.
There's Mr *Haveatall* is mad; hee'l spit you,
If he but know you are a Usurer.
    Cre. A plot, a plot to take away my life and Farm. [*Ex.*
    Have. Fight as I live with any one. Lieutenant
Do not come neer me now, nor yet thou *Caster*;
It works, 'fore *Mars* it works; I'l take my walk,
And if I do find any one by *Iove*. ——   *Ex. Haveatall.*
    Cast. What's he fox'd too? some drunken Planet raigns
And works upon the world; Provide my fancie
God Noble Patron: I'l win soberly,
I itch till I have beggard all the City.   *Exit Cast.*
    Hea. Till that you have undone your self you mean. *En. Mo.*
    Mo. Ey save you both: for derne love sayen soothly
Where is thylk amebly *Francklin*, cleped *Meanwel*?
    Hear. Hee's gone abroad.
    Mo. Lere me whylk way he wended.
    Slic. He is gon o'r the fields.
    Hear. To the Knights house.
    Mo. Why laugh you every dele? so mote I gone,
This goeth not aright; I dread some Covin.   *Exit Moth*
    Slic. Now will he meet with *Haveatall*; there'll be

A Combate worthy Chronicle. Let's go
And see how this grave motion will bestir him.   *Exeunt.*

ACT IV. SCEN. II.

Haveatall, after a while *Moth*, *Slicer* and
Hearsay watching.

  Ha. What, no man yet march by? who e'r comes next   [1690]
I'l give him one rap more for making me
Stay here so long.   *Enter Moth.*
                 So so here h'is; how shall
I do to know where he be a Gentleman,
Or Yeoman or Serving-man? I think
I'd best suppose him all, and beat him through   [1695]
Every degree, and so I shall not wrong him.
What? who goes there?
  Moth. Waes heal thou gentle Knight.
  Hav. Waes heal thou gentle Knight? speak what art thou?
Speak quickly doe: Villain know'st thou not me?
  Moth. Now by my troath I know not your Name;   [1700]
Whider I shall call you my Lord *Dan John*,
Or *Dan Thomas*, or *Dan Robert*, or *Dan Albon*:
I vow to God thou hast a full faire chine;
Upon my faith art some Officer.
  Hav. Have you the pox Sir? speak.
  Moth. No.
  Hav. No? nor yet   [1705]
An ach in your Bones!
  Moth. No.
  Hav. No? why then you are
No Gentleman; Lieutenant *Slicer* says so.
This cudgell then serves turn.
  Moth. You will not foyn?
  Hav. I will not foyn, but I will beat you Sir.
  Moth. Why intermete of what thou hast to done;   [1710]
So leteth me alone, 't shall be thy best.
  Hav. I fancy'd you a beating; you must have it.
'You shall not say but I will shew you favour.

Choose where you will be hacked with my sword,
Or bruis'd by my Batton.
   Moth. Dre not thy true, [1715]
And paynant *Morglay* out of Shete. Lo thus
Eftsoons Sir Knight, I greet thee lowting low.
   Hav. Downe lower yet.
   Moth. Rueth on my gray haires.
   Hav. Yet lower: so, then thus I do bestride thee.
   Moth. *Tubal* the sonne of *Lamech* did yfind [1720]
Musick by knocking Hammers upon Anviles;
Let go thine blows, thylke Art is no compleat.
   Hav. Dost thou make me a Smith thou Rogue? a *Tubal*?
   Moth. Harrow alas! flet *Englond*, flet *Englond*:
Dead is *Edmond*.
   Hav. Take that for history. [1725]
O brave Lieutenant now thy dinner works.
   Mo. I nis not *Edmond Ironside* God wot.
   Ha. More provocation yet? I'l seal thy lips.
   Mo. A twenty Devil way! So did the Saxon
Upon thylke plain of *Sarum*, done to death [1730]
By treachery, the Lords of merry *Englond*.
Nem esur Saxes.
   Have. Villain dost abuse me
In unbaptized language? do not answer;   [*Moth entreats*
If that thou dost, by *Iove* I'l strangle thee.   *by signs.*
Do you make mouths you Raskall thus at me? [1735]
You're at dumb Service now: why, this is more
Unsufferable than your old patch'd gibberish;
This silence is abuse. I'l send thee to
The Place of it, where thou shalt meet with *Oswald*,
Vortigern, *Harold*, *Hengist*, *Horsey*, *Knute*, [1740]
Alured, *Edgar*, and *Cunobeline*.   [*Slic. Hear. step in.*
Thus, thus I sheath my Sword.
   Slic. Redoubted Knight
Enough, 'tis thy foe doth vanquish'd lie
Now at thy mercy, mercy not withstand,
For he is one the truest Knight alive, [1745]
Though conquer'd now he lie on lowly ground.
   Ha. Thou ow'st thy life to my Lieutenant, Caitife.
Breath and be thankfull.

Mo. I reche not thine yeft;
Maugre thine head, algate I suffer none,
I am thine lefe, thine deere, mine *Potluck Jone*. [1750]

Exeunt.

Act. IV. Scen. III.

Andrew, Priscilla.

And. Fairest of things — tralucent creature — Hang me
If I do know what's next.
 Pris. This meant to mee?
 And. Fairest of things — tralucent creature — rather
Obscured Deity —— 'Tis gone again.
Lady will you eat a peece of Gingerbread? [1755]
 Pris. You might have better manners than to scoff
One of my breeding.
 An. Heark; indad I love you.
 Pris. Alas!
 An. I vow I burn in love, as doth
A penny Faggot.
 Pris. Hey ho!
 An. And I shall
Blaze out Sir reverence if ye do not quench me. [1760]
 Pris. Indeed now?
 An. Though I say't that should not say't,
I am affected towards you strangely.
 Pris. Now who'd have thought it?
 An. There's a thing each night
Comes to my Bedshead and cries Matrimony,
Matrimony *Andrew*.
 Pris. God forbid.
 An. It is [1765]
Some Spirit that would joyn us.
 Pri. Goodly, goodly.
 An. Then do I shake all over.
 Pris. Doth it so?
 An. Then shake again.
 Pris. I pray you now.

And. Then cry
Fairest of things —— tralucent creature —— rather
Obscured Deity, sweet Mrs *Jane*, [1770]
I come I come.
  Prisc. Sweet Sir you are deceiv'd:
I'm but her woeman; here she comes her self. [*En.* Mrs *Ja.*
  And. Now as my Father saith, I would I were
A Cucumber if I know what to doe.
  Jan. Why how now *Pris*? who's that that useth you [1775]
So lovingly?
  And. Fairest of things —— 'tis one
Tralucent Creature —— 'tis —— Ay that it is
One ——
  Pris. That would willingly run out of doores,
If that he had but Law enough.
  And. I say ——
  Jan. Nay ben't afraid: here's none shall doe you harm. [1780]
  An. 'Tis one that brought his Pigs to the wrong market.
You keep your woman here so fine, that I
Had like t' have made a proper businesse on't
Before I was aware. If any thing
Doe prove amisse, indeed-law you shall be [1785]
The Father on't. But know tralucent Creature
I am come off entire, and now am yours
Whole, *Andrew Credulous*, your servants servant.
  Jan. Methinks you contradict your self: how can you
Be wholly mine, and yet my servants servant? [1790]
  And. I doe but complement in that (I see
Downright's the best way here) if thou canst love
I can love too. Law thee there now. I'm rich.
  Jan. I use not to look after riches; 'tis
The person that I aime at.
  And. That is me; [1795]
I'm proper, handsome, faire, clean-limb'd: I'm rich.
  Jan. I must have one that can direct and guide me;
A Guardian rather than a Husband; for
I'm foolish yet.
  An. Now see the luck on't Lady
So am I too Ifaith.
  Jan. And who e'r hath me [1800]

Will find me to be one of those things which
His care must first reform.
   An. Do not doubt that;
I have a head for Reformation:
This noddle here shall do it. I am rich.
   Jane. Riches create no love; I fear you mean   [1805]
To take me for formality only,
As some staid peece of housholdstuff perhaps
Fit to be seen 'mong other ornaments:
Or at the best I shall be counted but
A name of dignity; not entertain'd   [1810]
For love but State; one of your train, a thing
Took to wipe off suspicion from some fairer
To whom you have vow'd Homage.
   An. Do not think
I've any Plots or Projects in my Head,
I will do any thing for thee that thou   [1815]
Canst name or think on.
   Pris. Pray you try him Mistris,
By my Virginity I think hee'l flinch.
   And. By my Virginity (which is as good
As yours I'm sure) by my Virginity
If that we men have any such thing (as   [1820]
We men haue such a thing) I do beleeve
I will not flinch. Alas! you don't know *Andrew*.
   Jan. Can you obtain but so much respite from
Your other Soverains service, as to keep
Your Eye from gazing on her for a while?   [1825]
   An. If I do look on any woman, nay,
If I do cast a sheeps eye upon any
But your sweet self, may I lose one of mine:
Marry I'l keep the other howsoe'r.
   Jane. I know not how I may beleeve you; you'l   [1830]
Swear you ne'r cast a glance on any, when
Your eye hath baited at each face you met.
   An. Blind me good now: being you mistrust, I will
Be blinded with this handkercheife; you shall
See that I love you now. So, let me have   [1835]
But any reasonable thing to lead me home,
I do not care though 't be a Dog, so that

He knows the way, or hath the wit t' enquire it.
   Jane. That care Sir shall be mine.   [*Ex. Iane, and Pris.*
   An. I doubt not, but
I shall be in the Chronicle for this,   [1840]
Or in a Ballad else. This handkercheif
Shall be hung up i'th' Parish Church insteed
Of a great silken flag to fan my grave:
With my Arms in't, pourtray'd in good blew thread
With this word underneath: *This, this was he*   [1845]
That shut his eyes because he would not see.
Hold who comes there?
                                [*Ent. Mean. Shape.*
   Mean. One Sir to lead you home.
   An. Who? Tutor *Meanwell*?
   Sha. Yes I do commit you   { *Shape counterfeits*
Unto your trusty friend, If you perform   { *Mrs Janes voice.*
This vow we may ——
   An. I'l say your sentence out,   [1850]
Be man and wife.
   Sha. If you'l do something else
That I'l propose.
   An. Pray make your own conditions.
   Sha. You'l promise me you'l not be jealous of me?
   An. Do what you will I'l trust you.
   Sha. Never hire
Any to tempt me?
   An. By this light (I would say   [1855]
By this darknesse) I never will.
   Sha. Nor mark
On whom I laugh? ——
   An. No.
   Sha. Nor suspect My smiles,
My nods, my winks? ——
   An. No, no.
   Sha. Nor yet keep count
From any Gallants visit?
   An. I'l ne'r reckon;
You shall do what you will.
   Sha. You'l never set   [1860]
Great Chests and Formes against my Chamber Door,

Nor pin my smock unto your shirt a nights,
For fear I should slip from you ere you wake?
  An. As I do hope for Day I will not.
  Sha. Give me
Some small pledge from you to assure your love;   [1865]
If that you yet prove false, I may have something
To witnésse your inconstancy. I'l take
This little Ruby: this small blushing stone
From your fair finger.
  An. Take it Sweet: there is
A Diamond in my Bandstring, if you have   [1870]
A mind to that I pray make use of 't too.
  Sha. In troth a stone of lustre, I assure you
It darts a pretty light, a veget spark;
It seems an Eye upon your Breast.
  An. Nay take it,
For loves sake take it then; leave nothing that   [1875]
Looks like an Eye about me.
  Sha. My good *Andrew*,
'Cause of thy resolution, I'l perform
This office for thee. Take my word for't, this
Shall ne'r betray thee.   *Ex. Shape.*
  An. Farewell honest *Jany*,
I cannot see to thank thee my sweet *Jany*.   [1880]
Tutor, your hand good Tutor, lead me wisely.
  Mea. Take comfort man; I have good news for thee:
Thine eyes shall be thine own before next morning.
                                                Exeunt.

Act IV. Scen. IV.

Shape, Chirurgion, Mercer.

  Sha. Hee's a good friend of mine, and I presume
Upon your secresie.
  Chi. O Sir —— the Deed   [1885]
By which it came was not more close. D'y' think
I would undo me self by twitting? 'twere
To bring the Gallants all about mine Ears,

And make me mine own Patient. I'm faithfull,
And secret, though a Barber.
   Sha. Nay, but hear me; [1890]
Hee's very modest: 'twas his first attempt
Procur'd him this infirmity; he will
Be bashfull I am sure, and won't be known
Of any such thing at the first; you must
Be sure to put him to't.
   Chi. Let me alone, [1895]
He knows not yet the world I do perceive.
It is as common now with Gentlemen,
As 'tis to follow fashion; only here
Lyeth the difference, that they keep in this
A little longer. I shall have so much [1900]
Upon your word Sir?
   Sha. If you do perform
The cure by that time (twenty peeces Sir.)
You are content?
   Mer. Yes Sir.
   Chi. It shall be done   *Ex. Shape.*
According to your own prescription.
Sit down I pray you Sir, this Gentleman [1905]
Is a good friend of yours.
   Mer. Indeed he is
A very honest man as any one
Can wish to deal with verily.
   Chi. Beleeve't
He loves you very well.
   Mer. I am most ready
To do him any service truly; pray you [1910]
Good Brother don't delay me, I'm in haste.
   Chi. Indeed, and truly, verily good Brother;
How could these milk-sop words e'r get him company
That could procure the Pox? where do you feel
Your grief most trouble you?
   Mer. I'm very well. [1915]
What mean you Brother?
   Chi. Nay, be not so modest;
'Tis no such hainous fault, as that you should
Seek thus to hide it: meer ill fortune only ——

Mer. Surely you do forget your self.
Chi. Come, come,
He told me you'ld be shamefac'd; you must be [1920]
Wary hereafter.
Mer. (I do perceive
He is a little mad indeed; the Gentleman
Told me so much just as I came along)
Yes, yes, I'l be wary, I'l take heed,
Come pray y' dispatch me.
Chi. So, I like you now. [1925]
It is the custome of most Gentlemen
Not to confesse untill they feel their bones
Begin t' admonish 'em.
Mer. You are i'th' right:
Good friend make haste; I've very urgent businesse.
Chi. Not rashly neither; Is your Gristle sound? [1930]
Me thinks 'tis very firm as yet to th' touch.
You fear no danger there as yet Sir, do you?
Mer. No, I'l assure you. (He must have his humour;
I see he is not to be cross'd.)
Chi. When did you
Feel the first grudging on't? 'tis not broke out [1935]
In any place?
Mer. No, no: I pray y' dispatch me.
Chi. These things desire deliberation;
Care is requir'd.
Mer. Good Brother go t' your Chest.
Chi. How can I know what Med'cines to apply,
If that you tell me not where lies your grief? [1940]
Mer. Nay good now let me go.
Chi. I must not Sir,
Nor will not truly: trust me you will wish
You had confess'd and suffer'd me in time,
When you shall come to dry burnt Racks of Mutton,
The Syren, and the Tub.
Mer. So now enough; [1945]
Pray fetch me what you promis'd.
Chi. Are you wild,
Or mad? I do protest I ne'r did meet

A Gentleman of such perversnesse yet.
I find you just as I was told you should [be].
   Mer. I lose the taking, by my swear, of taking   [1950]
As much, whiles that I am receiving this.
   Chi. I will not hinder you, if that you do
Prefer your gain before your health.
   Mer. Well then
I pray you tell it out; we Tradesmen are not
Masters of our own time.
   Chi. What would you have?   [1955]
   Mer. What would I have? as if you did not know;
Come come leave jesting now at last good Brother.
   Chi. I am in earnest Sir.
   Mer. Why, I would have
My money Sir, the twenty peeces that
The Gentleman did give you order now   [1960]
To pay me for the Velvet, that he bought
This morning of me.
   Chi. O! the Gentleman ——
   Mer. You should not make a laughing stock good Brother
Of one that wrongs you not; I do professe
I won't be fubb'd ensure your self.
   Chi. The Gentleman!   [1965]
Oh! oh! the Gentleman! is this the cure
I should perform? truly I dare not venture
Upon such desperate Maladies.
   Mer. You are
But merrily dispos'd?
   Chi. Indeed they are
Too high for my small Quality; verily   [1970]
Perhaps good Brother you might perish under
Mine hands truly; I do profess I am not
Any of your bold Mountebanks in this.
   Mer. You're still dispos'd ——
   Chi. To laugh at you good Brother.
Gull'd by my swear, by my swear gull'd; he told me   [1975]
You had a small infirmity upon you,
A griefe of youth, or two; and that I should
Have twenty peeces for the cure. He ask'd you
If that you were content, you answered yes.

I was in hope I'd gain'd a Patient more; [1980]
Your best way is to make haste after him.
  Mer. Now could I beat my self for a wise fool
That I was, thus to trust him.   *Exit.*
  Chi. ` B'w'y' Brother.
'Fore God a good one. O! the Gentleman.   *Ex. laughing.*

Act. IV. Scen. V.

Rimewell, Bagshot, Catchmey, Sir *Christopher*; A Song
at a window; congratulating (as they think)
Mr *Meanwels* Marriage.

1.
    Whiles early light springs from the skies, [1985]
    A fairer from your Bride doth rise;
    A brighter Day doth thence appear,
    And make a second morning there:
      Her blush doth shed
      All o'r the bed, [1990]
      Clean shamefac'd beames
      That spread in streames,
    And purple round the modest aire.

2.
    I will not tell what shreeks, and cries,
    What Angry Dishes, and what ties, [1995]
    What pretty oaths then newly born
    The listning Taper heard there sworn:
      Whiles froward she
      Most peevishly
      Did yielding fight [2000]
      To keep o'r night
    What shee'd have profer'd you ere morn.

3.
    Faire, we know, maids do refuse
    To grant what they do come to lose.
    Intend a Conquest you that wed; [2005]
    They would be chastly ravished.
      Not any kisse
      From Mrs Pris,

>   *If that you do*
>   *Perswade and woe,* [2010]
>   *Know pleasure's by extorting fed.*

4.
>   *O may her arms wax black and blew*
>   *Only by hard encircling you:*
>   *May she round about you twine*
>   *Like the easie twisting Vine;* [2015]
>   *And whiles you sip*
>   *From her full lip*
>   *Pleasures as new*
>   *As morning Dew,*
>   *Let those soft Tyes your hearts combine.* [2020]

Sing. God give you joy Mr *Meanwell*. God give your
      Worship good morrow.
Rim. Come let's be going.
Chr. Hold, a blow I'l have,
One jerk at th' times, wrap'd in a benediction
O' th' Spouses teeming, and I'l go with you. [2025]

A Song.

>   *Now thou our future Brother,*
>   *That shalt make this Spouse a Mother,*
>   *Spring up, and* Dod's *blessing on't.*
>   *Shew thy little sorrell Pate*
>   *And prove regenerate* [2030]
>   *Before thou be brought to the Font.*
>   *May the Parish Surplice be*
>   *Cut in peeces quite for thee,*
>   *To wrap thy soft body about;*
>   *So 'twill better service do* [2035]
>   *Reformed thus into*
>   *The state of an Orthodox Clout.*
>   *When thou shalt leave the Cradle,*
>   *And shalt begin to waddle,*
>   *And trudge in thy little Apron;* [2040]
>   *Mayst thou conceive a grace*
>   *Of half an hours space,*
>   *And rejoice in thy Friday Capon.*

For an errour that's the Flocks
Name Mr Paul, but urge St Knoxe; [2045]
   And at every reform'd Dinner,
Let cheese come in, and preaching,
And by that third Course teaching,
   Confirm an unsatisfi'd Sinner.
Thence grow up to hate a Ring, [2050]
And defie an offering:
   And learn to sing what others say.
Let Christ-tide be thy fast,
And lent thy good repast:
   And regard not an Holy day. [2055]

Enter Constable and Assistants.

Con. Lay hold on them; lay hold on them I say:
I'l hamper them.
   Cat. Hell take your headlong zeale;
You must be jerking at the times forsooth.
I am afraid the times will scape, and we
The men of them shall suffer now the scourge. [2060]
   Con. Let none escape.
   Chri. 'Twas godliness verily:
It was a Hymn I warbled.
   Con. Thou dost lye,
It was no Hymn, it was a Song. Is this
Your filthy Rendevow? you shall be taught
Another tune.
   Chr. I do beseech you shew [2065]
Mercifull cruelty, and as 'twere a kind
Of pittifull hardheartednesse. I'm strong.

They bring in Andrew, and Priscilla.

Con. I'm glad you told me so, I will provide
Your Ward accordingly. Drag 'em out both.
   An. Let me but send to th' Ordinary.
   Con. You shall not, [2070]
The Ord'nary hath sent to you: No Baile,
I will take none. I'l suffer no such sneaks
As you, t' offend this way. It doth belong
T'your Betters Sir.

An.   Here's a sufficient Man
I do assure you, take my word for that. [2075]
   Con.   This staff was made to knock down sin. I'l look
There shall be no Advowtry in my Ward
But what is honest. I'l see Justice done
As long as I'm in office. Come along.   *Exeunt.*

Act. V. Scene I.

Sir *Thomas Bitefig* as sick, *Iane*.

Sr *Tho.*   Now that I have made ev'n Girl, with Heav'n, [2080]
Though I am past the worst, and I perceive
My dinner only griev'd me, yet 'cause Life's
Frail, and uncertain, let me counsell thee,
'Tis good to be before hand still. First then
I charge thee lend no money; next serve God; [2085]
If ever thou hast Children teach 'em thrift;
They'l learn Religion fast enough themselves.
Nay, do not weep but hearken. When Heav'n shall
Please to call in this Weary Soul of mine,
Ben't idle in expence about my Burial; [2090]
Buy me a shroud, any old sheet will serve
To cloath corruption; I can rot without
Fine linnen; 'tis but to enrich the Grave,
And adorn stench, no reverence to the dead,
To make 'em crumble more luxuriously. [2095]
One Torch will be sufficient to direct
The footsteps of my Bearers. If there be
Any so kind as to accompanie
My body to the Earth, let them not want
For entertainment, prethee see they have [2100]
A sprig of Rosemary dip'd in common water,
To smell to as they walk along the streets.
Eatings and drinkings are no obsequies.
Raise no oppressing Pile to load my Ashes;
But if thou'l needs b' at charges of a Tomb, [2105]
Five or six foot of common stone engrav'd

With a good hopefull word, or else a couple
Of capital letters filled up with pitch,
Such as I set upon my Sheep, will serve;
State is not meet for those that dwell in dust. [2110]
Mourn as thou pleasest for me, plainness shews
True grief: I give thee leave to do it for
Two or three years, if that thou shalt think fit.
'Twill save expence in cloaths. And so now be
My blessing on thee, and my means hereafter. [2115]
   Jan. I hope Heav'n will not deal so rigidly
With me, as to preserve me to th' unwelcome
Performance of these sad injunctions.

Act V. Scen. II.

To them *Meanwell*.

   Mean. Good health unto you Sir.
   Sr *Tho.* I have the more
By reason of the care you took in sending [2120]
A Confessor unto me.
   Mean. I? a Confessor?
Sure there is some design, some trick or other
Put on you by those men, who never sleep
Unless they've cheated on that Day.
   Sir *Tho.* I hope
You do[n't] mean your Partners my good friends? [2125]
   Mean. They ne'r deserve the name of friends, they do
Covet, not love. If any came from them,
It was some Vulture in a holy habit,
Who did intend your Carkasse, not your safety;
Indeed I know not of't, I've all this while [2130]
Appear'd another to you than I am.   *Discloseth himself.*
Perhaps you know me now. I'm he whom you
Pleas'd to forbid your house, whom Mr *Credulous*
Takes leave to stile lost man, and Vagabond.
   Sr *Tho.* That I forbad you Sir my house was only [2135]
In care to my Daughter, not in hate to you.
   Mean. That I frequented it without your leave,

Was both in love to you, and to your Daughter;
That I have all this while liv'd thus disguis'd,
Was only to avert the snare from you, [2140]
Not to intrap you; that you might not be
Blinded by those, who like to venemous Beasts,
Have only sight to poyson; that you might not
Ruine your Daughter in a complement.

   Sr Tho. This may b' your plot, and this discoverie [2145]
Feign'd only to secure your own designs:
For 't cannot sink into me that they durst
Make mirth of my repentance, and abuse
My last devotion with a Scene of Laughter.

   Mean. They dare beyond your thought. When parted this [2150]
Your Confessor?

   Sr Tho. You could not chuse but meet him,
He is scarce yet at home.

   Mean. If that you dare
But venture with me home, I'l almost promise
I'l make it plain they've put a trick upon you.

   Sr Tho. Though every step were so much toward my grave [2155]
I'd tread them o'r with comfort that I might
Discover this religious villany.

                                               Exeunt.

Act V. Scen. III.

Hearsay, Slicer, and *Shape* in his Confessors habit.

   Hear. Come my good Vulture speak; what prey? what mirth?
   Slic. What income my dear holiness? what sport?
   Sha. Give me the Chair; imagine me the Knight [2160]
(When I sit down,) and (when I stand) the Confessor.

   {*As he is thus acting,* Meanwell *and Sir* Thomas
   discover themselves above.}

Thus I come in peace to thy soul good Son,
(Tis you must give it Father; I am ill,
I'm very ill; fit only now for Heav'n.
My Soul would fain be flying, were't not for [2165]
A Sin or two that clogs her.) But for a sin

Or two that clogs her? take heed, don't so neer
Your last deliverance play the Sophister
With Heav'n. A sin or two? why, I've heard say
You're wont to skrew your wretched Tenants up [2170]
To th' utmost farthing, and then stand upon
The third Rent Capon. Then he answers me
In the small dolfull tune of a Country wench
Examin'd by th' Officiall, for the mischance
Of a great belly caught at a Whitsonale; [2175]
(I could not help it.) Then it is your custome
When you invite, to think your meat laid out;
You write your Beef disburs'd, are wont to call
For the return of't just, as for a debt;
(True.) That two Chimneys ne'r yet smok'd at once [2180]
In all your Buildings; (All most true.) That you
Are wont to keep an untouch'd Capon, till
Corruption makes it able to walk out
And visit the Barn Door again: I could
Say much more, but I'd rather have you [2185]
Come so much nearer pardon, as t' accuse
Your self by your own mouth.
   Slic. How grave the Rogue was?
   Sha. (I'l do't as strictly as mine Enemy.)
   Sir *Tho.* I cannot hold; I'l break in as I am,
And take my vengeance whiles my furie's hot. [2190]
   Mean. Repress it Sir a while; h' hath but begun.
   Sha. Then thus he dralls it out. (I do confess
I've been addicted to frugality.)
Son do not mince; pray call it Covetousness.
(*Imprimis* It hath ever been my custome [2195]
To ride beyond an Inn to save my horse meat.
Item, When once I had done so, and found
No entertainment, I beguild the children
Of their parch'd pease, my Man being left to that
We make the embleme of mortality:) [2200]
What? grass you mean? (or sweet Hay which you please.)
   Hear. Me thinks this's truly coming to a Reckoning,
He doth account for's sins with *Item* so.
   Sha. (*Item* I've often bought a Cheapside Custard,
And so refresh'd my soul under my Cloak, [2205]

As I did walk the streets.) Cloaking of sins,
Although they be but eating sins, I do
Pronounce most dangerous. (I find this so,
I'd almost lost mine Eyes by't being justled.)
   Slic. O thou rich soul of Roguery.
   Shap. (Moreover [2210]
I once sung Psalmes with Servants where I lodg'd,
And took part with 'em in their lovely Reliques;
Truly my soul did lust, they were Temptations.)
What sing that you might eat? It is the sin
O'th' Brethren Son; but that their Reliques are [2215]
Whole widows houses.
   Hear. O thou preaching Devill!
   Sha. (*Item* I enter'd into a Chandlers shop,
And eat my bread in secret, whiles my man
Fed on the wholsome steem of Candle sewet.
Item, which grieves me most, I did make bold [2220]
With the Black Puddings of my needy Taylor;
Satan was strong, they did provoke me much.)
   Sr *Tho.* Wretch that I was to trust my bosome to
One so exactly bad, that if the book
Of all mens lives lay open to his view [2225]
Would meet no sin unpractis'd by himself.
I will rush in.
   Mean. Good Sir keep close a while.
   Sha. I see no tears, no penetentiall tears.
(Alas! I cannot weep, mine Eyes are Pumice.
But Alms I hope may yet redeem.) Alms giv'n [2230]
In a large manner Son. (Won't fifty pounds
Wipe off my score?) If doubled't may do something.
(Can I be sav'd no cheaper? take this then
And pray for me.) With that I thus dismiss'd him.
Blest Son, for now I dare pronounce thee blest, [2235]
Being thou'st powr'd thus out thy soul —— The wolf!
The wolf! 'sfoot peace, we're in the noose:
We are betrai'd, yon's *Meanwell* and the Knight ——
Truly he is as good a man as any
I ever yet confess'd —— don't look that way —— [2240]
A very honest charitable man,
Full of sincerity, and true devotion.

Act V, Scene iv] THE ORDINARY

 Sr Tho. Patience it self would now turn furious,
Let's for some Officers.
         Ex. Sir. Tho. and Mean.
 Sha. Discover'd all!
Religion is unluckie to me.
 Hear. Man!   [2245]
Perfidious man! there is no trust in thee!
 Slic. I never lik'd this *Meanwell*; I did alwaies
See treachery writ in's forehead: I well hop'd
H'ad been in Prison with his wench.
 Sha. Leave railing.
Along with me. There is left one way more;   [2250]
The Cat may yet perhaps light on all foure. *Exeunt.*

Act. V. Scen. IV.

Sir Thomas Bitefig, Meanwell, Constable, Watchmen.

 Sir *Tho.* What gone? upon my life they did mistrust.
 Mean. They are so beaten that they smell an Officer,
As Crows do Powder.
 Sr *Tho.* Watchman call you forth
The Mistris of the house, *Imprimis*, for *Ex. Officer.*
They have their lurking hole near hand most certain. [2256]
   Enter Moth, *and* Potluck *as Man and Wife.*
 Mo. *Denuncio vobis gaudium magnum,*
Robertus de Tinea electus est in sedem Hospitalem,
Et assumit sibi nomen Galfridi.
Joy comes to our house. I *Robert Moth* am   [2260]
Chesen into thylk Hospitall seat,
Thylk Bason of *Jone Potluck*, Vintners Widow,
And do transmue my name to Giffery.
New foysons byn ygraced with new Titles.
Come buss.
 Pot. Fie! Mr *Giffery* I swear   [2265]
You make m' asham'd 'fore all this Company.
 Sir *Tho.* Sir, if you be the Master of this house,
You've harbor'd here a company of cheating Villains,
Which we are come to apprehend.

Pot. Pray y' look,
Search every Corner, here's no cheats. I'm sure [2270]
The house was clear before your Worship entred.
  Con. Make fast the Doors for fear they do escape.
Let's in and ferret out these cheating Rakehels.
> *As the Watchmen go in and out about the Rooms*
> Hearsay, Slicer, *and* Shape *mingle themselves*
> *with 'em, being accounted Watchmen, and so*
> *pass without discovery.*

Enter 1. Watchman, and Hearsay.

1 Watch. 'Tis very certain they are not in the house.
Sr *Tho.* They had no time to get away.
Hear. Why then, [2275]
It may be being they are such cunning Fellows,
They have the trick of going invisible.

Enter 2. Watchman, and Slicer.

2 Watch. There's no place left unsearch'd but Pots and
    Mouseholes.
Slic. They're either gone or in the House that's certain.
2 Watchm. That cannot be; the Doors were shut I'm sure, [2280]
And so they could not get out; the Rooms then are
All search'd, and so they cannot be within.
Slic. I'l lay my neck to a farthing, then they're vanish'd.
Hear. Sunk like the Queen, they'l rise at Queenhive sure.

Enter Constable, and other Watchmen, and Shape, *among*
    'em, bringing in Credulous, *and* Caster.

Sha. Most certain these are two of them: for this [2285]
Old Knave, I'l take my Oath that he is one.
Con. Confess, confess, where are your other Comrads?
Cre. I am as honest as the skin that is
Between thy Brows?
Con. What skin between my Brows?
What skin thou knave? I am a Christian; [2290]
And what is more, a Constable; what skin?
Sr *Tho.* You are mistaken friends.
Con. I cry you mercy.
Sha. The Constable may call you any thing
In the Kings name upon suspicion.
Sr *Tho.* We're cheated friends; these men o'th' Ordnary [2295]
Have gull'd us all this while, and now are gone.

Cast. I am undon. Ne'r let me live if that
I did not think th' would gull me, I perceive
Fansie doth much; see how 'tis come to pass.
   Cred. Where is my Son God blesse him? where is   [2300]
       Andrew?
Pray God they have not taken him along;
He hath a perilous wit to be a cheat;
He'd quickly come to be his Majesties Taker.
   Con. I took one *Andrew Credulous* this morning
In dishonest Adultery with a Trull.   [2305]
And if he be your Son he is in Prison.
   Cred. Their villany o' my life. Now as I am
A Freeman and a Grocer, I had rather
Have found forty pounds; I pray go fetch him.   *Ex. officer.*
   Sr *Tho.* I'm sorry that your Son takes these lewd courses;   [2310]
He is not fit to make a Husband of.
   Cre. Do not condemn before you hear. I'l warrant
Though he be guilty yet hee's innocent.
                       Enter Haveatall.
   Mo. Hent him, for dern love Hent him; I done drad
His Visage foul yfrounct, with glowing eyn.   [2315]
   Have. I come t' excuse my ruder usage of you.
I was in drink when that I did it; 'twas
The Plot of those base Knaves, I hear are gone,
To teach me valour by the strength of Wine;
Naming that courage which was only fury.   [2320]
It was not wilfully.
   Mo. I do not reche
One bean for all. This Buss is a blive guerdon.
Hence Carlishnesse yferre. 'Tis a sooth saw,
Had I but venged all mine herme,
Mine Cloak had not been furred half so werme.   [2325]
   Enter Officers with Andrew, Priscilla, *and the four that*
     were taken at the Window singing.
   Cre. Now Sir you shall hear all. Come *Andrew* tell me,
How camst thou hither?
   An. Truly Mr *Meanwel*
Told me that I should meet with Mrs *Jane*,
And there I found her Chamber-maid.
   Cre. D'y' see?

Your Chamber-maid Sir *Thomas*; out you whore. [2330]
   An. Take heed what you say Father, shee's my wife.
   Cre. I would thou'rt in thy grave, then 'twere the better
Fortune o'th' two.
   Pris. Indeed this reverend Man
Joyn'd us i'th' Prison.
   Chr. Marriage is a Bond,
So no place fitter to perform it in. [2335]
   Sr *Tho.* Send for my Daughter hither, wee'l know all.
What are you Sir?
   Chr. A workman in the Clergie.
   Con. Yes, this is one I took at th' Window singing,
With these three other vagrant Fellows here.
   Chri. I was in body there, but not in mind, [2340]
So that my sin is but inchoately perfect,
And I though in a fault did not offend,
And that for three reasons. First, I did yield
Only a kind of unwilling consent.
Secondly, I was drawn as 'twere by their [2345]
Impulsive gentleness. Mark Sir I'm strong.
Thirdly, I deem'd it not a womans-shambles:
Fourthly and lastly, that I sung was only
An holy wish. Once more Beloved.
   Sr *Tho.* Peace!
Y'have said enough already. How came you [2350]
To sing beneath the Window?
   Rime. Mr *Hearsay*
Told us that Mr *Meanwell* was new married,
And thought it good that we should gratifie him,
And shew our selves to him in a Fescennine.
   Cre. That Raskall *Meanwel* was the cause of all, [2355]
I would I had him here.
   Sr *Tho.* Why? this is he,
Sr *Robert Littleworth* his Son, he hath
Disclos'd their vilanies; he is no cheat.
   Mean. God save you Mr *Credulous*; you have
Forgotten me perhaps, I'm somewhat chang'd. [2360]
You see your lost man's found; your Vagabond
Appears at last.
   Cre. Go, you are a gibing scab:

Leave off your flouting; you're a beardless Boy;
I am a Father of Children.
   Mean. And your Son
Will be so shortly, if he han't ill luck. [2365]
To vex you more, that hundred pounds you sent
To Mr *Caster, Shape* i'th' habit of
A Country fellow gull'd you of.
   Cred. That Raskall;
Thou shewst thy wit t' abuse an old man thus.
As God shall mend me I will hamper thee. [2370]
Thou'st been disguis'd here all this while, thou hast;
Would I were braid in mine own morter, if
I do not call th' in Question the next Terme
For counterfeiting of the Kings Subjects.
Come away from him Sirrah, come along. [2375]
                         Ex. Cred. And. Prisc.
   Mean. There's a Trunk they've left behind; I have
Seiz'd it for you; so that you'l be no loser.
   Sir *Tho.* If you can find a way whereby I may
Reward this courtesie of yours, I shall
Confess my self engaged doubly to you, [2380]
Both for the benefit and its requitall.   *Ent. Jane.*
   Mean. The appearance of your Daughter here suggests
Something to ask, which yet my thoughts call boldness.
   Sir *Tho.* Can she suggest yet any good, that is
So expert grown in this flesh Brokery? [2385]
   Mean. O do not blot that Innocence with suspicion,
Who never came so neere a blemish yet,
As to b' accus'd. To quit you of such thoughts
I did receive a tempting letter from
That Strumpet that's gone out (as sin is bold [2390]
To try even where no hope is). I made promise,
But to secure my self, and withall sound
Th' affections of young *Credulous* unto
Your vertuous Daughter, told him he should meet her
Where I agreed to meet her Chambermaid. [2395]
The blame must all be mine.
   Sr *Tho.* 'Tis her deliverance.
Shee hath escap'd two Plagues, a lustfull fool.
   Mean. I dare not challenge her I do confess,

As a reward due to my service, and
If you deny her me, assure your self [2400]
I'l never draw her from obedience:
I will not love her to procure her ruine,
And make m' affection prove her Enemy.
   Sr Tho. You speak most honestly, I never did
Think ill of your intents, but alwaies gave [2405]
A testimony to your life as large
As were your merits. But your fortunes are
Unequal, there's the want.
   Mean. What's there defective
Love shall supply: True, Mr *Credulous*
Is a rich man, but yet wants that which makes [2410]
His riches usefull, free discretion.
He may be something in the Eye o'th' World;
But let a knowing man that can distinguish
Between Possessions, and good parts, but view him,
And prize impartially, he will be rated [2415]
Only as Chests, and Caskets, just according
To what he holds. I valew him, as I
Would an Exchequer, or a Magazine.
He is not vertuous, but well stor'd, a thing
Rather well victuall'd then well qualified. [2420]
And if you please to cast your Eye on me,
Some moneys will call back my Fathers Lands
Out of his lime-twig fingers, and I shall
Come forth as gay as he.
   Sr Tho. I'l strive no longer
For fear I seem t' oppose felicity. [2425]
If shee'l give her consent y' are one.
   Jan. It is
The voice of Angels to me: I had thought
Nothing in all the store of nature could
Have added to that love, wherewith I do
Reverence that name, my Father, till that you [2430]
Spoke this.
   Sir Tho. I know your former Loves; grow up
Into an aged pair, yet still seem young.
May you stand fresh, as in your Pictures still,
And only have the reverence of the Aged.

I thank you for your pains Mr Constable, [2435]
You may dismiss your Watch now.
   Sha. A pox on't!
That after all this ne'r a man to carry
To Prison? must poor Tradesmen be brought out
And no body clap'd up?
   Mean. That you mayn't want
Employment, friends take this I pray and drink it. [2440]
   Sli. Sir, when y'are cheated next we are your servants —
                     Ex. all but Shape, Hear. Slic.

Act V. Scen. V.

Shape, Slicer, Hearsay.

   Sha. Lye thou there Watchman; how the knave that's look'd for
May often lurck under the Officer!
Invention I applaud thee.
   Hear. *London* aire
Me thinks begins to be too hot for us. [2445]
   Slic. There is no longer tarrying here, let's swear
Fidelity to one another, and
So resolve for *New England.*
   Hear. 'Tis but getting
A little Pigeon-hole reformed Ruff ——
   Slic. Forcing our Beards into th' Orthodox bent —— [2450]
   Sha. Nosing a little Treason 'gainst the King;
Bark something at the Bishops, and we shall
Be easily receiv'd.
   Hear. No fitter Place.
They are good silly People; Souls that will
Be cheated without trouble: One eye is [2455]
Put out with Zeal, th' other with Ignorance,
And yet they think they're Eagles.
   Sha. We are made
Just fit for that Meridian: no good work's
Allow'd there; Faith, Faith is that they call for,
And we will bring it 'em.
   Slic. What Language speak they? [2460]

Hear. English, and now and then a Root or two
Of Hebrew, which wee'l learn of some Dutch Skipper
That goes along with us this Voyage; Now
We want but a good Wind, the Brethrens sighs
Must fill our sailes. For what old *England* won't [2465]
Afford, *New England* will. You shall hear of us
By the next Ship that comes for Proselytes.
Each soyl is not the good mans Country only;
Nor is the lot his to be still at home:
    Wee'l claime a share, and prove that Nature gave [2470]
    This Boon, as to the good, so to the knave.   *Exeunt.*

The Epilogue.

Shap. *We have escap'd the Law, but yet do feare*
Something that's harder answer'd, your sharp Eare.
O for a present slight now to beguile
That, and deceive you but of one good smile!
'Tis that must free us; th' Author dares not look [5]
For that good fortune to be sav'd by's Book.
To leave this blessed soyle is no great woe;
Our griefe's in leaving you, that make it so.
   For if you shall call in those Beames you lent,
   'Twould ev'n at Home create a Banishment. [10]

FINIS.

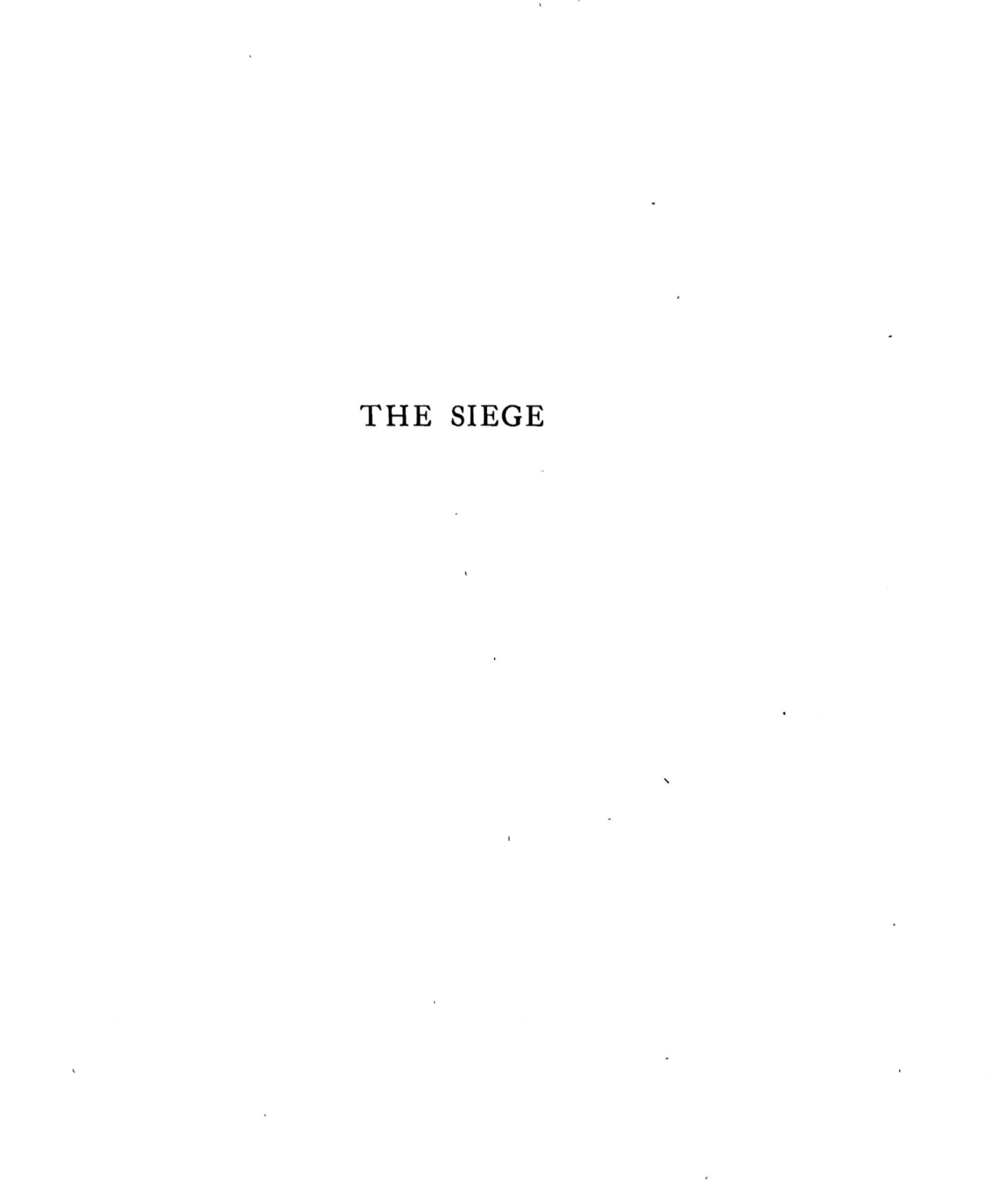

THE SIEGE

INTRODUCTION

1. The Text

THE SIEGE, OR LOVE'S CONVERT was printed for the first and last time in the *Works* (1651), having been entered on the Stationers' Register by Moseley on May 4, 1648. A transcription of the separate title-page and a signature collation may be consulted in the notes to the play. Two of the songs appeared in *The Marrow of Complements* (1655), and Mr. Goffin reprinted all the songs and the verse dedication in his edition of the *Poems* (1918). The variant readings of these texts will be found in the Textual Notes. The present text is based on the *Works* (1651), with occasional editorial changes. Four copies of the 1651 text have been collated. All changes are recorded in the Textual Notes.

2. Date of Composition and Stage History

Humphrey Moseley in his preface "To the Reader" states that Cartwright wrote almost nothing after he took holy orders in 1638. Although it is unadvisable to press this statement too closely when dealing with the occasional poems,[1] there is perhaps more reason to suppose that so far as the plays are concerned Moseley's remark can be taken in good faith. The year 1638, therefore, may be advanced as a provisional limit for the composition of *The Siege, or Love's Convert*.[2] We do not know how early the play was begun. Cartwright, in his dedication, tells us that an earlier and unfinished draught was only saved from the fire at the special instance of King Charles, who desired to see the work finished. One would suppose that *The Siege* was seen by Charles in 1636 during the royal progress, or a few months later in London on the occasion of the court performance of *The Royal Slave*. Perhaps Cartwright took the finished manuscript up to London with him as a gift for his royal patron. At any rate

---

1. See my note on Moseley's preface, p. 833.
2. Schelling suggests that Cartwright's play was given this double title to avoid confusion with D'Avenant's *Siege*, licensed in 1629. It should be noticed, however, that D'Avenant's play was not printed until 1673.—*Elizabethan Drama, 1558–1642* (1908), II, 47.

the play was known in London and disapproved of by the town wits. Our source of information is some lines in William Towers' commendatory poem:

> And thou, great Prince of Numbers, (like some Lord
> Fear'd for his Power, and for his Parts ador'd)
> Wert too great for Applause, a full Delight
> To th'taken Eare, but Envy to the Sight!
> How did the factious *London*-Wits first praise,
> And then with slanderous *But* maligne thy Bayes!
> How they arraign'd thy skill in Comædy,
> And before *Plutarch* su'd thy Play and Thee!
> *Sir, may This pass upon the Stage? may That?*
> *May Ghosts speak, Sir, or else I pray' say what?*[3]
> (So hardly could they speak, as if Ghosts grown
> Themselves, and turn'd into the Question:)
> *Nay but, good Sir,* Plutarch *himselfe saies Nay,*
> In what Tongue? *In our Mother Tongue, we say*:
> Do, p[i]n your faith upon an English sleeve
> For the Greek History; you'l not beleeve. . . .

Critical opinion, beginning with Langbaine, has been generally unanimous in affirming that *The Siege* was never produced. The above lines, therefore, are additionally important because they suggest an actual performance of the play.[4] An exact interpretation of the lines is difficult, but what Towers seems to say is this: "Although, Cartwright, the hearing of your plays was a delight, the seeing of them aroused envy. Witness the town wits, who at first praised and then began to limit your honor as a playwright. They also called in question your skill in comedy and tried you upon the touchstone of Plutarch's authority." Unfortunately it cannot be determined whether Towers is referring to *The Siege* or to *The Royal Slave* when he admits that the town wits first praised the play. If he means *The Siege*, the case for an actual stage production is strengthened; if not, the passage may indicate merely that *The Siege* circulated widely in manuscript. Whatever the case, Towers' lines show that the play was better known and more read by Cartwright's contemporaries than has hitherto been suspected.

There is one further fact worth noticing in connection with *The Siege*. It is, I believe, the only play before the Restoration dedicated

---

3. Compare *The Siege*, V, viii: "Captain you should not speak, you are a Ghost."

4. There is another reference to *The Siege* in Josias Howe's commendatory verses which might also perhaps be interpreted as an indication that the play received an actual London production.

directly to the reigning sovereign. The attitude towards the drama reflected in such a dedication is something new. It is a far cry from the early days of the century when polite authors were frankly apologetic in regard to their theatrical ventures. As the quality of drama degenerated, the status of play-writing seems to have risen.

3. Sources

Cartwright himself has seemingly recorded one of the principal sources of *The Siege* in a note prefixed to the 1651 edition of the play. While there is no actual proof that Cartwright is responsible for the note, it seems unlikely that anyone else would either have taken the trouble or have possessed the knowledge to suggest it. Under the heading "Occasio Fabulae," a passage from Plutarch's "Life of Cimon" follows in the original Greek, with a translation by Amyot in French—a queer confusion of tongues.[5] At the risk of adding to the confusion, I give the passage in North's translation of Amyot (ed. of 1676, p. 412):

... They say that King *Pausanias* being on a time in the City of Byzance, sent for *Cleonice*, a young maiden of a Noble house, to take his pleasure of her. Her parents durst not keep her from him, by reason of his cruelty, but suffered him to carry her away. The young gentlewoman prayed the Grooms of *Pausanias* Chamber to take away the lights, and thinking in the dark to come to *Pausanias* bed that was asleep, groping for the bed as softly as she could to make no noise, she unfortunately hit against the Lamp, and overthrew it. The falling of the Lamp made such a noise, that it waked him on the sudden, who thought straight therewithall that some of his enemies had been come traiterously to kill him, whereupon he took his dagger lying under his beds head, and so stabbed it in the young Virgin, that she died immediately upon it.

It is at once apparent that Cartwright has used Plutarch merely as a starting point. His setting is Byzantium and the tyrant Pausanias figures as Misander. He has also made partial use of Cleonice's midnight visit to the sleeping tyrant. Here the resemblance ceases. Cartwright has "ennobled" and "refined" all the leading characters in accordance with the dictates of heroic theory. A virgin who first morally yields and then dies, a parent who condones his daughter's shame, or a tyrant who remains a tyrant, was no food for capon-crammed Platonic appetites.[6]

---

5. The Greek and French passages from Plutarch have been omitted in this edition.

6. Ward (*English Dramatic Literature*, 1899, III, 139n) calls attention to a modern German treatment of the Pau-

The general theme of the "avenging virgin" has long been a popular one. The story of Judith immediately suggests itself, and another analogue may be found in George Rivers' *The Heroinae* (1639), the tale of Theutilla. Dramatic analogues are dealt with in the notes.

A suggested source for part of the comic underplot was long ago pointed out by Langbaine: "The Injunction which the Rich Widow *Pyle* laid upon her Lovers is borrow'd from *Boccace's Novels*. Day 9th, Nov. 1."[7] The title of this novella as it appears in the 1620–24 translation of the *Decameron* is as follows:

> Madam Francesca, a Widdow of Pistoya, being affected by two Florentine Gentlemen, the one named Rinuccio Palermini, and the other Alesandro Chiarmontesi, and she bearing no good will to eyther of them; ingeniously freed her selfe from both their importunate suites. One of them she caused to lye as dead in a grave, and the other to fetch him from thence: so neither of them accomplishing what they were enjoyned, fayled of obtaining his hoped expectation.

Although Langbaine's suggestion has been silently accepted, or appropriated, by all succeeding critics,[8] a glance at even the title will show that Boccaccio's story differs very materially from Cartwright's version. The differences, moreover, are not like those already noticed above in Cartwright's handling of Plutarch. They suggest, indeed, that not Boccaccio's novel but some other analogue of that novel was Cartwright's real source. Reference to A. C. Lee's *The Decameron, Its Sources and Analogues* (1909) is most instructive. Among the numerous analogues there cited,[9] two are particularly interesting for our present problem.[10] The first is a poem attributed by some to Lydgate, entitled "The Tale of the Lady Prioress and her Suitors";[11] the second is a short moralized story found in Pauli's

---

sanias story by H. Kruse, entitled *Das Mädchen von Byzanz* (1877). I have, unfortunately, not been able to see the play, so that I cannot say how Kruse's treatment agrees or disagrees with Cartright's.

7. *Account of the English Dramatick Poets* (1691), pp. 54-55.

8. Ward's (*English Dramatic Literature*, III, 139n) confusion with regard to the Boccaccio reference was caused by an ambiguous statement in Fleay's *Biographical Chronicle of the English Drama* (1891, I, 48).

9. Pp. 271-74.

10. Lee points out an analogue in Stigliani's *Mondo Nuovo*, 1628. Having some reason to suppose that Cartwright knew Stigliani's poetry (see my note to Cartwright's "Love inconcealable," p. 697), I found this reference interesting. Examination of the story in canto xxx shows, however, that Stigliani's version has no connection with Cartwright.

11. *Minor Poems of Dan John Lydgate*, ed. J. O. Halliwell (1840; Percy Society, II), pp. 107-17.

Schimpf und Ernst (1522), Number 220.[12] Although for several reasons it seems fairly certain that Lydgate's poem may be dismissed from our inquiry, it is much closer to Cartwright's than to Boccaccio's tale. In Lydgate, for example, as in Cartwright, there are *three* lovers involved, one of whom is disguised as a devil. Furthermore, the order of the climax is the same as in Cartwright—the devil frightens the priest and the supposed corpse, which in its turn, by coming to sudden life, frightens the devil. But all this is also true of the moral tale in Pauli's *Schimpf und Ernst*, which adds two important elements, parallel with Cartwright's version: first, the disguise of one of the lovers as an angel; second, the suggestion of a competition between the powers of good and evil for the soul of the "corpse." The important passages in Pauli are short enough to be given in full:

> Da nun der erst kam an den aben, da nam sie in in ir husz, ... vnd sprach zu im, du hoffierst mir, hetestu mich gern zu den eren, so wil ich dich beweren, ob du etwas vmb meinet willen darffest thun, so wil ich dir ein gute antwurt geben. ... Der iung gesel sprach, fraw was mir müglich ist zuthun das wil ich vmb euwert willen thun, vnd wil bisz in den dot gon. Die fraw sprach, leg das weisz kleid an vber die hosen, vnd gang zu dem gerner, da stot mein nachbuer in einem dottenbaum, vnd ist gestorben, schüt in vsz dem baum, vnd leg du dich daryn bisz man mettin lüt in der pfar an dem morgen, vnd nim den sack vnd stosz den dotten daryn, vnd bring mir in her, so wil ich dir ein gute antwurt geben, es musz ia sein. Der gut gesel sprach, das wil ich gern thun, ... Der ander hoffierer kam auch zu seiner stund, mit dem ret sie auch also, vnd legt im ein engelisch kleid an, vnd gab im ein geweichte kertzen[13] in sein hand, vnd schickt in auch anhin, er solt bei der leichen bleiben sitzen bisz an den morgen wan man mettin lütet, vnd wan ir den dotten bringen, so musz es ia sein. Er zohe also anhin vnd thet wie sie in bescheiden het. Der in dem baum lag der sahe durch die spelt vsz vnd sahe den engel kumen, vnd gedacht, da wil es sich machen, vnd der engel bleib also da sitzen. Die fraw schickt den dritten hoffierer auch dar, vnd gab im ein feüerhocken in die hend. ... Der tüffel wolt den engel mit dem hocken vber das ding ab ziehen, da segnet sich der engel, vnd stiesz im die gewecht kertz in das angesicht, vnd kempfften mit einander. Der in dem baum gedacht, es wer vmb sein seel zuthun, vnd wüst vff in den baum vnd stiesz den deckel vff, vnd zu dem baum hinusz. Der engel vnd der tüffel lieffen darvon, einer hierher, der ander dorthin, also kam die gut fraw der hoffierer ab. ...

It is impossible to say whether Cartwright knew the original German *Schimpf und Ernst*. Most probably he did not, since we have

---

12. Ed. H. Oesterley, Stuttgart (1866), pp. 145–47.

13. Compare *The Siege*, V, vi: "Prusias *drest like an Angell with a Caduceus in one hand, and a Taper in the other.*"

no record that he knew any German, a linguistic accomplishment not common in seventeenth-century England. According to Pauli's editor, Oesterley, the stories of the *Schimpf und Ernst* became extremely popular, and Cartwright may well have been familiar with some Latin translation or English version of the tale now untraced or lost.[14]

A word may be said about two of the principal characters. The type of the immoral and inhuman tyrant, which was to become so familiar in Restoration heroic drama, is well represented by Misander. He speaks with all the bombast and rant of a Maximin, without a Maximin's stature. Later, of course, under the influence of "true love" his nature undergoes a change and he becomes the type of the heroic lover—a strong and *not* silent man. The character of Pyle is also remarkable as a forerunner of another Restoration favorite—the proud, ambitious widow of comedy, who will go to any lengths to satisfy her desires.[15] Cartwright's conception of the type is on the whole well imagined and carried out with considerable vigor.

---

14. Miss Gebhardt (*The Ordinary*, p. xli) compares Pyle's trick to rid herself of her suitors with that employed by Facetia at the end of George Wilde's *Love's Hospital*, a play performed before the royal party on the same day, in the afternoon, as Cartwright's *Royal Slave*. The scenes, however, have nothing in common except the motive for the ruse.

15. Compare the character of Olympia in Massinger's *The Bondman* (1623).

THE SIEDGE:

Or,
Love's Convert,

A Tragi-Comedy.

Written by
Mr WILLIAM CARTVVRIGHT,
Late Student of *Christ-Church in*
Oxford, and Proctor of
the *University*.

LONDON,
Printed for *Humphrey Moseley*, and
are to be sold at his shop at the Sign of
the Princes Armes in St *PAVLS*
Churchyard. 1651.

The Dedication
To the late KING's Most Excellent MAJESTY.

May it please your Majesty,

The first Draught of this Trifle was so ill,
That 'twas the Crime, not Issue of the Quill,
Shape being wanting, to avoid the shame
The Spunge was destin'd Critick, or the Flame; [5]
My Mercy finding out this way alone
To mend it with one Blot, or make it none.
But touch'd with your Command, my Muse, like Steel
Kiss'd by the Loadstone, did new Motion feel;
Whence this redeem'd from Fire unto your Eye [10]
(Only perhaps to perish Royally)
Fears 'tis no Pardon, but Reprivall, and
Dreads the same Fate, though from another Hand:
So that the Change but little comforteth;
Sentence from you being but the *State* of Death. [15]
And that Fear comes from that Encrease of Ill,
That the last Errours are the greatest still.
Th'are Errours yet commanded, and plead this,
That by Injunction they have done amisse.
Two Names are due to't then; and some may ghesse [20]
That I obey, others that I transgresse:
The Prospect thus being Double-bounded, I
Hope that you'l put the first unto your Eye;
That, what th'Extent of Sight would stile offence,
The half-way Stop may call Obedience. [25]

Your Ma^{sties}
Most humble
Subject and Servant,
William Cartwright.

The Persons.

Misander	A Tyrant of *Thrace*.
Cleodemus, Timophilus	His Lords.
Prusias	A Courtier turn'd Captain.
Philostratus, Callimachus	Two other Captains.
Eudemus	A *Byzantine*, Father to *Leucasia*
Terpander, Scedasus, Patacion, Epigenes	Citizens of *Byzantium*.
Nicias	A Painter of *Byzantium*.
Leucasia	A Virgin of *Byzantium*, daug. to *Eudemus*.
Euthalpe	Her Attendant, Daughter to *Patacion*.
Chryse	Another Virgin of *Bizantium*.
Pyle	A rich haughty widdow of *Byz*.
Elpidia	Her Chamber-maid.
Priest. Souldier. Boy.	Mutes.
Five ancient Heroes & their five Ladyes.	Masquers.
Chirurgion	

The Scene, *Byzantium*.

ACT. I. SCEN. I.

*Scedasus, Patacion, Epigenes, Terpander, Eudemus,
Nicias* with the Pictures of three By-
zantine Virgins.

Sced. BUT there's no other way.
Epi. They must be sent
Or we must die.
Pat. Wee're no such subtile feeders
As to make Meals on Air, sup on a Blast,
And think a fresh Gale Second Course.
Terp. No verily; Let's see thy Pictures, *Nicias.* I [5]
would the Tyrant had a mind to all the Wenches in the
Citty, and would barter Bread in exchange: a Loaf a
Wench, have at him from one end o'th' Town to the
other.
Eud. Fond men! [10]
You strive to purchase a short Liberty
By means more infamous than Servitude;
If that a Tyrant's lust do burn, are we
Bound to supply that which may quench his fury?
If his unruly Passion, kindled by [15]
Report of Beauty, doth grow big with flames,
And saucily exact what e'r is fair
And eminently gracefull, as if Nature
Had sent it as a Tribute due to him,
Though't be the dowrie of another State, [20]
Shall we surrender it, and basely prize
Our Innocence below his haughty Anger?
Terp. I say the Pictures then shall not be sent.
Pat. Had we a Magazine well furnish'd, were
Our Granaries charg'd with Corn, there were some Plea [25]
Against his practice: but this tedious Siedge

Forceth our noble thoughts to other waies,
Whiles Famine cals that Lawful which is base.
   Terp.   Why then the Pictures must be sent how e'r.
   Eud.   Will you still owe your vertues to your Bellies?   [30]
And only then think nobly when y'are full?
Doth Fodder keep you honest? are you bad
When out of flesh? and think you't an excuse
Of vile and ignominious Actions, that
Y'are lean, and out of liking? for I must   [35]
Speak of you now as Cattle, whiles you thus
Enslave your selves unto the Paunch, enduring
A Tyranny beyond that you complain of.
   Terp.   I say he must speak of us now as Beasts;
Say what you will the Pictures sha'n't be sent.   [40]
   Sced.   'Tis better do't than starve.
   Eud.   Well rumbled Belly;
There spoke a stomack.
   Terp.   I, there spok a stomack.
   Sced.   We have not strength left to uphold our weapons;
Armour, that was e'r while a Garment only,
Is now a Burthen. Famine hath imprinted   [45]
Old age upon the Visages of Children,
And Youths appear like th' Ghosts of the deceas'd;
Or like some Creatures, whom the Destinies
Will not permit to dye; W'have scarce enough
Flesh to receive a Wound, no force to give one;   [50]
Would you have *Skelletons* maintain a fight
That will fall with th' Ayre of the passing Dart?
We have not vigour to defend our selves,
Nor yet a Sacrifice to win the Gods
Over unto our side.
   Eud.   To win the Gods?   [55]
Have you not Minds, and Pray'rs? 'tis not the Beasts
Heart that propitiates Heaven, but your own.
Think not that I engage my self in this
For a particular end, a private good;
'Tis common what I aime at: 'tis not that   [60]
My Daughter's liable to his choice
That I diswade. Whiles I deny the sending
Of these three faces, I deny your Wives,

Your Daughters, nay, perhaps your Sons; for that
Which now desires but one, will spread to all; [65]
Without distinguishing of Age, or Sexe.
Think what a Blot will stain our memory
To all Posterity, when't shall be said
Byzantium was a Pander to a Tyrant.
Let yet our miseries be honest; let us, [70]
If that the Gods deny us happinesse,
Persist unfortunate without Reproach.
    Terp. And that's considerable, wee'l be honest sure.
    Epi. We do approve your reasons; but if he
(As it is likely) conquer us, we shall [75]
'Mongst other our indignities, be sure
To suffer this too. Then consider with
What mind we do't; we yield up one to reskue
All other from abuse. Our own misfortunes
Are not as yet i'th' Catalogue. What can we [80]
Expect so mercifull as death? he won't
Indulge a killing torment; we shall be
Reserv'd to after miseries, and life
Only kept in to keep us longer dying.
    Terp. Marry God forbid; we will not be mangled sure. [85]
    Eud. Fear never wanted arguments; you do
Reason your selves into a Carefull bondage,
Circumspect only to your Misery:
I could urge Freedom, Charters, Country, Laws,
Gods, and Religion, and such precious names; [90]
Nay, what you value higher, Wealth; but that
You sue for Bondage, yielding to demands
As Impious, as th'are Insolent, and have
Only this sluggish aime, to perish full.
    Terp. Painter, budg not a foot, wee'l stand it out. [95]
    Nic. You speak most rightly Sir, but we are hungry.
    Pat. Hunger will be the least of evils, we
Shall not be found so Innocent, as only
To pine, and dye; our miseries will grow savage:
Man will refresh himself on man; the stronger [100]
Devour the weaker, till at last one pair
Be only left who must be call'd the Citty.
    Terp. Haste for thy life, we cannot stand it out.

Nic.   I hope your Worships will dispatch me with 'em.
'Tis my request my pains be only thus   [105]
Rewarded, to present 'em to the Tyrant.
   Sced.   Most fit, good *Nicias*. All agree?
   Epig. Pat.   Yes, all.
   Eud.   It is one happiness that he askes no more:
And we are blest in that a Tyrant's modest,
Being beholding to his wishes, that   [110]
They've put such limits to our Infamy.
There is no Beast more stubborn and unruly
Than is the Belly: Th' empty and the full
Are both alike in this, that they'll not listen.
The Brand be yours, if the Misfortune mine.   [115]
   Pat.   Sir, the misfortune cann't be only yours;
For I've a Daughter too, that in a love
To better education waits on yours;
Who hath from thence contracted such a tye
Unto her Ladies vertues, that she is   [120]
Resolv'd to run an equall hazard with her:
'Tis my *Euthalpe*; whom, were she anothers,
I would call fair, and vertuous, and deserving.
                                   Ex. Eud. Pat. Sced. Epig.
   Terp.   Go, go, go: follow and take order.
Nicias, come hither: I'l impart a secret to thee.   [125]
The truth is, one of us is much o'rseen: 'twas a most
improvident thing, who e'r 'twas did it, to go and beget
a fair Daughter, and nere aske the advice of the Com-
mon-Councel before hand. But let's be now judicious, and
weigh reasons.   [130]
Our Innocence priz'd below his Anger? —— Carry 'em
          not Painter.
Yet Famine cals that lawfull which is base. —— Thou must
          carry 'em Painter.
Still owe our Vertues to our Bellies? —— Stay Painter.
Yet no vigour left to defend our selves. —— Go Painter.
This sluggish aime to perish full? —— Stand Painter.   [135]
Yet the stronger will devour the weaker. —— Run Painter.
All these wisely consider'd, thou must not go, and thou
must go, and so I leave thee.   *Ex. Terp.*
   Ni.   Now I am Legat *Nicias*: th' only way

If you'd perform an Embassie with just [140]
And decent Ceremony, is to fast long;
This Siedge hath sterv'd me into so good Manners,
That when I'm feasted in the Tyrant's Tent
I shall not choose but make as many obeysances
Unto the Chine of Beef, as he that carrieth it [145]
Doth to the Chair of State. My lofty Widdow,
Who, if that I had dignity, hath promis'd
T' accept my Person, will be hence demerited:
For though I be abus'd, and made their mirth,
To suffer from a Prince is still thought worth. *Exit.* [150]

Act I. Scen. II.

Pyle, Elpidia.

Pyl. Three sent besides? have I so many Rivalls?
I'd thought I'd been the Phœnix of the Citty:
But men have left to judge, not I to be
What I was ever, fair, and smooth, and handsome;
Look we not bright *Elpidia*, and Maiestique? [155]
 Elpi. Truly sweet Mistris ——
 Pyl. How, you paltry Baggage?
Sweet Mistris? when we only want the Tyrants
Approving to be Queen? call us your Grace.
 Elp. Your Grace, me thinks, would make a very Queen,
But that you use to beat your servants so. [160]
 Pyl. Our Maids of Honour you do mean ——

Act. I. Scen. III.

To them *Nicias*.

—— Now Fellow!
 Nic. I hope your mind is chang'd, you will not lay
Such an Injunction on your willing Servant:
You punish, not command; what could you worse,
If you did hate me?

Pyl.   Dare you question what [165]
We please to will? or carry't, or you come not
So near hereafter, as to be commanded
Again by *Pyle*.
   Nic.   'Twere t'incense the Tyrant,
With these three Virgins to present your Picture.
   Pyl.   Why not our Picture Sir? we are a Widdow [170]
But of the first wrinkle; and yet no wrinkle
But that we please to say so. Wee're as faire
As any Shee in all *Byzantium*,
If that our Glass and Chambermaid tell truth:
Why not our Picture, Sawciness?
   Nic.   And 't please you, [175]
This is the very reason, why I say
It would incense the Tyrant, that we should
Keep so much Beauty so long from him.
   Pyl.   Dare you
Offer to daube it with your Commendations?
And make it less by your approving? know [180]
When you do ought but reverence, you disparage;
Wee're only to be prais'd by them that are
Worthy t' enjoy us, Kings.
   Nic.   I hope you will not
Suffer your thoughts to cut me out. Although
I am not o'th' Bloud Royall, yet I am [185]
Ambassadour, the first of my Trade, that
Ere yet obtain'd that Dignity.
   Pyl.   What? doth not
The least of our commands entitle you
To as much honour as the bigg'st Employment
Of the whole Citty can? If you do hope [190]
For our Affection, win't by doing this.
   Nic.   Though you are fit to be a sacred Consort
To Majesty, and yield all *Asia* Princes,
Yet give me leave, ev'n for that very reason
Not to perform this your Injunction. [195]
It were to lose you, while I strive to gain you.
   Pyl.   You are unmanner'd. Reason's for Mechanicks:
Stand we for Queen, and be disputed with?
   Nic.   I'm gon —— But pray y' suffer me ——

Pyl.   You're troublesome,
We do command you hence. That you may see   [200]
We do't in no great Anger (keep behind Sir,)
We do indulge our hand.
   Nic.   Good sweet *Elpidia*,
When that thy Mistris shall go o'r the Citty,
And aske thee what thou thinkst of him, and him,
Drop one good word for me. She is a Widdow;   [205]
Put her in mind of this my promising Nose;
That, and my long Foot, make up perfect Letters
Of Commendation to a Citty Widow.
   Elp.   If you have any other signs pray y' tell me;
I'l read her th' Inventory of your good Parts.   *Ex. Nicias.*   [210]
   Pyl.   The foolishness o'th' Man! But yet we cannot
Forbid these poor Mechanicks to affect us:
If that he had not undertook this charge,
I'd cast him off for daring to deny it;
And now he hath thus undertook it, he   [215]
Discards himself; for I do know that I
Must needs be chosen. To requite his love
I'l beg his pardon then, for daring to
Be Rivall to a Tyrant. How I scorn
All names below the Throne! I do feel something   [220]
That prompts my new-stamp'd thoughts to Majesty;
And saies I shall be Queen before I dye:
Shee's more than servile that desires not Rule.
Hold up our Train *Elpidia* as we pass.   *Exeunt.*

Act. I. Scen. IV.

Philostratus, Callimachus, Prusias.

   Phil.   Now who would live in peace good *Prusias*?
       tell me,   [225]
Is it not better far to seize your Prey
In open field, than to stand whimpring at
The Chamber door, like to the little Spaniel?
   Cal.   Or scratch upon the Wainscot like my Ladies
Black Cat to gain Admittance?

Phil. Here you do not [230]
With folded Arms embrace your self, because
You can't embrace your Mistris ——
   Pru. Right ——
   Cal. You do not
Stand in as many Postures, as a Painters
Servant, when that his Master is to daub
Some peopled Bus'ness in a Pyebald Canvass. [235]
   Phil. You do not lye Perdue under the shelter
Of an unmercifull Balcony, to
Get the Advouzon of an half kiss, when
Her first-born wrinkle shall indent her forehead.
   Call. You do not stand enchanted at her door, [240]
Gaping, and yawning, as if some Apothecary
Had hir'd your Mouth, and set it for stray Gnats,
And Vagabond Flies.
   Pru. Sweet Captain, prethee on.
   Cal. At home there's trick on trick. *Celadon* he
Loves *Amaryllis, Amaryllis Daphnis,* [245]
But *Daphnis Cloe, Cloe Melibæus,*
Fond *Melibæus Mopsa, Mopsa* at last
Some body, that loves some body, that I know not:
Affection goes like a Pedigree; Heart loves Heart
To th' end o'th' Chapter.
   Phil. No such Labyrinth here: [250]
No needles hanging at each others Tailes.
No *Cupid* here preserves the Tears of Lovers
To mix 'em with the Ashes of burnt Hearts,
To make a Lie to wash his Mothers smock in,
Which silly sighs must dry.
   Cal. You shall not have [255]
A wench cry pish, and puh. And is't not better
To clap the Bargain up for a brace of Drachma's,
Than to be bound to call all Women Nymphs,
And Goddesses, and Hamadryades;
That, when you are alone i'th' Woods, they'l please [260]
To be such willing Worms as Men call Milkmaids.
   Pru. Troth I ne'r thought 'em Deities: I was
Alwaies of this opinion, that they did
Consist of Flesh and Bloud. I now begin

To like all well in War, except the fighting. [265]
   Phil. The bravest sport is yet to come: The Ransack
O' th' Citty, that's the chiefest. You shall have
This Lord come profer you his Daughter, this
Burgesse his Wife, and that unskilfull youth
Pray you begin to him in 's trembling Bride. [270]
   Pru. I'm for your tender Maidenheads: I would not
Venture my self with a stale Virgin, or
A season'd Widow for a Kingdom.
   Cal. Shalt
Make choice among a thousand; let thy Affection
Fly at a Flock, a Cloud of Game: I'm tickled [275]
To think how we shall find one toothless Matron
Environ'd round, and cheerfully besiedg'd,
With her Strong-water Cellar; The other compass'd
With five or six good large deep-belly'd Bottles,
And both of them mumping for Consolation. [280]
   Phil. Then a step farther, and one fearfull Lady
Squatted among her Sweetmeats; th' other wedg'd
Between her Gally-pots and Fucusses;
A third perhaps doing her Devotions in
Potent Eringo's, or praying to her Gellies [285]
Against the good houre comes, and all to find
Grace in the Conquerours Eyes, Mine, Thine, or His.
   Call. Then, for the spoile, we shall come loaded home,
Gold, Silver, Garments, Pictures, Jewels, Statues,
Great massy Goblets, Chalices, and Gods, [290]
Women, and Boys, catch he that can, they are
His own that first laies hold on them. Dull Peace!
Hang her! she doth allow us nothing but
Those barren things Statutes, and Matrimony.
   Pru. I'l to the houses where I think I shall [295]
Meet with the best Conserves, and tenderst Virgins;
Sweetmeats and Maidenheads are all I aime at:
I shall not be so good at spoil as you,
Being I am but a new-made Captain: wherefore
If you *Callimachus*, or you *Philostratus* [300]
Meet with a handsome Perruke, pray y' reserve it
For your friend *Prusias* —— Peace, here comes *Misander.*

Act. I. Scen. V.

To them *Misander, Cleodemus, Timophilus.*

Mis. Hear you no News yet Captains from the City?
Phil. They slight your Majesty by their delaies,
Thinking to weary your desire by lingring. [305]
  Mis. I dealt too mildly with 'em, in that I
Did offer to request without the Sword:
They shall know what 'tis to delude him that
Ne'r threatned twice; whose anger then is base
When it admits that respite, as to give [310]
A second warning.
  Cleo. 'Tis below your Highness
Thus to expect: were you a private Man
It were past suff'rance.
  Mis. Do they mock me then?
I'l fall upon them like a Judgement. Plagues
And Famines shall be modest; what they count [315]
A visitation now, shall be my Custome,
One of my slightest punishments, and so
Reckon'd hereafter among ord'nary things.
  Cal. Please you but to give leave wee'l force admittance,
And ransack all the Citty ere Sunset. [320]
  Mis. Traytor, thou know'st not what thou wishest: there's
A Jewel in't, which if it should be touch'd
By any but my selfe, I should account
My Diadem guilty of offending Nature.
Be thankfull that I pardon thy request. [325]
  Tim. They are below your Anger; let no such
Vile, abject things disturb your higher thoughts,
Unto whose fame you'l add by Conquering;
Let them enjoy a Peace of your bestowing.
  Mis. Think not *Timophilus* to divert my Fury: [330]
I'l raze their City into a solitude;
Then, if they please, let 'em call that a Peace.
My Reconciliation is by Ruine.
  Tim. Me thinks y' have executed a Revenge
Sufficient by the Preparation to it: [335]
Anothers War carries less Miserie with it

Than your Provision for one; and they suffer
As Conquer'd, whiles that you do but approach.
  Mis. They do but grone divided yet; their sighs
Fly yet, as doth their smoak, here and there some;   [340]
I'l have them make one Cloud, wherein I will
Sit like a Deity in a softer Chariot,
Triumphing over Earth —— But I do ill
To menace such misfortunes to a City
That doth contain a Virgin of such sweetness   [345]
As makes each Place *Elysium* as she passeth:
I must be tender of their good —— Yet why,
Why shall they dare thus to deny her me
To whom all things of price are due? They're stubborn;
I'l bring those Buildings of that threatning height   [350]
As low as their Foundations, and their Minds
Lower than them. *Callimachus*, give order
Unto the Souldier for a sudden Assault.
  Cal. You thought it not excusable, but by
Your speciall Pardon, that I only ask'd it.   [355]
I will not dye for doing your Command.
  Mi. Am I neglected then? *Ph.* I'l go, and 't please you.
  Mis. Stay, Villain, or thou dy'st. Among the Throng
Of more ignoble Creatures, she perhaps
Might perish too; but that her Beauty will   [360]
Disarm ev'n Cruelty it self, and so
Work her escape by conquering with a Look.
Howe'r the Sin's too much, if that I should
Proceed but so far only, as to fright her.
Yet there's no other way of winning —— Go ——   [365]
Do not —— Why stir you not? —— Come back ——
To suffer thus, *Misander*, for that Blest one
(For sure she must be blest that is so fair)
Is chief of all thy Glories —— Captains, to
Your charges; what do you here? —— I am not well.   [370]
                        Ex. Mis. Cleo. Tim. Pru.
  Cal. He hath two Furies in him, Hate, and Love.
Killing, and Making Mortals wholly share him.
  Phil. A little Red i'th' Cheeks will melt him, when
A stream of bloud spilt by his own Command,
Moves him no more than if 'twere so much water.   [375]

    Call. This 'tis to have an hunting Eye; as he
Pass'd through *Byzantium*, he survey'd each Virgin
With a most eager and committing Look.
This one among the rest (who e'r she be)
He had no sooner spy'd, but his nimble Soul   [380]
Did visibly climb up unto her Eyes
By their own Beams.
    Phil. And he will hate as soon;
I'd rather be his Jument than his Mistresse:
Suspicion makes his Bed an Armory;
His head lyes never soft untill he hath   [385]
Guarded his Pillow with a brace of Daggers.
    Call. His Feare hath brought him to that custom too,
That let a Gnat but buzze, he stabs the Ayr,
Strikes out of Habit, and sleeps cruelly.
    Phil. Peace, let's withdraw, if that we mean to live.   [390]
                                        [*Exeunt.*]

Act I. Scen. VI.

*Misander, Patacion, Nicias, Timophilus,
Cleodemus, Prusias.*

    Mis. Do y' mock me with a shadow? and present
A Baby for a Goddesse? I'l proportion
Revenge unto your Crime, and leave nought else
To testifie the memory of your City,
But idle foolish Pictures, such as these.   [395]
    Pata. Our City sends them not in Policy
To keep you longer off. It is not, that
They may deny you, but that you may choose;
And if it please you but to stoop so low
As to design but one of them, and make her   [400]
More fair by such your choise, there shall be no
Delay in fetching her, but what you make
In giving the Command.
    Prus. They dare not mock you;
You need not doubt performance, I will warrant
The very Father will conduct her to   [405]
Your Bed, and be glad of th' emploiment too.

Tim. There's nothing wanting to them but the Life;
Did they but move you, th' had been very Virgins.
 Mis. How dare you look upon 'em, being I am
To make my choice of one? —— Let's see the Pictures.   [410]
 Nic. These are the very Stars that gild our City:
As for this other, 'tis the Picture of one
Whose very sight's an Epigram: to draw her
Is only lawfully to Libell her.
She is a good well-willer to your Majesty.   [415]
 Prus. A well-willer say you to his Majesty?
Let's see't.
 Nic. A Widdow, that I'm Sutor to;
I hope you'l scorn to take my leavings Sir.
 Mis. Whose Picture's this?
 Pat. 'Tis one *Leucasia's*,
The Daughter of *Eudemus*.
 Mis. That is she.   [420]
Along with them, *Timophilus*, and fetch her:
I love her in the Picture.
 Nic. O the Times!
Not bid me eat? there is no courtesie
I see in Tyrants. Please your Highnesse, I'd
Fain tell what house you keep when I come home.   [425]
 Mis. Goe, give him what the Camp affords.
 Nic. D'y' hear* Sir,   *To* Prusias.*
Be fair condition'd; use that Picture honestly
I pray y', and do not make my Pencill Cuckold.
         Exeunt Pat. Nic. Tim.
 Mis. I wonder his Affection would permit
His Art to shew it self in such a Piece.   [430]
Could he gaze so long on, as to pourtray,
And have so little flame, as not to love?   *As* Misan. *comtem-*
Shee's too exactly perfect to be brought   *plates* Leu. *Picture,*
Forth by a Woman: Nature sure her self   Pru. *contemplates*
Descending to conceive, travell'd with her.   *on the Widdows.* [435]
 Cle. Why do you fasten those large Eyes, which should
Shed light, as doth the Sun, on every place
Due to the World, upon a silly Tablet?
 Mis. Where the bare shadow's such, what is the Substance?
That face which carries Natures favours Printed   [440]

Upon it in such gracious Characters,
By a most lawfull captivating Power
Makes all our Senses hers. But take it hence:
I have her in my Mind, a Tablet that
Thine hands cannot remove; there I behold her [445]
Drawn by my Thoughts far better than the Pencill.
O! I do feel something that is not Lust;
A thing that is more subtle, more refin'd
Than to be stil'd Desire.
  Cleo. I hope you will not
Begin to yoak your self at last? It is [450]
The love of private men that doth descend
To Ceremonious Wedlock. You're t' enjoy
Without that idle knot of Matrimony.
  Mis. But that I have not leasure now to punish
I'ld —— Well; I'l suffer all. Say what you will. [455]
What Torrent is't hurries my Passions thus?
Here, hold my Sword —— Give me't again —— I am
Of Merits far too light to ballance hers;
She will refuse me sure —— Pray y' leave me Sirs ——
Yet now I think on't don't —— How every Limb [460]
Presents a Goddess! every part a Day
Darkning the neighbour Jewell! —— Let me have
Some Musick *Prusias* —— Prethee *Cleodemus*
Suffer not any to disturb my thoughts;
I would be quiet —— What a sacred vigor [465]
Dwels in each sprightfull Parcell! —— Low *Misander*,
    A shadow can thy larger Thoughts confine;
    Hiding a Power that's Tyrant over thine.
                      [*Exeunt.*]

ACT. II. SCENE I.

Callimachus, Philostratus, Prusias after them.

  Cal. Pox o'these easie Coxcombs! If he had [470]
Ask'd Wives and Children too he might have had 'em.
Could not their wise simplicities stand out,
And let us conquer 'em?

Phi. I feel mine Arms
Grow stiff again: I shall employ my strength
Only in carrying up of Pasties now. [475]
  Pru. (Is she not wondrous fair? not wondrous handsome?)
  Cal. We shall do nothing but drink Healths in Helmets
To him and his *Leucasia*, (as they call her)
Whiles he encircles her in amorous folds,
And practiseth sweet Battels in a Featherbed. [480]
  Pru. (What Torrent is't hurries my Passions thus?)
  Phi. Frailty of Man! These Vices are as proper
To your great Ones, as Feavers are, or Surfets:
Most Birds of Prey, you know, are still so subject
To wicked Cramps, they dare not sleep without [485]
A soft warm tender Lark all night i' their Talons.
  Pru. (And must a shadow thus my Thoughts confine?)
  Cal. His tender Lark hath made us lose our hopes
Of that tough Kite you wot of, the old Widdow
We thought to cast Dice for. Pox upon *Hymen*; [490]
I'd rather bear a Torch to fire the City
Than carry one in his Solemnities.   [*Pru. steps in to them.*
  Pru. Traytor, thou knowst not what thou wishest. There's
A Jewell in't, which if it should be lost
'Mong other spoils, I should account my self [495]
Guilty of an Offence 'gainst Heav'n, and Her.
  Cal. Must you be imitating of your Prince
In every thing forsooth? And 't please the gods,
Who is that worthy Jewell?
  Prus. 'Tis a Name
Fit to be sung by Angels, not profan'd [500]
By Mortall Tongues.
  Phil. Hast thou espous'd thy King's
Opinion too in Love? Thou that wert wont
To make a Dole of thine Affection
By scatter'd Lust, dost thou confine thy Dotage
Unto a single Face.
  Prus. She's too exact   { *He repeats* [505]
To be brought forth by Woman: Nature sure   { *what* Misan.
Descending to conceive travail'd with her.   { *said of Leu-*
                                                                                { casia's *Pict.*
  Cal. I will be hang'd if thou hast any brains;
Somthing there is perhaps that swims i'thy Noddle

Like to a little Curd in Poffet-drink; [510]
But for true Brain, 'tis gon.
   Prus. Low *Prusias*,
Sure thy deserts will never ballance hers.
Low *Prusias*, thou'rt unworthy.
   Phil. Pray y' who is't
That this low *Prusias* is unworthy of?
   Prus. O! do not vex me!
   Cal. This is like the reading [515]
Of a great swelling bumbast Coppy o' Verses,
And hiding of the Theam.
   Prus. T' your Charges, Captains.
What do you here?
   Cal. Faith laugh at you. Where is
Your Willow, and your Halter?
   Prus. Do not put me
To th' second Warning —— O! I am not well. *Ex. Prusias.* [520]
   Phil. Good faith, h' hath conn'd *Misander*, & we came
Just to the Repetition. Come, let's follow:
We will not lose this sport, although we have
Lost both our hopes, the Widdow, and the Spoyl.   *Ex.*

Act II. Scene II.

Pyle, Leucasia, Chryse, Euthalpe, Elpidia.

   [*Pyl.*] Do we appear, and yet no Reverence seen? [525]
Woman, you are unmanner'd.
   Euth. This directed
To me, or whom?
   Pyl. Is't not enough that you
Were thought so worthy by the City, as
To have your Face sent as a waiting Picture
'Mong ours, and so arrive to th' possibility [530]
Of lying she-perdieu with some old souldier,
To save the use of Furrs and Bearskins, but
Forgetfull of your own condition
(If it be any to be a Waiting-maid)
You must contemn us to our Face, and dare [535]
To stand upright, not bowing as we pass.

Euth.   But that I think this Humor (new put on
This Morning with that dresse) will set with th' Sun,
Being but a Pageant of one day, I would
Trouble my self to answer you good Widdow.   [540]
   Pyl.   Good Widdow! Y'are a Creature, who at best
Are but a living Utensill, a kind
Of Sensitive Instrument, grac'd with the Title
Of overseeing your Lady's dear delights:
What doe you else but feel the Monky's pulse,   [545]
And cater Spiders for the queasie Creature
When it refuseth Comfits? What doe y'else
But set perfidious wiles for simple Flyes
To keep game ready for the Parakeeto?
You'll tell me, that you place disorder'd hairs,   [550]
Rank some transgressing Curls, call in the Corner
Of some uncivill Ribband that starts out,
And will not keep the Discipline. You'l tell me,
Perhaps, that you manage the Pencill too,
Write white and red, and mend the faults of Nature;   [555]
Pray y' what of this? where you are best esteem'd
You only pass under the favourable Name
Of humble Cozens, that sit below the Salt.
   Eut.   This Creature you call Waiting-woman, were
She yours, perhaps were all you've said: but there   [560]
Is difference in Relations, and Things
Alter their Nature with their Places. Black
I'th' Teeth is Darkness, but i'th' Eye becomes
A colour of Resplendency: what is
Elsewhere unseemly, beams, and sparkles there.   [565]
That I obey this Lady (whom I cannot
Name without honour) comes not from the Meanness
Of Birth, or want of Fortunes, but from that
Desire I have to store my mind with good.
Endowments are an inbred Soveraignty;   [570]
Shee that hath more than I, hath more Rule too;
Which yet by fit degrees I do partake,
As I partake her Vertues. To serve thus,
Is but to light my Taper at Anothers,
That I see burns more cleer.
   Pyl.   This you have conn'd   [575]

Out of some wandring Story that you read
To make your Lady sleep.
   Eut. To wipe away
This, and what else remains; the Names, and Offices
We undergo, take not at all from worth.
The Sun doth dress your Gardens, will you stile   [580]
His Beams from thence Ignoble? Gentle winds
That wait upon your Flours, purge, and refine them,
And doing, what you please to misname Servile,
At once conveigh Perfumes to them, and borrow
A Tincture thence, which they had not before,   [585]
Which makes 'em flie more gratefull: Can you thence
Call those pure Blasts dishonourable? will you
Think 'em vile Instruments, and Utensils,
And rank them 'mongst the Pesantry of things?
Common Opinion blinds you. What is this,   [590]
But to unite good Qualities, and mix
Two better Natures to the making of
A third in each outshining both. To deal
Thus with the Vertuous then, cannot be Service,
But sweet Commerce: no Fate, or Force, but only   [595]
Our free Election. More I could repay
In a Comparison of this Condition,
And yours; were it not so Ingenuous,
As not to give Offence, though't be to those
Who do provoke it.
   Leuc. Pray you hear me too.   [600]
Those your dishonourable Offices, you please
To fasten on her, are a double wrong:
For you suppose that there is one so wanton
As to enjoyn 'em, when you say there is
One so ridiculously idle, as   [605]
To busie her self in the performance of 'em.
   Pyl. The first thing I'll do, when I'm chosen Queen
By that Judicious Tyrant, shall be to
Pronounce both of you Traitouresses.
   Chry. Pray y' let
The common thought of our ensuing Fate   [610]
Compose this strife. It was an hard Decree
Without our leaves to send our Pictures. I

Have pray'd unto *Diana*, that I may
Appear most ugly, and, me thoughts, the Image
Did seem to grant, and bow'd.
   Leuc. Some chaster God [615]
Cast an unshapen Cloud before his Eyes,
And make him loath, as soon as he shall see.
   Pyl. Come, come, y' are raw: you little think what 'tis
To be a Tyrant's Consort. You may get
This, or that head you hate, for every kisse. [620]
I would not clip him, unlesse 'twere to strangle
Some one I was offended with. Be not
So sad, I'l warrant you for being chosen.
Our Picture's sent; 'tis I must be your Queen.
   Chry. I hope 'twill be your fortune, being you wish it. [625]
   Pyl. Do you but hope? It must be so; you wrong us
If that you are not sure on't. We will give you
All Places in our Court: We will create
New Offices; *Elpidia*, you shall be
Lady o'th' Fan; You, *Chryse*, of the Colours; [630]
Leucasia, wiper of our Glasse; *Euthalpe*,
If she repent, may keep our Mercury water.
Some Grooms o'th' Teeth, and others of the hair;
Mistres o'th' Fricace, one, one of the Powders,
One of —— I know not what. Then there shall be [635]
A pair of Secretaries to the State
For Love-Letters to Forrain Princes, for
Whom we will found a Library, which shall
Be only stor'd with Play-books, and Romances.
   Elp. 'Twould be a labour worthy of your Highnesse [640]
To bind the liquorish Courtiers to the Peace,
As oft as we are drest for Masques and Playes.
We cannot keep a Pleat unrumpled, or
An Head-tire undisturb'd for them: what we
Have been two days in building, in a minute [645]
Is ruin'd by their boisterous Foppery.
   Pyl. Wee'l call a Parliament of women, choose
Burgesses out o'th' Matrons of the City:
Then wee'l reform all that we think Abuses,
Both Male and Female. Not a Courtier shall [650]
Dare to pretend to th' understanding of

Ought else besides a Play; nor learn a Language
Except it be in Fashion; write no Poetry,
Unlesse it be an Anagram upon
His Mistresses Name, or a thin Distich on [655]
Her little Spaniell. Then it shall be treason
T' appear with a full Calf before the Ladies.
No Lord shall be permitted then to trespasse
A bed with's Lady, but on Festivall Nights,
If that he be an Impotent convicted. [660]
Women shall be allow'd to tempt and wooe:
Especially if that the Man or is,
Or else hath lately been a Student in
Our Famous University of *Athens*.
Lastly, no Lord shall Authorize a Fashion, [665]
It being a Prerogative, that wee'l
Wholly reserve unto our self. I swell
With Axioms, Methods, Rules; I have as strong
A Modell in mine head of Reformation,
As they that are most factious ——

Act II. Scen. III.

To them *Epigenes, Scedasus, Terpander*.

—— How now Subjects. [670]
　Epig.　What? you expect to hear who 'tis that's chosen?
　Pyl.　God bless you my good People; I perceive
You're come to do us Homage: We are Queen.
You hear the Tyrant's wonderfully taken
With us: It was none of our seeking; Fortune [675]
Hath thrown the Dignity into our Lap.
Wee'l make your Yoak hereafter very easie.
　Sced.　How came your Mistris mad, *Elpidia*, thus?
　Elp.　I'm Lady of the Fan Sir; That's my Title.
　Terp.　Truly, good Mrs Tyrant, I'm glad on't, [680]
I hope you'l let's have Victuals cheap hereafter.
What price hath your Mistris put on Eggs yet, Lady?
　Pyl.　I'm studying now what Government is best;
Which of the Species goes on surest Maxims:

Democracy that runs int' Anarchy, [685]
And Aristocracy into Oligarchy;
The Transmigration's *Pythagoricall*;
I think the Common-wealth be best as 'tis.
Well, fare you well: they're come to fetch me here;
I must away with the Ambassadors —— [690]

Act. II. Scen. IV.

To them *Timophilus, Patacion, Nicias.*

——How fares the Partner of Our Throne, *Misander*?
  Tim. Most Noble Citizens, his Majesty
Accepteth of your profer, and by me
Demandeth one be sent that's nam'd ——
  Leu. O stay.
  Chr. O speak no further!
  Pyl. Speak it out aloud; [695]
We love to hear the Accent of our Name.
  Tim. He doth demand one nam'd *Leucasia*.
  Terp. O! goodwife *Pyle* you're not Mistris Tyrant.
  Pyl. Come, come, you forge.
  Pat. Truth is, *Leucasia*'s chosen. [700]
  Nic. Ne'r grieve for't, we shall live as merry as they.
  Terp. Troth, Gammer *Pyle*, I did even think so.
Now what you call'd your Throne's a Wicker chair;
Your Court's a Cottage, your Jewels twopenny Beads.
'Twas, as you say, none of your seeking; Fortune, [705]
Fortune hath thrown the Dignity' int' your Lap.
Pray y' make our Yoke hereafter very easie.
  Pyl. Are we not chosen then? I'l go and beat
All my Maids o'r for this: he had as good ——
I'l —— come away, you baggage —— what d' you gaze on [710]
You filthy Slut?   *Ex. Pyl. Elpi.*
  Terp. B'w'y' Lady of the Fan.
Now will she go and say her Prayers backward
Thrice, and turn Witch to be reveng'd upon him.
God save your Grace, *Leucasia*.
  Leu. O that word,

That word *Leucasia*! I did ne'r mislike [715]
My Name till now: I'm odious to my self,
'Cause I thus please another. Must it be
My punishment that some do call me fair?
Must I place Beauty 'mong the Injuries
Of spightfull Nature? did she only give it [720]
That there might not be wanting to our City
One to enrage a Tyrant?

   Terp. Let me tell you: saving your Tyrantship, you are a Fool. A Tyrant's Concubine's a pretty thing. You may live well on't if you will your self. 'Tis well you have light up- [725] on this Fortune, e'r you are able to judge of a good Leg & Foot. Good Lord to see! she had as fair a promising Table when she was in swadling-clouts as e'r I saw. As my Wife, her Nurse, was dressing her, come next *Quinquatria*, 'twill be just fifteen years, God bless the time! The Cat sate pur- [730] ring on the little stool, just in the Chimney corner I re- member. Saies I unto my Wife *Cyne*! Ay saies she; This child *Cyne* will be alive when we are dead & rotten! saies she to me again; the Child's a good Child Husband. Now see the luck on't; how things will come about! Don't [735] cry *Leucasia*.

   Leu. No other destiny, O heav'ns, but this?

   Tim. These froward Plaints do but prolong your Bondage: You onely doe defer your Liberty,
Grieving away that time should gain your freedome. [740]

   Leuc. Seeing that I must go, pray let me be
Conducted like a Sacrifice, for I
Am Offer'd, not Bestow'd. It is my Death,
(For so I think't) but given to my Countrey,
And to divert from her a punishment. [745]
Though th' Means be ill, 'tis Vertue to consent.   *Exeunt.*

Act II. Scen. V.

Prusias with the Picture of the Widdow, *Callimachus*
and *Philostratus* after him.

   Prus. Stay Villain, or thou dyest. Amongst the throng
Of more ignoble Creatures she might perish:
Yet there's no other way of winning her.

Call.   Hee's at it in the very same strain.
Prus.   Goe —— [750]
Doe not, —— Why stir you not? —— Come back —— To suffer
Thus, *Prusias*, for that blest one, is the chief
Of all thy Glories.
   Phil.   Look, the Widdows Picture!
   Prus.   I wonder his affection would permit
His Art to shew it self in such a Peece. [755]
Could he gaze so long on as to pourtray,
And have so little flame, as not to love?
                              Cal. and Phil. step in.
   Cal.   Yes verily I think he could. Must you
Be doting on a Picture too?
   Pru.   Take't hence.
I have her here.
   Phil.   Then thou'st a Fury there. [760]
   Pru.   O! I do feel something that is not Lust.
   Cal.   In good troth so do I; a perfect hate.
You are the Man for tender Maidenheads ——
   Ph.   ——That would not venture on a season'd Widdow ——
   Cal.   ——For a whole Kingdom Sir.
   Prus.   Say what you will. [765]
   Phi.   She is the verier Picture of the two.
   Cal.   She hath as many Colours in her face,
As that Board hath.
   Phi.   Thou err'st to call 'em Colours.
   Cal.   True! they turn Morter when th' are there.
   Pru.   Say on,
I'l suffer any thing.
   Phil.   Shee's —— let me see —— [770]
   Cal.   An Hag, a Witch, a Fury, ne'r stick at it.
   Pru.   Here, hold my Sword —— give't me again —— she hath
A fair white skin ——
   Phi.   —— A mangy gross thick hide.
   Pru.   Most Amber Tresses ——
   Cal.   A most ugly Maine.
   Pru.   Lips decent, and most fit ——
   Phil.   To sweep a Manger —— [775]
   Cal.   —— Which she doth open like a pair of Gates ——
   Phi.   —— And then claps down her teeth like a Percullis.

Pru. Neat Leg and Foot ——
Cal. Most durty Hocks, and Hoofs.
Pru. Descended from some King ——
Phi. Some antient Cart-horse.
Pru. A sprightly Goddess ——
Cal. A foule durty Beast. [780]
Pru. Her Eyes like Suns ——
Phi. —— Draw vapours from her Breath ——
Cal. —— Which in her Nose, as in the middle Region ——
Phi. —— Are turn'd to ominous Comets.
Pru. Pray leave me ——
Yet now I think on't don't —— How every smile
Shews us ——
Cal. —— The sign o'th' Mouth!
Pru. Let m' have some Musick [785]
Gentle *Callimachus* ——
Phi. How every gaping ——
Pru. Prethee *Philostratus* let me have none.
Cal. —— Betraies her Teeth, which stand one by another ——
Ph. —— As if that they were Cloves stuck in an Orenge.
Cal. Joy, *Prusias*, Joy: though thou be strucken blind —— [790]
Phi. —— Thou yet canst see her Picture in thy Mind.
                                                    Ex. severally.

Act II. Scen. VI.

Eudemus, Leucasia, Euthalpe.

   Eud. Ne'r murmur Girl, 't's a Service to thy Country.
   Leu. There was this only wanting to my evils,
That you too should approve; that, that good name
(Father) should yet inserted be in this [795]
My vile disgrace. Call 't you a service to
My Country, to turn Whore? What Brand will 't be
Unto your Liberty, when 't shall be said
'Twas purchas'd by a Strumpet?
   Eud. 'Tis not thou
Offend'st, but thine ill fortune, and the City: [800]
Rejoice that thou canst make the heavens guilty.
Come, thou must love him Girl.

Leu.   Can I love him
That thus will rob me of mine Honour?
   Eud.   'Tis
His tenderness unto thee.
   Leu.   If he be
Thus tender, how's he cruell? sure his Hate   [805]
Is something beyond Death, if he Love thus.
   Eud.   Alas! thou know'st not how to value Fortune;
What ever Nature of her own Accord,
Or Art by force can yeeld, will all be thine.
   Leuc.   But I shall lose mine Honour.
   Eud.   Thou shalt have   [810]
Th' Inventions of his Kingdome toyl to please thee;
A strife of Wits and Fancies to content thee;
And thou reward them amply by one smile:
The Silkworm shall spin only to thy Wardrobe;
The Sea yield Pearls unto thy Caskinet;   [815]
Thou shalt come forth loaded with Jewels, like
That Body with an hundred Eyes. Thou shalt
Take Coach to the next door, and as it were
An Expedition, not a Visit, be
Bound for an house but ten strides off, still carry'd   [820]
Aloof in indignation of the Earth.
Five hundred Asses shall be daily milk'd
To make a Bath for thee, which shall maintain
Thy skin in an unblemish'd tendernesse,
And make thine Age, in spight of Time, run back.   [825]
Nature her self shall joy to be thy Slave.
   Leuc.   But I shall lose mine Honour.
   Eud.   Hast a mind
To redeem that thou seem'st so tender of?
   Leuc.   I am so far engag'd to my disgrace,
That there's no means left for me to escape it;   [830]
Shew me but any except Death, and I
Will hearken to you with as much Religion,
As to some Reverend Auncestor, when he
In a shape more than Humane doth appear,
And dictate holy Oracles in Dreams.   [835]
   Eud.   The way, I'l shew thee, will preserve thy Life,
And that Life of thy Country, Liberty.
But thou'lt not do't I know.

    Leuc. Think not so ill
Of your good Daughter.
    Eud. Thou shalt kill this Tyrant.
    Leuc. Heavens forbid!
    Eud. I did suppose as much.   [840]
Goe, flye to his Embraces, there produce
Monsters, and Plagues: from him and thee there cannot
Spring any thing that's ord'nary in Nature.
    Leuc. Indeed I cannot kill him.
    Eud. When that he
Shall loath thy foul embraces, and avoid   [845]
Thy sight, as somthing that doth exprobrate
His sins unto him: When thou shalt be so
Unhappy, as to become fruitfull, and
Discarded from his Bed, walk despicable,
Loaded with spurious Brats, one in thy Bosome,   [850]
Another on thy Back, the third i' thine Hand,
Just like the Picture of Charity, thou'lt wish
Too late, thou'dst took the Counsell of thy Father.
    Leuc. Indeed I'l kill my self, if that you will.
    Eud. O! nourish no such thought my good *Leucasia*.   [855]
Take not to heart what I have said; my Passion
Carry'd my Tongue beyond my thoughts —— But —— Girle ——
Come, thou shalt kill him, and be famous for't.
    Leuc. But will you help me then?
    Eud. Why I'm thy Father.
Intreat that thou mayst come alone 'bout Midnight;   [860]
Pretend thy Modesty wo'nt suffer thee
To goe with solemn Pomp to thy disgrace:
And when thou'st opportunity strike home.
I will be ready when thou'st struck the blow
To rescue thee from danger. Fear no stain: [865]
A Tyrant's Bloud doth wash the hand that spils it.
    Leuc. Alas, *Euthalpe*, how am I distracted!   *Ex. Eudem.*
Either I must turn Homicide, or Whore;
And if I kill him, twill be said I did
Kindle the Flame, and then put out the Man;   [870]
If not, I kill my self; Shame waits on both;
And I (O cruell!) have this only Freedome
To choose the lesse offence.

Euth.   The straight is this,
Either you must ruine th' Effect, or else
Destroy the Cause; punish his Love, or lose [875]
Your Beauty by consenting. But Love is
A strong desire of being united to
That which is fair, by the most perfect means
That Nature yeelds, or Reason teacheth. Hee's
Deficient in the way then: Love is good [880]
Still in the Fountain, but offends i'th' stream.
But this will not be weigh'd by Common thoughts;
So that you will be said to punish him,
Because your self were fair, and he had Eyes.
  Leuc.   True, good *Euthalpe*; but yet put mine Honour [885]
Into the other Scale, which o'rweighs then?
  Euth.   Love's common unto all the masse of Creatures,
As Life and Breath; Honour to Man alone:
And amongst Men ('yet narrower) to the Prudent.
Honor being then 'bove Life, Dishonor must [890]
Be worse than Death: For Fate can strike but one,
Reproach doth reach whole Families; and in
Our Sex especiall, the chast Sphere of Vertue
Being to us as proper as the Aire
To winged Creatures. Yet I cannot bid you [895]
Strike to avoid a blow. Some Virgins Daggers
Have been deliver'd up to Fame by Penns;
But yet there goes a stain along, in that
Beauty could be so cruell.
  Leuc.   Some good God   [*Soft Mus. awhile.*
Direct me in my Dreams! But heark! I hear [900]
The Musick sounds sad Accents, and the Virgins
Are ready to conduct me; and I must
Depart without thy wonted Resolution.
Let me embrace thee yet; thou art no Tyrant.
Farwell, *Euthalpe*, and when e'r thou shalt [905]
Hear mention of me, pay a sigh, and say,
The Fate, if Bad, was not deserv'd.
  Euth.   The Gods
Leave me when e'r I dare be so ungratefull
As to leave you. Some Pow'r may look down yet
And help in pitty; we will tread one Path, [910]

Obey one Counsell, undergoe one Fate;
And resolutely in this mutuall Tye,
Either preserve our Honor, or else dye.   *Exeunt.*
                                               [*Soft Musick.*]

Act II. Scene VII.

*Leucasia with Euthalpe, and a Company of Virgins, and
others of Byzantium, solemnly conducting
her with this Song.*

1 Virg.	*Strow we these Flowers as we goe,*	
	Which trod by thee will sweeter grow.	[915]
2 Virg.	*Guard her, ye Pow'rs, if any be,*	
	That love afflicted Chastity.	
1 Virg.	*Her Mind deserves a Princely sway,*	
	But yet obtain'd another way.	
2 Virg.	*Her Vertues fit her for a Throne,*	[920]
	But of no Choice, except her own.	
1 Virg.	*O then look down on his Desires,*	
	And either quench, or clense his Fires.	
Chor.	*O then look down,* &c. *Exeunt.*	

ACT. III. SCEN. I.

Misander discover'd asleep, Leucasia to him.

Leu. All things are husht & laid, except my thoughts;   [925]
Somthing puls back my hand, methinks, and tels me
'Tis not a Virgin's Office to be cruell.
I would that he were dead, but not by me.
I am afraid. But do I only tremble?
Is that all I retain of Innocence?   [930]
Shee's too near guilt that only fears, and she
That's come so far as only to be stopp'd
By a misgiving Heart, hath don't already.
I cannot then retire me from the sin,
Though I do leave the Action unconsummate.   [935]

On then, *Leucasia*, on: that Tyrant hath
The same Design on thee, but that he will
Put it in practise by an easier way.
Prevent him then, and —— what? I am afraid
To hear it nam'd: I have decreed within me [940]
Somthing I dare not tell unto my self.
And truly 't hath been told me, that there is
A place, where after Death all sins are punish'd.
There be my wrongs Reveng'd —— But wilt thou then
Betray thine Honour to him, and bequeath [945]
Thy self to willing Infamy? Thy Deed
Hath Heav'n for its Defence; thine Innocence
Prompts thee to do it; it is Vertue strikes,
The Blow is none of thine —— Yet some do say
The Ghosts of those that are thus us'd do haunt [950]
The guilty after death, and I shall then
Be frighted every minute —— But thy Father,
Thy Father doth perswade thee; 'tis not thou,
It is *Eudemus* strikes —— Yet I shall never
Endure to see his bloud gush out in streams: [955]
'Twill be an hideous sight to view his wounds
Open, and gaping as it were for her
That newly made 'm. Can a Virgin this?
A Virgin wrong'd can more —— But I'm not safe;
All things, methinks, have Eyes: this wavering Taper [960]
Doth seem to watch, and listen what I say,
And trembles now to think what shall be done;
It is a Spy; first then extinguish that.
Darknesse belongs unto thy deed. Sin never
Yet wanted light; there's somthing that directs it [965]
Without a Day —— good Heav'n! how sound he sleeps!
I cannot do it for my heart —— 'Tis best
That I retire unseen ——

{ *As she puts out the Light, he starts out of his sleep, and snatching a Dagger from under his Pillow, stabs her.* }

Mis. So perish
All that do seek my life.
   Leuc. O! O!
   Mis. When Kings

Lye down, ev'n Darknesse doth become their Guard, [970]
And Night keeps watch. *Misander's* sleep hath Eyes.
Lights here, what lights ho! [*Phi. Cal. and Pru. with lights*
  Leuc. O!
  Mis. Is't thee my fair one?
(Quickly, a Surgeon ho! the hurt is mine:
Haste; every drop of Bloud's your Soveraigne's.)
Said I my sleep had Eyes! O, if it had, [975]
Thou ne'r hadst fall'n. This is a deed, that makes
Ev'n me asham'd, one, who they say ne'r blusht,
But only to cast out all Modesty.
Be husht, O Fame, in this part of my Life!
Oblivion, seize thou but this deed, and let me [980]
[Not] become the talk of all Posterity.
What e'r I did before was yet virile,
Having this plea at least, that 'twas to Man.
The Sex here is my shame, what shall I say
The Beauty of it is? That makes mine Act [985]
Deform'd beyond expression: 'Tis a sin
That puzzles all Invention to outstrip,
And comes a Novelty to History.
  Leu. Why have you us'd her thus, that could not wound you?
  Mis. And art thou kind yet, fair *Leucasia*? [990]
I dare not call thee mine. My Act's more hainous
In that thou still affect'st me, and thy Love
Makes me more wicked than the wrong I've done thee.
Thou hast found one way more t'augment my fault.
  Leuc. If I did please you, why am I thus wounded? [995]
If not, O why doe not you wound me more?
If thus you use those whom you love, your Subjects
Will make their pray'rs to heaven to be hated.
        [*Ent.* Phil. *with a Surgeon.*]
  Mis. Bind up her wound as tender as you can,
And be as Gentle, as I have been Cruell. [1000]
Here Health her self should come and work the Cure.
Nature lyes sick whiles she doth. O my Fate!
Y're idle O ye Gods! where is your Thunder?——

Act. III. Scen. II.

To them *Eudemus*.

Eud.   Not far off from thee most unhumane Tyrant.
Mis.   I am a Tyrant now indeed; this stroke   [1005]
Hath made that Name peculiarly mine.
Eud.   Was't this she pleas'd thee for? she did deserve it
In comming to thee. 'Tis a due that's paid her
For that offence. But if I'd thought thou hadst
Only requir'd her Bloud 't should have been spilt   [1010]
By me her Father, whiles she yet was honest,
Whiles not yet tainted with so near approach
Unto this Crime, as to Consent. I'm only
Sorry 'tis done so late.
Mis.   O do not think
This Sin, this Villany, call't what thou wilt,   [1015]
Was done with Counsell; 'Twas a meer Mistake;
Suspicion made me Cruell.
Eud.   Nay, I thank you,
I thank you for the Wound: I'm glad her Body
Hath only pleas'd to slaughter; you have been
Past expectation kind in striking thus.   [1020]
The wound had been far greater had you lov'd her.
Put this among your Deeds of Charity;
It is the only thing in which the Father,
Since thou didst first demand her, can rejoyce in.
Mis.   If yet thy Voice speak louder than thy Bloud   [1025]
Say this, *Leucasia*, only —— 'Twas his Error ——
O take revenge, *Eudemus*, whiles thy Fury
Yet prompts thine Arm —— O speak, *Leucasia*,
Curse me, *Leucasia*, so thou wilt but speak ——
O pardon me, *Eudemus*, 'tis a King,   [1030]
A King thus asks thee pardon —— By those Eyes,
Those Eyes, whose sight first Captivated mine,
By this thy present Beauty, though thus wounded,
Which makes me suppliant to thee, me, who do
Acknowledge no Superiour, I entreat   [1035]
Thou think not ill of me howe'r —— Blest Father,
Only unhappy by this Accident,

Remit mine Error —— Sweetest Virgin look,
Look once upon me, I've no Dagger now,
No such curs'd weapon —— If thou yet dar'st trust [1040]
Thy Daughter with me, all the helps that Art
Can yield shall be employ'd; there shall no Prayers
Be made to Heav'n but to recover her;
No Gums shall fly up in a pious smoak
But for her health, although the Gods I know [1045]
Favour her so, that she ne'r yet had need
T' employ a Sacrifice.
   Eud. Trust her with thee?
I'l trust her to Destruction as soon.
Give me my Daughter from thy loath'd Embraces.
You have done what you would: yet shee's not mine, [1050]
Whiles thus polluted by thy Love, and Anger.
When thou hast made her honest, and hast wrought
That cure upon her, then return her to me.
'Tis only Innocence that makes the Child.   *Ex. Eud.*
   Mis. Thou, unto whom I ow this curs'd misfortune, [1055]
Darkness, enwrap me. Though mine Eyes are blest
In viewing her, (too happy if not thus)
Yet that they may no longer share this guilt,
If thou canst hide one blacker than thy self,
Spread out thy Wings; O Night I fly to thee, [1060]
Strook deeper far, and wounded more than she.

                             { *Ex.* Mis. *and* Leuc. *convey'd in.* }
                             { *Manent* Phil. Cal. Prus. }

   Phil. Who is't would live in fear? Suspicion strikes
Those that intend no harm, insteed of Foes.
   Cal. This comes of Love forsooth —— They fool so long
Untill at last they ev'n kill one another. [1065]
The beastly Poets now will fall to work
And stab her o'r and o'r again; we shall
Have such *Leucasiads* now come forth I warrant,
And such *Misandriads* ——
   Pru. 'Twas no fault of his.
He did suspect some Treachery, some design [1070]
Upon his life; it was not meant to her.
   Phi. I would 't had been your Widdow, *Prusias.*

Cal. Faith, cut her throat in imitation too.
Phi. Sure you may do it safely; she hath no
Bloud left that will be spilt; 'twill only make [1075]
Another passage for her wind.
Cal. You may
When you have don't take her, and marry her
In Recompence: I'l warrant you shall find her
As warm then, and as moist, as she is now.
Pru. You never had that goodness, as to Love. [1080]
Keep in your Scoffs, or else ——
Cal. —— You'l beat me, won't you?
Pru. A man can't be a little Circumspect,
And carefull of himself, but you must twit him
With Cowardise. Sir, there's a King in *Thrace.*
Cal. Why, th' King shall know we love him Sir as well [1085]
As you, although we do not walk his Pace,
Eate not according to his Palate, Love not,
And hate not by Reflection.
Phi. There may be
True hearty Subjects, though they be not shadows
Cast from the Body Royal; and we may [1090]
Live very well; and yet not live by Rote.
Pru. Pray y' be not angry friends: you know wee're Mortals:
All have our faults.
Phi. And thine is Cowardize.
Why, now I see thou'rt coming: I perceive
There is some goodness in thee. Let's speak Treason. [1095]
Pru. Come, come, you're merry Captains: let m' alone;
What think you of this Action?
Cal. Though I don't
Commend it, yet, I'm glad 'tis done.
Pru. The King
Shew'd himself truly valiant, me thinks,
That he durst strike i'th' dark, he knew not whom. [1100]
Phi. No question but 'twas valiantly done:
Misander did it. Troth I like it well,
There'l be some trading now. This sneaking Peace
Stops all Commerce; a Man grows musty in't.
There is no dying out of Course.
Cal. Good faith, [1105]

I do ev'n long to cut a Throat: good Qualities
Are quickly lost, you know, for want of practice.
To them a Souldier.
 Sol. The City's up in Arms: away t' your Tents.
 Cal. This is the first thing that I lov'd 'em for.
Now you shall see the difference 'twixt us Captains [1110]
Train'd up i'th' Field, and you train'd up i'th' Court.
 Phi. Let's to our charges; how will you bestow
Your self most valiant *Prusias*?
 Pru. I'l along
Unto the King, and do as he doth. Pray you
For my sake spare the Widdow —— faith I love her. [1115]
Exeunt.

ACT. III. SCEN. III.

Misander on a Couch.

 Mis. Or Nature doth not make the Beautifull,
Or takes no care for their defence once made.
Where are those now say Beauty is a Guard
Sufficient without Weapons? Curs'd *Misander*:
Thou hast not that felicity of ill doing [1120]
As to offend the Common way. Thou dost
Act Crimes, that thwart receiv'd Opinions,
And contradict ev'n Truths agreed upon;
So that thy facts will be hereafter urg'd
As Proofs against Positions. Wretched Man! [1125]
If any shall hereafter strive t' express
A Mortall Malice, let him only say,
His Hate's as dangerous, as *Misander*'s Love.

ACT III. SCEN. IV.

To him *Cleodemus, Timophilus, Callimachus,*
Philostratus.

 Cle. Leave off this grief; The Citie's up in Arms Sir —
 Mis. How does *Leucasia*?
 Tim. — They're almost with us——— [1130]

Phi. — Their March is swift; *Eudemus* is their Captain—
Cal. — They are resolv'd to kill, or to be kill'd—
Mis. Hath she not slept as yet?
Cle. Do you sleep Sir?
Tim. Are you in such a Lethargy, that Thunder
Cannot awake you?
Mis. Doth her wound much grieve her? [1135]
Tim. You will be Butcher'd Sir within this half hour.
Mis. Ha!
Phil. You will have your throat cut presently.
Mis. Ay!
Cal. Pox upon this paltry nonsense Love.
Will you be made a Martyr by your slaves?
Mis. What is the matter Captain?
Cal. Why, the City [1140]
Is up in Arms, coming to kill you Sir.
Mis. Let 'em do what they will. You have not told
Whether *Leucasia* slept or no.
Cle. Come Sir,
On with this Sword; girt, and bestir your self.
Mis. What would you have me do?
Tim. Wee'd have you fight, [1145]
Or else give us directions how we shall.
Mis. I charge you make not any shew of Battel;
Let there be no resistance; give 'em free
And unmolested passage to me: all
Is safe I'm sure, if that you'l be contented. [1150]
He that shall first lift up his hand against 'em
Shall be the first that falls.
Cle. Then dye alone,
And perish sluggishly without resistance.
Tim. Come let's away, and each shift for himself.
Exeunt all but Misander.

Act III. Scen. V.

To him a Boy in the habit of a Virgin. Leucasia *discover'd in a Chair, and* Euthalpe *by her.*

Mis. I know, for my sake, that she hates all Men; [1155]
Who're therfore Miserable 'cause she hates them.

So that I've brought a Curse o'r half the world
By this one single Action. Prethee sing,
And try if in this habit thou canst wooe
Her weary thoughts into a gentle slumber. [1160]

Song.

Boy. *Seal up her Eyes, O Sleep, but flow*
Mild, as her Manners, too and fro:
Slide soft into her, that yet shee
May receive no wound from thee.
And ye, present her thoughts, O Dreams, [1165]
With hushing winds, and purling streams,
Whiles hovering silence sits without,
Carefull to keep disturbance out.
Thus seize her, Sleep, thus her again resign,
So what was Heavens gift, wee'l reckon thine. [1170]

{*As she fals asleep* Misander *seats himself just over against her, and looks immoveably upon her, not regarding any thing done in the next Scene.*}

Act. III. Scen. VI.

To them *Eudemus, Terpander, Scedasus, Epigenes, Patacion, Nicias,* Souldiers of *Byzantium.*

{*The Attendants flie all but* Euthalpe. *The* Byzantines *seeing* Misander *sit thus, fall off amaz'd.*}

Sced. What Policy is this and't please the Gods?
Ter.   The sign o'th' Tyrant gazing on the Virgin.
Nic.   Here's more work for my Pencill than my Sword.
Eud.   What? stand you fix'd as he? I thought there would
Have been that loyall strife who should have first [1175]
Let out that Bloud that covets yours.
  Epig.   Shall we
Fight with a Statue?
  Eud.   Flesh and bloud I warrant y',
No part is stone about him, but his Heart.
Through which, though hardned so, I'l find a Passage.
                    Eud. *makes at him.* Euth. *steps between.*

Eut. But through me first: the Sword hath more to do [1180]
Than you suspect.
   Eud. Will you dye too for Company?

{ Eud. *is stopt by* Sced. *and* Pata. Euthalpes *Father.*
Pat. *passeth over to defend his Daughter.* }

   Pat. You are my Enemy if you wrong my Daughter.
   Euth. This is a part of Fury, not of Valour.
Where heavy sadness hath quite tane away
All life and Soul, will you add more wounds yet, [1185]
And kill him that's already dead? you shall not
Disgrace your former deeds with such an Action.
   Eud. What? a she Champion?
   Eut. That I am a woman
Cannot take off from vertuous deeds; my Soul's
As Male as yours; there's no Sex in the mind. [1190]
   Eud. New Tenents to defend new Prodigies.
Was't this you went along for? Can you see him
Gazing upon these Wounds he made, and yet
Not give him one himself? Look how he takes
Delight in's Act ev'n to an Extasie. [1195]
   Sced. Wee'l strike when he may feel it: 'twere an Act
Of pitty to destroy him now; you see
He takes no notice, and makes no resistance.
   Eud. 'Tis only Beauty moves his wanton Eye;
Hee's blind to all besides. 'Tis not his time [1200]
To strike as yet, his Blow's at Midnight still.
Were't dark he would bestir himself; he dares
Do nothing when 'tis day: besides wee're Men;
He only shews his strength on feeble Virgins.
Were we but Women all our Blouds should run [1205]
Mixt in one common stream. You shall not stay me:
I'l sacrifice him to my wronged Daughter,
Whom he thus tortures.
   Euth. If that Love can torture
He is her punishment: hee's so tender of her
That he hath not once clos'd his Eyes, since first [1210]
He wounded her, but sits thus musing still,
Scarce breathing any time, except it be

To set a sigh at liberty: he is
Almost run Frantick for this hard mischance.
   Pat. You see, *Eudemus*, Heaven hath begun [1215]
To take revenge upon him, doe not interest
A mortall spight i'th'quarrell of the Gods.
Leave them to perfect what they've took in hand.
   Terp. Ne'r let me eat more if I could not cry
To see him how he looks —— yfaith he loves her. [1220]
   Eud. Think you that this is out of tendernesse
He thus takes care of her? he doth but strive
To make her fit to fall again; she must
Either endure his Anger, or his Lust
The worse Plague of the two. If that you love her, [1225]
Pray Heav'n she ne'r awake.
   Epig. You are too bitter;
You have too much o'th' Father in you; 'tis
Your Passion speaks.
   Eud. You are not Citizens,
That think this Injury my private one;
Not Souldiers, that let fall your swords, when that [1230]
Y' are come unto the point of Action;
Not Friends, in that you think 't my privat wrong,
And yet not strive to vindicate me: 'tis
Heaven's will my sword should only be ennobled
In this Designe. I will perform't ——
   Euth. You shall not. [1235]
   Pat. Keep off *Eudemus*.
   Eud. What *Patacion* turn'd
Misander's Bawd?
   Euth. Most passionate Man, you wrong
My Reverend Father, and your Daughter too;
I'm certain his Love's good; Lust never yet
Could look so quiet and so peaceable. [1240]
   Terp. Well, if it be a trick, he do's't as well
As e'r I saw one yet: yfaith hee'd make
A very pretty Actor in my Judgment.
Perhaps 'tis but his Image, there have been
Such tricks e'r now; pull him but by the Nose [1245]
And we shall quickly see —— But hold! who's here?

Act III. Scen. VII.

To them *Timophilus, Cleodemus, Callimachus, Philostratus, Prusias*, without weapons.

Tim. Most Noble Citizens, 'tis very kindly
Done of you, thus to visit your faire Virgin.
Eud. Perhaps you think to complement us out
Of our revenge; where are your Swords? your Weapons? [1250]
Tim. There, in that Chair.
Eud. This meerly is a Plot.
Cle. I would *Misander* did dissemble only!
Alas! the Passion is too true. I wrong it
When that I call it Passion: 'tis a Madness,
A Frensie rather. Would he lov'd us so [1255]
As he doth you, *Eudemus*, and your Daughter.
Eud. I would he did; I'm sure hee'd wound you then.
Cle. Heaven can witness, that was his mistake:
You must complain of Fortune, not of him.
Tim. You would do very nobly to conclude [1260]
A Truce between both parts till he recover.
I'm sure it is not your desire to end
The business of a Field in a Bedchamber.
Pat. We can't suspect that Treachery can have
A lodging in your Brest.
Pru. To wipe off all [1265]
Such thoughts, I am most willing to become
Hostage my self.
Cal. Phi. And we too if you please.
Pat. If you'l consent, *Eudemus*, I my self,
With *Scedasus*, and *Epigenes*, will be th' Exchange.
Eud. Being you'l have it so, I will.
Sced. Epig. And we. [1270]
Cle. May from these pledges spring such setled Peace
That we ne'r need these mutuall Offices
For its Assurance ——
Pat. And our strength hence grow
Weak to our selves, but potent to our Foe.

{ Misand. *desists his contemplation as* Leuc. *awakens.* }   { *They depart enterchangeably.*
Manent Mis. Euth. Leuc. }

Mis.   I am return'd again; I was transported, [1275]
And drunk in Revelations from the sight
Of your diviner Front. Me thoughts I saw
Venus, impregnate at one beck of *Jove*,
Deliver'd of a wing'd and star-like Infant;
At whose blest Birth the Spheres sung high, and loud, [1280]
And each thing else rejoyc'd; only a Soul
There was, which striving to destroy the Child
Presented it a Mixture made of Tears,
And Sighs, and Passions, instead of Nectar.
For this condemn'd to take it all her self, [1285]
She drank it, and grew Mad: Being thus distracted,
The Father of the World, and Love (that was
The little Infant) did forthwith confine her
Unto the Prison of an humane Body;
And only left her this way to regain [1290]
Her former Seat, by using the Child well.
   Euth.   Be your own Tutor then; Dyet that Child
With pure and simple Viandes; let no Passion
Trouble the Cup; or if some one slip in,
Purge and correct it, that it only give [1295]
A pleasing relish to the rest, and thence
Prove an Encitement only, no Disease.
   Mis.   Alas! you talk of streams fresh from the chaste
Resplendent Gravell of the purer Fountain.
The waters that I taste have journi'd through [1300]
All Minerals, and have stoln somewhat from each;
Straying as far in Qualities from the Fountain
As they've in space.
   Euth.   The Eye of Love, like that
O'th'Body, if distemper'd, is to be
Help'd by the Influx of some harmless Color. [1305]
If then your Soul see ill (for that's Love's Eye)
Cure it, by looking on her healing Vertues.
   Mis.   True, I must take those good Perfections
Only from her; I am my self as void
Of all, as Tables not yet lineate, [1310]
And only love to gain 'em.
   Euth.   You love them
In a desire of supplement.

Mis.   Had Heav'n
Given me all th' Endowments of my Saint,
I should rejoice as much in mine own Beauties
As now I sigh for hers. To love her would [1315]
Be a superfluous thing, my self sufficing
My self, as once *Narcissus* did *Narcissus*.
  Eut.   You seem to stray Sir from the Common Tenent
That Woman is but the defect of Man,
In that you make her thus his Complement. [1320]
  Mis.   And rightly: 'Tis she gives him operation.
Her Beauty 'tis that's Valorous, Liberall, Just:
Our Vertues only are but other Names
Of her Perfections; some good thing of hers
Disguis'd i'th' shape of Action. Thus at first [1325]
The Servant hath not that great Light and Beauty
Of better thoughts, that his blest Fair one hath;
But by conversing, and Example, grows
Up to the same vigor and force of honour;
As the weak Taper that is kindled from [1330]
The fuller light, shews first a fainter Beam,
But by the eager growth of Flames, casts forth
A Lustre still encreasing, till both, being
At the same measur'd brightness, do combine,
And twist by intermingled Beams, uniting [1335]
Themselves into one Circular flux of Glories.
  Leu.   Who hath inspir'd you thus? me thinks that mind
Which ere while like the place below the Moon
Had Thunders, Lightnings, Whirlwinds, and such other
Unruly Meteors, is now like the State [1340]
Of that above, where still one equall Calm,
One soft continued Quietness doth hush
All that wheels round about it, making things
Pass without Noise, and yet with Musick too.
Had you but ere while shewn such mildness, you [1345]
Had wounded my Soul then.
  Mis.   Unworthy Wretch!
By your instructions yet that name may be
Chang'd to a Title equalling ev'n Heav'n.
Speak, and I'l listen as some holy Priest
To the high Dictates of his whispering God. [1350]

Leu. Thus then. Love, whether he be found i'th' Fields
'Mong Beasts (where some think he was born, and as
He grew up practiz'd shooting upon them)
Or else 'mong Laws, and Men (where now his Temples,
His Altars, and his Statues are) is alwaies [1355]
Each where a thing Divine, and ought as such
Be worshiped by all that pretend to good.
Love having this Divinity in us
Far above other Creatures, in that he
Hath chosen out Man's Countenance to place [1360]
Two sparks of it, whence Hearts are easily kindled,
Man ought to cherish this fire by good Reason,
And make it burn more cleer, substracting from it
All grosser stuff: I banish not the Senses
When I name Reason; for as we must please [1365]
The Mind and Soul, so we must feed the Sight,
And sometimes too the Touch; in that we are
Not Reason only, but Eye too, and Hand.
  Mis. I do acknowledge all as Oracle,
Let me adore those Lips that utter'd it. [1370]
  Leuc. This doth not yet give way to your Embrace,
Or Authorize your Kiss: think not of any
Such thing, lest like the impatient *Orpheus*, you
By looking back lose what yo' have gain'd from Death.
You are not yet arriv'd at that perfection [1375]
As to participate those Sweets; your Merits
Must grow up to them: to transgress their bounds
Would be to wrong your self; for disproportion'd
Felicity, is a Misery. First, conceive
And think, and Fancy honourably within, [1380]
And then take leave t' embrace, & Crown those thoughts.
For they that love a Lip or Hand, love grosly:
Affection compasseth, not enters them;
Having, as th' Earth, the Surface scorch'd by th' Sun,
Whiles that the Center rests cold and benum'd. [1385]
Beasts and Plants move to propagate their like;
Our Love must then step higher, and contend
To make our selves Immortall: which is done
When each by dying in himself doth come
To live in something made of both these Deaths, [1390]

As doth the Voice and Lute in a third Musik,
Or Musk and Amber in a third Perfume.
And this the Gods and we call perfect Love.
   Mis. One Voice is Heav'n's and yours: now I perceive
That as the Earth enlightned by the Sun [1395]
Sends forth those fumes which after darken him;
So our Hearts kindled by our Reason first
Cloud the serenity of that by strange
And grosser Appetites. But you have drawn
The Veyl away that was before Love's Eyes. [1400]
Which Veyl yet was not his, but ours, he being
Said to want Eyes, because we walk in Secret,
And unknown Paths. Great Deity of Affections,
Thou art first fair and good thy self, and then
Mak'st others to be so. O pardon us [1405]
  Blasphemers then, who do the Blame transfer;
  And say that thou art blind, because we Err.   *Exeunt.*

Act. IV. Scen. I.

Philostratus, Callimachus, Pyle.

   Phi. Though I am sorry for that great misfortune
Leucasia hath receiv'd, yet in respect
I come t' enjoy your Countenance by it, [1410]
I cannot wish't undone.
   Pyl. It was a Judgment
From Heav'n upon her, 'cause she profer'd to
Ascend that Bed was only due to me.
   Cal. I do confess your Vertues do deserve
Rule, and Dominion; but they'l shew as fair [1415]
And gracefull in Despising it, as e'r
They could in Managing.   [*They whisper her by turns.*
   Phi. Don't hear him, Lady.
He would inveagle you: take it from me,
He is the notedst Flatterer in the Kingdom.
   Pyl. Can I be flatter'd then? I'd thought I had [1420]
Made all Praise Modest.

Cal. Whatsoe'r he saies,
Do not regard it Madam: I do know
He laies a wile to catch you, every word
Hath some device, some Engine in't.
   Pyl. Think you
My Wisdom can be caught?
   Cal. No; but hee'l try [1425]
To overreach you, though I'm sure he cannot.
He is the notedst Leacher in all *Asia*.
   Phi. I wonder you can speak with him: he hath
Something at this time very deep in's bones.
   Cal. You are in danger, Madam, from his Breath; [1430]
I look each word of his should be your Ruine,
He hath no part about him that is sound;
A very walking Hospitall.
   Pyl. I thank you.
   Phi. What e'r he saies beleeve him not; he cannot
Settle his heart on any single Face. [1435]
He is the Common Stallion of the Country,
Is sent for far and neer to cure Green-sicknesses;
H' hath times appointed for't in Market Towns,
And such a day 'tis said, *The Captain heals*.
   Cal. I know he Complements as soothingly [1440]
As if he spoke Perfumes; ne'r credit him.
I've heard him swear he only loves your Wealth.
   Pyl. Good!
   Phi. He hath told me he could ne'r affect you;
Y'are of too deep a Wrinkle, as he saies,
To be call'd old; y'are broken, and not Aged. [1445]
   Pyl. Your Servant Sir.
   Cal. I've heard him Vow he would
Ne'r Marry you, but that there's certain hope
You will be Carkas ere the Morning.
   Pyl. Well!
   Phi. He is in doubt whether you are not old
Deucalion's Widdow, and is sure you have [1450]
Only two Rags of Flesh instead of Breasts.
   Cal. He vows you had
No Parents, as he thinks, but are the first
Of all your Genealogy; one that

Knows not what that word Ancestor doth mean. [1455]
  Phi. He saies y' were moulded out of the first Earth
For an Essay, not meant for good and all;
But slipt out unawares from your Contriver;
And that e'r since you wear that durty Face,
As a true Badge of your early Creation. [1460]
  Pyl. I'm bound t'y' truly.
  Cal. Then he saies you are
So noisome, and so nasty, that he dares not
Come neer you in a Morning, till the Sun
Hath been upon you for a while.
  Phi. He means,
If that he hath the luck to marry you, [1465]
To shew you up and down for some strange Monster.
  Cal. He is resolv'd t' allow you for his ease
Something i'th' shape of a great lusty Groom
To save himself a Labour.
  Phi. He gives out
Hee'l take a Bedstaff, or an holy Wand [1470]
And baste you lustily two or three hours
Before you go to Bed, to make you limber.
You are too stark (he saies) to make a Spouse.
  Cal. 'Twould be a Curse, he saies, unto our Kingdom
Worse than the Tyrant is, if that he took [1475]
You to his Bed ——
  Phi. Then when you dye he swears
Hee'l take your skin and make a Coat of Armour.
  Cal. —— There were no other hope, but that we should
Have a most Rampant Petticoat born up
In Wars for th' Colours, and the low'st Tongu'd Woman [1480]
Whisper before the Army for a Trumpet.
  Pyl. I thank you heartily for your discovery.—— To *Cal.*
I'm bound to you for your Relation.—— To *Phi.*
I'l think upon your Sute assure your self.—— To *Cal.*
I will consider your request hereafter—— To *Phil.* [1485]
Pray let me see you oftner.—— *To them both*
     (Here's a brace
Of most notorious Villains; let me dye
A private Woman, if I fit you not.)   *Ex. Pyle.*
  Cal. I know you've got the Widdows promise Captain.

Phi. No doubt she gave it you, you did so whisper. [1490]
Cal. Good faith I spoke for thee most heartily.
I told her all thy Parts.
Phi. Troth now and then
I intermingled thy good Qualities too.
All that I did was honest; as I live
I ask'd her not the Question all the while. [1495]
Cal. I'l lay thee a brace of hundreds then shee's mine.
Phi. Win her and wear her then,. catch he that can.
Exeunt.

Act. IV. Scen. II.

Pyle, and *Prusias*.

Pyl. You have no hopes then to be King?
Pru. My Title
Is but infirm to th' Crown, All the bloud Royall
That I have in me came by sucking of [1500]
His Majesties finger when he cut it once.
But for Nobility I've all the Signs of 't.
Pyl. You rate your looks, perhaps, have faces of
All prizes, pay your debts with Countenance:
Put off your Mercer with your Fee-buck for [1505]
That season, and so forth; and then you write
Your Name in Characters that must be sent
About to the Professors, to discover
What Language they belong to: All, I take it,
Most certain Symptoms that y' are sick of Greatness. [1510]
Pru. I count your Judgment, Lady, most Authentick.
Pyl. Next, you are poor and needy, having been
So long a Courtier; you do spend your Pension
In oyntment for your Beard; by which cost when
You are arriv'd at th' easie Chambermaid, [1515]
You task your sharp Invention, to find out
A passage to her Lady, with as much
Care and Anxiety, as another would
To find a way beyond th' Herculean Pillars.
Prus. Your Ladiship, though young, speaks like a Sibyll. [1520]

Pyl.   That you may see I cannot Prophesie,
I must demand a subtle question of you.
What was the time that you began to love in?
  Prus.   My Love's Eternall; it did ne'r begin:
Tis not a thing subject to Generation.   [1525]
  Pyl.   I do not like it then.
  Prus.   I know, and 't please you,
The very instant; *June* the thirty one,
The Sun in's *Apogæum*, Moon in *Libra*,
First Quartile, Minutes twenty three, two Seconds,
Late in the Afternoon.
  Pyl.   What? you'r a Scholar.   [1530]
  Prus.   My Scholarship is at your service, Lady.
I'l make fine Anagrams upon your Name,
Or on your Dogg's; I'l give you a True-Love's Knot
In endlesse Verse; ask Questions of my Lute
In a most melting Tone, and make that ask   [1535]
Questions of me again, and all in Honour
To your fair Self.
  Pyl.   I've vow'd against all Scholars,
They ne'r come near to Kings, but when they have
A sullen fit o' Philosophy come upon 'em.
  Prus.   I hate a Scholar, I protest, as I   [1540]
Do the sharp Visage of my craving Taylor
At Quarter-day: that which I spoke ev'n now,
I conn'd out of an Almanack; I'm only
A *Philomath*, sweet Lady.
  Pyl.   I am all
For deeds of Prowesse.
  Prus.   Now you come to me.   [1545]
  Pyl.   What Squadrons do you lead besides your Creditors?
What Troups, but eager and despairing Tradesmen?
How many Towns, pray y', are you wont to take
'Twixt first and second Course? What Castles do y'
Demolish, besides Pye-crusts? What great Breaches   [1550]
Do y' make, and sally in, whiles that you pick
Your Ebony Teeth? then when you have bely'd
Old Captive Matrons suing t'y', how many
Young tender Virgins do you there deflowre
In eating of the other slice of Marmalad?   [1555]

Prus.   Your Ladiship hath a good grace in Mirth;
Your Jests do wear as new a dresse, as any.
I had a Feather quite struck off my Helmet
I'th' Tilt-yard once. Sweetest of Ladyes, speak,
Hath any one abus'd you?
   Pyl.   Yes, the King: [1560]
Dare you assault him?
   Prus.   For a world I would not
Offer to violate his Sacred Body,
Who is intended for your Loyall Husband.
   Pyl.   There are a brace of Captains here i'th' City,
Your Fellow-Hostages; I've suffer'd wrong [1565]
From them too, they'r below the Throne I'm sure.
   Prus.   In Words, or Deeds?
   Pyl.   Only in Words, that's all?
   Prus.   Fare-you-well Lady, they shall hear of it.
I'l go and rayl at 'em most heartily.   [*Exit Prusias.*
   Pyl.   I do beleeve your heart is in your Mouth, [1570]
Both wayes. If that I misse not of mine Aym,
You, and the Bumbast Captains shall be try'd.   [*Ex. Pyle*

Act. IV. Scen. III.

Timophilus, Patacion, Cleodemus, Scedasus; They
are met by *Eudemus*.

   Tim.   Most opportunely met, *Eudemus*; you
I know desire the common good, and never
Had a particular Interest that did [1575]
Run cross to that.
   Eud.   What is your Lordships meaning?
   Cleo.   If you'l preserve the Liberty of your City,
There is a way now profer'd you: *Misander*
Desires your Daughter.
   Eud.   Very likely Sir,
He hath a mind to wound her once again. [1580]
'Tis as the Sea looks smooth upon the Shipwrack'd,
He doth entice but for a second Booty.

Tim. 'Tis in the way of Marriage, honestly:
That he may make amends for this his wrong.
   Eud. Joyn her to him? I'l joyn her first unto   [1585]
A lustfull Satyr; I am sure the knot
Will be more innocent.
   Cleo. You do mistake:
His Flames are now as chaste, as erewhile foul.
Hee's carefull of Succession.
   Eud. Heav'n avert
The Prodigy! A Tyrant, and love honesty?   [1590]
Doth the great Rank and Line of Nephews now
Present it self to his Ambition?
I'l give her to my Slave first.
   Sced. Do not thwart
The publike good with a particular spleen.
   Pat. Hear Reason, good *Eudemus*.
   Eud. Will you speak it?   [1595]
   Pat. It is not his Sute only, 'tis ours too;
Your City asks it; there's a greater good
Preparing for us than your Anger sees.
Do not provoke those Evils, that are now
About to settle.
   Eud. If he hath a mind to't,   [1600]
I'l condiscend on this Condition
Hee'l promise hee'l not kill her the next Morning.
   Tim. That should be buried now.
   Eud. Do what you will,
My Title's least unto her now shee's publike.
   Cleo. 'Twill be the more by losing of her thus.   [1605]
   Tim. Let's to *Misander*, hee'l receive this News
With as much joy, as if another Kingdom
Were added to his Scepter by a Conquest.   *Exeunt.*

ACT. IV. SCEN. IV.

Pyle, Elpidia.

   Pyl. Now see you carry this as I have taught you,
And when I come to th' Throne I wil procure you   [1610]

An Husband to your Mind; some Elder Brother
That wants some six or seven Grains of Wit,
Besides his ord'nary Allowance.
  Elp. Truly
I never blab'd as yet you know; if they
Should offer but to question me, I would   [1615]
Look sweetly on 'em, & forswear it strongly.   [*One knocks*
I think there's one of them, and 't please your Grace.

Act. IV. Scen. V.

To them *Eudemus*.   [Elp. *fals off*.

  Pyl. *Eudemus*! You are welcome; I forestall
Your business, you are come t' invite me to
Your Daughters Marriage.
  Eud. Call it not her Marriage,   [1620]
It is her Death, her Execution.
You'd make a fitter Queen by far than she.
  Pyl. Nature, 'tis true, intended us for Queen;
And 'tis her wrong, not ours, that wee're neglected.
  Eud. I'd willingly promote your Cause, if that   [1625]
I knew but how; he hath done you more wrong
By his Refusall, than he hath my Daughter
By's Cruelty. I wonder you'r so slack:
Do you not dream of your Revenge? doth not
Your sleep each Night prompt you to right your Self?   [1630]
And ev'n that prove watchfull?
  Pyl. Alas! I
Have no Accesse; my Hate knows not to Reach him.
I might betray my Self by trying it,
Shewing an idle fruitlesse spight, and make
A Noise, not knowing where my sting might enter.   [1635]
  Eud. Will you assist me with your Secresie
And help, fair *Pyle*?
  Pyl. Any thing, *Eudemus*,
Loving *Eudemus*, any thing.
  Eud. You shall
Procure a trifle only, I'l apply it;

Somthing to kill a Rat, or some such Vermin. [1640]
    Pyl. Now you do put m' in mind of such a thing,
I can most readily furnish you; you must
Be sure to give 't him e'r he go to th' Temple.
'Twill cast him in a sleep; as soon as ever
He doth begin to Nod (I'l be in readinesse) [1645]
You shall conduct me to him, that I may
See how it works, and if it been't enough,
I'l second it. Let not your Daughter be
About him for a World: Walk in with me,
And I'l instruct you further. Wait you there [1650]
Till I return *Elpidia*.   [*Ex. Eud. Pyl.*
    Elp. Lord, to see
How many Husband's one may have that's rich!
They do swarm hither with their Verses, like
Town-Poets on some Lord's Son's Wedding-day.
Their Visits do save Oyl, and make the door [1655]
Turn easie. She (God bless her) 's cloy'd with 'em.
I've wash'd my face in *Mercury* water, for
A year and upwards; lain in Oyl'd Gloves still;
Worn my Pomatum'd Masks all night; each morning
Rang'd every Hair in its due rank and Posture; [1660]
Laid red amongst the white; writ o'r my face,
And set it forth in a most fair Edition;
Worn a thin Tiffeny only o'r my Breasts;
Kept Musk-plums in my Mouth continually;
Yet have not had one bite at all these baits, [1665]
But a poor single-sol'd thin meager Footman,
One that I could see through. I think I shall
Be sav'd by my Virginity, whether
I will or no, and lead an Ape in Heav'n.
Here she comes now with one of her Fopperies. [1670]
    [Elpid. *retires.*

Act IV. Scen. VI.

Pyle, Philostratus.

    Pyl. No, no, I sent your Plot; it is my Wealth
You aim at, not my Person. You've a mind
To join your self to twenty thousand Crowns.

Phi. Would ——

Pyl. —— Now you'l wish I know, you ne'r might wear [1675]
Foul Linnen more, never be lowzy agen,
Nor ly Perdue with the fat Sutlers Wife,
In the provoking Vertue of dead horse,
Your dear delights, and rare Camp Pleasures.

Phi. Widdow,
Would I might ne'r shed drop of bloud more, if [1680]
My Love hath any of these Vulgar Aimes.

Pyl. Next, you conceive I am so old and dry,
That Wenches troubled with Green Sicknesses
May long for Morsels of me, as they do
For bits of Mortar-wals and Cinders, whom [1685]
(To keep my body whole) in pity you
Will cure some other way: then passe from them
Into the Suburbs to seek out more Patients,
And by most provident Sin husband my Monyes,
Which now you gape for, in that way of Trade, [1690]
Which, when all fails, y' are sure will leave you that
That will intitle y' to th' King's Letters Patents,
As being maim'd in th' service of your Country.

Phil. To swear I were a Maid at these years now,
Would make you think I meant to keep so still. [1695]
By those our two Virginities we have lost,
And these two more, which we are yet to lose,
I am so far enamour'd on you, that
I think your wrinckles Beauty, count your Cough
Good Musick, and if e'r you come unto [1700]
A Palsey, will maintain it is a Motion
More pleasing to me than a Dance. More yet,
Shou'd you but spit a Tooth, I'd kisse you for't,
Untill you did spit more.

Pyl. I understand you ——
I am as God hath made me.

Phil. Half the City [1705]
Cann't say so much fair Lady: Do you think
It is your Wealth I aime at? Pray y' when heard you
Of any Souldier that would come so nigh
To commit with Gold, or fornicate with Silver,
As to intrust all Night a piece of either [1710]

In his incontinent Pockets? Not love you?
Command me any danger, if it be
Within the reach of Man, I'l compasse it.
   Pyl. Were it not that I should be said to task
Impossibilities, I'd bid you love me. [1715]
But being you ask a tryall of your heart,
Do what's contain'd but in this Paper only,   { *He takes the Pa-*
And as I live next Morn I'l marry you.   *per and reads.*
   Phi. No more? I'd thought you would have bid me pull
The *Parthian* King by th' Beard, or draw an Eye-tooth [1720]
From the Jaw Royall of the *Persian* Monarch.
You've thrown away your self too cheaply: were't
The killing of my Father, 'twere a Toy,
A silly trifle ——

ACT. IV. SCEN. VII.

To them *Prusias*.

——Save you valiant *Prusias*.
God give you joy Sir of your handsome Widdow; [1725]
Poor Soldiers can get nothing; your three legs
And five Similitudes have done the Deed.
I'l leave you to your Beauty.   *Exit Phil.*
   Pyl. How now Servant,
I see y' are Constant.
   Pru. 'Tis your Vertue makes me.
   Pyl. Do not you call my Gold my Vertue Sir? [1730]
Are not my Bags good Manners? and my Jewels
Cleanly Behaviour? You have laid your Trap,
Only to catch a Booty that may find you
Powders and Curling Irons.
   Pru. I shall have
No need of those, for you shall be my Head —— [1735]
   Pyl. ——'And your Brain too ——
   Pru. And understand for me.
   Pyl. Whiles out of Ignorance perhaps you'l keep
Some needy Poet in a politike Pension
Not to write Satyrs on you, and so rent

His wit, and Liberty of him, that you may [1740]
Vent Verses, and sin safely.
   Pru. I will turn
Poet my self, it is in fashion, Lady:
Hee's scarce a Courtier now, that hath not writ
His brace of Plaies. It is a Quality
That works more now upon the City Dames, [1745]
Than throwing of the Sledg, or Jumping well.
   Pyl. But Poets never yet prov'd vertuous Husbands.
   Pru. To please you then, I will speak only grave
Sad Morall Sentences; cough sager Proverbs;
And live your Yoakfellow in City Prose. [1750]
You shall not shake me off, although you beat me;
Nay, that shall make me love you more. I am
Your Spaniel, Lady.
   Pyl. 'Twere a good experiment
To try whe'r y' are true bred or no. *Elpidia*!
Bring me the holly Wand, with which I last [1755]
                            [*Elpid. brings the Wand.*
Did exercise. Come Sir, about: I'l try you.
What? shrink for this? you have no Metall Man;
'Twill be my dayly Practice, if you have me,
To keep my self in Breath: I'm us'd to do it,
I should grow Pursie else.
   Pru. No more o' your Wand! [1760]
You see my Patience Cudgell-proof; pray y' try
My sufferance, Lady, in another kind.
You shall find *Prusias* hardy.
   Pyl. Think you so?
Say that I have some Project in my head,
Some grand exployt, durst you perform your Part? [1765]
   Pru. Pray y' try me Madam.
   Pyl. By my hopes o'th' Throne,
If you perform what's in this little Schedule,
Wee're Man and Wife to Morrow.
   Pru. Were it to
Encounter with a Fury, I would do it.   *Exit Prus.*

Act. IV. Scen. VIII.

Callimachus to her.

Pyl.   O! I may languish here for ought you know.   [1770]
You are a proper Servant: I do fear
You but pretend Me onely, meane my Wealth.
I'm neer my Death, you think, something may fall,
And 'tis not good to be much out o'th' way.
You visit, and not wooe.
   Call.   I know this is   [1775]
That sneaking, fawning *Prusias* tells you so.
I'm truer than his haire, or teeth, or nose.
My meaning's honester than his, although
My words don't smell so well.
   Pyl.   You true? to what?
To your variety? your shift of Mistresses,   [1780]
When you have none of Shirts? I hope you will
Confesse y' have conquer'd Beauties, more than Towns.
   Call.   *Prusias* again upon my life. I doe
Confesse, that like the wandring foot o'th' Compasse,
I have been somewhat Mortall in that sort,   [1785]
But like the constant one hereafter will
Keep to the Center, onely move at home.
My Rings shall all b' engrav'd with holy Posies,
As, *Constant untill Death* —— *Endlesse as this* ——
So is my love —— *Not Hands but Hearts* —— all which   [1790]
I'll practice in my life and conversation.
Nay this wild Centaure on my sword here, shall
Be turn'd into a Turtle, and th' Inscription
(*Conquest and Maidenheads*) shall be blotted out
To give way to that tame word, *Chastity*.   [1795]
   Pyl.   For all my jesting I not doubted you:
I know you are as ready to performe,
As I am to command.
   Cal.   Would you could see
The Heart of your *Callimachus*: you'd wonder
To view your self full seated in the midst,   [1800]
And domineering over all my Bowels.

Performe what you command? I'l fight against
Heaven it self, and yet no Gyant neither,
No live *Collossus* as I take it.
   Pyl. Here
Within this Scrowl's prescrib'd what I would have you   [1805]
Do for my sake; a way will prove your faith.
And when 'tis prov'd call *Pyle* yours.
   Cal. —— Remember ——

Act IV. Scen. IX.

To them *Nicias*.

   —— Faith if thou hast a mind, good Painter, to
Our Chambermaid *Elpidia*, 'cause I see thee
Hanker so oft about our house here, tell me;   [1810]
I'l do thee all the good I can.
   Nic. I thank you.
   Cal. Prethee sweet Wife, abuse this busie fellow,
Put some fine trick upon him, that we may
Laugh at our Wedding: 'tis a sneaking Cockscomb.
   Pyl. *Nicias*, because I cannot see these Nuptials;   {*Exit* [1815]
Being so disdainfully refus'd, I prethee   *Cal.*
Take all the shew this night in *Juno's* Temple,
That I may see it at the second hand.
   Nic. I'l do it with that life, that you shall swear
You see the thing it self, excepting this,   [1820]
That you hear nothing spoken.
   Pyl. Thou'lt be secret:
I would not have it known.
   Nic. I'l stand behind
Some Pillar, or some Image, none shall see me.
   Pyl. This night's *Misander*'s Hymen, the next ——
   Nic. — Ours.   *Exit Nicias.*
   Pyl. So! I applaud my Wit for this my project: [1825]
Were not my Beauty such, that yet would be
Enough to recommend me to the Throne,
To be sure then I have two Stratagems,

If that *Misander* should not drink the Potion
I gave *Eudemus*, ere he go to th' Temple, [1830]
This yet may dash the Marriage; and *Leucasia*
That bold Usurpress of my Bed shall miss
Of being saluted Queen to night howe'r.
And it will be one comfort to my Fate,
If none b'advanc'd whom I may emulate. *Exit.* [1835]

Act. IV. Scen. X.

Leucasia with the Potion in a Glass.

Leu. I'm hurri'd still, and yet I know not whither,
But I am hurri'd —— O distracted thoughts!
Eudemus urgeth Poyson, but I love.
Is this a Fathers gift? and to be drank,
Before we go t' our Nuptials, that those Souls [1840]
Which should be join'd, may be divorc'd for ever?
'Twas meant for good *Misander*, but I'l drink it.
I have a thirst that's Loyall. My death will
Make no more alteration, than the adding
Of one neglected Marble to the Number [1845]
Of unregarded Sepulchers. His Fate
May draw the Veines of all the Kingdom dry,
And I commit a slaughter in one Person.
Drink then *Leucasia*; let it not be said
In after Histories that any ruine [1850]
Of a Republick ow'd it self to thee. *She drinks.*
So! now I am in health, and out of danger.
No Father now can urge. Ye Pow'rs who look
Upon th' Affections of those Hearts you wound,
How e're I fall, be you *Misanders* stay: [1855]
Wounded by him I cur'd his lawlesse Passions,
And by a better way did slay the Tyrant.
Some Virgin, who shall be so blest, as to
Enjoy his virtues, will perhaps for this
Sprinkle a flower or two upon my grave, [1860]
And wish me Rest. No tongue can blast my Name

With just Reproach, when after times shall know,
  That I, who when his Love was drossie, wou'd
  Have wrought his death, dy'd for him when 'twas
    good.   *Exit.*

ACT. V. SCEN. I.

Eudemus.

Eud.   With what Contrivance, and Deliberation   [1865]
Am I become a Paricide? whiles that
I seek to quit her from a Tyrant, I
Am proved one my self, one worse than he;
In that I'm Cruell out of Tendernesse.
Is this to save thine Honour my *Leucasia*,   [1870]
To take away thy Life? I would I had
Yeelded thee up without all tumult, then
Th' hadst liv'd at least. Now I desire thy Guilt.
Curs'd be that Fury that I dealt with ——

Act. V. Scen. II.

To him *Pyle.*

Pyl.   Come,
Make haste; conduct m', *Eudemus*; sleeps *Misander*?   [1875]
Hath he drunk deep and largely?
  Eud.   Hatefull Woman!
If thou hast any poison here about thee
Beside thy malice, doe one deed of Charity,
Infuse it into me: Shew here the vigor
Of that thy damned Art. Vile Sorceresse!   [1880]
Look me to death: for every glance of thine
Should carry Fate with it. Thou'rt slack, when that
Thou shouldst bestow it where it is deserv'd.
'Twas ready to destroy an innocent Virgin.
  Pyl.   What? hath *Leucasia* dranke it then?
  Eud.   I'm sorry   [1885]

Thou liv'st to aske the question, that thou dost not
Augment the number of the Furies, comming
A Plague ev'n unto them.
 Pyl. Be not so passionate,
My good *Eudemus*; take my Counsell with you,
If that your Daughter hath drank it her self,   [1890]
Remove all Company from her whatsoever.
Let not *Misander* see her for a world.
I will secure her life: it will not work
To death, these two days yet: I've that will cure her.
 Eud. Sweet *Pyle* pardon what my rage hath scatter'd: [1895]
I have not leisure now t' excuse my Fury.
For Heavens sake along with me unto her. *Exeunt.*

ACT. V. SCEN. III.

Leucasia discover'd sleeping, Misander, Cleodemus,
Timophilus, Patacion, Scedasus, Epigenes,
Terpander, Euthalpe.

 Mis. Is it still death if I begin to love?
 Euth. And can I live if she begin to dye?
To tear mine hair is Womanish; to forerun   [1900]
And lead the way t' *Elyzium* but a duty
She would not thank me for: if that some God,
Envious of honest fires, hath destin'd ruine
Unto this fairer Altar where they burn,
I'l see it be demolish'd decently,   [1905]
And then my self fall the last Sacrifice.
 Mis. Call for some Musick one of you; perhaps
That may infuse a Peace into her Senses:
Her Soul, I'm sure, 's awake. I would this kiss
Could suck out all the Poyson that torments thee. [1910]
 Euth. Hold! have you so forgot her sacred Dictates?
There is more Reverence due unto her Fate.
Had you gone so far now as to embrace,
Love would have told her in the other world,
And so your Spirits had been divorc'd for ever. [1915]
 Mis. Pardon, *Euthalpe*; Grief transported me.

Why do not Plants desert their Native soyl?
And powerfull Herbs put on new Motion, coming
Unforc'd unto her help? Nature, thou shouldst
Be factious to restore her: I accuse thee; [1920]
Where are thy Vertues? where thy remedies now?
   Terp. 'Twere good to knock an Horseshoe on the Threshold;
'T may be that Mother *Pyle* hath bewitch'd her:
Truly she looks as if she were bewhatled.
   Mis. Knew I but any that did mean her ill, [1925]
They should be sent to exercise their spight
'Mongst Ghosts and shadows. I'm resolv'd to watch her
Though this dull drowzie Pow'r should keep her in
His lazy chains, as long as heretofore   *Ent. Boy.*
He kept *Endymion*. Sleep's become my Rivall: [1930]
He loves her too. Softly, O softly, Boy!

                Song.

Boy.   *See how the Emulous Gods do watch*
      Which of them first her Breath shall catch,
      Ambitious to resign their Bliss,
      Might they but feed on Aire like this. [1935]
      Thus here protected she doth lie
      Hedg'd with a Ring of Majesty.
      And doth make Heaven all her own;
      Never more safe, than when alone.
      Thus whiles she sleeps Gods do descend, and kiss: [1940]
      They lend all other Breath, but borrow this.

Act. V. Scen. IV.

To them *Pyle, Eudemus.*

   Pyl. Make room for heaven's sake; pray y' quit the
                Place.
What, will you stifle her with this Multitude?
   Mis. Thunder it self shall not remove me hence.
[*Leucasia awakens and casts her Eye on* Misander.]
   Leuc. O! who disturbs the quiet of my Soul? [1945]
I'd been by this time at *Elysium*

Had none molested me. But I am glad
I am call'd back, being that I here enjoy
A pleasure far beyond all those below,
In only viewing you.
   Mis. Canst thou behold   [1950]
Him that did wound thee, and approve the sight?
   Leuc. It is a favour to me that you would
Take so much notice of me. I am not
Worthy of any thing that comes from you.
'T had been too great a Blessing to me, if   [1955]
Y' had only lov'd me without seasoning
That Happinesse with some Castigation
For my intruding boldnesse. I am blest,
In that I was once in those sacred Thoughts,
Which make all worthy that they think upon.   [1960]
   Mis. By what good Pow'r art thou so sudden chang'd?
Blest be the hand that laid thee in this sleep.
   Terp. I beleeve now, and't please your Majesty,
This Widdow ne'r had ought to do with her.
   Pyl. The Art was mine: her Father here came to me,   [1965]
And urging me to take Revenge upon you,
Intreated me to help him to a Poyson,
Which this *Leucasia* here was to have giv'n you.
I, carefull of your safety, gave him somthing
Which I call'd Poyson: but 'twas only an Essence   [1970]
Whose Virtue was to cast him that should take it
Into a sleep, and make him fall in Love
With the first Object that should offer it self
Unto him, as he wak'd; thinking indeed,
Because I lov'd you, to present my self.   [1975]
But envious Fates have cross'd my fair Intents,
And turn'd my means unto another's Ends,
Leucasia drinking it her self: which yet
Out of your Princely Grace you may correct.
   Eud. Th' hast done thou know'st not what: it is prov'd Poyson,
In that she dotes on him.
   Mis. O would some God   [1981]
Would make thee sleep too, to the same effect.
Is it too great a blessing to my Scepter
To have the love of good *Eudemus* too?

Eud.   Of good *Eudemus*? how can I deserve   [1985]
This Imputation? for I count all praise
From thee Aspersion.
  Leuc.   My most honour'd Father,
Think not so ill of blest *Misander*: for
I see him like a vigorous spark among
Things tumbling in the Common night o'th' world;   [1990]
Sent to make that we call a Pilgrimage
Deserve the name of life: without him, 'twere
Onely to stand without doors, till it pleas'd
The Gods to call us in.
  Mis.   Fairest of things,
And only like thy self, those pleasures, which   [1995]
The laden bosom of this lower world
Permits to carefull Mortalls, are too grosse,
Too earthy to be ours: Let's mount the wings
Of our desires, and take a flight into
Nature's sincerer Kingdome, where she mints   [2000]
And shapes refin'd delights, delights like thee.
  Leuc.   Wee'll to those places set a part for Love,
Where Trees kiss Trees, and Branch embraceth Branch;
Poplar to Poplar whispers there, and Myrtle
Doth sigh to Myrtle; Flow'rs erect themselves,   [2005]
And Boughs encline to meet 'em in salutes
With an unquestion'd freedome; no stalk being
Made yellow there by jealousie, no Tree
With'ring through sad suspition, that this Flower
Doth court that Bough, or that Bough serve this Flower.   [2010]
  Mis.   O! these are joys fresh from the Dugs of Nature.
There some Plants shew th' have fire, ev'n in their Colors:
Some Dialogues make; and some more passionate grieve;
Sweet Odors are their sighes; and Dew their teares.
Some Leaves, they say, have words of woe inscrib'd,   [2015]
As if that Flowers writ mutuall Letters too.
Our ancient Love-Priests say, that in that Garden
A Rose and Lilly (to whose sacred leaves
The neighboring Flowers do reverence) mingle Roots
In a most streight embrace, and thence produce   [2020]
Male Roses blanch'd with th' whiteness of the Lilly,
And Female Lillies dipt i'th' blush o'th' Rose;

Each borrowing others Beauty so, that 'tis
Thought Natures Prophecie of some future times,
Which shall fulfill it, and be happy.
   Leuc. As [2025]
'T hath types of things to come, so too 'tis said
That Ancient Stories are cut there in Trees;
And the mysterious Hedges are the Annals
Of former Ages: Thus each thing containing
Something that may be read, doth make the whole [2030]
But one fair Volume to instruct blest Souls.
   Mis. Among those pleasures we shall walk, and see
Here some Girl twisting of her Lovers locks,
Weaving, what caught her heart, into a Net;
There others making Dialogues with sighs [2035]
In a sad Parly; these from richer Banks, here
Culling out Flow'rs, which in a learned order
Do become Characters, whence they disclose
Their mutuall meaning, Garlands there and Nosegaies
Being fram'd into Epistles; yonder he [2040]
Watching his sleeping Lady, doth protect her
From Rivall Lyzards, and such loving Creatures,
And with a Bough of Myrtle guards her slumbers,
Lest the Bee should mistake her Beauteous Cheeks:
Others perhaps in a dissembled anger [2045]
Pursue their Coyer Loves, who at each turn
Fling Violets in their Faces, thus maintaining
Soft Love-fights, like the *Parthian*, who yet flie,
Not to escape, but to be caught.
   Leuc. And we
When we come there, what chaster pleasures shall we [2050]
Indulge to our Affections?
   Mis. Thou shalt sit
Queen of that Kingdom in a Chair of Light,
And Doves with ointed wings shall hover o'r thee,
Shedding Perfumes, as if blest Nature reign'd
Delights, and powr'd 'em on our tender Loves [2055]
To make 'em flourish: fresh, and well tun'd winds
Shall bring thee Viands in, and at each change
Of Service, alter their respectfull Musick.
Fountains shall walk upon thy Table, and

Birds singing to the fall of their soft waters [2060]
Shall by the Marriage of their mingled sounds
Create an Harmony shall make Syrens sleep.
Thence rising thou shalt walk, and view young Nymphs
In Currents gravell'd with transparent Amber,
Breaking their shapes at every step: thy self [2065]
Outshining both the Currents, and them too.
Then shalt thou sail in one entire rich Shell
Through Labyrinths of waters, whose perplex'd
And interwoven Banks shall be environ'd
With shady Trees charg'd with delightfull fruits, [2070]
Nature there making one continued Season.
  Leu. O! I am ravish'd with delight, and could
Live on the very thought: but all those joyes
Must, like a Morning Cloud pass into nought;
My incensed Father not permitting me [2075]
To enjoy you, who are your self all these.
  Mis. Consider, good *Eudemus*, do not nip
These buddings of our Souls: thou art that wall
That stands between our Hearts, let them but meet,
But meet, *Eudemus*, and the wheel of things [2080]
Shall turn another way; all that you shall
Complain of shall be only too much Joy.
All things shall flow according to your mind,
And yet before your wishes: when I do not
Prevent the earlinesse of your Desires [2085]
(Not staying so long as to meet 'm) say
They come too late, *Misander* is grown tardy.
  Eud. I will not dash these hopes. Be she then yours:
And be she fruitfull in her Vertues first,
Then in her Issue; that she may bring forth [2090]
Heirs to your Mind, as well as to your Throne.
  Mis. Thy Prayers must be heard; she is the only
Cause, that all Worth goes not upwards; Earth
Whiles it containeth her, hath somthing, which
The Heav'ns themselves adore. Let's to the Temple, [2095]
Which will be more a Temple, she being there:
                        [*Exeunt as to the Temple.*
  Pyl. I'm slighted then? I would 't had been true poison.
                                [*Exit Pyle.*

Act V. Scen. V.

Philostratus *in a Winding-sheet to perform the Injunction of the Widdow.*

Phil. I have not seen the inside of a Temple
These twelve Months til this time, & now I come
Commanded too: Hell's in this damned Widdow. [2100]
What doth she mean to make me lye in a Coffin?
I am not fit for Death, although I think
I'm very forward towards it: Somthing in
My Bones doth tell me so. But let that passe.
If Death should go to claim me now, I were [2105]
In a sweet case, he had eleven Points
O'th' Law, on's side, Possession. It would mad me
To lye Perdue i'th' Grave for a Womans pleasure.
Well, 't must be done: here lye *Philostratus*:
Enter a Coffin, to obtain a Carkasse. [2110]
[*He shuts himself in the Coffin.*]

Act. V. Scen. VI.

Prusias *drest like an Angell with a Caduceus in one hand, and a Taper in the other.*

Prus. Thou art an Angell, *Prusias*, therfore fit
To be receiv'd into her heav'nly Bosome.
She shapes thee in an Habit, that she'l wed thee.
Truly, I think all Courtiers would be Angels,
If that they were not giv'n so much to th' flesh, [2115]
That keeps 'em all from Heav'n'. But why should I
Be set to guard a Coffin? If there doe
Any ill Spirits use to haunt this Temple,
The Coffin must defend it self for *Prusias*.
This Rod yet, and this Candle have some Vertue [2120]
To fright away those Children of the Night.
Securely then I'l sit. What need I fear? {*He sets himself down on the Coffin.*}
Death is already under me. Heav'n blesse me!

I do begin to sweat; this Coffin rumbleth.
The Body's somthing noysome: 'tis a stale one; [2125]
Good troth it spurgeth very monstrously.

Act V. Scen VII.

*Nicias slinks in, and placeth himself as behind a Pillar to
take the sight;* Callimachus *after him
dress'd as a Fury.*

   Call. Well! a Male Fiend is fit for a She Fury;
Like must to like; so I unto this Widdow.
If any of my Coat should come and take
Acquaintance of me for a reall Fiend, [2130]
And find me tripping, I've no other way
But just to swear him down I am a true one
That have —— (let's see) —— lain Leiger in the Indies,
And so perhaps am grown out of his knowledge.
I wonder who 'tis that shee'l have me carry [2135]
Away i'th' Coffin; Sure some nasty Raskall.
   Nic. Lord! how my hand doth shake. I set down one thing,
Then blot it out again I know not how.
Pray *Jove* he doth not sent me! If he hath
But any Nose, he hath th' Advantage of me. [2140]
   Pru. Heav'n bless me! Yonder's one I'm sure's no Angel.
O my prophetick words! that I should promise
T' encounter with a Fury!
   Cal. Hold! yond's something
That is not one of us: I would I were
A very Fury now indeed, and had [2145]
All qualities belonging to my shape.
The first thing that I'd do, should be to make
My self invisible. Widdow, you must pardon me;
Sure I shall fall into a Thousand peeces
If that this shaking leave me not the sooner. [2150]
I vow I'm not afraid for all my fooling ——
I —— I —— must on ——
   Pru. Good heaven! hee's coming towards me:

How blew my Candle burns! I see his feet,
Th' are cloven ones for certain.
 Cal. Y —— y —— yet I dare not ——   [2155]
'Tis safest to retire, my joints are loose all,
And yet I can scarce move 'em.
 Nic. He hath found me,
He is upon the Train: how his Nose shakes
As he snuffs up the Ayre!
 Cal. My Teeth do ch —— ch —— ch —— chatter
As Schoolboys in cold weather.
 Pru. Heav'n defend me!   [2160]
How he doth gnash his Teeth, and make hell here!
I would I were i'th' Coffin at a Venture.
 Nic. All my left side's grown stupid. I'm half stone;
I feel a numness steal o'r all my limbs:
I shall augment the number of the Statues.   [2165]
It will be *Niobe Nicias* presently.
 Cal. Being it is an Angel, 'twill not hurt me.
I will make towards it however.
 Pru. Now,
Now he comes open-mouth'd; Lord, what a smoak
He belcheth like a Furnace! look! he claps   [2170]
His tail between his Legs, as dogs are wont
When they will do shrewd turns; 'tis a sly Spirit;
They'l never leave their cunning.
 Cal. Hee'l not suffer me
To talk long with him, hee's so us'd t' *Ambrosia*,
And to's Perfumes, which hee'l not find here sure.   [2175]
 Pru. O! —— *Cal.* O! ——
 Pru. You —— *Cal.* You ——
 Pru. Your Honour —— *Cal.* Blessed Spirit ——
 Pru. Yes —— *Cal.* I——must have——that——Body——there.
 Pru. You can ——
Lay no claime —— unto him —— he is not —— yours ——
 Cal. He is our due.
 Pru. How can you prove't?
 Cal. Dare you
Dispute with him that first invented Logick?   [2180]
 Pru. No, no, I am no Scholar, I'm a Captain.
 Cal. You must not guard the dead then, he must down.

Phi. *I am not he you come for, you're mistaken.

> *Philostratus *rising out of the Coffin, casts off* Prusias, *and frights 'em all; they disperse themselves to severall Places; he running out is met by* Misander *and the rest, who come to celebrate the Marriage there.*

Cal. Hoh!

Act. V. Scen. VIII.

Misander, Leucasia, Chryse, Euthalpe, Priest, Eudemus, Timophilus, Cleodemus, Patacion, Epigenes, Scedasus, Terpander.

Mis. Must there be something still to cross our joys?
What is the matter here? [2185]
  Phi. A Fury, a Fury!
Yonder he slinks.
  Cal. And 't please your Majesty
I am no Fury, I'm a Captain, one
They call *Callimachus* by daylight Sir;
The Angel Sir, the Angel!
  Pru. I'm the Angell,
Your Majesties Court-Captain you made last. [2190]
  Mis. Speak, what device is this?
  Terp. An Antick only
Prepar'd to grace your Marriage night, that hath
Mistook the place of entrance.
  Mis. Are you dumb?
  Terp. Angels may speak.
  Phi. The Widdow Sir I think ——
  Terp. Captain you should not speak, you are a Ghost. [2195]
  Phi. That damned Widdow hath abus'd us all.
  Terp. If she be damn'd, then she is yours grim Spirit.
  Phi. They call her *Pyle*; I confess I made
A little Love t' her, and profess'd I would
Do any thing that shee'd command me where- [2200]
Upon she set me to turn Ghost, and lye
All night i'th' Coffin there. I think that hee's
Her Angel too ——
  Terp. (Hee's her Angel.)

Phil. —— And he her Fury.
Pru. She transform'd me truly.
Cal. The trick was wholly hers.
Terp. She is in sight, [2205]
And looks on yonder.
Eud. Go, and fetch her hither.
Mis. Who's that behind the Pillar?
Nic. *Nicias* Sir;
He that did draw the Virgins. *Pyle* charg'd me,
As I did hope to marry her, that I should
Take all I saw this night here, and present her [2210]
With it betimes i'th' Morning.
Eud. Are you all
Sutors unto her then?
Cal. We do pretend
I'th' way of love; shee's wealthy.
Phi. But she hath sworn
To marry me.
Pru. Me.
Cal. Me Sir; you're deceiv'd.
Mis. How's that? to marry y' all?
Terp. Gramercy Widdow! [2215]
Seeing thou canst not have the King himself,
Thou wilt have all his Subjects.

[Enter *Pyle* and *Elpidia*.]

Mis. With what state
And pomp she stalks it?
Terp. This is she I told
Your Majesty I thought o'rlook'd *Leucasia*.
If you will let one of your Captains search her, [2220]
Hee'l find a Teat about her.
Eud. 'Cause you have
Abus'd these People in this sort, that did
Out of Affection visit you, we charge you
To take your choice out of 'em: if they will
Agree, 't shall be your punishment.
Cal. Phil. We do. [2225]
Nic. Pru. With all our Hearts.
Pyl. Well then, come forth, stand fair,
Let's see your faces all. First, *Nicias*, you

Being a Painter can create a Wife
With a few Colours whensoe'r you please.
I've sworn against all daubers.

   Elp. Please y' once [2230]
He bid me put y' in mind of's promising Nose,
And his long Foot.

   Pyl. But for your former service,
And being a Town-born Child, I care not if
I join you to my Chambermaid.

   Pru. Mark her Eye,
Mark but her Eye *Philostratus*, just on me. [2235]
I'm sure I am the Man.

   Pyl. For you, good Captain,
You are a Ghost, your winding sheet forbids
The tumbling in the Marriage one: 'tis said,
Let's live and love; the dead can claim no share.

   Pru. I told you so; mark but her Eye *Callimachus*. [2240]
Just upon me still.

   Pyl. Worthy Captain, I
Honour your Vertues and your Courage; but
Heav'n bless me from a Fiend; give me a Man,
A Man at least, nothing with cloven feet,
No *Incubus*; when I'm a Fury, claim me. [2245]

   Terp. Be rul'd by me, and take her at her word.

   Pru. Come my most constant Heart: (your Majesty
And I do sympathize most strangely in
Our Fortunes, that we should both of's be married
Just at one very instant.) Speak the word. [2250]

   Pyl. I do admire the Excellence of Angels;
They are to be ador'd.

   Pru. Thy love will serve.

   Pyl. 'Twere an unequall mixture for vile Earth
To join with Heav'n. Besides, I have heard say
That Angels have no Sex, I'l none of him. [2255]
Marriage respecteth Procreation.

   Pru. And 't please your Majesty she is a Traytor;
She would have had me kill you.

   Mis. We then confine you
To *Vesta*'s Temple, there to wait upon
The Virgins, and ne'r joyn in Wedlock more. [2260]

Pyl.   Although that Continence enjoyn'd, be only
A Death without the Pomp of shedding bloud;
Or at the best an holy Persecution;
Yet I would willingly embrace the doom,
But that I've vow'd my faith to *Nicias*.   [2265]
You won't adjudge me to a sin that may
Draw heav'ns revenge on you, as well as me?
   Nic.   (Pox o' your Craftiness) I humbly beg
That you'd remit her faults, and give her me
As a reward of my late Services.   [2270]
   Eud.   Thou ask'st a Torment, not a Gift; thou hast her.
Come, joyn those hands, *Sebaster*, that Religion
May perfect what Affection hath begun.

The Priest sings.

Be thou Hymen *present here,*
And ye O Marriage Gods, whoe'r: [2275]
Whiles I joyn these parts, joyn you such,
As know to meet without a touch.

   Euth.   We may not let this happy union pass
Without solemnity; 'tis no dishonour
To your great Valours, if you let a Siedge   [2280]
End in a Dance.
   Mis.   Although the only thing
I would deny you, be the honouring of me,
Yet for my good *Leucasia*'s sake, to whom
What e'r sounds joy and mirth is due, I will
Sit a Spectator, and think what is done   [2285]
A Sacrifice of thanks to Heav'n for her.

{ *They being all set, a Curtain being drawn discovers five valiant Generals standing in severall Postures, with fix'd Eyes like Statues.* }

   Mis.   Whose shapes are those?
   Euth.   They are the Statues Sir
Of five Commanders, the stout *Hercules,*
And he that trod his footsteps, the sage *Theseus,*
The next there *Pyrrhus*, and *Atrides* that,   [2290]
The outmost great *Achilles*.

{ *They continuing all this while in the Posture they first appear'd in, the Priest thus sings.* }

Priest. *Awake out of this senseless trance,*
And grace these Nuptials with a Dance.
Grow pliant O ye Marbles, Love
Is able to make Statues move. [2295]

> *The Priest having ended this Song, the Statues by the stealth of a slow Motion, do by little and little as it were assume life; and descending from their Pedestals walk about the Stage in a grave sad March to Trumpets, with their severall weapons in their hands, the Curtain in the mean time shutting: But making at last toward their former station, the Curtain flies aside, and they find five Ladies on their Pedestalls, in the Posture of Amorous Statues; at whose feet they having laid their weapons, conduct them down, and fall into a sprightly dance to Violins, and so depart.*

Euth. This only is the outward part o'th' feast:
The joyfull'st Dance is that you do not see.
Each Heart doth move as did those Bodies; were you
Spectator there a while, you would perceive
A full solemnity outshining this. [2300]

Mis. This was of your Contrivance, fair *Euthalpe*.
Y' have giv'n your Sex their due: Woman was born
To rule, and therefore each might justly change
Her Warriour int' a Lover, nay, each one
Change the whole five; for as they ought to rule, [2305]
So ought they to admit of many Servants,
As Kings do Subjects to encrease their Soveraignty.

Euth. You shew a soul most capable of Rule,
In that you thus will part with't to the weaker.

Mis. Nature compels me: 'tis the good man's Office [2310]
To serve and reverence Woman, as it is
The fire's to burn: for as our Souls consist
Of Sense and Reason, so do yours, more noble,
Of Sense and Love; which doth as easily calm
All your desires, as Reason quiets ours. [2315]

Euth. Some say we are Irrationall, and place us
'Mong Beasts, but you now carry us up too high.

Mis. Pardon the Vulgar, for they understand not,
Thinking that, where there is not Reason, there
The Composition's meerly Sensuall, [2320]
When that the difference is grand between
Being Irrationall, and working without Reason,

The former making Brute Beasts, but the latter
Agreeing to refin'd Intelligences;
'Mong which great Love is one, perhaps the Chief.' [2325]
Love then doth work in you, what Reason doth
Perform in us; here only lies the difference,
Ours wait the lingring steps of Age, and years,
But th' Woman's Soul is ripe when it is young;
So that in us what we call learning, is [2330]
Divinity in you, whose operations,
Impatient of delay, do outstrip time.
 Euth. You make us Sir veyl'd Goddesses, not Mortals.
 Mis. True! saw you not the Worthies there, though wise
And try'd, and Valiant; yet one clouded with [2335]
An Aged Beard, another wrincled, All
Subject to change and variation, when
Their Ladies, all of one bright constant clearnesse,
Smooth to the last Breath, stood immutable as
Some heav'nly thing, which Grace you carry up [2340]
Unto that place from whence you do descend
To make Men happy. But, no more, lest I
Be thought to flatter by the undiscerning.
Who was that Lady, *Euthalpe*, that subjected
The Great *Achilles* so?
 Euth. It was *Briseis*, [2345]
One of mine own Condition, an Attendant.
 Mis. Thou dost renew her honour'd Memory
More in thy merits far, than that Presentment.
 Leu. Sir, she hath been my Cabinet, my Tablet
In which I've writ my weightiest secrets; still [2350]
As faithful, and as silent too, as that:
And (if you prize such an unworthy purchase)
One, whom you owe *Leucasia* to.
 Mis. Fair Virgin,
If that my Kingdom hath a Soul that is
Worthy to meet with thine, I'l search him out, [2355]
And beg thee to accept him.
 Euth. 'Tis reward
Enough for me to see you happy thus,
There being no content in which I can
More rest, than viewing your joyn'd Excellencies.

Mis. Now we are one, my fair *Leucasia*; [2360]
Made dearer to each other by our dangers;
This Marriage sha'n't be single, I will joyn
Another Consort to thee. This knot shall
Strengthen both Equity, and Love, combine
My Throne, and Heart; and so one Tye shall be [2365]
My Marriage to *Byzantium*, and to Thee.

FINIS.

POEMS

Written by
Mr WILLIAM CARTVVRIGHT,
Late Student of *Chrift-Church* in
OXFORD, and Proctor of
the *Univerfity*.

The AYRES and SONGS fet by
Mr HENRY LAVVS, Servant to His
late MAJESTY in his Publick
and Private Mufick.

LONDON,
Printed for *Humphrey Mofeley*, and
are to be fold at his fhop at the Sign of
the Princes Armes in St *PAVLS*
Churchyard. 1651.

POEMS.

A Panegyrick to the most Noble
LUCY *Countesse of* Carlisle.

Madam,
       since Jewels by your self are worn,
Which can but darken, what they should adorn;
And that aspiring Incense still presumes
To cloud those Heavens towards which it fumes;
Permit the Injury of these Rites, I pray, [5]
Whose Darkness is increas'd by your full Day;
A day would make you Goddess did you wear,
As they of Old, a Quiver, or a Spear:
For you but want their Trifles, and dissent
Nothing in shape, but meerly Ornament; [10]
Your Limbs leave tracks of Light, still as you go;
Your Gate's Illumination, and for you
Only to move a step is to dispence
Brightness, and force, Splendor, and Influence;
Masses of Ivory blushing here and there [15]
With Purple shedding, if compared, were
Blots only cast on Blots, resembling you
No more than Monograms rich Temples do,
For being your Organs would inform and be
Not Instruments but Acts in Others, We [20]
What elsewhere is call'd Beauty, in You hold,
But so much Lustre, cast into a Mould;
Such a serene, soft, rigorous, pleasing, fierce,
Lovely, self-arm'd, naked, Majestickness,
·Compos'd of friendly Contraries, do young [25]
Poetique Princes shape, when they do long
To strik out *Heroes* from a Mortall Wombe,
And mint fair Conquerours for the Age to come.

But Beauty is not all that makes you so
Ador'd, by those who either see or know; [30]
'Tis your proportion'd Soul, for who ere set
A common useless weed in Christall yet?
Or who with Pitch doth Amber Boxes fill?
Balsom and Odors there inhabite still;
As Jewels then have Inward Vertues, so [35]
Proportion'd to that Outward Light they shew,
That, by their Lustre which appears, they bid
Us turn our sense to that which does lye hid;
So 'tis in you: For that Light which we find
Streams in your Eye, is Knowledge in your Mind; [40]
That mixture of bright Colours in your Face,
Is equall Temperance in another place;
That vigour of your Limbs, appears within
True perfect Valour, if we look but in;
And that Proportion which doth each part fill, [45]
Is but dispencing Justice in your Will.
Thus you redeem us from our Errour, who
Thought it a Ladies fame, neither to know
Nor be her self known much; and would not grant
Them Reputation, unless Ignorant; [50]
An *Heroïna* heretofore did pass
With the same faith as *Centaures*, and it was
A Tenet, that as Women only were
Nature's digressions, who did thence appear
At best but fair Mistakes, if they did do [55]
Heroic Acts, th'were faults of Custome too:
But you who've gain'd the Apex of your Kind,
Shew that there are no Sexes in the Mind,
Being so Candid, that we must confess
That Goodness is your Fashion, or your Dress. [60]
That you, more truly Valorous, do support
Virtue by daring to be good at Court;
Who, beyond all Pretenders, are alone
So much a friend to't, that with it y'are One,
And when We Men, the weaker Vessels, do [65]
Offend, we think we did it against you.
And can the thought be less, when that we see
Grace powrs forth Grace, Good Good, in one Pure, free,

And following Stream, that we no more can tell,
What 'tis you shew, than what true Tinctures dwel [70]
Upon the Doves bright Neck, which are so One,
And Divers, that we think them All, and None.
And this is your quick Prudence, which Conveys
One Grace into another, that who saies,
You now are Courteous, when you change the light, [75]
Will say you're Just, and think it a new sight;
And this is your peculiar Art, we know
Others may do like Actions, but not so:
The Agents alter things, and what does come,
Powerfull from these, flows weaker far from some; [80]
Thus the Suns light makes Day, if it appear,
And casts true Lustre round the Hemisphere;
When if projected from the Moon, that light
Makes not a Day, but only Colours Night;
But you we may still full, still perfect call, [85]
As what's still great, is equall still in all.

   And from this Largeness of your Mind, you come
To some just wonder, Worship unto some,
Whiles you appear a Court, and are no less
Than a whole Presence, or throng'd glorious Press; [90]
No one can ere mistake you. 'Tis alone
Your Lot, where e'r you come to be still known.
Your Power's its own Witness: you appeare
By some new Conquest, still that you are There.
But sure the Shafts your Vertues shoot, are tipt [95]
With consecrated Gold, which too was dipt
In purer Nectar, for where e'r they do
Print Love, they print Joy, and Religion too;
Hence in your great Endowments Church and Court
Find what t'admire; All wishes thus resort [100]
To you as to their Center, and are then
Sent back, as Centers send back lines agen.

   Nor can we say you learnt this hence, or thence,
That this you gain'd by Knowledge, this by Sence;
All is your own, and Native: for as pure [105]
Fire lends it self to all, and will endure
Nothing from others; So what you impart
Comes not from Others Principles, or Art,

But is Ingenite all, and still your Owne,
Your self sufficing to your self alone.   [110]
Thus your Extraction is desert, to whom
Vertue, and Life by the same Gift did come.
Your Cradle's thus a Trophe, and with us
'Tis thought a Praise confess'd to be born thus.
And though your Father's glorious Name will be   [115]
Full and Majestique in great History
For high designs; yet after Times will boast
You are his chiefest Act, and fame him most.
 Being then you're th'*Elixar*, whose least Grain
Cast into any Other, would maintain   [120]
All for true Worth, and make the piece Commence
Saint, Nymph, or Goddess, or what not from thence;
If when your Valorous Brother rules the Maine,
And makes the Flouds confess his powerfull Raign,
You should but take the Aire by in your Shell,   [125]
You would be thought Sea-born, and we might well
Conclude you such, but that your Deitie
Would have no winged Issue to set bye;
O had you Of-spring to resemble you,
As you have Vertues, then— But oh I do   [130]
Complain of our misfortunes, not your Own,
For are bless'd Spirits, for less happy known
Because they have not receiv'd such a Fate
Of Imperfection, as to Procreate?
Eternall things supply themselves; so we   [135]
Think this your Mark of Immortalitie.
 I now, as those of old, who once had met
A Deity in a shape, did nothing set
By lower, and less formes, securely do
Neglect all else, and having once seen you,   [140]
Count others only Natures Pesantry,
And out of Reverence seeing will not see.
 Hail your own Riches then, and your own store,
Who thus rule others, but your self far more;
Hail your own Glass and Object, who alone   [145]
Deserve to see your Own Reflection;
Persist you still the Faction of all Vowes,
A shape that makes oft Perjuries, and allows

Even broken faith's a Pardon, whiles men do
Swear, and reclaim what they have sworn seeing you. [150]
May you live long the Painters fault, and strife,
Who, for their oft not drawing you to life,
Must when their Glass is almost run out, long
To purchase Absolution for the Wrong;
But Poets, who dare still as much, and take [155]
An equal Licence, the same Errours make,
I then put in with them, who as I do
Sue for Release, so I may claime it too.
For since your Worth, and Modesty is such,
None will think this Enough, but You too Much. [160]

On the Imperfection of Christ-Church Buildings.

Arise thou Sacred Heap, and shew a Frame
Perfect at last, and Glorious as thy Name:
Space, and Torn Majesty, as yet are all
Thou hast: we view thy Cradle, as thy Fall.
 Our dwelling lyes half desert; The whole space [5]
Unmeeted and unbounded, bears the face
Of the first Ages fields, and we, as they
That stand on hills, have prospect every way:
Like *Theseus* Sonne, curst by Mistake, the frame
Scattred and Torn, hath parts without a Name, [10]
Which in a Landskip some mischance, not meant,
As dropping of the Spunge, would represent;
And (if no succour come) the Time's not far
When't will be thought no College, but a Quar.
Send then *Amphion* to these *Thebes.* (O Fates) [15]
W'have here as many Breaches, though not gates.
When any Stranger comes, 'tis shewn by us,
As once the face was of *Antigonus,*
With an half-Visage onely: so that all
We boast is but a Kitchin, or an Hall. [20]
Men thence admire, but help not, 't hath the luck
Of Heathen places that were Thunder-strook,
To be ador'd, not toucht; though the Mind and Will
Be in the Pale, the Purse is Pagan still:

Alas th'are Towr's that Thunder do provoke, [25]
We ne'r had Height or Glory for a stroke;
Time, and King *Henry* too, did spare us; we
Stood in those dayes both Sythe, and Scepter-free;
Our Ruines then were licenc'd, and we were
Pass'd by untouch'd; that hand was open here. [30]
Blesse we our Throne then! That which did avoid
The fury of those times, seems yet destroy'd:
So this breath'd on by no full Influence
Hath hung e'r since unminded in suspence,
As doubtfull whether't should Escheated be [35]
To Ruine, or Redeem'd to Majesty.
But great Intents stop seconds, and we owe
To Larger Wants, that Bounty is so slow.
A Lordship here, like *Curtius* might be cast
Into one Hole, and yet not seen at last. [40]
Two sacred Things were thought (by judging souls)
Beyond the Kingdomes Pow'r, *Christchurch* and *Pauls*,
Till, by a Light from Heaven shewn, the one
Did gain his second Renovation,
And some good Star ere long, we do not fear, [45]
Will Guide the Wise to Offer some gifts here.
But Ruines yet stand Ruines, as if none
Durst be so good, as *first to cast a Stone*.
Alas we ask not Prodigies: Wee'd boast
Had we but what is at one Horse-Race lost; [50]
Nor is our House, (as Nature in the fall
Is thought by some) *void and bereft of all*
But what's new giv'n: Unto our selves we owe
That Sculs are not our Churches Pavement now;
That that's made yet good way; that to his *Cup* [55]
And *Table Christ* may come, and not ride up;
That no one stumbling fears a worse event,
Nor when he bows falls lower than he meant;
That now our Windows may for Doctrine pass,
And we (as *Paul*) see Mysteries in a *Glass*; [60]
That something elsewhere is perform'd, whereby
'Tis seen we can adorn, though not supply.
   But if to all Great Buildings (as to *Troy*)
A God must needs be sent, and we enjoy

No help but Miracle; if so it stand [65]
Decreed by Heav'n, that the same gracious Hand
That perfected our *Statutes*, must be sent
To finish *Christ-Church* too, we are Content;
Knowing that he who in the Mount did give
Those Laws, by which his People were to live, [70]
If they had needed then, as now we do,
Would have bestow'd the *Stone* for *Tables* too.

A Continuation of the same to the Prince of Wales.

But turn we hence to you, as some there be
Who in the Coppy wooe the Deity;
Who think then most succesfull steps are trod
When they approach the Image for the God.
Our King hath shewn his Bounty, Sir, in you, [5]
By giving whom, h'hath giv'n us Buildings too.
For we see Harvests in a showre, and when
Heav'n drops a Dew, say it drops Flowers then,
Whiles all that blessed fatness doth not fall
To fill that Basket, or this Barn, but All. [10]
We know y"have Vertues in you now which stand
Eager for Action, and expect Command;
Vertues now ripe, Train'd up, and Nurtur'd so
That they wait only when you'l bid them flow.
Indulge you then, Our Rising Sun, we may [15]
Say your first Rayes broke here to make a Day:
For though the Light, when grown, powrs fuller streams,
'Tis yet more precious in it's Virgin Beams;
And though the third or fourth may do the Cure,
The Eldest Tear of Balsam's still most pure. [20]
'Tis only then our Pride that we may dwell
As Vertues do in you, compleat and well;
That when a College finish'd, is the sport
And Pastime only of your yonger Court,
An Act, to which some could not well arive [25]
After their fifty, done by you at five,
The late and Tardy Stock of Nephews may
Reading your Story, think you were born Gray;

This is the Thread weaves all our Hopes: for since
All Better Vertues now are call'd the *Prince* [30]
(As smaller Rivers lose their words, and beare
No name but Ocean when they come in there)
Thence we expect them, as these Streams we know
Can from no other Womb or Bosome flow;
Limne you our *Venus* then throughout, be she [35]
Christned, some Part at least, your Deity;
That when to take you Painters go about,
They be compell'd to leave some of you out;
Whiles you shew something here that won't admit
Colours and shape, something that cannot sit. [40]
Thus shall you nourish future Writers, who
May give Fame back those things you do bestow:
Where Merits too will be your work, and then
That Age will think you gave not stones, but Men.

On His Majesties recovery from the small Pox. 1633.

I doe confesse the over-forward tongue
Of publick duty turnes into a wrong,
And after-Ages, which could ne're conceive
Our happy CHARLES so fraile as to receive
Such a disease, will know it by the Noyse [5]
Which we have made, in shouting forth our Ioyes;
And our informing-duty onely be
A well-meant spight, or loyall injury.
Let then the name be alter'd, let us say
They were small Starres fixt in a Milky way; [10]
Or faithfull Turquoises, which Heaven sent
For a discovery, not a punishment;
To shew the ill, not make it; and to tell
By their paile lookes, the Bearer was not well.
Let the disease forgotten be, but may [15]
The Ioy returne, as yearely as the day.
Let there be new Computes, let reckoning be
Solemnely made from His Recovery:
Let not the Kingdomes Acts hereafter runne
From his (though happy) Coronation, [20]

But from his Health, as in a better straine;
That plac'd Him in his Throne, this makes Him Raigne.

To the King, On His Majesties Return from Scotland. *1633*.

We are a people now againe, and may
Style our selues Subjects: your prolong'd delay
Had almost made our jealousie engrosse
New feares, and rayse your absence into losse.
'Tis true the Kingdomes manners and the Lawe [5]
Retain'd their wonted vigour; the same awe
And loue still kept us loyall: but 'twas so
As Clocks once set in motion doe yet goe,
The hand being absent; or as when the Quill
Ceaseth to strike, the string yet trembles still. [10]
O count our sighs and feares! there shall not be
Againe such absence, though sure victorie
Would waite on every step, and would repay
A severall conquest for each severall day.
We doe not crowne your welcome with a Name [15]
Coy'nd from the Iourney, nor shall soothing fame
Call't an adventure: Heretofore when rude
And haughty Power was knowne by solitude,
When all that Subjects felt of Majesty
Was the oppressing yoke, and tyranny; [20]
Then it had pass'd for valour, and had beene
Thought Prowesse to haue dar'd to haue beene seen;
And the approaching to a neighbour Region
No Progresse, but an Expedition.
But her's no cause of a Triumphall dance, [25]
'Tis a Returne, not a Deliverance:
Your pious Raign secur'd your Throne, your Life
Was guard unto your Scepter: no rude strife,
No violence there disturb'd the Pompe, unlesse
Their eager Loue, and Loyalty did presse [30]
To see and know, whiles lawfull Majesty
Spread forth its Presence, and its Piety.
So hath the God, that lay hid in the voyce
Of his directing Oracle, made choyce

To come in Person, and untouch't hath crown'd [35]
The Supplicant with his Glory, not his sound.
Whiles that this Pompe was moving, whiles a fire
Shot out from you, did but provoke desire,
Not satisfie, how in loyalty did they
Wish an eternall Solstice, or a day [40]
That might make Nature stand, striving to bring
Ev'n by H E R wrong, more homage to the King!
But may'st Thou dwell with us, Iust C H A R L E S, and show
A Beame sometimes to Them: so shall we owe
To constant light, They to Posteritie [45]
Shall boast of this, that they were seene by Thee.

To the Queen on the same Occasion.

We doe presume our duty to no eare
Will better sound, then Yours, who most did feare.
We know Your busie eye perus'd the Glasse,
And chid the lazy Sands as they did passe:
We know no houre stole by with silent wing, [5]
But heard one Sigh dispatch'd unto your King.
We know His faith too; how that other faces
Were view'd as Pictures onely; how their graces
Did in this onely call His eye, that seene
They might present some parcell of his Queene. [10]
You were both maym'd, whiles sever'd; none could find
Whole Majesty: y'are perfect, when thus joyn'd.
We doe not thinke this Absence can adde more
Flames, but call forth those that lay hid before:
As when in thirsty flowers, a gentle dew [15]
Awakes the sent which slept, not gives a new.
As for our Ioy, 'tis not a suddaine heat
Starts into Noyse; but 'tis as true, as great:
We will be try'd by Yours: For we dare striue
Here, and acknowledge no Prerogatiue. [20]
We then proclaime this Triumph be as bright,
And large to all, as was your Marriage-night.
Cry we a second H Y M E N then, and sing,
Whiles You receiue the Husband, Wee the King.

On the Birth of the Duke of York.

The State is now past feare, and all that wee
Need wish besides is perpetuitie.
No gaudy traine of flames, no darkned Sunne,
No change inverting order did fore-runne
This Birth, no hurtlesse Natalitious fire [5]
Playing about Him made the Nurse admire,
And prophecie. Forc'd nature shewes these things
When Thraldome swels, when Bondmaids bring forth Kings.
And 'tis no favour: For Shee straight gives ore,
Paying these trifles, that She owe no more. [10]
Here She's reserv'd, and quiet, as if Hee
Were Her Designe, Her Plot, Her Policie:
Here the enquiring busie Common-eye
Onely intent upon new Majestie,
Nere lookes for further wonder, this alone [15]
Being sufficient, that Hee's silent showne.
What's Her intent, I know not: let it be
My pray'r, that Shee'll be modest, and that Hee
Have but the second honour, be still neere;
No imitation of the Father here. [20]
Yet let him, like to him, make Pow'r as free
From blot or scandall, as from poverty;
Count Blood and Birth no parts, but something lent
Meerely for outward grace, and complement;
Get safety by good life, and raise defence [25]
By better forces, Love, and conscience.
This likenesse wee expect; the Nurse may finde
Something in Shape, wee'll looke unto his Minde.
The forehead, Eye, and lip, poore humble parts
Too shallow for resemblance, shew the arts [30]
Of private guessings; action still hath beene
The Royall marke; those parts, which are not seene,
Present the Throne, and Scepter; and the right
Discoverie's made by judgement, not by sight.
I cannot to this cradle promise make [35]
Of actions fit for growth. A strangled snake,
Kill'd before knowne, perhaps 'mongst heathen hath

Beene thought the deed, and valour of the Swath.
Farre be such Monsters hence! the Buckler here
Is not the cradle, nor the dart, and speare [40]
The Infants Rattles: 'tis a Sonne of mirth,
Of peace and friendship, 'tis a quiet birth.
Yet if hereafter unfil'd people shall
Call on his sword, and so provoke their fall,
Let him looke backe on that admired Name, [45]
That Spirit of dispatch, that soule of fame,
His Grandsire *Henry*, tread his steps, in all
Be fully like to him, except his fall.
   Although in Royall births the Subjects lot
Be to enjoy what's by the Prince begot; [50]
Yet fasten, CHARLES, fasten those eyes You owe
Vnto a People, on this Sonne, to show
You can be tender too, in this one thing
Suffer the Father to depose the King.
See what delight Your Queene takes to peruse [55]
These faire unspotted Volumes, when She views
In Him that glance, in Her that decent grace,
In This sweet innocence, in All the face
Of both the Parents. May this blessing prove
A welcome Trouble, puzz'ling equall love [60]
How to dispense embraces, whiles that Shee
Strives to divide the Mother 'twixt all Three.

To Dr Duppa, *then Dean of* Christ-Church, *and Tutor to the* Prince *of* Wales.

Will you not stay then, and vouchsafe to be
Honour'd a little more Contractedly?
The Reverence here's as much, Though not the Prease;
Our Love as Tender, though the Tumult Less;
And your great Vertues in the narrow Sphere, [5]
Though not so Bright, shine yet as strong as there;
As Sun-Beams drawn into a point do flow
With greater force by being fettred so.
Things may a while in the same Order run,
As wheeles once turn'd continue Motion; [10]

And we enjoy a Light, as when the Eye
O'th' World is set all Lustre doth not dye:
But yet this Course, this Light, will so appear,
As only to Convince you have been here.
   He's Ours you ask (Great Soveraign) Ours, whom we   [15]
Will gladly ransome with a Subsidy.
Ask of us Lands, Our College, All; we do
Profer what's built, nay, what's intended too:
For he being Absent, 'tis an Heap, and we
Only a Number, no Society.   [20]
Hard Rival! for we dare Contest, and use
Such Language, now w' have nothing left to lose.
   Y' are only Ours, as some great Ship, that's gone
A Voyage i'th' Kings service, doth still run
Under the name o'th' Company: But we   [25]
Think it th' Indulgence of his Majesty
That y' are not whole engross'd, that yet you are
Permitted to be something that we dare
Call Ours, being honour'd to retain you thus,
That one Rule may direct the Prince, and us.   [30]
   Go then another Nature to him; go
A Genius wisht by all, except the Foe:
Fashion those ductile Manners, and inspire
That ample Breast with Clean and Active fire;
That when his Limbs shall write him Man, His Deeds   [35]
May write him yours; That from those Richer seeds
Thus sprouting we dividedly may ow
The Son unto our King, the Prince to you.
'Tis in the Power of your great Influence,
What *England* shall be fifty Harvests hence;   [40]
You'l do good to our Nephews now, and be
A Patron unto those you will not see;
Y' instruct a future Common-Wealth, and give
Laws to those People, that as yet don't live.
We see him full already; There's no fear   [45]
Of subtle Poyson, for good Axiomes, here,
All will be Health and Antidote, and one
Name will Combine State and Religion;
Heaven and We be Look'd on with one Eye,
And the same Rules guide Faith and Policy: [50]

The Court shall hence become a Church, and you,
In one, be Tutor to a People too.
He shall not now, like other Princes, hear
Some Morall Lecture when the Dinner's neer,
Learn nothing fresh and fasting, but upon [55]
This or that Dish read an instruction;
Hear *Livy* told, admire some Generals force,
And Stratagem, 'twixt first and second Course;
Then Cloze his Stomach with a Rule, and stay
'Mong Books perhaps to pass a Rainy day; [60]
Or his charg'd Memory with a Maxime task
To take up time before a Tilt or Masque:
No, you will Dictate wholesome grounds, and sow
Seeds in his Mind, as pure as that is now;
Breath in your Thoughts, your Soul, make him the true [65]
Resemblance of your Worth, Speak and live you:
That no old granted Sutour may still fear,
When't shall be one, to promise, and to swear.
That those huge Bulks, his Guard, may only be
Like the great Statues in the Gallery [70]
For Ornament not use; not to Afright
Th' Approachers Boldness, but afford a sight;
Whiles he, defended by a better Art,
Shall have a stronger Guard in every Heart,
And carrying your Vertues to the Throne, [75]
Find that his best defence, t' have need of none.
   May he Come forth your Work, and thence appear
Sacred and Pious, whom our Love may fear;
Discover you in all his Actions, be
'Bove Envy Great, Good above Flattery, [80]
And by a perfect fulness of each part,
Banish from Court that Torment, and this Art.
   Go O my Wishes with you: may they keep
Noise off, and make your Journey as your sleep,
Rather respose than Travell: May you meet [85]
No rough way, but in these unequall feet.
Good Fates take Charge of you; and let this be
Your sole Ill-luck, that Good is wisht by me.

*To the same immediately after the Publick
Act at* Oxon. *1634.*

And now (most worthy Sir) I've time to shew
Some Parcell of that Duty that I ow,
Which like late fruit, grows Vigorous by delay,
Gaining a force more lasting by its stay.
Had I presented you with ought, whiles here,   [5]
'T had been to sacrifice, the Priest not neer;
Forme rather than devotion, and a free
Expression of a Custome, not of me:
I was not then my self; Then not to err
Had been a trespass 'gainst the *Miniver*;   [10]
For, when our *Pumps* are on, we do dispence
With every slip, nay, every Crime, but Sense:
And we're encourag'd in't, the *Statutes* do't,
Which bind some Men to shew they cann't dispute.
   Suffer me, Sir, to tell you that we do   [15]
Owe these few daies solemnity to you;
For had you not among our Gowns been seen
Enlivening all, *Oxford* had only been
A Peopled Village, and our *Act* at best
A Learned *Wake*, or Glorious shepheards feast: [20]
Where (in my Judgement) the best thing to see
Had been *Jerusalem* or *Nineveh*,
Where, for true Exercise, none could surpass
The Puppets, and *Great Britaines Looking Glass*.
Nor are those Names unusuall; *July* here   [25]
Doth put forth all th' Inventions of the year:
Rare Works, and rarer Beasts do meet; we see
In the same street *Africk* and *Germany*.
Trumpets 'gainst Trumpets blow, the Faction's much,
These cry the Monster-Masters, Those the *Dutch*:   [30]
All Arts find welcome, all men come to do
Their Tricks and slights; Juglers, and *Curats* too,
Curats that threaten Markets with their Looks,
Arm'd with two weapons, Knives and Table-books;
Men that do itch (when they have eate) to note   [35]
The chief distinction 'twixt the *Sheep*, and *Goat*;

That do no questions relish but what be
Bord'ring upon the *Absolute Decree*,
And then haste home, lest they should miss the lot
Of venting *Reprobation*, whiles 'tis hot. [40]
But, above all Good sports, give me the sight
Of the Lay Exercise on Monday night,
Where a Reserved stomach doth profess
A zeal-prepared Hunger, of no less
Than ten days laying up, where we may see [45]
How they repair, how ev'ry man comes Three;
Where, to the envy of our Townsmen, some
Among the rest do by Prescription come,
Men that themselves do victuall twice a year,
At *Christmas* with their Landlords, and once here. [50]
None praise the *Act* more, and say less; they do
Make all Wine good by drinking, all Beer too;
This was their *Christian Freedom* here: nay we,
Our selves too then, durst plead a Liberty:
We reform'd Nature, and awak'd the Night, [55]
Making it spring as Glorious as the Light;
That, like the Day did dawn, and break forth here,
Though in a Lower, yet as bright a Sphere;
Sleep was a thing unheard of, unless 'twere
At Sermon after Dinner, all wink'd there; [60]
No Brother then known by the rowling White,
Ev'n they sate there as Children of the Night;
None come to see and to be seen; none heares,
My Lords fee-buck closeth bothe Eyes and Eares;
No Health did single, but our *Chancellors* pass, [65]
Viscounts and Earles throng'd seven in a Glass.
Manners and Language ne'r more free; some meant
Scarce one thing and did yet all Idioms vent;
Spoke *Minshew* in a Breath; the *Inceptors* Wine
Made *Latine* Native: Gray Coats then spoke fine, [70]
And thought that wiser Statute had done wrong
T'allot us four years yet to learn the Tongue.
   But *Oxford*, though throng'd with such People, was
A Court where e'r you only pleas'd to pass;
We reckon'd this your Gift, and that this way [75]
Part of the *Progress*, not your Journey lay.

I could relate you more, But that I fear
You'l find the Dregs o'th' time surviving here;
And that gets some Excuse: Think then you see
Some Reliques of the *Act* move yet in me. [80]

On the great Frost. 1634.

Shew me the flames you brag of, you that be
Arm'd with those two fires, Wine, and Poetry:
Y'are now benum'd spight of your Gods and Verse;
And may your Metaphors for Prayers rehearse;
Whiles you that call'd Snow *Fleece*, and *Feathers*, do [5]
Wish for true Fleeces, and true Feathers too.
   Waters have bound themselves, and cannot run,
Suff'ring what *Xerxes* fetters would have done;
Our Rivers are one Christall; Shoares are fit
Mirrours, being now, not like to Glass, but it: [10]
Our Ships stand all as planted, we may swear
They are not born up only, but grow there.
Whiles Waters thus are Pavements, firm as Stone,
And without faith are each day walk'd upon,
What Parables call'd folly heretofore, [15]
Were wisdome now, *To build upon the Shoare.*
There's no one dines among us with washt hands,
Water's as scarce here, as in *Africk* Sands;
And we expect it not but from some God
Opening a Fountain, or some Prophets Rod, [20]
Who need not seek out where he may unlock
A stream, what e'r he strook would be true Rock.
When Heaven drops some smaller Showers, our sense
Of Griefe's encreas'd, being but deluded thence;
For whiles we think those drops to entertain, [25]
They fall down Pearl, which came down half way Rain.
Green-Land's Removall, now the poor man fears,
Seeing all Waters frozen, but his Tears.
We suffer Day continuall, and the Snow
Doth make our Little Night become Noon now. [30]
We hear of some Enchristal'd, such as have
That, which procur'd their death, become their Grave.

Bodies, that destitute of Soul yet stood,
Dead, and not faln; drown'd, and without a Floud;
Nay we, who breath still, are almost as they, [35]
And only may be stil'd a softer Clay;
We stand like Statues, as if Cast, and fit
For life, not having, but expecting it;
Each man's become the *Stoick*'s wise one hence;
For can you look for *Passion*, where's no *Sense*? [40]
Which we have not, resolv'd to our first Stone,
Unless it be one Sense to feel w' have none.
Our very Smiths now work not, nay what's more,
Our Dutchmen write but five hours and give o'r.
We dare provoke Fate now: we know what is [45]
That last cold, Death, only by suff'ring this.
All fires are Vestall now, and we as they,
Do in our Chimneys keep a Lasting day;
Boasting within doores this domestique Sun,
Adored too with our Religion. [50]
We laugh at fire-Briefs now, although they be
Commended to us by his Majesty;
And 'tis no Treason, for we cannot guess
Why we should pay them for their happiness.
Each hand would be a *Scævola*'s: let *Rome* [55]
Call that a pleasure henceforth, not a doom.
A Feaver is become a wish: we sit
And think fall'n Angels have one Benefit,
Nor can the thought be impious, when we see
Weather, that *Bowker* durst not Prophesie; [60]
Such as may give new *Epochaes*, and make
Another *SINCE* in his bold Almanack;
Weather may save his doom, and by his foe
Be thought enough for him to undergo.
We now think *Alabaster* true, and look [65]
A suddain Trump should antedate his Book;
For whiles we suffer this, ought we not fear
The World shall not survive to a fourth year?
And sure we may conclude weak Nature old
And Crazed now, being shee's grown so Cold. [70]
   But Frost's not all our Grief: we that so sore
Suffer its stay, fear its departure more:

For when that Leaves us, which so long hath stood,
'Twill make a New Accompt *From th' second Floud.*

To the Right vertuous the Ladie Elizabeth Powlet

upon her Present to the Universitie of Oxon
being the Birth, Death, Ressurection and
Ascension of our Saviour, wrought by her
selfe in Needle-worke

Could wee iudge here Most vertuous Madam then
Your Needle might receave Praise from our Pen:
But this our want bereaves it of that Part,
Whiles to Admire, and Thanke is all our Art.
The Worke deserves a Shrine: I should rehearse [5]
Its Glories in a Storie, not a Verse.
   Colours are mixt so subt'ly, that thereby
The stealth of Art both takes and cheates the Eye;
At once a Thousand wee can gaze upon,
But are deceav'd by theire Transition: [10]
What toucheth is the same, Beame takes from Beame,
The Next still like, yet diffring in the extreame:
Here runnes This Track wee see, thither That tends,
But cann't say here This rose, or there that ends:
Thus whiles they creepe insensibly, wee doubt [15]
Whether the one powres not the other out.
   Faces so Quick and Livelie, that wee may
Feare, if wee turne our backs they'll steale away.
   Postures of Greife so true, that wee may sweare
Your Artfull fingers have wrought Passion there. [20]
   View wee the Manger and the Babe, wee thence
Believe the verie Threads have Innocence:
Then on the Cross such Love, such Griefe wee finde,
As 'twere a Transcript of our Saviours minde.
Each Parcell so Expressive, each so fitt, [25]
That the Whole seemes not so much wrought, as Writt.
'Tis Sacred Text all; wee may quote, and thence
Extract what may be press'd in our defence.
   Blest Mother of the Church, be in the List

Reckon'd from hence the Shee-Evangelist: [30]
Nor can the Style be Profanation, when
The Needle may convert more then the Pen;
When Faith may come by Seeing, and each Leafe
Rightly perus'd prove Gospell to the Deafe.
Had not St. Helen happ'ly found the Crosse, [35]
By this your worke you had repayr'd that Losse.
Tell me not of Penelope, Wee doe
See a Webb here more Chast, and Sacred too.
   Where are yee now, O Women, yee that sowe
Temptations, labouring to expresse the Bowe [40]
And the Blind Archer; yee that rarely sett
To please your Loves a Venus in a Nett?
Turne your Skill hither; then wee shall (no doubt)
See the Kings Daughter glorious too without.
   Women sow'd Idle Figg-leaves hitherto: [45]
Eve's Nakednesse is onlie cloth'd by you.

To Mr W.B. *at the Birth of his first Child.*

Y'are now transcrib'd, and Publike View
Perusing finds the Coppy true,
Without Erratas new crept in,
Fully Compleat and Genuine:
And nothing wanting can espy, [5]
But only Bulk and Quantity:
The Text in Letters small we see,
And the Arts in one Epitome.
O what pleasure do you take
To hear the Nurse discovery make, [10]
How the Nose, the Lip, the Eye,
The Forehead full of Majesty,
Shews the Father? how to this
The Mothers Beauty added is:
And after all with gentle Numbers [15]
To wooe the Infant into Slumbers.
   And these delights he yields you now,
The Swath, and Cradle, this doth shew:
But hereafter when his force

Shall wield the Rattle, and the Horse; [20]
When his ventring Tongue shall speak
All *Synalæphaes*, and shall break
This word short off, and make that two,
Pratling as *Obligations* do;
'Twill ravish the delighted Sense [25]
To view these sports of Innocence,
And make the wisest dote upon
Such pretty Imperfection.
   These hopeful Cradles promise such
Future Goodness, and so much, [30]
That they prevent my Prayers, and I
Must wish but for formality.
   I wish Religion timely be
Taught him with his *A B C*.
I wish him Good and Constant Health, [35]
His Father's learning, but more Wealth;
And that to use, not Hoard; a Purse
Open to bless, not shut to curse.
May he have many, and fast, friends,
Meaning Good-will, not private Ends, [40]
Such as scorn to understand,
When they name Love, a peece of Land.
May the Swath and Whistle be
The hardest of his Bonds. May he
Have no sad Cares to break his sleep, [45]
Nor other Cause, than now, to weep.
May he ne'r live to be again,
What he is now, a Child: May Pain
If it do visit, as a Guest
Only call in, not dare to rest. [50]

For a young Lord to his Mistris, who had taught him a Song.

Taught from your Artfull Strains, My Fair,
I've only liv'd e'r since by Air;
Whose Sounds do make me wish I were
Either all Voice, or else all Eare.

If Souls (as some say) Musick be [5]
I've learnt from you there's one in me;
From you, whose Accents make us know
That sweeter Spheres move here below;
From you, whose Limbs are so well met
That we may swear your Bodie's Set: [10]
Whose Parts are with such Graces Crown'd,
That th'are that Musick without sound.
I had this Love perhaps before,
But you awak'd and made it more:
As when a gentle Ev'ning Showre [15]
Calls forth, and adds, Sent to the Flower;
Henceforth I'l think my Breath is due
No more to Nature, but to you.
Sing I to Pleasure then, or Fame,
I'l know no Antheme, but your Name; [20]
This shall joy Life, this sweeten Death:
You, that have taught, may claim, my Breath.

On Mr Stokes *his Book on the Art of Vaulting*.

or,

In librum vere Cabalisticum de Ascensu Corporum
gravium h.e. in Tractatum de Arte Saliendi editum
a Gulillmo Stokes Almae Academiae Oxon Hipparcho,
et solo temporum horum Ephialte, Carmen desultorium

Reader, here is such a booke,
Will make you leape before you looke,
And shift, without being thought a Rooke.

The Author's aery, light, and thin;
Whom no man saw ere breake a Shin, [5]
Or ever yet leape out of's Skin.

When hee ere straind at horse, or bell,
Tom Charles himselfe who came to smell
His faults, still swore twas cleane and well.

His trickes are here in figures dimme,   [10]
Each line is heavier then his limbe
And shadowes weighty are to him.

Were Dee alive, or Billingsley,
We shortly shold each passage see
Demonstrated by A. B. C.   [15]

How would they vexe their Mathematicks,
Their ponderations, and their Statickes,
To shew the Art of these Volatickes?

Bee A. the horse, and the man B:
Parts from the girdle upwards C,   [20]
And from the girdle downwards D.

If the parts D proportiond weigh
To the parts C neither will sway,
But B lye equall upon A.

Thus would his horse and all his vectures,   [25]
Reduc'd to figures, and to sectures,
Produce new diagrams and Lectures.

And justly too: for the Pomado
And the most intricate Strapado
Heele do for naught in a Bravado.   [30]

Th' Herculean leape he can with sleight,
And that twice 50 times a night,
To please the Ladyes: Will is right.

The Angelica ne're puts him to't,
Then for the Pegasus, heele doe't   [35]
And strike a fountaine with his foot.

When he the Stags leape does, you'd sweare
The Stag himselfe, if he were there,
Would like th' unweildy Oxe appeare.

Hee'le fitt his strength, if you desire, [40]
Just as his horse, lower or higher,
And twist his limbes like nealed wire.

Had you, as I, but seene him once,
You'd sweare that Nature for the nonce,
Had made his body without bones. [45]

ffor Armes, sometimes hee'le hang on one,
Somtimes on both, somtimes on none,
And like a Meteor hang alone.

Let none henceforth our eares abuse,
How Daedalus scapt the twineing Stewes, [50]
Alas that is but flying newes.

Hee us'd wax'd plumes, as Ovid sings,
Will scornes to tamper with such things,
He is a Daedalus without wings.

Good faith, the Mewse had best looke to't [55]
Least they goe downe, and Sheene to boot,
Will and his woodden horse will doe't.

The Trojan steed let Souldiers scan,
And praise th' invention you that can,
Will puts 'um downe both Horse and man. [60]

At once sixe horses Theutobocchus
Leapt ore if fflorus doe not mocke us,
'Twas well: but let him not provoke us;

ffor were the matter to be try'd,
'Twere gold to Silver on Wills side, [65]
Heed quell that Theutobocchus pride.

Ile say but this to end the brawle,
Lett Theutobocchus in the fall
Cut a crosse-caper, and take all.

Then goe thy wayes, brave Will, for one [70]
By Jove 'tis thou must leap, or none,
To plucke bright honour from the Moone.

        Philippus Stoicus e Societate
          Portæ Borealis Oxon.

The Dreame.

I dream'd I saw my self lye dead,
   And that my Bed my Coffin grew;
Silence and Sleep this strange sight bred,
   But wak'd, I found I liv'd anew.
Looking next Morn on your bright face, [5]
   Mine Eyes bequeath'd mine Heart fresh pain;
A Dart rush'd in with every Grace,
   And so I kill'd my self again:
O Eyes, what shall distressed Lovers do,
If open you can kill, if shut you view. [10]

Love inconcealable. Stig.Ital.

Who can hide fire? If't be uncover'd, Light,
If cover'd, Smoake betraies it to the sight:
Love is that fire, which still some sign affords,
If hid, the'are Sighs; If open, they are Words.

The Teares.

If Souls consist of water, I
May swear yours glides out of your Eye:
If they may wounds receive, and prove
Festred through Grief, or ancient Love,
Then Fairest, through these Christall doores [5]
Teares flow as purgings of your Sores.
And now the certain Cause I know
Whence the Rose and Lilly grow

In your fair Cheeks, The often showres
Which you thus weep, do breed these flowers. [10]
If that the Flouds could *Venus* bring,
And warlike *Mars* from Flowers spring,
Why may not hence two Gods arise,
This from your Cheeks, that from your Eyes?

On one weepeing

Sawest thou not that liquid ball
Which from her tender eye did fall
Sure 'twas no obedient drop
Taught at will to flow or stopp
Such as the easy-tutour'd eye [5]
Now keepes in, then lets flye.
I know ith'midst of mirth, that there
Are spongie eyes can squeeze a teare.
I know there are of those that stand
At station and expect command [10]
Streames straind to march in ranke and file
The foolish lover to beguile.
But hers were true, and seeing there were
Of those before us did averre
The Soule was water may not I [15]
Sweare hers did glide out of her eye.
Soe upon the thirstye ground
Cleere and gentle, soft and round
ffalls the dew and makes the earth
Travaile with a fruitfull birth. [20]
So the bounty of the skie
Dropping fatnes doth supplie
Th' impoverisht plant with life and feeds
The tender infancy of seedes.
O now the certaine cause I know [25]
from whence the rose and Lilly grow
In her cheeke, the often showres
Which she weepes doth breede the flowers[.]
Did the enamoured moisture steale
Downe to her lippe in hope to seale [30]

That with a kisse? or would it faine
Salute her breast in hope to gaine
A wisht for entrance, there to sitt
With thoughts as innocent as it?
O tell mee what can wee deny [35]
Petitioning humilitie?
Or what suite can wee deferre
When the eye turnes Oratour[?]
A tear so true, soe faire, so good
Might have stopt Deucalions flood. [40]
If this barren age of ours
Would out of waters and of showres
Call a god, as they before
Did heaven with Mars and Venus store.
Heere better might two gods arise [45]
This from her cheekes, that from her eyes.

A Song of Dalliance

Heark, my *Flora;* Love doth call us
To that strife that must befal us:
He has rob'd his mothers Myrtles,
And hath pull'd her downy Turtles.
See, our genial posts are crown'd, [5]
And our beds like billows rise;
Softer combat's nowhere found,
And who loses, wins the prize.

Let not dark nor shadows fright thee;
Thy limbs of lustre they will light thee: [10]
Fear not any can surprise us,
Love himself doth now disguise us.
From thy waste thy girdle throw:
Night and darkness both dwell here:
Words or actions who can know, [15]
Where there's neither eye nor ear?

Shew thy bosome, and then hide it;
License touching and then chide it:

Give a grant, and then forbear it;
Offer something, and forswear it: [20]
Ask where all our shame is gone;
Call us wicked wanton men:
Do as Turtles, kiss and groan;
Say, We ne'er shall meet again.

I can hear thee curse, yet chase thee; [25]
Drink thy tears, yet still embrace thee.
Easie riches is no treasure:
She that's willing, spoils the pleasure.
Love bids learn the restless fight,
Pull and struggle whilst ye twine: [30]
Let me use my force to night,
The next conquest shall be thine.

Parchment.

Plain Shepherds Wear was only Gray,
And all Sheep then were cloath'd as they,
When Shepherds 'gan to write and think,
Some Sheep stole blackness from the Ink,
And we from thence found out the skill [5]
To make their Parchment do so still.

Falshood.

Still do the Stars impart their light
To those that travell in the night;
Still Time runs on, nor doth the Hand
Or Shadow on the Diall stand;
The streames still glide and Constant are: [5]
  Only thy Mind
  Untrue I find,
  Which carelesly
  Neglects to be
Like Stream, or Shadow, Hand, or Star. [10]

Fool that I am; I do recall
My words, and swear thou'rt like them all:
Thou seemst like Stars to nourish fire,
But O how cold is thy desire?
And like the Hand upon the Brass, [15]
   Thou point'st at me
   In mockery,
   If I come nigh,
   Shade-like thou'lt fly,
And as the Stream with Murmur pass. [20]

Thrice didst thou vow, thrice didst thou swear,
Whispring those Oaths into mine Eare,
And 'tween each one, as Seal of Bliss,
Didst interpose a sweeter kiss:
Alas that also came from Art, [25]
   For it did smell
   So fresh and wel,
   That I presume
   'Twas thy Perfume
That made thee swear, and not thy Heart. [30]

Tell me who taught thy subtile Eyes
To cheat true hearts with fallacies?
Who did instruct thy Sighs to Lie?
Who taught thy Kisses Sophistry?
Believe't 'tis far from honest Rigour; [35]
   O how I loath
   A tutor'd Oath!
   I'l ne'r come nigh
   A learned Sigh,
Nor credit Vows in Mood and Figure. [40]

'Twas *Venus* to me whisper'd this,
Swear and embrace, protest and kiss,
Such Oaths and Vows are fickle things,
My wanton Son does lend them wings:
The Kiss must stay, the Oath must fly: [45]
   Heav'n is the Schoole
   That gives this Rule:

>   I cann't prove true
>   To that and you,
>   The Goddess is in fault, not I.   [50]
>
>   Who for my wrong would thus much do,
>   For my Revenge may something too;
>   She, O She make thee true to all,
>   Marry an Army, and then fall
>   Through scornfull Hatred and disdain: [55]
>   But mayst thou be
>   Still false to me;
>   For if thy mind
>   Once more prove kind
>   Thou'lt swear thine Oaths all o'r again.   [60]

Beauty and Deniall.

> No, no, it cannot be; for who e'r set
> A Blockhouse to defend a Garden yet?
> Roses ne'r chide my boldness when I go
> To crop their Blush; why should your Cheeks do so?
> The Lillies ne'r deny their Silk to men;   [5]
> Why should your Hands push off, and draw back then?
> The Sun forbids me not his Heat; then why
> Comes there to Earth an Edict from your Eye?
> I smell Perfumes, and they ne'r think it sin;
> Why should your Breath not let me take it in?   [10]
> A Dragon kept the Golden Apples; true;
> But must your Breasts be therefore kept so too?
> All Fountains else flow freely, and ne'r shrink;
> And must yours cheat my Thirst when I would drink?
> Where Nature knows no prohibition,   [15]
> Shall Art prove Anti-Nature, and make one?
>   But O we scorn the profer'd Lip and Face;
> And angry Frowns sometimes add quicker Grace
> Than quiet Beauty: 'tis that melting kiss
> That truly doth distill immortall Bliss   [20]
> Which the fierce struggling Youth by force at Length
> Doth make the purchase of his eager strength;

Which, from the rifled weeping Virgin scant
Snatch'd, proves a Conquest, rather than a Grant.
    Beleeve't not: 'tis the Paradox of some One,   [25]
That in Old time did love an *Amazon*,
One of so stiff a Temper, that she might
Have call'd him Spouse upon the Marriage night;
Whose Flames consum'd him lest some one might be
Seduc'd hereafter by his Heresie: [30]
    That you are Fair and spotless, makes you prove
Fitter to fall a Sacrifice to Love:
On tow'rds his Altar then, vex not the Priest;
'Tis Ominous if the Sacrifice resist.
Who conquers still, and ransacks, we may say   [35]
Doth not Affect, but rather is in Pay.
But if there must be reall Lists of Love,
And our Embracing a true wrestling prove,
Bare, and Annoint you then: for, if you'l do
As Wrestlers use, you must be naked too.   [40]

Women.

Give me a Girle (if one I needs must meet)
Or in her Nuptiall, or her Winding Sheet;
I know but two good Houres that Women have,
One in the Bed, another in the Grave.
Thus of the whole Sex all I would desire,   [5]
Is to enjoy their Ashes, or their Fire.

To Cupid.

Thou, who didst never see the Light,
Nor knowst the pleasure of the sight,
But alwaies blinded, canst not say
    Now it is Night, or now 'tis Day,
So captivate her Sense, so blind her Eye,   [5]
That still she Love me, yet she ne'r know why.

Thou who dost wound us with such Art,
We see no bloud drop from the heart,

    And subt'ly Cruell leav'st no sign
      To tell the Blow or Hand was thine, [10]
O gently, gently wound my Fair, that Shee
May thence beleeve the Wound did come from thee.

To Venus.

Venus Redress a wrong that's done
    By that young spightfull Boy, thy Son,
He wounds, and then Laughs at the sore,
Hatred it self can do no more.
If I pursue, Hee's Small, and Light, [5]
    Both seen at once, and out of sight:
If I do flie, Hee's Wing'd, and then,
    At the third step, I'm caught agen:
Lest one day thou thy self mayst suffer so,
Or clip the Wantons Wings, or break his Bow. [10]

A Sigh sent to his absent Love.

I sent a Sigh unto my Blest ones Eare,
Which lost it's way, and never did come there;
I hastned after, lest some other Fair
Should mildly entertain this travelling Aire:
Each flowry Garden I did search, for fear [5]
It might mistake a Lilly for her Eare;
And having there took lodging, might still dwell
Hous'd in the Concave of a Christall Bell.
At last, one frosty morning I did spy
This subtile Wand'rer journeying in the Sky; [10]
At sight of me it trembled, then drew neer,
Then grieving fell, and dropt into a Tear:
I bore it to my Saint, and pray'd her take
This new born Of-spring for the Master's sake:
She took it, and prefer'd it to her Eare, [15]
And now it hears each thing that's whisper'd there.
O how I envy Grief, when that I see
My Sorrow makes a Gem, more blest than me!

Yet Little Pendant, Porter to the Eare,
Let not my Rivall have admittance there; [20]
But if by chance a mild access he gain,
Upon her tipp inflict a gentle pain
Only for Admonition: So when she
Gives eare to him, at least Shee'l think of Me.

Sadness.

Whiles I this standing Lake,
Swath'd up with Ewe and Cypress Boughs,
  Do move by Sighs and Vows,
  Let Sadness only wake;
That whiles thick Darkness blots the Light, [5]
My thoughts may cast another Night:
  In which double Shade,
  By Heav'n, and Me made,
    O let me weep,
    And fall asleep, [10]
  And forgotten fade.

Heark! from yond' hollow Tree
Sadly sing two Anchoret Owles,
  Whiles the Hermit Wolf howls,
  And all bewailing me, [15]
The Raven hovers o'r my Bier,
The Bittern on a Reed I hear
  Pipes my Elegy,
  And warns me to dye;
    Whiles from yond' Graves [20]
    My wrong'd Love craves
  My sad Company.

Cease *Hylas*, cease thy Call;
Such, O such was thy parting Groan,
  Breath'd out to me alone [25]
  When thou disdain'd didst fall.
Loe thus unto thy silent Tomb,
In my sad Winding Sheet, I come,

  Creeping o'r dead Bones,
  And cold Marble Stones, [30]
   That I may mourn
   Over thy Urn,
  And appease thy Groans.

    Corinna's *Tomb*.

Here fair *Corinna* buri'd lay,
Cloath'd and Lock'd up in silent Clay;
But neighb'ring Shepheards every morn
With constant tears bedew'd her Urn,
Untill with quickning moysture, she [5]
At length grew up into this Tree:
Here now unhappy Lovers meet,
And changing Sighs (for so they greet)
Each one unto some conscious Bough
Relates this Oath, and tels that Vow, [10]
Thinking that she with pittying sounds
Whispers soft Comfort to their Wounds:
When 'tis perhaps some wanton Wind,
That striving passage there to find,
Doth softly move the trembling leaves [15]
Into a voice, and so deceives.
Hither sad Lutes they nightly bring,
And gently touch each querulous string,
Till that with soft harmonious numbers
They think th' have woo'd her into Slumbers; [20]
As if, the Grave having an Eare,
When dead things speak the dead should hear.
Here no sad Lover, though of Fame,
Is suff'red to engrave his Name,
Lest that the wounding Letters may [25]
Make her thence fade, and pine away:
And so she withering through the pain
May sink into her Grave again.
O why did Fates the Groves uneare?
Why did they envy Wood should hear? [30]
Why, since *Dodona*'s holy Oake,

Have Trees been dumb, and never spoke;
Now Lovers wounds uncured Lye,
And they wax old in misery;
When, if true sense did quicken Wood, [35]
Perhaps shee'd sweat a Balsom floud,
And knowing what the World endures,
Would weep her moysture into Cures.

To the memory of a Shipwrackt Virgin.

Whether thy well-shap'd parts now scattred far
Asunder into Treasure parted are;
Whether thy Tresses, now to Amber grown,
Still cast a Softer day where they are shewn;
Whether those Eyes be Diamonds now, or make [5]
The Carefull Goddess of the Flouds mistake,
Chiding their lingring stay, as if they were
Stars that forgot t' ascend unto their Sphere;
Whether thy Lips do into Corall grow,
Making her wonder how't came red below; [10]
Whether those Orders of thy Teeth, now sown
In several Pearls, enrich each Channell one;
Whether thy gentle Breath in easie Gales
Now flies, and chastly fils the pregnant Sailes;
Or whether Whole, turn'd Syren, thou dost joy [15]
Only to Sing, unwilling to destroy;
Or else a Nymph far fairer dost encrease
The Virgin Train of the *Nereides*;
If that all Sense departed not with Breath,
And there is yet some Memory in Death, [20]
Accept this labour, sacred to thy Fame,
Swelling with thee, made Poem by thy Name.
   Hearken O Winds (if that ye yet have Eares
Who were thus deaf unto my Fair ones Tears)
Fly with this Curse; may Cavernes you contain [25]
Still strugling for Release, but still in vain.
   Listen O Flouds; black Night upon you dwell,
Thick Darkness still enwrap you; may you swell
Only with Grief; may ye to every thirst

Flow bitter still, and so of all be curst. [30]
    And thou unfaithfull, ill-Compacted Pine,
That in her Nuptials didst refuse to shine,
Blaze in her Pile. Whiles thus her death I weep
Swim down my murmuring Lute; move thou the deep
Into soft numbers, as thou passest by, [35]
And make her Fate become her Elegy.

To a Painters handsome Daughter.

Such are your Fathers Pictures, that we do
Beleeve they are not Counterfeits, but true;
So lively, and so fresh, that we may swear
Instead of draughts, He hath plac'd Creatures there;
People, not shadows; which in time will be [5]
Not a dead Number, but a Colony:
Nay, more yet, some think they have skill and Arts,
That th' are well-Bred, and Pictures of good Parts;
And you your Self, faire *Julia,* do disclose
Such Beauties, that you may seem one of those; [10]
That having Motion gain'd at last, and sense,
Began to know it Self, and stole out thence.
Whiles thus his æmulous Art with Nature strives,
Some think H' hath none, Others he hath two Wives.
If you love none, fair Maid, but Look on all, [15]
You then among his set of Pictures fall;
If that you look on all, and love all men,
The Pictures too will be your Sisters then,
For they as they have Life, so th' have this Fate
In the whole Lump either to Love or Hate; [20]
Your Choice must shew you're of another Fleece,
And tell you are his Daughter, not his Piece:
All other proofs are vain; Go not about;
We two'l Embrace, and Love, and clear the doubt.
When you've brought forth your Like, the world will know [25]
You are his Child; what Picture can do so.

Lesbia *On her Sparrow.*

Tell me not of Joy: there's none
Now my little Sparrow's gone;
   He, just as you
    Would toy and wooe,
He would chirp and flatter me, [5]
He would hang the Wing a while,
Till at length he saw me smile,
Lord how sullen he would be?

He would catch a Crumb, and then
Sporting let it go agen, [10]
   He from my Lip
    Would moysture sip,
He would from my Trencher feed,
Then would hop, and then would run,
And cry *Philip* when h' had done, [15]
O whose heart can choose but bleed?

O how eager would he fight?
And ne'r hurt though he did bite:
   No Morn did pass
    But on my Glass [20]
He would sit, and mark, and do
What I did, now ruffle all
His Feathers o'r, now let 'em fall,
And then straightway sleek 'em too.

Whence will *Cupid* get his Darts [25]
Feather'd now to peirce our hearts?
   A wound he may,
    Not Love conveigh,
Now this faithfull Bird is gone,
O let Mournfull Turtles joyn [30]
With Loving Red-breasts, and combine
To sing Dirges o'r his Stone.

The Gnat.

    A Gnat mistaking her bright Eye
For that which makes, and rules the Day,
Did in the Rayes disporting fly,
Wont in the Sun-Beams so to play.

    Her Eye whose vigour all things draws, [5]
Did suck this little Creature in,
As warmer Jet doth ravish straws,
And thence ev'n forc'd embraces win.

    Inviting Heat stream'd in the Rayes,
But hungry fire work'd in the Eye; [10]
Whose force this Captive Gnat obeys,
And doth through it her Martyr dye.

    The Wings went into Air; the Fire
Did turn the rest to Ashes there:
But ere death, strugling to retire, [15]
She thence enforc'd an easie Teare.

    Happy O Gnat though thus made nought,
We wreched Lovers suffer more,
Our Sonnets are thy Buzzings thought,
And we destroy'd by what w'adore. [20]

    Perhaps would she but our deaths mourn,
We should revive to dye agen:
Thou gain'dst a Tear, but we have scorn;
She weeps for Flies, but Laught at Men.

Love-Teares.

Brag not a Golden Rain O *Jove*; we see
Cupid descends in Showers as well as thee.

At a dry Dinner.

Call for what wine you please, which likes you best;
Some you must drink your Venison to digest.
Why rise you, Sir, so soon: you need not doubt,
He that I do invite sits my meal out;
Most true: But yet your Servants are gay men, [5]
I'l but step home, and drink, and come agen.

A Bill of Fare.

Expect no strange, or puzzling Meat, no Pye
Built by Confusion, or Adultery
Of forced Nature; No mysterious dish
Requiring an Interpreter, no Fish
Found out by modern Luxury: Our Corse Board [5]
Press'd with no spoyls of Elements, doth aford
Meat, like our Hunger, without Art, each Mess
Thus differing from it only, that 'tis less.
   Imprimis some Rice Porredge, sweet, and hot,
Three knobs of Sugar season the whole Pot. [10]
   Item, one pair of Eggs in a great dish,
So Ordered that they Cover all the Fish.
   Item, one gaping Haddocks Head, which will
At least afright the Stomach, if not fill.
   Item, one thing in Circles, which we take [15]
Some for an Eele, but th'Wiser for a Snake.
   We have not still the same, sometimes we may
Eat muddy Plaise, or Wheate; perhaps next day
Red, or White, Herrings, or an Apple Pye:
There's some variety in Misery. [20]
   To this come Twenty Men, and though apace,
We bless these Gifts, the Meal's as short as Grace.
Nor eat we yet in Tumult; but the Meat
Is broke in Order; Hunger here is neat;
Division, subdivision, yet two more [25]
Members, and they divided, as before.
O what a fury would your Stomach feel

To see us vent our Logick on an Eele?
And in one Herring to revive the Art
Of *Keckerman*, and shew the Eleventh part? [30]
Hunger in Armes is no great wonder, we
Suffer a Siedge without an Enemy.
  On *Midlent-Sunday*, when the Preacher told
The Prodigal's return, and did unfold
His tender welcome, how the good old man [35]
Sent for new Rayment, how the Servant ran
To kill the Fatling Calf, O how each Ear
List'ned unto him, greedy ev'n to hear
The bare Relation; how was every Eye
Fixt on the Pulpit; how did each man pry, [40]
And watch, if, whiles he did this word dispence,
A Capon, or a Hen would fly out thence?
  Happy the Jews cry we, when Quailes came down
In dry and wholsome Showers, though from the frown
Of Heaven sent, though bought at such a Rate; [45]
To perish full is not the worst of Fate;
We fear we shall dye Empty, and enforce
The Grave to take a Shaddow for a Corse:
For, if this Fasting hold, we do despair
Of life; all needs must vanish into Air; [50]
Air, which now only feeds us, and so be
Exhal'd, like Vapours to Eternity.
W'are much refin'd already, that dull house
Of Clay (our Body) is Diaphanous;
And if the Doctor would but take the pains [55]
To read upon us, Sinnews, Bones, Guts, Veines,
All would appear, and he might shew each one,
Without the help of a Dissection.
  In the aboundance of this want, you will
Wonder perhaps how I can use my Quill? [60]
Troth I am like small Birds, which now in Spring,
When they have nought to Eat do sit and Sing.

The Chambermaids Posset.

My Ladies young Chaplain could never arive
   More than to four points, or thereabout:
He propos'd fifteen, but was gravell'd at five,
   My Lady stood up and still preach'd 'em out.

The Red-hatted Vertue's in number but four, [5]
   With Grief he remembred, for one was not:
The Habit's divine, not yet in our Power,
   Were Faith, Hope, and (Brethren) the third I ha' forgot.

Sir *John* was resolved to suffer a Drench,
   To furnish his Spirit with better Provision [10]
A Posset was made by a Leviticall Wench,
   It was of the Chambermaids own Composition.

The Milk it came hot from an Orthodox Cow
   Ne'r rid by the Pope, nor yet the Popes Bull;
The heat of Zeal Boyled it, God knows how: [15]
   'Twas the Milk of the Word; Beleeve it who will.

The Ingredients were divers, and most of them new,
   No Vertue was judg'd in an Antient thing:
In the Garden of *Leyden* some part of them grew,
   And some did our own *Universities* bring. [20]

Imprimis two handfull of long Digressions,
   Well squeezed and press'd at *Amsterdam*,
They cured *Buchanan*'s dangerous Passions,
   Each Grocers Shop now will afford you the same.

Two ounces of *Calvinisme* not yet refin'd, [25]
   By the better Physicians not thought to be good;
But 'twas with the Seal of a Conventicle sign'd,
   And approv'd by the Simpling Brotherhood.

One Quarter of Practicall Piety next,
   With an Ounce and a half of *Histrio-mastix*, [30]

Three Sponfull of *T.C.*'s confuted Text,
    Whose close-noated Ghost hath long ago past *Styx*.

Next *Stript whipt Abuses* were cast in the Pot,
    With the worm eaten Motto not now in fashion;
All these in the Mouth are wondrous hot, [35]
    But approvedly Cold in operation.

Next *Clever* and *Doddisme* both mixed and fine,
    With five or six scruples of Conscience Cases,
Three Drams of *Geneva*'s strict Discipline,
    All steept in the sweat of the silenc'd faces. [40]

One Handfull of Doctrines, and Uses, or more,
    With the utmost Branch of the fifteenth point,
Then *Duties* enjoyn'd and *Motives* good store,
    All boyl'd to a Spoonfull, though from a siz'd Pint.

These all have astringent and hard qualities, [45]
    And for notable Binders received be,
To avoid the Costiveness thence might arise,
    She allay'd them with *Christian Liberty*.

The *Crumbs of Comfort* did thicken the Mess,
    'Twas turn'd by the frown of a sowre fac'd Brother, [50]
But that you will say converts wickedness,
    'Twill serve for the one as well as the Other.

An Ell *London*-measure of tedious Grace,
    Was at the same time Conceiv'd, and said,
'Twas eat with a spoon defil'd with no face, [55]
    Nor the Imag'ry of an Apostles head.

Sir *John* after this could have stood down the Sun,
    Dividing the Pulpit and Text with one Fist,
The Glass was Compell'd still Rubbers to run,
    And he counted the fift *Evangelist*. [60]

The Pig that for haste, much like a Devout
    Entranced Brother, was wont to Come in

With white staring Eyes, not quite roasted out,
    Came now in a Black Persecution skin.

Stale Mistris *Priscilla* her Apron-strings straite [65]
    Let down for a Line just after his Cure:
Sir *John* did not nibble, but pouch'd the deceit:
    An Advouzon did bait him to make all sure.

On a Gentlewomans Silk-hood.

Is there a Sanctity in Love begun
That every woman veils, and turns Lay-Nun?
Alas your Guilt appears still through the Dress;
You do not so much Cover as Confess:
To me 'tis a Memoriall, I begin [5]
Forthwith to think on *Venus* and the Gin,
Discovering in these Veyls, so subt'ly set,
At least her upper parts caught in the Net.
Tell me who taught you to give so much light
As may entice, not satisfie the Sight, [10]
Betraying what may cause us to admire,
And kindle only, but not quench desire?
Among your other subtilties, 'tis one
That you see all, and yet are seen of none;
'Tis the Dark-Lanthorn to the face; O then [15]
May we not think there's Treason against Men?
Whiles thus you only do expose the Lips,
'Tis but a fair and wantonner Eclipse.
Mean't how you will, At once to shew, and hide,
At best is but the Modesty of Pride; [20]
Either Unveil you then, or veil quite o'r,
Beauty deserves not so much; Foulness more.
    But I prophane, like one whose strange desires
Bring to Loves Altar foul and drossie Fires:
Sink O those Words t'your Cradles; for I know, [25]
Mixt as you are, your Birth came from below:
My Fancy's now all hallow'd, and I find
Pure Vestals in my Thoughts, Priests in my Mind.
    So Love appear'd, when, breaking out his way

From the dark Chaos, he first shed the Day; [30]
Newly awak'd out of the Bud so shews
The half seen, half hid, glory of the Rose,
As you do through your Veyls; And I may swear,
Viewing you so, that Beauty doth Bud there.
So Truth lay under Fables, that the Eye [35]
Might Reverence the Mystery, not descry;
Light being so proportion'd, that no more
Was seen, but what might Cause 'em to adore:
Thus is your Dress so Ord'red, so Contriv'd,
As 'tis but only Poetry Reviv'd. [40]
Such doubtfull Light had Sacred Groves, where Rods
And Twigs, at last did shoot up into Gods;
Where then a Shade darkneth the Beautuous Face,
May not I pay a Reverence to the place?
So under-water glimmering Stars appear, [45]
As those (but nearer Stars) your Eyes do here.
So Deities darkned sit, that we may find
A better way to see them in our Mind.
No bold *Ixion* then be here allow'd,
Where *Juno* dares her self be in the Cloud. [50]
Methinks the first Age comes again, and we
See a Retrivall of Simplicity;
Thus looks the Country Virgin, whose brown hue
Hoods her, and makes her shew even veil'd as you.
Blest Mean, that Checks our Hope, and spurs our Fear, [55]
Whiles all doth not lye hid, nor all appear:
O fear ye no Assaults from Bolder men;
When they assaile be this your Armour then.
A Silken Helmet may defend those Parts,
Where softer Kisses are the only Darts. [60]

A Dream Broke.

As *Nilus* sudden Ebbing, here
Doth leave a scale, and a scale there,
And somewhere else perhaps a Fin,
Which by his stay had Fishes been:
So Dreams, which overflowing be, [5]

Departing leave Half things, which we
For their Imperfectness can call
But Joyes i'th' Fin, or in the Scale.
If when her Teares I haste to kiss,
They dry up, and deceive my Bliss, [10]
May not I say the Waters sink,
And Cheat my Thirst when I would drink?
If when her Breasts I go to press,
Insteed of them I grasp her Dress,
May not I say the Apples then [15]
Are set down, and snatch'd up agen?
Sleep was not thus Death's Brother meant;
'Twas made an Ease, no Punishment.
As then that's finish'd by the Sun,
Which *Nile* did only leave begun, [20]
My Fancy shall run o'r Sleeps Themes,
And so make up the Web of Dreams:
In vain fleet shades, ye do Contest:
Awak'd how e'r I'l think the rest.

Loves Darts.

Where is that Learned Wretch that knows
What are those Darts the Veyl'd God throws?
O let him tell me ere I dye
When 'twas he saw or heard them fly;
   Whether the Sparrows Plumes, or Doves, [5]
   Wing them for various Loves;
     And whether Gold, or Lead,
     Quicken, or dull the Head:
I will annoint and keep them warm,
And make the Weapons heale the Harm. [10]

   Fond that I am to aske! who ere
Did yet see thought? or Silence hear?
Safe from the search of humane Eye
These Arrows (as their waies are) flie:
   The Flights of Angels part [15]
   Not Aire with so much Art;

    And snows on Streams, we may
      Say, Louder fall than they.
So hopeless I must now endure,
And neither know the Shaft nor Cure. [20]

    A sudden fire of Blushes shed
To dye white paths with hasty Red;
A Glance's Lightning swiftly thrown,
Or from a true or seeming frown;
    A subt'le taking smile [25]
    From Passion, or from Guile;
    The Spirit, Life, and Grace
    Of motion, Limbs, and Face;
These Misconceits entitles Darts,
And Tears the bleedings of our hearts. [30]

    But as the Feathers in the Wing,
Unblemish'd are and no Wounds bring,
And harmless Twigs no Bloodshed know,
Till Art doth fit them for the Bow;
    So Lights of flowing Graces [35]
    Sparkling in severall places,
    Only adorn the Parts,
    Till we that make them Darts;
Themselves are only Twigs and Quils:
We give them Shape, and force for Ills. [40]

    Beautie's our Grief, but in the Ore,
We Mint, and Stamp, and then adore;
Like Heathen we the Image Crown,
And undiscreetly then fall down:
    Those Graces all were meant [45]
    Our Joy, not Discontent;
    But with untaught desires
    We turn those Lights to Fires.
Thus Natures Healing Herbs we take,
And out of Cures do Poysons make. [50]

Parthenia *for her slain* Argalus.

    See thy *Parthenia* stands
Here to receive thy last Commands.
    Say quickly, say, for fear
Grief ere thou speaks, make me not hear.
    Alas, as well I may   [5]
Call to Flowers wither'd Yesterday.
    His Beauties, O th' are gone;
    His thousand Graces none.
This O ye Gods, is this the due
Ye pay to Men more just than you?   [10]
O dye *Parthenia*, Nothing now remains
Of all thy *Argalus*, but his Wounds and Stains.

    Too late, I now recall,
The Gods foretold me this thy fall;
    I grasp'd thee in my Dream,   [15]
And loe thou meltd'st into a Stream;
    But when They will surprise,
They shew the Fate, and blind the Eyes.
    Which Wound shall I first kiss?
    Here? there? or that? or this?   [20]
Why gave he not the like to me,
That Wound by Wound might answer'd be?
We would have joyntly bled, by Griefs ally'd,
And drank each other's Soul, and so have dy'd.

    In silent Groves below   [25]
Thy bleeding Wounds thou now dost shew;
    And there perhaps to Fame
Deliver'st up *Parthenia*'s Name;
    Nor do thy Loves abate.
O Gods! O Stars! O Death! O Fate!   [30]
    But thy Proud Spoyler here
    Doth thy snatch'd Glories wear;
And big with undeserv'd success
Swels up his Acts, and thinks Fame less;
And counts my Groans not worthy of Relief,   [35]
O Hate! O Anger! O Revenge! O Grief!

  Parthenia then shall live,
 And something to thy Story give.
  Revenge inflame my Breast
 To send thy wand'ring Spirit rest.   [40]
  By our fast Tye, our Trust,
 Our one Mind, our one Faith I must:
  By my past Hopes and Fears,
  My Passions, and my Tears;
 By these thy Wounds (my Wounds) I vow, [45]
 And by thy Ghost, my Griefe's God now,
I'l not revoke a Thought. Or to thy Tomb
My Off'ring He, or I his Crime will come.

  Ariadne *deserted by* Theseus, *as She sits upon a*
   Rock in the Island Naxos, *thus complains.*

Theseus! O *Theseus* heark! but yet in vain
 Alas deserted I Complain,
It was some neighbouring Rock, more soft than he,
 Whose hollow Bowels pittied me,
And beating back that false, and Cruell Name, [5]
 Did Comfort and revenge my flame.
 Then Faithless whither wilt thou fly?
 Stones dare not harbour Cruelty.

Tell me you Gods, who e'r you are,
Why, O why made you him so fair?   [10]
 And tell me, Wretch, why thou
 Mad'st not thy self more true?
Beauty from him may Copies take,
And more Majestique Heroes make,
 And falshood learn a Wile,   [15]
 From him too, to beguile.
  Restore my Clew
  'Tis here most due,
For 'tis a Labyrinth of more subtile Art,
To have so fair a Face, so foul a Heart.   [20]

The Ravenous Vulture tear his Breast,
The rowling Stone disturb his rest,

  Let him next feel
  Ixion's Wheel,
 And add one Fable more   [25]
 To cursing Poets store;
And then — yet rather let him live, and twine
His Woof of daies, with some thred stoln from mine;
 But if you'l torture him, how e'r,
 Torture my Heart, you'l find him there.   [30]

  Till my Eyes drank up his,
   And his drank mine,
  I ne'r thought Souls might kiss,
   And Spirits joyn:
   Pictures till then   [35]
  Took me as much as Men,
   Nature and Art
  Moving alike my heart,
But his fair Visage made me find
   Pleasures and Fears,   [40]
  Hopes, Sighs, and Tears,
As severall seasons of the Mind.
Should thine Eye, *Venus*, on his dwell,
Thou wouldst invite him to thy Shell,
  And Caught by that live Jet   [45]
  Venture the second Net,
And after all thy dangers, faithless he,
Shouldst thou but slumber, would forsake ev'n thee.

  The Streames so Court the yeelding Banks,
  And gliding thence ne'r pay their thanks;   [50]
   The Winds so wooe the Flow'rs,
   Whisp'ring among fresh Bow'rs,
  And having rob'd them of their smels,
  Fly thence perfum'd to other Cels.
This is familiar Hate to Smile and Kill,   [55]
Though nothing please thee yet my Ruine will.
  Death hover, hover o'r me then,
   Waves let your Christall Womb
   Be both my Fate, and Tomb,
  I'l sooner trust the Sea, than Men.   [60]

    Yet for revenge to Heaven I'l call
      And breath one Curse before I fall,
Proud of two Conquests *Minotaure*, and Me,
That by my Faith, This by thy Perjury,
Mayst thou forget to Wing thy Ships with White,   [65]
That the Black Sayl may to the longing sight
Of thy Gray Father, tell thy Fate, and He
Bequeath the Sea his Name, falling like me:
Nature and Love thus brand thee, whiles I dye
'Cause thou forsak'st, *Ægeus* 'cause thou drawest nigh.   [70]

    And yee O Nymphs below who sit,
      In whose swift Flouds his Vows he writ;
Snatch a sharp Diamond from the richer Mines,
And in some Mirrour grave these sadder Lines,
        Which let some God Convey   [75]
        To him, that so he may
      In that both read at once, and see
    Those Looks that Caus'd my destiny.
In *Thetis* Arms I *Ariadne* sleep,
Drown'd first by my own Tears, then in the deep;   [80]
Twice banish'd, First by Love, and then by Hate,
The life that I preserv'd became my Fate;
Who leaving all, was by him left alone,
That from a Monster freed himself prov'd one.

    Thus then I —— But look! O mine Eyes   [85]
      Be now true Spies,
      Yonder, yonder,
      Comes my Dear,
      Now my wonder,
      Once my fear,   [90]
    See Satyrs dance along
    In a confused Throng,
    Whiles Horns and Pipes rude noise
    Do mad their lusty Joyes,
    Roses his forehead Crown,   [95]
    And that recrowns the Flow'rs,
    Where he walks up and down
    He makes the desarts Bow'rs,

    The Ivy, and the Grape
      Hide, not adorn his Shape.   [100]
And Green Leaves Cloath his waving Rod,
'Tis either *Theseus*, or some God.

No drawing of Valentines.

Cast not in *Chloe*'s Name among
The Common undistinguish'd Throng,
    I'l neither so advance
    The foolish Raign of Chance,
    Nor so depress the Throne   [5]
    Whereon Love sits alone:
If I must serve my Passions, I'l not owe
Them to my fortune; ere I Love, I'l know.

Tell me what God lurks in the Lap
To make that Councel, we call Hap?   [10]
    What power Conveighs the name?
    Who to it adds the Flame?
    Can he raise mutuall fires,
    And answering desires?
None can assure me that I shall approve   [15]
Her whom I draw, or draw her whom I love.

No longer then this Feast abuse,
You choose and like, I like and choose;
    My flame is try'd and Just,
    Yours taken up on trust.   [20]
    Hail thus blest *Valentine*,
    And may my *Chloe* shine
To me and none but me, as I beleeve
We ought to make the whole year but thy Eve.

To Lydia *whom Men observ'd to make too much of me.*

I told you *Lydia* how 'twould be,
Though Love be blind, his Priests can see;

Your Wisdom that doth rule the Wise,
And Conquers more than your Black Eyes,
That like a Planet doth dispense, [5]
And Govern by its Influence
(Though to all else discreet you be)
Is blemish'd 'cause y' are fond of me.

Your Manners like a Fortress Bar
The Rough approach of Men of War; [10]
The *King's* and *Prince's* Servants you
Do use as they their Scrivenors do;
The Learned *Gown*, and City *Ruffe*,
Your Husband too, scurvy enough:
But still with me you meet and Close, [15]
As if that I were King of those.

You say, you ought how e'r to do
The same thing still; I say so too;
Let Tongues be free, speak what they will,
Say our Love's loud, but let's love still. [20]
I hate a secret stifled flame,
Let yours and mine have Voice, and Name;
Who Censure what twixt us they see
Condemn not you, but Envy me.

Go bid the eager flame Congeal [25]
To sober Ice, Bid the Sun steal
The Temper of the frozen Zone
Till Christall say, that Cold's its own.
Bid *Jove* himself, whiles the grave State
Of Heaven doth our Lots debate, [30]
But think of *Leda*, and be wise,
And bid Love have equall Eyes.

View Others *Lydia* as you would
View Pictures, I'l be flesh and bloud;
Fondness, like Beauty that's admir'd, [35]
At once is Censur'd and desir'd;
And they that do it will Confess,
Your Soul in this doth but digress:

But when you thus in Passions rise,
   Y' are fond to them, to me y' are wise. [40]

To Chloe *who wish'd her self young enough for me.*

Chloe, why wish you that your years
   Would backwards run, till they meet mine,
That perfect Likeness, which endears
   Things unto things, might us Combine?
Our Ages so in date agree, [5]
That Twins do differ more than we.

There are two Births, the one when Light
   First strikes the new awak'ned sense;
The Other when two Souls unite;
   And we must count our life from thence: [10]
When you lov'd me, and I lov'd you,
Then both of us were born anew.

Love then to us did new Souls give,
   And in those Souls did plant new pow'rs;
Since when another life we live, [15]
   The Breath we breath is his, not ours;
Love makes those young, whom Age doth Chill,
And whom he finds young, keeps young still.

Love, like that Angell that shall call
   Our bodies from the silent Grave, [20]
Unto one Age doth raise us all,
   None too much, none too little have;
Nay that the difference may be none,
He makes two not alike, but One.

And now since you and I are such, [25]
   Tell me what's yours, and what is mine?
Our Eyes, our Ears, our Taste, Smell, Touch,
   Do (like our Souls) in one Combine;
So by this, I as well may be
Too old for you, as you for me. [30]

A Valediction.

Bid me not go where neither Suns nor Show'rs
    Do make or Cherish Flow'rs;
Where discontented things in sadness lye,
    And Nature grieves as I;
  When I am parted from those Eyes, [5]
  From which my better day doth rise,
    Though some propitious Pow'r
    Should plant me in a Bow'r,
Where amongst happy Lovers I might see
    How Showers and Sun-Beams bring [10]
    One everlasting Spring,
Nor would those fall, nor these shine forth to me;
  Nature her Self to him is lost,
  Who loseth her he honour's most.
Then Fairest to my parting view display [15]
    Your Graces all in one full day;
Whose blessed Shapes I'l snatch and keep, till when
    I do return and view agen:
So by this Art Fancy shall Fortune Cross;
And Lovers live by thinking on their loss. [20]

No Platonique Love.

Tell me no more of Minds embracing Minds,
    And hearts exchang'd for hearts;
That Spirits Spirits meet, as Winds do winds,
    And mix their subt'lest parts;
That two unbodi'd Essences may kiss, [5]
And then like Angels, twist and feel one Bliss.

I was that silly thing that once was wrought
    To Practise this thin Love;
I climb'd from Sex to Soul, from Soul to Thought;
    But thinking there to move, [10]
Headlong I rowl'd from Thought to Soul, and then
From Soul I lighted at the Sex agen.

As some strict down-look'd Men pretend to fast,
   Who yet in Closets Eat;
So Lovers who profess they Spirits taste, [15]
   Feed yet on grosser meat;
I know they boast they Soules to Souls Convey,
How e'er they meet, the Body is the Way.

Come, I will undeceive thee, they that tread
   Those vain Aëriall waies, [20]
Are like young Heyrs, and Alchymists misled
   To waste their Wealth and Daies,
For searching thus to be for ever Rich,
They only find a Med'cine for the Itch.

Love but one.

See these two little Brooks that slowly creep
   In Snaky windings through the Plains,
I knew them once one River, swift and deep,
   Blessing and blest with Poets strains.

Then touch'd by Aw, we thought some God did powr [5]
   Those flouds from out his sacred Jar,
Transforming every Weed into a Flow'r
   And every Flower into a Star.

But since it broke it self, and double glides,
   The Naked Banks no dress have worn, [10]
And yon dry barren Mountain now derides
   These Valleys which lost glories mourn.

O *Chloris*! think how this presents thy Love,
   Which when it ran but in one Streame,
We hapy Shepheards thence did thrive and prove, [15]
   And thou wast mine and all Mens Theme.

But since't hath been imparted to one more,
   And in two Streams doth weakly creep,
Our Common Muse is thence grown low, and poor,
   And mine as Lean as these my Sheep. [20]

But think withall what honour thou hast lost,
   Which we did to thy full Stream pay,
Whiles now that Swain that swears he loves thee most,
   Slakes but his Thirst, and goes away?

O in what narrow waies our Minds must move!   [25]
We may not Hate, nor yet diffuse our Love!

Absence.

Fly, O fly sad Sigh, and bear
These few Words into his Ear;
Blest where e'r thou dost remain,
Worthier of a softer chain,
Still I live, if it be true   [5]
The Turtle lives that's cleft in two:
Tears and Sorrows I have store,
But O thine do grieve me more;
Dye I would, but that I do
Fear my Fate would kill thee too.   [10]

Consideration.

Fool that I was, that little of my Span
Which I have sinn'd untill it stiles me Man,
I counted life till now, henceforth I'l say
'Twas but a drowzy lingring, or delay:
Let it forgotten perish, let none tell   [5]
That I then was, to live is to live well.
Off then thou Old Man, and give place unto
The Ancient of daies; Let him renew
Mine Age like to the Eagles, and endow
My breast with Innocence, That he whom Thou   [10]
Hast made a man of sin, and subt'ly sworn
A Vassall to thy Tyranny, may turn
Infant again, and having all of Child,
Want wit hereafter to be so beguild;
O thou that art the way, direct me still   [15]

In this long tedious Pilgrimage, and till
Thy Voice be born, Lock up my looser Tongue,
He only is best grown that's thus turn'd young.

Vpon the Translation of Chaucer's Troilus *and*
Creseide *by Sir* Francis Kinaston.

Pardon me, Sir, this injury to your Bayes,
That I, who only should admire, dare Praise.
In this great Acclamation to your Name
I adde vnto the noise, though not the Fame.
'Tis to your Happy cares wee owe, that wee [5]
Read *Chaucer* now without a Dictionary;
Whose faithfull Quill such constant light affords,
That we now read his thoughts, who read his words,
And, though we know't done in our age by you,
May doubt which is the Coppy of the two. [10]
Rome in her Language here beginnes to know
Laws yet vntry'd, proud to be fetterd so;
And, taught our Numbers now at last, is thus
Growne Brittaine yet, and owes one change to vs.
The good is common. Hee, that hitherto [15]
Was dumbe to strangers, and's owne Country too,
Speakes plainely now to all; being more our owne
Eu'n hence, in that thus made to Aliens knowne.

A Translation of Hugo Grotius's *Elegy
on* Arminius.

Arminius Searcher of Truths deepest part,
High Soaring Mind, Pattern of quick-ey'd Art;
Soul big with Learning, Taken from this Blind
And Dusky Age, where Ignorant Mankind
Doth tremble hoodwink'd with uncertain Night; [5]
Thou now enjoy'st clear Fields of blessed Light,
And whether that the Truth ows much to thee,
Or as by Nature's Lot Man cannot see

All things, in some part thou didst slip (judge they
Who have that knowing Pow'r, that holy Key) [10]
Surely a frequent Reader of that high
Mysterious book, engaged by no tye
To Man's Decrees, Heav'n knows thou gain'st from thence
A wary and a Quiet Conscience.
Full both of Rest and Joy in that blest Seat [15]
Thou find'st what here thou sought'st, and seest how great
A Cloud doth muffle Mortals, what a small,
A vain and empty nothing is that All
We here call Knowledge, puff'd with which we Men
Stalk high, oppress, and are oppress'd agen. [20]
Hence do these greater Wars of *Mars* arise,
Hence lower Hatreds, mean while Truth far flies,
And that good friend of Holy Peace disdains
To shew her self where strife and tumult raigns:
Whence is this Fury, whence this eager Lust [25]
And itch of fighting setled in us? must
Our God become the Subject of our War?
Why sides, so new, so many? hath the Tare
Of the mischievous Enemy by Night
Been scatter'd in Christ's fields? or doth the spight [30]
Of our depraved Nature, prone to rage,
Suck in all kind of Fuell, and engage
Man as a Party in Gods Cause? or ought
The Curious World whiles that it suffers nought
To lye obscure, and ransakes every Room [35]
Block'd up from Knowledge justly feel this doom?
As that proud Number when they thought to raise
Insolent Buildings, and to reach new waies,
Spread into thousand Languages, and flung
Off the old Concord of their single Tongue. [40]
Alas what's our Intent poor little Flock
Cull'd out of all the world? we bear the Stock
Of new distractions dayly, daily new,
Scoft by the Turk, not pittied by the Jew;
Happy sincere Religion, set apart [45]
As far from Common Faction, as from Art;
Which being sure all Staines are wash'd away
By Christ's large Passion, boldly here doth lay

All Hope and Faith believing that Just One
Bestoweth life, but payes Confusion; [50]
Whose practice being Love, cares not to pry
Into the secrets of a Mystery;
Not by an over-anxious Search to know
If future things do come to pass or no,
By a defined Law; how God *wills* too, [55]
Void of't himself, how not, how far our will
Is sweyed by its Mover, what strict Laws
Exercis'd on it by the highest Cause:
And happy he, who free from all By-ends,
Gapes not for filthy Lucre, nor intends [60]
The noise of Empty Armour, but rais'd high
To better Cares, minds Heaven; and doth try
To see and know the Deity only there
Where he himself discloseth; and with fear
Takes wary steps in narrow waies, led by [65]
The Clew of that good Book that cannot ly;
Who in the midst of Jars walks equall by
An even freedom mix'd with Charity:
Whose pure refined Moderation
Condemn'd of all, it self condemneth none; [70]
Who keeping Modest Limits now doth please
To speak for truth, now holds his Tongue for Peace;
These things in Publike, these in private too,
These neer thine end, thou Counsail'dst still to do,
Arminius when ev'n suffering decay [75]
Under long Cares, weary of further stay
In an unthankfull froward Age, when found
Broke in that slighter part, i'th' better sound;
Thou wert enflam'd, and wholly bent to see
Those Kingdoms unto Thousands shewn by thee; [80]
And thou a Star now added to the Seat
Of that thy Fathers Temple, dost entreat
God that he give us as much Light as is fit
Unto his Flock, and grant Content with it;
That he give Teachers, such as do not vent [85]
Their private Fancies; give a full Consent
Of Hearts, if not of Tongues, and do away
By powerfull fire all dim and base Alay

Of mixt dissentions, that *Christs*'s City be
Link'd and united in one amity; [90]
Breath all alike, and being free from strife,
To Heav'n make good their faith, to Earth their life.

Martial lib.1. Epig.67.
Ad furem de libro suo.

Th' art out, vile Plagiary, that dost think
A Poet may be made at th' rate of Ink,
And cheap-priz'd Paper; none e'r purchas'd yet
Six or ten Penniworth of Fame or Wit:
Get Verse unpublish'd, new-stamp'd Fancies look, [5]
Which th' only Father of the Virgin Book
Knows, and keeps seal'd in his close Desk within,
Not slubber'd yet by any ruffer Chin;
A Book, once known, ne'r quits the Author; If
Any lies yet impolish'd, any stiff, [10]
Wanting it's Bosses, and it's Cover, do
Get that; I've such, and can be secret too.
    He that repeats stoln Verse, and for Fame looks,
    Must purchase Silence too as well as Books.

Martial. lib.7. Epig.59.
Ad Iovem Capitolinum.

Thou Swayer of the Capitoll, whom we
Whiles *Cæsar*'s safe, believe a Deity,
Whiles thee with wishes for themselves all tire,
And to be given, what Gods can give, require,
Think me not proud O *Jove*, 'cause 'mongst the rest [5]
I only for my self make no request:
To thee I ought for *Cæsar*'s wants alone
To make my Sute, to *Cæsar* for my own.

In Pompeios Juvenes.

Europe and Asia doth th' young Pompeys hold,
He lyes, if any where, in Lybian Mould:
No wonder if in all the world they dwell;
So great a Ruine ne'r in one place fell.

Si memini fuerant.
[*Ad Aeliam.*]

Thou hadst four Teeth, good Elia, heretofore,
But one Cough spit out two, and one two more:
Now thou mayst Cough all day, and safely too;
There's nothing left for the third Cough to do.

Martial lib.10. Ep.5.
In Maledicum Poëtam.

Who e'r vile slighter of the State, in more
Vile verse, hath libell'd those he should adore,
May he quite banish'd from the Bridge and Hill
Walk through the Streets, and 'mongst hoarse Beggars still
Reserved to the last even then entreat   [5]
Those mouldy harder Crusts that Dogs won't eat.
A long and wet December, nay, what's more,
Stewes shut against him, keep him cold and poor.
May he proclame those blest, and wish he were
One of the happy Ones, upon the Beer;   [10]
And when his slow houre Comes, whiles yet alive,
May he perceive Dogs for his Carcass strive;
And moving's rags fright eager Birds away:
Nor let his single torments in death stay;
But deep Gash'd now by *Æacus* whips, anon   [15]
Task'd with the restless *Sisyphus* his stone,
Then 'mongst the old blabbers waters standing dry;

Weary all Fables, tire all Poetry,
And when a Fury bids him on truth hit,
Conscience betraying him, cry out I writ. [20]

Martial lib. 11. Ep. 19.
In Lupum.

You gave m'a Mannour, *Lupus*, but I till
A larger Mannour in my Window still.
A Mannour Call you this? where I can prôve
One Sprig of Rew doth make *Diana*'s Grove?
Which a Grashopper's wing hides? and a small [5]
Emmet in one day only eats down all?
An half-blown Rose-leaf Circles it quite round,
In which our Common Grass is no more found,
Than *Cosmus* Leaf? or unripe Pepper? where
At the full length cann't lye a Cucumber, [10]
Nor a whole Snake inhabit? I'm afraid
'Tis with one Worm, one Earewick overlaid;
The Sallow spent the Gnat yet dies, the whole
Plot without Charge is tilled by the Mole,
A Mushroome cannot open, nor Fig grow, [15]
A Violet doth find no room to blow,
A Mouse laies waste the Bounds, my Bayliff more
Doth fear him than the *Caledonian Bore*;
The Swallow in one Claw takes as she flies
The Crop entire, and in her Nest it lies; [20]
No place for half *Priapus*, though he do
Stand without Syth, and t'other weapon too;
The harvest in a Cockleshell is put,
And the whole Vintage tunn'd up in a Nut,
Truly but in one Letter, *Lupus*, thou [25]
Mistaken wert; for when thou didst bestow
This Mead confirm'd unto me by thy Seal,
I'd rather far th'hadst given me a Meal.

Horat. Carm. lib.4. Ode 13.
Audivere Lyce.

My Prayers are heard, O *Lyce*, now
They're heard; years write thee Ag'd, yet thou
    Youthfull and green in Will,
    Putt'st in for handsome still,
And shameless dost intrude among   [5]
The Sports and feastings of the young.

There, thaw'd with Wine, thy ragged throat
To *Cupid* shakes some feeble Note,
    To move unwilling fires,
    And rouze our lodg'd desires,   [10]
When he still wakes in *Chia*'s face,
Chia, that's fresh, and sings with Grace.

For he (choice God) doth, in his flight,
Skip Sapless Oaks, and will not light
    Upon thy Cheek, or Brow,   [15]
    Because deep wrinkles now,
Gray Hairs, and Teeth decayed and worn,
Present thee fowl, and fit for Scorn.

Neither thy Coan Purples lay,
Nor that thy Jewels native day   [20]
    Can make thee backwards live,
    And those lost years retrive
Which Winged Time unto our known
And Publike Annals once hath thrown.

Whither is now that Softness flown?   [25]
Whither that Blush, that Motion gone?
    Alas what now in thee
    Is left of all that She,
That She that loves did breath and deal?
That *Horace* from himself did steal?   [30]

Thou wert a while the cry'd-up Face,
Of taking Arts, and catching Grace,
   My *Cynara* being dead;
   But my fair *Cynara*'s thread
Fates broke, intending thine to draw [35]
Till thou contest with th' Aged Daw.

That those young Lovers, once thy Prey,
Thy zealous eager Servants, may
   Make thee their Common sport,
   And to thy house resort [40]
To see a Torch that proudly burn'd
Now into Colder Ashes turn'd.

On the Birth of the King's fourth Child. 1635.

To the Queene.

Now that your Princely Birth, Great Queen's so showne,
That both Yeares may well clayme it as their owne,
That by this Early Budding we must hate
Times past, and thinke the spring fell out too late,
Corrected now by You: We aemulous too [5]
Bring forth, and with more pangs perhaps then You.
Our Birth takes life, and speech at once, whom we
Have charged here to want no Dictionary:
The former tongue's as hearty and as true;
But that's Your Courts, this onely meant to You. [10]

To the Queen on the same; being the Preface before the English Verses sent then from Oxford.

Blest Lady, You, whose Mantle doth divide
The flouds of time swelling on either side,
Your Birth so clos'd the past, yet came so true
A Ciment to that yeare that did ensue,
That *Ianus* did suspect *Lucina*, least [5]

Shee might entrench, & His become Her feast;
Whiles You may challenge one Day, and we doe
Make time have now two Daughters, Truth, and You.
   You bring forth now, great Queene, as you fore-saw
An Antiquation of the Salique Law: [10]
Y'have shewne once more a Child, whose ev'ry part
May gaine unto our Realme a severall Heart,
So giv'n unto Your King, so fitly sent,
As we may iustly call't your Complement.
O for an Angell here to sing! we doe [15]
Want such a voice, nay such a Ditty too:
This Cradle too's an Altar, whiles that one
Birth-time combines the Manger, and the Throne:
The very Nurse turnes Priestesse, and we feare
Will better sing then some grave Poets here. [20]
For, now that Royall Births doe come so fast,
That we may feare They'll Commons be at last,
And yet no Plague to cease, no starre to rise,
But those two Twinne-fires onely of Her eyes;
Wits will no more compose, but iust Rehearse, [25]
And turne the Pray'r of thanks into a Verse;
Some, their owne Plagiaries, will be read
In the Elder statue with a younger Head;
Or, to beare up perhaps an yeelding fame,
New-torture old words into Chronogramme: [30]
And there may be much concurse to this quill,
For silenc'd Preachers have most Hearers still.
But what dares now be barren, when our Queene
Transcrib'd is in Her second Copy seene?
Nor is the Father left out there: we may [35]
Say those small glasses snatch him ev'ry way:
Which too doe mutually represent
Themselves, as Element doth Element;
Whiles, here, there, yonder, All in All are showne
Casting each others Beauties, and their owne. [40]
   Your Sonnes, Great Sir, may fix your Scepter here,
But 'tis this sexe must make you raigne elsewhere.
And, though they All be shafts, 'twill yet be found
These, though the weaker, make the deeper Wound.
Come shee Munition then, and thus appease [45]

All clayme, and be the Venus of your Seas:
And henceforth looke we not t' espy from farre
A Guiding light. This be your Navies starre.

The Conclusion to the Queen.

And now perhaps You'll thinke a booke more fit,
That, like your Infants Soule, shewes nothing writ.
Yet deeme not all our heart spread in this Noise;
The booke would swell, should we but print blanke Ioyes:
For we have some that only can rehearse   [5]
In Prose, whom Age, and Christmas weanes from verse:
All cannot enter these Poetique lists;
This Swath's above the Fillets of some Priests;
And You're so wholly happy, that our Wreath
Must proclaime Blessings only, not Bequeath.   [10]

To Mrs Duppa, *sent with the Picture of the
Bishop of* Chichester (*her Husband*)
in a small peece of Glass.

A Shape for Temple windows fit,
Y'have here in half a Quarrell writ,
As Temples are themselves in Spots,
And fairer Cities throng'd in Blots.
Though't fill the World as it doth run,   [5]
One drop of Light presents the Sun;
And Angels, that whole Nations guide,
Have but a point where they reside.
Such Wrongs redeem themselves, Thus we Confess
That all expressions of him must be less.   [10]

Though in those Spots the bounded Sense
Cannot deny Magnificence,
Yet reaching Minds in them may guess
Statues, and Altars, Pyles and Press;

And Fancy seeing more than Sight, [15]
   May powre that drop to flouds of Light,
   And make that point of th' Compass foot
   Round, Round into a Center shoot;
The piece may hit to you then, though't be small,
True Love doth find resemblances in all. [20]

   By Conquer'd Pencils 'tis confess'd
   His Actions only draw him best,
   Actions that, like these Colours, from
   The trying fire more beamy come.
   Yet may He still like this appear [25]
   At one Just stand: Let not the year
   Imprint his Brow as it doth run,
   Nor known when out, nor when begun;
How ere the Shade be, may the Substance long
Confirm't, if right, Confute it, if't be wrong. [30]

      I was about to say,
      Ill Omens be away,
   All Beasts that Age and Art unlucky stile
      Keep from his sight a while;
   Let no sad Bird from hollow trees dare preach, [35]
      Nor Men, that know less, teach;
      And to my Self; do you not write,
      The whole year breaks in this daies Light;
   But I am bid blame Fancy, free the thing,
   To solid Minds these Trifles no fears bring. [40]

      I was about to pray,
      The years good in this day;
   That fewer Laws were made, and more were kept,
      The Church by Church-men swept;
   No reall Innovations brought about, [45]
      To root the seeming out;
      And Justice giv'n, not forc'd by those
      Who know not what they do oppose,
   But I am taught firme Minds have firmly stood,
   And good-wils work for good unto the Good. [50]

    I was about to Chide
    The Peoples raging Tide,
And bid them cease to cry the Bishops down
    When ought did thwart the Town,
Wish 'em think Prelates Men, till we did know [55]
    How it with Saints would go;
    But I conceiv'd that pious Minds
    Drew deepest sleeps in Storms and Winds;
And could from Tempests gain as quiet Dreams
As Shepheards from the Murmur of small Streams. [60]

    And you my Lord are he
    Who can all wishes free,
Whose round and solid Mind knows to Create
    And fashion your own Fate;
Whose firmness can from Ills assure success [65]
    Where Others do but guess;
    Whose Conscience holy Calms enjoys
    'Mid'st the loud Tumults of State-Noise;
Thus gather'd in your self, you stand your own,
Nor rais'd, by giddy changes, nor cast down. [70]

    And though your Church do boast
    Such (once thought pious) Cost,
That for each Month it shews a severall door,
    You yet do open't More;
Though Windows equal Weeks, you giv't a day [75]
    More Bright, more clear than they;
    And though the Pillers which stand there
    Sum up the many hours of th' Year,
The Strength yet, and the Beauty of that frame
Lies not in them so much as in your Name. [80]

    A Name that shall in Story
    Out-shine even *Jewel*'s glory,
A Name allowed by all as soon as heard,
    At once both Lov'd and Fear'd,
A Name above all Praise, that will stand high [85]
    When Fame it self shall dye,

Whiles thus your Mind, Pen, Shape, and fit,
Times to your Vertues will submit,
And Manners unto Times, May Heaven bless thus
All Seasons unto you, and you to us. [90]

To the King, on the Birth of the Princess Anne. March 17. 1636.

Great Sir,
Successe t'your Royall selfe, and us.
Wee're happy too, in that You're happy thus.
For where a Linkt Dependance doth States blesse,
The greaters fortune doth still name the lesse.
Can we be Loosers thought, when, for a Ray [5]
Or two subtracted, wee've receiv'd a Day?
When heav'n, for those few pieces of our Ore
It tooke, sends in th' Elixar to our Store?
And (Mighty S^r) one Graine of yours cast in
Turnes all our drossy copper, and our tinne, [10]
Hatching to Gold those Mettalls, which the Sunne
It selfe despair'd, and only left begunne.
'Tis then disloyall envy to repine:
W' have lost some Bullion, but have gain'd a Mine.
   If Scepters may have eyes, (as 'tis not much [15]
Amisse to grant them eyes, whose foresight's such)
This Birth so Soveraigne, scatt'ring health each where,
May well be styl'd your Scepters balsam teare.
Witnesse that griefe your *Queene* did late endure,
Blest be that pitty, which doth weep, and cure! [20]
   Your Issue shewes you now, as in due space
Five glasses iustly distant would your face;
Where one still flowing beame illustrates all,
Though by degrees the light doth weaker fall:
And we thus seeing them shall thinke w' have 'spi'd [25]
Your Highnesse only five times multipli'd.
And this proportion'd order makes each one
Only a severall step unto your throne.
Linke thus receiving Linke, may not we men

Say that the Golden Chain's let downe agen, [30]
Which by a still succeeding growth doth guide
Unto that Chaire, where the Chain's head is ty'd?
Th' are then Your Selfe lesse copy'd. For as some
By passe, as 'twere, doe send each Vertue home
Unto the Cause, and call it That: so wee [35]
Reducing Brookes to Seas, Fruit to the Tree,
Conclude that these are You, Who, when they grow
Up to a ripnesse, will such vertues shew,
That they'll be our example, our rule too;
For they hereafter must doe still as You. [40]
Be they then so receiv'd: 'Tis others lot
To have Lawes made; Yours (Greate S^r) are begot.

To the Queen.

And something too (great *Queene*) I was about
For You: but as it stuck, and would not out
(For wee, who have not wit propitious, doe
Travell with verse, and feele our Braine-pangs too)
A nest of Cupids hov'ring in one bright [5]
Cloud, did surprize my fancy, and my sight:
This flock hedg'd in her cradle, and Shee lay
More gracious, more divine, more fresh then they.
Each view'd her eyes, and in her eyes were showne,
Darts farre more pow'rfull, though lesse then their own. [10]
    These Venus eyes (says one) these are
    Our mothers sparkes, but chaster farre:
    And Thetis Sylver feete are these,
    The Father sure is Lord o' th' seas.
    Faire one (saith this) we bring you flowrs; [15]
    The Garden one day shall be Yours:
    Wear on your Cheekes these; and when you doe
    Venture at words, you'll speake 'em too.
    That veyle that hides great Cupids eyes
    (Saith that) must swath Her as shee lyes: [20]
    For certaine 'tis, that this is shee,
    Who destind is to make Love see.
    Let's pull our wings, that we may drowne

>   Her gracefull limbs in heavn'ly downe;
>   But they so soft are, that I feare [25]
>   Feathers will make impressions there.
>   May shee with love, and awe be seene,
>   Whiles ev'ry part presents a *Queene;*
>   And thinke, when first shee sees her face,
>   Her Mother's got behind the glasse. [30]
> This said, a stately maid appear'd, whose sight
> Did put the little Archers all to flight:
> Her shape was more then humane: such I use
> To fancy the most faire, the most chast Muse.
> And now by one swift motion being neare [35]
> My side, shee gently thus did pull mine eare;
> Th' emerit ancient warbling Priests, and you
> Nothing beyond Collect, or Ballad doe:
> Dare you salute a starre without try'd fire?
> Or welcome Harmony with an harsher Quire? [40]
> Raptures are due. Great Goddesse, I leave then:
> This subject only doth befit your penne.

In the memory of the most Worthy Beniamin Iohnson.

Father of *Poets*, though *thine* owne great day
Struck from *thy selfe*, scornes that a weaker *ray*
Should twine in *lustre* with *it*: yet my *flame*,
Kindled from *thine*, flies upwards tow'rds *thy* Name.
For in the acclamation of the lesse [5]
There's *Piety*, though from *it* no accesse.
And though my ruder *thoughts* make me of those,
Who hide and cover what they should disclose:
Yet, where the *lustre's* such, he makes it seene
Better to some, that drawes the *veile* betweene. [10]
  And what can more be hop'd, since that *divine*
Free filling *spirit* tooke its flight with *thine*?
Men may have *fury*, but no *raptures* now;
Like Witches, *charme*, yet not know whence, nor how.
And through distemper, grown not strong but fierce; [15]

In stead of *writing*, onely *rave* in *verse*:
Which when by *thy Lawes* judg'd, 'twill be confes'd,
'Twas not to be *inspir'd*, but be *posses'd*.
   Where shall we find a Muse like *thine*, that can
So well present and shew *man* unto *man*, [20]
That each one finds his *twin*, and thinkes *thy Art*
Extends not to the *gestures*, but the *heart*?
Where one so shewing *life* to *life*, that we
Think *thou* taughtst *Custome*, and not *Custome* thee?
Manners, that were Themes to *thy* Scenes still *flow* [25]
In the same *streame*, and are their *comments* now:
These times thus living o're *thy* Modells, *we*
Thinke them not so much *wit*, as *prophesie:*
And though *we* know the *character*, may sweare
A *Sybill's* finger hath bin busie there. [30]
   Things *common* thou speakst *proper*, which though known
For *publique*, stampt by *thee* grow thence *thine owne*:
Thy thoughts so *order'd*, so *expres'd*, that *we*
Conclude that *thou* didst not *discourse*, but *see*
Language so *master'd*, that *thy* numerous *feet*, [35]
Laden with *genuine words*, doe alwaies meet
Each in his *art; nothing* unfit doth fall,
Shewing the *Poet*, like the *wiseman*, All:
Thine equall skill thus wresting nothing, made
Thy penne seeme not so much to *write* as *trade*. [40]
   That *life*, that *Venus* of all things, which *we*
Conceive or shew, proportion'd *decencie*,
Is not found scattred in *thee* here and there,
But, like the *soule*, is wholly every where.
No strange perplexed *maze* doth passe for *plot*, [45]
Thou always dost *unty*, not *cut* the *knot*.
Thy Lab'rinths doores are open'd by one *thread*
That tyes, and runnes through *all* that's *don* or *said*.
No *power* comes down with learned *hat* and *rod*,
Wit onely, and *contrivance* is *thy god*. [50]
   'Tis easie to guild *gold*: there's small skill spent
Where ev'n the first rude *masse* is *ornament*:
Thy Muse tooke harder *metalls*, *purg'd* and *boild*,
Labour'd and *try'd*, *heated*, and *beate* and *toyld*,
Sifted the *drosse*, fil'd *roughnes*, then gave *dresse*, [55]

Vexing rude *subjects* into *comlinesse*.
Be it *thy* glory then, that *we* may say,
Thou run'st where th'*foote* was hindred by the *way*.

   Nor dost *thou* poure out, but dispence *thy* veine,
Skill'd when to spare, and when to entertaine: [60]
Not like our *wits*, who into one piece do
Throw all that they can say, and their *friends* too,
Pumping themselves, for one Termes *noise* so *dry*,
As if they made their *wills* in Poetry.
And such spruce *compositions* presse the *stage*,   [65]
When men transcribe *themselves*, and not the *age*.
Both sorts of Playes are thus like *pictures* showne,
Thine of the common *life*, theirs of their *owne*.

   Thy modells yet are not so fram'd, as we
May call them *libells*, and not *imag'rie*:   [70]
No name on any Basis; 'tis *thy* skill
To strike the *vice*, but spare the *person* still:
As he, who when he saw the Serpent wreath'd
About his sleeping sonne, and as he breath'd,
Drinke in his *soule*, did so the shoot contrive,   [75]
To kill the beast, but keepe the *child* alive.
So dost *thou* aime *thy darts*, which, ev'n when
They kill the *poisons*, do but wake the *men*.
Thy thunders thus but *purge*, and we endure
Thy launcings better then anothers *cure*;   [80]
And justly too: for th' *age* growes more unsound
From the *fooles balsam*, then the *wisemans wound*.

   No rotten talke brokes for a laugh; no *page*
Commenc'd man by th'instructions of *thy stage*;
No bargaining line there; no provoc'tive *verse*;   [85]
Nothing but what *Lucretia* might rehearse;
No need to make *good* count'nance *ill*, and use
The plea of *strict life* for a *looser Muse*:
No Woman rul'd *thy quill*: we can descry
No *verse* borne under any *Cynthia's* eye: [90]
Thy Starre was *judgement* onely, and right *sense*,
Thy selfe being to *thy selfe* an *influence*.
Stout *beauty* is *thy grace*: Sterne *pleasures* do
Present *delights*, but mingle *horrours* too:
Thy Muse doth thus like *Joves* fierce girle appeare,   [95]

With a faire *hand*, but grasping of a Speare.
  Where are they now that cry, *thy* Lamp did drinke
More *oyle* then th'Authour *wine*, while he did thinke?
We do imbrace their slaunder: *thou* hast *writ*
Not for *dispatch* but *fame*; no *market wit*: [100]
'Twas not *thy* care, that it might *passe* and *sell*;
But that it might endure, and be done *well*:
Nor would'st *thou* venture it unto the *eare*,
Untill the *file* would not make *smooth*, but *weare*:
Thy verse came season'd hence, and would not give; [105]
Borne not to feed the Authour, but to *live*:
Whence 'mong the choycer Judges rise a strife,
To make *thee* read as Classick in *thy life*.
Those that doe hence applause, and suffrage begge,
'Cause they can Poems forme upon one legge, [110]
Write not to *time*, but to the *Poets* day:
There's difference between *fame*, and sodaine *pay*.
These men sing Kingdomes falls, as if that fate
Us'd the same force t'a Village, and a State:
These serve *Thyestes* bloody supper in, [115]
As if it had onely a *sallad* bin:
Their Catilines are but Fencers, whose *fights* rise
Not to the fame of *battell*, but of *prize*.
But *thou* still put'st true passions on; dost *write*
With the same courage that try'd Captaines fight; [120]
Giv'st the right blush and colour unto things;
Low without *creeping*, *high* without losse of *wings*;
Smooth, yet not *weake*, and by a thorough-care,
Bigge without *swelling*, without *painting faire*:
They wretches, while they cannot stand to fit, [125]
Are not *wits*, but materialls of *wit*.
What though *thy* searching *wit* did rake the *dust*
Of *time*, and purge old *mettalls* of their *rust*?
Is it no *labour*, no *art*, thinke they, to
Snatch Shipwracks from the *deepe*, as *Dyvers* do? [130]
And rescue Jewells from the covetous *sand*,
Making the Seas hid wealth adorne the Land?
What though *thy* culling Muse did rob the store
Of Greeke, and Latine gardens to bring ore
Plants to *thy* native soyle? Their vertues were [135]

Improv'd farre more, by being planted here.
If *thy Still* to their *essence* doth refine
So many *drugges*, is not the *water thine*?
Thefts thus become just *works*: they and their *grace*
Are wholly *thine*: thus doth the *stampe* and *face* [140]
Make that the Kings, that's ravisht from the *mine*:
In others then 'tis *oare*, in *thee* 'tis *coine*.
   Blest life of Authours, unto whom we owe
Those that we have, and those that we want too:
Th'art all so *good*, that reading makes *thee worse*, [145]
And to have *writ* so well's *thine* onely curse.
Secure then of *thy* merit, thou didst hate
That servile base dependance upon *fate*:
Successe thou ne'r thoughtst *vertue*, nor that fit,
Which *chance*, and th'*ages* fashion did make hit; [150]
Excluding those from *life* in *after-time*,
Who into Po'try first brought *luck* and *rime*:
Who thought the peoples breath good ayre: sty'ld name
What was but *noise*; and getting Briefes for *fame*
Gathered the many's *suffrages*, and thence [155]
Made *commendation* a *benevolence*:
Thy thoughts were their owne Lawrell, and did win
That best applause of being crown'd within.
   And though th'exacting *age*, when deeper yeeres
Had interwoven *snow* among *thy haires*, [160]
Would not permit *thou* shouldst grow *old*, cause they
Nere by *thy* writings knew thee *young*; we may
Say justly, they're ungratefull, when they more
Condemn'd *thee*, cause *thou* wert so *good* before:
Thine Art was *thine Arts* blurre, and they'll confesse [165]
Thy strong *perfumes* made them not smell *thy* lesse.
But, though to *erre* with *thee* be no small skill,
And we adore the last *draughts* of *thy* Quill:
Though those *thy* thoughts, which the now queasie *age*,
Doth count but *clods*, and refuse of the *stage*, [170]
Will come up *Porcelaine-wit* some hundreds hence,
When there will be more *manners*, and more *sense*;
'Twas judgement yet to yeeld, and we afford
Thy silence as much *fame*, as once *thy* word:
Who like an aged *oake*, the *leaves* being gone, [175]

Wast *food* before, art now *religion*;
Thought still more *rich*, though not so richly *stor'd*,
View'd and *enjoy'd* before, but now *ador'd*.
    Great *soule* of *numbers*, whom we want and boast;
Like curing *gold*, most valu'd now *th*'art lost; [180]
When we shall feed on *refuse offalls*, when
We shall from *corne* to *akornes* turne agen;
Then shall we see that these two *names* are one,
JOHNSON and *Poetry*, which now are gone.

To My Honovr'd Friend Mr Thomas Killigrew, On these his Playes, the *PRISONERS* and *CLARACILLA*.

Worthy Sir,
    Manners, and Men, transcrib'd, Customes express'd,
The Rules, and Lawes Dramatique not transgress'd;
The Points of Place, and Time, observ'd, and hit;
The Words to Things, and Things to Persons fit;
The Persons constant to Themselves throughout; [5]
The Machin turning free, not forc'd about;
As Wheeles by Wheeles, part mov'd, and urg'd by part;
And choyce Materials workt with choycer Art;
Those, though at last begg'd from long sweate & toyle,
Fruits of the Forge, the Anvil, and the File, [10]
Snatch reverence from our Iudgements; and we doe
Admire those Raptures with new Raptures too.
    But you, whose thoughts are Extasies; who know
No other Mold, but that you'le cast it so;
Who in an even web rich fancies twist, [15]
Your selfe th' *Apollo*, to your selfe the Priest;
Whose first unvext conceptions do come forth,
Like Flowers with Kings Names, stampt with Native worth;
By Art unpurchas'd make the same things thought
Far greater when begot, than when they're Taught. [20]
So the Ingenuous fountaine clearer flowes
And yet no food besides its owne spring knowes.

Others great gathering wits there are who like
Rude Scholers, steale this posture from *Van Dike*,
That Hand, or eye from *Titian*, and doe than [25]
Draw that a blemish was design'd a Man;
(As that which goes-in Spoyle and Theft, we see
For th' most part comes out Impropriety)
But here no small stolne parcells slily lurke,
Nor are your Tablets such Mosaique worke, [30]
The web, and woofe are both your owne, the peece
One, and no sayling for the Art, or fleece,
All's from your Selfe, unchalleng'd All, All so,
That breathing Spices doe not freer flow.
No Thrifty spare, or Manage of dispence, [35]
But things hurld out with Gracefull Negligence,
A Generous Carriage of unwrested Wit;
Expressions, like your Manners freely fit:
No Lines, that wracke the Reader with such guesse,
That some interpret Oracles with lesse. [40]
Your Writings are all Christall, such as doe
Please Critickes palates without Critickes too:
You have not what diverts some Men from sense,
Those two Mysterious things, Greeke and Pretence:
And happily you want those shadowes, where [45]
Their Absence makes your Graces seeme more cleare.
   Nor are you he, whose vow weares out a Quill
In writing to the Stage, and then sits still;
Or, as the Elephant breeds, (once in ten yeares,
And those ten yeares but once) with labour beares [50]
A saecular play. But you goe on and show
Your veine is Rich, and full, and can still flow;
That this doth open, not exhaust your store,
And you can give yet two, and yet two more,
Those great eruptions of your beames do say, [55]
When others Sunnes are set, you'le have a Day.
And if Mens approbations be not Lot,
And my prophetique Bayes seduce me not;
Whiles he, who straines for swelling scenes, lyes dead
Or onely prays'd, you shall live prays'd, and read. [60]
    Thus, trusting to your selfe, you Raigne; and doe
    Prescribe to others, because none to you.

Vpon the Dramatick Poems of Mr John Fletcher.

Though when all *Fletcher* writ, and the entire
Man was indulged unto that sacred fire,
His thoughts, and his thoughts dresse, appear'd both such,
That 'twas his happy fault to do too much;
Who therefore wisely did submit each birth [5]
To knowing *Beaumont* e're it did come forth,
Working againe untill he said 'twas fit,
And made him the sobriety of his wit;
Though thus he call'd his Judge into his fame,
And for that aid allow'd him halfe the name, [10]
'Tis knowne, that sometimes he did stand alone,
That both the Spunge and Pencill were his owne;
That himselfe judg'd himselfe, could singly do,
And was at last *Beaumont* and *Fletcher* too;
   Else we had lost his *Shepherdesse*, a piece [15]
Even and smooth, spun from a finer fleece,
Where softnesse raignes, where passions passions greet,
Gentle and high, as floods of Balsam meet.
Where dress'd in white expressions, sit bright Loves,
Drawne, like their fairest Queen, by milkie Doves; [20]
A piece, which *Johnson* in a rapture bid
Come up a glorifi'd Worke, and so it did.
   Else had his Muse set with his friend; the Stage
Had miss'd those Poems, which yet take the Age;
The world had lost those rich exemplars, where [25]
Art, Language, Wit, sit ruling in one Spheare,
Where the fresh matters soare above old Theames,
As Prophets Raptures do above our Dreames;
Where in a worthy scorne he dares refuse
All other Gods, and makes the thing his Muse; [30]
Where he calls passions up, and layes them so,
As spirits, aw'd by him to come and go;
Where the free Author did what e're he would,
And nothing will'd, but what a Poet should.
   No vast uncivill bulke swells any Scene, [35]
The strength's ingenious, and the vigour cleane;

None can prevent the Fancy, and see through
At the first opening; all stand wondring how
The thing will be untill it is; which thence
With fresh delight still cheats, still takes the sence; [40]
The whole designe, the shadowes, the lights such
That none can say he shewes or hides too much:
Businesse growes up, ripened by just encrease,
And by as just degrees againe doth cease,
The heats and minutes of affaires are watcht, [45]
And the nice points of time are met, and snatcht:
Nought later then it should, nought comes before,
Chymists, and Calculators doe erre more:
Sex, age, degree, affections, country, place,
The inward substance, and the outward face; [50]
All kept precisely, all exactly fit,
What he would write, he was before he writ.
'Twixt *Johnsons* grave, and *Shakespeares* lighter sound
His muse so steer'd that something still was found,
Nor this, nor that, nor both, but so his owne, [55]
That 'twas his marke, and he was by it knowne.
Hence did he take true judgements, hence did strike
All pallates some way, though not all alike:
The god of numbers might his numbers crowne,
And listning to them wish they were his owne. [60]
    Thus welcome forth, what ease, or wine, or wit
    Durst yet produce, that is, what *Fletcher* writ.

Another on the same.

Fletcher, though some call it thy fault, that wit
So overflow'd thy scenes, that ere 'twas fit
To come upon the Stage, *Beaumont* was faine
To bid thee be more dull, that's write againe,
And bate some of thy fire, which from thee came [5]
In a cleare, bright, full, but too large a flame;
And after all (finding thy Genius such)
That blunted, and allayed, 'twas yet too much;
Added his sober spunge, and did contract
Thy plenty to lesse wit to make't exact: [10]

Yet we through his corrections could see
Much treasure in thy superfluity,
Which was so fil'd away, as when we doe
Cut Jewels, that that's lost is jewell too:
Or as men use to wash Gold, which we know [15]
By losing makes the streame thence wealthy grow.
They who doe on thy workes severely sit,
And call thy store the over-births of wit,
Say thy miscarriages were rare, and when
Thou wert superfluous, that thy fruitfull Pen [20]
Had no fault but abundance, which did lay
Out in one Scene what might well serve a Play;
And hence doe grant, that what they call excesse
Was to be reckon'd as thy happinesse,
From whom wit issued in a full spring-tide; [25]
Much did inrich the Stage, much flow'd beside.
For that thou couldst thine owne free fancy binde
In stricter numbers, and run so confin'd
As to observe the rules of Art, which sway
In the contrivance of a true borne Play: [30]
These workes proclaime which thou didst write retired
From *Beaumont*, by none but thy selfe inspired;
Where we see 'twas not chance that made them hit,
Nor were thy Playes the Lotteries of wit,
But like to *Durers* Pencill, which first knew [35]
The lawes of faces, and then faces drew:
Thou knowst the aire, the colour, and the place,
The simetry, which gives a Poem grace:
Parts are so fitted unto parts, as doe
Shew thou hadst wit, and Mathematicks too: [40]
Knewst where by line to spare, where to dispence,
And didst beget just Comedies from thence:
Things unto which thou didst such life bequeath,
That they (their owne Black-Friers) unacted breath.
Johnson hath writ things lasting, and divine, [45]
Yet his Love-Scenes, *Fletcher*, compar'd to thine,
Are cold and frosty, and exprest love so,
As heat with Ice, or warme fires mixt with Snow;
Thou, as if struck with the same generous darts,
Which burne, and raigne in noble Lovers hearts, [50]
Hast cloath'd affections in such native tires,

And so describ'd them in their owne true fires;
Such moving sighes, such undissembled teares,
Such charmes of language, such hopes mixt with feares,
Such grants after denialls, such pursuits [55]
After despaire, such amorous recruits,
That some who sate spectators have confest
Themselves transform'd to what they saw exprest,
And felt such shafts steale through their captiv'd sence,
As made them rise Parts, and goe Lovers thence. [60]
Nor was thy stile wholly compos'd of Groves,
Or the soft straines of Shepheards and their Loves;
When thou wouldst Comick be, each smiling birth
In that kinde, came into the world all mirth,
All point, all edge, all sharpnesse; we did sit [65]
Sometimes five Acts out in pure sprightfull wit,
Which flow'd in such true salt, that we did doubt
In which Scene we laught most two shillings out.
Shakespeare to thee was dull, whose best jest lyes
I'th Ladies questions, and the Fooles replyes; [70]
Old fashion'd wit, which walkt from town to town
In turn'd Hose, which our fathers call'd the Clown;
Whose wit our nice times would obsceannesse call,
And which made Bawdry passe for Comicall:
Nature was all his Art, thy veine was free [75]
As his, but without his scurility;
From whom mirth came unforc'd, no jest perplext,
But without labour cleane, chast, and unvext.
Thou wert not like some, our small Poets who
Could not be Poets, were not we Poets too; [80]
Whose wit is pilfring, and whose veine and wealth
In Poetry lyes meerely in their stealth;
Nor didst thou feele their drought, their pangs, their qualmes,
Their rack in writing, who doe write for almes,
Whose wretched Genius, and dependent fires, [85]
But to their Benefactors dole aspires.
Nor hadst thou the sly trick, thy selfe to praise
Vnder thy friends names, or to purchase Bayes
Didst write stale commendations to thy Booke,
Which we for *Beaumonts* or *Ben. Johnsons* tooke: [90]
That debt thou left'st to us, which none but he
Can truly pay, *Fletcher*, who writes like thee.

To the Right Reverend Father in God, Brian, *Lord Bishop of* Chichester, *Tutor to the Prince His Highness, my most gracious Patron,*

Many, and happy daies.

Syringus, Ergastus.

Syring.	Whether so fast *Ergastus*! say	
	Doth *Nysa*, or *Myrtilla* stay,	
	To meet thee now at Break of day?	
Ergast.	With Love, *Syringus*, I have done,	
	'Tis duty now that makes me run,	[5]
	To prevent the rising Sun.	
Syring.	What Star hath chill'd thy flames?	
	What Cross hath made thy fires take others names?	
Ergast.	Didst thou not last night hear	
	The *Dirge* we sung to the departed year?	[10]
	'Tis the daies early Prime	
	That gives new Feet, and Wings to Aged Time,	
	And I run to provide	
	Some Rurall present to design the Tide:	
Syring.	But to whom this Pious fear?	[15]
	To whom this opening of the year?	
Ergast.	To him, that by *Thames* flowry side,	
	Three Kingdoms Eldest Hopes doth guide,	
	Who his soft Mind and Manners Twines,	
	Gently, as we do tender Vines.	[20]
	'Tis he that sings to him the Course	
	Of Light, and of the Suns great force,	
	How his Beams meet, and joyn with Showers,	
	To awake the sleeping Flowers;	
	Where Hail, and Snow have each their Treasures;	[25]
	How wandring Stars tread equall Measures,	
	Ordered as ours upon the Plain,	
	And how sad Clouds drop down in Rain;	
	He tels from whence the Loud Wind blows,	
	And how the Bow of Wonder shews	[30]

            Colours mixt, as in a Loome,
            And where doth hang the Thunder's Womb;
            How Nature then Cloaths Fields and Woods,
            Heaps the high Hills, and powrs out Flouds;
            And from thence doth make him run,   [35]
            To what his Ancesters have done,
            Then gives some Lesson, which doth say,
            What 'tis to shear, and what to Flea,
            And shews at last, in holy Song,
            What to the Temple doth belong;   [40]
            What Offering suits with every Feast,
            And how the Altar's to be drest.

Syring.   Now Violets prop his Head,
              And soft Flowers make his Bed,
            These Blessings he for us prepares,   [45]
            The Joyes of Harvest Crown his Cares.

Ergast.   He labours that we may
              Not cast our Pipes away;
            That Swords to Plowsheares may be turn'd,
            And neither folds, nor Sheep-coats burn'd;   [50]
              That no rude Barbarous Hands
              May reap our well grown Lands,
            And that, sweet Liberty being barr'd,
            We not our Selves become the Heard;
              Heaven bless him, and his Books,   [55]
              'Tis he must gild our Hooks,
            And for his Charg's Birth-sake, *May*
            Shall be to me one Holy day.

Syring.   Come, I'l along with thee, and joyn,
              Some hasty Gift to thine;   [60]
            But we do Pearls, and Amber want,
              And pretious Stones are scant.
            And how then shall we enter, where
              Wealth Ushers in the year?

Ergast.   The Berries of the Misseltoe,   [65]
              To him will Orient shew;
            And the Bee's Bag as Amber come
              From the deep Oceans Womb;
            And Stones which murmuring Waters Chide,
              Stopt by them as they glide,   [70]

	If giv'n to him, will pretious grow;	
	Touch him, they must be so.	
Syring.	I know a Stream, that to the Sight	
	Betraies smooth Pebbles, Black, and White;	
	These I'l present, with which he may	[75]
	Design each Cross and Happy day.	
Ergast.	None, none at all of Blacker hue,	
	Only the White to him are due,	
	For Heaven, among the Reverend store	
	Of Learned Men, Loves no one more.	[80]
Syring.	Two days ago	
	My deep-fleec'd Ewe, should have her Lamb let fall,	
	Which if't be so,	
	I mean to offer't to him Dam and all;	
	And humbly say	[85]
	I bring a Gift as tender as the Day.	
Ergast.	Name not a Gift,	
	Who e'r bestows, he still returns him more;	
	That's but our Thrift	
	When he receives, he adds unto our store:	[90]
	Let's Altars trim,	
	Wishes are Lambs, and Kids, and Flocks to him.	
Syring.	Let's then the Sun arrest,	
	And so prolong our duties Feast,	
	Time will stay till he be blest.	[95]
Ergast.	Wish thou to his *Charge*, and then	
	I'l wish t' himself, and both agen,	
	Holy things to holy Men.	
Syring.	The unvext Earth Flowers to him bring,	
	And make the year but one great Spring;	[100]
	Let Nature stand, and serve, and wooe,	
	And make him Prince of Seasons too.	
Ergast.	And his learn'd Guide, no difference know,	
	But find it one, to Reap, and Sow;	
	Be Harvest all, and he appear	[105]
	As soon i'th' Soul, as in the Ear.	
Syring.	When his high *Charge* shall rule the State	
	(Which Heaven saies shall be, but late)	
	Let him no Thorns in Manners find,	
	And in the Many but one Mind;	[110]

	And Plenty pay him so much bliss,	
	That's Brothers Sheafs bow all to his.	
Ergast.	And he that fits him for that Seat,	
	May he Figs from *Thistles eat;	*Scotland.
	Like Ears of Corn let Men obey,	[115]
	And when he Breaths, bend all one way;	
	And if that any dare Contest,	
	Let his Rod still devour the rest.	
Syring.	Let Rams Change Colour, and behold	
	Their Fleeces Purple dy'd, or Gold:	[120]
	For this the holy Augur sayes,	
	Bodes unto Kingdoms happy daies.	
Ergast.	And his blest Guide like Fortune win,	
	And die his Flock too, but within;	
	And, where of Scarlet they be full,	[125]
	Wash he their Souls as white as Wooll.	
Syring.	Let his Great Scepter discords part,	
	As once the Staff made Flouds forbear,	
	And let him by diviner Art,	
	Those Tempests into Bulwarks rear;	[130]
	As he who lead Men through the deep,	
	As Shepheards use to Lead their Sheep.	
Ergast.	And his Rod sign the easie Flocks,	
	By being plac'd but in their Sight,	
	That all their young Ones shew their Locks	[135]
	Ringstreak'd, Speck'd and mark'd with White;	
	As that learn'd Man, who Hazell pill'd,	
	And so by Art his own Flock fill'd.	
Syring.	May his Rich Fleece drink Dew, and Lye	
	Well drench'd, though all the Earth be dry.	[140]
Ergast.	May his Rod bud, and Almonds shew,	
	Though all the rest do Barren grow.	
Syring.	May he not have a Subject look,	
	To please with murmuring, as the Brook,	
	And let the Serpent of the year	[145]
	Not dare to fix his sharp Teeth here.	
Ergast.	May his Guide pull them out, and so	
	Sow them that they never grow,	
	Or if in furrows Arm'd they spring,	
	Death to themselves their Weapons bring.	[150]

Syring. May he more Lawrels bring to us,
        Than he that set the Calender thus,
        New deeds of Glory will appear,
        And make his Deeds round as the Year.
Ergast. And may his Blessed Guide out-live [155]
        Years, and himself a new Thread give;
        And so his days still fresh transmit,
        Doing as time, and Conquering it.
Syring. May Vintage Joys swell both their Bowrs,
Ergast. And if they O'rflow, O'rflow on Ours. [160]
Syring. O would that We, that we, such Prophets were,
        As he that slew the Lyon and the Bear.
Ergast. Credit thy self, our Wishes must prove true,
        Far meaner Shepheards have ben Prophets too.

                The most faithfull Honourer of
                Your Lordships Vertues W.C.

A New-years Gift.

Although Propriety be Crost,
    By those that cry't up most,
No Vote hath yet pass'd to put down
      The pious fires
      Of good desires, [5]
Our wishes are as yet our own.

Bless'd be the day then, 'tis *New year's*,
    Nature knows no such fears
As those which do our hearts divide,
      In spight of Force [10]
      Times keep their Course,
The Seasons run not on their side.

I send (my Muse) to one that knows
    What each Relation ows,
One who keeps waking in his Breast [15]
      No other sense
      But Conscience,
That only is his Interest.

Though to be Moderate, in this time,
   Be thought almost a Crime, [20]
That vertue yet is his so much,
     That they who make
     All whom they take
Guilty, durst never Call him such.

He wishes Peace, that Publike Good, [25]
   Dry Peace, not bought with Bloud,
Yet such as Honour may maintain,
     And such the Crown
     Would gladly own.
Wish o'r that Wish to him again. [30]

He wishes that this Storm Subside,
   Hush'd by a turn of Tide,
That one fix'd Calm would smooth the Main,
     As Winds relent
     When Furie's spent. [35]
O wish that Wish to him again.

The Joys that Solemn Victories Crown,
   When we not slay our own,
Joys that deserve a generall Song
     When the day's gain'd [40]
     And no Sword stain'd,
Press on and round him in a Throng.

Thoughts rescue, and his danger kiss'd,
   Being found as soon as miss'd,
Wish him not taken as before, [45]
     Hazard can ne'r
     Make him more dear.
We must not fear so long once more.

Twist then in one most Glorious Wreath
   All Joys you can bequeath, [50]
And see them on the Kingdom thrown,
     When there they dwell
     He's pleas'd as well,
As if they sate on him alone.

    Go, and return, and for his sake   [55]
        Less noise and Tumult make,
    Than Stars when they do run their Rounds;
        Though Swords and Spears
          Late fill'd his Eares,
    He silence Loves, or Gentle Sounds.   [60]

A New-years-gift to Brian *Lord Bishop of* Sarum,
upon the Author's entring into holy Orders, 1638.

Now that the Village-Reverence doth lye hid,
    As *Ægypt*'s Wisdom did,
In Birds, and Beasts, and that the Tenants Soul,
    Goes with his New-year's fowl:
  So that the Cock, and Hen, speak more   [5]
  Now, than in Fables heretofore;
    And that the feather'd Things,
    Truly make Love have Wings;
Though we no flying Present have to pay,
A Quill yet snatch'd from thence may sign the Day. [10]

But being the Canon bars me Wit and Wine,
    Enjoyning the true Vine,
Being the Bayes must yeeld unto the Cross,
    And all be now one Loss,
  So that my Raptures are to steal   [15]
  And knit themselves in one pure Zeal,
    And that my each days breath
    Must be a dayly Death;
Without all Strain or Fury, I must than
Tell you this New-year brings you a new man.   [20]

New, not as th' year, to run the same Course o'r
    Which it hath run before,
Lest in the Man himself there be a Round,
    As in his Humor's found,
  And that return seem to make good   [25]
  Circling of Actions, as of Bloud;

      Motion as in a Mill
        Is busie standing still;
And by such wheeling we but thus prevaile,
To make the Serpent swallow his own Taile. [30]

Nor new by solemnizing looser Toyes,
        And erring with less Noyse,
Taking the Flag and Trumpet from the Sin,
        So to offend within:
    As some Men silence loud Perfumes, [35]
    And draw them into shorter Rooms,
        This will be understood
        More wary, not more Good.
Sins too may be severe, and so no doubt
The Vice but only sowr'd, not rooted out. [40]

But new, by th' Using of each part aright,
        Changing both Step and Sight,
That false Direction come not from the Eye,
        Nor the foot tread awry,
    That neither that the way aver, [45]
    Which doth tow'rd Fame, or Profit err,
        Nor this tread that Path, which
        Is not the right, but Rich;
That thus the Foot being fixt, thus lead the Eye,
I pitch my Walk low, but my Prospect high. [50]

New too, to teach my Opinions not t' submit
        To Favour, or to Wit;
Nor yet to Walk on Edges, where they may
        Run safe in Broader way;
    Nor to search out for New Paths, where [55]
    Nor Tracks nor Footsteps doth appear,
        Knowing that Deeps are waies,
        Where no Impression staies,
Nor servile thus, nor curious, may I then
Approve my Faith to Heaven, my Life to Men. [60]

But I who thus present my self as New,
        Am thus made New by You:

    Had not your Rayes dwelt on me, One long Night
        Had shut me up from Sight;
    Your Beams exhale me from among [65]
    Things tumbling in the Common Throng,
        Who thus with your fire burns
        Now gives not, but Returns;
    To Others then be this a day of Thrift
    They do receive, but you Sir make the Gift. [70]

To the Queen after her dangerous Delivery. 1638.

Great Madam,
   Though we could wish Your Issue so throng'd stood,
That all the Court were but one Royall Blood;
Though Your Young Iewels be of so much Cost,
That Your Least Spark of Light must not be lost:
Yet when t'Your Burthens Heaven not permits [5]
Quiets, as husht, as when the Halcyon sits;
And that Y'are thought so stor'd, that You may spare
Some Glories, and allow Blest Saints a share;
Contentedly we suffer such a Crosse,
T'endeare the Tablet by a Copies losse: [10]
And (as in urgent Tempests 'tis a Taught
Thrift, to redeeme the Vessell with the Fraught)
Wo doe halfe-willing with th' Elixir part
To keep th' Alembeck safe for future Art:
Our Treasure thus is shared by the Birth, [15]
Halfe unto Heaven, Halfe unto the Earth.
   Come Your Escape as Issue then, whiles we
Receive Your Safety as New Progeny:
Be You from henceforth to us a New Vow,
By Vertues Deare Before, by Danger Now. [20]
Twice giv'n, and yet no narrownesse of Thrift;
What ere is Great, may be a Second Guift:
Thus when the Best Act's done, there doth remaine
This only, to performe that Act againe.
   See how Your Great Iust Consort bears the Crosse! [25]
Your Safeties Gaine makes him oresee the Losse:
So that, although this Cloud stand at the Doore,

His Great Designes goe on still as before.
Thus stout Horatius being ready now   *Liv. Decad.*
To Dedicate a Temple, and by Vow   *1.lib.2.*   [30]
Settle Religion to his God, although
'Twas told his Child was dead, would not let goe
The Post o'th' Temple, but unmov'd Alone
Bid them take care o'th' funerall, and went on.

On the Death of the Right Honourable the Lord Viscount Bayning.

So when an hasty vigour doth disclose
An early flame in the more forward Rose,
That Rarenesse doth destroy it: Wonders owe
This to themselves still, that they cannot grow.
Such Ripenesse was His Fate: Thus to appear   [5]
At first, was not hereafter to stay here.
Who thither first steps, whither others tend,
When He sets forth is at the Iourney's end.
   But as Short things most vigour have, and we
Find Force the Recompence of Brevity;   [10]
So was it here: Compactednesse gave Strength,
The Life was Close, though not spun out at Length.
Nothing lay idle in't: Experience Rules,
Men strengthn'd Books, & Cities season'd Schools.
   Nor did he issue forth to come Home thence   [15]
(As some) lesse Man, then they goe out from hence:
Who think new Ayre new Vices may create,
And stamp Sinne Lawful in Another State;
Who make Exotick Customes Native Arts,
And Loose Italian Vices English Parts: [20]
He naturaliz'd Perfections only; gain'd
A round and solid mind, severely train'd,
And manag'd his desires; brought oft checkt Sense
Unto the sway of Reason, comming thence
His owne acquaintance, morgag'd unto none,   [25]
But was himselfe His owne possession.
Thus starres by journying still, gaine, and dispense,

Drawing at once, and shedding influence:
Thus Spheares by Regular Motion doe encrease
Their Tunes, and bring their Discords into Peace. [30]
    Hence knew He his owne value, ne're put forth
Honour for Merit; Pow'r instead of Worth:
Nor, when He poyz'd himselfe, would He prevaile
By Wealth, and make his Mannors turne the scale.
Desert was only ballanc'd; nor could we [35]
Say my Lord's Rents were only Weight, not He:
Only one slight he had; from being Small
Unto himselfe, He came Great unto all:
But Great by no mans Ruine: For who will
Say that his Seat e're made the next Seate ill? [40]
No Neighb'ring-village was unpeopled here
'Cause it durst bound a Noble Eye too neere.
Who could e're say my Lord, and the next Marsh
Made frequent Herriots? or that any harsh
Oppressive usage made Young Lives soone fall? [45]
Or who could His seven thousand bad Ayre call?
He blessings shed: Men knew not to whom more,
The Sun, or Him, they might impute their store.
No rude exaction, or licentious times
Made his Revenewes Others, or His Crimes: [50]
Nor are his Legacies poore-mens present teares,
Or doe they for the future raise their feares.
No such contrivance here as to professe
Bounty, and with Large Miseries feed the Lesse;
Fat some with their owne almes; bestow, and pill; [55]
And Common Hungers with Great Famines fill,
Making an Hundred Wretches endow Tenne,
Taking the Field, and giving a Sheafe then:
As Robbers, whom they spoile, perhaps will lend
Small summes to helpe them to their journey's end. [60]
All was untainted here, and th'Author such,
That every gift from Him grew twice as much.
    We, who erewhile did boast his presence, doe
Now boast a second grace, his bounty too;
Bounty, was judgment here; for he bestowes [65]
Not who disperseth, but who gives and knowes.
And what more wise designe, then to renew,

And dresse the brest, from which he knowledge drew!
Thus pious men, ere their departure, first
Would crown the fountain which had quencht their thirst. [70]
Hence strive we all his memory to engrosse,
Our Common Love before, but now Our Losse.

A New-years-gift to a Noble Lord. 1640.

My Lord,
Though the distemp'red Many cry they see
   The *Missall* in our Liturgie:
The Almanack that is before it set
   Goes true, and is not Popish yet.
     Whiles therefore none indites [5]
      This feast of Roman Rites,
   Whiles as yet *New-year* in Red Paint,
   Is not cry'd out on for a Saint;
Presents will be no Offrings, and I may
Season my duty safely with the day. [10]

Now an Impartiall Court, deaf to Pretence,
   Sits like the Kingdoms Conscience,
While Actions now are touch'd, and Men are try'd,
   Whether they can the day abide,
     Though they should go about [15]
      To track Offences out,
   In Deeds, in Thoughts, Without, Within,
   As Casuists, when they search out Sin;
When Others shake, how safe do you appear,
And a Just Patriot know no private fear? [20]

This you have gain'd from an unbiass'd Breast,
   Discharg'd of all Self Interest;
From Square, and solid Actions without flaw,
   That will in time themselves grow Law,
     Actions that shew you mean [25]
      Nought to the Common Scene,
   That you'l ne'r lengthen power by Lust,
   But shape and size it by your Trust,

That you do make the Church the Main, no Bye,
And chiefly mean what Others but Apply. [30]

Were every Light thus Regular as you,
   And to it's destin'd Motions true,
Did some not shine too short, but reach about,
   And throw their wholsome Lustre out,
     What danger then or fear, [35]
     Would seize this Sacred Sphere?
   Who would impute that Thriving Art
   That turns a Charge into a Mart?
We would enjoy, like you, a State Confess'd
Happy by all, still Blessing, and still Bless'd. [40]

But whether false suspicion, or true Crimes
   Provoke the Sowreness of the Times;
Whether't be Pride, or Glory call'd Pride, all
   Expect at least some sudden fall;
     And seeing as Vices, so [45]
     Their Cures may too far go,
   And Want of Moderation be
   Both in the Ill, and Remedy,
So that perhaps to bar th' Abuse of Wine,
Their Zeal may lead them to cut up the Vine. [50]

Pray'rs are Our Arms; and the time affords
   On a Good Day be said Good Words;
Could I shape Things to Votes, I'd wish a Calm,
   Soveraign and soft, as Flouds of Balm;
     But as it is, I square [55]
     The Vote to the Affair,
   And wish this Storm may shake the Vine,
   Only to make it faster twine;
That hence the Early Type may be made Good,
And our Ark too, rise higher with the Floud. [60]

As then Sick Manners call forth wholsome Laws,
   The Good effect of a bad Cause,
So all I wish must settle in this Sum,
   That more Strength from Laxations come.

, But how can this appear [65]
   To humor the New year?
When proper Wishes, fitly meant,
   Should breath his Good to whom they're sent.
Y'have a large Mind (my Lord) and that assures,
To wish the Publike Good, is to wish Yours. [70]

Vpon the Birth of the Kings sixth Child. 1640.

Great Mint of Beauties,
   Though all Your Royall Burthens should come forth
Dischargd by Emanation, not by Birth;
Though You could so prove Mother, as the Soule, [5]
When it doth most conceive without controule;
Though Princes should so frequent from You flow,
That we might thence say, Sun-Beames issue slow;
Nay, though those Royall Plants as oft should spring
From You, as great Examples from Your *King;*
None would repine, or, Narrow midst such Store, [10]
Thinke the Thrones Blessing made the Kingdome Poore.
Graynes, which are singly Rich, become not Cheape
Because th' are Many: Such grow from the Heape.
Where Five would Each for Number passe Alone,
The Sixt comes Their Improvement, and it's Owne. [15]
We see the Brothers Vertues, growing ripe
By just degrees, aspire to their Great Type;
We see the Father thrive in Them, and finde
W' have Heires, as to His Throne, so to His Mind:
This makes us call for More: the Parents Bloud [20]
Is great security, They will be Good.
   And These Your Constant Tributes to the State
Might make us stand up High, and trample Fate;
We might grow Bold from Conscience of just Good,
Had it the fortune to be Understood. [25]
But Some, that would see, dazzled by much light,
View only that which doth confound their sight:
Others, darke by Designe, doe veyle their eyes,
For feare by their own fault they should grow Wise,
And, what they cannot misse, by chance should finde: [30]

Injustice is, what Iustice should be, Blind.
Yet our Great Guide, carelesse of Common Voyce,
As Good by Nature rather, then by Choyce,
Sheds the same fruitfull Influence still on All,
As Constant Showrs on Thanklesse Desarts fall: [35]
And, like the Unmov'd Rock, though it doth heare
The Murmurs of Rude Waves, whose Rage breakes there;
He still gives Living Gemms, and doth present
To Froward Nations Wealth, and Ornament.
Some Stones there are, whose Colours doe betray [40]
The Face of Heaven, and that Scene of Day
That Nature shap'd them in, and thence come forth
Themselves th' Ingenuous Records of their Birth.
May then this Pearle (*Great Queene*) now bred from You,
Congeald, and fashiond of more Heavenly Dew, [45]
Shew forth the Temper of the Present State,
And Himselfe be to his owne Birth the Date:
That, as the solemne Trumpet's publique Blast
At the same time proclaim'd both Warre and Fast,
He may, Devoutly Valiant, praying stand, [50]
As th' Ancient *Hero's*, with a Speare in's hand;
And, mixing Vowes and Fights in one Concent,
Divide Himselfe between the Church, and Tent.
But if He be, by Milder Influence, borne
The Sonne of Peace, the Rose without a Thorne; [55]
What Once his *Grand-sires* Ripe Designes did boast,
And Now His Serious Father labours most,
Hee, as a Pledge sent to Both Nations, doe;
And cement Kingdomes, now againe call'd Two.
  And here some Genius prompts me, I shall see [60]
Him make Greeke Fables Brittish History;
And view, now such a Goddesse hath brought forth,
This Floating Island setled by the Birth.

Vpon the Death of the most hopefull
the Lord STAFFORD.

Mvst then our Loves be short still? Must we choose
Not to enjoy? onely admire, and loose?

Must Axioms hence grow sadly understood,
And we thus see, 'Tis dangerous to be good?
So Bookes begunne are broken off, and we [5]
Receive a fragment for an History;
And, as 'twere present wealth, what was but debt,
Lose that, of which we were not Owners yet;
But as in bookes, that want the closing line,
We onely can conjecture, and repine: [10]
So must we heere too onely grieve, and guesse,
And by our fancy make, what's wanting, lesse.
Thus when rich webs are left unfinished,
The Spider doth supply them with her thred.
For tell me what addition can be wrought [15]
To him, whose Youth was even the bound of thought;
Whose buddings did deserve the Robe, whiles we
In smoothnesse did the deeds of wrinckles see:
When his state-nonage might have beene thought fit,
To breake the custome, and allow'd to sit? [20]
His actions veil'd his age, and could not stay
For that which we call ripenesse, and just day.
Others may waite the staffe, and the gray-haire,
And call that Wisedome, which is onely Feare,
Christen a coldnesse, temp'rance, and then boast [25]
Full and Ripe Vertue, when all action's lost:
This is not to be noble, but be slacke:
A *Stafford* ne're was good by th' Almanacke.
He, who thus stayes the season, and expects,
Doth not gaine habits, but disguise defects. [30]
Heere Nature outstrips Culture: He came try'd;
Strait of himselfe at first, not rectifi'd:
Manners so pleasing, and so handsome cast,
That still that overcame, that was shewne last:
All mindes were captiv'd thence, as if't had beene [35]
The same to him, to have beene lov'd, and seene.
Had he not bin snatchd thus, what drive hearts now
Into his nets, would have driven Cities too:
For these his Essaies, which began to win,
Were but bright sparkes, which shew'd the Mine within, [40]
Rude draughts unto the picture; things we may
Stile the first beames of the encreasing day;

Which did but onely great discoveries bring,
As outward coolenesse shewes the inward spring.
Had he then liv'd; Pow'r ne'r had been thought short [45]
That could not Crush, taught only to support.
No Poor-mans Sighs had been the Lords Perfumes,
No Tenants Nakedness had hung his Rooms,
No Tears had sowr'd his wines, no tedious-Long-
Festivall-service been the Countri's wrong; [50]
A Wretch's Famine had been no dish then,
Nor Greatness thought to eat no Beasts, but Men;
Nor had that been esteem'd a Politick Grace
When Sutors came to shew a serious Face;
Or when an humble Cosen did pass by, [55]
Put saving Bus'ness in his frugall Eye;
Things of Injustice then and Potent Hate
Had not been done for th' profit of the State;
Nor had it been the Privilege of High Bloud
To back their Injuries with the Kingdoms good: [60]
Servants and Engines had been two things then,
And difference made 'twixt Instruments and Men.
Nor were his actions, to content the sight,
Like Artists Pieces, plac'd in a good light,
That they might take at distance, and obtrude [65]
Something unto the eye that might delude:
His deeds did all, most perfect then appeare,
When you observ'd, view'd close, and did stand neere.
For could there ought else spring from him, whose line
From which he sprung, was rule, & discipline, [70]
Whose Vertues were as Bookes before him set,
So that they did instruct, who did beget,
Taught thence not to be powerfull, but know,
Shewing he was their blood by living so.
For, whereas some are by their bigge lippe knowne, [75]
Others b'imprinted, burning swords were showne:
So they by great deeds are, from which bright fame,
Engraves free reputation on their name:
These are their Native markes, and it hath bin
The *Staffords* lot, to have their signes within. [80]
And though this firme Hereditary good,
Might boasted be, as flowing with the blood,

Yet he nere graspt this stay: But as those, who
Carry perfumes about them still, scarce doe
Themselves perceive them, though anothers sense   [85]
Sucke in th' exhaling odours: so he thence
Ne'r did perceive he carry'd this good smell,
But made new still by doing himselfe well.
T'embalme him then is vaine, where spreading fame
Supplies the want of spices; where the Name,   [90]
It selfe preserving, may for Ointments passe:
And he, still seene, lye coffind as in glasse.
Whiles thus his bud dims full flowres, and his sole
Beginning doth reproach anothers whole,
Comming so perfect up, that there must needes   [95]
Have beene found out new Titles for new deeds;
Though youth, and lawes forbid, which will not let
Statues be rais'd, or him stand Brasen: yet
Our mindes retaine this Royalty of Kings,
Not to be bound to time, but judge of things,   [100]
And worship, as they merit: there we doe
Place him at height, and he stands golden too.
A comfort, but not equall to the crosse,
A faire remainder, but not like the losse:
For he, that last pledge, being gone, we doe   [105]
Not onely lose the Heire but th' honour too.
Set we up then this boast against our wrong,
He left no other signe, that he was young:
And, spight of fate, his living vertues will,
Though he be dead, keepe up the Barony still.   [110]

On the Marriage of the Lady Mary *to the Prince of* Aurange *his Son.* 1641.

Amids such Heate of Businesse, such State-throng
    Disputing Right and Wrong,
And the sowre Iustle of Unclos'd Affayres;
    What meane those Glorious Payres?
  That Youth? That Virgin? Those All Dresst?   [5]
  The Whole, and every Face, a Feast?

   Great Omen! O ye Powr's,
    May this Your Knot be Ours!
  Thus while Cold things with Hott did jarre,
   And Dry with Moyst made Mutuall Warre,   [10]
    Love from that Masse did leap;
    And what was but an Heap
Rude and Ungatherd, swift as thought, was hurld
Into the Beauty of an Ordred World.

Goe then into His Arms, New as the Morne,   [15]
   Tender as Blades of Corne,
Soft as the Wooll, that Nuptiall Posts did crowne,
   Or th'Hallowd Quinces Downe,
  That Rituall Quince, which Brides did eate,
  When with their Bridegrooms they would treate.   [20]
    Though You are Young as th'Howres,
    Or This fresh Month's first Flowres:
  Yet, if Love's Preists can ought discerne,
   Fayrest, You are not now to learne,
    What Hopes, what Sighs, what Teares,   [25]
    What Ioyes are, or what Feares.
Ere Time to Lower Soules doth Motion bring,
The Great break out, and of Themselves take wing.

And You, Great Sir, 'mongst Speares and Bucklers borne,
   And by Your Father sworne   [30]
To worke the Webbe of His Designes compleate;
   Yield to this Milder Heate.
  Upon the same Rich Stock, we know,
  Valour, and Love, Both Planted grow:
   But Love doth first inspire   [35]
   The Soule with his soft Fire,
  Chafing the Brest for Noble Deeds;
  Then in That Seat True Valour breeds.
   So Rocks first yield a Teare,
   Then Gemms that will not weare.   [40]
So, oft, the Graecian's Sword did first divide
His Bridall Cake, then pierce the Enemies Side.

D'You see? or am I false? Your Tender Vine,
   Me thinks, on every twine

Tiaras, Scepters, Crownes, Spoyles, Trophies weares,   [45]
  And such Rich Burthens beares,
Which, hanging in their Beauteous shapes,
  Adorne her Bowghs like swelling Grapes:
    But Time forbids the Rites
      Of gathering these Delights,   [50]
  And onely Sighs allows, till he
  Hath better knitt, and spred Your Tree.
    Where Union would last Long,
    Shee fixeth in the Young,
And so grows up. Great Spirits with more Love   [55]
Differre their Ioyes, then Others doe them Prove.

But when Her Zone shall come to be unty'd,
  And She be Twice Your Bride;
When Shee shall Blush, and straight waxe Pale, and then
  By Turns doe Both agen;   [60]
  When Her owne Bashfullnesse shall prove
  The Second Nonage to Her Love;
    Then you will know what Blisse
    Angells both Have, and Misse;
  How Soules may mixe, and take fresh growth,   [65]
  In Neither Whole, and Whole in Both;
    Pleasures, that none can know,
    But such as have stayd so.
Wee from Long Loves at last to Hymen tend:
But Princes Fires beginne, where Subjects end.   [70]

To Philip, *Earl of Pembroke, upon his Lordships Election of Chancellor of the University of* Oxford

My Lord,
  When Studies now are blasted, and the times
Place us in false lights, and see Arts as Crimes,
When to heape knowledge is but thought to fil·
The mind with more Advantage to doe ill:
When all your honoured Brothers choyce and store   [5]

Of Learn'd Remaines with sweat and charge fetcht ore,
Are thought but uselesse Peeces: and some trust
To see our Schooles mingled with Abby dust.
That now you dare receive us, and professe
Your selfe our Patron, makes you come no lesse, [10]
Then a new Founder; whilst wee all allow,
What was Defence before, is Building now:
And this you were reserv'd for, set a part
For times of hazard; as the Shield and Dart
Laid up in store to be extracted thence, [15]
When serious need shall aske some try'd Defence;
And who more fit to manage the Gownes cause
Then you, whose even life may dare the Lawes,
And the Law-makers too: in whom the Great
Is twisted with the Good as Light with Heat; [20]
What though your sadder cares doe not professe
To find the Circles squaring, or to guesse
How many sands within a grayne or two
Will fill the world, these speculations doe
Steale man from man; You'r he that can suggest [25]
True Rules, and fashion manners to the best:
You can preserve our Charters from the wrongs
Of the untaught Towne, as farre as now the tongue
Doth from their understanding, You can give
Freedome to men, and make that freedome live; [30]
And divert hate from the now hated Arts,
These are your great endowments, these your parts,
And 'tis our honest Boast, when this wee scan,
Wee give a Title, but receive a Man.

Your Lordships most honoured
humble servant
William Cartwright.

On the Lady Newburgh, *who dyed of the small Pox.*

I now beleeve that Heaven once shall shrink
Up like a shrivell'd Scrole, and what we think,
Spread like a larger Curtain, doth involve
The Worlds Great Fabrick, shall at length dissolve

Into a sparing Handfull, and to be [5]
Only a Shrowd for its Mortality:
For her Disease Blest Soul, was but the same
Which alwaies raigneth in that upper Frame;
And hearing of her Fate, we boldly dare
Conclude that Stars, Sphears thicker Portions, are [10]
Only some Angry Pimples which foretell
That which at length must fall, now is not well.
   But why think we on Heav'n, when she is gone,
Almost as rich and fair a Mansion?
One who was good so young, that we from her [15]
Against Philosophy may well infer
That Vertues are from Nature; that the Mind
Like the first Paradise may unrefind
Boast Native Glories, and to Art not ow
That ought by Her it doth receive and show. [20]
I may not call her Woman, for she ne'r
Study'd the Glass and Pencill, could not swear
Faith to the Lover, and when he was gone
The same unto the next, and yet keep none;
She could not draw ill Vapours like the Sun, [25]
And drop them down upon some yonger One.
Alas her Mind was plac'd above these foul
Corruptions, still as high as now her Soul:
Nor had she any thought that e'r did fear
The open test of the Austerest Ear: [30]
For all of them were such as wretches we
May wish, not hope, for this felicity;
That when we think on Heaven we may find
Thoughts, like the worst of hers, burn in our Mind.
   Let not the Ancient glory that they found [35]
The Chain of Vertues, how they all were bound,
How met in one; We happier far did see
What they did either dream or Prophesie:
For since that She is gone, where can we find
A pair of Vertues met in all Mankind? [40]
Some one perhaps is Chaste, Another Just,
A Third is valiant, but we may not trust
To see them throng'd again, but still alone
As in a Ring One Spark, one pretious Stone.

I know some little Beauty, and one grain [45]
Of any Vertue doth to Others gain
The Name of Saint or Goddess: but the grace
Of every Limb in her, bright as the Face,
Presenting Chaster Beauties, did conspire
Only to stile her Woman: 'twas the fire [50]
Of a religious Mind that made her soar
So high above the Sex, Her faith was more
Then others stumbling blindness; only here
She was Immodest, only bold to fear,
And thence adore: for She I must Confess [55]
'Mongst all her Vertues had this one excess.
Forgive, thou all of goodness, if that I
By praising blemish, too much Majesty
Injures it self: where Art cannot express,
It veyls and leaves the rest unto a Guess. [60]
So where weak Imitation failes, enshrowd
The awfull Deity in an envious Cloud;
Hadst thou not been so Good, so Vertuous,
Heaven had never been so Covetous;
Each parcell of thee must away, and we [65]
Not have a Child left to resemble thee;
Nothing to shew thou wert, but what alone
Adds to our Grief, thy Ashes, or thy Stone:
And all our glory only can boast thus,
That we had one made Heaven Envy us; [70]
I now begin to doubt whether it were
A true disease or no; We well may fear
We did mistake: The Gods whom they'l bereave
Do blindfold first, then plausibly deceive:
The Error's now found out, we are beguil'd, [75]
Thou wert Enammel'd rather than Defil'd.

On Mrs Abigall Long, *who dyed of two Impostumes.*

So to a stronger guarded Fort we use
More battring Engines. Lest that death should loose

A nobler Conquest, Fates Conspiring come
Like Friendship payr'd into an Union.
 Tell me, you fatall Sisters, what rich Spoil, [5]
What worthy Honour, is it to beguile
One Maid by two Fates? while you thus bereave
Of life, you do not conquer, but deceive:
Me thinks an old decay'd and worn-out face,
A thing that once was Woman, and in Grace, [10]
One who each Night in Twenty Boxes lies
All took asunder: one w'hath sent her Eyes,
Her Nose, and Teeth, as Earnests unto Death,
Pawns to the Grave till she resign her Breath
And come her self, me thinks this Ruine might [15]
Suffice and glut the Envy of your spight;
Why aime you at the Fair? must you have one
Whose every Limb doth shew perfection?
Whose well Compacted Members harmony
Speaks her to be Natures Orthography? [20]
Must she appear your Rage? Why then farewell,
All, all the Vertue that on Earth did dwell.
Why do I call it Vertue? 'tis dishonour
Thus to bestow that Mortall little on her;
Something she had more Sacred, more Refin'd [25]
Than Vertue is, something above the Mind
And low Conceit of Man, something which Lame
Expression cannot reach, which wants a Name
'Cause 'twas ne'r known before; which I express
Fittest by leaving it unto a Guess; [30]
She was that one, lent to the Earth to shew
That Heavens Bounty did not only ow
Endowments unto Age, that Vertues were
Not to the Staff Confin'd, or the Gray-hair;
One that was fit ev'n in her Youth to be [35]
An Hearer of the best Philosophy;
One that did teach by Carriage; One whose looks
Instructed more effectually than Books,
She was not taught like Others how to place
A loose disordered Hair: the Comb and Glass, [40]
As curious Trifles, rather made for loose
And wanton softness than for honest Use;

She did neglect: no Place left for the Checks
Of Carefull Kindred; nothing but the Sex
Was womanish in her; She drest her Mind [45]
As others do their Bodies, and refin'd
That better part with Care, and still did wear
More Jewels in her Manners than her Ear;
The World she past through, as the brighter Sun
Doth through unhallowed Stews and Brothels run, [50]
Untouch'd, and uncorrupted; Sin she knew
As honest Men do Cheating, to eschew
Rather than practice; She might well have drest
All Minds, have dealt her Vertues to each Brest,
Enrich'd her Sex, and yet have still been one [55]
Fit for th' amazed Gods to gaze upon.
    Pardon, thou Soul of Goodness, if I wrong
Thine Ample Vertues with a sparing Tongue,
Alas, I am compell'd, speaking of thee,
To use one of thy Vertues, Modesty. [60]
    Blest Virgin, but that very Name which cals
Thee blest into an Accusation fals;
Virgin is Imperfection, and we do
Conceive Increase to so much Beauty due;
And alas Beauty is no Phenix; why, [65]
O why then wouldst thou not vouchsafe to try
Those Bonds of freedom, that when death did strike,
The World might shew, though not the same, the like?
Why wert not thou stamp'd in another Face,
That whom we now lament we might embrace? [70]
That after thou hadst been long hid in Clay
Thou might'st appear fresh as the early Day,
And seem unto thy wondring Kindred more
Young, although not more Vertuous than before?
    But I disturb thy Peace, sleep then among [75]
Thy Ancestors deceas'd, who have been long
Lockt up in Silence, whom thy carefull Love
Doth visit in their Urns, as if thou'dst prove
Friendship in the forgetfull dust, and have
A Family united in the Grave. [80]
    Enjoy thy death, Blest Maid, nay further do
Enjoy that Name, that very little too;

Some use there is in Ill; we not repine
Or grudge at thy Disease; it did refine
Rather than kill; and thou art upwards gone, [85]
Made purer even by Corruption.
   Whiles thus to Fate thou dost resign thy Breath,
   To thee a Birth-day 'tis, to us a Death.

An Epitaph on Mr. Poultney.

True to himself and Others, with whom both
Did bind alike a Promise and an Oath:
Free without Art, or Project; giving still
With no more Snare, or hope, than in his Will:
Whose mast'ring even Mind so ballanc'd all [5]
His Thoughts, that they could neither rise nor fall:
Whose train'd desires ne'r tempted Simple Health,
Taught not to vex but manage compos'd Wealth;
A season'd friend not tainted with Design,
Who made these words grow useless *Mine* and *Thine*; [10]
An equall Master, whose sincere Intents
Ne'r chang'd good Servants to bad Instruments:
A Constant Husband not divorc'd by Fate,
Loving, and Lov'd, happy in either State,
To whom the gratefull wife hath sadly drest [15]
One Monument here, Another in her Brest;
Poultney in both doth lye, who hitherto
To Others liv'd, to himself only Now.

To the Memory of the most vertuous Mrs Ursula Sadleir, who dyed of a Feaver.

Thou whitest Soul, thou thine own Day,
Not sully'd by the Bodies Clay,
   Fly to thy Native Seat,
   Surrounded with this Heat,
Make thy Disease which would destroy thee [5]
Thy Charriot only to conveigh thee;

And while thou soar'st and leav'st us here beneath,
Wee'l think it thy translation, not thy death.

But with this Empty feign'd Relief
We do but flatter our Just Grief, [10]
   And we as well may say
    That Martyr dy'd that day,
Ride up in flames, whom we saw Burn,
And into paler Ashes turn;
Who's he that such a Fate Translation calls [15]
Where the whole Body like the Mantle falls?

But we beguile our Sorrows so
By a false Scene of Specious Woe;
   Wee'l weigh, and count, and rate
    Our loss, then grieve the Fate. [20]
Wee'l know the measure of her worth,
Then mete and deal our Sadness forth:
And when the Sum's made up, and all is clos'd,
Say Death undid what Love himself Compos'd.

What Morns did from her smiling rise? [25]
What day was gather'd in her Eyes?
   What Air? what Truth? what Art?
    What Musick in each Part?
What Grace? what motion? and what skil?
How all by manage doubled still? [30]
Thus 'twixt her self and Nature was a strife,
Nature Materials brought, but she the Life.

The Rose when't only pleas'd the Sence,
Arm'd with no Thorns to give Offence,
   That Rose, as yet Curse-free, [35]
    Was not more mild than She,
Clear as the Tears that did bedew her,
Fresh as the Flowers that bestrew her,
Fair while She was, and when She was not, fair,
Some Ruines more than other Buildings are. [40]

Gardens parch'd up with Heat do so
Her Fate as fainter Emblems show.

    Thus Incense doth expire;
    Thus perfumes dye in fire;
      Thus did *Diana*'s Temple burn, [45]
    And all her Shrines to Ashes turn.
As She a fairer Temple far did waste
She that was far more Goddess, and more Chaste.

    Returning thus as innocent
    To Heav'n as she to Earth was lent, [50]
      Snatch'd hence ere she drank in
      The Taint of Age and Sin,
    Her Mind being yet a Paradise,
    Free from all Weeds of spreading Vice,
We may Conclude her Feaver, without doubt [55]
Was but the Flaming Sword to keep *Eve* out.

To the Memory of the Most Worthy,
Sir Henry Spelman.

Though now the Times perhaps be such that nought
Was left thee but to dye, and 'twill be thought
An Exprobration to rehearse thy Deeds,
Thriving as Flowers among these courser Weeds,
I cannot yet forbear to grieve, and tell [5]
Thy skill to know, thy Valour to do well.
    And what can we do less, when thou art gone
Whose Tenents as thy Manners were thine own;
In not the same Times both the same; not mixt
With th' Ages Torrent, but still clear and Fixt; [10]
As gentle Oyl upon the Streams doth glide
Not mingling with them, though it Smooth the Tide?
    What can we less, when thou art gone, whom we
Thought only so much living History?
Thou sifted'st long-hid Dust to find lost Ore [15]
And searchedst Rubbish to encrease our Store.
Things of that Age thou shew'dst, that they seem'd new,
And stand admir'd as if they now first grew;
Time in thy learned Pages, as the Sun
On *Ahaz* Diall, does thus backward run. [20]

Nor did'st thou this affectedly, as they
Whom Humour leads to know out of the Way:
Thy aym was Publike in't; thy Lamp and Night
Search'd untrod Paths only to set us right;
Thou didst consult the Ancients and their Writ,   [25]
To guard the Truth, not exercise the Wit;
Taking but what they said; not, as some do,
To find out what they may be wrested to;
Nor Hope, nor Faction, bought thy Mind to side,
Conscience depos'd all Parts, and was sole Guide.   [30]
So 'tis when Authors are not Slaves, but Men,
And do themselves maintain their own free Pen.
   This 'twas that made the Priest in every Line,
This 'twas that made the Churches Cause be thine;
Who perhaps hence hath suffer'd the less wrong,   [35]
And ows thee much because sh' hath stood so long;
That though her Dress, her Discipline now faints,
Yet her Endowments fall not with her Saints.
   This 'twas that made thee ransack all thy Store
To shew our Mother what she was before;   [40]
What Laws past, what Decrees; the Where, and When
Her Tares were sow'n, and how pull'd up agen;
A Body of that Building, and that Dress,
That *Councels* may Conspire and yet do less.
   Nor doth late Practise take thee, but old Rights,   [45]
Witness that Charitable Piece that lights
Our Corps to unbought Graves, though Custome led
So against Nature, as to tax the dead.
Though use had made the Land oft purchas'd be,
And though oft purchas'd keep Propriety;   [50]
So that the well Prepared did yet fear,
Though not to dye, yet to undo the Heyr.
   Had we what else thy Taper saw thee glean,
'Twould teach our Days perhaps a safer Mean;
Though what we see be much, it may be guess'd   [55]
As great was Shewn, so greater was suppress'd.
   Go then, go up, Rich Soul; while we here grieve,
Climb till thou see what we do but believe;
W' have not time to rate thee; thy Fate's such,
We know we've lost; our Sons will say how much.   [60]

On a vertuous young Gentlewoman that dyed suddenly.

When the old flaming Prophet climb'd the Sky,
Who, at one Glympse, did *vanish*, and not dye,
He made more Preface to a Death, than This,
So far from Sick, She did not *breath* amiss:
She who to Heaven more heaven doth annex, [5]
Whose lowest Thought was above all our Sex,
Accounted nothing Death, but t'be Repriev'd,
And dyed as free from sickness as she liv'd.
Others are dragg'd away, or must be driven,
She only saw her time and *stept* to Heaven; [10]
Where *Seraphims* view all her Glories o'r
As one Return'd, that had been there before.
For while she did this Lower World adorn,
Her Body seem'd rather *assum'd* than born;
So Rarifi'd, Advanc'd, so Pure and Whole, [15]
That Body might have been another's *Soul*;
And equally a Miracle it were
That she could Dye, or that she could Live here.

On the Death of the most vertuous Gentlewoman, Mrs Ashford, who dyed in Child-bed.

So when the great Elixar (which a Chast
And even Heat hath ripened) doth at last
Stand ready for the Birth, th' Alembick's Womb
Not able to discharge, becomes its Tomb;
So that that studied Stone is still Arts Cross, [5]
Not known by it's Vertue so much as his Loss,
And we may think some envious Fates Combine
In that one Ounce to rob us of a Mine;
And can our Grief be less, whiles here we do
Lose not the Stone, but the Alembick too? [10]
When Death Converts that hatching Heat to Cold,
And makes that Dust, which should make all else Gold.

If Souls from Souls be kindled as some sing,
That to be born and Light'ned is one Thing;
And that our life is but a tender Ray [15]
Snatch'd by the Infant from the Mothers Day;
And if the Soul thus kindled must have been
The framer of the Body, the Souls Inn;
Our Loss is doubled then, for that young flame
Flowing from hers, must have been for the same, [20]
As to have cast such Glories, shew'n such seeds,
Spread forth such matchless Vertues, done such deeds,
Moulded such beautious Limbs, that we might see
The Mother in each Grace, and think that she
Was but Reflected, whiles her Shape did pass [25]
As the snatch'd likeness doth into the Glass,
Which now in vain we look for, for our Streams
Of Light are but the Dawning of her Beams;
'Twas not her lot to lay up Deeds, and then
Twist them into one Vertue, as some Men [30]
Do hoord up smaller gains, and when they grow
Up to a Sum, into one Purchase throw;
Her Mind came furnish'd in, did charg'd appear,
As Trees in the Creation, Vertues were
Meer Natures unto her; Nor did she know [35]
Those Signs of our defects, to bud and grow;
Goodness her Soul, not Action, was; and She
Found it the same to do well and to be;
So perfect that her speculation might
Have made her self the bound of her own sight; [40]
And her Mind thus her Mind contemplating
In brief at once have been the Eye and thing.
Her Body was so pure that Nature might
Have broke it into Forms: That Buriall rite
Was here unfit, for it could not be said [45]
Earth unto Earth, Dust unto Dust was laid;
All being so simple that the quickest sight
Did judge her Limbs but so much fashion'd Light;
Her Eyes so beamy, you'ld have said the Sun
Lodg'd in those Orbs when that the day was done; [50]
Her Mouth that Treasure hid, that Pearls wer blots
And dàrkness, if Compar'd, no Gems but Spots.

Her Lips did like the Cherub's flames appear,
Set to keep off the bold for Coming there.
Her bosome such that you would guess 'twas this [55]
Way that departed Souls pass'd to their Bliss.
Her Body thus perspicuous; and her Mind
So undefil'd, so Beautious, so Refin'd,
We may Conclude the Lilly in the Glass
An Emblem, though a faint one, of her was. [60]
   What Others now count qualities and Parts
She thought but Complements, and meer By-Arts,
Yet did perform them with as perfect Grace
As they who do Arts among Vertues place.
   She dancing in a cross perplexed thread [65]
Could make such Labyrinths, that the guiding Thread
Would be it self at loss, and yet you'ld swear
A Star mov'd not so Even in its Sphere;
No looser flames but Raptures came from thence,
Her Steps stirr'd Meditations up, and Sense [70]
Resign'd delights to Reason, which were wrought
Not to Enchant the Eye, but catch the Thought.
   Had she but pleas'd to tune her Breath, the Winds
Would have been hush'd and listned, and those Minds
Whose Passions are their Blasts, would have been still, [75]
As when the Halcyon sits: So that her skill
Gave Credit unto Fables, whiles we see,
Passions like Wilder Beasts thus tamed be.
Her very looks were tune, we might descry
Consort, and Judge of Musick by the Eye: [80]
So that in Others that which we call Fair,
In her was Composition and good Air.
   When this I tell, will you not hence surmise
Death hath got leave to enter Paradise?
But why do I name death? for as a Star [85]
Which erewhile darted out a Light from far,
Shines not when neer the Brighter Sun; She thus
Is not extinct, but does lie hid to us.

On the Queens Return from the Low Countries.

Hallow the Threshold, Crown the Posts anew;
    The day shall have its due:
Twist all our Victories into one bright wreath,
    On which let Honour breath;
Then throw it round the Temples of our Queene;   [5]
'Tis Shee that must preserve those glories green.

When greater Tempests, then on Sea before,
    Receav'd Her on the shore,
When She was shot at, *for the King's own good*,
    By Villaines hir'd to Blood;   [10]
How bravely did Shee doe, how bravely Beare,
And shew'd, though they durst rage, Shee durst not feare.

Courage was cast about Her like a Dresse
    Of solemne Comelinesse;
A gather'd Mind, and an untroubled Face   [15]
    Did give Her dangers grace.
Thus arm'd with Innocence, secure they move,
Whose Highest Treason is but Highest Love.

As some Bright Starre, that runnes a Direct Course,
    Yet with Anothers force,   [20]
Mixeth its vertue in a full dispence
    Of one joynt influence,
Such was Her mind to th' Kings, in all was done;
The Agents Diverse, but the Action One.

Look on Her Enemies, on their Godly Lyes,   [25]
    Their Holy Perjuries,
Their Curs'd encrease of much ill gotten Wealth,
    By Rapine or by stealth.
Their crafty Friendships knit by equall guilt,
And the Crown-Martyrs blood so lately spilt.   [30]

Look then upon Her selfe; Beauteous in Mind,
    Scarce Angells more refin'd;

Her actions Blancht, Her Conscience still Her sway,
   And that not fearing Day:
Then you'l confesse Shee casts a double Beame,   [35]
Much shining by Her selfe, but more by Them.

Receive Her then as the new springing Light
   After a tedious Night:
As Holy Hermits doe Revealed Truth;
   Or Æson did his youth.   [40]
Her presence is our Guard, our Strength, our Store;
The cold snatch some flames thence, the valiant more.

But something yet, our Holy Priests will say,
   Is wanting to the Day:
'Twere sinne to let so Blest a feast arise   [45]
   Without a Sacrifice.
True, if our Flocks were full. But being all
Are gone, the Many-headed Beast must fall.

Vpon the death of the Right valiant
Sir Bevill Grenvill *Knight*.

Not to be wrought by Malice, Gaine, or Pride,
To a Compliance with the Thriving Side;
Not to take Armes for love of Change, or Spight,
But only to maintaine Afflicted Right;
Not to dye vainely in pursuit of Fame,   [5]
Perversely seeking after Voyce and Name;
Is to Resolve, Fight, Dye, as Martyrs doe:
And thus did He, Souldier, and Martyr too.
   He might (like some Reserved Men of State,
Who looke not to the Cause, but to its Fate)   [10]
Have stood aloof, engag'd on Neither Side,
Prepar'd at last to strike-in with the Tyde.
But well-weighd Reason told him, that when Law
Either is Renounc'd, or Misapply'd by th' awe
Of false-nam'd Common-wealths men; when the Right   [15]
Of King, and Subject, is suppress'd by Might;
When all Religion either is Refus'd

As meere Pretence, or meerly, as That, us'd;
When thus the Fury of Ambition swells,
Who is not Active, Modestly Rebells. [20]
Whence, in a just esteeme, to Church and Crowne
He offred All, and nothing thought his owne.
This thrust Him into Action, Whole and Free;
Knowing no Interest but Loyalty;
Not loving Arms as Arms, or Strife for Strife; [25]
Nor Wastful, nor yet Sparing of his Life;
A great Exactor of Himselfe, and then,
By faire Commands no lesse of Other men;
Courage, and Iudgement had their equall part,
Counsell was added to a Generous Heart; [30]
Affaires were justly tim'd; nor did He catch
At an Affected Fame of Quick Dispatch;
Things were Prepard, Debated, and then Done,
Nor rashly Brooke, nor vainely Over-spunne;
False Periods no where by Designe were made, [35]
As are by those, who make the Warre their Trade;
The Building still was suited to the Ground,
Whence every Action issu'd Full and Round.
We know who blind their Men with specious Lyes,
With Revelations, and with Prophecyes, [40]
Who promise Two things to obtaine a Third,
And are themselves by the like Motives stirr'd:
By no such Engines He His Souldiers drawes;
He knew no Arts, but Courage and the Cause;
With these he brought them on, as well train'd men, [45]
And with these too he brought them off agen.
  I should, I know, track Him through all the Course
Of his great Actions, shew their Worth and Force:
But, although all are Handsome, yet we cast
A more intentive Eye still on the last. [50]
  When now th' Incensed Rebell proudly came
Downe, like a Torrent without Bank, or Damm;
When Undeserv'd Successe urg'd on their force,
That Thunder must come downe to stop their Course,
Or Grenville must step in; Then Grenville stood, [55]
And with Himselfe oppos'd, and checkt the Flood.
Conquest, or Death, was all His Thought. So fire

Either Orecomes, or doth it selfe expire.
His Courage work't like Flames, cast heate about,
Here, there, on this, on that side; None gave out; [60]
Not any Pike in that Renowned Stand
But tooke new force from His Inspired Hand;
Souldier encourag'd Souldier, Man urg'd Man,
And He urg'd All: so much Example can.
Hurt upon Hurt, Wound upon Wound did call, [65]
He was the But, the Mark, the Ayme of All:
His Soule this while retir'd from Cell to Cell,
At last flew up from all, and then He fell.
But the Devoted Stand, enraged more
From that his Fate, ply'd hotter then before, [70]
And Proud to fall with Him, sworn not to yield,
Each sought an Honour'd Grave, and gain'd the Field.
Thus, He being fall'n, his Action fought anew;
And the Dead conquer'd, whiles the Living slew.

   This was not Natures Courage; nor that thing [75]
We Valour call, which Time and Reason bring;
But a Diviner Fury, Fierce, and High,
Valour transported into Ecstasie,
Which Angells, looking on Vs from above,
Use to conveigh into the Soules they love. [80]
You now that boast the Spirit, and its sway,
Shew Vs his Second, and wee'll give the Day.
We know your Politique Axiom—Lurk, or Fly.
Ye cannot Conquer, cause ye dare not Dye.
And though you thanke God, that you lost none there, [85]
Because Th' were such, who Liv'd not when they were;
Yet your great Generall (who doth Rise and Fall,
As his Successes doe; whom you dare call,
As fame unto you doth Reports dispense,
Either a Traitor, or His Excellence) [90]
How e'r he reignes now by unheard of Lawes,
Could wish His Fate together with His Cause.

   And Thou (Blest Soule) whose Cleare Compacted Fame,
As Amber Bodies Keeps, preserves thy Name,
Whose Life affords what doth content Both Eyes, [95]
Glory for People, Substance for the Wise;
Goe laden up with Spoyles, possesse That Seate

    To which the Valiant, when th' have Done retreat:
    And when Thou seest an happy Period sent
    To these Distractions, and the Storme quite spent; [100]
    Look downe, and say: I have my share in All,
    Much Good grew from my Life, Much from my Fall.

On the Nativity.
For the Kings Musick.

Omnes Heark,
1.   'Tis the Nuptiall Day of Heav'n and Earth;
2.   The Fathers Marriage, and the Sons blest Birth:
3.   The Spheres are giv'n us as a Ring; that Bliss,
    Which we call Grace is but the Deitie's Kiss,

Ch. And what we now do hear Blest Spirits sing, [5]
    Is but the happy Po'sie of that Ring.

1.   Whiles Glory thus takes Flesh, & th' Heav'ns are bow'd,
    May we not say God Comes down in a Cloud?
2.   Peace dropping thus on Earth, Good will on Men,
    May we not say that Manna fals agen? [10]

Ch. All Wonders we Confess are only his:
    But of these Wonders, He the greatest is.

1.   The Mother felt no pangs; for he did pass
    As subtle Sun-beams do through purer Glass.
2.   The Virgin no more loss of Name did find, [15]
    Than when her Vertues Issu'd from her Mind.

Ch. The Lilly of the Valleys thus did ow
    Unto no Gard'ners Hands that he did grow.

1.   Blest Babe, thy Birth makes Heaven in the Stall;
2.   And we the Manger may thy Altar call: [20]
3.   Thine and thy Mothers Eyes as Stars appear;
    The Bull no Beast, but Constellation here.

Ch. Thus Both were Born, the Gospell and the Law,
    Moses in Flags did lye, thou in the Straw.

    Open O Hearts,
1.   These Gates lift up will win [25]
2.   The King of Glory here to enter in;
3.   Flesh is his Veyl, and House: whiles thus we wooe,
    The World will dwell among, and in us too.

Ch. Flesh is his Veyl, *&c.*

On the Circumcision.

For the Kings Musick.

```
   1.   Gently, O Gently, Father, do not bruise
           That Tender Vine that hath no Branch to lose;
   2.   Be not too Cruel, see the Child doth Smile,
           His Bloud was but his Mothers Milk erewhile.
1 Lev.   Fear not the pruning of your Vine,                    [5]
           Hee'l turn your Water into Wine;
2 Lev.   The Mothers Milk that's now his Bloud,
           Hereafter will become her Food.
Chor.   'Tis done; so doth the Balsam Tree endure
           The Cruell Wounds of those whom it must Cure.       [10]
1 Lev.   'Tis but the Passions Essay: This young loss
           Only preludes unto his Riper Cross.
   1.   Avert, good Heav'n, avert that Fate
           To so much Beauty so much Hate.
2 Lev.   Where so great Good is meant                          [15]
           The Bloud's not lost, but spent.
Chor.   Thus Princes feel what People do amiss;
           The swelling's Ours, although the Lancing his.
   2.   When ye fair Heavens White Food bled,
           The Rose, say they, from thence grew Red,            [20]
           O then what more Miraculous good,
           Must spring from this diviner Floud?
2 Lev.   When that the Rose it self doth bleed,
           That Bloud will be the Churches Seed.
Cho.    When that the Rose, &c.                                [25]
```

On the Epiphany.

For the Kings Musick.

```
1 Mag.      See this is He, whose Star
              Did becken us from far;
2 Ma.      And this the Mother whom the Heavens do
              Honour, and like Her, bring forth New Stars too.
3 Ma.      I know not which my Thoughts ought first admire:   [5]
              Here Shew, O Heav'n, another guiding fire.
```

Cho.	Alas, this Wonder's so above our Skill,
	That though w'have found him, we may seek him still.
1 Ma.	Since that our own are Silenc'd, This Mouth be
	A more Inspired Oracle to me. [10]
2 Ma.	And these Eyes be my Stars, my Light,
3 Ma.	And this Hand wash an Ethiop white.
Cho.	Wisdom Commands the Stars (we say)
	But it was Ours thus to obey.
1 Ma.	He makes our Gold seem Pebble stone; [15]
2 Ma.	Sure 'tis their Greater *Solomon;*
1 Ma.	Our Myrrh and Frankinsence must not Contest;
3 Ma.	Diviner Perfumes breath from off her Breast.
2 Ma.	Blest Babe, receive our now disparag'd store:
3 Ma.	And where we cann't express, let us Adore. [20]
Cho.	Who against Policy will hence convince,
	That Land is blest, that hath so young a Prince.
To the King.	But as those Wise enrich'd his Stable, You
	Great Sovereign, have enrich'd his Temple too,
	The Inn by You hath not the Church beguil'd; [25]
	The Manger to the Altar's Reconcil'd:
	Since then their Wisdom is by Yours out-gone,
	Instead of Three Kings, Fame shall speak of One.
Cho.	Since then, *&c.*

November
or, Signal Dayes Observ'd in that Month in relation to the Crown and Royal Family.

Thou *Sun* that shed'st the Dayes, looke downe and see
A Month more shining by Events, than thee;
1. Day, is All Saints.
2. All Souls.
Departed *Saints* and *Souls* sign'd it before,
But now the living signe it more.
Persons and *Actions* meet, All meant for Joy, [5]
But some build up, and some destroy.
Bate us That Ushering Curse so dearly knowne
And then the Month is All our Owne.
So, at the First, Darkenesse was throwne about
Th' unshapen Earth, and Light was thence strooke out. [10]

3. Day, The Assembling of the unhappy Parliament. Draw the first Curtaine and the Scene is then
A Triple State of Cull'd and Trusted Men:
Men, in whose Hands 'twas once t'have giv'n us more
    Then our Bold Fathers Askd before:
Who, had they us'd their Prince's Grace, had got   [15]
    What no Armes could, and Theirs will not.
What more then Witchcraft did our Blessing Curse,
    And made the Cure make Evills worse?
'Tis the *Third* Day; throw in the Blackest Stone,
Mark it for Curs'd, and let it stand Alone.   [20]

4. Day, The Birth of the Princesse MARY. But, hold! speake gentler things! This *Fourth* was seene
The softest Image of our Beauteous *Queene*.
Bring me a Lambe, not us'd to Elder Food,
    That h'as as yet more Milke then Blood,
That to the Honour of this Early Bride   [25]
    (Like *Thetis* joynd to *Peleus* side,)
Some Tender Thing may fall; though none can be
    So White, so Tender, as is She.
Whiles we at home our Little Turfe debate,
She spreads our Glories to another State.   [30]

5. Day, Our Delivery from the Papists Conspiracy. Next view a Treason of the worst Intent,
Had not our Owne *done* more, then Strangers *meant*;
Religion is the Thing both sides pretend,
    But either to a different End:
They, out of Zeale, labour to reare their owne,   [35]
    These, out of Zeale to pull All downe.
Blesse Us from These, as Them! but yet compare
    Those in the Vault, These in the chayre.
Though the just Lot of unsuccessful sin
Fix their's Without, you'l finde Worse Heads within.   [40]

12. Day, The Kings Victory at Bramford. But hearke! What Thunder's that? and who those men
Flying tow'rds Heav'n, but falling downe agen?
Whose those Blacke Corps cast on the Guilty Shore?
    'Tis sin that swimmes to its owne Dore.
'Tis the Third scourge of Rebells, which allow'd   [45]
    Our Army, like the Prophets Cloud
Did from an Handfull rise, Untill at last
    Their Sky was by it Overcast.

      But (as Snakes Hisse after th'have lost their Sting)
      The Traytor call'd This Treachery in the King.   [50]

16. Day, The Birth of our gracious Q. MARY.
      Away, and view the Graces and the Houres
      Hov'ring aloofe and dropping mingled Flowres
      Upon a Cradle, where an Infant lay
          More Grace, more Goddesse then were they;
      Thrice did they destine Her to passe the seas;   [55]
          (Love made Her thrice to pass with ease)
      To raise a strength of Princes first, and then
          To raise Another strength of Men.
      Most Fruitful Queene! we boast Both Gifts, And thus
      The Day was meant to You, the Joy to Us.   [60]

17. Day, The beginning of Q Elizabeths Raigne.
      Next to this *Mother* stands a *Virgin Queene*,
      Courting and Courted wheresoever seen;
      The Peoples Love first from Her Troubles grew;
          Her Reigne then made That Love her Due.
      That Comely Order, which did then adorne   [65]
          Both Fabricks, now by Facion[']s torn;
      That Forme, by her allow'd, of *Common Pray'r*
          Is styl'd vaine Beating of the Ayre.
      How doe they Honour, how forsake Her Crowne!
      Her Times are still Cry'd up, but Practis'd Downe.   [70]

19 Day, The Birth of our gracious King CHARLES.
      Reach last, the Whitest Stone the World yet knew,
      White as the Soule, to whom the Day is due.
      Sonne of the Peaceful *Iames*, how is he blest
          With All his Blessings but His Rest!
      Though undeserved Times call All His Pow'rs,   [75]
          And Troubles season Other Hour's,
      Let this Day flow to Him as void of Care,
          As Feasts to Gods, and Poets are:
      The Wish is Just, O Heavens! As our strife
      Hath added to His *Cares*, adde Yee to His *Life*.   [80]

      And now, since His Large Heart with Hers is met,
      Whose Day the starres on purpose neare His set;
      NOVEMBER shall to me for ever shine,
          Red in its Inke, Redder in Wine.

And since the *Third* (which almost hath made shift
   T'Absolve the Treason of the *Fift*) [86]
Cannot be well Remembred, or Forgot
   By Loyall Hearts, as if 'twere not;
The *Last* extreame, against the *First* wee'l bring:
That gave us *Many Tyrants*, This a KING. [90]

Confession.

I do confess, O God, my wand'ring Fires
Are kindled not from Zeal, but loose desires;
   My ready Tears, shed from Instructed Eyes,
Have not been Pious Griefs, but Subtleties;
   And only sorry that Sins miss, I ow [5]
To thwarted wishes al the Sighs I blow:
   My Fires thus merit Fire; my Tears the fall
Of Showers provoke; my Sighs for Blasts do call.
   O then Descend in Fire; but let it be
Such as snatch'd up the Prophet; such as We [10]
Read of in *Moses* Bush, a Fire of Joy,
Sent to Enlighten, rather than Destroy.
   O then Descend in Showers: But let them be
Showers only and not Tempests; such as we
Feel from the Mornings Eye-lids; such as Feed, [15]
Not Choak the sprouting of the Tender Seed.
   O then Descend in Blasts: But let them be
Blasts only, and not Whirlwinds; Such as we
Take in for Health's sake, soft and easie Breaths,
Taught to Conveigh Refreshments, and not Deaths. [20]
   So shall the Fury of my Fires asswage,
And that turn Fervour which was Brutish Rage;
   So shall my Tears be then untaught to feign,
And the diseased Waters Heal'd again;
   So shall my Sighs not be as Clouds t' invest [25]
My Sins with Night, but Winds to purge my Brest.

DOUBTFUL POEMS

To Splendora not to be perswaded:

Still so obdurate, hast thou vowed to liue
still in contempt of mee, whose chaste thoughts giue
their burden to thy view? twixt euery line
conceiue a sighe, but would that make thee mine
Ide sighe so oft, so deepe, that who soere [5]
should heare me, should suppose my whole life were
but one continuate breath; Ide turne to ayre
so I might hover about thee my faire,
and fanne thy Rosy Cheeke, and now and then
steale a soft kisse from't, and retire againe, [10]
but by and by I should presume to sippe
ravishing sweetnesse from thy scarlett lipp;
would weeping winne thee, I would practise it
till thou shouldst thinke each line thou readst were writt
with dropps of eye-brine. I haue in my eyes [15]
a spring, which as it wastes still multiplyes;
Ide weepe till I became all but one teare,
then turne into a pearle, so thou wouldst weare
me in thy eye, pearles hurt the sight they say[;]
I would not thine my faire, but rather pray [20]
To Loues great Deity, and neuer cease
till thou wert brought in loue with thy disease;
I would be sighe, teare, any thing that might
come but so neere thee, as thy touch or sight;
nay lesse, I would be nothing, could I proue [25]
after my change that thou wouldst nothing loue;
Then I whom now the world doth something call
in being nothing, should be all in all.

To Splendora hauing seene and spoke with her through a window:

I looked, and through the window chanced to spye
my faire, I knew her by her sparckling eye,
from whence like lightning flew a flame so bright,
that it's reflection did amaze my sight;
shee lookt me thought, for she is all divine, [5]
Like Venus shaddowed with a Christall shrine[.]

She whisperd too, but oh now comes my death
the glasse denyed a passage to her breath,
which worthiest only to perfume the place
where her selfe is, flew backe upon her face; [10]
some catchd her haires, and hung dissolued like Dew
on floras Curles, when Summer is but new:

But hauing heard her talke, each sence was bound,
and her sweet voice strucke me into a swound;
Loues charmes at last were loosed, and I about [15]
to see how I did looke by chance looked out,
when hauing through the window spyed my blisse
giue me said I noe Looking-glasse but this.

To Splendora desiring to heare musick:

Chaunt aloud, yee shrill-mouthd quires
of the aire, our chastest fires,
pierce the clouds with sweetest notes
ravishd from your siluer throates:
By my faire's command, descend [5]
some harmonious spheare, and lend
thy Celestiall straines; returne
Thracian Orpheus from thy urne,
thou that couldst so sweetly warble,
as to force the sencelesse marble, [10]
to the topp of Thebes high towers,
and command heauens stronger powers

by the soule-inchaunting noyse
of thy sence-amazing voice,
touch thy Ivory Lute, let fall [15]
from its siluer strings a call,
that may beasts and birds assemble,
let thy nimble fingers tremble
on thy Instrument, and daunce
in Divisions, till a traunce [20]
possesse each vulgar eare, my faire
deserues your most harmonious ayre:
Murmure sweetly springs, and fountaines
gliding from the topps of mountaines,
into th'Vallies bosome; whistle [25]
milde favonius through some thistle,
or some bush, that may divide
thy perfumed breath, lay quite aside
your boystrous blasts, and call to minde
tis my Splendora bids the winde [30]
breathe its softest ayres; what feare yee
to obey, least Joue should heare yee?
and being angry should enquire
what proud mortall dares aspire
to be so prophane, as call [35]
winged Zephirus from his stall,
or command the windes to breathe
aires sweeter then the fragrant wreath
of vernall flora? tell proud Joue,
and the Gods, it is my loue [40]
Does enforce you to obey
what none could command but they:
And my Splendora, let them know
that here's a Goddesse dwells below,
for whom least earth should be too base [45]
her selfe makes heauen of the place;
and whose Divinity makes us all
Excorporate, and Angelicall;
what could be added to his Joy, whose life
were guilded ore with so divine a wife? [50]

To Splendora A morning Salutation:

1. Splendora blesse the morne and Sol's resort,
    each blossome yet unborne shall thanke thee for't;
        but theres noe sunne but in thine eyes.
            the flowers,
                and dew-bepearled bowers [5]
        shedd orient dropps till thou arise,
            which on the ground
            like pebbles round
    congealed appeare, each proud to beare thee lyes:

2. Pearch here then siluer Doue, and doe not flye mee, [10]
    if thou mis-doubtst my loue, sitt downe and trye mee,
        my soule is ravishd with thy sight
            Ide sippe
            Nepenthe from thy lipp,
        oh doe not kill me with thy flight, [15]
            should Joue withstand
            what I demaund
    Ide warre with heauen it selfe for my delight:

3. Mercurys charming Rodd, and powerfull numbers
    shall strike each prying God into deepe slumbers; [20]
        whilst we two solace in embraces
            none wakes,
            noe Deity partakes
        but Cupid sporting in our faces,
            the wanton boy [25]
            augments our Joy,
    Because he doates himselfe on thy sweet graces:

4. See what a louely bedd of fragrant Roses
    hath curteous flora spread, and deckd with posies
        to entertaine thy louelyer skinne, [30]
            sitt downe
            dis-roabe thy selfe, and crowne
        Desire with Joy, it is noe sinne;
            A sugred kisse,
            leades to my blisse, [35]
    Joue when he wakes will wish hee here had beene.

To Splendora weeping:

Oh now the certaine cause I know
whence the Rose, and Lillies grow
on your faire Cheeke, those often showers
which you doe weepe, produce those flowers;
if that the flouds could Venus bring, [5]
and warlike Mars from Juno spring,
why may not hence two Gods arise,
this from your Cheeke, that from your Eyes.

To Splendora on the Same occasion:

Why doe these orient drops distill
from those Imperious eyes, what still?
What canst thou finde in me, my choice,
but that may cause thee to reioyce?
Heauen and Earth shall both agree [5]
to worke thee all felicitie;
Joue shall send showers, whose euery dropp
congealed to Amber in thy lapp
shall precious bee, only in this
because so like thy teares it is: [10]
The fire shall turne its heate to light
for fairer prospect of thy sight,
but that the glances of thine eyes
would vanquish both its properties;
The greedy windes shall each one seeke [15]
gently to kisse thy Rosy Cheeke;
With perfumed blasts, and here's their strife
whose breath shall hold the longest life;
but when those windes haue spent their store
thy sweetest selfe shall yeeld them more. [20]
A prodigie, that silly Earth
should yeeld supply to heauens dearth;
the nimble ayre shall with the spheares
by subtle motions fill thine eares
with various harmonies; the Sunne [25]

shall cease his dayly course to runne,
and standing still should be amazed,
to see his radiant beames out-blazed,
supposing Daphne from her tree
re-metamorphosed into thee; [30]
The chirping birds in early quires
shall flocke to feede thy chaste desires,
with sugred tones; their widened bills
shall be a symptome of their wills;
each one shall straine their narrow throates [35]
till with their melodious notes
th' haue lulld thy fancy fast asleepe,
then shall they singe noe more, but weepe
in mournefull Elegies, to see
thy eares deafe to their harmony; [40]
But yet at last they should reioyce
to see thee slumber by their voice.

To his Mrs Walking in ye snow

See faire Splendora what a lovely bed
Of candid snow the courteous heavens have spread
O're Earths congealed face, to entertaine
Th' Impression of thy feet, ye downy Raine
O'recome with' whitenes of thy purer foote [5]
Melts into teares: ye beames of Phœbus shoote
A warmth into it, least its pierceing cold
Offend thy softer skin: so being controll'd
By Sols obsequious glances, it implies
A contradiction (warme snow) such as lyes [10]
Within ye curious Iland of thy palme
Softer then bruised spices, sweet as balme [.]
Stand then but still, & here will seeme to grow
A stately Cedar on a bed of snow.
Should rare Apelles see thee walke, his Ghost [15]
Would leave Elizium & review o^r coast
By whom as in a Landskip might be drawne
A Goddesse walkeing on a sheet of Lawne [.]
Observe Splendora how each amorous flaque

Hovers about thy bosome: how they'le make [20]
By their mild confluence a pure milky way
To run through y^t sleeke valley wch doth lay
Betweene ye two round hillockes, thy soft breasts
Whose native colours purity contests
With snow in whitenes, & excells, for marke [25]
How being compar'd with thine it waxes darke
And changes colour: being asham'd to lye
On earth so low & yet so neare ye sky
But banisht thence with whitenes, melts wth greife
Into a falling teare & seekes releife [30]
Within ye closure of thy garments hemme
Where it to decke thee freezes to a Gemme.

On the Prince Charles death. W.C.

Tis vayne to weepe; or in a riming spite
Abuse the Fates in some base Epithete.
Such griefe distills from every whining penne,
And proves those, which wee grieve, for to bee men,
Cause theyr memoriall smotherd in a verse [5]
Lives in a Distick pind to th mourning Herse.
Or in a patcht upp dolefull Elegy
The two houres griefe of idle Poëtry.
Ours was a Deity at least, or such a one
As amongst men composde of flesh & bone [10]
Finding none like himselfe, in hast hee left us,
Viewd the world, only dyde, & so bereaft us:
Yet past not silent, but lett some tears fall,
As only mourning his owne funerall.
Just like a babling loud Alar'me thats wound [15]
Vpp for an houre, which come foorth wth a sound
Tells, the Time's past: then having struck his fill,
As if that rung his owne last knell, stands still.
Hee was not th'error of deficient nature
But was produc't compleat in limbs & feature: [20]
Hee was no Heteroclite: twas Natures spight,
That hee departed, not her oversight.
Wee 'njoyde him not one Sunne: his life it was

Short as his litle selfe: who thus did passe
From one grave to another; as if h'had bin [25]
In hast to tell above, what here h'had seene.
Hee livd not to his cradle; scarce to's death:
That was his first, that was his latest breath.
Others are borne, & speake, & goe, then fall:
His birth disolvd into his funerall. [30]
Yet looseth hee no honour: every day
Some one or other goes the selfe same way.
Who seeing hee could not enjoy him here
Goes hence in hope to bee his subject there.
Hee knowes no change: but mongst the very hosts [35]
Of purer Shadowes lives the Prince of Ghosts.

CRITICAL NOTES

*Si quis emergat poetaster, vel criticus
Qui notas fecerit aut animadversiones aliquot,*
Deleatur d, alii legunt sic, codex meus sic habet,
Phoebus audit, literarum decus, sidus, oraculum.
—Burton, *Philosophaster*

THE LADY-ERRANT

Text: Works (1651), pages 1–81, plus, at the beginning, two unnumbered leaves, sigs. ²a and ²a2.

Title-page, sig. ²aʳ: THE / LADY-ERRANT. / A / Tragi-Comedy. / [rule] / Written by / Mr WILLIAM CARTVVRIGHT, / Late Student of *Christ-Church* in / OXFORD, and Proctor of / the Vniversity. / [rule] / LONDON, / Printed for *Humphrey Moseley*, and / are to be sold at his shop at the Sign of / the Princes Armes in St *PAVLS* / Churchyard. 1651.   *Format:* 8vo.   *Collation:* ²a–²b⁸, c–e⁸, f³.

THE PROLOGUE

23 *each Sex keeps to it's Part*. This and some later lines (27–28) seem to indicate definitely that *The Lady-Errant* was acted by both men and women. See the Introduction to the play.

ACT I, SCENES I and II

The situation in which Lerinus, Gynactor, and Iringus brag to each other of ladies' favors while the ladies in question overhear them may be compared with a scene in Sedley's *Mulberry Garden* (1668), IV, i. In Sedley's play, Wildish, after carefully placing Victoria and Olivia where they may hear but not be seen, leads on Modish and Estridge, two unconscionable fops, to make quite preposterous boasts of imaginary favors. As in Cartwright, the maligned women eventually discover themselves and soundly berate their would-be, aspiring servants. The first part of Sedley's scene was probably suggested by Jonson's *Silent Woman*, V, i, but the later development suggests that Sedley may well owe a hint to Cartwright. With the revenge threatened by Pandena, Cosmeta, and Rhodia upon the offending courtiers, both here and in II, ii, compare Dorimant's mock vow of revenge upon Bellinda in Etherege's *Man of Mode* (1676), II, ii. Cartwright's three cowards, Lerinus, Gynactor, and Iringus, seem to bear more than a family likeness to three figures in Jasper Mayne's *Amorous War* (printed 1648). These characters, Callias, Neander, and Artops, like Cartwright's, are cowards of the first water, who while their country is at war, prefer to remain at home to "comfort" the ladies (I, i). (We may also compare on this point the fops Saladine and Aleran in D'Avenant's *Fair Favourite*, I, i.) Again like Cartwright's cowards they boast of promised favors (III, v) and complain of being continually importuned for their love.

3-4 *Politique dore . . . hindges.* This is, I believe, a Latinism. Compare Shirley's *The Traitor*, I, ii: "When the hinge of State did faint under the burden."

23 *Rustick sents . . . Court nose.* Cartwright is poking fun at the courtier's habit of using too many and too heavy scents. See his second prologue to *The Royal Slave*, lines 11-12.

41 *Net . . . pitch it.* The Elizabethan practice of snaring birds in nets is nicely illustrated by a cut in Whitney's *Choice of Emblems* (1586), page 27.

119-21 *Demolish Castles . . . Gaine Sconces 'twixt . . . Course.* Compare *The Siege*, lines 1548-50:

> How many Towns, pray y', are you wont to take
> 'Twixt first and second Course? What Castles do y'
> Demolish, besides Pye-crusts?

122 *large* Cretan *Jar.* Perhaps Cartwright means the "great Jarres made of earth" found in Cyprus as described by Lithgow in his *Rare Adventures* (1632), page 163.

128-29 *Corruption of one Coward . . . Generation of another.* Compare Marmion's *Holland's Leaguer*, V, iii:

> The corruption of a cashiered serving-man
> Is the generation of a thief.

Saintsbury (*Minor Caroline Poets*, 1908, II, Introduction to Marmion's poems) suggests that these lines of Marmion will be specially significant to the student of Dryden. Saintsbury refers to the epigrammatic comment on Sir Robert Howard in Dryden's "Defence of *An Essay of Dramatic Poesy*" (1668): "The corruption of a Poet is the generation of a Statesman."

Act I, Scene iii

259 *Romancys.* This is a not uncommon variant form of "ro-

mances." Shadwell, in *The Lancashire Witches*, I, i, uses the word adjectivally in the phrase "Romancy Knights." See also Swift's "Cadenus and Vanessa" (*Poetical Works*, 1735, II, p. 88):

> For why such Raptures, Flights, and Fancies,
> To her, who durst not read Romances.

ACT I, SCENE IV

291–306 *Is there no secret . . . Grove . . . vow'd to dye.* The highly affected grief of Malthora and Florina is very reminiscent of Lysippus' description of Aspatia's grief in Beaumont and Fletcher's *Maid's Tragedy*, I, i.

298–301 *and Snow . . . without noise.* Coleridge copied the following version of these lines into his commonplace book:

> And snow whose hanging weight
> Archeth some still deep river, that for fear
> Steals underneath without a sound.

The lines were attributed to Coleridge (Fragment 113) by J. D. Campbell in his edition of the poems; identified as Cartwright's by E. H. Coleridge (*Complete Poetical Works*, 1912, II, 996).

314 *Ancient Poet* Linus. Linus was a purely mythical Greek poet who gained local habitation and name through popular etymology.

333–40 *To Walke . . . Souls Begin.* The last eight lines of Eumela's "Ode" are reprinted in *The Marrow of Complements* (1655), page 85, with the title "An Ode."

352–59 *These, Eumela, are not . . . Regular Motion.* With certain changes Coleridge copied these lines into his commonplace book. He read "Emmeline" for "Eumela" (line 352); "stand still, I trow," for "stand still. I know" (355); and "Passion" for "Passions" (356). The lines were attributed to Coleridge (Fragment 98) by J. D. Campbell in his edition of the poems; identified as Cartwright's by E. H. Coleridge (*Complete Poetical Works*, 1912, II, 996).

ACT II, SCENE I

381 *To fairer . . . Plains.* An obvious recollection of the opening line of the first canto of *The Faerie Queene*.

391 *Inch*. Compare Shirley's reference to a page as "this inch and a half" in *The Maid's Revenge*, III, ii. See also his *Gamester*, IV, i. The attendants of knights-errant were traditionally dwarfish; see Butler's *Hudibras*, Book I, Canto I, lines 373–76.

395 *Little-Sisters-Vows*. Cartwright was thinking perhaps of *1 Henry IV*, III, i, 250–60.

ACT II, SCENE II

438–39 Monster-quelling . . . Machessa. See the note to line 1612 of *The Ordinary*.

479–81 *keep you, As they doe Hawkes—Watching . . . inward*. To watch a hawk was "to prevent it from sleeping in order to tame it" (*NED*). Zachary Grey (*Notes on Shakespeare*, 1754, I, 199) cites this passage to illustrate *The Taming of the Shrew*, IV, i, 196–99.

481 *inward*. Used of a bird or beast, "inward" means "tame" or "domesticated" (*NED*).

483 *take a toy*. The phrase "to take a toy" means to conceive a sudden or unreasonable aversion (*NED*).

497 *Machin*. Cartwright seems to employ this word in the sense of "machination" or "scheme."

ACT II, SCENE III

509 *stroke*. "Stroke" here seems to mean "capacity" or "ability" (*Century Dictionary*).

514 *On the Greek Epigrams*. Compare the swearing upon Ovid in Shirley's *The Ball*, IV, ii.

ACT II, SCENE IV

554–55 *in the holy Rites Of . . . Venus*. Like Leander and Troilus, Lucasia receives the first glimpse of her lover during the celebration of a religious service.

ACT II, SCENE V

646 *unbody'd Essences*. Compare Cartwright's "No Platonique Love," line 5: "That two unbodi'd Essences may kiss."

ACT II, SCENE VI

Compare the situation in this scene with Massinger's *A New Way to Pay Old Debts* (about 1625), III, i.

657–58 *Have I deserted My Country.* Compare D'Avenant's *The Siege*, III, iv.

ACT III, SCENE II

This scene presents one of the most hallowed and hackneyed devices of Platonic drama—the duel of two sworn friends, incited by mistaken jealousy. To suggest any specific source for the scene would be absurd. The "matter" was in the air and contagious. Examples for comparison may be found in Randolph's *Jealous Lovers* (1632), II, xii; Brome's *Love-Sick Court* (1658), IV, ii; Carlell's *Deserving Favourite* (1629), IV, and *The Fool would be a Favourite* (1657), II; D'Avenant's *Fair Favourite* (1638), IV, i; and Chamberlayne's *Love's Victory* (1658), IV, vii. A forerunner of the situation may be studied in Beaumont and Fletcher's *Maid's Tragedy* (1611), III, ii. Aston Cokain's *Obstinate Lady* (1657), I, ii, varies the stock examples by contenting itself with a debate on love and friendship, so affecting that the impending combat is averted and the reader threatened not in vain with sleep.

873 *She hath a Mind.* All Platonic heroines seem to have been even more wise than beautiful, surely a parlous state in one who has just been described as having a face of "but one solid Light." Compare Carlell's *Osmond*, V, and Glapthorne's *Wit in a Constable*, I.

924–25 *in the mean Whiles he is absent.* I doubt whether this is even good seventeenth-century English, but the insertion of a second "while," following "mean," destroys the meter.

1006 *Let us embrace . . . yet.* Compare Sidney's *Arcadia* (ed. A. Feuillerat, 1912, p. 295).

1006–12 *The Fates. . . . I'l not be Jealous there.* Miss Kathleen M. Lynch (*Social Mode of Restoration Comedy*, 1926, p. 123) points out an interesting parallel in the Dryden-Howard *Indian Queen* (1664), V, i:

> Dear Montezuma,
> I may be still your friend, though I must die
> Your rival in her love: Eternity
> Has room enough for both; there's no desire,
> Where to enjoy is only to admire;
> There we'll meet friends, when this short storm is past.

As I point out in the General Introduction, Chapter IV, "Influence and Later Reputation," *The Indian Queen* seems to show the influence of *The Royal Slave*, a relationship which tends to strengthen the suggested influence of *The Lady-Errant* in the passage quoted above. Cartwright's situation and lines in turn suggest a memory of Beaumont and Fletcher's *Philaster*, IV, iii, 67–68; iv, 108–14.

Act III, Scene III

1021–22 *Dream . . . The reliques of your day-time thoughts.* This was a common explanation of dreams. Burton (*Anatomy of Melancholy*, 1638, Part 2, Sec. 2, Memb. 5) quotes from Cicero's *Somnium Scipionis*: ". . . for the most part our speeches in the day time, cause our phantasie to worke upon the like in our sleep." See also *The Phoenix Nest* (1593, p. 31): "A most rare, and excellent Dreame."

1034–59 *Wake my* Adonis, *do not dye*. This "ode," set to music by Dr. Coleman, was very popular. Other texts, with musical setting, appear in John Playford's *Select Musicall Ayres, and Dialogues* (1652, pp. 28–29; 1653, pp. 26–27); *Select Ayres and Dialogues* (1659, pp. 4–5; 1669, pp. 4–5—usually treated as a mere re-issue of *Select Ayres* 1659; hence not listed in the Textual Notes). Other texts of the lyric appear in Cotgrave's *Wits Interpreter* (1655, p. 105; 1662, p. 211; 1671, p. 211); and in *Parnassus Biceps* (1656, pp. 59–60). It was also reprinted, from *Parnassus Biceps* with the title "Venus *Lachrymans*," in Volume VI of Dryden's *Miscellany* (1716, p. 386; 1727, pp. 314–15).

1035 *thee and I*. Goffin points out that although this is not grammatically unexceptionable, similar uses, or misuses, of the pronouns can be instanced in other contemporaries of Cartwright and that even today, among his fellow Gloucestershire men, there are country people who would find the grammar impeccable. He quotes from Katherine Philips' "To Mrs. M. A. at parting":

> To part with thee I needs must die,
> Could parting sep'rate thee and I.

We may also recall Shakespeare's "Making we fools of nature" (*Hamlet*) and Shelley's "there is a holier judge than me" (*The Cenci*, III, i, 364). When used deliberately, in Cartwright's case for the sake of the rhyme, this figure was known as *enallage* by the Tudor grammarians. See Sister Miriam Joseph, *Shakespeare's Use of the Arts of Language* (1947), p. 61.

1042-43 *'twas this I feard . . . Ghost appear'd*. This is not a comforting sentiment to sing to a woman who has just dreamed of seeing her husband dead. The situation reminds one of a passage in Sidney's *Arcadia* (1590), Book III, Chapter 12: ". . . the beautiful *Parthenia* (who had that night dreamed shee sawe her husbande in such estate [i.e., dying], as she then founde him. . . ." Cartwright had already used, or was soon to use, this incident in his poem, "*Parthenia* for her slain *Argalus*."

ACT III, SCENE V

1101-2 *Love carries up* Eumela . . . *high as is her Princess*. Such a democracy in love was one of the tenets of Platonic love. Compare Glapthorne's *The Lady's Privilege*, II, i:

> Love's an unlimited passion, that admits
> No Ceremonious difference: this prerogative
> Should Queenes endevour, their unvalued Dowries
> Are not of worth to purchase: and tho here
> As it befits me, I observe the distance
> Due to your birth; yet in loves sacred Court,
> My place is high as yours.

See further, lines 1150-53 of *The Lady-Errant*.

1110-11 *same Metall that wounded both*. Eumela means that both she and Lucasia were wounded by Cupid's golden arrow, which kindles love, not his lead-tipped arrow, which creates an aversion to love. See Ovid's *Metamorphoses*, I, 468-76.

ACT IV, SCENE I

This, I assume, is the scene designated by Fleay (*Biographical Chronicle of the English Drama*, 1891, I, 48) and Hazlitt (*Play-Collector's Manual*, 1892, p. 127) as a borrowing from Aristophanes. They refer, presumably, either to the judgment of Euripides in the *Thesmophoriazusæ* or to the reported senate scene in the *Ecclesiazusæ*. Although I do not doubt that Cartwright's original inspiration for a female commonwealth came from Aristophanes, there is nothing in the present scene which might not better perhaps be referred to Erasmus' colloquy, "The Parliament, or Assembly, of Women." Erasmus' treatment combines the debate form used in the *Thesmophoriazusæ* and the idea of a female commonwealth found in the *Ecclesiazusæ*.

1178-87 *Grant me . . . our Modesty.* These lines, with some rephrasing, are used by D'Urfey in his *Commonwealth of Women* (1686), III, i, a poor alteration of Fletcher's *Sea Voyage*.

1192-95 *Now's the time . . . all one.* Compare these sentiments with those of the revolting slaves in Massinger's *The Bondman* (1623), II, iii, who likewise find an opportunity for insurrection offered by a war in which "our proud masters and all the able freemen of the city are gone unto the wars and old men and such as can make no resistance remain at home."

1206 *Primeve.* Obsolete form of "primeval" (*NED*).

1213 *Sibyl's Leaf.* Compare line 45.

1219 *one call'd us Dough-bak'd Men.* See Overbury's character of "A Very Woman": "A very *woman*, is a dow-bakt man, or a *she* meant well towards man, but fell two bowes short, *strength* and *understanding*." Compare the phrases "dough-bak'd men" in Donne's "A Letter to the Lady Carey" (l. 20) and "dough-baked creatures" in the anonymous "Character of a Fanatick" (1675; *Harleian Miscellany*, 1810, VIII, 79).

1232 *re-estate.* A very common seventeenth-century form of "reinstate" (*NED*).

1238 *cautelous.* The word is used here simply as a synonym for "cautious," not for "deceitful" as Cockeram's *English Dictionarie* (1623) defines it.

1275 *Sparks.* Small diamonds (*NED*).

1347 *To say I'l do't is lazy; it is done.* Compare a passage in *The Royal Slave*, lines 871-72; both would seem to be imitated from Seneca's *Hercules Furens*, III, ii:

> Si novi Herculem,
> Lycus Creonti debitas poenas dabit;
> Lentum est, dabit; dat: hoc quoque est lentum;
> dedit.

Act IV, Scene II

1423-25 *Jove . . . fit Husband . . . Got horns, and hoofs.* Cartwright's mythology seems to be a little doubtful here. Europa was not a "Cretan Lady," but was brought to Crete by Jupiter.

Act IV, Scene iii

1478 *I've both their Statues.* This bringing to life of the "statues" of Pæstanus and Philondas was probably suggested by *The Winter's Tale*, V, iii. See also, however, Massinger's *The City Madam* (1632), V, iii, and Jasper Mayne's *City-Match* (1637), V, vii.

Act IV, Scene vi

1611-12 *Wisdome and Love . . . never . . . Permitted to a God.* Compare the aphorism of Publilius Syrus: "Amare et sapere vix Deo conceditur."

1618 *first brake from out the Chaos.* According to one legend, Eros was the first born of all the gods. See Cartwright's poem, "On a Gentlewomans Silk-hood," line 29, and my note on the passage.

1625-26 *it self Hath Eyes.* Cartwright repeats this conceit in *The Siege*, lines 1399-1402.

1647-51 *Jealousie What art thou? . . . nought but Hate.* Compare Carew's "Song of Jealousy" (1633), lines 1-6:

> 'From whence was first this Fury hurl'd,
> This Jealousy, into the World?
> Came she from Hell?' *Answer.* 'No, there doth reign
> Eternal hatred, with Disdain;
> But she the daughter is of Love. . . .'

This song is dated 1633 on the authority of Thomas Killigrew, who claims in a note to the Second Part of his *Cicilia and Clorinda*, V, ii, that it was written for him by Carew as the result of a dispute with Mistress Cecily Crofts. Compare also "The description of Iealousie" in *The Phoenix Nest* (1593), page 91, and Sidney's *Arcadia* (ed. A. Feuillerat, 1912, p. 309).

1661-62 *Suffer that fear . . . springs from.* Coleridge copied these lines into his commonplace book in December, 1803, and added a line at the beginning: "My irritable fears all sprang from Love." All three lines were printed as Coleridge's (Fragment 64) by J. D. Campbell in his edition of the poems. They were identified as Cartwright's by E. H. Coleridge (*Complete Poetical Works*, 1912, II, 996).

1670-71 *Faith . . . Merit.* Compare Shakespeare's *Troilus and Cressida*, IV, iv:

>   Alas, a kind of godly jealousy . . .
>   In this I do not call your faith in question
>   So mainly as my merit.

Act V, Scene I

1714 *Queen o' th'* Amazons. Most of the classical lore concerning the Amazons may be found collected into a single narrative account in the first story of the second volume of Painter's *Palace of Pleasure* (1567). Much of the material in this scene connected with Amazons and Pygmies seems to be of Cartwright's own invention.

1715 *thou o'th'* Pigmies. The story of the queen of the Pygmies comes originally from Ovid's *Metamorphoses*, VI, 90–92, and from Aelian's *De Natura Animalium*, XV, xxix. Pliny's *Natural History* (trans. P. Holland, 1635 ed., I, 156) contains the most circumstantial account of the race. Lluellin (*Men-Miracles*, 1646, "Of Pigmies") cites twenty authorities. Dr. J. Ferriar in his essay "Of Certain Varieties of Man" (*Illustrations of Sterne*, 1812, II, 73–82) gives a complete discussion and criticism of all the sources of the Pygmy legend. See also Shirley's *The Opportunity*, IV, i, where Pisanio promises his page, Ascanio, that he shall be "prince of Pigmyland."

1722–28 *The King of* Monomotapa . . . *the* Agags . . . *look lovely*. It seems probable that the "Book" which Cartwright mentions in this passage as his authority was Peter Heylin's *Microcosmus*, which had gone through six editions by 1633. I quote from the edition of 1670 (by then called *Cosmographie*), pages 991–92:". . . a wilde and cruel people, called *Agag*, inhabiting on Lake *Zembre*, and the banks of the *Nilus*; dispersed about the fields in their homely cottages, black, *Cannibals*, and of an horrible aspect; more horrible than otherwise they would be, by drawing lines upon their cheeks with an iron-instrument, and forcing their eye lids to turn backwards. By the assistance of this people the King of *Moenhemage* hath hitherto preserved his Estate against the King of *Monomotapa*."

1750–51 *Quick-silver Is put into hot Loves*. A reference to the venereal disease, in the cure of which quicksilver or mercury was one of the most commonly used medicaments.

1755 *Hays*. Nets used for catching wild animals (*NED*).
1760 Chin, Chin. An Anglo-Chinese phrase of salutation. The earliest use recorded in the *NED* is 1795, over 150 years later than Cartwright's.
1769 *Ginger-bread Office*. A privy (*NED*).
1772 *stone-pots with Beards*. Cartwright is describing a large type of drinking mug-cum-jug, common in the seventeenth century, called a bellarmine. Compare *The Ordinary*, lines 1464–70:

> Thy belly looks like to some strutting hill,
> O'r shadow'd with thy rough beard like a wood.
>   *Chri.* Or like a larger Jug, that some men call
> A Bellarmine, but we a Conscience;
> Whereon the lewder hand of Pagan workman
> Over the proud ambitious head hath carv'd
> An Idoll large with beard Episcopal.

The jug was, of course, named after the famous Italian cardinal, Robert Bellarmine (1542–1621), a noted controversial writer.

1774 *Dorsers*. Panniers (*NED*).
1789–90 *They fly In a most war-like Figure naturally*. Under *Cranes*, Josua Poole (*English Parnassus*, ed. 1677, p. 283) quotes the following lines:

> Direct their flight on high,
> And cut their way, they in a Trigon fly:
> Which pointed figure may with ease divide
> Opposing blasts through which they swiftly glide.

1792–93 *Gentleman That bridles Stags . . . draw Caroches*. I have been unable to learn who this "Gentleman" was.
1799 *Yerk*. Lash or beat (*NED*).
1808 *twist*. The junction of the thighs (*NED*).
1810 *pall-mall*. Indiscriminately (*NED*). Cartwright's spelling is due to a confusion with the game called "pall-mall," which was sometimes spelled "pell-mell."
1821 *Teach 'em good Language by cleft sticks, and Bay-leaves*. Gifford in a note to Jonson's *Poetaster*, V, i (*Works*, ed. Gifford-Cunningham, I, 253–54) points out that "The bay was sacred to Apollo; hence perhaps the notion of the ancients, that a bay-leaf placed under the tongue was conducive to eloquence." (H. S. Mallory in his edition of *Poetaster*, 1905, p. 221, quotes

Juvenal, *Satire VII*, 18-19.) The allusion behind the reference to "cleft sticks" as a linguistic tool eludes me, though Gifford in the note already quoted (citing Cartwright's lines in illustration of Jonson) appears somehow to connect them with the "pilled rods" of Genesis 30 : 37; at least this is all I can deduce from his comment: "I do not suppose that Voltaire ever looked into Cartwright: but this [the proposals of Philænis] is nearly the way in which he recommended us to treat the revolted Caraibs." The only reference in Voltaire which seems to have any bearing correlates the Genesis passage with certain reports then current concerning the Caribs (*Œuvres Completes de Voltaire*, 1878, XI, 24-25). Cartwright uses the Genesis reference in *The Ordinary* (ll. 808-9) to illustrate the power of the imagination, and again in "To the Right Reverend *Father* in God, *Brian*" (ll. 133-38).

Act V, Scene ii

1829   *Souldier*. This is the common collective singular. See Fletcher's *Beggars' Bush*, I, ii, 70.

1870-71   Charistus *shall . . . Slave*. The "oracle machine," which, like a will-o'-the-wisp hangs about in the background and rather ineffectively motivates the principal action, is, of course, one of the commonest devices of Greek romance. In English it first becomes fashionable with Sidney's *Arcadia*. See F. W. Moorman's introduction to his edition of Shakespear's *Winter's Tale* (Arden edition, 1912).

1903   Cupid *hath his Cabinet*. Cartwright seems to mean that the affairs of Cupid are of a private or secret nature. See the scene of "Cupid's Cabinet" in Montague's *Shepherd's Paradise*.

Act V, Scene iv

1935   *Crisping Pins*. Curling pins.

1968   *seven Sages*. Cartwright is referring to the so-called "Seven Wisemen of Greece." See some verses, with an accompanying woodcut, concerning these Seven Sages in Whitney's *Choice of Emblems* (1586), page 130. Whitney records in his usual pedestrian verse the most famous "sentence" of each of the seven. There was a popular romance with the title, *The Proces of the Seuyn Sages*, which, however, seems to be concerned with seven Roman "wits."

Act V, Scene viii

2060 *Phœbus as Præsent shewes us future things.* I once thought it possible that Cartwright was using *Præsent* here in the sense of "prognosticator," from the Latin verb "prae-sentio." Compare, however, Milton, *Paradise Lost*, XI, 870-71:

> O thou who future things canst represent
> As present, . . .

Or Dryden, *Tyrannic Love*, I, i:

> I have consulted one, who reads heaven's doom,
> And sees, as present, things which are to come."

Goffin prints the phrase as "Phœbus at Present."

The Epilogue

1 *Neighbouring Plain.* I have suggested in the Introduction to the play that this phrase refers to Cambridge, and that the "Scrip and Crook" which "May worst our Poet's Book" (ll. 3-4) is a possible allusion to Montague's *Shepherd's Paradise*. There is a lightness of touch and a strain of genuine poetry in this epilogue which sets it apart from verse of the type.

THE ROYAL SLAVE

Printed Texts: The Royall Slave, Oxford, 1639; second edition, Oxford, 1640; third edition, *Works* (1651), pages 85–148.

Manuscript Texts: Bodleian Library, Arch. Seld. B. 26 (here collated, and designated as *S*); Folger MS. 7044, once in the possession of B. Dobell (here collated, and designated as *F*); British Museum, Addit. MS. 41, 616 (here collated, and designated as *P*); manuscript in the possession of the Duke of Bedford (here collated, and designated as *B*); Heber MS. 1043 (now untraced). For a full discussion of the printed and manuscript texts, see the Introduction to the play.

Title-page, 1639 edition: THE / ROYALL / SLAVE. / *A* / Tragi-Comedy. / Presented to the King and Queene / by the Students of *Christ-Church* / in Oxford. *August 30. 1636.* / Presented since to both their Ma- / jesties àt *Hampton-Court* by the / Kings Servants. / [double rule] / *OXFORD,* / Printed by William Turner for / Thomas Robinson. *1639.*   Format: 4to.   Collation: A–H⁴, I².

Title-page, 1640 edition: THE / ROYALL / SLAVE. / *A* / Tragi-Comedy. / Presented to the King and Queene / by the Students of *Christ-Church* / in Oxford. *August 30. 1636.* / Presented since to both their Ma- / jesties at *Hampton-Court* by the / Kings Servants. / [rule] / *The second Edition.* / [rule and ornament] / *OXFORD,* / Printed by William Turner for / Thomas Robinson. *1640.*   Format: 4to.   Collation: A–H⁴.

Title-page, Works (1651): THE / ROYALL / SLAVE. / A Tragi-Comedy. / [rule] / Presented to the King and Queen / by the Students of *Christ-Church* / in Oxford, *Aug. 30. 1636.* / Presented since to both their Majesties, at / *Hampton-Court,* by the Kings servants. / [rule] / The Third Edition. / [rule] / Written by / Mr William Cartvvright, / Late Student of *Christ-Church* in Oxford, and Proctor of / the *Vniversity.* / [rule] / London, / Printed for *T.R.* & *Humphrey Moseley,* and / are to be sold at his shop at the Sign of / the Princes

Armes in St *PAVLS* / Churchyard. *1651.*   *Format:* 8vo. *Collation:* g–k⁸.

THE PROLOGUE TO THE KING AND QUEENE

In addition to the manuscripts listed above, there is one in the British Museum (Egerton MS. 2725, fols. 115-16) which contains a copy of the first two prologues and the first two epilogues. This manuscript is included in the collation and is designated as *E*. It also contains the first stanza of the Priest's song, lines 167-72.

It seems likely that Cartwright received a hint for this prologue from the opening speech of Hymen in Jonson's *Hymenæi* (1606).

The first and second prologues to *The Royal Slave* may have suggested to D'Avenant the device of using a Priest of the Sun as a kind of chorus prologue to the third part of his *Play-House to be Let*—"The Cruelty of the Spaniards in Peru" (1658; *Dramatic Works*, ed. Maidment and Logan, IV, 78). Cartwright's priest, who first worships the sun and then turns to the king as being the greater light, seems to be quite clearly reflected in one of the choral songs in Shadwell's *Royal Shepherdesse* (1669; *Complete Works*, ed. M. Summers, I, 132). The song does not appear in John Fountain's *The Rewards of Vertue* (1661), of which Shadwell's play is a revision. That Shadwell was well acquainted with Cartwright's works is clear from his debt to *The Ordinary* in his adaptation of Molière's *L'Avare*, *The Miser* (1672).

THE PROLOGUE TO THE UNIVERSITY

11-12   *the Court Not smelt*. Cartwright has already referred to the courtiers' excessive use of perfumes (*The Lady-Errant*, line 23). Overbury in his character of "A Courtier" sums up the situation when he remarks, "He smels." See also *The Winter's Tale*, IV, iv, 757, and Henry King's poem, "To his friends of Christ Church upon the mislike of the marriage of the Artes, acted at Woodstocke" (quoted from Harl. MS. 6917, fol. 65):

> But is it true the Court mislikt the play, . . .
> Guests that are stronger farre in smell then witt.

17-18   *Majesty was seene . . . Spectators only made the Play*. Compare

"The Triumph of King Charles," 1641 (*Harleian Miscellany*, 1810, V, 86):

> Where e'er you go,
> All else are but spectators, not the show.

23 *late damn'd bookes*. Cartwright is thinking specifically, of course, of Prynne's *Histrio-mastix* (1633).

25 *little Ruffe*. A Puritan. Compare Cleveland's poem, "The Puritan" (*Works*, 1687, p. 355):

> With Pate cut shorter than the Brow,
> With little Ruff starch'd you know how.

See also Corbet's poem, "To Mr. Hammon Parson of Beadly, for pulling down the May-pole" (*Poems*, ed. O. Gilchrist, 1807, pp. 108–9):

> Oft hath a Sister grounded in a truth,
> Seeing the jolly carriage of the youth,
> Been tempted to the way thats broad and bad;
> And wert not for our private pleasures, had
> Renounced her little ruffe and goggle eye
> And quit her self of the fraternity.

See also *The Ordinary*, line 2449.

ACT I, SCENE 1

2–3 *I charm'd my fleas with 'em*. That is, I got drunk with them. Although Cartwright's meaning seems clear enough, I cannot illustrate the phrase from any other writer. Perhaps somewhat the same zoological activity lies behind the following line from Etherege's *Comical Revenge* (1664), IV, iii:

> Here's a Brimmer then to her, and all the Fleas
> About her.

4 *well to live*. Thoroughly drunk. Brand (*Popular Antiquities*, 1900, p. 495) quotes from Harris' *Drunkard's Cup* (1653): "One is *coloured*, another is *foxt*, a third is *gone to the dogs*, and a fourth is *well to live*."

14–19 *A pox on our Gaolor*. This lyric was set to music by William Lawes and appeared in *Catch that Catch can: or the Musical Companion* (1667), page 74, as an eight-line version, concluding with the two-line chorus from "Now, now, the Sunne is fled" (Act III, Scene i); the musical notation for these extra lines is not the same, however, as in the Henry Lawes setting for that song. The six-line version found in the play appeared in *The Musical Companion* (1673), page 53. The lyric was also set to music by John Hilton and published in his *Catch that Catch can, or A Choice Collection of Catches, Rounds, & Cannons* (1652), page 29; and again in *Catch that Catch can* (1658), page 28. The lyric (the eight-line version) occurs in *Merry Drollery, Complete* (1670), Part II, page 289, and in *The New Academy of Complements* (1671), page 120. An adapted version of the first two lines of Cartwright's lyric is used in "Hugh Peter's *Thanksgiving SPEECH for a Farewel to the City*" (in *Posthumous Works of Mr. Samuel Butler*, 1715, II, 170):

> A Pox on your *Butler*, and on his lean Jowl,
> There's Liberty lies in the Bottom o'th' Bowl.

Miss Willa McClung Evans ("Lovelace's Concept of Prison Life in 'The Vintage to the Dungeon,' " *Philological Quarterly*, XXVI [Jan., 1947], 62–68) suggests that Lovelace's drinking song, likewise set by William Lawes, received its suggestions for "typical" prison life not from his actual imprisonment in the Gatehouse (1642) but from the account of prison life in *The Royal Slave*. She also draws a parallel between the theme of Lovelace's "The Vintage to the Dungeon" and this song of Cartwright's. That Lovelace knew *The Royal Slave* seems clear from his imitation of the chorus lines in "Come from the Dungeon" (see note to lines 171–72).

19 *cry clinke in the Close*. Compare Jonson's *Silent Woman*, II, ii: ". . . how it chimes and cries tink in the close."

31 *her's a Persian line*. Compare "here's your compass," meaning a halter, in Heywood's *Fortune by Land and Sea* (1655), V, ii; and "your wedding ring" in *The Duchess of Malfi* (1614), IV, ii, 259.

39 *Web-errantry of highway-Inkle*. This is an extremely obscure phrase. "Highway-Inkle" is, I suppose, connected with "inkle-beggar," one who sells tape (*NED*). Cartwright means that Molops' wife has graduated from itinerant selling of cheap tapes to the twisting of hempen ropes. "Web-errantry" is unrecorded in the *NED*.

40 *turning and winding of home-bred Hempe*. The Elizabethan

method of making rope is well illustrated by a cut in Whitney's *Choice of Emblems* (1586), page 48.

41 *three-halfe-penny Legacy.* This seems for a long time to have been the standard price for the hangman's rope. See Francis Grose's *Dictionary of the Vulgar Tongue* (1785), under "Hangman's Wages."

45 *whiffle.* To blow with a puff of air (*NED*).

71 *custome of the Persian Kings.* See the Introduction to the play, page 187.

81 *'Tis a small fee.* In Cartwright's day and earlier it was the recognized custom for the hangman to take the clothes of his victims. See *I Henry IV*, I, ii, and Edwards' *Damon and Pithias* (ed. Hazlitt, *Old English Plays*, 1874, IV, 94).

95–97 *stand in your rankes . . . blow nothing on the Lords.* Compare Jasper Mayne's *Amorous War* (1638), V, ii:

> Come Gentlemen, now stand in Ranke, and keep
> Due distance from the *Lords;* Lest there passe
>   from you
> A creeping Entercourse, which may disturbe
> The sitting of the *Court.*

Mayne was one of Cartwright's best friends, a fact which makes the probability of influence here more likely. (See also lines 379–80 and 457–59.) Although we do not know which play was written first, it seems likely that *The Royal Slave* was the earlier.

Act I, Scene ii

The considerable borrowings from Theodorus Prodromus' *Rhodanthes et Dosiclis Amorum* in this scene are pointed out below. The situation and attitude of Cratander suggest a comparison with the situation and character of the prisoner, Sophocles, in Fletcher's *Four Plays in One* (about 1612). Compare also Gay's *Polly* (1729), II, viii. See the Introduction for a full discussion of Dryden's borrowing from this scene in his *Don Sebastian* (1690), I, i.

109 *conning a Hymne.* His neck-verse, usually Psalm 51:1.

111 *discourse o'th' Nature of the Soule.* Cartwright means perhaps Plato's *Phaedo.*

125 *next his heart.* Fasting, or on an empty stomach (*NED*). Although such is the accepted meaning of this phrase, the

present context seems to demand some meaning like "willingly" or "whole-heartedly."

131–36 *Contemne the Thunderer . . . rest is due.* Compare Theodorus Prodromus' *Rhodanthes et Dosiclis Amorum* (trans. from the Greek by Gilbertus Gaulminus, Paris, 1625), page 315: "Confestim indigenas Deos illustri ex praeda spoliisque sacrificio placaturus. Omnium enim rerum primitijs Numinum pacem exorare decet." See the Introduction to the play for a full discussion of Theodorus' novel in connection with *The Royal Slave*.

137–44 *True. Tell me . . . Natures trespasses.* Compare Theodorus, pages 320–23: "Verum age, si bovem sacrificare velles, an non opimum eligeres? *Dos.* Omnino eligerem. *Bry.* An non optimo mulso victimarum carnes irrigares? *Dos.* Ita facerem: nam optimum optimo tribui expedit. *Bry.* An pulchros Dei amant? *Dos.* Amant. *Bry.* An ipsa Pulchritudo, pulchrum quidpiam non est? Si pertendis, deformes igitur non amant. *Dos.* Non amant: Deformitas namque malum est."

148–52 *reasoned . . . Against thy selfe . . . to be spar'd.* Compare Theodorus, page 324: "*Bry.* Satius igitur formosos, ipsoque aetatis flore vernantes sacrificare. *Dos.* Ita est: verum quid ideo tibi concludendum videtur, ô Rex? *Bry.* Hoc omnino; vos uti spoliorum praedaeque primitias Dijs victoriae auctoribus sacrificandos. *Dos.* Bene, & si placet sacrifica."

152–58 *I could Tell you . . . destin'd Hecatombe.* Compare Theodorus, page 328: ". . . hoc unum, si concedis, addam. Dij taurorum sacrificia vitulorumque ac boum carnes, thurisque micam in ignem injectam gratissimas habent; humanas vero victimas, caedesque longe, ut puto, aversantur." And pages 336–39: "Adeo illi salutis nostrae amantes, hominum carnes, caedemque, elixa corpora, et foedum sanie aërem oderunt. Si secundum nos compositi essent, si lingua, dentibus, ventre, intestinis, & singulis quae nobis natura tribuit, instructi."

158–61 *this would be To deprecate my fate . . . Nuptialls.* Compare Theodorus, page 316: "At alius alacer intrepidusque mortem ut nuptias expectat."

167–69 *Come from the Dungeon to the Throne.* Lawes' complete musical setting has only recently been discovered (see the introduction to the play, p. 170). In *Select Ayres and Dialogues* (1659; reissued 1669), page 26, Lawes published a musical setting for the first six lines only. The play MSS. *S, F, P, B, E* also contain only the first six lines of the lyric (in *E* entitled "Chorus posterior"). Miss Evans notices a solo setting for this song in Lawes' autographed manuscript (p. 75, here collated), and another version, "probably copied from the original autographed version," in the British Museum (Addit. MS. 29,396). This last manuscript I have not seen. A version of the first six lines of this song, combined with the first six lines of the song in Act V, Scene vii (including, I believe, Lawes' setting of those lines) appeared in *Catch that Catch can: or the Musical Companion* (1667), pages 166–67, and in *The Musical Companion* (1673), sigs. [P5]v–[P6]. Cartwright's complete lyric is quoted in W. Beloe's *Anecdotes of Literature* (1812), VI, 179.

With the first line of Cartwright's song compare the opening line of a lyric in John Fountain's comedy, *The Rewards of Vertue* (1661): "Thus from the Prison to the Throne."

171–72 *So Beasts for sacrifice . . . crown'd . . . bleed.* Compare Lovelace's "Aramantha—A Pastoral" (*Poems*, ed. W. C. Hazlitt, 1864, pp. 69–70):

> She's for the Altar not the Skies
> Whom first you crowne, then sacrifice.

Compare also the following couplet in Settle's *Cambyses* (1671), II, i:

> This Night *Cambyses* dyes. Whilst *Smerdis* is
> Crown'd for our King, he for our Sacrifice.

200 *Jack-chaynes.* Chains each link of which consists of a double loop of wire, resembling a figure eight (*NED*). Cartwright's is the earliest use of the term recorded.

216–19 *still a Slave . . . Jewell . . . private man.* Compare the anonymous *Merry Devil of Edmonton* (1608), II, ii:

> She is no more disparag'd by thy basenes
> Then the most orient and the pretious iewell,
> Which still retaines his lustre and his beauty,
> Although a slaue were owner of the same.

ACT I, SCENE III

264 *tough fellow.* This is the reading of all the manuscripts and of the first two printed editions (1639, 1640); a note in the

Errata to the 1651 text tells us to read "rough fellow." The correction was probably the work of one of Moseley's press correctors. See Chaucer's *Troilus and Criseyde*, III, 87, for "tough" used in the sense of "pertinacious."

Act II, Scene III

370-96 *Come my sweet, whiles every strayne.* This song was set to music by Henry Lawes and appears in *Ayres and Dialogues* (1653), Part I, page 30, and (first stanza only) in *Select Ayres* (1659; reissued, 1669), page 26. A manuscript version of the setting and words (first two stanzas only) occurs in Lawes' autographed manuscript, page 74. The lyric also appears in *Wits Interpreter* (1655), page 113 (1662, p. 220, 1671, p. 220), and in *Marrow of Complements* (1655), pages 52-53. Beloe quotes the poem in full in his *Anecdotes of Literature* (1812), VI, 179.

370-73 *whiles every . . . they heare.* Josua Poole in *The English Parnassus*, prints these lines as follows (1657, p. 510; 1677, p. 552):

> Whilst every straine
> Calls the soul into the ears. Taking all ears captive.
> Which with a greedy listening fain
> Would turn into the sound it hears.

371 *Calls our Soules into the Eare.* Compare Traherne's "News," line 4: " 'Twas wont to call my Soul into mine Ear."

379-80 *conveigh Our Soules into each other's Brest.* Compare Jasper Mayne's lines in *The Amorous War* (1638), IV, vi:

> And Whil'st we try the Way,
> By which Love doth convey
>   Soule into Soule;
>   And mingling so,
> Makes them such Raptures know.

J. A. S. McPeek (*Catullus in Strange and Distant Britain*, 1939, p. 317) suggests that Cartwright here has a passage from Jonson's *Volpone* (III, vi) in mind, a passage itself based on Petronius, *Satyricon*, lxxix: "Et transfudimus hinc et hinc labellis Errantes animas."

389 *Shuffling so our soules.* Thomas Severne in his commendatory poem prefixed to the *Works* (1651) evidently recalled this phrase:

> He shuffles Souls with us,
> And Frames us Thus or Thus.

441 *knot.* A band or company of persons (*NED*).

Act II, Scene iv.

457–58 *send Tickets . . . to invite us to Their Lodgings.* In the same way one of the cowardly courtiers in Jasper Mayne's *Amorous War* (1638), III, i, says:

> Peace, here they come; Me thinks
> Yon'd two by sympathy already doe
> Send Tickets to invite us to their Tents.

Act II, Scene v

514–15 *stile Love-sport . . . misname An arguing out of* Plato. Although Cratander would not have admitted it, his own Platonic love doctrines were equally "misnamed an arguing out of Plato." As Buonateste in D'Avenant's *Platonic Lovers* (1636) says (II):

> My Lord, I still beseech you not to wrong
> My good old friend Plato, with this Court calumny;
> They father on him a fantastic love
> He never knew, poor gentleman.

530 *Reall.* Regal, or royal (*NED*). This is a late use of the word in this sense, though a later one can be found in D'Avenant's *Play-House to be Let* (1663), III.

548 *Exprobration.* A casting in one's teeth (Cockeram's *English Dictionarie*, 1623). See line 591.

Act II, Scene vi

This scene may have influenced Thomas Southerne in his stage version (1696) of Mrs. Aphra Behn's *Oroonoko, or, The Royal Slave.* The play contains a scene (III, ii), not found in the novel, in which Aboan, a fellow slave, tries to incite Oroonoko to head a revolt against his owners. Like Cratander, Oroonoko at first refuses, but is finally brought to promise his aid on condition that their aims may be compassed without bloodshed. Indeed, the whole conception of Southerne's character is much more like Cartwright's Cratander, with his Stoic philosophy and restraint, than like the savage and emotional Oroonoko of Mrs. Behn's novel. Is it perhaps significant that Southerne dropped the subtitle of the novel?

565 *you're not to be intreated.* That is, it won't be necessary to intreat you.

569 *contract.* Contracted. Such forms of the past participle, though rarer in the seventeenth century than in the sixteenth, are common enough before the Restoration. Its present use, of course, is adjectival.

589 *Errant.* This is a not uncommon variant spelling of "errand."

603 *Matron, and the Virgin.* Compare D'Avenant's *The Siege* (1629), II:

> Sir! I am eclips'd by the glory of your
> Merits. Virgins shall sing your praise, and the
> Matrons of the city commend your kindness
> In their prayers to Heaven.

See also Otway's *Venice Preserv'd* (1682), IV, i.

647-48 *Like to the doubtfull Needle . . . and neither.* Compare the strikingly similar image in Thomas Goffe's *The Careless Shepherdess* (written 1615-23, revived 1631, printed 1656), III, viii (p. 43):

> ". . . and does already make
> Me hinge like to a doubtfull needle drawn
> Betwixt two Loadstones, which at once inclines
> To both and neither."

ACT III, SCENE I

A drinking scene of this sort is a familiar commonplace of seventeenth-century plays, though the elaborate drinking ritual, reflecting contemporary practice among the societies of rufflers, is rather more difficult to parallel very closely. The "military" method, however, seems to have been a more or less regular accompaniment. (For various examples see the note on line 688, below.) The nearest parallel occurs in Shirley's *Honoria and Mammon* (1659), V, i, where the phrase "Draw home your arrow to the head" is used in drinking a health. Cartwright also seems to have had *The Cyclops* of Euripides in mind when he introduced the slaves initiating Molops, their jailer, into the divine mystery. In Euripides it is Silenus who inducts the Cyclops into the correct "manner" of drinking.

674-75 *drinke our Mistresses names . . . Alphabetically.* Howell

(*Familiar Letters*, 1705, pp. 352-53) mentions this method of drinking also in connection with Greeks: "The boonest companions for drinking are the *Greeks* and *Germans*: but the Greek is the merrier of the two, for he will sing and dance and kiss his next companion: but the other will drink as deep as he: if the Greek will drink as many glasses as there be letters in his Mistresses name, the other will drink the number of his years."

679 *Drinking such a Mystery*. Among the roarers and blades of Cartwright's day the art of drinking was indeed a "mystery." Most elaborate rituals and catchwords were invented to lend novelty to the sport, all of which was good material for dramatic satire. *Artes bibendi* abound. A good example of the type may be found in *Wits Interpreter* (1655) under the title, "Bacchus his Schoole, wherein he teaches the Art of drinking by a most learned method" (pp. 324-33). Brand (*Popular Antiquities*, 1900, pp. 491-507) gives extracts from many of these drinking manuals. See also such plays as Randolph's *Drinking Academy* (about 1626) and *Aristippus* (1630).

688 *Postures*. This military method of drinking is Cartwright's version of one of the many rituals mentioned in the last note. Other somewhat similar "military methods" may be found in Jonson's *The Silent Woman*, IV, i; Shirley's *The Opportunity*, III, i; *Love's Cruelty*, III, i; *The Royal Master*, II, i; *Honoria and Mammon*, V, i. Other drinking rituals appear in *Antony and Cleopatra*, II, vii; Suckling's *Brennoralt*, II, i (called the "Sacrifice"); Etherege's *Man of Mode*, IV, i (called the "Bachique"). Music was a regular accompaniment of these rituals.

689a Leo: *A match*. This speech has dropped out of the printed texts. It occurs in all four manuscripts (*F* here used).

699 *The Battle*. This "tune" is otherwise unrecorded. Perhaps it was written specially for the occasion by William or Henry Lawes. Shadwell in *The Woman-Captain*, III, ii, has the phrase "roar and have t'other Battel too, Boy," but any reference to Cartwright's "Battle" seems very doubtful.

702 *Gent*. This is merely an abbreviation for "gentlemen." See MSS. *S, F, P*, where the full form is used. Considerations of space forced the printer to use the slightly ambiguous form.

703 *nock 'em*. Fit the arrow to the bowstring (*NED*).

718-41 *Now, now, the Sunne is fled*. A manuscript version of this song, with Lawes' musical setting, may be found in Drexel MS. 4041 (New York Public Library). See Miss Evans' discussion of Lawes' setting in *Henry Lawes, Musician and Friend of Poets* (pp. 131–32). Another printed text appears in *The Marrow of Complements* (1655) pages 67–68, with the title. "Song. Sung by a Company of Cup-shaken Corybants." The original is quoted by Beloe in his *Anecdotes of Literature* (1812), VI, 180–81. With Cartwright's opening lines compare Shadwell's song in *The Woman-Captain* (1680), III, ii.

725–26 *Then laugh we . . . Roses.* See the note on lines 14–19. Compare Burns' "Wi quaffing and laughing" in *The Jolly Beggars*, line 11.

736–40 *With these . . . Beames.* The following version of these lines appears in Josua Poole's *English Parnassus* (ed. of 1677), page 599 (ed. of 1657, p. 557):

> Those Floods of light,
> Which with their sparkling Streams
> Darting diviner Graces,
> Casts glory round our faces,
> And dulls the Tapers with Majestick beams.

ACT III, SCENE II

More than a chance resemblance is suggested between this and the two following scenes and the second and third scenes in William Strode's *Floating Island* (1636), the play presented the night before *The Royal Slave*. In each the absent ruler is berated as a heavy philosophical spoil-sport, who places restrictions upon all the natural passions of man, and both scenes end with a solemn and formal oath to put the king to a sudden and bloody death; both plots, moreover, are overheard.

763–64 *fit To teach the Spartan boyes sobriety.* Thomas Heywood in *An Apology For Actors* (1612), sig. G1ʳ, writes:

> We present men with the vglinesse of their vices, to make them the more to abhorre them, as the *Persians* vse, who aboue all sinnes, loathing drunkennesse, accustomed in their solemne feasts, to make their seruants and captiues extremely ouercome with wine, and then call their children to view their nasty and lothsome behauiour, making them hate that sin in themselues, which shewed so grosse and abhominable in others.

Cartwright's attribution of the custom to Sparta is the commonly received one.

780 *immortall Canniballs*. Cartwright is referring to the Persian gods who demanded human sacrifice.

780–81 *there's no Ho with him*. There is no stopping him. Compare *The Knave in Graine* (1640), sig. F3ᵛ: "there's no ho with them."

797–98 *dares be so impudent . . . be good in a strange place*. It seems to have been taken almost as an axiom in Cartwright's day that an Englishman abroad was an Englishman morally "on the loose." Milton in his *Second Defense* congratulates himself a little priggishly perhaps on the fact that "in all the places in which vice meets with so little discouragement [Italy], and is protected with so little shame, I never once turned from the path of integrity and virtue, and perpetually reflected that though my conduct might escape the notice of men, it could not elude the inspection of God."

Act II. Scene iii

This scene of Cratander's temptation may have been suggested to Cartwright by some of the various anecdotes related of the remarkable continence of Alexander the Great. Two such stories are combined by Thomas Goffe in his *Courageous Turk* (1632) in a scene (sigs. C3ʳ-C3ᵛ) from which Cartwright may very well have taken a hint. Plutarch juxtaposes the two stories in his Life of Alexander; in his *Morals*, however, they are unconnected (see Philemon Holland's translation, 1603, pp. 1271, 1279).

825–26 *kill'd with . . . formality, As Quicksilver with fasting spittle*. Brand (*Observations on Popular Antiquities*, 1900, p. 723) quotes as follows from an anonymous work called *Secret Miracles of Nature* (1658):

> Divers experiments shew that power and quality there is in Man's fasting Spittle, when he hath neither eat nor drunk before the use of it: for it cures all tetters, itch, scabs, pushes, and creeping sores: and if venemous little beasts have fastened on any part of the body, as hornets, beetles, toads, spiders, and such like, . . . do but rub the places with fasting Spittle, and all those effects will be gone and discussed. Since the qualities and effects of Spittle come from the humours, . . . the reason may be easily understood why Spittle should do such strange things, and destroy some Creatures.

Since Howell (*Familiar Letters*, 1705 ed., p. 438) remarks that "morning spittle kills Dragons," we may accept its mortal effects upon mere quicksilver.

845 *in ure*. In use or practice (*NED*).

856 *put 'em streight in paste*. That is, make a pasty or deep pie out of them.

871-72 *'twere Lazynes . . . dead already*. See note to *The Lady-Errant*, line 1347.

ACT III, SCENE IV

874-960 *He must be more . . . so nobly, that*. These eighty-odd lines were recast in prose and printed as a dialogue in *The Marrow of Complements* (1655), under the title of "A Complementall Contestation" (pp. 54-56). The text of the dialogue is as follows:

> *The Lover being unwilling to part with a late received token, which his Mistresse (seemingly) is very earnest to recover, which occasioneth a sublime dispute.*
> *A Dialogue (supposed) betweene* Alberto *and* Sophrinda.

Alberto. He must be more the man that gaines it back without my will.
Sophrinda. Your justice must restore it, doe you delight to tryumph with soft spoiles of a Ladies cabinet.
Alberto. As I would not feigne favour, or belie a jewell, or a twist, to gaine the name of creature, or of a servant unto any, so by your beauty (if I may sweare by that) where honour is transmitted in a true mysterious gage of an Immaculate mind, I will defend it as some sacred Relique, or some more secret pledge dropt downe from heaven, to guard me from the dangers of the earth.
Sophrinda. But in that you make it common, you bereave it of all that you call divine.
Alberto. He that vaunts of a received favour ought to bee punished as sacrilegious persons are, because hee violates that sacred thing called spotlesse honour, but it may be seen, and yet not prostitute, I would not smother my joyes and make my happiness a stealth.
Sophrinda. Your thoughts doe flatter your deceived fancie into a state, which when you leave to think, dies as your thoughts which kept it up, what it is, that you call joy and happiness.
Alberto. I must confess I have no merits, whose just heart may extract ought from you called Love, yet when I doe consider that Affection cannot looke vertuously on any thing that is resplendent, but a subtile Image purely reflecting thence, must needs arise and pay that look againe, I doe take that leave to say, the carefull Deities provide that love shall ner'e be so unhappy as to want his brother.

Sophrinda. Why, I never spent a sigh for you, you never had a kisse for the reversion of one yet.

Alberto. Such Love is but Loves Idoll, and these soft tones [*sic*] that confine it to a kisse, or an embrace; doe as the superstitious did of old, contract the Godhead into a Bull or Goate, or some such lustfull creature; bee it farre from me to thinke that whensoever I see cleare streames of beautie, that I may presume to trouble them with quenching of my thirst, where a full splendour, where a bright effusion of immateriall Beames doe meet, for to make up one body of perfection, I should accompt my selfe injurious unto that Deity which hath let downe himselfe into those rayes, if that I should draw nigh without an awfull Adoration, which my religion payes to you, but being you like not the devotion, be content to slight the sacrifice, but spare the Altar.

Sophrinda. I am so farre from turning a beast, in which there lives a sparke of chaster honour, that I would hazzard this so priz'd a trifle, which men call life, that I might live there still, and prove that Love is but an Engine of the carefull powers invented for the safety and preservation of afflicted goodnesse, conceive not hence a passion burning towards you, for she that speakes like woman can be resolv'd like man.

Alberto. I can distinguish between Love and Love, between flames and good intents, nay between flames and flames themselves, the grosser now fly up, and now flie downe, still coveting new matter for food, consuming and consum'd, but the pure quicker flames that shoot up alwaies in one continued pyramid of lustre know no commerce with earth, but unmixt still, and still aspiring upwards (if that may be stil'd aspiring which is nature) have this property of immortality, still to suffice themselves, neither devowring nor yet devowred, which I acknowledge yours, on which I looke as on refin'd *Ideas* that knew no mixture or corruption being one eternall simpleness, that these should from the circle of their chaster glories, dart out a beame on me, is farre beyond all humane merit, and I may conclude, they have onely their owne nature for a cause, and that they are good, they are diffusive too.

Sophrinda. Your tongue hath spoke your thoughts so nobly, that I should esteeme my selfe the curse of all my sex, should I not gratifie such worth with Love, I here proclaime my selfe, yours to dispose of.

Alberto. And when I faile to manifest my gratitude, may Joves severest thunder strike me dead.

This is but one of nine such dialogues or drolls from Cartwright: one from *The Royal Slave*, six from *The Ordinary*, and two from *The Siege*, of which six are contained in *The Marrow of Complements* (1655) and three in *Wits Interpreter* (1655). In the light of Moseley's complaint in his preface "To the Reader" (*Works*, 1651) that Cartwright was being plundered by "certain *Plagiaries* (whereof this Great Town hath no small number, even now when 'tis empty)," it is not a little curious to find that *The Marrow of Complements* (entered on the Stationers' Register, December 20, 1653, as by Mr. Sheapard) was actually published by Moseley. In the face of such evidence Moseley's indignation rings a little hollow. Moseley, however, was not the only one at fault. Writing in his preface to *Wits Interpreter*, John Cotgrave, the editor of the collection, says:

> In a word, you may perceive it to be a *Collection* of all that for such a time could be ransackt from the private Papers of the *choicest Wits* of the three *Nations*, from which *Manuscripts* of theirs, if there be any *Copies* transcribed that are old, it was not the intention, but rather the misfortune of the *Insertor*, for upon the least intimation whilst I was in Town to attend the *Press*, I crossed out whatsoever I could hear had been formerly publisht.

With all due allowance made, this statement cannot be called disingenuous. *The Ordinary*, from which all three drolls are drawn, was published four years before Cotgrave's collection. Nobody, moreover, could for a moment suppose such obviously connected pieces as the first and third droll to be anything but parts of the same play. Finally, in spite of Cotgrave's reference to the "manuscripts" from which his collection had grown—a statement so far as he was concerned made perhaps in good faith—there seems to be little doubt that, without exception, these drolls and dialogues were based upon the text printed in the *Works* (1651), and not upon independent manuscripts. Unfortunately the liberties taken with Cartwright's text are so great and the general standard of the droll texts so corrupt, that it is impossible to be dogmatic on this point.

887a *But in that*. This stands as a broken line in all the printed texts. The manuscripts (*S, ?F, P, B*) expand to a complete metrical line: "But you doe ill to boast it, for in that."

944-51 *Flames . . . aspiring upwards . . . neither devouring, Nor yet devour'd*. The imagery here is, of course, the common property of all dealers in Neoplatonism. Compare Dante, *Purgatorio*, XVIII, 28-33, where he is describing the growth of love. The following lines from Suckling's *Aglaura* (1637), II, ii, 21-24 (*Works*, ed. A. H. Thompson, 1910, p. 100), which immediately precede a reference to the court Platonic love cult, seem to be a direct parody of Cartwright's lines:

> I had no sooner nam'd love to her, but she
> Began to talk of flames, and flames
> Neither devouring nor devour'd, of air
> And of chameleons.

945 *continued*. It seems probable that the reading of MSS. S, F, P, B, "continuall," is what Cartwright wrote.

951 *Nor yet devour'd; and such I acknowledge yours*. I have adopted the reading of the manuscripts in two places in this line: (1) "Nor yet" (S, F, P, B) for "And yet" (*1639, 1640, 1651*); (2) "acknowledge" (S, F, P) for "knowledge" (*1639, 1640, 1651*).

959 *that they're good, they are diffusive too*. According to Platonic philosophy it was of the very nature of the "Good" to be diffusive. See Plato's *Timaeus*: "He [the Creator] was good, and the good can never have any jealousy of anything. And being free from jealousy, he desired that all things should be as like himself as they could be."

984 *Scene is shut*. A technical expression, borrowed from the scenic machinery of the masque. It here means "after the play of life is done."

ACT III, SCENE V

1016–17 *breake the Streame . . . runne more weake*. See the note to Cartwright's poem, "Love but one," page 727.

ACT IV, SCENE II

1133 *plotting Destinies*. See the famous account of the Fates in "The Myth of Er," Plato's *Republic*, Book X.

ACT IV, SCENE III

SD *maunding people*. Itinerant beggars. For the best account of the cheats practiced by these rogues see Thomas Harman's *A Caveat or Warning for Common Cursetors* (1567; ed. by E. Viles and F. J. Furnivall in *Rogues and Vagabonds of Shakespeare's Youth*, 1907), and Greene's "Cony-catching" pamphlets. The disguises assumed by the four slaves are typical.

1142 *totter'd*. A common variant of "tattered."

1172 *the next Passenger is to decide it*. Cartwright seems to have been thinking of a situation in Fletcher and Massinger's *Beggars' Bush* (about 1622), II, i. See the Introduction to the play.

Act IV, Scene v

1233 *Tulipants.* An obsolete form of "turban" (*NED*).

Act V, Scene i

1263 *worthily admire.* An Elizabethan ellipsis. "Enough" is to be understood after "admire."

1266 *Man . . . Vertue.* Compare *The Lady-Errant*, lines 892–94.

Act V, Scene ii

Compare the situations in this and the next scene with *The Bondman* (1623), IV, ii (see W. G. Rice, "Sources of William Cartwright's *The Royal Slave*," MLN, XLV [1930], 515–18), and with Beaumont and Fletcher's *The Maid's Tragedy* (1611), V, ii.

1308 *expect.* The manuscripts all read "suspect," probably the correct reading.

Act V, Scene iii

1353–60 *Gods, Pitty's a Banquet . . . Architect.* Compare Theodorus, page 336: "Tua modo Numinibus sacrificij loco clementia erit. Etenim Immortales largis dapibus, meroque instructum convivium existimant, mutuum hominum amorem miserationemque: & siquis mortem evaserit, haec illis mensa, hoc poculum placet." Compare also, page 339: "Scilicet figulus qui vas suum contritum viderit, illo rupto, gaudebit? Artifex post erectas ad tertium usque fastigium aedes, si ingentem illae ruinam late dederint, non dolebit?"

1368 *He would be neare the Gods.* Compare Theodorus, page 327: ". . . ille ad sacrificium cum studio pergit: Et recte, quoniam Dijs proximus esse vult."

1377–78 *No heated rage . . . sacred Goblet . . . Altar.* Probably a topical allusion to Puritan treatment of sacramental cups is here intended.

1382 *Thunderer.* This, which is the reading of all the manuscripts, seems better than "Thunder," the reading of the printed editions.

1389 *hopelesse.* This is the reading of all the manuscripts. The printed copies read "hopefull," but Ephesus is the reverse of "hopefull" at this point in the action.

1396 *Your Majestie is not Rock.* Compare again Theodorus, page 340: "Non enim lapide aut quercu natus sum."

Act V, Scene iv

1448 *collogue*. To deal flatteringly or deceitfully (*NED*).

1464 *cases*. Clothes.

1465 *Gobline's Masque*. I do not know to what particular masque, if any, Cartwright is referring. Suckling's play, *The Goblins*, is, I believe, later than *The Royal Slave*. Perhaps he is thinking of the goblin disguises in Thomas Goffe's *The Careless Shepherdess* (revived 1631), a play which he seems to have known (see the note on lines 647-48 above).

Act V, Scene v

1487 *Dance*. This dance presented by the four slaves and the two whores serves as an antimasque to the dance by the "Company of younger Ladyes" which immediately follows. Miss Willa McClung Evans ("Lovelace's Concept of Prison Life in 'The Vintage to the Dungeon,' " *Philological Quarterly*, XXVI [Jan. 1947], 62-68) advances the theory that Lovelace's song, "The Vintage to the Dungeon," which was set to music by William Lawes, was perhaps written to be sung by the slaves during their dance. Earlier in the article Miss Evans had shown some reason for connecting Lovelace's verses with the drinking song in Act I, Scene i. Although the suggestion is most ingenious, I cannot see that there is any evidence for postulating a song at this point.

1496 SD *verses of* Claudian. The six verses (omitted in all the manuscripts) which the ladies "express" are from Claudian's *De Sexto Consulatu Honorii Augusti*, lines 625-30. The variations from the accepted modern text which appear in Cartwright's quotation are all based on genuine manuscript or emended readings. MS. *P* describes this dance by the "Company of younger Ladyes" as "a warlike Persian Daunce." This and the omission of the verses in all the manuscripts suggest that the Claudian dance was a refinement on the original conception.

1515 *Teare of some relenting Tree*. Drops of balsam were frequently described as "tears."

1545-46 *To speake more, were . . . to defer his suffrings*. Compare the anonymous *Nero*, IV, ii:

> But to be long in talk of dying would
> Show a relenting and a doubtful mind.

1551-52 *Witnesse yee Gods . . . My vowes.* Compare Theodorus, page 340: "Vellem patri seni longe ab hoc infortunio libero filium restitui: Deosque me vera dicere testor."

1555 *These teares I pay thee.* Compare Theodorus, page 324: "O fortissime Satraparum, tanta me huius adolescentis miseratio subit, ut ad lachrymas invitum cogat."

ACT V, SCENE VI

The "interrupted sacrifice," which forms the denouement of the play, has been a favorite device from the times of Abraham and Euripides, and received the special benediction of Greek romance in Heliodorus' *Aethiopica*. Miraculous omens had, of course, appeared on the English stage before Cartwright's play. See, for example, Fletcher's *Two Noble Kinsmen*, V, i; Jasper Fisher's *Fuimus Troes, or The True Trojans* (1633), II, vi; and Quarles' *The Virgin Widow* (printed 1649), V, i. But Cartwright, following his source in Theodorus' novel, seems to have been the first English playwright to draw upon other than human agency to effect his fateful interruption. Both Chamberlayne's *Love's Victory* (printed 1658), III, i, and Congreve's *Semele* (*Dramatic Works* [Old Dramatists Series], ed. Leigh Hunt, p. 291) seem to owe something to Cartwright's scene.

ACT V, SCENE VII

The manuscripts omit everything in this scene down to line 1574 (i.e. the sacrificial procession and the Priests' song). The general implications of these omissions are discussed in the Introduction to the play, but one or two additional points must be noticed here. That the procession and song are later interpolations is evident from the fact that line 1574 ("Hold, hold *Arsamnes*") completes the last line (1561) of Scene vi ("The Gods desire it not"). Moreover in MS. *F* the change of scene to the Temple takes place at the beginning of Scene vi ("The Temple appeers agayne"), thus definitely linking Scenes vi and vii. Finally, the concluding sentiment of the song contradicts the earlier demands of the Priests.

SD *Sagar.* Anglicised form of "sagaris," a two-edged cutting ax. The earliest recorded use in the *NED* is dated 1776.

4 Priests. The dramatis personae gives only three priests.

1562–73   *Thou ô bright Sun who seest all.* As noticed above, this song is omitted in all the play manuscripts, but a manuscript containing the words and setting by Henry Lawes has recently been discovered in the New York Public Library (see the introductory discussion, p. 170). The words and setting for the first stanza and chorus of this song are used to make up a second stanza (following the first six lines) for the song in Act I, Scene ii, in *Catch that Catch can: or the Musical Companion* (1667), pages 166–67, and in *The Musical Companion* (1673), sigs. [P5]v–[P6].

1568   *But thou ô Sun mayst set, and then.* This second stanza of the Priests' song is a free rendering of some lines of Catullus (Carmen V), which are translated as follows by Henry More in the preface to *Psychathanasia* (1642):

> The Sunne may set and rise again;
> If once sets our short light
> Deep sleep us binds with iron chain,
> Wrapt in eternall Night.

This poem of Catullus was a great favorite. There are English versions by Raleigh, Jonson, Campion, Alexander Brome, John Hall, and Crashaw.

1571   *Will make and have.* This is the reading of all the printed editions. Drexel MS.4041 (*L*) reads "will haue and make." Neither reading is very satisfactory. Cartwright means, perhaps, that Cratander's death will blanket the world and himself in eternal night.

1573 SD   *8th Appearance, the Sun eclipsed, and a showre of raine dashing out the fire.* Compare Theodorus Prodromus, page 343: "Nondum loquendi pausam fecerat, subitoque irruentis nimbi [rain storm] impetu extructa pyra deflagraverat, ut nec reliquum ignis superesset vestigium." Compare also the stage direction in Congreve's *Semele* (*Dramatic Works* [Old Dramatists Series], ed. Leigh Hunt, p. 291): *It lightens, and thunder is heard at a distance; then a noise of rain; the fire is suddenly extinguished on the altar: the Chief Priest comes forward.* A "shower of raine" follows the sacrifice of Busyris by Hercules in Heywood's *Brazen Age* (Pearson reprint, III, 183).

1592–93   *well wrought Picture . . . Behold both you, and that.* It was formerly believed that the eyes in a well painted picture should seem to look at the observer from whatever angle it is viewed.

THE EPILOGUE TO THE KING AND QUEENE

19-20 *We thinke you snatch'd . . . their day*. Lovelace reverses the conceit in his "Triumphs of Philamore and Amoret" (*Poems*, ed. W. C. Hazlitt, 1864, p. 217):

> When we shall be orewhelm'd in joy, like they
> That change their night for a vast half-year's day.

THE EPILOGUE TO THE UNIVERSITY

3-4 *Wee'd thought . . . live untill the morne*. Compare the sentiment in the following lines from Randolph's *Muses' Looking-Glass* (written before 1635), V, iii:

> Nor is the glass of so short life, I fear,
> As this poor labour: our distrustful author
> Thinks the same sun that rose upon her cradle
> Will hardly set before her funeral.

14 *fine for Poet*. Be considered a finished poet.

THE ORDINARY

Texts. Works (1651), pages 1–90, plus, at the beginning, two unnumbered leaves, sigs. [A] and A2. Modern reprints: *A Select Collection of Old Plays*, ed. R. Dodsley (1744), X, 163–244; *A Select Collection of Old Plays*, 2nd edition, ed. Isaac Reed (1780), X, 197–318; *The Ancient British Drama*, 1810, III, 142–78; *A Select Collection of Old Plays*, 3rd edition, ed. J. P. Collier (1826), X, 165–268; *A Select Collection of Old English Plays*, 4th edition, ed. W. C. Hazlitt (1875), XII, 203–318.

Title-page, 1651 edition: THE / ORDINARY, / [rule] / A Comedy, / [rule] / Written by / WILLIAM CARTVVRIGHT, / M.A. Ch.Ch. Oxon. / [rule] / LONDON, / Printed for *Humphrey Moseley*, and / are to be sold at his shop at the Sign of / the Princes Armes in St *PAVLS* / Churchyard. *1651.* *Format:* 8vo. *Collation:* A–E⁸, F⁷.

The following prologue and epilogue were presumably written for the London revival of *The Ordinary* in 1671 (see the Introduction to the play). They are printed in an anonymous anthology entitled, *A Collection of Poems Written upon several Occasions* (1673), pages 163–68 (misnumbered 178).

Prologue *to the Ordinary.*

From you grave men of business and of trade
Who were for industry, not pleasure, made
We seldom do implore, or hope for aid.
For we but rarely are oblig'd to you,
You come but when y'ave nothing else to do; [5]
Besides, our Wit to you needs no excuse,
For you all Wit do like a Mystriss use;
A thing you seldom see, while some are cloy'd
With Wit, as with a Wife too oft enjoy'd;
Nay, you will think that Wit which is not so, [10]
A Quibble, or a little Punn takes you;
Dullness does men for business prepare,
Whilst Wit delights in ease, and hates all care;
But to young brisk men who think it fit,

> To spend no Afternoon but in the Pit, [15]
> Whether we will or no we must submit.
> Some come with lusty *Burgundy* half-drunk,
> T'eat China Oranges, make love to Punk;
> And briskly mount a bench when th'Act is done,
> And comb their much-lov'd Periwigs to the tune, [20]
> And can sit out a Play of three hours long,
> Minding no part of't but the Dance or Song;
> These are our trusty friends, but some there are,
> Most bloody Judges, who no Poets spare;
> But I have heard some injur'd Authors say, [25]
> That these most parlous cens'rers of a Play.
> With little Wit which they so much employ,
> Which by Reflection only they enjoy,
> Would even those from whom they took't destroy.
> So does the fam'd Enlightner of the Night, [30]
> Eclipse the Sun, from whom sh'ad all her light;
> And these Mock Criticks hiss and whistle loud,
> And with their noise out-vie Bear-baiting Croud.
>   But Ladies, you are sweet, and soft, and fair,
> And will the Poet and the Actors spare; [35]
> But busy men and Sparks are welcome now,
> The little Misses and great Ladies too,
> You altogether make a Noble Show.
>   Y'ave paid for't, and whatever Poets say,
> Think or say what you please of this our Play. [40]

Compare lines 17–18 and 33 with the following couplets from a *Prologue at Oxford*, which immediately precedes the *Prologue to the Ordinary* (p. 161):

> No blustring Bullyes come in here half drunk,
> For *Chyna* Oranges and love to Punk,
> To fly at Vizard Masks talk Nonsense loud,
> And with their noise out-vye Bear-baiting Croud.

This *Prologue at Oxford* has been attributed to Dryden. See Hugh Macdonald, *John Dryden, A Bibliography* (1939), page 138n.

Epilogue *to the Ordinary*.

> Our Prologue huff'd, but we are humbler now,
> And fear the storme which hangs upon each brow,
> So in Sea-fights at first some have been bold,
> Who in the heat took Shelter in the Hold:
> But now the danger of your Thunder's nigh, [5]
> We have no refuge, but to mercy flie:

> We yield our selves, and you so gen'rous are,
> Submitting foes, though ne're so great, you'l spare.
>   Gallants, if y'are offended at our Play,
> And think w'have coursely treated you to day: [10]
> Think what a famine there is now of Wit,
> And that we bring the best that we can get;
> We are poor Farmers, and make homely fare,
> While our rich Landlords may great Feasts prepare;
> But their Revenue now is almost spent, [15]
> And you with little wit must be content:
> Nonsence shall wear the gay disguise of Rhime,
> And though not understood, shall sweetly chime:
> Now empty shows must want of sense supply,
> Angels shall dance, and *Macbeths* Witches fly: [20]
> You shall have stormes, thunder & lightning too
> And Conjurers raise spirits to your view:
> The upper Gall'rie shall have their desire,
> Who love a Fool, a Devil and a Friar:
> Damn'd Plays shall be adorn'd with mighty Scenes [25]
> And Fustian shall be spoke in huge Machines:
> And we wil purling streams and fire-works show
> And you may live to see it rain and snow,
> So Poets have their wit they care not how.
> This all our Scriblers can perform with ease. [30]
> Tickle the fools, though not the Witty please;
> If you expect true Comedy agen,
> That represents not Monsters, but shows men;
> Your expectation will be cross'd, we fear,
> For we have little hope to see such here. [35]

A line may have been omitted after line 22 of this epilogue, if we can trust the triplet bracket which appears in the original.

The Prologue

7 *Conversation*. Intimacy with the affairs of life (*NED*).

9 *by th' Poll*. By counting of heads, according to the *NED*. But such a meaning does not seem to fit the context. Perhaps the phrase might mean "according to the popular vote."

14 *Who make that* Person ... Name. This line is probably a reminiscence from Jonson's second prologue to *The Silent Woman* (1609):

> And that he meant, or him, or her, will say:
> They make a libel, which he made a play.

20   *drown'd Islands*. Cartwright is referring, I suppose, to the Atlantis myth as told in Plato.

DRAMATIS PERSONAE
   Simon Credulous. See the name Sir Simon Credulous, "the true Patron, honourer and lover of lying," in *Wits Interpreter* (1655), page 321.

ACT I, SCENE 1
   3-4   *sleep . . . in Chaine, and Skarlet At* Spittle-*Sermon*. Compare Jasper Mayne's *The City-Match*, I, iii:

>   Yes, and I
> To sleep the sermon in my chain and scarlet.

See the Introduction to the play.
   5   *of being*. In the hope, or with the intention, of being.
   18-19   Declaration, *or th'* Abolishing *O'th'*Common-Prayers. Charles had issued the "Declaration" reviving the so-called "Book of Sports" in 1633. This ill-advised action has been described as one of the "chief causes of the civil war," since it particularly outraged the most cherished doctrines of Puritanism. The magnificent liturgy of the Church of England, contained in the Book of Common Prayer, was particularly hated by the Puritans because of its "Popish" origins. During the early years of the Long Parliament, an act abolishing the use of the Book of Common Prayer was passed, and heavy penalties were assigned for using it surreptitiously. The Puritan attitude is amusingly satirized in an anonymous pamphlet entitled "Some Small and Simple Reasons" (*Harleian Miscellany*, 1809, IV, 177-83):

> My dear beloved and zealous brethren and sisters here assembled in this holy congregation, I am to unfold, unravel, untwist, untye, unloose, and undo, to your uncapable understandings, some small reasons, the matter, the causes, the motives, the grounds, the principles, the maxims, the why's and the wherefores, wherefore and why, we reject, omit, abandon, contemn, despise, and are and ought to be withstanders and opposers of the service-book, called by the hard name of Liturgy, or Common-Prayer, which hath continued in the church of England eighty-four years.

See also *The Souldiers Catechisme* (1644), pages 21-22.
   22   *Take heart of grace*. This phrase signifies "take courage," or "summon up resolution" (Reed).

27 *hal'd*. Dragged by force.
37 *well-appointed*. Completely accoutred (Reed).
70–71 *I will cast off This brood of Vipers*. Compare the tone of the last lines of Meanwell's soliloquy with that of Prince Hal in *1 Henry IV*, I, ii, 217–39.

ACT I, SCENE II

The character of the widow, Mistress Joan Potluck, particularly in this scene, seems to owe something to Chaucer's Wife of Bath. When, for example, she urges the scriptural advice that

> The holy blessing of all wedlock was
> T' encrease and multiply,

and murmurs invitingly that "woman was not made to be alone still," we catch perhaps far-off echoes of another widow. For some connection with Mistress Quickly, see below.

The scene itself owes important debts to at least three distinct sources. (1) For the "jeering" of the widow, Cartwright seems to have turned to the *Plutus* of Aristophanes—the scene between Chremylus, the Old Woman, and the Youth. The Old Woman, like Mistress Potluck, seeks to win back the favor of the Youth, while he and Chremylus seize the occasion to heap insults upon her with rude remarks about her age and physical appearance. A contemporary rendering of the scene, very much in Cartwright's vein, may be found in Randolph's *Hey for Honesty* (printed 1651), IV, iii. Compare the "jeering" of Truga in Cowley's *Love's Riddle* (printed in 1638), and the tone of the description in Skelton's "Tunning of Elynour Rumming." (2) *1 Henry IV*, III, iii, furnished further material for the "jeering." In this famous quarrel scene, Falstaff accuses Mistress Quickly of having had his pocket picked, and she retorts by threatening him with his back tavern reckonings and sundry unpaid loans. In the jeering which follows, Mistress Quickly is treated to most uncomplimentary remarks very similar to those heaped upon Mistress Potluck (see the note to ll. 200–1). In the meantime Prince Hal has appeared and admits to having picked Sir John's pockets, whereupon the wily old knight magnanimously cries, "Hostess, I forgive thee. . . . thou seest I am pacified." Compare the way in which Hearsay makes it appear that it was Mistress Potluck who was initially at fault and kindly agrees to take back his proffered rent money (ll. 260–66). Notice also in *2 Henry IV*, II, i, the promise of marriage which Mistress Quickly brings against Sir John—a claim no more successful than Mistress Potluck's. (3) Hearsay's method of placating Mistress Potluck by pretending that he has been planning an advantageous match for her suggests a scene in Jonson's *The Devil is an Ass* (1616), V, iii. Meercraft, who has been arrested at the suit of Master Gilthead and his landlord, Sledge, immediately claims that he has taken great "pains at court" to get them each a patent. Deceived, Gilthead and Sledge dismiss the sergeants, and Meercraft, like Hearsay, accepts the bail with an appearance of unwillingness, warning against the repetition of such an offense.

The two scenes in Mayne's *City-Match*, II, v, and Cowley's *Guardian*, I, i, comparable in part to this scene, have been noticed in the Introduction to the play (pp. 264–65).

73–171 *Now help good Heaven . . . My Husband dy'd*. The following dialogue, based on these lines, appears in John Cotgrave's *Wits Interpreter* (1655), pages 88–90 (misnumbered 88, 89, 88), here reprinted; (1662), pages 48–49; (1671), pages 48–49. In the 1662 and 1671 editions the dialogue is entitled, *The Widows Complaint*. No attempt at full collation has been made.

A DIALOGVE. Between Doll, *and* Furioso.

Dol. Now help me good Heavens! it is such an uncouth thing to be a Widdow out of Terme time, I do feel such aguish qualmes and dumps, and fits, and shakings still an end, J lately was a wife J do confess, but yet J had no Husband; he alass was dead to me, even when he liv'd unto the World, J was a Widdow while he had breath, his death only made others know so much:

Fur. Why so melancholy sweet.

Dol. How could I choose since thou wert not here; I hope the time is come that thou wilt be as good as thy word to me.

Fur. Nay hang me if I ere recant, you'l take me both wind and limb at a venture, will you not?

Dol. Ay good chuck every inch of thee she were no true woman that would not.

Fur. I must tell you one thing though, and yet I am loath.

Dol. I am thy rib, thon [thou 1662] must keep nothing from thy ribb good Chuck, thy yoak fellow must know all thy secrets.

Fur. Why I'le tell you sweet; I have nothing:

Dol. Heaven defend!

Fur. Tis true.

Dol. Now God for bid; and would you offer to undoe a Widdow woman so. I had as live the old Vintner were alive againe:

Fur. Nay I was not born with it I confess, but lying in *Turkie* for intelligence, the Great Turk being somewhat suspicious of me, lest I might entice some of the Seraglio gave command that I should be forthwith curbd.

Dol. Twas a heathen deed, ther's none but an infidell could have had the heart to have done it:

Fur. Now you know the worst that you you [*sic*] must trust to come lets to Church, besides there is another thing which doth something trouble me. Ere now J have had a spice of the Pox or so too.

Dol. I do not ask thee about these diseases my question is if thou hast all thy parts.

Fur. Faith you will not be answered, I have lost a joynt or two, for there are few Souldiers come off whole unlesse it be the generall, and some few sneaks.

Dol. I but my meaning is, whether that something is not wanting that should write thee Husband.

Fur. Nere feare that wench for all my talk, but I am jealous least the memory of your Husband should extinguish all flames that tend to kindling of any love fire.

Dol. J do confess I do beare him in memory, but when I remember what your promise was when he lay sick, it takes something from the bitterness of my sorrows I tell thee woman was not made to be alone.

Fur. Tender things at seventeen may use that plea but you are now arriv'd at *Marton* [*Matron* 1662] I suppose these young sparks are rak'd up in sager embers.

Dol. Nay do not abuse her that must be your wife, you might have pitty and not come with your nick-names, have I deserv'd this?

Fur. If you once hold merits, I have done, I am glad, I know of what Religion you are?

Dol. What's my Religion? tis well known there hath been no Religion in my house ere since my Husband dy'd. Yet if you can leave me I can leave you, there are other men enough that won't refuse a fortune when tis profferd.

Fur. Well I must be gone think ont, and so farewell.

Thine to the end, that is perhaps
a Moneth or two.

It will be noticed that the adaptor has combined the parts of Hearsay and Slicer and thus made complete nonsense of the whole scene. See my discussion of these drolls in a note to *The Royal Slave*, line 874.

76 *still an end.* Constantly, continuously (*NED*).

81-113 *How now? So melancholy . . . women of the Parish.* The following dialogue, based on these lines, occurs in *The Marrow of Complements* (1655), pages 72-73 (compare the dialogue quoted above, line 73, from *Wits Interpreter*, 1655):

> *A Sportive Complementall Interlocution* (*The Adolescent being willing for ever to frustrate her hopes whom he hath (seemingly) assented to Marry*.)
> *A Dialogue supposed betweene* Juvenillio *and* Thais.

Juvenillio. How now, so melancholy sweete.

Thais. How could I chuse, being thou wert not here, the time is come I hope now, that thou wilt be as good unto me as thy word.

Juvenillio. Nay, hang me if I ere repent, you will take mee both wind and limbe at the venture, will you not?

Thais. Yes good chuck every inch of thee, shee were no woman that would not.

Juvenillio. I must tell you one thing, and yet I am loth.

Thais. Pray thee tell me.

Juvenillio. When then Ile tell you sweet, I was not borne with it I confesse, but lying in Turky with a late Embassadour (one of whose meniall traine I boast my selfe) the great Turke somewhat suspitious of mee lest I might entice some of his Seraglio, did command I should be forthwith cut.

Thais. A heathen deed it was; none but an Infidell could have the heart to doe it.

Juvenillio. Now you know the worst of me, that you must trust to; come let us to Church.

Thais. Good Sir excuse me, nature never intended one woman should be joyned to another, the holy blessing of wedlock was increase and multiply, I will doe nothing against Gods word, and therefore I here release you of your promises.

Iuvenillio. Since you needs will cast cast [*sic*] me off; let me intreate this one thing of you, that you would not make me your table-talke at the next Gossipping.

Thais. Never feare it, indeed I pittie thee, poore thing, or rather poore *Nothing*, I shall get you a contribution (perhaps) of the women of the Parish next Sunday, farewell poore main'd man.

See my discussion of these drolls in a note to *The Royal Slave*, line 874.

89-91 *I am thy Rib . . . Thy yoak-fellow.* Compare Beaumont and Fletcher's *Knight of the Burning Pestle* (1611), III, v: ". . . for your wife is your own flesh, the staff of your age, your yokefellow, . . . nay, she's your own rib."

92 *Why then I'l tell you sweet.* Hearsay's pretense of impotence may have been suggested by Jonson's *Silent Woman*, V, i.

92 *defend.* Forbid.

96 *I was not born with it.* Hazlitt suggests omitting "not," but this is not necessary, and it changes the meaning.

123 *Art thou intire and sound in all thy limbs?* Mistress Potluck's solicitude in this and the succeeding enquiries rather reminds one of the Widow Wadman's similar concern.

171–266 *How now sweet* Shape? . . . *Marriage for ever.* The following droll, based on these lines, appears in John Cotgrave's *Wits Interpreter* (1655), pages 81–83 (here reprinted); (1662), pages 42–44; (1671), pages 42–44. No attempt at full collation has been made.

The old Widdow.

A How now what so close about the Widdow, and alone too.

B. Troth tis not my suit, for this thing whose prayer hath bin these ten years, that she may obtaine the second tooth, and the third haire dotes on me, on me that refuse all that are past sixteen.

A. Why faith this was her suit to me just now.

B. I had the first on't then, but a Coach-man or a Groom were much fitter for her.

A: You honour her too much to think she deserves a thing that can lust moderately, give her the Sorrell stallion my [in my 1662] Lords long Stable.

B: Or the same coloured Brother, which is worse.

W. Why Gentlemen?

A. Foh, foh, she hath let flye:

W. Do you think I have no more manners then so?

B. Nay faith I can excuse her for that, but I confesse she spoke which is all one.

A. Her breath would rout an Army sooner then that of a Canon.

B. It would lay a Devil sooner then all *Trithemius* charms.

A. Hark how it blusters in her Nostrills like a wind in a foule Chimney.

W. Out you base Companions, you stinking Swabbers.

B. For her gate that's such as if her Nose did strive to outrun her heels.

A. Shee's just six yards behind when that appears, it saves an Usher Madam.

W. You are most foule mouth'd knaves to use a woman thus.

A. Your playsterd mouth doth drop against foule weather.

B. Fye how you writh it, now it looks just like a ruffled Boot.

A Or an oyld paper Lanthorn:

B Her nose the candle in the midst of it:

A How bright it flames? put out your Nose good Lady, you burn day-light.

W Come up you lousie Raskalls:

A Not upon you for a Kingdome good *Ione*. The great Turk *Jone*—The great Turk.

B Kiss him Chuck, kisse him Chuck, open mouth'd and be reveng'd.

W Hang you base cheating varlet.

A Don't you see *December* in her face?

B Sure the Survayor of the high wayes wil have to do with her for not keeping her countenance passable.

A There lyes a hoare frost on her head, and yet a constant thaw in her Nose:

B She's like a peece of fire-wood, dropping at one end, and yet burning ith' midst:

A O that endeavouring face! when will your costiveness have done good Madam?

B Do you not heare her gutts already squeak like Kit-strings.

A They must come to that with in this two or three years by that time shee'l be true perfect Catt. They practise before hand:

B I can endure no longer though I should throw off my Woman-hood: [*This speech belongs to W; so assigned 1671 ed.*]

A No need, that's done already, nothing left thee that may stile thee woman, but lust and tongue, no flesh but what the vices of the Sex exact to keep them in heart.

B Thou art so leane and out of case, that it were very absurd to call the [thee 1662] Devill incarnate:

A Thou art a drye Devill troubled with the lust of that thou hast not, flesh:

W. Rogue, Rascall, Villaine, I'le shew you cheating tricks ifaith, all shall be now laid open; have I suffered you thus received long in my house, and never took one peny Rent for this? I'le have it all by this good blessed light I will.

B. You may if you please undo your self, I will not strive to hinder you, but there is something contriving for you which perhaps may be yet brought about a match, or so [about, a Match or so, 1662] a proper fellow, 'tis a trifle that [that, 1662] a thing *J* know you care not for, have I plotted to match you in good sort, and am I us'd so? as for the Rent you ask, here taken [take 1662] it, take your mony, perhaps you had better nere have taken it, it may stop some proceedings.

W, Alas you know you may have the heart out of my belly as they say, if you will take the paines to reach it out, I am sometimes peevish I confesse, here take your mony.

A. No.

W. Good Sir.

A. No, keep it, and hoard it up, for my purse is no safe place for it.

W. Let me request you to be pleased to take it.

A. Alas twill only trouble mee, I can as well go light as be your Treasurer.

W. Good speak to him to take it.

R. [B. 1671] Come be once overuled by a woman, come, you shall take it.

W. Nay faith you shall, here put it up good Sir.

A. Well upon intreaty, I am content for once, but make no custome of it, you do presume upon my easie foolishnesse tis, [foolishness, 'tis 1662] that you make so bold, but mark me, if ere I find you in this mood again. [again, 1662] I'le dash your hopes of marriage for ever:

The tiresome mud-slinging which characterizes this scene was a favorite device of Caroline comedy. It was technically known as "jeering" (see Jonson's *Staple of News* (1625), II, i). See my discussion of these drolls in a note to *The Royal Slave*, line 874.

179–226 *You doe Honour her . . . Devill incarnate.* The following dialogue, based on these lines, occurs in *The Marrow of Complements* (1655), pages 59–61 (compare the dialogue quoted above, in the note to line 171, from *Wits Interpreter*, 1655):

Two Gentlemen willing to paint forth some
Letcherous old Crone.
A Dialogue between Olyndro *and* Gioto.

Olyndro. You do her too much honor to think shee deserves a thing that can lust moderately, give her the Sorrel Gelding in my Lords long stable.

Gioto. Or the same colour'd brother which is worse.

Olyndro. Her breath would rout an Army sooner then that of a Cannon.

Gioto. It would lay a Devill sooner then all *Tytremius* Charmes.

Olyndro. How her breath blusters in her nostrills, just like the wind in a fowle Chimney.

Gioto. For her Gate, that is such as if her nose did strive to outrun her heeles.

Olyndro. Her playster'd face doth drop against moist weather.

Gioto. Which when she writes [*sic*] it, lookes just like a rufled boot.

Olyndro. Or an old paper-Lanthorn.

Gioto. Her nose the candle in the midst of it.

Olyndro. Sure the Surveyer of the High-waies will have to do with her, for not keeping her countenance passable.

Gioto. There lies a hoar-frost on her head, and yet a constant thaw in her nose.

Olyndro. She is like a piece of firewood dropping at one end, and yet burning in the midst.

Gioto. You may hear her guts squeak like Kitlings.

Olyndro. They must come to that within this two or three years, by that time she will bee a true perfect Cat, they practise before hand.

Gioto. Nothing is left her that may stile her woman, but lust and tongue, no flesh but what the vices of the Sex exact to keep them in heart.

Olyndro. She is so lean, and out of —— case, that 'twere absurd, to call her Devill incarnate.

182–83 *The sorrell Stallion . . . Or the same colour'd Brother.* Miss Gebhardt (Thesis, *The Ordinary*) compares *Bartholomew Fair*, (1614), III, ii, where Justice Busy is described as a "stone-puritane, with a sorrell head, and beard" (1640 ed.).

190 Trithemius *charmes*. Trithemius (1462–1516) is called by Thevet a "subtle philosopher, an ingenious mathematician, a famous poet, an accomplish'd historian, a very eloquent orator, and eminent divine." See Reed's long note. His reputation as a magician was probably founded upon the mistaken attribution to him of a book entitled *Veterum Sophorum sigilla et imagines magicae* (1612).

195–96 *She's just six yards behind . . . saves an Usher Madam.* Compare Buckingham's "Advice to a Painter" (*Dramatick Works*, 1715, II, 212–13):

> *Povey* the Wit, and *R*—— the Beau-garzon,
> Who at his Entering shews a foot of Chin,
> To let you know his Face is coming in.

200 *ruffled boot.* Compare Jonson's *Every Man out of his Humour*, I, i: "and ruffle your brow like a new boot."

200–1 *Lanthorn. Her nose the candle.* Compare *1 Henry IV*, III, iii: ". . . thou art our admiral, thou bearest the lanthorn in the poop, but 'tis in the nose of thee." Similar witticisms at the expense of the nose were not, of course, uncommon. See *The Chronicle History of King Leir*, V, v; *Jack Drum's Entertainment*, I, i; Dekker's *Wonderful Year* (1603; Bodley Head Quartos, p. 76); W. Elderton's *A New Merry Newes* (1606), sig. [A7]ᵛ; Randolph's *Hey for Honesty*, II, iv; Glapthorne's *Wit in a Constable*, V, i; Killigrew's *Parson's Wedding*, V, iv; and Cleveland's "Midsummer Moon" (*J. Cleaveland Revived*, 1662, pp. 171–72).

203 *burn day-light.* A proverbial phrase for doing anything in waste or with no advantage (Reed).

208–10 *the Surveyer Of the high-waies . . . her countenance passable.*

Miss Gebhardt (Thesis, *The Ordinary*, p. 95) compares *Comedy of Errors*, III, ii, 104–7. Although the parallel is not very close, it seems probable that Shakespeare's lines may have been in the back of Cartwright's mind since later in *The Ordinary* (lines 413–18) he appears to borrow again from this same scene.

217   *Kitstrings*. Fiddle strings.

222–23   *nothing left thee . . . but Lust, and Tongue*. Compare Cowley's *Love's Riddle* (printed in 1638, but written while Cowley was still a student at Westminster), I, i, where one of the characters is describing Truga (a character type like Potluck):

> . . . yet you must talk,
> For thou hast nothing left thee of a Woman
> But Lust and Tongue.

There is, I suppose, a common classical source for this elevating comment.

257   *joyne with him*. Collier suggests that we should read "joyne with me," "as she is asking Shape to unite his solicitations with hers." The change is unnecessary, since "him" refers quite properly to Slicer who has just been addressed in the line before.

ACT I, SCENE III

Compare Jonson's *Cynthia's Revels* (1600), III, iii. In both scenes the "scholar" enters and his manner of presenting himself is criticised by his "tutor."

284–85   *a piece Of service for a Gentleman to caper*. Hazlitt has changed the text to read: "no piece Of service for a gentleman, to caper." The emendation is uncalled for and changes the sense of the passage. "A piece of service" is part of a series which begins with "an adventure, an exploit."

294   *extemporary*. Arising at the moment (*NED*). Cockeram's *English Dictionarie* (1623): "*Extempore*. Out of hand."

295   *was strait read on*. That is, his skeleton was used to illustrate an anatomical lecture. Hazlitt's note to the effect that "a lecture, probably, was delivered on the phenomenon," suggests more than Cartwright means.

301   *A Churle, a Hind*. By Cartwright's time these words are synonymous and mean a "rustic, or boor" (*NED*).

319-20 *Proofes, No Doctrines, nor no Uses.* See my note on "The Chambermaids Posset," line 41.

323-24 *Labell out o'your mouth . . . In* Foxes *Book.* Cartwright is referring, of course, to the illustrations in John Foxe's *Actes and Monuments* (1562/3), which picture the unfortunate victims with long scrolls, containing pious ejaculations, issuing from their mouths. In effect they look not unlike our modern comic strips.

Act I, Scene iv

Gerber (*Sources*, pp. 62, 73) draws attention to two Jonsonian passages, one in *Every Man out of His Humour*, V, ii, and the other in *The Magnetic Lady* (1632), I, i, as possible sources of suggestion for this rather amusing scene between Slicer, Hearsay, and old Simon Credulous, in which the two rogues, with outrageous "mutual adulations," persuade Credulous that they are, respectively, a great military hero and secret agent. See Gerber's monograph for a full discussion of the passages. Two other apposite sources may be suggested. (1) Jonson's epigram entitled *Captain Hungry* (Epigram CVII, *Works*, ed. Gifford-Cunningham, 1903, III, 249) sketches, in language very similar to Cartwright's, the portrait of the common political agent who pretends to possess the confidence of great states, gained in traveling all over the world on important missions. Here in miniature is a portrait of the magnificent Hearsay. (2) In Shackerley Marmion's *Holland's Leaguer* (1632), II, i, Argurtes is extolling his confederate Autolicus (in an attempt to cheat Trimalchio):

> O! 'tis Autolicus!
> My noble friend and brother of the sword.
> His stomach and his blade are of one temper,
> Of equal edge, and will eat flesh alike. . . .
> He is the shrewdest pated fellow breathing,
> The only engineer in Christendom,
> Will blow you up a carak like a squib,
> And row under water: the Emperor
> And Spinola by secret intelligence
> Have laid out for him any time this ten years,
> And twice he has escaped them by a trick.
> He is beyond Daedalus, or Archimedes,
> He lies concealed like a seminary,

> For fear the state should take notice of him.
> Machavill for policy was a dunce to him,
> And had he lived in Mahomet's days he had been
> His only counsellor for the Alcoran!
> He is newly come from Holland.

Here we have a character of the noble Slicer, with overtones of the subtle Hearsay.

Also compare with this scene Chamberlayne's *Love's Victory* (printed 1658), II, i, where Creon tries to impress upon Aeratus what a great soldier he has been and how siutable he is as a tutor for Creon's nephew.

338-51 *I did not hold the* University . . . *High noble thoughts*. Gerber (*Sources*, p. 80) suggests a comparison with Shirley's *The Gamester* (acted 1634), I, i. Compare also Jonson's *The Devil is an Ass*, III, i (also noted by Gebhardt, Thesis, *The Ordinary*, p. 97).

343-44 *A naked shorn thing . . . thin dockt top, . . . cut into a Logick mode*. Miss Gebhardt (Thesis, *The Ordinary*, p. 97) suggests that Cartwright is here probably having a fling at the University regulations on haircuts. The Laudian Statutes (issued 1634, in a kind of provisional form) under Title XIV, "Of the Scholastic Dress and Costume," read: "There must be, also, a mean observed in the dressing of the hair; and they are not to encourage the growth of curls, or immoderately long hair" (translated G. R. M. Ward, 1845, I). She also quotes an amusing anecdote concerning the infringement of this warning from Thomas Crosfield's *Diary* (ed. F. S. Boas, 1935) under January 24, 1635. In the phrase "Logick mode" it seems to me that Cartwright was probably thinking of the circular figures sometimes used in books on logic to illustrate the various figures of the syllogism.

361-69 *But for your deeds of Valour . . . mast and saile*. Combining these lines with lines 392-97, Zachary Grey (*Notes on Shakespeare*, 1754, I, 219), not too convincingly, suggests that Cartwright has here "improv'd" a passage in *All's Well*, IV, iii, 161-65, describing "Monsieur Parolles, the gallant militarist."

364 *Strabo*. A philosopher of Crete, and a geographer, in the time of Augustus (Reed).

Ptolomy. The celebrated astronomer, geographer, and mathematician of Alexandria, who flourished in the first half of the second century A.D.

Stafford. Robert Stafford was born in Dublin and educated at Exeter College, Oxford. In 1607 he published a *Geographical and Anthological description of all the Empires and Kingdomes . . . in this terrestrial Globe.* Wood reports that Stafford's tutor, John Prideaux, had the chief hand in the work (Reed).

365 *Lithgoe.* William Lithgow, the author of *Rare Adventures and Painefull Peregrinations* (1632) reports that his "Paynefull feet traced over (beside my passages of Seas and Rivers) thirty-six thousand and odde miles, which draweth neare to twice the circumference of the whole Earth." His book makes extremely entertaining reading. See Reed's note.

naked. Unarmed (Hazlitt).

366 *Coriat.* Thomas Coriat, like Lithgow above, was a great traveler on foot. He published his observations in 1611 under the title *Coryats Crudities hastily gobled up in five Moneths Travells in France, Savoy, . . . and the Netherlands.* More commendatory poems were written for this book than for any other in the seventeenth century. Cartwright's *Works* (1651) has the doubtful honor of being second in the list of too-much-commended books.

367 *Jack Mandevil.* Cartwright is referring to the supposed author of the famous *Travels* (first printed 1568).

371-75 *I've worn some Leather . . . that passe.* Quoted as a motto to "An Old Soldier" in Washington Irving's *Bracebridge Hall* (1822).

377 *that meer word,* Slicer. Compare the effect of Talbot's name, *1 Henry VI,* II, i, 79-81.

381-84 *Counsels of moment . . . very strongly.* Gerber (*Sources,* p. 73) suggests a comparison with Jonson's *Magnetic Lady,* I, i:

> Will screw you out a secret from a statist. . . .
> *Sir. Moth.* And lock it in the cabinet of his memory—
> *Compass.* Till it turn a politic insect or a fly.

385-91 *Distinguish each . . . by severall sents . . . fatall steame.* Compare Middleton's *Your Five Gallants,* IV, viii, where Frippery, the broker-gallant, is described as "a fellow of several scents and steams, French, Dutch, Italian, English" because he wears the clothes of so many different people.

388 *broken beer.* Apparently "broken beer" means beer made up from the leavings of half-drunk cans (Reed). See Reed's note for other uses of the term.

395 *Pagan.* Collier suggests very plausibly that the true reading is "Paynim." The confusion of *y* and *g*, and *u* and *n* is an easy error to make in setting up from an early seventeenth-century hand. The *Errata* (1651) reads: "Pageant r. Pagan."

397 *Bandeleers.* Broad belts, worn over the shoulder and across the breast, by which a wallet, or cartridge case, might be suspended (*NED*).

404 *a lay.* A layer (*NED*).

405 *Prester-Johnion whispers.* Cartwright speaks of "whispers" because nobody was very sure just where the land of the famous Prester John lay.

408 *H'hath with his breadth supplyd a breach.* Collier first suggested reading "breadth" for the original "breath," and I have adopted his emendation. Miss Gebhardt (Thesis, *The Ordinary*, pp. liv, 100), however, ingeniously supports the 1651 text by a quotation from Shirley's *The Young Admiral* (licensed 1633), III, i (Gifford-Dyce ed. III, 129): ". . . thy head shall be an anvil, and break all the swords that light upon't, and for the shot, thy breath shall damp a cannon, it shall fall off like one of thy buttons." As she points out, the possibility of Cartwright's borrowing here is strengthened by what looks like another borrowing from the same play in Act II, Scene iii (see the note to that scene).

413–18 *Turkey in's bloudy Liver . . . reek in all.* Koeppel ("Shakespeare's Wirkung auf zeitgenössische Dramatiker," in W. Bang's *Materialien*, IX, 84) first pointed out that these lines seemed to be a clear echo of the Syracusean Dromio's description of the kitchen-wench, Nell, in *The Comedy of Errors*, III, ii, 116–44. Compare also, however, the following passage from Burton's *Anatomy of Melancholy* (1638 ed., Pt. III, Sec. 2, Memb. 5, Subs. 3, p. 557):

> Let her head be from *Prage*, paps out of *Austria*, belly from *France*, back from *Brabant*, hands out of *England*, feet from *Rhine*, buttocks from *Switzerland*, let her have the *Spanish* gate, the *Venetian* tyre, *Italian* complement and endowments. [Described by Burton as a German adage of Bebelius.]

And compare Richard Brome's *The City Wit* (1653), in *Dramatic Works* (1873), I, 340:

> Oh, hee's an absolute spirit! He has an English face, a French tongue, a Spanish heart, an Irish hand, a Welch Leg, a Scotch beard, and a Dutch buttock.

417–18 *Ragioni Di Stato.* Reasons or politics of state (Hazlitt). Miss Gebhardt (Thesis, *The Ordinary*, p. 101) quotes Gifford's note to Jonson's *Cynthia's Revels*, I, i (Gifford-Cunningham, I, 154): "This 'choice remnant of Italian,' (which no Italian could pronounce,) or something like it, seems to have been proverbial for the politics of different countries. It is used by Cartwright, (and many others,) '*Ragioni di stato* generally reek in all.' —*Ordinary*, act i, sc. 4."

422 *Divert the Torrent of the Turkish rule.* When Cartwright composed this play the threat of Turkish supremacy in a large part of Europe seemed very real to most people. Something of the common state of mind can be seen in the following quotation from a pamphlet entitled "The Strangling and Death of the Great Turk," 1642 (*Harleian Miscellany*, 1810, V, 183):

> I am very loth to trouble you with a preface, yet, at this time, you must pardon me, for it is for God's cause, to exemplify his glory and providence, that hath put an hook in the nostrils of Leviathan, and kept him from devouring poor Christians, who yet are in arms to devour one another; that hath thrown a stone from heaven, to strike the golden image to powder, which was stretching itself to overlook and overtop the provinces of Europe; that hath put an ax to the great tree, and felled it at a blow, which was beginning to overspread the earth, and be a shadow for the beasts of the field.... Where are your dreaming gazettes and coranto's now, that talked of such formidable preparation, and so many hundred-thousand in an army? Where is the threatening of Poland, and terrifying the Cossacks with so many thousand Tartarians? Where is their coming into Hungary, to begin a new war there? What, all hushed, and quiet? Why, then, thine be the honour, O God.... This, then, is all I would say unto you, by the way of introduction, to give God the praise, that the great Turk is dead so opportunely, whereby there is hope, that Europe shall be preserved from their invasion, and those affrightings.

428 *Governour of some new little Island.* Is Cartwright thinking, perhaps, of Sancho's island in *Don Quixote*?

435 *uxorious showre.* Cartwright refers, of course, to Jupiter's seduction of Danaë in the form of a golden shower.

Act I, Scene v

453 *Colour ... for.* Give a specious appearance of (*NED*).

463 *Emerit.* Retired from active service (*NED*). Cartwright uses

the word again in the second part of his poem "To the King, on the Birth of the Princess *Anne*," line 37.

464 *German clock*. These clocks were much used in England about Cartwright's time (Reed). When Cartwright says that Moth, "like An Image in a German clock, doth move, Not walke," he is referring to the peculiarly stiff and awkward movements of the various figures which, in this type of clock, came out to announce the hours. Compare Ned Ward's *London Spy* (1703; ed. A. L. Hayward, n.d.), page 78.

466 *Hee'l surely love her . . . like some Old ruin'd peece*. Compare John Earle's character of "An Antiquary" (*Microcosmographie*, 1628): "He is one that hath that unnatural disease to be enamoured of old age and wrinkles, and loves all things (as Dutchmen do cheese,) the better for being mouldy and wormeaten."

488 *purchase*. Prize (Collier).

490–91 *barren Wives . . . do to St* Antholins. The Church of St. Antholins in London was a haunt of the Puritans. Cartwright is making the usual sneer at Puritan morality.

ACT II, SCENE I

SD The 1671 prompt copy adds the stage direction, "3 Baylifes fighting," and gives the scene as "Coven [*sic*] Garden."

521–24 *There is a way . . . The design is by a dinner*. The metamorphosis of Have-at-all through the magical effects of a dinner suggests the transformation wrought on Trincalo in *Albumazar* (1614), II, iii.

521 *though*. Altered from "that" by Dodsley, who is followed by all subsequent editors except Miss Gebhardt. Some change is necessary since the line as it stands contains two direct objects.

534 *Bagpudding*. A pudding boiled in a bag (*NED*).

544 *hardest*. Most vigorous, or most inured (*NED*). Hazlitt altered to "hardiest."

545 *Juments*. Beasts of burden (*NED*). Cartwright is referring specifically to the so-called beefeaters, who are the traditional Tower of London guards.

552 *After a crown a meal*. Collier (followed by Hazlitt) reads "After a crown meal." The emendation is, I believe, unnecessary. Cartwright says that gallants would owe their increased

valor to their ordinaries and would fight at the rate of a crown a meal, i.e., would fight with very great bravery. In Cartwright's London a crown was considered an extremely high price for an ordinary meal.

557 *No dish but must present Artilery.* Gifford (*Works of Ben Jonson,* ed. Gifford-Cunningham, III, 178) was the first to suggest Jonson's *Neptune's Triumph* (1624) as the original source of Cartwright's "military dinner." (See also Ward, *English Dramatic Literature,* III, 140n.; Koeppel, "Ben Jonson's Wirkung auf zeitgenössische Dramatiker," in *Anglistische Forschungen,* XX, 190-91; Gerber, *Sources,* pp. 74-77.) Jonson, repeating his conceit almost verbatim in *The Staple of News* (1625), IV, i, suggests that a cook may teach "the whole art military" and "all the tactics at one dinner," and, as Gifford observes, Cartwright "has reduced this into practice in his *Ordinary* and furnished out a military dinner with great pleasantry." Some other examples of "military dinners" may also be noticed: Fletcher's *The Bloody Brother* (1621), II, ii (see the discussion in the General Introduction, Chapter II, of Cartwright's suggested connection with this play); Randolph's *Aristippus* (1630); Fisher's *The True Trojans* (1633), III, vii; Heywood's *The English Traveller* (1633), II, i; Shirley's *The Lady of Pleasure* (1635), IV, ii; Killigrew's *The Parson's Wedding* (after 1650), III, ii; and, outside the drama, Earle's *Microcosmographie* (1628), "A Cook." The most striking parallel, however, to Cartwright's particular version of the "military dinner" occurs in *The London Chanticleers* (about 1636; Hazlitt-Dodsley, *Collection of Old English Plays,* XII, 341):

> *Curds.* What shall we have at our wedding dinner? We'll be sure of a plum-pudding, that shall be the very flower of the feast.
> *Heath.* Then a leg of beef shall walk round the table, like a city captain with a target of lamb before it: a snipe, with his long bill, shall be a serjeant, and a capon carry the drumsticks. Thou shalt be lady-general, and pick out the choicest of every dish for thy life-guard.

568 *Marchpanes.* Marchpane was a confection made of pistachio nuts, almonds, and sugar, etc., formerly in high esteem (Reed).

572 *Swiming in whitebroth.* Gerber (*Sources,* p. 76) calls attention to Jonson's isle "floating in now, In a brave broth" in

Neptune's Triumph. We may also compare the "standing lake of white broth" in *The Bloody Brother,* II, ii.

577–78 *Breast of Mutton, stuff'd With Pudding.* The following note, by Pegge, is given by Reed: "This is called a St. Stephen's Pudding; it used formerly to be provided at St. John's College, Cambridge, uniformly on St. Stephen's Day."

579 *Perdues.* Outposts stationed in a hazardous position (*NED*).

581 *fennell.* A fragrant perennial umbellifer having yellow flowers, made use of in sauces (*NED*).

588 *Petronels.* Large pistols or carbines used especially by horse-soldiers (*NED*).

590 *Caveari.* This word was pronounced as a trisyllable in Elizabethan English. The eating of caviar was considered a foreign affectation by the earlier Elizabethan writers. See Reed's note.

594 *long Spitchcock.* Cartwright's phrase seems to be a contradiction in terms. The *NED* defines a "spitchcock" as "an eel cut into short pieces, dressed with bread-crumbs and chopped herbs, and broiled or fried." See line 681.

597 *Malecotoons.* The malacoton is one of the late peaches (Reed).

620 *Aligant.* A Spanish wine made at Alicante (*NED*).

621 *Tent.* A Spanish red wine of low alcoholic content (*NED*).

629 *My word.* That is, my motto.

633 *Beware you say 'tis yours.* The way in which Slicer plays Have-at-all and Credulous off against each other in the matter of the dinner seems reminiscent of Jonson's *Silent Woman,* III, iii.

659 *trunck-hose Justices.* That is, justices with old-fashioned ideas. By Cartwright's time trunk-hose were considered entirely outmoded.

678 *breath to dust.* Gerber (*Sources,* p. 63) compares Jonson's *Every Man out of his Humour,* V, iii: "Carlo will rack your sinews asunder, and rail you to dust."

679 *Templers.* That is, the members and students of the Inner Temple.

681 *Oliv'd.* A term in cookery, used to describe beef or veal cut into thickish slices and rolled up with onions and herbs (*NED*).

Act II, Scene ii

The character of Moth, the antiquary, who here appears for the first time, is one of Cartwright's most original efforts, a rather typically academic creation. The peculiar jargon which Moth speaks, a sort of bastard Middle English, has been shown by Reed (*Select Collection of Old Plays*, 1780, X, 234), Ballmann ("Chaucers Einfluss auf das englische Drama," *Anglia*, XXV, 63–66), Lounsbury (*Studies in Chaucer*, 1892, III, 116–18), Gerber (*Sources*, pp. 53–58), and Gebhardt (Thesis, *The Ordinary*, pp. lxvi–lxxxvi) to be a patchwork of phrases and lines from Chaucer, culled here and there from six of the principal works. Miss Gebhardt's study is extremely detailed, giving among other things a complete text of all the Chaucerian lines (from Speght's edition of 1602) which Cartwright weaves into his verse, and attempting to show exactly how much (or rather how little) Middle English Cartwright knew. She also adds an interesting section on the state of Middle English studies in Cartwright's day (pp. lxxxvi–c). That Cartwright was interested in Chaucer we know from his commendatory poem to Kynaston's *Amorum Troili et Cresseidae* (1635), but the speeches of Moth prove how carefully and enthusiastically he had studied the poet. In treating Cartwright's numerous mistakes in using Middle English, one should always keep this clearly in mind. They show a sad lack of philological knowledge, but no lack of a thorough knowledge of Chaucer's poetry. Moreover, as Miss Gebhardt points out (pp. lxxxiv–lxxxv), linguistic error in a character which prided himself on antiquarian learning added satirical point to the treatment, especially before an academic audience which might be supposed to be in the know. One should also not forget the typesetter who in several instances has presented us with strange forms of which even Cartwright may be declared innocent.

Miss Gebhardt further suggests that Cartwright may have been influenced in his method of constructing Moth's peculiar jargon by the Chaucerian imitation which was composed by one of the characters in *The Returne from Parnassus, Part One* (about 1600), IV, i. It is, of course, barely possible that Cartwright knew this play, but on the whole it is improbable since it was a Cambridge play and remained in manuscript until the nineteenth century. Nor is there in *The Returne* any suggestion of a dramatic use of Chaucer. Moreover, it must be remembered that Chaucer had been laid under contribution by dramatists long before Cartwright's Moth, notably by John Heywood in *The Pardoner and the Friar* (1533) and by Ben Jonson in *The Alchemist*, though in both his language has been modernized. Heywood's borrowing is particularly interesting since his Pardoner speaks many lines lifted directly from Chaucer's *Prologue* and *Pardoner's Prologue*. A borrowing of some lines from *The Prologue* may be noticed in Randolph's *Aristippus* (1630; ed. Hazlitt, *Works*, 1875, I, 21); also a short poem, "Imitatio Chauceri altera, In eundem" in *Musarum Deliciae* (1655), pages 74–75.

After all has been said, however, the conception of a character who spoke only "Middle English"—an attempt to emphasize his passion for antiquity—was Cartwright's own. There is no connection between Marmion's Veterano in *The Antiquary* (acted 1636) and Cartwright's Moth, other than obvious features common to the character type (see Earle's *Microcosmographie*, 1628, "An Antiquary").

It is possible that Butler may have had Cartwright's Moth in mind when, in his character of "An Antiquary," he wrote:

> He has a great veneration for words that are stricken in years, and are grown so aged that they have outlived their employments. These he uses with a respect agreeable to their antiquity and the good services they have done.

In dealing with Moth's Chaucerisms I have not thought it worth while either to gloss the majority of his words, most of which are a matter of common knowledge to anyone likely to read Cartwright, or to point out word for word or line for line the exact Chaucerian source for Cartwright's pilferings. The Chaucer *Concordance* (1927) has rendered this second task unnecessary. I have, however, pointed out the most flagrant examples of Cartwright's philological errors.

686 *Golierdis*. Reed quotes Tyrwhitt: "This jovial sect seems to have been so called from Golias, the real or assumed name of a man of wit, toward the end of the 12th century, . . . In several authors of the 13th century, quoted by Du Cange, the Goliardi are classed with the *joculatores* and *buffones*." Cartwright took the name from line 560 of Chaucer's *Prologue*.

687 *two* Janus *heads*. That is, two bronze Roman asses.

690 *Nad be*. An impossible construction for the context. Cart-

wright says, "It had not been," when he means, "It may not be." Even for the first meaning the form would have to be "Nad ben."

693 *I kissen.* Another impossible construction.

696 *lytherly.* Cartwright's sense requires the adjectival "lither," meaning "wicked" or "unpleasant." But Miss Gebhardt (Thesis, *The Ordinary*, p. 106) notes that Speght had glossed "litherly" as meaning "slouthfull."

702 *unwenned.* Cartwright means "unwemmed," that is, "unspotted."

714-15 *Lore me o thing mere. Abouten what.* A parlous passage in the original, which reads, "Lore me o thing mere Alouten, what." By "Lore" Cartwright means "lere," the imperative of the verb "to teach." "Mere" stands for some form of "more," the correct Middle English form being "mo." "Alouten" is, so far as I can find, an otherwise unknown word. It is, I believe, merely the compositor's error for "abouten," which, with a full stop after "mere" and the deletion of the following comma, makes excellent sense of the passage.

715 *brendle.* Cartwright's form for "brenne," meaning "to burn."

728 *y'eke.* Perhaps meant for "ye also," the original reads "yeke."

ACT II, SCENE III

This scene represents one of Cartwright's principal borrowings from Jonson's *Alchemist*, I, i (see *Works of Ben Jonson*, ed. Gifford-Cunningham, II, 13; Koeppel, "Ben Jonson's Wirkung auf zeitgenössische Dramatiker," *Anglistische Forschungen*, XX, 162-64; Gerber, *Sources*, pp. 64-66). In Jonson's play, Dapper, like Caster, wishes to become a successful gambler. He approaches Subtle, who, with much show of reluctance—a move which satisfactorily produces money from the victim—finally agrees to furnish Dapper with a "familiar" or "fly." In the same way Hearsay, playing the role of Subtle, at first pretends reluctance to initiate Caster into the mystery, until with the aid of Shape (compare Jonson's Face) he has separated the stupid gull from all but a fraction of his money. At this point Cartwright leaves Jonson for a moment. With possibly a hint from Shirley's *The Young Admiral* (1633), IV, i, where the importance of the imagination is especially stressed in rendering Pazzorello "slick and shot free" (also noted by Gebhardt, Thesis, *The Ordinary*, p. liv), he invents his own method of making Caster gambling-proof. For the conclusion of the scene, where Caster becomes filled with grandiose visions of the future and makes vast promises of building cathedrals and renovating colleges, he turns once again to *The Alchemist*, II, i, and draws upon the richly teeming source of Sir Epicure Mammon's dreams of approaching affluence. Gerber (*Sources*, p. 66) also notices two other passages which promise a pious use of wealth: Shirley's *The Bird in a Cage*, II, i, and Beaumont and Fletcher's *The Night-Walker*, IV, v. To these may be added a satirical passage in D'Avenant's *The Wits*, I, ii.

747 *new* Atlantis. Presumably a reference to Bacon's *New Atlantis*, first published in 1635.

762 *Ames Ace.* Double ace, the lowest throw at dice (*NED*).

765–75 *Your high And low men . . . open to the eye.* Gifford (*Works of Ben Jonson*, II, 18) points out that Cartwright is here imitating a passage in Jonson's *Alchemist* II, ii:

> You shall no more deal with the hollow dye,
> Or the frail card.

Cartwright's terms of "art" may be best studied in Cotton's *Compleat Gamester* (1674) pages 11–16. Wilson in *The Cheats* (1664), IV, i, repeats most of Cartwright's terms and adds some new ones:

> Did not I, if you are yet cool enough to hear truth, teach you your top, your palm, and your slur? Shew'd you the mystery of jack-in-a-box, and the frail die? Taught you the use of up-hills, down-hills, and petars? the wax'd, the grav'd, the slipt, the goad, the fullam, the flat, the bristle, the bar; and generally, instructed you from prick-penny to long-lawrence?

802–4
> *The little Æthiop Infant had not been*
> *Black in his Cradle, had he not been first*
> *Black in the Mothers strong Imagination.*

These lines have caused the editors much trouble. Following the suggestion of Steevens in a note to Reed's edition, Hazlitt prints the lines as follows:

> The little Ethiop infant would have been
> Black in his cradle, had he not been first
> White in the mother's strong imagination.

Reed refers to Digby's *A Late Discourse* (1658) as the source of Cartwright's story, but, as Hazlitt points out, this little book did not appear until several years after Cartwright's death. It is remarkable, however, that the anecdote concerning St. John the Baptist which immediately follows (ll. 805-7) is also found in Digby's book, coupled with the account of the Queen of Ethiopia, who gave birth to a white child. Hazlitt suggests a common source. At any rate Cartwright cannot have known Digby's *Discourse* even in manuscript, since the *Discourse* was first delivered in French in the form of a lecture in 1657. It was printed in French from notes taken at the lecture and then translated into English by Robert White in 1658. In spite of the coincidence afforded by Digby's *Discourse*, it is still possible, I believe, to defend the original reading of the 1651 text. Cartwright is speaking of white parents to whom a black child (Æthiop Infant) has been born. This interpretation finds considerable support in the following lines from Cleveland's "Mixt Assembly" (*Works*, 1687, p. 32):

> She that conceiv'd an *Æthiopian* Heir
> By Picture, when the Parents both were fair,
> At sight of you had born a dapled Son,
> You chequering her Imagination.

Compare also the story in Head and Kirkman's *English Rogue*, *Part Three* (1674), Chapter II, of the woman who "is after marriage gotten with Child by a *Moor*, and perswades her Husband it was his, notwithstanding, it being conceived so by the strength of imagination."

813 *Wounds*. Reed refers to page 6 of Digby's *Discourse* (1658) noticed above, where the remarkable cure effected on James Howell by the "powder of sympathy" is recounted. The reference, however, has no point here, since it is by a powder that the cure is wrought. The mistake arose perhaps through a misprint on page 5, where the arsenical powder is spoken of as the "Power of Sympathy." In the same way Collier misquotes the title of Digby's work as "Sir Kenelm Digby's Discourse, touching the Cure of Wounds by the Power of Sympathy." He is followed by Hazlitt.

823 *Who 'tis they do believe*. Collier suggests we should read "Why

'tis they so believe," while Hazlitt, adopting part of Collier's reading, gives "Why 'tis they do believe." I am not sure that any change is necessary.

843   *I'l take up for't*. That is, I'll raise money by mortgages.

862   *That pleasure that I'l baulk*. All the modern editors, following Dodsley, read "but I'l baulk," a reading which completely alters the sense of the passage. Caster clearly means to say that there are no pleasures which he will hesitate to enjoy.[1]

876   *forty thousand unto* Pauls. See the note to lines 42–44 of "On the Imperfection of *Christ-Church* Buildings."

877   *Cathedral . . . in* Banbury. Reed refers to Corbet's "Iter Boreale," where Banbury is one of the towns visited. It was a puritan stronghold, hence the humor in Caster's suggestion.

882–84   *build up All Colleges . . . left unperfect*. A reference to the unfinished state of parts of Christ Church. See Cartwright's two poems on this subject, "On the Imperfection of *Christ-Church* Buildings" and "A Continuation of the same to the Prince of *Wales*."

891   *happy*. Characterized by or involving good fortune (*NED*). This use of the word is a Latinism and can be here taken as synonymous with "wealthy."

Act II, Scene iv

903   *Pies take him*. *Pies* or *pize* is an oath, the origin of which is uncertain (*NED*).

904   *Fly*. That is, a familiar spirit.

918–19   *wit . . . will be th' undoing of you*. Gerber (*Sources*, p. 72) compares Jonson's *Bartholomew Fair*, I, i: "Come, John, this ambitious wit of yours, I am afraid, will do you no good in the end."

Act II, Scene v

972   *picking meat*. Trifling fare. The *NED* quotes the phrase from R. Harvey (1589) and Bunyan (1678).

979   *canst not complement, but in Caparisons*. That is, Andrew cannot pay compliments unless he is properly dressed for the occasion.

---

[1] The phrase "All the modern editors" here, and elsewhere in the notes to this play, must not be interpreted to include Miss Gebhardt unless she is specifically mentioned. If Miss Gebhardt has a comment on the passage in question, that comment has been worked into the note.

ACT III, SCENE I

999–1000 *Harrow alas!* . . . *Cupido*. These two lines are used in a droll which appeared in *The Marrow of Complements* under the title "An Amorovs Dialogve, Managed betweene John Medlay a Tyler. and Jone Simper-Sudds a Farmers Daughter," page 48:

> *Ione.* Doe you love me then *Iohn*?
> *Medlay.* Harrow, Alas I swelt as I goe, brenning in Love of little Cupido, wee'll be marryed to morn, *Ione*.

1005 *wendeth*. An impossible word in the context. Cartwright means "woneth."

1006–13 *Saint* Francis, *and Saint* Benedight. Four lines of this lyric appeared in *The Marrow of Complements* page 61, under the title "The Consecration of a new Built Fabrick." As Gerber (*Sources*, p. 54) points out, Cartwright takes his first two lines almost literally from Chaucer (*Canterbury Tales*, T, 3483–84). The remainder, Gerber suggests, may be compared with a "counter-spell" in Fletcher's *Monsieur Thomas*, IV, vi. See also, of course, Spenser's "Epithalamion," lines 340–52, and the following lines in *The Troublesome Reign of John, King of England*, Part I (1591), sig. [E4]ᵛ:

> A pardon, O *parce*, Saint *Fraunces* for mercie,
> Shall shield thee from nightspells and dreaming
>   of diuells.

Goffin (*Poems*, pp. 167–68) prints these lines as if they were part of the Prologue. Washington Irving (*Sketch Book*, 1820) uses the verses as a motto for his essay, "Christmas Eve."

1014 *Bryd*. That is, bird. Collier and Hazlitt both read "bride."

1018 *lycand*. That is, pleasing. Moth suddenly breaks into Northern dialect.

1026 *deignous*. Cartwright probably means "worthy." Actually the word means "bumptious" or "disdainful."

1034 *the* Titius *in Hell*. There is a strong temptation to emend this reading by the usually accepted text of the Chaucerian original ("he, Ticius, in helle;" *Troilus and Criseyde*, I, 786). Skeat, however, records that two of the manuscripts actually read "the." Is this mere coincidence, or does it indicate that Cartwright had access to Chaucer manuscripts? Speght (ed. of 1602) reads "he Tityus" (Gebhardt, Thesis, *The Ordinary*, p. lxxvii).

1042–46 *now* Aldersgate . . . *from* Aluredus. Compare Stow's *Survey of London* (ed. of 1603, edited by H. B. Wheatley, Everyman Library, p. 33):

> The next is Ældresgate, or Aldersgate, so called not of Aldrich or of Elders, that is to say, ancient men, builders thereof; not of Eldarne trees, growing there more abundantly than in other places, as some have fabled, but for the very antiquity of the gate itself, as being one of the first four gates of the city. . . .

Stow does not mention the Aluredus etymology.

1045 *growden.* An impossible form based on analogy with the past participles of weak verbs, plus the plural ending.

1050–54 *By* Woden *God of Saxons* . . . *My Sepulchre.* Quoted as a motto to Chapter VI of Scott's *The Antiquary*; also used as a motto to introduce Irving's story, "Rip Van Winkle," in *The Sketch Book* (1820).

1053 *thylke [day] in which.* Miss Gebhardt (Thesis, *The Ordinary*, pp. lxxviii, 37) shows that the reading "day" (the reading of all the modern editors) is justified by line 1045 (Skeat's ed.) of Chaucer's "Chanouns Yemannes Tale" which Cartwright is imitating.

1058 *this tenth of our King.* As Pegge pointed out (in Reed's Dodsley, 1780), this reference to the tenth year of Charles' reign would suggest that Cartwright was engaged on *The Ordinary* in 1634, or at least before March 26, 1635.

1059 *crumpe Ring.* Or more properly, "cramp ring." These rings were formerly worn, after being blessed by the king, in the belief that they cured the cramp. See Reed's long note.

1060 *I bequeathen.* Another impossible form.

1062–63 *witnesse that this . . . my tooth.* Pegge (in Reed's Dodsley, 1780) observes that this refers to the old custom of biting the wax, usually red, in sealing deeds. The form generally used was:

> And to witness this is sooth,
> I bite the wax with my wang tooth.

ACT III, SCENE II

Gerber (*Sources*, p. 60) points out the resemblance between the "joy old Credulous anticipates in getting Caster's farm" and the behavior of the usurious woolen-draper, Quomodo, in Middleton's *Michaelmas Term* (1607), II, iii; III, iv; IV, i.

1103 *sneaksbill.* A sharp-nosed, lean, sneaking fellow (*Century Dictionary*). A "wretched fellow, one out of whose nose hunger drops" (Cotgrave).

1119 *flinch for th' wetting.* An allusion to the effects of water on cloth ill woven (Reed).

1123–25 *He sent . . . For . . . hundred pound, by the same token, That you invited him to th' eating house.* I am not at all sure of the meaning here. Collier omits the comma after "token," and Hazlitt omits both commas. The phrase "by the same token that" may perhaps be taken to mean "in evidence of which I advance the fact that." It does not even seem very clear that old Credulous has asked Caster to dine at the ordinary.

1137 *considerable.* That is, to be considered.

ACT III, SCENE III

Gerber (*Sources*, p. 79) compares with this scene an episode in Shirley's *Bird in a Cage* (1633), IV, ii. Compare somewhat later analogues in Killigrew's *Claricilla* (1636), I, i; Glapthorne's *The Hollander* (1635), IV; and Chamberlayne's *Love's Victory* (printed 1658), III, ii. Gerber further suggests a parallel between Priscilla's behavior toward Meanwell and Abigail's advances to her mistress's suitor, Welford, in Beaumont and Fletcher's *The Scornful Lady* (1610), I, i; III, i. I do not feel that this parallel has much bearing in the present case.

1263–86 *Come, o come, I brook no stay.* This song, set to music by Henry Lawes, appears in *Select Ayres and Dialogues* (1659, reissued 1669), page 61 [mispaged 55]; and in John Playford's *Musick's Delight on the Cithren* (1666), Number 91. Cartwright's lyric also appears in *Westminster Drollery*, Part II (1672), page 79 (where the second stanza is omitted). There are three manuscript versions: (1) British Museum, Harl. MS. 3511, fol. 9ᵛ; (2) Bodleian Library, Rawl. MS. D.1092; (3) Lawes' autographed MS., page 103. The Harleian MS. (fols. 9ᵛ–10ʳ) contains an "Answer" to Cartwright's lines by Thomas (?) May:

Answer.

Goe o goe be gon away
He cannot love that cannot stay
  See how the ugly night
  Is banisht by the light
And conquiring Sol has got the day.

> To 'b unwilling's to be chast
> And every gallant that's in hast
> > Comits a reall fault
> > Desire will write him naught
> Although the act be never past.
>
> Blasting tapours I wish gon
> Since such a flame is worst [*sic*] than none
> > The long-a-kindling fire
> > Is gon befor't expire
> I'le lie still warme & still alone.
>
> Learne to vanquish then those powers
> The will unbridled's none of ours
> > Who in a Mrs Cheeke
> > Kisseth chimes all the weeke
> For bells and baubles sells his howres.

The subject of Cartwright's lyric is the common classical and Elizabethan theme, "Gather ye rosebuds while ye may." Gerber (*Sources*, p. 78) compares Cloe's song in Fletcher's *Faithful Shepherdess*, I, iii. Compare also the last stanza of Herrick's "Corinna's going a-maying" and Stanley's translation of a poem of Guido Casoni entitled "Time Recovered." Perhaps Cartwright's version was suggested in part by the following lines from Jonson's *Cynthia's Revels*, I, i:

> Witness thy youth's dear sweets here spent untasted,
> Like a fair taper, with his own flame wasted.

1270 *Is fourscore at fifteen*. It seems scarcely necessary to point out that fourteen or fifteen was considered a good marriageable age to the seventeenth-century mind for any girl that was not going to "lead apes in hell." Robert Jones states the case for three of the parties concerned in his lyric "My father faine would have me take" (*Muses Gardin for Delights*, 1610, No. XV). While the gallant's attitude may be suggested by lines 15-17 of Suckling's "Lutea Allison."

ACT III, SCENE IV

As Gerber suggests (*Sources*, p. 61) Cartwright seems to have taken some hints for the general handling of his scene from Middleton's *A Fair Quarrel* (1617), IV, i. For a good contemporary account of "roisterers" and "roarers" and their

ACT III, SCENE V

1327 *Qualities.* That is, professions. Compare line 1297.

1330-31 *'tis pitty Professions . . . slighted thus.* Cartwright may have taken a hint for Sir Kit's speech on the bad state of "business" from Fletcher's *The Spanish Curate* (1622), II, i.

1355 Pauci . . . amavit [Iupiter]. See Virgil's *Æneid*, VI, 129–30. "Iupiter" seems to have dropped out of Cartwright's text.

1356 *Quadragessimall wits.* Steevens notes that this refers to "those who write the customary verses during the Lent season at Oxford." It means here perhaps only "starved" wits.

1367 *Ridles, and Clouds are very lights of speech.* Sir Kit's desire to keep "these two In desperate hope of understanding" him by his riddles and clouds rather reminds one of Stephen Hawes' rhetorically serious promise in the verse dedication of his *Pastime of Pleasure* (1509):

> The lyght of trouth I lacke cunnying to cloke,
> To drawe a curtayne I dare not to presume,
> Nor hyde my matter with a misty smoke,
> My rudenes cunnying doth so sore consume:
> Yet as I may I shall blowe out a fume
> To hyde my mynde underneth a fable,
> By covert coloure well and probable.

With Sir Kit's method of speaking in contrarieties, a common Elizabethan figure, compare Romeo's first set speech, *Romeo and Juliet*, I, i, 180–87.

1375 *froth, and barme.* Probably a reminiscence of Jonson's satire on Marston's phrase "barmy froth" in *The Poetaster*, V, i.

1378 *Bilke.* A statement having nothing in it (*NED*).

1386 *transmiss'd.* That is, transmitted. This is the only example of the word quoted by the *NED*.

1387 *Trencher Analects.* That is, as Steevens points out, scraps left over from other people's plates. Gifford in a note to *The Old Law* (*Massinger's Works*, 1840, p. 502) says that the phrase refers to the moral sayings which were formerly carved on the large wooden trenchers, something on the order of Mr. Dick's "moral pocket-handkerchiefs" (compare Milton, *Apology for Smectymnuus*, Bohn ed., 1848, III, 135). Gifford

1398 *good dozen of pacificall Beere*. Gerber (*Sources*, p. 61) compares the beer with the stock of wine kept on hand to compose the mock quarrels of the roarers in Middleton's *A Fair Quarrel* (1617), IV, i, and suggests that this reflects an actual practice of the times. The only other evidence for such an assumption which I have been able to find occurs in Ford's *The Lover's Melancholy*, I, ii, where after a typical exchange of roaring "courtesies" Rhetias, one of the combatants, suddenly, for no very good reason unless in reference to this custom, enquires: "Are thy bottles full?" and Corax, the physician, answers: "Of rich wine, let's all suck together."

1406 *humble Sir*. Hazlitt suggests that we should read "noble sir," but Sir Kit speaks such nonsense anyway, usually saying just the opposite of what he means, that the original reading is quite likely to be correct. It is barely possible that "humble" is to be taken in an adverbial sense with the preceding verb "levell," in which case a comma would be necessary before "Sir."

1412 *Kit*. That is, a fiddle.

1414–20 *It is the holy cause . . . thy Betters*. Quoted by Walter Scott in *The Fortunes of Nigel*, II, 299 (adapted).

1415–16 *Thou Son of Parchment . . . Buckram bag*. Miss Gebhardt (Thesis, *The Ordinary*, p. 122) compares Peter Hausted's *Rival Friends* (1632), V, ix, where a Puritan suitor is described as "A whoreson *Inkbottle*, and *two skins of parchment*." On "Buckram bag" she quotes Nares: "The lowest class of attorneys appear to have carried bags of this material. 'To Westminster Hall I went, and made a search of enquirie, from the blacke gowne to the buckram bag . . .' Nash, *Pierce Penilesse*, 1592."

1428 *Sternolds, or Wisdoms Meteer*. Bagshot is referring to two metrical versions of the Psalms, both very much favored by the puritan factions. In *The Assembly-Man* (1647; *Harleian Miscellany*, 1810, VI, 62), John Berkenhead describes the state of affairs as follows:

> Yet he has mercy on Hopkins and Sternhold because their meetres are sung without authority (no statute, canon, or injunction at all) only, like himself, first crept into private houses, and then into churches. Mr. Rous moved those meetres might be sequestered, and his own rhimes to

enjoy the sequestration; but was refused, because John Hopkins was as ancient as John Calvin, besides, when Rous stood forth for his trial, Robin Wisdom was found the better poet.

Reed refers to Wood's *Athenae* for an account of Robert Wisdom. See also Corbet's poem "To the Ghost of Robert Wisdome" (*Poems*, ed. Gilchrist, 1807, p. 229). Hazlitt refers the reader to Warton's *History of English Poetry*.

1429 *'Tis my cause*. Hazlitt alters to " 'Tis by cause," a change which is unwarranted, since when Rimewell claims the cause as his he is referring to the defense of Sternhold and Wisdom as poets, a profession which, as it is his own, he feels called upon to champion.

1432 London *measure Beard*. See the note to line 53 of "The Chambermaids Posset."

1440 Lopez. The following account of Lopez appears in a pamphlet called *Robert Earl of Essex's Ghost* (1624; *Harleian Miscellany*, 1809, III, 518):

In the year 1594, Roderick Lopez, doctor of physick, a Portuguese by birth, and entertained physician in ordinary to Queen Elizabeth, being instigated by Christofero de Moro, a special counsellor of King Philip's, covenanted to take away the life of her sacred Majesty, by a poisoned potion; for the performance of which deed of darkness, the said De Moro promised him fifty thousand crowns, and he had earnest given him, a jewel of gold, with a diamond and ruby of rich value, but that plot was detected by God's providence, and Lopez received condign punishment.

A long modern study of the Lopez case may be found in A. S. Hume's *Treason and Plot* (1901), pages 115–64. I fail to see the exact applicability of Sir Kit's remark. Presumably to call a person a "Lopez" was to call him a "villain." Perhaps, however, Cartwright is referring to Lopez in Fletcher's *Spanish Curate*, a character which certainly deserves the title "rascal" if not "villain."

1443 [*un*]*sanctified Rithmes*. I have adopted Hazlitt's reading in part, though it is possible that to the zealous Puritan, Sir Kit, the word "sanctified" had a Popish and unhallowed flavor. All the modern editors read "rhymes" for the original "Rithmes." Since the two words were frequently confused under the single meaning of "rhyme," it is impossible to be sure which Cartwright really intended. See Puttenham's *Arte of English Poesie* (1589), Book II, Chapter V (ed. Arber, 1869,

1450–52 *A judgment shewn . . . A pill . . . death of* Katherin Stubs. The first pamphlet mentioned by Catchmay is at present unknown, the second, "A Pill to Purge Out Popery" by John Mico, was first published in 1623, and the third, "the life And death of *Katherin Stubs*," was a popular and edifying work, written by her husband, Philip Stubs, and was published first in 1592. See Reed's and Collier's notes.

pp. 90–91), for a contemporary discussion of the problem presented by these two metrical concepts. The present context seems to favor the "rhyme" meaning.

1467 *A Bellarmine.* That is, a large drinking jug, named after the Jesuit theologian, Roberto Bellarmino (1542–1621). Gifford (*Works of Ben Jonson*, II, 345) and Gerber (*Sources*, pp. 72–73) compare Christopher's description of Catchmey as a "Bellarmine" with Jonson's *The New Inn*, I, i, where Lovel similarly describes the Host.

1471 *Tyrant* Eglon. Miss Gebhardt (Thesis, *The Ordinary*, p. 126) notes this as a reference to Judges 3:17, where Eglon, king of the Moabites, is described as "a very fat man."

1512 *future-now.* It is necessary to insert the hyphen here to make Sir Kit's meaning clear.

1518 *stickled.* That is, acted as umpire or mediator.

1534–61 *Then our Musick is in prime.* Three later versions of this song appeared in *The Marrow of Complements* (1655, p. 46), in *Wits Interpreter* (1655, p. 51; 1662, p. 157; 1671, p. 157), and in *The New Academy of Complements* (1671, pp. 127–28).

1538 *Quest.* The modern editors all read "guest," except Goffin, who, however, does not attempt to explain the original reading. The word here seems to be used in an active sense, that is, as "something seeking" instead of as "something sought."

1541–44 *A Mooting Night . . . A Reading-Day.* Reed refers the reader for an explanation of these law terms to Sir William Dugdale's *Origines Juridiciales* (1666). The so-called Reading Days took place in Lent and in August and lasted for three weeks (2nd ed., pp. 159–60, 247–48). The whole procedure and the various ceremonies involved are extremely complicated. On a mooting night the students exercised their wits by discussing hypothetical law cases.

1546 *The Benchers dare speak Latin.* Does this have any reference to "the benchers' phrase; *pauca verba, pauca verba,*" in *Every Man in his Humour*, IV, ii (*Jonson's Works*, ed. Gifford-Cunningham, I, 39), or is "bencher" to be taken in the sense of "one of the senior members of the Inns of Court" (*NED*)?

1558 Sutcliffs *Wit*. Dr. Matthew Sutcliffe was Dean of Exeter during the reign of James I. He was a strong champion of the reformed religion and founded a college at Chelsea to encourage the study of polemics. In his "Letter to Ben Jonson," Beaumont writes:

> 'Tis liquor that will find out Sutcliffe's wit,
> Lie where it will, and make him write worse yet.

Professor H. E. Rollins suggests that "Numph Crouch," who does duty for Sutcliffe in the line as it appears in *The Marrow of Complements*, is an error for Humph[rey] Crouch, the prolific ballad maker (see H. E. Rollins, *Cavalier and Puritan*, 1923, pp. 144-45). See Reed's note.

ACT III, SCENE VI

1580 *liquorous*. That is, greedy or wanton (*NED*). "Liquorish," the reading of all the modern editors, is merely a variant form of the same word.

ACT IV, SCENE I

1600-1 Tribulation, *Nor holy* Ananias. Tribulation Wholesome and Ananias, a pastor and deacon of Amsterdam, are two characters in Jonson's *Alchemist*.

1603 *hold Bias*. That is, observe the orthodox method.

1605 *by yea and nay*. That is, at all events. This phrase was a favorite among the Puritans.

1610 *I would I were a pepper corn*. Reed compares *I Henry IV*, III, iii:

> An I have not forgotten what the inside of a church is made of, I am a peppercorn, a brewer's horse.

1612-13 *Great* Andrew Mahomet *Imperious* . . . Credulous. Compare Dekker's *Satiro-Mastix* (1602; ed. T. Hawkins, *Origin of the English Drama*, 1773, III, 115):

> . . . you must be call'd *Asper*, and *Criticus*, and *Horace*; thy title's longer o'reading than the stile o'the big *Turk's*: *Asper, Criticus, Quintus, Horatius, Flaccus.*

Gerber (*Sources*, p. 63) suggests a comparison with Jonson's *Every Man out of His Humour* (1599), I, i, and Beaumont and Fletcher's *Knight of the Burning Pestle* (1611), I, iii. See also Jonson's *The Devil is an Ass* (1616); II, i, Cowley's *Love's Riddle* (1638), III, i, and Cartwright's own *Lady-Errant*, II, i. James Howell in his *Familiar Letters* (ed. of 1705, p. 256) gives an interesting discussion of these "tremendous titles", and Thomas Goffe imitates the original in *The Raging Turk* (1631), sig. I1ᵛ.

1619–20 *The Sign o' th' half Moon . . . at your door, Is not for nought*. We may recall the wonderful sign made by Subtle for Abel Drugger in *The Alchemist*, II, i.

1622–23 *noise Of Fidlers*. That is, a consort of fiddlers. Reed illustrates the phrase by a number of examples. Gifford in his notes to *The Silent Woman*, III, ii, glossing the same phrase, refers to "Mr. Spindle's noise," which he says is to be found in Cartwright. I know of no such passage.

1623 *The Great Turk loves no Musick*. Gerber (*Sources*, pp. 78–79) compares Beaumont and Fletcher's *Knight of the Burning Pestle*, I, iv.

1635–62 *The Devill take all Fortunes . . . An idle hundred*. It is interesting to compare Alcippe's account of his bad luck at piquet in Molière's *Les Fâcheux*, II, ii.

1638 *one to bear*. This is a phrase used in backgammon, meaning to have only one piece to remove at the end of the game (*NED*).

1654 *Coranti*. That is, news-sheets. The *NED* does not record a plural in "i." The regular form is "corantos." In the next line old Credulous uses "Coranti" as a singular, but this, I suppose, is done simply to show his ignorance. Compare, however, Jonson's use of "gazetti" in *Volpone*, V, ii.

1676 *fox'd*. That is, drunk.

1677–78 *fancie God*. All the modern editors read "fancy, Good," but the original text is perfectly correct. Caster is referring to his "Fancy-man" (l. 1658), whom he likens to a "fly," or familiar spirit. See Jonson's *Alchemist*, III, ii.

1682 *amebly*. No such word as this is recorded. Presumably Cartwright means some form of "amiable."

1689 *grave motion*. That is, pompous puppet.

ACT IV, SCENE II

Cartwright perhaps received a suggestion for this scene from *The Fary Knight* (V, ii, 1405–1506), a play recently attributed to Thomas Randolph. See the Introduction to the *The Ordinary*, pp. 263–64n for a discussion of the problem.

1708 *foyn.* That is, to make a thrust with a pointed weapon (*NED*).

1710 *Why intermete of what thou hast to done.* Miss Gebhardt (Thesis, *The Ordinary*, p. 131) quotes Skeat's paraphrase of the line from Chaucer's *Troilus and Criseyde*, I, 1026: " 'Why, meddle with that which really concerns you,' i. e. mind your own business."

1716 *paynant* Morglay *out of Shete*. That is, piercing sword out of its scabbard. Hazlitt, perhaps rightly, changes "paynant" to "poynant." As Reed explains, "Morglay," although actually the sword of Sir Bevis of Southampton, later became a generic term for "sword." The spelling "Shete" probably represents Cartwright's own pronunciation of the word.

1720–21 Tubal *the sonne of* Lamech *did yfind Musick by knocking Hammers upon Anviles*. As Gerber points out (*Sources*, p. 57), this passage is almost certainly borrowed from Chaucer's *Book of the Duchesse* (ll. 1161–65), but Cartwright has corrected Chaucer's error of Tubal for Jubal. On the other hand, Cartwright himself seems to have gone just as far astray by making Tubal and Jubal one person.

1722 *no compleat.* That is, now complete. Reed remarks: "The passage requires this explanation, or poor Moth's argument seems to want force: his present hopes being founded on a supposition, that all possible discoveries to be made by beating, have been already made."

1724–25 *flet* Englond, *flet* Englond: *Dead is* Edmond. The event here referred to took place in 1016. In Howes' continuation of Stow's *Annales* (1615), page 91, the defeat of the English is described as follows:

After this, King *Edmund* determining manfully to give battel unto *Canute*, . . . The next day the King had overthrowne the Danes, but for Edrike of Straton, who seeing the Englishmen have the better hand, hee cutte off the head of a certaine man, named *Osmearus*, like to King *Edmund* in face and hayre, and holding it uppe, cryed out, that the Englishmen fought in vaine, and held up the head, saying: Your maister king *Edmund* is dead, flie as fast as you can: which the Englishmen had no sooner heard, but they were readie to flie.

See Reed's note, which quotes an account from another authority.

1732 *Nem esur Saxes*. This tag is a corruption of "Nemath eowre Seaxas" (Take your knives), the watchword used by Hengist when he treacherously slew some three hundred Britons and their king, Vortigern, A.D. 476, on the plains of Salisbury. Numerous historical accounts of the massacre exist, and the scene has been dramatised in Middleton's *Mayor of Queenborough* (about 1618), IV, iii. There is a bewildering variety in the different forms which this tag takes: Nennius gives "Nimed eure Saxes"; Robert of Gloucester, "Nymeth oure saxes" and a side-gloss reads "Nymeth owre sexes"; Hardyng, "Nemyth your sexes"; Verstegan (quoted by Reed), "Nem cowr [*sic*] seaxes"; and Fielding quotes the phrase in *Jonathan Wild* as "Nemet eour Saxes." As quoted in Middleton's play, the phrase is "Nemp your Sexes." It is not surprising that Moth's version is a peculiar one, though some of the peculiarity is, I suspect, due to the printer. What Cartwright probably wrote was "Nemet ur Saxes," or "Nem eour Saxes."

1742 *Redoubted Knight*. All the modern editors, rightly I think, read this in preference to the original "Redoubled Knight," though it is possible to torture sense into the original by paraphrasing as follows: "Thou hast redoubled sufficient blows, O Knight; it is thy foe, etc."

1749 *Maugre thine head, algate I suffer none*. That is, in spite of your efforts, I have suffered no hurt.

ACT IV, SCENE III

As Gerber points our (*Sources*, pp. 66–70), this scene is borrowed in part from Jonson's *Alchemist*, III, ii. Subtle, disguised as a Priest of Fairy, abetted by Dol Common, blinds Dapper's eyes with a scarf, and, under pretense of gaining the favor of his aunt, the Fairy Queen, strips him of all his money. In *The Ordinary* Andrew is likewise blindfolded, and Shape, pretending to be his hoped-for mistress, induces him to part gladly with two jewels of value. With this, however, the parallel ceases, and I do not feel that the "congruities in the two scenes" are quite so "numerous and lucid" as Gerber seems to feel. Jonson's scene is also even more closely imitated by Shirley in *The Young Admiral* (1637), IV, i, where one of the mulcts lifted from the victim is a diamond, as in Cartwright.

For the motive which leads up to the blinding, Cartwright seems to owe more to Massinger's *The Bondman* (1623), II, i, than to Jonson. In *The Bondman* Cleora binds up her eyes so that she may not look upon the face of man until her lover, Leosthenes, returns; so Andrew asks to be blindfolded that he may not look upon any woman's face except that of his mistress.

Andrew's foolish set speeches were probably suggested by the scene between Amorphus and Asotus in Jonson's *Cynthia's Revels* (1600), III, iii.

Finally, in the "conditions" which Shape (as Mistress Jane) imposes upon Andrew before "she" will consent to marriage we may see an obvious forerunner of the famous scene in Congreve's *Way of the World* (1700) when Millamant finally agrees "to dwindle into a wife." See also Crowne's *Sir Courtly Nice* (1685; ed. Maidment and Logan, 1874, III, 351). See Miss Kathleen M. Lynch's article, "D'Urfé's *L'Astrée* and the 'Proviso' Scenes in Dryden's Comedy" (*Philological Quarterly* IV [Oct., 1925], 302-8). She fails, however, to notice either the Cartwright or Crowne scenes.

1751–1844 *Fairest of things . . . my Arms in't.* These lines were converted into a droll-dialogue and printed in John Cotgrave's *Wits Interpreter* (1655), pages 84-87 (here reprinted); (1662), pages 45-47; (1671), pages 45-47. In the 1662 and 1671 editions the dialogue is entitled, *The fantastick Schollar.* No attempt at full collation has been made.

              Will.   *Rebeccahs* [*sic*]

Wil. Fairest of things — translucent creature — hang me if I know what's next:
Reb. This meant to me?
Will. Fairest of all things — translucent creature — rather obsured [obscur'd 1662] Deity — tis gone againe, Lady will you eat apeice of Ginger bread.
Reb. You might have better manners then to scoff one of my breeding.
Will. Heark, indeed I love you.
Reb. Alas.
Will. I vow I burn in Love as doth a penny Faggot.
Reb. Heigh ho!
Will. And I shall blaze out sir reverence if you do not quench me.

Reb. Jndeed now, [*sic*]

Will. Though J say't that should not say't, I am affected toward you strangely.

Reb. Now who would have thought it?

Will. Theres a thing each night, and [that 1662] cries matrimony matrimony *Will.*

Reb. Godforbid.

Will. It is some Spirit that would joyn us.

Reb. Goodly, goodly.

Will. Then do I shake all over.

Reb. Doth it so?

Will. Then shake again.

Reb. I pray you now:

Will. Then cry fairest of things — translucent creature, rather obscured Deity, sweer [sweet 1662] Mistresse, *Rebeccah*, I come, I come.

Reb. Alas I pitty you truly.

Wil. Now as my Father saith, I would I were a Cowcumber if I know what to do. Fairest of things, — tis one translucent Creature — tis — .

Reb. Ay, that is one.

Wil. That would willingly run out of dores if hee had Law enough.

Reb. I say —

Will. Nay be not afraid, here's none shall do you harme know then translucent creature, I am whole your *William.*

Reb. Lack wit, your Servants Servant.

Wil. Me thinks you contradict your self, how can you be wholy mine and yet my servants servant. [*This speech belongs to Rebeccah, and the speech before should be part of Will's speech; so given in 1671 ed.*]

Wisl. [*sic*] I do but complement in that I see down right's the best way here, if thou canst love, I can love too, law you there now, J am rich.

Reb. I use not to look after Riches, tis the person I aime at.

Will. That's me, I am proper, handsome, faire, cleane-limm'd; I am rich.

Reb. I must have one that can direct and guid me, a Guardian rather then a Husband, for I am foolish yet.

Will. Now see the luck ont Lady, so am I too ifaith.

Reb. And who ere hath me will find me to be one of those things which his care must first reforme.

Wil. Do not doubt that, I have a head for Reformation. This noddle shall do it. I am rich.

Reb. Riches create no love, I feare you meane to take me for formality only, as some staid peece of Housholdstuffe fitt to be seen, perhaps among other Ornaments, or all [at 1662] the best I shall be counted but a name of dignity, nor entertained for Love but state; one of your traine, a thing took to wipe of [off 1662] suspicion from some person fairer to whom you have vowed homage:

Will. Do not think I have any Plots or Projects in my head, I will do any thing for thee that thou canst name or think on.

Reb. I doubt you'l flinch.

Will. By my Virginity which is as good as yours, I am sure [sure; 1662] by my Virginity, if that wee men have any such thing, I do beleive, I will not flinch. Alas you dont know, *Richard.*

Reb. Can I obtaine so much respite from your other Soveraigns service, as to keep your eye from gazing on her for a while.

Will. If I do look on any woman nay if I do cast a sheeps eye upon any but your sweet selfe may I loose one of mine, marry I'le keep the other howsoever.

Reb. I know not how I may beleive you, you will sweare you never cast a glance upon any when your eye hath baited at each face from me.

Will. Blind me good now, being you mistrust, I will be blinded with this hand-kirchife, you shall see that J love you now. So, now let me have any reasonable thing to lead the way home; J care not though it be a Dogg, so he knows the way and can enquire it out.

Reb. Jle have a care of that Sir.

Will. I doubt not but shall [but I shall 1662] be in the Chronicle for this, or in a Ballad else. This handkirchife shall be hung up in the Parish Church instead of a great silken Flagge to fanne my Grave with my Armes in it. So for the present farewell deare Paragon of beauty. I cannot now see to thank thee my deare Mistress *Rebecca.*

See my remarks on these drolls in the notes to *The Royal Slave*, line 874.

1751 *tralucent.* A variant form of "translucent." See Marlowe's *Hero and Leander*, First Sestiad, line 296.

1753-1838 *Fairest of things . . . wit t'enquire it.* The following droll based on these lines appeared in *The Marrow of Complements* (1655), pages 88-91 (compare the preceding droll based on lines 1751-1844):

> *A sportive complementall Colloquie (for the solace of the reader, (supposed) between* Didaco *and* Mamilla.

Didaco. Fairest of all things, will you eat a piece of Ginger-bread.

Mamilla. You might have better manners, or at least more civilitie, then to scoffe her never injur'd you.

Didaco. Indad, I love you, I vow I burn in love like some penny faggot.

Mamilla. Saint *Winifrid* forbid it.

Didaco. And I shall blaze out sir reverence, if you do not quench me.

Mamilla. May I credit it?

Didaco. Credit it? may I never eat more else.

Mamilla. Though I say it that should not, I am affected towards you strangely, there's a thing comes each night to my beds head, every jot as swarthy, and much resembling thy selfe.

Didaco. And to me every morning a voice utters these words, *Matrimony, Matrimony, Didaco.*

Mamilla. Now God forbid it.

Didaco. Then do I shake all over, but I beleeve it is some spirit that would joyne us.

Mamilla. Goodly, goodly, may I beleeve this also?

Didaco. What? not beleeve *Don Didaco Doloso.* Lady, I am wholly entirely yours, yea more, your Servants Servant.

Mamilla. Me thinks you contradict your selfe, how can you be wholly mine, and yet my Servants Servant?

Didaco. I doe but complement in that, if thou canst love, I can love too, law thee there now. I am rich.

Mamilla. I use not to look after riches, 'tis the person that I aime at.

Didaco. That's me, I am proper, handsome, faire, clean-limb'd, I am rich.

Mamilla. I must have one that can direct and guide me, a Guardian rather then a Husband, for I am foolish, yet.

Didaco. Now see the luck on't Lady, I am so too, I faith.

Mamilla. Who ere hath me, will find me to be one of those things which his care must reforme.

Didaco. Doe not doubt that I have a head for reformation, this nodle here shall doe it. I am rich.

Mamilla. Riches create no love, I fear you take me for formality only.

Didaco. Do not think I have any plots or projects in my head, I will doe any thing for thee that thou canst name or think on.

Mamilla. By my virginity, I fear you'l flinch.

Didaco. By my virginity (which is as good as yours I am sure) by my virginity, if we men have any such thing (as we men have such a thing) I will not flinch.

Mamilla. My desire is then, that for the time to come you shall not so much as cast a sheeps eye upon any woman save my selfe.

Didaco. If I look upon any but your sweet selfe, may I lose one of mine, marry Ile keep the other howsoever.

Mamilla. I know not how I may beleeve you.

Didaco. Blind me good now with this handkerchief, let me have but any reasonable thing to lead me home, I do not care though it be a dog, so that he knowes the way, or hath the wit to enquire it.

Mamilla. Well Sir, ile take your own word. Farewell.

See my remarks on these drolls in the notes to *The Royal Slave*, line 874.

1779   *Law.* That is, a headstart (*NED*).

1785   *indeed-law.* The ejaculation "law" was frequently attached or hyphenated to an adverb or noun. Compare "ifaithlaw" and "heart-law" in Cowley's *The Guardian* (ed. A. R. Waller, 1906, pp. 162, 215, 228; 233, 235).

1788   *servants servant.* Compare Shakespeare's *Twelfth Night*, III, i, 114.

1833   *Blind me good now.* Compare the motive for Andrew's blindfolding himself with that of Cleora in Massinger's *The Bondman*, II, i. The subsequent cheating of the blindfolded Andrew by the "complices" seems to be borrowed from Jonson's *Alchemist*, III, ii (see Gerber, *Sources*, pp. 66-70). See my discussion in the introductory note to this scene.

1873   *a veget spark.* Reed glosses as "a lively spark." The word "spark," however, here means a "small diamond or ruby" (*NED*). See *The Lady-Errant*, line 1275.

ACT IV, SCENE IV

Genest (*Some Account of the English Stage*, 1832, IV, 110; X, 115) first pointed out the close resemblance between this scene and two scenes in *The Knave in Graine* (1640) by J. D. Miss Gebhardt (Thesis, *The Ordinary*, pp. lvi-lxii) discusses the problem in detail (see my Introduction to the play). The caste of characters—a Mercer's Man, a Barber, and Julio (i.e., Shape)—and the situation in the fourth act of *The Knave in Graine* almost exactly parallel Cartwright's characters and situation. Miss Gebhardt has collected a number of persuasive verbal echoes between the two scenes, some of which are pointed out below. The second scene from *The Knave in Graine* (the last of Act IV) employs Shape's trick in making the Mercer verbally agree to his own deluding.

It should be noticed that there are a number of nondramatic analogues, most of them earlier than Cartwright's play. The earliest in English occurs in *A C. Mery Talys* (about 1525), Number XXXIX, "Of the gentylman that promysed the scoler of Oxforde a sarcanet typet." This story, like all but two of the nondramatic analogues, deals with a cheater, a cheated, and a priest, although in the present case there is no question of money involved. The role of the priest, like Cartwright's Chirurgion or J.D.'s Barber, is to act as interference while the cheater makes good his escape. Two similar stories appear in *Scoggin's Jests* (about 1565; ed. W. C. Hazlitt in *Shakespeare Jest Books*, 1864, II, 134-40). Hazlitt (p. 137) refers to another analogue in *The Conceits of Old Hobson* (1607), but I can find no such story in that collection. The second of the stories in *Scoggin's Jests*, "How *Scogin* deceived the Draper," affords the closest early nondramatic parallel to Cartwright. A late analogue, contained in Theophilus Lucas' *Lives of the Gamesters* (1714; ed. C. H. Hartmann in *Games and Gamesters of the Restoration*, 1930, pp. 135-36) is so close to both Cartwright's and J.D.'s scenes, even to verbal echoes, that it is either based on one or the other, or—and this is more likely—related to the common source upon which Cartwright and J.D. may be supposed to have drawn. An Italian version of the tale occurs in Straparola's *Piacevoli Notti* (1550), Notte Decimaterza, Favola ii.

1887 *twitting*. Cartwright seems to employ this word in the sense of "tattling" or "telling tales out of school." The present passage is the only example of this meaning quoted in the *NED*.

1891-94 *Hee's very modest . . . first*. Miss Gebhardt (Thesis, *The Ordinary*, p. lix) compared *The Knave in Graine*, sig. I1v:

> *Julio.* A pretty handsome youth, and will be loath to discover himselfe, being extreamly bashfull, and will make it strange. . . .

1916-18 *Nay, be not so modest; . . . ill fortune only*. Miss Gebhardt (Thesis, *The Ordinary*, p. lx) compares *The Knave in Graine*, sig. I2v: "be not ashamed, you are not the first, nor shall be the last, that meet with these disasters."

1920 *He told me you'ld be shamefac'd*. Miss Gebhardt (Thesis, *The Ordinary*, p. lix) compares *The Knave in Graine*, sig. I2v: ". . . the Gentleman your Kinsman, told mee before, how bashfull you would be."

1945 *Syren*. The modern editors all read "syringe." Cartwright's form "Syren" probably represents his pronunciation of the word (see the *NED*). Miss Gebhardt (Thesis, *The Ordinary*, p. 134) suggests that the true reading should be "Sering" and quotes from the analogous scene in *The Knave in Graine* (1640), sig. [I3]r: "My meaning was to give you a Sering, or an incision Knife." If by "Sering" Miss Gebhardt means us to understand "searing" or "burning" I think she is mistaken, though "Sering" as a variant form of "syringe" is very plausible.

1949 *as I was told you should [be]*. All modern editors read "as I was told I should" for the original "as I was told you

1950–51 *the taking, . . . of taking As much*. Hazlitt wishes to omit the second "taking," since "it spoils the sense, and is not essential to the metre, such metre as it is." The sense is a little improved by the omission, but the meter, even such as it is, is ruined. The passage makes a certain amount of sense as it stands, and there is no reason to disturb it. The devil of emendation pricks, however, and suggests that we might read "I lose by talking, by my swear, of taking As much."

1950 *by my swear*. That is, by my oath. Hazlitt observes that this is an unusual expression. The *NED* gives this passage as the earliest use of "swear" in the sense of "oath." See below, line 1975.

1965 *I won't be fubb'd ensure your self*. That is, I won't be cheated, you may be convinced of that. Compare *The Knave in Graine*, sig. D1ʳ.

1970 *small Quality*. That is, unassuming profession.

ACT IV, SCENE V

It seems probable that Thomas Killigrew took a hint from this scene for part of his plot involving the Widow and Mistress Pleasant in the fourth and fifth acts of *The Parson's Wedding*.

1985–2020 *Whiles early light springs from the skies*. A later version of this lyric appeared in *The Marrow of Complements* (1655), pages 83–84. Cibber quotes this song in his *Lives of the Poets* (1753), I, 280–81. His version is based on Dodsley's edition of *The Ordinary* (1744) and is full of errors. J. B. Emperor (*Catullian Influence in English Lyric Poetry, Circa 1600–1650*, University of Missouri Studies, 1928, p. 74) suggests two possible Catullan influences on Cartwright's lyric.

1995 *Angry Dishes and . . . ties*. All the modern editors read "Angry pishes and . . . fies." The emendation seems inevitable; at least I can find no evidence to support the original reading.

2007–11 *Not any kisse . . . by extorting fed*. In paraphrase these lines mean: "If by wooing and persuasion you fail to win a kiss from Mistress Pris, you must realize that true pleasure is gained by extortion."

2025 *Spouses*. That is, the Church's.

2026-55 *Now thou our future Brother*. A later version of this song appeared in *The Marrow of Complements* (1655), pages 68-69, with the title "A Blessing Bestowed upon the Bantling of a Brownist." The 1655 text omits one line and adds a couplet at the end (see the variant readings). Compare Killigrew's satire on the offspring of a Brownist in *The Parson's Wedding*, III, v.

2028 Dod's *blessing*. John Dod was a Puritan divine. See my note to "The Chambermaids Posset," line 37.

2077-78 *no Advowtry in my Ward But what is honest*. Shades perhaps of Dogberry!

Act V, Scene 1

Cartwright's scene reminds one of the Laird of Milnwood's dying instructions to his housekeeper in Scott's *Old Mortality* (Vol. II, Chap. xxxix):

He had been gieing me preceeze directions anent the bread, and the wine, and the brandy, at his burial, and how often it was to be handed round the company—(for dead or alive, he was a prudent, frugal painstaking man), and then he said, said he, "Ailie," (he aye ca'd me Ailie—we were auld acquaintance)—"Ailie, take ye care and haud the gear weel thegither; for the name of Morton of Milnwood's gane out like the last sough of an auld sang." And sae he fell out o'ae dwam into another, and ne'er spak a word mair, unless it were something we cou'dna mak out, about a dipped candle being gude eneugh to see to dee wi';—he could ne'er bide to see a moulded ane, and there was ane, by ill luck, on the table.

It is barely possible that Scott was thinking of Cartwright. We know that he was familiar with *The Ordinary* since he quotes lines 1050-54 in *The Antiquary* and lines 1414-20 in *The Fortunes of Nigel*.

2101 *A sprig of Rosemary*. Compare D'Avenant's *The Wits* (1634), IV, i:

Engine. And what to entertain them, sir?
Thrift. A little rosemary, which thou mayst steal
From the Temple garden.

Compare also Thrift's remarks about funeral torches and after-funeral drinking.

2114 *save expence in cloaths*. Compare Wilson's *The Projectors*, IV:

But suppose, sir, I kept her always in mourning, would it not do well, think ye, to save linen and washing?

Act V, Scene ii

2124-25 *I hope You do[n't] mean your Partners.* This is the reading of the Restoration prompt copy. Some change seems necessary, though the modern editors all read, as in the original, "do mean."

2144 *Ruine your Daughter in a complement.* That is, spoil your daughter's happiness in a bad husband. Cartwright uses "complement" in a very similar sense in *The Siege*, lines 1319-20:

> That Woman is but the defect of Man,
> In that you make her thus his Complement.

The last three editors read "in a compliment," a reading from which I can extract no meaning.

Act V, Scene iii

Gerber (*Sources*, pp. 70-71) thinks this scene "shows markedly Jonson's influence," particularly that of *The Alchemist*, IV, iii, where Sir Epicure Mammon, confessing his voluptuous mind to "father" Subtle, and blaming himself for the ruin of all their "golden" hopes, gives a hundred pounds to Bethlem Hospital (via Subtle) as a penance. I fail to see any essential connection between the two scenes, apart from the mulct of a hundred pounds. There is no question of a specially assumed disguise in Jonson and the actual business of confession can scarcely be compared. The device of obtaining a confession under disguise as a friar or priest is not so common in English drama as one might expect. Peele's *Edward I* contains such a scene, and the situation in Shakespeare's *Measure for Measure* is fairly close. A late example may be found in Shirley's *The Gentleman of Venice* (1639), V, ii, where Cornari disguises himself as a friar to extort a confession from Florelli. None of these, however, shows any particular evidence of connection with Cartwright, whose scene seems an unusually happy effort.

2180 *two Chimneys ne'r yet smok'd at once.* Compare Jonson's *The Staple of News*, II, i. See note on line 2229 below.

2219 *Fed on the . . . steem of Candle sewet.* Gerber (*Sources*, p. 70) compares Jonson's *Alchemist*, I, i, where Face reminds Subtle how he used to take his "meal of steam in, from cooks' stalls."

2229 *cannot weep, mine Eyes are Pumice*. Compare Jonson's *Staple of News*, II, i:

> *Madrigal.* I've heard you have offered, sir, to lock up smoke ...
> And wept when it went out, sir, at your chimney.
> *Fitton.* And yet his eyes were drier than a pumice.

Jonson is imitating Plautus' *Aulularia* (see Gifford's note to the passage), but Cartwright seems to have borrowed from Jonson rather than directly from Plautus, since Plautus, though he mentions pumice, does not connect it with the eyes. Compare a not unsimilar passage abusing the meanness of misers in Jasper Mayne's *The City-Match*, III, iii.

2231-32 *Won't fifty pounds Wipe off my score*. Gerber (*Sources*, pp. 70-71) compares Jonson's *Alchemist*, IV, iii.

ACT V, SCENE IV

As Gerber emphasizes (*Sources*, p. 71), Cartwright has again borrowed heavily from Jonson's *Alchemist* for the denouement of his comedy. As Face disguises himself as the caretaker Jeremy and deceives the irate dupes of Subtle's ingenuity right under their very noses, so Slicer, Hearsay, and Shape disguise themselves as watchmen and take part in the search for themselves, offering from time to time helpful suggestions and criticisms. The final escape of the whole gang scot free is also reminiscent of Jonson's comedy.

Compare the situation created by Andrew's marriage to Priscilla, through a trick of Meanwell's, to the predicament of Sir Nicholas Treedle, another booby, in Shirley's *The Witty Fair One* (1628), V, v.

2236 *The wolf*. Imitated from Terence, *Adelphi*, IV, i.

2253-54 *smell ... As Crows do Powder*. I cannot explain this allusion.

2256 *They have ... most certain*. Following this line the Restoration prompt copy introduces lines 2376-2434. Thus after old Credulous says, "Sirrah, come along" (l. 2375), Sir Thomas says, "I thank you for your pains" (l. 2435). See my remarks on this alteration in the Introduction to the play.

2262 *Bason*. I do not understand what Moth means by "Thylk Bason of *Jone Potluck*, Vintners Widow," a phrase which he seems to make appositional with "thylk Hospitall seat" in the line before. Possibly the "sign" of Mistress Potluck's shop was a basin.

2264 *foysons*. Plenty or abundance. Miss Gebhardt (Thesis, *The Ordinary*, p. 136) notes Nares comment that "Cartwright, whose play of *The Ordinary* was published in 1651, puts foison into the mouth of Moth, the antiquary, as an obsolete word, which in Shakespeare's time it certainly was not." She adds: "Nares takes Cartwright's attempts at obsolete English too seriously!"

2265 *Come buss*. As Miss Gebhardt points out (Thesis, *The Ordinary*, p. 136), "buss" is also (like "foysons" above) an Elizabethan word and Chaucer would have written "come ba me."

2284 *Sunk like the Queen, they'l rise at Queenhive sure*. This is a reference to the old story of Queen Elinor, the wife of Edward I, "who sunck at Charingcrosse, and rose againe at Potters-hith, now named Queenehith" (quoted from the title-page of Peele's *Edward I*). Milton in *Animadversions upon the Remonstrant's Defence* (ed. J. A. St. John, *Prose Works*, 1848, III, 73) refers to the story as "that old wife's tale." Middleton in his *Witch*, I, i, also refers to it. Dyce, in his edition of Peele, includes an old ballad on the same subject. See Reed's note.

2288-89 *as honest as the skin . . . thy Brows*. Gerber (*Sources*, p. 64) suggests Jonson's *Every Man out of his Humour*, II, i, as a possible source for this expression. It is, however, proverbial (see Reed's note to Shakespeare's *Much Ado about Nothing*, III, v). See also *Comedy of Errors*, II, ii, 140.

2291 *what skin*. Hazlitt observes that "the Constable's ideas had become confused, and he thought that *Credulous* was taxing him with having been circumcised."

2309 *Have found forty pounds*. That is, raised forty pounds (to have prevented the disgrace).

2315 *Visage foul yfrounct, with glowing eyn*. In spite of what Steevens says in his note to this passage, the word "yfrounct" means "wrinkled," nor is the passage "unmeaning jargon." Cartwright took the first three words from line 155 of *The Romaunt of the Rose* (Gerber, *Sources*, p. 57). All that is necessary to make good sense of the passage is to place the comma after "yfrounct" instead of after "foul" where it falls in the original (pointing suggested by Steevens).

2354 *Fescennine*. Corrected from "Festennine" by all the modern editors. According to Steevens a "fescennine" is "a nuptial ditty: from *Fescennia*, or *Fescennium*, a town in Italy, where these kinds of songs were first practised."

2365-66 *ill luck. To vex you more, that.* The modern editors, except Reed, make nonsense out of this passage, which is correctly pointed in the original.

Act V, Scene v

2442 *Lye thou there Watchman.* That is, Shape throws aside his disguise as one of the Watch. Miss Gebhardt (Thesis, *The Ordinary*, p. 139) thinks there may be here a sly allusion to Bishop Corbet, which would have been quickly picked up by an Oxford audience. Aubrey ('Brief Lives,' ed. A. Clark, 1898, I, 186) on the authority of Josias Howe, a friend of Cartwright's who contributed verses to the *Works* (1651), relates the anecdote as follows:

> His chaplain, Dr. Lushington, was a very learned and ingeniose man, and they loved one another. The bishop sometimes would take the key of the wine-cellar, and he and his chaplaine would goe and lock themselves in and be merry. Then first he layes downe his episcopall hat, — "*There lyes the Dr.*" Then he putts of his gowne, — "*There lyes the Bishop.*" Then 'twas, — "*Here's to thee, Corbet,*" and "*Here's to thee, Lushington.*"

Compare also the story of Sir Christopher Hatton, Lord Chancellor to Elizabeth, who, at the marriage of his son, "danced the measures at the solemnity," and "left the gown in the chair, saying, 'Lie thou there, Chancellor.'" (quoted from a contemporary letter in Sir Harris Nicholas' *Life and Times of Sir Christopher Hatton*, 1847, pp. 478-79).

2448 *So resolve for* New England. At the end of Peter Hausted's *Rival Friends* (1632), V, xi, it is suggested that the way to dispose of a group of gulls is to "Barrell them vp and send them for *new England.*" The suggestion is vetoed, however, because "there's fooles enow already there."

2449 *little Pigeon-hole reformed Ruff.* See the note to *The Royal Slave*, Second Prologue, line 25.

2458 *work's.* Probably intended as a plural form; "are" understood.

The Epilogue

Cartwright's device of making Shape speak the epilogue seems to have been suggested by Jonson's *Alchemist*, where the epilogue is delivered by the rogue, Face.

THE SIEGE, OR, LOVE'S CONVERT

Text. Works (1651), pages [91]-180.

Title-page, 1651 ed.: THE / SIEDGE: / or, / Love's Convert, / A TRAGI-COMEDY. / [rule] / Written by / Mr WILLIAM CART-VVRIGHT, / Late Student of *Christ-Church in* / OXFORD, and Proctor of / the *Vniversity*. / [rule] / LONDON, / Printed for *Humphrey Moseley*, and / are to be sold at his shop at the Sign of / the Princes Armes in St *PAVLS* / Churchyard. *1651.* *Format:* 8vo. *Collation:* [F8], G–L⁸, M⁴.

THE DEDICATION
   The dedication of a printed play directly to the king is at least most unusual before the Restoration.

16-17   *And that Fear comes from that Encrease of Ill,*
         That the last Errours are the greatest still.

   Although the general meaning of this couplet is clear enough, I do not understand the syntax of the whole in relation to the phrase "Encrease of Ill."

ACT I, SCENE I
   5   *Let's see thy Pictures.* With this device of sending pictures of various virgins of Byzantium for Misander's choice compare Massinger's *Emperor of the East*, II, i.
   79 *All other.* The use of "other" in the singular with a plural meaning is common. See E. A. Abbott, *Shakespearian Grammar* (1897), p. 24.
   148 *demerited.* The *NED* notices the present passage as the latest use of this verb in the sense of "to deprive of merit, to disparage."

ACT I, SCENE III
   206 *my promising Nose.* For the implication here, consult Slawkenbergius! Compare Randolph's *Jealous Lovers*, II, ii:

> I do not know where the enchantment lies,
> Whether it be the magic of mine eyes,
> Or lip, or cheek, or brow: but I suppose
> The conjuration chiefly in my nose.

ACT I, SCENE IV

236 *lye Perdue*. That is, lie sentinel.

238 *Advouzon*. See my note on line 68 of "The Chambermaids Posset."

251 *No needles hanging at each others Tailes*. I am not sure what Cartwright means here. I suppose "needles" must be taken in the sense of "magnetic needles," in which case the line may mean that in the sort of free-love which Philostratus is describing there are no troublesome interattractions among lovers of the sort that Callimachus has just criticized. Or, perhaps, "needles" should be taken as "stings."

270 *begin to him*. That is, make an essay for him.

275 *a Cloud of Game*. A cloudlike body of birds, hence a multitude (*NED*).

280 *mumping*. Begging (*NED*).

283 *Gally-pots*. Small earthen glazed pots, used by apothecaries for ointments (*NED*).

283 *Fucusses*. Paints or cosmetics for beautifying the skin (*NED*).

ACT I, SCENE V

312 *to expect*. That is, to wait.

ACT I, SCENE VI

400 *to design*. That is, to indicate or designate.

431 *Could he gaze so long on, as to pourtray*. We would prefer to read "so long on['t]," but see line 756, where Prusias repeats Misander's speech.

466 *Parcell*. Part.

ACT II, SCENE I

503 *Dole*. Distribution (*NED*).

517 *Theam*. Subject of discourse (*NED*).

ACT II, SCENE II

541–600 *Y'are a Creature . . . do provoke it*. Professor Greenough (*A Bibliography of the Theophrastan Character in English*, 1947, p.

67) suggests that the character of a "waiting woman" sketched in these lines is in the Theophrastan character tradition. He sees the same influence at work in lines 626-70, in which Pyle describes her "ideal state," and again, in II, iv, lines 723-26, the character of a "tyrant's concubine" (I fail to see much influence here and suspect the reference should be to II, vi, 810-25). There is, I think, no doubt that passages like these owe much to the Theophrastan character, but to imply that these three references (all occurring within a few pages) exhaust Cartwright's debt in this direction is misleading. Equally striking examples can be produced from either *The Lady-Errant* (IV, i, 1163-1233, the character of "women"; 1314-45, the character of a "lady-errant") or *The Ordinary* (I, iv, 352-418, the characters of the "military man" and the "politician"; I, v, 472-83, the character of the "miser"). And in *The Siege* itself we may note a further example in the character of the "unwilling virgin" (IV, v, 1657-70).

542 *a living Utensill*. Compare Aphra Behn's *The City Heiress* (1682), IV, ii: "Therefore, thou sometimes necessary Utensil, withdraw" (addressed to a waiting woman).

598-600 *were it not . . . do provoke it*. Paraphrased, these lines seem to mean: ". . . if it were not thus well bred, not to give offense, although it may be to those who have provoked reprisal." I suspect that as they stand these lines are corrupt; both "so" and "as" seem to be superfluous.

623 *warrant you for being*. That is, guarantee you against.

634 *Fricace*. Frication or rubbing. The *NED* quotes this passage as the last recorded use of the word.

647-67 *Wee'l call a Parliament of women . . . unto our self*. Pyle's whole idea here seems a little reminiscent of Cartwright's earlier play, *The Lady-Errant*. He is fond of playing with this notion of women politicians. As a description of how an individual intends to run a new order in the Commonwealth, compare Shirley's *Love in a Maze*, IV, ii, and Shakespeare's *The Tempest*, II, i.

664 *University of* Athens. Although there actually was such an institution as the University of Athens, Cartwright is probably glancing at his own Oxford, which was frequently called the Athens of England.

Act II, Scene iii

683–86 *what Government is best . . . Oligarchy.* Pyle is weighing the relative merits of aristocracy, oligarchy, and democracy as discussed by Plato in *The Republic*, Book VIII.

Act III, Scene iv

715–16 Leucasia! *I did ne'r mislike My Name till now.* Perhaps a general reminiscence of *Romeo and Juliet* (see ll. 727–35, below).

725 *have light.* A past participle in "t" instead of "ted" was common in verbs ending in a dental. See E. A. Abbott, *Shakespearian Grammar* (1897), pp. 242–43.

727–35 *Good Lord to see! . . . will come about.* Compare *Romeo and Juliet*, I, iii, 16–57. See also the garrulous old nurse, Polish, in Jonson's *Magnetic Lady*, I, i.

727 *Table.* The quadrangular space between certain lines in the palm of the hand; a term in palmistry (*NED*).

Act II, Scene vi

815 *Caskinet.* A form made up of "casket" and "carcenet," perhaps originally a misprint. Here used in the former sense (*NED*).

846 *exprobrate.* That is, cast in one's teeth.

852 *the Picture of Charity.* Cartwright is referring to one of two statues on the Aldgate in London. Stow describes the statue of Charity as follows: "On the north side standeth Charity, with a child at her breast, and another led in her hand" (quoted from Gifford's note to Jonson's *Silent Woman*, I, i). In *The London Chaunticleers*, Scene ii, Nancy Curdwell remarks: "O, how like the picture of Charity should I look with two sucklings at my breast!"

Act II, Scene vii

915 *Which trod by thee will sweeter grow.* Compare Drayton's *Endimion and Phoebe* (1595; ed. J. W. Hebel, 1925, p. 22):

> Hee kist the flowers depressed with her feete,
> And swears from her they borrow'd all their sweet.

See also Jonson's famous lyric "Drink to me only with thine eyes."

ACT III, SCENE I

Compare the famous scene in Beaumont and Fletcher's *Maid's Tragedy* (1611), V, i, where Evadne avenges her lost honor by slaying the King. See also Suckling's *Aglaura* (1637), V, ii, and Fletcher's *Bloody Brother* (1621), V, ii.

949-51 *Yet some do say . . . guilty after death.* Leucasia's fearful remark was probably suggested by Plutarch, where the spirit of Cleonice haunts Pausanias until his death.

963 *first then extinguish that* [the taper]. Compare Othello's famous phrase, uttered under very similar circumstances, "Put out the light, and then put out the light" (V, ii, 7). So too Aglaura, in a scene which may be considered an analogue to Cartwright's, is careful to "put out the light" (Suckling's *Aglaura*, V, ii). It may, however, have been suggested by the Pausanias story in Plutarch.

984-85 *The Sex here is my shame, what shall I say The Beauty of it is?* That is, since the sex is my shame, what shall I call the beauty?

ACT III, SCENE II

1106 *Qualities.* Accomplishments or abilities (*NED*).

ACT III, SCENE III

1124 *facts.* Acts or deeds.
1125 *As Proofs against Positions.* That is, as exceptions to general rules.

ACT III, SCENE IV

1130 *How does* Leucasia. Misander's lethargy in the face of a threatened revolt and his preoccupation with Leucasia may be compared with a scene in Carlell's *Osmond, the Great Turk* (1638), II.

ACT III, SCENE V

1161-70 *Seal up her Eyes, O Sleep, but flow.* This little song later appeared in *The Marrow of Complements* (1655), pages 62-63, entitled "A Song. On a Lady sleeping." Both the song and the situation in which it is used bear considerable resemblance to a scene and lyric in Fletcher's *Valentinian*, V, ii. Compare (?)Fletcher's lyric:

> Care-charming Sleep, thou easer of all woes,
> Brother to Death, sweetly thyself dispose
> On this afflicted prince; fall, like a cloud,
> In gentle showers; give nothing that is loud
> Or painful to his slumbers; easy, light
> And as a purling stream, thou son of Night,
> Pass by his troubled senses; sing his pain,
> Like hollow murmuring wind or silver rain;
> Into this prince gently, oh, gently slide,
> And kiss him into slumbers like a bride!

Fletcher's lines, of course, owe much to Samuel Daniel's sonnet, "Care-charmer sleep, son of the sable night."

ACT III, SCENE VI

1191 *Tenents.* An obsolete form of "tenets" (*NED*).

1196–97 *Wee'l strike when . . . him now.* Compare *Hamlet*, III, iii, 73–95, and Beaumont and Fletcher's *Maid's Tragedy*, V, i.

1216 *doe not interest.* That is, do not mingle.

1277–91 *Me thoughts I saw . . . by using the Child well.* I do not know the source, if there is one, for this rather pretty little myth of the birth of Love and the fall of the Soul. The form "methoughts" is used twice by Shakespeare and is formed, as Abbott suggests (*Shakespearian Grammar*, 1897, p. 210), by analogy with the present form "methinks." Cartwright uses the same form in line 614.

1338 *the place below the Moon.* Most ancient writers agree in placing the region of the nine classes of evil spirits in the region of the "middle air," that is, "below the moon." The sixth class "are those aëriall devils that corrupt the aire and cause plagues, thunders, fiers, etc." See Burton's *Anatomy of Melancholy*, Part I, Section 2, Member 1, Subsection 2 (1638 ed., p. 44).

1355 *Statues.* The 1651 text reads "Statutes." The confusion is a common one; compare the 1651 edition of *The Royal Slave*, line 406.

1401 *Which Veyl yet was not his* [Love's], *but ours.* Compare *The Lady-Errant*, lines 1625–26.

ACT IV, SCENE I

1417 SD [*They whisper her by turns.* Gifford (*Plays of Philip Massinger*, 1840, p. 275n) suggests that Cartwright is imitating a scene in Massinger's *The Picture* (1629), IV, ii. Here, as in Cartwright, the wooing and abusing of the rival suitors is carried on simultaneously in alternate speeches, and the fortunate recipient of these attentions sets each aspirant an absurd task as a test of his affection. Compare also a similar scene in Cowley's *The Guardian* (1642), I, iv and v (retained in the recension, *Cutter of Coleman Street*, I, vi.).

1470 *Bedstaff*. Apparently the exact nature of a "bedstaff" is not known. The *NED* rather vaguely defines it as "a stick used in some way about a bed, formerly handy as a weapon."

1473 *stark*. Stiff or rigid (*NED*).

ACT IV, SCENE II

1504 *prizes*. That is, prices.

1505 *Fee-buck*. See page 685, the note to line 64 of "To the same [Dr. Duppa] immediately after the Publick Act at *Oxon*. 1634."

1533-34 *a True-Love's Knot In endlesse Verse*. An actual example of such verse may be found at the end of Book I, Song 3, of Browne's *Britannia's Pastorals* (1613).

1544 Philomath. A lover of learning. Of course, Prusias means just the opposite.

1548-50 *How many Towns . . . Pye-crusts*. Cartwright copies these lines almost verbatim from his earlier play, *The Lady-Errant*, lines 119-21. In saying that Cartwright copies here from *The Lady-Errant*, I am conscious, of course, that the process may well have been reversed. At any rate the several links between the two plays (see ll. 647, 1401) suggest that the original draft of *The Siege* (whenever completed) was written about the same time as *The Lady-Errant*.

1572 *Bumbast Captains*. That is inflated, puffed-up captains.

ACT IV, SCENE III

1590 *A Tyrant, and love honesty*. We should probably read "love honestly" (see l. 1583, above). "Honest" is here used, of course, in the common sense of "chaste."

ACT IV, SCENE V

The poison potion which after all turns out to be a harmless drug or love philter is a favorite dramatic device. See Beaumont and Fletcher's *Four Plays in One* (before 1616), Part II, "The Triumph of Love"; Shakespeare's *Romeo and Juliet* and *Cymbeline*; Phineas Fletcher's *Sicelides* (1614), V, ii; and Barclay's *Lost Lady* (1637), IV, iii, and V, i.

1647 *been't*. This form was, I believe, even in Cartwright's time considered dialectal. See also *The Ordinary*, line 2090.

1664 *Musk-plums*. Dried raisins or plums, scented with musk, eaten to keep the breath sweet.

1669 *lead an Ape in Heav'n*. This is a variation on the usual phrase "to lead apes in hell." Both mean "to die an old maid." Mr. Ernest Kuhl ("Shakspere's 'Lead Apes in Hell' and the Ballad of 'The Maid and the Palmer,'" *Studies in Philology*, XXII [1925], 453–66) traces the origin of the phrase to the mediaeval custom of punishing adultery by making the criminal "lead an ape by the neck" as part of his or her penance (p. 462). Referring to Cartwright's use of the proverb, he writes: "Cartwright gave one solution [i.e., of what happened after the punishment in hell was over] when he wrote that women on ceasing to be old maids left hell to lead apes in heaven" (p. 456). Presumably Mr. Kuhl saw the passage out of its context. At any rate his explanation seems to me wholly mistaken. In his reference to "Heaven" Cartwright may well have been thinking of Beatrice's retort (*Much Ado about Nothing*, II, i, 45–51) when threatened with the like fate (Mr. Kuhl later quotes this passage, p. 466):

> *Leonato.* Well then, go you into hell?
> *Beatrice.* No; but to the gate; and there will the devil meet me, like an old cuckold, with horns on his head, and say, "Get you to heaven, Beatrice, get you to heaven, here's no place for you maids:" so deliver I up my apes, and away to Saint Peter for the heavens.

1670 *one of her Fopperies*. That is, one of her suitors.

Act IV, Scene vi

Compare the situation in this and the three scenes following with Shirley's *The Ball* (1632), III, iii.

1678 *provoking Vertue*. Stimulating power or efficacy (*NED*).

1692 *Letters Patents*. The form "patents" reflects, of course, the origin of the phrase in the French "lettres patentes."

1714–15 *to task Impossibilities*. That is, to impose impossible things upon. Although the present reading makes good sense, I suspect that Cartwright wrote "to ask Impossibilities."

1719-21 *bid me pull . . .* Persian *Monarch.* Zachary Grey (*Notes on Shakespeare,* 1754, I, 126-27) compares *Much Ado,* II, i, 273-78, but a nearer source for Cartwright's lines seems to be Middleton and Rowley's *Spanish Gypsy* (1623), II, i: "Anything; kill the great Turk, pluck out the Mogul's eye-teeth."

ACT IV, SCENE VII

1726-27 *your three legs and five Similitudes.* Cartwright's meaning is not at all clear to me. By "three legs" Philostratus is probably referring to the courtier's affectation of carrying a cane, but what he means by "five Similitudes" I cannot guess. Perhaps we should read "fine Similitudes," a reading which at once solves the difficulty.

1731 *good Manners.* Here used with the inevitable pun on "manors."

1743-44 *Hee's scarce a Courtier now, that hath not writ His brace of Plaies.* Unfortunately, this "playful" remark of Cartwright's is almost literally true.

1752-56 *I am Your Spaniel . . . holly Wand . . . I'l try you.* This situation, in which Prusias offers himself as his mistress' spaniel and Pyle gets a switch to test his resolution, reminds one quite forcibly of a similar scene, now famous, in Otway's *Venice Preserv'd,* III, i. It is not unlikely that Otway took a hint from this scene.

ACT IV, SCENE VIII

1788 *My Rings . . . with holy Posies.* These little mottos, of which Callimachus gives several examples, were very popular in Cartwright's day. Special collections of them were gathered and published. Their use was not limited to rings. Almost anything in the way of wearing apparel or jewelry might be so decorated. See the collection called *Love's Garland* published in 1624.

1803-4 *no Gyant neither, No live* Collossus *as I take it.* Callimachus means that he will fight against Heaven in spite of the fact that he is neither a giant nor a colossus.

ACT IV, SCENE IX

1817 *Take all the shew.* That is, make a sketch of all the wedding festivities.

1825 *So! I applaud my Wit for this my project.* Various analogues for Pyle's device of cheating her four suitors are discussed in the Introduction to the play. The closest analogue is that quoted from Pauli's *Schimpf und Ernst* (1522), Number 220.

1835 *emulate.* That is, be jealous of (*NED*).

Act V, Scene iii

1920 *factious.* Active or zealous.

1922 *'Twere good to knock an Horseshoe on the Threshold.* Brand (*Observations on Popular Antiquities*, 1900, p. 597) observes:

> Touching the common practice of nailing horse-shoes on the thresholds of doors, Aubrey certifies that it is "to hinder the power of Witches that enter into the House. Most Houses of the West End of London have the Horse-shoe on the Threshold."

1924 *bewhatled.* Bewildered or out of one's wits. The *NED* marks the word as "rare," and quotes only this passage as an example of its use.

1930 *He kept* Endymion. According to some versions of the legend Endymion slept on Latmus for thirty years. See E.K.'s gloss to the July eclogue of *The Shepheards Calender* and Drayton's *Endimion and Phoebe*, ed. J. W. Hebel (1925), page 50.

1932–41 *See how the Emulous Gods do watch.* This lyric appeared later in *The Marrow of Complements* (1655), page 63, entitled "Song. 2. On the same occasion."

Act V, Scene iv

The overwrought and extravagant descriptions of love's garden, a sort of earthly and very un-Platonic paradise, which distinguish this scene are direct, if illegitimate descendants of similar word-paintings in Tasso and Spenser, especially of their gardens of Armida and Acrasia; though perhaps an even closer parallel is afforded by the descriptions of the Mohammedan heaven in the *Koran* (Chapters lv and lvi), a book which Cartwright might have known in French or Latin translation. Shirley in his *Lady of Pleasure* (1635), V, i, has left us an excellent burlesque of this essentially false and vicious style. What sounded false to Shirley, however, rang clear and high to other ears, for a dialogue in prose and a verse rhapsody in rhymed couplets were extracted from the scene and published in *The Marrow of Complements* (1655).

1970-74 *an Essence . . . fall in Love . . . first Object . . . as he wak'd.*
Compare Oberon's magic potion in *A Midsummer Night's Dream*, through the power of which he makes Titania fall in love with the metamorphosed Bottom and works havoc among the four lovers.

1994-2031 *Fairest of things . . . instruct blest Souls.* These lines appear in the form of a prose dialogue in *The Marrow of Complements* (1655), pages 65-67:

> *A Platonick Inter-locution (supposed) between*
> Parismus *and* Placentia.
>
> *Parismus.* Fairest of things, and onely like thy self, those pleasutes [*sic*] which the laden bosome of this lower world permits to carefull mortalls, are too grosse, too earthy to be ours; let us mount the wings of our desires, and take a flight into Natures sincere Kingdome, where she mints, and shapes refin'd delights, delights like thee.
>
> *Placentia.* Wee'l to those places set apart for love, where Trees kisse trees, and Branch embraceth branch, Poplar to Poplar whispers there, and Myrtle to Myrtle doth sigh to Myrtle [*sic*]; Flowers erect themselves, and boughs encline to meet them in salutes, with an unquestion'd freedome, no stalk being made yellow there by jealousie, no Tree whithering through sad suspition, that this Flower doth court that bough, or that bough serve this Flower.
>
> *Parismus.* O these are joyes fresh from the Dug of nature, there some plants shew they have fire even in their colours, some Dialogues, make, and some more passionate grieve, sweet odours are their sighs, and dew their tears. Some leaves they say, have words of woe inscrib'd; as if that Flowers writ mutuall letters too, our antient Love-Priests say, that in that Garden a Rose, and Lillie (to whose sacred leaves the neighbouring Flowers do reverence) mingle roots, in a most streight embrace, and then produce Male Roses blanched, with the whitenesse of the Lillie, and Female Lillies dipt in the Roses blush, each borrowing others beauty, so that 'tis thought Nature prophesies of some future times which shall fulfil it and be happy.
>
> *Placentia.* As they are types of things to come, so too 'tis said, that antient stories are cut there in Trees, and the mysterious hedges are the Annals of former Ages, thus each thing contained something that may be read, doth make the whole but one fair volume to instruct blest soules.
>
> *Parismus.* But first my dear 'twere no Impietie for us to mingle limbs while here on earth.
>
> *Placentia.* For that, my womans temper not allowes I should encourage, or dehort you (dearest) our soules united are, our bodies then need no more happy union.

See my remarks on these dialogue-drolls in the notes to *The Royal Slave*, line 874.

2003-10 *Where Trees kiss Trees . . . Bough serve this Flower.* For some account of the "loves of the plants" we cannot do better than to turn to Burton's *Anatomy of Melancholy.* In Part III, Section 1, Member 1, Subsection 2 (1638 ed., p. 411), we read:

> 'Tis [i.e *Love*] more eminent in Plants, Hearbs, and is especially observed in vegetals; as betwixt the Vine and Elme a great Sympathy, betwixt the Vine & the Cabbage, betwixt the Vine and Olive, . . . betwixt the Vine and Baies a great antipathy, the Vine loves not the Bay, *nor his smell, and will kill him, if he grow neare him;* the Burre and the Lintle cannot endure one another; the Olive and the Mirtle embrace each other, in roots and branches if they grow neere. [A list of Latin authorities follows.]

Again, in Part III, Section 2, Member 1, Subsection 1 (1638 ed., pp. 431-32):

> In vegetall creatures what soveraignty Love hath, by many pregnant proofes and familiar examples may be proved, especially of palme trees, which are both he and she, and expresse not a sympathy but a love-passion, as by many observations have been confirmed.
>
> *Vivunt in venerem frondes, omnisque vicissim*
> *Felix arbor amat, nutant & mutua palmæ*
> *Fœdera, populeo suspirat populus ictu,*
> *Et Plantano Platanus, alnoque assibilat alnus.* [Claudian]
>
> *Constantine* . . . gives an instance out of *Florentius* his Georgicks, of a Palme tree that lov'd most fervently, *and would not be comforted untill such time her love applied her selfe unto her, you might see the two trees bend, and of their own accords stretch out their boughs to embrace and kisse each other.*

There seems no doubt that Cartwright had the above verses of Claudian in mind when he wrote the present passage.

2015 *Some Leaves . . . have words of woe inscrib'd.* See Ovid's *Metamorphoses,* X, 214-16, the story of Hyacinthus, whose flower was inscribed with "the letters of lamentation, AI, AI."

2032-62 *Among those pleasures . . . make Syrens sleep.* These lines appear in *The Marrow of Complements* (1655), pages 71-72, in the form of an epistle in rhymed couplets, the original being very considerably altered and expanded:

> *A Complementall Rhapsody, Meriting presentation*
> *to any Noble Mistresse, the Lover desirous to*
> *illustrate the Beatitude of the (feigned) Elyzium.*
>
> Dearest,
> For that our hearts to Loves soft pleasure yeelds,
> Love shall conduct us to th' Elyzian Fields;

> Among those pleasures we shall walke and see,
> Here some Gyrle dallying on her Lovers knee.
> Weaving what caught her heart into a net,
> Another into a twisted Anulet
> Of fagrant [*sic*] flowers, dancing before her Deare,
> Presenting all the pleasures of the yeare.
> There others making Dialogues with sighs
> In a sad parly, wooing with their eyes,
> Garlands and Nosegaies int'Epistles framd,
> There others sleeping (with late actions tam'd)[;]
> There with a bough of Myrtle one doth guard
> His sleeping Mistresse, taking his reward
> Oft from her Rosie lips, while others runne
> (In a dissembled anger) as to shunne
> Their zealous votaries, and at each turne,
> Fling Violets in their faces, here forlorne
> His Armes a-crosse a pensive Lover sits
> And raves, and smiles and teares his face by fits;
> Till in conclusion he desert his mone,
> Grasping the slender wast of's loved one;
> Queene of the Kingdome, in a chaire of light,
> Thou shalt enthroned be (my deare delight)
> While Doves with oynted wings o're thee shal hover,
> And hourely tribute payd thee by each Lover
> As a due homage, each upon his Knee,
> Offering his heart, to be dispos'd by thee.
> Fountaines shall walke upon thy table, and
> Birds singing to the waters fall shall stand
> In crowds together on Ambrosiac Trees,
> Drawing the Spheres downe with their melodies,
> And by the marriage of their mingled sounds,
> Make the three Syrens sleepe, the charmed grounds
> Yeelding both Myrrhe and Cassia, every where,
> The bounteous soyle shall blushing Roses beare.
> All this (my dearest) doubt not to enjoy
> Hereafter, if thou here wilt sport and toy.

This rhetorical rigmarole constitutes one of the most barefaced plagiarisms which I have encountered in an age notorious for much "picking and stealing."

2037-39 *Flow'rs . . . in a learned order . . . disclose Their mutuall meaning.* The so-called "language of the flowers" is known and practiced even today. Tables of the various significations of each flower are frequently found in cheap late nineteenth-century dictionaries. See Steevens and Malone's notes to *Hamlet*, IV, v, 173-84.

2053 *ointed.* Anointed (*NED*).
2059 *Fountains shall walk upon thy Table.* Compare the notorious lines in Crashaw's "Saint Mary Magdalene, or the weeper":

> He's followed by two faithful fountains,
> Two walking baths, two weeping motions,
> Portable and compendious oceans.

2085 *Prevent.* That is, anticipate.

ACT V, SCENE V

2106-7 *he had eleven Points O'th' Law, on's side, Possession.* This seems to have been the Elizabethan form for our modern proverb, "Possession is nine points of the law." See John Ray's *Collection of English Proverbs* (1678), page 191.

ACT V, SCENE VI

2113 *She shapes thee in an Habit, that she'l wed thee.* We should read, I think, "in the Habit."
2121 *Children of the Night.* Fairies or spirits.
2126 *spurgeth.* That is, ferments (*NED*).

ACT V, SCENE VII

2131 *find me tripping.* That is, catch me making mistakes.
2146 *shape.* Disguise.
2154 *How blew my Candle burns.* Cartwright is referring to the popular superstition that upon the approach of an evil spirit the flame of a candle would begin to turn blue and finally go out.
2162 *at a Venture.* Even considering the risks.
2180 *him that first invented Logick.* That is, the devil, the "father of lies."

ACT V, SCENE VIII

2195 *you should not speak, you are a Ghost.* See W. Towers' commendatory poem, sig. [*10]^r.
2219 *o'rlook'd.* That is, cast the evil eye upon.
2221 *Hee'l find a Teat about her.* It was a common belief that witches had extra teats with which they suckled their familiars. See, for example, *The Wonderfull Discoverie of Witches in the Countie of Lancaster* (1613; ed. G. B. Harrison, 1929), pages 21-22.
2274-95 *Be thou Hymen present here.* Goffin omits this lyric in his edition of the *Poems*. It is admittedly very inferior.

2280-81 *let a Siedge End in a Dance.* With this masque dance, in which statues come alive, compare Beaumont's *Inner Temple Masque* (1612) and Shadwell's *Psyche* (1675), IV. Like Holofernes' "show" of the Worthies, in which four had to do duty for nine, Cartwright's masque contents itself with but five.

THE POEMS

I have based my text of the poems on the *Works* (1651), except where an earlier edition or special manuscript exists. All such departures from the 1651 text are noted in each case under the notes to each poem.

References in the notes are to line numbers.

A Panegyrick . . . Carlisle

    Text.—*Works* (1651), pages 183–88. Fragments of this poem are found in Rawl. MS. D.951. These excerpts, which are included in a general sampling (fols. 62–69) from the whole range of Cartwright's poetry, are nothing more than transcriptions from the *Works* (1651). Curiously enough, in these fragments the poem is entitled, "To the Queene." In the notes to the remaining poems no further reference will be made to this manuscript.

    Lady Lucy Percy, who was the daughter of the ninth Earl of Northumberland, married James Hay, first Earl of Carlisle, in 1617. Her husband died in 1636. Nearly all the poets of the time, including Donne, Carew, Herrick, Suckling, and D'Avenant, offered tributes at the shrine of "Lucinda," who "has been rightly styled, by Bishop Warburton, the 'Erinnys of England;' since her wanton fascination and heartless treachery wrought evil widely" (*Poems and Masque of Thomas Carew*, ed. J. W. Ebsworth, 1893, p. 218). In view of the lady's too evident reputation, it is a little difficult to credit the scholar Cartwright with complete disinterestedness in the fulsome compliments which overload every line of this poem.

18 *Monograms.* Goffin suggests that the word here means a preliminary sketch or outline for a picture and quotes Ben Jonson's use of the word in this learned sense ("Underwoods," LXXI, *Works*, ed. Gifford-Cunningham, 1903, III, 331):

    You were not tied by any painter's law
    To square my circle, I confess, but draw
    My superficies: that was all you saw.

>   Which if in compass of no art it came
>   To be described by a monogram,
>   With one great blot you had formed me as I am.

Cartwright, indeed, may well have had these lines of Jonson's in mind. In line 17, compare the phrase, "Blots only cast on Blots."

33 *Amber Boxes.* Boxes of ambergris, sweet perfume (Goffin).

51 *An* Heroïna. I do not understand the reason for Goffin's alteration to *As Heroins*. The Latin form of *heroine* was not uncommon in the seventeenth century. See, for example, Cleveland's "Mount Ida" (*Works*, 1687, p. 230):

>   Next *Pallas* that brave *Heroina* came,
>   The thund'ring Queen of Action, War and Fame.

Compare, also, G. Rivers' book *The Heroinae* (1639).

109 *Ingenite.* Innate, native (*NED*).

115 *your Father's glorious Name.* Lady Lucy's father, Henry Percy, was a prisoner in the Tower for sixteen years. Here he surrounded himself with a group of well-known scholars and amused himself with various literary and scientific pursuits. For several years Lady Lucy shared her father's imprisonment.

119 *th'*Elixar. Goffin believes this refers to the "ideal *elixir vitae* of the alchemists, which was to vanquish death." More likely, however, the other, and more common, meaning of "philosopher's stone" is intended, since Cartwright stresses the "transmuting" qualities of the Lady Lucy in her relations with other mortals not so blessed as she.

123 *your Valorous Brother.* This is the Algernon Percy, tenth Earl of Northumberland, who was made Lord High Admiral of England in 1638. During the Civil War his sympathies caused him to side with the Parliament, under which he served in an official capacity.

138 *shape.* That is, a disguise.

ON THE IMPERFECTION . . . BUILDINGS

Texts.—Harl. MS. 6931, fols. 53–55; Addit. MS. 22,602, fol. 26ᵛ (signed "T. Cartwright," but with the "T" crossed out); *Works* (1651), pages 188–90.

As evidence of the sorry state of Christ Church buildings

at the time Cartwright wrote his appeal, Goffin cites a quotation from Thomas Baskerville's *Account of Oxford:*

> [Christ Church] has of late years been much beautified by Bryan Duppa and Samuel Fell, Deans, who also built the fine porch and Stayr-Case to the hall anno 1630. Nevertheless the Roof of the northern and part of the western Square were not covered till after ye Restoration of the King, but lay exposed to ye injury of all kinds of weather.

Cartwright's poem reminds one of Chaucer's *Somnour's Tale* (D.2099-2106):

> 'Yif me thanne of thy gold, to make oure cloystre,'
> Quod he, 'for many a muscle and many an oystre,
> Whan othere men han been ful wel at eyse,
> Hath been oure foode, our cloystre for to reyse;
> And yet, God woot, unnethe the fundement
> Parfourned is, ne of our pavement
> Nys nat a tyle yet withinne oure wones,
> By God, we owen fourty pound for stones!'

14 *Quar.* The word is still used in Gloucestershire and west country dialects for *quarry*. It frequently occurs in Sylvester's *Du Bartas* (Goffin). See M. Lluellin, *Men-Miracles* (1646), page 114, and Cleveland, *Works* (1687), page 206.

35 *Escheated.* Perhaps a pun is intended on the two meanings of escheat: (a) to be forfeit or confiscated; (b) to revert to the lord, king, or state (*NED*).

37 *seconds.* Things of inferior importance. *Seconds* is rare as a plural noun in this sense.

42-44 *Pauls, . . . second Renovation.* As Goffin observes, the spire of St. Paul's was struck by lightning and destroyed in 1561. Though immediate measures were taken to restore the damage, the spire was never rebuilt, and much of the other renovation work remained uncompleted. It was not, indeed, until shortly after 1628, when Laud became Bishop of London, that a serious attempt was made, under the direction of Inigo Jones, to finish the work of restoration. (See Waller's verses "On the Repairing of St. Pauls," 1633.) Cartwright is referring, therefore, to this seemingly miraculous renovation, which after so many years of delay, had been visited on St. Paul's, and hopes that similar good fortune may eventually fall to the lot of Christ Church.

Goffin points out that "Renovation" (l. 44) must here be

pronounced as a word of five syllables, giving the full disyllabic value to the suffix "ion." He adds that such a pronunciation was possible "only at the end of the line." This is an unwise generalization. It would, perhaps, be true to say that *usually* this pronunciation was confined to the end of the line, but numerous examples of internal use could be quoted from almost any of Cartwright's contemporaries, among whom Lovelace, perhaps, uses the device most frequently. A single example from Cartwright himself will serve all purposes, however (second poem to Fletcher, "Another on the Same," l. 11):

> Yet we through his corrections could see
> Much treasure in thy superfluity.

A Continuation . . . Prince of Wales

Texts.—MSS., see preceding poem; *Works* (1651), pages 190–91.

15 *Indulge.* To bestow or grant a favor. An early use of the verb. The earliest citation in *NED* is 1638, while, from internal evidence, this poem can be dated 1635. The whole couplet is difficult syntactically. We may paraphrase as follows: May you then grant, you who are our Rising Sun, that we may say it was here [i.e., Christ Church] that your first rays broke to bring a day. The reading of the first line is somewhat clearer in Harl. MS. 6931:

> Indulge you then (our King's Sonne) that we may . . .

20 *The Eldest Tear of Balsam.* Goffin suggests that here *balsam* "is made to stand for the *tree* from which the healing juice is extracted."

26 *done by you at five.* As Goffin points out, this line enables us to date the poem 1635. Prince Charles was born May 29, 1630.

27 *Nephews.* Grandsons or descendants, a common contemporary meaning.

40 *sit.* Goffin and Chalmers print *fit*, but *sit* is correct and receives the support of both manuscripts. Compare Ben Jonson's "Eupheme" IV, "Underwoods" (*Works*, ed. Gifford-Cunningham, 1903, III, 359):

> Beside, your hand will never hit,
> To draw a thing that cannot sit.

On His Majesties . . . small Pox. 1633

    Texts.—*Pro Rege suo Soteria* (1633), sig. G3ʳ (here reprinted); *Works* (1651), page 192. *Pro . . . Soteria* also contains a Latin poem (sig. D1) by Cartwright.

    This poem is reprinted from *Works* (1651) in T. H. Ward's *English Poets* (1881, II, 230). Compare Carew's poem "Upon the King's Sickness" (*Poems and Masque of Thomas Carew*, ed. J. W. Ebsworth, 1893, p. 32).

10   *Starres.* Ward (*English Poets*, II, 227) writes that Dryden later made use of the central conceit in this poem, but with less success. He refers, I suppose, to Cartwright's comparison of the smallpox scars to turquoise stones, and to the following lines from Dryden's poem, "Upon the Death of the Lord Hastings" (*Poems of John Dryden*, ed. J. Sargeaunt, 1929, pp. 175–76):

    Was there no milder way but the Small Pox . . .
    Or were these Gems sent to adorn his Skin,
    The Cab'net of a richer Soul within?

If anyone considers Cartwright's conceit farfetched or too curious, let him read Bishop Corbet's thoughts on the same theme in his "Elegie upon the Death of the Lady Haddington" (*Poems*, ed. O. Gilchrist, 1807, p. 128):

    O thou deform'd unwoman-like disease,
    That plowst up flesh and bloud, and there sow'st
        pease,
    And leav'st such printes on beauty, that dost come
    As clouted shon do on a floore of lome;
    Thou that of faces hony-combes dost make . . . .

11–14   *Turquoises . . . paile lookes . . . not well.* Cartwright evidently had Donne's "First Anniversary" (1621 ed., p. 32) in mind:

    As a compassionate Turcoyse which doth tell
    By looking pale, the wearer is not well.

Others besides Cartwright seem to have remembered Donne's conceit. See Kynaston's *Cynthiades* (1642) (ed. G. Saintsbury, *Minor Poets of the Caroline Period*, 1906, II, 161), "To Cynthia":

    . . . as a turquois[e] bought, . . .
    Whose love and bounty doth such virtue lend

>   As makes it to compassionate, and tell
>   By looking pale, the wearer is not well.

In a footnote to this passage Saintsbury compares the following lines from Benlowes' *Theophila* (1652), Canto V, Stanza xcii:

>   No sympathizing turkise there, to tell
>   By paleness th' owner is not well,

and judges them as "almost too close in phrase not to be borrowed, though the *materies* is *publicissima*."

TO THE KING . . . SCOTLAND. 1633

Texts.—*Solis Britannici Perigaeum* (1633), sig. L3ʳ (here reprinted); *Works* (1651), pages 193–94. *Solis . . . Perigaeum* also contains a Latin poem by Cartwright (sigs. [B4]ᵛ–C1ʳ), signed "*Guil. Cartwright A.B. ex Aede Christ.*"

7–10 *but 'twas . . . still.* These lines are quoted, without acknowledgment and with small changes, by David Lloyd in his account of Sir Rowland Berkley (*Memoires*, 1668, p. 121).

9 *Quill.* A plectrum formed of the quill of a feather (*NED*).

30 *eager Loue, and Loyalty.* Goffin pertinently notices that it is rather Cartwright who "shows his own eager loyalty, for Charles's visit to Scotland comprised a long series of diplomatic mistakes, chiefly in regard to religious policy; even his coronation was carried out in the manner most likely to upset Scottish prejudice."

TO THE QUEEN . . . OCCASION

Texts.—*Solis Britannici Perigaeum* (1633), sig. [L4]ʳ (here reprinted); *Works* (1651), pages 194–95.

ON THE BIRTH . . . YORK

Texts.—*Vitis Carolinae Gemma Altera* (1633), sig. I3 (here reprinted); *Works* (1651), pages 197–98. *Vitis . . . Altera* also contains a Latin poem by Cartwright (sigs. [C4]ʳ–D1ʳ), The variant issues of the 1633 edition are identical for Cartwright's poem.

James, Duke of York, was born October 13, 1633. Poems

celebrating his birth were, of course, legion; Jonson alone seems to have varied the monotony a little by writing on his christening.

36–38 *A strangled snake . . . Swath.* Contrast Dryden's use of the same Hercules legend, also with reference to James, in his *Threnodia Augustalis,* lines 446–54.

43 *unfil'd.* Goffin observes that this word occurs more than once in Cartwright with the sense of "unpolished," but that in the present context it means "uncultured."

47 *Grandsire* Henry. Henry IV, king of France and Navarre. He was assassinated by a Roman Catholic fanatic in 1610.

57–58 *In Him . . . in Her . . . In This.* Cartwright refers in turn to Prince Charles, Princess Mary, and the new-born Prince James.

To Dr Duppa . . . Tutor to the Prince of Wales
Text.—*Works* (1651), pages 199–201.

Bryan Duppa, to whom this poem is addressed, was a good friend and patron to Cartwright. Born at Greenwich in 1588, Duppa received his education first at Westminster and later at Oxford. Always apparently in favor, his rise was rapid. Appointed Dean of Christ Church in 1629, an office which he retained until 1638, he was also made Vice-Chancellor of the university (1632), then Chancellor of Salisbury (1634), royal tutor (about 1635?), Bishop of Chichester (1638), Bishop of Salisbury (1641), and, finally, Bishop of Winchester (1660). He died at Richmond in 1662. The importance of Cartwright's connection with Duppa is considerable. In his notes to *Jonsonus Virbius* (1638) Gilchrist, the eighteenth-century scholar and champion of Jonson, writes: "The patron of learning [Duppa] when learning was proscribed,—for the greater part of what is beautiful and useful in the writings of Mayne, Cartwright, and many others, religion and literature are indebted to the fostering protection of Doctor Bryan Duppa."

Goffin thinks these verses were written immediately after Duppa's appointment as royal tutor. Certainly the opening lines seem to support this view, and the later reference to a journey—presumably the trip to London—which Duppa is about to make, would seem to set the matter beyond doubt.

32 *A Genius.* See Cockeram, *The English Dictionarie* (1623): "*Genius.* A good angell, or a familiar evill spirit, the soule."

55 *fresh and fasting.* That is, on an empty stomach, or when the mind is sharp-set, not dulled by too much eating. Charles, unlike "other Princes," will not receive instruction only at meal time or when the attention is otherwise engaged.

To the same . . . Publick Act at Oxon. 1634

Text.—*Works* (1651), pages 202–4.

In John Ayliffe's *Ancient and Present State of the University of Oxford*, 1723 (II, 131ff.), we find some account of the Oxford Act:

> There is a general Commencement once every Year in all the Faculties of Learning, which is called the *Act* at *Oxford*, and the *Commencement* at *Cambridge;* which *Act* is opened on the *Friday* following the *7th* of *July*, and Exercises perform'd in the Schools on *Saturday* and *Monday* ensuing the Opening thereof; and also in the publick Theatre, with great Solemnity. . . . At the equal Expence of all the Inceptors, there is a sumptuous and elegant Supper at the College or Hall of the *Senior* of each Faculty, for the Entertainment of the Doctors, called the *Act-Supper*. . . . And after the End of the *Act*, the Vice-Chancellor, with the Regents of the foregoing Year, immediately assemble in the Congregation-House; where, at the Supplication of the Doctors and Masters newly created, they are wont to dispense with the wearing of *Boots* and *Slop Shoes*, to which the Doctors and Masters of the *Act* are oblig'd, during the *Comitia*.

Goffin notices the following passages in Evelyn's *Diary* under July, 1654:

> 8th. Was spent in hearing several exercises in the scholes, and after dinner the Proctor opened the Act at St. Marie's (according to custome) and the Prevaricators their drolery. Then the Doctors disputed.
>
> 10th. On Monday I went againe to the Scholes to heare the severall Faculties, and in the afternoone tarried out the whole Act in St. Marie's, the long speeches of the Proctors, the Vice-Chancellor, the severall Professors, creation of Doctors by the cap, ring, kisse, &c, these antient ceremonies and institution being as yet not wholy abolish'd.

Goffin also refers the reader to July 10, 1669, of the *Diary*, which deals with the occasion on which Evelyn was presented with an honorary doctor's degree by Oxford, in recognition of his scientific studies.

11 Pumps. Then, as now, a kind of light shoe, or slipper for indoor use (*NED*). Cartwright makes the wearing of pumps

a symbol of the loosening of the reins of reason and academic propriety. There may be some allusion intended to the practice of removing the doctor's *boots* and *slop shoes* at the end of the Act (see the quotation above from Ayliffe).

22–24 Jerusalem *or* Nineveh . . . Great Britaines Looking Glass. Both "Jerusalem" and "Nineveh," as Goffin points out, were well-known motions, or puppet plays. He quotes the familiar reference to both these motions in Jonson's *Bartholomew Fair*, V, i, and notices "the Widow, who ne'er saw any Shew yet, but the Puppet-play o' *Ninive*," in Cowley's *Cutter of Coleman Street*, V, xi. "Great Britaines Looking Glass" Goffin identifies with a puppet-play version of Lodge and Greene's *A Looking Glass for London and England* (printed in 1594). Since *A Looking Glass for London and England* deals allegorically with the Ninevah story, the motions of "Ninevah" and "Great Britaines Looking Glass" were probably the same play under different names, in spite of the fact that Cartwright seems to speak of them as separate productions. Cartwright was not perhaps so conversant with "the motions" as he would have us think.

It does not appear very clear whether the general gaiety and festival appearance of the town was the direct result of the Act, or whether merely the summer was to blame. Certainly Cartwright's account reads more like "the circus come to town," than the description of an annual academic exercise. Probably, however, the Act, with the many visitors and potential customers which flocked to it, was the original cause. That a very similar atmosphere prevailed in Cambridge during their Commencement is witnessed to by Cleveland in his satirical poem, "How the Commencement grows new" (*Works*, 1687, pp. 68–70).

30 *These cry the Monster-Masters, Those the* Dutch. Goffin prints a dash between "Monster" and "Master," which changes the construction of the sentence. Paraphrasing Cartwright's line we get: the Monster-Masters cry up these [rare animals], the Dutch cry up those [rare animals].

38 Absolute Decree. Cartwright is referring to one of the most commonly used of the theological terms in the long-continued debate between the Calvinist and Arminian positions in the church. The "decree" of God, said Arminius, is "absolute"

with regard to His own actions, but only conditional with regard to man's. Prynne in *Anti-Arminianisme* (1630) declared that the doctrine of his opponents "makes man an absolute, an independent creature" (Goffin). It should be noticed that Cartwright was not unnaturally an Arminian, denying the doctrine of election and predestination, believing in the freedom of the will. See his translation of Hugo Grotius' "Elegy on Arminius."

40 Reprobation. The Calvinistic opposite of "election." Cockeram's *Dictionarie* (1623) gives the following definition of a "reprobate": "One past grace, a castaway."

42 *Lay Exercise on Monday night.* Goffin notes that "Evelyn speaks of the 'magnificent entertainment at Wadham Hall' which he attended on a similar occasion."

53 Christian Freedom. An expression often found on the lips of Puritans (Goffin). See a later note to line 48 of "The Chambermaids Posset."

61 *Brother then known by the rowling White.* Goffin illustrates this line by a quotation from the song of Cock Lorrel in Jonson's *The Gipsies Metamorphosed* (1621):

> His stomach was queasy . . .
> To help it he called for a puritan poacht,
>   That used to turn up the eggs of his eyes.

Cartwright is trying to say that even the Puritan visitors went to sleep during the after-dinner sermon, hiding their "white starring eyes" and becoming temporarily blind, that is, "Children of the Night." Actually this last phrase is one of the numerous terms for spirits or fairies; see line 2121 of *The Siege*.

64 *My Lords fee-buck closeth bothe Eyes and Eares.* The term "fee-buck" is very rare and apparently does not occur outside of Cartwright. *NED* defines "fee-buck" as "? a buck received as a perquisite." The word is found again in *The Siege*, IV, ii: "Put off your Mercer with your Fee-buck for / That season, and so forth." Goffin very neatly illustrates the meaning of the term from the opening lines of Dryden's Prologue to *Amboyna* (1673):

> As needy Gallants in the Scriv'ners hands
> Court the rich Knave that gripes their Mortgag'd Lands,

> The first fat Buck of all the Season's sent,
> And Keeper takes no Fee in Complement;
> The doteage of some *Englishmen* is such
> To fawn on those who ruine them, the *Dutch*.

Goffin further points out that the " 'Courtier turn'd Captain' in *The Siedge* and the 'needy gallant' of Dryden make a curious coincidence."

69 *Spoke* Minshew. Cartwright is referring to John Minsheu's *The Guide into the Tongues, viz. English, Welsh, Low Dutch, High Dutch, French, Italian, Spanish, Portuguez, Latine, Greeke, Hebrew, &c.* (1617). To "Speak Minshew in a Breath" must have taken more than a single glass of the "Inceptors wine."

69–70 *the* Inceptors *Wine Made* Latine *Native*. Was Cartwright perhaps thinking of Chaucer's Somnour (*Prologue*, ll. 637–38)?

71 *wiser Statute*. "The statutes of the University had been undergoing revision for some time. A book containing the new rules was published during Dr. Duppa's Vice-Chancellorship, on the 22nd July, 1634. These statutes were distasteful to the Anti-Arminians (v. Wood, *Antiq.* I, 390 et seq.): 'Statutum est, quod qui ad Doctoratum in S. Theologia aspirat, post susceptum Baccalaurei in Theologia Gradum, per quatuor Annos integros publicum Theologiae Praelectorem audiat, priusquam ad Incipiendum in eadem Facultate admittatur.' " (Goffin).

ON THE GREAT FROST. 1634

Texts.—Harl. MS. 6931, fols. 78–79; Mal. MS. 21, fols. 71–72 (dated by Malone, "about 1644"); *Works* (1651), pages 204–6; *The English Parnassus: or, A Helpe to English Poesie*, by Josua Poole (1657), pages 315–16; (1677), pages 357–58.

This frost seems to have raised much discussion at the time and to have lingered in the memory for many years after. Numerous references to it may be found in contemporary literature. See, for example, D'Avenant's *The Temple of Love* (1634) (*Dramatic Works*, ed. Maidment and Logan, 1872, I, 293); Jasper Mayne's *The City-Match* (written about 1635–37), V, ii; an anonymous manuscript poem entitled, "On the dissolution of the great frost" (Egerton MS. 2725, fols. 148–49).[1] Goffin quotes as follows from Laud's *Diary* (Dec. 10,

---

1. This poem occurs again in Malone MS. 21, fols. 70–71 (where it is attribu-

1634): "That night the frost began, the Thames almost frozen; and it continued until the Sunday, sevennight after." And again (Jan. 5, 1634/5): "Monday night being Twelfth Eve, the frost began again; the Thames was frozen over, and continued so till Feb. 3."

"On the Great Frost," a burlesque poem by Charles Cotton (1630–87), has no connection with the present occasion. Cotton's verses, which are greatly inferior to Cartwright's in point of wit, show no evidence of influence by the earlier poem.

The following poem, signed "H:C:," occurs in Harleian MS. 6931, fols. 80–81, directly following Cartwright's verses (see the note on the texts, above). As the poem so far as I know has never been printed, I give the complete text.

> On the Hott Summer following the Great Frost, in
>   imitation of the Verses made upon it by W:C:
>
> Where is the Cold you quak't [with], you that be
> Shooke with two Palseyes, Age, & Poverty,
> Court not Flames, now no Promethean art
> Neede steale from Phaebus (what we feele) his dart,
> He is too bounteous, he hath bent his bow[;]   [5]
> Scatter'd his flaming arrowes, as if now
> There were new Pythons, & the new drown'd earth
> Had bred some Serpent fearfull beyond dearth.
> The quarter hath bin Noone-tyde, the whole night
> Felt the like heate with day, if not like light[;]   [10]
> Birds in the Aire feare stifling; poor men blow
> Water as t'were theire Pottage, we scarce know
> Charewell from Grice's, Arissotle's [sic] brinke
> Yields liquor, senjors might account good drinke[;]
> All Tauernes are discommon'd, tis soe hott   [15]
> Our Dutch-men thrice (?) well drunk forsake the pott.
> We all live Portia's death, our very meate
> Is roasted soone as 'tis layd downe, we eate
> Nothing but heat, that which is coldest fish
> Comes boyld unto the Shore as to the Dish.   [20]
> The Floud Sunk not, but vanish't, the Sun's lust
> Thaw'd the cold snow, not into drops, but dust[;]
> The earth now suffers Barnabyes hard fate

---

ted to "Dudley Diggs") and in a Huntington Library MS. (HM.116, pp. 103–5). Another poem entitled "To A freind in yͤ greate frost" appears in a second Huntington MS. (HM.198, pp. 191–92).

    More thirsty for her drinking, & too late   [24]
    Yawnes after drinke; the loth'd, the angry'ed clouds
    For theire Complain'd of bounty Feed noe Flouds,
    Scarce squeez'd afford a dew, & that they give
    To Fertalize her lipps, & make her live.
    Amidst this heate there moysture none appeares
    But the fatt Rich man's Sweate, & poormans teares: [30]
    Our gliding Chanells are become Firme Land
    Resembling Rivers only by theire Sand;
    Without a prophetts mantle to devide,
    We through our Jordan safely walke & ride.
    We have forgott the floud, begin to doubt   [35]
    The Element of Water at this Drought:
    For the firy Element, we justly dare
    (Spight of Philosophie) swear's below the Ayre,
    If there be any Ayre, for doubt we must
    That as the other, we find nought but dust.   [40]
    We are confirm'd i'th faith, that the world shall
    From fire, not water take it's Farewell fall;
    Two Elements are spent, the duller left
    Is become fewell, of it's cold bereft,
    Couer'd with flaming dust will soone be brought   [45]
    To Ashes, if some God quench not this drought.
    Agues forgett theire cold fitts, frozen Limbes
    Thaw at a Feavers Fire, now noe man swimmes
    Unto his grave, we all with Envy thinke
    The river out of mercy from's false brinke   [50]
    Stole those two lovely brothers, while that we
    Survive to feele on Earth [our] Purgatory[.]
    If as Eliah's body our Soules rise
    Hurried in flaming raptures to the skyes,
    This comfort[s], we'ld bid none take care to burne   [55]
    Our bones; each Grave it selfe will prove an urne.

This metaphysical *tour de force*, though lacking some of the polish of Cartwright's verses, compares very favorably with them in an ingenious display of wit.

10–12 *Glass . . . Ships . . . planted . . . grow*. Compare Donne, "The Calm" (*Poems*, ed. E. K. Chambers, n.d., II, ll. 8–10):

    Smooth as thye mistress' glass, or what shines there,
    The sea is now, and, as these isles which we
    Seek, when we can move, our ships rooted be.

31–32 *We hear . . . their Grave*. The essential meaning of this couplet is easy enough to understand: those who were drowned in water are now buried in that same water, but water which has become ice. Syntactically the sentence is impossible. The sense of Cartwright's thought is well illustrated by the following lines from William Browne's "On One Drowned in the Snow" (*Poems*, ed. G. Goodwin, 1894, II, 290, ll. 3-6):

> That which exil'd my life from her sweet home,
> For grief straight froze itself into a tomb.
> One only element my fate thought meet
> To be my death, grave, tomb, and winding-sheet.

42 *one Sense*. Compare Donne, "The Calm" (*Poems*, ed. E. K. Chambers, II, ll. 55-56):

> We have no power, no will, no sense; I lie
> I should not then thus feel this misery.

46 *last cold, Death*. Both Goffin and the Malone MS. give the line a different meaning. The emphasis is on the terrible state of *cold* which the "Great Frost" has produced and which Cartwright believes is as painful as the last great coldness of very death. By omitting the comma after *cold* Goffin entirely changed the meaning of the passage, while the Malone MS shifted the emphasis to *last*: "That last, call'd Death."

51 *fire-Briefs*. Circular letters asking for assistance for sufferers by fire (*NED*). Though the compound word is rare—this passage from Cartwright is the only one cited—the custom behind the word can be more readily illustrated. See, for example, some lines in A. Gill's bitter lines, "Upon Ben Johnsons Magneticke Lady. 1632" (Egerton MS. 2725, fol. 130):

> Let Thomas Purfoot, or John Trundle doe it
> In such dull Characters, as for reliefes
> Of fires, and wracke, we find in begging briefes.

See also Thomas Harman, *A Caveat or Warning for Common Cursetors*, 1567 (ed. E. Viles and F. J. Furnivall, *Rogues and Vagabonds of Shakespeare's Youth*, 1907, p. 61):

These Demaunders for glymmar be for the moste parte wemen; for glymmar, in their language, is fyre. These goe with fayned lycences and counterfayted wrytings, having the hands and seales of suche gentlemen as dwelleth nere to the place where they fayne them selves to have bene burnt, and their goods consumed with fyre.

57 *A Feaver.* Compare Shadwell, *The Woman-Captain* (*Complete Works*, ed. M. Summers, 1927, IV, 28):

> I have heard your Servants in Winter wish for the Plague or any hot Disease; and I for my part could be contented with a Feaver.

60 Bowker. John Bowker, or Booker, was one of the numerous almanac makers of the time. Goffin, presumably quoting from his almanac for 1634, says he had indeed prophesied "much snow, fierce winds, hard frost" for December. By way of excusing any mistakes in his prognostications Booker adds: "It is sufficient for an Artist though he attaine not the End, always to perform so much as the rules of Art require, which our common Almanacke-writers never do." A good, if not unbiased, account of Booker may be found in *Mr. William Lilly's History of His Life and Times* (2nd. ed. 1715), pp. 28–29: "He was a very honest Man, abhorred any Deceit in the Art he studied; had a curious Fancy in judging of Theft, and as successful in resolving Love-Questions." He became famous, says Lilly, in the years 1632 and 1633 "for a Prediction of his upon a Solar Eclipse." With Cartwright's reference compare some lines in Cleveland's "Dialogue between two Zealots" (*Works*, 1687, p. 26).

65 Alabaster. William Alabaster (1567–1640), now principally remembered for his neoclassical Latin tragedy *Roxana* (1632), was also the author of cabalistic and mystical books. His *Ecce Sponsus Venit* (1633) treats of the end of the world. This is the same Alabaster, or Alablaster, whom Cromwell, in his first speech to Parliament (1629), accused of preaching "flat Popery at Paul's Cross" (Thomas Carlyle, *Oliver Cromwell's Letters and Speeches* [Boston, 1845], I, 62.) See also Herrick's "To Doctor Alablaster," *Hesperides*, No. 764. *Allestree*, the reading of the Malone MS, was the name of another almanac writer who published between 1619 and 1640.

To . . . LADIE ELIZABETH POWLET

Texts.—Bod. MS. 22 (here printed; the title of the poem in both Goffin's and my text is actually the title for the whole collection, in which Cartwright's poem happens to come first); *Works* (1651), pages 195–96; *Parnassus Biceps* (1656), pages 146–47; *J. Cleaveland Revived: Poems, Orations, Epistles,*

. . . with Some other Exquisite Remains of the most eminent Wits of both the Universities that were his Contemporaries (1659), pages 62–64; (1662), pages 86–88; *Works of Mr. John Cleveland* (1687), pages 359–60 (reissued in 1699 with a new title-page).

The explanation of how Cartwright's poem came to be included among Cleveland's poems is as follows. Williamson, the editor of *J. Cleaveland Revived*, notices in his epistle "To the Reader" (sigs. [A6]ᵛ–[A7]ʳ):

> Some other Poems are intermixed, such as the Reader shall find to be of such persons, as were for the most part Mr. *Cleavelands* Contemporaries; some of them no lesse eminently known to the three Nations. I hope the World cannot be so far mistaken in his Genuine Muse, as not to discern his pieces from any of the other Poems; . . . some of their Poems, contrary to my expectation, I being at such a distance, I have since heard, were before in print: but as they are excellently good, and so few, the Reader (I hope) will the more freely accept them.

In the third edition (1662), however, Cartwright's verses are still included in spite of Williamson's claim (sig. [A5]ʳ): ". . . in this third Edition I have crossed them [i.e., the poems he had earlier discovered to be in print] out, only reserving those that were excellently good, and never before extant." By the edition of 1687, Williamson's preface has been superseded, but Cartwright's poem is still retained, although the editors, "J.L." and "S.D.," fulminate against "late Editions . . . wherein is scarce one or other Poem of his own to commute for all the rest" ("The Epistle Dedicatory," sig. A3ᵛ). This last collection (1687) is probably one of the most heterogeneous gatherings ever published under one man's name.

Cartwright's poem is the first in a collection of verses presented in manuscript to the Lady Elizabeth Paulet in Convocation on July 9, 1636, in recognition of her gift to the university—a piece of needle-work depicting the birth, death, and resurrection of Christ. Goffin suggests that it is identical with "A curious piece of needlework," which was "formerly No. 346 on the list of curiosities kept in the Anatomy School at Oxford."

As Goffin observes, the Lady Elizabeth Paulet, or Pawlet, must be carefully distinguished from the Lady Jane Pawlet, who died in 1631. The exact identity of the Lady Elizabeth seems a little doubtful. Goffin thinks she was either the second wife of John Pawlett, who died in 1649; and daughter of Christopher Ken, or a daughter of the third marquis of Winchester. Two other possibilities may be suggested, perhaps: (a) Elizabeth, daughter of Edward Paulet, who married George Paulet (born 1565), third son of Sir Amias Paulet; (b) Elizabeth, third daughter of Sir Amias Paulet, who died unmarried.

G. Thorn-Drury in his edition of *Parnassus Biceps* (1927) writes that he "cannot accept the suggestions which have been made" regarding the identity of Lady Elizabeth. Although Mr. Thorn-Drury is unable to make any definite statement, he thinks it most likely that she was a member of the "well-known Hampshire noble family," since the Winchester carrier was paid twelve shillings for bringing them to Oxford. His search, however, has been without result. Mr. Thorn-Drury adds two other small facts of interest, though without giving any source: (a) the piece of needlework was really two pieces; (b) the university spent five shillings and eight pence "for 2 greene sey curtaines for the two needleworke peeces," which have since disappeared.

14 *rose ... ends.* Compare William Browne (*Britannia's Pastorals*, Bk. II, Song iii, ll. 402-3) where he is speaking of the blending of colors in the dove's neck:

> Where none can say (though he it strict attends)
> Here one begins, and there the other ends.

26 *wrought, as Writt.* As Goffin points out the past tense of the verb *write* was sometimes confused with the past of *work*. Cartwright doubtless intended a pun.

To Mr W. B. ... first Child
Text.—*Works* (1651), pages 207-8.

The identity of Mr. W.B. seems as mysterious, if not as important, as that of Mr. W.H. Goffin suggests two possibilities: first, William Backhouse (1593-1662), a Rosicrucian philosopher, who studied at Christ Church and was the father of two sons; second, Will Burton (1609-57), the antiquary, not the elder brother of Robert Burton, who was forced to leave Oxford on account of poverty (line 36 might possibly refer to this misfortune). It is not unnatural, perhaps, to suppose that the "W.B." here addressed would take the opportunity afforded by the publication of Cartwright's works in 1651 to repay his debt by contributing some commendatory verses. Although no poems by either Backhouse or Burton appear, two other men bearing the initials W.B. did write such verses. They were W. Barker and William Bell. Considerations of age at once dismiss Bell, and of Barker nothing further seems to be known. Other "W.B.'s" might easily be added, but the list is sufficiently inconclusive and confusing as it stands.

Cartwright's verses may owe something to an earlier poem by Richard Corbet entitled "To his Son *Vincent Corbet*, 1630" (see below, ll. 35-40). The similarity was first pointed out by Gilchrist in his edition of Corbet's *Poems* (1807, p. 151). Another poem by Henry King called "Wishes to my sonne John, for this new, and all succeeding yeares: Jan. 1. 1630" (*Poems*, ed. L. Mason, 1914, pp. 181-83) somewhat resembles both Corbet's and Cartwright's verses.

10-14 *To hear the Nurse . . . added is.* Compare William Strode's poem, "A Letter" (*Poetical Works*, ed. B. Dobell, 1907, pp. 100-1):

> As in a child the nurse descryes
> The mother's lippes, the father's eyes,
> The uncle's nose; and doth apply
> An owner to each part.

22 *Synalæphaes.* The coalescence or contraction of two syllables into one (*NED*).

24 *Pratling as* Obligations *do.* Cartwright uses *Obligations* in the sense of written legal agreements, a common meaning, comparing the clipped speech of the child to the many abbreviations which appeared in the barbarous Latin of such documents.

35-40 *I wish him . . . Health . . . Ends.* Compare the following lines from Corbet's poem "To his Son *Vincent Corbet*, 1630" (see the introductory note):

> I wish thee, Vin, before all wealth,
> Both bodily and ghostly health. . . .
> I wish thee all thy mothers graces,
> Thy fathers fortunes, and his places.

> I wish thee friends, and one at court
> Not to build on, but support.

43 *Whistle.* Small silver whistles seem to have been one of the two *sine qua non* of seventeenth-century babyhood. Trinculo adds the other when (Dryden, *The Tempest*, III, iii) he cries: "It shall be a Whistle for our first Babe, and when the next Shipwreck puts me again to swimming, I'll dive to get a Coral to it."

FOR A YOUNG LORD . . . TAUGHT HIM A SONG

Texts.—Lawes' autographed MS., page 247; *Works* (1651), pages 208-9.

This lyric was set to music by Henry Lawes. Lawes' setting divides the poem into five stanzas of four lines, the last two lines (21-22) serving as a chorus to be repeated after each stanza.

Goffin notes that this poem is quoted in full in the *Retrospective Review*, IX (1824), 162-63. It is a delicate and altogether charming lyric, showing Cartwright at his courtly best.

15-16 *As when . . . Sent to the Flower.* Goffin compares lines 15-16 in Cartwright's poem "To the Queen" (1633):

> As when in thirsty flowers, a gentle dew
> Awakes the sent which slept, not gives a new.

ON MR STOKES . . . ART OF VAULTING

Texts.—Mal. MS. 21, fols. 55ʳ-56ᵛ (here printed); *Works* (1651), pages 209-12.

This poem was apparently written to celebrate the composition of William Stokes' *The Vaulting Master: or, The Art of Vaulting reduced to a Method* (1641). Goffin notices the following remarks from Evelyn's *Diary* (Jan. 22, 1637): "I would needs be admitted into the dancing and vaulting schools, of which late activity one Stokes, the master, did afterwards set forth a pretty book, which was published, with many witty elogies before it." Curiously, Cartwright's verses do not appear in either the first or the second (1652) edition of this book. Since the Malone MS. seems to offer a better text than the *Works* (1651), I have, following Goffin, made it the basis of the present text.

The title "Ephialtes," which Cartwright bestowed upon the miraculous Stokes, Goffin takes to mean "flying- or nightmare." This sense of "incubus" was a well-known one, but it does not fit the present context, where a rather more complimentary meaning is called for. Though Cartwright may have intended some sort of double meaning in his use of the word, he was undoubtedly employing it in its etymological sense of "one who leaps or springs up" (from the verb ἐφάλλομαι, "to leap or spring up," particularly used of mounting horses). The whole phrase, "et solo temporum horum Ephialte," may, therefore, be rendered, "the only (i.e., best) vaulter of his times."

The significance of the signature "Philippus Stoicus e Societate Portæ Borealis Oxon." is lost to us, unless possibly it refers to some athletic society, situated near the North Gate, of which Cartwright was an earnest member.

3 *Rooke.* Goffin thinks the word is here used "in the old disparaging sense, applied to persons." While probably some play on this meaning was at the back of Cartwright's mind, he is primarily thinking of the rook, or castle, in chess, which can only move in a vertical, or horizontal, straight line. The efficacy of Master Stokes' handbook is so great that it enables the individual to move suddenly in any direction—not, like a rook, always in a straight line.

8 *Tom Charles.* Identity unknown. Possibly the same as "that great French rider" referred to in Massinger and Rowley's *The Old Law*, III, ii. The name *Charles*, either as a surname or Christian name, was not at all common in England at this time. A Mr. Thomas Charles set to music Lovelace's song called "The Scrutinie."

10 *trickes . . . figures dimme.* As Goffin notices, each of the various vaulting positions was carefully illustrated in Stokes' manual by individual engravings, e.g., the *Pomado*, *Strapado*, and *Herculean leap*. Goffin further quotes the following passage from *Cynthia's Revels* (*Jonson's Works*, ed. Gifford-Cunningham, 1903, I, 157–58): "He courts ladies with how many great horse he hath rid that morning, or how oft he hath done the whole, or half the pommado in a seven-night before."

13 *Dee . . . Billingsley.* John Dee (1527-1608) was the great

mathematician and famous sorcerer in the time of Queen Elizabeth. Sir Henry Billingsley, Lord Mayor of London, who died in 1606, first translated Euclid into English (Goffin).

18 *Volatickes.* Winged creatures (*NED*).

25 *vectures.* "Carriages" or positions (Goffin). Bacon uses the word in his essay "Of Seditions and Troubles": "There be but three things which one nation selleth unto another; the commodity as nature yieldeth it; the manufacture; and the vecture, or carriage."

50 *Daedalus . . . twineing Stewes.* Why Cartwright should term the Cretan labyrinth a "stews," I cannot guess. The adjective "twining" is natural enough. See Ovid, *Metamorphoses*, VIII, 183 ff.

52 *wax'd plumes.* Both the 1651 text and Goffin read "wax plumes." The Malone MS. is undoubtedly correct. Compare the following passage in Whitney's *Choice of Emblems* (1586), page 28:

> Heare, *Icarus* with mountinge vp alofte,
> Came headlonge downe, and fell into the Sea:
> His waxed winges, the sonne did make so softe,
> They melted straighte, and feathers fell awaie.

56 *Sheene.* Referring to the royal mews there (Goffin).

61–62 *Theutobocchus . . . fflorus.* The *Works* (1651) gives a marginal reference to [Florus] "Lib.3. c.3." Goffin quotes the passage as follows: "Certe rex ipse Theutobocchus quaternos, senosque equos transilire solitus, vix unum, quum fugeret, ascendit, proximoque in saltu comprehensus, insigne spectaculum triumphi fuit."

71–72 *leap . . . plucke bright honour . . . Moone.* As Goffin points out, these lines are a reminiscence of Hotspur's lines in Shakespeare's *I Henry IV*, I, iii, 201–2:

> By Heaven, methinks it were an easy leap
> To pluck bright honour from the pale-faced moon.

It is possible, however, that Cartwright did not associate these lines with Shakespeare at all, but took them at second hand from the Induction to Beaumont and Fletcher's *The Knight of the Burning Pestle* (*Works of Beaumont and Fletcher*, ed. A. Dyce, 1843, II, 135), where they are quoted verbatim.

THE DREAME
     Text.—*Works* (1651), page 213.

LOVE INCONCEALABLE
     Text.—*Works* (1651), page 213.

  The title of this epigram is followed by the double abbreviation "Stig. Ital." Rather hesitatingly I suggest that the phrase means "from the Italian of Stigliani." Tommaso Stigliani, who was alive about 1600, was the author of a large number of poems, of which an edition appeared in 1625 under the title *Il Canzoniero del Sig. Cavalier Fra 'Tomaso Stigliani*. In this collection (p. 22) a poem with the heading "Amore incelabile" actually occurs, but its contents seem to bear no relation to Cartwright's verses.

  The central conceit of Cartwright's poem, whether original or translated, was probably suggested by a passage in Ovid's "Epistle of Paris to Helen" from the *Heroides*. Heywood (*Troia Britanica*, 1609, p. 197; *Passionate Pilgrim*, 1612, sig. [D5]ʳ) translates the lines as follows:

>   When I would rather in my thoughts desire
>   To hide the smoke, til time display the fire:
>   Time that can make the fire of Love shine cleare,
>   Vntroubled with the misty smoke of feare:
>   But I dissemble it, for who I pray
>   Can fire conceale, that will it selfe betray?

THE TEARES
     Text.—*Works* (1651), page 214.

  This poem is a much shorter and improved version of "On one Weepeing" (see below). Goffin relegates "The Teares" to his notes, but, as the version which finally appeared in the collected *Works* (1651), it deserves a place in the standard text.

  7–14 *And now the certain . . . from your Eyes?* These eight lines were set to music by Henry Lawes and published in his *Ayres and Dialogues* (1653), page 21, with the title, "To a Lady weeping." There are also three manuscript versions of this eight-line form: (1) Lawes' autographed MS., page 105; (2) Harl. MS. 3511, fol. 1ᵛ; (3) Harl. MS. 6917, No. 147 (see my comments on the "Splendora" poems in the General Introduction, Chapter V, "The Text"). Goffin confuses these lines with some similar ones in "On one Weepeing" (see his note to line 25 of that poem).

ON ONE WEEPEING

Text.—Mal. MS. 21, fol. 52. This manuscript was printed for the first time in Goffin's edition of the *Poems* (1918). My text, which differs in a number of important readings from Goffin's, is also based on the manuscript.

I am not altogether satisfied that "On one weepeing" should be ascribed to Cartwright. The evidence for assigning it to him is essentially the same as that advanced for the "Splendora" group (see General Introduction, Chapter V, "The Text," pp. 75-76). Moreover, the way in which a short poem like "The Teares" has here been expanded bears a suspicious resemblance to the method of composition of the last of the "Splendora" poems, "To his Mrs Walking in ye snow," which is little more than an expanded version of Strode's (or Carew's) "On a Gentlewoman Walking in the Snow." And a further link between the two poems is suggested by the fact that both appear in the same manuscript (Malone 21). It is also remarkable that one of the very few examples of a double epithet (a characteristic of the "Splendora" poems) in Cartwright occurs in this poem (l. 5, "easy-tutor'd").

5 *easy-tutour'd.* Goffin observes that Cartwright is fond of the image expressed by the word "tutored." He compares the "tutor'd Oath" in line 37 of "Falshood" and the "Tears, shed from Instructed Eyes" in line 3 of "Confession."

26 *whence the rose and Lilly grow.* I refer the reader to Goffin's excellent note—too long to quote here—in which he discusses, with illustrations, the rise of this favorite conceit in English poetry.

A SONG OF DALLIANCE

Texts.—*Sportive Wit* (1656), sigs. [c6]^v–[c7]^r (here reprinted); *Parnassus Biceps* (1656), pages 136-37.

These verses were reprinted from *Parnassus Biceps* (1656) with the title "Love's Courtship" in Volume VI of Dryden's *Miscellany* (1716), pages 405-6; (1727), pages 333-34.

A. H. Bullen reprinted this poem in his *Speculum Amantis* (1902), pages 10–12. He praises the verses in the highest terms, calling them (p. x) "magnificent" and the "finest of all Cartwright's poems." He goes on to suggest that if Cartwright indeed wrote more poems of this order—not of course for publication!—his extraordinary contemporary reputation is more easy to understand. Grierson (*Metaphysical Lyrics and Poems of the Seventeenth Century*, 1921, p. xxxvi) writes: "His [Carew's] *Ecstasy* is the most daring and poetically the happiest of the imitations of Donne's clever if outrageous elegies; Cartwright's *Song of Dalliance* its nearest rival."

PARCHMENT

Text.—*Works* (1651), page 214.

1 *Shepherds Wear . . . only Gray.* Goffin quotes from Greene's *Friar Bacon and Friar Bungay:*

> Proportion'd as was Paris, when, in grey,
> He courted Oenon in the vale by Troy.

In the *Gentleman's Magazine* (March, 1833, p. 216) the Reverend J. Mitford gives two other quotations, one from Greene and one from Peele, to show that such "was the phrase for a homely shepherd's garb." See Dyce's note to the above passage from *Friar Bacon and Friar Bungay*, where he notices Mitford's article and adds another example, also dealing with Paris and his love for Oenone, from Greene's *Orlando Furioso* (*Dramatic and Poetical Works of Greene and Peele*, ed. A. Dyce, 1861, p. 158). We should not forget, however, Milton's "uncouth Swain" who rose and "twitch'd his Mantle blew."

FALSHOOD

Texts.—Addit. MS. 19,268, fol. 9; Folger MS. 2071.6, pages 90–91; *Works* (1651), pages 215–16.

The two manuscript versions of this poem deserve special notice since they offer a text which differs radically at times from that of 1651 (see the variant readings). There is no question, however, of the superiority of the 1651 text considered as poetry.

Goffin styles this poem "One of the most living of Cartwright's pieces," and notices that the first two stanzas were recently quoted in the *Daily Mirror* (May 21, 1912).

53 *make thee true to all*. Compare the reversal of this conceit in "A Song" in *A Crew of Kind London Gossips* (1663), page 79:

> Since thou hast been false to many
> Be not constant now to any.

Beauty and Deniall

Text.—*Works* (1651), pages 217-18.

Women

Text.—*Works* (1651), page 218.

Compare Thomas Brown's epigram (*The Remains of Mr. Thomas Brown*, 1720, p. 240):

> In Marriage are two Things allow'd,
> A Wife in Wedding Sheets, and in a Shroud:
> How can a Marry'd State then be a-curst
> Since the last Day's as happy as the first?

Both Cartwright's and Brown's lines are adaptations of an epigram from the Greek Anthology (XI, 381): "Every woman is a source of annoyance, but she has two good seasons, the one in her bridal chamber and the other when she is dead." See K. McEuen, *Classical Influence upon the Tribe of Ben* (1939), page 244.

2 *Nuptial, or her Winding Sheet*. Compare Dryden's "Upon the Death of the Lord Hastings" (l. 4): "To bring a winding for a wedding sheet."

To Cupid

Texts.—*Works* (1651), pages 218-19; Henry Lawes, *Ayres and Dialogues* (1655), page 8.

To Venus

Texts.—Lawes' autographed MS., page 152; *Works* (1651), page 219; Henry Lawes, *Ayres and Dialogues* (1653), page 7; (1669), pages 8-9. Goffin appears to make the 1653 Lawes edition the basis of his text.

2 *spightfull Boy*. I have adopted the reading of the Lawes autographed MS.; the "sprightfull" of all the printed texts,

though suitable enough as an epithet for Cupid, seems wrong in the present context.

9-10 *Lest one day . . . clip the Wantons wings . . . Bow*. Compare Lyly's *Gallathea* (ca. 1585), III, iv: "As for thee *Cupid*, I will breake thy bowe, and burne thine arrowes, binde thy handes, clyp thy wings, and fetter thy feete"; and Spenser's *Faerie Queene*, III, vi, 21 and 24:

> The like that mine, may be your paine another tide. . . .
> Ile clip his wanton wings, that he no more shall flye.

While all three passages probably reflect the influence of the first *Idyllium* of Moschus, some other more immediate common source seems to be indicated.

A SIGH SENT TO HIS ABSENT LOVE

Texts.—Addit. MS. 19,268, fol. 7ᵛ (printed below); Folger MS. 2071.6, pages 86-87; Shakespeare, *Poems* (1640), sig. [L7]ʳ (agrees closely with the British Museum manuscript version); *Works* (1651), pages 219-20.

Since one of the manuscript versions (Addit. MS. 19,268, fol. 7ᵛ) differs considerably from the text of the *Works* (1651), I print it, collated with the printed copy in Shakespeare's *Poems* (1640), in full.

A sigh sent to his Mistresse
I sent a sigh into my mistresse eare[,]
Which went her way and never cam there[;]
I hastned after least som other fayre
Shold mildly entertayne this travelling ayre[:]
Each flowrie garden I did search for fear   [5]
it might mistake a lilie for her eare[,]
and having ther tooke lodginge might still dwel
housed in the concave of a christall bell[;]
I sought amongst the birds[,] thinking it might
resort for companie to the winged flight[,]   [10]
and soe play trewant, but alasse each note
they merrily did warble in the throate
told me it was not there, by that mirths signe[,]

1 into] unto *1640*
2 never] ne're *1640*
3 hastned] hasted *1640*
7 might still] still might *1640*
8 housed] Hous'd *1640*

a] *Omitted 1640*
10 winged] wing'd *1640*
13 was not . . . signe] was but the mirthy signe *1640*

> if one were there[,] I knew twas none of mine.
> at last on[e] frostie morning I did spy   [15]
> this subtle wanderer iourneying in the sky,
> At sight of me it trembled, And for feare
> It greivinge fell & dropt into a teare[.]
> I bore it to my St and prayd her take
> this new borne of spring for the m^rs sake[,]   [20]
> which she receavinge granted me her lipp
> and soe preferrd it to her softer tippe[:]
> and now this pendant burthen pleasd her [placed here]
> heares each thinge that is whisperd in her eare[:]
> I grive 'cause I have lost a teare & shee   [25]
> With sorow is more happie far then me[;]
> Yet ther is on[e] remedie left, let her to ease me
> give me but on[e] of hers & soe she'l please me.

Poems of this type and theme were common among Cartwright's contemporaries. Compare, for example, three poems by William Strode, "A Song on a Sigh," "To his Paper," and "To the Same," in all of which the general development of the thought is similar, though there are no actual verbal parallels (*Poetical Works*, ed. B. Dobell, 1907, pp. 6, 135, 136). See also John Day's "The Parliament of Bees" (1641), Character VIII, and Henry Vaughan's "The Sigh." A more interesting parallel, however, is offered by William Browne's "A Sigh from Oxford" (*Poems*, ed. G. Goodwin, 1894, II, 201–8), from which Cartwright seems to have taken several hints for his own poem. Compare with Cartwright's verses the following lines of Browne:

> When that office thou hast done,
> And the lady lastly won,
> Let the air thou left'st the girl,
> Turn a drop, and then a pearl;
> Which I wish that she should wear
> For a pendant in her ear;
> And its virtue still shall be,
> To detect all flattery.
>   (45–52)

---

14   mine.] thine? *1640*
16   this] The *1640*
     iourneying] *Omitted 1640*
18   *Omitted 1640*
19   bore] bare *1640*
20   of spring] off-spring *1640*
21   receavinge] perceiving *1640*
23   pleasd her] now doth heare *1640*
24   heares] *Omitted 1640*
     that is] thats *1640*
26   happie] happier *1640*
27   Yet ther . . . ease me] Yet there is remedy left to ease me *1640*

> If thou meet a Sigh, which she
> Hath but coldly sent to me,
> Kiss it, for thy warmer air
> Will dissolve into [? it to] a tear.
>   *(103–6)*
>
> With that Regent, from that hour,
> Leiger lie Ambassador:
> Keep our truce unbroke, prefer
> All the suits I send to her.
>   *(143–46)*

And compare R. Fletcher, "A Sigh" (*Martial His Epigrams*, 1656, pp. 149–51):

> Fly thou pretty active part
> To the Mistris of my heart. . . .

This poem also concludes with the inevitable reference to metamorphosis into a tear:

> Return to me my pretty dear,
> And I will hide thee in a tear.

See also "To his Mrs Walking in ye snow" in the Doubtful Poems, p. 569.

1   *I sent a Sigh.* Goffin compares the first line of Cartwright's "Absence":

> Fly, O fly, sad Sigh, and bear. . . .

12   *Then grieving fell . . . Tear.* Compare "On a Gentlewoman Walking in the Snow" (*Poetical Works of William Strode*, ed. B. Dobell, 1907, p. 41):

> And overcome with whiteness there,
> For griefe it thaw'd into a teare.

21–24   Compare the conceit in these lines with stanzas 9 and 10 of Donne's "A Valediction of My Name, in the Window."

22   *Upon her tipp.* I have adopted the reading of the Folger MS. in preference to "Lip" of the 1651 text.

SADNESS

   Text.—*Works* (1651), pages 220–21.
   This poem is quoted in full in the *Retrospective Review*, IX (1824), 164–65. The first two stanzas show Cartwright at his best in the subtle handling of rhythms to express a mood.

7-11 *In which double Shade, . . . fade.* Coleridge copied the following version of these lines into his commonplace book:

> There in some darksome shade
> Methinks I'd weep
> Myself asleep,
> And there forgotten fade.

These lines have always been considered one of Coleridge's own metrical experiments (No. 10). Professor Earl Wasserman drew my attention to their origin.

CORINNA'S TOMB

Text.—*Works* (1651), pages 221-22.

See an adaptation of parts of Cartwright's poem in Aaron Hill's "Belinda's *Grave*" (*Works*, 1754, III, 313).

TO THE MEMORY OF A SHIPWRACKT VIRGIN

Text.—*Works* (1651), pages 223-24.

This poem is quoted in full in the *Retrospective Review*, IX (1824), 165-66, where, as Goffin notices, it is referred to as an example of Cartwright's "fanciful and perhaps somewhat conceited style." A comparison of Cartwright's lines with two other contemporary poems, both written on a similar occasion, Milton's "Lycidas" and Cleveland's "On the Memory of Mr. *Edward King* drown'd in the *Irish* Seas" (*Works*, 1687, pp. 61-62), makes an interesting and enlightening study. It is pointless to carry coals to the praise of Milton's "Lycidas," but Cartwright's and Cleveland's verses are not so well known. Each is an excellent example of the author's school. "Lycidas," of course, apart from its classical associations, defies classification except as "Miltonic," but the other two poems, both alike lacking Milton's philosophical seriousness, are more readily pigeonholed. Cleveland's lines, an intellectual orgy run to seed, are a terrible warning to the so-called metaphysical poet. Conceit upon conceit, couplet upon couplet of arid, wire-drawn subtleties is the unpleasant result. Cartwright's poem, on the other hand, though by no means free from conceits, employs them with all the simple sensuous temper of the Cavalier poets, chastened with the clarity and polish of a Son of Ben. I cannot agree with Mr. Paul

Saunders (*Anathema*, 1935, Vol. I, No. 2) who thinks the poem "fails somewhat toward the end." Indeed the finest lines in the poem are the last four, lines not unworthy of the author of *Lycidas*:

> Whiles thus her death I weep
> Swim down my murmuring Lute; move thou the deep
> Into soft numbers, as thou passest by,
> And make her Fate become her Elegy.

In view of their common subject it is worth observing the "whether" series in Milton's *Lycidas* (ll. 154-62) and in the opening lines (1-6) of Cartwright's poem. Again this same "whether" series seems to link Cartwright's poem with Dryden's "Ode to Mrs. Anne Killigrew." The implied "whether" sequence in Dryden's poem has been attributed to the influence of *Lycidas*, in as much as the poem as a whole gives evidence of a careful study of Milton's handling of elegiac form (see Miss Ruth Wallerstein, "On the Death of Mrs. Killigrew: The Perfecting of a Genre," *Studies in Philology*, XLIV [July, 1947], p. 525). I would like to suggest however, that the development of the thought in the first stanza, the series of "suggested locations" for the departed soul leading up to a statement that the poet wishes to address her, follows closely the structure of Cartwright's introductory lines and suggests very strongly that in this part of the poem it is Cartwright, more than Milton, whom Dryden is recalling.

TO A PAINTERS HANDSOME DAUGHTER

Texts.—*Works* (1651), pages 224-25; *Parnassus Biceps* (1656), pages 45-46.

LESBIA ON HER SPARROW

Text.—*Works* (1651), pages 225-26.

Cartwright's lines are suggested by Catullus' lyrics (Loeb ed., Nos. II and III) which lament the death of a sparrow belonging to his mistress, Lesbia. Goffin, ignoring Catullus, says that Cartwright was "probably thinking of Skelton's *Phylyp Sparrow*." Though, of course, Skelton's poem is in the Catullan tradition, it seems more than probable that Cartwright knew the earlier English poem, since it is possible to detect several verbal echoes of Skelton in the later poet's work. For a full account of Cartwright's debt to Catullus see J. A. S. McPeek, *Catullus in Strange and Distant Britain* (1939, pp. 65-67), and J. B. Emperor, *The Catullian Influence in English Lyric Poetry, Circa 1600-1650*, University of Missouri Studies (1928, pp. 70-71). Mr. McPeek notes that Cartwright's poem belongs "in its main development to the Skeltonian tradition (p. 65)."

In the eighteenth century Aaron Hill adapted Cartwright's lyric, calling it "*Lesbia's Lamentation*, on the Death of her Sparrow; altered from *Mr. Cartwright*" (*Works*, 1754, III, 153-54). Hill's version appeared again in *The Public Advertiser* (1787), No. 16622. Cartwright's poem was quoted in full in the *Retrospective Review*, IX (1824), 166-67.

THE GNAT

Text.—*Works* (1651), pages 226-27.

The central conceit of this poem—the destruction of a fly or other small insect in the radiance of a lady's eye—was a favorite among the poets of the time. Jonson uses it in his "Hour-Glass" (*Works*, ed. Gifford-Cunningham, 1903, III, 285), where it occurs as the one original thought in a poem which is otherwise only a translation of two short Latin poems by Jerom Amaltheus (see Gifford's note). We may also notice Carew's "A Fly that Flew into his Celia's Eye" (*Poems*, ed. J. W. Ebsworth, 1893, pp. 34-35) and Cleveland's "Upon a Fly that flew into a Lady's Eye, and there lay buried in a Tear" (*Works*, 1687, pp. 231-32). Shadwell threatens to throw some light upon the origin of the conceit, but unfortunately credits his readers with more knowledge than most of us in the present day possess (*The Amorous Bigotte*, *Works*, ed. M. Summers, 1927, V, 61):

> I am so dazled with your radiant Eye,
> That like the silly, and unheedful flye,
> As sweetly the Heroick Poet sings,
> At that bright flame I've sing'd m' advent'rous wings.

It is not at all impossible that by the "Heroick Poet" Shadwell is only referring to his favorite, Jonson.

Aaron Hill makes use of Cartwright's verses in his poem also called "The Gnat" (*Works*, 1754, III, 160-61).

1-2 *A Gnat mistaking . . . rules the Day.* Compare Cleveland's poem, cited above, lines 5-6:

> Or didst thou foolishly mistake
> The glowing Morn in that Day-break?

4 *Wont in the Sun-Beams so to play.* Compare Carew's poem, cited above, lines 1-2:

> While this Fly lived, she used to play
> In the bright sunshine all the day.

7 *Jet doth ravish straws.* Jet, like amber, when rubbed, generates sufficient electrical energy to attract light objects. Goffin notices Sir Thomas Browne's discussion in *Pseudodoxia Epidemica* (1646), Book II, Chapter iv.

16 *She thence enforc'd an easie Teare.* Compare Carew's poem, cited above, line 16:

> She fell; and with her dropp'd a tear.

LOVE-TEARES

Text.—*Works* (1651), page 227.

AT A DRY DINNER

Text.—*Works* (1651), page 227.

Although the title sufficiently explains the point of this epigram, the text itself is not very clear.

A BILL OF FARE

Text.—*Works* (1651), pages 227-29.

Goffin (*Poems*, xviii-xix) thinks this poem was occasioned by Laud's prohibition of the "Westminster supper" held annually on a Friday night by those members of Christ Church who, like Cartwright, were old Westminster boys. I feel a little doubtful on this point, but have no better suggestion to offer.

30 Keckerman. "Keckerman (1573-1609) was a German scholar who systematized many branches of knowledge. He was evidently commonly regarded as a standard of intellectual subtlety." (Goffin).

61-62 *like small Birds, . . . sit and Sing.* For some reason, not very clear to anybody else perhaps, these lines always remind me of the following stanza in Tennyson's *In Memoriam* (XXI):

> Behold, ye speak an idle thing:
> Ye never knew the sacred dust:
> I do but sing because I must,
> And pipe but as the linnets sing.

THE CHAMBERMAIDS POSSET

Texts.—*Works* (1651), pages 229-32; *Marrow of Complements* (1655), pages 49-51.

Goffin's suggestion that Cartwright's verses were meant to be sung to the tune of "Cock Lorrel" is plausible, since the metrical scheme in both this and Jonson's song (from *The Gipsies Metamorphosed*, 1621) is the same. The device that gives this stanza form its peculiar lilt and rough force is the regular use of a double, or at least feminine, rhyme at the end of every second and fourth line.

3 *He propos'd fifteen.* Cartwright, here as elsewhere, is ridiculing the interminable sermons of the Puritan faction. Even in the Anglican church it was not uncommon in those days to see "the glass turned," but, as Cartwright later humorously remarks, under a Puritan Poundtext "The Glass was Compell'd still Rubbers to run." Walter Scott in *Old Mortality* (Vol. I, Ch. xviii) describes one of these Marathon sermons, delivered by a certain Gabriel Kettledrummle, a Presbyterian dissenter:

> The discourse which he pronounced upon this subject was divided into fifteen heads, each of which was garnished with seven uses of application, two of consolation, two of terror, two declaring the causes of backsliding and of wrath, and one announcing the promised and expected deliverance. . . . At times he was familiar and colloquial — now he was loud, energetic, and boisterous. Some parts of his discourse might be called sublime, and other sunk below burlesque.

3 *gravell'd.* Nonplussed. Goffin gives several examples of the word used in this sense.

5 *Red-hatted Vertue's.* The so-called cardinal virtues of ancient philosophy: justice, prudence, fortitude, and temperance. By the "one" which "was not," Cartwright means, I suppose, temperance. I have retained the apostrophe in "Vertue's"

19 *Garden of* Leyden. Cartwright is thinking of the strong Anabaptist faction raised by John of Leyden in the city of Münster about 1533. A readable account of the whole matter, written, of course, by the opposing party, was published in 1642 under the title, *A Warning for England* (*Harleian Miscellany*, 1810, V, 253–64).

20 *some did our own* Universities *bring*. This is a bob at Cambridge, particularly Emmanuel College, founded in 1585, which was a hotbed of Puritanism.

23 Buchanan'*s dangerous Passions*. George Buchanan (1506–82), one-time instructor of Montaigne and later (1570) tutor to James VI, was the author of a number of important historical works. Since he was a supporter of the reformed church, his books found favor among the Puritan factions, particularly *De Jure Regni apud Scotos* (1579), in which he advocated kingship by election and the justice of tyrannicide under certain conditions. The book was naturally one of the mainstays of the Long Parliament. In the phrase "dangerous Passions" Cartwright may intend some reflection upon the personal character of Buchanan, who is reputed to have been of an irascible temper.

29 *Practicall Piety*. Probably the title of one of the myriad Puritan devotional pamphlets. Perhaps an error for Lewis Bayly's *Practice of Piety* (1619, eleventh ed.).

30 Histrio-Mastix. A book by William Prynne, published in 1633, the full title of which runs: *Histrio-Mastix, The Player's Scourge, or Actors Tragedie*. At the time of its publication, the work raised a storm of protest in court circles because of a supposed slur upon the person of the Queen for taking part in court masques. With this "libel" as a lever, the Star Chamber proceeded with unusual severity against the author, sentencing Prynne to pay a fine of five thousand pounds to the King, to forfeit his position as a lawyer, to lose both his ears, and to be exposed in the pillory. Among Royalist writers of the time, the book was made a butt for all wits, the name alone being sufficient to summon up all the hated attributes of Puritanism. That it should form part of a "Leviticall

Wench's" posset was in the nature of things inevitable. Goffin notes that Prynne was expelled from Oxford in 1634 and suggests that "Prynne's continual praise of that 'other Mr Cartwright,' referred to in this poem as *T.C.*," may have been "an additional cause of irritation" to the poet.

31 *T. C's confuted Text.* As Goffin points out, *T.C.* refers to the Puritan divine, Thomas Cartwright. Goffin also notices the following couplet from Monmouth's commendatory verses, prefixed to the *Works* (1651), sig. [¹a7]ʳ:

> Yet *Cartwright* makes amends by his cleer Wit
> For all the Schismes the other *Cartwright* writ.

32 *close-noated.* Having the hair cut short. See Rider's *Dictionarie* (1633): "To notte, or cut the haire away. Notted or clipped." Cartwright is poking fun at the Puritan practice of cropping the hair.

33 Stript whipt Abuses. As Goffin observes, Cartwright is referring to George Wither's *Abuses Stript and Whipt* (1613), a book for which the author was imprisoned in the Marshalsea for several months. Though Wither was a Puritan, it was not until 1642 that he actually declared himself for the Parliament.

34 *Motto not now in fashion.* Cartwright is again aiming at Wither, whose *Motto* (1621) bore the following "word": "Nec habeo, nec careo, nec curo." Goffin points out that Wither here pictures the "hero," himself, as one "who lacks worldly but not spiritual possessions, and fears no mere terrestrial assaults." John Taylor, the Water Poet, wrote an answer to Wither's poem (1621).

37 Clever *and* Doddisme. John Dod (1549?–1645) was a Puritan minister, best remembered as the author of the "Sermon on Malt," but known principally to his contemporaries for his *Exposition of the Commandments* (1632), a work which gained him the nickname of "Decalogue Dod." Lowndes (*Bibliographer's Manual*, 1858, II, 654) writes: "The sayings of this puritan divine were once proverbial, and were often printed in a small tract or broad sheet." Dod published most of his writings in collaboration with a certain Richard Cleaver, about whom nothing further seems to be known. This fact alone, however, sufficiently explains Cartwright's meaning.

Corbet in his "Iter Boreale" (*Poems*, ed. O. Gilchrist, 1807, p. 175) again pairs them:

> And if you have no orders 'tis the better,
> So you have Dods Praecepts, or Cleavers Letter.

41 *Doctrines, and Uses.* Terms commonly used by the Puritans in dividing their long-winded scriptural expositions. Compare Cleveland's "The Puritan" (*Works*, 1687, p. 357):

> With running Text, the Nam'd forsaken,
> With *For* and *But*, both by Sense shaken,
> Cheap Doctrines forc'd, wild Uses taken,
> Both sometimes one, by Mark mistaken,
> With any thing to any shapen.

See also Cleveland's "The Schismatick" (*Works*, 1687, p. 378) and Cartwright's *The Ordinary*, I, iii.

44 *siz'd Pint.* A standard pint measure.

48 Christian Liberty. One of the favorite cant expressions of the Puritan sects. See Calvin's *Institutes* (1561), Book III, Chapter 19, "Of Christian libertie." The phrase was naturally very frequently made fun of by writers on the Anglican side. The following, for example, is a typical fling at it (*Merry Drollerie*, Part II, n.d., "New *England* described," p. 105):

> Loe in this Church all shall be free
> To Enjoy their Christian liberty;
> All things made common, void of strife,
> Each man may take anothers wife,
> And keep a hundred maids, if need,
> To multiply, increase, and breed.

See also Etherege's *She Wou'd if She Cou'd*, 1668 (1735 ed., p. 9).

49 Crumbs of Comfort. "There were many editions of *The Crumbs of Comfort*, a pious and non-partisan book of meditation and prayer. 'A Prayer for God's protection of his Church in respect of the present Troubles in it' is an example of one of the prayers" (Goffin). In spite of Goffin's view that the book was nonpartisan, I suspect that *The Crumbs of Comfort* was not much to the taste of the strong Anglican party. Cartwright's reference is certainly not complimentary, and compare the following extract from one of Cleveland's letters (*Works*, 1687, p. 98): "Is it not pity, that the pure Extract

of sanctified *Emmanuel*, parboil'd there in the Pipkin of Predestination, and since well read in the Sick-man's Salve and the Crums of Comfort, and liberally fed with all the Minced Meat in Divinity?" Old Foresight, in Congreve's *Love for Love* (1695), III, xiii, asks for this book in a repentant moment. See also Robert South's uncomplimentary description of the book as "furniture of old women's closets" (*Sermons Preached upon Several Occasions*, 1843, I, 67).

53 *An Ell* London-*measure*. It was apparently the custom for London merchants to give a little over and above standard measure. Cartwright again speaks of a "*London* measure Beard" in *The Ordinary*, III, v, and Suckling in the first Prologue to *Aglaura* writes:

> As in all bargains else — men ever get
> All they can in; will have London measure,
> A handful over in their very pleasure.

Goffin, while correctly explaining the phrase, destroys the sense of the text by printing "Ell-London measure."

59 *Rubbers*. Although common in the technical sense of a set of three or five games, "Rubbers" is here used with a rather broader sense. It is the only example of such usage in the *NED* (Goffin).

61–64 *The Pig . . . Black Persecution skin*. As Goffin observes, the eyes of a roasted pig, when it was "done to a turn," dropped out. We may compare Shadwell's words (*The Humourists, Works*, ed. M. Summers, 1927, I, 195): "Eyes staring like Pigs half roasted." Massinger, however, seems to tell a slightly different tale (*The Old Law*, III, ii):

> Methinks your luck's good that your eyes are in
>   still,
> Mine would have dropt out like a pig's half
>   roasted.

Whatever the culinary niceties of the question, Cartwright's meaning is clear enough: the roast pig, which, before Sir John had "suffer'd his drench," used to come to the table in a half-cooked state, now, because of the interminable length of his discourse, arrives burnt to a cinder. The implied comparison of an underdone pig to a "half-baked" Puritan aspirant was made specially apposite by the reference to the "white staring Eyes" of the former. For some reason, perhaps because they spent so much time with eyes upcast in meditation, Puritans were frequently distinguished by their opponents as having white eyes. Cartwright, as Goffin observes, has already referred to this characteristic in his poem to Bryan Duppa "After the Publick Act at *Oxon.* 1634" (l. 61). Mayne (*The City-Match*, 1637, IV, i), writing of a Puritan, observes: "No, I'll never trust again / A woman with white eyes." And Cleveland, in his invaluable poem "The Puritan" (*Works*, 1687, p. 355), begins his description as follows:

> With Face and Fashion to be known,
> For one of sure Election,
> With Eyes all white, and many a Groan,
> With Neck aside to draw in Tone,
> With Harp in's Nose, or he is none.

67 *pouch'd the deceit.* Swallowed the bait. "To pouch" in this technical sense means "to take into the stomach" and is used only of fishes and certain types of birds (*NED*). The earliest recorded use of the term in this special sense is 1653, several years later than Cartwright's.

68 *An Advouzon did bait him to make all sure.* Although the general meaning of this line seems clear enough, I cannot explain the use of "advowson" in its present context. Cockeram's *English Dictionarie* (1623) correctly defines "advowson" as the "Right which a man hath to present a Clergieman to a spirituall Benefice." In Cartwright, however, the word seems to mean the "promise" or "bestowal" of a church living. Cleveland also seems to give a similar turn to it in the opening lines of his poem, "To *Julia* to expedite her Promise" (*Works*, 1687, p. 6):

> Since 'tis my Doom, Love's Undershrieve,
>   Why this Reprieve?
> Why doth my She Advowson fly
>   Incumbency?

On a Gentlewomans Silk-hood

Texts.—Addit. MS. 22,602, fols. 14-15 (signed "T. Cartwright"); Harl. MS. 7319, fol. 23 (this is a late manuscript and bears the date 1675); Mal. MS. 21, fols. 75-76; Folger

MS. 452.1, pages 54–55 (before 1661); *Works* (1651), pages 232–34.

A much shortened and garbled version of Cartwright's verses appeared in *The Marrow of Complements* (1655), page 70:

> *The presentation of a Sylke Hood.*
> So Love appear'd breaking his way
> When from the Chaos he brought Day,
> Drawne from the tender bud, so showes
> The halfe-seene glory of the Rose,
> As you when veyl'd, and I may sweare [5]
> (Viewing your beauty) buddeth there,
> Such doubtfull life had groves, where Rods
> And twigs, at last did shoote up Gods,
> When shade then darkeneth the face,
> May I not reverence the place. [10]
> Accept this vaile then (sweete) for I
> Affect a clouded Deitie.

Goffin observes that Cartwright's poem has been altered to suit the requirements of the presentation, and that even the meter has been changed from pentameter to tetrameter.

Compare Corbet's poem "On Ladies Veils" (*Poems*, ed. O. Gilchrist, 1807, p. 232). This poem is usually accompanied by "An Answer" (British Museum, Addit. MS. 22,602; Bodleian Library, Malone MS. 21, fols. 46–47). See also a short poem by James Howell (*Familiar Letters*, 1705, p. 204) entitled "Upon *Clorindas* Mask," and another set of verses by Edmund Prestwick, called "To a Lady refusing to unvaile" (*Hippolitus . . . Together with divers other Poems*, 1651, p. 92). See also Basse's *Three Pastoral Elegies* (1602), Elegy II (*Poetical Works*, ed. R. W. Bond, 1893, p. 54).

It seems to me likely that Farquhar's "Poetical Dialogue between you and I" (printed in one of his letters, *Complete Works*, ed. Charles Stonehill, 1930, II, 305) owes some hints to Cartwright's verses.

The manuscript version of Cartwright's poem in Folger MS. 452.1 is followed (No. 69, p. 56) by some verses entitled "Vpon the same." The first seven lines, obviously a separate poem, may be found in substantially the same form in *Witts Recreations* (1650), sig. [Q7]r, but the remaining lines I have not been able to identify:

Vpon the same.
Like to the selfe-inhabiting snaile
Or like a Squirrell penthous'd with her owne tayle
Such is my Mistresse hid in her veyle.
Or like a Carpe that is lost in the mudding
Or more like to a great bagg-pudding
For as the pudding the bagg is within
Soe is she lost in her taffety Ginne.

There is not halfe soe warme a fire
In the fruition as desire;
When we have reap'd the fruite of paine
Possession makes vs poore againe:
Sense is too nigardly for blisse
And payes vs dully with what is,
But Fancy's liberall she gives all
That can within her largenesse fall.
Veyle therefore still whilst I diuine
The richnesse of that hidden myne;
Ile make imagination tell
All wealth that can in beauty dwell;
And thus the highly valewed ore
Earth's darke Exchecquer keepes in store.
Our eyes, our apprehensions theefe,
They binde vnlimited beleefe;
We see all while we nothing see
Disclosure oft proues Robberie:
For if you shine not fayrest being showne
I made this Cabbinet for a Bristow stone.

29 *So Love appear'd.* Cartwright is referring to one of the ancient Greek legends which made the God of Love first-born of all the gods. See Plato, "The Symposium" (*Works*, trans. B. Jowett, III, 301):

Phaedrus began by affirming that Love is a mighty god, and wonderful among gods and men, but especially wonderful in his birth. For that he is the eldest of the gods is an honour to him; and a proof of this is, that of his parents there is no memorial; neither poet nor prose-writer has ever affirmed that he had any.

Goffin says that both the manuscripts (Harl. MS. 7319 and Folger MS. 452.1 were unknown to him) read "Jove" instead of "Love." This is not the case, however; none of the manuscripts reads "Jove."

31-32 *Newly awak'd . . . half seen, half hid, . . . Rose.* Compare

Fairfax's translation (1600) of Tasso's *Jerusalem Delivered*, XVI, 14:

> The gently budding rose, quoth she, behold,
> That first scant peeping forth with virgin beams,
> Half ope, half shut, her beauties doth upfold
> In their dear leaves, and less seen, fairer seems.

See also Spenser's version of Tasso's lines in *The Faerie Queene*, II, xii, 74. Quarles has his own version of the conceit in *Argalus and Parthenia*, 1629 (*Works*, ed. A. Grosart, 1881, III, 270):

> ... a milke-white *vaile* did hide
> Her blushing face; which, nere the lesse discloses
> Some glimpse of red, like *lawne* ore-spredding *roses*.

52 *Retrivall.* A return to, or reestablishment of, something; the earliest use of the word recorded in the *NED*. See Rider's *Dictionarie* (1633): "Retrive, i. a seeking againe."

A Dream Broke

Text.—*Works* (1651), pages 234-35.

1-4 *As* Nilus *sudden Ebbing, . . . Fishes been.* Probably suggested by Ovid's *Metamorphoses*, I, 422-433. See the long note in the Variorum Spenser, *The Faerie Queene*, Book I, pages 184-187. Also compare *The Faerie Queene*, III, vi, 8.

21-24 *My Fancy shall . . . I'l think the rest.* Compare with the title of Cartwright's poem and with these lines Donne's "The Dream," lines 6-10:

> My Dreame thou brok'st not but continued'st it,
> Thou art so truth, that thoughts of thee suffice,
> To make dreames truths; and fables histories;
> Enter these armes, for since thou thoughtst it best,
> Not to dreame all my dreame, let's act the rest.

Loves Darts

Text.—*Works* (1651), pages 235-36.

5 *Whether . . . Doves.* The line is unmetrical, containing four instead of three major stresses.

38 *Till we that make them Darts.* This is the reading of the 1651 text and of both editors, but it is certainly corrupt. Either one

of two emendations restores the sense, however: transpose "we" and "that," or, read " 'Tis" for "Till."

PARTHENIA FOR HER SLAIN ARGALUS

Text.—*Works* (1651), pages 237-38.

As Goffin observes, the story of Argalus and Parthenia is originally to be found in Sidney's *Arcadia* (1590), Books I, 5, 7, 8, and III, 12, 16, but was adapted by Francis Quarles in his long poem, *Argalus and Parthenia* (1629). Although Cartwright was very likely acquainted with Quarles' poem, there is nothing in his verses which may not equally well have been suggested by Sidney's account. Indeed, in lines 19-24, it is possible perhaps to trace Sidney's hand (see below). Quarles follows Sidney with almost slavish care, changing almost nothing and making only two important additions. Over all, however, he casts a mantel of almost intolerably embroidered expansiveness. Whatever the source of the poem, it is not one of Cartwright's happiest efforts.

The Parthenia whom Fletcher in his *Purple Island* (Cantos x–xii) celebrates as the type of "chastity in the single" has no connection, apart from her name, with the heroine of Sidney's romance.

19-24 With these lines compare Sidney's *Arcadia* (1590), III, 12 (ed. A. Feuillerat, 1912, p. 427), which I quote from a contemporary edition of 1627, page 276:

> But while the other sought to stanch his remediles wounds, she with her kisses made him happy: for his last breath was delivered into her mouth.

Quarles omits this circumstance.

31-36 This account of Amphialus, whom Cartwright calls the "Proud Spoyler," does not agree with either Sidney's or Quarles' accounts, in both of which, after the moving intervention of Parthenia, he appears in a repentant and sympathetic role.

ARIADNE DESERTED BY THESEUS ... THUS COMPLAINS

Texts.—Lawes' autographed MS., pages 254-[60] (see note to l. 85); Harl. MS. 6931, fols. 88-90; *Works* (1651), pages 238-42; Lawes, *Ayres and Dialogues* (1653), pages 1-7.

This poem, reprinted from *Works* (1651), appears in Volume I of Dryden's *Miscellany* (1716, pp. 236–38; 1727, pp. 228–30).

The story of Theseus and Ariadne has come down to us in a variety of forms, almost none of them agreeing in the essential matters concerning her desertion by Theseus and the manner of her death. Plutarch, in his "Life of Theseus" (*Plutarch's Lives*, tr. North, ed. of 1676, p. 8), gives a good summary of the case:

> They report many other things also touching this matter, and specially of *Ariadne*: but there is no troth nor certainty in it. For some say, that *Ariadne* hung her self for sorrow, when she saw that *Theseus* had cast her off. Others write, that she was transported by mariners into the Isle of Naxos, where she was married unto *Œnarus* the Priest of *Bacchus*: and they think that *Theseus* left her, because she was in love with another, . . . Others hold opinion, that *Ariadne* had two children by *Theseus*: the one of them was named *Œnopia*, and the other *Staphylus*. . . . But one *Paenon* . . . reciteth this clean after another sort, and contrary to all other: saying, that *Theseus* by tempest was driven with [*sic*] the Isle of Cyprus, having with him *Ariadne*, which was great with child, and so sore sea-sick, that she was not able to abide it. In so much as he was forced to put her aland, and himself afterwards returning aboard, hoping to save his ship against the storm, was compelled forthwith to loose into the sea. The women of the countrey did courteously receive and intreat *Ariadne*: . . . they did their best by all possible means to save her, but she died notwithstanding in labour, and could never be delivered: So she was honourably buried by the Ladies of Cyprus. *Theseus* not long after returned thither again, who took her death marvellous heavily, and left money with the inhabitants of the Countrey, to sacrifice unto her yearly: . . . And yet there are of the Naxians, that report this otherwise: saying, There were two *Minoes*, and two *Ariadnes*, whereof the one was married to *Bacchus* in the Isle of Naxos, of whom *Staphylus* was born: and the other the youngest, was ravished and carried away by *Theseus*, who afterward forsook her, and she came into the Isle of Naxos with her Nurse called *Corcyna*, . . . The second *Ariadne* died there also . . . .

Although Plutarch's account does not by any means exhaust all the stories of Ariadne's fortunes, it will serve to give some idea of the wealth of material which lay ready to the poet's hand. Cartwright's own version seems to be a combination of the legend as told by Ovid (*Heroides*, X) and by Catullus (No. LXIV); the opening stanza showing strong marks of Ovid's hand, the conclusion, of Catullus'. The body of the poem, however, and by far the major part, is so far as we know the work of Cartwright's own imagination, though

Mr. McPeek (*Catullus in Strange and Distant Britain*, 1939, pp. 20-23) questions Cartwright's originality and suggests (p. 273) that he is giving a free rendering of some hypothetical French poem. Apart from this, which I consider an unnecessary reservation, Mr. McPeek's account of the sources of the poem is excellent. I quote his conclusion (p. 23):

> It is hard to draw any positive conclusion from so confused a mass of detail. The method of narration is Ovidian; the themes of the punishment of Theseus, and the main elements of the Bacchic procession are apparently drawn from Catullus. It is to be doubted that Cartwright was the first to effect this curious bit of mortising.

J. B. Emperor (*The Catullian Influence in English Lyric Poetry, Circa 1600-1650*, University of Missouri Studies, 1928, pp. 72-73) ignores the strong Ovidian influences, stating that "the whole poem is obviously inspired by the episode of Ariadne in *Carm.* lxiv."

In addition to these Latin sources, it seems likely that Cartwright also had in mind the second idyll of Theocritus.

Miss Willa McClung Evans raises some interesting points in connection with this poem in *Henry Lawes, Musician and Friend of Poets* (1941), pages 161-65. Though admitting the possibility that Cartwright may have taken up the Ariadne theme on his own initiative, she suggests that it is not unlikely that Henry Lawes, inspired by Monteverdi's *Lamento d'Arianna* (perhaps through the influence of Milton), approached Cartwright with the suggestion that he should compose a kind of aria-libretto for him. She further suggests that both poem and music were actually composed during the Oxford siege, though any direct evidence for this assumption is lacking. Such a view clashes, of course, with Moseley's statement ("To the Reader") that he composed but "one Sheet" after he took holy orders in 1638, but, as we have seen before, this statement must not be taken too seriously.

Robert Shafer (*The English Ode to 1660*, 1918, p. 138) discusses this poem as an early example of irregular verse, in which "one is wholly at a loss to distinguish any difference in principle between Cartwright's practice as here illustrated and Cowley's." No mention is made of Cartwright's poem in George N. Shuster's *The English Ode from Milton to Keats* (1940)—surely an unwarranted omission. The following summary was prefixed to the text of the poem in Henry Lawes' *Ayres and Dialogues* (1653), page 1:

> The Story of *Theseus* and *Ariadne*, as much as concerns the ensuing Relation, is this.

Theseus going over into *Creet* to fight with the *Minotaure*, made his Father *Ægeus* this promise, that if he came off with Life and Victory, he would set up white sailes at his comming back, the Ship as he went out having black sailes in token of griefe: being come into *Creet*, *Ariadne* the Kings Daughter there fell in love with him, and gave him a Clew of thread, by which after he had slain the *Minotaure* he extricated himselfe out of that perplexed Labyrinth: having thus obtained the Victory, he carryed her along with him into the Island *Naxos*, where he tooke occasion to leave her as she was a sleep, and so hasting homeward, forgot to hoist the white sailes; his Father *Ægeus*, therefore, who stood upon a Rock, expecting his return, as soon as he perceived the black sailes, cast himselfe headlong into the Sea, from whom it was called the *Ægean* Sea. In this while, *Ariadne* complaining of *Theseus* his Infidelity, resolving to destroy her selfe, having made her own Epitaph, was comforted by *Bacchus*, who comming thither was enamoured of her Beauty, and took her to his protection.

Lawes' setting of Cartwright's verses seems to have been one of the most successful and popular of his more ambitious works. John Phillips and John Cobb, in the commendatory verses prefixed to the *Ayres and Dialogues*, both single out this song for special praise. More important than these, however, Milton makes particular mention of it in his sonnet "To Mr. H. Lawes, on his Aires," which appeared first in Henry and William Lawes' *Choice Psalmes Put into Musick for Three Voices* (1648):

> Thou honour'st Verse, and Verse must lend her wing
> To honour thee, the Priest of *Phœbus* Quire
> That tun'st their happiest lines in Hymn, or Story.

Goffin remarks that "story" here probably refers to Cartwright's poem on Ariadne. There is, however, no question about it, since in *Choice Psalmes* (1648) the word "story" is starred and the marginal comment reads: "The story of Ariadne set by him in Music." To find Milton referring thus appreciatively to Cartwright's poetry is worth a volume of lesser men's praise. Miss Evans (p. 214) notices an article by J. S. Smart ("The Italian Singer in Milton's Sonnets,"

Musical Antiquary, IV [Jan., 1913], pp. 91–97) in which he suggests that Cartwright's and Lawes' *Ariadne* (performed in character) was one of the songs by which "Emilia" caught Milton's interest.

This song of Ariadne also found favor with Pepys. In the *Diary*, under November, 1665, we find the following record:

> 19th (Lord's Day). Up, and after being trimmed, alone by water to Erith, all the way with my song book singing of Mr. Lawes's long recitative song in the beginning of his book.

Goffin notices that Cartwright's poem is reprinted in John Nichols' *Collection of Poems* (1780–82), I, 58–63.

1–5 *Theseus! . . . Rock . . . beating back . . . Name.* Compare Ovid, *Heroides*, X, 21–22:

> Interea toto clamanti litore "Theseu!"
> reddebant nomen concava saxa tuum.

See also Chaucer, *Legend of Good Women*, line 2193.

3 *Rock, more soft than he.* Compare the following lines from Phineas Fletcher's *Sicelides* (1614), III, vi:

> In rocks and seas I finde more sense and louing,
> The rocke lesse hard then he, the sea lesse mouing.

And from Pope's "Summer: The Second Pastoral," lines 17–18:

> The hills and rocks attend my doleful lay,
> Why art thou prouder and more hard than they?

7 *Faithless whither wilt thou fly.* Compare Ovid, *Heroides*, X, 35:

> "quo fugis?" exclamo; "scelerate revertere Theseu!"

20 *so fair a Face, so foul a Heart.* This line, and the idea in the preceding lines, were perhaps suggested by Catullus' poem (No. LXIV), lines 175–76:

> nec malus hic celans dulci credelia forma
> consilia. . . .

28 *Woof of daies.* Mitford, in his edition of Gray, compares line 98 of "The Bard."

61–62 *for revenge to Heaven I'l call, . . . before I fall.* Compare Catullus' poem (No. LXIV), lines 188–91:

> non tamen ante mihi languescent lumina morte
> nec prius a fesso secedent corpore sensus,
> quam iustam a divis exposcam prodita multam,
> caelestumque fidem postrema comprecer hora.

64 *That by my Faith.* I have here adopted the reading of the manuscripts and the 1653 text, obviously correct, in preference to "thy Faith" of the 1651 text.

71 *And yee O Nymphs.* This, the reading of the manuscripts and 1653 text, seems a better reading than "And yet" of the 1651 text.

85–102 Cartwright appears to depend largely upon Catullus for his ending, although Ovid in his *Metamorphoses* (VIII, 176-79) likewise ascribes Ariadne's salvation to Bacchus. There are, however, unmistakable echoes of the following lines (No. LXIV, ll. 251-55) of Catullus' poem:

> At parte ex alia florens volitabit Iacchus
> cum thiaso Satyrorum et Nysigenis Silenis,
> te quaerens, Ariadna, tuoque incensus amore.
> . . . .
> qui tum alacres passim lymphata mente furebant
> euhoe bacchantes, euhoe capita inflectantes.

Ariadne's error in supposing the approaching god to be the returning Theseus, if not exactly classical in conception, gives a happy turn to the end of the poem, superior to either of its classical predecessors. Compare also with Cartwright (ll. 85-90) the opening lines of Dryden's "Song of a Scholar and his Mistress."

85 *Thus then I.* I give here the reading of the manuscripts and the 1653 text. "That then I" of the 1651 text looks like an obvious misreading. Lawes' autographed manuscript and the 1653 text further expand the line by reading "Thus then I f———," the dramatic change in the situation being emphasized by the truncated form of "fall" (the "f———" is allowed for in the musical setting).

NO DRAWING OF VALENTINES

Text.—Works (1651), page 242.

A full discussion of St. Valentine's Day and the various folk ceremonies connected with it may be found in Brand's

Popular Antiquities (1900), pages 28–31. Goffin notices the following quotation from Henry Bourne's *Antiquitates Vulgares* (1725), quoted by Brand (p. 28):

> It is a ceremony never omitted among the vulgar to draw lots, which they term Valentines, on the eve before Valentine Day. The names of a select number of one sex are, by an equal number of the other, put into some vessel; and after that, every one draws a name, which for the present is called their Valentine, and is looked upon as a good omen of their being man and wife afterwards.

See D'Avenant's song, "Run to love's lott'ry," in *The Unfortunate Lovers* (1673 ed.), III. i; Henry King's "St. Valentine's Day" (*Poems*, ed. L. Mason, 1914, pp. 34–35); James Howell's "On my *Valentine*, Mistress *Frances Metcalf* (now Lady Robinson) at York" (*Familiar Letters*, 1705, pp. 201–2); and an anonymous poem, "The Drawing of Valentines," in *Westminster Drollery* (1671), pages 35–37.

To Lydia whom Men observ'd to make too much of me
    Text.—*Works* (1651), pages 243–44.

One of the best of Cartwright's amorous lyrics, though lacking some of the spirit of "A Song of Dalliance" or "To Chloe."

To Chloe who wish'd her self young enough for me
    Text.—*Works* (1651), pages 244–45.

It is unexpected, but pleasant, to find some lines from this poem quoted in a detective novel, *Dancers in Mourning* (1937), by Margery Allingham.

A comparison of Cartwright's verses with Donne's "The Good-Morrow" or "A Valediction Forbidding Mourning," both of which show points of similarity with Cartwright's, does not by any means reveal Cartwright at a disadvantage. Indeed there is a certain tenderness in the former which is lacking in Donne's perhaps more forceful verses.

Coleridge copied the second stanza of this poem into one of his commonplace books and the lines were published as Coleridge's own in 1893, with the title "The Second Birth." The error was corrected in the Oxford *Complete Poetical Works*, ed. E. H. Coleridge (1912), Introduction, page iv.

A Valediction
    Text.—Works (1651), pages 245-46.

This is one of the most frequently quoted of Cartwright's lyrics.

No Platonique Love
    Texts.—Works (1651), pages 246-47; *Marrow of Complements* (1655), page 70.

Cartwright's connection with the Platonic love cult, so fashionable at court about 1634 and for years after, may be found fully treated in the General Introduction, Chapter II. Here it will be sufficient to observe that much poetic dust was raised by champions pro and con, with, on the whole, the advantage leaning to the side of the con's, of which "motes in the sun's eye" Cartwright's poem may be taken as one of the best examples. Of other "contra" poems we may notice two by Cowley, "Platonick Love" and an "Answer to the Platonicks"; three by Cleveland, "Platonick Love" and two called "The Anti-Platonick"; one by Suckling, "To Mrs. Cicely Crofts"; and one by Sedley, "The Platonick." Those on the side of the angels are perhaps fewer. Mistress Katherine Philips, a devout follower of Cartwright, allows most of her verse to be permeated with Neoplatonic love doctrines, but has no particular poem defending Platonic love. Herbert of Cherbury, John Hall, and Philip Ayres all have poems entitled "Platonic Love" which treat the theme sympathetically, and two other sympathetic treatments in anonymous poems may be found in "The Platonick Lover" (*Marrow of Complements*, 1655, p. 112) and "Platonicke Love" (Egerton MS. 2725, fol. 128). George Daniel's series of poems entitled "Love Platonicke" argues the question from both sides and at the same time takes a hit at the so-called Platonic love cult. In the late Caroline drama, particularly in Cartwright's plays, the doctrine of Platonic love was treated with a wearisome reverence and "damnable iteration," though even here it did not escape scot free; witness D'Avenant's *The Platonic Lovers* (1636), the anonymous *Lady Alimony* (1659), Shirley's *The Lady of Pleasure* (1635), and the Duchess of Newcastle's somewhat later *Sociable Companions; or, the Female Wits* (1668).

1 *Tell me no more.* Goffin thinks it possible that these words suggested the form for Carew's famous lyric beginning, "Ask me no more where Jove bestows." This seems improbable, since Carew's poem is supposed to have been written as an answer to an anonymous set of verses, entitled "A Question," which first appeared in *Wit Restor'd* (1658) and is immediately followed by Carew's lines under the title, "The Reply." Although I know of none earlier than Cartwright's and Carew's poems, there are a number of lyrics which employ the "ask" or "tell" formula. Ebsworth, in his note to Carew's poem (*Poems*, 1893, pp. 231–37), quotes a number of examples, all more or less connected with Carew's verses. To these we might add Alexander Brome's "Tell me not of a face that's fair," Henry King's "Tell me no more how fair she is," Dryden's "Ask not the cause, why sullen spring," an anonymous "Tell me no more you love" (*A Collection of Poems Written Upon several Occasions*, 1673, p. 54), another anonymous poem, entitled "On Lesbia" (Harl. MS. 6917, fol. 41), beginning

> Aske me noe more whether doth stay
> The sooty night when it is day,

a third anonymous poem beginning "Tell me no more of Constancy," and a fourth, "Tell me no more you love, unless" (*Last and Best Edition of New Songs*, 1677, sig. D1ʳ and [C6]ᵛ). Cartwright's own "Tell me not of Joy," the opening line of his lyric "*Lesbia* On her Sparrow," should not be forgotten.

1–6 *Tell me no more . . . feel one Bliss.* See Cleveland's "A Letter to a Friend disswading him from his Attempt to marry a Nun" (*Works*, 1687, p. 120): "Sure at this Grate those Chrisom Lovers, call'd Platonicks, had their first Training. Those Queasie Gamesters that diet themselves with the very Notion of Mingling Souls, without putting the Body to farther Brokage, than kissing of Hands and twisting of Eyebeams." Goffin compares lines 31–34 in Cartwright's own "Ariadne Deserted by Theseus." A kind of rebuttal is offered by John Hall in "The Lure," lines 79-84.

17–18 *I know they boast . . . Body is the Way.* Goffin gives the following quotation from Thomas Watson: "Siquidem opinati sunt aliqui, in osculo fieri animarum combinationem" (*Hekatompathia*, 1582, Sonnet xx). The sentence occurs in the form of a footnote to line 11. The following lines from Kynaston's "To Cynthia" (*Cynthiades*, 1642, ed. Saintsbury, in *Minor Poets of the Caroline Period*, 1906, II, 160) refer perhaps to these lines of Cartwright's poem:

> Know 'twas well said that spirits are too high
> For bodies, when they meet to satisfy.

24 *They only find a Med'cine for the Itch*. This last unfortunate line almost ruins an otherwise perfect poem. Some such blot, however, was nearly always the inevitable result of running a conceit to death. Donne, for example, "quells" his "Farewell to Love"—not one of his best but a very presentable love lyric—with the following couplet:

> Each place can afford shadows; if all fail
> 'Tis but applying worm-seed to the tail.

Love but one

Text.—Works (1651), pages 247–48.

A considerably altered version of Cartwright's poem appears in *Examen Poeticum: being the Third Part of Miscellany Poems* (1693), pages 326–27, entitled "Love but one." The variants for the first twelve lines are given in the variant readings, but lines 13–24 are quite distinct from Cartwright's and are given below:

> 4.
> Such, *Chloris*, is thy Love; which, while it ran,
>   Confin'd within a single Stream,
> Fir'd every tuneful Son of mighty *Pan*;
>   And thou wert mine, and all Mens Theam.

> 5.
> But when imparted to one Lover more,
>   It in two Streams did faintly creep;
> The Shepherds common Muse grew low and poor,
>   And Mine, as lean as these my Sheep.

> 6.
> Alas! that Honour, *Chloris*, thou hast lost,
>   Which we to thy full Flood did pay!

> While now, that Swain, that swears he loves thee most,
>   Slakes but his thirst, and goes away!

This same version was reprinted in the third volume of the so-called Dryden *Miscellany*, 1716 (pp. 120-21) and 1727 (p. 119).

Cartwright's conceit, not an uncommon one perhaps, seems to have struck the fancy of his ardent admirer, Katherine Philips. Compare the following lines from "To Rosania, now Mrs. Montague" (*Poems*, 1678, p. 56):

> Divided Rivers lose their name;
> And so our too unequal flame
> Parted, will Passion be in me,
> And an Indifference in thee.

And the same writer's "A Dialogue of Friendship multiplyed" (p. 144):

> Friendship (like Rivers) as it multiplies
> In many streams, grows weaker still and dies.

Compare also the theme of Cowley's "Leaving Me and then loving Many" (*The Mistress*, 1671 ed., p. 14).

In *The Royal Slave* (ll. 1015-24) Cartwright, using the same figure, argues the case in the opposite direction, for "this is not to destroy, / But to enlarge the streame."

ABSENCE

Texts.—*Works* (1651), page 248; *Wits Interpreter* (1655), page 54; (1662), page 160; (1671), page 160; *The New Academy of Complements* (1671), pages 132-33.

1 *Fly, O fly sad Sigh, and bear.* Goffin compares the opening lines of Carew's "A Prayer to the Wind" (*Poems*, ed. J. W. Ebsworth, 1893, p. 9):

> Go, thou gentle whispering wind,
> Bear this Sigh!

Compare also Philip Ayres' "To the Winds," lines 13-16:

> Go, gentle Air, fly to my Dear,
>   That thus with love inflames my breast,
> And whisper softly in her ear,
>   'Tis she that robs my soul of rest: . . .

The suggestion for this type of opening probably comes from the first stanza of Meleager's "The Gnat." See also Cartwright's "A Sigh sent to his absent Love."

9–10 *Dye I would . . . would kill thee too.* The Ohio State University copy of the *Works* (1651) has a manuscript note which compares these lines with two in Shenstone's "Elegy XXVI":

> To die I languish, but I dread to die,
>   Lest my sad fate should nourish pangs for you.

Consideration

Text.—*Works* (1651), page 249 (misprinted 259).

Goffin observes that these verses "touch a graver note" and serve "as an introduction to the more serious poems which follow." The possible use of this poem as a means of dating the poems which precede it in the *Works* (1651) is discussed in the General Introduction, Chapter III (pp. 38–39n).

8–9 *renew Mine Age like to the Eagles.* Cartwright is quoting Psalm 103, but with a difference. All versions agree in reading "youth" instead of "age." Strictly speaking Cartwright's reading is the more logical. Compare Jonson's *Alchemist*, II, i (*Works*, ed. Gifford-Cunningham, 1903, II, 19).

8–19 These lines are strongly suggestive of the "philosophy of the child" which we find so prominently voiced in the later poems of Henry Vaughan and Thomas Traherne. In the expression of this doctrine, latent of course in the Scriptures, Cartwright anticipates these men by at least thirty years. He again employs the idea in his poem "To the Memory of the Most vertuous Mrs *Ursula Sadleir*."

Vpon the Translation of Chaucer's *Troilus and Creseide*

Texts.—Francis Kynaston, *Amorum Troili et Cresseidae* (1635), sig. **1ʳ (here reprinted); *Works* (1651), pages 249 (misprinted 259)–50.

Sir Francis Kynaston (1587–1642), the author of this translation of the first three books of Chaucer's *Troilus and Criseide*, was one of the leading literati of the court. In 1635 he founded the "Musaeum Minervae," a society to give instruction to "our gentlemen before their taking long journeys into foreign parts." The institution did not outlive its founder. His translation, published at Oxford, was hailed, as Goffin observes, by fifteen poems, like Cartwright's, all from the pens of Oxford men.

9-10 *know't done . . . by you . . . which is the Coppy of the two.* Compare Pope's similar remark on Johnson's translation of his *Messiah*.

A TRANSLATION OF HUGO GROTIUS'S ELEGY ON ARMINIUS
    Text.—*Works* (1651), pages 250-53.

The original of Cartwright's translation may be consulted in Hugo Grotius' *Poemata Omnia* (1645), page 221, "In mortem Jacobi Arminii." Goffin suggests that Cartwright may have used an edition which was published in London in 1639.

The very high percentage of run-on lines in this poem, much higher than in any of Cartwright's other rhymed verse, might seem to throw some doubt upon his claims of authorship. The manner, however, is distinctly Cartwright's own.

55-56   *By a defined Law; how God wills too,*
        Void of't himself, how not, how far our will.
As it stands this couplet is apparently corrupt: "it" has no referent, and "will" stands without a rhyme. In the Latin of Grotius, which Cartwright was translating, the lines appear as follows (*Poemata Omnia*, 1645, p. 222; London 1639, p. 310):

    An lege certa . . .
    Exsors *malorum* quomodo *malum* nolit
    Velitque Rector.

I have italicized the two words which solve the difficulty. Through some fault, probably of the manuscript, the direct object of "wills" or "velit," which in Latin is "malum," has been omitted. If we translate "malum" as "evil," the natural rendering, both sense and syntax are restored, and the couplet will read:

    By a defined Law; how God wills evil
    Void of't himself, how not, how far our will . . . .

Such a change necessitates the omission of "too." The presence of this word in the text can best be explained, I think, as an attempt on the part of the printer or copier to botch up a manuscript which he was unable to read. As it stood, "too" rhymed with the rhyme-words of the preceding couplet, "know" and "no."

82-84   *. . . dost entreat*
God that he give us as much Light as is fit
Unto his Flock.

There is some difficulty here in the grammatical structure. "Us" in the second line is redundant, since the indirect object of "give" is really "Flock," and the two can scarcely be taken in apposition. The omission of "us" would not only improve the sense, but give a metrically better line.

MARTIAL LIB. 1. EPIG. 67
Text.—Works (1651), page 253.

The modern editions of Martial, and Goffin, number this epigram 66, but Cartwright's numbering, in this and the following translations, agrees with the seventeenth-century texts. Although I am scarcely qualified to judge, Cartwright's translations of Martial seem to me, in point of accuracy and poetic verve, superior to any of the other English translations.

8   *slubber'd.*   Soiled or sullied (*NED*).

MARTIAL LIB. 7. EPIG. 59
Text.—Works (1651), page 254.

IN POMPEIOS JUVENES
Text.—Works (1651), page 254.

As Goffin points out, this epigram is taken from Martial, Book V, Number 75, where it is entitled, "De Pompeio & filiis."

SI MEMINI FUERANT
Text.—Works (1651), page 254.

As Goffin points out, this epigram is taken from Martial, Book V, Number 20, where it is entitled, "Ad Aeliam."

4   *There's nothing left for the third Cough to do.*   R. Fletcher in his *Martial His Epigrams* (1656), page 4, renders the line word for word the same.

MARTIAL LIB. 10. EP. 5
    Text.—*Works* (1651), page 255.

MARTIAL LIB. 11. EP. 19
    Text.—*Works* (1651), pages 255–56.

27–28 *Mead . . . Meal.* Goffin observes that Cartwright here very cleverly preserves the original play on words between Martial's "praedium" and "prandium." Cartwright's version may be compared with an unsigned translation in Harleian MS. 6917, fol. 86, which, although it shows some similar phrasing elsewhere, fails to preserve the play on words in this passage.

HORAT. CARM. LIB. 4. ODE 13.
    Texts.—*Works* (1651), pages 256–58; Alexander Brome, *The Poems of Horace, . . . Rendered in English Verse by Several Persons* (1666), pages 148–49; (1671), pages 152–53; (1680), pages 154–55.

    J. L. Brooks ("Alexander Brome: Life and Works" [unpublished doctoral thesis, Harvard, 1932], Appendix A, p. 294) provisionally attributes this translation to Dr. William Chamberlyne on the evidence of the initials "W.C." by which it is signed in Brome's *Horace* (1666).

    Cartwright's version also occurs in the "Chandos Classics" edition (1889) of Horace in translation. The editor here dates it 1638, but upon what evidence I do not know. He may perhaps have been led to this conclusion by Moseley's statement ("To the Reader") that "here is but one Sheet was written after he entered *Holy Orders*," which was, indeed, in 1638. Moseley's statement, however, will not stand the test of facts, since a number of poems can be shown to be certainly later than that year.

    Goffin observes that the *Quarterly Review* (1895), CLXXX, 121, quotes the sixth stanza of this "admirable version" of Horace's "Audivere Lyce."

ON THE BIRTH OF THE KING'S FOURTH CHILD. 1635
    Texts.—*Coronae Carolinae Quadratura* (1636), sigs. ²A1ʳ, ²A1ᵛ–²A2ʳ, ²D1ᵛ (here reprinted); *Works* (1651), pages 260–62.

This poem is in three parts in the 1636 and 1651 editions: "To the *Queene*," "To the Queen on the same; being the Preface before the English Verses sent then from *Oxford*" (title, 1651), and "The Conclusion to the Queen." Only the second of these is signed with Cartwright's name in the 1636 text; the first and third are assigned to Cartwright on the strength of their inclusion in the *Works* (1651). Goffin combines "The Conclusion to the Queen" with the second part of the poem, a position all the more unfortunate as Cartwright is there addressing King Charles. In the 1636 edition "The Conclusion to the Queen" is separated from the second part by almost all the other commendatory verses.

To the Queen on the same

Texts.—See the preceding poem.

10 *Antiquation.* The action of making antiquated. (*NED*). Cartwright's is the earliest use cited.

28 *In the Elder statue with a younger Head.* The 1651 edition has the following marginal note to this line: "Marcellus *was accused for taking off* Augustus *his head, and putting the Head of* Tiberius *upon the same Statue.*" I believe this same gloss appears in the Bodleian copy of the 1636 edition, but neither of the Folger copies has it.

30 *Chronogramme.* A phrase, sentence, or inscription, in which certain letters (distinguished from the rest) express by their numerical values a date or epoch (*NED*). This type of learned toying was very popular in the middle of the seventeenth century. John Berkenhead in his *Assembly-Man* (1647; *Harleian Miscellany*, 1810, VI, 59) remarks:

> Of late they are much in love with chronograms, because, if possible, they are duller than anagrams. O how they have torn the poor bishops names, to pick out the number six hundred sixty-six! little dreaming, that a whole baker's dozen of their own assembly have that beastly number in each of their names, and that as exactly as their solemn league and covenant consists of six-hundred sixty-six words.

The following is an example of the chronogram from *Britannia Natalis*, Oxford (1630):
  Chronogramma: MDCXXX:
    Mat. 2. 2.
  NatVs est ReX, VIDI steLLaM eIVs In orIente.

THE CONCLUSION TO THE QUEEN
   Texts.—See the two preceding poems.

TO MRS DUPPA, SENT WITH THE PICTURE OF THE BISHOP OF CHICHESTER (HER HUSBAND)
   Text.—*Works* (1651), pages 263–66

   If we may judge from the title, this poem was written before 1641 and after 1638, during which years Duppa was Bishop of Chichester. It is almost certain, however, that lines 71–80 refer specifically to Salisbury Cathedral, which Cartwright calls "your Church." If this is so, Moseley has probably telescoped two poems. Note the sudden change of stanza form and of person addressed following line 30, and the suggestion of birthday wishes in lines 38 and 42.

2   *Quarrell.* A square or, more usually, a diamond-shaped pane of glass, of the kind used in making lattice-windows (*NED*).

71–78   *your Church.* Goffin takes "your Church" to refer to Christ Church Cathedral in Oxford, in the restoration of which Duppa had interested himself. The description, however, which immediately follows in the next few lines does not apply to Christ Church as Cartwright knew it. If, on the other hand, we suppose that Cartwright is speaking of Salisbury Cathedral, the description, except for a single detail, fits perfectly. Compare with Cartwright's lines "the local rhyme in which the Cathedral is celebrated. . . . it is attributed by Godwin, who gives a Latin version of it, to a certain Daniel Rogers" (*Handbook to the Cathedrals of England*, 1861, Pt. I, p. 70):

> As many days as in one year there be,
> So many windows in this church you see.
> As many marble pillars here appear
> As there are hours through the fleeting year.
> As many gates as moons one here doth view,
> Strange tale to tell, yet not more strange than true.

   Camden prints a very similar version in his *Britannia* (1586) (see Holland's translation, *Britain*, 1610). It will be noticed that Cartwright only mentions as many windows as weeks in the year and not, as in the above doggerel, as many windows as days. Day's *Parliament of Bees* (1641), Character II, makes use of a similar rhyme in describing a bee-hive.

82 *Jewel's glory.*   Goffin misunderstands the reference here, printing "*Jewel's*" without the apostrophe and unitalicized. Cartwright is referring, of course, to John Jewell (1522–71), Bishop of Salisbury. This mention of a famous Salisbury divine immediately following lines 71–80 strengthens the case for the identification of "your Church" with Salisbury Cathedral.

To the King, on the Birth of the Princess Anne

Texts.—*Flos Britannicus . . . Filiola Carolo & Mariae* (1636) sigs. 2[1ᵛ]–2[3ʳ] (each signature has four leaves and is numbered in the upper right-hand corner; the arrangement of the signatures in the second part [English verses] is very confused; sig. 2, which has eight leaves, comes first), here reprinted; *Works* (1651), pages 266–69. *Flos Britannicus* also contains a Latin poem by Cartwright (sigs. 5 [2ᵛ]–5 [3ʳ]).

The *Works* (1651) reads "Princess Elizabeth" for "Princess Anne." The error is corrected by Goffin.

5–6 *we be Loosers thought . . . receiv'd a Day.*   These lines refer to the death of the Queen's first child, which was born on May 13, 1629, and died two hours later. See a poem doubtfully attributed to Cartwright entitled "On the Prince Charles death."

To the Queen

Texts.   See preceding poem.

With the exception of the four weak opening lines this address to the queen is one of the most pleasing of its kind that I know.

36 *thus did pull mine eare.*   Imitated from the sixth *Bucolic* of Virgil, lines 3–4:

> Cum canerem reges et proelia, Cynthius aurem
> Vellit, et admonuit.

37 *emerit.*   Retired from active service. Cartwright again uses the word in *The Ordinary*, I, v:

> To win that old Emerit thing, that like
> An Image in a German clock, doth move,
> Not walke, I meane that rotten Antiquary.

IN THE MEMORY OF THE MOST WORTHY BENIAMIN IOHNSON

Texts.—*Jonsonus Virbius* (1638), pages 34-39 (here reprinted); *Works* (1651), pages 311-17.

This poem was reprinted from *Jonsonus Virbius* (1638) in Volume II of Dryden's *Miscellany* (1716), pages 168-73; (1727), pages 165-70.

In this poem Cartwright reveals himself as a critic of considerable insight. Further evidence of his critical ability may be found in his two commendatory poems on Fletcher, and, to a lesser degree, in his poem on Killigrew. Cartwright's views on Jonson and Fletcher may be found discussed at length in the General Introduction, Chapter III. "The Poems."

31 *Things* common *thou speakst* proper. Headley (*Select Beauties of Ancient English Poetry*, 1787, II, 157) points out that Cartwright is here echoing Horace's *Ars Poetica*, line 128: "Difficile est propriè communia dicere." Compare Jonson's translation: " 'Tis hard to speak things common properly" (not published until 1640).

31-124 The following prose version of some of these lines occurs in David Lloyd's *Memoires* (1668), in his "Life of Dudley Digges," page 426:

> Yea, common things grew proper in his Charms, rather than Speeches, wherein his thoughts were so ordered, so expressed, as if he did not discourse, but see; words and things falling into their order, so naturally and easily, as nothing fell amiss; as if the Scholar, as well as the Wiseman, were all things.
>
> That life, that *Venus* of all things which we conceive or shew, proportioned. Decency [*sic*] was not found scattered in him here or there, but like the soul wholly every where; exercises wherein he spake not only phancy to please, but reason to convince; vexing and filing the roughest subject, by the Chimistry and heat of a great spirit into comelinesse; not pouring in the Ore or Grosse, but in fair Coin, and choice distillations, dispensing his learning, well skilled when to spare, and when to entertain. He gave the right blush and colour unto things, low without creeping, high without losse of wings[,] smooth, yet not weak, and by a through care, big without swelling, without Painting fair.

40   trade. To exercise (*NED*).

41-42 *That* life, *that* Venus *of all things . . . proportion'd* decencie. Headley (*Select Beauties of Ancient English Poetry*, 1787, II, 157) observes that Cartwright has the following line (l. 42) from Horace's *Ars Poetica* in mind: "Ordinis haec virtus erit, et Venus, aut ego fallor."

45-50 plot . . . knot . . . *No* power *comes down* . . . god. Compare Cleveland, "An Elegy on Ben. Johnson" (*Works*, 1687, p. 313):

> Thy Scene was free from Monsters, no hard Plot
> Call'd down a God t'unty th'unlikely Knot.

See Horace, *Ars Poetica*, lines 191-92.

59 *Nor dost* thou *poure out, but dispence* thy *veine*. Compare Dryden, "Essay of Dramatick Poesy" (*Critical Essays*, ed. J. C. Collins, 1903, p. 87): "One cannot say he wanted Wit; but rather, that he was frugal of it."

70 libells. Cartwright is scarcely being too ingenuous here. Certainly Jonson was ever being plagued, and not without reason, for his satirical personal portraits. In the second prologue to *The Silent Woman* (1609) he defends himself:

> If any yet will with particular sleight
> Of application, wrest what he doth write;
> And that he meant, or him, or her, will say:
> They make a libel, which he made a play.

See also *The Magnetic Lady* (1632), II, i (end of scene).

72 *To strike the* vice, *but spare the* person *still*. This line is translated from Martial's tag: "Parcere personis, dicere de vitiis." Also Pliny, in a letter to Atrius Clemans, writes: "He points his eloquence against the vices, not the persons of mankind, and without chastising reclaims the wanderer." Jonson himself uses the sentiment in "An Epitaph on Mr. Vincent Corbet" (*Works*, 1903, III, 287):

> His looks would so correct it, when
> It chid the vice yet not the men.

Like Cartwright, Cleveland applies it to Jonson, "An Elegy on Ben. Johnson" (*Works*, 1687, p. 314):

> We know thy free Vein had this Innocence,
> To spare the Party, and to brand th' Offence.

See also a commendatory poem signed "T. S." in Richard Brome's *Five New Playes* (1659), sig. [A8].

83 *brokes.* Bargains. Goffin compares line 85: "No bargaining line there."

86 *Nothing but what* Lucretia *might rehearse.* Compare Henry King, "To my dead friend Ben: Johnson" (*Poems*, ed. L. Mason, 1914, p. 82):

> Thy Comick Sock induc'd such purged sence,
> A *Lucrece* might have heard without offense.

108 *To make* thee *read as Classick in* thy life. Compare Cleveland, "An Elegy on Ben. Johnson" (*Works*, 1687, p. 333):

> Thou shalt be read as Classick Authors; and
> As Greek and Latine taught in every Land.

118 prize. A fencing bout (*NED*).

122–24 Low *without* creeping ... *without* painting faire. Goffin quotes from "J.A.G." (*Notes and Queries*, IV, 4, 511), who compares these verses with the famous lines in Denham's "Cooper's Hill" (ll. 189–92) describing the Thames:

> O could I flow like thee, and make thy stream
> My great example as it is my theme!
> Though deep, yet clear; though gentle, yet not dull;
> Strong without rage; without o'erflowing, full.

It may be observed that "J. A. G." was anticipated by Henry Headley (*Select Beauties of Ancient English Poetry*, 1787, II, 158), who also notices Pope's parody in *The Dunciad*.

Goffin further points out that these lines do not occur in the first edition of "Cooper's Hill" (1642), but were added in the edition of 1655. The case for Cartwright's influence seems good, and Cartwright receives a little reflected glory in Dryden's praise of Denham's verses in his "Dedication of the Aeneis," 1697 (*Essays of John Dryden*, ed. W. P. Ker, 1926, II, 217), but it is only fair to observe that Denham might have found other and earlier models. Compare, for example, the following lines from Thomas Randolph's poem, "To Master Feltham, on his book of Resolves" (*Works*, ed. W. C. Hazlitt, 1875, II, 575):

> I mean, the style being pure, and strong and round;
> Not long, but pithy; being short-breath'd, but sound,

> Such as the grave, acute, wise Seneca sings —
> That best of tutors to the worst of kings.
> Not long and empty; lofty, but not proud;
> Subtle, but sweet; high, but without a cloud.
> Well-settled, full of nerves — in brief 'tis such,
> That in a little hath comprised much.

The general similarity in verse rhythms and construction is unmistakable. Or again, compare Francis Quarles' description of Parthenia in his "Argalus and Parthenia," 1629 (*Works*, ed. A. Grosart, 1881, III, 242):

> Merry yet modest; witty, and yet wise:
> Not apt to toy, and yet not too too nice;
> Quick, but not rash; Courteous, and yet not common;
> Not too familiar, and yet scorning no man.

See also E.K.'s epistle to *The Shepheards Calender* (1579), where, describing Spenser's style, he speaks of it as "round without roughnesse, and learned without hardnesse"; and compare *Love's Labour's Lost*, V, i, 3–5.

If indeed Denham was imitating Cartwright—and it seems most likely, in spite of the other possible sources—then the imitators of Denham (or Cartwright) have a sort of second-hand interest for us. Wycherley (*Posthumous Works*, 1728, II, 29, "An Epistle to Mr. Dryden") describing Dryden's style writes:

> In Smoothness, Measure, Majesty and Force;
> A safe, tho' high; a swift, yet easie Flight;
> Discreet, tho' daring; lofty, yet in Sight.

Pope's imitation in *The Dunciad*, III, lines 169–72, need not be quoted. David Mallet, in his satire, "Of Verbal Criticism," lines 227–28, echoes the form:

> Great without swelling, without meanness plain,
> Serious, not silly; sportive, but not vain.

Again in a London newspaper, in a contemporary poem on George Washington, we find the following couplet:

> Great without pomp, without ambition brave,
> Proud, not to conquer fellow-men, but save.[1]

---

1. After the above note had been written, my attention was drawn to the long and detailed discussion and illustration of these lines in Mr. T. H.

127-41 These lines, omitting lines 137-38, are quoted in a slightly different version by Langbaine in *English Dramatick Poets* (1691), pages 148-49, and according to Malone (*Shakspeare, Ford, and Jonson* [*Plays of Shakspeare*, 1790, I, Pt. i, 410-11]) served the actor, Macklin, in connection with his forgeries concerning Ford's *Lover's Melancholy*. See the lines which Macklin attributes to Thomas May.

Denham took a rather different view of Jonson's "borrowings" from the classics. See his poem, "On Mr Abraham Cowley, His Death" (ll. 32-38):

> Nor, with Ben Jonson, did make bold
> To plunder all the Roman stores
> Of poets, and of orators:
> Horace's wit, and Virgil's state,
> He did not steal, but emulate!
> And when he would like them appear,
> Their garb, but not their clothes, did wear.

139-40 *Thefts . . . they and their* grace *are wholly* thine. Compare Cleveland, "An Elegy upon Ben. Johnson" (*Works*, 1687, p. 314):

> And hadst not chosen rather to translate
> Their learning into English, not their Rate;
> Indeed this last, if thou hadst been bereft
> Of thy Humanity, might be call'd Theft,
> The other was not, whatsoe'er was strange,
> Or borrowed, in thee did grow thine by th' Change.

152 luck *and* rime. See Jonson's "A Fit of Rhyme Against Rhyme" (*Works*, ed. Gifford-Cunningham, 1903, III, 311-12).

167 *to* erre *with* thee . . . *skill*. We are reminded of Byron's well-known line in "English Bards and Scotch Reviewers": "Better to err with Pope, than shine with Pye." Both lines were probably suggested by the anonymous tag: "Mallem cum *Scaligero* errare quam cum *Clavio* rectè sapere."

169-71 thy *thoughts . . . Will come up* Porcelaine-wit. As Goffin observes, Cartwright is referring to the common belief that "porcelain or china dishes . . . are made of earth, which lieth in preparation about an hundred years under ground" (Sir

---

Banks' edition of *The Poetical Works of Sir John Denham* (1928), pp. 52-54, 342-50. Since, however, my note adds a number of points to Mr. Banks' discussion, I have decided to let it remain.

Thomas Browne, *Pseudodoxia Epidemica*, II, 5). In his preface "To the Reader" to *Argalus and Parthenia* (1629), Francis Quarles has the following striking passage:

> In this discourse, I have not affected to set thy understanding on the Rack, by the tyranny of strong *lines*, which (as they fabulously report of *China-dishes*) are made for the third *Generation* to make use of, and are the meere itch of wit.

Cartwright's lines simply reverse Quarles' conceit.

In his Prologue to *The Virtuoso* (1676), Shadwell seems to recall Cartwright's verses:

> For Wit, like China, should long buri'd lie,
> Before it ripens to good Comedy;
> A thing we ne'r have seen since Johnson's days,
> And but a few of his were perfect Plays.

Compare also J. Marsh's lines in his commendatory poem "To Mr. Congreve, on *The Old Bachelor*":

> Some vainly striving honour to obtain,
> Leave to their heirs the traffic of their brain,
> Like china under ground, the ripening ware,
> In a long time, perhaps grows worth our care.

181–82   *When we shall feed on* refuse offalls, *when*
         We shall from corne *to* akornes *turne agen.*

Cartwright was probably thinking of Jonson's own lines in the second stanza of his "Ode to Himself" (*Works*, ed. Gifford-Cunningham, 1903, II, 385):

> Say that thou pour'st them wheat,
>   And they will acorns eat;
> 'Twere simple fury still thyself to waste
>   On such as have no taste!

Compare the concluding lines of Herrick's "Upon M. Ben. Johnson" (*Hesperides*, No. 383):

> Oh fie upon 'em! Lastly too, all witt
> In utter darkenes did, and still will sit
> Sleeping the lucklesse Age out, till that she
> Her Resurrection ha's again with Thee.

TO MY HONOVR'D FRIEND MR THOMAS KILLIGREW

Texts.—Thomas Killigrew, *The Prisoners and Claracilla* (1641), sigs. [A5]ʳ–[A6]ʳ (here reprinted); *Works* (1651), pages 258-60. *The Prisoners* (1641) also contains a Latin poem by Cartwright (sig. [A6]).

The little octavo in which this poem of Cartwright's first appeared is one of the worst printed books I have ever seen. Although written in prose, the two plays are hacked up into a blank verse which defies reading, let alone scansion. Both plays are bad, *Claracilla*, perhaps, a little less so than *The Prisoners*. Beside them Cartwright's three tragicomedies appear as miracles of plot construction and finish. Occasionally, however, as in the description of the sea storm in *The Prisoners*, Killigrew achieves an effect by sheer force and hurry of expression for which we look in vain in Cartwright's work.

35 *Manage.* Management, administration, control. A term borrowed from horsemanship (*NED*). A favorite word of Cartwright's. See Goffin's note.

49 *Elephant breeds, (once in ten yeares.* Goffin quotes from Pliny: "The vulgar notion is that the elephant goes with young ten years."

Vpon the Dramatick Poems of Mr John Fletcher

Texts.—Beaumont and Fletcher, *Comedies and Tragedies* (1647), sigs. ¹d^v–¹d2^r (here reprinted); *Fifty Comedies and Tragedies* (1679), sig. A2^v; *Comedies and Tragedies* [Tonson's ed.] (1711), I; *Works* (1651), pages 269-71.

The appearance of this and the following poem in the Beaumont and Fletcher folio of 1647 affords, indirectly, some information about the conditions under which that volume was published. The title of Cartwright's first poem there reads: "Upon the report of the printing of the Dramaticall Poems of Master *John Fletcher*, collected before, and now set forth in one Volume." From this it seems that an edition of Fletcher alone was in the air probably as early as 1638. Confirmation of part of this statement may be found in Humphrey Moseley's preface, "The Stationer to the Readers" ([A4]^v): "It was once in my thoughts to have Printed Mr. *Fletcher's* workes by themselves, because single & alone he would make a *Just Volume.*" (See also ll. 31-32 of Cartwright's second poem.) The date 1638 I mention very tentatively, since I have already discredited Moseley's remark that almost none of Cartwright's poems was written after he entered holy orders (1638). (See my note on Moseley's preface, p. 833.) In this particular case, however, since Moseley was the publisher of both Beaumont and Fletcher's and Cartwright's works, he may be supposed to have known when these verses came into his hands. Therefore, unless we are willing to brand Moseley's statement as a conscious lie, a lie, moreover, which won him no particular business advantage, we should, under the circumstances, give this date more than passing consideration.

In connection with the poems themselves, it is interesting to see that Cartwright is the only writer honored by the inclusion of two sets of verses—this in spite of the fact that he had been dead four years when the folio was published. (It is possible that Jasper Mayne also has two poems included, if a short poem signed "I.M.," which immediately precedes his own verses, is from his hand.) Although the fact that Moseley published the volume must be allowed due weight, it is not too extravagant to suppose that this honor accorded to Cartwright reflects the genuine regard in which his poetical, and particularly perhaps his critical, powers were held by his contemporaries. The value which was attached to his name as an incentive to the book-buying public is even better illustrated, however, by the following example. In 1650 the fifth edition (so called on the title, but no fourth edition can be traced) of Barten Holyday's *Aulas Persius Flaccus His Satires* was published containing among others a commendatory poem signed "W. Cartwright." Unfortunately for the reputation of Holyday, who apparently was personally responsible for this edition of the *Satires*, later research (see J. L. Brooks, "Alexander Broome: Life and Works" [unpublished doctoral thesis, Harvard, 1932]: p. 237) has shown that the same verses, which here appear with Cartwright's name, originally appeared in the earlier editions of Holyday's translation (1616, 1617, 1635) under the name of I. Knight. Although Brooks does not notice it, Cartwright was not the only one to suffer exploitation. A poem, which in all the earlier editions is signed with the initials "T.G.," now is announced as the work of "Brian Duppa. *Bishop of Salisbury*."

The choice of Cartwright and Duppa is, I think, significant.

Cartwright devotes a part of each poem to combating the apparently popular belief that Fletcher, without the sage advice and blue-penciling of Beaumont, was incapable of producing a finished play, because " 'twas his happy fault to do too much." This view of Beaumont as a sort of glorified city-editor has been thoroughly "laid" by modern criticism. Cartwright himself seems to look upon Beaumont as little better than a usurper of Fletcher's just renown:

> Though thus he call'd his Judge into his fame,
> And for that aid allow'd him halfe the name.

Again modern criticism has reversed the verdict and hails Beaumont as the greater poet, if not the greater dramatist. In defense of Fletcher, Cartwright brings forward the large number of plays which that poet produced after the early death of Beaumont (1616). However, he either forgets, or did not know of, Fletcher's later collaborators—an oversight which rather weakens his argument, since the total of Fletcher's collaborations with Massinger alone is greater than the number of plays which connects his name with Beaumont. Pope echoes Cartwright's view of Beaumont in his imitation of Horace, Book II, Epistle I, line 84.

3-4 *His thoughts ... too much.* With a single slight change this couplet is quoted, without attribution by David Lloyd in his *Memoires* (1668), p. 426.

15 *his* Shepherdesse. Fletcher's *The Faithful Shepherdess* (about 1608). Cartwright triumphantly instances this play as the unaided work of Fletcher.

21-22   *A piece, which* Johnson *in a rapture bid*
         Come up a glorifi'd Worke, and so it did.

As Goffin points out, Cartwright is referring to some lines in Jonson's commendatory poem, "To Mr. John Fletcher, upon his *Faithful Shepherdess*" (*Works*, ed. Gifford-Cunningham, 1903, III, 290-91):

> ... which shall rise
> A glorified work to time, when fire
> Or moths shall eat what all these fools admire.

ANOTHER ON THE SAME

Texts.—Beaumont and Fletcher, *Comedies and Tragedies* (1647) sig. [d2] (here reprinted); *Comedies and Tragedies* [Tonson's ed.] (1711), I; *Works* (1651), pages 271–73.

This second poem to Fletcher, on the whole superior to the first, is omitted in the Beaumont and Fletcher second folio (1679).

4 *To bid thee be more dull, that's write againe.* If we may trust Moseley ("The Stationer to the Readers" sig. [A4]ᵛ), Fletcher, like Shakespeare, was not accustomed to "write againe":

> What ever I have seene of Mr. *Fletcher's* owne hand is free from interlining; and his friends affirme he never writ any one thing twice: it seemes he had that rare felicity to prepare and perfect all first in his owne braine; to shape and attire his *Notions*, to adde or loppe off, before he committed one word to writing, and never touched pen till all was to stand as firme and immutable as if ingraven in Brasse or Marble.

Taken in connection with what has already been said concerning Fletcher and his dependence upon Beaumont, the charge so strongly combated by Cartwright, this statement of Moseley's is of considerable importance.

44 *That they (their owne Black-Friers) unacted breath.* Dyce in his edition of Beaumont and Fletcher (1843, I, xliv), where he reprints Cartwright's poem, has a note to the effect that Cartwright is here referring to the closing of the theatres (1642). If this were true it would immediately dispose of all the arguments in favor of dating the poem earlier than 1638. Such an interpretation, however, does not seem to be at all necessary. All Cartwright really says is that these plays are so life-like and lively that, without the advantage of a theatre, they act themselves in the mere perusal.

51–60 Shirley seems to have had these lines in mind when in his preface "To the Reader" (sig. [A3]ᵛ) he wrote:

> You may here find passions raised to that excellent pitch and by such insinuating degrees that you shall not chuse but consent; & go along with them, finding your self at last grown insensibly the very same person you read, and then stand admiring the subtile Trackes of your engagement.

59 *And felt such shafts steale through their captiv'd sence.* Goffin omits "steale" and prints "captived," drawing attention, in a footnote, to the fact that "All editions print *captiv'd.*"

60 *made them rise Parts.* That is, made them assume the actual characteristics of the different roles. Compare Jasper Mayne's poem in *Jonsonus Virbius* (1638), page 33:

> And were made judges, not bad parts by th'ear.
> For thou ev'n sin did in such words array,
> That some who came bad parts, went out good play.

69-76 Shakespeare *to thee was dull, whose best jest lyes*
I' th Ladies questions, and the Fooles replyes;
Old fashion'd wit, . . .

These are probably the best-known lines in all Cartwright's works. They are, moreover, not infrequently quoted as evidence of a general tendency on the part of Cartwright and his immediate contemporaries to discountenance Shakespeare as dramatist and poet. I must confess myself unable to understand Mr. Goffin in his note to this passage. He writes:

> These famous lines and the preceding judgment on Ben Jonson are valuable for the history of criticism, valuable because they are discerning and reasonable, because, too, of the fame of the critic. We see from the lines quoted how the Elizabethan imagination was out of date for "correct" poets: though Cartwright will yet concede that Shakespeare was certainly capable of good clownish repartee, simple natural human stuff. It is a point of view; and I am reminded of an Indian student who recorded similar and somewhat refreshing "first impressions of Shakespeare." "Shakespeare's humorous characters," he wrote, "reveal great truths in the form of witty and amusing remarks. These amusing remarks and repartees are full of interest."

In the first place I must agree with Goffin that Cartwright's judgment has at least a considerable grain of truth to recommend it. When, however, he says, in one and the same sentence, that Cartwright both repudiates Elizabethan "imagination" as dull and admits that Shakespeare was good at "clownish repartee," I am lost. Pretty certainly Cartwright does neither. No question of "imagination" is raised at all. Cartwright is speaking solely of comic wit, and "wit" here seems to be used almost exclusively in the modern sense. All that Cartwright really says is that the best "jest" of which Shakespeare was capable lies in the type of wit combat which, for example, we find in *All's Well that Ends Well*, II, ii. Although Goffin here speaks of Cartwright's criticism as "discerning and reasonable," in a note to an earlier poem

(p. 183) he writes: "Cartwright does not disdain the imaginative ideas of 'dull' Shakespeare." Evidently in Goffin's case, as among most critics, Cartwright's lines have been interpreted as a wholesale criticism of Shakespeare as a dramatist and poet. Nothing it seems to me was farther from Cartwright's mind. He is very specifically attacking one aspect of Shakespeare's comic powers, an aspect which all will agree has suffered more than any other by the passage of time. Wit, as it is generally distinguished from true humor, is the special delight of its own age and the butt and wonder of the immediately succeeding age. Cartwright stood in the same relation to the wit of Shakespeare's time as we stand to that of the Victorian era. (In this connection it is interesting to compare Dryden's arraignment of wit in the early English dramatists, including Fletcher, in his "Defense of the Epilogue" appended to the second part of *The Conquest of Granada*, 1670.) Finally, it should be observed that on the two occasions when Cartwright mentions Shakespeare it is to couple his name with that of Jonson—a high compliment from a Son of Ben.

In lines 73–78 Cartwright terms Shakespeare's wit "obsceanesse" and "Bawdry" in comparison with Fletcher's, which is "cleane, chast, and unvext." I cannot now take the space to discuss the relative "moral tone" of comic wit under Elizabeth and Charles. It must be sufficient to observe that present-day taste has generally tended to reverse Cartwright's dictum. As a matter of fact, in this last moral judgment of Shakespeare's wit, Cartwright seems to be little more than echoing Jonson's remarks on "The wit of the old comedy" in *Timber*, which first appeared in the folio of 1640/41. If Cartwright did indeed have this passage from Jonson before him, it would be almost necessary to date the poem sometime after that year. It is possible, however, that Cartwright is simply recalling Jonson's source in the *Ad Horatii de Plauto et Terentio judicium* of Heinsius (see *Discoveries*, ed. Maurice Castelain [1906], p. 134).

The tone of Cartwright's lines may well be compared with the following lines from the "Praeludium" (probably by Shirley) to the revival in 1631 of Thomas Goffe's *The Careless Shepherdess:*

> As your Forefathers, whose dull intellect
> Did nothing understand but fools and fighting, ...
> The Motly Coat was banish'd with Trunk Hose,
> And since their wits are sharp, the Swords are sheath'd. ...
> Then playing upon words is as much out
> Of fashion here, as Pepper is at Court.

72 *In turn'd Hose.* This was altered by Theobald to "In trunk-hose" on the analogy of a phrase in Berkenhead's poem, prefixed to the 1647 folio:

> ... you two thought fit
> To wear just robes, and leave off trunk-hose wit.

(See Dyce's note in his edition of Beaumont and Fletcher, 1843, I, xlv.) Certainly Berkenhead's phrase seems more natural, and it turns up again in ? Shirley's "Praeludium" to the revival (1631) of Thomas Goffe's *The Careless Shepherdess* (p. 5), and in Edward Phillips' *Theatrum Poetarum* (1675), when he refers to "the Trunk-Hose Fancy of Queen Elizabeth's days." No change, however, is really demanded.

75 *Nature was all his Art.* In this particular criticism of Shakespeare, Cartwright is following rather Milton than Jonson, who apart from a passing remark in his *Conversations*, "That Shakspeer wanted arte," very distinctly voices the opposite view in his commendatory poem to the first folio (1623):

> Yet must I not give Nature all; thy Art,
> My gentle Shakespeare, must enjoy a part.

Cartwright's view, however, was the one gradually to gain favor, and we find Denham, for example, in his poem "On Mr Abraham Cowley, His Death" (ll. 22-25) repeating it and—the irony of criticism—coupling Fletcher with Shakespeare:

> Old mother Wit, and Nature, gave
> Shakespeare and Fletcher all they have;
> In Spenser, and in Jonson, Art
> Of slower Nature got the start.

See also Sedley's "Prologue to *The Wary Widdow*" (*Works*, ed. V. de Sola Pinto, 1928, I, 50) and Fuller's *Worthies* (1662), page 126, where he remarks that "*nature* it self was all the *art* which was used upon him."

To the Right Reverend Father in God, Brian, Lord Bishop of Chichester

Text.—Works (1651), pages 274–79.

Goffin suggests that this poem was probably written in 1638 when Duppa was made Bishop of Chichester. Compare Herrick's poem called "A Pastorall upon the birth of Prince *Charles*."

107–8   *When his high* Charge *shall rule the State*
         (Which Heaven saies shall be, but late)

Cartwright is referring to Prince Charles, to whom Duppa acted as royal tutor. He prophesied more truly than he knew.

A New-years Gift

Text.—Works (1651), pages 279–81.

Although it is impossible to be sure to whom this excellent poem was addressed, general internal evidence seems to point to King Charles himself (see ll. 25–30, 37–42, 49–54).

43–44   *Thoughts rescue, and his danger kiss'd,*
         Being found as soon as miss'd.

Although this is the reading of all editions, I can get no meaning from the lines as they stand. I suggest that the first two words, "Thoughts rescue," are a mistake for "Though he's rescu'd." Such a change will make excellent sense, though the force of the contemporary allusion is lost on us.

A New-years-gift to Brian Lord Bishop of Sarum, upon the Author's entring into holy Orders, 1638

Text.—Works (1651), pages 284–86.

Goffin points out that Brian Duppa's title as "Bishop of Sarum" must be an error, since Duppa did not become Bishop of Salisbury until 1641. I hope Goffin is correct and that this, and not the date 1638, is really at fault. Unfortunately, so far as I know, this poem is the sole authority for that date. If, indeed, the date 1638 is a mistake and Cartwright did not actually enter holy orders until Duppa was Bishop of Salisbury (1641), it will be necessary to treat with greater respect Moseley's statement, so often referred to, that Cartwright wrote almost nothing (one sheet) after entering the church.

Taking a number of other points into consideration, however, I must declare in favor of the earlier date (1638). The present confusion may be easily enough explained as an attempt on Moseley's part to give Duppa his correct title at the time the poem was actually printed (1651). A reverse case has already been noticed in connection with the poem "To Mrs *Duppa*," in the title of which Duppa is styled "Bishop of Chichester," though that may probably be explained by supposing that Moseley combined two separate poems.

This poem is given in T. H. Ward's *English Poets* (1881), II, 231-33.

27-28   *Motion as in a Mill*
        Is busie standing still.
A good example of the hyperconceit. Compare Cleveland, "An Answer to a Pamphlet written against the Lord *Digby's* Speech" (*Works*, 1687, pp. 107-8): "The Judges Circuit would be like the wheeling of a Mill, move continually, but never nearer their Journey's end."

To the Queen after her dangerous Delivery. 1638

Texts.—*Musarum Oxoniensium pro serenissima Regina Maria* (1638), sig. [a4] (here reprinted); *Works* (1651), pages 286-87. *Musarum . . . Maria* also contains a Latin poem by Cartwright (sig. B3ᵛ).

Goffin quotes from Madan, *Oxford Books* (1912), II, 139:

> The infant princess Catherine (born and died Jan. 29th, 1638/9), who is commemorated in these verses, seems to have lived a few hours only, and to be unnoticed in ordinary pedigrees and histories.

29 *Horatius*. The 1651 edition omits the marginal note: "Liv. Decad.1. lib.2." In Baker's translation of Livy (London, 1814, I, 121) the anecdote may be found in Book II, Chapter viii. The comparison is a particularly happy one.

On the Death of the Right Honourable the Lord Viscount Bayning

Texts.—*Death repeal'd by a thankful Memorial sent from Christ Church in Oxon.* (1638), pages 5-6 (here reprinted); *Works* (1651), pages [2]304-6. *Death repeal'd* (1638) also contains a Latin poem by Cartwright (pp. 47-48).

"Paul Bayning became heir to the Viscounty of Sudbury in 1629. He died July 11th, 1638, without heirs, the title becoming extinct" (Goffin).

As Goffin points out, the contributors to *Death repeal'd* (1638) were without exception Oxford men. Christ Church was Bayning's college.

39-40 *no mans Ruine . . . made the next Seate ill.* Compare Jonson's poem, "To Penshurst" (*Works*, ed. Gifford-Cunningham, 1903, III, 263):

> And though thy walls be of the country stone,
> They're reared with no man's ruin, no man's groan;
> There's none that dwell about them wish them down.

41-42 *No Neighb'ring-village was unpeopled here*
'Cause it durst bound a Noble Eye too neere.

See Evelyn's *Diary* under September 7, 1649:

> Take it altogether, the meadows, walkes, river, forest, corne-ground, and vineyards, I hardly saw any thing in Italy exceede it. The yron gates are very magnificent. He has pulled downe a whole village to make roome for his pleasure about it.

See also, Sir Thomas Elyot, *The Governour* (1531), Book I, Chapter xii:

> . . . finally was sodaynely slayne by the shotte of an arowe, as he was huntynge in a forest, whiche to make larger and to gyue his deere more lybertie, he dyd cause the houses of lii parisshes to be pulled downe, the people to be expelled, and all beyng desolate to be tourned in to desert, and made onely pasture for beestes sauage.

And Sidney's *Arcadia* (ed. A. Feuillerat, 1912), page 393.

A NEW-YEARS-GIFT TO A NOBLE LORD. 1640
Text.—*Works* (1651), pages 281-83.

The identity of the person to whom this poem is addressed is unknown.

66 *To humor the New year.* I suspect that we should read "honor" instead of "humor," although some meaning can be extorted from the line as it stands.

UPON THE BIRTH OF THE KINGS SIXTH CHILD. 1640
Texts.—*Horti Caroli*n*i Rosa Altera* (1640), sigs. ²a1ᵛ–²a2ᵛ (here

reprinted); *Works* (1651), pages 287-89. The 1640 edition exists in two issues, but Cartwright's poem is identical in both.

The "Kings sixth Child," Prince Henry, was born July 8, 1640.

63 *This Floating Island.* England, made unsteady and drifting by internal dissensions. The other "Floating Island," as Goffin observes was Delos, which, according to Spenser (*Faerie Queene*, II, xii, 13), "firmely was established" by the birth of Latona's "fayre twins," Apollo and Artemis. Thus Cartwright speaks of Prince Henry's birth as "settling" England.

VPON THE DEATH OF THE MOST HOPEFULL, THE LORD STAFFORD

Texts.—*Honour and Virtue, Triumphing over the Grave* (1640), sigs. P2ʳ–P3ᵛ [misnumbered P2] (here reprinted); *Works* (1651), pages [2]306-9; *Parnassus Biceps* (1656), pages 137-41.

The Lord Henry Stafford here celebrated was the grandson of Edward Stafford, third son of the first Baron Stafford (1501-63). He died in 1637. *Honour and Virtue* (1640), in which Cartwright's poem first appeared, was published as a memorial life of Lord Henry by his kinsman Anthony Stafford (1587-?1645). Goffin refers the reader to the articles on Anthony Stafford and the first Baron Stafford in *DNB*.

45-62 These eighteen lines are omitted in both *Honour and Virtue* (1640) and *Parnassus Biceps* (1656); they appear therefore only in the *Works* (1651). Goffin places them after line 26, a position which destroys the sense and breaks into the middle of a verse paragraph, thus departing from the line arrangement of the only complete text we possess (1651).

49-50 *No Tears had sowr'd his wines, no tedious-Long-*
Festivall-service been the Countri's wrong.

This type of run-on line was affected as a Latinism by even the best writers, e.g., Jonson and Milton. A single example from Shirley's *The Cardinal* (1652 ed., p. 5) will suffice:

> His talk will fright a lady: War and grim-
> Faced honour are his Mistress; he raves.

Examples of this metrical device in rhymed verse are rare. See, however, the concluding couplet of Herrick's "Farewell unto Poetry."

89–102 These lines are quoted, without attribution, by David Lloyd in his *Memoires* (1668), page 114. He applies them to Sir William Berkley.

On the Marriage of the Lady Mary to the Prince of Aurange his Son. 1641

Texts.—*Proteleia Anglo-Batava* (1641) sigs. a2ᵥ–a3ᵥ (here reprinted); *Works* (1651), pages 289–91. *Proteleia* (1641) also contains a Latin poem by Cartwright (sigs. A3ʳ–[A4]ʳ).

Goffin observes that Princess Mary, eldest daughter of Charles I, was not yet ten when the marriage was contracted. The ceremony took place on May 2, 1641.

To Philip, Earl of Pembroke, upon his Lordships Election of Chancellor of the University of Oxford

Texts.—Two broadside editions: (1) Luttrell (British Museum), Vol. I, fol. 120, "Printed for T.W. 1641," no woodcut, single sheet (here reprinted); (2) British Museum 669, fol. 4, dated 1641, full-length woodcut of ?Pembroke with label reading "My reward is from above," single sheet. Cartwright's verses also appear in SECVNDA VOX POPVLI / OR, / The Commons gratitude to the most / Honorable Philip, Earle of Pembroke / and Montgomery, for the great affection which / hee alwaies bore unto them. / With some verses upon his Lordships Election of / Chancellor of the University of *Oxford*. / By Willian [*sic*] Cartwright. /[full-length woodcut of ?Pembroke in a square] / Printed in the yeare 1641 (4 leaves, [A1], [A2], A3, [A4], unpaged; Cartwright's verses occur on [A2]ᵥ, followed by Thomas Herbert's verses [long form] on A3ʳ–[A4]ᵥ); and in *Works* (1651), pages 292–93 (misnumbered 593).

The discovery of a copy of the *Secunda Vox Populi* (in the Huntington Library, 145891) with the Cartwright verses as described by Hazlitt (*Collections and Notes*, 1876, I, 210) solves all the bibliographical difficulties raised by Goffin in his notes.

Both the broadside editions preface Cartwright's verses with the following imposing list of Pembroke's titles:

To the Right Honourable / PHILIP / Earles of Pembroke and Mountgomery, Baron Herbert of / Cardiffe and Shurland, Lord Par and Rosse of

Kendall, / Lord Fitzhugh Marmion, and Saint Quintine, Lord Warden of the / Staneries, in the countie of Devon and Cornewall, Lord High Steward / of the Duchie of Cornewall, Chancellour of the University of / Oxford, lord Lieutenant of the counties of Kent, / Cornewall and Wilts, Lord Chamberlaine of his / Majesties most honourable Household, Knight of the / most noble order of the Garter, and one of his / Majesties most honourable privie Counsell.

ON THE LADY NEWBURGH, WHO DYED OF THE SMALL POX

    Text.—*Works* (1651), pages 293 (misnumbered 593)–95 (misnumbered 592).

1–2 *Heaven once shall shrink / Up like a shrivell'd Scrole.* The general image is, of course, borrowed from Isaiah, 34:4 or Revelations, 6:14. I cannot, however, find the least authority for the translation "shrivel" in any of the versions I have consulted (Greek, Vulgate, Bishops', Geneva, Rheims, Calvin, Authorized). Apparently, nevertheless, there was some common authority for such a translation, since I find two other writers employing it in the same context. See Hooker's sermon, "A Remedy against Sorrow and Fear" (*Works*, ed. J. Keble, 1845, III, 646): ". . . in the day when the heavens shall shrival as a scroll and the mountains move as frighted men out of their places." And R. Fletcher, "Good Friday" (*Martial His Epigrams*, 1656, p. 156): "Or must yᵉ shrivell'd heavens in one dread fire / Rowle up in flames?"

44 *Spark.* A small diamond or ruby. Compare Cartwright's *The Lady-Errant*, IV, i:

    Crysolits, Jaspers, Diamonds, two whereof
    Do double the twelfth Caract: besides Sparks
    Enough to stick the Roof o'th' Banquetting House.

57–59   *. . . if that I*
    By praising blemish, too much Majesty
    Injures it self.
Although all editions punctuate as above, a semicolon or colon is needed after "blemish."

73–74 *The Gods whom they'l bereave / Do blindfold first.* This thought has, I believe, a classical origin. Compare Katherine Philips, "In Memory of F. P. who died at Acton" (*Poems*, 1678, p. 40):

> In these vast hopes we might thy change have found
> But that Heav'n blinds whom it decrees to wound.

Dryden has a variation of the theme in *The Hind and the Panther* (III, 1094-95).

On Mrs Abigall Long, who dyed of two Impostumes

Text.—*Works* (1651), pages 295 (misnumbered 592)-98.

11-15 *One who each night . . . her self.* One is here unpleasantly reminded of Swift's verses on "A Beautiful Young Nymph Going to Bed." I presume that a common source, probably classical, will explain the parallel.

29-30
> *. . . which I express*
> *Fittest by leaving it unto a Guess.*

Cartwright has a similar conceit in his verses "On the Lady Newburgh" (ll. 59-60):

> . . . where Art cannot express,
> It veyls and leaves the rest unto a Guess.

Compare Middleton's Prologue to *The Roaring Girl* (1611):

> Yet what need characters, when to give a guess
> Is better than the person to express?

An Epitaph on Mr. Poultney

Text.—*Works* (1651), page 298.

Goffin observes that the *Retrospective Review*, IX (1824), 169, quoting the poem in full, terms it "sensible, feeling, and concise."

15-16
> *To whom the gratefull wife hath sadly drest*
> *One Monument here, Another in her Brest.*

Compare Dryden, "Upon the Death of the Lord Hastings" (*Poems*, ed. J. Sargeaunt, 1929, p. 176):

> Erect no *Mausolæums:* for his best
> Monument is his Spouses Marble brest.

To the Memory of the most vertuous Mrs. Ursula Sadleir, who dyed of a Feaver

Text.—*Works* (1651), pages 299-300.

There is a little wall tablet to the memory of Ursula Sadleir, in Salisbury Cathedral. She was the daughter of

George and Katherine Sadleir and died in the second year of her age, July 18, 1641. She was followed to the grave seven days later by her younger sister (sorocula) Katherine.

8 *Wee'l think it thy translation, not thy death.* M. Lluellin, who was apparently a very close friend of Cartwright's, has a similar conceit in "An Elegie on the Most Reverend Father in God William, Lord Archbishop of Canterbury" (*Men-Miracles*, 1646, p. 138):

> He like old *Enoch* to His Blisse is gone,
> 'Tis not his Death, but his Translation.

Compare also two lines in an anonymous epitaph, dated 1644, "On James Whitehall, *Rector*" (in James Jones' *Sepulchrorum Inscriptiones*, 1727, I, 104-5):

> One that could live and dye as he hath done,
> Suffer'd not death, but a Translation.

The opening line of the epitaph ("White at [*sic*] his Name and whiter than this Stone") makes a curious coincidence with Cartwright's opening line.

55-56 *We may Conclude her Feaver, without doubt*
Was but the Flaming Sword to keep Eve *out.*

Cartwright, having said that Mistress Sadleir was as free from taint of sin when she died as when she was first born, concludes with the above couplet, which makes up for any lack of poetry by the positive brilliance of its application. In comparison, the following similar conceit from Donne's poem "A Fever" (*Poems*, ed. E. K. Chambers, I, ll. 13-16) is trite:

> O wrangling schools, that search what fire
>   Shall burn this world, had none the wit
> Unto this knowledge to aspire,
>   That this her fever might be it?

To the Memory of the Most Worthy, Sir Henry Spelman

Text.—*Works* (1651), pages 309-11.

Sir Henry Spelman (1564?-1641) was a well-recognized historian and antiquary. He has been called the true founder of the philological science in England. The work which particularly won him this distinction was his *Glossarium Archai-*

ologicum, the first volume of which appeared in 1626. Goffin also observes that in 1635 he wrote to a friend in Cambridge suggesting the foundation of an Anglo-Saxon lectureship at that university. Cartwright, as we know from other sources, was likewise interested in the older stages of English, a common ground which may, in part, explain his connection with Spelman. Besides his philological studies, Spelman also published several works in connection with the church, to one of which, *De Sepultura* (1641), Cartwright specifically refers in line 46.

3   *Exprobration.* "A casting in ones teeth" (Cockeram, *English Dictionarie*, 1623). As Goffin points out Cartwright uses the word in *The Royal Slave*, II, v, and the verb "to exprobrate" occurs in *The Royal Slave*, II, vi, and in *The Siege*, II, vi.

5-60   The following condensation of these lines appears in David Lloyd's "Life and Death of Sir John Bramston" (*Memoires*, 1668, p. 85):

> It's Pity none undertook thy Worth to tell,
> They Skill to know, thy Valour to do well;
> And what could Men do less when thou art gone,
> Whose Tenents, as thy Manners, were thine own.
> In not the same times both the same; not mixt,
> With the Ages Torrent, but still clear and fixt;
> As gentle Oyl upon the Stream doth glide,
> Not mingling with them, though it smooth the Tide.
> Nor didst thou thus affectedly, as they
> Whom humor leads to know, out of the way.
> Thy Aim was publick in it, thy Lamp and Night
> Searched untrod Paths, only to set us right.
> Thou didst consult the Ancients, and their Writ,
> To guard the Truth, not exercise thy Wit;
> Taking but what they say, not as some do,
> To find out what they may be wrested to;
> Nor Hope, nor Faction, bought thy Mind to side,
> Conscience deposed all Parts, and was sole guide.
> We have not time to rate thee, thy Fate's such,
> We know we've Lost, our Sons will say how much.

What useful things commendatory poems might be made; almost as good as an open letter of recommendation!

20   Ahaz *Diall.* As Goffin points out the reference is to 2 Kings, 20:11. The conceit seems to have been a favorite one. See, for example, Phineas Fletcher, *The Purple Island*, Canto VIII

(Chalmers, *English Poets*, 1810, VI, 116); William Strode, "Of Death and Resurrection" (*Poetical Works*, ed. B. Dobell, 1907, p. 50); Dryden, *The Hind and the Panther*, III, 538.

37 *That though her Dress, her Discipline now faints.* This is the reading of all editions, but something is obviously wrong. Perhaps the simplest solution is to consider "faints" as a singular verb used with a plural subject for the sake of the rhyme.

46 *that Charitable Piece.* As Goffin points out, this is a reference to Spelman's *De Sepultura* (1641). In illustration of Cartwright's next few lines, Goffin quotes from this work: "[The money] was first given for praying for Souls and such like, but that being abolished and given to the king, the Parsons, it seemeth, take it for the Grave." Spelman strives to show that the practice of paying for burial ground was no longer lawful.

On a vertuous young Gentlewoman that dyed suddenly

Text.—*Works* (1651), page [1]306 (exists in two states; see the introductory note to "On the *Queens* Return").

This poem is quoted in T. H. Ward, *English Poets* (1881) II, 233. Compare the first eight lines of Cartwright's poem with Dryden's *Eleonora* (1692), lines 301–16.

On the Death of ... Mrs Ashford, who dyed in Child-bed

Text.—*Works* (1651), pages [2]301–3.

6 *Not known by it's Vertue so much as his Loss.* Goffin remarks: "A second 'by' before 'Loss' would destroy the metre, but the line, as it stands, falls away badly after the first half." I cannot defend the line poetically, but, as it now reads, it is merely an example of the typical Elizabethan ellipsis and needs no emendation.

78 *Passions like Wilder Beasts thus tamed be.* Goffin points out that Lloyd seems to recall this line, when, in his "Life and Death of Mr. William Cartwright" (*Memoires*, 1668, p. 423), he describes Cartwright's metaphysical lectures on the passions:

> ... especially his Lectures on the Passions, which in his Descriptions seem but variated reason; those wild beasts being tuned and composed to tameness and order, by his sweet and harmonious language.

With this and the five preceding lines of Cartwright's poem compare also Carew, "On Celia Singing to her Lute" (*Poems*, ed. J. B. Ebsworth, 1893, p. 35), and Shadwell, *Psyche* (*Works*, ed. M. Summers, 1927, II, 291-92).

On the Queens Return from the Low Countries

Texts.—Musarum Oxoniensium . . . : Epibateria . . . Mariae ex Batavia Feliciter Reduci (1643), sigs. D1ᵛ–D2ʳ (here reprinted); *Works* (1651), pages [1]301-2 (exists in two states). *Epibateria* (1643) also contains a Latin poem by Cartwright (sig. Aa1).

This collection of congratulatory verses was occasioned by Henrietta Maria's return (February, 1643) from her mission to the continent, where she had gone in 1642 in an attempt to raise arms and money for the royal cause.

In most copies of the *Works* (1651) the second and fifth stanzas of this poem have been censored, leaving blanks on the pages where the lines were deleted. Some copies, however, contain the poem in its original uncensored form. Actually these two states represent two distinct settings of type. See my discussion of this matter in the General Introduction, Chapter V, "The Text."

9 *When She was shot at*, for the King's own good. As Goffin observes, this is a reference to "the cannonade fired on the Queen at her landing in Burlington. One of the Parliament captains responsible for this was seized and condemned, but graciously pardoned by the Queen. He was so touched by this kindness that he and several comrades came over to the King's side. Hence the episode was 'for the King's own good.' " The incident is referred to by Cowley in his poem "The Puritan and the Papist" (1643): "That you dare *shoot* at *Kings*, to *save* their *life*." See also Henry King, "An Elegy upon King Charles the First" (*Poems*, ed. L. Mason, 1914, p. 153).

13-16 *Courage was cast . . . grace*. Compare Margaret Cavendish's account in her biography of the Duke of Newcastle (ed. M. A. Lower, 1872, p. 30): ". . . she her self, and her Attendants, were forced to leave the same [a house], and to seek Protection from a Hill near that place, under which they retired; and all that while it was observed that Her Majesty shewed as much Courage as ever any person could do; for her undaunted and Generous spirit was like her Royal Birth. . . ." Goffin notices that these four "beautiful lines of Cartwright" are quoted in the *Quarterly Review*, XIII (1815), 488, from a life of Wellington, where they are used to describe the behavior of the Duchess of Angoulême at Waterloo.

30 *the Crown-Martyrs blood so lately spilt.* A writer in *Notes and Queries* (first series, I, 108-9) objects that this stanza of the poem, at least, could not be by Cartwright, since he died in 1643 and Charles was not executed until 1649. The "Crown-Martyr" here referred to was, of course, as Goffin observes, the Earl of Strafford, who was executed on May 12, 1641. The critic in *Notes and Queries* did not apparently know that the poem in its entirety had been published six years before the death of Charles. Another anonymous writer in the same volume of *Notes and Queries* (p. 151) draws attention to this fact.

Vpon the death of the Right valiant Sir Bevill Grenvill Knight

Texts.—Folger MS. 2071.7, fols. 262ᵛ-263ᵛ; *Verses on the death of the Right Valiant Sʳ Bevill Grenvill, Knight* (1643), pages 8-11 (here reprinted); another edition (1644), pages 5-8; *Works* (1651), pages [1]303-6 (exists in two states); *Verses by the Vniversity of Oxford On the Death of . . . Sir* Bevill Grenvill, *alias* Granvill, *Kt.* (1684, printed at London), pages 6-9; Lloyd, *Memoires* (1668), pages 470-71 (through line 80).

The Folger MS. (2071.7) gives no title to Cartwright's verses but includes them as second in a series under the title "Vpon Sʳ Richard Greenfield." Cartwright's verses are divided into stanzas of eight lines, the last couplet of each being indented. Both Lloyd (*Memoires*, 1668, pp. 470-71) and the manuscript omit lines 47-50. Otherwise Lloyd, as is his custom, seems to use the 1651 text, with one or two trifling variations. In view of the common omission, however, it is possible that Lloyd used a manuscript source.

Goffin bases his text on the London reprint of 1684. Chalmers (*English Poets*, 1810, VI) restores the deleted lines (see below), also from the 1684 text.

Goffin gives the following account of Sir Bevil Grenville:

Sir Bevill Grenville, who was a grandson of the Commander of the *Revenge*, was born in Cornwall in 1596. He went to Exeter College, Oxford, became a close friend of Sir John Eliot, and assisted at the latter's popular re-election to Parliament. He himself was a member of both the Short and Long Parliaments. He accompanied Charles against the Scots in 1639 and so obtained his knighthood. He opposed the death of Strafford and did not sign the Protestation. In February, 1643, at the outbreak of the war, he wrote to his wife: "God's will be done. I am satisfied I cannot expire in a better cause." He was at the Royalist victory at Stratton, May, 1643, but was killed at Lansdown on July 5th. "The bloody and tedious battle lasted from break of day until very late at night, when Sir Beville Grenville, bravely behaving himself, was killed at the head of his stand of pikes."

73-74 *Thus, He . . . the Living slew.* These are described as "noble lines" by George Granville, the grandson of Sir Bevil, in the notes to his poem entitled an "Essay Upon Unnatural Flights in Poetry."

81-92 These lines are deleted in most copies of the *Works* (1651), but a few copies contain the censored passage. See my discussion of the matter in the Introduction, Chapter V, "The Text."

90 *Traitor.* The writer already quoted in the notes to "On the Queens Return" objects (*Notes and Queries*, first series, I, 109) that, since this is a reference to Cromwell, the passage must be a later interpolation by some other hand. As in the former case he is again corrected by the other anonymous critic, who points out that the "Traitor" here meant is probably either the Earl of Essex or Sir William Waller (p. 151). Goffin is wrong in saying that "*Traytor* in the 1684 reprint fills the blank of the earlier editions." The 1643 edition also reads "Traitor."

On the Nativity

Text.—Works (1651), pages 317-18.

This and the two following poems were all, according to the *Works* (1651), composed "For the Kings Musick." The musical settings were probably by Henry Lawes.

On the Circumcision

Text.—Works (1651), pages 318-19.

Compare the two songs composed by Herrick on the same occasion (*Poetical Works of Robert Herrick*, ed. F. W. Moorman,

1915, pp. 365–67). Like Cartwright's(?) they were set to music by Henry Lawes. The first of Herrick's songs (*The New-yeeres Gift, or Circumcisions Song*) contains a blood-rose image (ll. 22–23) very similar to the conceit in lines 19–22 of Cartwright's poem. See also Miss Ruth Wallerstein's comments on the influence of religious music on the metrical form of these verses (*Richard Crashaw, A Study in Style and Poetic Development*, 1935, p. 49).

ON THE EPIPHANY

Texts.—*Works* (1651), pages 319–20.

NOVEMBER, OR, SIGNAL DAYES

Texts.—Broadside (undated), British Museum, 669, fol. 11, Bodleian Library, Wood, 416 (here reprinted); *November* (1671, printed in London).

Goffin gives a confusing note on the text of this poem, which is admittedly a rather confusing matter. In the first place he talks of a 1643 broadside edition, on which one would suppose he had based his text. The text which Goffin reprints, however, is the London edition of 1671—at least insofar as he reprints any specific text. Moreover, the 1643 edition, which he says is preserved in the Bodleian Library, does not seem to exist—at any rate neither the attendants nor I could discover it. There is, however, an undated broadside of the poem, copies of which may be found in both the Bodleian Library and the British Museum. The British Museum copy (669, fol. 11) is dated "November. 6. 1647" in a nearly contemporary hand. Since it is possible to show by internal evidence of the marginal commentary, that the broadside, whatever its date, is earlier than the dated London edition of 1671, I have made this particular British Museum copy the basis of my text. Goffin further complicates matters by stating that the poem was reprinted "at Oxford" in 1671. The only 1671 edition which I have found was printed not in Oxford, but in London, "In the Savoy, . . . by T. N. for *Henry Herringman.*" Goffin may possibly have been misled by a copy of the undated broadside in the Bodleian Library which is dated "1671" in a seventeenth-century hand (see *Texts* above).

It is probable, as Goffin observes, that Moseley is referring to "November" when in his preface "To the Reader" he writes:

> And (take it on his word who never *subscrib'd* to a Lye) there's nothing kept from you but only one short Paper of Verses: what that is, and why it is not here, we need not tell you; for it hath been twice already Printed, though above our Power to bring it with its fellows.

It should be noticed that Moseley here says that the poem has already (1651) been twice printed. If this is true, and there does not seem to be any good reason for doubting it, one of the editions has left "not a rack behind"—except in Goffin's note.

The marginal commentaries in the London edition (1671) are considerably fuller than those in the undated broadside version. They are as follows:

> [Stanza i] *First Day* All-Saints; *Second Day* All Souls.
> [Stanza ii] *Third Day Began the* Long Parliament 1640 *and* Mahomet *began his Reign* Anno 622. *and* Cautionary Towns *restored to the* States 1616.
> [Stanza iii] *Fourth Day The Birth of the Princess Royal* MARY (*P of* Aurange) 1632. *and of her Son the now Prince of* Aurange 1650.
> [Stanza iv] *Fifth Day, The* Gun-powder-Plot 1605.
> [Stanza v] *Twelfth and Thirteenth Day,* Brainford *Fight* 1642.
> [Stanza vi] *Sixteenth Day Queen* HENRIETTE MARIA *born.*
> [Stanza vii] *Seventeenth Day Queen* ELIZABETH *began her Reign* 1558.
> [Stanza viii] *Nineteenth Day The Birth of* K. CHARLES *the First* 1600.

11 *Draw the first Curtaine and the Scene is then.* Cartwright here employs the image of the court masque and treats each succeeding anniversary as a new scene in such an entertainment.

CONFESSION

Text.—Works (1651), page 320.

This to me is one of the most unpleasing of all Cartwright's poems—cold and artificial, when it should be simple and sincere.

The following lines from R. Fletcher's "Whitsunday" (*Martial His Epigrams*, 1656, pp. 162-63) may have some connection with Cartwright's verses:

> Are men like *Moses* bush? can bodyes burn
> Insensible? and not to ashes turn?
>
> . . . .
>
> Descend on me *Great God*! but in such fire
> May not consume, but kindle my desire.
> Descend on me in flames, but such as move
> Wing'd by th' inspiration of the Dove.
> Descend on me in *Cloven Tongues*! such as dispense
> No double meanings in a single sense.

THE DOUBTFUL POEMS

To Splendora not to be perswaded
Text.—The text of this and the following five poems is based directly on Harleian MS. 6917, fols. 75ʳ–77ᵛ. This poem is Number 143, fol 75. They were first ascribed to Cartwright and published by Miss Willa McClung Evans (*PMLA*, LIV [June, 1939], 406–11). My transcription will be found to differ from Miss Evans' in a number of readings. Capital "S" and "E" are almost indistinguishable from lower case "s" and "e."

For a full discussion of the attribution and authenticity of these poems see the General Introduction, Chapter V, "The Text," pp. 75-77.

Compare in general Cartwright's poem entitled "A Sigh sent to his absent Love." See also the notes to that poem.

To Splendora hauing seene and spoke with her through a window
Text.—Harleian MS. 6917, No. 144, fol. 75ᵛ.

This is perhaps the most original of the Splendora poems.

To Splendora desiring to heare musick
Text.—Harleian MS. 6917, No. 145, fols. 75ᵛ–76ᵛ.

To Splendora A morning Salutation
Text.—Harleian MS. 6917, No. 146, fols. 76ᵛ–77ʳ.

To Splendora weeping
Text.—Harleian MS. 6917, No. 147, fol. 77ʳ.

These eight lines are in fact part of Cartwright's acknowledged poem "The Teares." See the note to lines 7-14 of that poem. Several readings which are peculiar to this version are given among the variants to "The Teares."

To Splendora on the Same occasion
    Text.—Harleian MS. 6917, No. 148, fol. 77.

To his Mʳˢ Walking in yᵉ snow
    Text.—Malone MS. 21, fols. 78–79.

This poem seems to be little more than a considerably expanded and inferior version of Strode's (or Carew's) "On a Gentlewoman Walking in the Snow":

> I saw fair Cloris walke alone
> Where feather'd rayne came softly downe,
> And Jove descended from his tower
> To court her in a silver shower;
> The wanton snowe flewe to her breast   [5]
> Like little birds into their nest,
> And overcome with whiteness there
> For greife it thaw'd into a teare,
> Thence falling on her garment's hemme
> For greife it freez'd into a gemme.   [10]
> Or: [Which trickling down her garments hemme
>   To deck her freezd into a gemme.]

See *Poetical Works of William Strode*, ed, B. Dobell (1907), page 41.

1–3 *See . . . what a lovely bed . . . heavens have spread . . . to entertaine.* Compare the first three lines of "To Splendora A morning Salutation."

3 *congealed.* This is a favorite word with the Splendora poet. See line 9 of "To Splendora A morning Salutation" and line 8 of "To Splendora on the Same occasion." I can recall only two uses in Cartwright's acknowledged poems ("To *Lydia*," l. 25; and "Vpon the Birth of the Kings sixth Child," l. 45).

4 *yᵉ downy Raine.* Compare "feather'd rayne" in Strode's poem quoted above (line 2).

5–6 *O'recome with' whitenes . . . Melts into teares.* Compare lines 7 and 8 in Strode's poem. Compare also lines 11 and 12 of Cartwright's "A Sigh sent to his absent Love." See lines 29 and 30 below.

10 *A contradiction (warme snow).* This conceit also appears in Drummond's "Love Suffereth No Parasol" (*Poetical Works*, ed. W. B. Turnbull, 1890, p. 95).

19–20 *each amorous flaque . . . thy bosome.* Compare line 5 of Strode's poem.

20–25 *how they'le make . . . milky way . . . sleeke valley . . . breasts . . . in whitenes.* The imagery in these lines was the common property of the followers of the Petrarchan pastoral school. See, for example, Phineas Fletcher's *Brittain's Ida* (1628), Canto VI, Stanza 7; or Basse's *Three Pastoral Elegies* (1602), Elegy II (*Poetical Works of William Basse*, ed. R. Warwick Bond, 1893, pp. 57–59). The Fletcher and Basse passages are somehow connected (see Bond's note). See also *The Description of Woman* in *Witts Recreations* (1650), sigs. V2^r–V3^v.

29–30 *banisht . . . with whitenes, melts wth Greife . . . teare.* See the note to lines 5–6, above.

31–32 *thy garments hemme . . . decke thee freezes . . . Gemme.* Compare lines 9 and 10 (particularly the second version) of Strode's poem. Compare also *Samson Agonistes*, lines 728–30.

ON THE PRINCE CHARLES DEATH. W.C.

Text.—Folger MS. 646.4, pages [158]–59.

Cartwright's claim to these lines rests entirely on the initials "W.C.," though the general style of the verse may also be taken into account. The poem appears in a manuscript commonplace book which contains a large number of poems assigned to "W.S." [William Strode] and others assigned to Corbet, Carew, Donne, etc. It is, however, the only poem in the volume attributed to "W.C." So far as I know it has never been printed.

The occasion for these verses was the premature birth, and death, on May 13, 1629, of the first child born to Charles I and Henrietta Maria. Poems commemorating the event are not common. See one by Ben Jonson in "Underwoods," No. LXXXI, one, unsigned, in Folger MS. 2071.6, page 140, and another, also unsigned, in Sir Richard Cholmley's Commonplace Book (Harvard MS.), page 95.

8 *The two houres griefe.* The child lived only two hours.

TEXTUAL NOTES

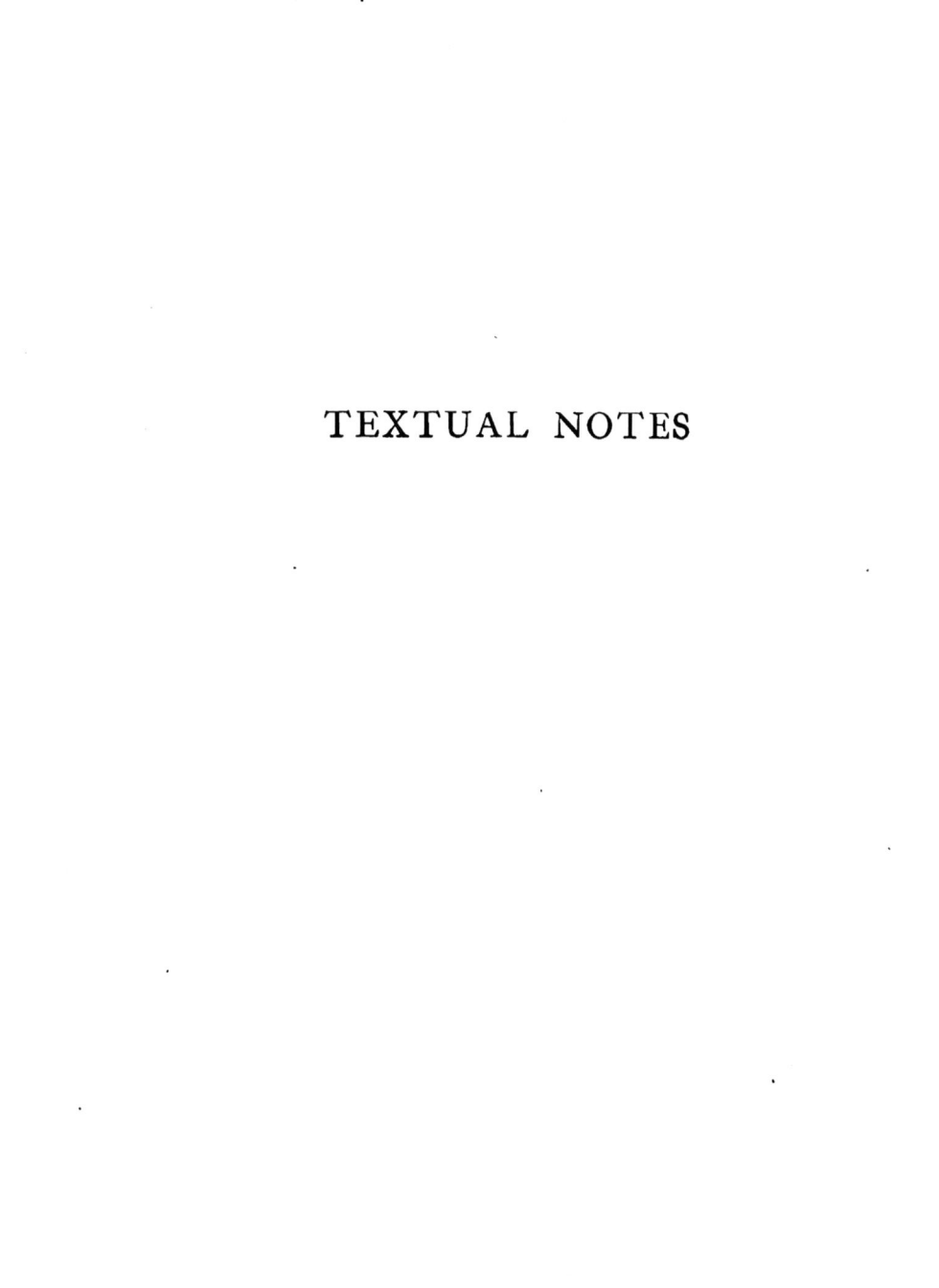

The Lady-Errant

In the prompt copy of *The Lady-Errant* two principal methods of deletion can be readily distinguished: (1) words, phrases, lines, and groups of lines crossed through with a single pen stroke; and (2) groups of lines, sometimes whole scenes, circled. The first method is used sometimes by Herbert (or his deputy) and sometimes by the playhouse reviser (the agent can usually be determined by the nature of the cut), and is designated in the notes which follow as "Deleted PC"; the second method, used only by the playhouse reviser, is designated as "Deleted PC reviser." Any other methods of deletion are specially noted.

THE PROLOGUE

13 *here*] here, **Goffin**
21 *conceive,*] conceive **Goffin**

THE PERSONS

PC distinguishes the principal characters (9) by a small cross preceding and following the name; less important characters (9) marked with a single cross following. This division, however, leaves *Eumela* as a minor character. *Philænus* and *3 Priests* are not marked with crosses.

ACT I

SCENE 1 **PC adds the following regie note: a Letter for olind: in 1st act. particular for Cosmeta in 4 Act a Roll: for Cosmet[a] a Letter for Eumela in 2 Ac[t] 2 Napkins in 3 Act**
3 Politique dore] gates of State **PC**
9 advis'd] most easy **PC**
21-25 They'd have ... them.] **Deleted PC reviser**
25 them.] them, **1651**
25-26 I believe They'd] I believe they would have smelt so rank I would **PC**
58-60 (as if ... 'em there)] but now **PC**
62 Poet.)] Poet. **1651**
64 wheels o'th'State] gouernment **PC**
66 How does ... now] is his Lordship **PC**
76 or ... Stairs.] **Originally deleted in PC; stet later written in margin** Stairs.] Stairs, **1651**
92 (*Cos.* ... on.)] *Cos.* ... on. **1651**
96-97 and ... still.] **Deleted PC**
109-10 Crest ... Boot] Scarfê **PC**
111 *Pan.*] *Pan* **1651**
120 at once] **Deleted PC**
126 Madam!] Madam? **1651**
147 Embraces?] Embraces. **1651**
156 Manner] grace **PC**
164 to] of **PC**
166 Man ... Romance] heroe in some brave Romance **PC**
169 that] my **PC**
  us] me **PC**
173 Eccho's] Eccho's and wood Nymphs **PC**
174-76 Send ... Nymphs] **Deleted PC reviser**
185 Give ... Drugs.] **Deleted PC**
193 in spight of you] **Deleted PC**
196 SD *Ler.*] *Ler,* **1651**
207 God] **Deleted PC**
208-14 as City ... Prescription still?] **Deleted PC reviser who then adds as freely as knigh[t] errants do kingdomes to their Squire[s.]**
223-24 in History ... Turtles] chronicled **PC**

229-30	and so ... Garments] **Deleted PC**	411	read?] read? that Ladies-errant kept Pages **PC**
232-33	the Ladies ... Lords.] **Deleted PC**	414	like you.] **PC adds prompter's note:** Knock read[y.]
239-42	Their Tapers ... Faces;] **Deleted PC reviser**	421	deliverance] deliverer **PC**
240	And] Aud **1651**	428	deliverance] deliverer **PC**
243	This] that **PC**	430	if it were] **PC adds SD:** *Knoc[k.]
244	to] ro **1651**	443	Why] why **1651**
257	Your ... not.] **Deleted PC**	452	The plumpest Bulbi?] **Deleted PC**
261	take rest] take our rest **PC**	462	share ... meat] eate at their tabl[e] **PC**
	as then] **Deleted PC**		
280-83	without ... self alone] Our thoughts our secret thoughts Eumela **PC**	465	good Comedies] **PC here adds a prompter's note: Call Mal[thora] & fflorina ? deoo: sher & Burf-[ord] Bamfei[ld.]**
284	Trouble ... World] Trouble and Tumult **PC**	466	Park—] Park.—**1651**
297-99	whose cold ... yet] **Deleted PC (it is possible that the whole of line 299 was meant to be deleted)**	472	With ... next y'] **Deleted PC**
		481	and prove inward.] **Deleted PC**
		485	Our thanks] **PC adds SD:** Ent: fflo: Maltho.
325	Take ... there] touch thy Lute **PC**	486	Will be] **PC adds SD in left margin: Dance [o]f 8.**
326	That thou ... sad] thy mournfull Ode Malthora **PC**		Will ... Recompence.] **PC inserts here the following speech: Ler. And to show our joy if they please we'l join with 'em in a dance.**
SD	Eumela] Malthora **PC**		
333	Live,] Live **Goffin**		
334	Why;] why **1655**		
336	Truth] truths **1655**		
	suspect,] suspect. **1655**	SD	Gan.] Gon. **1651 (some copies)**
341-44	Thou art ... like.] **Deleted PC**	508-9	Paria ... Chamber.] **Deleted PC**
354-55	That being ... still.] **Deleted PC reviser**	519	Of Loaves and Wine] Of strong Greek Wine **PC**
		537	I'l] **Deleted PC**
Act II		SD	Eumela.] Eumela. a Letter **PC**
Scene I	**PC here first indicates the setting as Hall.**	543	Mars ... you.] **Deleted PC**
		561	and Achme] **Deleted PC**
373 SD	Cosmeta] Cosmeta with a particula[r] **PC**	567	after] **Deleted PC**
375	Ladyes] Ladys **1651**	577	that] **Deleted PC**
376 SD	Rho.] Rho **1651**	582	permit] leave **PC**
381	To fairer ... pricking] To Ladyes in Romances riding **PC**	596	I go.] I go. they are neare in y° Groue Mad: **PC**
384	and young Bodkins] or Bodkins **PC**	DESIGNATION	Act. II.] Act. III. **1651**
385	You wear ... Delights.] **Deleted PC**	Scene v	**This scene is deleted by PC reviser**
400	generous] **Deleted PC**	Scene vi	**PC indicates the setting as Grove.**
403	'Vantage ... thou] **Deleted PC**	655	words return'd] very words **PC**

657 I'l]Ile 1651 (B)
660 As an Intelligence] Deleted PC
661 To move . . . it?] Deleted PC
662 Prince?] Prince, 1651 (B)
665 last?] last, 1651 (B)
666 She] she 1651 (B, C)
668 wise.] wise; 1651 (B, C)
669 only] onely 1651 (B)
671 Forbid] Forbids 1651 (A, B, C)
674 doe] do 1651 (B, C)
679 accesse] access 1651 (C)
680 lesse] less 1651 (C)
  goe] go 1651 (B, C)
681 doe] do 1651 (B, C)
685 self . . . self] selfe . . . selfe 1651 (B)
  art.] art: 1651 (B, C)
686 goe . . . goe] go . . . go 1651 (B, C)
688 CATCHWORD Olyndus] Olyn. 1651 (B, C)
689 Olyndus,] Olyndus 1651 (B, C)
690 informe] inform 1651 (B, C)
693 that] Deleted PC
  She . . . She] she . . . she 1651 (B, C)
696 however] however 1651 (A)
  She] she 1651 (B, C)
697 you,] you 1651 (B, C)
  one] one. 1651 (B)
699 Bodies,] Bodies. 1651 (B, C)
703 be] bee 1651 (B)
704 Beautiful] Beautifull 1651 (C)
  &] and 1651 (B, C)
706 self . . . fair] selfe . . . faire 1651 (B)
709-10 But doth . . . Nature.] Deleted PC
712 I'l] Ile 1651 (B)
716 do] doe 1651 (B)
  Lucasia] Calanthe 1651 (A)
718 Lover,] Lover 1651 (B)
SD Exeunt.] Exeunt 1651 (A)

ACT III
719 May't] M May't 1651
  May't . . . Highness,] Deleted PC

726 Will be . . . Ears;] here, is safe. PC
736-38 Ev'n . . . dangers.] Deleted PC
743 Amorous] Deleted PC
751 Headlong] Headstrong PC
774-75 they have . . . Eyes:] Deleted PC
783-806 Though I . . . yeeld.] Deleted PC reviser
798 That;] That 1651
807 love his] like his PC
817 Spend, and disburse] and disclose PC
819-20 'till . . . Triumph] Deleted PC
841 Doom.] Doom 1651
850-54 With . . . people.] With rapture PC
858 Flowers] angells PC
859-61 Eyes . . . Lustre.] Deleted PC
872 Achme] Acme 1651 (altered in Errata)
874-76 and makes . . . her] Deleted PC
882-97 Conceive . . . Glories?] Deleted PC reviser
901 Dote] Doat 1651 (B)
  and . . . Bloud] with Bloud PC
905 Spark] spark 1651 (B)
  She] she 1651 (B)
909 bids you when y'have] bids when you have 1651 (B)
910 her Subjects] his Subjects 1651 (B)
911 Her] His 1651 (B)
  Kingdom] Kingdome 1651 (B)
  Conquer] conquer 1651 (B)
912-15 If I . . . Affection.] Deleted PC
917 Tyranny,] Tyranny: 1651 (B)
918 She] she 1651 (B)
922 She] she 1651 (B)
924 Charistus] Charistus, 1651 (A)
925 him,] him 1651 (A)
  She] she 1651 (B)
926 I'l] I'll 1651 (B)
928 that Fire] the Fire 1651 (B)
929 self] selfe 1651 (B)
931 The bent of] your PC
933 self,] self; 1651 (B)
938 Lucasia!] Calanthe! 1651 (A)

943   that's Masculine] that is not noble PC
944   Treachery] [t]raytor PC
      anger] Anger 1651 (B)
945   lazie] lazy 1651 (B)
946   And] Aud 1651 (B)
947   here] here, 1651 (B)
949   Pray] 'Pray 1651 (B)
955   'Tis] 'Iis 1651 (B)
957-59 which hath ... War.] which is now fighting against yor. country. PC
962   Clasp'd in Embraces] in a friends arm[s] PC
964   The Bosome ... Father] your Fathers house PC
965   Eyes,] Eyes; 1651 (B)
968   Thunder] Thunder, 1651 (A)
974   untye] unty 1651 (B)
981   proclam'st] proclaim'st 1651 (B)
983 SD retire,] retire? 1651 (A)
      Myrtle] Myrtl 1651 (A)
984   Oly.] Olyn. 1651 (B)
987   is] has PC
988   Reverence] reverence 1651 (B)
      Lucasia] Calanthe 1651 (A)
990   whom (but] hear me PC
      with)] with you PC
991   Lucasia] Calanthe 1651 (A)
996   Lucasia] Calanthe 1651 (A)
998   Men] men 1651 (B)
1000 Lucasia] Calanthe 1651 (A)
1002 Heavens forbid] Heaven forbid 1651 (B)
1005 SD sinks.] sinks 1651 (B)
      embrace.] embrace 1651 (A)
1014 some good] somegood 1651
SCENE IV PC indicates the setting as grove Continu[ed.]
1023 b'your] by'our 1651
1028 one] Deleted PC
      Wee'l divert] PC adds here a prompter's note: Call Nicias in to dance a Jigg.
1029 Reach me] Reach her PC
1030 Have ... heard] let's heare PC

complain] PC adds here a prompter's note: Jigg
1031-33 The young ... these.] Deleted PC.
TITLE The Ode.] Venus *lamenting her lost* Adonis 1652, 1659; *Venus lachrimans* 1656; Venus for her belov'd Adonis **Goffin**
1034 *Luc.*] *Cal.* 1651
1036 *words*] looks 1652, 1653, 1655, 1659
1037 *Loves*] fears 1652, 1653, 1655, 1659
1039 *'em*] them 1652, 1653, 1655, 1656, 1659
1040 *that*] thy 1656
1041 *those*] these 1655
1044 *thund'ring*] thundering 1656
1049 *did hang*] first hung 1652, 1653, 1655, 1659
1056 *Sorrow*] sorrŏws 1656
1058 *no Fates can*] the Fates shan't 1652, 1653, 1655, 1659
      whiles] whilst 1652, 1653, 1655, 1659
1059 *Grieve, and*] Grieve. and 1651; weep but 1656
1064 From ... Myrtles.] here from the ground. PC
1072 lean'd] fell PC
1073 Trees] ground PC
1077 O Heav'ns,] Deleted PC
1092 He was ... lov'd him.] a Princess lov'd him. **PC (this is the final reading; an earlier alteration read** He had a Princess's love; 'twas I that lov'd him.**)**
1094 And signs ... Soveraign] Deleted PC
1108-9 O Nature ... Hearts?] O Nature were not our Hearts [th]e same? PC
1115-62 Would some ... own Foe.] **These lines (pages 43 through 44) are missing in PC**
1146 forget] forge 1651 (corrected in the *Errata*).

Act IV

SCENE I   **PC indicates the setting as Hall. a Table and 10 Chaires with ye great.**

1163   My Lady ... Mercuriall] most wise, most valliant, & most politick Ladies **PC**

1166-70   A Peece ... forth us;] **Deleted PC**

1170   howsoever] howsoeve **1651** (corrected in some copies)

1176   Being ... Grossness:] **Deleted PC**

1178-79   grant me ... more fit] & fit **PC**

1180-82   Which some ... Slaves;] **Deleted PC reviser**

1182   our] yet our **PC**

1183-86   t'assume ... Imperiall, hath] to Challenge a Soverainty in Arts, and Arms, hath **PC**

1189   Envious of her] **Deleted PC**

1191-92   Let us ... Creation.] **Deleted(?) PC reviser**

1196   selves into] **Deleted PC**

1201   Mistris Speaker] Eumela **PC**

1213   *Sibyl's ... Juno!*] **Deleted PC**

1215-19   man hath ... Dough-bak'd Men.] man ever had halfe that cunning, in mannageing an intrigue, as wee haue, haue they not learnt the best of their state policy, their wise dissimulation [from us (?) ?] **PC**

1218   Dough-bak'd] Dough bak'd **1651**

1221   greater] greater of their owne **PC**

1223-24   they being ... spit.] **Deleted PC**

1278   more] embost **PC**

1279-82   The one ... More yet,] **Deleted PC**

1283   less engraven] engraven **PC**

1286   Furs] Fur gownes **PC**

1303   that's all] bodkins & a bushel of thimbles **PC**

1307   disburse.] disburse this treasure. **PC**

1309   Perhaps] **Deleted PC**

1313   as yet] **Deleted PC**

1323   Suburb brangles.] **PC adds SD: here Antick.**

1325   and Be.] **Deleted PC**

1327   own.] own **1651**

1328   *Luc.*] *Cal.* **1651**

1331   were ... Thunder] were hid in Thunder **PC**

1338   I look to her,] I court her, and **PC**

1339   to] **Deleted PC**

1343-45   for ever? ... Natives] for ever? and be at once the Natives **PC**

1359   propos'd] popos'd **1651**

1393   *Eumela,*] What looks like the word all, followed by a d (the rest shaved) appears in the upper right corner of PC. Perhaps all is a carelessly written call, and d the initial letter of an actor's name.

1411   very] **Deleted PC**

1418   Dames.] Dames for beauty. **PC**

1419-21   Yes to ... They say] **Deleted PC**

1420   *Phil.*] *Phil,* **1651**

1433-34   as a hungry ... rich Heir] as a rich Heir **PC**

1443   are in] supply **PC**

1448-50   How can ... Confident.] **Deleted PC reviser**

1454-57   They're to ... they come.] look they are coming hith[er] the Queene is wth em too **PC**

1457 SD   *Ex. ... Phi.*] **Deleted PC** Phi.] Phi– **1651**

SCENE III   **This scene is deleted by PC reviser**

1472-73   'twas young ... went.] **Deleted PC** (this and the following deletion were made before the whole scene was cut)

1474-75   and endeavour ... come out.] **Deleted PC**

SCENE IV   **This scene is deleted by PC reviser**

1496   Now] Perhaps we should read How

1506 SD   To them ... *Pæstanus.*] To

them *Adraste,* Florina, Malthora PC
1506 *Charistus,*] You are welcome home my L^{ds}. *Charistus,* PC
1507 Kingdom ... you?] Kingdom's lost they say PC
1515-27 This blast ... in breath.] Deleted PC reviser
1537 And dust] Deleted PC
1563-78 Father ... *Crete.*] Deleted PC reviser (certain passages in these lines were first separately deleted)
1565 in] it 1651 (corrected in the *Errata* and in PC)
1573-76 Honour ... write] Honour is Justice Temperance and Prudence and doth write PC
1578-79 If he ... them;] Deleted PC
1586-97 And yet ... deserve her.] Deleted PC reviser (lines 1589-90 mark an earlier separate cut)
1588 could stoop] could stould stoop 1651 (corrected in some copies)
1589-90 Or if ... Prince?] Deleted PC
1604-5 drinks ... suspicion] drinks ye poyson of suspicion PC
1617-21 What Though ... Advis'd;] Deleted PC
1624 of Instinct, and Diety] of ye Diety PC
1625-44 Alas! it ... preserve it.] Deleted PC reviser
1646-47 Or who ... cracking?] Deleted PC
1655 *Luc.*] *Luc.* 1651
1655-63 These preserve ... Center.] Deleted PC reviser
1663 What ... not] Deleted PC
1664 it] you PC
Defect in one] Deleted PC
1690 Errours] Deleted PC
1692 which] while PC

ACT V
SCENE I This scene is deleted by PC reviser

1708 Metamorphosis] Metamophosis 1651
1725 *Cos.*] *Cas.* 1651
1742 such] snch 1651 (some copies)
1748 *Rho.*] *Pho.* 1651
1777 know't, there] know't there 1651
1778 *Mach.*] *Mach* 1651
1787 Service.] Service 1651
1814 *Philænis*] *Philenis* 1651
SCENE II PC adds stage setting and prompter's note: Pallace for Church [?to] be read[y.]
1837 Queen, your] Queen tho your PC
1838-43 Are greater ... of Vertue] Deleted PC
1881 any] euerie PC
1882 That ... discern.] Deleted PC
1884 and pare] lessen PC
1888 Scepters] kingdomes PC
1890-95 you ne'r ... them on.] Deleted PC reviser (first through line 1893 only)
1900 *Luc.*] *Cal.* 1651 (corrected in the *Errata*); *Mal.* PC
1900-1 If it ... Trust;] Deleted PC
1901 Injustice] Injustice Madam, PC
1903 Cabinet] Cabinet, council too, PC
SCENE III This scene seems to be deleted by PC reviser
1934 what Forks ... Carving?] we have? PC
1935 Crisping Pins] Crisping iron[?s] PC
1960-68 Pray y'allow ... Sages.] Deleted PC reviser
1984 Impertinent] Impertinen 1651
1997 a peece of Chrystall] such brittle ware PC
1999 Crystal] glass PC
2005 Though ... Native.] Deleted PC
2023 Among your selves.] Deleted PC
2031 *Cos.*] *Cos* 1651
2049 stand off.] Deleted PC
2050 1 Priest.] 1 Priest, 1651
2051 true;] true **Goffin**
2052 *Bright*;] *Bright,* **Goffin**

2059	Cho.] *Cho.* **1651**
2060	*as Præsent*] at Present **Goffin**
2065	*Loves*] Love's **Goffin**
2069	*Doves,*] *Doves* **1651**
2071	Chorus.] **Omitted Goffin**
2077	though happy] **Deleted PC**
2101	spoke it,] **PC adds SD: Grand dance.**
2109	**Following this line in PC appears Sir Henry Herbert's license (the signature only in his autograph):** March: 9: 1671: This Play Called The Lady Errant may bee Acted by the Dukes Company of Actors as Lycenced by
	Henry Herbert Millb: Westm^r M.R.

The Royal Slave

PROLOGUE TO THE KING AND QUEEN
TITLE THE PROLOGVE ... QVEENE.]
　　To the Kinge & Queene/theire Maj:^{ts}/The Prologue P; The Prologue to the Royall slave presented to his Majestie at X^{ts} Church in Oxford. E
SD *The first ... Sun.*] **Omitted S, B, P**; At the first discouery of the scene appeerd a Temple of the Sunn. The prologue (a preest of the Sunn) worshipping &c. F
　　Appearance,] *Appearance* 1639, 1640, 1651
　　One ... discover'd] The Curtaine drawne, a Priest is discovered E
　　in a Temple ... new] worshipping theyr Sunne in his Temple, upon ye sight of new S; worshippinge their Sunne, upon the sight of a new F; worshiping their King in his temple upon sight of the new B; worshippinge their Sunne, upon the sight of a New P; worshippinge at the Altar of the Sunne, whe [sic] as soon as he espyed the E
　　Majesty] King & the Queene E
　　addresseth ... Throne.] speaks as followeth E
　　to] towards, S, B
1　From my] Mag: From my F, P
2　by] from P (by in margin)
　　Sun.] Sun, 1651
4　yond] yon F, P
5-6　your ... yours] **These two words are underlined and** our **written in the left margin in P**
6　its] it's 1651, Goffin; i'ts F
8　but confesse] but to confesse (reading of proof sheet A of 1639 quarto, corrected)
9　Art,] Art (reading of proof sheet A of 1639 quarto, corrected); Art. S; Art: F, P
10　still] farre E
11　Whiles] Whilst E
　　Majesty ... is] Ma:^{ty} our Sceanes are P; Majesty scenes are E
12　Entertainer] Entertainer, 1640, 1651, Goffin

PROLOGUE TO THE UNIVERSITY
TITLE THE PROLOGVE ... VNIVERSITY.] **Omitted in P**; The Prologue to the University, after the *King's departure.* 1651, Goffin; The Prolouge to the Vniversity, by a Preist discouer'd at his Deuotions, as before. F; The Prologue to the same presented to the Vniversity. E
SD A Priest ... before.] **Omitted in Goffin, S, B, E**
1　*our Rites*] *the Rites* (reading of proof sheet A of 1639 quarto, corrected)
　　the] yor S, B; our F
2　*Devotion's*] Deuotion's S; Devotions 1639, 1640, 1651, F, P
3　*But ... wish*] But now I would S, F, B; But I would E
　　Question] Questions B
　　hung up] bring up E
　　there] here 1651, E
4　*eare.*] *eare:* 1651
5　*Building*] Buildings S, B, E
6　*th'*] the B
　　into a] int'a S
8　*Professour,*] Professour E

9 *th'*] the **B**
   we] you **1651**
14 *Sinne*] Singe **E**
15 *then*] there **Goffin**
19 *Expect no*] **No paragraph in S**
21 *sent*] lent **S, F, B**
23 *We ... none*] Here's none wee hope **S, B**
   from] by **E**
24 *sowre it into*] sowre't into a **E**
   with] by **E**
25 *or*] the **E**
27 *There's ... shot*] No Man is shott **S, F, B, E**
   Person's] Person **S, F, B, E**
29 *And such ... adventures*] And such the first Adventures should still **S, F, B**; And such the adventures should still **E**
31 *or*] nor **S, F, B**
32 *is*] are **E**
33 *The Stage*] **Paragraph in S**; The State **E**
34 *lay*] ley **Goffin**
36 *Mercenary*] Merc'nary **(reading of proof sheet A of 1639 quarto, corrected)**
   Guise] Quire **E**
   fits] fit **1640**
   Gowne] Crowne **B (F seems to have been altered from** Crowne to Gowne**)**
37 *Applause,*] Applause **1651, Goffin**

PROLOGUE TO THEIR MAJESTIES AT HAMPTON COURT
TITLE THE PROLOGUE ... *Hampton-Court.*] **Omitted in all MSS**
SALUTATION *Most mighty ... Queene:*] Most mighty ... Queen, **1651**; **omitted Goffin**
4 *they'are*] th'are **1640, 1651, Goffin**
11 *yet*] **Omitted Goffin**
16 *chaf'd*] chas'd **Goffin**
19 *this;*] this: **1640**
20 *now.*] now: **1651, Goffin**

THE PERSONS OF THE PLAY
It has not been considered worth while to record here the many unimportant variations in the lists of the dramatis personae which appear in the four manuscripts, no two of which agree. The variations are largely those of character order and descriptive title. The more interesting readings, with those of the printed texts, follow.
Praxaspes] Paraxaspes **1651 (corrected in** *Errata***)**
His Lords.] His Nobles **S, P, B**
Orontes] Oronates **B**
3. Magi ... Priests.] Magi 3—— Preists of theyr God Mithra **P**
Queene to Arsamnes.] Queene to Arsames. **1640**
Masquers, 6. Ladyes.] 6 other Ladyes attendants **F**

ACT I
SD *2ᵈ Appearance ... side.*] The Second Appearance ... side. **1640, 1651; omitted S, P, B**; 1ˢᵗ. Act: 1 Scene appeereth the Cytty Sardis in Front and on one syde a prison. **F**
Philotas] Philotus **1651**
singing in the Prison,] within the Prison. **P**
1 *Captives,*] Captives **1651**
   most] more **(underlined and** most **written above) P**
3 *'em*] them **B**
3-4 *too ... live*] I'me sure well to liue too **S, F, B**
4 *and*] **Omitted S**
   they're] they are **S, F, P**
6-7 *our Gaolor, &c.*] **1651**; our Gaolor. &c. **1639, 1640**; our &c. **S, P, B**; &c. **F**
8 *So! now*] Soe now **S, P, B**; So, now **F**
   they're] they are **S, F, P**

11 Hymne] Hymns **B**
in the prayse] in honour **S**; in the honoʳ **B**; omitted **P**
12 their] the **B**
great ... Tunbellyed] greate, huge, rowling, Tun-belly'd **F**; Huge tunnebelly'd **P**
14 our] the **1652, 1658, 1670, 1671**
Jowle;] **1640, 1651, 1671**; Jowle **1639**; Goales, **1652, 1658**; Jole, **1670**; Jowle: **F**; Jowle—**P**
14 SD *That's I. That's I.*] **F, S, P**; *That's that's I.* **1639, 1640, 1651**
15 o'th'Bowle.] *o'th'Bowl,* **1651**; of Bowles: **1652, 1658**; of th' Bole, **1670**
16 what ... Raskall] the Raskall what e're he **1652, 1658**
ever] e're **1652, 1658**; ere **S, F, P, B**
16 SD *Mol.*] **S, F, P, B**; omitted **1639, 1640, 1651**
againe:] agayne. **F**; again? **P**
good, good] **S, F**; *good good* **1639, 1640, 1651**; good **P**
17 Our Dungeon is] his Dungeons are **1652, 1658**
but ... too] so are our Cups too **1652, 1658**
but] First written **as** and in **B**, but later corrected to **but**
Cup's] Cups are **1667, 1670, 1671, 1673**
18 a round] a health **1652, 1658**; round **1670**
19 hard] cold **1652, 1658, 1671**
Irons] Iron **1671**
21 there is] there's **S, F, B**
22 of] Omitted **B**
22-23 I have ... it] I remember **S, B**
24 voyces] voice **P**
29 SD *He ... enter.*] (Hee opens yᵉ Dore.) **S, B**; (he opens yᵉ Prison doore.) **P** (follows my Friends, line 25 above, in these MSS
and] Omitted **F**
30 SD *shews ... halter.*] Omitted **S, F, P, B**

31 hand will] hand that will **P**
33 halfe-breeches] half breeches **1651**
what's] what is **S, P, B**
35 Sir] Sʳˢ **P**
words:] words Sʳ **S**
36 you] yee **P**
here] Omitted **S, F, B**
37 owne] **1640, 1651**; one **1639**
39 Web-errantry] Web errantry **1640, 1651**
40 turning and winding] turnings and windings **S, F, P, B**
43 And] Then **S, F, P, B**
44 of thine] Omitted **S, F, P, B**
45 whiffle] whiffe **S, P, B**
51 I'd] I doe **B**
53 mak'st] makest **S**
55 gon, and don't] gon doe not **P**
don't] doe not **B**
loves] love's **1640, 1651** (the apostrophe is specially added by the proof-corrector of the 1640 quarto)
56 Garbidge-tubbes] Garbidge tubs **1651**
57 shall be] shalbe **P**
words you] words that you **P**
59 won't let us] won't let's **F**; will not let us **P**
61 what's] what is **S, F, P**
62 his] the **P**
63 some] Omitted **S, P**
64 take] bringe **P**
65 and ... him] that he may be **F, P**
70 to make] make **S**
71 Kings] Kings, **1651**
73 for ... dayes] Omitted **S, F, P, B**
74 will, and] will for 3 dayes, and **S, F, P, B**
be certainly] certainely be **P**
76 I'd] I doe **B**
78 reasonably] **F** read **nobly**, altered to **reasonably**; reasonable **B**
I'd] I had **F, B**
79 liffe] 'lieve **1651**

82 an't] and S; &'t P
84 their] these 1651
   brave with] braue here with S, F, P, B
   meanes.] meanes elce. P
85 Well, what] ? what P (the question mark, which equals a mark of exclamation in this MS, seems to indicate that Well has simply dropped out in copying)
86 have] ha' S, F
   old] Omitted S, B
89 the Stratocles] the Stratocles's P; Stratocles B
90 of't] on't S, F; of it B
   Revell it] reuell't S, F, P
   night] the night B
91 of the] of theire S, F, B
   people.] people 1651
93 and] Omitted S, P
   sure ... none] sure that shee lett not any S, F, B; sure that you lett not any P
94 of the Law] in Law S, F, P, B
   Market] Mercat F; Marketts P, B
95 approaches] approacheth S, F, P
96-97 be ... Lords.] blow nothing upon ye Lords be sure S, F, P, ?B
97 SD To them] Omitted S, B
   Hydarnes, Masistes] Masistes, Hydarnes S, F, P
   Orontes, Priests] Preist, Orontes S; Orontes. Three Preists with the Royall Robes P
   Cratander.] Cratander, 1640, 1651
100 apart] a part S
101 he's] hee is S, F
102 thought him unfit] conceivd him not fitt S, F, P, B
   honour.] P here adds SD: Exit Mol:
103-5 Goe call ... sword.] Not divided as verse in S, P
103 all] Omitted P
   these has] these that ha's S; these that hath P; these that has B

105 if't] if it B
105 SD Enter ... Cratander.] Enter ... Cratander, 1651; to them Molops wth Cratander. S, F, B; To them Molops wth Cratander readinge. P
108 We've] W'haue S, F, P; (?W') haue B
109 conning a Hymne] cunning an Hymne P
112 the well inclin'd] th'well-inclin'd, 1651; th'well inclin'd F; the well-enclin'd P
113 conquer'd] Conquered F
   dost speake] speakst F
115 Conquest,] Conquest. P
116 entitle't yours] entitle yours P
122 subdued] subdu'd F, P
123 deservings] deserving's 1651
127 flesh'd] flesh't 1640
   Conscience] Conscience, 1651
129 Lawrell's planted] Lawrells plated P
   ev'n] even S, P
130 safe-protecting] safe protecting 1651
   will not] Begins next line in F
132 strength] strenght F
134 Heav'n] Heauen S, P
135 fruits] Wealth S, F, B; fruit P
137 True.] True, 1651
   vowes,] vows. 1651
138 wouldst] would F
141 th'Deity] ye Deity S, P
142 maymed, or mishapen] maymd or ye misshapen S, F, P, B
143 A thing] Omitted P
   himselfe] it selfe S, F, B
144 Natures] Nature's 1651
146 specious] spatious P
148 (t's pitty)] ('t's pitty) 1651; ('ts pitty) S, F; ('tis pitty) B
   reasoned] reasond S, F, P
151 prov'd] prov'd, 1640, 1651
153 the] yt S, P
   appetite] appetite, 1640, 1651
163 Heav'n] Heauen S

165 the Robes] 1640, 1651; Robes 1639; the Robes F (Robes **written above** Crowne), S, P
166 faithfull] Loyall P
166 SD (*He kisseth*] (Kisses S, F; (Kisseth P; (Kisse B
   The Priest's] The Preistes S; A Preist P
   song] sings P
   whiles he puts] while he puts 1651; whiles he is putting S, P, B
167 Throne] *Throne*, 1651
169 then a while] then a while then a while 1667
   mayst] *may'st* 1651; maiest S; mayest LA
170 to fall] to fall to fall 1667
171 *Cho:*] Cho. 1651; **omitted** S, F, P, B, E
   sacrifice] Sacrifiee 1651
172 bleed.] bleed, they bleed. 1659, 1667, 1669, 1673
173-79 Wash ... Beasts: &c.] **Omitted 1659, 1667, 1669, 1673, S, F, P, B, E (replaced by lines 1562-67 in 1667, 1673)**
175 That as ... see] And when thou fallest maye wee see LA
178 Whiles] Whilst LA
   pleasures ripen] pleasure ripens **Beloe (1812)**
179 *Cho:*] Cho. 1651
   Beasts:] *Beasts*, 1651
184 SD *Ex. Arsam.*] **Omitted S, B**
190 Off with] Strike off P
191 quickly] **Omitted 1640, 1651**
193 Royall] **Omitted S**
194 Battle] **Part of previous line in P**
195 safe] safe, 1640, 1651
196 his] it's S; its B
198 SD (*Ex. Crat.*] **Omitted S, B**
199 you'l] you would P
   I've] I haue S, F, P
200 Jack-chaynes at] Jack chains at 1651; Jack chaines y^t art at S, F, P, B

service:] service.. 1639 (a half-turned colon); service. 1640, 1651
   Gentlemen] Gent: F
201 your] **Omitted P**
202 foot] feete P
202-3 liberty to kicke thee.] libertie thee P (thee **crossed through**)
203 thee.] thee 1651
203 SD (*Ex. ... Slaves.*] (Exeunt *Slaues & Mol:*) S; (Ex: 4 Slaues and Molops.) F; Exeunte Captiues & *Molops*. P
204 Whether] Whither 1651
205 large] vast F
206 Hee'd] Hee'ld P
209 A] **Part of previous line in P**
210 they that] those who S, B; those that F; they who P
212 the] our S, F, B
214 Slave.] Slave; 1640, 1651
216 sullying] suffering B
220 Sun, my Lord,] 1640, 1651; Sun my Lord 1639
221 Though't] Though it S, P, B
222 Hart] Heart F, B
   Lyon] Lyons S, P, B; Lyon's F
223 thwart] th'wart P
225 to] of 1651
226 Comicke folly] Comickfolly 1651
228 But ... Queene.] **Omitted S, B**
   Oron.] Oran. 1651
230 pray see] pray y'see P
231 SD (*Ex. Oron. Hyd.*] Exeunt *Oront: & Hyd:* S, F, P (**following carriage., line 229, in P**)
231 Y'have] You haue B
233 th'Miseries] the miseries S, B; th'-Misery P
236 looke] looking 1651
   awhile] a while 1640
239 Male wits] Male-wits F
240 You'd] Y'de F; You'ld P
241 she wit] shee-wit F
246 A] **Part of previous line in F**
250 You'd] You'ld F, P
251 some] a P

252 knew] saw **S, F, P, B**
253 yet 'twixt] betwixt **F**
255 Councels] Counsels **1651**; Councell **S**
259 exercise, your wits] exercise your wits, **1651**; exercise: your wits **P**
260 sharpes?] sharpes. **S, F, P, B**
      how] which way **S, P, B**
261 poynts] points, **1651**
262 Lords?] Lord? **S, F, P**
263 vertues has] vertue has **1651**; Vertues h'as **S**; Vertu's has **F, B**; Vertues hath **P**
264 tough] **The 1651 Errata corrects to rough; 1640 and all MSS read tough**
267 mysterious] mysterous **1651**
268 can] that can **B**
269 SD To them ... *Orontes*.] Enter Orontes & *H*ydarnes **S, B**; To them Orontes, Hydarnes **P**
269 Lords] Lord **P**
275 Beauty] Honour **P**
      seasoned] season **S, F, P**
276 are] **Omitted B**
281 turne] change **P**
284 you're] your'e **1651**
286 you'd] you'le **S, ?F, P, B (reading badly shaved in F)**
288 overpoysing] ouer-poysed **S, B**
290 Th'] The **B**
      prayses] prayers **B**
291 th'] the **B**
      only] one **B**
295 thought] though **P**
      an] a **S, F**
297 I've] Iu'e **S, P**; I'haue **F**; I haue **B**
298 againe;] againe: **1640, 1651**
302 SD To them *Arsamnes*.] *A*rsamnes to ye 4 Nobles. **S, F, B**
304 thus] this **P**
305 your] our **?B**
      He is] Hee's **S**
      growne the talke] grownehe t talke **1640**
306 h'hath] hath **S, F, P, B**

309 turnes] turne **B**
311 my] the **B**
316 Those] The **P**
      numbers] **1640, 1651, S, F, P**; number **1639**
317 minde] man **S**
324 on] & **P**
327 Choaking]**P seems to have read Cheking originally; corrected to Choking in left margin**
      ev'n] euen **S**
      which ... life] which gave 'em life **1640, 1651**; y^t gaue them Birth **S, F**; that gaue em Birth **P**; that gaue Birth **B**
335 but] yet **S, P**; but yet **F**
336 the] those **F, P**
338 Kings] Kings, **1651**
340 creepe] creepe, **1640, 1651**
341 SD (*Exeunt*.] (Exeunt O*es*) **S**; omitted **P**; Exeunt omnes **B**
      Finis Act. I.] Omitted **1651, S**; Finis Act: j^mi. **F**

ACT II
SD *3^d Appearance ... Palace.*] **Omitted S, P, ?B**; 2: Act: 2 Scene appeeres a Royal palace. **F (first line of SD badly shaved)**
      Appearance,] Appearance **1639, 1640, 1651**
342 *Cra.*] *Cra* **1640**; omitted **S, F, P**
343 delights,] delights **1651**
345 I'le] **P first read I'll; this crossed through and Il'e put in left margin**
347 subtle,] subt'le **1651**; subtile **S**; subtle **F, P**
350 'em] them **F**
351 The] That **S, F, P**
      groveling] grou'linge **P**
352 Beyond] Aboue **S, F, P, B**
354 SD *Praxaspes,*] Praxaspes & **S, F**
355 still] sill **P**
358 Country-man] Countryman **S, F, P**
361 the] **Omitted 1640, 1651**

362	taste] 1640, 1651; taste, 1639	383-86	*Then . . . content*] Given as two lines in P
363	*Best*] Part of previous line in P		
364	*Prax. . . . in.*] Speech omitted in P	384	*them*] vs S, B
DESIGNATION	Act. 2.] Omitted S; follows line 365 in P	387	*Youthfull*] As youthfull LA
			early] earthly MC 1655
364 SD	To them . . . *above.*] To them *Atossa Mandane Ariene* appearinge aboue as the boy is singinge *Two Strumpets* steele in. P (follows line 365 in P)	388	*Then*] Hee. Then MC 1655
		389	*Shuffling*] Suffering MC 1655
			soules,] soules MC 1655, Goffin
		391	*be.*] be: 1651, 1653, MC 1655, WI 1655, Goffin
366	*Atos.*] Opposite this line, in left margin, F reads aboue.	392-95	*Then . . . fire*] Given as two lines in P
	where] how 1651		
	see] see, ?1640	392	*smother*] smother, 1640, 1651, 1653, MC 1655, WI 1655, Goffin
367	*vow'd*] vowe'd F		
368	*try*] rry 1651	393	*the other*] th'other S, B
369	*Prax.*] Mas: S, F, P, B	395	*fire*] fire, 1653
	begin.] 1651; begin 1639, 1640; beginne Boy. P	396	*Scorning*] Swiming Beloe (1812)
		400	*our*] P first read of corrected to our
SD	*Boy singes.*] Songe. F	401	*Lords?*] Lord? 1651
370-96	*Come . . . Lake.* Title Love and Musick 1653, 1669; *The Kiss.* WI 1662 and 1671; A Song. *Between two Lovers Sung in two parts.* MC 1655	402	*you*] you, 1651
		403	*Thought*] Though P
		405	*thought*] thoughts 1651
			about] abought 1640
		406	*Statue*] Statute 1651; statua B
370	*Come*] Hee. Come MC 1655	408	*th'*] the B
	whiles] whilst 1653, MC 1655, WI 1655, LA; whilest 1669	409	*one*] once 1651
		410	*one*] on F
371	*into*] unto Goffin	412	*into*] in 1640, 1651
	Eare;] Eare, 1651	413	*Loosing*] Losing 1651
372	*they*] the 1640, 1651, 1653, MC 1655, 1669, Goffin		*selfe*] thoughts S, F, P, B
			joy] Joyes S, F, P, B
	listning] listing 1651 (altered in Errata to listening), MC 1655; list'ning S, ?B	414	*'tis,*] 1640, 1651; 'tis 1639 (possible comma in Huntington copy, 1639; what looks like a slipped comma in Library of Congress copy, 1639)
373	*the*] that S, F, P, B		
	sound] Sounds LA		*colder*] cooler F
	heare;] hear, 1651	419	*wines*] Wine S
374-77	*Lest . . . Harmony,*] Given as two lines in P	422	*Pow'r?*] power? S, F, P
		423	*punish*] punih 1640
379	*Now*] She. Now MC 1655	424	*abase*] abuse P
380	*into*] unto Goffin		*honour*] Honours S, P
381	*interchanged*] enterchanged 1651, Goffin; enterchang'd S	426-28	*you shall . . . Treason.*] P telescopes these lines as follows: you shall perceaue that to a Kings/ How short soe ere you stile it this
382	*Slumbring*] Slumb'ring 1651, 1653 LA; Slumbering Goffin		

	is flatt Treason. (to a and this are written above, their places of insertion marked with carets)
427	Reignes] raigne S, F, B
428	stile] stile, B
429	abus'd] betrayd F, P
SD	two] Omitted S, F
	women] Strumpets P (the whole SD begins opposite line 431 in P)
431	so long] Omitted S, B
434	tempt] Omitted S, B
	Ho!] F and P opposite this read: Ent: Ser[:] F; Enter Servants P
435	without] without there S
437	them] 'em F, P
	doe] Omitted B
439	vices] vices. 1651
440	Only] Alone S, B
441	Carry'd] Carried S
	the] that F, P
442	or] & P
443	or] and S, B; & P
444	hit] fitted P (P originally read hit)
445 SD	Exit.] Omitted S, F
446	Mandane] Madane B
DESIGNATION	Act. 2.] Omitted S
SD	Philotas ... Archippus] Stratocles, Leocrates, Philotas, Archippus S, F, P
	in ... Habits.]Omitted S, F, B; attired like Persian Lords. P
453	'm at] them on S, F; em on P; them at B
	Mandane] Madane B
454	'em] them S, B,
456 SD	descend] desend 1651
457	yet] Omitted B
	they'le] theyl'e 1639, 1640; they'l 1651
459	it Man] Omitted S, F, P, B
460 SD	(Ent. ... Arie.] Omitted S, F, B; (To them Mand & Ariene) P (following end of line 459)
461	Phil. Str. Arch.] Om: S, B; Phil: Arc: Str: F, P
464	disguised] disguisd S
466	sure.] sure 1651
467	in one] in a P (a inserted above with a caret)
469	don't] doe n't S, P; doe not B
470	'em] them B
474	backward] backwards S, P, B
476	y'] you S, P, B
	Tumblers ... Jugglers?] Juglers or Tumblers? F
478	Ribbon] Ribband 1651; Ribben F; Ribbin P
480	cheekes] lipps F (corrected to cheekes)
481	Up?] Part of last line in S, F, P
482	you have] yon have 1651; you ha' S; y'haue F
483	grant] giue P
485-88	Phil. I perceive ... so too.] Omitted B
485	I perceive] Come, come, I now perceiue F
488	not] you B
489	snore] snort 1651
490	proclaime] proclame 1651; complayne F (altered to proclayne)
	'Tis] Tis 1651
491	Instrument.] 1640, 1651; Instrument, 1639
492	'tis somewhat] it lookes somewhat S, F; 't lookes somethinge P
	love] love. 1640
495	Favour's] savours S
	genuinely] Omitted B
500	awhile] a while 1640, 1651
	pray speake] pray y'speake S, F, P
503	Arch.] Phil P
504	of us] of's S
505	seeke] offer S, F, P, B
506	too ... too] to ... too 1651; too ... to F
508	shan't] cha'nt P
DESIGNATION	Act. 2.] Omitted S
509 SD	As they ... them.] As they carry out the Ladyes Cratander meets them. 1651; As they are carrying

the Ladies out, *Crantander* meets them. S, F, B; Cratander meets them as they are carryinge the ladyes out. P
509 Yee] You F
hold.] hold! 1651
510 What is] What's B
511 Love-sport] sport B
512 *Pro,*] *Pro* 1651
are now] now are S, B
516 downe-right] downe right 1640; down-ripe 1651 (corrected in *Errata* to right)
518 That] Who S, F, P
miseries] Misery's F
520 set] sets F, P
Torture] Tortures F
521 hunger] Hunge: ?P
522 midst] middest F
524 Recreations] Relaxations P
527 Dungeon] Dungeons S
527 SD (*Ex. 4. Slaves.*] (*Ex. foure Slaves* 1640, 1651; (Exeunt Slaues.) S, B
529 beyond] deyond 1640
533 SD (*Ex. . . . Arie.*] (Exeunt *A*ri: Man:) S; (Exeunt *M*and & *A*riene.) P
535 transpose] transport S, F, B
536 them] em S, P
537 might] shall S, B; may F, P
Besides] Perhapps F (altered to Besides)
538 path] place S, B
542 cōtemplate] contemplate 1651
Beauties] Vertues F (altered to ·Beautys)
542 SD (*As he . . . gold chayne.*] Follows line 544 in 1651; (*A*tos: throwes him a chayne. S, B; ([As he is musing Atossa] aboue throughs down [a] gold chayne to him F (first line of SD shaved off); As he is Musing *A*tossa from aboue throwes downe a chayne unto him. P
543 strength] strenght F

546 heav'ns] Heauens S, P
drop] shower S, P, B; dropt F
547 out of] of out F
cloudes] cloud S, F, B
548 Exprobration] exprobation 1651, F
550 It cannot] 1640, 1651; I' cann't 1639; It can't S, P, B (the t in It has been inserted with a caret in P); 'T can't F
552 Mettle] Metal 1651; Meddall P (altered from Mettall)
555 from my shoulders] Omitted S, B; from me P
DESIGNATION *Act. 2.*] Omitted S
556 SD *Hippias,*] *H*ippias & S, F, P
559 *Hippias,*] Hippias & P
how] Begins next line in S, F, P
564–66 for We . . . good.] Arranged as follows in P: for wee doe presume/You are not to be entreated to doe vs good.
565 you're] you are S, F, P, B
566 doe] Omitted S
569 for] to S, F, P, B
573 that] wch. P
579 it did grow] it grow P (originally the reading also of F, but some word, presumably it (since shaved) has been inserted with a caret)
580 then] the F
582 us] Omitted S, B
587 into our] int'our S, F (some indications of correction in S)
591 *Hip.*] Speech heading here and in line 593 inserted in margin of S
592 Though] P originally read They altered to Though, then crossed out and though written in left margin
hath] haue F
Persians] Persian S, F, P
595 the] a S, P
y',unlesse] y'vnlesse F; y'.vnlesse P
598 honours,] honours 1651
599 numerous] numerons 1651

602	th'] the **B**		in 1651 text capitalize the first word in each line, suggesting some attempt at verse arrangement; the MSS treat the lines correctly as prose.
	aged,] aged **1651**		
603	Matron,] Matron **1651**		
604	in] by **F**		
610	the] these **S, B**		
611	*Hippias*] Phocion **P**	653	out sleepe] sleepe out **P**
	pow'r] power **S**; powre **F**	656	May] But may **P**
613	*Arsamnes*] Arsamnes's **F**	659	thou] **Omitted B**
	I've] I haue **B**	659-60	sinnes ... we] sinnes, in proofe we **P**
615	his] him **S, F, P, B**		
	e're] before **S**	660	we will] weele **B**
	Country] subiects **S, F, P, B**	661	Jarres] fflagons **P**
616	You're] y'are **S, F, P**; you are **B**	663	for a] for an **P**
618	ratify'd] Ratifyed **P**	666	selves,] selues **1640**; selues a little **S, B**
	that's] that is **B**		
620	fortune,] fortune; **1651**		presently] you presently **F**
626	measur'd] Measured **P**	667	thy] yor **B**
627	t'your] to your **P**	668	the] our **S, B**
629	Pow'rs] Powers **S**	672	What?] **Omitted F**
630	them] em **F**	673	Cup?] Cup. **1651**
632	cannot tell] doe not know **S, F, P**	674	Mistresses] Mistresse **S**
639	Pray stay] Pray y'stay **P**	675	Alphabetically] **It is possible that F read Alphabetica[ll]; otherwise the word runs unusually far into what was the right margin**
	consider.] **1640, 1651**; consider, **1639**		
640	streightned] straightend **S**	678	begin] come **S, F, P, B**
641	th'] y^e **B**	680	blockhead] block-head **1640, 1651**
643	loose] lose **1651**	684	and ... still] **Omitted P**
645	I'm] I am **B**		still,] **Some copies of 1639 seem to read still;**
647	the] a **S**		
648	unto both] to both parts **S, P, B**		will] doe **S, F, P, B**
651	Death] fate **F, P**	685	that that] that w:^ch **F, P, B**
652	Betwıxt] Betweene **S, P**	687	Still-snoutes.] Still spowts. **P**
652 SD	(*Exeunt.*] **Omitted S**	688	noblest] noblest way of **S, B**; Nobler way of **P**
	Finis Act. 2.] **Omitted 1651, S**; Finis Act: 2^d^. **F, P**		
		689	'em.] **1651**; 'em **1639, 1640**
ACT III		689a	*Leo: A match.*] **This speech is supplied from F; it occurs also in S, P, B; omitted in all the printed texts**
SD	*Philotas, ... Leocrates*] Philotas, Stratocles, Leocrates, Archippus **F, P**		
		690	the Pots] the Cans **S, B**; the rest of the pots **F**; the Flagons **P**
	in] All in **P**		
	after ... manner.] according to ye Custome of ye Greekes. **S, F, P, B**		play.] play, **1651**; play then, **P**
		690-91	wenches, ... you] Musicke and ye wenches y^t you **S, P**; wenches, and the fidlers, that you **F**
653-57	Set a watch ... *Stratocles.*] **The printed editions, except line 655**		

692 will . . . any] will yeeld none S, B
693-94 and I . . . all.] Omitted S, B
  amongst . . . all.] amongst all of you. F, P
694 For] As for S, F, P, B
696 *Leoc.* Call . . . *Molops.*] Omitted P
  Molops.] S and F here add the following SD: (Enter Fidlers)
697 Well, what] Well now what S, B; Well now; what F; Well then what P
  those Raskalls] they S, P, B
  whiles] whilest S, F
699 Battle] battle 1640, 1651
  SD *Ent. Mus.*] Omitted S, B (see line 696); Enter Fidlers F
700 Thinke] Now Gentlemen/Thinke F; begins a new line in P
700-1 all . . . now] now in seruice all S, B; all in Seruice F
702 your] the F
  Gent:] Gentlemen S, F, P
  SD They . . . hands.] They take theire canns S, B; They take their flagons in [?their] left hands F; They take their Cups P
703 now] Omitted S, B
  SD They . . . & fill.] They take their cups in their right hands, to fill. 1640; They take their cups in their right hands to fil. 1651; they fill them S, B; They take their cups in their right hands, & fill them F; They take their Flagons & fill theire Cups P
709 Here] To thee F
710 you] yee S, F, P, B
711 SD *all together.*] alltogether. 1640; altogether. 1651; off together S; off all together. F, P, B
714 Fidlers] Squeakers P
  Throats . . . awhile;] Throats and sing a while; 1640, 1651; throats a while & singe; F
715 'em] them P, B
716 seasonable] reasonable P
717 enough.] P here adds the following SD: (Enter 2. ffidlers)
  SD *Song*] Title Song. Sung by a Company of Cup-shaken Corybants. MC
718 *Now, now*] Now L
719 *into*] unto S, F, P; to L
  Tethys] Thetis MC; teths L
720 *Ceasing*] P originally read Ceasinge or beasinge (W. W. Greg); altered to leauing in another hand in the left margin
721 2.] Placed opposite line 722 in MC and Goffin; Lawes' musical score brings the second singer (bass) in at line 721.
722 *sleepe,*] sleepe 1640
724 *mad*] made MC
  sometimes,] sometimes 1651
725 *Then laugh we*] then laugh wee then laugh wee L
  quaffe we] quaffe MC, S
727 *whence may*] where shall L
729 *set*] sit F
  till] tell L
730. 2.] Placed opposite line 731 in MC
  Here see] Here see. Goffin; he sees L
731 *does arise*] doth arise S, F, P; doth rise L
733 *than hee.*] than hee Goffin; omitted P; then his L
735 *1.2.*] MC places 1. preceding this line, 2. preceding line 736; then 1. again preceding line 737, and 2. again preceding line 740.
  we chase] we chase we chase L; we chuse Beloe (1812)
  the] thee P
736 *these true*] these thestrew L
739 *Cast's Glories*] Casts glories Goffin; Casts A glorie L
740 *dulls*] dull P; dimes L
  with] Omitted MC
741 *Then . . . &c.*] P repeats complete chorus

744 Cyclops] Cylops **1651 (corrected in the** Errata); Cyclopses S; Cyclops's P
745 Braines] Brayne S, P
746 our] O P
747 SD *Cratander*.] Cratande. **1651**
749 Some thing] Something **1651**
    more] worse S, F, P, B
    misfortunes?] misfortune? F
750 Innocence] innocency B
752 not] noe F, P
754 that] yet F, P
756 spend] spasse S; passe F, P, B
759 wreathes] very wreathes S, P, B
762 hundreth] hundredeth S
763 warre] warrs S, F, P
    you're] Y'are S, F, P; you are B
765 how e're] howeuer S, F, P, B
766 if] though S, B
768 'em] them S, F, P, B
769 into] in B
770 even] eu'n F
771 SD (*Ex. Crat.*] (Exit)S, P
772 Speakes well] **Part of line 771 in F, P;** speakes true F, P, B
    a good] an honest S, F, P, B
773 dissembling] dislembling **1651**
    Raskall] Villayne S, F, P, B
774 faction?] **1651**; faction. **1639, 1640**
775 don't] doe not S, F, P, B
776 (*Ex. Mol.*] (Exit) S
778 but a] but S, B
    hee's insufferable.] He is vnsufferable. S, P
779 hee's] he is S, P, B
780 the] th' P
    there's] there is P, B
    Ho] whoe S, F, B; who P
782 have beene] be S, B
783 womanish,] womanish **1651**
    have ... himselfe,] have been chast himself; **1651**; keepe himselfe chast S, B
    uncivill] uncivill, **1651**
788 meerely] **Omitted S, B**
    a] **Omitted B**

791 very scurvily] vere scurvily **1651**; wondrous ill S, F, P, B
792 I'd] I had F
793 villanies] villaines P
796 knew] perceiu'd F, P
    any] what S
797 in] in a P
797-98 so ... be] Omitted S, B
798 place.] State! F, P
799 not you] you not F, P
800 at.] at **1651**
802 hundreth] hundredth S
803 warre] warrs S, F, P
DESIGNATION *Act. 3.*] Omitted S
804 SD *Praxaspes*,] Praxaspes & S, F, P
805 are] What are S
806 your] yᵉ S
808 you come] thou comest P
810 an't] and't S, P
814-15 But You ... on] But you/Think vpon F; But you/Thinke on P
817 Discreetly, looke] discreetly/And looke S (discreetly part of preceding line); Discreet, & looke F, B; Discreetely, & looke P
819 feet] heeles S, F, P, B
    we ... off] w'haue onely left off S, B; Wee'ue only left our F; wee'ue onely left off P
820 fetterd] fettred P
822 th'] the S, P
828 your] our S, B
833 Heav'n] heauen S, P
834 b'as] be as S, P, B
836 *Mas.*] *Mas* **1651**
    me;] me, **1651**
842 which] as S, F, B
    Market-townes] Mercat Townes F
843 Thou 'wert] Th'wert **1651**; Thou wert S, F, P, B
845 ure] vse P
846 weazen] Weazand P
847 You] Yee S
848 should] shoul **1651**
850 be] were F

852-53 Must ... then?] **Given as one line in S**
854 require't] require it **S, P**
855 them,] them. **1640;** 'em **P**
856 'em] them **F**
　　Gods.] **1651;** Gods **1639, 1640**
　　Who e're] **Begins line 857 in P**
859 Unlawfull] **1640, 1651;** Uulawfull **1639**
　　and] or **P**
860 Arch. ... Leoc.] *A*r: *Le*: *Str*: **S**
　　Leoc.] **Omitted P**
　SD *Cratander ... them.*] **Omitted S, P, B;** Crat: appear[es] ouer-hearing t[hem.] **F (opposite lines 858, 859)**
861 this] this: **P**
863 Liberty,] **1640, 1651;** Liberty **1639, S, F, P**
865 th'] yᵉ **S, P, B**
867 run] be runne **P**
868 thē] then **1651**
　SD (*powrs ... ground*)] **Omitted S, P, B**
869 just angers] great Anger **P**
　SD (*he drinkes.*] **Omitted S, P, B**
870 thickned] thickn'd **P**
873 SD all] **Omitted S, P, B**
　　(*Exeunt.*] Exeunt Omnes. **P**
DESIGNATION *Act. 3.*] **Omitted S**
874 Man] mortall **S, B**
　　gaynes it] gaines't **S**
876 triumph,] triumph. **1651**
877 With] With yᵉ **S**
　　of ... Cabinet?] of Ladyes Cabinets? **P**
878 Favour] favours **P**
　　and] or **S, P, B**
880 of] of a **1651**
882 well may] may well **S, F, P, B**
886 more] new **S, B**
　　Heav'n] Heaven **1651**
887a But in that] But you doe ill to boast it, for in that **S, ?F, P, B** (the reading in F very badly shaved)

889 that] **Omitted F**
890 received] receiu'd **P**
895 my] myne **P**
896 deceived] deceiu'd **F, P** (altered from deceiued in F)
899 call] stile **S, F, P, B**
903 on] or **P**
905 Purely ... thence,] (Purely ... thence) **S, F, P**
906 againe;] again, **1651**
　　doe] dare **S, F, B;** may **P**
910 you;] you: **1651**
912 Is] s **1651**
　　these] those **S, F, P, B**
　　that] who **S, F, P, B**
913 it] **Omitted P**
　　kisse,] kiss **1651**
915 Contract] **Opposite this word, in left margin, P has a small mark like a clover leaf (see also lines 932 and 939)**
　　Bull, or Goat] goate or Bull **S, B**
917 Be't far] Be it far **S;** omitted **P**
919 them] 'em **S, B**
921 immateriall] subtle Immateriall **F**
　　to] **Begins next line in S, F, P, B**
922 up] **Omitted S, F, P, B**
　　perfection;] perfection, **1651**
924 that] the **B**
　　which] yᵗ **S, B;** who **P**
925 Himselfe] It selfe **P**
926 Adoration;] adoration; **1651;** Adoration. **1639, 1640**
929 but] and **S, F, B**
931 there] their **1651**
932 That] **Opposite this word, in left margin, P has a small mark like a clover leaf (see line 915 above)**
933 it] **S, F, P, B;** I **1639, 1640, 1651**
　　still;] still, **1651**
935 Pow'rs] Powers **S**
937 toward] towards **S, P**
　　you;] you, **1651**
939 Crat.] **Opposite this speech-heading, in the left margin, P has a**

small mark like a clover leaf (see line 932 above)
betwixt Love,] between Love 1651
942 cov'ting] coueting S, P
943 food] good B
945 continued] continuall S, F, P, B
947-48 And still ... have] And still Aspireinge (wch is Nature) haue P
951 Nor yet] S, F, P, B; And yet 1639, 1640, 1651
acknowledge] S, F, P (P reads 'acknowledge); knowledge 1639, 1640, 1651
953 or] nor P
958 They've] Th'haue S, P; Th'ue F; They haue B
960 nobly] noble S, P, B
962 night] nights P
shed] shedds S, F, P
Poppy] Poppies S, F, P
twice o're] thrice on S, B
th'weary'd] th'wearyed S, F; the wearied P
963 Registers;] Registers, 1651
964 contrive,] contrive 1651
968-70 Can ... have] Half-quotes are placed in the left margin in P, opposite these lines, presumably to mark an aphoristic passage (see lines 1037 and 1038)
973 two] to 1651
974 both.] both 1640
980 Your selfe] Part of previous line in P
that's] 1640, 1651; thats 1639
my 'intent is] m'intent 1651; my intent's S, B; my intent is P
981 Arsamnes] Arsamnes's F
985 I'le] P first read I'll, crossed out and Il'e written in left margin (compare line 345)
t'Elysium] to Elysium F, P, B
joyfull] gratefull P
989 designes] 1640, 1651; designes. 1639
SD (Ex. Crat.] Omitted P

990 helps] doth P
DESIGNATION Act. 3.] Omitted S
990 SD To her Arsamnes.] Arsamnes meetes Atossa and brings her backe. S, P, B
992 And ... follies] Omitted P
Eyes] Ey S, F, B
993 cast] send S, B
994 'Tis] It is S, F, P, B
1001 Chayne.] Chain 1651
Do 'y'] d'you S, B; do y' F; Doe ye P
1003 (the Sun] (y^t Sun S, P
1004 Send] Lend S, F, P, B
others] other S, P
those] these P
1005 loose] lose 1651
light, nor heat] Heate nor light P
1008 enjoyne] Copyist in F repeated confine from line above; this has been crossed out, but corrected reading shaved off
1009 Flow'r] Flower S, F, P
smell] smells S, F
1010 Flower.] Flower: 1651; Honour, P
1012 streams,] streames 1651
1013 Flow'rs] Flowers S, P
1014 toward] towards S, P, B
1017 make it] mak't P
1019 there,] there 1640
1021 destroy,] destroy 1651
1022 But ... up] Omitted P
1023 destitute, indeed] Destitute then indeed P (then has been inserted above with a caret)
1024 You'd] You had S, B; Y'had F, P
1027 (As ... ground)] Parentheses omitted P
flow] run S, F, P, B
1030 An] Opposite this word, in left margin, P has a small mark like a clover leaf (see line 939 above)
1033 an] a S, F (F originally read an, but n crossed out)
1034 whole] Omitted S, F, P, B
1037-38 To shew ... away] Half-quotes

	are placed in the left margin in P opposite these lines, presumably to mark an aphoristic passage (see lines 968-70 above)	1084	*Mandane*] Mandane, **1651**; Madane B
		1085	our] yᵉ S, F, P, B
		1086	Away, away, to] Away, Away, Away, to S, P
1038	The Almes] But th'Almes P	SD	(*Exeunt.*] [*Exe.* **1651**; omitted S, B; Exit Omnes P
1041	methinkes] methinks, **1651**		
1042	may] might S, F, P, B	DESIGNATION	*Act. 4.*] Omitted S
1044	wholly] allwaies S, B	1087	no more] on more **1651**; no further S, F, P, B
1045	*Arsam.*] Opposite this speech heading, in the left margin, P has a small mark like a clover leaf (see line 1030 above)		I am] I'me S, B
		1088	not] no **1640, 1651**
			Perjury.] Perjury **1651**
1049	'bout] about B	1092	t'expresse] to expresse S, F, P, B
1051	neighbouring] neighbring S	1093	Persia] Persin P
	bough] Bow P	1094	alike] a like P
	prove,] prove **1651**	1095	Wee're] W'are S; wee'ere P
1052 SD	(*Exeunt.*] *Exeu.* **1651**; omitted P	1100	dreades] dread's **1651**
			slavery] Slau'ry F
	Finis Act. 3.] Omitted **1651**, S; Finis Act: 3ᵗⁱʲ. F, P	1101	And ... nay] Nay Colophon F
			Magnesia] Magnasia P; Magnessa B
		1104	Liberty:] Liberty; **1651**
ACT IV		1107	weakned] weaken'd F
DESIGNATION	*Act. 4. Sce. 1.*] Act: 4: Scen: 5 S	1108	shelter:] shelter, **1651**
			preserving] preservin **1651**
SD	*Mandane, Ariene*] Ariene. Mandane S, P	1109	Liberties] Liberty S, F, P, B
	Ladyes,] Ladies **1651**	1114	Army:] Army; **1651**
	and ... sorts.] Omitted P		tell] shew S, F, P, B
	sorts] sorte S, F	1115	that] w:ᶜʰ F
1056	Corrupt,] Corrupt **1651**		head] heades S, F, P, B
1058	t'your] to your S, F, P	1116	Persian] Pesian P
1059	I'm so assur'd] I am s'assur'd F; I'm so assured P; I am soe assurd B		them] em S, F, P, B
		1117	them] em S, F, B
1067	Castle.] Castle, **1651**	1118	Towards] Toward F, P
1070	shall] still P	1119	And Ladyes] Part of last line in P
1074	our] your S, B		now] Doe now P
	Epitaph,] Epitaph S; Epitaph: P	1120	within] within yᵉ S
1075	History.] History S; History, P	1122	meanes, for] meanes so P
1076-78	The sacred ... Dreames,] The sacred gods of marriage night by night, for this/And personally thank you in your Dreames. S, B	1127	th'] yᵉ S, P
		1128	wee're] w'are S
		1130	*Pho.Hip.*] Hip: Phoc: S, F, P
			it.] it **1651**
1081	flight] fight P	SD	(*Ex. Hip. Pho.*] Exeunt Hip: & Phoc) P
	doe] shall P		So; my] Soe, my S; So 'my F; So! my P

1131 who] whome S, F, P, B
1132 Have ... life.] Vngratefull wretches, swere my death, P
1134 Councell] Counsell 1651
1136 SD (*Exit Cratander.*] **Omitted** S; Exit. F, P
4ᵗʰ Appearance, a Wood.] **Omitted** S, P, B; Act 4. Sce: 3: here appeeres (with variation of the Scene) a wood and a landschap. &c. F
after a while] after a while, 1651; afterwards S, P, B; afterward F
Stratocles ... places.] Stratocles comminge out of a wood at seuerall places, disguised in Beggers Habits P
disguis'd] disguised S, P
counterfeiting] counterfeyte S, F, B
maunding] maimed B
and] **Omitted** S
out of ... side] out of yᵉ side of a wood S, P, B
severall] seu'rall F
1137 Holla!] So. Ho, P
1138 Holla!] So: Ho: P
1139 *Archippus?*] Archippus P
1140 *Leocrates?*] Leocrates P
1142 forth] **Omitted** S, F, P, B
1142-43 tot-/ter'd] tottred P
1143 thee] the 1651
Actæon] 1640, 1651; Acteon 1639
newly reviv'd] **Omitted** S, B
1146 They're] They are S, P, B
1149 Holla!] So. Ho, P
1150 Holla!] So: Ho! P
1151 'em] them F
they ... by;] **Omitted** S, B
1152 'em.] em againe. S; them. F; them againe. B
Holla!] So. Ho? P
1153 you there?] **Following these words F gives the following SD**: Ent: Stra: Phil:
1155 wordes:] words yet, P
I'm] I am B

1156 punctuall.] punctuall 1640
1157 D'ye] Do y' F, P; Doe you B
we have] wee'ue S, F
1159 to] towards S, B
1160 by] **Omitted** F, B
1162 wee've] we haue F, B
done ill] done wondrous ill P
1163 he ... houre] he's wont to passe this howre B
1164 agree] agreed B
1168 thou then] thou doe't then S, F; thou then doe't B
1169 No] Nay P
of it] on't S
to] **Omitted** P
1170 an] any P
it:] it; 1651
1171 not] I am not B
1172 it] **Omitted** F
hee] & he F
1173 judg'd] iudgd by him S, P; iudg'd be him B
the] **Omitted** F
must] shall S, B
1175 dost thou] Doe you S, P; Doe yee F, B
we will] wee'le S, F, P, B
1177 You] But you S, P
to bee] for P
1179 you not] not you S, F, B
1182 be all] all be P
1183 broke] broken F
1184 among us to—.] among us to— 1640, 1651, S; amongst to— F; among us to. P; **B omits** among us
SD *Cratan. ... them.*] **Omitted** P
Cratan.] C. 1651
discover'd] discouered S
them.] em S
1186 here] yonder F, P, B
1188 not] nor 1640, 1651, ?B
us] **Omitted** P
1189 wood] woods S, P
now] **Omitted** F

1190 unlucky] **1640, 1651;** unluckly **1639**
 againe:] againe **1640**; again, **1651**
1191 toward] towards **S, F, P**
1192 howe're] how e'r **1651**; how'ere **S, F;** How ere **P**
DESIGNATION *Act. 4. Sce. 4.*] *Act. 2. Sce. 3.* **1640**
1193 *Leoc.*] *Phil.* **S**
1194 poore] **Omitted S, F, P, B**
1195 cloaths;] cloaths, **1651**
1195-96 thy/Judgement] **Omitted S, B**
1198 *Leoc.*] *Phil.* **S**
 great] **Omitted B**
1199 Thou'd'st] thoud'st **S;** thou'ldst **P**
 pleas'd] pleased **P**
1201 SD *As Cra. ... Postures.*] As Cratander narrowly lookes on them some counterfeyte Lamnes, others Dumbnes &c **S, B (B omits &c); SD follows line 1200 in P**
 views] obserues **P**
 thē] them **1640, 1651**
 Postures.] seuerall postures. **F;** Postures all. **P**
1202 Man] men **S, F, P, B**
1203 Temple] Temples **P**
1205 *Sisarmes,*] *Sisarmes* **1651**
1206 Ho!] **Omitted P**
 nigh] neere **S, F, P, B**
 seize] Come seizne **P**
1209 Nor] Or **S**
 arme] Armes **P**
1210 mine eye. I] my. I **S;** eye, why I **P;** my I **B**
1211 were] are **S, P**
1212 You now would] You'd now **S, B;** You'ld now **P**
 who's] who is **P**
1213 Priest] Preirst **P**
1214 Is it not] Is not it **S, B;** Is't not **F**
 as to] to **F**
1215 Is fitt'st] is fittest **F (part of preceding line)**
1216 I live] **Part of preceding line in F**

 and will ... to] And shall do still vnto **F**
 Punishment] punishments **S, P**
1217 them] em **S, F, P, B**
 are.] are, ?**1651**
1218 'em] them **P**
1220 so,] so **1640, 1651**
1221 our] my **F**
 farther] further **S, P**
1222 your] our **1640**
1225 your Pate] thy head **S;** y:ʳ head **F, P, B**
 for it.] for't. **F, P**
SD (*Ex. ... Slaves.*] (Exeunt) **S;** Exeunt Ser: & 4 Slaues. **F;** omitted **P**
DESIGNATION *Act. 4.*] *Act. 2.* **1640;** omitted **S**
1226 Wee're] W'are **S;** We'ere **P**
 of't] o'n't **F**
1227 *Prax.*] *Prax* **1640**
1229 Pow'r] power **S;** Pow'er **F**
1230 man] in't **S, F, B;** omitted **P**
 all] they all **P**
 vanish'd] ravisht **B**
1231 *Mas.*] **1640, 1651, S, F, B, D;** *Hyd.* **1639**
1232 have] ha' **S, F, B**
1235 Eunuches] Enuches **1651**
1235-37 My Lords, This ... they say.] My Lords, this is not to discouer, what's/Become of them, they'ue taken weapons too **F**
1236 discover] find **P**
 'em] them **S, B**
1238 that] as **S, P, B**
1240 armes] armes wth em **S, F, B;** armes with them **P**
1244 They now are] They are **S, F;** Th'are **P**
 to be surpriz'd] to be surprized **F;** to be forth wᵗʰ· surprized **P**
1245 Greekes.] Greeke. **1651**
 Cratander,] *Cratander.* **1640**
1246 'em] them **S, B**

1247 t'] to **P, B**
Let us] Lett's **B**
1250 SD (*Exeunt.*] Omitted **S, P**
Finis Act. 4.] Omitted **1651**; Finis Act: 4^(ti.) **F, P**

ACT V
SD *5th ... Castle.*] Omitted **S, P, B**; Act: 5: Sc: 1: the Scene agayne changing, appeers a Castell. **F**
with ... midst.] & other Ladyes all in warlike Habits discouered on the walls of Arsamnes Castle w^(th.) Cratander seated in the midst of them. **P**
women] Women all **S, F, B**
habits,] habits: **1640, 1651**
discover'd] discouered **S, P**
Castle] Omitted **S, F, B**
walls, with] Walls; **F**
midst.] middle of them. **S**; middst of them. **F, P, B**
1252 the] this **S, F, P, B**
prize;] prize, **1651**
1253-54 whose ... value,] (whose ... valew,) **F** (parentheses added over commas)
1254 under value] undervalew **S**
1259 Your] The **B**
1261 you] me **P**
1268 "Twould] Itwould **P**
1269 danger hence:] danger hence; **1651**; Danger, here. **S, B**; danger hence. **F**; dainger. Here: **P**
1270 You're] Y'are **S, F, P**
1282 While] Whiles **S, F, P, B**
thus] this **S, F, P**
1284 my] our **S, F, P, B**
1285 to] vnto **S**
1286 we] **1640, 1651, S, F, P, B**; me **1639**
DESIGNATION *Act 5.*] Omitted **S**
1286 SD To them below] Omitted **B**
Hydarnes ... Masistes] Praxaspes, Masistes, Orontes, Hydarnes **S**;

Praxaspes, Masistes, Hydarnes, Orontes **F, P**
others in] others all in **S, F, P, B**
1291 Captive] Captaine **B**
1292 began,] began **1651**
1293 King] Kings **S, P**
1296 invisible Plague] invisible Plauge **F**; consuminge fire **P**
1297-98 Hee ... So] Hee's is seated soe/Soe **S**
1300 Nation.] Nation **1640**
1308 expect] suspect **S, F, P, B**
1309 wrested] wretched **P**
1310 witnesse] witnesse, **1640, 1651**
1312 have] Omitted **P**
1313 but what I've] for what Iu'e **S**; for what Iu'ue **P**
1315 something] somewhat **S, F, P**
1315-16 If then ... me] One line in **S**
1316 still] Omitted **S, B**; stile **P**
1317 to] vnto **S, F, P, B**
1319 needes must] must needs **P**
1320 it cannot] for it cannot **S**; for it can't **F, P, B**
1321 Th'] The **B**
o'th'] of th' **S, P**; of the **B**
1322 say] speake **S, F, P, B**
On] Omitted **B**
1323 they're] Th'are **F, P**
1324 scatter'd] scattered **P**
1325 The ... meale] Part of preceding line in **P**
that] Omitted **S**
1329 SD *Sould. within.*] Sol: **S, F, P**
arme.] Fourth arme omitted **S, F, P**; following this line **S, F, B** insert the SD: (A shout from ye Enemy & some running to ye King)
Ex. ... Battle.] (Ex. Ars: & Lords) **S, P, B**; *Ex: Arsamnes, Lords, & Soldiers.* **F** (follows second half of line 1329 in MSS)
Lords, &c.] Lords, **1651**
1330 Let us] Lets **B**
now] now, **1640, 1651**

1333	they're] th'are S, F, P	1382-84	I may . . . to take.] But I/may not afflict him with a Courtesy/ 'T can't be a Guift that he must be compelld/To take. S
1334	Let's prepare.] Omitted S, B		
DESIGNATION	Act. 5.] Omitted S		
SD	To them . . . Chase.] To them Arsamnes & y⁰ Rest as from y⁰ Chase S; Arsam: etc returne as from the Chase. F, B (precedes act and scene division in F); To them Arsamnes & y⁰ Lords as from the Chase P	1382	I] But I S, F, P, B
		1383	Court'sie; it can't] Courtesy/'T can't S; Curtesy, 't can't F; Curtesy 't cannot P
		1385	are most] Begins next line in S
		1388	Pray'rs] prayers S, P
			gaining] giuing B
SD	Chase.] Pursute. 1651	1389	hopelesse] S, F, P, B; hopefull 1639, 1640, 1651
1335	to 'appeare] to appear 1651; t'appeare S, F, P, B		
1338	gates] Gate S, P, B	1391	h'] he P
1341	an't] and't 1651	1395	I aske you] I aske it S, B (part of preceding line in S)
1342	Pow'r] power S, F, P		
1349	aske;] aske, 1651	1396	Majestie] Majecty 1651
1352	solemne Feast and] feast and solemne S, F, P, B	1397	up] Omitted 1640, 1651, ?B
		1402	Soules] Soule ?P
1353	'em.] 'em; 1651; them. S, F, P	1404	last] late F, P
1354	Innocent and Vertuous] Vertuous and y⁰ Innocent S, B	1407	Society] Societies S
		1409	war] warrs S, F, P, B
1355	Festivall.] Festivall; 1640, 1651		and to] Omitted P
1357	Do y'] D'you S, B	1411	all are] are all S
1358	steame] stream 1651	1412	Ev'n] Euen S, P
1359	Deities] Diety's P		others] Other S
	e're did] did ere P	1414	pow'r] power S, F, P
1364	While] Whiles S, F, P	1415	meanest:] meanest; 1640, 1651
	permit it to] permit to S (possibly the second t of permitt is meant to be taken as an elided form of it)	1417	(Since . . . Pow'r)] Parentheses omitted S, F, P
			put it in] putt in S (see line 1364) Pow'r] Power S
1366	the] th' S, P, B	1418	give it] giue't you S, F, B; giue it you P
1370	Mandane.] Mandane, 1651		
1372	our Husbands] your Nobles S, F, P, B	1419	the Ephesian] th'Ephesians S; th' Ephesian F; the Ephesians P
	we] wedd B		safety:] safety; 1651
1373	unlike] unlikt B		the Altar] th' Altar S, F, P
1374	your] Omitted F	1421	City] Country S
1375	Wee're] We are P	1427	Pow'r unto] power to S, B
1377	hath snatch'd] did snatch S, F, P, B	1429	undergoe] undergo, 1651
		1431	strangers.] S; strangers, 1639, 1640, 1651, P; Strangers: F
1380	Eares] Cares P		
	you've] y'haue S, P, B		
1382	Thunderer] S, F, P, B; Thunder 1639, 1640, 1651	1433	comming.] comming, 1640; comming; 1651

1435	Victory,] Victory **1651** that's] that is **F**		1471	do y'heare?] doe you. **S**; omitted **B**
1436	The sluggish] **Part of preceding line in S**		1473	remember you] remember y^t you **S, F, B**

1435 Victory,] Victory **1651**
      that's] that is **F**
1436 The sluggish] **Part of preceding line in S**
1437 when] wen **1651**
      wee've] we haue **S**
      joyn'd] joyned **1651**
1438 combining so,] combineinge, so **P**
1439 th'] the **S**
1442 subdu'd] subdued **1651**
 SD   (*Ex. . . . Ladyes.*)] Omitted **P**
DESIGNATION *Act. 5.*] Omitted **S**
 SD   *Stratocles . . . Archippus*] *A*rchippus, *L*eocrates, *S*tratocles **S, F, P**
1444 *Molops,*] *Mol.* **1651**
1445 thou hadst] th'hadst **S**; thou hasdst **P**
1446 Pot-quarrels] Can quarrells **S**
1447 By my . . . humour.] **Not distinguished as a separate line in 1651**
1448 Well] Will **B**
      say I] say then I **S, F, P, B**
1449 *Arsamnes*] *Arsamnes,* **1651**
1450 their returne] theire victorious returne **S, F, P, B**
      that] and **B**
1452 Yes] Omitted **S, P**
      againe.] againe, **1640**; again **1651**
1453 thou] Omitted **S**
1455 you know] for you know **F, P**
      Cratanders] *Cratander's* **1651**
1457 thou] Omitted **S**
      into] in **S, P**
1458 We] Why wee **S, F, P, B**
      study'd] studyed **S, P**
1461 They are] they're **S, P**; Th're **F**
1462 doe] Omitted **S, F, P, B**
1463 under] into **S, B**
      that] Omitted **S**
1464 to] Omitted **S, F, P**
      into] in **S, B**
      most] Omitted **P**
1466 they will] they'le **S**
      if] **1640, 1651**; If **1639**
1467 thing] whitt **F, P**
1470 thing,] thing **1651**

1471 do y'heare?] doe you. **S**; omitted **B**
1473 remember you] remember y^t you **S, F, B**
1474 SD (*Exeunt.*)] Omitted **S, P**
      6th Appearance . . . againe.] Omitted **S, P, B**; Act: 5: Sce: 5: the royal palace or Court appeers agayne. **F**
      Lords . . . as] *Praxaspes, Orontes, Hydarnes, Masistes* returning as **S, F, B**; *Praxaspes, Orontes, Hydarnes, Masistes, Mandane, Ariene,* returninge as **P**
      Ladyes] *Ladies,* **1651**
1475 Whiles] While **S**
      we're] wee are **S**; w'are **P**
1476 Heav'n] Heauen **S, P**
1478 swiftly away] swiftly 'away **F**
1479 sports] sporte **B**
1480 doe shew] expresse **P**
1485 which your] you **S**; your **P, B**
      refus'd] refused **S**
1486 'em] them **S, P, B**
1487 'em] them **B**
1490 We will] wee'll **S, B**
1491 All] **Part of preceding line in S**
 SD   *The foure . . . Postures.*] The 4 *Slaues* and ye 2 *Strumpetts* presented by *Molops* dance in theire Cripple postures **S, F, B**; To them *Molops* vsheringe in the fower *Slaues* & the two *Whores*, who daunce in their Cripple Postures **P**
      Postures.] *Postures* **1651**
1492 I hope . . . Majesty] Your Ma^{ty} I hope **S, F**; Yo:^{r.} I hope **P**
1494 like] same **F**
      eye.] eye? **1651**
1496 their] this **1640, 1651**; ?**B**
 SD   *The Ladyes . . . Claudian.*] To them *Six Ladyes* attird in their Military Habits who present them wth. a warlike Persian Daunce. **P**
      war-like] military **S, F, P, B**

and dance] and soe dance **S, F, B**
the whole ... Claudian.] **Omitted S, F, P, B**
Insonuit ... ictu.] **These verses from Claudian are omitted in all the MSS**
Insonuit ... magister,] **Omitted 1640, 1651**
Mutatosque] Mutatos **1640, 1651**
grave parma sonat] gravè parma sonat, **1640, 1651**
plauditur] clauditur **1640, 1651**

DESIGNATION *Act. 5.*] **Omitted S; F inserts the following SD: The Temple appeers agayne (this change of scene does not come until Act V, Scene vii in printed editions)**

1498 SD *1. Priest.*] A Priest **S**; the first Preist **P**
1499 *1. Priest.*] *1. Priest* **1651**; Pr: **S**; Preist **P**
1500 All in] In all **S, F, B**
1503 into] vnto **S, F, P, B**
eares] Eare **F**
1504 I've] I haue **B**
1. Priest.] Pr: **S**; Preist. *1.* **P**
1507 an] a **P**
Hecatombe] Hecatombe? **S**
1509 Destiny's] Destinies **S, B**; Destinyes **P**
1510 fire with] fires of **S**; fires with **F, P**
1511 into] vnto **S, F, P, B**
1512 In one] **Reading of S not clear: In tone** *or* **In tond** *or* **In fond**
continued] continude **S, F, P**
1513 *1. Priest.*] Pr: **S**; Preist. *1.* **P**
1515 Teare] Peare **P**
1516 *Cratander,*] *Cratander.* **1640**; Cratander yͤ **S (line 1517 begins, however, The Gods)**
1518 Heav'n] Heauen **S, F, P**
1520 that thou hadst] yᵗ wouldst **S**; that thou wouldst **F, P, B**
1521 Heav'n] Heauen **S, F, P**

1523 Statues] Statutes **P**
may] will **F**
thinkst] think'st **1640, 1651**
1525 thy Images] th'Images
1527 Who] That **S, F, P**
1528 you] ye **P**
1529 'T will] T'will **P**
foule.] foul; **1651**
1531 Pray you] Pray y' **S, F, P**
a while] awhile **S, F**
1535-36 T'accuse ... would] If I'accuse/ Or Gods, or Men it's the part of him that would **P. The If has been inserted below with a caret and the it's above with a caret; Men has been altered from Men's. It looks as though the scribe mistook his T' for an I' (easily confused) and altered the passage accordingly.**
1535 T'accuse] To accuse **S, B**
1536 's the part] were but yᵉ part **S, B**
that would] **Begins next line in S**
1537 desires] **Begins next line in S**
1538 whensoever] whensoe're **S**
1540 the] th' **S, F, P**
I've] I haue **P**
1542 mine] my **S**
and] on **S, B**
1543 by] by **P (altered from** my**)**
prays'd.] prays'd **1640**; prais'd; **1651**
1546 Policy,] Policy **1651**
suffrings] sufferings **1651, S, P**; Suff'rings **F**
1549 henceforth] hence forth **1651**
1551 Witnesse] Witness, **1651**
1553-54 (Worthy ... presence,)] **Parentheses omitted P**
1553 Heav'n] Heauen **S, P**
1558 *Arsamnes,* on.] Arsamnes one? **P**
1560 arme] hand **P**
thee. Sure] thee sure. **S**; thee Sure **F**; thee: Sure. **P**
1561 desire] require **S**
SD (*Exeunt.*] **Omitted S, F, P, B**

DESIGNATION *Act 5. Sce. 7.*] **Act designation omitted S**; Act: 5. Scen: vltim: **P**

SD *7th Appearance ... thereon.*] **Omitted S, P, B**; Act. 5: Sce. 7; appeereth the Sunn Eclypsed and a shoure of rayne falling on the Altar puts out the fyre. **F** (appears opposite line 1574, in left margin)

1561-73 SD *Enter Molops ... by the Priest.*] **The stage business and song omitted by S, F, P, B; the scene begins with line 1574**
discover'd,] 1640, 1651; discover'd 1639
2 by 2;] 2 by 2, 1651
Queene,] Queen; 1651

1562-73 *Thou ô bright ... backe the Man.*] **Headed Song. 1640, 1651**

1562 *Thou ô*] O thou 1667, 1673

1563 *Looke down*] look down, look down 1667, 1673, L

1566 *Cho.*] **Omitted 1667, 1673, L**
While thus] Thus while 1673; Whilst thus L
thankes,] thanks Goffin
be;] be, Goffin

1567 *grant*] give 1667, 1673, L

SD *Altar;*] Altar, 1651

1569 *agen.*] agen, Goffin

1570 *leave*] lowse L

1571 *make and have*] haue and make L

1573 *Vertues*] vertue L
Man.] Man Goffin

SD *8th Appearance, ... fire.*] **Omitted S, P, B**; the sunn appears ecllypsed in the Scene. **F** (in right margin, opposite line 1574)
eclipsed,] eclipsed 1640, 1651
is singing] in singing 1651

1574 *2. Priest.*] **Before this speech of the Second Priest's the MSS have the following SD: To them 2: Preist S; To Them 2d Preist F; To them** yᵉ second Preist. **P**; To them two Prests **B**
Hold, hold] Stopp, Stopp S, F, P, B

1575 Heav'n] Heauen S, P
your] the F, P

1578 put out] extinguisht S, B; extinguis't F; extinguish'd P

1579 now,] now 1640, 1651

1581 Heav'ns] Heauens S, P

1582 justify'd] iustifyed S

1584 pow'r] Power S, P

1589 they] you S

1590 Ephesus's] Ephesus'es S
mine] my S

1592 well wrought] well-wrought S

1593 'T] It P (originally read I)

1597 stayd] stay'd 1640, 1651

1602 rul'd] rule S

1603 them] 'em P

1605 Vertues] Vertu's F

1607 warre] warrs S
end] end, 1651

1608 SD FINIS.] Finis Act: 5ti. P

THE EPILOGUE TO THE KING AND QUEENE
TITLE THE EPILOGVE...QVEENE.]
To the Kinge & Queene their Ma:ts The Epilogue. **P**; The Epilogue spoke by the slaue. **E**

1 Crat.] **Omitted Goffin**
glorious] Solemne S, F, P, B, E

2 sport.] sport: 1651

3 though] heere S, F, P, B
th'] the E
Priest] Preists P

4 till] tell P

7 our] a E

8 These] Those S, F, P, E
your] the E

9 Great joy] S and F indent this line

11 Can you] S, F, and P do not indent this line
expect then] require then P; require the E

12 only] out Goffin
Spheare] Spheare, 1651

13 *course*] Court F
14 *it's*] its 1651, Goffin
15 *O were*] F indents this line; Were E
    to it] to't P
16 *Court*] Court: 1651
17 *wee've*] we haue E
19 *snatch'd*] snatch P, E
    grieve,] grieue 1640, 1651
20 *an*] a F
    yeare's] yeares 1651
    part . . . day.] doe wish the day: E
21-22 *though . . . still,*] In parentheses S, P, E
21 *your*] you 1651, Goffin
22 *favours*] favor B, E
23 *will*] shal E
    yet] still E
    rise] arise E
24 *Great Sir,*] In parentheses E

THE EPILOGUE TO THE UNIVERSITY
    This epilogue is omitted in P.
TITLE THE EPILOGVE . . . *VNIVERSITY.*] The Epilouge To the Vniversity. By Arsamnes. F
1 *Arsam.*] Omitted Goffin, S
    wee've] w'haue E
2 *Errours*] arrowes E
    weighing Eare] neighing eares E
3 Wee'd] Wee S, F, B, E
    they'd have] th' would haue S, F, B, E

4 doe seldome] scarce euer E
    untill] vnto S, F, B
6 The one expecteth] Th'one expecte E
    th'other] the other E
7 Parts] Part E
9 those] some F, B, E
10 Doth] Doe E
    Schooles] Schoole E
11 thence] then E
12 May] Doe E
    those] the E
13-14 We are . . . fine] Who are not yet train'd to the trade, none fitt/ To find E (after train'd the scribe has written up and then crossed it through)
14 Poet, . . . Player] for Player, or for Poet S, F, B, E
15 rough fil'd] rough-fil'd S
17 The Slave (then] Our Captiue S; The Captiue F, B; A Captaiue E (the reading is possibly Captaine)
19 so] for E
22 his] the E

THE EPILOGUE TO THEIR MAJESTIES AT HAMPTON-COURT
    This epilogue is omitted in all manuscripts.
3 *Feare's*] Fears 1651
    doe] do, 1651; doe, Goffin
18 *you*] yee 1651

The Ordinary

In the prompt copy of *The Ordinary* two principal methods of deletion can be readily distinguished: (1) words, phrases, lines, and groups of lines crossed through with a single pen stroke; and (2) groups of lines, sometimes whole scenes, circled. The first method is used sometimes by Herbert (or his deputy) and sometimes by the playhouse reviser (the agent can usually be determined by the nature of the cut), and is designated in the notes which follow as "Deleted PC"; the second method, used only by the playhouse reviser, is designated as "Deleted PC reviser." Any other methods of deletion are specially noted.

THE PROLOGUE
13 to] too 1651
14 meant] means **Goffin**

DRAMATIS PERSONAE
 Shape] **Through a misinterpretation of the large bracket in the 1651 edition all the modern editors have failed to include Shape among the Complices in the Ordinary (see Gerber, *Sources*, p. 40n).**
 The Scene, LONDON.] **Above this PC adds a regie note: Wooden Cup.**

ACT I
DESIGNATION Act. I. Scene. I.] **PC indicates the setting as** New hall.
4 *Shap.*] **Deleted PC**
5 of] on **D, R**
16 y' be] you, be **D, R, C, H**
24-25 meets . . . Cogitations] **Deleted PC**
27 unto . . . hal'd] **Deleted PC**

32-49 why should . . . confin'd] **Deleted PC reviser**
44 kill] killed **H**
63-69 I'le count . . . Duty.] **Deleted PC reviser**
64 that's] thats 1651
72 meane] meant **H**
DESIGNATION Act. I. Scen. II.] **PC indicates setting as** New Ord[i]nary **and adds a regie note:** A purse for Hearsay
80 whiles] whilst **D, R, C, H**
81 SD *Enter Hear.*] **PC marks a double cross in left margin (compare line 118)**
87-88 she . . . not.] **One line H**
88-89 I must . . . loth.] **One line D, R, C, H**
96 not born] born **H**
107-9 As Mr *Christopher* . . . Gods word.] **Deleted PC (this is the only deletion in the play made in Herbert's characteristic manner, that is, by underlining and placing a cross in the left margin)**
118 SD *En Slic.*] **PC marks a double cross in right margin (compare line 81)**
121 Lieutenant] Lieuteuant 1651
124-28 To tell . . . parts.] **Deleted PC reviser (line 125 had been deleted earlier and the phrase o'th' Pox scratched out by Herbert)**
126 Bell. (Hem) Was't] Bell (Hem) wast 1651
129 Faith] **Deleted PC**
132 something] somethlng 1651
149 beleeve] beleeve it & **PC**
150-52 The memory . . . Love-fire:] **Deleted PC**

155-63   I doe...Embers.] **Deleted PC reviser**
171-72   so close Alone w'] so close/Alone wi' **D, R, C;** so close alone/Wi' **H**
177   faith] **Deleted PC**
183   Or...worse.] **Deleted PC**
   same colour'd] same-colour'd **D, R, C, H**
184-87   Foh, foh!...all one.] **Deleted PC**
185   Doe y'] D'you **D, R, C, H**
188-203   Her breath...day-light.] **D** prints a number of these lines as prose.
189-92   It would...Chimney.] **Deleted PC reviser**
190   *Trithemius*] Trithemius's **D**
195-96   She's...Madam.] **Deleted PC**
200   paper Lanthorn] paper-lanthorn **D, R**; paper-lantern **C, H**
202   Lady;] Lady **1651**
204-5   Not...great Turk.] **Deleted PC**
206   open-mouth'd] **D, R, C, H;** open'd mouth'd **1651;** open mouth'd **G**
210   countenance] countenace **H**
214-15   O that...Madam?] **Deleted PC**
216-19   Do you...hand.] **Deleted line by line in PC and then circled by reviser**
223-25   no...heart.] **Deleted PC**
225   *Sha.*] Sli: **PC**
226   incarnate.] incarnate for **PC**
229   Ifaith] **Deleted PC**
233   By...light] **Deleted by Herbert and later restored by the reviser as indicated by** stet **in the margin**
245   took it.] took **1651** (corrected in *Errata*); took——**D**
259   Faith] **Deleted PC**
268   smell,] smell; **R, C;** smell **H**
271-384   Advantage...very strongly;] **These lines (pp. 11 through 14) are missing in PC**
284   a piece] no piece **H**

302   ne're] never **D, R, C, H**
306   descent] dissent **1651** (corrected in *Errata*)
308-10   live honest,...we do] live honest,/And...did./If that you...time,/We do **D;** live/Honest, and...did./If that you...time, we do **H**
313   honest] honost **1651**
328   Glyster] clyster **D, R, C, H**
370   Lieutenant] Leiutenant **1651**
394-95   Carves...venison:] **Deleted PC**
395   Pagan] **R, C;** Paguim **1651** (the *Errata* reads "*p.* 15, *l.* 11. Pageant *r.* Pagan."), **D;** paynim **H** (following a suggestion of **C**)
400-5   Here lies...whispers——] **Indications of deletion by PC reviser**
408   breadth] **C, H;** breath **1651, D, R, G**
421   Troth] **Deleted by Herbert and later restored by the reviser, as indicated by** stet **in the margin**
423   Tract] track **D, R, C, H**
433   We have got] There is **PC**
439   ten] then **1651** (corrected in *Errata* and by PC reviser)
SD   *Shape.*] **Deleted PC**
442-43   The Prey...Politick.] **Deleted PC**
459   *Sha.*] Sli. **PC**
463   Emerit] eremite **D, R, C, H**
476   keeps] keep **H**
482   Moyties] moyeties **D;** moieties **R, C, H**
486   assurance] assurance[s] **H**

ACT II
SCENE 1   **PC adds the following SD: 3 Baylifes fighting. and indicates the setting as Coven[*sic*] Garden.**
498   hast] has't **D, R, C, H**
499   hast] Has't **D, R, C, H**
501   No.] No, **1651**

506	Title's] Titles 1651		691	writeth my much] writeeth much my C, H
507	Pox!] **Deleted PC**			I wis;] I wis 1651; I wis, D, R, C; i-wis H
521	though] D, R, C, H: that 1651, G		714	Lore me o thing] Lore me nothing D, R; Love me o'thing C; Lore me o'thing H
544	hardest] hardiest H			
545	Juments] yeomen D			
547-50	my Lord ... Bodkin:] **First deleted by reviser in PC; later restored as indicated by** stet **in the margin**		714-15	mere. Abouten what] mere Alouten, what 1651
			717	Ycliped] Ycleped D, R, C, H
			719	day;] day 1651
552	a crown a meal] a crown meal C, H		723 SD	*Meanwel.*] *Meanwel,* 1651
563	formalitie;] **Cross in right margin of PC**		727	Fawny] fauns D, R, C, H
			728	y'eke] yeke 1651
567	Fife;] **Cross in right margin of PC**		731 SD	*Exit.*] *Exeunt.* 1651, D, R, C, H
575	Lieutenant] Leiutenant 1651		SCENE III	**PC indicates the setting as** new Ordinary
576	Bustard] buzzard D, R, C, H			
588	Petarrs] petards D, R, C, H		735-857	And solitudes ... I warrant him.] **These lines (pp. 27 through 30) are missing in PC**
596	heaven] **Deleted PC**			
	Apricocks] apricots D, R, C			
613	to] too 1651		741-42	On ... informer.] One line D, R, C, H
623-25	Some ... in't.] **Deleted line by line in PC and then circled by reviser**		757	Monies] Money D, R, C, H
			759	discover,] discover 1651
632-35	It works ... valour.] **Deleted PC reviser**		782	Terme by Art, as] Terme, by Art as 1651
650	Pox!] **Deleted PC**		802-3	had not been Black] had not been White R, C; would have been black H
656	scape] 'scape D, R, C, H			
657	win off] win of D, R, C, H			
658	serv'd] sign'd D, R, C, H		804	Black] White R, C, H
663	'em] them C, H		812	clos'd] clos' 1651
669-73	when ... Cudgels.] **Deleted PC**		815	that's] thats's 1651
681-82	Oliv'd ... fury.] **Deleted PC (the last word probably not meant to be included in the deletion)**		819	must: good Sir, I pray] must, good Sir I pray 1651; must, good Sir; I pray D; must, good Sir. I pray R, C, H
681	Powder'd———] D, R, C, H, G; powder'd. 1651			
683	false] falss 1651		823	Who 'tis they do] Why 'tis they so C; Why 'tis they do H, G
684	I nas] I na'as D; I na's R, C; I was H			
			838	b' abus'd] be abus'd D, R, C; he abus'd H
684-85	Depardieux you Snyb] depardieus/You snyb D, R, C; depardieu/You snyb H			
			862	that I'l] but I'll D, R, C, H
			865	Heav'n] **Deleted PC**
687	these two *Janus*] those two Janus' D, R, C, H		884-85	'Twil/Never] 'Twill ne'er D, R
			887	Thing] **Omitted H**
688	these] those D, R, C, H		SCENE IV	**PC indicates the setting as** ordin: Continues **(The setting**
690	is me] is in me D, R; is to me C, H			

was first marked as Coven Garden, but this has been crossed out)
903 cloaks] clothes D
905 this,] this 1651 (perhaps the reading should be this ['s]), D, R, C, H
911 'Tis ... Decoy.] Given, wrongly I think, as an [Aside] by H
920 Faith] Deleted PC
926 *Sha.*] *Sha* 1651
927 Sim] Sim. D, R, C
955 he's noble] he's only noble PC
956-63 men ... Revenues.] Deleted PC
963 pithy] pithly D
976 *Andrew*] Simon PC
    to] too 1651
977 'Slid] Deleted PC
978 As God ... me] Deleted, but later restored (stet in margin), in PC
981 can't, my] can't my 1651
994 Ord'naries] Ordinaries D, R, C, H

Act III
1005 wendeth.] wendeth 1651
1014 Bryd] bride C, H
1053 Unto thylke [day] in] D, R, C, H, G; Unto thylke in 1651
1058 tenth] tenth [year] H
1068 mine] my C, H
Scene II PC indicates the setting as Redlyon feilds (Coven G was first written in and then smudged out; and ? New hall written below, also crossed out.)
1098 'Slid] Deleted PC
1100-1 this Land ... brain.] Marked as [Aside] by H
1117 Faith] Deleted PC
1118 wast] was't D, R, C
1120 And't] An't D, R, C, H (H marks this line as [Aside], although Shape is obviously addressing Credulous)
1127 Ordnary] Ordinary D, R, C, H
1139 is't] is it H

Scene III PC indicates the setting as New hall
1180 (And ... Virgin)] Deleted PC
1201 expectation's] expectations 1651
1225-26 Doth ... him——] One line D, R, C, H
1246-49 If ... thee.] Deleted PC
1247 worse] worse, 1651
1250 send] sent D
1261-1301 Peace ... you Sir.] Deleted PC reviser with pen marks diagonally across the page (faith in line 1289 had earlier been separately deleted)
1263-86 *Come, o come ... the Hours.*] Title Love admits no Delay 1659; An Invitation to enjoyment 1672
1264 *He*] She 1659, 1666, Harl. 3511, Rawl. D. 1092, LA
    doth not] cannot Harl. 3511
1268-72 *To be ... unfold*] Omitted 1672
1269 *that*] the Harl. 3511, Rawl. D. 1092
1271 *Desires do write us*] Desires, do wright her 1666
1272 *youth*] youths Harl. 3511
1275 *See*] Omitted Harl. 3511
    See ... gone] See the Tapers almost done Rawl. D. 1092
1276 *Thy ... that*] And the flame like it Harl. 3511
1277 *as*] like Rawl. D. 1092
1282 *O let ... Powr's*] Let us then cherish these our powers 1666; let vs cherrish then these powres LA (an O seems to have been crossed out before let)
    O let us] Come let's Harl. 3511; Come let us Rawl. D. 1092
    these] those Harl. 3511
1283 *Whiles ... may*] Whiles we yet 1666; Whilst we may yet 1672; Whilst that we may Harl. 3511 Whiles as we yet may Rawl. D. 1092
    call] stile Rawl. D. 1092

1285 *Chime,*] Chime **Goffin**; crime Harl. 3511
1286 *Hours*] hour **1659**
1290 'Twould] 'T could **D, R, C, H**
1292 *Sappho*] *Sahpho,* **1651** (some copies)
SCENE IV PC indicates the setting as Coven-Garden (the word Ordinary had been written in earlier and then crossed out)
1302 You're] Your **1651**
1317 military,] **D, R, C, H**; military **1651**
1318 Lieutenant.] Lieutenant **1651**
SCENE V PC indicates the setting as Ordinary. Also adds a regie note: with a Lette[r] Table and 4 Chaires.
1323 [I] see] see **1651**
1337 they, by] they [did], by **H**
1355 *amavit [Iupiter].*] *amavit.* **1651**
1383 kill'd] killed **H**
1383 SD *passing by*] passing by wth a Lette[r] **PC** (the addition in PC shows some signs of having been crossed out)
1394 You'r] Your **1651** (some copies)
1395 pray y'send] Pray, send **D, R, C, H**
1396 out now;] **R, C, H**; out, now **1651**; out; now **D**
1398 pacificall] pacifick **D, R, C**
1406 humble] noble **H**
1419 Couzen remov'd] cousin [once] remov'd **H**
1429 my] by **H**
1430 *Catchmey.*] *Catchm.* **1651**
1430-31 I/Too forward?] I too forward! **D, R, C, H**
1437 'twixt] betwixt **D, R, C, H**
1443 Defil'd with [un]sanctified Rithmes] Defil'd with sanctified Rithmes **1651**; Defiled with sanctified rithmes **D**; Defiled with sanctified rhimes **R, C**; Defiled with [un]sanctified rhymes **H**
1449-52 Buy a good ... *Stubs*] Given in italics by **D, R, C, H**
1449 Buy] **D, R, C, H**; By **1651**

1457 some] same **R, C, H**
1459 office.] office, **1651**
1465 O'rshadow'd] O'r shadow'd **1651**
1470 beard Episcopal] Deleted **PC**
1484 holy] Deleted **PC**
1493 Drink t' 'em] Drink to 'em **D, R, C, H**
1496 presence,] presence. **1651**
1502 abstemious *Rimewel*] abstemious, Rimewell **D, R**
1512 future-now] future now **1651 D, R, C, H**
    I'l] I **D, R, C, H**
1516 O'] O **1651**
1518 bloud-shed] blood shed **D, R, C, H**
1526 never] ne'er **D, R, C, H**
1532 we will] we'll **D, R, C, H**
1534 1. Catch.] **MC 1655, WI 1655, AC 1671**, and **Goffin** omit all the stanza headings and choruses.
1538 *Quest*] guest **AC 1671, D, R, C, H**
1542 *John an Okes*] John-a-Nokes **D, R, C, H**
1545 *Frights*] Frightens **AC 1671**
1546 dare] doe **MC 1655**
1549 *Hunger*] Hunting **MC 1655**
1550 *discard*] discart **WI 1655**; discharge **AC 1671**
1555 *break Fast*] breakfast **MC 1655, D, R, C, H, Goffin**
1558 *Old* Sutcliffs] *Numph Crouches* **MC 1655**; Old *Suckcliffs* **WI 1655, AC 1671**
1559 *Did*] Doth **MC 1655**
1563 Let us] Let's **D, R, C, H**
SCENE VI PC indicates the setting as Hall
1568 Chambermaid;] Chambermaid, **1651**; chambermaid! **D, R**; chambermaid. **C, H**
1575 For Gods] Deleted **PC**
1580 Pox] Deleted **PC**
    liquorous] liquorish **D, R, C, H**

ACT IV
SCENE I PC indicates the setting as Ordin:

1611 do'st] Does't **D, R, C, H**
1612 else:] else, **C**; else **H**
1622 give's] give us **D, R, C, H**
1624 Does] Doe's **1651**
1632 'Snigs ... News.] **Correctly printed as one line D, R, C, H**
1635 all Fortunes,] ill fortune **D, R, C**
1636 Heaven] **Deleted PC**
1647 impertinencies] impertinences **H**
1650 Heaven] **Deleted PC**
1651 faith] **Deleted PC**
1654 Coranti Dotard] Corant, dotard **D**
1658 ventring] venturing **D, R, C, H**
1660 Pox!] **Deleted PC**
1675 SD *Ex.*] **D, R, C, H**; En. **1651**
1677-78 fancie/God] fancy,/Good **D, R, C, H, G**
1682 amebly] amebly, **1651**
SCENE II **PC indicates the setting as** Red Lyon feild **(the word ffeild is again written below and crossed out)**
1691 one rap] onerap **1651**
1692 h'is] he is **D, R, C, H**
1693 where] whether **D, R**; whe'r **C, H**
1700 troath] **Deleted PC**
1703 to God] **Deleted PC**
1704 faith] **Deleted PC**
faith art] **So substantially all editions; the correct reading is probably** faith th'art
1705 pox] **Probably deleted PC**
1705-6 No? nor ... Bones!] No! nor yet an ach in your bones? **D, R**; No, nor yet/An ache in your bones? **C, H**
1714 where] whether **R, C, H**
1716 paynant] poynant **H**
1718 Downe] Done **1651**
1731 *Englond.*] *Englond* **1651**
1742 Redoubted] **D, R, C, H**; Redoubled **1651**
1743 'tis] it is **D, R, C, H**
1750 SD *Exeunt.*] **Omitted D, R, C, H**
SCENE III **PC indicates the setting as** Hall.
1757 indad] indeed **D, R, C, H**

1762-63 strangely. Now who'd] strangely. Now,/Who'd **C, H**
1765 God] **Deleted PC**
1772 SD *En. Mrs Ja.*] **PC reviser double scores above and below this SD and places a heavy crisscross in left margin**
1785 indeed-law] indeed law **R, C**; indeed, la **H**
1807 staid] stay'd **D, R**
1808 'mong] 'mongst **H**
1854 Never] never **1651**
1855 I would say] **Opposite this line PC has a prompter's note** call Rim. Bagsh. S' Kit. Catchm:
SCENE IV **PC omits this scene with the note** leave out this scene. (God in line 1984 separately deleted)
1887 me self] myself **D, R, C, H**
1902 time (twenty ... Sir.)] time (twenty pieces, sir,) **C**; time, twenty pieces, sir: **H**
1906-8 Indeed ... verily.] Indeed ... man,/As ... verily. **D, R, C, H**
1908-9 Beleeve't ... well.] **One line D, R, C, H**
1912 Indeed ... Brother;] *Indeed-and-truly-verily-good brother!* **H**
1914 procure the Pox?] **H marks this as** [Aside]
1915 Your] **D, R, C, H, G**; You **1651**
1920 you'ld] you'd **D, R, C, H**
1931 th'] the **D, R, C, H**
1945 Syren] syringe **D, R, C, H**; Sering **G**
1949 you should [be].] you should. **1651**; I should. **D, R, C, H**
1950 of taking] **H omits** taking
1968-69 You ... dispos'd?] **One line D, R, C, H**
1980 I'd] I had **D, R, C, H**
1984 SD *Ex.*] *Ex* **1651**
SCENE V **PC indicates the setting as** Coven Garden.
1985 *Whiles*] While **Cibber**
1988 *make*] makes **C, H**

1991 Clean] Clear **Cibber**
shamefac'd] shame-faced **Goffin**
1992 spread] spreads **MC 1655**
1995 Dishes] pishes **D, Cibber, R, C, H**
ties] fies **D, Cibber, R, C, H**
1996 then . . . born] **In parentheses MC 1655**
1997 listning] listening **MC 1655**
Taper] bridegroom **Cibber**
1998 Whiles] While **Cibber**
2003 Faire] For **Cibber**
2008 Mrs Pris] Mistresse Cis **MC 1655**
2010 woe,] woe. **1651**
2011 Know] No **Cibber**
2016 whiles] while **Cibber**
2020 Let] Like **Cibber**
2021 God . . . God] **Both words deleted PC**
2026-55 Now thou . . . Holy day.] **Given in a five-stanza form MC 1655, D, R, C, H**
2027 That . . . Mother,] That hast tane forme from thy mother; **MC 1655**
2048 And by . . . teaching] **Omitted MC 1655**
2050 grow] grown **MC 1655**
2055 And . . . Holy day.] **After this line MC 1655 adds the following couplet:** Mayst thou talke thou knowst not what,/And be a prettie prick-eard Brat.
2064 Rendevow] rendezvous **D, R, C, H**
2070 Con.] **D, R, C, H;** Pri. **1651**
2073 you, t'offend] you to offend **D, H;** you, to offend **R, C**

ACT V
SCENE I **PC reviser deletes this scene with pen marks, diagonally across the page**
2080 ev'n] even **D, R, C, H**
2085 next serve God] **Deleted PC (before deletion of entire scene)**
2086 'em] them **D, R, C, H**

2095 'em] them **D, R, C, H**
2105 thou'l] thou'lt **D, R, C, H**
2116 Heav'n] heaven **C, H**
2117 unwelcome] unmelcome **1651**
SCENE II **PC indicates the setting as Hall**
2125 do[n't] mean] do mean **1651;** don't mean **PC**
2129 not] **D, R, C, H, G;** nor **1651**
2135 Sir] **Omitted D, R, C, H**
2144 in a complement] by compliment **D;** in a compliment **R, C, H**
2145 b'your] be your **D, R, C**
SCENE III **PC adds the following regie note: a Table & 4 Chaires. The setting is indicated as Ordinary**
2157 SD Slicer, and Shape] Shape and Slicer **PC (The speeches of Shape and Slicer are usually interchanged throughout this scene. The whole scene is rather confusingly cut up; apparently at one time it was intended to omit everything from line 2170 to line 2227, but this passage was restored, as indicated by a number of stet's in the margins.)**
2158 speak; what] **R, C, H;** speak what **1651, D**
2161 SD As . . . above.] **PC reviser places a cross in left margin**
2169-70 I've heard say You're] **PC reviser adds below this three lines, first crossed out, then marked Stet: one of the G[ ] liest and guilty one [?s] that lives especially of that (?)worst (?)of Sins (?)Covetise (Several of these readings are very questionable.)**
2176 custome] costome **1651**
2177 out;] out, **1651**
2185 I'd] I had **D, R, C, H**
2190 whiles] whilst **D, R, C, H**
2192 dralls] drawls **D, R, C, H**
2202 this's] this is **D, R, C, H**
2217 enter'd] entered **D, R, C;** entered **H**
2218 whiles] whilst **D, R, C, H**

2227 while.] whıle, 1651
2228 *Sha. I see no*] **Before these words PC inserts** ? & yett
2230 giv'n] given **D, R, C, H**
2240 that way——] **PC reviser places a cross in right margin**
2242 Full ... devotion.] **A line drawn across the page under this line in PC**
2249 H'ad] H'had **H**
      Leave] leave 1651
2256 most certain.] **PC places an asterisk after this line (see line 2375 SD)**
2263 Giffery] Geffery **D, R, C, H**
2265 Come buss.] **H adds the SD Kisses her**
      Giffery] Geffery **D, R, C, H**
2269 Which] **Omitted H**
      to apprehend] t'apprehend **D, R, C**
2273 SD *with 'em*] *with them* **H**
2274 *1 Watch.*] Heari: **PC**
2280 *2 Watchm.*] Heari: **PC**
2295 Ordnary] Ordinary **D, R, C, H**
2298 th'would] they would **D, R, C, H**
2308-9 rather/Have] rather have **H**
2309 SD *Ex. officer.*] Ex. officer. Slicer etc **PC**
2315 foul yfrounct, with] foul, yfrounct with **1651, D, R, C, H**
2333-34 Indeed ... Prison.] **One line D, R, C, H**
2336 Send ... hither] Come hither daughter **PC** (come hither written again in left margin and crossed out)
2338 th'] the **C, H**
2354 Fescennine] **D, R, C, H**; Festennine 1651
2357 his Son, he] his Son & now my son in law **PC**
2360 chang'd.] **R, C, H**; chang'd, **1651, D**
2365-66 ill luck./To ... more,] ill luck./To vex you more; **D**; ill luck/To vex you more, **C**; ill-luck/To vex you more: **H**
2375 SD *Ex. Cred.*] **Opposite this SD PC reviser adds This Scene comes in at this* (see line 2256)**
2388 b' accus'd] be accus'd **D, R, C, H**
2391 is).] is) 1651
2395 her] your **D, R, C, H**
2403 m' affection] my affection **D, R**
2412-18 He may ... Magazine.] **Deleted PC reviser**
2412 the Eye] th'eye **D, R, C, H**
2427-31 I had ... this.] **Deleted PC reviser**
2434 of the Aged.] **Opposite this line PC reviser adds the following SD: ent Moth Pot.**
2435 I thank you] **Before this line PC reviser inserts Come along, the last two words of line 2375, to serve as a connective.**
2436 *Sha.*] **H, following Shapes's name, notes: [Disguised as a Constable.]; Hear. PC**
2441 *Sli.*] **H, following Slicer's name, notes: [Disguised]**
2442 *Sha.*] Slic: **PC**
2457 Sha.] Slic: **PC**
2460 *Slic.*] Sh: **PC**
2471 **Following this line in PC appears Sir Henry Herbert's license (wholly in his autograph):**
      This Comedy, called th Ordinary the Reformations obserued nay [*sic*] bee Acted, not otherwise January 15. 1671
                                    Henry Herbert
                                    M R.

EPILOGUE

5 free] **Omitted Goffin**

The Siege

The Dedication
TITLE   The   Dedication ... MAJESTY.]
         The Dedication to the King
         Goffin
  1   May ... Majesty,] **Omitted Goffin**
  23 Sight] Light **Goffin**
SUBSCRIPTION   Your ... William Cart-
         wright.] **Omitted Goffin**

OCCASIO FABULAE
         The two quotations from Plu-
         tarch's *Life of Cimon*, one Greek
         and a translation of the Greek into
         French by Amyot, occupy sig. G2ʳ
         in *Works* (1651). They have been
         omitted in this edition. North's
         translation of the passage is quoted
         in the Introduction to the play. See
         also the General Introduction,
         Chapter V, "The Text," page 72,
         where the several states in which
         this page appears are noticed.

ACT I
    1   *Sced.*] *Sced* **1651**
    8   Wench,] Wench **1651**
   51   *Skelletons*] **Altered, wrongly, to**
         Skeleton **in the** Errata
  192   Consort] Consorr **1651**
  202   hand.] hand, **1651**
  255   dry.] dry, **1651**
  265   well in] wellin **1651**
  271   *Pru.*] *Pri.* **1651**
  277   besiedg'd,] besiedg'd **1651**
  282   Sweetmeats] Sweet.meats **1651**
  283   Between] Beeween **1651**
  302   *Prusias*] *Prucias* **1651**
  304   your] you **1651**
  313   suff'rance.] suff'rance **1651**
  370 SD   *Pru.*] *Pru* **1651**
  377   he] be **1651**
  383   Jument] Jnment **1651**
  387   to that] too that **1651**
  389   cruelly.] cruelly, **1651**
  390 SD   [*Exeunt.*]] **Omitted 1651**
  458   too light] to light **1651**
  468 SD   [*Exeunt.*]] **Omitted 1651**

ACT II
  487   confine?)] confine? **1651**
  521   *Phil.*] *Ph l.* **1651** (the *i* has failed to print)
  525   [*Pyl.*]] **Omitted 1651**
  600   hear] bear **1651**
  859   *Eud.*] *End.* **1651**
  895   Creatures.] Creatures **1651**
  919   *obtain'd*] obtained **Goffin**
  923   *Fires.*] Fires **Goffin**
  924   Chor. *O ... down,* &c.] **Omitted Goffin**

ACT III
  981   [Not] become] Become **1651**
 1052   and hast] and has **1651**
 1166   *streams,*] streams **Goffin**
 1170   *what*] **Omitted 1655**
 1170 SD   *fall off*] *full off* **1651**
 1181   suspect.] suspect **1651**
 1274 SD   *depart enterchangeably*] *depart-enterchangeably* **1651**
 1355   Statues] Statutes **1651**
 1357   worshiped] worship'd **1651**

ACT IV
 1483   your] you **1651**
 1520   *Prus.*] *Prns.* **1651**
 1582   but] bnt **1651**
 1653   Verses] Veases **1651**
 1734   Irons.] Irons **1651**
 1741   *Pru.*] *Pru* **1651** (some copies)
 1757   Metall Man;] Mettle Man, **1651** (some copies)

1771 I] ! 1651 (some copies)
1773 fall,] fall. 1651 (some copies)
1783 again] ogain 1651 (some copies)
1864 'twas] twas' 1651 (some copies)

Act V
1866 Paricide] Parricide 1651 (some copies)
1933 shall] should 1655
1935 on] an 1655
1940 whiles] while 1655
      descend, and kiss:] ascend and kiss, 1655; descend and kiss. Goffin
1971 Virtue] Vertue 1651 (some copies)
1977 another's] anothers 1651 (some copies)
2003 kiss] like 1651 (some copies)
2005 Myrtle;] Myrtle. 1651 (some copies)
2012 fire,] Comma doubtful 1651
2015 inscrib'd] inscrib d 1651
2097 SD *Injun-/ction*] *Injun-/junction* 1651 (some copies)
2116 'em] e'm 1651
2117 Coffin?] Coffin. 1651 (some copies)
2122 SD *He*] *he* 1651
2126 monstrously] monstruously 1651 (some copies)
2291 SD *continuing*] *continuiug* 1651

The Poems

A PANEGYRICK ... CARLISLE
- 51 An *Heroina*] As Heroins **Goffin**
- 75 now are] are now **Rawl. D. 951**
- 76 Will] Wee'l **Rawl. D. 951**
- 93 Power's] Powers **Goffin**
- 142 see.] see, **1651**

ON THE IMPERFECTION ... BUILDINGS
- 5 half desert] half-desert **Addit. 22,-602**
- 7 fields] Field **Harl. 6931**
- 10 hath] both **Goffin**
- 12 of] off **Addit. 22,602**
  represent;] represent. **Addit. 22,-602**; represent, **Goffin**
- 15 then *Amphion*] them Alphion **Harl. 6931**
- 16 though] if **Harl. 6931**
- 20 an] a **Harl. 6931**
- 21 not,] not. **Goffin**
- 22 were] are **Harl. 6931**
- 23 toucht] touch't **Goffin**
- 25 th'are] they're **Harl. 6931**; theire **Addit. 22,602**
- 26 or] nor **Addit. 22,602**
- 27 too] roo **1651**
- 30 untouch'd;] untouch'd, **1651** (corrected by **Goffin**)
- 33 So] See **Harl. 6931**
- 35 whether't] whether t' **Harl. 6931**; whither'it **Addit. 22,602**
  Escheated] encheated **Harl. 6931**
- 40 yet not] not be **Addit. 22,602**
- 41-42 Two ... *Pauls,*] So that two Sacred things were thought by alle/Beyond the Kingdomes Power, Christchurch & Paul. **Addit. 22,602**; Or that ... Paul **Harl. 6931**
- 44 his] the **Harl. 6931**
- 46 some gifts] their giufts **Harl. 6931**; their Courses **Addit. 22,602**
- 49 not] no **Addit. 22,602**
  Wee'd] wee'ld **Harl. 6931, Addit. 22,602**
- 50 at] Omitted **Harl. 6931**
- 52-53 *void ... giv'n*] void ... giv'n **Goffin**
- 53 *what's*] what **Harl. 6931**
- 54 Pavement] Pavements **Harl. 6931, Addit. 22,602**
- 67 That] Which **Addit. 22,602**
  sent] lent **Harl. 6931**
- 69 in] on **Addit. 22,602**
- 70 his] the **Harl. 6931**
- 71 then] them **Goffin**
- 72 *Stone*] Stones **Addit. 22,602**

A CONTINUATION ... PRINCE OF WALES
- TITLE *A Continuation ... Wales.*] A Diversion to the Prince of Wales. **Harl. 6931**; To the most Hopefull Charles Prince of Wales. **Addit. 22,602**
- 1 hence] now **Addit. 22,602**
- 5 shewn] shed **Harl. 6931, Addit. 22,602**
- 6 Buildings too.] Building, too? **Addit. 22,602**
- 7 Harvests] Harvest **Harl. 6931, Addit. 22,602**
- 15 Our ... we] (our King's Sonne) that we **Harl. 6931**
- 28 Story] history **Harl. 6931, Addit. 22,602**
  were] Omitted **Harl. 6931**
- 29 the] that **Harl. 6931**
- 30 call'd the *Prince*] call'd, the Prince; **Addit. 22,602**
- 33 these Streams] those beames **Harl. 6931**

34 or] noe **Harl. 6931**
35 then] when **Harl. 6931**
   throughout] thoroughout **Addit. 22,602**
36 some . . . least] at last some part **Harl. 6931**
39 something] nothing **Harl. 6931**
   won't] w'ont **Addit. 22,602**
40 Colours and shape] Colour and Shape **Harl. 6931, Addit. 22,602**
   sit] fit **Chalmers, Goffin**
42 you do] you did **Harl. 6931**; which you **Addit. 22,602**
43 Where Merits] Whose meritts **Harl. 6931**; Whose Meritt **Addit. 22,602**
   work] Works **Addit. 22,602**

ON HIS MAJESTIES . . . SMALL POX, 1633
TITLE *On His . . . Pox. 1633*] **No title 1633**
17 be] by **1633 (Goffin)**; any copies I have seen read be

TO THE KING . . . SCOTLAND. 1633
TITLE *To the . . . Scotland. 1633.*] *To the King.* **1633**
6 vigour] rigour **1651, Goffin**
7 but 'twas so] But it was so **Lloyd (see Notes)**
10 trembles] trembleth **Lloyd**
19 Majesty] Majesty, **1651, Goffin**
20 oppressing] oppressiug **1633**
24 Progresse] prowesse **1651 (corrected in** *Errata* **to Progress)**; *Progress* **Goffin**
25 Triumphall] triumphant **1651**
27 Raign] Altered in *Errata* to Faith **1651**; followed by **Goffin**
28 strife,] strife **Goffin**
40 Wish] With **Goffin**
42 the] a **1651**

TO THE QUEEN . . . OCCASION
TITLE *To the . . . Occasion.*] *To the Queene.* **1633**; *Yo the . . . Occasion.* **1651**
5 silent] present **1651**
8 view'd] viewed **Goffin**
22 Marriage-night.] Marriage-night **Goffin**

ON THE BIRTH . . . YORK
TITLE *On the . . . York*] **Omitted 1633**; **Goffin adds 1633 to title.**
7 Forc'd] Fond **1651**
15 wonder] wonders **Goffin**
19 neere;] neere, **Goffin**
22 From] from **1633**
27 likenesse] likewise **1651**
   expect;] expect, **Goffin**
56 These] Those **1651**

TO DR. DUPPA . . . TUTOR TO THE PRINCE OF WALES
3 Prease] Presse **Goffin**
5 the] this **Goffin**
65 true] true, **1651 (corrected by Goffin)**

TO THE SAME . . . PUBLICK ACT AT OXON. 1634
6 sacrifice,] Sacrifise **1651 (comma supplied in** *Errata***)**
28 Germany.] Germany **Goffin**
30 Monster-Masters] Monster—Masters **Goffin**
44 zeal-prepared in Hunger] zeal prepared-Hunger **1651 (corrected in** *Errata***)**
46 Three;] Three, **1651**; Three. **Goffin**
48 Among . . . come,] **Omitted Goffin**
60 Sermon] Sermou **1651**
78 You'l] You'd **Goffin**

ON THE GREAT FROST. 1634
1 the] your **Mal. 21**; those **1657**
   of] on **1657**
2 two] **Omitted 1657**
3 Y'are] You are **1657**

Gods] God **Mal. 21, Harl. 6931**; god **1657**
4 may] doe **Mal. 21, Harl. 6931, 1657**
5 Whiles] whilst **Mal. 21, 1657, Goffin**
6 Fleeces,] Fleeces; **1651 (corrected by Goffin)**
7-8 Waters ... done;] Omitted here **1657**; quoted as a couplet earlier (p. 314)
10 being ... like to] being not now like to **Harl. 6931**; not being now like **1657**
12 not ... only] not onely born up **1657**
13 Whiles] Whilst **Mal. 21**; while **1657** thus] they **1657**
14 And ... each day] And are each day without faith **Harl. 6931**
16 Were wisdome now] Were now discreete **Mal. 21, Harl. 6931**; Was now discreet **1657**
17 There's no one] Here's no one **Mal. 21**; There's not one **1657** among] amongst **Harl. 6937, 1657**
18 Water's as] Water is **1657**
20 a Fountain, or] some fountaines, or **Mal. 21**; a fountain by **1657**
21 need] needs **1657** may] should **1657**
22 he] be **Goffin**
23-24 When Heaven ... encreas'd] When heaven dropt some smaller showre our sence/Our greifes increased'd **Mal. 21**; When as heaven drops some smaller drops, our sense/Of Griefe's encreas'd **1657**
25 whiles] while **Mal. 21, Harl. 6931**; whilst **1657**
think those] seeke those **Mal. 21**; think the **Harl. 6931**
26 Pearl] pearles **Mal. 21, 1657**
came down half way] half-way came down **Goffin**
27 Removall] removing **Mal. 21**

28 Waters] water **1657**
30 our] one **Mal. 21**; a **1657**
Noon] none **Harl. 6931**
34 and not faln] and not fell **Mal. 21, Harl. 6931**; and fell not **1657**
and without] without **Mal. 21**; yet without **1657**
36 stil'd] call'd **Mal. 21, Harl. 6931, 1657**
39 one] man **1657**
40 For ... for] ffor how can there be **Mal. 21**
41 not] now **Mal. 21**
42 Unless] Except **Harl. 6931**
43 nay what's more,] And (what's more), **Harl. 6931**
44 Dutchmen] Dutch **Mal. 21**
45 Fate] faith **1657**
what is] what 'tis **1657**
46 That last cold, Death,] That last, calld Death, **Mal. 21**; To feel cold Death, **1657**; That last cold Death, **Goffin**
49 this] our **1657**
50 too] it **1657**
53 no] not **1657**
54 Why] That **1657**
55 be a] be as **Harl. 6931**
58 one] a **Mal. 21, 1657**
59 the thought] For **Mal. 21 Goffin reads** your thought; the thoughts **1657**
60 that] which **Harl. 6931**
61 Such ... give] Wheather may give **Mal. 21, 1657**; Wheather to give **Harl. 6931**
63 by his] by hy his **1657**
65 now ... *Alabaster*] now do think Allestree **Mal. 21**
67 whiles] while **Mal. 21, Harl. 6931**; whilst **1657**
ought we] we ought **1657**
68 shall not] should not **Harl. 6931**; cannot **1657**
70 Crazed] crazie **1657**
being ... so] when that she's grown

so **Mal. 21**; being she's grown thus **Harl. 6931**; being she is grown thus **1657**
72 Suffer] Sffer **1657**
73 Leaves us, which] leaves which **Mal. 21, 1657**
74 make ... second] make us count from since the second **1657**

To ... LADIE ELIZABETH POWLET
TITLE *To the* ... Needle-worke] *To the Lady* Pavvlet, *upon her Present sent to the Vniversity, being the Story of the Nativity and Passion of our Saviour, wrought by her self in Needle-work.* **1651**; Upon the Lady Paulets Gift to the University of Oxford: Being an exact piece of Needle-work presenting the whole story of the Incarnation, Passion, Resurrection, and Ascension of our Saviour. **1656**; *To a Lady that wrought a story of the Bible in needle-work.* **1659, 1660, 1662, 1687, 1699**
2 our] the **1651**
4 Whiles] Whilst **1656**; Whil'st **1659-1699**
6 Glories] glory **1656-1699**
8 stealth] strength **1656-1699**
   both takes and cheates] doth take and cheat **1656-1699**
11 toucheth] touches **1660-1699**
12 diffring] differing **1656**; diff'ring **1659-1699, Goffin**
13 Track wee see, thither] this tract, thither we see **1656, 1659**; tract, whither we see **1660-1699**
14 But cann't ... there] But cannot say here this or there **1656-1699**
15 whiles] while **1656-1699**
18 our backs] aside **1651**
20 fingers] finger **1660-1699**
21 wee the] me the **1651** (corrected in the *Errata*)
23 such Griefe] and Grief **1651**
24 a] the **1659-1699**
25 each so] and so **1651, Goffin**
27 Text all; wee] text, all we **1656**
28 press'd] pass'd **1659-1699**
30 from hence the] with th'four a **1656**; with four, a **1659-1699**
32 then] than **1651, Goffin**
34 Deafe.] Deafe **Goffin**
35 St. Helen happ'ly] that Helen haply **1656-1699**
39 yee that] you that **1651**
41 And] Of **1656-1699**
   yee] you **1651**
43 (no doubt)] no doubt **1659-1699**
45 sow'd] sew'd **1651, Goffin**
   Idle] onely **1656-1699**
46 onlie] truly **1651**

To MR W. B. ... FIRST CHILD
22 *Synalæphaes*] Synaloephoes **Goffin**
28 Imperfection] **According to Goffin the 1651 text reads** Imperfections **I have seen no copy with this reading.**

FOR A YOUNG LORD ... TAUGHT HIM A SONG
TITLE *For a young Lord ... a Song.*] **No title, LA**
2 I've only ... since] I euer since haue liu'de **LA**
12 th'are that] tis but **LA**
13 I had ... perhaps] I had in part this loue **LA**
14 awak'd and] a wakde, and **LA**
16 Flower] flowre **LA**

ON MR STOKES ... ART OF VAULTING
TITLE *On Mr* Stokes ... or,] **Not in Mal. 21; from 1651**
Tractatum] *Tractatu* **1651, Goffin**
Gulıllmo] Guil. **1651, Goffin**
Oxon] Omitted **1651, Goffin**
et] & **1651**; omitted **Goffin**
temporum] **Mal. 21 reads** temporum

    nostrorum but nostrorum has been crossed through
    desultorium] *de sultorium* 1651
7 hee ere] e'r he 1651, **Goffin**
16 would they] they would **Goffin**
21 downwards] downward 1651
34 puts] put 1651, **Goffin**
37 Stags leape] *Stag-Leap* 1651, **Goffin**
40 his ... desire] **Bracketed Mal. 21**
46 hang] lye 1651
52 wax'd] wax 1651, **Goffin**
60 'um] 'em 1651, **Goffin**
69 Cut a crosse-caper] Cut *Will's* Cross Caper 1651, **Goffin**
72 plucke] pull 1651, **Goffin**
SUBSCRIPTION **Not in Mal. 21; from** 1651

LOVE INCONCEALABLE. STIG. ITAL.
1 fire] fear **Goffin**

THE TEARES
    7-14 **See lines 25-28, 42-46 of "On one weepeing."**
7 And] O **LA, Harl. 3511, Harl. 6917,** 1653
8 Whence] From whence **Harl. 3511**
    Lilly] Lillies **Harl. 6917**
    grow] 1653, **Harl. 6917**; grow, 1651; grow; **Harl. 3511**
9 In ... Cheeks] on ... Cheeke **Harl. 6917**
    The] those **Harl. 3511, Harl. 6917**
    showres] showers **Harl. 3511, Harl. 6917**; showr's 1653
10 thus] doe **Harl. 6917**
    do breed] doe cause **LA** (altered to breede); doe bring **Harl. 3511**; produce **Harl. 6917**
    these] those **LA, Harl. 3511, Harl. 6917,** 1653
    flowers] flowres **LA**; Flow'rs 1653
12 And] Or 1653
    Flowers] Juno **Harl. 6917**
14 Cheeks] Cheeke **Harl. 6917**

ON ONE WEEPEING
3 Sure 'twas] Sure't'was **Goffin**
7 know ith'midst] know the midst **Goffin**
11 straind] traind **Goffin**
17 Soe] See **Goffin**
30 seale] steale **Goffin**; the MS has steale crossed out and seale written over it
37 Or ... deferre] O ... deterre **Goffin**; the reading Or is a little doubtful, but improves the sense
38 the] your **Goffin**
40 Deucalions] Deucalion's **Goffin**
41 If] In **Goffin**

A SONG OF DALLIANCE
TITLE *A Song of Dalliance*] **Goffin**; *Cartwright's* Song of Dalliance Never printed before. 1656; *Loves Courtship.* **PB 1656**
2 that] the **PB 1656**
3 has] hath **PB 1656**
5 posts] hosts **Goffin**
7-8 Softer ... prize.] Softer lists are no where found,/And the strife its selfe's the prize. **PB 1656**
9-10 Let not ... thee:] Let not shades and dark affright thee,/Thy eyes have lustre that will light thee: **PB 1656**
11 Fear not] Think not **PB 1656**
13 thy] that **PB 1656**; the **Bullen (see Notes)**
14 darkness both dwell] silence both wait **PB 1656**
19-20 Give a ... it:] Profer something and forbear it,/Give a grant and then forswear it: **PB 1656**
21 our] my **PB 1656**
22 wicked wanton] wanton wicked **PB 1656**
24 Say, We ... again.] Say thou ne're shalt joy againe. **PB 1656**; Say "We ne'er shall meet again." **Bullen, Goffin**

27 is] are **PB 1656**
29 restless fight] wrestlers slight **PB 1656, Bullen, Goffin**
30 whilst ye twine] when we twine **PB 1656**

FALSHOOD
TITLE *Falshood*] To his M^ris that proude false **Addit. MS, Folger MS**
2 those] them **Addit. MS, Folger MS**
3 doth] death **Folger MS**
4 Or . . . the] Uppon the clocke or **Addit. MS**
5 The . . . are:] **Omitted in Addit. MS**
6-10 Only thy . . . or Star.] **Addit. MS reads:**
    all doe obey
    natures greate sway
    onely her minde
    untrue I finde
and soe forlorne I suffer wronge
10 Star.] Star, **1651 (corrected Goffin)**
11-20 Fool that I . . . Murmur pass.] **Omitted in Addit. MS**
12 thou'rt] thou art **Folger MS**
19 Shade-like thou'lt] Shad'like tho'lt **Folger MS**
21 didst thou . . . didst thou] did shee . . . did shee **Addit. MS**
22 Whispring those] Whisperinge soft **Addit. MS, Folger MS**
mine] my **Folger MS**
23 'tween each one, as] tweene each one a **Addit. MS**; t'weene each oath, as **Folger MS**; t'ween each one, as **Goffin**
24 Didst interpose] Shee interpresd **Addit. MS**
sweeter] sweete **Addit. MS**
29 thy] her **Addit. MS**
30 thee . . . thy] her . . . her **Addit. MS**
33 instruct] mistrust **Addit. MS, written over another word**
35 Believe't 'tis] Beleeve 'tis **Addit. MS**
38 ne'r] never **Addit. MS**
41-53 'Twas *Venus* . . . true to all,] Both MSS omit these lines. In their place the Addit. MS reads:

Alasse unfaithfull they are gone
as is the day shee sware uppon
they were but vow'd alas I finde
Each kisse outlived, the oath it signd
they never knew a second morne
    they found the wombe
    a suddayne tombe
    her verie breath
    did give them death
twas fatall to them to be borne

But singe [*sic*] shee boasts her self divine
O may shee like the stars still shine
Equall to all; impart her lights
To smyths, & Tinkers as to [and such crossed out] wights
of finer mould & softer stone
    O May her light
    each spangled night
    seeme to the eye
    to fall and Die
enioyed of all but loved of none.

May she still groane not without cause
May shee still sigh without a pause
May shee proue constant unto all

The Folger MS reads:

Alas their' fledd, vaine idle thinges
As yf thy lightnes lent them winges:
They were but vow'd; and wretch I find
Each kisse out liu'd ye oath it sign'd;
They never knew a second morne
But found ye wombe

   A suddaine tombe
   Thy very breath
   Did giue them death
  T'was fatall to them to be borne.

  May'st thou still groane not wthout cause,
  May'st thou still sigh, wthout a pause,
  May'st thou prooue constant unto all,
56 mayst thou] may shee **Addit. MS**
58 thy] her **Addit. MS**
59 Once] one **Addit. MS**
60 thine] her **Addit. MS**; thy **Folger MS**
  o'r] over **Addit. MS**

BEAUTY AND DENIALL
23 Which] Wich **1651 (corrected by Goffin)**
33 On] Oh **Goffin**

TO CUPID
TITLE *To* Cupid.] A Prayer to *Cupid*. **1655**
1 Thou ... Light] *Cvpid* who didst ne're see light **1655**
3 alwaies] ever **1655**
6 yet ... know] though she know not **1655**
7 Thou ... such] Thou that woundest with such **1655**
12 thence] hence **1655**

TO VENUS
TITLE *To* Venus.] **No title, LA**; A Complaint against *Cupid*. **1653, 1669**
2 spightfull] **LA**; sprightfull **1651, 1653, 1669**
4 can] could **LA, 1653, 1669**
7 Wing'd] Winged **Goffin**
8 third] first **1653, 1669**
9 mayst] maiest **LA**
10 Bow.] Bow, **1651**

A SIGH SENT TO HIS ABSENT LOVE
TITLE *A Sigh ... Love.*] A Sigh. **Folger MS**
1 Blest ones] Mistres **Folger MS** (so also **Addit. MS** and **1640**; see the Notes); Blestones **1651**
10 journeying] iourning **Folger MS**
11 then drew neer] and for feare **Folger MS** (so also **Addit. MS** and **1640**)
12 Then] It **Folger MS** (so also **Addit. MS**)
18 a] this **Folger MS**
22 tipp] **Folger MS**; Lip **1651**

SADNESS
25 alone] alone. **1651 (some copies)**

TO A PAINTERS HANDSOME DAUGHTER
TITLE *To a*] On a **1656**
2 Counterfeits] counterfeit **1656**
4 plac'd] placed **1656**
7 Nay, more yet,] Nay more; yet **1656**
8 That ... Pictures] That they are well bred, pictures **1656**
11 last] least **1656**
12 out] from **1656**
13 Whiles] Whilst **1656**
19-20 For they ... Hate;] **Omitted 1656**
21 you're] you are **1656**
23 vain;] vain: **1651 (some copies)**
24 two'l] two will **1656**
25 you've] you have **1656**

LESBIA ON HER SPARROW
18 though] thongh **1651 (some copies)**
22 all] all, **1651 (some copies)**

THE GNAT
20 detroy'd] destroyed **Goffin**
24 Laught] Laughs **Goffin**

AT A DRY DINNER
1 you please] your please **1651 (corrected by Chalmers)**

A Bill of Fare
- 2 Adultery] Adultery, 1651 (corrected by Goffin)
- 16 th'Wiser] the Wiser Goffin
- 22 Meal's] Meals Goffin
- 34 return,] return; Goffin
- 38 unto] uuto 1651
- 42 thence?] thence! Goffin

The Chambermaids Posset
- 1 Ladies] Lady 1655
- 5 Vertue's] vertues 1655; Virtues Goffin
- 6 he remembred] be remembered Goffin
- 7 Habit's] habits 1655
- 8 I ha'] is 1655
- 10 furnish] punish Goffin
- 15 God] A blank left in 1655
- 21 handfull] handfulls 1655, Goffin
- 22 squeezed] squeexed 1651 (corrected by Chalmers and Goffin)
- 26 better] berter 1651
- 27 'twas] t'was Goffin
- 30 a] Omitted 1655
  Histrio-mastix] Histrio-mastrix 1651 (corrected Goffin)
- 31 Three] Two 1655
  Sponfull] spoonfulls 1655; Sponfulls Goffin
  T.C.'s] T.C. 1655
  confuted] confused 1655
- 32 close-noated] close noated Goffin
  ago] since Goffin
- 33-48 Next . . . Liberty.] Omitted 1655
- 34 fashion;] fashion, Goffin
- 39 Geneva's] Genevah's 1651 (some copies)
- 52 'Twill] And will 1655
- 53 An Ell London-measure] An Ell, London measure 1655; An Ell-London measure Goffin
- 54 Conceiv'd] conceived 1655
- 56 Imag'ry] Image 1655
- 61-68 The Pig . . . sure.] Omitted 1655

On a Gentlewomans Silk-hood
- title On . . . Silk-hood.] Gentlewomen's black hoods Addit. 22,602; The Veil. Harl. 7319
- 1 Sanctity] chastity Mal. 21
- 2 veils,] veils Goffin
  Lay-Nun?] Lay-Nun. Goffin
- 3 your] the Mal. 21
  through] thorough Addit. 22,602
  the] this Addit. 22,602, Harl. 7319, Folger 452.1
- 5 I] to Mal. 21
- 6 on] of Mal. 21
  and] an Mal. 21
- 7 these] those Mal. 21, Harl. 7319, Folger 452.1
  subt'ly] subtly (corrected from closely) Addit. 22,602; wisely Harl. 7319
  set,] set Goffin
- 8 her] the Addit. 22,602
  the] a Mal. 21.
- 10 may] will Mal. 21
- 11 may] will Mal. 21
- 12 desire] the fire Mal. 21
- 13 your other] the Mal. 21
  'tis] this is Addit. 22,602, Harl. 7319, Folger 452.1
- 15 Dark-Lanthorn] Dark Lanthorn Goffin
  face] Fear Harl. 7319
- 16 May . . . think] I may conclude Mal. 21, Addit. 22,602, Harl. 7319, Folger 452.1
  Men?] Men. Addit. 22,602; Men Goffin
- 17 Whiles] Whilst Mal. 21; While Harl. 7319; new paragraph Addit. 22,602
  the] your Addit. 22,602
  Lips,] Lips? Goffin
- 18 Eclipse.] Eclipse Goffin
- 19 Mean't . . . will,] (Mean't . . . will) Addit. 22,602
  hide,] hide Goffin
- 21 o'r,] o'r Goffin

22 much;] **Harl. 7319**; much, **Folger 452.1**; much **1651, Goffin**
23 No paragraph **Folger 452.1**
   I] Omitted **Mal. 21**
   strange] strong **Addit. 22,602**
24 Bring] Brings **Addit. 22,602, Harl. 7319, Folger 452.1**
   Altar] Altars **Addit. 22,602, Harl. 7319**
25 O] Omitted **Harl. 7319**
   t'your Cradles] to the **(followed by a blank) Mal. 21**; to your Cradles **Harl. 7319**
26 Mixt] Foule **Addit. 22,602**
   your] the **Mal. 21**
27 Fancy's . . . hallow'd] Fancy now is Hallow'd **Harl. 7319**
   and] Omitted **Mal. 21**
29 out] forth **Mal. 21**
30 shed] shewd **Mal. 21**
31 Bud] bed **Mal. 21**
32 half . . . hid] half-hid, half-seen **Harl. 7319**
33 through] thorough **Addit. 22,602**
   Veyls] Veil **Harl. 7319**
34 doth] does **Harl. 7319**
35 New paragraph **Folger 452.1**
   lay] layes **Mal. 21**
38 might] may **Mal. 21**
   'em] them **Mal. 21, Addit. 22,602, Harl. 7319, Folger 452.1**
39 Thus is your] This is the **Mal. 21**; Thus is the **Addit. 22,602**
   Contriv'd,] Contriv'd. **Goffin**
41 Light] Lights **Mal. 21, Addit. 22,602, Harl. 7319**
   Groves] Defective **Mal. 21**
   where] whose **Harl. 7319**
42 at last] at first **Addit. 22,602**
   Gods] Defective **Mal. 21**
43 darkneth] darkens **Addit. 22,602, Harl. 7319, Folger 452.1**
   Face,] Face **Goffin**
44 May not I] Shall I not **Mal. 21**; Shall not I **Addit. 22,602, Folger 452.1**

a] Omitted **Mal. 21**
45 New paragraph **Folger 452.1**
46 those . . . Stars)] those (but neerer) Stars **Addit. 22,602**; those; but nearer Stars **Harl. 7319**; those but . . . starrs, **Folger 452.1**
   your] the **Mal. 21**
   here] bear **Harl. 7319**
47 New paragraph **Folger 452.1**
   darkned] darkened **Folger 452.1**
   we] Men **Harl. 7319**
48 our] their **Harl. 7319**
49 allow'd,] allow'd **Goffin**
50 Where] When **Mal. 21, Goffin**
   the] that **Mal. 21**
51 New paragraph **Folger 452.1**
52 Retrivall] revivall **Mal. 21**
54 shew even] looke as **Mal. 21**; shew ev'n **Harl. 7319, Folger 452.1**
55 our . . . our] the . . . the **Mal. 21**
56 Whiles] Whilst **Mal. 21**; Where **Addit. 22,602, Harl. 7319**
   doth] does **Harl. 7319**
57 New paragraph **Folger 452.1**
   ye no Assaults] ye not assaults **Mal. 21**; you no Assault **Addit. 22,602, Harl. 7319**
58 assaile] assault **Mal. 21**
59 Parts,] Parts **Goffin**
60 only] Sharpest **Harl. 7319**

A DREAM BROKE
23 fleet] sweet **Goffin**

LOVES DARTS
2 throws?] throw **1651 (some copies)**
16 Not] For **1651 (some copies)**

PARTHENIA FOR HER SLAIN ARGALUS
28 *Parthenia's*] *Patheuia's* **1651**

ARIADNE DESERTED BY THESEUS . . . THUS COMPLAINS
TITLE Ariadne *deserted . . . complains.*]. Ariadne deserted by Thesevs sit-

tinge vppon a Rock in ye Island Naxos thus Complaines **LA**
1 O *Theseus*] ô theseus! **LA**; O *Theseus,* **1653**
2 deserted] forsaken **LA**
3 neighbouring] Neighb'ringe **LA, 1653**
9 you . . . you] yee . . . yee **LA, 1653**; yee . . . you **Harl. 6931**
10 you] yee **LA, 1653**; the **Harl. 6931**
13 may] might **LA**
19 Labyrinth] labrinth **LA, 1653**
21 Ravenous Vulture] Rav'nous Vultre **LA**; rav'nous Vulter **1653**
28 stoln] stolen **Goffin**
29 him] **Omitted Harl. 6931**
31 **No stanza break indicated in LA; numbered 4 in Harl. 6931**
 my] myne **LA, 1653**
41 Hopes . . . Tears] **LA originally read** sighes hopes & feares **but this was later changed (by the same hand) to** hopes sighes & teares
43 **Goffin indicates a stanza break at this line.**
 Eye] Eyes **Harl. 6931**
47 he] ?flee **Harl. 6931 (reading very doubtful)**
48 Shouldst] ?& **Harl. 6931 (reading very doubtful)**
 ev'n] **Omitted Harl. 6931**
49 yeelding] guilding **Harl. 6931**
50 gliding thence] gilding them **Harl. 6931**
51 Flow'rs] flowers **1653**
62 Bow'rs] bowers **1653**
57 Death] death! **LA**
61 Heaven] heau'n **LA, 1653**
62 fall,] fall; **LA**
64 my] **LA, Harl. 6931, 1653**; thy **1651**
65 Mayst] maiest **LA**; Mayt **Harl. 6931**
66 Sayl] Sailes **LA, 1653**
68 the] that **LA, Harl. 6931, 1653**

69 whiles] whylst **LA, 1653**
70 *Ægeus*] Eugevs **LA**
 drawest] drawst **LA, Harl. 6931**; draw'st **1653**
71 yee] **LA, Harl. 6931, 1653**; yet **1651**
73 the] yor **LA**; your **1653**
79-84 In *Thetis* . . . prov'd one.] **Marked as a new stanza in LA; entitled** Her Epitaph **in 1653**
80 by my] in myne **LA, 1653**; in my **Harl. 6931**
81 banish'd] **1653**; Banishd **LA**; banished **1651**
82 The] That **Harl. 6931**
83 him] hem **Harl. 6931**
 alone,] alone **Goffin**
84 freed] fre'd **1653**
85 Thus] **LA, Harl. 6931, 1653**; That **1651**
 then I——But look!] then I f—— but look **LA (the MS breaks off at this point)**; then I F—— but looke, **1653**
88 Dear,] Dear. **Goffin**
93 Whiles] Whilst **Harl. 6931, 1653**
96 Flow'rs] flowers **1653**
98 Bow'rs] Bowers **1653**
100 his] ?this **Harl. 6931 (reading very doubtful)**
101 Rod,] Rod. **Goffin**
102 'Tis either] 'tis he; 'tis either **1653**

TO CHLOE WHO WISH'D HER SELF YOUNG ENOUGH FOR ME
2 backwards] backward **Goffin**

NO PLATONIQUE LOVE
5 unbodi'd] unbodied **1655**
15 profess] protest **1655**
19 Come . . . that] Let all beleeve this truth that those that **1655**
21 Heyrs] Hares **1655**
24 Med'cine] medicine **1655**

LOVE BUT ONE
2 windings] Writhings **1693**

3   River,] River 1693
6   from out] out of 1693
7   into] unto Goffin
13-24 O Chloris!...away?] **For the 1693 version of these lines see the Notes.**
20 Sheep.] Sheep 1651
25-26 O in...Love!] Omitted 1693

ABSENCE
TITLE *Absence*] The Sigh. 1655; no title AC 1671
1   Sigh] Sighs AC 1671
2   his] her 1655, AC 1671
3-10 Blest...too.] "Blest...too." Chalmers; 'Blest...too! Goffin
4   chain,] chain. 1655; chain AC 1671
6   that's] that AC 1671
7   Sorrows] sorrow AC 1671

UPON THE TRANSLATION OF CHAUCER'S TROILUS AND CRESEIDE
TITLE *Vpon the...Kinaston.*] To the worthy Author on this his *Approved Translation.* 1635
14 change] Charge 1651

MARTIAL. LIB. 7. EPIG. 59
TITLE *Martial*] Matial 1651

SI MEMINI FUERANT
TITLE *Si...fuerant*] *Si memini fuerunt* 1651 (corrected Goffin)

MARTIAL LIB. 10. EP. 5
3   he] be Goffin
7   nay] may Goffin

HORAT. CARM. LIB. 4. ODE 13
6   Sports and feastings] feasts and sportings 1666
7   thaw'd] sham'd 1666
    ragged] ragg'd 1666
10 rouze our lodg'd] cross our long'd 1666
11 wakes] awakes 1666

15 Cheek] cheeks 1666
17 decayed] decay'd 1666
19-24 Neither thy...hath thrown.] Omitted 1666
31 a while] awhile 1666
36 contest] confess 1666
39 Make thee] *Make thee* 1666

ON THE BIRTH OF THE KING'S FOURTH CHILD
TITLE *On the Birth...1635.*] Goffin; *On the Birth...2636.* 1651; *To the Queene.* 1636
1   Queen's] Queen',s 1636
6   then] than 1651

TO THE QUEEN ON THE SAME
TITLE To the Queen on] Omitted Goffin; no title 1636
    then] them Goffin
11 Y'have] T'have Goffin
20 then] than 1651, Goffin
24 Her] h r 1651
25 iust] first Goffin
33 now be] now to be Goffin
37 too] to Chalmers
43 'twill] t'will Goffin
45 shee Munition] Shee-Munition 1651

TO THE KING, ON THE BIRTH OF PRINCESS ANNE
TITLE *To the King...1636.*] Omitted 1636
    Anne] Elizabeth 1651; corrected by Goffin
2   thus.] thus Goffin
3   States] Sates 1636; corrected by Goffin from 1651 ed.
4   greaters] greater 1651
8   Store?] Store. Goffin
15 as 'tis] as't is Goffin
21 Issue] 1651; Yssue 1636
25 w' have 'spi'd] we've spi'd 1651; w'have spi'd Goffin
26 Highnesse only] Majesty but 1651
38 will] with Chalmers

TO THE QUEEN
TITLE *To the Queen*] Omitted **1636**
10 then] than **1651, Goffin**
17 Wear on] We are **1636 (corrected by Goffin from 1651 ed.)**
. and] Omitted **1651**
21 'tis] 't is **Goffin**
24 limbs] wings **Goffin**
  heavn'ly] heav'nly **Goffin**
31 sight] Light **1651**
39 you] your **1651**

IN THE MEMORY OF ... BENIAMIN IOHNSON
TITLE *In the* ... Iohnson] *To the Memory of* Ben Johnson. *Laureat.* **1651**; In Memory ... Johnson **Goffin**
12 tooke] takes **1651**
25 *Manners ... Themes*] Manners were Themes, and **1651**
29 may sweare] may and swear **1651**
31 known] showne **Goffin**
34 not] nor **1651**
  see] see: **1651**
37 *art;*] Art, **1651**
38 *wiseman*] wise men **1651**
43 and] or **1651**
46 dost] doth **Goffin**
48 That] Which **1651**
49 and] or **1651**
62 too,] too. **Goffin**
70 *imag'rie:*] imag'rie. **Goffin**
83 brokes] breaks **1651**
107 rise] rose **1651**
108 as] a **1651**
116 *sallad*] ballad **Goffin**
119 put'st] puts **1651**
  passions] passion **Goffin**
127 *wit*] Muse **1651, Langbaine (see Notes)**
128 Of ... of] Oft ... from **Langbaine**
129 Is it] It is **Goffin**
133 culling] calling **Goffin**
134 ore] o'r **1651** (Goffin states that 1638 text reads ore followed by a period; this is not true of the copies I have seen.)
137 *Still*] Skill **Goffin**
150 and] or **1651**
165 *Arts*] Acts **1651**
166 *thy* lesse.] thee lesse, **Goffin**
169 those] these **Goffin**
176 art] and **1651, Goffin**

TO MY HONOUR'D FRIEND MR THOMAS KILLIGREW
TITLE To My Honovr'd ... *CLARACILLA*] *To Mr* Thomas Killegrew *on his two Playes, the Prisoners, and* Claracilla. **1651**
  these] Omitted **Goffin**
2 Dramatique] Dragmatique **1651**
6 free] fire **1651**
9 Those] These **Goffin**
24 *Van Dike,*] *Van Dick,* **1651**; *Van Dike* **1641**; Van Dike. **Goffin**
27 which goes-in] wich goes in **1651**; which goes in **Goffin**
57 approbations] approbation **Goffin**
58 prophetique] prophetiquet **1641**

VPON THE DRAMATICK POEMS OF MR JOHN FLETCHER
TITLE *Vpon ... Fletcher.*] **1651**; Upon the report of the printing of the Dramaticall Poems of Master *John Fletcher,* collected before, and now set forth in one Volume. **1647, 1679**
2 indulged] indulg'd **1679**
3 appear'd] **1651, 1679**; appeared **1647**
13 judg'd] **1651, 1679**; judged **1647**
21 bid] bid. **Goffin**
26 Language] Learning **1651**
31 Where] When **Goffin**
  up] forth **1651**
33 Where] When **Goffin**
36 ingenious] ingenuous **1651**
40 delight] delights **1651, 1679, Goffin**
42 much] much **1647**

44 cease,] cease. **1651, Goffin**
46 the] these **1679**
50 face;] face, **1651, Goffin**

ANOTHER ON THE SAME
TITLE *Another . . . same.*] Another. **1647**
30 true borne Play:] true-borne Play, **1651, Goffin**
31 These] Those **Dyce**
37 knowst] knew'st **Dyce**
38 a] the **1651**
41 where] were **1651, Chalmers**
47 exprest] express **Dyce**
52 fires;] fires, **1651, Goffin**
59 steale] Omitted **Goffin**
64 mirth,] mirth. **Goffin**
67 flow'd] **1651**; flowed **1647**
72 In turn'd Hose] In trunk-hose **Theobald**
92 pay] **Goffin** states: "Most editions have play." (I have seen no copies with that reading.)

TO THE RIGHT REVEREND FATHER IN GOD, BRIAN, LORD BISHOP OF CHICHESTER
8 others] other **Goffin**
17 flowry] flowing **Goffin**
20 as] and **1651** (corrected **Chalmers**)
29 He] She **Goffin**
62 pretious] pretions **1651**
73 Sight] Light **Goffin**
155 out-live] unt-live **1651**
156 Years] Tears **Goffin**

A NEW-YEARS GIFT
8 Nature] Natures **1651** (corrected by **Goffin**); Nature's **Chalmers**
13 (my Muse)] my (Muse) **1651**
27 Yet] Let **Goffin**
35 Furie's] Furies **Goffin**
45 Wish] With **Goffin**

A NEW-YEARS-GIFT TO BRIAN LORD BISHOP OF SARUM
12 Enjoyning] Enjoying **Goffin**

63 your] you're **1651** (corrected **Goffin**)

TO THE QUEEN AFTER HER DANGEROUS DELIVERY. 1638
TITLE *To the Queen . . . 1638.*] To the Queene. **1638**
1 Great Madam,] Omitted **1651**
5 Yet] But **1651**
6 Quiets] Quiet **1651**
10 T'endeare] To endear **1651**
12 the Fraught] **Goffin** claims that **1651** reads a Fraught I have not found the reading in any of the copies of **1651**. Chalmers' edition (1810), however, reads a Fraught
16 Halfe . . . Earth] th'other half to Earth **1651**
17 Come] Came **1651**
21 Twice] Well **1651**
22 What ere] What he **1651**

ON THE DEATH OF . . . THE LORD VISCOUNT BAYNING
TITLE *the Lord Viscount*] the Lord **1651**; Viscount **Goffin**
1 when] where **1651**
2 forward] froward **1651**
12 Life] like **1651**
22 round] Square **1651**
23 oft checkt] oft-checkt **1651**
24 of] **1651**; of, **1638**
30 Tunes] times **Goffin**
40 ill?] ill: **Goffin**
56 Famines] Famine **1651**
59 they spoile] they've spoyl'd **1651**
68 which] whence **1651**
70 which] that **1651**

A NEW-YEARS-GIFT TO A NOBLE LORD. 1640
53-54 Calm, Soveraign and soft,] Calm Soveraign, and soft **1651**
57 wish] with **Goffin**
69 Y'have] T'have **Goffin**

Vpon the Birth of the Kings sixth
   Child. 1640
title   *Vpon ... Child. 1640.*] *To the
     Queene.* **1640**
  3 Dischargd] Discharg'd **1651**; Dis-
     charged **Goffin**
 10 or, Narrow] or murrow **1651**
 14 Where] When **Goffin**
 15 Sixt] Sixth **1651, Goffin**
 26 by] with **1651**
 31 Injustice] In Justice **1651**
 33 then] than **1651, Goffin**
 43 Ingenuous] Ingenious **1651**
 45 fashiond] fashioned **Goffin**
 60 prompts] prompt **Goffin**
 62 hath] that **1651**

Vpon the Death of ... the Lord Stafford.
title   *Vpon ... STAFFORD.*] *On the
     ... Stafford.* **1640. 1651**; Upon
     the death of the Lord *Stafford,
     the last of his name.* **1656**
  4 dangerous ... good]   dangerosu
     1640; *dangerous ... good* **1651**;
     "dangerous ... good" **Goffin**
  8 were] are **1656**
 11 must we] we must **1651**
 14 her] his **1651**
 22 which] Omitted **1656**
 23 gray-haire] **Hyphen doubtful 1656**;
     omitted **1651, Goffin**
 26 Vertue] Vertues **1651**
 27-44 This is ... inward spring.] **Mis-
     placed by Goffin (see the Notes)**
 28 A ... good] And to be good only
     1651 (comma after slacke)
 31 outstrips] outstrip'd **1651**; outslips
     1656
 32 rectifi'd] rectified **Goffin**
 34 that was shewne] that was shewne
     1640 (similar turned t in **1640,**
     lines **98** Statues and **106** to **100**);
     which was shewn **1656**
 35 if't had] if 'thad **Goffin**

 37 snatchd] snatched **Goffin**
     drive] drove **1651**
 40 which shew'd] that shew **1651**
 45-63 **Omitted 1640, 1656; supplied
     from 1651; misplaced by Goffin
     as lines 27-44 of his text.**
 68 neere.] neer: **1651**; neere, **Goffin**
 70 which] whence **1651**
     discipline,] Discipline? **1651**; disci-
     pline. **Goffin**
 76 b'imprinted,] by imprinted **1656**
 81 Hereditary] hereditatry **1656**
 86 odours] odour **1656**
 89 T'embalme] To imbalme **1656**; To
     embalm **Lloyd (see the Notes)**
     is] were **1651, Lloyd**
     where] when **Lloyd**
 91 It] Its **Lloyd**
     Ointments] oyntment **1651, 1656,
     Lloyd**
 93 Whiles] While **Lloyd**
     bud dims full flowres] Bud is full
     Flower **1651**; Bud's full Flower
     Lloyd
 98 him] he **1651, Lloyd**
     Brasen: yet] brazen yet, **1651**
 99 retaine] retaines **1656**
100 Not ... time] *Not ... Time* **1651,
     Lloyd**; "Not ... time" **Goffin**
105 that] the **1651**

On the Marriage of the Lady Mary
title   *On the ... Son. 1641.*] **No title
     1641**; The Marriage of Lady
     Mary ... Son, **1641 Goffin**
  3 sowre Iustle] fierce Justle **1651**;
     sowre tustle **Goffin**
     Unclos'd] Unclosed **Goffin**
  9 while] where **1651**
 18 th' Hallowd] the hallow'd **1651**
 26 Feares.] Feares; **1651**; Feares
     Goffin
 32 Yield] Yeld **Goffin**
 34 Both] doth **1651**
 37 Chafing] Chasing **Goffin**

41 Graecian's Sword] Grecian Swords 1651; Groecian's Sword **Goffin**
42 His] The 1651
43 Your] yond 1651
52 Tree.] Tree; 1651; Tree **Goffin**
57 Zone] Tone 1651 (corrected in the *Errata*)
65 may] do 1651
69 tend:] send, 1651; tend **Goffin**

To Philip, Earl of Pembroke
TITLE *To* Philip...Oxford] *To the Cancellour of the Vniversity of Oxford, then newly chosen. 1641.* 1651; *With some Verses upon his Lordships Election of Chancellor of the Vniversity of* Oxford. **Secunda Vox**
2 Arts] Acts 1651
8 Abby dust.] Alby-dust: 1651; Abby dust, **Goffin**
11 whilst] whiles 1651
13 a part] apart 1651, **Goffin**
20 Good] Good, Brit. Mus. 669, fol. 4, *Secunda Vox,* 1651
25 Steale] Heale **Goffin**
27 wrongs] Wrong 1651, **Goffin** (probably the correct reading)
31 divert] divest 1651
 from the now] now, from the 1651
SUBSCRIPTION *Your Lordships...Cartwright.*] *Your Lordships most humble Servant,* William Cartwright. **Secunda Vox**; omitted 1651

On the Lady Newburgh
10 Portions, are] Portions are. 1651; Portions are **Goffin**
38 Prophesie] Phophesie **Goffin**
53 Then] Than **Goffin**
68 Grief] Brief **Goffin**
69 only] Omitted **Goffin**

On Mrs Abigall Long
31 lent] but **Goffin**
79 the] that **Goffin**

An Epitaph on Mr. Poultney
15 wife] wife. 1651 (some copies)

To the Memory...Spelman
15 sifted'st long-hid] siftedst long hid **Goffin**
52 Heyr.] Heyr, 1651 (corrected **Goffin**)

On a vertuous young Gentlewoman that dyed suddenly
1 Sky,] Sky 1651 (censored issue)
7 Death,] Death 1651 (censored issue)
 Repriev'd] Repriv'd 1651 (censored issue)
11 o'r] o're 1651 (censored issue)
14 assum'd] afsum'd 1651 (censored issue)
16 Soul;] Soul. 1651 (censored issue)

On the Death of...Mrs Ashford
46 Earth...laid] "Earth...laid" **Goffin**

On the Queens Return from the Low Countries
TITLE *On the...Countries.*] 1651; no title 1643
7-12 When greater...not feare.] Omitted, leaving blank, in 1651 (censored issue)
10 Villaines] Legions 1651 (uncensored issue)
19 Direct] diverse 1643
25-30 Look on...lately split.] Omitted, leaving blank, in 1651 (censored issue)
29 Friendships] Friendship 1651 (uncensored issue)
36 more] none **Goffin**
 Them.] Them, 1643

Upon the death of...Sir Bevill Grenvill
TITLE *Vpon the ...Knight.*] 1651; no

	title in 1643, 1644, 1684, Folger MS
2	Thriving] Triving 1668
12	strike-in] strike in 1644, Goffin
13	well-weighd] well weigh'd Goffin
14	Either is] Either's 1651; or is Folger MS
	th'awe] awe Folger MS
15	false-nam'd] false nam'd Goffin
	Common-wealths men] Patriots, that 1651, 1668
26	Nor . . . nor] Not . . . not Goffin
34	Nor . . . nor] Not . . . or 1651, 1668
36	who] that 1651
42	stirr'd] mou'd Folger MS
43	Souldiers] Shoulders Chalmers
46	these too] those two 1651, 1668
47-50	I should . . . the last] Omitted Folger MS, 1668
51	Incensed] inclosed Folger MS
	Rebell] Legions 1651, 1668
53	Undeserv'd] understood 1668
55	Grenville . . . Grenville] *Greenevill . . . Greenvill* 1651 (uncensored issue); *Greenvill . . . Greenvill* 1651 (censored issue); Granville . . . Granville Goffin
57	Thought] thoughts 1668
62	Inspired] inspiring 1651, 1668
63	Man,] Man. Goffin
64	Example] Examples Goffin
72	and] so 1651, 1668
73	being] ?bene Folger MS
	anew] a new ?1684, Goffin
74	conquer'd] conquered Folger MS
77	Diviner] diver Folger MS
78	Ecstasie,] Extasie. Goffin
80	1668 omits all after this line.
81-93	These twelve lines omitted in 1651 (censored issue)
81	You now that] you y^t doe Folger MS
82	give the] giue you the Folger MS
84	Ye] Yet 1644
	ye dare] you dare Folger MS
86	Because Th' were] 'Cause they were 1651
	Th'were . . . they were] they were . . . the were Folger MS
90	Traitor] **Omitted and space filled by a dash in 1651 (uncensored issue)**
94	preserves] preserved Goffin
98	th'have] they've 1651 (uncensored issue); they'ave 1651 (censored issue); th'a Folger MS
99	an] a Folger MS
101	All,] All Goffin

ON THE NATIVITY

19	1. Blest] 1 Blest 1651
24	Open O Hearts] 1. Open, O Hearts Goffin

ON THE CIRCUMCISION

4	erewhile.] erewhile, 1651
17	amise] amuse Goffin
18	his.] his Goffin

ON THE EPIPHANY

16	2 Ma.] 2 Ma, 1651
25	Inn] Sun Goffin

NOVEMBER OR SIGNAL DAYES

TITLE	*November . . . Family.*] 1671; November. 1647
1	shed'st] shew'st 1671
	Dayes] Day 1671, Goffin
5	meet] met 1671
7	so . . . knowne] (so . . . known) 1671, Goffin
10	thence] then 1671, Goffin
17	then] than 1671, Goffin
24	h'as] hath 1671, Goffin
	then] than 1671, Goffin
26	joynd] come 1671
28	So . . . She.] So tender or so white as She: 1671
29	Whiles] While 1671, Goffin
30	Glories] Glory 1671, Goffin

35	They ... reare] They Covenant out of zeal to rear **1671, Goffin**	76	And ... season] All troubles seize on **1671**
42	but ... agen] but soon fall down again **1671, Goffin**	79	As] and **1671**
47	an] a **1671, Goffin**	80	*Cares*] Care **1671, Goffin** Yee] **Omitted 1671**
48	Their ... Overcast] By it their Sky was overcast **1671, Goffin**	82	neare His] neer have **1671**
50	Traytor] Traytors **1671, Goffin**	85	*Third* ... shift] Third Day (which hath now made shift **1671, Goffin**
51	Houres] Powers **1671, Goffin**		
54	then were] than are **1671, Goffin**	86	Treason] Treasons **1671, Goffin**
66	Facion[']s] Faction's **1671, Goffin**		
72	the] his **1671, Goffin**		
75	call] cloud **1671**		

CONFESSION

18 we] wc **1651**

APPENDIX

A. MOSELEY'S PREFACE

To the Reader.

The Book in your hand, were the *Author* living, should say nothing *to the Reader:* And here we but tell you, how we have us'd Him in publishing his *Poems.* You will do him wrong to call them his *Works*; they were his *Recreation;*[1] we found not these Sheets among his *Books*: so strangely scatter'd were these excellent Peeces that till now they never met all together. Had you miss'd this *Impression,* 'tis odds you had seen none, or none entire: for, certain *Plagiaries* (whereof this Great Town hath no small number, even now when 'tis empty) began to plunder Him; which would have forc'd us to an *Action of Trover* for recovery of stollen *Wit.* They knew he was dead; and therefore One had the Forhead to affirm, that himself made Verses this last Summer, which our *Author* wrote (and whereof we had Coppies) Ten years since. Were his name worth spelling, you should have it. But he read not all, when he pilfer'd some, else our *Author* had* told him out of *Martial,*

*Page 253

> He that repeats stoln Verse, and for Fame look's,
> Must purchase Silence too, as well as Books.

Such Pick-Poets hereafter may rob, but cannot steal, for now this Book is every *Reader's*: And (take it on his word who never *subscrib'd* to a Lye) there's nothing kept from you but only one short Paper of Verses: what that is, and why it is not here, we need not tell you; for it hath been twice already Printed, though above our Power to bring it with its fellows. We hope you will not imagine here is a Line but what was the *Author's* own: for, though this be a *Posthume Edition,* here is no false *Codicill,* begotten after the Father was buried: he were a bold man (to say no worse) would go about to *impose* on this *Author*; from whose own Manuscripts you have this *Impression.* If you ask, why its crowded in so scant a Volume? 'tis

---

1. Lloyd, *Memoires,* p. 422: "Whose very *Recreations* hath above fifty of the choicest Pens to applaud them."

for your own sakes; we see it is such weather that the most ingenious have least money; else the Lines are as long as in *Folio*, and would equall those of trebble its price. You look not here we should praise our *Author*; 'tis better done by much better hands: if you think He hath too many *Commenders*, it is a sign you knew him not: we grant here are more than before other Books, and yet we give you not all we have. The truth is, His high Abilities were accompanied with so much Candor and Sweetness that they made him equally *lov'd* and *admir'd*: for it is a debt due to vertuous Modesty, that those receive most Honour who least seek it.[2] Some perhaps may quarrell with the *Frontispeece* (a man in a *Gown* before a Book of *Poems*:) Such may know 'twas done on purpose: we could have dress'd him with *Chaplets* and *Laurel*, *Cloak'd*, and *Embroyder'd*, as well as others: but, since he first went to the *King's* Schoole at *Westminster* till he went out of the World, he was ever in a *Gown*: give them a Cloak whose Works need one; he writ nothing contrary to the Lawes of *Art* or *Vertue*;[3] nothing but what the *Gown* may own, which (as it is the Emblem of *Science* and the Robe of *Honour*, in all Orders, from the *Emperour* to the *Attorney*) can displease none but those in *Buff*. If any suppose Him no Master in *Poetry* because a *Scholar*, (as some who are *not Scholars* use to talk) we wish them a little of the *Author's* Modesty: they often see Verses, written perhaps by the youngest sort, and by those they judge the whole *University*. There is a wide distance 'twixt *Iudging* and *Censuring*; for they who know least, do censure deepest; as the most cruell *Iudges* have least *Law*. But though all *Scholars* are not *Poets*, every *Poet* must be a *Scholar*, let him live where he will. And we need not go far to instance, that the best *Poems* of these later Ages were written by the best *Scholar*, the immortall *Hugo Grotius*. A great *Phansie*, with judgement to ballance it, may do and be what it will: for (as *Aristotle* said of

2. *Ibid.*, p. 422: "his high abilities were accompanyed with so much candor and sweetness, that they made him equally *loved*, and admired, his vertuous modesty attaining the greatest honor by avoiding *all* [*sic*]." Wood, *Athenae Oxonienses*, 1721 ed., II, 35: "But that which is most remarkable, is that these his high parts and abilities were accompanied with so much candour and sweetness, that they made him equally beloved and admired by all Persons." Finally in Langbaine, *Account of the English Dramatick Poets* (p. 53), this becomes: "In a word he was of so sweet a disposition, and so replete with all Virtues, that he was beloved by all Learned Men that knew him, and admired by all Strangers."

3. Lloyd, *Memoires*, p. 423: "dropping not a line against the Laws either of Art or Vertue."

Æschron the Poet) *he could not tell what Æschron could not do.*⁴ If *Ovid* were no Lawyer, 'twas because he would not, he might have been, as well as *Grotius*. But the greatest *Orator* (no less a man than *Cicero*) tuggd and sweat for a little *Poetry*, and prov'd at last he was not *born* to it.⁵ We speak this for our *Author's* sake, who was so full and absolute in both, that those who best knew him, knew not in which he was more excellent.⁶ There are can witness, that our ablest Judge & Professor of *Poesie*, said with some passion, *My Son Cartwright writes all like a Man*: You'l soon guess 'twas *Ben Iohnson* spake it: What had *Ben* said had he read his own eternity in that lasting *Elegy* given him by our *Author*, or that other Latine one by our *Author's* Friend Mr *Robert Waring*, neither of which Peeces are easie to be imitated.⁷ It may seem strange the same man should be *Tully* and *Virgil*;⁸ but stranger to such as heard Him when *Metaphysick Reader* to the *Vniversity*, (for in those daies *Oxford* was a *Vniversity*)[.] And clearly we may say, since that *Lecture's* Foundation, it was never perform'd better than by our *Author*, and by his learned Predecessor Mr *Thomas Barlow* of *Queens* Colledge.⁹ We have not yet told you He was a *Divine*, some body will like his *Poems* the worse for it; but such will mistake both Him and his Book: for as

4. *Ibid.*, p. 422: "in fine a great fansie, with as great judgment, that could do and be what it would: no man can tell (as *Aristotle* said of *Æschron* the Poet) *what this prodigious man could not do.*" Langbaine, *Account of the English Dramatick Poets*, p. 53: "And One fitly applied to our Author, that saying of *Aristotle* concerning *Aeschron* the Poet, that *He could not tell what* Aeschron *could not do.*"

5. Langbaine, *Account of the English Dramatick Poets*, p. 52: "He was an excellent Orator, and yet an admirable Poet, a Quality which *Cicero* with all his pains could not attain to."

6. Wood, *Athenae Oxonienses*, 1721 ed., II, 35: "in which Faculties, as also in the *Greek* Tongue, he was so full and absolute, that those that best knew him, knew not in which he most excelled."

7. Lloyd, *Memoires*, p. 423: "So just a Poet that *Ben. Johnson* our ablest Judge and Professor of Poetry, said with some Passion: *My Son* Cartwright *writes all like a man*, (What had *Ben.* said, had he read his own Eternity in that lasting Elegy given him by Mr. *Cartwright*, or that other by his good friend Mr. *Robert Waring*, neither of which pieces are easily to be imitated)." Langbaine, *Account of the English Dramatick Poets*, p. 53: "To speak of his Poetry, there needs no other Character of it in general, than that the ablest Judge of Poetry at that time, I mean *Ben Johnson*, said with some Passion, *My Son* Cartwright *writes all like a Man.*"

8. Wood, *Athenae Oxonienses*, 1721 ed., II, 35: "He was another *Tully* and *Virgil*."

9. Lloyd, *Memoires*, p. 423: "(where no performance ever like his, and his learned Predecessor Mr. *Tho. Barlow* of *Queens*)." Wood, *Athenae Oxonienses*, 1721 ed. II, 35. "the exposition of them

here is nothing his *Function* need blush at, so here is but one Sheet was written after he entred *Holy Orders*: some before He was twenty years old, scarce any after five and twenty, never his Business, only to sweeten and releeve deeper Thoughts. There are make it a Trade, though (compared to Him) are but as those Tradesmen now-adaies make *Sermons*. The highest Poet our Language can boast of (the late *Dean* of St *Paul's*) you'l grant was afterwards an excellent Preacher; and in the judgement of (then) a most Learned *University*, our *Author* was so too. If the Witts read his *Poems*, Divines his *Sermons*, Philosophers his *Lectures* on *Aristotle's Metaphysicks*, they will scarce beleeve He dyed at *thirty*.[10] What strange height he would have risen to, we cannot imagine; for He was a Student of most *growing* Parts; and therefore his Patron (that eminent example of *Piety* and *Learning* the Lord Bishop of *Sarum* Doctor *Duppa*) would not deprive *Oxford* of Him, nor of his other Chaplain Mr *Iohn Gregory*, who now also is gone after him to Heaven. You will be deceiv'd to expect such hereafter; for you cannot but have heard of the *Oxford Visitours*. Had our *Author* liv'd he had felt them too; but a fatall choice *Feaver* (seven years since) prevented their *Visitation*:[11] which Feaver then robb'd us of Mr *Masters* of *New-Colledge*, Mr *Diggs* of *All-Souls*, with many other most hopefull Gentlemen. But since we lost our *Author*, let us save what we can of him: his *Poems* you see come first to hand, as in a great Shipwrack the lightest Treasure swims uppermost: You may gain more, of higher use, hereafter. In the interim pardon his Zeal (to the *Author*) who was loth to let any thing perish which is immortall. *Farewell*.

---

was never better performed than by him and his Predecessor *Tho. Barlow* of *Qu. Coll.*" Langbaine, *Account of the English Dramatick Poets*, p. 52: "and those who heard his Metaphysical Lectures, gave him the Preference to all his Predecessors, the present Bishop of *Lincoln* excepted."

10. Lloyd, *Memoires*, p. 424: ". . . and all this at thirty years of age." Lloyd thus simply repeats Moseley in spite of the fact that he has himself already given 1615 as the year of Cartwright's birth. Wood, *Athenae Oxonienses*, 1721 ed., II, 35: "So that if the Wits read his Poems, Divines his Sermons, and Philosophers his Lectures on *Aristotle's* Metaphysics, they would scarce believe that he died at a little above thirty Years of Age."

11. Lloyd, *Memoires*, p. 426: In his *Life and Death of Mr. Dudley Digges*, who likewise died in 1643, Lloyd writes: "A choice Feaver, called a New Disease in *Oxford* Garrison, seizing on him, and other persons of pure spirits, and nobly tempered bodies, 1643/4, prevented him in those great services he was qualified for in his generation, which indeed deserved him not, being likely to have turned him out of the University, by a Malignant Visitation, if he had not been called out of the world by a Malignant disease."

A NOTE ON MOSELEY'S PREFACE

A few inaccuracies in Moseley's account should be noticed. (1) Moseley's statement "from whose own Manuscripts you have this *Impression*" is probably correct, so far as manuscripts are involved, for everything except *The Royal Slave*, which is printed from the second (Oxford, 1640) edition. How many of the manuscripts were actually Cartwright's own, we have no means of knowing, though the generally excellent quality of Moseley's text seems to favor his assertion. (2) The description of the frontispiece as "a man in a *Gown* before a Book of *Poems*" is only half true. The book is actually a copy of Aristotle's *Metaphysics*. (3) The statement that "here is but one Sheet was written after he entred *Holy Orders*" (i.e., 1638) cannot be taken too seriously. At least ten poems can be shown to have been composed after this date. Moseley goes on to say that he wrote "scarce any after five and twenty," a remark which is only another way of repeating that he wrote very little after taking holy orders in 1638, since, according to Moseley's method of reckoning his age, Cartwright was born in 1613. (4) For a full discussion of Moseley's statement that "He dyed at *thirty*," see the Introduction, Chapter I, pp. 4n, 6–7n.

B. METRICAL ANALYSIS OF STANZA FORMS

In the following analysis letters refer to the rhyme scheme, numbers to the number of major stresses in the line.

			PAGE
I	*Twenty-line stanza*		
		a5 a3 b5 b3 c4 c4 d3 d3 e5 f3 f3 e5 g4 g4 h5 h4 i5 i4 j5 j5	494
II	*Eighteen-line stanza*		
		a4 a2 b2 c2 b2 c2 d3 d3 e3 e3 f3 f3 g3 g3 h3 h3 i4 i4	490
		a3 b2 a3 b2 c2 c3 d2 d3 e4 f2 f2 e4 g4 g4 h3 h3 i5 i5	489
III	*Fourteen-line stanza*		
		a5 a3 b5 b3 c4 c4 d3 d3 e4 e4 f3 f3 g5 g5	539
		a4 a4 b5 b5 c3 c3 d4 d4 e5 e5 f5 f5 g5 g5	490
		a4 b4 a4 b4 c3 c3 d4 d4 e4 e4 f3 f3 g4 g4	103
		a4 a4 b3 b3 c4 c4 d4 d3 e4 e3 f4 f3 g4 g4	162
IV	*Twelve-line stanza*		
		a4 a4 b3 b3 c4 c4 d5 d5 e4 f3 f3 e4	489
		a4 a4 b3 b3 c4 c4 d3 d3 e2 e2 f5 f5	488
		a3 a4 b3 b4 c3 c4 d3 d3 e4 e4 f5 f5	487
V	*Eleven-line stanza*		
		a3 b4 b3 a3 c4 c4 d3 d3 e2 e2 d3	473
VI	*Ten-line stanza*		
		a5 a5 b5 b4 c5 c4 d5 d4 e5 e5	560
		a5 a4 b5 b4 c3 c3 d4 d4 e5 e5	533
		a5 a3 b5 b3 c4 c4 d3 d3 e5 e5	528
		a4 a4 b5 b5 c5 c5 d5 d5 e5 e6	490
		a4 a4 b4 b4 c4 c4 d4 d4 e5 e5	400, 424, 472, 506
		a4 b4 a4 b4 c4 d4 c4 d4 b5 b5	465
		a4 a4 b4 b4 c4 d2 d2 e2 e2 c4	468
		a4 a4 b2 b2 c3 c3 d5 d5 e4 e4	488
		a4 a4 b4 b4 c3 c3 d3 d3 e4 e4	485
		a3 a3 b5 b3 c5 c3 d4 d4 e5 e5	507
VII	*Nine-line stanza*		
		a4 a4 b4 b4 c2 d2 d2 b4 b4	335
		a4 b3 a4 b3 c2 c2 d2 d2 a4	212

834

METRICAL ANALYSIS

VIII   *Eight-line stanza*

     $a_5\ a_4\ b_5\ b_4\ c_5\ c_4\ d_4\ d_4$ 488
     $a_4\ a_4\ b_3\ b_3\ c_4\ c_4\ d_5\ d_5$ 547
     $a_4\ a_4\ b_4\ b_4\ c_4\ d_4\ c_4\ d_4$ 467
     $a_4\ a_4\ b_4\ b_4\ c_3\ c_3\ d_3\ d_3$ 127
     $a_4\ a_4\ b_3\ b_3\ c_3\ c_3\ d_5\ d_5$ 491
     $a_4\ a_4\ b_2\ b_2\ c_4\ d_4\ d_4\ c_4$ 477
     $a_4\ a_4\ b_3\ b_3\ c_3\ c_3\ d_4\ d_4$ 126
     $a_4\ a_4\ b_3\ b_3\ c_4\ c_4\ d_4\ d_3$ 162
     $a_4\ a_4\ b_4\ b_4\ c_4\ c_4\ d_2\ d_2$ 303
     $a_3\ a_4\ b_3\ b_4\ c_4\ c_4\ d_4\ d_4$ 91
     $a_3\ a_3\ b_4\ b_4\ c_4\ c_4\ d_3\ d_3$ 126

IX   *Six-line stanza*

     $a_5\ b_3\ a_5\ b_3\ c_5\ c_5$ 494
     $a_5\ a_3\ b_5\ b_3\ c_5\ c_5$ 559
     $a_4\ a_4\ b_5\ c_3\ c_3\ b_5$ 223
     $a_4\ a_4\ b_4\ b_4\ c_5\ c_5$ 249, 471
     $a_4\ b_4\ a_4\ b_4\ c_4\ c_4$ 493
     $a_4\ a_4\ b_4\ c_2\ c_2\ b_4$ 320
     $a_4\ a_4\ b_3\ c_4\ c_3\ b_3$ 336
     $a_4\ a_4\ b_3\ c_3\ c_3\ b_3$ 336
     $a_4\ a_4\ b_3\ c_2\ c_2\ b_3$ 320
     $a_4\ a_4\ b_3\ b_3\ c_4\ c_4$ 503
     $a_4\ a_3\ b_4\ c_2\ c_2\ b_4$ 526
     $a_4\ a_3\ b_4\ b_3\ c_4\ c_4$ 162
     $a_3\ a_3\ b_3\ c_4\ c_4\ b_3$ 336
     $a_3\ a_3\ b_3\ c_3\ c_3\ b_3$ 336

X   *Five-line stanza*

     $a_4\ a_4\ b_3\ b_3\ a_4$ 311

XI   *Four-line stanza*

     $a_5\ b_4\ a_5\ b_4$ 495
     $a_4\ b_4\ a_4\ b_4$ 478, 481

XII   *Three-line stanza*

     $a_4\ a_4\ a_4;\ b_4\ b_4\ b_4;\ c_4\ c_4\ c_4$ 462

C. BIBLIOGRAPHY OF CARTWRIGHT PUBLICATIONS, 1630–1700

The following bibliography is arranged chronologically.

I. SEPARATE PUBLICATIONS
- *1639*   *The Royall Slave*, Oxford.
- *1640*   *The Royall Slave*, Oxford (2nd. edition).
- *1641*   *To the Right Honourable Philip Earle of Pembroke*, London (two different broadside editions).

        Secunda Vox Populi, [?London] (another edition of the above).
- *1651*   *Comedies, Tragi-Comedies, With other Poems*, London.
- *1652*   *An Off-spring of Mercy*, London.
- *1671*   *November, or, Signal Days*, London (this poem also appears in an earlier, undated broadside).

II. PUBLICATIONS CONTAINING POEMS BY CARTWRIGHT
- *1630*   *Britanniae Natalis*, Oxford, p. 46 (Latin).
- *1631*   *Ad . . . Iohannem Cirenbergium*, Oxford, one Latin poem.
- *1633*   *Pro Rege suo Soteria*, Oxford, sigs. D (Latin), G3^r.

        Solis Britannici Perigaeum, Oxford, sigs. [B4]^v–C^r (Latin), L3^r–[L4]^r.

        Vitis Carolinae Gemma Altera, Oxford, sigs. [C4]^r–D^r (Latin), I3.
- *1635*   *Amorum Troili et Cresseidae*, by Sir Francis Kynaston, Oxford, sig. **^{r}.

        Parentalia . . . Rolando Cottono, London, sig. C2 (Latin).
- *1636*   *Coronae Carolinae Quadratura*, Oxford, sigs. ^{2}A^r, ^{2}A^v–^{2}A2^r, ^{2}D^v.

        Flos Britannicus . . . Filiola Carolo & Mariae, sigs. 5[2^v]–5[3^r] (Latin), 2[1^v]–2[3^r].
- *1638*   *Death repeal'd by a thankful Memorial sent from Christ Church in Oxon.*, Oxford, pp. 4–6, 47–48 (Latin).

        Musarum Oxoniensium pro serenissima Regina Maria, Oxford, sigs. B3^v (Latin), [a4].

        Jonsonus Virbius, London, pp. 34–38.

1640 *Horti Carolini Rosa Altera*, Oxford, sigs. ²a ᵛ–²a2 ᵛ.
Honour and Virtue, Triumphing over the Grave, by Anthony Stafford, London, sigs. P2 ʳ–P3 ᵛ (missigned P2).
Poems, by William Shakespeare, London, sig. [L7] ʳ.

1641 *Proteleia Anglo-Batava*, Oxford, sigs. A3 ʳ–[A4] ʳ (Latin), a2 ᵛ–a3 ᵛ.
The Prisoners and Claracilla, by Thomas Killigrew, London, sigs. [A5] ʳ–[A6] ʳ, [A6] (Latin).

1643 *Epibateria . . . Mariae ex Batavia Feliciter Reduci*, Oxford, sigs. Aa (Latin), D ᵛ–D2 ʳ.
Verses on the death of the Right Valiant S ʳ Bevill Grenvill, Knight, Oxford, pp. 8–11.

1644 *Verses on the death . . . S ʳ Bevill Grenvill*, Oxford (2nd. edition), pp. 5–8.

1647 *Comedies and Tragedies*, by Beaumont and Fletcher, London, 1647, sigs. d ᵛ–[d2] ʳ, [d2].

1652 *Select Musicall Ayres and Dialogues*, collected by John Playford, London, pp. 28–29.
Catch that Catch can, or A Choice Collection of Catches, Rounds, & Cannons, collected by John Hilton, London, p. 29.

1653 *Ayres and Dialogues*, by Henry Lawes, London, pp. 1–7, 7, 30.
Select Musicall Ayres and Dialogues, collected by John Playford, London, pp. 26–27.

1655 *The Marrow of Complements*, London, pp. 46, 48, 49–51, 52–53, 54–56, 59–61, 61, 62–63, 63, 65–67, 67–68, 68–69, 70, 71–72, 72–73, 83–84, 88–91.
Wits Interpreter, collected by John Cotgrave, London, pp. 51, 54, 81–83, 84–87, 88–90, 105, 113 (later editions, 1662, pp. 42–44, 45–47, 48–49, 157, 160, 211, 220; 1671, same pagination as in 1662).
Ayres and Dialogues, by Henry Lawes, London, p. 8.

1656 *Parnassus Biceps*, London, pp. 45–46, 136–37, 137–41, 146–47.
Sportive Wit, London, sigs. [c6] ᵛ–[c7] ʳ.

1657 *The English Parnassus*, collected by Josua Poole, London, pp. 315–16, 510 (later edition, 1677, pp. 357–58, 552).

1658 *Catch that Catch can*, collected by John Hilton, London, p. 28.

1659   *J. Cleaveland Revived*, London, pp. 62–64 (later editions, 1662, pp. 86–88; 1687, pp. 359–60).

Ayres and Dialogues, by Henry Lawes, London (reissued in 1669), pp. 4–5, 8–9, 26, 61.

1666   *The Poems of Horace*, collected by Alexander Brome, London, pp. 148–49 (later editions, 1671, pp. 152–53; 1680, pp. 154–55).

Musick's Delight on the Cithren, collected by John Playford, London, No. 91.

1667   *Catch that Catch can: or the Musical Companion*, edited by John Playford, London, pp. 74, 166–67.

1668   *Memoires of the Lives, Actions, Sufferings and Deaths of . . . Personages That Suffered . . . for the Protestant Religion*, by David Lloyd, London, pp. 85, 121, 426, 470–471.

1670   *Merry Drollery, Complete*, Part II, London, p. 289.

1671   *The New Academy of Complements*, London, pp. 120, 127–28, 132–33.

1672   *Westminster Drollery*, Part II, London, p. 79.

1673   *The Musical Companion*, collected by John Playford, London, p. 53 and sigs. [P5]ᵛ–[P6].

1679   *Fifty Comedies and Tragedies*, by Beaumont and Fletcher, London, sig. A2ᵛ.

1684   *Verses by the Vniversity of Oxford . . . On the Death of . . . Sir Bevill Grenvill, alias Granvill, Kt.*, London (3rd. edition), pp. 6–9.

1693   *Examen Poeticum: being the Third Part of Miscellany Poems*, London, pp. 326–27.

D. LIST OF MANUSCRIPTS

THE ROYAL SLAVE

BODLEIAN LIBRARY
   Arch. Seld. 26, fols. 103-35

FOLGER SHAKESPEARE LIBRARY
   MS. 7044

BRITISH MUSEUM
   Addit. 29,396 (musical setting for one song)
   Addit. 41,616
   Egerton 2725, fols. 115-17 (first two prologues and epilogues, and one song)

BEDFORD MS. (collation by Thorn-Drury in Widener Library)

NEW YORK PUBLIC LIBRARY
   Drexel 4041 (musical settings for three songs)

THE POEMS

BODLEIAN LIBRARY
   Rawl. D. 951, fols. 62-69 (scattered extracts from the *Works*, 1651)
   Rawl. D. 1092, fols. 270-71.
   Bod. MS. 22
   Malone 21, fols. 52, 71-72, 75-76, 78-79

BRITISH MUSEUM
   Harl. 3511, fols. 1, 9-10
   Harl. 6917, fols. 75-77
   Harl. 6931, fols. 53-55, 55-56, 78-79, 88-90
   Harl. 7319, fol. 23
   Addit. 19,268, fols. 7, 9
   Addit. 22, 602, fols. 14-15, 26

Folger Shakespeare Library
    MS. 452.1, pp. 54–55
    MS. 646.4, pp. [158]–59
    MS. 2071.6, pp. 86–87, 90–91
    MS. 2071.7, fols. 262–63

Lawes' Autographed MS. (in the possession of Miss Naomi Church), pp. 74, 75, 103, 105, 152, 254–60

INDEX

The index is intended to serve as a general index, combining subject, author, title, first-line, and note entries. Short poem titles and first lines of poems and songs from the plays are given in quotation marks. Bold-faced page references are used to refer to pages where an actual text appears. Page references to the Critical Notes are preceded by CN; to the Textual Notes by TN.

Although a reasonable completeness has been aimed at, certain entries are selective, especially in connection with the Critical Notes, where nothing is to be gained by noting every reference to Cartwright or to Cartwright's former editors. The following are the selective entries: CARTWRIGHT, COLLIER, DODSLEY, GERBER (not an editor), GOFFIN, HAZLITT, and REED. However, all references to Miss Gebhardt's unpublished edition of *The Ordinary* are noted. Again, only a selection of the words and phrases glossed in the Critical Notes is included in the Index.

Individual works, except in special cases, are indexed only under the author. The most obvious exception to this rule, apart from anonymous works, is the indexing by first lines of Cartwright's poems and songs in the general index instead of in the main CARTWRIGHT entry. Full page references for each poem, however, will be found only under the poem title in the main CARTWRIGHT entry.

INDEX

ABBOTT, E. A., *Shakespearian Grammar*, 661, 664, 666
Absolute decree, Calvinist doctrine of, 684–85
Act, the (at Oxford), 683–86
ADAMS, J. Q., *The Dramatic Records of Sir Henry Herbert*, 29n, 31n, 85n, 182n, 184n
Addit. MS. 19,268 (B.M.), 699, 701–2, 839
Addit. MS. 22,602 (B.M.), 677, 679, 713, 714, 839
Addit. MS. 29,396 (B.M.), 594, 839
Addit. MS. 41,616 (B.M.), 588, 839
Ad . . . Iohannem Cirenbergium, 836
advowson, *n.*, 662, 713
AELIAN, 584
AESCHYLUS, *The Persians*, 190n
"After our Rites done to the King, we doe" (second prologue, *Royal Slave*), 196–97, 259n, CN 589–90, TN 776–77
Ahaz dial, 756–57
ALABASTER (or ALABLASTER), William, 690
alicant (Aligant), *n*, 630
ALLINGHAM, Margery, *Dancers in Mourning*, 60, 723
alouten (?), 633
"Although Propriety be Crost," 526–28
AMALTHEUS, Jerom, 706
Amazons, Cartwright's use of Amazon lore, 88, 584
amber boxes, 677
amebly (?), 646
"Amids such Heate of Businesse, such State-throng," 539–41
AMYOT, Jacques, 357
Ancient British Drama, The (containing *The Ordinary*), 257
ANDERSON, Robert, *The British Poets*, 58n
"And now (most worthy Sir) I've time to shew," 455–57
"And now perhaps You'll thinke a booke more fit," 506
"And something too (great *Queene*) I was about," 510–11
antiquation, *n.*, 732
"*Apollo*, who foretell'st what shall ensue" (*Lady-Errant*), 159–60, CN 587, TN 774–75

Architypographus, duties of, 13; Cartwright suggested for the office, 13–15
Arch. Seld. MS B.26 (Bod.), 167, 588, 839
"Arise thou Sacred Heap, and shew a Frame," 445–47
ARISTOPHANES, 60, 88; *Ecclusiazusae*, 87, 581–82; *Lysistrata*, 87; *Plutus*, 614, *Thesmophoriazusae*, 87, 581–82
"*Arminius* Searcher of Truths deepest part," 497–500
Arsamnes, character in *The Royal Slave*, 188
ASHFORD, Mrs., 757, Cartwright's poem on, 551–53
"As *Nilus* sudden Ebbing, here," 484–85
ATHENAEUS, 188
Athens, a name for Oxford, 663
ATKYNS, Sir Robert, 6n
Atossa, character in *The Royal Slave*, 186n, 190n
AUBREY, John, 'Brief Lives,' 4–5, 6n, 7, 9, 12n, 15–16, 18n, 20, 21, 660, *Remaines of Gentilisme and Judaisme*, 166n
AYLIFFE, John, *Ancient and Present State of the University of Oxford*, 683
AYRES, Philip, 724, 727

B, H. (Henry Bold), 63n
B., I., 65 See John Berkenhead
B.J., 47n
B., W., 51, 692–93
BACKHOUSE, William, 692–93
Bacon, Francis, 47, 634, 696
BAGNEL, Pope's error for Robert Speed, 55
bagpudding, *n*, 628
BAINES, Thomas, 63n
BALDWIN, T. W., 29n
balsam, *n*, 679
BANKS, T. H., 738–39n
BARKER, G. F. R., *The Record of Old Westminsters*, 7n, 9n
BARKER, W., 63n, 693
BARLOW, Thomas, 18n, 831
BASKERVILL, C. R., *The Elizabethan Jig*, 172
BASKERVILLE, Thomas, *Account of Oxford*, 678

843

BASSE, William, 714, 766
BATHURST, Ralph, 15n, 30n, 37, 63n, 185n
Battle, The, ? a ballad tune, 598
Bay leaves, the use of, 585
BAYNING, Paul, 750, Cartwright's poem on, 531-33
BEAUMONT, Francis, First Folio (1647), 49, 63n, 741-42; 837, connections with John Fletcher, 741-44; *Four Plays in One*, 592, 667-68, *The Inner Temple Masque*, 675; *The Knight of the Burning Pestle*, 88, 265, 617-18, 646, 696; *The Maid's Tragedy*, 86, 577, 579, 605, 665, 666, *The Night-Walker*, 634; *Philaster*, 580; *The Scornful Lady*, 639, mentioned, 57n, 645
BEAUMONT, ? Sir John, 52n
BEDDOES, Thomas L., 10
Bedford MS. of *The Royal Slave*, 168-69, 588
bedstaff, *n.*, 667
begin to, to, 662
BEHN, Aphra, *The City Heiress*, 663; *Oroonoko*, 596
BELL, William, 63n, 185n, 693
bellarmine, *n.*, 585, 644
BELOE, William, *Anecdotes of Literature*, 594, 595, 599
bencher, *n.*, 644-45
BENLOWES, Edward, *Theophila*, 681
BENTLEY, G. E., *Shakespeare and Jonson*, 15n; *The Jacobean and Caroline Stage*, 182n
BERKENHEAD, John, commendatory poem in *Works* (1651), 4n, 7n, 63n, 65, 81n, 185, *The Assembly-Man*, 642, 732; mentioned, 11, 21n, 52, 747
BERKLEY, Sir Rowland, 681
"Be thou *Hymen* present here" (*Siege*), 435-36, CN 674
BEVIS of Southampton, 647
bewhatle, to, 670
bias, to hold, 645
Bible, versions of, 753; Genesis, 586; Isaiah, 753; Judges, 644; 2 Kings, 756-57, Psalm CIII, 728; Revelations, 753
"Bid me not go where neither Suns nor Show'rs," 494
bilke, *n*, 641
BILLINGSLEY, Sir Henry, 695-96
Biographia Britannica, 6n, 56
Biographie Universelle, 57
BIRCH, Thomas, *Court and Times of Charles the First*, 184n
Bitefigg, Sir Thomas, character in *The Ordinary*, 259, 261, 265n, 267
"Blest Lady, You, whose Mantle doth divide," 504-6

BLISS, Philip, ed. of Wood's *Athenae*, 5n, 9n, 68
BOAS, F. S., *Shakespeare and the Universities*, 59n
BOCCACCIO, Giovanni, *Decameron*, analogue for the subplot of *The Siege*, 358
Bodleian MS. (Arch. Seld. B.26) of *The Royal Slave*, 167, 588, 839
Bod. MS 22, 690-91, 893
BOLD, Henry, 63n
BOURNE, Henry, *Antiquitates Vulgares*, 723
BOWERS, F. T., 263-64n
BOWKER, John, 690
BRADNER, Leicester, *A History of Anglo-Latin Poetry, 1500-1925*, 50n
"Brag not a Golden Rain O *Jove*; we see," 478
BRAMSTON, Sir John, 756
BRAND, John, *Observations on Popular Antiquities*, 590, 598, 600, 670, 722-23
BRATHWAITE, Richard, 641
brendle, to, 633
BRISSONIUS, Barnabe, *De Regio Persarum Principatu*, 188
Britanniae Natalis, 38n, 732, 836
British Museum (Petworth) MS. of *The Royal Slave*, 168, 588
broke, to, 737
broken beer, 626
BROME, Alexander, 47, 63n, 608, 725, 731, 838
BROME, Richard, *The City Wit*, 626; *The Court Beggar*, 85; *The Damoiselle*, 262; *A Jovial Crew*, 46-47n, *The Love-Sick Court*, 579; *Five New Playes*, 737
Brooks, J.L., *Alexander Brome: Life and Works*, 731, 742
BROWN, Thomas, 700
BROWNE, Sir Thomas, 33, 707, 739-40
BROWNE, William, *Britannia's Pastorals*, 667, 692. quoted, 689, 702-3
bryd, *n.*, 637
BUCHANAN, George, 50n, 709
BUCKINGHAM. *See* VILLIERS, G.
BULLEN, A. H., account of Cartwright in *DNB*, 6, 20n; *Speculum Amantis*, 43-44, 73, 699
bumbast, *adj.*, 667
BUNYAN, John, 636
burn day-light, to, 621
BURNS, Robert, 599
BURTON, Robert, 692; *The Anatomy of Melancholy*, 580, 626, 666, 672
BURTON, Will, 692-93
BUSBY, Richard, 53, 175, 176n
BUTLER, Samuel, 591, 632; *Hudibras*, 88, 578

"But turn we hence to you, as some there be," 447-48
BYRON, George Gordon, Lord, 739

C., B., 15n, 63n
C., H., 687
C., I. (John Castilion), 63n
C., J., 51
C. Merry Talys, A, 653
C., T. (Thomas Cartwright), 710
C., W., 766
Calanthe (in *The Lady-Errant*), the problem of the name, 67, 82-83, reference to by K. Philips, 52n
Calendar of State Papers, Domestic Series, 11n, 171n, 181
'Call for what wine you please, which likes you best," 479
CALVIN, John, 711
CAMDEN, William, 733
CAMPBELL, J. D., 58, 577, 583
CAMPBELL, L. B., *Scenes and Machines on the English Stage*, 177
CAMPBELL, Thomas, *Specimens of the British Poets*, 6, 58
CAMPION, Thomas, 608
CAREW, Thomas, 24n, 35, 40, 75, 583, 676, 680, 698, 699, 706, 707, 725, 727, 758, 765, 766
CARLELL, Lodowick, *The Deserving Favourite*, 579; *The Fool would be a Favourite*, 579, *Osmond, the Great Turk*, 579, 665, mentioned, 28
CARLISLE, Lucy, Countess of, 676; Cartwright's poem to, 441-45
CARLYLE, Thomas, 690
CARNARVON, Lord, 172n
CARTE, T., *Collection of Letters, 1641-1660*, 20n
CARTWRIGHT, John, *The Preachers Travels*, 10, 188n
CARTWRIGHT, Thexton, the poet's uncle, 10
CARTWRIGHT, Thomas, Puritan divine, 710
CARTWRIGHT, Thomas, brother of poet, 7n
CARTWRIGHT, William, father of poet, 7, 10
CARTWRIGHT, William, date and place of birth, 6; brothers and sisters, 7n; genealogical table, 8; family reverses, 9, sent to free school at Cirencester, 9; king's scholar at Westminster, 9; student of Christ Church, Oxford, 9; matriculation (1631/32), 9n; B.A. (1632) and M.A. (1635), 12, *Royal Slave* performed before the King, 12-13; suggested for office of Architypographus of Oxford press, 13-15; entered holy orders, 15; made succentor at Salisbury, 15; voice and eye-sight, 15n; preached "victory" sermon after Edgehill, 15-16; style as a preacher, 15-17, imitated by Wright, 17, effectiveness as lecturer, 17-18; made Reader in Metaphysics, 17-18, member of the "Council of War," 18-19; imprisonment, 19; appointed Junior Proctor, 20; death from "camp disease," 20, burial, 20; general mourning for, 20-21

—Literary characteristics and affiliations, formative influences on plays, 22-26, 262-64; as Cavalier dramatist, 26-28, blank verse, 28, suggested hand in *Bloody Brother*, 30-32; formative influences on poetry, 33-36; place among contemporaries as poet, 36, use of stanza forms, 36-37, 834-35, use of the couplet, 37; occasional verse, 37-42; his criticism in verse, 40-42; love poetry, 42-44, humorous verse, 44, translations, 44; contemporary reputation, 46-49; characteristics as a writer in general, 48, later reputation, 49-50, 54-60, influence on contemporaries, 50-53; on later writers, 53-56; as writer of comedy, 258-59

—The *Works* (1651), commendatory poems prefixed to, 46-48, 63n; textual principles followed in present edition, 61-62; bibliographical study of, 62-72; Moseley's entry on Stationers' Register, 62-63; copies used in establishing text, 62; treatment of poem texts, 62, 72-75. *See also* Commendatory poems

—*The Lady-Errant*, Restoration revival by the Duke's men, 28-30, 54, 81, 85-87; survival of prompt copy, 28-29; deletions by Revels Office, 29, 86; changes made by playhouse reviser, 29-30, 86, Katherine Philips' knowledge of, 52-53n; Coleridge's acquaintance with, 58; text of, 61, 72, 81, 575; mention, 13, 22, 58, 62, 67, 70n, 184, 257, 260, 261, 262n, 589, 646, 663, 667

—*The Ordinary*, Restoration revival of, 28-30, 54, 258, 260-62; prompt copy of, 28-29; special debt to Jonson, 34, 263-64; the text, 61, 62, 72, 257-58, date of composition, 259; probable presentation of, 259; droll dialogues based on, 259-60; licensing of, 260; playhouse reviser of, 261; deletions by Revels Office, 260-61, scenery in Restoration revival, 261-62; Restoration prologue and epilogue, 262, 610-12, sources, 262-68 mention, 13, 23, 44n, 45, 56, 59, 62, 70n, 71, 81, 82, 84, 85n, 86, 171, 184, 586, 589, 602, 603, 663, 712, 734

—*The Royal Slave*, the Hampton Court performance, 12-13, 180-84, corrected proof sheets of early text, 13n, 165-66; metrical features, 28; the text, 62, 72, 165-70, 588-89; printed copies, 62, 165, 588-89, not entered on Stationers'

Register, 165; manuscript copies of, 166-70, 588, relation of MSS. to printed text, 169-70; parts of, in other MSS., 170, reception of, 171; collaboration of Jones and Lawes on, 171-72; relation with masque, 172-73, date of composition, 174, Oxford performances of, 174-80; the "appearances," 176n, 177-78; staging of, 177, 183, problem of "interludes," 178-79; second performance, before the University, 180; honorarium from Charles I to C. for, 182, droll dialogue based on, 184; later influence of, 185-86, 596-97, 608; sources, 186-91; Greek history in, 188, use of Theodorus Prodromus' *Rhodanthes et Dosiclis Amorum*, 188-90, influence of *Beggars' Bush*, 191, list of separate publications of, 836; mentioned, 22, 23n, 24, 27n, 31, 39, 50, 53, 54, 58n, 59, 61, 62, 70n, 81, 82, 84, 86, 259n, 355, 356, 360n, 580, 582, 727, 756, 833

—*The Siege, or Love's Convert*, the text, 62, 72, 355, 561; date of composition, 355, attitude of town wits, 356, question of actual production of, 356; dedicated to Charles I, 356-57; sources, 357-60; forerunner of Restoration heroic tragedy, 36c; droll dialogue based on, 602; mention, 22, 23, 38n, 46n, 53n, 57, 58n, 62, 70n, 71, 81n, 82, 86, 257, 576, 583, 685, 686, 756

—The Poems, alphabetized by title·

Absence, 496, 703, CN 727-28, TN 819
Another on the same [John Fletcher], 40, 41-42, 49, 57n, 63n, 519-21, 679, 735, CN 744-47, TN 821
Ariadne deserted by *Theseus*, 36, 488-91, CN 717-22, 725, TN 817-18.
At a dry Dinner, 479, CN 707, TN 815
Beauty and Deniall, 470-71, CN 700, TN 815
Bill of Fare, A, 44, 479-80, CN 707-8, TN 816
Chambermaids Posset, The, 44, 481-83, 623, 643, 656, 662, 685, CN 708-13, TN 816
Conclusion to the Queen, The [on birth of King's fourth child], 506, CN 733
Confession, 40, 563, 698, CN 762-63, TN 825
Consideration 39, 39-40n, 496-97, CN 728
Continuation of the same [imperfection of Christ-Church buildings] to the Prince of *Wales*, A, 447-48, 636, CN 679, TN 809-10
Corinna's Tomb, 55, 474-75, CN 704
Dream Broke, A, 484-85, CN 716, TN 817
Dreame, The, 465, CN 697
Epitaph on Mr. *Poultney*, An, 38, 53n, 547, CN 754, TN 823

Falshood, 43, 75, 468-70, 698, CN 699-700, TN 814-15
For a young Lord to his Mistris, who had taught him a Song, 461-62, CN 694, TN 812
Gnat, The, 55, 478, CN 706-7, TN 815
Horat. Carm lib. 4 Ode 13. Audivere Lyce, 44, 503-4, CN 731, TN 819
In Pompeios Juvenes [Martial], 56, 501, CN 730
In the memory of the most Worthy *Beniamin Iohnson*, 4n, 40-41, 42, 56, 57n, 511-16, CN 735-40, TN 820
Lesbia On her Sparrow, 43, 55, 57n, 477, CN 705-6, TN, 815
Love but one, 495-96, 604, CN 726-27, TN 818-19
Love inconcealable *Stig. Ital.*, 44n, 358n, 465, CN 697, TN 813
Loves Darts, 485-86, CN 716-17, TN 817
Love-Teares, 478, CN 707
Martial lib. 1. Epig 67. Ad furem de libro suo, 500, CN 730
Martial lib. 7. Epig. 59. Ad Iovem Capitolinum, 500, CN 730, TN 819
Martial lib. 10 Ep. 5 In Maledicum Poëtam, 501-2, CN 731, TN 819
Martial lib. 11. Ep. 19 In Lupum, 502, CN 731
New-years Gift, A, 526-28, CN 748, TN 821
New-years-gift to a Noble Lord. 1640, A, 533-35, CN 750, TN 821
New-years-gift to *Brian* Lord Bishop of *Sarum*, A, 39n, 40, 528-30, CN 748-49, TN 821
No drawing of *Valentines*, 491, CN 722-23
No Platonique Love, 43, 494-95, 578, CN 724-26, TN 818
November or, Signal Dayes, 5n, 73, 560-63, CN 761-62, TN 824-25, 836
On a Gentlewomans Silk-hood, 483-84, 583, CN 713-16, TN 816-17
On a vertuous young Gentlewoman that dyed suddenly, 38, 62, 69, 551, CN 757, TN 823
On His Majesties recovery from the small Pox. 1633, 448-49, CN 680-81, TN 810
On Mr *Stokes* his Book on the Art of Vaulting, 39n, 40, 44, 462-65, CN 694-96, TN 812-13
On Mrs *Abigall Long*, who dyed of two Impostumes, 39, 544-47, CN 754, TN 823
On one weepeing, 73, 76, 466-67, CN 698, TN 813
On the Birth of the Duke of *York*, 451-52, CN 681-82, TN 810
On the Birth of the King's fourth Child. 1635, 504-6, CN 731-32, TN 819

On the Circumcision, 40, 559, CN 760-61, TN 824

On the Death of the most vertuous Gentlewoman, Mrs *Ashford*, who dyed in Child-bed, 551-53, CN 757-58, TN 823

On the Death of the Right Honourable the Lord Viscount *Bayning*, 531-33, CN 749-50, TN 821

On the Epiphany, 40, 559-60, CN 761, TN 824

On the great Frost. 1634, 44, 265n, 457-59, CN 686-90, TN 810-12

On the Imperfection of *Christ-Church* Buildings, 445-47, 636, CN 677-79, TN 809

On the Lady *Newburgh*, who dyed of the small Pox, 38, 39, 542-44, CN 753-54, TN 823

On the Marriage of the Lady *Mary* to the Prince of *Aurange* his Son. *1641*, 539-41, CN 752, TN 822-23

On the Nativity, 40, 558, CN 760, TN 824

On the Prince Charles death. W. C., 38n, 77, 570-71, 734, CN 766

On the *Queens* Return from the Low Countries, 38, 69, 554-55, CN 758-59, TN 823

Panegyrick to the most Noble Lucy Countesse of *Carlisle*, A, 38, 441-45, CN 676-77, TN 809

Parchment, 468, CN 699

Parthenia for her slain *Argalus*, 478-88, 581, CN 717, TN 817

Sadness, 473-74, CN 703-4, TN 815

Sigh sent to his absent Love, A, 75, 472-73, CN 701-3, 728, 764, 765, TN 815

Si memini fuerant [Martial], 501, CN 730, TN 819

Song of Dalliance, A, 43, 73, 467-68, CN 698-99, 723, TN 813-14

Teares, The, 44, 73, 75, 76, 456-66, CN 697-98, 764, TN 813

To a Painters handsome Daughter, 476, CN 705, TN 815

To *Chloe* who wish'd her self young enough for me, 43, 493, CN 723, TN 818

To *Cupid*, 44, 471-72, CN 700, TN 815

To Dr *Duppa*, then Dean of *Christ-Church*, 452-54, CN 682-83, TN 810

To his Mrs Walking in ye snow, 75, 569-70, 698, 703, CN 765

To *Lydia* whom Men observ'd to make too much of me, 491-93, CN 723, 765

To Mr *W.B* at the Birth of his first Child, 38, 460-61, CN 692-94, TN 812

To Mrs *Duppa*, sent with the Picture of the Bishop of *Chichester* (her Husband), 506-9, CN 733-34, 749

To My Honovr'd Friend M^r. Thomas Killigrew, 40, 42, 516-17, 735, CN 740-41, TN 820

To *Philip*, Earl of Pembroke, 541-42, CN 752-53, TN 823

To Splendora A morning Salutation, 76, 567, CN 764, 765

To Splendora desiring to heare musick, 565-66, CN 764

To Splendora hauing seene and spoke with her through a window, 76, 565, CN 764

To Splendora not to be perswaded, 564, CN 764

To Splendora on the Same occasion [weeping], 568-69, CN 765

To Splendora weeping, 75, 568, CN 764

To the King, On His Majesties Return from *Scotland*, 1633, 449-50, CN 681, TN 810

To the King, on the Birth of the Princess *Anne*. March 17. 1636, 38, 509-10, 628, CN 734, TN 819

To the memory of a Shipwrackt Virgin, 38, 54, 475-76, CN 704-5

To the Memory of the most vertuous Mrs *Ursula Sadleir*, who dyed of a Feaver, 40n, 547-49, 728, CN 754-55

To the Memory of the Most Worthy, Sir *Henry Spelman*, 40, 42, 549-50, CN 755-57, TN 823

To the Queen [on the birth of Princess Anne], 38n, 510-11, CN 734-35, TN 820

To the Queen after her dangerous Delivery. 1638, 530-31, CN 749, TN 821

To the Queen on the same [birth of the King's fourth child], 504-6, CN 732, TN 819

To the Queen on the same Occasion [Charles' return from Scotland], 450, CN 681, 694, TN 810

To the Right Reverend Father in God, *Brian*, Lord Bishop of *Chichester*, 522-26, 586, CN 748, TN 821

To the Right Vertuous the Ladie Elizabeth Powlet, 459-60, CN 690-92, TN 812

To the same [Dr. Duppa] immediately after the Publick Act at *Oxon* 1634, 455-57, 667, CN 683-86, 713, TN 810

To *Venus*, 44, 472, CN 700-1, TN 815

Translation of *Hugo Grotius's* Elegy on *Arminius*, A, 37n, 44n, 497-500, 685, CN 729-30

Vpon the Birth of the Kings sixth Child. 1640, 38, 535-36, CN 750-51, 765, TN 822

Vpon the Death of the most hopefull the Lord Stafford, 536-39, CN 751-52, TN 822

Vpon the death of the Right valiant Sir *Bevill Grenvill* Knight, 38, 69, 555–58, CN 759–60, TN 823–24
Vpon the Dramatick Poems of Mr John Fletcher, 40, 41–42, 49, 57n, 63n, 518–19, 735, CN 741–43, TN 820–21
Vpon the Translation of *Chaucer's Troilus* and *Creseide* by Sir *Francis Kinaston*, 40, 42, 497, 631, CN 728–29, TN 819
Valediction, A, 43, 494, CN 724
Women, 471, CN 700

—Other works, Latin poems, 38n, 680, 681, 734, 741, 749, 752, 758, 836–37; *An Off-spring of Mercy, Issuing out of the Womb of Cruelty*, 16–17, 836, "a treatise of metaphysique," 18n
case, *n*., 606
caskinet, *n*., 664
CASONI, Guido, 640
CASTILION, John, 63n
"Cast not in *Chloe*'s Name among," 491
CATULLUS, Caius Valerius, influence on Cartwright, 608, 655, 705–6, 718–19, 721–22
cautelous, *adj*., 582
caveari, *n*, 630
CAVENDISH, Margaret, Duchess of Newcastle, biography of her husband, 184, 758–59; *The Sociable Companions*, 724
CERVANTES, Miguel de, 88, 627
CHALMERS, Alexander, *The English Poets*, 6, 17n, 58, 73–74, 679, 759
CHALMERS, George, *Apology for the Believers in the Shakespeare-Papers*, 182n
CHAMBERLAYNE, William, *Love's Victory*, 27, 579, 624, 639; poem attributed to, 731
Character of a Fanatick, The, 582
Charistus, character in *The Lady-Errant*, 52, 54
CHARLES, Prince, son of Charles I, died at birth, Cartwright's poem on, 570–71, 734, 766
CHARLES, Prince, later Charles II, Cartwright's poem to, 447–48, 679, 748, mention, 682, 683
CHARLES, Tom, 695
CHARLES, Thomas, 695
CHARLES THE FIRST, admired Cartwright, 21, 355; poems addressed to, 448–49, 449–50, 509–10, 748, mentioned, 38n, 359, 681, 746, 758, 766
charm my fleas, to, 590
CHAUCER, Geoffrey, Cartwright's use of, 614, 637, 638, 647, 678, 686, dramatists indebted to, 631–32; mentioned, 51, 595, 721, 728
"Chaunt aloud, yee shrill-mouthd quires," 565–66
children of the night, 674, 685

chin, chin, *n*., 585
"*Chloe*, why wish you that your years," 493
CHOLMLEY, Sir Richard, Commonplace Book (Harvard MS.), 766
Christian Freedom, 658
Christian Liberty, 711
Christopher, Sir, character in *The Ordinary*, 263
Chronicle History of King Leir, The, 621
chronogramme, *n*., 732
CHURCH, Naomi, 170
CIBBER, Theophilus, *Lives of the Poets*, 6, 56, 655
CICERO, Marcus Tullius, 580
Citty Cozener, The, 257, 258n
CLAUDIAN, Claudius, 606, 672
CLEAVER, Richard, 710–11
cleft sticks, 585–86
CLEVELAND, John, *J. Cleaveland Revived*, 690–91, 838, quoted, 590, 621, 635, 677, 707, 711–12, 713, 725, 736, 737, 739; mentioned, 36, 50, 55, 678, 684, 690, 704, 706, 724, 749
Clevelandism, 44, 49
close-noated, *adj*., 710
cloud of game, 662
COBB, John, 720
COBBE, J., 63n
COCKERAM, Henry, *The English Dictionarie*, 582, 596, 622, 683, 685, 713, 756
COKAIN, Aston, *The Obstinate Lady*, 579
COLE, Thomas, 63n
COLE family, 7
COLEMAN, Charles, 44, 58c
COLEMAN, George, 56, 57
COLERIDGE, E. H., 58n, 577, 583, 723
COLERIDGE, Samuel Taylor, 58, 577, 583, 704, 723
COLERIDGE, Sara, 58n
Collection of Poems Written upon Several Occasions, A, (1673), 28n, 185n, 262, 610–12, 725
COLLIER, J. P., *Select Collection of Old Plays*, 257, 258
collogue, to, 606
COLLOP, John, *Poesis Rediviva*, 49n, 73
colour for, to, 627
"Come, o come, I brook no stay" (*Ordinary*), 311–12, CN 639–40, TN 802–3
"Come from the Dungeon to the Throne" (*Royal Slave*), 169, 170, 205, 589, CN 593–94, TN 780
"Come my sweet, whiles every strayne" (*Royal Slave*), 44, 170, 212–13, CN 595, TN 782
Commendatory poems to *Works* (1651), as source of information, 46–48; contributors, 63n; bibliographical discussion of, 64–67; quoted, 17, 36, 37, 41n, 45, 75n, 81n, 356, 595–96, 710; mentioned, 21, 40, 44n, 55n, 63, 185, 674, 693

Conceits of Old Hobson, The, 653
CONGREVE, William, *Love for Love*, 712; *Semele*, 27n, 607, 608; *The Way of the World*, 649; mention, 50
considerable, *adj.*, 639
conversation, *n.*, 612
CONWAY, Viscount, 171n, 172n
Coranti, 646
CORBET, Richard, quoted, 590, 680, 693-94, 711; mentioned, 10, 36, 55, 636, 643, 660, 714, 766
CORIAT, Thomas, 625
CORNEILLE, Pierre, 60
Coronae Carolinae Quadratura, 731, 836
COTGRAVE, John, *Wits Interpreter*, 49, 259, 580, 595, 598, 602, 603, 613, 615-16, 617, 618-20, 644, 649-51, 727, 837
COTTON, Charles, 634, 687
"Could wee iudge here Most vertuous Madam then," 459-60
Counter-Scuffle, The, 55
COWLEY, Abraham, *Cutter of Coleman Street*, 265n, 667, 684; *The Guardian*, 264, 265, 615, 652, 667; *Love's Riddle*, 614, 622, 646; mentioned, 10, 36, 50, 60, 724, 727, 758
CRASHAW, Richard, 55, 608, 674
Cratander, character in *The Royal Slave*, 52, 53, 81n, 173, 175, 185, 186n, 189, 190, 191
Credulous, Andrew, and Simon, characters in *The Ordinary*, 260, 264n, 265n, 266, 267, 268
CREED, William, 63n
Crew of Kind London Gossips, A, 700
CRICHTON, James, the Admirable, 59
crisping pins, *n. pl.*, 586
CROFTS, Cecily, 583
CROMWELL, Oliver, 690
CROSFIELD, Thomas, *Diary*, 11n, 171, 174n, 624
CROUCH, Humphrey, 645
CROWNE, John, *Sir Courtly Nice*, 649
Crumbs of Comfort, The, 711-12
crumpering, 638
CUNNINGHAM, G G , *Lives of Eminent and Illustrious Englishmen*, 6
CUNNINGHAM, Peter, *Extracts from the Accounts of the Revels at Court*, 182

D., J., *The Knave in Graine*, 600; its connection with *The Ordinary*, 266, 653, 654, 655
D. S , 691
Daily Mirror, The, 700
DANIEL, George, 52n, 724
DANIEL, Samuel, 666
DANTE ALIGHIERI, 603
DANTON, J. P., 62n, 68n

D'AVENANT, Sir William, *The Fair Favourite*, 567, 579; *The Platonic Lovers*, 596, 724; *The Play-House to be Let*, 589, 596; *Salmacida Spolia*, 178; *The Siege*, 355n, 579, 597; *The Tempest*, 694; *The Temple of Love*, 178, 686; *The Unfortunate Lovers*, 723; *The Wits*, 634, 656; mentioned, 28. 29n, 30, 55, 676
DAVISON, Henry, 63n, 65
DAY, John, *The Parliament of Bees*, 702, 734
Death repeal'd (1638), 749, 836
DEE, John, 695-96
defend, to, 618
deignous, *adj.*, 637
DEKKER, Thomas, 24n, 621; *Satiro-Mastix*, 645
demerit, to, 661
DENHAM, Sir John, 55, 737-38, 739, 747
DERING, Sir Edward, 52n, 63n
Description of Woman, The, 766
design, to, 662
Dialogue drolls. See Droll dialogues
DICKENS, Charles, 60, 258n
DIGBY, Sir Kenelm, 635
DIGGES, Dudley, 4n, 20, 686-87n, 735, 832
DIO CHRYSOSTOM, 187-88
DOD, John, 656, 710-11
DODSLEY, Robert, *Select Collection of Old Plays*, 56, 257
dole, *n.*, 662
DONNE, John, influence on Cartwright, 34; "The Calm," 688, 689; "The Dream," 716, "Farewell to Love," 726, "A Fever," 755; "The First Anniversary," 680; "The Good-Morrow," 723; "A Letter to the Lady Carey," 582; "A Valediction Forbidding Mourning," 723; "A Valediction of My Name, in the Window," 703; mentioned, 36, 40, 55, 656, 699, 766, 832
dorsers, *n. pl.*, 585
Double epithet, in Cartwright, 76, 698
DOWNES, John, Roscius Anglicanus, 86
"Drawing of Valentines, The," 723
DRAYTON, Michael, 664, 670
Drexel MS. 4041 (New York Public), 599, 608, 839
Drinking rituals in drama, 597, 598
Droll dialogues, show popularity of Cartwright, 49; from *Royal Slave*, 184, 601-2, 602-3, from *The Ordinary*, 615-16, 617, 618-20, 620-21, 649-51, 651-52, from *The Siege*, 671, 672-73
DRUMMOND, William, 765
DRYDEN, John, knowledge of Cartwright, 53-54; "Ask not the cause why sullen spring," 725; *Dedication of the Aeneis*, 737; *Defence of An Essay of Dramatic Poesy*, 576, "Defense of the Epi-

logue," 746, *Don Sebastian*, 54, 185-86, 592; *Eleonora*, 757; *An Essay of Dramatic Poesy*, 736; *The Hind and the Panther*, 754, 757; *The Indian Queen*, 53, 185-86n, 579-80, *Miscellanies*, 54, 580, 698, 718, 727, 735; "Prologue at Oxford," 611; "Prologue to *Amboyna*," 685-86; "Prologue to the University of Oxford," 41n; "Song of a Scholar and his Mistress," 722, *The State of Innocence*, 179n, *The Tempest*, 694, *Threnodia Augustalis*, 682; "To the Memory of Mrs Killigrew," 54, 705, *Tyrannic Love*, 587; "Upon the Death of the Lord Hastings," 53, 680, 700, 754, mentioned, 37, 50, 738

DUGDALE, Sir William, 644

Duke's Company, Oxford performances by, 37n, mentioned, 29, 87, 260, 261

DUPPA, Brian, Cartwright's poems to, 452-54, 455-57, 522-26, 528-30, sketch of, 682; poem attributed to, 742-43, as Bishop of Salisbury, 748-49, mentioned, 15, 73, 686, 713, 832

DUPPA, Mrs, Cartwright's poem to, 506-9

Du PORT, James, *Musae Subsecivae*, 50

D'URFÉ, Honoré, *L'Astrée*, 27n, 190-91n

D'URFEY, Thomas, *The Commonwealth of Women*, 50, 582

DYCE, Alexander, 57n, 744, 747

EARLE, John, *Microcosmographie*, 628, 629, 632

EDWARDS, Richard, *Damon and Pithias*, 592

Egerton MS. 2725 (B M), 589, 686, 689, 724, 839

EGLON, king of the Moabites, 644

ELDERTON, W, 621

ELLIS, George, *Specimens of the Early English Poets*, 57

ELYOT, Sir Thomas, 750

emerit, adj , 627, 734

EMPEROR, J. B., *Catullian Influence in English Lyric Poetry, Circa 1600-1650*, 655, 706, 719

emulate, to, 670

Enallage, a rhetorical figure, 581

Ephialtes, 695

Epibateria . . . Maria ex Batava . . . Reduci, 7n, 758, 837

ERASMUS, Desiderius, 87, 581-82

ESSEX, Robert Devereux, Third Earl of, 760

escheat, to, 678

ETHEREGE, George, *The Comical Revenge*, 590, *The Man of Mode*, 575, 598; *She Wou'd if She Cou'd*, 711

Eucharistica Oxoniensia, 38

Eumela, character in *The Lady-Errant*, 86

EURIPIDES, *The Cyclops*, 597, mentioned, 607

"*Europe* and *Asia* doth th'young *Pompeys* hold," 501

EVANS, Willa M., on "To Splendora," 75, 764; *Henry Lawes*, 170, 173, 174n, 594, 599, 719, 720; mentioned, 591, 606

Examen Poeticum (1693), 726, 838

'Expect no strange, or puzzling Meat, no Pye," 479-80

exprobrate, to, 664; exprobration, n., 596, 756

extemporary, adj., 622

Factious, adj., 670

FAIRFAX, Edward, 716

FARMER, Richard, 56

FARQUHAR, George, 714

Fary Knight, The. See RANDOLPH, T.

'*Father* of *Poets*, through *thine* owne great day," 511-16

FEATLY, Daniel, 166n

fee-buck, n., 667, 685

FELL, John, 5, 15n, 17, 21n, 63n

FERRIAR, John, "Essay on the Dramatic Writings of Massinger," 27n, 57, 263n; on Pygmy legend, 584

FIELDING, Henry, 648

FINCH, Francis, 52n, 63n

FINCH, John, 48, 63n

fine for, to, 609

fire-briefs, n. pl., 689

"First Draught of this Trifle was so ill, The" (dedication, *Siege*), 363, CN 661, TN 807

FISHER, Jasper, *Fuimus Troes, or The True Trojans*, 607, 629

FLETCHER, John, his tragicomedy, 22-24; Cartwright's poems on, 518-19, 519-21, First Folio (1647), 49, 63n, 741-42, 837, *Beggars' Bush*, 586, Cartwright's debt to, 191, 604, *The Bloody Brother*, 30-31, 629, 630, 665; *The Custom of the Country*, 187, *The Faithful Shepherdess*, 640, 743; *Four Plays in One*, 592, 667-68; *The Knight of the Burning Pestle*, 265, 617-18, 646, 696; *The Laws of Candy*, 187, *Love's Cure*, 88n, *The Maid's Tragedy*, 86, 577, 579, 605, 665, 666; *Monsieur Thomas*, 637; *The Night-Walker*, 634, *Philaster*, 580, *The Scornful Lady*, 639; *The Sea-Voyage*, 87, 582, *The Spanish Curate*, 641, 643, *The Two Noble Kinsmen*, 607, *Valentinian*, 665-66, mentioned, 31, 46, 50, 57, 747

FLETCHER, Phineas, *Sicelides*, 668, 721, *Purple Island*, 717, 756; *Brittains Ida*, 766

FLETCHER, R., *Martial his Epigrams*, 703, 730, 753, 763

"*Fletcher*, though some call it thy fault, that wit," 519-21
FLEAY, F. G., *Biographical Chronicle of the English Drama*, 30-32, 84, 85n, 87n, 259, 358n, 581; mentioned, 31n
flinch for the wetting, not to, 639
FLORUS, 696
Flos Britannicus, 734, 836
FLOYD, Humphrey, 19n
fly, *n.*, 636
"Fly, O fly sad Sigh, and bear," 496
Folger MS. 452.1, 713-14, 714-15, 839
Folger MS. 646 4, 766, 839
Folger MS. 2071.6, 699, 701, 703, 766, 839
Folger MS. 2071.7, 759, 839
Folger MS. 7044 of *The Royal Slave*, 167-68, 588, 839
"Fool that I was, that little of my Span," 496-97
FORD, John, *The Broken Heart*, 82; *The Lover's Melancholy*, 642, 739
"For that our hearts to Loves soft pleasure yeelds," 672-73
FOSTER, J., *Alumni Oxonienses*, 7n, 10n, 12n
FOUNTAIN, John, *The Rewards of Vertue*, 589, 594
fox'd, to be, 646
FOXE, John, 623
FRAZER, Sir James, *The Dying God*, 187, 188n
fricace, *n*, 663
"From my Devotions yonder am I come" (first prologue, *Royal Slave*), 195, CN 589, TN 766
"From you grave men of business and of trade" (Restoration prologue, *Ordinary*), 610-11
fubb'd, to be, 655
fucuss, *n.*, 662
FULLER, Thomas, 747

G., E., 51
G., J. A., 737
G., T., 742
gally-pots, *n. pl.*, 662
GARDINER, Robert, 63n
GAY, John, *Polly*, 592
GAYLEY, C. M, *Beaumont, the Dramatist*, 32
GAYTON, Edmund, 14n
GEBHARDT, Erma R., "An Edition of William Cartwright's *The Ordinary*," 13n, 18, 46n, 60n, 61n, 64n, 67n, 82, 257n, 258n, 259n, 262, 264n, 266, 360n, 621, 622, 624, 626, 627, 628, 631, 633, 634, 636n, 637, 638, 642, 644, 647, 653, 654, 659, 660
GENEST, John, *Some Account of the English Stage*, 82, 87n, 266, 653

gent. (abbreviation), 598
Gentleman's Magazine, The, 699
"Gently, O Gently, Father, do not bruise," 559
GERBER, Friedrich, *The Sources of William Cartwright's Comedy "The Ordinary,"* 6, 20, 262, 265, 629, 631, 633, 638, 639, 640, 642, 647, 648, 657, 658
GERRARD, George, 171, 172n
GIFFORD, William, edition of Jonson, 43, 585-86, 629, 634, 644, 646, edition of Massinger, 57, 641, 666-67, mentioned, 267n
GILCHRIST, Octavius, 15n, 57n, 682, 693
GILDON, Charles, 5, 54n
GILL, A., 689
ginger-bread office, 585
"Give me a Girle (if one I needs must meet)," 471
GLAPTHORNE, Henry, *The Hollander*, 639; *The Lady's Privilege*, 581; *Wit in a Constable*, 579, 621
"Gnat mistaking her bright Eye, A," 478
GODOLPHIN, Sidney, 52n
"Goe o goe be gon away," an answer, by Thomas (?) May, to Cartwright's "Come, o come," in *The Ordinary*, 639-40
GOFFE, Thomas, *The Careless Shepherdess*, 597, 606, 746, 747; *The Courageous Turk*, 600; *The Raging Turk*, 646; mention, 24n
GOFFIN, R. Cullis, *The Life and Poems of William Cartwright*, 6, 7n, 9n, 11, 12n, 20n, 35, 37n, 39, 57n, 73, 74, 76, 81, 165, 166n, 170, 258, 355, 745-46
GOLDSMITH, Oliver, *Beauties of English Poesy*, 57
GOODRIDGE, Richard, 63n
GRANVILLE, George, 760
gravell'd, to be, 708
GRAY, Thomas, 721
Great Britaines Looking Glass, 684
"*Great Sir*, Successe t'your Royall selfe, and us," 509-10
GREENE, Robert, "cony-catching" pamphlets, 604; *A Looking Glass for London and England*, 684; *Friar Bacon and Friar Bungay*, 699; *Orlando Furioso*, 699
GREENOUGH, C. N., *Bibliography of the Theophrastan Character in English*, 662-63
Greek Anthology, The, 700
GREG, W. W., *Dramatic Documents, Commentary*, 168n
GREGORY, John, 10n, 11, 12n, 832
GRENVILLE, Sir Bevil, Cartwright's poem on, 555-58; 759-60
GREY, Zachary, *Notes on Shakespeare*, 56, 578, 624, 669

GRIERSON, Sir Herbert, *Metaphysical Lyrics and Poems of the Seventeenth Century*, 35, 699
GRIFFITH, William, 21
GROSE, Francis, *A Classical Dictionary of the Vulgar Tongue*, 592
Grosses vollständiges Universal Lexicon, 57
GROTIUS, Hugo, Cartwright's translation from, 497–500, 729–30, mentioned, 830, 831

HABINGTON, William, *The Queen of Aragon*, 178
HALL, John, 36, 47n, 608, 724, 725
"Hallow the Threshold, Crown the Posts anew," 554–55
happy, *adj*, 636
HARBAGE, Alfred, *Annals of English Drama*, 83n; *The Cavalier Drama*, 22n, 23, 24, 258n, 264, *Thomas Killigrew*, 22n, mentioned, 167
hardest, *adj*, 628
HARDING, Samuel, *Sicily and Naples*, 82
HARDYNG, John, 648
"Hark . . . ." *See* "Heark . . ."
Harl. MS 3511 (B M.), 639–40, 697, 839
Harl MS. 6917 (B.M), 589, 697, 725, 731, 764–65, 839
Harl. MS. 6931 (B.M.), 677, 679, 686, 687–88, 717, 839
Harl. MS 7319 (B.M), 713, 715, 839
HARMAN, Thomas, 604, 689
HARRIS, R , *The Drunkard's Cup*, 590
HARVEY, R., 636
HATTON, Sir Christopher, 660
HAUSTED, Peter, *The Rival Friends*, 642, 660
Have-at-all, character in *The Ordinary*, 264n
HAWES, Stephen, 641
HAY, James, Earl of Carlisle, 676
hays, *n pl*, 585
HAYWARD, Edward, deputy to Sir Henry Herbert, 261
HAZLITT, W. C., 653; *Collections and Notes*, 752; *Play-Collector's Manual*, 87n, 175n, 581, *Select Collection of Old English Plays* (containing *The Ordinary*), 257, 258
HEAD, Richard, *The English Rogue*, 635
HEADLEY, Henry, *Select Beauties of Ancient English Poetry*, 35n, 41n, 57, 735, 736, 737
"Heark, my *Flora*, Love doth call us," 467–68
"Heark, 'Tis the Nuptiall Day of Heav'n and Earth,"558
HEARNE, Thomas, 13n
Hearsay, character in *The Ordinary*, 264n, 268n
heart of grace, to take, 613
Heber MS. of *The Royal Slave*, 167, 588

HEINSIUS, Daniel, 746
HELIODORUS, *Aethiopica*, 189n, 607
HENRIETTA MARIE, Queen, acted in Court masques, 84, 790, commended *The Royal Slave*, 171, letter about *Royal Slave*, 180–81, Cartwright's poems to, 450, 504–6, 510–11, 530–31, 535–36, 554–55, 758–59, mentioned, 766
HENRY, Prince, sixth child of Charles I, 59, 751
HENRY THE FOURTH, of Navaare, 682
HERBERT, Sir Henry, as Master of Revels, 29–30; license for *The Lady Errant*, 85, fee for licensing, 85n; licensed *The Royal Slave*, 185, license for *The Ordinary*, 260, method of cutting, 260–61, mentioned, 32n, 184n
HERBERT, Sir Thomas, 188n
HERBERT OF CHERBURY, Edward Lord, 724
Herculean leap, 695
"Here fair *Corinna* buri'd lay," 474–75
HERRICK, Robert, 640, 676, 690, 740, 748, 751, 760–61
HEYLIN, Peter, 584
HEYLIN, ?Peter, 166n
HEYWOOD, John, *The Pardoner and the Friar*, 632
HEYWOOD, Thomas, *The Brazen Age*, 608; *The English Traveller*, 629; *Fortune by Land and Sea*, 591; quoted, 599, 697
highway-Inkle, 591
HILL, Aaron, use of Cartwright's poems, 55–56, 57n, 704, 706, 707
HILL, George, 63n
HILL, R., 63n, 185n
HILTON, John, *Catch that Catch can* (1652 and 1658), 591, 837
HOLLAND, Philemon, 600, 733
HOLLAND, Samuel, *Romancio-Mastix*, 24n, 88
HOLYDAY, Barten, 49, 742
HOOKER, Richard, 33, 753
HORACE, Cartwright's translation from, 44, 503–4, 731; echoes of, in Cartwright, 735, 736
Horti Carolini Rosa Altera, 750–51, 837
HOPKINS, John, versifier of Psalms, 642–43
HOWARD, Edward, *The Woman's Conquest*, 187
HOWARD, Sir Robert, *The Indian Queen*, 53, 185–86n, 579–80
HOWE, Josias, 63n, 356n, 660
HOWELL, James, 47, 63n, 635; *Familiar Letters*, 597–98, 600–1, 646, 714, 723
HOWES, Dorothy, Cartwright's sister, 12n
HOWES, E., his continuation of Stow's *Annales*, 647
HUC, Peter le, 181
HUME, A. S , *Treason and Plot*, 643
HUNT, Leigh, 27n

HUNTER, Joseph, *Chorus Vatum Anglicanorum*, 6, 50
Huntington MS. HM 116, 687
Huntington MS. HM 198, 687

I do confess, O God, my wand'ring Fires," 563
"I doe confesse the over-forward tongue," 448-49
"I dream'd I saw my self lye dead," 465
"I looked, and through the window chanced to spye," 565
"I now beleeve that Heaven once shall shrink," 542-44
"I sent a Sigh unto my Blest ones Eare," 472-73
"I sent a sigh into my mistresse eare," 701
"I told you *Lydia* how 'twould be," 491-93
"If Souls consist of water, I," 465-66
ILES, Richard, 63n
indeed-law, an exclamation, 652
indulge, to, 679
ingenite, *adj.*, 677
interest, to, 666
inward, *adj*, 578
IRVING, Washington, 59, 625, 637, 638
"Is there a Sanctity in Love begun," 483-84

Jack-chaynes, *n. pl.*, 594
Jack Drum's Entertainment, 621
JACKSON, William A., 62n
JAMES, Duke of York (later James II), 681-82; Cartwright's poem to, 451-52
Jane, Mistress, character in *The Ordinary*, 260, 261, 266
JEFFREYS, John, 63n
Jerusalem, a puppet play, 684
JEWELL, John, 734
JOHNSON, Doctor Samuel, 38, 56, 729
JONES, Inigo, 171, 174n, 176n, 178, 179
JONES, James, *Sepulchorum Inscriptiones*, 755
JONES, Robert, *The Muses Gardin for Delights*, 640
JONSON, Benjamin, Cartwright's poem on, 4n, 40, 511-16, 735-40, influence on Cartwright, 34, 36, 37, 50, 51, 263-64, *The Alchemist*, 60, 263-64, 632, 633-34, 645, 646, 648, 653, 657, 658, 660, 728; *Art of Poetry*, 735; *Bartholomew Fair*, 621, 636, 684; Epigram cvii (*Captain Hungry*), 623; *The Case is Altered*, 267; *Cynthia's Revels*, 622, 627, 640, 649, 695; *The Devil is an Ass*, 615, 624; "Drink to me only with thine eyes," 664; "An Epitaph on Mr. Vincent Corbet," 736, *Every Man in his Humour*, 645; *Every Man out of his Humour*, 621, 623, 630, 646, 659, "A Fit of Rhyme Against Rhyme," 739; *The Gipsies Metamorphosed*, 685, 708; "The Hour-Glass," 706; *Hymenaei*, 589; *The Magnetic Lady*, 623, 625, 664, 689, 736, *Neptune's Triumph*, 32n, 629-30; *The New Inn*, 9n, 644; "Ode to Himself," 740; *The Poetaster*, 585, 641; *The Silent Woman*, 264n, 575, 591, 598, 612, 630, 646, 664, 736; *The Staple of News*, 620, 629, 657, 658; *Timber*, 746; "To Mr. John Fletcher upon his *Faithful Shepherdess*, 743; "To Mr. William Shakespeare," 747; "To Penshurst," 750; "Underwoods," LXXI, 676-77; "Underwoods," LXXXI, 766; "Underwoods," CII, No iv, 679, *Volpone*, 595, 646; mentioned, 24, 31, 57, 190, 608, 682, 746, 751, 831
Jonsonus Virbius, 15n, 57n, 682, 735, 745, 836
JOSEPH, Sister Miriam, *Shakespeare's Use of the Arts of Language*, 581
Judgment shewn upon a Knot of Drunkards, A, 644
Judith, the story of, 358
juments, *n. pl.*, 628
JUVENAL, Decimus Junius, 586

K., E., in epistle to *Shepheards Calender*, 738
KECKERMANN, Bartholomaeus, 707
KERR, Mina, *Influence of Ben Jonson on English Comedy, 1598-1642*, 262n
KILLIGREW, Henry, 11n
KILLIGREW, Thomas, *Cicilia and Clorinda*, 583, *The Parson's Wedding*, 621, 629, 655, 656, *The Prisoners* and *Claracilla*, 639, 740-41, 837; Cartwright's poem to, 516-17; 740-41; mentioned, 29n
KING, Henry, 36, 589, 693, 723, 725, 737, 758
KINGSLEY, Charles, *Plays and Puritans*, 59-60, 258n
King's Men, 181, 182-83, 184n
KIRKMAN, Francis, *The English Rogue*, 635
kit, *n.*, 642
kitstrings, *n. pl*, 622
Knave in Graine, The. See D., J.
KNIGHT, I., 49, 742
knot, *n.*, 596
KOEPPEL, Emil, 626, 629, 633
Koran, the, 670
KRUSE, H, *Das Mädchen von Byzanz*, 578n
KUHL, Ernest, 668
KYNASTON, Sir Francis, "To Cynthia," 680-81, 726, *Amorum Troili et Cresseidae*, 631, 728, 836; Cartwright's poem to, 497, 728-29

L., J., 691
Lady Alimony, 724
LAMB, Charles, *Specimens of English Dramatic Poets*, 57

LANGBAINE, Gerard, *Account of the English Dramatick Poets*, 5, 9n, 54, 56, 180n, 258, 356, 358, 739, 830n, 831n, 832n
LANGBAINE, Gerard, a friend of Cartwright, 5n
Last and Best Edition of New Songs (1677), 725
LAUD, William, 5n, 14, 166n, 171, 174-75, 176, 180n, 181, 184n, 678, 686-87, 707
Laudian Statutes (Oxford), 14, 624, 686
law, *n.*, 652
LAWES, Henry, friend of Cartwright, 15n; set Cartwright's work to music, 40, 44, 171, 591, 593-94, 598, 599, 608, 694, 721, 760; contributed commendatory poem o *Works* (1651), 47, 52n, 63n; suggested collaboration with Cartwright, 173-74, 719, autographed MS., 170, 595, 639, 694, 697, 700, 717, 722, 839, comment on *The Royal Slave*, 174n, *Ayres and Dialogues* (1653), 36, 75, 595, 697, 700, 717, 719-20, 837, *Ayres and Dialogues* (1655), 700, 837; *Choice Psalmes*, 720; *Select Ayres and Dialogues* (1659), 174n, 580, 593, 595, 639, 838
LAWES, William, 590, 591, 598, 606, *Choice Psalmes*, 720
LAWRENCE, W. J., 30n, 179n, *Pre-Restoration Stage Studies*, 32n
lay, *n.*, 626
lead an ape in heaven, to, 668
LEE, A. C., *The Decameron, Its Sources and Analogues*, 358
LEE, Sir Sidney, 265n
LEIGH, J., 63n, 185n
LESSING, Gotthold Ephraim, 57
LEUCASIA, character in *The Siege*, 53n, 81n, 82, 83
LEYDEN, JOHN OF, 709
"Like to the selfe-inhabiting snaile," 715
LILLY, William, *History of his Life and Times*, 690
LINUS, mythical Greek poet, 577
liquorous, *adj.*, 645
LITHGOW, William, 576, 625
LIVY, 749
LLOYD, David, *Memoires*, 4, 6n, 7n, 10, 18, 21, 54, 171n, 681, 735, 743, 752, 756, 757, 759, 829n, 830n, 831n, 832n, 838, his plagiarism of Cartwright, 4, plagiarism of the commendatory poems to the *Works* (1651), 4
LLUELLIN, Martin, 51, 63n; *Men-Miracles*, 19, 51-52, 259n, 548, 678, 755
LOCKE, John, 33
LODGE, Thomas, *A Looking Glass for London and England*, 684
London Chanticleers, The, 629, 664
London-measure, 643, 712

LONG, Mrs. Abigall, CARTWRIGHT'S poem on, 544-47, 754
LOPEZ, Roderigo, 643
LOUNSBURY, T. R., *Studies in Chaucer*, 631
LOVELACE, Lord, 19n
LOVELACE, Richard, 35, 50, 185, 591, 594, 606, 609, 679, 695
Love's Garland, 669
LOWNDES, W. T., *Bibliographer's Manual*, 710
LUCAS, Theophilus, *Lives of the Gamesters*, 266, 654
LUCASIA, character in *The Lady-Errant*, 52, 67, 81n, 82
LUSHINGTON, Thomas, 660
lycand, *adj.*, 637
LYDGATE, John, 358, 359
LYLY, John, *Gallathea*, 701
LYNCH, K. M., on Platonic drama, 22n, 23, 26n, on D'Urfé's *L'Astrée*, 649; *The Social Mode of Restoration Comedy*, 22n, 579
lytherly, *adj.*, 633

M., I., 742
McCARTHEY, William, 67n, 70n
MACDONALD, Hugh, *John Dryden, A Bibliography*, 611
McEUEN, K., *Classical Influence upon the Tribe of Ben*, 700
MACHESSA, character in *The Lady-Errant*, 88
machin, *n*, 578
MACKLIN, Charles, 56, 739
McPEEK, J. A. S., *Catullus in Strange and Distant Britain*, 595, 706, 719
"Madam, since Jewels by your self are worn," 441-45
MADAN, F, *Oxford Books*, 749
"Mallem cum *Scaligero . . . sapere*," 739
MALLET, David, 738
Mal. MS. 21 (Bod.), 76, 686, 689, 690, 694, 696, 698, 713, 714, 765, 839
MALONE, Edmund, *Historical Account of the English Stage*, 177, 182n; mentioned, 56, 167, 739
manage, *n.*, 741
MANDEVIL, Jack, the fictitious Sir John Mandeville, 625
"Manners, and Men, transcrib'd, Customes express'd," 516-17
MARLOWE, Christopher, 651
MARMION, Shackerley, 9n; *The Antiquary*, 632; *A Fine Companion*, 29n, *Holland's Leaguer*, 576, 623
Marrow of Complements, The, 49, 184, 260, 355, 577, 595, 599, 601-2, 603, 617, 620-21, 637, 644, 645,

651-52, 655, 656, 665, 670, 671, 672-73, 708, 714, 724, 837
MARSH, J., 740
MARSTON, John, 641
MARTIAL, Marcus Valerius, Cartwright's translations from, 500-2, 730-31, 829, mentioned, 736
MARY, Princess, eldest daughter of Charles I, 682, 752
MASON, R , 63n
MASSINGER, Philip, *Beggar's Bush*, 191, 586, 604; *The Bondman*, 186n, 360n, 582, 605, 649, 653; *The City Madam*, 267n, 583, *The Emperor of the East*, 661; *A New Way to Pay Old Debts*, 578; *The Old Law*, 187, 641, 695, 712; *The Picture*, 667; mentioned, 24n, 28, 31, 59, 743
MASTER, Thomas, 9n, 11, 20, 51, 832
Master of the Revels. *See* HERBERT, Sir Henry
Matchless Orinda, The. *See* PHILIPS, K.
MAY, Thomas, 739
MAY, ?Thomas, 639
MAYNE, Jasper, Cartwright's friendship with, 17, 51; commendatory poem in *Works* (1651), 21n, 36, 63n, *The Amorous War*, 51, 265n, 576, 592, 595, 596; *The City Match*, 51, 171n, 264, 265, 583, 613, 615, 658, 686, 713, quoted, 745; mentioned, 11n, 49n, 185n, 682
Meanwell, character in *The Ordinary*, 261, 265, 266, 267n
MELEAGER, 728
Memories. *See* Lloyd, D.
Men and Armour for Gloucestershire in 1608, 7n
Merry Devil of Edmonton, The, 594
Merry Drollerie, Part II, 711
Merry Drollery, Complete (1670), 591, 838
MICO, John, *A Pill to Purge Out Popery*, 644
MIDDLETON, Thomas, *A Fair Quarrel*, 640, 642; *The Mayor of Queenborough*, 648; *Michaelmas Term*, 638; *The Roaring Girl*, 754, *The Spanish Gypsy*, 669; *The Witch*, 659; *Your Five Gallants*, 265-66, 625, mentioned, 31
military dinner, as dramatic device, 32n, 629
MILLER, A., publisher of Cartwright's sermon, 16n, 49
MILLES, Robert, 166n
MILTON, John, compared to Cartwright, 33-34, 35, 747, and Cartwright's *Ariadne*, 36-37, 719, 720, 721; 751, *Animadversions*, 659, *An Apology*, 641; *Comus*, 34n, 174n, *Lycidas*, 699, 704-5; *Paradise Lost*, 34, 46, 587; *Poems* (1645), 46; *Samson Agonistes*, 766, *Second Defense*, 600
MITFORD, J., 699, 721
MINSHEU, John, 686

Misander, character in *The Siege*, 357, 360
MOLIÈRE, Jean Baptiste Poquelin de, *L'Avare*, 267, 589; *Les Fâcheux*, 646; *Les Précieuses Ridicules*, 267n; *Tartuffe*, 267n
MONMOUTH, Henry Carey, Earl of, 63n, 710
monograms, n.pl., 676
MONTAGUE, Walter, *The Shepherd's Paradise*, 23, 83-84, 85, 586, 587
MONTAGUE, (?)Walter, 52n
MONTEVERDI, Claudio, 719
MOORMAN, F. W , 586
MORE, Henry, Psychanthanasia, 608
Morglay, a sword, 647
MORTON, Thomas, *Columbus*, 186n
MOSCHUS, 701
MOSELEY, Humphrey, preface to *Works* (1651), 3, 6n, 18n, 20, 21, 34n, 35, 39n, 63, 73n, 75, 355, 602-3, 719, 731, 741-42, 762, 829-32, ownership right in Cartwright's plays, 29n, 63; activities as publisher, 47n; promised edition of Cartwright's Latin poems, 49, 73; entry on Stationers' Register for publication of Cartwright's plays, 53n, 62-63, 81, 257, 258n; textual value of his edition, 73; mentioned, 82, 595, 744
Moth, character in *The Ordinary*, 59, 60, 258n, 261, 263, 264n, 630-32
mump, to, 662
Musarum Deliciae, 632
Musarum Oxoniensium . . . Maria, 749, 836
"Mvst then our Loves be short still? Must we choose," 536-39
"My Ladies young Chaplain could never arive," 481-83
MYLLES, John, 11n
"My Prayers are heard, O *Lyce*, now," 503-4

NARES, Robert, 642, 659
NASH, Thomas, 642
NAU, Estienne, 181
NEEDHAM, F., 165-65
"Nem esur Saxes," an Anglo-Saxon tag, 648
Neoplatonism, its connections with the drama, 23; in Cartwright's plays, 25-26
nephew, n., 679
Nero, 606
NEVILL, E., 4n, 7n, 63n
New Academy of Complements, The (1671), 591, 644, 727, 838
NEWBURGH, Lady, Cartwright's poem on, 542-44, 753
NEWCASTLE, Duchess of. *See* CAVENDISH, M.

NEWMAN, Mr, 11
next his heart, 592
NICHOLAS, Sir Harris, *Life and Times of Sir Christopher Hatton*, 660
NICHOLS, John, *Collection of Poems*, 57, 721
Nicias, character in *The Siege*, 86n
NICIAS, dancer in Restoration revival of *The Lady Errant*, 86
NICOLL, Allardyce, *Stuart Masques*, 84, 85, 177, 178
Nineveh, a puppet play, 684
"No, no, it cannot be, for who e'r set," 470–71
nock, to, 598
NORTH, Sir Thomas, 357
Notes and Queries, 737, 759, 760
"Not to be wrought by Malice, Gaine, or Pride," 555–58
"Now, now, the Sunne is fled" (*Royal Slave*), 223, 590–91, CN 598–99, TN 786
"Now that your Princely Birth, Great Queen's so showne," 504–6
"Now thou our future Brother" (*Ordinary*), 44n, 336–37, CN 656, TN 805

O'erlook, to, 647
OESTERLEY, H., 359n, 360
"Oh now the certaine cause I know," 568
oint, to, 674
OLDYS, William, manuscript notes to Langbaine's *Account*, 6, 21n, 258
OLIPHANT, E. H. C., *The Plays of Beaumont and Fletcher*, 30–31, 31n
olive, to, 630
Olyndus, character in *The Lady-Errant*, 54
one to bear, 646
OSBALDSTONE, Lambert, 9
OTWAY, Thomas, *Venice Preserv'd*, 597, 669
"Our Prologue huff'd, but we are humbler now" (Restoration epilogue, *Ordinary*), 611–12
OVERBURY, Sir Thomas, 582, 589
OVID, 578, 581, 584, 672, 696, 697, 716, 718–19, 721, 722
OWEN, Mrs. Anne, 52
OWEN, John, 52
Oxford press, the, 13

P., K. *See* Philips, K.
P., T, Baronet, 63n, 64
pall-mall, adv., 585
PALMER, Francis, 63n
"Pardon me, Sir, this injury to your Bayes," 497
Parentalia . . Rolando Cottono, 836
Parnassus Biceps, 580, 690, 692, 698, 705, 751, 837

PATTERSON, Charles, 58n
PAULET, Lady Elizabeth, 691–92; Cartwright's poem to, 459–60
PAULI, Johannes, *Schimpf und Ernst* and subplot in *The Siege*, 358–60, 670
PEELE, George, *The Arraignment of Paris*, 191n; *Edward I*, 657, 659
PEGGE, S., 257, 259n, 630, 638
PEMBROKE, Philip Earl of, Cartwright's poem to, 541–42, 752–53
PEPYS, Samuel, 37, 721
PERCY, Lady Lucy, later Countess of Carlisle, 676, Cartwright's poem to, 441–45
PETRONIUS, Gaius, 595
PETTUS, Sir John, 63n
PHILIPOTT, Thomas, 63n, 185n
PHILIPS, Katherine, 50, 51, 52–53, 185, 580, 724, 727, 753–54; *Letters from Orinda to Poliarchus*, 52–53
PHILLIPS, Edward, *Theatrum Poetarum*, 4, 747
PHILLIPS, John, 720
Phillipus Stoicus, pseudonym of Cartwright, 695
Philosophy of friendship, Cartwright's influence on Katherine Philips', 52
Philosophy of the child, 39–40
Phoenix Nest, The, 580, 583
picking meat, 636
PIERRE, Sebastian la, 181
pies, an oath, 636
"Plain Shepherds Wear was only Gray," 468
PLATO, 592, 604, 613, 664, 715
Platonic drama, 22–27, 172
Platonic love cult, 23–24, 27n, 83–84, 724
PLAYFORD, John, *Catch that Catch can* (1667), 590, 594, 608, 838, *The Musical Companion* (1673), 591, 594, 608, 838, *Musick's Delight on the Cithren* (1666), 639, 838; *Select Musicall Ayres* (1652), 580, 837, (1653), 580, 837
Playhouse Pocket-Companion, The, 56–57, 74n
PLAUTUS, *Aulularia*, 267, 658
PLINY, 584, 736, 741
PLUTARCH, 356, 357, 600, 665, 718
POINTER, John, *Oxoniensis Academia*, 13n
poll, by the, 612
pomado, n., 695
POOLE, Josua, *The English Parnassus*, 585, 595, 599, 686, 837
POPE, Alexander, 27, 37, 55n, 721, 729, 737, 738, 743
PORTMAN, George, 181
possession eleven points of the law, 674

INDEX

POTLUCK, Mistress Joan, character in *The Ordinary*, 260, 614-15
pouch, to, 713
POULTNEY, Mr. 754, CARTWRIGHT'S poem on, 547
POWLET. *See* PAULET
"Pox on our Gaolor, and on his fat Jowle, A" (*Royal Slave*), 200, CN 590-91, 606, TN 778
Practical Piety, ? a book title, 709
PRESTWICK, Edmund, *Hippolitus*, 714
Priscilla, character in *The Ordinary*, 261, 267, 268
Private Formes of Prayer, 16n
PRODROMUS. *See* THEODORUS PRODROMUS
Pro Rege suo Soteria, 680, 836
Proteleia Anglo-Batava, 752, 837
PRYNNE, William, 85, 590, 685, 709-10
Public Advertiser, The, 57n, 706
PUBLILIUS SYRUS, 583
PUCKERING, Sir Thomas, 184n
pumps, *n pl.*, 683-84
PUTTENHAM, George, 643-44
Pygmies, Cartwright's use of Pygmy lore, 584
Pyle, character in *The Siege*, 363

Quadragessimall wits, 641
quality, *n.*, 641, 655, 665
quar, *n.*, 678
QUARLES, Francis, 46; *Argalus and Parthenia*, 716, 717, 738, 740; *The Virgin Widow*, 607
quarrell, *n.*, 733
Quarterly Review, The, 731, 759
quest, *n.*, 644
quill, *n.*, 681

RABELAIS, François, 60
RACINE, Jean, 60
ragioni di stato, 627
RALEIGH, Sir Walter, *History of the World*, 188n, 190, 608
RANDOLPH, Thomas, *Aristippus*, 598, 629, 632; *The Drinking Academy*, 598; *The Fary Knight*, 263-64n, 647; *Hey for Honesty*, 614, 621; *The Jealous Lovers*, 88n, 579, 661; *The Muses' Looking-Glass*, 609, poem to Feltham, 737-38, mentioned, 36, 50, 51, 55
Rawl. MS. D. 951 (Bod.), 676, 839
Rawl. MS. D 1092 (Bod.), 639, 839
RAY, John, *Collection of English Proverbs*, 674
RAYMOND, John, 63n
"Reader, here is such a booke," 462-65
reall, *adj.*, 596
REED, Isaac, *Select Collection of Old Plays*, 257, 258, 259n, 631

REED, J. C., 63
re-estate, to, 582
Reprobation, doctrine of, 685
retrivall, *n.*, 716
Retrospective Review, The, 10n, 58, 694, 703, 704, 706, 754
Returne from Parnassus, Part One, The, 631
Revels Office, 81, 85, 185
RICE, W. G., 186-87n, 605
RIDER, John, 716
RISTINE, F. H., *English Tragi-comedy*, 23n
"Rites and Worship are both old, but you, The," (third prologue, *Royal Slave*). 198, TN 777
RIVERS, George, *The Heroinae*, 185, 358, 677
Robert Earl of Essex's Ghost, 643
ROBERT OF GLOUCESTER, *Chronicle*, 648
ROBINSON, Thomas, publisher, 63
ROGERS, Daniel, 733
ROLLINS, H. E , *Cavalier and Puritan*, 645
romancys, *n. pl.*, 576
Romaunt of the Rose, The, 659
rooke, *n.*, 695
ROSSINGHAM, Edward, 183-84
ROWLEY, William, *The Old Law*, 187, 641, 695, 712; *The Spanish Gypsy*, 669
rubbers, *n. pl.*, 712
RUDDER, S., *A New History of Gloucestershire*, 6n
RUPERT, Prince, 84

S., I. M., 51
S , T., 737
S., W. (William Strode), 766
"Sacred to your Delight" (prologue, *Lady-Errant*), 91, CN 575, TN 769
SADLEIR, Ursula, Cartwright's poem on, 547-49, 754-55
sagar, *n* , 607
"Saint *Francis*, and Saint *Benedight*," (*Ordinary*), 59, 303, CN 637
SAINTSBURY, George, 76, 576, 681
SAUNDERS, Paul, 35n, 43, 704-5
"Sawest thou not that liquid ball," 466-67
SCHELLING, F. E., *Elizabethan Drama, 1558-1642*, 84, 87, 355n
Scoggin's Jests, 166, 653
SCOTT, Sir Walter, 34n, 638, 642, 656, 708
"Seal up her Eyes, O Sleep, but flow" (*Siege*), 400, CN 665-66, TN 807
seconds, *n. pl.*, 678
Secret Miracles of Nature, 600
Secunda Vox Populi, 752, 836

SEDLEY, Sir Charles, *The Mulberry Garden*, 575; mentioned, 50, 724, 747
"See faire Splendora what a lovely bed," 569-70
"See how the Emulous Gods do watch" (*Siege*), 424, CN 670, TN 808
"See these two little Brooks that slowly creep," 495-96
"See this is He, whose Star," 556-60
"See thy *Parthenia* stands," 487-88
SENECA, Lucius Annaeus, *Hercules Furens*, 582
SETTLE, Elkanah, 50; *Cambyses*, Cartwright's influence on, 185, 191n, 594; *The Empress of Morocco*, epilogue to, 185n
SEVERNE, Thomas, 63n, 595
SHADWELL, Thomas, *The Amorous Bigotte*, 706; *Bury Fair*, 49-50, *The Humourists*, 712; *The Lancashire Witches*, 577, *The Miser*, debt to Cartwright, 267-68, 589; *Psyche*, 675, 758, *The Royal Shepherdesse*, 263n, 589; *The Scowrers*, 268n, *The Virtuoso*, 740; *The Woman-Captain*, 598, 599, 690
SHAFER, Robert, *The English Ode to 1660*, 719
SHAKESPEARE, William, Cartwright's comparison of, to Fletcher, 745-47; *All's Well*, 624, 745; *Antony and Cleopatra*, 598; *The Comedy of Errors*, 622, 626, 659; *Cymbeline*, 668, *Hamlet*, 580, 666, 673; *I Henry IV*, 578, 592, 614, 621, 645, 696; *II Henry IV*, 615, *I Henry VI*, 625, *Love's Labour's Lost*, 675, 738, *Macbeth*, 612, *Measure for Measure*, 187, 657; *A Midsummer Night's Dream*, 187, 671; *Much Ado*, 656, 659, 668, 669, *Othello*, 665, *The Passionate Pilgrim*, 697, *Poems* (1640), 701-2, 837; *Romeo and Juliet*, 641, 664, 668; *The Taming of the Shrew*, 578, *Troilus and Cressida*, 583-84, *Twelfth Night*, 653, *The Winter's Tale*, 583, 586, 589, 663; mentioned, 24n, 36, 41
Shape, character in *The Ordinary*, 261, 268n
shape, n., 674, 677
"Shape for Temple windows fit, A," 506-9
SHEAPARD, Mr., 603
Shene (Sheene), 696
SHELLEY, P. B., *The Cenci*, 580-81
SHERBURNE, Edward, 47, 63n
"Shew me the flames you brag of, you that be," 457-59
SHIRLEY, James, *The Ball*, 88n, 578, 688, *The Bird in a Cage*, 634, 639; *The Cardinal*, 751; *The Gamester*, 578, 624; *The Gentleman of Venice*, 657; *Honoria and Mammon*, 597, 598, *The Lady of Pleasure*, 629, 670, 724, *Love in a Maze*, 663; *Love's Cruelty*, 598; *The Maid's Revenge*, 578, *The Opportunity*, 584, 598; *The Royal Master*, 598; *The Sisters*, 29n; *The Traitor*, 264n, 576; *The Witty Fair One*, 12, 47n, 658, *The Young Admiral*, 264n, 626, 633, 648-49; quoted, 47n, 744, 746-47; mentioned, 28
"Show...," See "Shew..."
SHUSTER, G N., *The English Ode from Milton to Keats*, 719
SIDNEY, Sir Philip, 34, *The Arcadia*, 579, 581, 583, 586, 717, 750
SIMPSON Percy, *Proof-Reading in the Sixteenth, Seventeenth, and Eighteenth Centuries*, 13n, 14, 165
"Since Jewels by your self are worn, Madam," 441-45
siz'd Pint, 711
SKEAT, W. W., 637, 647
SKELTON, John, 614, 705-6
Slawkenbergius, 661
SLICER, character in *The Ordinary*, 261, 264n, 268n
slubber, to, 730
SMALWOOD, Matthew, 63n, 185n
SMART, J. S, 720-21
SMITH, Robert, 712
sneaksbill, n., 639
Solis Britannici Perigaeum, 681, 836
"So Love appear'd breaking his way," 714
Some Small and Simple Reasons, 613
"So to a stronger guarded Fort we use," 544-47
SOUERS, P. W., *The Matchless Orinda*, 35, 38, 52, 53, 54
Souldiers Catechisme, The, 613
Sources. See GERBER, F.
SOUTHERNE, Thomas, 50; *Oroonoko*, 596-97
"So when an hasty vigour doth disclose," 531-33
"So when the great Elixar (which a Chast," 551-53
spark, n., 582, 653, 753
SPEGHT, Thomas, his edition of Chaucer, 631, 637
SPELMAN, Sir Henry, *De Sepultura*, 757; Cartwright's poem on, 549-50, 755-56
SPENCE, Joseph, 55
SPENSER, Edmund, *The Faerie Queene*, 577, 670, 701, 716, 751; mentioned, 33, 51, 637, 670, 738
spitchcock, n., 630
"Splendora blesse the morne and Sol's resort," 567
"Splendora" poems, attribution of, discussed, 75-77, use of double epithet in, 76, 698; texts of, 564-70, CN 764-66
Sportive Wit, 698, 837
spurge, to, 674
STAFFORD, Anthony, *Honour and Virtue*, 751, 837
STAFFORD, Lord Henry, Cartwright's poem on, 536-39, 751

STAFFORD, Robert, 625
STANLEY, Thomas, 55, 640
STANTON, William, 41n, 63n
STAPYLTON, Sir Robert, 7n, 63n
"State is now past feare, and all that wee, The," 451-52
Stationers' Register, 16n, 31, 53n, 62-63, 73n, 81, 165, 257, 258n, 355, 603
STEELE, M.S., *Plays and Masques at Court*, 184n
STEEVENS, George, 56n, 257
STENNING, A. H., *The Record of Old Westminsters*, 7n, 9n
STERNE, Lawrence, reference to Widow Wadman, 618
STERNOLD, Thomas, versifier of Psalms, 642-43
stickle, to, 644
STIGLIANI, Tommaso, 44n, 358n, 697
still an end, 617
"Still do the Stars impart their light," 468-70
"Still so obdurate, hast thou vowed to liue," 564
STOKES, William, Cartwright's poem to, 462-65, 694-95; *The Vaulting Master*, 694
STOPES, C. C., 181n, 182n
STOTEVILE, Mr., 11
STOW, John, *Annales*, 647; *Survey of London*, 638, 664
STRABO, 188n
STRAFFORD, Thomas Wentworth, Earl of, 759
Strangling and Death of the Great Turk, The, 627
strapado, n , 695
STRAPAROLA, Francesco, 654
Stratocles, character in *The Royal Slave*, 190n
STRODE, William, *The Floating Island*, 21n, 172, 177, 178, 599, quoted, 693, 765; mentioned, 36, 75, 698, 702, 703, 757, 766
stroke, n., 578
"Strow we these Flowers as we goe" (*Siege*), 392, CN 664, TN 807
STUBS, Philip, *Life and Death of Katherine Stubs*, 644
"Successe t'your Royall selfe, and us, Great Sir," 509-10
"Such are your Fathers Pictures, that we do," 476
SUCKLING, Sir John, *Aglaura*, 603, 665, 712, *Brennoralt*, 598; *The Goblins*, 606, mentioned, 24n, 28, 35, 640, 676, 724
SUGGE, Mr., 11
SUTCLIFFE, Matthew, 64;
SWANNE, Nicklis, 166n
swear, by my, 655
SWIFT, Jonathan, 577, 754
SWINBURNE, A. C., 59
SYLVESTER, Joshua, 55, 678
synalaephaes, n. pl , 693

syren, n., 654

Table, n., 664
take up for, to, 636
TASSO, Torquato, 670, 716
"Taught from your Artfull Strains, My Fair," 461-62
TAYLOR, John, 710
"Tell me no more of Constancy," 725
"Tell me no more of Minds embracing Minds," 494-95
"Tell me no more you love," 725
"Tell me no more you love, unless," 725
"Tell me not of Joy: there's none," 477
tenents, n. pl., 666
TENNYSON, Alfred, Lord, 708
tent, n., 630
TERENCE, *Adelphi*, 658
TERRENT, Jerumael, 10
"Th'art out, vile Plagiary, that dost think," 500
"Then our Musick is in prime" (*Ordinary*), 320, CN 644, TN 803
THEOCRITUS, 719
Theophrastan character, 663
THEODORUS PRODROMUS, *Rodanthes et Dosiclis Amorum*, principal source of *The Royal Slave*, 189-90, 592, 593, 605, 607, 608
"There is not halfe soe warme a fire," 715
"*Theseus*! O *Theseus* heark! but yet in vain," 488-91
THEUTOBOCCHUS, 696
THOMPSON, H. L, Christ Church, 11n, 12n
THORNDIKE, A. H., *Shakespeare's Theater*, 177n
THORN-DRURY, G., 165, 167, 169, 692
"Those glorious Triumphs of the Persian Court" (first epilogue, *Royal Slave*), 251, CN 609, TN 797-98
"Thou, who didst never see the Light," 471-72
"Thou art . . . ." *See* Th'art . . ."
"Though all Your Royall Burthens should come forth," 535-36
"Though now the Times perhaps be such that nought," 549-50
"Though the distemp'red Many cry they see," 533-35
"Though we could wish Your Issue so throng'd stood," 530-31
"Though we well know the Neighbouring Plain" (epilogue, *Lady-Errant*), 162, CN 587
"Though when all *Fletcher* writ, and the entire," 518-19

"Thou hadst four Teeth, good Elia, heretofore," 501
"Thou ô bright Sun who seest all" (*Royal Slave*), 170, 183, 249, CN 608, TN 797
"Thou *Sun* that shed'st the Dayes, looke downe and see," 560–63
"Thou Swayer of the Capitoll, whom we," 500
"Thou whitest Soul, thou thine own Day," 547–49
"Thus cited to a second night, wee've here" (second epilogue, *Royal Slave*), 252, CN 609, TN 798
"Tis vayne to weepe, or in a riming spite," 570–71
"To carve our Loves in Myrtle rinds" (*Lady-Errant*), 103–4, CN 577, TN 770
TOMKIS, Thomas, *Albumazar*, 628
TOPP, Henry, 9
"To the Reader, Preface to *Works* (1651). *See* MOSELEY, Humphrey
totter'd, *adj*, 604
TOWERS, William, 15n, 56n, 63n, 185n, 356, 674
toy, to take a, 578
TRAHERNE, Thomas, 40, 595, 728
transmiss, to, 641
trencher analects, 641
TREVOR, Arthur, 20n
TRITHEMIUS, 621
Triumph of King Charles, The, 590
Troublesome Reign of John, King of England, The, 63
True News from Oxford, 19n
"True to himself and Others, with whom both," 547
trunck-hose, *adj.*, 630, 747
tulipants, *n. pl.*, 605
turn'd hose, in, 747
twist, *n.*, 585
twitting, *n.*, 654
"'Twould wrong our Author to bespeake your Eares" (prologue, *Ordinary*), 271, CN 612–13, TN 799
TWYNE, Brian, 19n

Unfil'd, *adj.*, 682
"Unfil'd Author, though he be assur'd, The" (third epilogue, *Royal Slave*), 253, TN 798
University (Oxford) *Register*, R., 180n, 181n
unwenned, *adj.*, 633
ure, keep in, 601
Uses, doctrines and, 623, 711

VAN DOREN, Mark, *The Poetry of John Dryden*, 50, 53n
VAN LENNEP, W. B, 28, 260n
VAUGHAN, Francis, 63n, 75n
VAUGHAN, Henry, 40, 45, 47, 51, 52n, 63n, 66, 702, 728
VAUGHAN, Thomas, 63n
vectures, *n. pl.*, 696
veget, *adj*, 653
venture, at a, 674
"*Venus* Redress a wrong that's done," 472
Verses by the Vniversity of Oxford on Death . . . Grenvill (1684), 759, 838
Verses on the death of . . . Grenvill, Knight (1643), 759, 837; (1644), 759, 837
VERSTEGAN, Richard, 648
vertue, *n.*, 668
VILLIERS, George, Duke of Buckingham, 621
VIRGIL, 641, 734
Visitation of Gloucestershire, 1623, 7
Visitation of the County of Gloucester, 1682–1683, 7n
Vitis Carolinae Gemma Altera, 681, 836
volaticks, *n. pl.*, 696
VOLTAIRE, François Arouet de, 58

W., C. (Christopher Ware), 63n
"Wake my *Adonis*, do not dye" (*Lady-Errant*), 44, 126–27, CN 580, TN 772
WALLER, Edmund, 50, 55, 678
WALLER, Sir William, 760
WALLERSTEIN, Ruth, 705, *Richard Crashaw*, 761
WALTON, Izaak, 47, 48, 55n, 63n, 66
WARBURTON, William, 676
WARD, G. R. M., *Oxford University Statutes*, 14n, 624
WARD, Ned, *The London Spy*, 628
WARD, T. H., *The English Poets*, 680, 749, 757
WARD, W. A., *English Dramatic Literature*, 85n, 87, 258, 357n, 358n, 629
WARE, Christopher, 63n
WARING, Robert, 11, 63n, 831; *Amoris Effigies*, 21n
WARING, William, 63n
Warning for England, A, 709
WASHBOURNE, Thomas, 15n
WASHINGTON, George, 738
WASSERMAN, E. R, 54n, 58n, 704; *Elizabethan Poetry in the Eighteenth Century*, 55n
WATKINS, Richard, 63n, 65
WATSON, Thomas, 725–26
"We are a people now againe, and may," 449–50
web-errantry, *n.*, 591
WEBSTER, John, 24n; *The Duchess of Malfi*, 591
"We doe presume our duty to no eare," 450

"We have escap'd the Law, but yet do feare" (epilogue, *Ordinary*), 351, CN 660, TN 806
well-appointed, *adj.*, 614
Westminster Drollery (1671), 723; *Part II* (1672), 639, 838
Westminster Supper, the, 11n, 707
"When Studies now are blasted, and the times," 541–42
"When the old flaming Prophet climb'd the Sky," 551
"Where is that Learned Wretch that knows," 485–86
"Where is the Cold you quak't [with], you that be," 687–88
"Whether so fast *Ergastus!* say," 522–26
"Whether thy well-shap'd parts now scattred far," 475–76
whiffle, to, 592
"Whiles early light springs from the skies" (*Ordinary*), 335–36, CN 665, TN 804–5
"Whiles I this standing Lake," 473–74
"Whither . . . ." *See* "Whether . . ."
WHITNEY, Geffrey, *Choice of Emblems*, 576, 586, 592, 696
"Who can hide fire? If't be uncover'd, Light," 465
"Who e'r vile slighter of the State, in more," 501–2
"Why doe these orient drops distill," 568–69
WILDE, George, *Love's Hospital*, 176, 360n
WILLIAMSON, E., 691
"Will you not stay then, and vouchsafe to be," 452–54

WILMOT, John, Earl of Rochester, 33
WILMOT, Lord, 19n
WILSON, John, *The Cheats*, 634, *The Projectors*, 656
WINSTANLEY, William, 5n
WISDOM, Robert, 642–43
WITHER, George, 710
Wit Restor'd, 725
Wits Interpreter See COTGRAVE, J.
Witts Recreations, 714, 766
Wonderfull Discoverie of Witches in the Countie of Lancaster, The, 674
WOOD, Anthony, *Athenae Oxonienses*, 5, 6n, 9n, 15n, 20n, 54, 68, 643, 830n, 831n, 832n; *City of Oxford*, 20n, *Fasti*, 12n, 20n; *Historia et Antiquitates*, 4, 6n, 9n, 175n, 176n, 179, 180n; *History and Antiquities*, 19, 171n, 172, 176, 177, 179, 180, 265, *Life and Times*, 19
WOODWARD, William, 167
word, *n.*, 630
Works (1651). See CARTWRIGHT, W.
WRIGHT, Abraham, *Five Sermons in Five several Styles*, 17, 51
wrought, *p. p.*, 692
WYCHERLEY, William, 738

Yea and nay, by, 645
yerk, to, 585
"Y'are now transcrib'd, and Publike View," 460–61
"You gave m'a Mannour, *Lupus*, but I till," 502

CPSIA information can be obtained at www.ICGtesting.com
Printed in the USA
BVOW062348170413

318479BV00011B/235/P